GENERAL MOTORS

CHEVY NOVA/GEO PRIZM
1985-93 REPAIR MANUAL

CHILTON'S

President, Chilton Enterprises	David S. Loewith
Senior Vice President	Ronald A. Hoxter
Publisher & Editor-In-Chief	Kerry A. Freeman, S.A.E.
Managing Editors	Peter M. Conti, Jr., W. Calvin Settle, Jr., S.A.E.
Assistant Managing Editor	Nick D'Andrea
Senior Editors	Debra Gaffney, Ken Grabowski, A.S.E., S.A.E.
	Michael L. Grady, Richard J. Rivele, S.A.E.
	Richard T. Smith, Jim Taylor
	Ron Webb
Project Managers	Martin J. Gunther, Jeffrey M. Hoffman
Director of Manufacturing	Mike D'Imperio

CHILTON BOOK COMPANY

ONE OF THE **DIVERSIFIED PUBLISHING COMPANIES**,
A PART OF **CAPITAL CITIES/ABC, INC.**

Manufactured in USA
© 1993 Chilton Book Company
Chilton Way, Radnor, PA 19089
ISBN 0-8019-8422-X
Library of Congress Catalog Card No. 92-054897
1234567890 2109876543

Contents

Contents

SAFETY NOTICE

Proper service and repair procedures are vital to the safe, reliable operation of all motor vehicles, as well as the personal safety of those performing repairs. This manual outlines procedures for servicing and repairing vehicles using safe, effective methods. The procedures contain many NOTES, CAUTIONS, and WARNINGS which should be followed along with standard procedures to eliminate the possibility of personal injury or improper service which could damage the vehicle or compromise its safety.

It is important to note that the repair procedures and techniques, tools and parts for servicing motor vehicles, as well as the skill and experience of the individual performing the work vary widely. It is not possible to anticipate all of the conceivable ways or conditions under which vehicles may be serviced, or to provide cautions as to all of the possible hazards that may result. Standard and accepted safety precautions and equipment should be used when handling toxic or flammable fluids, and safety goggles or other protection should be used during cutting, grinding, chiseling, prying,or any other process that can cause material removal or projectiles.

Some procedures require the use of tools specially designed for a specific purpose. Before substituting another tool or procedure, you must be completely satisfied that neither your personal safety, nor the performance of the vehicle will be endangered.

Although information in this manual is based on industry sources and is complete as possible at the time of publication, the possibility exists that some car manufacturers made later changes which could not be included here. While striving for total accuracy, Chilton Book Company cannot assume responsibility for any errors, changes or omissions that may occur in the compilation of this data.

PART NUMBERS

Part numbers listed in this reference are not recommendation by Chilton for any product by brand name. They are references that can be used with interchange manuals and aftermarket supplier catalogs to locate each brand supplier's discrete part number.

SPECIAL TOOLS

Special tools are recommended by the vehicle manufacturer to perform their specific job. Use has been kept to a minimum, but where absolutely necessary, they are referred to in the text by the part number of the tool manufacturer. These tools can be purchased, under the appropriate part number, from your Honda dealer or regional distributor, or an equivalent tool can be purchased locally from a tool supplier or parts outlet. Before substituting any tool for the one recommended, read the SAFETY NOTICE at the top of this page.

ACKNOWLEDGMENTS

The Chilton Book Company expresses appreciation to the General Motors Corp. for their generous assistance.

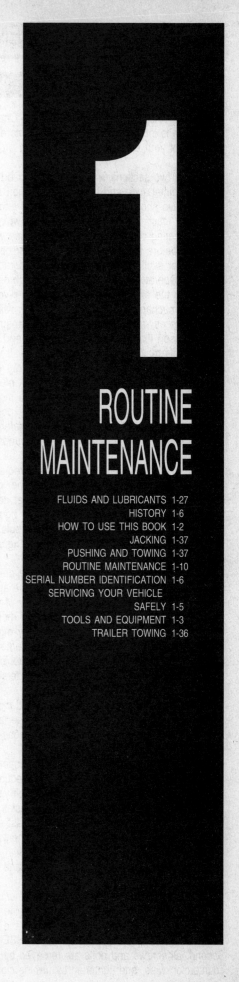

1

ROUTINE MAINTENANCE

HOW TO USE THIS BOOK

Chilton's Total Car Care manual for the Chevrolet Nova and Geo Prizm is intended to help you learn more about the inner workings of your car and save you money on its upkeep and operation.

The first two sections will be the most used since they contain maintenance and tune-up information and procedures. Studies have shown that a properly tuned and maintained car can get at least 10% better gas mileage (which translates into lower operating costs); periodic maintenance will catch minor problems before they turn into major repair bills.

The other sections deal with the more complex systems of your car. Operating systems from engine through brakes are covered to the extent that the average do-it-yourselfer becomes mechanically involved. This book will not explain such things as rebuilding the automatic transmission for the simple reason that the expertise required and the investment in special tools make this task uneconomical. It will give you the detailed instructions to help you change your own brake pads and shoes, tune the engine, replace spark plugs and filters, and do many more jobs that will save you money, give you personal satisfaction and help you avoid expensive problems.

A secondary purpose of this book is a reference guide for owners who want to understand their car and/or their mechanics better. In this case, no tools at all are required. Knowing just what a particular repair job requires in parts and labor time will allow you to evaluate whether or not you're getting a fair price quote and help decipher itemized bills from a repair shop. Simply reading through the book about a particular repair will introduce you to vocabulary and part names; this will allow you to 'speak the language' better when discussing the car and its repair.

Before attempting any repairs or service on your car, read through the entire procedure outlined in the appropriate section. This will give you the overall view of what tools and supplies will be required. There is nothing more frustrating than having to walk to the bus stop on Monday morning because you were short one gasket on Sunday afternoon. So read ahead and plan ahead. Each operation should be approached logically and all procedures thoroughly understood before attempting any work.

Some special tools that may be required can often be rented from local automotive jobbers or places specializing in renting tools and equipment. Check the yellow pages of your phone book.

All sections contain adjustments, maintenance, removal and installation procedures, and overhaul procedures. When overhaul is not considered practical, we tell you how to remove the failed part and then how to install the new or rebuilt replacement. In this way, you at least save the labor costs. Backyard overhaul of some components (such as the alternator or water pump) is just not practical, but the removal and installation procedure is often simple and well within the capabilities of the average car owner.

Two basic mechanic's rules should be mentioned here. First, whenever the LEFT side of the car or engine is referred to, it is meant to specify the DRIVER'S side of the car. Conversely, the RIGHT side of the car means the PASSENGER'S side. Second, all screws and bolts are removed by turning counterclockwise, and tightened by turning clockwise.

Safety is always the most important rule. Constantly be aware of the dangers involved in working on or around an automobile and take proper precautions to avoid the risk of personal injury or damage to the vehicle. See the paragraph in this Section, Servicing Your Vehicle Safely and the SAFETY NOTICE on the acknowledgment page before attempting any service procedures and pay attention to the instructions provided. There are 3 common mistakes in mechanical work:

1. Incorrect order of assembly, disassembly or adjustment. When taking something apart or putting it together, doing things in the wrong order usually just costs you extra time; however it CAN break something. Read the entire procedure before beginning disassembly. Do everything in the order in which the instructions say you should do it, even if you can't immediately see a reason for it.   When you're taking apart something that is very intricate (for example a carburetor), you might want to draw a picture of how it looks when assembled at one point in order to make sure you get everything back in its proper position. A sketch or diagram is also highly recommended before removing vacuum hoses or wiring connectors.   We will supply exploded views whenever possible, but sometimes the job requires more attention to detail than an illustration provides. When making adjustments (especially tune-up adjustments), do them in order. One adjustment often affects another and you cannot expect satisfactory results unless each adjustment is made only when it cannot be changed by any other.

2. Over- or under-tightening nuts and bolt. The amount of rotational force applied to a bolt is called torque and can be measured in numerical units. In this country, the most common unit of measure is the foot-pound (ft.lb.); you may also encounter inch-pounds and Newton-meters.   While it is more common for overtorquing to cause damage, undertorquing can cause a fastener to vibrate loose and cause serious damage, especially when dealing with aluminum parts. Pay attention to torque specifications and use a torque wrench in assembly. If a torque figure is not available, remember that if you are using the right tool to do the job, you will probably not have to strain yourself to get a fastener tight enough. The pitch of most threads is so slight that the tension you put on the wrench will be multiplied many times in actual force on what you are tightening.   A good example of critical torque can be seen in the case of spark plug installation, especially where you are putting the plug into an aluminum cylinder head. Too little torque can fail to crush the gasket, causing leakage of combustion gases and consequent overheating of the plug and engine parts. Too much torque can damage the threads or distort the plug, which changes the spark gap to the electrode. Since more and more manufacturers are using aluminum in their engine and chassis parts to save weight, a torque wrench should be in any serious do-it-yourselfers tool box.   There are many commercial chemical products available for ensuring that fasteners won't come loose, even if they are not torqued just right (a very common brand is Loctite®). If you're worried about getting something together tight enough to hold, but loose enough to avoid mechanical damage during assembly, one of these products might offer substantial insurance. Read the label on the package and make sure the product is

compatible with the materials, fluids, etc.. involved before choosing one.

3. Crossthreading. This occurs when a part such as a bolt is screwed into a nut or casting at the wrong angle and forced, causing the threads to become damaged. Crossthreading is more likely to occur if access if difficult. It helps to clean and lubricate fasteners and to start threading the nut or bolt with your fingers. If you encounter resistance, unscrew the part and start over again at a different angle until it can be inserted and turned several times without much effort. Keep in mind that many parts, especially spark plugs, use tapered threads so that gentle turning will automatically bring the part you're threading to the proper angle if you don't force it. Don't put a wrench on the part until it's been turned in a couple of times by hand. If you suddenly encounter resistance and the part has not seated fully, don't force it. Pull it back out and make sure it's clean and threading properly. Always take your time and be patient; once you have some experience, working on your car will become an enjoyable hobby.

TOOLS AND EQUIPMENT

▶ **See Figure 1**

Naturally, without the proper tools and equipment it is impossible to properly service you vehicle. It would be impossible to catalog each tool that you would need to perform every operation in this book. It would also be unwise for the amateur to rush out and buy any expensive set of tools on the theory that he may need one or more of them at sometime.

The best approach is to proceed slowly, gathering together a good quality set of those tools that are used most frequently. Don't be misled by the low cost of bargain tools. It is far better to spend a little more for better quality. Forged wrenches, 6 or 12 point sockets and fine tooth ratchets are by far preferable to their less expensive counterparts. As any good mechanic can tell you, there are few worse experiences than trying to work on a car with bad tools. Your monetary savings will be far outweighed by frustration and mangled knuckles.

Begin accumulating those tools that are used most frequently; those associated with routine maintenance and tune-up. In addition to the normal assortment of screwdrivers and pliers you should have the following tools for routine maintenance jobs (your Chevrolet Nova or Prizm uses mostly metric fasteners):

1. SAE/Metric wrenches, sockets and combination open-end/box-end wrenches in sizes from ⅛ in. (3mm) to ¾ in. (19mm); and a spark plug socket (¹³/₁₆ in.)If possible, buy various length socket drive extensions. One break in this department is that the metric sockets available in the U.S. will all fit the ratchet handles and extensions you may already have (¼ in., ⅜ in., and ½ in. drive). Many retail chain stores have periodic sales on sets of wrenches and sockets. Much like a set of fine dinnerware, once you have the starter set, you can add individual pieces as needed.

2. Jackstands for support. These are absolutely required for any undercar work. Make sure each stand is rated at least to the total weight of your vehicle.

3. Oil filter wrench

4. Oil filter spout for pouring oil

5. Grease gun for chassis lubrication

6. Hydrometer for checking the battery.

7. A container for draining oil and fluids.

8. Many rags for wiping up the inevitable mess.

In addition to the above items there are several others that are not absolutely necessary, but handy to have around. These include oil-dry, a transmission funnel and the usual supply of lubricants, antifreeze and washer solvent, parts cleaners and hand cleaners, although these can be purchased as needed. This is a basic list for routine maintenance, but only your personal needs and desires can accurately determine your list of necessary tools. After you've been working on your car for a while, you'll be amazed at the number of non-automotive tools living in your tool box. A small mirror can see up and under a component, wooden golf tees plug vacuum lines perfectly and a kitchen turkey baster is excellent for removing overfilled fluids.

The second list of tools is for tune-ups. While the tools involved here are slightly more sophisticated, they need not be outrageously expensive. There are several inexpensive tach/dwell meters on the market that are every bit as good for the average mechanic as a $400.00 professional model. Just be sure that it goes to at least 1,200-1,500 rpm on the tach scale and that it works on 4, 6 and 8 cylinder engines. A basic list of tune-up equipment could include:

9. Tach-dwell meter

10. Spark plug wrench

11. Timing light (a DC light that works from the car's battery is best, although an AC light that plugs into 110V house current will suffice at some sacrifice in brightness)

12. Spark plug gauge/adjusting tools

13. Set of feeler blades

In addition to these basic tools, there are several other tools and gauges you may find useful. These include:

14. A compression gauge. The screw-in type is slower to use, but eliminates the possibility of a faulty reading due to escaping pressure

15. A manifold vacuum gauge

16. A test light and/or a volt-ohm meter (VOM). The test light will show that power is (or is not) present in an electrical circuit. The VOM will do the same, but can also be used for checking how much power (voltage), continuity and resistance. An inexpensive VOM can be a valuable tool when chasing electrical gremlins.

17. An induction meter. This is used for determining whether or not there is current in a wire. These are handy for use if a wire is broken somewhere in a wiring harness.

As a final note, you will probably find a torque wrench necessary for all but the most basic work. The beam type models are perfectly adequate, although the newer click (breakaway) type are more precise, and you don't have to crane your neck to see a torque reading in awkward situations. The breakaway torque wrenches are more expensive and should be recalibrated periodically.

Special Tools

Special tools are occasionally necessary to perform a specific job or are recommended to make a job easier. Their

Fig. 1 You need only a basic assortment of hand tools for most maintenance and repair jobs

use has been kept to a minimum. When a special tool is indicated, it will be referred to by manufacturer's part number, and, where possible, an illustration of the tool will be provided so that an equivalent tool may be used. Before substituting another tool, you must be fully satisfied that neither your safety nor the performance of the car will be compromised by its use. A list of tool manufacturers and their addresses follows:

- Your local Chevrolet dealer
- General Motors Service Tool Division   Kent-Moore Tools   29784 Little Mack Rd.   Roseville, MI. 48066
- Snap-on Tools Corp.   Kenosha, Wisconsin 53141
- CP/Matco Tools   4403 Allen Rd.   Stow, Ohio 44224

SERVICING YOUR VEHICLE SAFELY

It is virtually impossible to anticipate all of the hazards involved with automotive maintenance and service, but care and common sense will prevent most accidents.

The rules of safety for mechanics range from 'don't smoke around gasoline' to 'use the proper tool for the job.' The trick to avoiding injuries is to develop safe work habits and take every possible precaution.

Do's

▶ See Figure 2

- Do keep a fire extinguisher and first aid kit within easy reach. Know how to use them before you need them.
- Do wear safety glasses or goggles when cutting, drilling, grinding or prying, even if you have 20/20 vision. If you wear glasses for the sake of vision, they should be made of hardened glass that can serve also as safety glasses, or wear safety goggles over your regular glasses.
- Do shield your eyes whenever you work around the battery. Batteries contain sulfuric acid. In case of contact with the eyes or skin, flush the area with water or a mixture of water and baking soda and get medical attention immediately.
- Do work neatly. A few minutes spent clearing a workbench or setting up a small table for tools is well worth the effort. Make yourself put tools back on the table when not in use; doing so means you won't have to grope around on the floor for that wrench you need right now. Protect your car while working on it with fender covers. If you don't wish to buy a fender cover, an old blanket makes a usable substitute.
- Do use safety stands for any undercar service. Jacks are for raising vehicles; safety stands are for making sure the vehicle stays raised until you want it to come down. Whenever the car is raised, block the wheels remaining on the ground and set the parking brake.
- Do use adequate ventilation when working with any chemicals or hazardous materials. Like carbon monoxide, the asbestos dust resulting from brake lining wear can be poisonous in sufficient quantities.
- Do disconnect the negative battery cable when working on the electrical system. The secondary ignition system can contain up to 40,000 volts.
- Do follow manufacturer's directions whenever working with potentially hazardous materials. Both brake fluid and antifreeze are poisonous if taken internally. Housepets and small animals are attracted to the odor and taste of engine coolant (antifreeze). It is a highly poisonous mixture of chemicals; special care must be taken to protect open containers and spillage. If a housepet drinks any amount of coolant, it is a 'drop everything' emergency — seek immediate veterinary care.

- Do properly maintain your tools. Loose hammerheads, mushroomed punches and chisels, frayed or poorly grounded electrical cords, excessively worn screwdrivers, spread wrenches (open end), cracked sockets, slipping ratchets, or faulty droplight sockets can cause accidents. Working on your own car is not supposed to be a painful experience.
- Do use the proper size and type of tool for the job being done.
- Do, when possible, pull on a wrench handle rather than push on it, and adjust your stance to prevent a fall.
- Do use socket, open-end or box-end wrenches where possible. They are made to a precise measurement and will fit the hardware exactly. If you must use an adjustable wrench, be sure that the jaws are tightly closed on the nut or bolt and pulled so that the face is on the side of the fixed jaw.
- Do select a wrench or socket that fits the nut or bolt. The wrench or socket should sit straight, not cocked.
- Do strike squarely with a hammer; avoid glancing blows.
- Do set the parking brake and block the drive wheels if the work requires the engine running.

Fig. 2 Always use jackstands when working under the car

Don'ts

• Don't run an engine in a garage or anywhere else without proper ventilation — EVER! Carbon monoxide is poisonous; it takes a long time to leave the human body and you can build up a deadly supply of it in your system by simply breathing in a little every day. You may not realize you are slowly poisoning yourself. Always use power vents, windows, fans or open the garage doors.

✳✳CAUTION

Carbon monoxide is odorless and colorless. Your senses cannot detect its presence. Early symptoms of monoxide poisoning include headache, irritability, improper vision (blurred or hard to focus) and/or drowsiness. When you notice any of these symptoms in yourself or your helpers, stop working immediately and get to fresh, outside air. Ventilate the work area thoroughly before returning to the car.

• Don't work around moving parts while wearing a necktie or other loose clothing. Short sleeves are much safer than long, loose sleeves; hard-toed shoes with neoprene soles protect your feet and give a better grip on slippery surface. Jewelry (watches, fancy belt buckles, beads or body adornment of any kind) is not safe working around a car. Long hair should be hidden under a hat or cap.

• Don't use pockets for toolboxes. A fall or bump can drive a screwdriver deep into your body. Even a wiping cloth hanging from the back pocket can wrap around a spinning shaft or fan.

• Don't smoke when working around gasoline, cleaning solvent or other flammable material. Assume that all liquids and sprays are flammable unless specifically labeled otherwise.

• Don't disconnect either terminal from the battery while the engine is running. Modern cars contain many solid-state components and 'black-box' computers. You will not get a second chance with solid-state failures; you will get to buy some very expensive replacement parts.

• Don't smoke when working around the battery. When the battery is being charged, it gives off explosive hydrogen gas.

• Don't use gasoline, kerosene or solvents to wash your hands; there are excellent soaps available. Gasoline contains lead, and lead can enter the body through a cut, accumulating in the body until you are very ill. Gasoline also removes all the natural oils from the skin so that bone-dry hands will suck up oil and grease.

• Don't service the air conditioning system unless you are equipped with the necessary tools and training. The refrigerant, R-12, is extremely cold when compressed, and when released into the air will instantly freeze any surface it contacts, including your eyes. Although the refrigerant is normally non-toxic, R-12 becomes a deadly poisonous gas in the presence of an open flame. One good whiff of the vapors from burning refrigerant can be fatal.

HISTORY

Built in Freemont, California, by the New United Motor Manufacturing, Inc., and bought by Chevrolet under the terms of a joint venture agreement between General Motors and Toyota Motors, the Nova borrows its dimensions and many mechanical components from the Toyota Corolla.

Toyota was responsible for designing and engineering the manufacturing layout, coordinating the acquisition and installation of equipment and the implementation of the production system. Production management is handled jointly by Toyota and Chevrolet; Chevrolet handles the distribution and marketing the products of the joint venture.

Built in two body styles only, the 4-door sedan and the 5-door hatchback originally came equipped with the 1587 cc 4A-LC engine. This engine is virtually ideal for a car of this size, offering reasonable performance in a front wheel drive package, economy and simplicity of repair. Additionally, the cars have independent suspension at all four wheels, front disc brakes, and a list of interior amenities. The Novas could be had in either the base or CL levels; the CL package included further niceties such as remote fuel door release, tilt-wheel steering column and velour interior.

For 1988, the 4-door sedan was given an optional twin-cam 16 valve motor. This 4A-GE motor is derivative of the original, but gives noticably more horsepower due to better 'breathing' of the engine and better fuel control from the new fuel injection system.

Beginning in 1989, the Nova was restyled completely and christened Prizm. The product line was brought under the Geo banner, under which Chevrolet has grouped its foreign and import products.

SERIAL NUMBER IDENTIFICATION

Vehicle

▶ See Figures 3 and 4

The Vehicle Identification Number (VIN) or serial number is a 17 digit format and is located on a stamped plate which is attached to the left side of the instrument panel. This plate is visible through the windshield.

Engine

▶ See Figures 3, 4 and 5

The eighth digit of the Vehicle Identification Number (VIN), located on a stamped plate attached to the left side of the instrument panel, identifies the engine code. Engine serial numbers are also are also stamped on the engine block and consist of an engine series identification number, followed by a seven digit production number.

VEHICLE IDENTIFICATION CHART

It is important for servicing and ordering parts to be certain of the vehicle and engine identification. The VIN (vehicle identification number) is a 17 digit number visible through the windshield on the driver's side of the dash and contains the vehicle and engine identification codes. The tenth digit indicates model year and the eighth digit indicates engine code. It can be interpreted as follows:

Engine Code

Code	Liters	Cu. In. (cc)	Cyl.	Fuel Sys.	Eng. Mfg.
4	1.6	97 (1600)	4	Carb	Toyota
5	1.6	97 (1600)	4	EFI	Toyota
6	1.6	97 (1600)	4	EFI	Toyota
8	1.8	107.5 (1800)	4	EFI	Toyota

EFI—Electronic Fuel Injection
Carb—Carburetor

Model Year

Code	Year
F	1985
G	1986
H	1987
J	1988
K	1989
L	1990
M	1991
N	1992
P	1993

ENGINE IDENTIFICATION

Year	Model	Engine Displacement Liters (cc)	Engine Series (ID/VIN)	Fuel System	No. of Cylinders	Engine Type
1985	Nova	1.6 (1600)	4	Carb	4	SOHC
1986	Nova	1.6 (1600)	4	Carb	4	SOHC
1987	Nova	1.6 (1600)	4	Carb	4	SOHC
1988	Nova	1.6 (1600)	4	Carb	4	SOHC
	Nova	1.6 (1600)	5	EFI	4	DOHC
1989	Prizm	1.6 (1600)	6	EFI	4	DOHC
1990	Prizm	1.6 (1600)	6	EFI	4	DOHC
	Prizm ②	1.6 (1600)	5	EFI	4	DOHC
1991	Prizm ①	1.6 (1600)	5	EFI	4	DOHC
	Prizm ②	1.6 (1600)	6	EFI	4	DOHC
1992	Prizm ①	1.6 (1600)	5	EFI	4	DOHC
	Prizm ②	1.6 (1600)	6	EFI	4	DOHC
1993	Prizm	1.6 (1600)	6	EFI	4	DOHC
	Prizm ③	1.8 (1800)	8	EFI	4	DOHC

Carb—Carburetor
EFI—Electronic Fuel Injection
SOHC—Single Overhead Cam
DOHC—Double Overhead Cam
① Base/LSi
② GSi
③ Optional on LSi only

Fig. 3 Vehicle Identification Number (VIN) location

Transaxle

▶ See Figures 6 and 7

The manual and automatic transaxle identification numbers are stamped into the top of the casing, on the clutch/torque converter housing end of the transaxle.

Fig. 4 Explanation of the Vehicle Identification Number (VIN)

Fig. 5 Engine identification number locations

TRANSMISSION APPLICATION CHART

Year	Model	Transmission Identification	Transmission Type
1985	Nova	MM5	5-speed manual
	Nova	(MX1) A131L	3-speed automatic
1986	Nova	MM5	5-speed manual
	Nova	(MX1) A131L	3-speed automatic
1987	Nova	MM5	5-speed manual
	Nova	(MX1) A131L	3-speed automatic
1988	Nova	MM5	5-speed manual
	Nova ①	(MX1) A131L	3-speed automatic
	Nova ②	(MS7) A240E	4-speed automatic
1989	Prizm	MM5	5-speed manual
	Prizm	(MX1) A131L	3-speed automatic
1990	Prizm	MM5	5-speed manual
	Prizm	(MX1) A131L	3-speed automatic
	Prizm (GSi)	(MS7) A240E	4-speed automatic
1991	Prizm	MM5	5-speed manual
	Prizm	(MX1) A131L	3-speed automatic
	Prizm (GSi)	(MS7) A240E	4-speed automatic
1992	Prizm	MM5	5-speed manual
	Prizm	(MX1) A131L	3-speed automatic
	Prizm (GSi)	(MS7) A240E	4-speed automatic
1993	Prizm	NA	5-speed manual
	Prizm	A131L	3-speed automatic
	Prizm (LSi)	A245E	4-speed automatic

NA—Not available
① Carbureted
② Fuel Injected

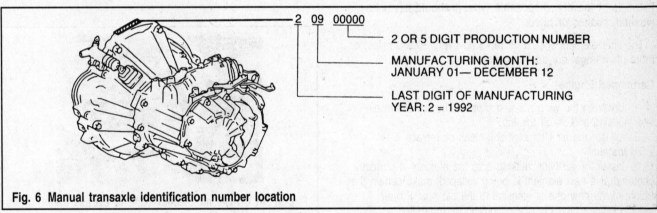

2 09 00000

2 OR 5 DIGIT PRODUCTION NUMBER

MANUFACTURING MONTH:
JANUARY 01— DECEMBER 12

LAST DIGIT OF MANUFACTURING
YEAR: 2 = 1992

Fig. 6 Manual transaxle identification number location

2 K Y 00000

4 OR 5 DIGIT PRODUCTION NUMBER

MODEL IDENTIFICATION
Y : 3-SPEED
Z : 4-SPEED

MANUFACTURING MONTH: A THRU M
(I NOT USED) A = JAN, B = FEB, C = MAR ....

LAST DIGIT OF MANUFACTURING
YEAR: 2 = 1992 OR A THRU N (I NOT USED)
M = 1991, N = 1992.......

Fig. 7 Automatic transaxle identification number

ROUTINE MAINTENANCE

❋❋CAUTION

While not every maintenance operation requires you to get under the car, many do. Even if you're not working under the car, it may be necessary to remove a wheel or gain access to a low component. Proper support of the car is critical to your safety during these operations. Refer to 'Jacking' at the end of this Section.

Air Cleaner

REMOVAL & INSTALLATION

▶ **See Figures 8, 9 and 10**

All the dust and grit present in the air is kept out of the engine by means of the air filter element. Proper maintenance is vital, as a clogged element not only restricts the air flow and thus the power, but can also cause premature engine wear.

The filter element should be cleaned or replaced every 7,500 miles, or more often if the car is driven under dry, dusty conditions. Remove the filter element and using low pressure compressed air, blow the dirt out.

➡**The filter element used on the Chevrolet Nova/Geo Prizm is of the dry, disposable type. It should never be washed, soaked or oiled.**

The filter element should be replaced every 30,000 miles, or more often under dry dusty conditions.

Carbureted Engine

1. Unfasten the wing nut and clips on the top of the air filter housing and lift off the top.
2. Lift out the air filter element; clean or replace it.
   To install:
3. Install the air filter, making sure the element is correctly centered. If a new element is being installed, make certain the height of the new one is identical to the old one. Proper sealing between the top of the housing and the filter is essential.

Fig. 8 Unhook the air cleaner case retaining clips to release the top cover of the air cleaner housing — 1992 VIN code 6 engine shown

4. Reinstall the top of the housing and attach the clips. Install the wing nut and tighten it snugly with your fingers.

Fuel Injected Engines

1. The air cleaner housing is located on the left front fender, just ahead of the shock tower. Locate and carefully remove the screws or unhook the clips, holding the top half to the bottom half of the housing.
2. Lift the top of the casing just enough to remove the old filter. Be careful of other wires and hoses in the area.
   To install:
3. Install the new filter, making sure it is properly positioned in the housing.
4. Reinstall the cover and install the retaining screws.

Fuel Filter

REMOVAL & INSTALLATION

The fuel filter is located on the firewall. The element inside the filter reduces the flow speed of the fuel causing dirt particles that are heavier than gasoline to settle to the bottom. The lighter particles are filtered by the element.

Fig. 9 Lift off the air cleaner case to access the element — 1992 VIN code 6 engine shown

Fig. 10 Lift the air cleaner element out of the bottom case — 1992 VIN code 6 engine shown

Carbureted Engine

▶ See Figure 11

Gasoline is hazardous and extremely flammable. Remove the hoses slowly and contain spillage. Observe no smoking/no open flame precautions. Have a Class B-C (dry powder) fire extinguisher within arm's reach at all times.

1. Remove the fuel filler cap.
2. Note the routing of inlet and outlet lines and the direction of flow as marked by the arrow on the filter. With a pair of pliers, shift the clips on the inlet and outlet hoses back and well away from the connections on the filter.
3. Disconnect the fuel lines, using a twisting motion to break them loose. Pull the filter out of its retaining clip. Plug the lines immediately to prevent spillage.

To install:

4. Install the filter in the holder. When reconnecting the fuel lines, make sure the hoses are connected to the correct ports on the filter. The arrow on the filter indicates direction of flow and points towards the carburetor.
5. Install the hose clips to the inside of the bulged sections of the fuel filter connections, and not right at the ends of the fuel lines. Start the engine and check for leaks.
6. Install the fuel filler cap.

Fuel Injected Engines

▶ See Figures 12 and 13

The fuel system is under pressure. Release pressure slowly and contain spillage. Observe no smoking/no open flame precautions. Have a Class B-C (dry powder) fire extinguisher within arm's reach at all times. Perform this procedure only on a cold motor.

1. Disconnect the negative battery cable.
2. Relieve the pressure in the fuel line as follows:
   a. Fit a wrench of the exact size onto the upper line connection and fit a second wrench on the flats of the filter. This counter holding arrangement will prevent the filter and lines from turning during removal.

b. Wrap the upper filter area in layers of rags to absorb spray and spillage.
   c. Slowly loosen the bolt holding the line to the filter. When the pressure is equalized, remove the bolt and the line. Plug the line immediately.
3. Again using two wrenches, disconnect the lower line to the filter. Be prepared to deal with fuel spillage. Be very careful not to crimp or bend the fuel line. Plug the line immediately.
4. Remove the filter from its holder.

To install:

5. Install a new filter. Apply a thin coat of oil to the threads and connect the bottom fuel line to the filter. Always begin the threads by hand, then tighten to 22 ft.lbs.
6. Install the upper line with NEW gaskets. Make sure the line is held within the forked bracket on the filter and begin the bolt by hand to insure proper threading.
7. Tighten the bolt to 22 ft.lbs. Reconnect the negative battery cable.
8. Start the engine and check for leaks. (The engine may require a longer period of cranking until it starts due to loss of fuel pressure.)

PCV Valve

The Positive Crankcase Ventilation (PCV) valve regulates crankcase (oil pan) ventilation during the various engine operating conditions. At high vacuum (idle speed and partial load range) it will open slightly and at low vacuum (full throttle) it will open fully. This causes vapor to be removed from the crankcase by the engine vacuum and then sucked into the combustion chamber where it is burned.

REMOVAL & INSTALLATION

▶ See Figures 14, 15, 16, 17 and 18

Carbureted Engines

1. Check the ventilation hoses for leaks or clogging. Clean or replace as necessary.
2. Locate the PCV valve in the valve cover. Remove the valve.

1. Fuel filter
2. Bracket
3. Direction of flow

Fig. 11 Carbureted engine fuel filter and mounting bracket

New Gasket

Fig. 12 Replacing the fuel filter for the fuel injection system — 1988

1. Union bolt
2. Gasket
3. Fuel line
4. Gasket
5. Filter
6. Gasket
7. Fuel line
8. Gasket
9. Union bolt

Fig. 13 Replacing the fuel filter for the fuel injection system — 1989-92

← —BLOW-BY GAS

← - - - —FRESH AIR

1. Air cleaner
2. Carburator
3. Positive crankcase ventilation valve

Fig. 14 Positive crankcase ventilation system — carbureted engines

3. Blow into the engine end of the valve. There should be a free passage of air through the valve.

✳✳CAUTION

Do not suck air through the PCV valve. Petroleum substances inside the valve may be harmful to your health.

4. Blow through the intake manifold side of the valve. There should be little or no passage of air through the valve.
5. If the PCV valve failed either of the preceding two checks, it will require replacement.
To install:
6. Install the valve firmly into the valve cover. Connect the hose(s) and make sure there are no leaks around the hose connections.

Fuel Injected Engines

1. The PCV is easily checked with the engine running at normal idle speed (warmed up).
2. Remove the PCV valve from the valve cover or intake manifold, but leave it connected to its hose.
3. Place your thumb over the end of the valve to check for vacuum. If there is no vacuum, check for plugged hoses or ports. If these are open, the valve is faulty.
4. With the engine off, remove the PCV valve completely. Shake it end to end, listening for the rattle of the needle inside

TO INTAKE MANIFOLD SIDE

Fig. 15 Air should pass through the PCV valve when blowing into the crankcase side — carbureted engines

INTAKE MANIFOLD SIDE

Fig. 16 Air should not pass through the PCV valve when blowing through the intake side

1. PCV valve
2. PCV hose

BLOW-BY GAS ⟶
FRESH AIR - - - ⟶

Fig. 17 Positive crankcase ventilation system — fuel injected engines

Fig. 18 Removing the PCV valve — 1992 VIN code 6 engine shown

the valve. If no rattle is heard, the needle is jammed (probably with oil sludge) and the valve should be replaced.

➡ **An engine which is operated without crankcase ventilation can be damaged very quickly. It is important to check and change the PCV valve at regular maintenance intervals.**

Evaporative Canister

OPERATION

The basic evaporative emission control system used on all vehicles is the charcoal canister storage method. This method transfers fuel vapor from the fuel tank to an activated carbon (charcoal) storage device (canister) to hold the vapors when the vehicle is not operating. When the engine is running, the fuel vapor is purged from the carbon element by intake air flow and consumed in the normal combustion process.

TESTING

Check the evaporation control system every 15,000 miles. Check the fuel and vapor lines and the vacuum hoses for proper connections and correct routing, as well as condition. Replace clogged, damaged or deteriorated parts as necessary, using only hoses marked fuel resistant or 'EVAP'. If the charcoal canister is clogged, it may be cleaned using low pressure compressed air. The entire canister should be replaced every 5 years/60,000 miles.

REMOVAL & INSTALLATION

1985-88

VIN CODE 4 ENGINE (CARBURETED)

▶ **See Figures 19 and 20**

1. Diagram or label the hoses running to the canister. Incorrect reassembly will affect driveability. Remove the hoses from the canister.
2. Remove the charcoal canister from the vehicle.
3. Visually check the charcoal canister for cracks or damage.
4. Check for a clogged filter and stuck check valve. Using low pressure compressed air, blow into the tank pipe and check that the air flows freely and without resistance from the other pipes. If the airflow is not free and unrestricted, replace the canister.
5. Clean the filter in the canister by blowing 43 psi of compressed air into the pipe to the outer vent control valve (see illustration) while holding the other upper canister pipes closed.

➡ **Do not attempt to wash or flush the charcoal canister. Also be sure that no activated carbon comes out of the canister.**

6. Reinstall the canister on its mounts and connect the hoses to their proper ports.

1. Tank pipe
2. Purge pipe

Fig. 19 Checking the charcoal canister — 1985-88 VIN code 4 carbureted engine

Fig. 20 Cleaning the charcoal canister — 1985-88 VIN code 4 carbureted engine

1989-90

VIN CODE 6 ENGINE

1. Remove the air cleaner assembly.
2. Label and disconnect the 2 vacuum hoses from the canister.
3. Disconnect the bracket holding the canister to the firewall and remove the canister.

To install:

4. Install the canister to the fenderwell bracket.
5. Install the 2 vacuum hoses.
6. Install the air cleaner.

1990-92

VIN CODE 5 ENGINE

1. Remove the air cleaner duct assembly as follows:
   a. Loosen the 2 clamps on the duct.
   b. Disconnect the 2 vacuum hoses from the air duct assembly.
   c. Disconnect the duct from the throttle body and MAP sensor.
2. Remove the air cleaner/mass air flow assembly as follows:
   a. Unclamp the 4 clamps.
   b. Remove the 1 bolt from the idle up VSV.
   c. Disconnect the electrical connector from the mass air flow meter.
   d. Remove the air cleaner/mass air flow assembly.
3. Label and disconnect the 2 vacuum hoses from the canister.
4. Remove the clamp holding the canister and remove the canister from the vehicle.

To install:

5. Install the canister to the bracket.
6. Install the 2 vacuum hoses.
7. Install the air cleaner.

VIN CODE 6 ENGINE

1. Remove the air cleaner assembly.
2. Label and disconnect the 2 vacuum hoses from the canister.
3. Disconnect the bracket holding the canister to the firewall and remove the canister.

To install:

4. Install the canister to the fenderwell bracket.
5. Install the 2 vacuum hoses.

6. Install the air cleaner.

Valve Clearance Adjustment

Every 60,000 miles or 72 months the valve clearance should be adjusted. Please refer to Section 2 for the procedure.

Timing Belt Replacement

Every 60,000 miles the timing belt should be replaced. Failure to replace the timing belt could result in serious engine damage. Please refer to Section 3 for the procedure.

Battery

All Novas and Prizms are equipped with maintenance free batteries, which do not require normal attention as far as fluid level checks are concerned. However, the terminals require periodic cleaning, which should be performed at least once a year.

The sealed top battery cannot be checked for charge in the normal manner, since there is no provision for access to the electrolyte.

FLUID LEVEL

▶ See Figure 21

1. If the indicator eye on top of the battery is dark, the battery has enough fluid. If the eye is light, the electrolyte level is too low and the battery must be replaced.
2. If the green dot appears in the middle of the eye, the battery is sufficiently charged. If no green dot is visible, charge the battery at a low rate. The green dot will appear when the battery is at 65% of full charge; in some cases the battery may need charging even if the green dot is visible.

➡**Do not charge the Nova battery for more than 50 amp/hours or the Prizm battery for more than 75 amp/hours. (Number of charging amps x number of hours on charger = amp/hours. Example: Charger set for 10 amp rate of charge — do not charge longer than 5 hours. 10 x 5 = 50.)   If the green dot appears, or if the electrolyte squirts out of the vent hole stop the charge.   It may be necessary to tip the battery from side to side to get the green dot to appear after charging.**

Fig. 21 Examples of battery 'eye' on maintenance free batteries. A flashlight may be needed to determine the color in low light conditions

CABLES AND CLAMPS

▶ **See Figures 22, 23 and 24**

At least twice a year, clean the side terminals and cable ends. Loosen the clamp bolts (you may have to brush off any corrosion with baking soda and water solution if they are really messy) and remove the cables, negative cable first.

There is a special cleaning tool available for cleaning side terminal batteries. When using this tool, make sure you get the terminal and the cable ends clean and shiny. Any oxidation, corrosion or foreign material will prevent a sound electrical connection and inhibit either starting or charging.

Check the battery tray and wash it off with warm soapy water, rinse and dry. Any rust should be sanded away, and the tray given at least two coats of a quality anti-rust paint.

Drive Belts

INSPECTION

The drive belts are used to transfer power from the crankshaft at the bottom of the engine to another component which needs to be turned. The belts are generally made of rubber and fabric layers and are subject to deterioration from wear, heat, and chemicals.

To inspect the belts, make sure the engine is off and the key removed from the ignition. (This eliminates any chance of surprises while you've got your hands on potentially moving parts). Select a long section of a belt and examine it closely.

Fig. 23 Clean the battery posts with a wire brush, or the special tool shown

Fig. 24 Clean the inside of the clamps with a wire brush, or the special tool

Fig. 22 Special pullers are available to remove cable clamps

There should be no signs of fraying, cracking or chunking on either the top surface or the working faces.

Continue checking all the belts in the same fashion. If you're checking the longest sections, you're seeing a representative section of the belt. If you wish, start the engine and shut it off again; the belts will come to rest in another position and other sections may be viewed.

Considering the speed at which the belts turn, and the importance of what they drive (alternator, water pump, power steering, etc..), any flaw found in a belt should be viewed as a potential for failure. Replace the belt before it chooses to break on a cold, rainy night.

CHECKING TENSION AND ADJUSTMENT

▶ **See Figures 25, 26, 27, 28 and 29**

The belt tension on most driven components is adjusted by moving the component (alternator, power steering pump, etc..) within the range of a slotted bracket. Some late model air conditioner compressor drive belts are adjusted by varying the number of discs between the halves of the crankshaft pulley.

Check the belt tension every 6 months or 10,000 miles. Push in on the drive belt about midway between the crankshaft pulley and the driven component. If the belt deflects more than 9/16 inch or less than 3/8 inch, adjustment is required.

1. Loosen the adjustment nut and bolt in the slotted bracket. Slightly loosen the pivot bolt(s).

2. Pull (don't pry) the component outward (away from the engine) to increase tension. Push inward to reduce tension. Tighten the adjusting nut and bolt and the pivot bolt.

3. Components such as the power steering pump and some air conditioner compressors, may be mounted with a double slotted adjusting bracket using a threaded bolt or bolts and locknuts to adjust and maintain tension. Loosen the locknut(s) and slightly loosen the bolt(s) in the slotted groove(s), turn the threaded adjustment bolt(s) in or out to gain correct tension. Tighten locknuts and slotted bracket bolts.

4. Recheck the drive belt tension, readjust if necessary.

REPLACEMENT

If a belt must be replaced, the driven unit must be loosened and moved to its extreme loosest position, generally by moving it toward the center of the engine. After removing the old belt, check the pulleys for dirt or built-up material which could affect belt contact. Carefully install the new belt, remembering that it is new and unused — it may appear to be just a little too small to fit over the pulley flanges. Fit the belt over the largest pulley (usually the crankshaft pulley at the bottom center of the engine) first, then work on the smaller one(s). Gentle pressure in the direction of rotation is helpful. Some belts run around a third or idler pulley, which acts as an additional pivot in the belt's path. It may be possible to loosen the idler pulley as well as the main component, making your job much easier. Depending on which belt(s) you are changing, it may be necessary to loosen or remove other interfering belts to get at the one(s) you want.

When buying replacement belts, remember that the fit is critical according to the length of the belt ('diameter'), the width of the belt, the depth of the belt and the angle or profile of the V shape. The belt shape should exactly match the shape of the pulley; belts that are not an exact match can cause noise, slippage and premature failure.

After the new belt is installed, draw tension on it by moving the driven unit away from the motor and tighten its mounting bolts. This is sometimes a three or four-handed job; you may find an assistant helpful. Make sure that all the bolts you loosened get retightened and that any other loosened belts also have the correct tension. A new belt can be expected to stretch a bit after installation so be prepared to re-adjust your new belt, if needed, within the first hundred miles of use.

Fig. 26 Loosen the pivot bolt

Fig. 25 Drive belt tension checking locations

Fig. 27 Push the component inwards

Fig. 28 Slip the old belt off and the new one on

Fig. 29 Pull outwards to tension the belt

Hoses

▶ **See Figure 30**

Replacing hoses requires draining the cooling system. Have a large drain pan or bucket available along with a generous supply of rags. Be prepared to deal with fluid spills immediately. See the previous list of Do's and Don'ts for other hints.

1. Drain the cooling system. This is always done with the engine cold. Attempting to drain hot coolant is very foolish; you can be badly scalded.

   a. Remove the radiator cap.

   b. Position the drain pan under the drain cock on the bottom of the radiator. Additionally, the Nova/Prizm engines have a drain cock on the side of the engine block, near the oil filter. This may be opened to aid in draining the cooling system. If for some reason the radiator drain cock can't be used, you can loosen and remove the lower radiator hose at its joint to the radiator.

   c. If the lower hose is to be used as the drain, loosen the clamp on the hose and slide it back so it's out of the way. Gently break the grip of the hose on its fitting by twisting or prying with a suitable tool. Do not exert too much force or you will damage the radiator fitting. As the hose loosens, you can expect a gush of fluid to come out — be ready.

   d. Remove the hose end from the radiator and direct the hose into the drain pan. You now have fluid running from both the hose and the radiator.

   e. When the system stops draining, proceed with replacement of the damaged hose.

Housepets and small animals are attracted to the odor and taste of engine coolant (antifreeze). It is a highly poisonous mixture of chemicals; special care must be taken to protect open containers and spillage.

2. Loosen the hose clamps on the damaged hose with a screwdriver and slide the clamps either off the hose altogether or in toward center.

3. Break the grip of the hose at both ends by prying it free with a suitable tool or by twisting it with your hand.

4. Remove the hose.

5. Install a new hose. A small amount of soapy water on the inside of the hose end will ease installation.

➡**Radiator hoses should be routed with no kinks and, when installed, should be in the same position as the original. If other than specified hose is used, make sure it does not rub against either the engine or the frame while the engine is running, as this may wear a hole in the hose. Contact points may be insulated with a piece of sponge or foam; plastic wire ties are particularly handy for this job.**

6. Slide the hose clamps back into position and retighten. When tightening the clamps, tighten them enough to seal in the coolant but not so much that the clamp cuts into the hose or causes it internal damage. If a clamp shows signs of any damage (bent, too loose, hard to tighten, etc.) now is the time

ENGINE DRAIN PETCOCK

RADIATOR DRAIN PETCOCK

Fig. 30 Location of draincocks for the cooling system. Never drain hot coolant — wait for the engine to cool

to replace it. A good rule of thumb is that a new hose is always worth new clamps.

➡**Make sure that the hose clamps are beyond the bead and placed in the center of the clamping surface before tightening them.**

7. Either reinstall the lower radiator hose and secure its clamp or close the drain cocks on the side of the engine block and bottom of the radiator.

8. Fill the system with coolant. Chevrolet strongly recommends the coolant mixture be a 50/50 mix of antifreeze and water. This mixture gives best combination of anti-freeze and anti-boil characteristics for year-round driving.

9. Replace and tighten the radiator cap. Start the engine and check visually for leaks. Allow the engine to warm up fully and continue to check your work for signs of leakage. A very small leak may not be noticed until the system develops internal pressure.

➡**Leaks at hose ends are generally clamp related and can be cured by snugging the clamp. Larger leaks may require removing the hose again — to do this you MUST WAIT UNTIL THE ENGINE HAS COOLED DOWN, GENERALLY A PERIOD OF HOURS. NEVER UNCAP A HOT RADIATOR. After all leaks are cured, check the coolant level in the radiator (with the engine cold) and top up as necessary.**

Air Conditioning

SAFETY PRECAUTIONS

R-12 refrigerant is a chlorofluorocarbon which, when released into the atmosphere, contributes to the depletion of the ozone layer in the upper atmosphere. Ozone filters out harmful radiation from the sun.

Consult the laws in your area before servicing the air conditioning system in your vehicle. In some states, it is illegal to perform repairs involving refrigerant unless the work is done by a certified technician.

There are two particular hazards associated with air conditioning systems and they both relate to refrigerant gas.

The refrigerant (generic designation: R-12, trade name: Freon, a registered trademark of the DuPont Co.) is an extremely cold substance. When exposed to air, it will instantly freeze any surface it comes in contact with, including your eyes.

The other hazard relates to fire. Although normally non-toxic, refrigerant gas becomes highly poisonous in the presence of an open flame. One good whiff of the vapor formed by refrigerant can be fatal. Keep all forms of fire (including cigarettes) well clear of the air conditioning system.

Further, since it has been established that the chemicals in R-12 (dichlorodifluoromethane) contribute to the damage occurring in the upper atmosphere, sophisticated recovery equipment will be necessary to prevent the release of this gas when working on an air conditioning system. DO NOT, under any circumstances, attempt to loosen or tighten any fittings or perform any work other than that outlined here.

SYSTEM CHECKS

A lot of A/C problems can be avoided by simply running the air conditioner at least once a week, regardless of the season. simply let the system run for at least 5 minutes a week (even in the winter), and you'll keep the internal parts lubricated as well as preventing the hoses from hardening.

Checking For Oil Leaks

Refrigerant leaks show up only as oily areas on the various components because the compressor oil is transported around the entire system along with the refrigerant. Look for oily spots on all the hoses and lines, and especially on the hose and tube connections. If there are oily deposits, the system may have a leak, and you should have it checked by a qualified repairman.

A small area of oil on the front of the compressor is normal and no cause for alarm.

Check the Compressor Belt

The compressor drive belt should be checked frequently for tension and condition. Refer to 'Drive Belts' in this section.

Keep the Condenser Clear

The condenser is mounted in front of the radiator. It serves to remove heat from the air conditioning system and cool the refrigerant. Proper air flow through the condenser is critical to the operation of the system.

Periodically inspect the front of the condenser for bent fins or foreign material (dirt, bugs, leaves, etc..). If any cooling fins are bent, straighten them carefully with needle nose pliers. You can remove any debris with a stiff bristle brush or hose.

Refrigerant Level Check
▶ **See Figures 31 and 32**

The first order of business when checking the refrigerant is to find the sight glass. It is located in the head of the receiver/drier. On Novas, it's located to the left of the radiator, just behind the left headlights. On the Prizm, it's still behind the headlight, but in front of the condenser. Once you've found it, wipe it clean and proceed as follows:

1. With the engine and the air conditioning system running, look for the flow of refrigerant through the sight glass. If the air conditioner is working properly, you'll be able to see a continuous flow of clear refrigerant through the sight glass, with perhaps an occasional bubble at very high temperatures.

2. Cycle the air conditioner on and off to make sure what you are seeing is refrigerant. Since the refrigerant is clear, it is possible to mistake a completely discharged system for one that is fully charged. Turn the system off and watch the sight glass. If there is refrigerant in the system, you'll see bubbles during the off cycle. If you observe no bubbles when the system is running and the air flow from the unit in the car is delivering cold air, everything is OK.

3. If you observe bubbles in the sight glass while the system is operating, the system is low on refrigerant. Have it checked by a professional.

4. Oil streaks in the sight glass are an indication of trouble. Most of the time, if you see oil in the sight glass, it will appear

Fig. 31 Location of receiver-drier and sight glass on 1989-92 Prizm

Fig. 32 Oil streaks (A), constant bubbles (B) or foam (C) indicate there is not enough refrigerant in the system. Occasional bubbles during initial operation is normal. A clear sight glass indicates a proper charge of refrigerant or no refrigerant at all, which can be determined by the presence of cold air at the outlets in the car. If the glass is clouded with a milky white substance, have the receiver/drier checked professionally

as series of streaks, although occasionally it may be a solid stream of oil. In either case, it means that part of the charge has been lost. This is almost always accompanied by a reduction in cold air output within the car.

GAUGE SETS

▶ See Figure 33

Before attempting any charge-related work, you will need a set of A/C gauges. These are generally available from good parts suppliers and automotive tool suppliers. Generally described, this tool is a set of two gauges and three hoses. By connecting the proper hoses to the car's system, the gauges

can be used to 'see' the air conditioning system at work. The gauge set is also used to discharge and recharge the system.

Additionally, if a component must be removed from the system, a vacuum pump will be needed to evacuate (draw vacuum) within the system to eliminate any moisture which has entered during repairs. These pumps can be purchased outright; many find it easier to rent one from a supplier on an as-needed basis.

Refrigerant will be needed; make sure you purchase enough meet the capacity of the system. Since the refrigerant is measured by weight (generally in ounces), you'll need a small scale to weigh the refrigerant container as the system is recharged.

DISCHARGING THE SYSTEM

▶ See Figures 34, 35 and 36

❄❄CAUTION

Wear protective goggles and gloves before proceeding with repairs.

Connecting and disconnecting the gauges should always be done with the engine off to prevent injury from moving parts. To hook up the gauges, first make sure that the valves on the gauges are turned to the closed (off) position. The hose from the low-pressure gauge will attach to the low pressure side (suction) of the A/C system.

The Prizm has this connection on the compressor; it's labeled 'S'. The fuel-injected Nova's low pressure connector is

Fig. 33 A typical set of manifold gauges for the air conditioning system

found in the piping on the firewall — it's the line that does NOT connect to the receiver-drier. Carbureted Novas have the low pressure connection in a vertical section of the A/C tubing on the right side of the engine near the fender; it's the line that couples to another short piece running to the compressor.

Discharging and Recovering Refrigerant

When any refrigeration system component except the pressure cycling switch is replaced, all of the Refrigerant-12 in the refrigeration system must be completely discharged and recovered by using an approved air conditioning refrigerant recovery system. The system must always be discharged at the low-pressure side service fitting to control the loss of refrigerant oil. Oil loss will occur if the high-pressure side service fitting is used.

1. With the ignition switch in the **OFF** position, remove the protective cap from the low-pressure side service fitting.

2. The refrigerant recovery station should be connected, following the equipment manufacturer's instructions.

3. With the low-pressure side of the refrigeration system fully discharged, the high-pressure side service fitting should be checked for any remaining pressure.

4. If refrigerant under pressure remains in the high-pressure side of the system, an attempt should be made to discharge the high-pressure side of the system by using the same procedure as used for the low-pressure side service fitting. Noticeable residual pressure in the system indicates a restriction in the high-pressure side of the system. The cause for this pressure must be diagnosed and corrected before evacuating and charging the system.

5. When the system is completely discharged and the refrigerant stored in the recovery tank, the technician should measure, record the amount and discard the refrigerant oil that was collected in the recovery system accumulator.

6. If the measured quantity of oil is 0.5 fl. oz. (15 ml) or more, the same amount of new 525 viscosity refrigerant oil must be added to the system, plus any quantity in the removed parts. This must be done before evacuating the system and charging it with Refrigerant-12. For the specific quantity of oil normally retained in the removed part, refer to 'Refrigerant Oil Distribution' later in this section.

Adding Oil

Refrigerant oil must be added after the refrigeration system has been discharged and before it is evacuated. To add oil, the refrigeration system suction hose should be disconnected at the receiver/dryer outlet pipe connection. The correct quantity should be poured into the hose. The hose should then be connected to the pipe. For specific quantity instructions, refer to 'Refrigerant Oil Distribution' later in this section.

Refrigerant Oil Distribution

The refrigeration system requires a total of 6.0 fl.oz. (180 ml) of 525 viscosity refrigerant oil. New oil quantities must be added to the system during component replacement.

With no signs of excessive oil leakage, oil should be added in the following prescribed manner:

1. If the compressor is removed, drain the oil from both the defective compressor and the new replacement compressor. Measure the amount removed for the defective compressor. If the measure amount is less than 1.0 fl.oz. (30 ml), add 2.0

fl.oz. (60 ml) to the new replacement compressor. If more than 1.0 fl.oz. (30 ml), is drained from the defective compressor, add the same amount to the new compressor.

2. If the evaporator is removed, 3.0 fl.oz. (90 ml) of new oil must be added to the system.

3. If the condenser is removed, drain and measure the oil in it. If more than 0.5 fl.oz. (15 ml) is collected, add the same amount to the refrigeration system.

4. If the receiver/drier is removed, 3.5 fl.oz. (100 ml) of oil must be added to replace the oil trapped in the desiccant of the original receiver/drier.

With signs of excessive oil leakage, only the receiver/drier should be removed. The oil in the receiver/drier should be drained, measured and recorded. It is not necessary to remove and drain the compressor because it retains only a minimum quantity of oil. With signs of excessive oil leakage, oil should be added in the following prescribed manner:

5. If less than 3.0 fl.oz. (90 ml) of oil was retained in the receiver/drier, 3.0 fl.oz. (90 ml) of new oil should be added to the system.

6. If more than 3.0 fl.oz. (90 ml) of oil was retained, an equal amount of new oil should be added.

Refrigerant Loss from an Abrupt Leak

If the refrigerant charge is abruptly lost due to a large refrigerant leak, approximately 3.0 fl.oz. (90 ml) of refrigerant oil will be carried out of the system suspended in the refrigerant. Any failure that causes an abrupt refrigerant discharge will result in this oil loss. Failures that allow the refrigerant to seep or bleed off over time do not cause this oil loss.

Upon replacement of a component which caused a large refrigerant leak, add 3.0 fl.oz. (90 ml) of new 525 viscosity refrigerant oil plus the required amount of oil for the particular component.

Add the oil directly to the replaced component if possible. If the oil cannot easily be added to the replaced part, add the oil to the receiver/drier.

EVACUATING AND CHARGING THE REFRIGERATION SYSTEM

The charging instructions provided with the charging station should be adhered to with the following exceptions:

1. The high-pressure line should not be connected to the refrigeration system.

2. The high-pressure valve on the charging station should remain closed at all times.

3. The entire evacuating and charging procedure should be done through the low-pressure side service fitting.

Following these procedures will prevent high-pressure side system pressure from getting to the charging station. This fact can become crucial if an error is made in the valve sequence during the compressor operation to pull in the Refrigerant-12.

Refrigerant Drum Method

The Refrigerant-12 drum should be placed on a scale and the total weight noted before charging. During charging, the scale should be monitored to determine the amount of refrigerant used.

The low-pressure gage of the J 23575-01 Manifold Gage Set should be connected at the low-pressure side service fitting. The high-pressure gage should be connected to the J 34119 Vacuum Pump. The J 23575-01 Manifold Gage Set center gage hose should be connected to the Refrigerant-12 drum. A J 23390 Control Valve must be connected to the 5.4 kg (12 lb.) drum to control the flow of refrigerant. The 13.6 kg (30lb.) drum incorporates its own control valve.

To begin evacuating the refrigeration system, the high-pressure side and low-pressure side gage valves should be opened slowly and the vacuum pump should be started. The system should be pumped until the low-pressure side gage reaches a vacuum reading of 94.6-97.9 kPa (28-29 in. Hg) at sea level. For each 305m (1,000 ft.) above sea level, this specification should be lowered by 3.38 kPa (1.0 inch). At 1,525m (5,000 ft.) elevation, a vacuum reading of only 77.7-81.1 kPa (23-24 in. Hg) is required.

If the specified vacuum cannot be reached, the vacuum control valve should be closed and the pump should be shut off. Then the pump and connection should be checked for a leak.

When the low-pressure side gage reaches the specified vacuum reading, the system is fully evacuated. The high-pressure side gage valve should be closed and the vacuum pump should be shut off.

The low-pressure side gage should be watched to be sure the vacuum holds for five minutes. If vacuum is held for five minutes, the vacuum hose should be disconnected at the high-pressure side gage and charging should begin. If vacuum does not hold for five minutes, the system should be charged with 0.23 kg (0.5 lb.) of Refrigerant-12 and a check made for refrigerant leaks. The system should be discharged and the refrigerant recovered before repairing the leak(s). Then the evacuation procedure should be repeated.

Charging

To prepare for charging the refrigeration system, the engine should be started and run until it reaches operating temperature. The air conditioning mode lever should be in the OFF position.

With the engine at operating temperature and the Refrigerant-12 drum inverted, the refrigerant source valve should be opened to allow 0.23 kg (0.5 lb.) of liquid Refrigerant-12 to flow into the system through the low-pressure side service fitting.

As soon as this quantity of refrigerant enters the refrigeration system, the compressor should be engaged by pressing the A/C switch and moving the blower speed switch to any position by 'OFF'.' This will draw in the remainder of the total refrigerant charge. The total charge is 1.59 kg (3.50 lbs.).

Charging speed can be increased by placing a large volume fan in front of the vehicle to pass more air over the condenser. If condenser temperature is maintained below the temperature of the charging drum, Refrigerant-12 will enter the system more rapidly.

When the full charge is added, the Refrigerant-12 source valve should be turned off and the engine allowed to run for 30 seconds to clear the lines and gages.

✳✳CAUTION

A gage line should never be removed from its adapter when the line is connected to the refrigeration system. The line adapter from the service fitting always should be removed to disconnect a line. The charging hose at the gage set should not be removed while the hose is attached to the low-pressure side service fitting. This may result in complete discharge of the system and may cause personal injury from escaping Refrigerant-12.

With the engine running, the low-pressure side charging hose adapter should be removed from the low-pressure side service fitting. It must be unscrewed rapidly to avoid releasing excessive refrigerant from the system.

After replacing the protective cap on the low-pressure side service fitting and turning OFF the engine, a leak test should be performed using the J 29547 Electronic Leak Detector. With the refrigeration system fully charged and leak-tested, the air conditioning system should be tested to ensure proper performance. Refer to 'Refrigeration System Checks' earlier in this section.

Windshield Wipers

Intense heat and ultra-violet rays from the sun, snow, ice and frost, road oils, acid rain, and industrial pollution all combine quickly to deteriorate the rubber wiper refills. One

REAR VIEW

1. Accumulator pressurizing valve
2. Oil drain valve
3. Red hose (vapor)
4. Blue hose (liquid)
5. Tank
6. Oil drain
7. Oil drain measured container

FRONT CUT-AWAY VIEW

8. Control panel
9. Accumulator separator
10. Compressor
11. Filter drier
12. Refrigerant pump
13. Yellow hose (air purge)

Fig. 34 Air conditioning refrigerant recovery/recycling station J38100-B or C, component locations

1. Refrigerant recovery
   and recycling station
2. Station inlet
3. Yellow hose
4. Manifold gauge set

Fig. 35 Air conditioning refrigerant recovery/recycling station hookup

pass on a frosty windshield can reduce a new set of refills to an unusable condition. The refills should be replaced about twice a year or whenever they begin to streak or chatter on wet glass.

Blade life can be prolonged by frequent cleanings of the glass with a rag and a commercial glass cleaner. The use of an ammonia based cleaner will ease the removal of built-up road oils and grease from the glass. Ammonia based cleaners are harmful to painted surfaces. Be careful when applying them and don't fill the washer jug with an ammonia based solvent; when used it will run onto the painted bodywork.

WINDSHIELD WASHER ADJUSTMENT

The washer spray direction can be adjusted by inserting a pin into the nozzle and turning it to the desired position.

WIPER BLADE REPLACEMENT

▶ **See Figure 37**

Normally, if the wipers are not cleaning the windshield properly, only the refill has to be replaced. The blade and arm usually require replacement only in the event of damage. It is not necessary (except on Tridon refills) to remove the arm or the blade to replace the refill (rubber part), though you may have to position the arm higher on the glass. You can do this by turning the ignition switch on and operating the wiper. When they are positioned where they are accessible, turn the ignition switch off.

There are several types of refills and your vehicle could have any kind, since aftermarket blades and arms may not use exactly the same type refill as the original equipment.

1. Lift the wiper arm off the glass.
2. Depress the release lever on the center bridge and remove the blade from the arm.
3. Lift the tab and pinch the end bridge to release it from the center bridge.
4. Slide the end bridge from the wiper blade and the wiper blade from the opposite end bridge.
5. Install a new element and be sure the tab on the end bridge is down to lock the element in place. Check each release point for positive engagement.

Most Trico styles use a release button that is pushed down to allow the refill to slide out of the release jaws. The new refill slides in and locks in place. Some Trico refills are removed by locating where the metal backing strip or the refill is wider. Insert a small screwdriver blade between the frame and the metal backing strip. Press down to release the refill from the retaining tab.

The Anco style is unlocked at one end by squeezing two metal tabs, and the refill is slid out of the frame jaws. When the new refill is installed, the tabs will click into place, locking the refill.

The polycarbonate type is held in place by a locking lever that is pushed downward out of the groove in the arm to free the refill. When the new refill is installed, it will lock in place automatically.

The Tridon refill has a plastic backing strip with a notch about an inch from the end. Hold the blade (frame) on a hard surface so that frame is tightly bowed. Grip the tip of the backing strip and pull up while twisting counterclockwise. The backing strip will snap out of the retaining tab. Do this for the remaining tabs until the refill is free of the arm. The length of these refills is molded into the end and they should be replaced with identical types.

No matter which type of refill you use, be sure that all of the frame claws engage the refill. Before operating the wipers, be sure that no part of the metal frame is contacting the windshield.

Tires and Wheels

▶ **See Figures 38, 39, 40, 41, 42, 43, 44 and 45**

Common sense and good driving habits will afford maximum tire life. Fast starts, sudden stops and hard cornering are hard on tires and will shorten their useful life span. If you start at normal speeds, allow yourself sufficient time to stop, and take corners at a reasonable speed, the life of your tires will increase greatly. Also make sure that you don't overload your vehicle or run with incorrect pressure in the tires. Both of these practices increase tread wear.

Inspect your tires frequently. Be especially careful to watch for bubbles in the tread or side wall, deep cuts, or underinflation. Remove any tires with bubbles. If the cuts are so deep that they penetrate to the cords, discard the tire. Any cut in the sidewall of a radial tire renders it unsafe. Also look for uneven tread wear patterns that indicate that the front end is out of alignment or that the tires are out of balance.

A. Compressor delivery
   hose
B. Suction hose
C. Evacuating
D. Charging
1. Manifold gauge set
2. Low pressure gauge
3. High pressure gauge

4. Vacuum pump
5. Refrigerant drum
6. Condenser
7. Compressor
8. Evaporator
9. Receiver/drier
10. Expansion valve
11. Service valve

Fig. 36 Charging the air conditioning system

TIRE ROTATION

So that the tires wear more uniformly, it is recommended that the tires be rotated every 7,500 miles. This can only be done when all four tires are of the same size and load rating capacity. Any abnormal wear should be investigated and the cause corrected.

Radial tires may be cross-switched; newer production methods have eliminated the need to keep them on one side of the car. Studded snow tires will lose their studs if their direction of rotation is reversed. Mark the wheel position or direction of rotation on radial studded snow tires before removal.

➡ **Avoid overtightening the lug nuts or the brake disc or drum may become permanently distorted. Alloy wheels can be cracked by overtightening. The specified lug nut torque is 76 ft. lbs. for Nova and Prizm cars. Always tighten the nuts in a crisscross pattern.**

TIRE DESIGN

When buying new tires, you should keep the following points in mind, especially if you are switching to larger tires or a different profile series.

1. All four tires should be of the same construction type. Radial, bias, or bias-belted tires should not be mixed. Radial

Fig. 37 The rubber element can be changed without replacing the entire blade assembly

tires are highly recommended for their excellent handling and fuel mileage characteristics. All Novas and Prisms are delivered with radial tires as standard equipment.

2. The wheels must be the correct width for the tire. Tire dealers have charts of tire and wheel compatibility. A mismatch can cause sloppy handling and rapid tread wear. The tread width should match the rim width (inside bead to inside bead) within an inch. For radial tires the rim width should be 80% or less of the tire (not tread) width. The illustration gives an example of a tire size designation number.

3. The height (mounted diameter) of the new tires can change speedometer accuracy, engine speed per given road speed, fuel mileage, acceleration, and ground clearance. Tire manufacturers furnish full measurement specifications to their dealers.

4. The spare tire should be usable, at least for low speed operation, with the new tires. Novas and Prizms use a space-saving spare tire mounted on a special wheel. This wheel and tire is for emergency use only. Never try to mount a regular tire on a special spare wheel.

5. There shouldn't be any body interference when the car is loaded, on bumps or in turning through maximum range.

TIRE INFLATION

The importance of proper tire inflation cannot be overemphasized. A tire employs air under pressure as part of its structure. It is designed around the supporting strength of air at a specified pressure. For this reason, improper inflation drastically reduces the tire's ability to perform as it was intended. A tire will lose some air in day-to-day use; having to add a few pounds of air periodically is not necessarily a sign of a leaking tire.

Fig. 38 Tread wear indicators will appear when the tire is worn out

Fig. 39 Tread depth can also be checked with an inexpensive gauge

Fig. 40 A penny works as well as anything for checking tread depth; when the top of Lincoln's head is visible, it's time for new tires

Fig. 41 Tire rotation patterns. 'A' is recommended, 'B' is acceptable. Note that the spare tire is not used in the rotation

METRIC TIRE SIZES

P 155   80 R 13

TIRE TYPE
P – PASSENGER
T – TEMPORARY
C – COMMERCIAL

ASPECT RATIO
$\dfrac{\text{(SECTION HEIGHT)}}{\text{(SECTION WIDTH)}} \times 100$

70
75
80

RIM DIAMETER
(INCHES)
12
13
14

SECTION WIDTH
(MILLIMETERS)
145
155
ETC.

CONSTRUCTION TYPE
R – RADIAL
B – BIAS-BELTED
D – DIAGONAL (BIAS)

SECTION WIDTH

SECTION HEIGHT

Fig. 42 Common (P-Metric) tire coding. A performance code such as H or V may appear before the R; the designation 'M+S' may appear at the end of the code to indicate a snow or all-season tire

- DRIVE WHEEL HEAVY ACCELERATION
- OVERINFLATION

- HARD CORNERING
- UNDERINFLATION
- LACK OF ROTATION

Fig. 43 Examples of inflation-related tire wear patterns. As little as two pounds under specification can induce premature wear

PROPERLY INFLATED   IMPROPERLY INFLATED

RADIAL TIRE

Fig. 44 Radial tires have a characteristic sidewall bulge; don't try to measure tire pressure by looking at the tire. Use a quality air gauge

Tire pressures should be checked regularly with a reliable pressure gauge. Too often the gauge on the end of the air hose at your corner garage is not accurate enough because it suffers too much abuse. Always check tire pressure when the tires are cold, as pressure increases with temperature. If you must move the vehicle to check the tire inflation, do not drive more than a mile before checking. A cold tire is one that has not been driven for a period of about three hours.

➡Never exceed the maximum tire pressure embossed on the tire. This maximum pressure is rarely the correct pressure for everyday driving. Consult your owners' manual for the proper tire pressures for your vehicle.

CARE OF SPECIAL WHEELS

If you have invested money in magnesium, aluminum alloy or sport wheels, special precautions should be taken to make

"Letter" sizes			Inch Sizes	Metric-inch Sizes		
"60 Series"	"70 Series"	"78 Series"	1965–77	"60 Series"	"70 Series"	"80 Series"
			5.50-12, 5.60-12	165/60-12	165/70-12	155-12
		Y78-12	6.00-12			
		W78-13	5.20-13	165/60-13	145/70-13	135-13
		Y78-13	5.60-13	175/60-13	155/70-13	145-13
			6.15-13	185/60-13	165/70-13	155-13, P155/80-13
A60-13	A70-13	A78-13	6.40-13	195/60-13	175/70-13	165-13
B60-13	B70-13	B78-13	6.70-13	205/60-13	185/70-13	175-13
			6.90-13			
C60-13	C70-13	C78-13	7.00-13	215/60-13	195/70-13	185-13
D60-13	D70-13	D78-13	7.25-13			
E60-13	E70-13	E78-13	7.75-13			195-13
			5.20-14	165/60-14	145/70-14	135-14
			5.60-14	175/60-14	155/70-14	145-14
			5.90-14			
A60-14	A70-14	A78-14	6.15-14	185/60-14	165/70-14	155-14
	B70-14	B78-14	6.45-14	195/60-14	175/70-14	165-14
	C70-14	C78-14	6.95-14	205/60-14	185/70-14	175-14
D60-14	D70-14	D78-14				
E60-14	E70-14	E78-14	7.35-14	215/60-14	195/70-14	185-14
F60-14	F70-14	F78-14, F83-14	7.75-14	225/60-14	200/70-14	195-14
G60-14	G70-14	G77-14, G78-14	8.25-14	235/60-14	205/70-14	205-14
H60-14	H70-14	H78-14	8.55-14	245/60-14	215/70-14	215-14
J60-14	J70-14	J78-14	8.85-14	255/60-14	225/70-14	225-14
L60-14	L70-14		9.15-14	265/60-14	235/70-14	
	A70-15	A78-15	5.60-15	185/60-15	165/70-15	155-15
B60-15	B70-15	B78-15	6.35-15	195/60-15	175/70-15	165-15
C60-15	C70-15	C78-15	6.85-15	205/60-15	185/70-15	175-15
	D70-15	D78-15				
E60-15	E70-15	E78-15	7.35-15	215/60-15	195/70-15	185-15
F60-15	F70-15	F78-15	7.75-15	225/60-15	205/70-15	195-15
G60-15	G70-15	G78-15	8.15-15/8.25-15	235/60-15	215/70-15	205-15
H60-15	H70-15	H78-15	8.45-15/8.55-15	245/60-15	225/70-15	215-15
J60-15	J70-15	J78-15	8.85-15/8.90-15	255/60-15	235/70-15	225-15
	K70-15		9.00-15	265/60-15	245/70-15	230-15
L60-15	L70-15	L78-15, L84-15	9.15-15			235-15
	M70-15	M78-15				255-15
		N78-15				

Note: Every size tire is not listed and many size comparisons are approximate, based on load ratings. Wider tires than those supplied new with the vehicle, should always be checked for clearance.

Fig. 45 Tire size comparison chart

sure your investment is not wasted and that your special wheels look good for the lifetime of the car.

Special wheels are easily scratched and/or damaged. Occasionally check the rims for cracking, impact damage or air leaks. If any of these are found, replace the wheel. In order to prevent this type of damage, and the costly replacement of a special wheel, observe the following precautions:

• Use extra care not to damage the wheels during removal, installation, balancing, etc.. After removal of the wheels from the car, place them on a mat or other protective surface. If they are to be stored for any length of time, support them on strips of wood. Never store tires upright — the tread will develop flat spots.

• While driving, watch for sharp obstacles.

• When washing, use a mild detergent and water. Avoid cleansers with abrasives or the use of hard brushes. There are many cleaners and polishes for special wheels. Use them.

• If possible, remove your special wheels from the car during the winter months. Salt and sand used for snow removal can severely damage the finish.

• Make sure that the recommended lug nut torque is never exceeded or the wheel may crack. Never use snow chains on special wheels; severe scratching will occur.

FLUIDS AND LUBRICANTS

Fluid Disposal

▶ See Figures 46 and 47

Used fluids such as engine oil, transaxle fluid, antifreeze and brake fluid are hazardous wastes and must be disposed of properly. Before draining any fluids, consult with local authorities; in many areas, waste oil, etc.. is being accepted as a part of recycling programs. A number of service stations and auto parts stores are also accepting waste fluids for recycling.

Be sure of the recycling center's policies before draining any fluids, as many will not accept different fluids that have been mixed together, such as oil and anti-freeze.

Fuel and Engine Oil Recommendations

FUEL

All Chevrolet Novas and Geo Prizms use unleaded fuel of 91 research octane (RON) or higher. Regular leaded fuel may not be used in these models because they are equipped with a catalytic converter for emission control purposes. Leaded fuel will render the converter useless, raising the emission content of the exhaust to illegal and environmentally unacceptable levels. It will also block the converter passages, increasing exhaust back pressure; in extreme cases, exhaust blockage will be raised to the point where the engine will not run.

Fig. 46 Engine compartment fluid check locations — 1985-88 VIN code 4 carbureted engine

1. Power steering fluid reservoir
2. Engine oil filler cap
3. Engine oil dipstick
4. Brake fluid reservoir
5. Air filter
6. Fuse block
7. Coolant recovery tank
8. Battery
9. Fusible links
10. Radiator cap
11. Transmission fluid level dipstick
12. Oil filter
13. Distributor
14. Windshield washer reservoir

Fig. 47 Engine compartment fluid check locations — 1988-92 VIN code 5 and 6 engines

Fuels of the same octane rating have varying anti-knock qualities. Thus if your engine knocks or pings, try switching brands of gasoline before trying a more expensive higher octane fuel.

Your engine's fuel requirements can change with time, due to carbon buildup which changes the compression ratio. If switching brands or grades of gas doesn't work, check the ignition timing.

ENGINE OIL

▶ See Figure 48

The SAE (Society of Automotive Engineers) grade number indicates the viscosity of the engine oil, or its ability to lubricate under a given temperature. The lower the SAE grade number, the lighter the oil; the lower the viscosity, the easier it is to crank the engine in cold weather.

Oil viscosities should be chosen from the oils recommended for the lowest anticipated temperatures during the oil change interval. Multi-viscosity oils (5W-30, 10W-30 etc..) offer the important advantage of being adaptable to temperature extremes. They allow easy starting at low temperatures, yet they give good protection at high speeds and engine temperatures. This is a decided advantage in changeable climates or in long distance touring. For recommended oil viscosities, refer to the engine oil viscosity chart.

The API (American Petroleum Institute) designation indicates the classification of engine oil for use under given operating conditions. Only oils designated for Service SG/SC, SG/CD or just SG, should be used. These oils provide maximum engine protection. Both the SAE grade number and the API designation can be found on the top of a can of oil.

Non-detergent or straight mineral oils should not be used. Oil viscosities should be chosen from those oils recommended for the lowest anticipated temperatures during the oil change interval.

Fig. 48 Oil viscosity chart

Engine

OIL LEVEL CHECK

▶ **See Figures 49, 50 and 51**

❋❋CAUTION

Prolonged and repeated skin contact with used engine oil, with no effort to remove the oil, can be harmful.

Always follow these simple precautions when handling used motor oil:
- Avoid prolonged skin contact with used motor oil.
- Remove oil from skin by washing thoroughly with soap and water or waterless hand cleaner. Do not use gasoline, thinners or other solvents.
- Avoid prolonged skin contact with oil soaked clothing.

The engine oil should be checked on a regular basis, ideally at each fuel stop. If the car is used for trailer towing, or for heavy-duty use, it would be wise to check it more often.

When checking the oil level, it is best that the oil be at operating temperature, although checking the level immediately after stopping will give a false reading because not all of the oil will have drained back into the crankcase. Be sure that the car is on a level surface, allowing time for all of the oil to drain back into the crankcase.

1. Open the hood and locate the dipstick. It is located on the right hand (passenger's side) of the engine.

2. Remove the dipstick and wipe it clean with a rag.

3. Insert the dipstick fully into the tube and remove it again. Hold the dipstick horizontally and read the oil level on the dipstick. The level should be between the F (Full) and L (Low) marks. If the oil level is at or below the L mark, sufficient oil should be added to restore the level to the proper place. Oil is added through the capped opening in the top of the valve cover.

4. Replace the dipstick and check the level after adding oil. Be careful not to overfill the crankcase.

Fig. 49 Typical oil dipstick

ENGINE OIL AND FILTER CHANGE

▶ **See Figures 52, 53, 54, 55 and 56**

The engine oil and oil filter should always be changed together. To skip an oil filter change is to leave a quart of contaminated oil in the engine as well as a contaminated filter. Engine oil and filter must be changed at least as specified in the Maintenance Intervals chart.

➡**Certain operating conditions may warrant more frequent changes. If the vehicle is used for short trips, water condensation and low-temperature deposits may make it necessary to change the oil sooner. If the vehicle is used mostly in stop-and-go city traffic, corrosive acids and high-temperature deposits may necessitate shorter oil changing intervals. The shorter intervals are also true for industrial or rural areas where high concentration of dust contaminate the oil. Cars used for carrying heavy loads, pulling trailers, or in mountainous areas may also need more frequent oil and filter changes.**

The type of engines used in the Nova and Prism — overhead camshaft — are particularly sensitive to proper lubrication with clean oil. Don't risk an expensive repair by neglecting the easiest maintenance on the car. Change the oil and filter regularly — it's cheap insurance.

To change the engine oil and filter, the car should be parked on a level surface and the engine should be at operating temperature. This is to ensure that foreign matter will be drained away with the oil and not left behind in the engine to form sludge, which will happen if the engine is drained cold. Oil that is slightly brownish when drained is a good sign that the contaminants are being drained away.

You should have available a container that will hold at least five quarts, a wrench to fit the oil drain plug, a spout for pouring in new oil and some rags to clean up the inevitable mess. If the filter is being replaced, you will also need a band wrench to fit the filter.

1. Position the car on a level surface and set the parking brake or block the wheels. Slide a drain pan under the oil drain plug.

2. From under the car, loosen, but do not remove the oil drain plug. Cover your hand with a heavy rag or glove and slowly unscrew the drain plug. Push the plug against the threads to prevent oil from leaking past the threads.

❋❋CAUTION

The engine oil will be hot. Keep your arms, face and hands away from the oil as it drains out.

3. As the plug comes to the end of the threads, whisk it away from the hole, letting the oil drain into the pan, which hopefully is still under the drain plug. This method usually avoids the messy task of reaching into a tub full of hot, dirty oil to retrieve a usually elusive drain plug. Crawl out from under the car and wait for the oil to drain.

4. When the oil is drained, install the drain plug and tighten it.

5. Loosen the filter with a band wrench and spin the filter off by hand. Be careful of the one quart of hot, dirty oil that inevitably overflows the filter.

Fig. 50 Engine oil dipstick location — 1992 VIN code 6 engine shown

Fig. 51 The engine oil should be between the 'L' and the 'F' marks on the dipstick — 1992 VIN code 6 engine shown, other engines similar

Fig. 52 By keeping an inward pressure on the drain plug as you unscrew it, the oil won't escape past the threads

Fig. 53 Remove the oil filter with a strap wrench

Fig. 54 Lubricate the gasket on the new filter with clean engine oil. A dry gasket may not make a good seal and will allow the filter to leak

Fig. 55 Install the new oil filter by hand

Fig. 56 Add oil through the cylinder head cover only

6. Coat the rubber gasket on a new filter with clean engine oil and install the filter. Screw the filter onto the mounting stud and tighten according to the directions on the filter. Do not overtighten the filter; it may rupture under pressure and instantly deliver 5 quarts of oil onto the ground.

7. Refill the engine with the specified amount of clean engine oil. Be sure to use the proper viscosity. Pour the oil in through the opening in the valve cover.

8. Run the engine for several minutes, checking for oil pressure and leaks. The oil warning light on the dash should go out after a few seconds of engine operation. A few minutes

after the engine is shut off, check the level of the oil and add if necessary.

➡**Please dispose of used motor oil properly. Do not throw it in the trash or pour it on the ground. Take it to your dealer or local service station for recycling.**

Manual Transaxle

FLUID RECOMMENDATIONS

The specified gear lubricant for all Nova and Prizm cars is SAE 75W-90 or SAE 80W-90 GL-5 gear lubricant.

FLUID LEVEL CHECK

▶ **See Figure 57**

The oil in the manual transaxle should be checked at least every 15,000 miles and replaced every 25,000-30,000 miles.

1. With the car parked on a level surface, remove the filler plug from the side of the transaxle housing.

2. If the lubricant begins to trickle out of the hole, there is enough lubricant. Otherwise, carefully insert your fingers (watch out for sharp threads) and check to see if the oil is up to the edge of the hole.

❋❋CAUTION

Used oil may cause skin cancer if repeatedly left in contact with the skin for prolonged periods. Although this is unlikely unless you handle oil on a daily basis, it is wise to thoroughly wash your hands with soap and water immediately after handling used oil.

3. If not, add oil through the hole until the level is at the edge of the hole. Most gear lubricants come in a plastic squeeze bottle with a nozzle, making additions simple. Refer to the Recommended Lubricants chart for the proper oil.

4. Replace the filler plug, run the engine and check for leaks.

Fig. 57 Checking the oil level with your finger

DRAIN AND REFILL

▶ **See Figure 58**

The manual transmission oil should be changed at least every 30,0000 miles. To change, proceed as follows:

1. The manual transmission oil should be hot before it is drained. If the car is driven until the engine is at normal operating temperature, the oil should be hot enough.

2. Remove the cover under the left hand side of the engine. You may wish to jack and support the car to gain access and make the work easier. The car will need to be lowered onto level ground before refilling the transaxle with fresh oil.

3. Remove the filler plug to provide a vent. If the car is elevated, you may encounter spillage as the fill plug is removed.

4. Locate the drain plug on the bottom of the transaxle. Place a large container underneath the transaxle and remove the plug.

❋❋CAUTION

The oil will be hot. Protect your hands and arms.

5. Allow the oil to drain completely. Clean off the plug and reinstall it. Tighten it until it is just snug. If the car is elevated, lower it to a level position.

6. Fill the transaxle with SAE 75W-90 or 80W-90 gear oil. This usually comes in a plastic squeeze bottle with a long nozzle; otherwise you can use an oil siphon gun available at most auto parts stores. Refer to the Capacities Chart for the proper amount of oil to put in.

7. Add new oil until it begins to run out of the filler hole.

8. Replace the filler plug, drive the car for a few minutes, stop, and check for leaks.

➡**Please dispose of used oil properly. Do not throw it in the trash or pour it on the ground. Take it to your dealer or local service station for recycling.**

Fig. 58 Manual transaxle refill

Automatic Transaxle

FLUID RECOMMENDATIONS

The correct automatic transmission fluid for all Nova and Prizm cars is Dexron® II. There are no acceptable substitutes; internal damage may result if other fluids are used.

FLUID LEVEL CHECK

▶ **See Figures 59 and 60**

Check the automatic transmission fluid level at least every 5,000 miles (more often if possible). The dipstick is in the engine compartment between the battery and the distributor.

The fluid level should be checked only when the transmission is hot (normal operating temperature). The transmission is considered hot after about 20 miles of highway driving.

1. Park the car on a level surface with the engine idling. Shift the transmission into Neutral and set the parking brake.

2. Remove the dipstick, wipe it clean and reinsert it firmly. Be sure that it has been pushed all the way in. Remove the dipstick and check the fluid level while holding it horizontally. With the engine running, the fluid level should be between the notches in the 'HOT' range on the dipstick.

3. If the fluid level is below the second notch, add Dexron® II automatic transmission fluid through the dipstick

Fig. 59 Always check automatic transmission fluid when fully warmed up. The fluid level should always be between the notches

Fig. 60 Automatic transmission fluid dipstick location — 1992 VIN code 6 engine shown

tube. This is easily done with the aid of a long-necked funnel. Check the level often as you are filling the transmission. Be extremely careful not to overfill it. Overfilling will cause slippage, seal damage and overheating. Approximately one pint of ATF will raise the level from one notch to the other.

✳✳WARNING

The fluid on the dipstick should always be a bright red color. If it is discolored (black or brown), or smells burnt, serious transmission troubles, probably due to overheating, should be suspected. The transmission should be inspected by a qualified service technician to locate the cause of burnt fluid.

DRAIN AND REFILL

The automatic transmission fluid should be changed at least every 30,000 miles. If the car is normally used in severe service, such as stop-and-go driving, trailer towing or the like, the interval should be halved. The fluid should be hot before it is drained; a 20 minute drive will accomplish this.

The automatic transmission has a drain plug so that if you're in a hurry, you can simply remove the plug, drain the fluid, replace the plug, and then refill the transaxle. Although this method is fine, a slightly longer procedure may be more effective on Novas and is required for Prizms.

1. Remove the plug and drain the fluid. When the fluid stops coming out of the drain hole, loosen the pan retaining screws until the pan can be pulled down at one corner. If the pan is stuck, tap the edges lightly with a plastic mallet to loosen it; don't pry it or wedge a screwdriver into the seam. Lower the corner of the pan and allow the remaining fluid to drain out.

2. After the pan has drained completely, remove the pan retaining screws and then remove the pan and gasket.

3. Clean the pan thoroughly and allow it to air dry. If you wipe it out with a rag you run the risk of leaving bits of lint in the pan which will clog the tiny hydraulic passages in the transaxle.

4. With the pan removed on Prizm vehicles, the transmission filter is visible. The filter should be changed any time the transmission oil is drained. Remove the three bolts holding the filter and remove the filter.

✳✳WARNING

The bolts are three different lengths and must be reinstalled in their correct locations. Take great care not to interchange them.

5. Clean the mating surfaces for the oil pan and the filter; make sure all traces of the old gasket material is removed.

6. On Prizms, install the new filter. Install the three bolts in their correct locations and tighten only to 89 inch lbs.

7. Install the pan using a new gasket.

8. Install the drain plug.

9. It is a good idea to measure the amount of fluid drained from the transaxle to determine the correct amount of fresh

fluid to the be added. This is because some parts of the transaxle may not drain completely.

➡**Do not overfill the transaxle. The automatic transaxle and the differential are separate units.**

10. With the engine off, add new Dexron® II fluid through the dipstick tube. The refill capacity is 2.4 quarts.

11. Start the engine and shift the gear selector into all positions from P through L, allowing each gear to engage momentarily. Shift into P. DO NOT race the engine.

12. With the engine idling, check the fluid level. Add fluid up to the COOL level on the dipstick.

➡**Please dispose of used oil properly. Do not throw it in the trash or pour it on the ground. Take it to your dealer or local service station for recycling.**

A13L 3-Speed Automatic Transaxle Differential (Final Drive Unit)

FLUID RECOMMENDATIONS

The correct automatic transmission differential fluid for all Nova and Prizm cars is Dexron® II. There are no acceptable substitutes; internal damage may result if other fluids are used.

FLUID LEVEL CHECK

▶ **See Figure 61**

The oil in the differential should be checked at least every 5,000 miles and replaced every 20,000 miles.

1. With the car parked on a level surface, remove the filler plug from the SIDE of the differential.

➡**The plug on the bottom of the differential is the drain plug. Do not confuse the differential filler plug with the filler plug for the transaxle.**

2. If the lubricant begins to trickle out of the hole, there is enough lubricant. Otherwise, carefully insert your finger (watch out for sharp threads) and check to see if the oil is up to the edge of the hole.

3. If the oil is not up to level, add oil through the hole until the level is at the edge of the hole. Most gear lubricants come in a plastic squeeze bottle with a nozzle, making additions simple. The differential uses Dexron® II automatic transmission fluid.

4. Replace the filler plug, run the engine and check for leaks.

DRAIN AND REFILL

The fluid in the differential should be changed at least every 20,000 miles.To drain and fill the differential, proceed as follows:

1. Park the vehicle on a level surface. Set the parking brake.

2. Remove the filler (upper) plug. Place a container which is large enough to catch all of the differential fluid under the drain plug.

3. Remove the drain (lower) plug and allow all of the oil to drain into the container.

4. Install the drain plug. Tighten it so that it will not leak, but do not overtighten.

5. Refill with 1.5 quarts of Dexron® II automatic transmission fluid. Be sure that the level reaches the bottom of the filler plug.

6. Replace the filler plug, run the engine and check for leaks.

➡**Please dispose of used oil properly. Do not throw it in the trash or pour it on the ground. Take it to your dealer or local service station for recycling.**

Cooling System

FLUID RECOMMENDATIONS

▶ **See Figure 62**

The correct coolant for the Nova and Prizm is any permanent, high quality ethylene glycol antifreeze mixed in a 50/50 concentration with water. This mixture gives the best combination of anti-freeze and anti-boil characteristics within the engine. Do not run the system filled with straight antifreeze or straight water; temperature extremes could damage the engine. For example, undiluted antifreeze will freeze at -8°F while a 50/50 mixture of antifreeze and tapwater freezes at -34°F.

Fig. 61 Filler and drain plug locations on the front differential

Fig. 62 The freezing protection rating can be checked with an antifreeze tester

FLUID LEVEL CHECK

▶ See Figure 63

❊❊CAUTION

Always allow the car to sit and cool for an hour or so (longer is better) before removing the radiator cap. To avoid injury when working on a warm engine, cover the radiator cap with a thick cloth and turn it slowly counterclockwise until the pressure begins to escape. Never remove the radiator cap until the expansion tank cap is removed. After the pressure is completely removed, remove the cap. Never remove the cap until the pressure is gone.

It's best to check the coolant level when the engine is cold. The radiator coolant level should be between the LOW and the FULL lines on the expansion tank when the engine is cold. If low, check for leakage and add coolant up to the FULL line but do not overfill it. There must be room in the jug for normal expansion of hot fluids.

DRAIN AND REFILL

The engine coolant should be changed every 30,000 miles or three years, whichever comes first. Replacing the coolant is necessary to remove the scale, rust and chemical by-products which build up in the system. This is a potentially messy job so have a large drain pan or bucket available along with a

Fig. 63 Check the coolant level in the expansion tank

healthy supply of rags. Be prepared to deal with fluid spills immediately. See the previous list of Do's and Don'ts for other hints.

1. Draining the cooling system is always done with the engine cold. Attempting to drain hot coolant is very foolish; you can be badly scalded.
2. Remove the radiator cap.
3. Position the drain pan under the drain cock on the bottom of the radiator. Additionally, the Nova/Prizm engines have a drain cock on the side of the engine block, near the oil filter. This should be opened to aid in draining the cooling system completely. If for some reason the radiator drain cock can't be used, you can loosen and remove the lower radiator hose at its joint to the radiator.
4. If the lower hose is to be used as the drain, loosen the clamp on the hose and slide it back so it's out of the way. Gently break the grip of the hose on its fitting by twisting or prying with a suitable tool. Do not exert too much force or you will damage the radiator fitting. As the hose loosens, you can expect a gush of fluid to come out — be ready. Remove the hose end from the radiator and direct the hose into the drain pan. You now have fluid running from both the hose and the radiator.

❊❊WARNING

Housepets and small animals are attracted to the odor and taste of engine coolant (antifreeze). It is a highly poisonous mixture of chemicals; special care must be taken to protect open containers and spillage.

5. When the system stops draining, close both draincocks.
6. In a bucket or similar large container, mix a 50/50 solution of antifreeze and water. Using a funnel, fill the radiator with this solution. Allow time for the fluid to run through the hoses and into the engine.
7. Fill the radiator to just below the neck. With the radiator cap off, start the engine and let it idle; this will circulate the coolant and begin to eliminate air in the system. Top up the radiator as the level drops.
8. When the level is reasonably stable, shut the engine off, and replace the radiator cap. Fill the expansion tank to a level halfway between the LOW and FULL lines and cap the expansion tank.
9. Drive the car for 10 or 15 minutes; the temperature gauge should be fully within the normal operating range. It is helpful to set the heater to its hottest setting while driving — this circulates the coolant throughout the entire system and helps eliminate air bubbles.
10. After the engine has cooled (2-3 hours), check the level in the radiator and the expansion tank, topping up as necessary.

CLEANING AND FLUSHING THE COOLING SYSTEM

Proceed with draining the system as outlined above. When the system has drained, reconnect any hoses close the radiator draincock. Move the temperature control for the heater to its hottest position; this allows the heater core to be flushed as well. Using a garden hose or bucket, fill the radiator and allow the water to run out the engine drain cock. Continue until the water runs clear. Be sure to clean the expansion tank as well.

If the system is badly contaminated with rust or scale, you can use a commercial flushing solution to clean it out. Follow the manufacturer's instructions. Some causes of rust are air in the system, failure to change the coolant regularly, use of excessively hard or soft water, and/or failure to use the correct mix of antifreeze and water.

After the system has been flushed, continue with the refill procedures outlined above. Check the condition of the radiator cap and its gasket, replacing the cap if anything looks improper.

Brake and Clutch Master Cylinders

FLUID RECOMMENDATIONS

Both the hydraulic brake system and the hydraulic clutch system use brake fluid in the lines. Select a quality fluid meeting DOT 3 or DOT 4 specifications. DO NOT use brake fluid from previously opened containers which have been sitting around for any length of time — it will have absorbed enough moisture from the air to make it useless.

FLUID LEVEL CHECK

▶ **See Figures 64 and 65**

The brake and clutch master cylinders are located under the hood in the left rear section of the engine compartment. They are made of translucent plastic so that the levels may be checked without removing the tops. The fluid level in both reservoirs should be checked at least every 5,000 miles. The fluid level should be maintained at the uppermost mark on the side of the reservoir. Any sudden decrease in the level indicates a possible leak in the system and should be checked out immediately.

➡ **Normal brake wear will cause the fluid level to drop over a period of time. The fluid isn't leaking — it's simply relocated within the system.**

When making additions of brake or clutch fluid, use only fresh, uncontaminated brake fluid meeting or exceeding DOT 3

or 4 standards. Be careful not to spill any brake fluid on painted surfaces, as it eats paint.

Before removing the caps to either reservoir, wipe off the cap area with a rag. This helps prevent dirt from entering the system. Do not allow the master cylinder reservoir to remain open any longer than necessary; brake fluid absorbs moisture from the air, reducing its effectiveness and causing corrosion in the lines.

Power Steering Pump

FLUID RECOMMENDATIONS

The correct fluid for the power steering system is Dexron® II automatic transmission fluid. There are no acceptable substitutes; any other fluid may damage the system.

FLUID LEVEL CHECK

▶ **See Figures 66 and 68**

The fluid level in the power steering reservoir should be checked at least every 5,000 miles. The vehicle should be parked on level ground, with the engine warm and running at normal idle. Remove the filler cap and check the level on the dipsticks; it should be within the HOT area on the dipstick. If the level is low, add Dexron® II ATF until the proper level is achieved.

Fig. 65 Master cylinder reservoir location — 1992 VIN code 6 engine shown

Fig. 64 Always fill the master cylinder slowly so as not to create air bubbles in the system

IF COLD ADD
IF COLD O.K.
COLD HOT
IF HOT O.K.
IF HOT ADD

Fig. 66 Power steering pump dipstick

Fig. 67 Power steering pump reservoir and dipstick location — 1992 VIN code 6 engine shown

Look down in the reservoir and check for evidence of foaming or which indicates the existence of air in the system. The power steering system does not 'consume' fluid in normal use; any sign of fluid loss or air in the system should be treated as a potential problem.

The power steering fluid does not require replacement during the normal life of the car.

Chassis Greasing

The Nova and Prizm do not require routine chassis lubrication. All of the suspension joints are permanently lubricated and sealed during assembly.

Fig. 68 Foaming or emulsification indicates air in the system

TRAILER TOWING

General Recommendations

When towing a trailer, your car will handle differently than without the trailer. The three main causes of trailer-related accidents are driver error (notably failure to anticipate and react earlier than usual), excessive speed and improper loading.

Since the Nova and Prizm are front wheel drive cars, attaching the load of a trailer to the rear bumper creates special problems. As the weight of the trailer is hooked to the rear, the rear of the car is forced downwards. At the same time the front of the car rises, resulting in less weight on the drive wheels. This lightened, nose-up attitude has a definite effect on the 'go, stop and turn' functions of the tires. Wet

Body Lubrication

There is no set period recommended for body lubrication; however, it is a good idea to lubricate the following body points at least once a year with the recommended lubricant, especially in the fall before cold weather:

Key lock cylinders — multi-purpose lubricant GM 12345120 or equivalent, or synthetic SAE 5W-30 engine oil.

Weather-strips — silicone dielectric grease GM 12345579 or equivalent.

Hood latch and pivot points — engine oil.

Hatchback, hood and door hinges — engine oil.

After lubricating a body part, be sure that all the excess lubricant has been wiped off, especially in any area of the car which may come in contact with clothing.

Wheel Bearings

REMOVAL, INSTALLATION AND REPACKING

The wheel bearings at both the front and rear of the car are permanently sealed and pressed into place. They are considered life-of-the-car components and are only replaced in the event of mechanical failure. There is no maintenance required on the wheel bearings.

Replacement of the bearings — a difficult task involving several special tools and a hydraulic press — is discussed in Section 8.

and/or slippery roads compound this problem since the tires have already lost some of their grip. You must alter your driving style when towing; moderate speeds and anticipation of problems are required.

Always check the trailer lighting before departing. Double check the hitch and its safety chains. Remember that the trailer makes the car tail-heavy; braking distances are increased and acceleration is slower. Chevrolet states that you should not exceed 45 mph when towing with these cars due to the increase in trailer sway at higher speeds.

Simply being conscious of the trailer at all times will go a long way to making your trip a safe one. Wider turns, extra length and a greater exposure to cross-winds need to be in your mind every minute.

When parking the car with the trailer, seek level ground if possible. If the unit must be parked on a slope, make sure the parking brake is firmly set and the transmission is set either in PARK (automatic) or first or reverse (manual). Always use wheel chocks on at least one vehicle wheel and one trailer wheel when parking, whether on a slope or not.

Necessary Equipment

Use only a hitch which is recommended by the manufacturer for your car and conforms to the weight requirements of the trailer. The hitch should be firmly bolted to the rear bumper but should not interfere with the motion of the energy absorbing bumper. Do not use axle-mounted hitches as they will place undue loads on the rear suspension, wheel bearings and tires. It is recommended by Chevrolet that the hitch be removed when not in use to prevent additional damage in the event of a rear end collision.

Wiring connections will need to be made from the car to the trailer. Minimum lighting requirements include tail lights, brake lights and turn signals. Some trailers now include sidemarker and reverse lights as well.

➡**The additional turn signals may cause the system to flash very slowly or not at all. this can be cured by installing a heavy-duty turn signal flasher.**

PUSHING AND TOWING

Push Starting

Although Chevrolet recommends against it, all Novas and Prizms equipped with a manual transaxle can be pushed started, although more than one car has received a dented fender or bumper from this operation. Push starting can develop extremely hot exhaust pulses which can damage the catalytic converter.

If push starting is the last resort, turn the ignition switch to the ON position, push in the clutch pedal, put the gear shift lever in second or third gear and partially depress the gas pedal. As the car begins to pick up momentum while being pushed, release the clutch pedal. Be prepared for the engine to start and the car to accelerate. As soon as the engine is running, push in the clutch and stop the car, keeping the engine running until it has smoothed out and warmed up a bit. As a rule, if the car hasn't started after two or three tries at pushing, it isn't going to.

✳✳CAUTION

Never attempt to push start the car while it is in reverse.

JACKING

▶ **See Figures 69 and 70**

The car should only be lifted with a proper jack. While the scissors jack in the trunk may be used, a floor (hydraulic) jack is recommended for its additional load-carrying capability. An added benefit is that the floor jack can be used to lift one end

Electric trailer brakes are recommended for any trailer over 1000 lbs. Your local laws may require brakes on trailers over a specific weight. Consult your dealer or a reputable repair facility for the correct wiring hook-ups.

TRAILER AND TONGUE WEIGHT

The total weight of the trailer and its load must NOT exceed 1400 lbs. The tongue weight (weight on the hitch) must not exceed 140 lbs or 10% of the total trailer weight, whichever is less.

The trailer must be loaded so that about 60% of the total load is in the front half of the trailer. Make sure that any load is secured in place; a sudden weight shift can radically upset the handling of the trailer and the tow vehicle.

As a further caution, the TOTAL weight of the vehicle and trailer (including passengers, luggage, hitch, trailer and cargo) cannot exceed the Gross Vehicle Weight Rating (GVWR) shown on the manufacturer's plate on the left door jamb.

Novas and Prizms that are equipped with an automatic transmission cannot be push started no matter how far or how fast they are pushed. Attempting to do so will severely damage the transmission and possibly the catalytic converter.

Towing

Novas and Prizms should be towed with the front (drive) wheels in the air. Do not tow the vehicle with the front wheels or all four wheels on the ground; transmission damage will result. In the event of wheel, tire or suspension damage to the rear, the car must be transported on a flatbed carrier.

Additionally, care must be taken not to damage the driveshafts, boots or suspension when hooking up towing equipment.

of the car; the scissors jack can only raise one corner at a time. When purchasing a floor jack, make sure its weight rating is at least equal to the TOTAL weight of your car. Since the Nova/Prizm cars are currently in the 2300 lb. range, a 1½ ton capacity jack will suffice.

Correct placement of the jack is essential to the success of the project. Only lift the car at the designated jacking points on the body or frame. These reinforced locations will support the weight of the car during the elevation. Any other points, such as the floor pan, engine oil pan or suspension will not.

Before lifting the car, make sure the surrounding area is clear. If any wheels are to be removed, loosen the wheel lugs two or three turns while the wheel is on the ground. Place a wheel chock behind a wheel on the opposite side (or at the opposite end) of the car. Once the car is elevated, immediately place jackstands under the support points. Make sure the stands are on a firm, level footing and will not shift under load. Lower the jack until the weight of the car is supported on the stand, not on the jack.

These simple preliminary steps cannot be stressed often enough. Each year many people are maimed or killed because

their car fell on them. A hydraulic jack cannot be trusted to stay elevated — always use jackstands, even for a quickie repair.

The following are certain safety precautions which should always be observed when jacking the vehicle. They are as follows:

1. Always jack the car on a level surface.

2. Set the parking brake if the front wheels are to be raised. This will keep the car from rolling backward off the jack.

3. If the rear wheels are to be raised, block the front wheels to keep the car from rolling forward.

4. Block the wheel diagonally opposite the one which is being raised.

5. If the vehicle is being raised in order to work underneath it, support it with jackstands. DO NOT place the jackstands

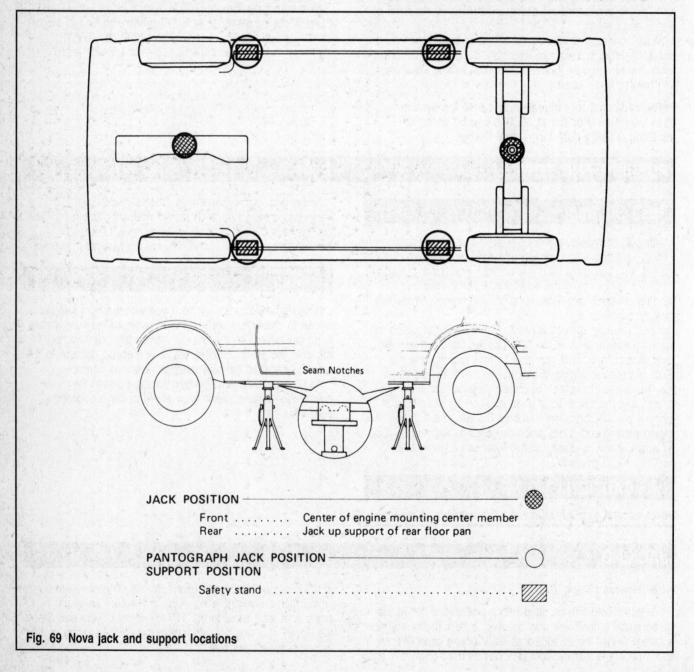

Seam Notches

JACK POSITION ⎯⎯⎯⎯⎯⎯⎯⎯⎯⎯⎯⎯⎯⎯⎯⎯⎯⎯⎯
    Front .... Center of engine mounting center member
    Rear .... Jack up support of rear floor pan

PANTOGRAPH JACK POSITION ⎯⎯⎯⎯⎯⎯⎯⎯⎯⎯⎯
SUPPORT POSITION

    Safety stand ....

Fig. 69 Nova jack and support locations

SUSPENSION CONTACT HOIST

FRAME CONTACT HOIST/SAFETY STAND

FLOOR JACK
FRONT. . .ENGINE LOWER CROSSMEMBER
REAR . . .REAR SUBFRAME

Fig. 70 Prizm jack and support locations

against the sheet metal panels beneath the car or they will become distorted.

✳✳CAUTION

Do not work beneath a vehicle support only by a jack. Always use jackstands.

6. Do not use a bumper jack to raise the vehicle; the bumpers are not designed for this purpose.

CAPACITIES

Year	Model	Engine ID/VIN	Engine Displacement Liters (cc)	Engine Crankcase with Filter	Transmission (pts.)		Drive Axle (pts.)	Fuel Tank (gal.)	Cooling System (qts.)
					5-Spd	Auto.			
1985	Nova	4	1.6 (1600)	3.5	5.4	11.6 ①	3.0	13.2	6.4
1986	Nova	4	1.6 (1600)	3.5	5.4	11.6 ①	3.0	13.2	6.4
1987	Nova	4	1.6 (1600)	3.5	5.4	11.6 ①	3.0	13.2	6.4
1988	Nova	4	1.6 (1600)	3.5	5.4	11.6 ①	3.0	13.2	6.4
	Nova	5	1.6 (1600)	3.9	4.8	16.3 ②	—	13.2	6.3
1989	Prizm	6	1.6 (1600)	3.4	4.8	11.6 ③	3.0	13.0	6.3
1990	Prizm	5	1.6 (1600)	3.4	5.4	15.2	—	13.2	6.0
	Prizm	6	1.6 (1600)	3.4	5.4	11.6 ③	3.0	13.0	6.3
1991	Prizm	5	1.6 (1600)	3.9	5.4	11.6 ③	3.0	13.2	6.0
	Prizm	6	1.6 (1600)	3.4	5.4	15.2	—	13.2	6.0
1992	Prizm	5	1.6 (1600)	3.9	5.4	11.6 ③	3.0	13.2	6.0
	Prizm	6	1.6 (1600)	3.4	5.4	15.2	—	13.2	6.0
1993	Prizm	6	1.6 (1600)	3.4	5.4	③	3.0	13.2	6.2
	Prizm	8	1.8 (1800)	4.3	5.4	④	—	13.2	6.4

① Drain and refill: 4.8 pts.
② Drain and refill: 6.6 pts.
③ Drain and refill: 5.2 pts.
④ Drain and refill: 7.0 pts. (includes differential)

Maintenance Intervals Chart

Miles x 1000 or months of age	5	10	15	20	25	30	35	40	45	50	55	60
Engine oil and filter	R	R	R	R	R	R	R	R	R	R	R	R
Body lubrication		T		T		T		T		T		T
Engine idle speed		I				I						I
Engine coolant						R						R
Spark plugs						R						R
Air filter		I		I		R		I		I		R
Valve clearance						I						I
Engine drive belts		I				I						I
Charcoal canister												I
Fuel lines and connections			I			I		I				I
Fuel filter cap gasket												R
Exhaust system			I			I		I				I
Engine timing belt												R
Wheels and tires	I	I	I	I	I	I	I	I	I	I	I	I
Brakes	I	I	I	I	I	I	I	I	I	I	I	I
Fluid levels check		T		T		T		T		T		T
Transmission fluid	I	I	I	I	I	R	I	I	I	I	I	R
Adjust clutch free play		T		T		T		T		T		T

R: Replace
T: Interval shown or at least twice a year
I: Inspect and clean, adjust, repair, service or replace as necessary
REMINDER: These are maximum intervals, not to be exceeded. More frequent maintenance and inspection may be required depending on usage of the vehicle.

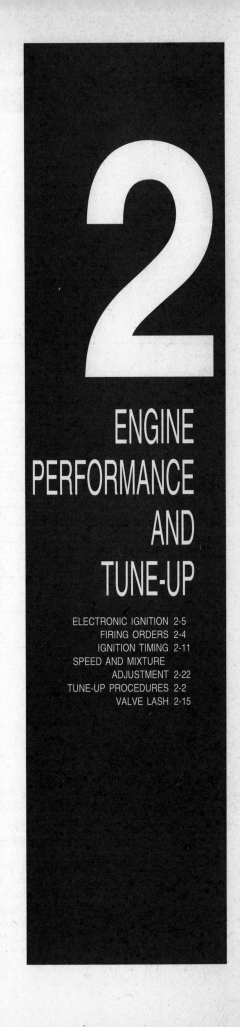

2

ENGINE PERFORMANCE AND TUNE-UP

TUNE-UP PROCEDURES

GASOLINE ENGINE TUNE-UP SPECIFICATIONS

Year	Engine ID/VIN	Engine Displacement Liters (cc)	Spark Plugs Gap (in.)	Ignition Timing (deg.) MT	Ignition Timing (deg.) AT	Fuel Pump (psi)	Idle Speed (rpm) MT	Idle Speed (rpm) AT	Valve Clearance In.	Valve Clearance Ex.
1985	4	1.6 (1600)	0.043	0	0	7.6	650	800	0.008	0.012
1986	4	1.6 (1600)	0.043	0	0	7.6	650	750	0.008	0.012
1987	4	1.6 (1600)	0.043	0	0	7.6	650	800	0.008	0.012
1988	4	1.6 (1600)	0.043	0	0	7.6	650	750	0.008	0.012
	5	1.6 (1600)	0.043	—	10B①	②	800	800	0.008	0.010
1989	6	1.6 (1600)	0.031	10B①	10B①	②	700	700	0.008	0.010
1990	5	1.6 (1600)	0.031	10B①	10B①	②	700	700	0.008	0.010
	6	1.6 (1600)	0.031	10B①	10B①	②	700	700	0.008	0.010
1991	5	1.6 (1600)	0.031	10B①	10B①	②	700	700	0.008	0.010
	6	1.6 (1600)	0.031	10B①	10B①	②	700	700	0.008	0.010
1992	5	1.6 (1600)	0.031	10B①	10B①	②	700	700	0.008	0.010
	6	1.6 (1600)	0.031	10B①	10B①	②	700	700	0.008	0.010
1993	6	1.6 (1600)	0.031	10B①	10B①	②	700	700	0.008	0.010
	8	1.8 (1800)	0.031	10B①	10B①	②	700	700	0.008	0.010

NOTE: The underhood specifications sticker often reflects tune-up specification changes in production. Sticker figures must be used if they disagree with those in this chart.
B—Before Top Dead Center
① See text: "Ignition Timing Adjustment"
② Refer to Section 5: Electronic Fuel Pump-
"Pressure Testing"

Neither tune-up nor troubleshooting can be considered independently since each has direct bearing on the other.

➡**The procedures contained in this section are specific procedures applicable to your Nova or Prizm.**

An engine tune-up is a service designed to restore the maximum power, performance, economy and reliability in an engine, and at the same time, assure the owner of a complete check and lasting results in efficiency and trouble-free performance. Engine tune-up becomes increasingly important each year, to ensure that pollutant levels are in compliance with federal emissions standards.

It is advisable to follow definite and thorough tune-up procedures. Tune-up consists of three separate steps:

1. Analysis, the process of determining whether normal wear is responsible for performance loss, and whether parts require replacement or service

2. Parts Replacement or Service

3. Adjustment, where engine adjustments are returned to the original factory specifications after the installation and/or servicing of parts.

The extent of an engine tune-up is usually determined by the mileage or length of time since the previous service, although the type of driving and the general mechanical condition of the engine must be considered. Specific maintenance should also be performed at regular intervals, depending on operating conditions.

The first job is to locate the problem and cause. Once the problem has been isolated, refer to the appropriate section for repair, removal or adjustment procedures.

It is advisable to read the entire section before beginning a tune-up, although those who are more familiar with tune-up procedures may wish to go directly to the instructions.

Spark Plugs

A typical spark plug consists of a metal shell surrounding a ceramic insulator. A metal electrode extends downward through the center of the insulator and protrudes a small distance. Located at the end of the plug and attached to the side of the outer metal shell is the side electrode. The side electrode bends in at a 90° angle so that its tip is even with, and parallel to, the tip of the center electrode.

The distance between these two electrodes (measured in thousandths of an inch) is called the spark plug gap. The spark plug in no way produces a spark but merely provides a gap across which the current can arc. The coil produces anywhere from 20,000 to 40,000 volts which travels to the distributor where it is sent through the spark plug wire to the spark plug. The current passes along the center electrode and jumps to the gap to the side electrode, and, in so doing, ignites the air/fuel mixture in the combustion chamber.

SPARK PLUG HEAT RANGE

▶ See Figure 1

Spark plug heat range is the ability of the plug to dissipate heat. The longer the insulator (or the farther it extends into the engine), the hotter the plug will operate; the shorter the insulator the cooler it will operate. A plug that absorbs little heat and remains too cool will quickly accumulate deposits of oil and carbon since it is not hot enough to burn them off. This leads to plug fouling and consequently to misfiring.

A plug that absorbs too much heat will have no deposits, but, due to the excessive heat, the electrodes will burn away quickly and in some instances, preignition may result. Preignition takes place when plug tips get so hot that they glow sufficiently to ignite the fuel/air mixture before the actual spark occurs. This early ignition will usually cause a pinging during low speeds and heavy loads.

The general rule of thumb for selecting the correct heat range is if most of your driving is long distance, high speed travel, use a colder plug; if most of your driving is stop-and-go or short trips, use a hotter plug. Original equipment plugs are a compromise, but most people never have occasion to change their plugs from the factory-recommended heat range.

REPLACING SPARK PLUGS

▶ See Figures 2, 3, 4 and 5

A set of spark plugs usually requires replacement after about 30,000 miles, depending on your style of driving. In normal operation, plug gap increases about 0.001 in. for every 1,000-2,500 miles of use. As the gap increases, the plug's voltage requirement also increases. It requires a greater voltage to jump the wider gap and about two or three times as much voltage to fire a plug at high speeds than at idle.

When you're removing spark plugs, you should work on one at a time. Don't start by removing the plug wires all at once; unless you number them, they may become mixed up. Take a minute before you begin and number the wires with tape. The best location for numbering is near where the wires come out of the cap.

1. Grasp the boot firmly, twist to loosen it on the plug and remove the wire from the plug. Do not pull on the wire itself as this will ruin the wire.

2. If possible, use a brush or rag to clean the area around the spark plug. Make sure that all of the dirt is removed so that none will enter the cylinder after the plug is removed.

Fig. 2 When removing the spark plug wire, always grasp it by the rubber boot

Fig. 1 Spark plug heat range

Fig. 3 Removing the spark plug on the EFI engines

3. Remove the spark plug using the proper size socket. Make sure the socket is firmly seated on the hex faces of the plug. Turn the socket counterclockwise to remove the plug. Be sure to hold the socket straight on the plug to avoid breaking the plug.

4. Use a round-wire feeler gauge to check the plug gap. The correct size gauge should pass through the electrode gap with a slight drag. If you're in doubt, try one size smaller and one larger. The smaller gauge should go through easily while the larger one shouldn't go through at all.   If the gap is incorrect, use the electrode bending tool on the end of the gauge to adjust the gap. When adjusting the gap, always bend the side electrode. The center electrode is non-adjustable.

5. Squirt a drop of penetrating oil on the threads of the new plug; don't oil the threads too heavily. Install it by hand, turning the plug in clockwise until it is snug.

6. When the plug is finger tight, tighten it with a wrench to 22 ft. lbs. DO NOT overtighten the plug. The threads in aluminum heads are easily damaged or stripped.

7. Install the plug boot firmly over the plug. Proceed to the next plug.

Fig. 4 Always use a wire gauge to check the electrode gap

Fig. 5 Adjust the electrode gap by bending the side electrode

Spark Plug Cables

CHECKING AND REPLACING

Visually inspect the spark plug cables for burns, cuts, or breaks in the insulation. Check the spark plug boots and the nipples on the distributor cap and coil. Replace any damaged wiring. If no physical damage is obvious, the wires can be checked with an ohmmeter for excessive resistance.

When installing a new set of spark plug cables, replace the cables one at a time so there will be no mixup. Getting the cables crossed up during installation may prevent the car from starting. Replace the longest cable first. Install the boot firmly over the spark plug. Route the wire exactly the same as the original, paying close attention to any clips or holders. Insert the nipple firmly into the tower on the distributor cap. Repeat the process for each cable.

FIRING ORDERS

▶ **See Figures 6, 7 and 8**

➡**To avoid confusion, spark plug wires should be replaced one at a time. Distributor terminal position may differ slightly from that which is illustrated.**

Fig. 6 1.6L SOHC (VIN Code 4) Engine Engine Firing Order 1-3-4-2 Distributor Rotation: Counterclockwise

Fig. 7 1.6L DOHC (All 1988 & 1991-92 VIN Code 5) Engine Firing Order 1-3-4-2 Distributor Rotation: Clockwise

Fig. 8 1.6L DOHC (1990 VIN Code 5, 1989-93 VIN Code 6 & 1993 VIN Code 8)
Engine Firing Order 1-3-4-2
Distributor Rotation: Clockwise

ELECTRONIC IGNITION

Electronic ignition systems offer many advances over the conventional breaker point ignition system. By eliminating the points, maintenance requirements are greatly reduced. An electronic ignition system is capable of producing much higher voltage, which in turn aids in starting, reduces spark fouling and provides better emission control.

The system on the Nova consists of a distributor with a signal generator, an ignition coil and an electronic igniter. The signal generator is used to activate the electronic components of the ignition. It is located in the distributor and consists of three main components; the signal rotor, the pick-up coil and the permanent magnet. The signal rotor (not to be confused with the ignition rotor) revolves with the distributor shaft, while the pickup coil and the permanent magnet are stationary. As the signal rotor spins, the teeth on it pass a projection leading from the pickup coil. As they pass, voltage is allowed to flow through the system, firing the spark plugs. There is no physical contact and no electrical arcing, hence no need to replace burnt or worn parts.

Service consists of inspection of the distributor cap, rotor and the ignition wires, replacing them as necessary. In addition, the air gap between the signal rotor and the projection on the pickup coil should be checked periodically.

Diagnosis and Testing — Nova

ENGINE CRANKS BUT DOES NOT START

Check For Spark

1. Disconnect the high tension spark plug wire from the spark plug.
2. Hold the end about ½ inch from the body of the car.
3. Crank the engine and see if spark occurs.

➡**NOTE:Do not crank for more than 1 or 2 seconds at a time on the 1988 EFI (VIN Code 5) engine.**

4. If spark does not occur, perform the following test:

Check Power Source Line Voltage
▶ See Figure 9

1. Remove the distributor cap.

2. Set the ignition switch to the **ON** position.
3. Using a voltmeter, connect the positive probe to the ignition coil positive terminal and the negative probe to the body ground. The voltage reading should be approximately 12 volts.

Signal Generator (Pick-up Coil)

1985-88 VIN CODE 4 CARBURETED ENGINE
▶ See Figure 10

1. Set the ignition switch to the **OFF** position.
2. Remove the distributor cap.
3. Disconnect the signal generator (pick-up coil) wire from the ignitor (module).
4. Measure the resistance between across the signal generator (pick-up coil). If the resistance is not 140-180 ohms, replace the pick-up coil and breaker plate.

1988 VIN CODE 5 FUEL INJECTED ENGINE
▶ See Figure 11

1. Set the ignition switch to the **OFF** position.
2. Remove the distributor cap.
3. Disconnect the signal generator (pick-up coil) wire from the ignitor (module).
4. Measure the resistance between the positive (+) and negative (-) terminals of the two signal generators (pick-up coils). If the resistance is not 140-180 ohms, replace the distributor.

Fig. 9 Ignition line voltage test — 1985-88 VIN Code 4 engines

Fig. 10 Pickup coil resistance test — 1985-88 VIN Code 4 engines

Fig. 11 Pickup coil resistance — 1988 VIN Code 5 engine

Fig. 12 Checking the air gap — 1985-88 VIN Code 4 engines

Air Gap Adjustment

VIN CODE 4 CARBURETED ENGINE

▶ See Figure 12

1. Remove the distributor cap. Inspect the cap for cracks, carbon tracks or a worn center contact. Cracks in the cap can be very hard to see. They are usually hairline thin and run in odd directions within the cap. Replace the cap if necessary, transferring the wires one at a time from the old cap to the new one.

2. Pull the ignition rotor (not the signal rotor) straight up and remove it. Replace it if the contacts are worn, burned or pitted. Do not file the contacts.

3. Turn the engine over (you may use a socket wrench on the front pulley bolt to do this) until the projection on the pickup coil is directly opposite the signal rotor tooth.

4. Get a non-ferrous (paper, brass, or plastic) feeler gauge of 0.012 in. (0.3mm), and insert it into the pick-up air gap. DO NOT use an ordinary metal feeler gauge! The gauge should just touch either side of the gap. The permissible range is 0.008-0.016 in. (0.20-0.40mm).

➡ The air gap on the Nova is not adjustable. If the gap is not within specifications, the pick-up coil (igniter) must be replaced.

1988 VIN CODE 5 FUEL INJECTED ENGINE

▶ See Figure 13

The electronically controlled fuel injection system relies on the Electronic Control Module (ECM) for proper operation. Because the ECM needs to receive information from the distributor (and to control its function), there are two pickup coils in the distributor. Make sure you measure the gap to each coil.

1. Remove the distributor cap. Inspect the cap for cracks, carbon tracks or a worn center contact. Cracks in the cap can be very hard to see. They are usually hairline thin and run in odd directions within the cap. Replace the cap if necessary, transferring the wires one at a time from the old cap to the new one.

2. Pull the ignition rotor (not the signal rotor) straight up and remove it. Replace it if the contacts are worn, burned or pitted. Do not file the contacts.

3. Turn the engine over (you may use a socket wrench on the front pulley bolt to do this) until the projection on the pickup coil is directly opposite a signal rotor tooth.

4. Get a non-ferrous (paper, brass, or plastic) feeler gauge of 0.012 in. (0.3mm), and insert it into the air gaps between

Fig. 13 Measuring the air gap — 1988 VIN Code 5 engine

the signal rotor and the pickup coil projections on each side. DO NOT use an ordinary metal feeler gauge! The gauge should just touch either side of the gap. The permissible range for all models is 0.008-0.016 in. (0.2-0.4mm).

5. The air gap is not adjustable. Should it be out of specification, the entire distributor must be replaced.

Diagnosis and Testing — Prizm

ENGINE CRANKS BUT DOES NOT START

1989-92

▶ **See Figures 14, 15, 16, 17 and 18**

1. Check for spark at each spark plug with a spark tester. Check at least 2 plug wires.

2. If spark is only detected at some plugs, check for a faulty distributor cap or rotor. Also check the spark plugs and plug wires. Replace, if necessary.

3. If no spark is detected, with the ignition switch at the **ON** position, check for voltage at the ignition coil positive (+) terminal, using a digital voltmeter.

4. If battery voltage is not indicated, repair the open circuit between the battery and the ignition coil.

5. If battery voltage is detected, check the ignition coil resistance.

   a. Turn the ignition switch to the **OFF** position.

   b. Check that the primary coil resistance is between 1.28-1.56 ohms.

   c. Check that the secondary coil resistance is between 10,400-14,000 ohms.

6. If the coil resistance is not within specification, replace the ignition coil.

7. If the coil resistance is within specification, disconnect the pickup coil connector. Measure the resistance between terminals 2 and 3 (1989-90 vehicles) or terminals 5 and 6 (1990-92 VIN Code 6 engines) or either terminal (1990-92 VIN Code 5 engines). If the resistance is not 140-180 ohms, replace the distributor.

8. If the resistance is within 140-180 ohms, measure the resistance between the pickup coil connector terminals 1 and 3 (1989-90 vehicles), terminals 2 and 5 (1991-92 VIN Code 6 engines) or either terminal (1990-92 VIN Code 5 engines). If the resistance is not 140-180 ohms, replace the distributor.

9. If the resistance is within 140-180 ohms, reconnect the pickup coil connector and check the signal rotor air gap. If the signal rotor air gap is not 0.008-0.016 inch (0.2-0.4 mm), replace the distributor.

10. If the signal rotor air gap is within 0.008-0.016 inch (0.2-0.4 mm), substitute a known good igniter.

11. If the vehicle starts, install an igniter.

12. If the vehicle still does not start, reinstall the original igniter. The problem is in the wiring between the ignition system and the ECM or with the ECM itself.

1993

▶ **See Figures 19 and 20**

1. Check for spark at each spark plug with a spark tester. Check at least 2 plug wires.

Fig. 14 Measuring the pickup coil resistance — 1989-90 VIN Code 6 engine

Fig. 15 Measuring the pickup coil resistance — 1991-92 VIN Code 6 engines

2. If spark is only detected at some plugs, check for a faulty distributor cap or rotor. Also check the spark plugs and plug wires. Replace, if necessary.

3. Measure the resistance of the distributor connector **C1** when cold, between terminals 3 and 6, using a digital voltmeter. If the camshaft position (CMP) sensor resistance is not between 185-275 ohms, replace the distributor housing.

4. Measure the resistance of the distributor connector **C1** when cold, between terminals 2 and 5, using a digital voltmeter. If the camshaft position (CMP) sensor resistance is not between 370-550 ohms, replace the distributor housing.

5. Measure the resistance of the distributor connector **C1** when hot, between terminals 3 and 6, using a digital voltmeter. If the camshaft position (CMP) sensor resistance is not between 240-325 ohms, replace the distributor housing.

6. Measure the resistance of the distributor connector **C1** when hot, between terminals 2 and 5, using a digital voltmeter. If the camshaft position (CMP) sensor resistance is not between 475-650 ohms, replace the distributor housing.

7. Measure the air gap between the signal rotor and the camshaft position (CMP) sensor. If the air gap is not 0.008-0.016 inch (0.2-0.4 mm), replace the distributor housing.

Component Replacement

The two most commonly replaced parts in the distributor (aside from the cap and rotor as maintenance) will be the

1 PICKUP COIL
2 SIGNAL ROTOR

Fig. 16 Checking the air gap on the 1989-92 VIN Code 6 engines

A 0.2-0.4 mm (0.008-0.016")
B 0.2-0.4 mm (0.008-0.016")

Fig. 17 Measuring the air gap — 1990-92 VIN Code 5 engines

Fig. 18 Pickup coil connectors — 1990-92 VIN Code 5 engines

signal generator and the igniter. Replacement of any internal piece requires removal of the distributor from the engine.

➡The distributor on the 1989-90 VIN Code 6 (Prizm) engine contains no replaceable parts except the ignition coil. Any other failed item in the distributor requires replacement of the complete unit.

Fig. 19 Measuring the Camshaft Position (CMP) sensor resistance — 1993 engines

Fig. 20 Measuring the air gap — 1993 engines

IGNITER AND SIGNAL ROTOR

Removal & Installation

1985-88 VIN CODE 4 AND VIN CODE 5 ENGINES

▶ See Figures 21, 22, 23 and 24

1. Remove the distributor as outlined in Section 3. Make certain the negative battery cable is disconnected before beginning the work.
2. Remove the packing and distributor rotor.
3. Remove the dust cover over the distributor components and remove the dust cover over the ignition coil.
4. Remove the nuts and disconnect the wiring from the ignition coil.

5. Remove the four screws and remove the ignition coil from the distributor.
6. At the igniter terminals, disconnect the wiring from the connecting points.
7. Loosen and remove the two screws holding the igniter and remove it from the distributor.
8. If the signal rotor is to be replaced, use a screwdriver and CAREFULLY pry the rotor and spring up and off the shaft. When replacing the rotor, use a small bearing driver or long socket to fit over the shaft on top of the signal rotor. Tap gently; the force will be equally distributed and the rotor will slide evenly into place.
9. Install the igniter and connect its wiring. Pay particular attention to the correct routing of the wiring within the housing. There is one correct position only; any other wiring placements risk damage.
10. Install the ignition coil and secure its wiring. Again, watch the wiring positions.
11. Reinstall the dust covers, the packing and distributor rotor.
12. Reinstall the distributor and set the engine timing.

1990-92 VIN CODE 5 ENGINE

1. Disconnect the negative battery cable.
2. Remove the distributor from the engine as outlined in Section 3.
3. Remove the distributor cap, cap seal and rotor.
4. Remove the dust cover from the igniter.
5. Remove the igniter and pickup coil retaining screws.
6. Separate the pickup coil from the igniter and disconnect the electrical connections from the igniter.

Fig. 21 The coil is easily removed with the distributor off the car

Fig. 22 Removing the igniter

Fig. 23 Carefully pry the signal rotor off the shaft. Don't damage the shaft or distributor housing

CORRECT   WRONG

1– YELLOW WIRE
2– GREEN WIRE
3– BROWN WIRE
4– RED WIRE

Fig. 24 Correct wiring placement is required during reassembly. The spinning rotor can cut a wire almost instantly. Above: wiring path for igniter; below: color code and placement for ignition coil wiring

To install:

7. Reconnect the electrical connections between the igniter and pickup coil and assemble the pickup coil to the igniter.
8. Install the igniter and pickup coil to the distributor.
  a. Adjust the signal rotor air gap to 0.008-0.016 (0-2 mm).
9. Install the igniter dust cover.
10. Install the rotor, cap seal and cap.
11. Reconnect the negative battery cable.

1991-92 VIN CODE 6 ENGINE

▶ See Figures 25, 26 and 27

1. Disconnect the negative battery cable.
2. Remove the distributor cap, cap seal and rotor.
3. Remove the dust cover from the igniter.
4. Remove the ignitor retaining screws and remove the ignitor assembly from the distributor.

To install:

5. Install the ignitor assembly to the distributor housing. Then, install the retaining screws.
6. Install the ignitor assembly dust cover.
  a. Align a signal rotor ridge with the ridge on the generator assembly. Then, adjust the signal rotor air gap to 0.008-0.016 (0-2 mm).
7. Install the distributor rotor, cap seal and cap.
8. Reconnect the negative battery cable.

1993 VIN CODE 6 AND VIN CODE 8 ENGINES

1. Disconnect the negative battery cable.
2. Remove the distributor from the vehicle.
3. Remove the distributor cap, cap seal and rotor.
4. Remove the dust cover from the igniter.

Fig. 25 Removing the ignition coil

Fig. 26 Removing the igniter

Fig. 27 Installing the igniter

5. Remove the 3 screws and 3 wires from the ignitor terminals.

6. Remove the 2 ignitor retaining screws and remove the ignitor assembly from the distributor housing.

To install:

7. Install the ignitor assembly to the distributor housing. Then, install the retaining screws and wire terminals.

8. Install the ignitor assembly dust cover.

9. Install the distributor rotor, cap seal and cap.

10. Reconnect the negative battery cable.

IGNITION TIMING

Ignition timing is the measurement (in degrees) of crankshaft position at the instant the spark plug fires. Ignition timing is adjusted by loosening the distributor locking device and turning the distributor in the engine.

It takes a fraction of a second for the spark from the plug to completely ignite the mixture in the cylinder. Because of this, the spark plug must fire before the piston reaches TDC (top dead center, the highest point in its travel), if the mixture is to be completely ignited as the piston passes TDC. This measurement is given in degrees (of crankshaft rotation) before the piston reaches top dead center (BTDC). If the ignition timing setting for your engine is seven degrees BTDC, this means that the spark plug must fire at a time when the piston for that cylinder is 7 degrees before top dead center of its compression stroke. However, this only holds true while your engine is at idle speed.

As you accelerate from idle, the speed of your engine (rpm) increases. The increase in rpm means that the pistons are now traveling up and down much faster. Because of this, the spark plugs will have to fire even sooner if the mixture is to be completely ignited as the piston passes TDC. To accomplish this, the distributor incorporates means to advance the timing of the spark as the engine speed increases.

The distributor in your carbureted Nova has two means of advancing the ignition timing. One is called centrifugal advance and is actuated by weights in the distributor. The other is called vacuum advance and is controlled by the large circular housing on the side of the distributor.

In addition, some distributors have a vacuum-retard mechanism which is contained in the same housing on the side of the distributor as the vacuum advance. The function of this mechanism is to retard the timing of the ignition spark under certain engine conditions. The causes more complete burning of the air/fuel mixture in the cylinder and consequently lowers exhaust emissions.

Because these mechanisms change ignition timing, it is necessary to disconnect and plug the vacuum lines from the distributor when setting the basic ignition timing.

The fuel injected Nova and all Prizm have neither a centrifugal advance nor a vacuum unit. All the timing changes are controlled electronically by the ECM. This solid state "brain" receives data from many sensors (including the distributor), and commands changes in spark timing (and other functions) based on immediate driving conditions. This instant response allows the engine to be kept at peak performance and economy throughout the driving cycle. Basic timing can still be checked and adjusted on these engines.

If the ignition timing is set too far advanced (BTDC), the ignition and expansion of the air/fuel mixture in the cylinder will try to force the piston down while it is still traveling upward.

This causes engine ping, a sound which resembles marbles being dropped into an empty tin can. If the ignition timing is too far retarded (after, or ATDC), the piston will have already started down on the power stroke when the air/fuel mixture ignites and expands. This will cause the piston to be forced down only a portion of its travel. This results in poor engine performance and lack of power.

Ignition timing adjustment is checked with a timing light. This instrument is connected to the number one (No. 1) spark plug wire. The timing light flashes every time an electrical current is sent from the distributor through the No. 1 spark plug wire to the spark plug. The crankshaft pulley and the front cover of the engine are marked with a timing pointer and a timing scale.

When the timing pointer is aligned with the 0 mark on the timing scale, the piston in the No. 1 cylinder is at TDC of it compression stroke. With the engine running, and the timing light aimed at the timing pointer and timing scale, the stroboscopic (periodic) flashes from the timing light will allow you to check the ignition timing setting of the engine. The timing light flashes every time the spark plug in the No. 1 cylinder of the engine fires. Since the flash from the timing light makes the crankshaft pulley seem to stand still for a moment, you will be able to read the exact position of the piston in the No. 1 cylinder on the timing scale on the front of the engine.

If you're buying a timing light, make sure the unit you select is rated for electronic or solid-state ignitions. Generally, these lights have two wires which connect to the battery with alligator clips and a third wire which connects to no. 1 plug wire. The best lights have an inductive pick-up on the third wire; this allows you to simply clip the small box over the wire. Older lights may require the removal of the plug wire and the installation of an inline adapter. Since the spark plugs in the twin-cam engines (4A-GE and 4A-FE) are in deep wells, rigging the adapter can be difficult. Buy quality the first time and the tool will give lasting results and ease of use.

CHECKING AND ADJUSTMENT

1985-88 VIN Code 4 Carbureted Engine
▶ **See Figure 28**

This engine requires a special tachometer hook-up to the service connector wire coming out of the distributor. As many tachometers are not compatible with this hook-up, we recommend that you consult with the manufacturer or salesman before purchasing a certain type.

✳✳WARNING

NEVER allow the ignition coil terminal to become grounded; severe and expensive damage can occur to the coil and/or igniter!

1. Warm the engine to normal operating temperature. Do not attempt to check timing or idle on a cold engine — all the readings will be different. Connect a tachometer and check the engine idle speed to be sure it is within the specification given in the Tune-Up Specifications chart at the beginning of this Section. Adjust the idle if needed and shut the engine off.

2. If the timing marks are difficult to see, use a dab of paint or chalk to make them more visible.

3. Connect a timing light according to the manufacturer's instructions.

4. Label and disconnect the vacuum line(s) from the distributor vacuum unit. Plug it (them) with a pencil or golf tee(s).

5. Be sure that the timing light wires are clear of the fan and start the engine.

6. Allow the engine to run at the specified idle speed with the gearshift in Neutral.

✳✳CAUTION

Be sure that the parking brake is set and the wheels are blocked to prevent the car from rolling in either direction.

7. Point the timing light at the marks on the tab alongside the crank pulley. With the engine at idle, timing should be at the specification given on the Tune-Up Specification Chart at the beginning of the section.

8. If the timing is not at the specification, loosen the bolts at the base of the distributor just enough so that the distributor can be turned. Turn the distributor to advance or retard the timing as required. Once the proper marks are seen to align with the timing light, timing is correct.

9. Stop the engine and tighten the bolts. Start the engine and recheck the timing. Stop the engine; disconnect the tachometer and the timing light. Connect the vacuum line(s) to the distributor vacuum unit.

1988 VIN Code 5 Engine — Fuel Injected Nova

▶ **See Figures 29 and 30**

This engine requires a special tachometer hook-up to the service connector wire coming out of the distributor. As many tachometers are not compatible with this hook-up, we recommend that you consult with the manufacturer or salesman before purchasing a certain type.

✳✳WARNING

NEVER allow the ignition coil terminal to become grounded; severe and expensive damage can occur to the coil and/or igniter.

1. Warm the engine to normal operating temperature. Do not attempt to check timing or idle on a cold engine — all the readings will be different.

2. Using a small jumper wire, short both terminals of the Check Engine connector located near the wiper motor.

3. Connect a tachometer and check the engine idle speed to be sure it is within the specification given in the Tune-Up Specifications chart at the beginning of this section. Adjust the idle if needed and shut the engine OFF.

4. If the timing marks are difficult to see, use a dab of paint or chalk to make them more visible.

5. Connect a timing light according to the manufacturer's instructions.

6. Start the engine and use the timing light to observe the timing marks. With the jumper wire in the connector the timing should be 10° BTDC with the engine fully warmed up and the transmission in Neutral. If the timing is not correct, loosen the bolts at the distributor just enough so that the distributor can be turned. Turn the distributor to advance or retard the timing as required. Once the proper marks are seen to align with the timing light, timing is correct.

7. Without changing the position of the distributor, tighten the distributor bolts and double check the timing with the light.

8. Disconnect the jumper wire at the Check Engine connector.

9. Check the timing again with the light. Manual transmission cars should now show timing in excess of 16° BTDC and automatic transmission cars more than 12° BTDC. If necessary, repeat the timing adjustment procedure.

10. Shut the engine OFF and disconnect all test equipment.

Fig. 28 Ignition timing adjustment and mark location, 1985-88 VIN Code 4 carbureted Nova

Fig. 29 Jumper wire must be installed to check the timing on fuel injected Novas, 1988 VIN Code 5 engines

Fig. 30 Ignition timing marks on the 1988 VIN Code 5 and all 1991-93 engines. Note the small notch on the pulley; this is the mark to align with the degree scale

1989-92 VIN Code 6 Engine — Fuel Injected Prizm

▶ See Figures 30, 31, 32 and 33

This engine requires a special tachometer hook-up to the service connector port on the left shock tower. As many tachometers are not compatible with this hook-up, we recommend that you consult with the manufacturer or salesman before purchasing a certain type.

✳✳WARNING

NEVER allow the tachometer terminal to become grounded; severe and expensive damage can occur to the coil and/or igniter.

1. Warm the engine to normal operating temperature. Turn all electrical accessories OFF.
2. Connect a tachometer and check the engine idle speed to be sure it is within the specification given in the Tune-Up Specifications chart at the beginning of this section. Adjust the idle if needed and shut the engine OFF.
3. Connect a timing light according to the manufacturer's instructions.
4. Remove the cap on the diagnostic connector. Using a small jumper wire, short terminals E1 and T together.
5. Start the engine and use the timing light to observe the timing marks. With the jumper wire in the connector, the timing should be at the specification listed on the Vehicle Emissions Label located under the hood. If the timing is not correct, loosen the bolts at the distributor just enough so that the distributor can be turned. Turn the distributor to advance or retard the timing as required. Once the proper marks are seen to align with the timing light, timing is correct.
6. Without changing the position of the distributor, tighten the distributor bolts to 14 ft. lbs. and double check the timing with the light.

7. Remove the jumper wire from the diagnostic connector and reinstall the cap.
8. On 1989-90 VIN code 6 engines, disconnect the air control valve (ACV) connector at the intake manifold.
9. Recheck the timing; it should be 10° BTDC.
10. On 1989-90 VIN code 6 engines, reconnect the ACV connector.
11. Shut the engine OFF and disconnect all test equipment.

1991-92 VIN Code 5 and All 1993 Engines

▶ See Figures 30, 31, 32, 33 and 34

This engine requires a special tachometer hook-up to the service connector port on the left shock tower. As many tachometers are not compatible with this hook-up, we recommend that you consult with the manufacturer or salesman before purchasing a certain type.

✳✳WARNING

NEVER allow the tachometer terminal to become grounded; severe and expensive damage can occur to the coil and/or igniter.

1. Warm the engine to normal operating temperature. Turn all electrical accessories OFF.
2. Connect a tachometer and check the engine idle speed to be sure it is within the specification given in the Tune-Up Specifications chart at the beginning of this section. Adjust the idle if needed and shut the engine OFF.
3. Connect a timing light according to the manufacturer's instructions.
4. Remove the cap on the diagnostic connector. Using a fused jumper wire, connect terminals E1 and TE1 together.
5. Start the engine and use the timing light to observe the timing marks. With the jumper wire in the connector, the timing should be at the specification listed on the Vehicle Emissions Label located under the hood. If the timing is not correct, loosen the bolts at the distributor just enough so that the distributor can be turned. Turn the distributor to advance or retard the timing as required. Once the proper marks are seen to align with the timing light, timing is correct.
6. Without changing the position of the distributor, tighten the distributor bolts to 14 ft. lbs. and double check the timing with the light.
7. Remove the jumper wire from the diagnostic connector and reinstall the cap.
8. Shut the engine OFF and disconnect all test equipment.

1. E1 terminal
2. T terminal
3. Service wire
4. Diagnostic connector

Fig. 31 Checking the timing requires shorting the E1 and T terminals at the diagnostic connector, 1989-92 VIN Code 6 and 1990 VIN Code 5 engines — see text for details

1. IG terminal
2. Tachometer
3. Battery
4. Diagnostic connector

Fig. 32 Correct tachometer hook-up — 1989-92 Prizm

1 ACV CONNECTOR

Fig. 33 Use care when handling the air control valve wiring. The connector has a locking device which must be released before removal

Fig. 34 Checking the timing requires shorting the E1 and TE1 terminals at the diagnostic connector, 1991-92 VIN Code 5 and all 1993 engines — see text for details

VALVE LASH

Valve lash is one factor which determines how far the intake and exhaust valves will open into the cylinder. If the valve clearance is too large, part of the motion of the camshaft will be used up in removing excessive clearance, thus the valves will not be opened far enough. This condition has two effects, the valve train components will emit a tapping noise as they take up the excessive clearance, and the engine will perform poorly, due to a smaller amount of air/fuel mixture admitted to the cylinders. The less the exhaust valves open, the greater the back pressure in the cylinder.

If the valve clearance is too small, the intake and exhaust valves will not fully seat on the cylinder head when they close. When a valve seats on the cylinder head it does two things, sealing the combustion chamber so none of the gases in the cylinder can escape and cooling itself by transferring some of the heat it absorbed from the combustion process. Therefore, if the valve clearance is too small, the engine will run poorly (due to gases escaping from the combustion chamber), and the valves will overheat and warp.

➡While all valve adjustments must be as accurate as possible, it is better to have the valve adjustment slightly loose than slightly tight, as burnt valves may result from overly tight adjustments.

ADJUSTMENT

1985-88 VIN Code 4 Carbureted Engine

♦ See Figures 35, 36 and 37

1. Start the engine and run it until it reaches normal operating temperature.
2. Stop the engine. Remove the air cleaner assembly. Remove the valve cover.

✳✳CAUTION

Be careful when removing components; the engine will be hot.

3. Turn the crankshaft until the pointer or notch on the pulley aligns with the **O** or the **T** mark on the timing scale.

This will ensure that the engine is at TDC. Turning the engine (with a wrench on the crankshaft bolt) is much easier if the spark plugs are removed.

➡**Check that the rocker arms on the No. 1 cylinder are loose and those on the No. 4 cylinder are tight. If not, turn the crankshaft one complete revolution (360°).**

4. Using a feeler gauge, check the clearance between the bottom of the rocker arm and the top of the valve stem. This measurement should correspond to the one given in the Tune-Up Specifications Chart in this section. Check only the valves listed under First in the accompanying illustrations for your engine.

5. If the clearance is not within specifications, the valves will require adjustment. Loosen the locknut on the rocker arm and, still holding the nut with an open end wrench, turn the adjustment screw to achieve the correct clearance. This is a detail-oriented job; work for exact clearance.

6. Once the correct clearance is achieved, keep the adjustment screw from turning with your screwdriver, and then tighten the locknut. Recheck the valve clearance. If it's proper, proceed to the next valve as shown on the diagram.

7. After the correct four valves have been adjusted, turn the engine one complete revolution (360°) and adjust the remaining valves. Follow steps 4-6 and use the valve arrangement illustration marked Second.

Fig. 35 Adjust these valves first on the 1985-88 VIN Code 4 carbureted engines

Fig. 36 Adjust these valves second on the 1985-88 VIN Code 4 carbureted engines

Fig. 37 Checking the valve lash

1. Valves—number 1 cylinder
2. Valves—number 2 cylinder
3. Intake camshaft
4. Exhaust camshaft
5. Valves—number 3 cylinder

Fig. 38 First pass when checking valve clearance on the 1988-93 fuel injected engines

8. Use a new gasket and then install the valve cover. Install any other components which were removed for access to the cover.

9. Start the engine. Listen for any excessive tapping (indicating a loosened rocker) and check the valve cover for any signs of oil leaks.

1988 VIN Code 5 Fuel Injected Engine All 1989-93 Engines

▶ See Figures 38, 39, 40, 41, 42, 43, 44 and 45

❋❋WARNING

The use of the correct special tools or their equivalent is REQUIRED for this procedure. The valve adjustment requires removal of the adjusting shims (Tool kit J-37141 or equivalent) and accurate measurement of the shims with a micrometer. A selection of replacement shims is also required. Do not attempt this procedure if you are not equipped with the proper tools.

➡Valves on this motor are adjusted with the engine cold. Do not attempt adjustment if the engine has been run within the previous 4 hours. An overnight cooling period is recommended.

1. Remove the valve cover following procedures discussed in Section 3.

2. Turn the crankshaft to align the groove in the crankshaft pulley with the **0** mark on the timing belt cover. Removing the spark plugs makes this easier, but is not required.

1. Valves—number 1 cylinder
2. Valves—number 2 cylinder
3. Intake camshaft
4. Exhaust camshaft
5. Valves—number 3 cylinder

Fig. 39 Second pass when checking valve clearance on the 1988-93 fuel injected engines

Fig. 40 Use the correct tools to depress and hold down the valve lifter

Fig. 41 Carefully remove the shim to be replaced (above) with a small screwdriver and magnetic tools. Clean and dry the shim before measuring with the micrometer (below)

3. Check that the lifters on No. 1 cylinder are loose and those on No. 4 are tight. If not, turn the crankshaft pulley one full revolution (360°).

4. Using the feeler gauge, measure the clearance on the four valves shown in the diagram labeled First Pass. Make a WRITTEN record of any measurements which are not within specification.

5. Rotate the crankshaft pulley one full turn (360°) and check the clearance on the other four valves. These are shown on the diagram labeled Second Pass. Any measurements not within specification should be added to your WRITTEN record.

6. For ANY given valve needing adjustment:

a. Turn the crankshaft pulley until the camshaft lobe points upward over the valve. This takes the tension off the valve and spring.

b. Using the forked tool, press the valve lifter downward and hold it there. Some tool kits require a second tool for holding the lifter in place, allowing the first to be removed.

c. Using small magnetic tools, remove the adjusting shim from the top of the lifter.

d. Use the micrometer and measure the thickness of the shim removed. Determine the thickness of the new shim using the formula below or the selection charts. For the purposes of the following formula, T = Thickness of the old shim; A = Valve clearance measured; N = Thickness of the new shim.

- For the intake side (camshaft nearest to the intake manifold): N = T + (A - 0.20mm or 0.008 in.)
- For the exhaust side (camshaft nearest to the exhaust manifold): N = T + (A - 0.25mm or 0.010 in.)

e. Select a shim closest to the calculated thickness. Use the lifter depressor tool to press down the lifter and install the shim. Shims are available in 17 sizes from 2.50mm (0.0984 in.) to 3.30mm (0.1299 in.). The standard increment is 0.05mm (0.002 in.)

f. Repeat Steps **a** through **e** for each valve needing adjustment.

7. Reinstall the valve cover, following the procedures outlined in Section 3.

8. Check and adjust the timing and idle speed, following the procedures outlined in this section.

Exhaust valve adjusting shim selection chart

Removed Shim Thickness (mm) column headers: 2.500, 2.525, 2.550, 2.575, 2.600, 2.620, 2.640, 2.650, 2.660, 2.680, 2.700, 2.720, 2.740, 2.750, 2.760, 2.780, 2.800, 2.820, 2.840, 2.850, 2.860, 2.880, 2.900, 2.920, 2.940, 2.950, 2.960, 2.980, 3.000, 3.020, 3.040, 3.050, 3.060, 3.080, 3.100, 3.120, 3.140, 3.150, 3.160, 3.180, 3.200, 3.225, 3.250, 3.275, 3.300

Measured Clearance (mm) ranges:
Measured Clearance (mm)
0.000 — 0.009
0.010 — 0.025
0.026 — 0.040
0.041 — 0.050
0.051 — 0.070
0.071 — 0.090
0.091 — 0.100
0.101 — 0.120
0.121 — 0.140
0.141 — 0.150
0.151 — 0.170
0.171 — 0.190
0.191 — 0.199
0.200 — 0.300
0.301 — 0.320
0.321 — 0.325
0.326 — 0.340
0.341 — 0.350
0.351 — 0.370
0.371 — 0.375
0.376 — 0.390
0.391 — 0.400
0.401 — 0.420
0.421 — 0.425
0.426 — 0.440
0.441 — 0.450
0.451 — 0.470
0.471 — 0.475
0.476 — 0.490
0.491 — 0.500
0.501 — 0.520
0.521 — 0.525
0.526 — 0.540
0.541 — 0.550
0.551 — 0.570
0.571 — 0.575
0.576 — 0.590
0.591 — 0.600
0.601 — 0.620
0.621 — 0.625
0.626 — 0.640
0.641 — 0.650
0.651 — 0.670
0.671 — 0.675
0.676 — 0.690
0.691 — 0.700
0.701 — 0.720
0.721 — 0.725
0.726 — 0.740
0.741 — 0.750
0.751 — 0.770
0.771 — 0.775
0.776 — 0.790
0.791 — 0.800
0.801 — 0.820
0.821 — 0.825
0.826 — 0.840
0.841 — 0.850
0.851 — 0.870
0.871 — 0.875
0.876 — 0.890
0.891 — 0.900
0.901 — 0.925
0.926 — 0.950
0.951 — 0.975
0.976 — 1.000
1.025 — 1.001
1.026 — 1.050
1.051 — 1.075

AVAILABLE SHIM NUMBERS AND THICKNESSES

mm (in.)

SHIM NO.	THICKNESS	SHIM NO.	THICKNESS
02	2.500 (0.0984)	20	2.950 (0.1161)
04	2.550 (0.1004)	22	3.000 (0.1181)
06	2.600 (0.1024)	24	3.050 (0.1201)
08	2.650 (0.1043)	26	3.100 (0.1220)
10	2.700 (0.1063)	28	3.150 (0.1240)
12	2.750 (0.1083)	30	3.200 (0.1260)
14	2.800 (0.1102)	32	3.250 (0.1280)
16	2.850 (0.1122)	34	3.300 (0.1299)
18	2.900 (0.1142)		

Specified exhaust valve clearance (cold):
0.20–0.30 mm (0.008–0.012 in.)
Example: A 2.800 mm shim is removed
and the measured clearance
is 0.450 mm.
Replace the 2.8000 mm shim
with shim NO. 22 (3.000 mm).

Fig. 42 Exhaust valve adjusting shim selection chart — 1988-92

Removed Shim Thickness (mm) — column headers:

Measured Clearance (mm)	2.500	2.525	2.550	2.575	2.600	2.620	2.640	2.650	2.660	2.680	2.700	2.720	2.740	2.750	2.760	2.780	2.800	2.820	2.840	2.850	2.860	2.880	2.900	2.920	2.940	2.950	2.960	2.980	3.000	3.020	3.040	3.050	3.060	3.080	3.100	3.120	3.140	3.150	3.160	3.180	3.200	3.225	3.250	3.275	3.300
0.000 – 0.009															02	02	04	04	04	06	06	08	08	08	10	10	12	12	12	14	14	16	16	16	18	18	20	20	20	22	22	24	24	26	26
0.010 – 0.025													02	02	02	04	04	04	06	06	08	08	08	10	10	12	12	12	14	14	16	16	16	18	18	20	20	20	22	22	24	24	26	26	28
0.026 – 0.029											02	02	02	04	04	04	06	06	06	08	08	10	10	10	12	12	14	14	14	16	16	18	18	20	20	20	22	22	24	24	26	26	28		
0.030 – 0.040							02	02	02	04	04	04	06	06	06	08	08	10	10	10	12	12	14	14	14	16	16	18	18	18	20	20	20	22	22	24	24	26	26	28					
0.041 – 0.050								02	02	02	04	04	06	06	06	08	08	10	10	10	12	12	14	14	14	16	16	18	18	18	20	20	22	22	22	24	24	26	26	28					
0.051 – 0.070						02	02	02	02	04	04	06	06	06	08	08	08	10	10	12	12	12	14	14	14	16	16	18	18	18	20	20	22	22	22	24	24	26	26	28	28				
0.071 – 0.075					02	02	02	02	04	04	04	06	06	08	08	08	10	10	12	12	12	14	14	14	16	16	18	18	18	20	20	22	22	22	24	24	26	26	28	28					
0.076 – 0.090					02	02	02	02	04	04	06	06	08	08	08	10	10	12	12	12	14	14	16	16	16	18	18	20	20	20	22	22	24	24	26	26	28	28	30						
0.091 – 0.100				02	02	04	04	04	06	06	06	08	08	10	10	10	12	12	14	14	14	16	16	18	18	18	20	20	20	22	22	24	24	26	26	28	28	30							
0.101 – 0.120			02	02	02	04	04	04	06	06	08	08	08	10	10	12	12	12	14	14	16	16	16	18	18	20	20	22	22	22	24	24	26	26	28	28	30	30							
0.121 – 0.125		02	02	02	04	04	06	06	06	08	08	08	10	10	12	12	14	14	14	16	16	18	18	18	20	20	22	22	22	24	24	26	26	28	28	30	30								
0.126 – 0.140		02	02	04	04	06	06	06	08	08	08	10	10	12	12	14	14	14	16	16	18	18	18	20	20	20	22	22	24	24	26	26	28	28	30	30	32								
0.141 – 0.149		02	02	04	04	06	06	06	08	08	10	10	10	12	12	14	14	14	16	16	18	18	18	20	20	22	22	22	24	24	26	26	28	28	30	30	32								
0.150 – 0.250																																													
0.251 – 0.270	04	06	06	08	08	10	10	10	12	12	14	14	14	16	16	18	18	18	20	20	22	22	22	24	26	26	26	28	28	30	30	30	32	32	34	34									
0.271 – 0.275	04	06	06	08	08	10	10	10	12	14	14	16	16	16	18	18	20	20	20	22	22	24	24	24	26	26	28	28	28	30	30	32	32	34	34										
0.276 – 0.290	06	06	08	08	10	10	10	12	12	14	14	16	16	16	18	18	20	20	22	22	22	24	24	26	26	28	28	30	30	30	32	32	34	34											
0.291 – 0.300	06	06	08	08	10	10	12	12	12	14	14	16	16	16	18	18	20	20	22	22	22	24	24	26	26	28	28	28	30	30	32	32	32	34	34										
0.301 – 0.320	06	08	08	10	10	12	12	12	14	14	16	16	16	18	18	20	20	20	22	22	24	24	24	26	26	28	28	28	30	30	32	32	32	34	34										
0.321 – 0.325	06	08	08	10	10	12	12	14	14	16	16	18	18	18	20	20	22	22	24	24	24	26	26	28	28	30	30	30	32	32	34	34												
0.326 – 0.340	08	08	10	10	12	12	14	14	24	16	16	18	18	20	20	20	22	22	24	24	26	26	28	28	28	30	30	32	32	32	34	34	34											
0.341 – 0.350	08	08	10	10	12	12	14	14	14	16	16	18	18	18	20	20	22	22	22	24	26	26	26	28	28	30	30	30	32	32	34	34	34											
0.351 – 0.370	08	10	10	12	12	14	14	14	16	16	18	18	18	20	20	22	22	22	24	24	26	26	26	28	28	30	30	30	32	34	34	34	34											
0.371 – 0.375	08	10	10	12	12	14	14	16	16	18	18	20	20	22	22	22	24	24	26	26	28	28	28	30	30	30	32	34	34	34	34													
0.376 – 0.390	10	10	12	12	14	14	16	16	16	18	18	20	20	22	22	24	24	24	26	26	28	28	30	30	32	32	32	34	34															
0.391 – 0.400	10	10	12	12	14	14	16	16	16	18	18	20	20	20	22	22	24	24	24	26	26	28	28	30	30	32	32	32	34	34														
0.401 – 0.420	10	12	12	14	14	16	16	16	18	18	20	20	20	22	22	24	24	24	26	26	28	28	30	30	30	32	32	34	34															
0.421 – 0.425	10	12	12	14	14	16	16	18	18	20	20	22	22	22	24	24	26	26	28	28	28	30	30	32	32	34	34																	
0.426 – 0.440	12	12	14	14	16	16	18	18	20	20	22	22	22	24	24	26	26	28	28	30	30	30	32	32	34	34																		
0.441 – 0.450	12	12	14	14	16	16	18	18	18	20	20	22	22	22	24	24	26	26	26	28	30	30	30	32	32	34	34	34																
0.451 – 0.470	12	14	14	16	16	18	18	18	20	20	22	22	22	24	24	26	26	26	28	28	30	30	32	32	32	34	34	34																
0.471 – 0.475	12	14	14	16	16	18	18	20	20	22	22	24	24	24	26	26	28	28	30	30	32	32	32	34	34																			
0.476 – 0.490	14	14	16	16	18	18	20	20	20	22	22	24	24	26	26	26	28	28	30	30	32	32	32	34	34																			
0.491 – 0.500	14	14	16	16	18	18	20	20	20	22	22	24	24	26	26	26	28	28	30	30	32	32	32	34	34																			
0.501 – 0.520	14	16	16	18	18	20	20	20	22	22	24	24	24	26	26	28	28	28	30	30	32	32	32	34	34																			
0.521 – 0.525	14	16	16	18	18	20	20	22	22	24	24	26	26	26	28	28	30	30	32	32	34	34																						
0.526 – 0.540	16	16	18	18	20	20	22	22	24	24	26	26	26	28	28	30	30	32	32	34	34																							
0.541 – 0.550	16	16	18	18	20	20	22	22	22	24	24	26	26	28	28	30	30	30	32	32	34	34	34																					
0.551 – 0.570	16	18	18	20	20	22	22	22	24	24	26	26	26	28	28	30	30	30	32	32	34	34	34																					
0.571 – 0.575	16	18	18	20	20	22	22	24	24	26	26	28	28	30	30	30	32	32	34	34																								
0.575 – 0.590	18	18	20	20	22	22	24	24	26	26	28	28	30	30	32	32	32	34	34																									
0.591 – 0.600	18	18	20	20	22	22	24	24	24	26	26	28	28	30	30	32	32	32	34	34																								
0.601 – 0.620	18	20	20	22	22	24	24	24	26	26	28	28	28	30	30	32	32	32	34	34																								
0.621 – 0.625	18	20	20	22	22	24	24	26	26	28	28	30	30	32	32	34	34	34																										
0.626 – 0.640	20	20	22	22	24	24	26	26	28	28	30	30	30	32	32	34	34	34																										
0.641 – 0.650	20	20	22	22	24	24	26	26	26	28	28	30	30	32	32	34	34	34																										
0.651 – 0.670	20	22	22	24	24	26	26	26	28	28	30	30	30	32	32	34	34	34																										
0.671 – 0.675	20	22	22	24	24	26	26	28	28	30	30	32	32	34	34																													
0.676 – 0.690	22	22	24	24	26	26	28	28	28	30	30	32	32	34	34																													
0.691 – 0.700	22	22	24	24	26	26	28	28	28	30	30	32	32	32	34	34																												
0.701 – 0.720	22	24	24	26	26	28	28	28	30	30	32	32	32	34	34																													
0.721 – 0.725	22	24	24	26	26	28	28	30	30	32	32	34	34	34																														
0.726 – 0.740	24	24	26	26	28	28	30	30	30	32	32	34	34	34																														
0.741 – 0.750	24	24	26	26	28	28	30	30	30	32	32	34	34	34																														
0.751 – 0.770	24	26	26	28	28	30	30	30	32	32	34	34	34																															
0.771 – 0.775	24	26	26	28	28	30	30	32	32	34	34																																	
0.776 – 0.790	26	26	28	28	30	30	32	32	32	34	34																																	
0.791 – 0.800	26	26	28	28	30	30	32	32	32	34	34																																	
0.801 – 0.820	26	28	28	30	30	32	32	32	34	34																																		
0.821 – 0.825	26	28	28	30	30	32	32	34	34																																			
0.826 – 0.840	28	28	30	30	32	32	32	34	34																																			
0.841 – 0.850	28	28	30	30	32	32	34	34	34																																			
0.851 – 0.870	28	30	30	32	32	34	34	34																																				
0.871 – 0.875	28	30	30	32	32	34	34	34																																				
0.876 – 0.890	30	30	32	32	34	34	34																																					
0.891 – 0.900	30	30	32	32	34	34																																						
0.901 – 0.925	30	32	32	34	34																																							
0.926 – 0.950	32	32	34	34																																								
0.951 – 0.975	32	34	34																																									
0.976 – 1.000	34	34																																										
1.001 – 1.025	34																																											

AVAILABLE SHIM NUMBERS AND THICKNESSES

mm (in.)

SHIM NO.	THICKNESS	SHIM NO.	THICKNESS
02	2.500 (0.0984)	20	2.950 (0.1161)
04	2.550 (0.1004)	22	3.000 (0.1181)
06	2.600 (0.1024)	24	3.050 (0.1201)
08	2.650 (0.1043)	26	3.100 (0.1220)
10	2.700 (0.1063)	28	3.150 (0.1240)
12	2.750 (0.1083)	30	3.200 (0.1260)
14	2.800 (0.1102)	32	3.250 (0.1280)
16	2.850 (0.1122)	34	3.300 (0.1299)
18	2.900 (0.1142)		

Specified intake clearance (cold):
0.15–0.25 mm (0.006–0.010 in.)

Example: A 2.800 mm shim is removed and the measured clearance is 0.450 mm. Replace the 2.800 mm shim with shim NO. 24 (3.050 mm).

Fig. 43 Intake valve adjusting shim selection chart — 1988-92

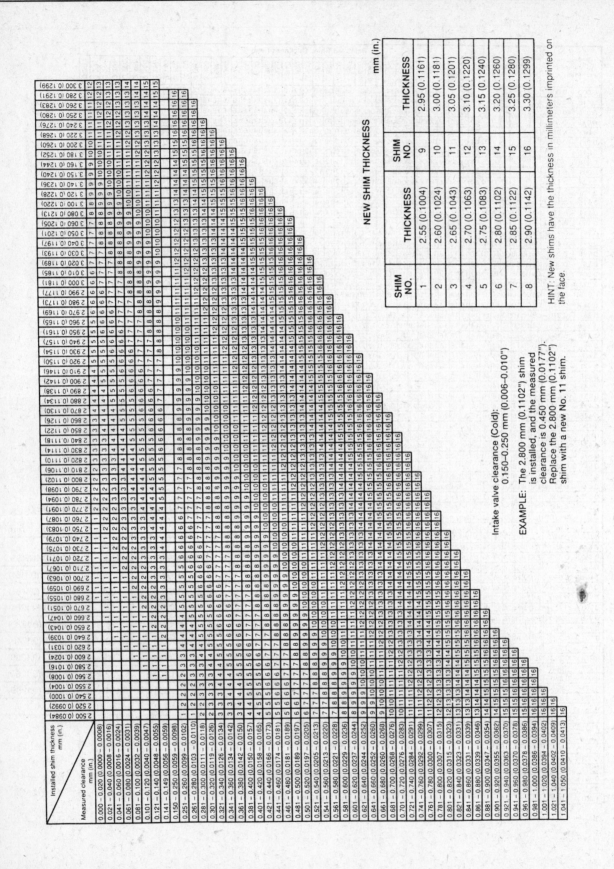

NEW SHIM THICKNESS

SHIM NO.	THICKNESS	SHIM NO.	THICKNESS mm (in.)
1	2.55 (0.1004)	9	2.95 (0.1161)
2	2.60 (0.1024)	10	3.00 (0.1181)
3	2.65 (0.1043)	11	3.05 (0.1201)
4	2.70 (0.1063)	12	3.10 (0.1220)
5	2.75 (0.1083)	13	3.15 (0.1240)
6	2.80 (0.1102)	14	3.20 (0.1260)
7	2.85 (0.1122)	15	3.25 (0.1280)
8	2.90 (0.1142)	16	3.30 (0.1299)

HINT: New shims have the thickness in millimeters imprinted on the face.

Intake valve clearance (Cold):
0.150–0.250 mm (0.006–0.010")

EXAMPLE: The 2.800 mm (0.1102") shim is installed, and the measured clearance is 0.450 mm (0.0177"). Replace the 2.800 mm (0.1102") shim with a new No. 11 shim.

Fig. 44 Intake valve adjusting shim selection chart — 1993

NEW SHIM THICKNESS

mm (in.)

SHIM NO.	THICKNESS	SHIM NO.	THICKNESS
1	2.55 (0.1004)	9	2.95 (0.1161)
2	2.60 (0.1024)	10	3.00 (0.1181)
3	2.65 (0.1043)	11	3.05 (0.1201)
4	2.70 (0.1063)	12	3.10 (0.1220)
5	2.75 (0.1083)	13	3.15 (0.1240)
6	2.80 (0.1102)	14	3.20 (0.1260)
7	2.85 (0.1122)	15	3.25 (0.1280)
8	2.90 (0.1142)	16	3.30 (0.1299)

HINT: New shims have the thickness in millimeters imprinted on the face.

Exhaust valve clearance (Cold): 0.25–0.35 mm (0.010–0.014")

EXAMPLE: The 2.800 mm (0.1102") shim is installed, and the measured clearance is 0.450 mm (0.017"). Replace the 2.800 mm (0.1102") shim with a new No. 9 shim.

Fig. 45 Exhaust valve adjusting shim selection chart — 1993

SPEED AND MIXTURE ADJUSTMENT

Carbureted Nova

▶ **See Figures 46, 47, 48, 49 and 50**

This section contains only adjustments as they normally apply to engine tune-up. Descriptions of the carburetor and fuel systems and complete adjustment procedures can be found in Section 5.

When the engine in your Nova is running, air/fuel mixture from the carburetor is being drawn into the engine by a partial vacuum created by the downward movement of the pistons. The amount of air/fuel mixture that enters the engine is controlled by the throttle plates in the bottom of the carburetor. When the engine is not running, the throttle plates are closed, completely blocking off the bottom of the carburetor from the inside of the engine.

The throttle plates are connected, through the throttle linkage, to the gas pedal inside the car. What you actually are doing when you depress the gas pedal is opening the throttle plate in the carburetor to admit more air/fuel mixture to the engine. The further you open the throttle plates in the carburetor, the higher the engine speed becomes.

To keep the engine idling, it is necessary to open the throttle plates slightly. To prevent having to keep your foot on the gas pedal when the engine is idling, an idle speed adjusting screw is included on the carburetor. This screw has the same effect as keeping your foot on the gas pedal — it holds the throttle plate open just a bit. When the screw is turned in, it opens the throttle, raising the idle speed of the engine. This screw is called the curb idle adjusting screw, and the procedures in this section will tell you how to adjust it.

When you first start the car after an overnight period, the cold motor requires a different air-fuel mixture to run properly. Because of the different mixture, the idle speed must be higher during cold engine operation. This high idle (sometimes called cold idle or fast idle) speed is also adjustable and should be checked periodically. If the high idle is too low, the car will bog and stall until it warms up. If the high idle is set too high, the engine is wasting fuel and suffering increased and premature wear.

Before performing any carburetor adjustments, ALL of the following conditions must be met:
- All accessories are switched off
- Ignition timing is set correctly and all vacuum lines are connected
- Transmission in Neutral and engine warmed up to normal operating temperature
- Choke opened fully
- Fuel level in carburetor sight glass at the correct level. If the level is too high or low, adjust the float level as explained in Section 5.
- Tachometer installed with the positive (+) connector running to the service connector.

CURB IDLE SPEED ADJUSTMENT

Once all the above conditions are met, the curb idle can be adjusted by turning the adjusting knob at the rear of the carburetor. It has a knurled plastic head that may be gripped with the fingers (no screwdriver required) but may be hard to get at under the air cleaner housing. Turn the knob clockwise to raise the idle and counter-clockwise to lower it. Keep a close eye on the tachometer while turning the knob; sometimes a small change in the adjustor causes a big change in the idle speed. Adjust the idle speed to the rpm shown in the Tune-Up Specifications chart at the beginning of this section.

IDLE MIXTURE ADJUSTMENT

To conform with Federal regulations, the idle mixture adjusting screw is adjusted at the factory and plugged with a steel plug by the manufacturer. Under normal conditions there should be no need to remove this plug.

When troubleshooting rough idle, check all other possible causes before attempting to adjust the idle mixture. Only if no other factors are found to be at fault should the idle mixture be adjusted. Since this repair involves removal of the carburetor, it is recommended that the car be thoroughly

Fig. 46 Check the fuel level in the float bowl

Fig. 47 Special service connector required for tachometer hook-up

1. FAST IDLE ADJUSTING SCREW
2. IDLE ADJUSTING SCREW

Fig. 48 Curb idle and fast idle adjusting screws are located on the firewall side of the carburetor

Fig. 50 Seating the adjusting screw

checked on an exhaust emissions analyzer as part of the diagnostic procedure before committing to the repair. If you perform this repair incorrectly or if the idle mixture is not the cause of your problem, you may cause the car to become uncertifiable under Federal and State or Provincial emission laws.

1. Following the procedures given in Section 5, remove the carburetor.

2. Using the following procedure, remove the Mixture Adjusting Screw plug (MAS plug).

a. Plug all of the carburetor ports to prevent the entry of steel particles when drilling.

b. Mark the center of the plug with a punch.

c. Drill a 6mm hole in the center of the plug. As there is only 1mm clearance between the plug and the screw below it, drill carefully and slowly to avoid drilling onto the screw. The drill may force the plug off at any time.

d. Through the hole in the plug, fully screw in the mixture adjusting screw with a screwdriver.

➡**NOTE: Be careful not to damage the screw tip by tightening the screw too tight.**

e. Use a 7mm drill to force the plug off.

3. Inspect the mixture adjusting screw as follows:

a. Blow off any steel particles with compressed air.

b. Remove the screw and inspect it. If the drill has gnawed into the screw top or if the tapered portion is damaged, replace the screw.

1. Drill bit
2. Idle mixture screw
3. 0.04 in. (1mm)

Fig. 49 Drilling the mixture adjusting screw plug

4. Reinstall the mixture adjusting screw. Fully seat the idle mixture adjusting screw and then back it out 3¼ turns.

➡**Be careful not to damage the screw tip by tightening the screw too tight.**

5. Reinstall the carburetor on the engine. Reconnect the vacuum hoses to their proper locations.

6. Reinstall the air cleaner.

7. Adjust the idle speed and mixture as follows:

a. Check the following initial conditions:
• The air cleaner is installed
• The engine is at normal operating temperature
• The choke is fully open
• All accessories are switch off
• All vacuum lines are connected
• The ignition timing is correct
• The transaxle is in neutral (N)
• The float level is correct
• The front wheels are pointed straight ahead (power steering equipped vehicles)

b. Start the engine

c. Turn the mixture adjustment screw slowly until the maximum idle speed is obtained. The preliminary adjustment of 3¼ turn should be fairly close.

d. Set the idle speed by turning the idle speed adjusting screw. The idle mixture speed should be as shown on either the underhood Emissions Label or the Tune-Up Specifications chart at the beginning of this section.

e. Before moving to the next step, repeat adjustments (c) and (d) until the maximum speed will not raise any further no matter how much the idle mixture adjusting screw is adjusted.

f. Final adjust to 650 rpm by turning the mixture adjusting screw.

g. Final adjust the idle speed to specification by turning the idle adjusting screw.

8. Reinstall the mixture adjusting screw plugs. Remove the air cleaner and the EGR vacuum modulator bracket. With the tapered end of the plug facing inward, tap in the plug until it is even with the carburetor surface.

9. Reinstall the EGR vacuum modulator bracket and the air cleaner.

HIGH IDLE SPEED ADJUSTMENT

1. Stop the engine and remove the air cleaner and its housing.

2. Plug the hot idle compensator hose. It's the hose that runs from the lower front part of the carburetor body to a small valve on the air cleaner housing. If not plugged, it will create a vacuum leak causing either a rough idle or stalling.

3. On the left side of the engine, between the block and the firewall, find the vacuum valve with five hoses connected to it. One hose will be in a separate position and four will be in line. This is the thermo vacuum switching valve (TVSV). Of the four hoses in line, one will be labeled " M "; it's usually the second one from the upper or outer end of the valve.

4. Give the hose on the M port a half-turn and remove it from the port. Plug the port (not the hose) with an airtight plug to prevent vacuum leaks.

5. Hold the throttle plate open slightly (you can move the linkage with your fingers or pull gently on the accelerator cable) and move the choke plate to its fully closed position. Hold the choke closed as you release the throttle cable.

6. Start the engine but DO NOT move the gas pedal or the accelerator cable. The engine has been fooled into thinking it's cold — the choke is set and the high idle is engaged. If you move the accelerator, you'll undo everything set up in the previous 5 steps.

7. Adjust the high idle by turning the Fast Idle adjusting screw; it's located just to the left and below the curb idle adjusting screw. You'll need a short, narrow screwdriver to adjust the screw. Set the fast idle to 3000 rpm.

✷✷CAUTION

The engine is running at high speed. Beware of moving parts and hot surfaces.

8. When the fast idle is set correctly, shut the engine off. Remove the plug from the M port of the TVSV and reconnect its hose. Remove the plug from the hot idle compensator hose.

9. Reinstall the air cleaner housing and the filter; connect the hose.

Fuel Injected Nova and Prizm

IDLE SPEED ADJUSTMENT

▶ **See Figures 51 and 52**

One of the merits of electronic fuel injection is that it requires so little adjustment. The computer (ECM) does most of the work in compensating for changes in climate, engine temperature, electrical load and driving conditions. The curb idle on the fuel injected Nova and Prizm should be checked periodically but not adjusted unless off spec by more than 50 rpm. If you are a compulsive tinkerer who feels that "the idle can be adjusted, therefore it must be adjusted", please don't.

If the idle is too far outside its normal range, the computer will see it as a problem (too much or too little air being taken in for the speed of the engine) and attempt to compensate by changing the amount of fuel being delivered. This can lead to wild surging and extremely bizarre idle behavior, making the car virtually undrivable. This is one area in which the old rule of Don't fix it if it isn't broken, applies.

On 1988-90 models, the idle speed adjusting screw is located on the side of the throttle body. You can find the throttle body by following the accelerator cable to its end. The adjusting screw may have a cap over it to prevent casual meddling. If so, pop the cap off with a small screwdriver.

With the engine fully warmed up, properly connect a tachometer. Make sure that all the electrical accessories on the car are turned off and remove the cap over the adjustor screw, if there is one. Start the engine and use a screwdriver to turn the screw. The idle speed should be as shown on the underhood Emissions Label or in the Tune-Up Specifications chart at the beginning of this section.

Fig. 51 Idle adjuster location, fuel injected Nova

Fig. 52 Location of idle adjusting screw, fuel injected Prizm

If for any reason the idle cannot be brought into specification by this adjustment, return the screw to its original setting and follow other diagnostic procedures to find the real cause of the problem. Do not try to cure other problems with this adjustment.

MIXTURE ADJUSTMENT

The air/fuel ratio burned within the engine is controlled by the ECM, based on information delivered by the various sensors on the engine. It is not adjustable as a routine maintenance item. The easiest way to check the air/fuel mixture is to put the car through a tailpipe emissions test. Whether or not this is required in your area, it's a good way of putting numbers on the combustion efficiency of the engine. The engine can only burn so much fuel; if too much is being delivered, it will show up on the test as unburned hydrocarbons (HC).

Putting the car through this test once a year from the time it is newly acquired can provide an excellent baseline for diagnosing future problems.

TORQUE SPECIFICATIONS		
Component	U.S.	Metric
Spark plugs		
1985–88 VIN Code 4 engine	13 ft. lbs.	18 Nm
1988 VIN Code 5 engine	13 ft. lbs.	18 Nm
1989–90	21 ft. lbs.	28 Nm
1991–92		
VIN Code 5 engine	21 ft. lbs.	28 Nm
VIN Code 6 engine	13 ft. lbs.	18 Nm
1993	13 ft. lbs.	18 Nm
Distributor hold-down bolts		
1985–88	14 ft. lbs.	20 Nm
1989–90	89 inch lbs.	10 Nm
1991–92		
VIN Code 5 engine	14 ft. lbs.	20 Nm
VIN Code 6 engine	89 inch lbs.	10 Nm
1993	89 inch lbs.	10 Nm

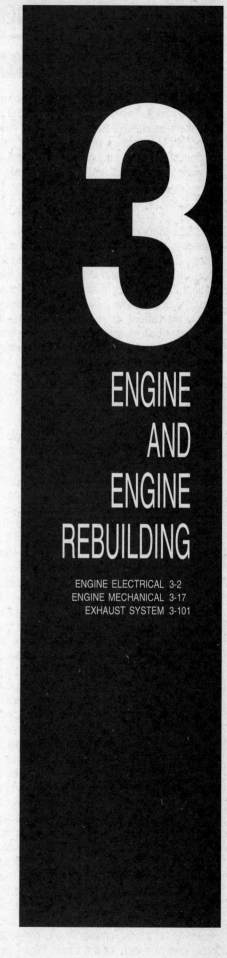

3

ENGINE AND ENGINE REBUILDING

ENGINE ELECTRICAL

For any electrical system to operate, it must make a complete circuit. This simply means that the power flow from the battery must make a complete circle. When an electrical component is operating, power flows from the battery to the components, passes through the component (load) causing it to function, and returns to the battery through the ground path of the circuit. This ground may be either another wire or the actual metal part of the car upon which the component is mounted.

Perhaps the easiest way to visualize this is to think of connecting a light bulb with 2 wires attached to it to the battery. If one of the two wires was attached to the negative (-) post of the battery and the other wire to the positive (+) post, the light bulb would light and the circuit would be complete. Electricity could follow a path from the battery to the bulb and back to the battery. Its not hard to see that with longer wires on our light bulb, it could be mounted anywhere on the car. Further, one wire could be fitted with a switch so that the light could be turned on and off at will. Various other items could be added to our primitive circuit to make the light flash, become brighter or dimmer under certain conditions or advise the user that it's burned out.

Some automotive components don't use a wire to battery — they ground to the metal of the car through their mounting points. The electrical current runs through the chassis of the vehicle and returns to the battery through the ground (-) cable; if you look, you'll see that the battery ground cable connects between the battery and the body of the car.

Every complete circuit must include a load — something to use the electricity coming from the source. If you were to connect a wire between the 2 terminals of the battery (DON'T do this) without the light bulb, the battery would attempt to deliver its entire power supply from one pole to another almost instantly. This is a short circuit. The electricity is taking a short-cut to get to ground and is not being used by any load in the circuit. This sudden and uncontrolled electrical flow can cause great damage to other components in the circuit and can develop a tremendous amount of heat. A short in an automotive wiring harness can develop sufficient heat to melt the insulation on all the surrounding wires and reduce a multi-wire cable to one sad lump of plastic and copper. Two common causes of shorts are broken insulation (thereby exposing the wire to contact with surrounding metal surfaces) or a failed switch (the pins inside the switch come out of place, touch each other and reroute the electricity).

Some electrical components which require a large amount of current to operate also have a relay in their circuit. Since these circuits carry a large amount of current (amperage or amps), the thickness of the wire in the circuit (wire gauge) is also greater. If this large wire were connected from the load to the control switch on the dash, the switch would have to carry the high amperage load and the dash would be twice as large to accommodate wiring harnesses as thick as your wrist. To prevent these problems, a relay is used. The large wires in the circuit are connected from the battery to one side of the relay and from the opposite side of the relay to the load. The relay is normally open, preventing current from passing through the circuit. An additional, smaller wire is connected from the relay to the control switch for the circuit. When the control switch is turned on, it grounds the smaller wire to the relay and completes its circuit. The main switch inside the relay close, sending power to t he component without routing the main power through the inside of the car. Some common circuits which may use relays are the horn, headlights, starter and rear window defogger systems.

It is possible for larger surges of current to pass through the electrical system of your car. If this surge of current were to reach the load in the circuit, it could burn it out or severely damage it. To prevent this, fuse and/or circuit breakers and/or fusible links are connected into the supply wires of the electrical system. These items are nothing more than a built-in weak spot in the system. It's much easier to go to a known location (the fusebox) to see why a circuit is inoperative than to dissect 15 feet of wiring under the dashboard, looking for what happened.

When an electrical current of excessive power passes through the fuse, the fuse blows and breaks the circuit, preventing the passage of current and protecting the components.

A circuit breaker is basically a self-repairing fuse. It will open the circuit in the same fashion as a fuse, but when either the short is removed or the surge subsides, the circuit breaker resets itself and does not need replacement.

A fuse link (fusible link or main link) is a wire that acts as a fuse. It is normally connected between the starter relay and the main wiring harness under the hood. Since the starter is the highest electrical draw on the car, an internal short during starter use could direct about 130 amps into the wrong places. Consider the damage potential of introducing this current into a system whose wiring is rated at 15 amps and you'll understand the need for protection. Since this link is very early in the electrical path, it's the first place to look if nothing on the car works but the battery seems to be charged and is properly connected.

Electrical problems generally fall into one of 3 areas:

1. The component that is not functioning is not receiving current.

2. The component is receiving power but not using it or using it incorrectly (component failure).

3. The component is improperly grounded.

The circuit can be can be checked with a test light and a jumper wire. The test light is a device that looks like a pointed screwdriver with a wire on one end and a bulb in its handle. A jumper wire is simply a piece of wire with alligator clips on each end. If a component is not working, you must follow a systematic plan to determine which of the 3 causes is the villain.

4. Turn on the switch that controls the item not working.

➡**Some items only work when the ignition switch is turned on.**

5. Disconnect the the power supply wire from the component.

6. Attach the ground wire on the test light to a good metal ground.

7. Touch the end probe of the test light to the power wire; if there is current in the wire, the light in the test light will

come on. You have now established that current is getting to the component.

8. Turn the ignition or dash switch off and reconnect the wire to the component.

If the test light does not go on, then the problem is between the battery and the component. This includes all the switches, fuses, relays and the battery itself. Next place to look is the fusebox; check carefully either by eye or by using the test light across the fuse clips. The easiest way to check is to simply replace the fuse. If the fuse is blown, and upon replacement, immediately blows again, there is a short between the fuse and the component. This is generally (not always) a sign of an internal short in the component. Disconnect the power wire at the component again and replace the fuse; if the fuse holds, the component is the problem.

If all the fuses are good and the component is not receiving power, find the switch for the circuit. Bypass the switch with the jumper wire. This is done by connecting one end of the jumper to the power wire coming into the switch and the other end to the wire leaving the switch. If the component comes to life, the switch has failed.

✳✳WARNING

Never substitute the jumper for the component. The circuit needs the electrical load of the component. If you bypass it, you cause a short circuit.

Checking the ground for any circuit can mean tracing wires to the body, cleaning connections or tightening mounting bolts for the component itself. If the jumper wire can be connected to the case of the component or the ground connector, you can ground the other end to a piece of clean, solid metal on the car. Again, if the component starts working, you've found the problem.

It should be noted that generally the last place to look for an electrical problem is in the wiring itself. Unless the car has undergone unusual circumstances (major bodywork, flood damage, improper repairs, etc.) the wiring is not likely to change its condition. A systematic search through the fuse, the connectors and switches and the component itself will almost always yield an answer. Loose and/or corroded connectors — particularly in ground circuits — are becoming a larger problem in modern cars. The computers and on-board electronic (solid state) systems are highly sensitive to improper grounds and will change their function drastically if one occurs.

Remember that for any electrical circuit to work, ALL the connections must be clean and tight.

Battery and Starting System

BASIC OPERATING PRINCIPALS

The battery is the first link in the chain of mechanisms which work together to provide cranking of the automobile engine. In most modern cars, the battery is a lead/acid electrochemical device consisting of six 2v subsections (cells) connected in series so the unit is capable of producing approximately 12v of electrical pressure. Each subsection consists of a series of positive and negative plates held a short distance apart in a solution of sulfuric acid and water.

The two types of plates are of dissimilar metals. This causes a chemical reaction to be set up, and it is this reaction which produces current flow from the battery when its positive and negative terminals are connected to an electrical appliance such as a lamp or motor. The continued transfer of electrons would eventually convert the sulfuric acid to water, and make the 2 plates identical in chemical composition. As electrical energy is removed from the battery, its voltage output tends to drop. Thus, measuring battery voltage and battery electrolyte composition are 2 ways of checking the ability of the unit to supply power. During the starting of the engine, electrical energy is removed from the battery. However, if the charging circuit is in good condition and the operating conditions are normal, the power removed from the battery will be replaced by the generator (or alternator) which will force electrons back through the battery, reversing the normal flow, and restoring the battery to its original chemical state.

The battery and starting motor are linked by very heavy electrical cables designed to minimize resistance to the flow of current. Generally, the major power supply cable that leaves the battery goes directly to the starter, while other electrical system needs are supplied by a smaller cable. During starter operation, power flows from the battery to the starter and is grounded through the car's frame and the battery's negative ground strap.

The starting motor is a specially designed, direct current electric motor capable of producing a very great amount of power for its size. One thing that allows the motor to produce a great deal of power is its tremendous rotating speed. It drives the engine through a tiny pinion gear (attached to the starter's armature), which drives the very large flywheel ring gear at a greatly reduced speed. Another factor allowing it to produce so much power is that only intermittent operation is required of it. Thus, little allowance for air circulation is required, and the windings can be built into a very small space.

The starter solenoid is a magnetic device which employs the small current supplied by the start circuit of the ignition switch. This magnetic action moves a plunger which mechanically engages the starter and closes the heavy switch connecting it to the battery. The starting switch circuit consists of the starting switch contained within the ignition switch, a transmission neutral safety switch or clutch pedal switch, and the wiring necessary to connect these in series with the starter solenoid or relay.

The pinion, a small gear, is mounted to a one-way drive clutch. This clutch is splined to the starter armature shaft. When the ignition switch is moved to the **start** position, the solenoid plunger slides the pinion toward the flywheel ring gear via a collar and spring. If the teeth on the pinion and flywheel match properly, the pinion will engage the flywheel immediately. If the gear teeth butt one another, the spring will be compressed and will force the gears to mesh as soon as the starter turns far enough to allow them to do so. As the solenoid plunger reaches the end of its travel, it closes the contacts that connect the battery and starter and then the engine is cranked.

As soon as the engine starts, the flywheel ring gear begins turning fast enough to drive the pinion at an extremely high rate of speed. At this point, the one-way clutch begins allowing the pinion to spin faster than the starter shaft so that the starter will not operate at excessive speed. When the ignition switch is released from the starter position, the solenoid is de-energized, and a spring pulls the gear out of mesh interrupting the current flow to the starter.

Some starters employ a separate relay, mounted away from the starter, to switch the motor and solenoid current on and off. The relay replaces the solenoid electrical switch, but does not eliminate the need for a solenoid mounted on the starter used to mechanically engage the starter drive gears. The relay is used to reduce the amount of current the starting switch must carry.

Charging System

BASIC OPERATING PRINCIPLES

The automobile charging system provides electrical power for operation of the vehicle's ignition and starting systems and all the electrical accessories. The battery services as an electrical surge or storage tank, storing (in chemical form) the energy originally produced by the engine driven generator. The system also provides a means of regulating generator output to protect the battery from being overcharged and to avoid excessive voltage to the accessories.

The storage battery is a chemical device incorporating parallel lead plates in a tank containing a sulfuric acid/water solution. Adjacent plates are slightly dissimilar, and the chemical reaction of the 2 dissimilar plates produces electrical energy when the battery is connected to a load such as the starter motor. The chemical reaction is reversible, so that when the generator is producing a voltage (electrical pressure) greater than that produced by the battery, electricity is forced into the battery, and the battery is returned to its fully charged state.

The vehicle's generator is driven mechanically, through V-belts, by the engine crankshaft. It consists of 2 coils of fine wire, one stationary (the stator), and one movable (the rotor). The rotor may also be known as the armature, and consists of fine wire wrapped around an iron core which is mounted on a shaft. The electricity which flows through the 2 coils of wire (provided initially by the battery in some cases) creates an intense magnetic field around both rotor and stator, and the interaction between the 2 fields creates voltage, allowing the generator to power the accessories and charge the battery.

There are 2 types of generators: the earlier is the direct current (DC) type. The current produced by the DC generator is generated in the armature and carried off the spinning armature by stationary brushes contacting the commutator. The commutator is a series of smooth metal contact plates on the end of the armature. The commutator plates, which are separated from one another by a very short gap, are connected to the armature circuits so that current will flow in one direction only in the wires carrying the generator output. The generator stator consists of 2 stationary coils of wire which draw some of the output current from the generator to form a powerful magnetic field and create the interaction of fields which generates the voltage. The generator field is wired in series with the regulator.

Newer automobiles use alternating current generators or alternators, because they are more efficient, can be rotated at higher speeds, and have fewer brush problems. In an alternator, the field rotates while all the current produced passes only through the stator winding. The brushes bear against continuous slip rings rather than a commutator. This causes the current produced to periodically reverse the direction of its flow. Diodes (electrical one-way valves) block the flow of current from traveling in the wrong direction. A series of diodes is wired together to permit the alternating flow of the stator to be rectified back to 12 volts DC for use by the vehicles's electrical system.

The regulator consists of several circuits. Each circuit has a core, or magnetic coil of wire, which operates a switch. Each switch is connected to ground through one or more resistors. The coil of wire responds directly to system voltage. When the voltage reaches the required level, the magnetic field created by the winding of wire closes the switch and inserts a resistance into the generator field circuit, thus reducing the output. The contacts of the switch cycle open and close many times each second to precisely control voltage. On many newer cars, the regulating function is performed by solid-state (rather than mechanical) components. The regulator is often built in to the alternator; this system is termed an integrated or internal regulator.

While alternators are self-limiting as far as maximum current is concerned, DC generators employ a current regulating circuit which responds directly to the total amount of current flowing through the generator circuit rather than to the output voltage. The current regulator is similar to the voltage regulator except that all system current must flow through the energizing coil on its way to the various accessories.

Ignition Coil

TESTING

▶ **See Figures 1 and 2**

➡ **This test requires the use of an ohmmeter. When using this tool, make sure the scale is set properly for the range of resistance you expect to encounter during the test. Always perform these tests with the ignition OFF.**

1. Disconnect the distributor cap and set it aside. The spark plug wires may be left attached to the cap. Remove the rotor and the dust cover(s).
2. Using the ohmmeter, measure the resistance between the positive (+) and negative (-) terminals on the coil. The resistance on the primary side of the coil (when cold) should be:
   - 1985-88 VIN Code 4 engine: 0.3-0.5ω
   - 1986-88 VIN Code 4 engine: 0.4-0.5ω
   - 1988 VIN Code 5 engine: 0.5-0.7ω
   - 1989-90 VIN Code 6 engine: 1.28-1.56ω
   - 1990 VIN Code 5 engine: 0.4-0.5ω
   - 1991-92 VIN Code 5 engine: 1.28-1.56ω
   - 1991-92 VIN Code 6 engine: 0.4-0.5ω
   - 1993 All engines: 1.11-1.75ω
3. Using the ohmmeter, measure the resistance between the positive terminal and the center (high tension) terminal.

(This is the terminal to which the coil attaches in the cap.) The resistance on the secondary side should be:
- 1985 VIN Code 4 engine: 7,500-10,500ω
- 1985- 88 VIN Code 4 engine: 7,500-10,400ω
- 1988 VIN Code 5 engine: 0.4-0.5ω
- 1988 VIN Code 5 engine: 11,000-16,000ω
- 1990 VIN Code 5 engine: 10,200-13,800ω
- 1989-90 VIN Code 6 engine: 10,400-14,000ω
- 1991-92 VIN Code 5 engine: 10,400-14,000ω
- 1991-92 VIN Code 6 engine: 10,200-13,800ω
- 1993 All engines: 9,000-15,700ω

4. Coils measuring outside either of these ranges must be replaced.

REMOVAL & INSTALLATION

▶ See Figure 3

External Coil

External coils (coils which are not built into the distributor) are easily replaced by the following procedure:
1. Make certain the ignition is off and the key is removed.
2. Disconnect the high tension wire (running between the coil and the distributor) from the coil.
3. Label and disconnect the low tension wires from the coil.
4. Loosen the coil bracket and remove the coil. Install the new coil and tighten the bracket.
5. Attach the low tension wires first, then the coil wire.

Fig. 1 Checking the coil primary resistance

Fig. 2 Checking the coil secondary resistance

Fig. 3 The coil is easily removed with the distributor out of the engine

Internal Coil

The internal coils found within the distributor can be changed without removing the distributor. A selection of various short screwdrivers may be required for access to the screws.
1. Disconnect the negative battery cable.
2. Remove the distributor cap with the wires attached and set it aside.
3. Remove the rotor and the dust cover(s).
4. Remove the nuts and disconnect the wires from the terminals on the coil.
5. Remove the 4 retaining screws and remove the coil. Note that later cars have a gasket below the coil — remove it carefully to avoid damage.
6. Install the coil, paying close attention to the gasket and its placement.
7. Connect the wiring to the coil and be careful of the routing of the wires.
8. Install the dust cover(s), the rotor and the cap.
9. Reconnect the battery.

Distributor

REMOVAL & INSTALLATION

✳✳WARNING

 Once the distributor is removed, the engine should not be turned or moved out of position. Should this occur, please refer to the end of this section.

1985-88 VIN Code 4 Engine

▶ See Figure 4

1. Disconnect the negative battery cable.
2. Disconnect the distributor wire at its connector.
3. Label and disconnect the vacuum hoses running to the vacuum advance unit on the side of the distributor.
4. Remove the distributor cap (leave the spark plug wires connected) and swing it out of the way.
5. Carefully note the position of the distributor rotor relative to the distributor housing; a mark made on the casing will be helpful during reassembly. Use a marker or tape so the mark doesn't rub off during the handling of the case.
6. Remove the distributor hold-down bolts.

Fig. 4 Distributor removal — 1985-88 VIN Code 4 engine

Fig. 5 Distributor removal — 1988 VIN Code 5 engine

7. Carefully pull the distributor out until it stops turning counterclockwise.

To install:

8. If the engine has not been moved out of position, align the rotor with the mark you made earlier and reinstall the distributor. Position it carefully and make sure the drive gear engages properly within the engine. Install the holding bolts.

9. Install the distributor cap and re-attach the vacuum lines to their correct ports.

10. Install the wiring to the distributor, and connect the battery cable.

11. Check and adjust the timing as necessary.

1988 VIN Code 5 Engine

▶ See Figure 5

1. Disconnect the negative battery cable.

2. Label and disconnect the coil and spark plug wiring at the distributor cap.

3. Disconnect the distributor wire at its connector.

4. Remove the distributor hold-down bolts. Before moving or disturbing the distributor, mark the position of the distributor relative to the engine and the position of the rotor relative to the case. Use a marker or tape so the mark doesn't rub off during the handling of the case.

5. Remove the distributor from the engine.

6. Remove the O-ring from the distributor shaft.

To install:

7. If the engine has not been moved out of position, align the rotor with the mark you made earlier and reinstall the distributor. Position it carefully and make sure the drive gear engages properly within the engine. Install the holding bolts.

8. Reconnect the wiring and the spark plug wires. Connect the negative battery cable.

9. Check and adjust the timing as necessary.

1989-93 All Engines

▶ See Figures 6, 7 and 8

1. Disconnect the negative battery cable.

2. Disconnect all electrical connections at the distributor, including the plug wires.

3. Remove the distributor cap.

4. Mark the position of the distributor case relative to the engine. Use a marker or tape so the mark doesn't rub off during the handling of the case. Also mark the position of the distributor rotor relative to the case.

5. Remove the distributor mounting bolts.

6. Remove the distributor from the engine and remove the O-ring from the distributor shaft.

7. If the engine has not been moved out of position, align the rotor with the mark you made earlier and reinstall the distributor. Position it carefully and make sure the drive gear engages properly within the engine. Install the holding bolts.

8. Reconnect the wiring and the spark plug wires. Connect the negative battery cable.

9. Check and adjust the timing as necessary.

Installation - Timing Lost

If the engine has been cranked, dismantled or the timing otherwise lost while the distributor was out, proceed as follows:

Fig. 6 Distributor removal — 1989-90 VIN Code 6 and 1990-92 VIN Code 5 engines

Fig. 7 Distributor removal — 1991-92 VIN Code 6 engine

Fig. 8 Distributor removal — 1993 all engines

1985-88 VIN CODE 4 ENGINE

▶ See Figure 9

1. Remove the No. 1 spark plug.
2. Place your finger over the spark plug hole and rotate the crankshaft clockwise to TDC (Top Dead Center). Watch the timing marks on the pulley; as they approach the zero point, you should feel pressure (compression) on your finger. If not, turn the crankshaft another full rotation and line up the marks.
3. Install the spark plug.
4. Observing the alignment marks made during removal, reinstall the distributor.

➡Align the protrusion on the housing with the pin on the spiral gear drill mark side.

1988 VIN CODE 5 ENGINE 1991-92 VIN CODE 6 ENGINE

▶ See Figure 10

1. Remove the No. 1 spark plug.
2. Place thumb over the spark plug hole. Crank the engine slowly until compression is felt. It will be easier to have someone rotate the engine by hand, using a wrench on the crankshaft pulley.

➡The spark plugs on the fuel injected engines are in deep wells; use a screwdriver handle to plug the hole and feel the compression.

3. Align the timing mark on the crankshaft pulley with the **0** degrees mark on the timing scale attached to the front of the

engine. This places the engine at TDC of the compression stroke.

➡Verify that the timing marks are aligned properly by, removing the oil filler cap and check to see the cavity in the camshaft. If necessary turn the crankshaft pulley 1 complete revolution.

4. Turn the distributor shaft until the rotor points to the No. 1 spark plug tower on the cap.
5. Install the distributor into the engine. Be sure to align the distributor-to-engine block mark made earlier.

➡Align the drilled marks on the driven gear with the cavity of the housing. Install the distributor into the engine and align the center of the flange with the center of the bolt hole in the cylinder head.

6. Install spark plug and wire.
7. Connect battery negative cable. Check and/or adjust ignition timing.

1989-90 VIN CODE 6 ENGINE 1990-92 VIN CODE 5 ENGINE

▶ See Figures 11 and 12

1. Crank the engine and align the timing mark on the crankshaft pulley with the **0** degrees mark on the timing scale attached to the front of the engine. This places the engine at TDC of the compression stroke.

➡This can be accomplished by cranking the engine until the exhaust camshaft is in the position shown in the illustration.

2. Turn the rotor until the distributor alignment marks match.
3. Install the distributor into the engine.
4. Connect battery negative cable. Check and/or adjust ignition timing.

1993 ALL ENGINES

▶ See Figure 13

1. Crank the engine and align the timing mark on the crankshaft pulley with the **0** degrees mark on the timing scale attached to the front of the engine. This places the engine at TDC of the compression stroke. This can be accomplished as follows:
2. Remove the circuit opening relay.
  a. Remove the radio.

Fig. 9 Setting the No. 1 cylinder — 1985-88 VIN Code 4 engine

Fig. 10 Distributor installation — 1988 VIN Code 5 and 1991-92 VIN Code 6 engines

Fig. 11 Positioning the exhaust camshaft — 1989-90 VIN Code 6 and 1991-92 VIN Code 5 engines

Fig. 12 Positioning the distributor alignment marks — 1989-90 VIN Code 6 and 1991-92 VIN Code 5 engines

b. Disconnect the circuit opening relay electrical connector from the center console.

c. Remove the circuit opening relay from the center console.

3. Remove the No. 1 spark plug.

4. Install a compression gauge into the spark plug cavity.

5. Crank the engine and observe the compression gauge. The TDC of the cylinder's compression stroke occurs when the compression reading is highest.

6. Align the timing mark on the crankshaft pulley with the **0** degrees mark on the timing scale attached to the front of the engine. This places the engine at TDC of the compression stroke.

7. Position the rotor to the No. 1 cylinder position.

8. Install the distributor.

9. Remove the compression gauge and install the spark plug.

10. Install the opening circuit relay by reversing the removal procedure.

11. Set the ignition timing.

Igniter (Ignition Module)

REMOVAL & INSTALLATION

For testing and replacement of distributor ignitor, please refer to Section 2, 'Engine Performance And Tune-Up'.

Fig. 13 Removing the circuit opening relay — 1993 models

Alternator

ALTERNATOR PRECAUTIONS

Several precautions must be observed with alternator equipped vehicles to avoid damaging the unit. They are as follows:

1. If the battery is removed or disconnected for any reason, make sure that it is reconnected with the correct polarity. Reversing the battery connections may result in damage to the one-way rectifiers.

2. When utilizing a booster battery as a starting aid, always connect it as follows: positive to positive, and negative (booster battery) to a good ground on the engine of the car being started.

3. Never use a fast charger as a booster to start a car with an alternator.

4. When servicing the battery with a fast charger, always disconnect the car battery cables.

5. Never attempt to polarize an alternator.

6. Never apply more than 12 volts when attempting to jump start the vehicle. Many road service vehicles use 2 batteries connected in series to provide power — this 24 volt surge can destroy an electrical system instantly.

7. Do not use test lamps of more than 12 volts (V) for checking diode continuity.

8. Do not short across or ground any of the terminals on the alternator.

9. The polarity of the battery, alternator, and regulator must be matched and considered before making any electrical connections within the system.

10. Never disconnect the alternator or the battery with the engine running.

11. Disconnect the battery terminals when performing any service on the electrical system. This will eliminate the possibility of accidental reversal of polarity.

12. Disconnect the battery ground cable if arc welding (such as body repair) is to be done on any part of the car.

Noise from an alternator may be caused by a loose drive pulley, a loose belt, loose mounting bolts, worn or dirty bearings or worn internal parts. A high frequency whine that is heard at high engine speed or full alternator output is acceptable and should not be considered a sign of alternator failure.

TESTING — ON VEHICLE INSPECTION

1. Inspect the battery specific gravity and electrolyte level. Check the specific gravity of each cell. The standard specific gravity of each cell is 1.25-1.27 when fully charged at 68°F. On a Delco battery with a 'maintenance eye' look for a GREEN DOT which means the battery is fully charged. The DARK eye (GREEN DOT NOT VISIBLE) means the battery must be charged. The CLEAR or LIGHT YELLOW eye means replace the battery.

2. Make sure the battery terminals are not loose or corroded. Check the fusible link for continuity.

3. Inspect the drive belt for excessive wear. Check the drive belt tension. If necessary adjust the drive belt.

4. Check the following fuses for continuity: ENGINE, CHARGE, IGN fuses.

5. Visually check alternator wiring and listen for abnormal noises.

6. Check that the discharge warning light comes ON when the ignition switch is turned ON. Start the engine. Check that the warning light goes out.

7. Check the charging circuit WITHOUT A LOAD. Connect a battery/alternator tester according to the manufacturer's instructions.

8. Check the charging circuit WITH A LOAD (turn on high beams and heater fan). Connect a battery/alternator tester according to the manufacturer's instructions.

9. Replace the necessary parts. Recheck the charging system. The standard amperage with a load on the system should be 30 amps. If a battery is fully charged, sometimes the indication will be less than 30 amps.

REMOVAL & INSTALLATION

1985-90 Except 1990 VIN Code 5 Engine

▶ See Figures 14 and 15

1. Disconnect the negative battery cable.

✳✳CAUTION

Failure to disconnect the battery can cause personal injury and damage to the car. If a tool is accidentally shorted at the alternator, it can become hot enough to cause a serious burn.

2. Disconnect the large connector from the alternator.

3. Remove the nut and the single wire from the alternator.

4. Loosen the adjusting lock bolt (Prizm, lower bolt) and pivot (upper) bolt. Remove the drive belt.

➡**It may be necessary to remove other belts for access.**

5. Remove the lower bolt first, support the alternator and remove the upper pivot bolt. Remove the alternator from the car.

6. Installation is reverse of the above procedure. When reinstalling, remember to leave the bolts finger tight so that the belt may be adjusted.

7. Make sure that the plugs and connectors are properly seated and secure in their mounts.

Fig. 14 Alternator mounting — 1985-88

Fig. 15 Alternator mounting — 1989-90 and 1991-92 base and LSi models

1991-92 All Engines and 1990 VIN Code 5 Engine

▶ See Figures 15 and 16

1. Disconnect the negative battery terminal from the battery.

➡**Failure to disconnect the negative cable may result in injury from the positive battery lead at the alternator and may short the alternator and regulator during the removal process.**

2. Remove the rubber protector, nut and wire from the battery **B** terminal on the alternator.

3. Remove the 3-wire alternator connector.

4. On the Prizm Base and LSi models use the following steps;

  a. Remove the upper and lower alternator bolts and nuts.

  b. Remove generator.

5. On the Prizm GSi models use the following steps;

  a. Raise and support the vehicle safely.

  b. Remove the power steering and air conditioning drive belts.

  c. Remove the lower mounting bolt and nut from the alternator bracket.

  d. Remove the alternator drive belt from the pulley.

  e. Remove the lower alternator mounting bracket (1 nut and 2 bolts).

➡**Removal of the alternator mounting bracket is necessary because of the extremely proximate nature of the engine compartment design. There is no way of getting the alternator out of the vehicle with the mounting bracket in place.**

f. Remove the alternator from the vehicle through the space between the right splash shield and the oil pan.

6. Installation is reverse of the above procedure. When reinstalling, remember to leave the bolts finger tight so that the belt may be adjusted.

7. Make sure that the plugs and connectors are properly seated and secure in their mounts.

1993

▶ See Figure 17

1. Disconnect the negative battery terminal from the battery.

➡**Failure to disconnect the negative cable may result in injury from the positive battery lead at the alternator and may short the alternator and regulator during the removal process.**

2. Loosen the pivot bolt and the adjusting lock bolt.
3. Remove the drive belt.
4. Remove the alternator connector from the back of the alternator.
5. Remove the 1 nut and alternator wire.
6. Remove the 2 clips and the wire harness.
7. Remove the 2 bolts and 1 nut, and remove the alternator from the mounting bracket.

To install:

8. Place the alternator in its brackets and install the mounting bolts. Do not tighten them yet.
9. Slip the belt back over the pulley. Pull outwards on the unit and adjust the belt tension. Tighten the mounting and adjusting bolts. Tighten the generator pivot mounting bolt to 26

ft. lbs. (35 Nm) and the adjusting lock bolt to 17 ft. lbs. (23 Nm).

10. Install the electrical leads and the negative battery cable.

Regulator

REMOVAL & INSTALLATION

▶ See Figures 18, 19, 20 and 21

The voltage regulator is contained within the alternator. It is called an IC type (Integrated Circuit). The alternator must be removed to replace the regulator.

1. Disconnect the negative battery cable.
2. Remove the alternator.

Fig. 17 Alternator mounting — 1993 all models

1. Upper adjustment nut
2. B terminal
3. Three-wire connector
4. Lower alternator mounting bracket
5. Lower mounting bolt
6. Lower mounting nut

Fig. 16 Alternator mounting — 1990-92 GSi models

3. Support the alternator on a workbench, pulley end down but not resting on the pulley.

4. At the side of the alternator, remove the nut and the plastic terminal insulator.

5. Remove the 3 nuts and remove the end cover.

6. Remove the 5 screws and carefully remove the brush holder and then the IC regulator. Be careful to keep track of various small parts (washers, etc.) — they will be needed during reassembly.

7. When reinstalling, place the cover over the brush holder. Install the regulator and the brush holder onto the alternator and secure them with the 5 screws. Make sure the brush holder's cover doesn't slip to one side during installation.

8. Before reinstalling the rear cover, check that the gap between the bush holder and the connector is at least 1mm. After confirming this gap, install the rear alternator cover and its 3 nuts.

9. Install the terminal insulator and its nut. Hold the alternator horizontally and spin the pulley by hand. Make sure everything turns smoothly and there is no sign of noise or binding.

Battery

REMOVAL & INSTALLATION

▶ See Figure 22

1. Disconnect the negative battery cable.

2. Disconnect the positive battery cable.

3. On Nova, remove the bolt holding the battery retainer and remove the retainer. On Prizms, remove the front retainer bolt first, then the rear retainer bolt and the retainer.

4. Remove the battery. You are reminded that the battery is a fairly heavy item. Use care in lifting it out of the car.

5. The new battery is installed in the reverse order of removal. Make certain that the retainer is correctly placed and its bolts are tight. Connect the positive cable first, then the negative cable.

➡Removing the battery may require resetting various digital equipment such as radio memory and the clock.

Starter

TESTING

▶ See Figure 23

1. Inspect the battery specific gravity and electrolyte level. Check the specific gravity of each cell. The standard specific gravity of each cell is 1.25-1.27 when fully charged at 68°F. On a Delco battery with a 'maintenance eye' look for a GREEN DOT which means the battery is fully charged. The DARK eye (GREEN DOT NOT VISIBLE) means the battery must be charged. The CLEAR or LIGHT YELLOW eye means replace the battery.

2. Check the battery terminals are not loose or corroded. Check the fusible link for continuity.

3. For further starting system troubleshooting, refer to the troubleshooting chart to find the problem and possible cause and remedy. Replace or repair the necessary items.

REMOVAL & INSTALLATION

1985-90

▶ See Figure 24

1. Disconnect the negative battery cable.

2. Disconnect all the wiring from the starter terminals.

3. On Nova, remove the transaxle cable and bracket from the transaxle.

4. Remove the starter mounting bolts.

5. Remove the starter.

6. Reassemble in reverse order of disassembly.

1991-92 Prizm

▶ See Figure 24

BASE AND LSi MODELS

1. Disconnect the negative battery cable.

2. Disconnect the positive battery cable from the starter solenoid by removing the nut from terminal 30 stud.

3. Disconnect the ignition switch lead from terminal 50.

4. Remove the 2 starter assembly retaining bolts and remove the starter assembly.

5. To install, reverse the removal procedures. Torque the starter-to-engine bolts to 26 ft. lbs. (35 Nm).

GSi MODEL

1. Disconnect the negative battery cable.

2. Remove the rear cooling fan assembly.

3. Raise and safely support the vehicle safely.

4. Remove the right and left splash shields.

5. Disconnect the oxygen sensor connector from the front exhaust pipe.

6. Disconnect the front exhaust pipe.

7. Remove the starter assembly mounting bolts.

8. Disconnect the positive battery cable from the starter solenoid by removing the nut from terminal 30 stud.

9. Disconnect the ignition switch lead from terminal 50. Remove the starter assembly from the vehicle.

10. To install, reverse the removal procedures. Torque the starter-to-engine bolts to 29 ft. lbs. (39 Nm).

1993

▶ See Figure 25

1. Disconnect the negative battery cable.

2. Disconnect the intake air temperature (IAT) sensor from the air cleaner (ACL). Loosen the (ACL) hose clamp bolt.

3. Remove the 4 ACL cap clips, hose ACL cap from the lower housing and throttle body.

4. Disconnect the wire clamp from the starter motor.

5. Disconnect the starter motor electrical connector.

6. Remove the 1 nut and the positive battery cable from the starter motor terminal.

7. Remove the 2 bolts and the starter motor from the vehicle.

1. Pulley
2. Drive end frame
3. Retainer
4. Rotor
5. Bearing cover
6. Front bearing
7. Rear bearing
8. Terminal insulator
9. Rubber insulator
   IC regulator
10. Brush holder
11. Rear end cover
12. Rear end frame
13. Cover
14. Spring
15. Brush
16. Rectifier holder

Fig. 18 Exploded view of the Nova alternator

To install:

8. Install the starter motor and tighten the 2 retaining bolts to 29 ft. lbs. (39 Nm).

9. Install the 1 nut and the positive battery cable to the starter motor terminal.

10. Connect the starter motor electrical connector.

11. Connect the wire clamp to the starter motor.

12. Connect the hose ACL cap to the lower housing and throttle body and secure with the 4 ACL cap clips.

13. Connect the intake air temperature (IAT) sensor to the air cleaner (ACL). Tighten the (ACL) hose clamp bolt.

14. Connect the negative battery cable.

SOLENOID REPLACEMENT

▶ **See Figure 26**

The starter solenoid or magnetic switch is an integral part of the starter. It cannot be replaced without complete disassembly of the starter.

1. Remove the starter from the car.

2. Disconnect the wire lead from the magnetic switch terminal.

3. Remove the 2 long, through bolts holding the field frame to the magnetic switch. Pull out the field frame with the armature from the magnetic switch.

4. On 1.0kw (1000 watt) starters, remove the felt seal. On 1.4kw starters, remove the O-ring.

1. Pulley nut
2. Pulley
3. Drive end frame assembly
4. Insulator
5. Front bearing
6. Front bearing retainer
7. Rotor
8. Rear bearing cover
9. Rear bearing
10. End cover
11. Brush holder
12. Brush
13. IC regulator
14. Terminal insulator
15. Rectifier
16. Rectifier end frame
17. Wave washer

Fig. 19 Exploded view of the Prizm alternator

Fig. 20 Removing the IC regulator from the alternator

Fig. 21 Maintain the minimum clearance between the brush holder and the connector when reassembling.

Fig. 22 Battery installation — 1989-93 shown

5. To remove the starter housing from the magnetic switch assembly:

   a. For 1.0 kw starters, remove the 2 screws and remove the starter housing with the idler gear and clutch assembly.

   b. For 1.4kw units, remove the 2 screws and remove the starter housing with the pinion gear, idler and clutch assembly.

6. Using a magnetic tool, remove the spring and steel ball from the clutch shaft hole.

7. Remove the end cover from the field frame.

8. On 1.4kw units, remove the O-ring.

9. Use a small screwdriver or steel wire to separate the brush springs and remove the brushes from the holder.

10. Pull the brush holder off the field frame.

11. Remove the armature from the field frame.

12. Perform testing and repairs as necessary:

   a. Measure the length of the brushes. If they are less than the acceptable minimum length, replace them with new brushes.**Standard Length:**
   - 1.0kw — 13mm
   - 1.4kw — 15mm

Minimum Length:
   - 1.0kw — 8.5mm
   - 1.4kw — 10mm

   b. Check the magnetic switch by performing the pull-in coil open circuit test. Using an ohmmeter, check for continuity between terminal 50 and terminal C. If there is no continuity, replace the magnetic switch.

   c. Check the hold in coil of the magnetic switch. Use the ohmmeter to check for continuity between terminal 50 and the body (case) of the unit. If there is no continuity, replace the switch.

13. To reassemble the starter, apply high-temperature grease to the armature bearings and insert the armature into the field frame.

14. Use a screwdriver or a steel wire to hold the brush spring back and install the brushes into the holder(s).

✳✳WARNING

Make certain the positive wires to the brushes are not grounded or touching surrounding parts.

15. For 1.4kw starters, install the O-ring on the field frame.

16. Install the end cover on the field frame.

17. Apply grease to the ball and spring and insert them into the clutch shaft hole.

18. Install the gears and clutch assembly to the starter housing. Apply grease to the gear and clutch assemblies and:

   a. For 1.0kw starters, place the clutch assembly, idler gear and bearing in the starter housing.

   b. For 1.4kw starters, place the clutch assembly, idler gear, bearing and pinion gear in the starter housing.

19. Insert the spring into the clutch shaft hole and place the starter housing onto the magnetic switch. Install the 2 screws.

20. On 1.0kw units, install the felt seal on the armature shaft. On 1.4kw units, install the O-ring on the field frame.

21. Install the field frame with armature onto the magnetic switch assembly and install the 2 through bolts.

➡There is a protrusion or tab on each part; make sure you line them up correctly.

22. Connect the wire to the terminal on the magnetic switch.

23. Reinstall the starter on the vehicle.

Problem	Possible cause	Remedy
Engine will not crank	Battery charge low	Check battery specific gravity
		Charge or replace battery
	Battery cables loose, corroded or worn	Repair or replace cables
	Neutral start switch faulty (A/T)	Replace switch
	Fusible link blown	Replace fusible link
	Starter faulty	Repair starter
	Ignition switch faulty	Replace ignition switch
Engine cranks slowly	Battery charge low	Check battery specific gravity
		Charge or replace battery
	Battery cables loose, corroded or worn	Repair or replace cables
	Starter faulty	Repair starter
Starter keeps running	Starter faulty	Repair starter
	Ignition switch faulty	Replace ignition switch
	Short in wiring	Repair wiring
Starter spin – engine will not crank	Pinion gear teeth broken or faulty starter	Repair starter
	Flywheel teeth broken	Replace flywheel

Fig. 23 Starter troubleshooting chart

Fig. 24 Starter installation — 1985-92

Fig. 25 Starter installation — 1993

Fig. 26 Exploded view of starter motors

ENGINE MECHANICAL

Understanding the Engine

The piston engine is a metal block containing a series of round chambers or cylinders. The upper part of the engine block is usually an iron or aluminum - alloy casting. The casting forms outer walls around the cylinders with hollow areas in between, through which coolant circulates. The lower block provides a number of rigid mounting points for the crankshaft and its bearings. The lower block is referred to as the crankcase.

The crankshaft is a long, steel shaft mounted at the bottom of the engine and free to turn in its mounts. The mounting points (generally 4 to 7) and the bearings for the crankshaft are called main bearings. The crankshaft is the shaft which is made to turn through the function of the engine; this motion is then passed into the transmission/transaxle and on to the drive wheels.

Attached to the crankshaft are the connecting rods which run up to the pistons within the cylinders. As the air/fuel mixture explodes within the tightly sealed cylinder, the piston is forced downward. This motion is transferred through the connecting rod to the crankshaft and the shaft turns. As one piston finishes its power stroke, its next upward journey forces the burnt gasses out of the cylinder through the now-open exhaust valve. By the top of the stroke, the exhaust valve has closed and the intake valve has begun to open, allowing the fresh air/fuel charge to be sucked into the cylinder by the downward stroke of the piston. The intake valve closes, the piston once again comes back up and compresses the charge in the closed cylinder. At the top (approximately) of this stroke the spark plug fires, the charge explodes and another power stroke takes place. If you count the piston motions in between power strokes, you'll see why automotive engines are called 4-stroke or 4-cycle engines.

While one cylinder is performing this cycle, all the others are also contributing; but in different timing. Obviously, all the cylinders cannot fire at once or the power flow would not be steady. As any one cylinder is on its power stroke, another is on its exhaust stroke, another on intake and another on compression. These constant power pulses keep the crank turning; a large round flywheel attached to the end of the crankshaft provides a stable mass to smooth out the rotation.

At the top of the engine, the cylinder head(s) provide tight covers for the cylinders. They contain machined chambers into which the fuel charge is forced as the piston reaches the top of its travel. These combustion chambers contain at least one intake and one exhaust valve which are opened and closed through the action of the camshaft. The spark plugs are screwed into the cylinder head so that the tips of the plugs protrude into the chamber.

Since the timing of the valve action (opening and closing) is critical to the combustion process, the camshaft is driven by the crankshaft via a belt or chain. The valves are operated either by pushrods (called overhead valves — the valves are above the cam) or by the direct action of the cam pushing on the valves (overhead cam).

Lubricating oil is stored in a pan or sump at the bottom of the engine. It is force fed to all the parts of the engine by the oil pump which may be driven off wither the crank or the cam shaft. The oil lubricates the entire engine by travelling through passages in the block and head. Additionally, the circulation of the oil provides 25-40% of the engine cooling.

If all this seems very complicated, keep in mind that the sole purpose of any motor — gas, diesel, electric, solar, etc. — is to turn a shaft. The motion of the shaft is then harnessed to perform a task such as pumping water, moving the car, etc. Accomplishing this shaft-turning in an automotive engine requires many supporting systems such as fuel delivery, exhaust handling, lubrication, cooling, starting, etc. Operation of these systems involve principles of mechanics, vacuum, electronics, etc. Being able to identify a problem by what system is involved will allow you to begin accurate diagnosis of the symptoms and causes.

Engine Overhaul Tips

Most engine overhaul procedures are fairly standard. In addition to specific parts replacement procedures and complete specifications for your individual engine, this section also is a guide to accepted rebuilding procedures. Examples of standard rebuilding practice are shown and should be used along with specific details concerning your particular engine.

Competent and accurate machine shop services will ensure maximum performance, reliability and engine life.

In most instances it is more profitable for the do-it-yourself mechanic to remove, clean and inspect the component, buy the necessary parts and deliver these to a shop for actual machine work.

On the other hand, much of the rebuilding work (crankshaft, block, bearings, piston rods, and other components) is well within the scope of the do-it-yourself mechanic. Patience, proper tools, and common sense coupled a basic understanding of the motor can yield satisfying and economical results.

TOOLS

The tools required for an engine overhaul or parts replacement will depend on the depth of your involvement. With a few exceptions, they will be the tools found in a mechanic's tool kit (see Section 1). More in-depth work will require any or all of the following:

- A dial indicator (reading in thousandths) mounted on a universal base
- Micrometers and telescope gauges
- Jaw and screw-type pullers
- Gasket scrapers; the best are wood or plastic
- Valve spring compressor
- Ring groove cleaner
- Piston ring expander and compressor

- Ridge reamer
- Cylinder hone or glaze breaker
- Plastigage®
- Engine stand

Occasionally, the use of special tools is called for. See the information on Special Tools and Safety Notice in the front of this book before substituting another tool.

INSPECTION TECHNIQUES

Procedures and specifications are given in this section for inspecting, cleaning and assessing the wear limits of most major components. Other procedures such as Magnaflux® and Zyglo® can be used to locate material flaws and stress cracks. Magnaflux® is a magnetic process applicable only to ferrous (iron and steel) materials. The Zyglo® process coats the material with a fluorescent dye penetrant and can be used on any material. Checks for suspected surface cracks can be more readily made using spot check dye. The dye is sprayed onto the suspected area, wiped off and the area sprayed with a developer. Cracks will show up brightly.

OVERHAUL TIPS

Aluminum has become extremely popular for use in engines, due to its low weight. Observe the following precautions when handling aluminum parts:
- Never hot tank aluminum parts (the caustic hot tank solution will eat the aluminum.)
- Remove all aluminum parts (identification tag, etc.) from engine parts prior to the tanking.
- Always coat threads lightly with engine oil or anti-seize compounds before installation to prevent seizure.
- Never overtighten bolts or spark plugs especially in aluminum threads.

Stripped threads in any component can be repaired using any of several commercial repair kits (Heli-Coil®, Microdot®, Keenserts®, etc.).

When assembling the engine, any parts that will be in frictional contact must be prelubed to provide lubrication at initial start-up. Any product specifically formulated for this purpose can be used, but engine oil is not recommended as a prelube.

When semi-permanent (locked, but removable) installation of bolts or nuts is desired, threads should be cleaned and coated with Loctite® or other similar, commercial non-hardening sealant.

REPAIRING DAMAGED THREADS

▶ **See Figures 27, 28, 29, 30 and 31**

Several methods of repairing damaged threads are available. Heli-Coil® (shown here), Keenserts® and Microdot® are among the most widely used. All involve basically the same principle — drilling out stripped threads, tapping the hole and installing a prewound insert — making welding, plugging and oversize fasteners unnecessary.

Two types of thread repair inserts are usually supplied: a standard type for most Inch Coarse, Inch Fine, Metric Course and Metric Fine thread sizes and a spark plug type to fit most spark plug port sizes. Consult the individual manufacturer's catalog to determine exact applications. Typical thread repair kits will contain a selection of prewound threaded inserts, a tap (corresponding to the outside diameter threads of the insert) and an installation tool. Spark plug inserts usually differ because they require a tap equipped with pilot threads and a combined reamer/tap section. Most manufacturers also supply blister-packed thread repair inserts separately in addition to a master kit containing a variety of taps and inserts plus installation tools.

Before effecting a repair to a threaded hole, remove any snapped, broken or damaged bolts or studs. Penetrating oil can be used to free frozen threads. The offending item can be removed with locking pliers or with a screw or stud extractor. After the hole is clear, the thread can be repaired, as shown in the series of accompanying illustrations.

Engine Compression

A noticeable lack of engine power, excessive oil consumption and/or poor fuel mileage measured over an extended period are all indicators of internal engine wear. Worn piston rings, scored or worn cylinder bores, leaking head gaskets, sticking or burnt valves and worn valve seats are all possible culprits here. A check of each cylinder's compression will help you locate the problems.

Fig. 27 Damaged bolt holes can be repaired with thread repair inserts

Fig. 28 Standard thread repair insert (left) and spark plug thread insert (right)

Fig. 29 Drill out the damaged threads with specified drill. Drill completely through the hole or to the bottom of a blind hole

Fig. 30 With the tap supplied, tap the hole to receive the thread insert. Keep the tap well oiled and back it out frequently to avoid clogging the threads

Fig. 31 Screw the threaded insert onto the installation tool until the tang engages the slot. Screw the insert into the tapped hole until it is ¼-½ turn below the top surface. After installation break off the tang with a hammer and punch

As mentioned in the Tools and Equipment section of Section 1, a screw-in type compression gauge is more accurate that the type you simply hold against the spark plug hole, although it takes slightly longer to use. It's worth it to obtain a more accurate reading. Follow the procedures below.

TESTING

Gasoline Engines

1. Warm up the engine to normal operating temperature.
2. Remove all the spark plugs.
3. Disconnect the high tension lead from the ignition coil.
4. Fully open the throttle either by operating the carburetor throttle linkage by hand or by having an assistant floor the accelerator pedal.
5. Screw the compression gauge into the No.1 spark plug hole until the fitting is snug.

✳✳WARNING

Be careful not to crossthread the plug hole. On aluminum cylinder heads use extra care, as the threads in these heads are easily ruined.

6. Ask an assistant to depress the accelerator pedal fully on both carbureted and fuel injected vehicles. Then, while you read the compression gauge, ask the assistant to crank the engine 2 or 3 times in short bursts using the ignition switch.
7. Read the compression gauge at the end of each series of cranks, and record the highest of these readings. Repeat this procedure for each of the engine's cylinders. As a general rule, new motors will have compression on the order of 150-170 pounds per square inch (psi). This number will decrease with age and wear. The number of pounds of pressure that your test shows is not as important as the evenness between all the cylinders. Many cars run very well with all cylinders at 105 psi. The lower number simply shows a general deterioration internally. This car probably burns a little oil and may be a bit harder to start, but based on these numbers doesn't warrant an engine tear-down yet.   Compare the highest reading of all the cylinders. Any variation of more than 10% should be considered a sign of potential trouble. For example, if your compression readings for cylinders 1 through 4 were: 135 psi, 125 psi, 90 psi and 125 psi, it would be fair to say that cylinder number 3 is not working efficiently and is almost certainly the cause of your oil burning, rough idle or poor fuel mileage.
8. If a cylinder is unusually low, pour a tablespoon of clean engine oil into the cylinder through the spark plug hole and repeat the compression test. If the compression comes up after adding the oil, it appears that the cylinder's piston rings or bore are damaged or worn. If the pressure remains low, the valves may not be seating properly (a valve job is needed), or the head gasket may be blown near that cylinder. If compression in any 2 adjacent cylinders is low, and if the addition of oil doesn't help the compression, there is leakage past the head gasket. Oil and coolant in the combustion chamber can result from this problem. There may be evidence of water droplets on the engine dipstick when a head gasket has blown.

GENERAL ENGINE SPECIFICATIONS

Year	Engine ID/VIN	Engine Displacement Liters (cc)	Fuel System Type	Net Horsepower @ rpm	Net Torque @ rpm (ft. lbs.)	Bore × Stroke (in.)	Compression Ratio	Oil Pressure @ rpm
1985	4	1.6 (1600)	Carb	70 @ 4800	85 @ 2800	3.19 × 3.03	9.0:1	34 @ 2000
1986	4	1.6 (1600)	Carb	70 @ 4800	85 @ 2800	3.19 × 3.03	9.0:1	34 @ 2000
1987	4	1.6 (1600)	Carb	70 @ 4800	85 @ 2800	3.19 × 3.03	9.0:1	34 @ 2000
1988	4	1.6 (1600)	Carb	70 @ 4800	85 @ 2800	3.19 × 3.03	9.0:1	34 @ 2000
	5	1.6 (1600)	EFI	88 @ 6600	98 @ 4800	3.19 × 3.03	9.4:1	57 @ 3000
1989	6	1.6 (1600)	EFI	102 @ 5800	101 @ 4800	3.19 × 3.03	9.5:1	57 @ 3000
1990	5	1.6 (1600)	EFI	102 @ 5800	101 @ 4800	3.20 × 3.00	9.5:1	56 @ 3000
	6	1.6 (1600)	EFI	102 @ 5800	101 @ 4800	3.19 × 3.03	9.5:1	57 @ 3000
1991	5	1.6 (1600)	EFI	130 @ 6800	105 @ 6000	3.20 × 3.00	10.3:1	56 @ 3000
	6	1.6 (1600)	EFI	102 @ 5800	101 @ 4800	3.20 × 3.00	9.5:1	56 @ 3000
1992	5	1.6 (1600)	EFI	130 @ 6800	105 @ 6000	3.20 × 3.00	10.3:1	56 @ 3000
	6	1.6 (1600)	EFI	102 @ 5800	101 @ 4800	3.20 × 3.00	9.5:1	56 @ 3000
1993	6	1.6 (1600)	EFI	108 @ 6000	105 @ 4800	3.18 × 3.03	9.5:1	56 @ 3000
	8	1.8 (1800)	EFI	115 @ 5600	115 @ 4800	3.18 × 3.37	9.5:1	56 @ 3000

NOTE: Horsepower and torque are SAE net figures. They are measured at the rear of the transmission with all accessories installed and operating. Since the figures vary when a given engine is installed in different models, some are representative rather than exact.
Carb—Carburetor
EFI—Electronic

VALVE SPECIFICATIONS

Year	Engine VIN	Engine Displacement Liters (cc)	Seat Angle (deg.)	Face Angle (deg.)	Spring Test Pressure (lbs. @ in.)	Spring Installed Height (in.)	Stem-to-Guide Clearance (in.)		Stem Diameter (in.)	
							Intake	Exhaust	Intake	Exhaust
1985	4	1.6 (1600)	45	44.5	46 @ 1.52	1.52	0.0031	0.0039	0.2744–0.2750	0.2742–0.2748
1986	4	1.6 (1600)	45	44.5	46 @ 1.52	1.52	0.0031	0.0039	0.2744–0.2750	0.2742–0.2748
1987	4	1.6 (1600)	45	44.5	46 @ 1.52	1.52	0.0031	0.0039	0.2744–0.2750	0.2742–0.2748
1988	4	1.6 (1600)	45	44.5	46 @ 1.52	1.52	0.0031	0.0039	0.2744–0.2750	0.2742–0.2748
	5	1.6 (1600)	45	44.5	32 @ 1.36	1.36	0.0031	0.0039	0.2350–0.2356	0.2748–0.2354
1989	6	1.6 (1600)	45	45.5	32 @ 1.36	1.36	0.0031	0.0039	0.2350–0.2356	0.2748–0.2354
1990	5	1.6 (1600)	NA	NA	NA	NA	0.0010–0.0024	0.0012–0.0026	0.2350–0.2356	0.2748–0.2354
	6	1.6 (1600)	45	45.5	32 @ 1.36	1.36	0.0031	0.0039	0.2350–0.2356	0.2748–0.2354
1991	5	1.6 (1600)	45	45.5	NA	NA	0.0031	0.0039	0.2350–0.2356	0.2748–0.2354
	6	1.6 (1600)	NA	NA	NA	NA	0.0010–0.0024	0.0012–0.0026	0.2350–0.2356	0.2748–0.2354
1992	5	1.6 (1600)	45	45.5	NA	NA	0.0010–0.0024	0.0012–0.0026	0.2350–0.2356	0.2748–0.2354
	6	1.6 (1600)	NA	NA	NA	NA	0.0010–0.0024	0.0012–0.0026	0.2350–0.2356	0.2748–0.2354
1993	6	1.6 (1600)	45	NA	NA	NA	0.0010–0.0024	0.0012–0.0026	0.2350–0.2356	0.2748–0.2354
	8	1.8 (1800)	45	NA	NA	NA	0.0010–0.0024	0.0012–0.0026	0.2350–0.2356	0.2748–0.2354

NA—Not available

CAMSHAFT SPECIFICATIONS

All measurements given in inches.

Year	VIN	Engine Displacement Liters (cc)	Journal Diameter					Lobe Lift		Bearing Clearance	Camshaft End Play
			1	2	3	4	5	In.	Ex.		
1985	4	1.6 (1600)	1.1015–1.1022	1.1015–1.1022	1.1015–1.1022	1.1015–1.1022	—	1.5409	1.5409	0.0015–0.0029	0.0031–0.0071
1986	4	1.6 (1600)	1.1015–1.1022	1.1015–1.1022	1.1015–1.1022	1.1015–1.1022	—	1.5409	1.5409	0.0015–0.0029	0.0031–0.0071
1987	4	1.6 (1600)	1.1015–1.1022	1.1015–1.1022	1.1015–1.1022	1.1015–1.1022	—	1.5409	1.5409	0.0015–0.0029	0.0031–0.0071
1988	4	1.6 (1600)	1.1015–1.1022	1.1015–1.1022	1.1015–1.1022	1.1015–1.1022	—	1.5409	1.5409	0.0015–0.0029	0.0031–0.0071
	5	1.6 (1600)	1.0610–1.0616	1.0610–1.0616	1.0610–1.0616	1.0610–1.0616	1.0610–1.0616	1.3998–1.4002	1.3998–1.4002	0.0014–0.0028	0.0031–0.0075
1989	6	1.6 (1600)	1.9822	0.9035	0.9035	0.9035	0.9035	1.3700	1.3590	0.0014–0.0028	0.0043
1990	5	1.6 (1600)	1.0610–1.0616	1.0610–1.0616	1.0610–1.0616	1.0610–1.0616	1.0610–1.0616	1.3941–1.3980	1.3941–1.3980	0.0014–0.0028	0.0031–0.0075
	6	1.6 (1600)	1.9822	0.9035	0.9035	0.9035	0.9035	1.3700	1.3590	0.0014–0.0028	0.0043
1991	5	1.6 (1600)	1.9822	0.9035	0.9035	0.9035	0.9035	1.3700	1.3590	0.0014–0.0028	0.0043
	6	1.6 (1600)	1.0610–1.0616	1.0610–1.0616	1.0610–1.0616	1.0610–1.0616	1.0610–1.0616	1.3941–1.3980	1.3941–1.3980	0.0014–0.0028	0.0031–0.0075
1992	5	1.6 (1600)	1.9822	0.9035	0.9035	0.9035	0.9035	1.3700	1.3590	0.0014–0.0028	0.0043
	6	1.6 (1600)	1.0610–1.0616	1.0610–1.0616	1.0610–1.0616	1.0610–1.0616	1.0610–1.0616	1.3941–1.3980	1.3941–1.3980	0.0014–0.0028	0.0031–0.0075
1993	6	1.6 (1600)	0.9035–0.9041	0.9035–0.9041	0.9035–0.9041	0.9035–0.9041	0.9035–0.9041	1.6500–1.6539	1.6520–1.6560	0.0014–0.0028	0.0043
	8	1.8 (1800)	0.9035–0.9041	0.9035–0.9041	0.9035–0.9041	0.9035–0.9041	0.9035–0.9041	1.6500–1.6539	1.6520–1.6560	0.0014–0.0028	0.0043

CRANKSHAFT AND CONNECTING ROD SPECIFICATIONS

All measurements are given in inches.

Year	VIN	Engine Displacement Liters (cc)	Crankshaft				Connecting Rod		
			Main Brg. Journal Dia.	Main Brg. Oil Clearance	Shaft End-play	Thrust on No.	Journal Diameter	Oil Clearance	Side Clearance
1985	4	1.6 (1600)	1.8992–1.8898	0.0008–0.0020	0.0008–0.0073	2	1.5742–1.5748	0.0008–0.0020	0.0059–0.0098
1986	4	1.6 (1600)	1.8992–1.8898	0.0008–0.0020	0.0008–0.0073	2	1.5742–1.5748	0.0008–0.0020	0.0059–0.0098
1987	4	1.6 (1600)	1.8992–1.8898	0.0008–0.0020	0.0008–0.0073	2	1.5742–1.5748	0.0008–0.0020	0.0059–0.0098
1988	4	1.6 (1600)	1.8992–1.8898	0.0008–0.0020	0.0008–0.0073	2	1.5742–1.5748	0.0008–0.0020	0.0059–0.0098
	5	1.6 (1600)	①	0.0006–0.0013	0.0008–0.0087	3	1.6529–1.6535	0.0008–0.0020	0.0059–0.0098
1989	6	1.6 (1600)	1.8991–1.8898	0.0006–0.0013	0.0008–0.0087	3	1.5742–1.5748	0.0008–0.0020	0.0059–0.0098
1990	5	1.6 (1600)	1.8992–1.8998	0.0006–0.0013	0.0008–0.0087	3	1.5742–1.5748	0.0008–0.0020	0.0059–0.0098
	6	1.6 (1600)	1.8991–1.8898	0.0006–0.0013	0.0008–0.0087	3	1.5742–1.5748	0.0008–0.0020	0.0059–0.0098
1991	5	1.6 (1600)	1.8992–1.8898	0.0006–0.0013	0.0008–0.0087	3	1.6529–1.6535	0.0008–0.0020	0.0059–0.0098
	6	1.6 (1600)	1.8992–1.8998	0.0006–0.0013	0.0008–0.0087	3	1.5742–1.5748	0.0008–0.0020	0.0059–0.0098
1992	5	1.6 (1600)	1.8992–1.8898	0.0006–0.0013	0.0008–0.0087	3	1.6529–1.6535	0.0008–0.0020	0.0059–0.0098
	6	1.6 (1600)	1.8992–1.8998	0.0006–0.0013	0.0008–0.0087	3	1.5742–1.5748	0.0008–0.0020	0.0059–0.0098
1993	6	1.6 (1600)	①	0.0006–0.0013	0.0008–0.0087	3	1.5742–1.5748	0.0008–0.0020	NA
	8	1.8 (1800)	①	0.0006–0.0013	0.0008–0.0087	3	NA	0.0008–0.0020	NA

NA—Not available

① Marked 0: 1.8895–1.8898
  Marked 1: 1.8993–1.8995
  Marked 2: 1.8991–1.8893

PISTON AND RING SPECIFICATIONS

All measurements are given in inches.

Year	Engine VIN	Engine Displacement Liters (cc)	Piston Clearance	Ring Gap			Ring Side Clearance		
				Top Compression	Bottom Compression	Oil Control	Top Compression	Bottom Compression	Oil Control
1985	4	1.6 (1600)	0.0035–0.0043	0.0098–0.0185	0.0059–0.0165	0.0118–0.0402	0.0016–0.0031	0.0012–0.0028	—
1986	4	1.6 (1600)	0.0035–0.0043	0.0098–0.0185	0.0059–0.0165	0.0118–0.0402	0.0016–0.0031	0.0012–0.0028	—
1987	4	1.6 (1600)	0.0035–0.0043	0.0098–0.0185	0.0059–0.0165	0.0118–0.0402	0.0016–0.0031	0.0012–0.0028	—
1988	4	1.6 (1600)	0.0035–0.0043	0.0098–0.0185	0.0059–0.0165	0.0118–0.0402	0.0016–0.0031	0.0012–0.0028	—
	5	1.6 (1600)	0.0039–0.0047	0.0098–0.0138	0.0078–0.0118	0.0059–0.0157	0.0016–0.0031	0.0012–0.0028	—
1989	6	1.6 (1600)	0.0024–0.0031	0.0098–0.0138	0.0059–0.0118	0.0039–0.0236	0.0016–0.0031	0.0012–0.0028	—
1990	5	1.6 (1600)	0.0039–0.0047	0.0098–0.0185	0.0079–0.0165	0.0059–0.0205	0.0012–0.0028	0.0012–0.0028	—
	6	1.6 (1600)	0.0024–0.0031	0.0098–0.0138	0.0059–0.0118	0.0039–0.0236	0.0016–0.0031	0.0012–0.0028	—
1991	5	1.6 (1600)	0.0024–0.0031	0.0098–0.0138	0.0059–0.0118	0.0039–0.0236	0.0016–0.0031	0.0012–0.0028	—
	6	1.6 (1600)	0.0039–0.0047	0.0098–0.0185	0.0079–0.0165	0.0059–0.0205	0.0012–0.0028	0.0012–0.0028	—
1992	5	1.6 (1600)	0.0024–0.0031	0.0098–0.0138	0.0059–0.0118	0.0039–0.0236	0.0016–0.0031	0.0012–0.0028	—
	6	1.6 (1600)	0.0039–0.0047	0.0098–0.0185	0.0079–0.0165	0.0059–0.0205	0.0012–0.0028	0.0012–0.0028	—
1993	6	1.6 (1600)	0.0008–0.0015	0.0098–0.0138	0.0138–0.0234	0.0039–0.0177	0.0018–0.0035	0.0012–0.0028	—
	8	1.8 (1800)	0.0008–0.0015	0.0098–0.0138	0.0138–0.0234	0.0039–0.0177	0.0018–0.0035	0.0012–0.0028	—

TORQUE SPECIFICATIONS

All readings in ft. lbs.

Year	VIN	Engine Displacement Liters (cc)	Cylinder Head Bolts	Main Bearing Bolts	Rod Bearing Bolts	Crankshaft Damper Bolts	Flywheel Bolts	Manifold Intake	Manifold Exhaust	Spark Plugs	Lug Nut
1985	4	1.6 (1600)	43	44	29	87	58	20	18	13	76
1986	4	1.6 (1600)	43	44	29	87	58	20	18	13	76
1987	4	1.6 (1600)	43	44	29	87	58	20	18	13	76
1988	4	1.6 (1600)	43	44	29	87	58	20	18	13	76
	5	1.6 (1600)	①	44	36	101	58	20	18	13	76
1989	6	1.6 (1600)	44	44	36	87	③	14	18	21	76
1990	5	1.6 (1600)	44	44	36	87	③	20	18	13	76
	6	1.6 (1600)	44	44	36	87	③	14	18	21	76
1991	5	1.6 (1600)	44	44	36	87	③	14	18	21	76
	6	1.6 (1600)	44	44	36	87	③	20	18	13	76
1992	5	1.6 (1600)	44	44	36	87	③	14	18	21	76
	6	1.6 (1600)	44	44	36	87	③	20	18	13	76
1993	6	1.6 (1600)	①	44	②	87	③	14	25	13	76
	8	1.8 (1800)	①	44	②	87	③	14	25	13	76

① 22 ft. lbs. plus 90°, plus an additional 90°
② 22 ft. lbs. plus 90°
③ Manual trans.—58 ft. lbs.
   Automatic trans.—47 ft. lbs.

Engine

REMOVAL & INSTALLATION

1985-88 VIN Code 4 Engine

→All wires and hoses should be labeled at the time of removal. The amount of time saved during reassembly makes the extra effort well worthwhile.

1. Disconnect the negative battery cable.
2. Drain the cooling system and save the coolant for reuse.

✳✳CAUTION

When draining the coolant, keep in mind that cats and dogs are attracted by the ethylene glycol antifreeze, and are quite likely to drink any that is left in an uncovered container or in puddles on the ground. This will prove fatal in sufficient quantity. Always drain the coolant into a sealable container. Coolant should be reused unless it is contaminated or several years old.

3. Drain the engine oil and the transmission oil.

✳✳CAUTION

Used motor oil may cause skin cancer if repeatedly left in contact with the skin for prolonged periods. Although this is unlikely unless you handle oil on a daily basis, it is wise to thoroughly wash your hands with soap and water immediately after handling used motor oil.

4. With the help of an assistant, remove the hood from the car. Be careful not to damage the paint finish.
5. Remove the air cleaner assembly from the carburetor.
6. Disconnect the upper radiator hose from the engine and remove the overflow hose.
7. Remove the coolant hose at the cylinder head rear coolant pipe and remove the coolant hose at the thermostat housing.
8. Remove the fuel hoses from the fuel pump.
9. Loosen the adjustor(s) and remove the alternator belt, the power steering and/or air conditioning drive belts depending on equipment.
10. Label and remove all wiring running to the motor. Be careful when unhooking wiring connectors; many have locking devices which must be released.
11. Label and disconnect vacuum hoses. Make sure your labels contain accurate information for reconnecting both ends of the hose. Make sure the labels will stay put on the hoses.
12. Disconnect the wiring at the transaxle.
13. Disconnect the speedometer cable at the transaxle.
14. Safely elevate and support the vehicle on jackstands.

15. Disconnect the exhaust pipe from the manifold. Be ready to deal with rusty hardware.

16. Disconnect the air hose at the converter pipe, if so equipped.

17. Loosen and remove the transaxle cooler lines at the radiator.

18. Remove the left and right undercovers (splash shields) under the car.

19. If so equipped, remove the power steering pump from its mounts and lay it aside. Leave the hoses attached. The pump may be hung on a piece of stiff wire to be kept out of the way.

20. If so equipped, remove the air conditioning compressor from its mounts and position out of the way. DO NOT loosen any hoses or fittings — simply move the compressor out of the way. It may be hung from a piece of stiff wire to be kept out of the way.

21. Disconnect the cable and bracket from the transaxle.

22. Disconnect the steering knuckles at the lower control arms.

23. Have an assistant step on the brake pedal while you loosen the nuts and bolts holding the driveshafts to the transaxle. Let the disconnected shafts hang down clear of the transaxle.

24. Remove the flywheel cover. If equipped with an automatic transmission, remove the flexplate-to-torque converter bolts.

25. Disconnect the front and rear mounts at the crossmember by first removing the 2 bolt covers and removing the 2 bolts at each mount. Remove the center crossmember under the engine.

26. Remove the clip and washer holding the shift cable; disconnect the cable at the outer shift lever or outer selector lever.

27. Lower the vehicle to the ground. Remove the radiator and fan assembly.

28. Install the engine hoist to the lifting bracket on the engine. Keep the wiring harness in front of the chain. Draw tension on the hoist enough to support the engine but no more. Double check the hoist attachments before proceeding.

29. Remove the through bolt to the right side engine mount.

30. Remove the left side transaxle mount bolt and remove the mount.

31. Lift the engine and transaxle assembly out of the engine compartment, proceeding slowly and watching for any interference. Pay particular attention to not damage the right side engine mount, the power steering housing and the neutral safety switch. Make sure wiring, hoses and cables are clear of the engine.

32. Support the engine assembly on a suitable stand; do not allow it to remain on the hoist for any length of time.

To install:

33. Lower the engine and transaxle into the car, paying attention to clearance and proper position.

34. Install the left side transaxle mount and its bolt.

35. Install and tighten the right side through bolt for the motor mount.

36. When the engine is securely mounted within the car, the lifting devices may be removed. Replace the radiator and fan assembly.

37. Safely elevate and support the vehicle on jackstands.

38. Install the center crossmember and connect the shift cable.

39. Connect the front and rear mountings for the crossmember and reinstall the bolt covers.

40. Install the flywheel-to-torque converter bolts. Tighten them to the final specification in 3 steps: first, all to 20 ft. lbs; next, all to 40 ft. lbs. and finally all to 58 ft. lbs.

41. Replace the flywheel cover.

42. Connect the driveshafts to the transaxle; correct tightness is 27 ft. lbs.

43. Reconnect the steering knuckles to the lower control arms.

44. Reattach the cable and bracket to the transaxle.

45. Depending on equipment, reinstall the power steering pump and/or the air conditioning compressor. Tighten the mounting bolts enough to hold the unit in place but no more; the belts will be installed later.

46. Install the left and right splash shields (under covers).

47. Reconnect the transmission cooler lines to the radiator and connect the air hose at the converter pipe.

48. Connect the exhaust pipe to the manifold and tighten the bolts to 46 ft. lbs.

49. Lower the vehicle to the ground; reconnect the speedometer cable at the transaxle.

50. Paying close attention to proper routing and labeling, connect the wiring and vacuum hoses to the engine.

51. Install the drive belts (alternator, power steering and air conditioning) and make sure the belts are properly seated on the pulleys. Adjust the belts to the correct tension and tighten the bolts.

52. Connect the fuel hoses at the fuel pump. Use new clamps if necessary.

53. Attach the coolant hoses: at the thermostat housing, at the cylinder head rear pipe, at the overflow, and at the outlet for the upper hose. Insure that the hoses are firmly over the ports; use new clamps wherever needed.

54. Install the air cleaner assembly onto the carburetor.

55. Have an assistant help reinstall the hood. Make sure its is properly adjusted and secure.

56. Refill the transmission with the proper fluid.

57. Refill the engine oil to the proper level.

58. Refill the engine coolant with the proper amount of fluid.

59. Double check all installation items, paying particular attention to loose hoses or hanging wires, untightened nuts, poor routing of hoses and wires (too tight or rubbing) and tools left in the engine area.

1988 VIN Code 5 Engine

▶ **See Figures 32 and 33**

➡ **All wires and hoses should be labeled at the time of removal. The amount of time saved during reassembly makes the extra effort well worthwhile.**

1. Disconnect the negative battery cable.

2. With a helper remove the hood from the car. Use care not to damage the paint finish on the bodywork.

3. Drain the engine oil.

❋❋CAUTION

Used motor oil may cause skin cancer if repeatedly left in contact with the skin for prolonged periods. Although this is unlikely unless you handle oil on a daily basis, it is wise to thoroughly wash your hands with soap and water immediately after handling used motor oil.

4. Drain the cooling system. Save the coolant for reuse.

❋❋CAUTION

When draining the coolant, keep in mind that cats and dogs are attracted by the ethylene glycol antifreeze, and are quite likely to drink any that is left in an uncovered container or in puddles on the ground. This will prove fatal in sufficient quantity. Always drain the coolant into a sealable container. Coolant should be reused unless it is contaminated or several years old.

5. Drain the transaxle oil.
6. Remove the air cleaner assembly.
7. Remove the coolant reservoir tank and remove the PCV hose.
8. Remove the heater hoses from the water inlet housing.
9. Disconnect the fuel inlet hose from the fuel filter.

❋❋CAUTION

The fuel system is under pressure. Release pressure slowly and contain spillage. Observe no smoking/no open flame precautions. Have a Class B-C (dry powder) fire extinguisher within arm's reach at all times.

10. Disconnect the heater and air hoses from the air valve.
11. Remove the fuel return hose from the pressure regulator.
12. If equipped with a manual transaxle, remove the slave cylinder from the housing. Loosen the mounting bolts and move the cylinder out of the way but do not loosen or remove the fluid hose running to the cylinder.
13. Disconnect the vacuum hose running to the charcoal cannister.
14. Disconnect the shift control cable, the speedometer cable (at the trans) and the accelerator cable (at the throttle body).
15. If the car has cruise control, disconnect the cables. Remove the cruise control actuator by:
   a. Disconnecting the vacuum hose,
   b. Removing the cover and the 3 bolts,
   c. Disconnecting the actuator connector and removing the actuator.
16. Remove the ignition coil.
17. Remove the main engine wiring harness in the following steps:
   a. Inside the car, remove the right side cowl (kick) panel.
   b. Disconnect the connectors at junction block 4.
   c. Remove the cover over the Electronic Control Module (ECM) and carefully disconnect the ECM plugs.
   d. Pull the main wiring harness into the engine compartment.

18. Disconnect the wiring at the number 2 junction block in the engine compartment.
19. Remove the engine and transaxle ground straps.
20. Disconnect the washer change valve connector.
21. Remove the wiring at the cruise control vacuum pump connector and the vacuum switch connector.
22. Remove the hose from the brake vacuum booster.
23. Depending on equipment, remove the air conditioning compressor and/or the power steering pump. Note that the units are to be removed from their mounts and placed out of the way — hoses and lines DO NOT disconnect from the units.
   a. Remove the power steering pump pulley nut.
   b. Loosen the idler pulley adjusting bolt and pulley bolt.
   c. Remove the 4 compressor mounting bolts.
   d. Move the compressor aside and suspend it from stiff wire out of the way.
   e. Loosen the compressor bracket bolts.
   f. Disconnect the oil pressure connector.
   g. Loosen the power steering pump lock bolts and pivot bolts.
   h. Remove the pump and its bracket; suspend it out of the way with a piece of stiff wire.
24. Safely elevate the vehicle and support on jackstands. Double check the stands and make sure the vehicle is solidly supported.
25. Remove the splash shields under the car.
26. Disconnect the oil cooler hoses.
27. Disconnect the exhaust pipe from the exhaust manifold.
28. Carefully disconnect the wiring from the oxygen sensor.
29. Remove the cover under the flywheel.
30. Remove the front and rear motor mounts from the center crossmember.
31. Remove the center crossmember.
32. Disconnect the right side control arm at the steering knuckle.
33. Disconnect the driveshafts from the transaxle.
34. Lower the vehicle to the ground. Install the engine hoist to the lifting bracket on the engine. Hang the engine wires and hoses on the lift chain. Take tension on the hoist sufficient to support the motor; double check all hoist attaching points.
35. Disconnect the right side engine mount by removing the bolt.
36. Disconnect the left side motor mount from the transaxle bracket.

Fig. 32 Removing the engine mounts from the crossmember — 1988 VIN code 5 engine

Fig. 33 Removing the left side engine mount at the transaxle — 1988 VIN code 5 engine

37. Lift the engine and transaxle from the vehicle.

✴✴WARNING

Be careful to avoid hitting the steering box and the throttle position sensor.

38. Support the engine assembly on a suitable stand; do not allow it to remain on the hoist for any length of time.

39. Disconnect the radiator fan temperature switch connector.

40. Disconnect the start injector time switch.

41. Remove the vacuum hoses from the Bimetal Vacuum Switching Valves (BVSV).

42. Remove the hoses from the water bypass valves and remove the water inlet housing assembly.

43. Label and remove the wiring connectors from the reverse switch, the water temperature sensor, and the water temperature switch. On cars with automatic transmissions remove the wiring to the neutral safety switch and the transaxle solenoid.

44. If equipped with automatic transmission, remove the 6 torque converter - to-flexplate bolts.

45. Remove the starter along with its cable and connector.

46. Support the transaxle, remove the retaining bolts in the case and remove the transaxle from the engine. Pull the unit straight off the engine; do not allow it to hang partially removed on the shaft. Keep the automatic transaxle level; if it tilts forward the converter may fall off.

To install:

47. Before reinstalling the engine in the car, several components must be reattached or connected. Install the transaxle to the engine; tighten the 12mm bolts to 47 ft. lbs and the 10mm bolts to 34 ft. lbs.

48. Install the starter, its cable and connector. Tighten the mounting bolts to 29 ft. lbs.

49. Install the 6 torque converter-to-flexplate bolts on automatic transaxles. Tighten the bolts to 20 ft. lbs

50. Attach the wiring to the reverse light switch, the water temperature sensor and the water temperature switch.

51. Connect the hoses to the water bypass pipes and the wiring to the start injector time switch and the radiator fan temperature switch.

52. On automatic transaxle vehicles, connect the wiring to the neutral safety switch and the transmission solenoid.

53. Reinstall the water inlet housing assembly and connect the vacuum hoses to the BVSVs.

54. Attach the lifting mechanism to the engine; drape the hoses and wires on the chain.

55. Lower the engine and transaxle into place in the vehicle. Be careful not to hit the power steering gear housing or the throttle position sensor.

56. Install the right motor mount and through bolt; tighten it to 58 ft. lbs.

57. Install the left mount and attach it to the transaxle bracket. When the engine is securely mounted in the car, the lifting equipment may be removed.

58. Safely elevate and support the vehicle on jackstands.

59. Connect the driveshafts to the transaxle. Tighten the bolts to 27 ft. lbs.

60. Attach the right side control arm to the steering knuckle and tighten the bolts and nuts to 47 ft. lbs.

61. Replace the cover under the flywheel.

62. Install the engine mount center crossmember, tightening the bolts to 29 ft. lbs.

63. Install the front and rear mounts onto the crossmember. Tighten the mount bolts to 35 ft.lbs and the front and rear through bolts to 58 ft. lbs.

64. Using new gaskets and nuts, connect the exhaust pipe to the exhaust manifold; correct torque is 46 ft. lbs.

65. Connect the wiring to the oxygen sensor and attach the oil cooler lines.

66. Lower the vehicle from its stands to the ground.

67. Install the power steering pump and pulley with its bracket. Tighten the lock bolt and the pivot bolt.

68. Connect the wiring to the oil pressure unit.

69. Install the compressor bracket, the compressor and the belt. Tighten the pulley bolt on the power steering pump to 28 ft. lbs.

70. Install the drive belts and adjust them to the proper tension. Make certain each belt is properly fitted on its pulleys.

71. Connect the vacuum hose to the brake booster.

72. Install the wiring to the No. 2 junction block. Connect the cable from the starter to the positive battery terminal and connect the engine and transaxle ground straps. DO NOT connect the negative battery cable at this time.

73. Attach the connectors for the washer change valve, and, if equipped, the cruise control vacuum pump and vacuum switch.

74. Connect the main engine wiring harness by:

    a. Feeding the 2 connectors from the engine compartment back into the passenger compartment,

    b. Connecting the ECM connector(s) and replacing the cover,

    c. Connecting the wiring to the No. 4 junction block.

    d. Replacing the right side kick panel.

75. Reinstall the ignition coil.

76. If so, equipped install the cruise control actuator.

77. Connect or reinstall the cables for the accelerator, the cruise control, the speedometer and the shifter.

78. Install the vacuum hose to charcoal cannister.

79. On cars with manual transaxles, attach the clutch slave cylinder to the bell housing.

80. Attach the fuel return hose to the pressure regulator, the heater and air hoses to the air valve and the fuel hose to the fuel filter.

81. Connect the heater hoses to the water inlet housing.

82. Reinstall the PCV hose, the coolant reservoir and the air cleaner assembly.

83. Fill the transaxle with the correct amount of fresh oil, and fill the engine with fresh oil.

84. Fill the cooling system with the proper amount of fluid.

85. Double check all installation items, paying particular attention to loose hoses or hanging wires, untightened nuts, poor routing of hoses and wires (too tight or rubbing) and tools left in the engine area.

86. Connect the negative battery cable.

87. Start the engine and allow it to approach normal operating temperature. Check carefully for leaks. Shut the engine off.

88. Elevate the front end of the car, support on jackstands and install the splash shields below the car.

89. Lower the car to the ground. With your helper, install the hood and adjust it for proper fit and latching.

1989-90 VIN Code 6 Engine

▶ See Figures 34, 35 and 36

1. Remove the hood. Have a helper assist you and be careful not to damage the painted bodywork.

2. Disconnect the negative battery cable, then the positive battery cable and remove the battery.

3. Raise the vehicle and safely support it on jackstands.

4. Remove the left and right splash shields.

5. Drain the engine oil and the transmission oil.

✳✳CAUTION

Used motor oil may cause skin cancer if repeatedly left in contact with the skin for prolonged periods. Although this is unlikely unless you handle oil on a daily basis, it is wise to thoroughly wash your hands with soap and water immediately after handling used motor oil.

6. Drain the engine coolant and save it in closed containers for reuse.

✳✳CAUTION

When draining the coolant, keep in mind that cats and dogs are attracted by the ethylene glycol antifreeze, and are quite likely to drink any that is left in an uncovered container or in puddles on the ground. This will prove fatal in sufficient quantity. Always drain the coolant into a sealable container. Coolant should be reused unless it is contaminated or several years old.

7. Remove the air cleaner hose and the air cleaner assembly.

8. Remove the coolant reservoir. Remove the radiator and fan assembly.

9. Disconnect the accelerator cable and if equipped with automatic transaxle, the throttle cable.

10. Disconnect and remove the cruise control actuator.

11. Label and disconnect the main engine wiring harness from its related sensors and switches.

12. Remove the ground strap connector and its bolt. Disconnect the wiring to the vacuum sensor, the oxygen sensor and the air conditioning compressor.

13. Label and disconnect the brake booster vacuum hose, the power steering vacuum hose, the charcoal cannister vacuum hose and the vacuum switch vacuum hose.

14. Carefully disconnect the fuel inlet and return lines.

✳✳CAUTION

The fuel system is under pressure. Release pressure slowly and contain spillage. Observe no smoking/no open flame precautions. Have a Class B-C (dry powder) fire extinguisher within arm's reach at all times.

15. Disconnect the heater hoses.

16. Loosen the power steering pump mounting bolt and through bolt. Remove the drive belt.

17. Remove the 4 bolts holding the air conditioner compressor and remove the compressor. DO NOT loosen or remove any lines or hoses. Move the compressor out of the way and hang it from a piece of stiff wire.

18. Disconnect the speedometer cable from the transaxle.

19. On cars with manual transmissions, unbolt the clutch slave cylinder from the bell housing and move the cylinder out of the way. Don't disconnect any lines or hoses. Disconnect the shift control cables by removing the 2 clips, the washers and retainers.

20. On cars with automatic transmissions, remove the clip and retainer and separate the control cable from the shift lever.

21. Elevate the car and support it safely on jackstands.

22. Remove the 2 bolts from the exhaust pipe flange and separate the pipe from the exhaust manifold.

23. Remove the nuts and bolts and separate the driveshafts from the transaxle.

24. Remove the through bolt from the rear transaxle mount.

25. Remove the nuts from the center transaxle mount and the rear mount.

26. Lower the vehicle to the ground and attach the lifting equipment to the brackets on the engine. Take tension on the hoist line or chain just enough to support the motor but no more. Hang the engine wires and hoses on the chain or cable.

27. Remove the 3 exhaust hanger bracket nuts and the hanger. Remove the 2 center crossmember-to-main crossmember bolts. Remove the 3 center crossmember-to-radiator support bolts.

✳✳CAUTION

Support the crossmembers with a jack or jackstands when loosening the bolts. The pieces are heavy and could fall on you.

Fig. 34 Fuel inlet line — 1989-90 VIN code 6 engine

28. Remove the 8 crossmember-to-body bolts, then remove the 2 bolts holding the control arm brackets to the underbody. Remove the 2 center mount-to-transaxle bolts and remove the mount. Carefully lower the center mount and crossmember and remove from under the car.

29. At the left engine mount, remove the 3 bolts and the bracket, then remove the bolt, 2 nuts, through bolt and mounting. Remove the 3 bolts and the air cleaner bracket.

30. Loosen and remove the 5 bolts and disconnect the mounting bracket from the transaxle bracket. Remove the through bolt and mounting.

31. Carefully and slowly raise the engine and transaxle assembly out of the car. Tilt the transaxle down to clear the right engine mount. Be careful not to hit the steering gear housing. Make sure the engine is clear of all wiring, lines and hoses.

Fig. 35 Removing the engine mount-to-bracket bolt — 1989-90 VIN code 6 engine

1. Front transaxle mount
2. Rear transaxle mount
3. Main crossmember
4. Center support
5. Center transaxle mount
6. Mount bolt shields

Fig. 36 Detail of the crossmember and center support — 1989-90 VIN code 5 & 6 engine

32. Support the engine assembly on a suitable stand; do not allow it to remain on the hoist for any length of time.

33. With the engine properly supported, disconnect the reverse light switch and the neutral safety switch (automatic trans).

34. Remove the rear end cover plate.

35. For automatic transaxles, remove the 6 torque converter mounting bolts.

36. Remove the starter.

37. Support the transaxle, remove the retaining bolts in the case and remove the transaxle from the engine. Pull the unit straight off the engine; do not allow it to hang partially removed on the shaft. Keep the automatic transaxle level; if it tilts forward the converter may fall off.

To install:

38. Before reinstalling the engine in the car, several components must be reattached or connected. Install the transaxle to the engine; tighten the 12mm bolts to 47 ft. lbs and the 10mm bolts to 34 ft. lbs

39. Install the starter, its cable and connector. Tighten the mounting bolts to 29 ft. lbs.

40. Install the 6 torque converter-to-flexplate bolts on automatic transaxles. Tighten the bolts to 20 ft. lbs.

41. Install the rear cover plate and connect the wiring to the reverse light switch and the neutral safety switch (automatic trans.).

42. Attach the chain hoist or lift apparatus to the engine and lower it into the engine compartment. Before it is completely in position, attach the power steering pump and its through bolt to the motor.

➡**Tilt the transaxle downward and lower the engine to clear the left motor mount. As before, be careful not to hit the power steering housing (rack) or the throttle position sensor.**

43. Level the engine and align each mount with its bracket.

44. Install the right mounting insulator (bushing) to the engine bracket with the 2 nuts and bolt. Tighten the bolt temporarily.

45. Align the right insulator with the body bracket and install the through bolt and nut. Temporarily tighten the nut and bolt.

46. Align the left mounting insulator with the transaxle case bracket. Temporarily install the 3 bracket bolts.

47. With the engine held in place by these mounts, repeat steps 44, 45 and 46, tightening the bolts to the following tightness. Step 44: 38 ft. lbs.; step 45: 64 ft. lbs.; step 46: 35 ft. lbs.

48. Install the left sidemounting support with its 2 bolts; tighten them to 15 ft. lbs.

49. With the engine securely mounted in the car, the lifting equipment may be removed. Elevate the car and support it on jackstands.

50. Install the center mount to the transaxle with its 2 bolts and tighten them to 45 ft. lbs.

51. Position the center mount over the front and rear studs and start 2 nuts on the center mount only. Loosely install the 3 center support-to-radiator support bolts.

52. Loosely install the 2 front mount bolts. Raise the main crossmember into place over the rear studs and align all the underbody bolts.

53. Install the 2 rear mount nuts; leave them loose.

54. Loosely install the 8 underbody bolts, the lower control arm bracket bolts, the 2 center support-to-crossmember bolts and the exhaust hanger bracket and nuts.

55. With everything loose, but in place, make a second pass over all the nuts and bolts tightening them to the following specifications:
- Crossmember-to-underbody bolts: 152 ft. lbs.
- Lower control arm bracket-to-underbody bolts: 94 ft. lbs.
- Center support-to-radiator support: 45 ft. lbs.
- Center support-to-crossmember: 45 ft. lbs.
- Front, center and rear mount bolts: 45 ft. lbs.
- Exhaust hanger bracket nuts: 9 ft. lbs. (115 INCH lbs.)

56. Install the rear transaxle mount and tighten its bolt to 64 ft. lbs.

57. Install the nuts on the center transaxle mount and tighten them to 45 ft. lbs.

58. Reconnect the driveshafts to the transaxle.

59. Using a new gasket, connect the exhaust pipe to the manifold and install the exhaust pipe bolts, tightening them to 18 ft. lbs.

60. Lower the vehicle to the ground.

61. Either connect the control cables to the shift outer lever and selector lever and attach the control cables to manual transaxles or reconnect the control cable to the shift lever and install the clip and retainer on automatic transaxles. If equipped with manual transaxle, reattach the clutch slave cylinder to its mount.

62. Attach the speedometer cable to the transaxle.

63. Install the air conditioning compressor and drive belt if so equipped.

64. Install the power steering pump, pivot bolt and drive belt if so equipped. Adjust the belts to the correct tension.

65. Install the fuel inlet and outlet lines.

66. Connect the heater hoses. Make sure they are in the correct positions and that the clamps are in sound condition.

67. Connect the vacuum hoses to the vacuum switch, the charcoal canister, the vacuum sensor, the power steering and the brake booster.

68. Connect the wiring to the air conditioning, the oxygen sensor and the vacuum sensor.

69. Observing the labels made at the time of disassembly, reconnect the main engine harness to its sensors and switches. Work carefully and make sure each connector is properly matched and firmly seated.

70. Install the ground strap connector and its bolt; connect the wiring at the No. 2 junction block in the engine compartment.

71. Install the cruise control actuator if so equipped.

72. Connect the accelerator cable and throttle cable (automatic) to their brackets.

73. Install the radiator and cooling fan assembly. Install the overflow reservoir.

74. Install the air cleaner assembly and the air intake hose.

75. Install the battery. Connect the positive cable to the starter terminal, then to the battery. DO NOT connect the negative battery cable at this time.

76. Fill the transmission with the correct amount of fresh fluid.

77. Refill the engine coolant.

78. Fill the engine with the correct amount of fresh oil.

79. Double check all installation items, paying particular attention to loose hoses or hanging wires, untightened nuts, poor routing of hoses and wires (too tight or rubbing) and tools left in the engine area.

80. Connect the negative battery cable. Start the engine and allow it to idle. As the engine warms up, shift the automatic transmission into each gear range allowing it to engage momentarily. After each gear has been selected, put the shifter in PARK and check the transmission fluid level.

81. Shut the engine off and check the engine area carefully for leaks, particularly around any line or hose which was disconnected during removal.

82. Elevate and support the front end of the car on jackstands. Replace the left and right splash shields and lower the vehicle.

83. With the help of an assistant, reinstall the hood. Adjust the hood for proper fit and latching.

1990 VIN Code 5 Engine 1991-92 All Engines

▶ See Figure 37

1. Disconnect the negative terminal from the battery.

2. Using a scratch awl, scribe the hood hinge-to-hood outline. Disconnect the windshield washer fluid lines from the hood. Remove the 4 hood hinge bolts (2 on each side) disengaging the hood from the hinge. Using an assistant remove the hood.

3. Properly relieve the fuel system pressure.

4. Raise and safely support the vehicle.

5. Remove the left and right stone shields.

6. Drain the engine oil and the cooling system.

7. Drain the transaxle fluid. Lower the vehicle.

8. Remove the air cleaner hose and air cleaner assembly. Remove the radiator, cooling fan and cooling overflow reservoir.

9. Disconnect the accelerator cable and throttle cable from the bracket.

10. Remove the cruise control actuator.

11. Disconnect and tag all electrical component connectors.

12. Disconnect and tag all the necessary vacuum lines.

13. Remove the fuel inlet and outlet lines.

14. Remove the heater hoses from the engine.

15. Remove the power steering pump and bracket from the engine and set it off to the side. Leave the power steering hydraulic lines hook up to the pump.

16. Remove the air conditioning compressor and bracket bolts from the engine and set it off to the side. Leave the freon lines hooked up to the compressor.

17. Remove the speedometer cable from the transaxle.

18. Disconnect the clutch release cylinder without disconnecting the line and hose (manual transaxles only).

19. On the manual transaxle models, disconnect the transaxle control cables by removing the 2 clips, washers and retainers. Disconnect the control cables from the shift outer lever and select outer lever.

20. Disconnect the control cable from the shift lever (automatic transaxle only).

21. Raise and safely support the vehicle.

22. Disconnect the front exhaust pipe from the exhaust manifold.

23. Remove the transaxle mounts. Lower the vehicle.

24. Remove the engine mounts.

25. Attach a suitable chain hoist to the lifting device on the engine. Slowly lift the engine/transaxle assembly out of the vehicle and place it in a suitable engine stand.

To install:

26. Attach a suitable chain hoist to the lifting device on the engine. Slowly lift the engine/transaxle assembly into the vehicle.

27. Tilt the transaxle downward to clear the left mount.

28. Raise and safely support the vehicle. Install the engine and transaxle mounts.

29. Install the drive axles.

30. Install the exhaust pipe to the exhaust manifold.

31. Install the right and left and stone shields. Lower the vehicle.

32. Install the control cable to the shift lever (automatic transaxle).

33. On vehicles equipped with manual transaxles, install the control cables to the shift outer lever and select outer lever. Install the clutch release cylinder.

34. Install the air conditioner compressor bracket, compressor and bolts.

35. Install the power steering pump and bracket to the engine.

36. Install the heater hoses to the engine.

37. Install the fuel inlet and outlet lines.

38. Reconnect the disconnected vacuum lines.

39. Reconnect the disconnected electrical connectors.

40. Install the cruise control actuator.

41. Install the accelerator and throttle cable to the bracket.

42. Install the radiator, cooling fan and overflow reservoir. Refill the cooling system.

43. Install the air cleaner hose and air cleaner assembly.

44. Refill the transaxle.

45. Refill the engine with the recommended oil.

46. Reconnect the battery.

47. Install the hood assembly.

48. Start the engine and check for leakage of any kind. Make all necessary repairs and adjustments.

49. Torque the center transaxle mount-to-center crossmember nuts 45 ft. lbs. (61 Nm)

50. Torque the rear transaxle mount-to-main crossmember nuts 45 ft. lbs. (61 Nm).

51. Torque the right engine mount through bolt 64 ft. lbs. (87 Nm).

52. Torque the right engine mount support bolts 35 ft. lbs. (47 Nm).

53. Torque the right engine mount support bolts 35 ft. lbs. (47 Nm).

54. Torque the engine mount-to-engine bracket nuts 45 ft. lbs. (61 Nm).

55. Torque the engine mount-to-bracket bolt 45 ft. lbs. (61 Nm).

56. On vehicles equipped with an automatic transaxle, torque the flywheel retaining bolts to 47 ft. lbs. (64 Nm).

57. On vehicles equipped with a manual transaxle, torque the flywheel retaining bolts to 58 ft. lbs. (78 Nm).

1993

1. Disconnect the negative terminal from the battery.

2. Using a scratch awl, scribe the hood hinge-to-hood outline. Disconnect the windshield washer fluid lines from the

Fig. 37 Engine alignment with mounts — 1991-92

hood. Remove the 4 hood hinge bolts (2 on each side) disengaging the hood from the hinge. Using an assistant remove the hood.

3. Properly relieve the fuel system pressure.

4. Raise and safely support the vehicle.

5. Remove the 12 bolts and remove the left and right stone shields.

6. Drain the engine oil and the cooling system.

7. Drain the transaxle fluid. Lower the vehicle.

8. Disconnect the accelerator cable from the accelerator bracket.

9. Disconnect the accelerator cable and kickdown cable (with auto. trans.) from the accelerator bracket.

10. Remove the radiator and cooling fan assembly.

11. Disconnect and label the following electrical connectors:
- Throttle position (TP) sensor.
- Idle air control (IAC) valve.
- Throttle opener solenoid vacuum (TP SV) valve.
- Manifold absolute pressure (MAP) sensor.
- Intake air temperature (IAT) sensor.
- Engine coolant temperature (ECT) sensor.
- ECT sensor sending unit.
- Data link connector (DLC).
- A/C ECT switch (A/C equipped vehicles only).
- Exhaust gas recirculation (EGR) temperature sensor (California specification vehicles).
- Wiring harness from retaining clamps on fenders.
- Engine ground wires from intake manifold, right hand fender and left hand fender.

12. Disconnect and tag the following vacuum hoses:
- TP SV Valve.
- Solenoid purge (SP) valve.
- EGR valve.

13. Disconnect the hose clamp and air hose from the air cleaner(ACL).

14. Disconnect the 4 clips and the air cleaner upper case.

15. Remove air the cleaner element from the air cleaner.

16. Remove the air cleaner retaining harness, the 3 bolts and the air cleaner lower case.

17. Remove the battery.

18. Remove 2 bolts and coolant reservoir support bracket.

19. Remove the 1 bolt, and the windshield washer reservoir from the vehicle; disconnecting the electrical connector and hose.

20. Pry off the cruise control actuator cover (if equipped).

21. Remove the 3 bolts and the cruise control actuator.

22. Remove the 2 hose clamps and heater hose from the thermostat housing and coolant inlet pipe.

23. Disconnect the fuel feed pipe from fuel rail and intake manifold.

24. Disconnect the fuel return hose from fuel pressure (FPR) regulator.

25. Remove the clutch release cylinder (manual transaxle equipped vehicles).

26. Disconnect the transaxle control cable(s) from transaxle.

27. Remove the scuff plates from left and right side.

28. Remove the shift lever knob (manual transaxle equipped vehicles).

29. Remove the knee bolster, glove box door, instrument panel trim bezel, front and rear console and left hand cowl side trim panel.

30. Remove the radio.

31. Disconnect the 3 engine control module (ECM) connectors.

32. Disconnect the cowl wire harness connector.

33. Pull the engine wire harness from the cowl panel.

34. Remove the A/C compressor, if equipped, without disconnecting hoses. Remove drive belt and relocate compressor, temporarily suspending it from the radiator support bracket.

35. Remove the power steering pump, if equipped.

36. Raise and safely support the vehicle.

37. Remove the front pipe (Federal specification vehicles).

   a. Disconnect the Oxygen (O2) sensor.

   b. Remove the 2 front pipe to support bolts.

   c. Remove the 2 front pipe to exhaust manifold nuts and bolts.

   d. Remove the 2 front pipe mount nuts and front pipe with 2 gaskets from the vehicle.

38. Remove the front pipe (California specification vehicles).

   a. Disconnect the Oxygen (O2) and sub-Oxygen (O2) sensor connectors.

   b. Remove the 2 front pipe to warm up 3-way catalytic converter (WU-TWC) bolts and nuts.

   c. Remove the 2 front pipe to support bolts.

   d. Remove the 2 front pipe to exhaust manifold nuts.

39. Remove the left and right drive axles from the transaxle.

➡ **It is not necessary to remove the drive axle from the steering knuckle for engine or transaxle removal.**

40. Lower the vehicle.

41. Attach an engine hoist.

42. Disconnect the transaxle mounts.

43. Disconnect the engine mounts.

44. Make sure all the wires and hoses are disconnected and remove the engine and transaxle from the vehicle, ensuring clearance on all sides.

To install:

45. Install the engine and transaxle to the vehicle, ensuring clearance on all sides.

46. Connect the transaxle mounts.

   • Tighten the 2 mounting bolts to 45 ft. lbs. (61 Nm).

   • Tighten the mount through bolt to 64 ft. lbs. (87 Nm).

47. Connect the engine mounts and tighten the through bolts to 47 ft. lbs. (64 Nm).

48. Remove the engine hoist.

49. Raise and safely support the vehicle.

50. Install the left and right drive axles to the transaxle.

51. Install the front pipe (Federal specification vehicles).

   a. Install the 2 front pipe mount nuts and the front pipe with the 2 gaskets to the vehicle.

   b. Install the 2 front pipe to exhaust manifold nuts and bolts but do not fully tighten at this time.

   c. Connect the Oxygen (O2) sensor.

   d. Install the 2 front pipe to support bolts.

   e. Tighten all bolts as follows:

   • Front pipe to exhaust manifold nuts and bolts to 46 ft. lbs. (62 Nm).

   • Front pipe to support bolts to 14 ft. lbs. (19 Nm).

52. Install the front pipe (California specification vehicles):

   a. Install 2 new gaskets to the front pipes.

   b. Install the front pipe to TWC, secure with the bolts and nuts, but do not fully tighten at this time.

   c. Connect the Oxygen (O2) and sub-Oxygen (O2) sensor connectors.

   d. Install the 2 front pipe to warm up 3-way catalytic converter (WU-TWC) bolts and nuts, but do not tighten at this time.

   e. Install the 2 front pipe to support bolts.

   f. Tighten all bolts as follows:

   • Front pipe to WU-TWC nuts and bolts to 46 ft. lbs. (62 Nm).

   • Front pipe to TWC bolts and nuts to 32 ft. lbs. (43 Nm).

   • Front pipe to support bolts to 14 ft. lbs. (19 Nm).

53. Lower the vehicle.

54. Install the power steering pump (if equipped).

55. Install the A/C compressor, if equipped.

56. Push the engine wire harness through the cowl panel and connect the connector.

57. Connect the 3 engine control module (ECM) connectors.

58. Install the radio.

59. Install the knee bolster, glove box door, instrument panel trim bezel, front and rear console and left hand cowl side trim panel.

60. Install the scuff plates to the left and right side.

61. Install the shift lever knob (manual transaxle equipped vehicles).

62. Connect the transaxle control cable(s) from transaxle.

63. Install the clutch release cylinder (manual transaxle equipped vehicles).

64. Connect the fuel feed pipe to fuel rail and intake manifold and tighten to 22 ft. lbs. (29 Nm).

65. Connect the fuel return hose to the fuel pressure (FPR) regulator.

66. Install the 2 hose clamps and heater hose to the thermostat housing and coolant inlet pipe.

67. Install the 3 bolts and the cruise control actuator. Tighten to 19 ft. lbs. (25 Nm)

68. Install the cruise control actuator cover.

69. Install the 1 bolt, and the windshield washer reservoir to the vehicle; connecting the electrical connector and hose.

70. Install the 2 bolts and coolant reservoir support bracket.

71. Install the battery.

72. Install the air cleaner retaining harness, the 3 bolts and the air cleaner lower case. Install a new element.

73. Connect the 4 clips and the air cleaner upper case.

74. Connect the hose clamp and air hose to the air cleaner(ACL).

75. Install the radiator and cooling fan assembly.

76. Connect the following electrical connectors:
- Throttle position (TP) sensor.
- Idle air control (IAC) valve.
- Throttle opener solenoid vacuum (TP SV) valve.
- Manifold absolute pressure (MAP) sensor.
- Intake air temperature (IAT) sensor.
- Engine coolant temperature (ECT) sensor.
- ECT sensor sending unit.
- Data link connector (DLC).
- A/C ECT switch (A/C equipped vehicles only).
- Exhaust gas recirculation (EGR) temperature sensor (California specification vehicles).
- Wiring harness from retaining clamps on fenders.
- Engine ground wires from intake manifold, right hand fender and left hand fender.

77. Connect the following vacuum hoses:
- TP SV Valve.
- Solenoid purge (SP) valve.
- EGR valve.

78. Connect the accelerator cable to the accelerator bracket.

79. Connect the accelerator cable and kickdown cable (with auto. trans.) to the accelerator bracket.

80. Fill the transaxle fluid.

81. Install the 12 bolts and the left and right stone shields.

82. Fill the engine oil and the cooling system.

83. Install the oil drain plug and gasket.

84. Lower the vehicle.

85. Connect the battery terminals to the battery.

86. Install the 4 hood hinge bolts (2 on each side) engaging the hood to the hinge. Use an assistant to install the hood.

87. Fill the engine oil and the cooling system.

Cylinder Head Cover

REMOVAL & INSTALLATION

1985-88 VIN Code 4 Engine

1. Disconnect the negative battery cable.
2. Remove the air cleaner assembly.
3. Disconnect the PCV hose.
4. Disconnect the accelerator cable.
5. Disconnect the wire harness.
6. Remove the upper timing belt cover bolts and the cover. Remove the 2 valve cover bolts.
7. Remove the valve cover and its gasket.

➡If the cover is stuck in place, tap a corner with a plastic or rubber mallet. Don't pry the cover up; it will deform and leak.

To install:

8. Clean the mating surfaces on the head and the cover; install a new gasket.

9. Place the cover and gasket in position on the head. Make sure the cover is straight and that the rubber bushings are on the studs.

10. Install the cover nuts and the upper belt cover with its bolts. Tighten the cover nuts to 15 ft. lbs.

11. Connect the wiring harness, the accelerator cable and the PCV hose.

12. Install the air cleaner assembly and connect the negative battery cable.

13. Start the engine and check for leaks after the engine has warmed up. Minor leaks may be cured by slightly snugging the cover bolts and the timing belt cover bolts. Any leak that is still present after about a ¼ turn CANNOT be cured by further tightening. Remove the cover again and either reposition or replace the gasket.

1988 VIN Code 5 Engine 1990 VIN Code 5 Engine 1991-92 VIN Code 6 Engine

▶ See Figure 38

1. Disconnect the negative battery cable.
2. Disconnect or remove the PCV valve, the accelerator cable and the wiring harness.
3. Disconnect the spark plug wires at the plugs and disconnect the wiring to the noise filter.
4. Disconnect the oil pressure sender wire and, if equipped with air conditioning, the wire to the compressor.
5. Remove the center cover (between the cam covers) and its gasket.
6. Remove the cap nuts, the rubber seals and remove the valve covers.

➡If the cover is stuck in place, tap a corner with a plastic or rubber mallet. Don't pry the cover up; it will deform and leak.

To install:

7. Clean the mating surfaces of the head and the covers.

8. Apply RTV sealant to the cylinder head before reassembly. This step is REQUIRED to prevent oil leakage.

9. Install the covers with new gaskets. Install the seals and the cap nut, making sure everything is properly seated. tighten the cap nuts to 15 ft. lbs. (20 Nm).

10. Install the center cover with its gasket.

11. Connect the wiring to the oil pressure sender and the compressor, if equipped.

12. Connect the wiring to the noise filter and install the spark plug wires.

13. Connect, in this order, the wiring harness, the accelerator cable, the PCV valve and the negative battery cable.

14. Start the engine and check for leaks after the engine has warmed up. Minor leaks may be cured by slightly snugging the cover bolts. Any leak that is still present after about a ¼ turn CANNOT be cured by further tightening.

Fig. 38 Apply sealant to these points before reinstalling the valve cover — 1988 VIN Code 5 engine

Remove the cover again and either reposition or replace the gasket.

1989-90 VIN Code 6 Engine 1991-92 VIN Code 5 Engine

▶ **See Figure 39**

1. Disconnect the negative battery cable.
2. Disconnect the PCV and the vacuum hose.
3. Loosen the engine wiring harness running over the upper timing belt cover for easier access to the valve cover.
4. Remove the spark plug wires from the spark plugs.
5. Remove the 3 cap nuts, the seals below them and remove the valve cover.

To install:

6. Clean the mating surfaces of the head and the cover. Install a new gasket before installing the valve cover.
7. Apply RTV sealant to the cylinder head as illustrated before reassembly. This step is REQUIRED to prevent oil leakage.
8. Install the covers with new gaskets. Install the seals and the cap nut, making sure everything is properly seated. Tighten the cap nuts to 15 ft. lbs. (20 Nm).
9. Reconnect the spark plug wires and reposition the wiring harness over the timing belt cover.
10. Connect the vacuum hose, the PCV and the negative battery cable.
11. Start the engine and check for leaks after the engine has warmed up. Minor leaks may be cured by slightly snugging the cover bolts. Any leak that is still present after about a ¼ turn CANNOT be cured by further tightening. Remove the cover again and either reposition or replace the gasket.

1993 All Engines

1. Disconnect the negative battery cable.
2. Disconnect the PCV and the 2 vacuum hoses.
3. Loosen the engine wiring harness running over the upper timing belt cover for easier access to the valve cover.
4. Remove the spark plug wires from the spark plugs.
5. Remove the 4 cap nuts, the seals below them and remove the cylinder head cover.

To install:

6. Clean the mating surfaces of the head and the cover. Install a new gasket before installing the valve cover.
7. Apply RTV sealant to the cylinder head before reassembly. This step is REQUIRED to prevent oil leakage.

Fig. 39 Apply sealant to these points before reinstalling valve cover — 1989-90 VIN Code 6 and 1991-92 VIN Code 5 engines

8. Install the covers with new gaskets. Install the seals and the cap nut, making sure everything is properly seated. Tighten the cap nuts to 53 inch lbs. (6 Nm).
9. Reconnect the spark plug wires and reposition the wiring harness over the timing belt cover.
10. Connect the vacuum hoses, the PCV and the negative battery cable.
11. Start the engine and check for leaks after the engine has warmed up. Minor leaks may be cured by slightly snugging the cover bolts. Any leak that is still present after about a ¼ turn CANNOT be cured by further tightening. Remove the cover again and either reposition or replace the gasket.

Rocker Arms and Shafts

REMOVAL & INSTALLATION

1985-88 VIN Code 4 Engine

▶ **See Figures 40, 41 and 42**

1. Remove the valve cover as described previously.
2. Loosen each rocker support bolt little-by-little, in 3 steps, in the proper sequence.
3. Remove the bolts and remove the rocker assembly from the head. Inspect the valve contacting surfaces for wear. Inspect the rocker-to-shaft clearance by wiggling the rocker on the shaft. Play should be virtually none; any noticeable motion requires replacement of the rocker arms and/or the shaft.
4. Disassemble the rockers from the shaft. Check the contact surfaces for signs of visible wear or scoring.
5. Using either an inside micrometer or a dial indicator, measure the inside diameter of the rocker arm. Using a regular micrometer, measure the diameter of the shaft. Maximum allowable difference (oil clearance) between the 2 measurements is 0.06mm.
6. After replacing any needed parts, loosen the adjusting screw locknuts.
7. The rocker shaft has oil holes in it. When assembling the rockers onto the shaft, make sure the holes point to the left, the right and down. (Said another way, when viewed from the end of the shaft, the oil holes are at 3, 6 and 9 o'clock.)

✳✳WARNING

Failure to observe this positioning will cause the rockers to starve for oil, causing expensive and premature wear.

8. Install the rocker assembly on the head. Tighten the retaining bolts in 3 steps and in the correct sequence. Torque the bolts to 18 ft. lbs. on the third pass.
9. Set the motor to TDC and adjust the valves, using the procedures discussed in Section 2.

1988-93 All Twin Camshaft Engines

The twin camshaft motors (one cam for the intake valves and one for the exhaust valves) use direct-acting cams; that is, the lobes of the camshaft act directly on the valve mechanism. These engines do not have rocker arms.

Fig. 40 Rocker support bolt loosening sequence — 1985-88 VIN Code 4 engine

Fig. 41 Oil hole positioning — 1985-88 VIN Code 4 engine

Fig. 42 Tighten the rocker support bolts in this sequence — 1985-88 VIN Code 4 engine

Thermostat

REMOVAL & INSTALLATION

All Models

▶ **See Figures 43 and 44**

The thermostat and its built-in by-pass valve is installed on the inlet side of the water pump. Its purpose is to prevent overheating of the coolant by controlling the flow into the engine from the radiator. During warm up, the thermostat remains closed so that the coolant within the engine heats quickly and aids the warming up process.

As the coolant temperature increases, the thermostat gradually opens, allowing a supply of lower temperature coolant (from the radiator) to enter the water pump and circulate through the engine.

✳✳WARNING

A thermostat with an internal by-pass should never be removed as a countermeasure to overheating. Removing the thermostat actually makes the problem worse because more coolant bypasses the radiator, thereby reducing cooling even more.

1. Drain the cooling system and save the coolant for reuse.

✳✳CAUTION

When draining the coolant, keep in mind that cats and dogs are attracted by the ethylene glycol antifreeze, and are quite likely to drink any that is left in an uncovered container or in puddles on the ground. This will prove fatal in sufficient quantity. Always drain the coolant into a sealable container. Coolant should be reused unless it is contaminated or several years old.

2. Remove the water inlet housing and remove the thermostat. Carefully observe the positioning of the thermostat within the housing.
3. Install the new thermostat in the housing, making sure it is in correctly. It is possible to install it backwards. Additionally, make certain that the air bleed valve aligns with the protrusion on the water inlet housing. Failure to observe this placement can result in poor air bleeding and possible overheating.
4. Install the water inlet housing cover with a new gasket. Install the 2 hold down bolts and tighten them to 20 ft. lbs. Do not overtighten these bolts!
5. Refill the cooling system with coolant.
6. Start the engine. During the warm up period, observe the temperature gauge for normal behavior. Also during this period, check the water inlet housing area for any sign of leakage. Remember to check for leaks under both cold and hot conditions.

Fig. 43 Thermostat assembly. Prizm shown, Nova similar

Fig. 44 Correct placement of the air bleed valve during thermostat replacement

Combination Manifolds

REMOVAL & INSTALLATION

1985-88 VIN CODE 4 Engine
▶ See Figures 45 and 53

The intake and exhaust manifolds on the 4A-LC engine are a 1-piece or combination design. They can not be separated from each other or removed individually.

1. Disconnect the negative battery cable.
2. Remove the air cleaner assembly.
3. Label and disconnect all vacuum hoses at the carburetor.
4. Disconnect the accelerator cable and, for automatic transmissions, the throttle cable.
5. Label and disconnect the electrical connections at the carburetor.
6. Disconnect the fuel line at the fuel pump.
7. Carefully loosen and remove the carburetor mounting bolts and remove the carburetor.

✳✳CAUTION

The carburetor bowls contain gasoline which may spill or leak during removal. Observe no smoking/no open flame precautions. Have a Class B-C (dry powder) fire extinguisher within arm's reach at all times.

➡**Keep the carburetor level during removal and handling. As soon as it is off the car, wrap or cover it with a clean towel to keep dirt out.**

8. Remove the Early Fuel Evaporation (EFE) gasket.
9. Remove the vacuum line and dashpot bracket.
10. Carefully remove the heat shields on the manifold; don't break the bolts.
11. Safely elevate and support the vehicle on jackstands.
12. Disconnect the exhaust pipe at the manifold and exhaust bracket at the engine.
13. Remove the hose at the converter pipe.

14. Lower the car to the ground and remove or disconnect the vacuum hose to the brake booster.
15. Remove the bracket for the accelerator and throttle cables.
16. Evenly loosen and then remove the bolts and nuts holding the manifold to the engine. Remove the manifold and its gaskets.
17. Using a precision straight edge and a feeler gauge, check the mating surfaces of the manifold for warpage. If the warpage is greater than the maximum allowable specification, replace the manifold.**Maximum permitted warpage:**
    Intake 0.2mm;
    Exhaust 0.3mm
To install:
18. When reinstalling, always use new gaskets and make sure they are properly positioned. Place the manifold in position and loosely install the nuts and bolts until all are just snug. Double check the placement of the manifold and in 2 passes tighten the retaining nuts and bolts to 18 ft. lbs.
19. Reinstall the bracket for the accelerator and throttle cables and connect the vacuum hose to the brake vacuum booster.
20. Elevate and safely support the car on jackstands.
21. Reconnect the hose at the converter pipe. Install the exhaust bracket at the engine and, using new gaskets, connect the exhaust pipe to the manifold.
22. Lower the vehicle to the ground. Install the heat shield onto the manifold.
23. Reinstall the vacuum line and the dashpot bracket.
24. Install the EFE gasket.
25. Reinstall the carburetor. Slowly and evenly tighten the mounting nuts and bolts to 8-10 ft. lbs. Connect the electrical connectors to the carburetor.
26. Connect and secure the fuel line to the fuel pump.
27. Attach the accelerator cable and throttle valve cable (automatic trans.).
28. Observing the labels made earlier, install the vacuum lines. Be careful of the routing and make sure that each line fits snugly on its port. double check each line for crimps or twists.
29. Install the air cleaner assembly and connect the negative battery cable.

Fig. 45 Measuring the manifold for warpage — 1985-88 VIN Code 4 engine

Intake Manifold

REMOVAL & INSTALLATION

1988 VIN Code 5 Engine

▶ See Figures 46, 47 and 54

1. Disconnect the negative battery cable.
2. Drain the cooling system.

✳✳CAUTION

When draining the coolant, keep in mind that cats and dogs are attracted by the ethylene glycol antifreeze, and are quite likely to drink any that is left in an uncovered container or in puddles on the ground. This will prove fatal in sufficient quantity. Always drain the coolant into a sealable container. Coolant should be reused unless it is contaminated or several years old.

3. Remove the air cleaner assembly.
4. Remove the upper radiator hose at the engine.
5. Disconnect the accelerator cable and, on automatic transmissions, the throttle valve cable.
6. Label and disconnect vacuum hoses at the manifolds.
7. Disconnect and remove the fuel delivery pipe (fuel rail) and remove the injectors. During removal, be careful not to drop the injectors.

✳✳CAUTION

The fuel system is under pressure. Release pressure slowly and contain spillage. Observe no smoking/no open flame precautions. Have a Class B-C (dry powder) fire extinguisher within arm's reach at all times.

8. Disconnect the vacuum hose to the brake booster and remove the heat shield(s) from the manifold(s).
9. Safely raise the car and support it on jackstands.
10. Disconnect the wire for the water temperature sensor and remove the water outlet housing (thermostat housing) and the bypass pipe.
11. Remove the exhaust bracket and disconnect the exhaust pipe at the manifold. Remove the support bracket for the intake manifold.

12. Lower the vehicle to the ground.
13. Remove the intake manifold with the air control valve and gaskets and/or remove the exhaust manifold with its gaskets.
14. Using a precision straight edge and a feeler gauge, check the mating surfaces of the manifolds for warpage. If the warpage is greater than the maximum allowable specification, replace the manifold. **Maximum allowable warpage:**
   - Intake Manifold: 0.05mm
   - Exhaust Manifold: 0.3mm
   - Air Control Valve: 0.05mm

   To install:
15. When reinstalling, always use new gaskets and make sure they are properly positioned. Place the manifold(s) in position and loosely install the nuts and bolts until all are just snug. Double check the placement of the manifold(s) and in 2 passes tighten the retaining nuts and bolts. The exhaust manifold retaining bolts should be tightened to 18 ft. lbs. (25 Nm) and the intake manifold bolts should be tightened to 20 ft. lbs. (27 Nm). The bolts for the intake support bracket should also be tightened to 20 ft. lbs. (27 Nm)
16. With the manifold(s) in place, elevate and support the vehicle; install the support bracket for the intake manifold and connect the exhaust pipe to the exhaust manifold. Attach the exhaust bracket.
17. Install the bypass pipe, the water outlet housing and connect the wiring to the water temperature sensor.
18. Lower the car to the ground and install the heat shield(s) on the manifolds.
19. Connect the vacuum hose for the brake vacuum booster.
20. Install the fuel delivery pipe and the injectors. Tighten the mounting bolts to 13 ft. lbs.
21. Observing the labels made earlier, install the vacuum lines. Be careful of the routing and make sure that each line fits snugly on its port.
22. Double check each line for crimps or twists.
23. Connect the accelerator cable and throttle valve cable (automatic trans.)
24. Reconnect the upper radiator hose.
25. Install the air cleaner assembly.
26. Refill the coolant.
27. Connect the negative battery cable.

1989-90 VIN Code 6 Engine

▶ See Figures 48 and 49

1. Disconnect the negative battery cable.

Fig. 46 Removing the fuel rails and injectors — 1988 VIN Code 5 engine

Fig. 47 Check for warpage in three positions — 1988 VIN Code 5 engine

2. Drain the cooling system.

✳✳CAUTION

When draining the coolant, keep in mind that cats and dogs are attracted by the ethylene glycol antifreeze, and are quite likely to drink any that is left in an uncovered container or in puddles on the ground. This will prove fatal in sufficient quantity. Always drain the coolant into a sealable container. Coolant should be reused unless it is contaminated or several years old.

3. Remove the air cleaner assembly.
4. Label and disconnect the vacuum hoses at the manifold.
5. Label and disconnect the wiring to the throttle position sensor, the cold start injector, the injector connectors, the air control valve and the vacuum sensor.
6. Disconnect the cold start injector pipe.

✳✳CAUTION

The fuel system is under pressure. Release pressure slowly and contain spillage. Observe no smoking/no open flame precautions. Have a Class B-C (dry powder) fire extinguisher within arm's reach at all times.

7. Disconnect the water hose from the air valve.
8. Raise and safely support the car on jackstands.
9. Remove the intake manifold support bracket. Lower the car to the ground.
10. Remove the 7 bolts, 2 nuts and the ground cable. Remove the intake manifold and its gaskets.

Fig. 48 Removing the cold start injector line at the intake manifold — 1989-90 VIN code 6 engine

Fig. 49 Intake manifold assembly — 1989-90 VIN code 6 engine

11. Measure the intake manifold mating surface with a precision straight edge and a feeler gauge. If the warpage exceeds 0.2mm, the manifold must be replaced.
   To install:
12. To reassemble, install the manifold with new gaskets in position. Attach the 7 bolts, 2 nuts and the ground cable connector.
13. Raise and safely support the car; install the manifold support bracket and its bolts. Lower the car to the ground.
14. Tighten the manifold mounting nuts and bolts evenly to 14 ft. lbs. (19 Nm).
15. Connect the water hose to the air valve.
16. Connect the fuel line to the cold-start injector.
17. Connect the wiring to the throttle position sensor, the cold start injector, the injector connectors, the air control valve and the vacuum sensor.
18. Observing the labels made earlier, install the vacuum lines. Be careful of the routing and make sure that each line fits snugly on its port. Double check each line for crimps or twists.
19. Connect the accelerator and throttle valve (automatic trans.) cables to their brackets.
20. Refill the coolant.
21. Install the air cleaner assembly and connect the negative battery cable.

1990 VIN Code 5 Engine 1991-92 All Engines
▶ See Figure 54

1. Disconnect the negative battery cable.
2. Drain the cooling system.
3. Remove the air cleaner assembly.
4. Remove the upper radiator hose at the engine.
5. Disconnect the accelerator cable and, on automatic transaxles, the throttle valve cable.
6. Label and disconnect vacuum hoses at the manifolds.
7. Disconnect and remove the fuel delivery pipe (fuel rail) and remove the injectors. During removal, be careful not to drop the injectors.

✳✳CAUTION

The fuel system is under pressure. Release pressure slowly and contain spillage. Observe no smoking/no open flame precautions. Have a Class B-C (dry powder) fire extinguisher within arm's reach at all times.

8. Disconnect the vacuum hose to the brake booster and remove the heat shield(s) from the manifold(s).
9. Raise the vehicle and support it safely.
10. Disconnect the wire for the water temperature sensor and remove the water outlet housing (thermostat housing) and the bypass pipe.
11. Remove the exhaust bracket and disconnect the exhaust pipe at the manifold. Remove the support bracket for the intake manifold.
12. Lower the vehicle to the ground.
13. Remove the intake manifold with the air control valve and gaskets and/or remove the exhaust manifold with its gaskets.
14. Using a precision straight edge and a feeler gauge, check the mating surfaces of the manifolds for warpage. If the

warpage is greater than the maximum allowable specification, replace the manifold. **Maximum allowable warpage:**

Intake Manifold: 0.05mm
Exhaust Manifold: 0.3mm
Air Control Valve: 0.05mm.

To install:

15. When reinstalling, always use new gaskets and make sure they are properly positioned. Place the manifold(s) in position and loosely install the nuts and bolts until all are just snug. Double check the placement of the manifold(s) and in 2 passes tighten the retaining nuts and bolts. The exhaust manifold retaining bolts should be tightened to 18 ft. lbs. (25 Nm) and the intake manifold bolts should be tightened to 20 ft. lbs. (27 Nm). The bolts for the intake support bracket should also be tightened to 20 ft. lbs. (27 Nm).

16. With the manifold(s) in place, elevate and support the vehicle; install the support bracket for the intake manifold and connect the exhaust pipe to the exhaust manifold. Attach the exhaust bracket.

17. Install the bypass pipe, the water outlet housing and connect the wiring to the water temperature sensor.

18. Lower the vehicle to the ground and install the heat shield(s) on the manifolds.

19. Connect the vacuum hose for the brake vacuum booster.

20. Install the fuel delivery pipe and the injectors. Tighten the mounting bolts to 13 ft. lbs. (18 Nm).

21. Observing the labels made earlier, install the vacuum lines. Be careful of the routing and make sure that each line fits snugly on its port.

22. Double check each line for crimps or twists.

23. Connect the accelerator cable and throttle valve cable (automatic trans.)

24. Reconnect the upper radiator hose.

25. Install the air cleaner assembly.

26. Refill the coolant.

27. Connect the negative battery cable.

1993 All Engines

➡On the 1993 engines, the upper intake air chamber and intake manifold can be separated. A metal gasket is used to improve sealing performance. No cold start injector assembly is used on the 1993 vehicles.

1. Relieve the fuel pressure. Disconnect the negative battery cable.

2. Remove the air cleaner assembly. Drain the coolant.

3. Tag and remove all wires, hoses or cables in the way of intake manifold removal. Remove the intake manifold stay (bracket).

4. Remove the cold start injector pipe, if equipped.

5. Disconnect the electrical connectors and remove the fuel delivery pipe (fuel rail) and remove the injectors. During removal, be careful not to drop the injectors.

✳✳CAUTION

The fuel system is under pressure. Release pressure slowly and contain spillage. Observe no smoking/no open flame precautions. Have a Class B-C (dry powder) fire extinguisher within arm's reach at all times.

6. Remove the intake manifold retaining bolts. Remove the intake manifold from the vehicle.

To install:

7. Clean the gasket mating surfaces being careful not to damage them. Check the mating surfaces for warpage with a straight edge. The specification for maximum warpage on the intake manifold is 0.0079 in. (0.20mm). If warpage is greater than maximum, replace the manifold.

8. Match the old gasket with the new one for an exact match. Use a new gasket when installing the manifold and tighten the bolts evenly and in several passes from the center outward to 20 ft. lbs. Install the intake manifold stay (bracket).

9. Install the cold start injector pipe, if equipped. Torque the cold start injector union bolt to 18 ft. lbs.

10. Install all necessary wires, hoses or cables. Install the air cleaner assembly.

11. Refill the cooling system. Connect the negative battery cable. Start the engine. Check for leaks and road test for proper operation.

Exhaust Manifold

REMOVAL & INSTALLATION

1988 VIN Code 5 Engine

▶ **See Figure 54**

1. Disconnect the negative battery cable.
2. Drain the cooling system.

✳✳CAUTION

When draining the coolant, keep in mind that cats and dogs are attracted by the ethylene glycol antifreeze, and are quite likely to drink any that is left in an uncovered container or in puddles on the ground. This will prove fatal in sufficient quantity. Always drain the coolant into a sealable container. Coolant should be reused unless it is contaminated or several years old.

3. Remove the air cleaner assembly.
4. Remove the upper radiator hose at the engine.
5. Disconnect the accelerator cable and, on automatic transmissions, the throttle valve cable.
6. Label and disconnect vacuum hoses at the manifolds.
7. Disconnect and remove the fuel delivery pipe (fuel rail) and remove the injectors. During removal, be careful not to drop the injectors.

✳✳CAUTION

The fuel system is under pressure. Release pressure slowly and contain spillage. Observe no smoking/no open flame precautions. Have a Class B-C (dry powder) fire extinguisher within arm's reach at all times.

8. Disconnect the vacuum hose to the brake booster and remove the heat shield(s) from the manifold(s).
9. Safely raise the car and support it on jackstands.

10. Disconnect the wire for the water temperature sensor and remove the water outlet housing (thermostat housing) and the bypass pipe.

11. Remove the exhaust bracket and disconnect the exhaust pipe at the manifold. Remove the support bracket for the intake manifold.

12. Lower the vehicle to the ground.

13. Remove the intake manifold with the air control valve and gaskets and/or remove the exhaust manifold with its gaskets.

14. Using a precision straight edge and a feeler gauge, check the mating surfaces of the manifolds for warpage. If the warpage is greater than the maximum allowable specification, replace the manifold. **Maximum allowable warpage:**

    Intake Manifold: 0.05mm;

    Exhaust Manifold: 0.3mm;

    Air Control Valve: 0.05mm.

To install:

15. When reinstalling, always use new gaskets and make sure they are properly positioned. Place the manifold(s) in position and loosely install the nuts and bolts until all are just snug. Double check the placement of the manifold(s) and in 2 passes tighten the retaining nuts and bolts. The exhaust manifold retaining bolts should be tightened to 18 ft. lbs. and the intake manifold bolts should be tightened to 20 ft. lbs. The bolts for the intake support bracket should also be tightened to 20 ft. lbs

16. With the manifold(s) in place, elevate and support the vehicle; install the support bracket for the intake manifold and connect the exhaust pipe to the exhaust manifold. Attach the exhaust bracket.

17. Install the bypass pipe, the water outlet housing and connect the wiring to the water temperature sensor.

18. Lower the car to the ground and install the heat shield(s) on the manifolds.

19. Connect the vacuum hose for the brake vacuum booster.

20. Install the fuel delivery pipe and the injectors. Tighten the mounting bolts to 13 ft. lbs.

21. Observing the labels made earlier, install the vacuum lines. Be careful of the routing and make sure that each line fits snugly on its port.

22. Double check each line for crimps or twists.

23. Connect the accelerator cable and throttle valve cable (automatic trans.)

24. Reconnect the upper radiator hose.

25. Install the air cleaner assembly.

26. Refill the coolant.

27. Connect the negative battery cable.

1989-90 VIN Code 6 Engine

▶ **See Figure 50**

1. Disconnect the negative battery cable.

2. Remove the 5 bolts and remove the upper heat shield (insulator) from the manifold.

3. Raise and safely support the vehicle on jackstands.

4. Disconnect the exhaust pipe from the exhaust manifold and remove the manifold support and its 2 bolts.

5. Lower the vehicle to the ground. Disconnect the oxygen sensor wire.

6. Remove the 2 nuts and 3 bolts holding the manifold to the engine. Remove the manifold and its gaskets. When the manifold is clear of the car, remove the lower heat shield.

7. Measure the exhaust manifold mating surface with a precision straight edge and a feeler gauge. If the warpage exceeds 0.28mm, the manifold must be replaced.

To install:

8. Before reinstalling, attach the lower heat shield to the manifold with the 3 bolts. Tighten the bolts to 18 ft. lbs.

9. Install the manifold with new gaskets and tighten its bolts and nuts to 18 ft. lbs.

10. Raise the car and safely support in on jackstands. Install the manifold support and tighten the bolts to 18 ft. lbs.

11. Connect the exhaust pipe to the manifold with new gaskets and tighten the bolts to 18 ft. lbs.

12. Lower the car to the ground. Install the upper heat shield on the manifold and tighten its 5 bolts to 18 ft. lbs.

13. Connect the wiring to the oxygen sensors.

14. Connect the negative battery cable.

1990 VIN Code 5 Engine 1991-92 All Engines

▶ **See Figures 50 and 54**

1. Disconnect the negative battery cable.

2. Drain the cooling system.

3. Remove the air cleaner assembly.

4. Remove the upper radiator hose at the engine.

5. Disconnect the accelerator cable and, on automatic transaxles, the throttle valve cable.

6. Label and disconnect vacuum hoses at the manifolds.

1. Exhaust manifold
2. Nut
3. Bolt

Fig. 50 Location of exhaust manifold attaching hardware — 1989-90 VIN code 6, 1991-92 VIN code 5 and all 1993 engines

7. Disconnect and remove the fuel delivery pipe (fuel rail) and remove the injectors. During removal, be careful not to drop the injectors.

✳✳CAUTION

The fuel system is under pressure. Release pressure slowly and contain spillage. Observe no smoking/no open flame precautions. Have a Class B-C (dry powder) fire extinguisher within arm's reach at all times.

8. Disconnect the vacuum hose to the brake booster and remove the heat shield(s) from the manifold(s).

9. Safely raise the vehicle and support it.

10. Disconnect the wire for the water temperature sensor and remove the water outlet housing (thermostat housing) and the bypass pipe.

11. Remove the exhaust bracket and disconnect the exhaust pipe at the manifold. Remove the support bracket for the intake manifold.

12. Lower the vehicle to the ground.

13. Remove the intake manifold with the air control valve and gaskets and/or remove the exhaust manifold with its gaskets.

To install:

14. Using a precision straight edge and a feeler gauge, check the mating surfaces of the manifolds for warpage. If the warpage is greater than the maximum allowable specification, replace the manifold. Maximum allowable warpage: Intake Manifold: 0.05mm; Exhaust Manifold: 0.3mm; Air Control Valve: 0.05mm.

15. When reinstalling, always use new gaskets and make sure they are properly positioned. Place the manifold(s) in position and loosely install the nuts and bolts until all are just snug. Double check the placement of the manifold(s) and in 2 passes tighten the retaining nuts and bolts. The exhaust manifold retaining bolts should be tightened to 18 ft. lbs. (25 Nm) and the intake manifold bolts should be tightened to 20 ft. lbs (27 Nm). The bolts for the intake support bracket should also be tightened to 20 ft. lbs (27 Nm).

16. With the manifold(s) in place, elevate and support the vehicle; install the support bracket for the intake manifold and connect the exhaust pipe to the exhaust manifold. Attach the exhaust bracket.

17. Install the bypass pipe, the water outlet housing and connect the wiring to the water temperature sensor.

18. Lower the vehicle to the ground and install the heat shield(s) on the manifolds.

19. Connect the vacuum hose for the brake vacuum booster.

20. Install the fuel delivery pipe and the injectors. Tighten the mounting bolts to 13 ft. lbs. (18 Nm).

21. Observing the labels made earlier, install the vacuum lines. Be careful of the routing and make sure that each line fits snugly on its port.

22. Double check each line for crimps or twists.

23. Connect the accelerator cable and throttle valve cable (automatic trans.)

24. Reconnect the upper radiator hose.

25. Install the air cleaner assembly.

26. Refill the coolant.

27. Connect the negative battery cable.

1993 All Engines
▶ See Figure 50

1. Disconnect the negative battery cable.

2. Disconnect the oxygen sensor electrical connector.

3. Remove the 2 exhaust pipe to exhaust manifold bolts and 2 front pipe to exhaust manifold nuts (front pipe to warm up 3 way catalytic converter WU TWC on Calif. spec. vehicles).

4. Remove the 5 bolts and the upper heat insulator.

5. Remove the 3 bolts and the exhaust manifold brace (2 bolts on Calif. spec. vehicles).

6. Remove the 5 nuts, exhaust manifold (WU TWC on Calif. spec. vehicles) and gasket from the cylinder head.

7. Remove the 3 bolts and the lower heat insulator from the exhaust manifold.

8. Remove the 4 nuts and 2 WU TWC heat insulators (Calif. spec. vehicles, if required).

9. Remove the 2 bolts, 2 nuts and WU TWC from exhaust manifold (Calif. spec. vehicles, if required).

To install:

10. Clean the exhaust manifold and cylinder head mating surfaces.

11. Install the 2 bolts, 2 nuts and WU TWC to the exhaust manifold (Calif. spec. vehicles, if removed, and tighten to 22 ft. lbs. (29 Nm)).

12. Install the 4 nuts and 2 WU TWC heat insulators (Calif. spec. vehicles, if removed) and tighten to 80 inch lbs. (9 Nm).

13. Install the 3 bolts and the lower heat insulator to the exhaust manifold and tighten to 80 inch lbs. (9 Nm).

14. Install a new gasket and exhaust manifold (WU TWC on Calif. spec. vehicles) to the cylinder head and tighten the 5 nuts to 25 ft. lbs. (34 Nm).

15. Install the 3 bolts and the exhaust manifold brace (2 bolts on Calif. spec. vehicles) and tighten to 29 ft. lbs (39 Nm).

16. Install the 5 bolts and the upper heat insulator and tighten to 80 inch lbs. (9 Nm).

17. Install the 2 exhaust pipe to exhaust manifold bolts and 2 front pipe to exhaust manifold nuts (front pipe to warm up 3 way catalytic converter WU TWC on Calif. spec. vehicles) and tighten to 46 ft. lbs. (62 Nm).

18. Connect the oxygen sensor electrical connector.

19. Connect the negative battery cable.

Radiator

REMOVAL & INSTALLATION

Nova

1. Drain the coolant by opening the engine block and radiator drain cocks. Collect the coolant in a clean container and save for reuse.

✳✳CAUTION

When draining the coolant, keep in mind that cats and dogs are attracted by the ethylene glycol antifreeze, and are quite likely to drink any that is left in an uncovered container or in puddles on the ground. This will prove fatal in sufficient quantity. Always drain the coolant into a sealable container. Coolant should be reused unless it is contaminated or several years old.

2. Unplug the wiring to the cooling fan(s).
3. Remove the fan shroud, the 4 bolts on the top of the radiator tank and, if equipped with air conditioning, the 2 bolts on the bottom radiator tank.
4. If equipped with automatic transmission, disconnect the oil cooler lines running to the radiator. Use a clean container to collect the oil which runs out. Cap the lines immediately to prevent dirt form entering the system.
5. Disconnect the overflow hose at the radiator neck.
6. Disconnect the upper and lower radiator hoses from the radiator.
7. Remove the 2 radiator hold-down brackets and lift the radiator out of the engine compartment.
8. After reinstalling the radiator, attach the holddown brackets.
9. Connect the upper and lower radiator hoses and the coolant overflow hose.
10. If equipped with automatic transmission, remove the plugs from the lines and connect the oil cooler lines to the radiator.
11. Reinstall the 4 bolts at the top tank and, on automatics, install the 2 bolts at the lower tank.
12. Connect the wiring for the fan(s).
13. Confirm that the draincocks on the engine and radiator are closed. Refill the cooling system with the proper amount of engine coolant.
14. Add automatic transmission fluid in an amount equal to that lost from the oil cooler during removal.
15. Start the engine and check hose and line connections for leaks. Allow the engine to warm up to normal operating temperature. Check carefully for leaks under both cold and hot conditions.
16. Check the automatic transmission fluid and add if necessary.

Prizm

1. Disconnect the negative battery cable.

2. Drain the coolant by opening the engine block and radiator drain cocks. Collect the coolant in a clean container and save for reuse.

✳✳CAUTION

When draining the coolant, keep in mind that cats and dogs are attracted by the ethylene glycol antifreeze, and are quite likely to drink any that is left in an uncovered container or in puddles on the ground. This will prove fatal in sufficient quantity. Always drain the coolant into a sealable container. Coolant should be reused unless it is contaminated or several years old.

3. Remove the coolant overflow reservoir.
4. Disconnect the upper radiator hose from the radiator and the lower radiator hose from the thermostat housing.
5. If equipped with automatic transmission, disconnect the oil cooler lines running to the radiator.
6. Remove the upper radiator brackets.
7. Disconnect the wiring running to the fan(s).
8. Remove the radiator and fan assembly from the car. If the radiator is to be worked on or replaced, the fan and shroud assembly, the lower hose and the lower rubber mounts must be removed. Don't forget to install them on the new unit before installing it.
9. With the necessary parts mounted on the radiator, install the radiator in the car. Install the upper mounting brackets. Tighten them to 7.5 ft. lbs. (89 inch lbs.)
10. Install the oil cooler hoses to the radiator if equipped with automatic transmission.
11. Connect the electrical lead(s) to the fan(s).
12. Replace the coolant overflow reservoir and connect the hose.
13. Install and secure the upper and lower radiator hoses. Use new clamps.
14. Connect the negative battery cable.
15. Confirm that the draincocks on the engine and radiator are closed. Refill the cooling system with the proper amount of engine coolant.
16. Add automatic transmission fluid in an amount equal to that lost from the oil cooler during removal.
17. Start the engine and check hose and line connections for leaks. Allow the engine to warm up to normal operating temperature. Check carefully for leaks under both cold and hot conditions.
18. Check the automatic transmission fluid and add if necessary.

Electric Cooling Fan

TESTING

1. Disconnect the electrical connector from the cooling fan.
2. Using an ammeter and jumper wires, connect the fan motor in series with the battery and ammeter. With the fan running, check the ammeter reading, it should be 3.4-5.0A on all 1985-88 vehicles, 5.8-7.4A on 1989-92 vehicles and 5.7-7.7A on 1993 vehicles. If the amp readings are not within specifications, replace the motor.

3. Reconnect the fan's electrical connector. Start the engine, allow it to reach temperatures above 194°F and confirm that the fan runs. If the fan doesn't run, replace the temperature switch.

REMOVAL & INSTALLATION

1. Disconnect the negative terminal from the battery.
2. Label and disconnect the electrical connector from the cooling fan motor.
3. Remove the fan shroud-to-radiator frame bolts and the fan/shroud assembly from the vehicle.
4. Remove the fan blade-to-motor nut, fan blade and washer.
5. Remove the fan-to-shroud bolts and the fan motor from the shroud.
6. Test the fan motor and replace it, if necessary.
7. To install, reverse the removal procedures and check the fan operation.

Water Pump

REMOVAL & INSTALLATION

1985-88 All Engines
▶ **See Figures 51 and 52**

1. Drain the engine coolant by opening the radiator and engine block draincocks. Collect the coolant in clean containers and save for reuse.

✳✳CAUTION

When draining the coolant, keep in mind that cats and dogs are attracted by the ethylene glycol antifreeze, and are quite likely to drink any that is left in an uncovered container or in puddles on the ground. This will prove fatal in sufficient quantity. Always drain the coolant into a sealable container. Coolant should be reused unless it is contaminated or several years old.

2. On the 1988 VIN Code 5 engine, remove the power steering drive belt.
3. Loosen the water pump pulley bolts.
4. Loosen the alternator locking bolt and the pivot nut.
5. Move the alternator to its loosest position and remove the belt.
6. On the 1985-88 VIN Code 4 engine, remove the power steering drive belt.
7. Remove the 4 bolts on the water pump pulley and remove the pulley.
8. Disconnect the water inlet and the water bypass hoses from the water inlet pipe.
9. Disconnect and remove the water inlet pipe by removing the 2 clamp bolts and the 2 nuts at the back of the pump. Remove the O-ring from the back of the pump.

10. Remove the mounting bolt for the dipstick tube; remove the tube and dipstick. Immediately plug the hole in block to prevent fluid from polluting the oil.

✳✳WARNING

During the following steps, if coolant should get by the plug in the dipstick hole and run into the motor, the engine oil MUST be changed before starting the motor. Failure to do so can damage the engine bearings.

11. On 1985-88 VIN Code 4 engine, remove the No. 1 (upper) timing belt cover. On 1988 VIN Code 5 engines, both the No. 2 (lower) and No. 3 (middle) timing belt covers must be removed.
12. Remove the water pump bolts and the water pump.
To install:
13. Place the water pump gasket (O-ring) on the block and install the pump. Tighten the mounting bolts to 11 ft. lbs.
14. Install the timing belt cover(s), making sure they are properly seated and not rubbing on the belt or other moving parts.
15. Install a new seal (O-ring) on the dipstick tube and lightly coat it with engine oil. Remove the plug and install the dipstick tube and dipstick; secure the mounting bolt.
16. Using a new O-ring, install the inlet pipe to the water pump.
17. Attach the clamps and bolts to hold the pipe in place.
18. Connect the water inlet and water bypass hoses to the inlet pipe.
19. Install the water pump pulley and tighten the 4 pulley bolts finger tight.
20. For 1985-88 VIN Code 4 engines, install the power steering drive belt.
21. Install the drive belts on all the pulleys and adjust all of them to the correct tension.
22. With the belts in place and adjusted, the water pump pulley will now resist turning. Tighten the pulley bolts to 16-18 ft. lbs.
23. For the 1988 VIN Code 5 engine, install the power steering belt and adjust to the proper tension.
24. Confirm that the draincocks are closed on the engine block and radiator. Refill the engine coolant.
25. Start the engine and check for leaks.

Fig. 51 Water pump components — 1985-88 VIN Code 4 engine

Fig. 52 Water pump components — 1988 VIN Code 5 engine and 1989-90 VIN code 6 engine

1989-92 All Engines
▶ See Figure 52

1. Remove the radiator cap. Drain the engine coolant by opening the radiator and engine block draincocks. Collect the coolant in clean containers and save for reuse.

✳✳CAUTION

When draining the coolant, keep in mind that cats and dogs are attracted by the ethylene glycol antifreeze, and are quite likely to drink any that is left in an uncovered container or in puddles on the ground. This will prove fatal in sufficient quantity. Always drain the coolant into a sealable container. Coolant should be reused unless it is contaminated or several years old.

2. Raise and safely support the vehicle on jackstands.
3. Remove the 2 nuts for the rear motor mount.
4. Lower the vehicle to the ground.
5. Remove the windshield washer fluid container.
6. If so equipped, remove the cruise control bracket with the control module.
7. Remove the through bolt for the right motor mount.
8. Place a jack under the engine. Use a piece of wood between the engine and the jack.
9. Raise the engine slowly and carefully. Keep a close watch on lines and cables. The engine need only be raised enough to gain access to various nuts and bolts.
10. Loosen the water pump pulley bolts, but leave them in place.
11. Loosen the alternator lock bolt and pivot nut; swing the alternator towards the engine and remove the drive belt.
12. Loosen the pivot bolts and the lock bolt for the power steering pump and move it towards the engine; remove the power steering belt.
13. With the belts removed, the water pump pulley may be removed from the pump.
14. Lower the jack, allowing the engine to return to place.
15. Remove the water inlet and water bypass hoses from the water inlet pipe.
16. Remove the clamp holding the water inlet pipe to the engine. Loosen and remove the 2 nuts holding the inlet pipe to the water pump. Remove the pipe and its O-ring.

17. Remove the mounting bolt for the dipstick tube; remove the tube and dipstick. Immediately plug the hole in block to prevent fluid from polluting the oil.

✳✳WARNING

During the following steps, if coolant should get by the plug in the dipstick hole and run into the motor, the engine oil MUST be changed before starting the motor. Failure to do so can damage the engine bearings.

18. Remove the upper timing belt cover.

➡The timing belt is exposed with the cover(s) removed. Do not allow oil or coolant to contact the belt. This includes any fluid which may be accidentally transferred through rags, fingerprints, etc.

19. Remove the 3 water pump bolts and remove the water pump.
   To install:
20. Position a new O-ring on the engine and fit the water pump. Tighten the 3 bolts to 11 ft. lbs.
21. Install the upper timing belt cover.
22. Install a new O-ring on the dipstick tube.
23. Remove the plug in the engine and install the tube. Tighten the mounting bolt.
24. Using a new O-ring, install the water inlet pipe at the back of the water pump. Tighten the 2 nuts to 14. ft. lbs.
25. Connect the water inlet and water bypass hoses to the water inlet pipe.
26. Following the same jacking procedure as before, elevate the motor with the floor jack.
27. Install the water pump pulley and tighten the bolts finger tight. It will be easier to do the final tightening when the belts are installed.
28. Install the power steering belt and adjust its tension.
29. Install the alternator drive belt and adjust its tension.
30. Tighten the water pump pulley bolts to 17 ft. lbs.
31. Lower the jack, allowing the engine to return to its normal place.
32. Install the through bolt for the right motor mount. Tighten it to 64 ft. lbs.
33. Reinstall the cruise control module and the bracket, if so equipped.
34. Raise and safely support the vehicle on jackstands.
35. Install the 2 nuts for the rear mount and tighten them to 38 ft. lbs.
36. Lower the vehicle to the ground.
37. Replace the washer fluid container.
38. Confirm that the draincocks on the radiator and engine block are closed. Refill the cooling system with coolant.
39. Start the engine and check for leaks. Pay particular attention to any hose or fitting which was disassembled during the repair.
40. After the engine is shut off, double check the drive belts for proper tension and adjust as necessary.

1993

1. Disconnect the negative battery cable. Drain the engine coolant from the radiator.
2. Remove all drive belts.

3. Support the engine using suitable equipment. Place a wooden block between the jack and engine. Remove the right engine mount and insulator.

4. Remove the No. 3 (upper) and No. 2 (middle) timing belt covers.

5. If equipped with power steering, raise and safely support the vehicle. Remove the front transaxle mount. Lower the vehicle, remove the cooling fan assembly.

6. Remove the mounting bolt for the dipstick tube; remove the tube and dipstick. Immediately plug the hole in the block to prevent fluid from contaminating the oil.

7. Remove the electrical connector for the coolant temperature sending unit.

8. Remove the 2 nuts securing the engine coolant pipe to the cylinder block.

9. Loosen the hose clamp and remove the coolant inlet pipe from the vehicle.

10. Loosen the hose clamp and remove the coolant inlet hose from the water pump.

11. If equipped with power steering, raise the engine and remove the mounting bolts for the water pump. Remove the water pump and O-ring from the vehicle.

To install:

12. Install a NEW O-ring to the vehicle. Install the water pump and torque the retaining bolts EVENLY to 11 ft. lbs.

13. Lower the engine if necessary, and connect the coolant hose to the water pump. Reconnect the engine coolant inlet pipe to the vehicle and secure to hose with clamp and secure to block with 2 nuts. Tighten the engine coolant inlet pipe nuts to 11 ft. lbs.

14. Connect the electrical connector for the coolant temperature sending unit.

15. Install the oil guide tube and torque the retaining bolt to 84 inch lbs. Install the oil level indicator to the guide tube.

16. Install the radiator fan assembly, if necessary.

17. If equipped with power steering, raise and safely support the vehicle. Install the front transaxle mount. Torque the through bolt nut to 64 ft. lbs. and 2 mount nuts to 47 ft. lbs.

18. Lower the vehicle (if necessary) and install the No. 3 (upper) and No. 2 (middle) timing belt covers.

19. Support the engine using suitable equipment. Install the right engine mount and insulator.

20. Remove all engine lifting equipment.

21. Install and adjust all drive belts.

22. Reconnect the negative battery cable. Fill the cooling system. Start the engine and check for coolant leaks.

Cylinder Head

REMOVAL & INSTALLATION

1985 — 88 VIN Code 4 Engine

▶ See Figures 53 and 56

➡All wires and hoses should be labeled at the time of removal. The amount of time saved during reassembly makes the extra effort well worthwhile.

1. Disconnect the negative battery cable.

2. Drain the cooling system and save the coolant in clean containers.

✴✴CAUTION

When draining the coolant, keep in mind that cats and dogs are attracted by the ethylene glycol antifreeze, and are quite likely to drink any that is left in an uncovered container or in puddles on the ground. This will prove fatal in sufficient quantity. Always drain the coolant into a sealable container. Coolant should be reused unless it is contaminated or several years old.

3. Remove the air cleaner assembly.

4. Elevate and safely support the vehicle on jackstands.

5. Drain the engine oil.

✴✴CAUTION

Used motor oil may cause skin cancer if repeatedly left in contact with the skin for prolonged periods. Although this is unlikely unless you handle oil on a daily basis, it is wise to thoroughly wash your hands with soap and water immediately after handling used motor oil.

6. Disconnect the exhaust pipe from the exhaust manifold and the exhaust bracket from the engine.

7. Disconnect the hose at the converter pipe.

8. If equipped with power steering, loosen the pivot bolt at the power steering pump.

9. Lower the vehicle to the ground.

10. Disconnect the accelerator and throttle control cables at the carburetor and bracket.

11. Label and remove the wiring at the cowl, the oxygen sensor and the distributor.

12. Label and disconnect the vacuum hoses.

13. Disconnect the fuel hoses at the fuel pump.

14. Remove the upper radiator hose from the engine.

15. Remove the water outlet assembly from the head. Remove the heater hose.

16. If equipped with power steering, remove the adjusting bracket.

17. Label and disconnect the vacuum hoses and spark plug wires at the distributor. Remove the distributor.

18. Remove the PCV from the valve cover.

19. Reposition or disconnect the wiring harness running along the head.

20. Remove the upper timing belt cover bolts.

21. Remove the valve cover and its gasket.

22. Remove the water pump pulley bolts and the pulley.

23. Remove the alternator belt.

24. Matchmark the camshaft pulley and the cylinder head so that the marks can be realigned during reinstallation. With chalk or crayon, mark the timing belt with an arrow showing the direction of rotation and mark the belt-to-pulley alignment as well.

25. Loosen the bolt holding the timing belt idler pulley; move the idler to release tension on the belt and snug the bolt to hold the idler in the loosened position.

26. Carefully pull or slide the timing belt off the cam pulley. Do not crimp the belt and do not force it off the pulley with tools.

Fig. 53 Cylinder head exploded view — 1985-88 VIN Code 4 engine

27. Loosen and remove the head bolts gradually, in 3 passes and in the order shown in the illustration.

❋❋WARNING

Head warpage or cracking can occur if the correct removal procedure is not followed.

28. Remove the cylinder head with the manifolds and carburetor attached. If the head is difficult to lift off, gently pry it up with a suitable tool placed between the head and the projection on the block. If prying is needed, be careful not to score or gouge the mating surfaces of the head and/or the block.

29. Keeping the head upright, place it on wooden blocks on the workbench. If the head is to receive further work, the various external components will need to be removed. If the head is not to be worked on, the mating surface must be cleaned of all gasket and sealant material before reinstallation.

30. Clean the engine block mating surface of all gasket and sealant material. Use plastic or wooden scrapers so as not gouge the metal. Remove all traces of liquids from the surface and clean out the bolt holes.

To install:

31. Install the new head gasket on the block with the sealer facing upwards.

32. Place the head in position and make sure it is properly seated and aligned.

33. Install and tighten the cylinder head bolts. Tighten then gradually, evenly, and in 3 passes in the order shown. On the first pass, tighten all the bolts to 14 ft. lbs. On the second

1. EGR valve
2. Camshaft bearing cap
3. Adjusting shim
4. Valve lifter
5. Valve keepers
6. Valve spring retainer
7. Valve spring
8. Snap ring
9. Valve guide bushing
10. Valve stem oil seal
11. Valve spring seal
12. Delivery pipe
13. O-ring
14. Injector

15. Cylinder head rear cover
16. Cylinder head
17. Cyllinder head gasket
18. Valve
19. Upper exhaust manifold insulator
20. Exhaust manifold
21. Lower exhaust manifold insulator
22. Distributor
23. No. 2 timing belt cover
24. Engine mounting bracket
25. No. 3 timing belt cover
26. Exhaust camshaft timing pulley
27. Intake camshaft timing pulley
28. No. 4 timing belt cover

29. Gasket
30. Water outlet
31. Intake manifold stay
32. Intake manifold
33. Cold start injection pipe
34. Gasket
35. Air control valve
36. Gasket
37. Exhaust valve camshaft
38. Intake valve camshaft
39. Cylinder head center cover
40. Cylinder head cover

Fig. 54 Cylinder head exploded view — 1988 VIN Code 5, 1990 VIN Code 5 and 1991-92 VIN Code 6 engines

1. Camshaft snapring
2. Wave washer
3. Camshaft sub-gear
4. Camshaft gear spring
5. Valve cover (cylinder head cover)
6. Spark plug tube gasket
7. Valve cover gasket
8. Camshaft bearing cap
9. Instake camshaft
10. Exhaust camshaft
11. Adjusting shim
12. Valve lifter
13. Valve keepers
14. Valve spring retainer
15. Valve spring
16. Valve spring seat
17. Valve stem oil seal
18. Valve guide bushing
19. Valve
20. Distributor
21. Water inlet housing
22. Water outlet housing
23. Head gasket
24. Exhaust manifold upper insulator (heat shield)
25. Exhaust manifold gasket
26. Exhaust manifold
27. Exhaust manifold lower insulator (heat shield)
28. Center timing belt cover
29. Upper timing belt cover
30. Camshaft timing gear
31. Fuel rail
32. Cold-start injector pipe
33. Intake manifold gasket
34. Intake manifold

Fig. 55 Cylinder head exploded view — 1989-90 VIN Code 6 and 1991-92 VIN Code 5 engines

Fig. 56 Mark the timing belt rotation before removal — 1985-88 VIN Code 4 engine

Fig. 57 Cylinder head loosening sequence — 1985-88 VIN Code 4 engine

pass the bolts are tightened to 30 ft. lbs. and on the last pass the bolts are tightened to their final setting of 43 ft. lbs.

✳✳WARNING

Failure to follow this procedure exactly may cause either premature gasket failure or head damage.

34. Align the camshaft pulley mark(s) made during disassembly with the marks on the head and or block.

35. Install the timing belt onto the cam pulley, being careful not to allow the belt to become mispositioned on the lower (crank) pulley. Handle the belt carefully and avoid getting fluids or lubricants on the belt.

36. Loosen the holding bolt for the timing belt idler pulley and allow it to tension the belt.

Fig. 58 Cylinder head torque sequence — 1985-88 VIN Code 4 engine

37. Turn the crankshaft clockwise through at least 2 full revolutions; finish the rotation by aligning the timing marks at TDC. Double check that the small triangular mark on the cam pulley is at the top and pointing up.

38. Tighten the bolt for the timing belt idler pulley to 27 ft. lbs.

39. Using a belt tension gauge such as GM-23600-B or equivalent, check the timing belt tension. Correct tension is 0.6mm at 4.4 lbs.

40. If the head was disassembled during the repair, adjust the valves at this time. If the head was not disassembled, the valves need not be adjusted.

41. Install the valve cover and the upper timing cover.

42. Install the water pump pulley and bolts; install the alternator belt and adjust it to the correct tension.

43. Correctly position or reconnect the wiring harness running along the head.

44. Install the PCV valve in the valve cover.

45. Correctly install the distributor and connect the wiring, vacuum lines and spark plug wires.

46. Install the power steering adjusting bracket if so equipped.

47. Install the heater hose, the water outlet at the head and connect the upper radiator hose to the engine.

48. Connect the fuel lines to the fuel pump.

49. Observing the labels made earlier, connect the vacuum hoses to their ports. Make sure the hoses fit securely on the fittings and are not crimped or twisted.

50. Connect the wiring at the cowl, the oxygen sensor and the distributor.

51. Connect the accelerator and throttle control cables at the bracket and at the carburetor.

52. Safely raise and support the vehicle.

53. If equipped with power steering, tighten the pivot bolt for the pump.

54. Connect the hose at the converter pipe.

55. Connect the exhaust bracket to the engine and connect the exhaust pipe to the manifold.

56. Lower the vehicle to the ground.

57. Install the air cleaner assembly.

58. Add the correct amount of fresh engine oil.

59. Confirm that the radiator and engine draincocks are closed and fill the cooling system with the correct amount of coolant. Install the radiator cap.

60. Double check all installation items, paying particular attention to loose hoses or hanging wires, untightened nuts, poor routing of hoses and wires (too tight or rubbing) and tools left in the engine area.

61. Connect the negative battery cable.

62. Start the engine; during the warm up period, check carefully for any signs of fluid leaks or engine overheating.

63. When the engine has reached normal operating temperature, check the ignition timing and adjust the idle speed as necessary.

1988 VIN Code 5 Engine

▶ See Figures 54, 59, 60, 61, 62, 63 and 64

➡**All wires and hoses should be labeled at the time of removal. The amount of time saved during reassembly makes the extra effort well worthwhile.**

1. Disconnect the negative battery cable

2. Open the draincocks on the engine and radiator. Collect the coolant in clean containers.

✳✳CAUTION

When draining the coolant, keep in mind that cats and dogs are attracted by the ethylene glycol antifreeze, and are quite likely to drink any that is left in an uncovered container or in puddles on the ground. This will prove fatal in sufficient quantity. Always drain the coolant into a sealable container. Coolant should be reused unless it is contaminated or several years old.

3. Remove the air cleaner assembly.
4. Disconnect the cruise control cable if so equipped.
5. Disconnect the throttle cable from the throttle linkage.
6. Remove the heater hose from the cylinder head rear cover.
7. Label and remove the vacuum hoses from the throttle body.
8. If equipped with cruise control, remove the actuator and bracket assembly.
9. Remove the ignition coil.
10. Remove the upper radiator hose from the cylinder head and the radiator.
11. Remove the brake booster vacuum hose.
12. Remove the PCV hose.
13. Unbolt and remove as a unit the fuel pressure regulator.
14. Unbolt and remove the EGR valve with the lines attached.
15. Remove the cold start injector hose.

✳✳CAUTION

The fuel system is under pressure. Release pressure slowly and contain spillage. Observe no smoking/no open flame precautions. Have a Class B-C (dry powder) fire extinguisher within arm's reach at all times.

16. Remove the No. 1 fuel line.
17. Remove the first and second water bypass hoses from the auxiliary air valve.
18. Remove the vacuum pipe and the cylinder head rear cover.
19. Remove, disconnect or reposition the wiring harness(es) around the head as necessary.
20. Remove the distributor.
21. Remove the exhaust manifold and its gaskets.
22. Remove the fuel delivery pipe and the injectors. DO NOT drop the injectors.
23. Remove the intake manifold support bracket; remove the intake manifold and the intake air control valve.
24. Remove the power steering drive belt.
25. Remove the upper timing belt cover and the valve covers.
26. Remove the water outlet fitting with the bypass pipe and the belt adjusting bar.
27. Remove the spark plugs.
28. Turn the crankshaft clockwise, stopping so that the groove in the crank pulley aligns with the idler pulley bolt. Additionally, check that the valve lifters on No. 1 cylinder are loose (the cam lobes are NOT depressing the lifters). If the

valves are under tension, rotate the crank 1 full revolution and check again. The engine is now on TDC/compression.
29. Remove the right motor mount.
30. Remove the water pump pulley.
31. Remove the lower and middle (Nos. 2 and 3) timing belt covers.

✳✳WARNING

The bolts are different lengths. Label or diagram the correct location of each bolt as it is removed. Improper placement during reassembly can cause engine damage.

32. Place matchmarks on the timing belt and the belt pulleys. Make sure that you mark each pulley and the belt clearly. Additionally, mark an arrow on the belt showing the direction of rotation.
33. Carefully slide the timing belt off the camshaft pulleys. Do not pry on the belt with tools. Keep the belt under light upward tension so that the bottom (crankshaft) end doesn't shift position on its pulley.
34. Remove the camshaft pulleys. Use an adjustable wrench to counterhold the cams during removal. Look for the flats on the cam and fit the wrench to them.
35. With the pulleys removed, the end plate (otherwise called No. 4 timing cover) may be removed.
36. Loosen the head bolts in the order shown in the diagram. Make 3 complete passes, loosening them slowly, evenly and in order.
37. Remove the cylinder head. If it is difficult to remove, it may be pried up gently with a suitable tool. Be very careful

Fig. 59 Examples of matchmarks on timing belt and pulleys. Don't forget an arrow showing the direction of rotation. The belt will break if put on backwards

Fig. 60 Remove the head bolts in this sequence — 1988 VIN Code 5 engine

not to scratch or gouge the mating surfaces when prying the head up.

38. Keeping the head upright, place it on wooden blocks on the workbench. If the head is to receive further work, the various components will need to be removed. If the head is not to be worked on, the mating surface must be cleaned of all gasket and sealant material before reinstallation.

39. Clean the engine block mating surface of all gasket and sealant material. Use plastic or wooden scrapers so as not gouge the metal. Remove all traces of liquids from the surface and clean out the bolt holes.

To install:

40. Install the new head gasket on the block. Make sure it is properly placed and that all the holes and passages in the block line up with the holes in the gasket.

41. Place the head in position and make sure it is properly seated and aligned.

42. Apply a light coat of oil to the threads of the cylinder head bolts.

43. Install the 10 cylinder head bolts.

➡**The bolts for the exhaust side are 108mm long; the bolts for the intake side are 87.5mm long.**

44. Tighten the cylinder head bolts in 3 passes and in sequence. The first pass should tighten them to 8-10 ft. lbs., the second pass to 16. ft. lbs. and the third pass to 22 ft. lbs.

45. Mark the front (towards the front of the car) of each bolt with a dot of paint.

46. In the specified order, tighten each bolt through exactly 90° of rotation.

47. Repeat the procedure, tightening each bolt an additional 90°. Check that the paint marks on each bolt are now facing rearward.

48. Apply RTV sealer or equivalent to the cylinder head. Install new cam end seals and coat them lightly with multi-purpose grease.

49. Install the end plate or No. 4 timing cover.

50. Install the right side engine mount bracket and tighten its bolts to 18 ft. lbs.

51. Install the camshaft pulleys. Be sure to align the camshaft knock pin and the camshaft pulley. Tighten the pulley bolts to 34 ft. lbs.

52. Install the lower and middle (Nos. 2 and 3) timing belt covers. Remember that the bolts are different lengths; make certain the correct bolt is in the correct location.

53. Install the water pump pulley.

54. Install the right engine mount. Tighten the through bolt to 58 ft. lbs.

55. Install the spark plugs. Correct tightness is 13 ft. lbs.

56. Reinstall the water outlet with the bypass pipe and the belt adjusting bar.

57. Install the valve covers.

58. Install the alternator and power steering drive belts. Adjust the belts to the correct tension.

59. Install the intake manifold and intake air control valve. Tighten the bolts to 20 ft. lbs

60. Install the bracket and support for the intake manifold.

61. Install the fuel delivery pipe and the injectors. Make sure the insulators and spacers have been placed properly. Make sure the injectors rotate smoothly in their seats.

62. Tighten the delivery pipe retaining bolts to 13. ft. lbs.

Fig. 61 Tighten the head bolts in this sequence — 1988 VIN Code 5 engine

Fig. 63 Sealant must be applied to the head before reinstalling the valve cover — 1988 VIN Code 5 engine

Fig. 62 Apply a dot of paint to the front of each head bolt. Apply 90 degree of rotation in the correct sequence. After all are set, repeat the pattern, tightening each bolt through an additional 90 degree — 1988 VIN Code 5 engine

A	MATCHMARK
B	KNOCK PIN
26	EXHAUST CAMSHAFT TIMING PULLEY
27	INTAKE CAMSHAFT TIMING PULLEY

Fig. 64 Align the cam pulleys before installing the timing belt — 1988 VIN Code 5 engine

63. Install the exhaust manifold tighten its nuts and bolts to 18 ft. lbs.

64. Reinstall the distributor.

65. Attach, reposition or connect the wiring harness(es) around the head. Make sure that all retaining clips are used and are secure. Double check the wiring to eliminate any contact with moving parts.

66. Install the vacuum pipe and the cylinder head rear cover with a new gasket.

67. Connect the first and second bypass hoses to the auxiliary air valve.

68. Connect the No. 1 fuel line.

69. Use new gaskets and connect the cold start injector line. Tighten the bolts to 13 ft. lbs.

70. Replace the EGR valve and use a new gasket.

71. Use a new O-ring and attach the fuel pressure regulator. Tighten the regulator bolts to 6.8 ft. lbs (82 inch lbs.)

72. Install the PCV hose and the brake vacuum hose.

73. Install the radiator hose at the radiator and the cylinder head.

74. Install the ignition coil.

75. Install the cruise control actuator and bracket assembly if so equipped.

76. Observing the labels made earlier, connect the vacuum hose to the throttle body.

77. Attach the heater hose to the cylinder head rear cover.

78. Connect the throttle valve and accelerator cables.

79. Connect the cruise control cable, if so equipped.

80. Install the air cleaner assembly.

81. Confirm that the draincocks on the radiator and engine block are closed. Fill the cooling system with coolant.

82. Double check all installation items, paying particular attention to loose hoses or hanging wires, untightened nuts, poor routing of hoses and wires (too tight or rubbing) and tools left in the engine area.

83. Connect the negative battery cable.

84. Start the engine. During the warm up period, check for any sign of leakage or overheating. Check engine timing and adjust the idle speed if necessary.

85. After the engine is shut off, check the drive belts and adjust the tension if necessary.

1989-90 VIN Code 6 Engine, 1991-92 VIN Code 5 Engine
▶ **See Figures 55, 65, 66, 67 and 68**

➡**All wires and hoses should be labeled at the time of removal. The amount of time saved during reassembly makes the extra effort well worthwhile.**

1. Disconnect the negative battery cable.

2. Open the draincocks on the engine and radiator. Collect the coolant in clean containers.

✳✳CAUTION

When draining the coolant, keep in mind that cats and dogs are attracted by the ethylene glycol antifreeze, and are quite likely to drink any that is left in an uncovered container or in puddles on the ground. This will prove fatal in sufficient quantity. Always drain the coolant into a sealable container. Coolant should be reused unless it is contaminated or several years old.

3. Raise the vehicle and safely support it on jackstands.

4. Remove the lower right splash (stone) shield.

5. Remove the 2 covers for the rear engine mount nuts and studs.

6. Remove the 2 rear transaxle mount-to-main crossmember mounting nuts.

7. Remove the 2 center mount-to-center crossmember nuts.

8. Lower the vehicle to the ground.

9. Remove the air cleaner assembly.

10. Disconnect or remove throttle cable, the transmission kick-down cable (automatic) and, if equipped, the cruise control actuator cable.

11. Label and disconnect the vacuum lines. Loosen, disconnect or reposition the wiring harnesses running to the head.

12. Disconnect the fuel inlet line.

✳✳CAUTION

The fuel system is under pressure. Release pressure slowly and contain spillage. Observe no smoking/no open flame precautions. Have a Class B-C (dry powder) fire extinguisher within arm's reach at all times.

13. Remove the cold start injector line.

14. Remove the coolant hoses by disconnecting their junctions at the head.

15. Disconnect the heater hoses.

16. Remove the water outlet housing and the water inlet housing.

17. Label and remove the spark plug wires.

18. Remove the PCV valve.

19. Loosen the air conditioning compressor, power steering pump and alternator brackets as necessary; remove the valve cover.

20. Remove the drive belts.

21. Remove the air conditioning idler pulley.

22. Disconnect the wiring at the cruise control actuator (if so equipped); remove the actuator and its bracket.

23. Remove the windshield washer reservoir.

24. Support the engine with a support fixture such as GM J 28467-A or a chain hoist. Alternatively, a floor jack may be placed below the engine; use a piece of wood on the jack to distribute the load.

25. Remove the right engine mount through bolt.

26. Raise the engine enough to gain access to the water pump pulley bolts.

27. Remove the water pump pulley.

28. Lower the engine back to its normal position. Remove the wiring harness from the upper timing belt cover.

29. Raise the vehicle and safely support it on jackstands.

30. Remove the cylinder head-to-cylinder block bracket.

31. Remove the exhaust pipe support bracket and disconnect the exhaust pipe from the exhaust manifold.

32. Remove the upper timing belt cover and then the center timing belt cover.

➡**The timing belt is exposed with the cover removed. Do not allow the belt to become contaminated with fluids or lubricants. This includes accidental contact by rags, fingerprints, etc.**

33. Remove the right engine mount bracket.

34. By turning the crankshaft clockwise, set the engine to TDC/compression. Align the timing mark at zero (on the crank) and check that the valve lifters for No. 1 cylinder are NOT under compression from the camshafts; the cam lobes should be pointed up. The small hole in the exhaust camshaft pulley should be aligned with the mark on the camshaft cap.

35. Remove the distributor.

36. Remove the plug from the lower timing belt cover.

37. Matchmark the timing belt and pulleys at the crankshaft and both camshafts. Mark an arrow on the belt showing the direction of rotation.

38. Loosen the idler pulley bolt and push the pulley into its loosest position. Tighten the bolt to hold the idler in this loosened position.

39. Holding the timing belt with a clean cloth, slide the belt off the camshaft pulleys. Keep light upward tension on the belt so that it does not change its position on the lower (crankshaft) pulley.

✳✳WARNING

Do not pry on the belt with tools. Do not crease or crimp the belt. Be careful not to drop anything into the lower belt cover. Keep the timing belt clean and free of fluids and lubricants.

40. Using a 10mm, 12-point deep socket wrench, loosen the cylinder head bolts in the proper sequence. It is recommended that the tension be released in 2 or even 3 passes.

✳✳WARNING

Head warping or cracking can result from improper removal procedures.

41. Remove the cylinder head with the manifolds attached. If the head is difficult to lift off, carefully pry with a suitable tool between the head and a projection on the block. Be careful not to scratch or gouge the mating surfaces of the head or block.

42. Place the head on wooden blocks on the workbench. If the head is to be disassembled, the external parts will need to be removed. If the head is to be reused intact, the mating surface must be cleaned of all gasket and sealant material. Clean the mating surface on the block of all traces of gasket material and fluids. Clean the bolt holes, removing all fluid and solid material.

Fig. 65 Loosen the idler pulley and move it to its loosest position — 1989-90 VIN Code 6 and 1991-92 VIN Code 5 engines

Fig. 66 Remove the cylinder head bolts in this order — 1989-90 VIN Code 6 and 1991-92 VIN Code 5 engines

To install:

43. When reassembling, place the new head gasket in position on the block. Make sure it is placed correctly and that all the holes line up.

44. Carefully install the cylinder head in position on the block. Make sure the head is seated over the guide dowels.

45. Apply a light coat of engine oil to the threads of the head bolts and under the caps of the bolts. Place the bolts in their holes.

46. Tighten the bolts in the proper sequence. Repeat the pattern 3 times, tightening the first pass to 14 ft. lbs., the second pass to 28 ft. lbs. and the third pass to the final setting of 44 ft. lbs.

47. If the camshafts have not been turned while the head was removed, double check their placement against the marks on the head. If the cams were moved, they must be turned into the TDC/compression position.

48. Double check that the crankshaft is still in its TDC position. Carefully reinstall the timing belt over the cam pulleys, making sure the matchmarks align exactly. The slightest error in placement can greatly reduce engine performance and possibly damage the engine. With the belt correctly installed, loosen the bolt holding the idler pulley in the loosened position. The pulley will spring against the belt, providing tension on it. Turn the crankshaft pulley clockwise 2 full revolutions (from TDC to TDC) and double check that all the components are properly aligned. Tighten the idler pulley bolt to 27 ft. lbs.

49. Reinstall the distributor.

50. Attach the right side engine mount bracket.

51. Install the air conditioning idler pulley.

Fig. 67 Install the cylinder head bolts in this order — 1989-90 VIN Code 6 and 1991-92 VIN Code 5 engines

52. Install the center timing belt cover and the upper timing belt cover.

53. Raise the vehicle and safely support it on jackstands.

54. Using new gaskets and bolts, connect the exhaust pipe to the exhaust manifold. Tighten the bolts to 18 ft. lbs. Install the exhaust manifold support bracket.

55. Install the cylinder head-to-cylinder block bracket.

56. Lower the vehicle to the ground. Connect or reinstall the wiring harness to the upper timing belt cover.

57. Raise the engine enough to gain access to the water pump. Install the water pump pulley and lower the engine into its normal position.

58. Install the right engine mount through bolt and tighten it to 64 ft. lbs. When this bolt is secured, the engine lifting apparatus may be removed from the car.

59. Install the windshield washer reservoir.

60. If equipped with cruise control, reinstall the actuator and its bracket and connect the wiring to the actuator.

61. Install the drive belts and adjust them to the proper tension.

62. Place sealant on the valve cover in the proper locations and install the valve cover. Tighten the retaining nuts to 15 ft. lbs.

63. Install the PCV valve.

64. Install the spark plugs, and connect the water inlet housing and the water outlet housing.

65. Reinstall the heater hoses and the coolant hoses.

66. Install the fuel rail and injectors.

67. Connect the cold start injector pipe.

68. Connect the fuel inlet line.

69. Observing the labels made earlier, carefully connect the vacuum lines and electrical leads. Make sure the vacuum hoses are properly seated on their ports and are not kinked or twisted. Electrical connectors must be clean and firmly attached at all points. Double check the routing of lines and wires to avoid any contact with moving parts.

70. Depending on equipment, connect the transaxle kick-down cable (automatic), the cruise control actuator cable and/or the accelerator cable.

71. Install the air cleaner assembly.

72. Raise the vehicle and safely support it on jackstands. Attach the 2 rear mount-to-main crossmember nuts and tighten them to 45 ft. lbs. Install the 2 center mount-to-center crossmember nuts and tighten them to 45 ft. lbs. Install the covers on the nuts and studs.

73. Install the lower right splash shield.

74. Lower the vehicle to the ground.

Fig. 68 Apply sealant to these points before reinstalling the valve cover — 1989-90 VIN Code 6 and 1991-92 VIN Code 5 engines

75. Confirm that the radiator and engine block draincocks are closed and refill the cooling system.

76. Double check all installation items, paying particular attention to loose hoses or hanging wires, untightened nuts, poor routing of hoses and wires (too tight or rubbing) and tools left in the engine area.

77. Connect the negative battery cable.

78. Start the engine. During the warm up period, check for any sign of leakage or overheating. Check engine timing and adjust the idle speed if necessary.

79. After the engine is shut off, check the drive belts and adjust the tension if necessary.

1990 VIN Code 5 Engine 1991-92 VIN Code 6 Engine

▶ **See Figures 54, 69 and 70**

1. Disconnect the negative battery cable

2. Open the drain cocks on the engine and radiator. Collect the coolant in clean containers.

3. Remove the air cleaner assembly.

4. Disconnect the cruise control cable if so equipped.

5. Disconnect the throttle cable from the throttle linkage.

6. Remove the heater hose from the cylinder head rear cover.

7. Label and remove the vacuum hoses from the throttle body.

8. If equipped with cruise control, remove the actuator and bracket assembly.

9. Remove the ignition coil.

10. Remove the upper radiator hose from the cylinder head and the radiator.

11. Remove the brake booster vacuum hose.

12. Remove the PCV hose.

13. Unbolt and remove as a unit the fuel pressure regulator.

14. Unbolt and remove the EGR valve with the lines attached.

15. Remove the cold start injector hose.

✳✳CAUTION

The fuel system is under pressure. Release pressure slowly and contain spillage. Observe no smoking/no open flame precautions. Have a Class B-C (dry powder) fire extinguisher within arm's reach at all times.

16. Remove the No. 1 fuel line.

17. Remove the first and second water bypass hoses from the auxiliary air valve.

18. Remove the vacuum pipe and the cylinder head rear cover.

19. Remove, disconnect or reposition the wiring harness(es) around the head as necessary.

20. Remove the distributor.

21. Remove the exhaust manifold and its gaskets.

22. Remove the fuel delivery pipe and the injectors. Do not drop the injectors.

23. Remove the intake manifold support bracket; remove the intake manifold and the intake air control valve.

24. Remove the power steering drive belt.

25. Remove the upper timing belt cover and the valve covers.

26. Remove the water outlet fitting with the bypass pipe and the belt adjusting bar.

27. Remove the spark plugs.

28. Turn the crankshaft clockwise, stopping so that the groove in the crank pulley aligns with the idler pulley bolt. Additionally, check that the valve lifters on No. 1 cylinder are loose (the cam lobes are not depressing the lifters). If the valves are under tension, rotate the crank 1 full revolution and check again. The engine is now on TDC/compression.

29. Remove the right motor mount.

30. Remove the water pump pulley.

31. Remove the lower and middle (Nos. 2 and 3) timing belt covers.

➡**The bolts are different lengths. Label or diagram the correct location of each bolt as it is removed. Improper placement during reassembly can cause engine damage.**

32. Place matchmarks on the timing belt and the belt pulleys. Make sure to mark each pulley and the belt clearly. Additionally, mark an arrow on the belt showing the direction of rotation.

33. Carefully slide the timing belt off the camshaft pulleys. Do not pry on the belt with tools. Keep the belt under light upward tension so that the bottom (crankshaft) end doesn't shift position on its pulley.

34. Remove the camshaft pulleys. Use an adjustable wrench to counter hold the cams during removal. Look for the flats on the cam and fit the wrench to them.

35. With the pulleys removed, the end plate (otherwise called No. 4 timing cover) may be removed.

36. Loosen the head bolts in the proper sequence. Make 3 complete passes, loosening them slowly, evenly and in order.

37. Remove the cylinder head. If it is difficult to remove, it may be pried up gently with a suitable tool. Be very careful not to scratch or gouge the mating surfaces when prying the head up.

38. Keeping the head upright, place it on wooden blocks on the workbench. If the head is to receive further work, the various components will need to be removed. If the head is not to be worked on, the mating surface must be cleaned of all gasket and sealant material before reinstallation.

39. Clean the engine block mating surface of all gasket and sealant material. Use plastic or wooden scrapers so as not gouge the metal. Remove all traces of liquids from the surface and clean out the bolt holes.

To install:

40. Install the new head gasket on the block. Make sure it is properly placed and that all the holes and passages in the block line up with the holes in the gasket.

41. Place the head in position and make sure it is properly seated and aligned.

42. Apply a light coat of oil to the threads of the cylinder head bolts.

43. Install the 10 cylinder head bolts.

➡**The bolts for the exhaust side are 108mm long; the bolts for the intake side are 87.5mm long.**

44. Tighten the cylinder head bolts in 3 passes and in sequence. The first pass should tighten them to 8-10 ft. lbs. (11-14 Nm), the second pass to 16 ft. lbs. (22 Nm) and the third pass to 44 ft. lbs. (60 Nm).

45. Apply RTV sealer or equivalent to the cylinder head. Install new camshaft end seals and coat them lightly with multi-purpose grease.

46. Install the end plate or No. 4 timing cover.

47. Install the right side engine mount bracket and tighten its bolts to 64 ft. lbs. (87 Nm).

48. Install the camshaft pulleys. Be sure to align the camshaft knock pin and the camshaft pulley. Tighten the pulley bolts to 34 ft. lbs. (47 Nm).

49. Install the lower and middle (No. 2 and 3) timing belt covers. Remember that the bolts are different lengths; make certain the correct bolt is in the correct location.

50. Install the water pump pulley.

51. Install the right engine mount. Tighten the through bolt to 64 ft. lbs. (87 Nm).

52. Install the spark plugs. Correct tightness is 13 ft. lbs. (18 Nm).

53. Reinstall the water outlet with the bypass pipe and the belt adjusting bar.

54. Install the valve covers.

55. Install the alternator and power steering drive belts. Adjust the belts to the correct tension.

56. Install the intake manifold and intake air control valve. Tighten the bolts to 20 ft. lbs. (27 Nm).

57. Install the bracket and support for the intake manifold.

58. Install the fuel delivery pipe and the injectors. Make sure the insulators and spacers have been placed properly. Make sure the injectors rotate smoothly in their seats.

59. Tighten the delivery pipe retaining bolts to 13 ft. lbs. (18 Nm).

60. Install the exhaust manifold tighten its nuts and bolts to 18 ft. lbs. (25 Nm).

61. Reinstall the distributor.

62. Attach, reposition or connect the wiring harness(es) around the head. Make sure that all retaining clips are used

Fig. 69 Cylinder head bolt loosening sequence — 1990 VIN Code 5 and 1991-92 VIN Code 6 engine

Fig. 70 Cylinder head bolt tightening sequence — 1990 VIN Code 5 and 1991-92 VIN Code 6 engine

and are secure. Double check the wiring to eliminate any contact with moving parts.

63. Install the vacuum pipe and the cylinder head rear cover with a new gasket.

64. Connect the first and second bypass hoses to the auxiliary air valve.

65. Connect the No. 1 fuel line.

66. Use new gaskets and connect the cold start injector line. Tighten the bolts to 13 ft. lbs. (18 Nm).

67. Replace the EGR valve and use a new gasket.

68. Use a new O-ring and attach the fuel pressure regulator. Tighten the regulator bolts to 6.8 ft. lbs (82 in. lbs.)

69. Install the PCV hose and the brake vacuum hose.

70. Install the radiator hose at the radiator and the cylinder head.

71. Install the ignition coil.

72. Install the cruise control actuator and bracket assembly if so equipped.

73. Observing the labels made earlier, connect the vacuum hose to the throttle body.

74. Attach the heater hose to the cylinder head rear cover.

75. Connect the throttle valve and accelerator cables.

76. Connect the cruise control cable, if so equipped.

77. Install the air cleaner assembly.

78. Confirm that the drain cocks on the radiator and engine block are closed. Fill the cooling system with coolant.

79. Double check all installation items, paying particular attention to loose hoses or hanging wires, loosened nuts, poor routing of hoses and wires (too tight or rubbing) and tools left in the engine area.

80. Connect the negative battery cable.

81. Start the engine. During the warm up period, check for any sign of leakage or overheating. Check engine timing and adjust the idle speed if necessary.

82. After the engine is shut off, check the drive belts and adjust the tension if necessary.

1993

▶ **See Figures 71 and 72**

1. Disconnect the negative battery cable and relieve the fuel system pressure.

2. Remove the timing belt and tensioner as outlined in this section.

3. Remove the camshafts as outlined in this section.

4. Disconnect and label the hoses from the intake chamber.

5. Disconnect the A/C actuator electrical connector, if so equipped.

6. Disconnect the hoses and the electrical connector and remove the EGR SV valve.

7. Remove the engine wire clamp.

8. Remove the 3 bolts and the intake manifold brace.

9. Disconnect the hose clamp and fuel return hose from the pressure regulator.

10. Remove the 1 bolt and nut and the air pipe from the intake manifold.

11. On California vehicles, remove the EGR valve and vacuum modulator.

12. Remove the throttle body from the manifold.

13. Remove the fuel inlet hose clamp bolt and the air intake chamber brace with gasket.

14. Disconnect the 2 PCV hoses from the cylinder head cover.

15. Disconnect the vacuum hose from the pressure regulator.

16. Remove the 3 bolts and 2 nuts and the air intake chamber cover with gasket.

✳✳CAUTION

The fuel system is under pressure. Release pressure slowly and contain spillage. Observe no smoking/no open flame precautions. Have a Class B-C (dry powder) fire extinguisher within arm's reach at all times.

17. Remove the union bolt, 2 gaskets and disconnect the fuel inlet pipe from the fuel rail.

18. Disconnect the injector electrical connectors.

19. Remove the 2 bolts and the fuel rail with the 4 injectors attached.

20. Remove the 4 insulators and 2 spacers from the cylinder head.

21. Remove the 7 bolts, ground strap, 2 nuts and the intake manifold with the gasket from the cylinder head.

22. Disconnect the oxygen sensor electrical connector.

23. Remove the 2 exhaust pipe to exhaust manifold bolts and 2 front pipe to exhaust manifold nuts (front pipe to warm up 3 way catalytic converter WU TWC on Calif. spec. vehicles).

24. Remove the 5 bolts and the upper heat insulator.

25. Remove the 3 bolts and the exhaust manifold brace (2 bolts on Calif. spec. vehicles).

26. Remove the 5 nuts, exhaust manifold (WU TWC on Calif. spec. vehicles) and gasket from the cylinder head.

27. Remove the cylinder head bolts in sequence using a 10mm, 12 point deep well socket.

28. Keeping the head upright, place it on wooden blocks on the workbench. If the head is to receive further work, the various components will need to be removed. If the head is not to be worked on, the mating surface must be cleaned of all gasket and sealant material before reinstallation.

29. Clean the engine block mating surface of all gasket and sealant material. Use plastic or wooden scrapers so as not gouge the metal. Remove all traces of liquids from the surface and clean out the bolt holes.

To install:

30. Install the new head gasket on the block. Make sure it is properly placed and that all the holes and passages in the block line up with the holes in the gasket.

31. Place the head in position and make sure it is properly seated and aligned.

32. Apply a light coat of oil to the threads of the cylinder head bolts.

33. Install the 10 cylinder head bolts.

➡**The bolts for the exhaust side are 108mm long; the bolts for the intake side are 90mm long.**

34. Tighten the cylinder head bolts in several passes and in sequence to 22 ft. lbs. (29 Nm). Tighten the cylinder head

bolts in sequence another 90 degrees. Then tighten the cylinder head bolts an additional 90 degrees.

➡️**If the correct tightening sequence is not followed, warpage or leakage may result.**

35. Install a new gasket and the exhaust manifold (WU TWC on Calif. spec. vehicles) to the cylinder head and tighten the 5 nuts to 25 ft. lbs. (34 Nm).

36. Install the intake manifold with a new gasket to the cylinder head and secure with the 2 nuts, 7 bolts and ground strap. Tighten the bolts and nuts to 14 ft. lbs. (19 Nm).

37. Install 4 new insulators and 2 spacers to the cylinder head.

38. Install the fuel rail with injectors to the intake manifold and secure with the 2 bolts, but do not fully tighten. Make sure the injectors rotate smoothly, if not replace the O-rings. Make sure the electrical connector is pointed upward. Tighten the fuel rail bolts to 11 ft. lbs. (15 Nm).

39. Install the injector electrical connectors.

40. Install the union bolt, 2 new gaskets and connect the fuel inlet pipe to the fuel rail. Tighten the bolt to 22 ft. lbs. (29 Nm).

41. Install the 3 bolts and 2 nuts and the air intake chamber cover with a new gasket. Tighten to 14 ft. lbs. (19 Nm).

42. Connect the vacuum hose to the pressure regulator.

43. Connect the 2 PCV hoses to the cylinder head cover.

44. Install the air intake chamber brace with a new gasket and tighten the bolt to 21 ft. lbs. (28 Nm).

45. Install the fuel inlet hose clamp bolt and tighten to 89 inch lbs. (10 Nm).

46. Install the throttle body to the manifold using a new gasket and tighten the nuts and bolts to 17 ft. lbs. (23 Nm).

47. Attach the accelerator to the throttle body and tighten the 2 bolts to 11 ft. lbs. (15 Nm).

48. Connect the TP sensor electrical connector.

49. On California vehicles, using new gaskets, install the EGR valve and vacuum modulator. Tighten the EGR to manifold bolts and nuts to 115 inch lbs (13 Nm) and the EGR valve to EGR pipe bolts to 43 ft. Lbs. (59 Nm).

50. On California vehicles, install the 2 vacuum hoses to the throttle body.

51. Install the air pipe to the manifold and tighten the bolt to 80 inch lbs. (9 Nm).

52. Connect the hose clamp and fuel return hose to the pressure regulator.

53. Install the 3 bolts and the intake manifold brace and tighten to 14 ft. lbs. (9 Nm).

54. Install the engine wire clamps.

55. Install the EGR SV valve and connect the hoses and the electrical connector. Tighten the EGR SV valve retaining bolts 115 inch lbs. (13 Nm).

56. Connect the A/C actuator electrical connector, if so equipped.

57. Connect the hoses to the intake chamber.

58. Install the camshafts as outlined in this section.

59. Install the timing belt and tensioner as outlined in this section.

60. Connect the negative battery cable.

Fig. 71 Cylinder head bolt loosening sequence — 1993 VIN Code 6 & 8 engines

Fig. 72 Cylinder head bolt tightening sequence — 1993 VIN Code 6 & 8 engines

CYLINDER HEAD CLEANING AND INSPECTION

1985-88 VIN Code 4 Engine
▶ See Figures 73, 74, 75, 76 and 77

1. With the head removed from the car, remove the carburetor, the fuel pump and the intake and exhaust manifolds.

2. Remove the rocker arm assembly, following procedures outlined earlier in this section.

3. Use a dial indicator to measure the camshaft end-play (axial end-play or thrust clearance). Standard play is 0.08-0.18mm. Maximum allowable free play is 0.25mm. Free-play at or beyond the maximum requires replacement of the head.

Fig. 73 Use of a dial indicator and check the camshaft end-play. — 1985-88 VIN Code 4 engine

4. Remove the camshaft, following procedures outlined later in this section.

5. Remove the valves, following procedures outlined later in this section.

6. Using a wire brush chucked into an electric drill, remove all the carbon from the combustion chambers in the head. Be careful not to scratch the head surface.

7. Use a gasket scraper and remove all material from the manifold and head surfaces, again being careful not to scratch the surface.

8. Use a valve guide brush or a fine-bristled rifle bore brush with solvent to clean the valve guides.

9. Use a clean cloth and a stiff bristle brush with solvent to thoroughly clean the head assembly. Make sure that no material is washed into the bolt holes or passages. If possible, dry the head with compressed air to remove fluid and solid matter from all the passages.

✴✴WARNING

Do not clean the head in a hot tank or chemical bath. Parts of the head will dissolve.

10. With the head clean and dry, use a precision straight-edge and a feeler gauge to measure the head for warpage. Also measure the manifold faces. Any warpage in excess of the maximum requires replacement of the head.

11. If all is well with the head to this point, it is highly recommended that it be taken to a professional facility such as a machine shop for sophisticated crack testing. The various procedures are much more reliable than simple examination by

Fig. 74 Removing combustion chamber carbon; make sure it is removed and not merely burnished

Fig. 75 Do not scratch the head mating surface when removing old gasket material

Fig. 76 Checking the cylinder head for warpage

Fig. 77 Cylinder head warpage clearances

eye. The cost is reasonable and the peace of mind is well worth the cost. If any cracks are found, the head must be replaced.

12. While the head is being checked, carefully scrape the carbon from the tops of the pistons. Don't scratch the metal of the piston tops and don't damage the cylinder walls. Remove all the carbon and fluid from the cylinder.

13. If repairs are needed to the valves, camshaft or other components, follow the appropriate procedures outlined in this section.

1988 VIN Code 5 Engine
▶ **See Figures 74, 75, 76, 77 and 78**

1. With the head removed from the car, remove the camshafts following procedures outlined later in this section.

2. Remove the valve lifters and the adjusting shims following procedures outlined later in this section.

3. Remove any external fittings, brackets, cables, etc.

4. Remove the valves following procedures outlined later in this section.

5. Carefully scrape the carbon from the tops of the pistons. Don't scratch the metal of the piston tops and don't damage the cylinder walls. Remove all the carbon and fluid from the cylinder.

6. Clean all the gasket material from the block, manifold and head surfaces. If possible, use compressed air to blow the carbon and oil from the bolt holes and passages.

7. Using a wire brush chucked into an electric drill, remove all the carbon from the combustion chambers in the head. Be careful not to scratch the head surface.

Fig. 78 Removing carbon from the piston tops; do not scratch the pistons

1. Half circle plug
2. Cylinder head

Fig. 79 Remove the half circle plug from the cylinder head

8. Use a valve guide brush or a fine-bristled rifle bore brush with solvent to clean the valve guides.

9. Use a clean cloth and a stiff bristle brush with solvent to thoroughly clean the head assembly. Make sure that no material is washed into the bolt holes or passages. If possible, dry the head with compressed air to remove fluid and solid matter from all the passages.

※※WARNING

Do not clean the head in a hot tank or chemical bath. Parts of the head will dissolve.

10. With the head clean and dry, use a precision straightedge and a feeler gauge to measure the head for warpage. Also measure the manifold faces. Any warpage in excess of the maximum requires replacement of the head.

Maximum allowable warpage:
- Cylinder block face: 0.05mm
- Intake manifold face: 0.05mm
- Exhaust manifold face: 0.10mm

11. If all is well with the head to this point, it is highly recommended that it be taken to a professional facility such as a machine shop for sophisticated crack testing. The various procedures are much more reliable than simple examination by eye. The cost is reasonable and the peace of mind is well worth the cost. If any cracks are found, the head must be replaced.

1989-90 VIN Code 6 Engine 1991-92 VIN Code 5 Engine 1993 All Engines

▶ **See Figures 74, 75, 76, 77 and 79**

1. With the head removed from the engine, remove the intake and exhaust manifolds, following procedures outline earlier in this section.

2. Remove the camshafts, following procedures outlined later in this section.

3. Remove the valve lifters and the adjusting shims.

4. Remove the spark plug tubes.

5. Remove the engine hoist hooks.

6. Remove the valves, using procedures outlined later in this section.

7. On 1989-92 engines, remove the half-circle plug at the end of the head.

8. Using a wire brush chucked into an electric drill, remove all the carbon from the combustion chambers in the head. Be careful not to scratch the head surface.

9. Use a valve guide brush or a fine-bristled rifle bore brush with solvent to clean the valve guides.

10. Use a clean cloth and a stiff bristle brush with solvent to thoroughly clean the head assembly. Make sure that no material is washed into the bolt holes or passages. If possible, dry the head with compressed air to remove fluid and solid matter from all the passages.

※※WARNING

Do not clean the head in a hot tank or chemical bath. Parts of the head will dissolve.

11. With the head clean and dry, use a precision straightedge and a feeler gauge to measure the head for warpage. Also measure the manifold faces. Any warpage in excess of the maximum requires replacement of the head.**Maximum allowable warpage:**
- Cylinder block face: 0.05mm
- Intake manifold face: 0.10mm
- Exhaust manifold face: 0.10mm

12. If all is well with the head to this point, it is highly recommended that it be taken to a professional facility such as a machine shop for sophisticated crack testing. The various procedures are much more reliable than simple examination by eye. The cost is reasonable and the peace of mind is well worth the cost. If any cracks are found, the head must be replaced.

1990 VIN Code 5 Engine 1991-92 VIN Code 6 Engine

▶ **See Figures 74, 75, 76 and 77**

1. With the head removed from the engine, remove the intake and exhaust manifolds, following procedures outline earlier in this section.

2. Remove the camshafts, following procedures outlined later in this section.

3. Remove the valve lifters and the adjusting shims.

4. Remove the spark plug tubes.

5. Remove the engine hoist hooks.

6. Remove the valves, using procedures outlined later in this section.

7. Remove the half-circle plug at the end of the head.

8. Using a wire brush chucked into an electric drill, remove all the carbon from the combustion chambers in the head. Be careful not to scratch the head surface.

9. Use a valve guide brush or a fine-bristled rifle bore brush with solvent to clean the valve guides.

10. Use a clean cloth and a stiff bristle brush with solvent to thoroughly clean the head assembly. Make sure that no material is washed into the bolt holes or passages. If possible, dry the head with compressed air to remove fluid and solid matter from all the passages.

✳✳WARNING

Do not clean the head in a hot tank or chemical bath. Parts of the head will dissolve.

11. If all is well with the head to this point, it is highly recommended that it be taken to a professional facility such as a machine shop for sophisticated crack testing. The various procedures are much more reliable than simple examination by eye. The cost is reasonable and the peace of mind is well worth the cost. If any cracks are found, the head must be replaced.

CYLINDER HEAD RESURFACING

The Nova and Prizm cylinder heads from all engines may be resurfaced by a reputable machine shop. Resurfacing is recommended if the engine suffered a massive overheating, such as from a failed head gasket.

The heads are manufactured to be as light as possible; consequently, there is not much excess metal on the face. Any machining must be minimal. If too much metal is removed, the head becomes unusable. A head which exceeds the maximum warpage specification CANNOT be resurfaced. The machine shop will have a list of minimum head thicknesses; at no time may this minimum be exceeded.

Valve Springs and Valves

REMOVAL & INSTALLATION

▸ **See Figures 80, 81 and 82**

➥**This procedure requires the use of a valve stem compressor. This common tool is available at most auto supply stores. It may also be possible to rent one from supplier.**

✳✳WARNING

It is absolutely essential that all components be kept in order after removal. Old ice trays make excellent holders for small parts. The containers should be labeled so that the parts may be reinstalled in their original location. Keep the valves in numbered order in a holder such as an egg carton or an inverted box with holes punched in it. Label the container so that each valve may be replaced in its exact position. (Example: Exhaust #1, #2 etc.)

1985-88 VIN Code 4 Engine

1. Remove the head from the engine and remove the rocker arm and cam shafts, following procedures outlined in this section.

Fig. 80 Typical valve and related components

2. Using a valve spring compressor, compress the valve spring and remove the keeper at the top of the valve shaft.
3. Slowly release the tension on the compressor and remove it. Remove the spring retainer (upper cap), the valve spring, the valve stem oil seal and the lower spring seat.
4. The valve is then removed from the bottom of the head.
5. Repeat steps 2-5 for each valve in the head, keeping them labeled and in order.
6. Thoroughly clean and decarbon each valve. Inspect each valve and spring as outlined later in this section.
7. Lubricate the valve stem and guide with engine oil. Install the valve in the cylinder head and position the lower spring seat.
8. Coat the valve face and seat with a light coat of valve grinding compound. Attach the suction cup end of the valve grinding tool to the head of the valve (it helps to moisten it first).
9. Rotate the tool between the palms, changing position and lifting the tool often to prevent grooving. Lap in the until a smooth, evenly polished surface is evident on both the seat and face.
10. Remove the valve from the head. Wipe away all traces of grinding compound from the surfaces. Clean out the valve guide with a solvent-soaked rag. Make sure there are NO traces of compound in or on the head.
11. Proceed through the remaining valves, lapping them one at a time to their seats. Clean the area after each valve is done.
12. When all the valves have been lapped, thoroughly clean or wash the head with solvent. There must be NO trace of grinding compound present.
13. Lubricate the new valve stem seal with engine oil and install it onto the valve stem over the lower seat.
14. Install the valve spring and the upper seat, compress the spring and install the 2 keepers. Relax tension on the compressor and make sure everything is properly placed. Tap on the installed valve stem with a plastic mallet to ensure proper locking of the retainers.
15. Install the half-circle plug at the end of the head. Coat it with a silicone sealer before installation.
16. Complete the reassembly of the head by installing the camshafts and the manifolds.

Except 1985-88 VIN Code 4 Engine

1. Remove the head following procedures outlined earlier in this section.

Fig. 81 Installing the valve

Fig. 82 Lapping a valve in by hand

2. On 1989-90 VIN Code 6 engine and 1991-92 VIN Code 5 engine, remove the intake and exhaust manifolds.

3. Remove the camshafts following procedures outlined later in this section. Label the shafts and their retainers.

4. Remove the valve lifters and the adjusting shims.

5. On the 1988 VIN Code 5 engine and 1991-92 VIN Code 6 engine, remove the bond cable and the right engine hoist hook. Remove the temperature sensor bracket and the left engine hoist hook. For the 1989-90 VIN Code 6 engine, 1991-92 VIN Code 5 engine and all 1993 engines, simply remove the engine hoist hook(s).

6. Remove the spark plug tubes from the head, if so equipped.

7. Attach the spring compressor. For the 1988 VIN Code 5 engine and 1991-92 VIN Code 6 engine, use GM tool J-37134 or equivalent, and for the 1989-90 VIN Code 6 engine, 1991-92 VIN Code 5 engine and all 1993 engines, use J-8062 with a J-37979 adaptor or equivalent tools.

8. Compress the valve spring and remove the keepers at the top of the valve shaft.

9. Slowly release the tension on the compressor and remove it. Remove the spring retainer (upper cap), the valve spring, the valve stem oil seal and the lower spring seat. The valve is then removed from the bottom of the head.

10. Repeat steps 2-5 for each valve in the head, keeping them labeled and in order. On 1991-92 VIN Code 5 engine, remove the half-circle plug at the end of the head on.

11. Thoroughly clean and decarbon each valve. Inspect each valve and spring as outlined later in this section.

12. Lubricate the valve stem and guide with engine oil. Install the valve in the cylinder head.

13. Coat the valve face and seat with a light coat of valve grinding compound. Attach the suction cup end of the valve grinding tool to the head of the valve (it helps to moisten it first).

14. Rotate the tool between the palms, changing position and lifting the tool often to prevent grooving. Lap in the until a smooth, evenly polished surface is evident on both the seat and face.

15. Remove the valve from the head. Wipe away all traces of grinding compound from the surfaces. Clean out the valve guide with a solvent-soaked rag. Make sure there are NO traces of compound in or on the head.

16. Proceed through the remaining valves, lapping them one at a time to their seats. Clean the area after each valve is done.

17. When all the valves have been lapped, thoroughly clean or wash the head with solvent. There must be NO trace of grinding compound present. Lubricate the new valve stem seal with engine oil and install it onto the valve stem over the lower seat.

18. Install the valve spring and the upper seat, compress the spring and install the 2 keepers. Relax tension on the compressor and make sure everything is properly placed. Tap on the installed valve stem with a plastic mallet to ensure proper locking of the retainers.

19. On the 1988 VIN Code 5 engine, install the spark plug tubes, the engine hangers, the temperature sensor bracket and the bond cable. For the 1989-90 VIN Code 6 engine, 1991-92 VIN Code 5 engine and all 1993 engines, install the tubes and the hanger(s).

20. Install the valve lifters and the adjusting shims. Don't attempt to adjust the valves until after the head is bolted onto the engine.

21. On the 1991-92 VIN Code 5 engine, coat the half-circle plug with silicone sealant and install it in position.

22. Complete the reassembly of the head by installing the camshafts and the manifolds for the 1989-90 VIN Code 6 engine and 1991-92 VIN Code 5 engine, following procedures outlined in this section.

INSPECTION AND MEASUREMENT

▶ **See Figures 83, 84, 85, 86 and 87**

➡**Accurate measuring equipment capable of reading to 0.0001 (ten thousandths) inch is necessary for this work. A micrometer and a hole (bore) gauge will be needed.**

Inspect the valve faces and seats for pits, burned spots, and other evidence of poor seating. If the valve face is in such poor shape that the head of the valve must be cut to true the contact face, discard the valve.

The correct angle for the valve face is given in the Valve Specifications Chart at the beginning of this section. It is recommended that any reaming or refacing be done by a reputable machine shop.

Check the valve stem for scoring and/or burned spots. If the stem and head are in acceptable condition, clean the valve thoroughly with solvent to remove all gum and varnish.

Use the micrometer to measure the diameter of the valve stem. Use the hole gauge to measure the inside diameter of the valve guide for that valve. Subtract the stem diameter from

Fig. 83 Valve refacings should be handled by a reputable machine shop

Fig. 84 Measure the diameter of the valve guide and the valve stem. The difference is the stem clearance

Fig. 85 Checking the valve spring for squareness

Fig. 86 Checking the spring free height

the guide diameter and compare the difference to the chart. If not within specifications, determine the cause (worn valve or worn guide) and replace the worn part(s).

Using a steel square, check the valve spring for correct height and squareness. If the squareness is not within 2mm, replace the spring. If the free height of the spring is not within specification, replace the spring. The installed height of the spring must be measured with the spring under tension in the head. Assemble the valve and spring with the retainers and clips into the head; modify a small steel ruler to fit and record the distance from the bottom spring seat to the upper retainer. If not within specification, shim washers (one or more) any be added between the lower spring seat and the spring.

➡Use only washers designed for this purpose.

Valve Seats

The valve seats for all Nova and Prizm engines are not replaceable. A failed seat (which cannot be recut) requires replacement of the head. Seat recutting is a precise art and is best performed by a machine shop. Seat concentricity should also be checked by a professional facility.

Fig. 87 Measure the valve spring installed height (A) with a modified steel ruler

Valve Guides

▶ See Figure 88

INSPECTION

Valve guides should be cleaned as outlined earlier and checked when the stem-to-guide clearance is measured. As a general rule, if the engine admits oil through the guides (and the oil seals are in good condition), the guides are worn.

Valve guides which are not excessively worn or distorted may, in some cases, be knurled rather than replaced. Knurling is a process in which metal inside the valve guide is displaced and raised by a cutter, making a very fine crosshatched pattern. This raised pattern reduces the clearance to the valve stem and provides excellent oil control. The possibility of knurling rather than replacing the valve guides should be discussed with a machinist.

REMOVAL & INSTALLATION

▶ See Figures 89, 90 and 91

✳✳CAUTION

Replacing the valve guides requires heating the head to high temperatures and the use of special tools. Do not attempt this repair if you are not equipped with the proper heating and handling equipment. Do not attempt this repair unless equipped with the correct valve guide tools and a reamer. When handling the heated head, always use heavy gloves and tongs.

1985-88 VIN Code 4 Engine

1. Heat the cylinder head evenly to 194°F.
2. Carefully remove the head from the heat source and support it upright on the workbench.
3. Using valve guide tool such as J-25367-1 or similar, and a hammer, drive the guide out of the head.
4. Reheat the head to 194°F (90°C) and support it on the workbench.
5. Use the guide tool and a hammer to drive in the new guide until it projects 14.5-15.0mm.

Fig. 88 Cross-section of a knurled valve guide

Fig. 89 Correct installation of guides. GM special tool shown — 1985-88 VIN Code 4 engine

6. Allow the head and guide to air cool. Do not attempt to quick-cool the metal with any water or fluid.
7. Measure the inner diameter of the guide. Compare this to the stem diameter of the new valve. If the stem to guide clearance is insufficient, ream the new guide with a sharp 7mm reamer until the correct clearance is obtained.

1988 VIN Code 5 Engine

1. Break off the upper part of the old bushing. Wrap an old valve stem in tape to prevent the stem from dropping too far into the guide. Pad the surrounding area with rags. Insert the old valve into the guide and strike the valve with a hammer.

✳✳WARNING

Be careful not to damage the surrounding area in which the lifter sits.

2. Heat the cylinder head gradually, in water, to 212°F.
3. Carefully remove the head from the water. Use tool J-37133 or similar and a hammer to drive out the guide.
4. With the guide removed, measure the bore (in the head) into which the guide fits. If the bore is greater than 10.9mm, have the bore ground to 11.05-11.08mm and install a 0.05mm oversize guide. If the bore is greater than 11.08mm, the head must be replaced.
5. Reheat the head in water to 212°F (100°C), then carefully remove it from the water.
6. Using the removal and installation tool (J-37133), drive in the new guide until the snapring makes contact with the cylinder head.

Fig. 90 A quick and handy method for breaking off the tops of valve guides before removal — 1985-88 VIN Code 4 engine

7. Measure the inner diameter of the guide. Compare this to the stem diameter of the new valve. If the stem to guide clearance is insufficient, ream the new guide with a sharp 6mm reamer until the correct clearance is obtained.

1989-90 VIN Code 6 Engine 1991-92 VIN Code 5 Engine

1. Gradually heat the cylinder head to 212°F.
2. Carefully remove the head from the heat source.
3. Using tool J-37133 or similar and a hammer to drive out the guide.
4. With the guide removed, measure the bore (in the head) into which the guide fits. If the bore is greater than 10.9mm, have the bore ground to 11.05-11.08mm and install a 0.05mm oversize guide. If the bore is greater than 11.08mm, the head must be replaced.
5. Reheat the head to 212°F (100°C) and then remove it from the heat.
6. Using the REMOVAL & INSTALLATION tool (J-37133) and an adapter such as J 38277, drive in the new guide until it projects 12.5-13.0mm above the head.
7. Measure the inner diameter of the guide. Compare this to the stem diameter of the new valve. If the stem to guide clearance is insufficient, ream the new guide with a sharp 6mm reamer until the correct clearance is obtained.

1990 VIN Code 5 Engine 1991-92 VIN Code 6 Engine

1. Using tool J-37133 or similar and a hammer to drive out the guide.
2. With the guide removed, measure the bore (in the head) into which the guide fits. If the bore is greater than 11.027 mm, have the bore ground to 11.05-11.08mm and install a 0.05mm oversize guide. If the bore is greater than 11.08mm, the head must be replaced.
3. Using the removal and installation tool (J-37133).
4. Measure the inner diameter of the guide. Compare this to the stem diameter of the new valve. If the stem to guide clearance is insufficient, ream the new guide with a sharp 6mm reamer until the correct clearance is obtained.

1993

1. Using tool J-37133 or similar and a hammer to drive out the guide.
2. With the guide removed, measure the bore (in the head) into which the guide fits. If the bore is greater than 11.27mm, have the bore ground to 11.05-11.077mm and install a

Fig. 91 Use a precision reamer to enlarge new valve guides if necessary

0.05mm oversize guide. If the bore is greater than 11.077mm, the head must be replaced.
3. Using the removal and installation tool (J-37133) and an adapter such as J 38277, drive in the new guide until it projects 12.7-13.1mm above the head.
4. Measure the inner diameter of the guide. Compare this to the stem diameter of the new valve. If the stem to guide clearance is insufficient, ream the new guide with a sharp 6mm reamer until the correct clearance is obtained.

Oil Pan

REMOVAL & INSTALLATION

1985-88 VIN Code 4 Engine

1. Disconnect the negative battery cable.
2. Safely raise and support the vehicle on jackstands.
3. Drain the engine oil and replace the drain plug when the pan is empty.

✳✳CAUTION

Used motor oil may cause skin cancer if repeatedly left in contact with the skin for prolonged periods. Although this is unlikely unless you handle oil on a daily basis, it is wise to thoroughly wash your hands with soap and water immediately after handling used motor oil.

4. Remove the right splash shield.
5. Remove the oil pan bolts.
6. Remove the oil pan. If the pan is difficult to remove, tap it gently with a rubber or plastic mallet. Do not use a pry bar to release it.

✳✳WARNING

Do not bend or deform the edge (flange) of the oil pan during removal.

To install:
7. Clean the pan thoroughly and remove all sludge and solid matter. Clean the mating surfaces of the pan and the engine, removing all traces of old gasket material and sealer. During the cleaning, remove the drain bolt and clean the threads. Install a new gasket on the bolt and install the bolt in the pan.
8. Apply a new gasket and/or sealant to the pan and install the pan to the engine.
9. Install and tighten the pan bolts to 4 ft. lbs. (48 inch lbs.)
10. Install the right splash shield.
11. Lower the vehicle to the ground.
12. Refill the engine oil and connect the negative battery cable.
13. Start the engine and check for leaks.

1988 VIN Code 5 Engine

1. Disconnect the negative battery cable.
2. Safely raise and support the vehicle on jackstands.

3. Drain the engine oil and replace the drain plug when the pan is empty.

❉❉CAUTION

Used motor oil may cause skin cancer if repeatedly left in contact with the skin for prolonged periods. Although this is unlikely unless you handle oil on a daily basis, it is wise to thoroughly wash your hands with soap and water immediately after handling used motor oil.

4. Remove the right splash shield.
5. Remove the front exhaust pipe. Disconnect it at the manifold and the catalytic converter.
6. Remove the exhaust bracket.
7. Remove the oil pan bolts. Remove the oil pan. If the pan is difficult to remove, tap it gently with a rubber or plastic mallet. Do not use a pry bar to release it.

❉❉WARNING

Do not bend or deform the edge (flange) of the oil pan during removal.

To install:
8. Clean the pan thoroughly and remove all sludge and solid matter. Clean the mating surfaces of the pan and the engine, removing all traces of old gasket material and sealer. During the cleaning, remove the drain bolt and clean the threads. Install a new gasket on the bolt and install the bolt in the pan.
9. Apply a new gasket and/or sealant to the pan and install the pan to the engine.
10. Install and tighten the pan bolts to 4 ft. lbs. (48 inch lbs.).
11. Install the front exhaust pipe and its bracket.
12. Install the right splash shield.
13. Lower the vehicle to the ground.
14. Refill the engine oil and connect the negative battery cable.
15. Start the engine and check for leaks.

1989-90 VIN Code 6 Engine 1991-92 VIN Code 5 Engine

1. Disconnect the negative battery cable.
2. Elevate and safely support the vehicle on jackstands.
3. Remove the right and left splash shields.
4. Drain the oil.

❉❉CAUTION

Used motor oil may cause skin cancer if repeatedly left in contact with the skin for prolonged periods. Although this is unlikely unless you handle oil on a daily basis, it is wise to thoroughly wash your hands with soap and water immediately after handling used motor oil.

5. Disconnect the sensor to the oxygen sensor.
6. Remove the front exhaust pipe. Disconnect the pipe at the catalytic converter and the exhaust manifold.

7. Remove the 2 nuts and the 19 bolts from the oil pan. Remove the oil pan from the engine.

❉❉WARNING

Use caution when removing the oil pan. The oil pump at the front of the engine may be damaged during removal. Use caution not to damage the edge of the pan.

8. Remove the 2 nuts and 2 bolts holding the oil pick-up and strainer to the engine. Remove the pick-up assembly and its gasket.
To install:
9. Clean the mating surfaces of the pan and cylinder block of all sealant and gasket material. Remove any traces of oil on these surfaces.
10. Thoroughly clean the pick-up and screen assembly and allow it to air dry.
11. Install the pick-up and strainer assembly with a new gasket. Tighten the nuts and bolts to 90 inch lbs. (10 Nm).
12. Apply a continuous bead of GM Sealant 1050026 or similar to both sides of the new oil pan gasket and place the gasket in position on the pan.
13. Install the pan onto the engine with all the nuts and bolts finger tight.
14. Tighten the nuts and bolts to 44 inch lbs. (5 Nm).
15. Connect the exhaust pipe to the catalytic converter and to the exhaust manifold.
16. Connect the wiring to the oxygen sensor.
17. Install the left and right splash shields.
18. Lower the vehicle to the ground.
19. Refill the engine oil and connect the negative battery cable.
20. Start the engine and check for leaks.

1990 VIN Code 5 Engine 1991-92 VIN Code 6 Engine

1. Disconnect the negative battery cable.
2. Safely raise and support the vehicle on jackstands.
3. Drain the engine oil and replace the drain plug when the pan is empty.

❉❉CAUTION

Used motor oil may cause skin cancer if repeatedly left in contact with the skin for prolonged periods. Although this is unlikely unless you handle oil on a daily basis, it is wise to thoroughly wash your hands with soap and water immediately after handling used motor oil.

4. Remove the right splash shield.
5. Remove the front exhaust pipe.
6. Remove the oil pan bolts. Remove the oil pan. If the pan is difficult to remove, tap it gently with a rubber or plastic mallet. Do not use a pry bar to release it.

❉❉WARNING

Do not bend or deform the edge (flange) of the oil pan during removal.

To install:
7. Clean the pan thoroughly and remove all sludge and solid matter. Clean the mating surfaces of the pan and the

engine, removing all traces of old gasket material and sealer. During the cleaning, remove the drain bolt and clean the threads. Install a new gasket on the bolt and install the bolt in the pan.

8. Apply a new gasket and/or sealant to the pan and install the pan to the engine.

9. Install and tighten the pan bolts to 53 inch lbs. (6 Nm).

10. Install the front exhaust pipe.

11. Install the right splash shield.

12. Lower the vehicle to the ground.

13. Refill the engine oil and connect the negative battery cable.

14. Start the engine and check for leaks.

1993 Except VIN Code 8 Engine

1. Disconnect the negative battery cable.

2. Disconnect the oxygen sensor electrical connector.

3. Raise and support the vehicle safely.

4. Drain the engine oil and replace the drain plug when the pan is empty.

❋❋CAUTION

Used motor oil may cause skin cancer if repeatedly left in contact with the skin for prolonged periods. Although this is unlikely unless you handle oil on a daily basis, it is wise to thoroughly wash your hands with soap and water immediately after handling used motor oil.

5. Remove the both splash shields.

6. Separate the front exhaust pipe from the exhaust manifold and the catalytic converter.

7. Remove the 2 hanger bolts and remove the front pipe from the vehicle.

8. Remove the 2 bolts from the lower the front end of the center support.

9. Remove the 3 lower engine reinforcement brace to transaxle bolts.

10. Remove the 2 lower engine reinforcement brace to cylinder block bolts and remove the engine reinforcement brace from the vehicle.

11. Remove the 19 bolts, 2 nuts and using a screwdriver, pry between the engine oil pan and lower cylinder block reinforcement brace.

12. If the pan is difficult to remove, tap it gently with a rubber or plastic mallet.

❋❋WARNING

Do not bend or deform the edge (flange) of the oil pan during removal.

13. Remove the 3 bolts oil strainer and gasket.

To install:

14. Clean the pan thoroughly and remove all sludge and solid matter. Clean the mating surfaces of the pan and the engine, removing all traces of old gasket material and sealer. During the cleaning, remove the drain bolt and clean the threads. Install a new gasket on the bolt and install the bolt in the pan.

15. Apply a new gasket and/or sealant to the pan and install the pan to the engine.

16. Install and tighten the pan bolts to 44 inch lbs. (5 Nm).

17. Install the lower engine reinforcement brace to cylinder block and tighten the bolts to 47 ft. lbs. (64 Nm).

18. Install the lower engine reinforcement brace to the transaxle and tighten the bolts to 47 ft. lbs. (64 Nm).

19. Install the front exhaust pipe.

20. Install the both splash shields.

21. Install the lower the front end of the center support and tighten the 2 bolts to 45 ft. lbs. (61 Nm).

22. Lower the vehicle.

23. Connect the negative battery cable.

1993 VIN Code 8 Engine

➡**This procedure also includes removal of the lower cylinder block reinforcement brace.**

1. Disconnect the negative battery cable.

2. Disconnect the oxygen sensor electrical connector.

3. Raise and support the vehicle safely.

4. Drain the engine oil and replace the drain plug when the pan is empty.

❋❋CAUTION

Used motor oil may cause skin cancer if repeatedly left in contact with the skin for prolonged periods. Although this is unlikely unless you handle oil on a daily basis, it is wise to thoroughly wash your hands with soap and water immediately after handling used motor oil.

5. Remove the both splash shields.

6. Separate the front exhaust pipe from the exhaust manifold and the catalytic converter.

7. Remove the 2 hanger bolts and remove the front pipe from the vehicle.

8. Remove the 2 bolts and lower the front end of the center support.

9. Remove the 13 bolts, 2 nuts and using a screwdriver, pry between the engine oil pan and lower cylinder block reinforcement brace.

10. If the pan is difficult to remove, tap it gently with a rubber or plastic mallet.

❋❋WARNING

Do not bend or deform the edge (flange) of the oil pan during removal.

11. Remove the 2 bolts, 2 nuts and the baffle plate.

12. Remove the 3 bolts oil strainer and gasket.

13. Remove the 3 transaxle mounting bolts from the engine rear end plate side.

14. Remove the 14 bolts from the lower cylinder block reinforcement brace.

15. Remove the 6 Torx® bolts from the lower cylinder block reinforcement brace.

To install:

16. Clean the pan thoroughly and remove all sludge and solid matter. Clean the mating surfaces of the pan and the engine, removing all traces of old gasket material and sealer. During the cleaning, remove the drain bolt and clean the threads. Install a new gasket on the bolt and install the bolt in the pan.

17. Apply sealant to the lower cylinder block reinforcement brace to cylinder block mating surface.

18. Install the 14 bolts to the lower cylinder block reinforcement brace and tighten to 71 inch lbs. (8 Nm).

19. Install the 6 Torx® bolts to the lower cylinder block reinforcement brace and tighten to 11 ft. lbs. (15 Nm).

20. Install the 3 transaxle mounting bolts to the engine rear end plate side and tighten to 17 ft. lbs. (23 Nm).

21. Install the 3 bolts, oil strainer and gasket and tighten to 62 inch lbs. (7 Nm).

22. Apply a new gasket and/or sealant to the oil pan mating surface.

23. Install the engine oil pan to the lower cylinder block reinforcement brace and tighten the pan nuts and bolts to 44 inch lbs. (5 Nm).

24. Install the front exhaust pipe.

25. Install the both splash shields.

26. Install the center support and tighten the 2 bolts to 45 ft. lbs. (61 Nm)

27. Connect the oxygen sensor.

28. Lower the vehicle.

29. Connect the negative battery cable.

Oil Pump

REMOVAL & INSTALLATION

1985-88 VIN Code 4 Engine

▶ See Figures 92 and 93

➡This procedure requires special-purpose tools which may not be in your everyday tool set. Snapring pliers (internal and external) and pulley removers of various sizes are available at most reputable tool outlets.

1. Disconnect the negative battery cable.
2. Remove the oil pan as previously outlined.
3. Drain the cooling system.

✳✳CAUTION

When draining the coolant, keep in mind that cats and dogs are attracted by the ethylene glycol antifreeze, and are quite likely to drink any that is left in an uncovered container or in puddles on the ground. This will prove fatal in sufficient quantity. Always drain the coolant into a sealable container. Coolant should be reused unless it is contaminated or several years old.

4. Loosen the water pump pulley bolts.
5. Remove the alternator bolts.
6. If equipped with power steering, remove the drive belt.
7. If equipped with air conditioning, loosen the air conditioning idler pulley and the adjustor. Remove the drive belt and then remove the idler pulley and adjustor.
8. Remove the alternator bolts and remove the alternator; place it or suspend it out of the way.
9. Remove the water pump pulley.
10. Disconnect the upper radiator hose at the engine.
11. Label and disconnect the vacuum hoses running through the work area.

12. Remove the No. 1 (upper) timing belt cover and its gasket.

13. Remove the No. 3 (middle) timing belt cover and its gasket.

14. Rotate the crankshaft to the TDC/compression position.

15. Elevate and safely support the vehicle on jackstands. Double check the placement of the stands and the stability of the car on the stands.

16. Remove the right splash shield.

17. Remove the flywheel cover.

18. Remove the crankshaft pulley. Block the flywheel to prevent the crank from turning.

19. Remove the No. 2 (lower) timing belt cover.

20. Mark the position of the camshaft and crankshaft timing pulleys on the timing belt and mark an arrow on the belt showing the direction of rotation.

21. Loosen the timing belt idler pulley bolt, move the pulley to release tension on the belt and tighten the bolt. This holds the pulley in the loosened position.

22. Slip the timing belt off the crankshaft timing pulley.

23. Remove the crankshaft timing pulley.

24. Remove the dipstick tube.

25. Remove the timing belt idler pulley.

26. Remove the bolts in the oil pump case and carefully remove the oil pump. It may require gentle tapping to loosen it; use only a plastic or rubber mallet.

To install:

27. When reinstalling, place the new gasket against the block and install the oil pump to the crankshaft with the spline teeth of the drive gear engaged with the large teeth of the crankshaft. Tighten the bolts to 18 ft. lbs.

28. Install the timing belt idler pulley.

29. Install the dipstick tube.

30. Install the crankshaft timing pulley.

31. Install the timing belt. (Refer to: Timing Belt — REMOVAL & INSTALLATION later in this section.).

32. Install the lower belt cover.

33. Install the crankshaft pulley and tighten it to 87 ft. lbs.

34. Install the flywheel cover.

35. Install the right splash guard and lower the vehicle to the ground.

36. Install the middle and upper timing belt covers with their gaskets.

37. Reconnect the vacuum hoses.

38. Attach the water pump pulley; leave the bolts finger tight.

39. Position and secure the alternator.

Fig. 92 Exploded view of the oil pump — 1985-88 VIN Code 4 engine

Fig. 93 Aligning the oil pump drive gear with the crankshaft — 1985-88 VIN Code 4 engine

40. If so equipped, install the air conditioning adjusting bolt, idler pulley and belt. Install the belt and adjust it to the proper tension.

41. Install the power steering belt and adjust it if so equipped.

42. Tighten the water pump bolts.

43. With a new gasket, install the oil pick-up and strainer assembly. Tighten the nuts and bolts to 6.8 ft. lbs.

44. Refill the cooling system.

45. Install the oil pan following procedures outlined previously.

46. Start the engine and check for leaks. Allow the engine to warm up fully and check the work area carefully under warm and cold conditions.

1988 VIN Code 5 Engine

▶ See Figures 94, 95, 96 and 97

1. Disconnect the negative battery cable.
2. Remove the oil pan as previously outlined.
3. Remove the oil pick-up and strainer.
4. Remove the oil pan baffle plate.
5. Drain the cooling system.

✳✳CAUTION

When draining the coolant, keep in mind that cats and dogs are attracted by the ethylene glycol antifreeze, and are quite likely to drink any that is left in an uncovered container or in puddles on the ground. This will prove fatal in sufficient quantity. Always drain the coolant into a sealable container. Coolant should be reused unless it is contaminated or several years old.

6. Disconnect the accelerator cable or linkage.
7. Remove the cruise control actuator if so equipped.
8. Remove the washer tank.
9. Remove the upper radiator hose at the engine block.
10. Remove the power steering and/or the air conditioning drive belt(s).
11. Loosen the bolts to the water pump pulley and then remove the alternator drive belt.
12. Remove the spark plugs.
13. Rotate the crankshaft and position the engine at TDC/compression. The crankshaft mark aligns at zero and the camshaft, when viewed through the oil filler cap, has a small cavity pointing upward.
14. Use a floor jack and a piece of wood to slightly elevate the engine. Remove the right engine mount; then remove the 3 bolts and remove the right reinforcing plate for the engine mount.
15. Remove the water pump pulley.
16. Remove the crankshaft pulley. Counterhold the crankshaft or block the flywheel to prevent the crank from turning.

Fig. 94 Aligning the engine at TDC/compression for No. 1 cylinder — 1988 VIN Code 5 engine

Fig. 95 Arrows indicate the nuts and bolts holding the right engine mount and the reinforcing plate — 1988 VIN Code 5 engine

17. Remove the timing belt covers.

18. Remove the timing belt guide.

19. Loosen the idler pulley bolt, push it all the way to the left and tighten the bolt. This removes tension from the belt.

20. Matchmark the belt and all the pulleys so that the belt may be reinstalled exactly as it was before. Mark an arrow on the belt showing direction of rotation.

21. Remove the timing belt from the lower pulley (crankshaft timing pulley). If you are careful, the belt may remain undisturbed on the camshaft pulleys.

22. Remove the idler pulley and spring.

23. Remove the crankshaft timing pulley.

24. Remove the PCV hose.

25. Remove the dipstick and tube.

26. Remove the 7 bolts in the oil pump and carefully remove the pump. If it is difficult to remove, tap it lightly with a plastic or rubber mallet. Do not pry it off or strike it with a metal hammer.

To install:

27. When reinstalling, place a new gasket on the block. Install the oil pump to the crankshaft with the spline teeth to the drive gear engaged with the large teeth of the crankshaft.

28. Install the 7 retaining bolts and tighten them to 16 ft. lbs.

29. Install the dipstick tube and dipstick.

30. Install the crankshaft timing pulley.

31. Install the timing belt idler pulley.

32. Install the timing belt. (Refer to Timing Belt — REMOVAL & INSTALLATION procedures in this section.)

33. Install the timing belt guide. It should install with the cupped side facing outward.

34. Make sure the gaskets are properly seated in the timing belt covers and reinstall the covers. Make sure each bolt is in the correct hole.

35. Install the crankshaft pulley. Again using a counterholding device, tighten the bolt to 101 ft. lbs.

36. Install the water pump pulley and tighten the bolts finger tight. Install the valve covers.

37. Install the right side engine mount. Tighten the nut to 38 ft. lbs. and the through bolt to 64 ft. lbs.

38. Install the reinforcement for the right motor mount and tighten the bolts to 31 ft. lbs.

39. Install the spark plugs.

40. Install the alternator drive belt and tighten the water pump pulley bolts.

41. Install and adjust the power steering and/or the air conditioner drive belts.

42. Connect the upper radiator hose.

43. Install the windshield washer reservoir.

44. If equipped with cruise control, reinstall the cruise control actuator.

45. Connect the accelerator cable or linkage.

46. Install the oil pan baffle plate. Clean the contact surfaces thoroughly, apply a bead of sealer to the baffle plate and press the baffle plate into position. Be very careful not to get any sealant into the oil passages.

47. Install the oil pick-up and strainer assembly. Install the PCV hose.

48. Install the oil pan, following procedures discussed in this section.

49. Using new gaskets, reconnect the exhaust pipe. Tighten the bolts to the catalytic converter to 32 ft. lbs. and the bolts to the exhaust manifold 46 ft. lbs.

50. Install the flywheel cover.

51. Install the stiffener plate and the center engine mount.

52. Refill the engine with oil.

53. Refill the coolant system.

54. Start the engine and check for leaks. Allow the engine to warm up to normal operating temperature and check the work area carefully for signs of seepage.

55. With the engine shut off, check the tension of the drive belts and adjust if necessary. Reinstall the splash guards under the car.

1989-92 All Engines

▶ See Figure 96

1. Disconnect the negative battery cable and elevate the vehicle. Safely support it on jackstands. Remove the splashshield(s).

2. Remove the protectors from the 2 center engine mount nuts and studs.

3. Remove the 2 center transaxle mount-to-center crossmember nuts.

4. Remove the 2 rear transaxle mount-to-main crossmember nuts.

5. Drain the engine oil.

6. Remove the oil pan. Remove the oil pick-up and strainer assembly.

7. Lower the vehicle to the ground.

8. Depending on equipment, loosen the air conditioning compressor bracket, the power steering pump bracket and the alternator bracket as applicable. Remove the drive belts.

Fig. 96 Correct positions for installation of the oil pump — 1988 VIN Code 5 engine and 1989-90 VIN Code 6 engine

Fig. 97 Detail of the oil pump system — 1988 VIN Code 5 engine

9. Remove the alternator from its mounts and place it out of the way. The wiring may be left attached.

10. Lift out the windshield washer fluid reservoir.

11. Support the engine. This may be done from above with tool J 28467-A or a chain hoist or from below with a floor jack. Be very careful of the jack 12.

12. Remove the through bolt in the right engine mount.

13. Remove the water pump pulley.

14. Lower the engine to its normal position.

15. Remove the crankshaft pulley.

16. Remove the timing belt covers.

17. Remove the timing belt guide from the crank pulley.

18. Loosen the idler pulley bolt, push it all the way to the left and tighten the bolt. This removes tension from the belt.

19. Matchmark the belt and all the pulleys so that the belt may be reinstalled exactly as it was before. Mark an arrow on the belt showing direction of rotation.

20. Remove the timing belt from the lower pulley (crankshaft timing pulley). If you are careful, the belt may remain undisturbed on the camshaft pulleys.

21. Remove the idler pulley and spring.

22. Remove the dipstick and dipstick tube.

23. Remove the crankshaft timing pulley.

24. Raise the vehicle and safely support it on jackstands.

25. Remove the 7 bolts holding the oil pump.

26. Remove the 7 bolts in the oil pump and carefully remove the pump. If it is difficult to remove, tap it lightly with a plastic or rubber mallet. Do not pry it off or strike it with a metal hammer.

To install:

27. When reinstalling, place a new gasket on the block. Install the oil pump to the crankshaft with the spline teeth to the drive gear engaged with the large teeth of the crankshaft.

28. Install the 7 retaining bolts and tighten them to 16 ft. lbs.

29. Lower the vehicle to the ground.

30. Install the timing belt idler pulley.

31. Install the dipstick tube and dipstick.

32. Install the timing belt. (Refer to Timing Belt — REMOVAL & INSTALLATION procedures in this section.)

33. Install the timing belt guide. It should install with the cupped side facing outward.

34. Make sure the gaskets are properly seated in the timing belt covers and reinstall the covers. Make sure each bolt is in the correct hole.

35. Install the crankshaft pulley. Tighten the bolt to 87 ft. lbs.

36. Elevate the motor to gain access to the water pump.

37. Install the water pump pulley.

38. Install the right engine mount through bolt. Tighten the through bolt to 64 ft. lbs. When the bolt is secure, the engine lifting apparatus may be removed.

39. Position and install the alternator.

40. Reinstall the drive belts for the alternator, power steering and air conditioning as applicable. Adjust the belts to the correct tension.

41. Raise the vehicle and safely support it on jackstands.

42. Install the oil pick-up and strainer assembly.

43. Apply a continuous bead of sealer (GM 1050026 or similar) to both sides of the new pan gasket.

44. Place the gasket on the pan and install the pan to the block. Tighten the bolts and nuts to 3.6 ft. lbs. (44 inch lbs.)

45. Install the 2 rear transaxle mount-to-main crossmember nuts and tighten them to 45 ft. lbs. Install the 2 center transaxle mount-to-center crossmember nuts and tighten them to 45 ft. lbs.

46. Install the protectors over the nuts and studs for the mounts.

47. Lower the vehicle to the ground.

48. Install the windshield washer fluid reservoir.

49. Refill the engine with the correct amount of fresh oil.

50. Connect the negative battery cable.

51. Start the engine and check for leaks. Allow the engine to warm up to normal operating temperature and check the work area carefully for signs of seepage.

52. With the engine shut off, check the tension of the drive belts and adjust if necessary. Reinstall the splash guard(s) under the car.

1993

▶ See Figure 98

1. Disconnect the negative battery cable.

2. Remove the timing belt and tensioner as outlined in this section.

3. Remove the oil pan and strainer as outlined in this section.

4. Remove the 1 bolt and the guide tube with the oil level indicator from the oil pump.

5. Remove the 7 bolts and the oil pump with the gasket from the cylinder block. If necessary, tap on the back side of the oil pump with a plastic or rubber faced hammer to break it loose from the cylinder block.

6. Remove the oil seal from the oil pump.
To install:
7. Apply clean engine oil to the new oil seal.
8. Install the new oil seal to the oil pump using tool J 35403 or equivalent. Coat the inside of the new oil seal with wheel bearing lubricant.
9. Install a new gasket to the cylinder block and install the oil pump to the crankshaft, engaging the spline teeth during installation. Tighten the bolts to 16 ft. lbs. (21 Nm).

➡**The oil pump bolts are 2 lengths. Make sure the 2 longer bolts are installed in the correct position to prevent leaks.**

10. Install the timing belt and belt tensioner as outlined in this section.
11. Install the engine oil pan and strainer as outlined in this section.
12. Install the guide tube and oil level indicator to the oil pump. Tighten the guide tube bolt to 80 inch lbs. (9 Nm)
13. Connect the negative battery cable.

INSPECTION AND OVERHAUL

1989-93 All Engines
▶ **See Figures 99, 100, 101 and 102**

1. Remove the pump body cover.
2. Using a feeler gauge, measure the clearance between the driven gear and the pump body. If the clearance is greater than 0.0079 in. (0.20mm), replace the oil pump.
3. Using a feeler gauge, measure the clearance between both gear tips. The clearance should be a maximum of 0.012 in. (0.35mm).
4. If the clearance is greater than the maximum, replace the oil pump gear set.
5. Using a feeler gauge and a straightedge, measure the side clearance. The clearance should be a maximum of 0.004 in. (0.10mm).
6. If the clearance is greater than the maximum, replace the oil pump gear set and/or the pump body.

Fig. 99 Oil pump cover

Fig. 100 Removing the snap ring

Fig. 101 Measuring the clearance between the driven gear and pump body

Fig. 98 Oil pump assembly — 1993 models

Fig. 102 Measuring the gear to pump body clearance

Timing Belt Covers

REMOVAL & INSTALLATION

1985-88 VIN Code 4 Engine

▶ **See Figure 103**

1. Disconnect the negative battery cable.
2. Remove the right side splash shield under the engine.
3. Loosen the water pump pulley bolts and remove the alternator belt. Remove the power steering drive belt if so equipped.
4. Remove the bolts and remove the water pump pulley.
5. Loosen the air conditioning idler pulley mounting bolt. Loosen the adjusting nut and then remove the air conditioning drive belt if so equipped. Remove the idler pulley.
6. Rotate the crankshaft clockwise and set the engine to TDC/compression on No. 1 cylinder. Loosen the crankshaft pulley mounting bolt and remove the crank pulley.

➡ **Before removing the pulley, check that the rockers on the No. 1 cylinder are loose and that the timing marks on the crankshaft align at the zero setting. If the rockers are not loose, rotate the crankshaft 1 full revolution, stopping again at the zero point.**

7. Remove the mounting bolts and the No. 1 (upper) cover.
8. Remove the 4 bolts and remove the center engine mount.
9. Place a block of wood on a floor jack and position it under the motor. Raise the engine slightly, remove 2 bolts and then remove the right engine mount.
10. Lower the engine and then remove the No. 2 (lower) and the No. 3 (center) covers with their gaskets.
11. When reinstalling, make certain that the gaskets and their mating surfaces are clean and free from dirt and oil. The gasket itself must be free of cuts and deformations and must fit securely in the grooves of the covers.
12. Install the No. 3 cover with its gasket, then install the No. 2 cover and its gasket. Before tightening the bolts fully, check that the gaskets have not fallen out of place.
13. Raise the engine slightly and install the right engine mount.
14. Lower the engine into place and install the center engine mount. Tighten the bolts to 29 ft. lbs.
15. Install the upper timing belt cover.
16. Install the crankshaft pulley; tighten the bolt to 87 ft. lbs.
17. Install the water pump pulley and tighten the bolts finger tight.
18. Reinstall the idler pulley for the air conditioning belt. Install the belt and adjust it by turning the adjustor into position.
19. Tighten the water pump pulley bolts.
20. Install the power steering drive belt if so equipped.
21. Install the splash shield.
22. Connect the negative battery cable.

1988 VIN Code 5 Engine

▶ **See Figures 104 and 105**

1. Disconnect the negative battery cable.
2. Elevate the vehicle and safely support it on jackstands.
3. Remove the right front wheel.
4. Remove the splash shield from under the car.
5. Drain the coolant into clean containers. Close the draincocks when the system is empty.

❋❋CAUTION

When draining the coolant, keep in mind that cats and dogs are attracted by the ethylene glycol antifreeze, and are quite likely to drink any that is left in an uncovered container or in puddles on the ground. This will prove fatal in sufficient quantity. Always drain the coolant into a sealable container. Coolant should be reused unless it is contaminated or several years old.

6. Lower the car to the ground. Disconnect the accelerator cable and, if equipped, the cruise control cable.
7. Remove the cruise control actuator if so equipped.
8. Carefully remove the ignition coil.
9. Disconnect the radiator hose at the water outlet.
10. Remove the power steering drive belt and the alternator drive belt.
11. Remove the spark plugs.
12. Rotate the crankshaft clockwise and set the engine to TDC/compression on No. 1 cylinder. Align the crankshaft marks at zero; look through the oil filler hole and make sure the small hole in the end of the camshaft can be seen.
13. Raise and safely support the vehicle. Disconnect the center engine mount.
14. Lower the vehicle to the ground.
15. Support the engine either from above or below. Disconnect the right engine mount from the engine.

Fig. 103 Timing belt and related components — 1985-88 VIN Code 4 engine

1. No.2 Timing belt cover
2. No.3 timing belt cover
3. Exhaust camshaft timing pulley
4. Intake camshaft pulley
5. Gasket
6. Idler pulley
7. Crankshaft timing pulley
8. Timing belt
9. Tension spring
10. Timing belt guide
11. No.1 timing belt cover
12. Crankshaft pulley
13. Drive belt
14. Water pump pulley

Fig. 104 Timing belt, cover and related components — 1988 VIN Code 5 engine and 1991-92 VIN Code 6 engine

16. Raise the engine and remove the mount.
17. Remove the water pump pulley.
18. Remove the crankshaft pulley. The use of a counterholding tool such as J-8614-01 or equivalent, is highly recommended.
19. Remove the ten bolts and remove the timing belt covers with their gaskets.

✳✳WARNING

The bolts are different lengths; they must be returned to their correct location at reassembly. Label or diagram the bolts during removal.

20. When reinstalling, make certain that the gaskets and their mating surfaces are clean and free from dirt and oil. The gasket itself must be free of cuts and deformations and must fit securely in the grooves of the covers.
21. Reinstall the covers and their gaskets and the 10 bolts in their proper positions.
22. Install the crankshaft pulley, again using the counterholding tool. Tighten the bolt to 101 ft. lbs.
23. Install the water pump pulley.
24. Install the right engine mount. Tighten the through bolt to 58 ft. lbs.
25. Reinstall the spark plugs and their wires.
26. Install the alternator drive belt and the power steering drive belt. Adjust the belts to the correct tension.
27. Connect the radiator hose to the water outlet port.
28. Install the ignition coil.
29. Install the cruise control actuator and the cruise control cable if so equipped.

Fig. 105 Timing cover bolts must be installed in the correct locations. Bolt lengths shown are in millimeters (mm) — 1988 VIN Code 5 engine

30. Connect the accelerator cable.
31. Refill the cooling system with the correct amount of anti-freeze and water.
32. Connect the negative battery cable.
33. Start the engine and check for leaks. Allow the engine to warm up and check the work areas carefully for seepage.
34. Install the splash shield under the car.
35. Install the right front wheel.

1989-90 VIN Code 6, 1990 VIN Code 5 and All 1991-92 Engines

▶ **See Figures 104 and 106**

1. Disconnect the negative battery cable.
2. Elevate the vehicle and safely support it on jackstands.
3. Remove the right splash shield under the car.

4. Lower the vehicle. Remove the wiring harness from the upper timing belt cover.

5. Depending on equipment, loosen the air conditioner compressor, the power steering pump and the alternator on their adjusting bolts. Remove the drive belts.

6. Remove the crankshaft pulley. The use of a counterholding tool such as J 8614-01 or similar is highly recommended.

7. Remove the valve cover.

8. Remove the windshield washer reservoir.

9. Elevate and safely support the vehicle.

10. Support the engine either from above (Tool 28467-A or chain hoist) or below (floor jack and wood block) and remove the through bolt at the right engine mount.

11. Remove the protectors on the mount nuts and studs for the center and rear transaxle mounts.

12. Remove the 2 rear transaxle mount-to-main crossmember nuts. Remove the 2 center transaxle mount-to-center crossmember nuts.

13. Carefully elevate the engine enough to gain access to the water pump pulley.

14. Remove the water pump pulley. Lower the engine to its normal position.

15. Remove the lower center and upper timing covers.

To install:

16. If further work is to be done, the car may be lowered to the ground but the engine must remain supported until the mount(s) are reinstalled.

17. When reinstalling, make certain that the gaskets and their mating surfaces are clean and free from dirt and oil. The gasket itself must be free of cuts and deformations and must fit securely in the grooves of the covers.

18. Install the covers and the bolts; tighten the bolts to 3.6 ft. lbs. (44 INCH lbs.)

19. Elevate the engine and install the water pump pulley.

20. Lower the engine to its normal position. Install the through bolt in the right engine mount and tighten it to 64 ft. lbs. With the bolt secure, the engine lifting apparatus may be removed.

21. Install the valve cover.

22. Install the crankshaft pulley and tighten its bolt to 87 ft. lbs.

23. Reinstall the air conditioning compressor, the power steering pump and the alternator. Install their belts and adjust them to the correct tension.

24. Reconnect the wiring harness to the upper timing belt cover.

25. Raise the vehicle and safely support it on jackstands.

26. Install the 2 nuts on the center transaxle mount and the rear transaxle mount. Tighten all the nuts to 45 ft. lbs.

27. Install the protectors on the nuts and studs.

28. Install the splashshield under the car.

29. Lower the vehicle to the ground.

30. Install the windshield washer reservoir and connect the negative battery cable.

1993 All Engines

For removal and installation procedure of the front timing belt covers on all 1993 models, please refer to 'Timing Belt, Tensioner and Gears' procedure, outlined in this section.

1. Upper timing belt cover	6. Camshaft timing pulley	11. Crankshaft pulley
2. Bolt	7. Crankshaft timing gear	12. Bolt
3. Idler pulley	8. Tension spring	13. Inspection plug
4. timing belt	9. Timing belt guide	14. Center timing belt cover
5. Bolt	10. Lower timing belt cover	15. Bolt

Fig. 106 Timing covers, belt and related components — 1989-90 VIN Code 6 engine and 1991-92 VIN Code 5 engine

Timing Belt, Tensioner and Gears

REMOVAL & INSTALLATION

➡Timing belts must always be handled carefully and kept completely free of dirt, grease, fluids and lubricants. This includes any accidental contact from spillage, fingerprints, rags, etc. These same precautions apply to the pulleys and contact surfaces on which the belt rides.   The belt must never be crimped, twisted or bent. Never use tools to pry or wedge the belt into place. Such actions will damage the structure of the belt and possibly cause breakage.

1985-88 VIN Code 4 Engine

▶ **See Figures 107, 108, 109, 110, 111 and 112**

1. Remove the timing belt covers using procedures described earlier in this section.

2. If not done as part of the cover removal, rotate the crankshaft clockwise to the TDC/compression position for No. 1 cylinder. Insure that the crankshaft marks align at zero and that the rocker arms on No. 1 cylinder are loose.

3. Loosen the timing belt idler pulley to relieve the tension on the belt.

4. Make matchmarks on the belt and both pulleys showing the exact placement of the belt. Mark an arrow on the belt showing its direction of rotation.

5. Carefully slip the timing belt off the pulleys.

✳✳WARNING

Do not disturb the position of the camshaft or the crankshaft during removal.

6. Remove the idler pulley bolt, pulley and return spring.

7. Use an adjustable wrench mounted on the flats of the camshaft to hold the cam from moving. Loosen the center bolt in the camshaft pulley and remove the pulley.

8. Check the timing belt carefully for any signs of cracking or deterioration. Pay particular attention to the area where each tooth or cog attaches to the backing of the belt. If the belt shows signs of damage, check the contact faces of the pulleys for possible burrs or scratches.

9. Check the idler pulley by holding it in your hand and spinning it. It should rotate freely and quietly. Any sign of grinding or abnormal noise indicates replacement of the pulley.

10. Check the free length of the tension spring. Correct length is 38.5mm measured at the inside faces of the hooks. A spring which has stretched during use will not apply the correct tension to the pulley; replace the spring.

11. If you can test the tension of the spring, look for 8.4 lbs. of tension at 50mm of length. If in doubt, replace the spring.

12. Reinstall the camshaft timing belt pulley, making sure the pulley fits properly on the shaft and that the timing marks align correctly. Tighten the center bolt to 34 ft. lbs.

13. Before reinstalling the belt, double check that the crank and camshafts are exactly in their correct positions. The alignment mark on the end of the camshaft bearing cap should

Fig. 108 Always measure the free length of the idler pulley tensioning spring. The correct length is 1.512 in — 1985-88 VIN Code 4 engine

Fig. 109 Make sure the cam is firmly held when removing the timing belt sprocket — 1985-88 VIN Code 4 engine

Fig. 107 Always matchmark the belt and both pulleys before removing the timing belt. Mark an arrow on the belt showing direction of rotation — 1985-88 VIN Code 4 engine

show through the small hole in the camshaft pulley and the small mark on the crankshaft timing belt pulley should align with the mark on the oil pump.

14. Reinstall the timing belt idler pulley and the tension spring. Pry the pulley to the left as far as it will go and temporarily tighten the retaining bolt. This will hold the pulley in its loosest position.

15. Install the timing belt, observing the matchmarks made earlier. Make sure the belt is fully and squarely seated on the upper and lower pulleys.

16. Using the equipment installed during the removal of the timing covers, elevate the engine enough to gain access to the work area.

17. Loosen the retaining bolt for the timing belt idler pulley and allow it to tension the belt.

18. Temporarily install the crankshaft pulley bolt and turn the crank clockwise 2 full revolutions from TDC to TDC. Insure that each timing mark realigns exactly.

19. Tighten the timing belt idler pulley retaining bolt to 27 ft. lbs.

20. Measure the timing belt deflection (Tool 23600 B or similar), looking for 6-7mm of deflection at 4.4 pounds of pressure. If the deflection is not correct, readjust the idler pulley by repeating steps 15 through 18.

21. Remove the bolt from the end of the crankshaft.

22. Lower the engine into position and install the right engine mount.

23. Install the timing belt guide onto the crankshaft and install the lower timing belt cover.

24. Continue reassembly of the timing belt covers as outlined previously in this section.

1988 VIN Code 5 Engine

▶ See Figures 113, 114 and 115

1. Remove the timing belt covers following procedures explained previously in this section.

2. Remove the timing belt guide from the crankshaft pulley.

3. Loosen the timing belt idler pulley, move it to the left (to take tension off the belt) and tighten its bolt.

4. Make matchmarks on the belt and all pulleys showing the exact placement of the belt. Mark an arrow on the belt showing its direction of rotation.

5. Carefully slip the timing belt off the pulleys.

❉❉WARNING

Do not disturb the position of the camshafts or the crankshaft during removal.

6. Remove the idler pulley bolt, pulley and return spring.

7. Remove the PCV hose and the valve covers.

8. Use an adjustable wrench to counterhold the camshaft. Be careful not to damage the cylinder head. Loosen the center bolt in each camshaft pulley and remove the pulley. Label the pulleys and keep them clean.

9. Check the timing belt carefully for any signs of cracking or deterioration. Pay particular attention to the area where each tooth or cog attaches to the backing of the belt. If the belt shows signs of damage, check the contact faces of the pulleys for possible burrs or scratches.

Fig. 110 Make sure the camshaft alignment mark shows through the small hole in the pulley — 1985-88 VIN Code 4 engine

Fig. 112 After the timing belt is reinstalled, always check for the correct tension. See text for correct procedure — 1985-88 VIN Code 4 engine

Fig. 111 The crankshaft and oil pump marks must be aligned before reinstalling the timing belt — 1985-88 VIN Code 4 engine

Fig. 113 Examples of matchmarks on timing belt and pulleys. Don't forget an arrow showing the direction of rotation. The belt will break if put on backwards — 1988 VIN Code 5 engine

10. Check the idler pulley by holding it in your hand and spinning it. It should rotate freely and quietly. Any sign of grinding or abnormal noise indicates replacement of the pulley.

11. Check the free length of the tension spring. Correct length is 43.5mm measured at the inside faces of the hooks. A spring which has stretched during use will not apply the correct tension to the pulley; replace the spring.

12. If you can test the tension of the spring, look for 22 lbs. of tension at 50mm of length. If in doubt, replace the spring.

13. Align the camshaft knock pin and the pulley. Reinstall the camshaft timing belt pulleys, making sure the pulley fits properly on the shaft and that the timing marks align correctly. Tighten the center bolt on each pulley to 34 ft. lbs. Be careful not to damage the cylinder head during installation.

14. Before reinstalling the belt, double check that the crank and camshafts are exactly in their correct positions. The alignment marks on the pulleys should align with the cast marks on the head and oil pump.

15. Reinstall the valve covers and the PCV hose.

16. Install the timing belt idler pulley and its tensioning spring. Move the idler to the left and temporarily tighten its bolt.

17. Carefully observing the matchmarks made earlier, install the timing belt onto the pulleys.

18. Slowly release tension on the idler pulley bolt and allow the idler to take up tension on the timing belt. DO NOT allow the idler to slam into the belt; the belt may become damaged.

19. Temporarily install the crankshaft pulley bolt. Turn the engine clockwise through 2 complete revolutions, stopping at TDC. Check that each pulley aligns with its marks.

20. Using tool J 23600-B or similar, check the tension of the timing belt at a point halfway between the 2 camshaft sprockets. The correct deflection is 4mm at 4.4 lbs. pressure. If the belt tension is incorrect, readjust it by repeating steps 19 and 20. If the tension is correct, tighten the idler pulley bolt to 27 ft. lbs.

21. Remove the crankshaft pulley bolt.

22. Install the timing belt guide onto the crankshaft timing pulley.

23. Reinstall the timing belt covers, following procedures outlined previously in this section.

1989-90 VIN Code 6 Engine 1991-92 VIN Code 5 Engine
▶ **See Figure 116**

1. Remove the timing belt covers using procedures described earlier in this section.

A MATCHMARK
B KNOCK PIN
26 EXHAUST CAMSHAFT TIMING PULLEY
27 INTAKE CAMSHAFT TIMING PULLEY

Fig. 114 Align the cam pulleys before installing the timing belt — 1988 VIN Code 5 engine

Fig. 115 Make certain all the timing marks (A) are aligned before timing belt is installed — 1988 VIN Code 5 engine

2. If not done as part of the cover removal, rotate the crankshaft clockwise to the TDC/compression position for No. 1 cylinder.

3. Loosen the timing belt idler pulley to relieve the tension on the belt, move the pulley away from the belt and temporarily tighten the bolt to hold it in the loose position.

4. Make matchmarks on the belt and both pulleys showing the exact placement of the belt. Mark an arrow on the belt showing its direction of rotation.

5. Carefully slip the timing belt off the pulleys.

✳✳WARNING

Do not disturb the position of the camshafts or the crankshaft during removal.

6. Remove the idler pulley bolt, pulley and return spring.

7. Use an adjustable wrench mounted on the flats of the camshaft to hold the cam from moving. Loosen the center bolt in the camshaft timing pulley and remove the pulley.

8. Check the timing belt carefully for any signs of cracking or deterioration. Pay particular attention to the area where each tooth or cog attaches to the backing of the belt. If the belt shows signs of damage, check the contact faces of the pulleys for possible burrs or scratches.

9. Check the idler pulley by holding it in your hand and spinning it. It should rotate freely and quietly. Any sign of grinding or abnormal noise indicates replacement of the pulley.

10. Check the free length of the tension spring. Correct length is 38.5mm measured at the inside faces of the hooks. A spring which has stretched during use will not apply the correct tension to the pulley; replace the spring.

11. If you can test the tension of the spring, look for 8.4 lbs. of tension at 50mm of length. If in doubt, replace the spring.

12. Reinstall the camshaft timing belt pulley, making sure the pulley fits properly on the shaft and that the timing marks align correctly. Tighten the center bolt to 43 ft. lbs.

13. Before reinstalling the belt, double check that the crank and camshafts are exactly in their correct positions. The alignment mark on the end of the camshaft bearing cap should show through the small hole in the camshaft pulley and the small mark on the crankshaft timing belt pulley should align with the mark on the oil pump.

14. Reinstall the timing belt idler pulley and the tension spring. Pry the pulley to the left as far as it will go and temporarily tighten the retaining bolt. This will hold the pulley in its loosest position.

15. Install the timing belt, observing the matchmarks made earlier. Make sure the belt is fully and squarely seated on the upper and lower pulleys.

16. Loosen the retaining bolt for the timing belt idler pulley and allow it to tension the belt.

17. Temporarily install the crankshaft pulley bolt and turn the crank clockwise 2 full revolutions from TDC to TDC. Insure that each timing mark realigns exactly.

18. Tighten the timing belt idler pulley retaining bolt to 27 ft. lbs.

19. Measure the timing belt deflection (Tool 23600 B or similar), looking for 5-6mm of deflection at 4.4 pounds of pressure. If the deflection is not correct, readjust the idler pulley by repeating steps 15 through 18.

20. Remove the bolt from the end of the crankshaft.

21. Install the timing belt guide onto the crankshaft and install the lower timing belt cover.

22. Continue reassembly of the timing belt covers as outlined previously in this section.

1990 VIN Code 5 Engine 1991-92 VIN Code 6 Engine

▶ **See Figure 117**

1. Remove the timing belt covers.
2. Remove the timing belt guide from the crankshaft pulley.
3. Loosen the timing belt idler pulley, move it to the left (to take tension off the belt) and tighten its bolt.
4. Make matchmarks on the belt and all pulleys showing the exact placement of the belt. Mark an arrow on the belt showing its direction of rotation.

Fig. 116 Correct alignment of the camshaft before reinstallation of the timing belt — 1989-90 VIN Code 6 engine and 1991-92 VIN Code 5 engine

5. Carefully slip the timing belt off the pulleys.

➡**Do not disturb the position of the camshafts or the crankshaft during removal.**

6. Remove the idler pulley bolt, pulley and return spring.
7. Remove the PCV hose and the valve covers.
8. Use an adjustable wrench to counter hold the camshaft. Be careful not to damage the cylinder head. Loosen the center bolt in each camshaft pulley and remove the pulley. Label the pulleys and keep them clean.
9. Check the timing belt carefully for any signs of cracking or deterioration. Pay particular attention to the area where each tooth or cog attaches to the backing of the belt. If the belt shows signs of damage, check the contact faces of the pulleys for possible burrs or scratches.
10. Check the idler pulley by holding it and spinning it. It should rotate freely and quietly. Any sign of grinding or abnormal noise indicates replacement of the pulley.
11. Check the free length of the tension spring. Correct length is 41.09mm measured at the inside faces of the hooks. A spring which has stretched during use will not apply the correct tension to the pulley; replace the spring.
12. Test the tension of the spring, look for 22 lbs. of tension at 50mm of length. If in doubt, replace the spring.

To install:

13. Align the camshaft knock pin and the pulley. Reinstall the camshaft timing belt pulleys, making sure the pulley fits properly on the shaft and that the timing marks align correctly. Tighten the center bolt on each pulley to 34 ft. lbs. (46 Nm). Be careful not to damage the cylinder head during installation.
14. Before reinstalling the belt, double check that the crank and camshafts are exactly in their correct positions. The alignment marks on the pulleys should align with the cast marks on the head and oil pump.
15. Reinstall the valve covers and the PCV hose.
16. Install the timing belt idler pulley and its tensioning spring. Move the idler to the left and temporarily tighten its bolt.
17. Carefully observing the matchmarks made earlier, install the timing belt onto the pulleys.
18. Slowly release tension on the idler pulley bolt and allow the idler to take up tension on the timing belt. Do not allow the idler to slam into the belt; the belt may become damaged.
19. Temporarily install the crankshaft pulley bolt. Turn the engine clockwise through 2 complete revolutions, stopping at TDC. Check that each pulley aligns with its marks.
20. Using tool J 23600-B or similar, check the tension of the timing belt at a point halfway between the 2 camshaft sprockets. The correct deflection is 4mm at 4.4 lbs. pressure. If the belt tension is incorrect, readjust it by repeating steps 19 and 20. If the tension is correct, tighten the idler pulley bolt to 27 ft. lbs. (37 Nm).
21. Remove the crankshaft pulley bolt.
22. Install the timing belt guide onto the crankshaft timing pulley.
23. Reinstall the timing belt covers, following procedures outlined previously in this section.

1993

▶ **See Figure 118**

1. Disconnect the negative battery cable.

A. Valve timing marks
1. Exhaust camshaft timing pulley
2. Intake camshaft timing pulley
3. Idler pulley
4. Crankshaft timing pulley
5. Timing belt

Fig. 117 Examples of matchmarks on timing belt and pulleys. Don't forget an arrow showing the direction of rotation. The belt will break if put on backwards — 1990 VIN Code 5 engine and 1991-92 VIN Code 6 engine

2. Remove 1 bolt, hose connector, electrical connector and windshield washer reservoir from the engine compartment.
3. Remove the cruise control actuator cover, if equipped.
4. Remove the cruise control electrical connector, if equipped.
5. Remove the cruise control cable, if equipped.
6. Remove the 3 bolts and cruise control actuator from the vehicle, if equipped.
7. Raise and support the vehicle safely.
8. Remove the right front wheel and tire assembly.
9. Remove the 10 bolts, 2 plastic clips and right-front wheelhousing.
10. Loosen the coolant pump pulley adjusting bolt, pivot bolt and lock bolt and remove the alternator/coolant pump drive belt.
11. Lower the vehicle.
12. Remove the air conditioning (A/C) compressor without disconnecting the hoses and relocate, if equipped.
13. Remove the 4 bolts and A/C compressor mounting bracket, if equipped.
14. Loosen the power steering pump pivot and lock bolts, if equipped.
15. Relocate the power steering pump toward the engine and remove the drive belt, if equipped.
16. Remove the following electrical connectors: alternator electrical connector, alternator lead wire and the oil pressure switch electrical connector.
17. Remove the 2 bolts and the engine wiring harness cover.
18. Remove the wiring harness from the cylinder head cover.

19. Remove the secondary (spark plug) wires.
20. Remove the spark plugs from the cylinder head.
21. Remove the 2 hose clamps and the positive crankcase ventilation (PCV) hoses from the cylinder head cover.
22. Remove the 4 cap nuts, the seal washers and the cylinder head cover with gasket from the cylinder head.
23. Turn the crankshaft to align the timing mark on crankshaft pulley at **O**, setting No. 1 cylinder at top dead center (TDC) of compression stroke. Check that the valve lifters on the No. 1 cylinder are loose. If not, turn crankshaft pulley 1 complete revolution (360 degrees).
24. Remove the engine ground wire from the right fender apron.
25. Install a J 28467-A.
26. Remove the engine mount.
27. Remove the 4 bolts and coolant pump pulley from coolant pump.
28. Remove the crankshaft pulley using a J 8614-01 and a J 1859-03.
29. Remove the 9 bolts and timing belt covers from the engine.
30. Slide the timing belt guide from crankshaft.
31. Set camshaft and crankshaft timing gears to align marks as indicated.

➡Do not turn crankshaft or camshaft independently after removal of timing belt. Binding or damage to engine components could result. If timing belt is to be reused, mark timing belt with arrow showing direction of engine revolution. Put matchmarks where timing belt meets with crankshaft timing gear and camshaft timing gear to ensure installation in the same position.

32. Remove the idler pulley bolt, idler pulley and tension spring.
33. Remove the timing belt from camshaft and crankshaft timing gears.

✳✳WARNING

Do not bend, twist or turn the timing belt inside out. Do not allow the belt to come in contact with oil, coolant or steam.

34. Remove the camshaft timing gear bolt while holding camshaft by the hexagonal wrench head section.

✳✳WARNING

Be careful not to damage the cylinder head when holding camshaft in place.

35. Remove crankshaft timing gear using 2 flat bladed screwdrivers to pry off.
To install:
36. Check the camshaft and crankshaft timing gears to align marks as indicated. Do not turn crankshaft or camshaft independently before installation of the timing belt.
37. Install the camshaft timing gear. Align the camshaft key with the groove on the gear and slide the gear on the camshaft; secure with the camshaft timing gear bolt. Hold the camshaft at hexagonal wrench head portion to prevent rotation

and tighten the camshaft timing gear bolt to 43 ft. lbs. (59 Nm).

➡**Inspect the camshaft timing gear to ensure mark is still aligned as indicated.**

38. Install the crankshaft timing gear. Align the crankshaft key with the groove on the gear and slide the gear on the crankshaft.

➡**Inspect the crankshaft timing gear to ensure mark is still aligned as indicated.**

39. Reinstall the timing belt idler pulley and the tension spring. Pry the pulley to the left as far as it will go and temporarily tighten the retaining bolt. This will hold the pulley in its loosest position.

40. Install the timing belt, observing the matchmarks made earlier. Make sure the belt is fully and squarely seated on the upper and lower pulleys.

41. Loosen the retaining bolt for the timing belt idler pulley and allow it to tension the belt.

42. Temporarily install the crankshaft pulley bolt and turn the crank clockwise 2 full revolutions from TDC to TDC. Insure that each timing mark realigns exactly.

43. Tighten the timing belt idler pulley retaining bolt to 27 ft. lbs.

44. Measure the timing belt deflection at the SIDE point, looking for 5-6mm of deflection at 4.4 pounds of pressure. If the deflection is not correct, readjust the idler pulley by repeating steps 15 through 18.

45. Install the timing belt guide, with the cup side facing outward, onto the crankshaft and install the timing belt covers from the lowest to the highest. Tighten the 9 cover bolts to 62 inch lbs. (7 Nm).

46. Install the crankshaft pulley to the crankshaft after aligning the pulley key with the slot on the pulley; secure with the 1 bolt while holding the crankshaft pulley with tool J 8614-01 or equivalent, and tighten the pulley bolt to 87 ft. lbs (118 Nm).

47. Install engine mount to body; secure with 4 bolts. Do not tighten fully.

48. Raise and safely support the vehicle.

49. Install the mounting bracket(s) to engine mount; secure with 1 bolt (2 if equipped with power steering) and 2 nuts.

50. Tighten the mounting bracket-to-engine mount bolt to 47 ft. lb. (64 Nm).

51. Tighten the mounting bracket-to-engine mount nuts to 38 ft. lb. (52 Nm).

52. Tighten the engine mount-to-body bolt 'A' to 19 ft. lb. (25 Nm).

53. Tighten the engine mount-to-body bolts 'B' to 19 ft. lb. (25 Nm).

54. Tighten the engine mount-to-body bolt 'C' to 19 ft. lb. (25 Nm), if equipped with cruise control.

55. Install right-side wheelhousing; secure with 10 bolts and 2 plastic clips.

56. Tighten the wheelhousing bolts to 11 ft. lb. (15 Nm).

57. Install the tire and wheel assembly.

58. Lower the vehicle.

59. Remove tool J 28467-A or its equivalent.

60. Install the A/C pipe bracket (2 pieces, if equipped, and secure with 1 bolt and 1 screw.

61. Tighten the A/C pipe bracket bolt to 89 inch lbs. (10 Nm).

62. Install the engine ground wire to the right fender apron.

63. Install the new cylinder head cover gasket to the cylinder head.

64. Install new seal washers to the cylinder head cover.

65. Install the cylinder head cover to the cylinder head; secure with 4 cap nuts.

66. Tighten the cylinder head cap nuts to 53 inch lbs. (6 Nm).

67. Install 2 PCV hoses to the cylinder head cover; secure with hose clamps.

68. Install the secondary (spark plug) wires and spark plugs.

69. Install engine wiring harness to the cylinder head cover.

70. Install the engine wiring harness cover; secure with 2 bolts.

71. Tighten the wiring harness cover bolts to 53 in. lb. (6 Nm).

72. Install the following electrical connectors: alternator electrical connector, alternator lead wire, and the oil pressure switch electrical connector.

73. Install the power steering pump, if equipped, and move back to original position.

74. Install the A/C compressor, if equipped, and move back to original position.

75. Adjust the power steering pump drive belt.

76. Adjust the A/C compressor drive belt.

77. Install the cruise control actuator, if equipped, and adjust.

78. Install the windshield washer reservoir to fender; secure with 1 bolt.

79. Tighten the windshield washer reservoir bolt to 53 in. lb. (6 Nm).

80. Install the hose connector and electrical connector to the windshield washer reservoir.

81. Install the negative (-) battery cable.

82. Tighten the negative (-) battery cable-to-negative (-) battery terminal retainer to 11 ft. lb. (15 Nm).

Fig. 118 Setting crankshaft and camshaft positions — 1993 engines

Camshaft and Bearings

REMOVAL & INSTALLATION

➡Camshaft end play (thrust clearance) must be checked before the cam is removed. Please refer to the 'Inspection' section for details of this check.

1985-88 VIN Code 4 Engine

▶ See Figures 119, 120 and 121

1. Remove the valve cover.
2. Drain the cooling system.

✳✳CAUTION

When draining the coolant, keep in mind that cats and dogs are attracted by the ethylene glycol antifreeze, and are quite likely to drink any that is left in an uncovered container or in puddles on the ground. This will prove fatal in sufficient quantity. Always drain the coolant into a sealable container. Coolant should be reused unless it is contaminated or several years old.

3. Loosen the water pump pulley bolts.
4. Remove the alternator belt.
5. Raise the vehicle and safely support it on jackstands.
6. Remove the power steering pivot bolt, if so equipped.
7. Remove the bolt which goes through both the upper and lower timing belt covers.
8. Lower the vehicle to the ground. Remove the power steering pump belt if so equipped.
9. Remove the water pump pulley.
10. Disconnect the upper radiator hose at the engine water outlet.
11. Label and disconnect vacuum hoses.
12. Remove the upper timing belt cover and its gasket.
13. At the distributor, label and disconnect the spark plug wires, the vacuum hoses and the electrical connections. Remove the distributor.
14. Disconnect the hoses at the fuel pump and remove the fuel pump.
15. Remove the distributor gear bolt.
16. Remove the rocker arm assembly.
17. Rotate the crankshaft clockwise and set the engine to TDC/compression on No. 1 cylinder. Make sure the rockers for cylinder No. 1 are loose. If not, rotate the crankshaft 1 full turn.
18. Matchmark and remove the timing belt from the camshaft pulley. Support the belt so that it doesn't change position on the crankshaft pulley.
19. Loosen the camshaft bearing cap bolts a little at a time and in the correct sequence. After removal, label each cap.

Fig. 119 Loosen and remove the bearing caps in this order — 1985-88 VIN Code 4 engine

20. Remove the camshaft oil seal (at the pulley end) and then remove the camshaft by lifting it straight out of its bearings.

✳✳WARNING

Although reasonable in weight, the cam is brittle in nature. Handle it gently and do not allow it to fall or hit objects. It may break into pieces.

To install:
21. When reinstalling, coat all the bearing journals with engine oil and place the camshaft in the cylinder head.
22. Place bearing caps Nos. 2, 3 and 4 on each journal with the arrows pointing towards the front of the engine.
23. Apply multi-purpose grease to the inside of the oil seal. and apply liquid sealer on the outer circumference of the oil seal.
24. Install the seal in position, being very careful to get it straight. Do not allow the seal to cock or move out of place during installation.
25. Install the bearing cap for bearing No. 1 and apply silicone sealant to the lower ends of the of the seal.
26. Tighten each bearing cap little at a time and in the correct sequence. Tighten the bolts to 9 ft. lbs.
27. Hold the camshaft with an adjustable wrench and tighten the drive gear to 22 ft. lbs.
28. Install the timing belt as previously outlined.
29. Install the rocker arm assembly.
30. Install the fuel pump with a new gasket and connect the hoses.

Fig. 120 Apply sealant to these points before reinstalling the Nova valve cover — 1985-88 VIN Code 4 engine

Fig. 121 Tighten the bearing caps in this order — 1985-88 VIN Code 4 engine

Fig. 122 Remove the camshaft bearing caps in this order — 1988 VIN Code 5 engine

31. Replace the distributor and connect its vacuum hoses, electrical connections and the spark plug wires.

32. Install the upper timing belt cover but don't install the bolt which holds both the upper and the lower covers yet.

33. Connect the vacuum hoses.

34. Connect the upper radiator hose to the water outlet.

35. Install the water pump pulley and tighten the bolts finger tight.

36. Install the power steering drive belt if so equipped.

37. Elevate the vehicle and safely support it on jackstands.

38. Install the bolt which connects the upper and lower timing belt covers.

39. Install the power steering pump pivot bolt and the belt; adjust the belt tension.

40. Lower the vehicle. Install the alternator belt and adjust it to the correct tension.

41. Tighten the water pump pulley bolts.

42. Refill the cooling system.

43. Install the valve cover with a new gasket.

1988 VIN Code 5, 1990 VIN Code 5 and 1991-92 VIN Code 6 Engines

▶ See Figures 122, 123, 124 and 125

1. Remove the valve covers and the timing belt cover following procedures outlined previously in this section.

2. Make certain the engine is set to TDC/compression on No. 1 cylinder. Remove the timing belt following procedures outlined earlier in this section.

3. Remove the crankshaft pulley if so desired.

4. Remove the camshaft timing belt pulleys.

5. Loosen and remove the camshaft bearing caps in the proper sequence. It it recommended that the bolts be loosened in 2 or 3 passes.

6. With the bearing caps removed, the camshaft(s) may be lifted clear of the head. If both cams are to be removed, label them clearly — they are not interchangeable.

❋❋WARNING

Although reasonable in weight, the cam is brittle in nature. Handle it gently and do not allow it to fall or hit objects. It may break into pieces.

To install:

7. When reinstalling, place the camshaft(s) in position on the head. The exhaust cam has the distributor drive gear on it. Observe the markings on the bearing caps and place them

according to their numbered positions. The arrow should point to the front of the engine.

8. Tighten the bearing cap bolts in the correct sequence and in 3 passes to a final tightness of 115 inch lbs. (13 Nm)

9. Position the camshafts so that the guide pins (knock pins) are in the proper position. This step is critical to the correct valve timing of the engine.

10. Install the camshaft timing pulleys and tighten the bolts to 34 ft. lbs. (47 Nm). Double check the positioning of the camshaft pulleys and the guide pin.

11. Double check the positioning of the camshaft pulleys and the guide pin.

12. Install the crankshaft pulley if it was removed. Tighten its bolt to 101 ft. lbs. and double check its position to be on TDC.

13. Install the timing belt and tensioner. Adjust the belt according to procedures outlined previously in this section.

14. Install the timing belt covers.

A   I = INTAKE   E = EXHAUST
B   I = INTAKE   E = EXHAUST
C   FRONT MARK
D   I.D. FOR BEARING
    NO. 2 THRU NO. 5

Fig. 123 Examples of markings on camshaft bearing caps. Note that the bearing on the right is for position No. 1 only — 1988 VIN Code 5 engine

Fig. 124 Tighten the bearing caps (intake and exhaust) in this order — 1988 VIN Code 5 engine

Fig. 125 Correct position of guide pins — 1988 VIN Code 5 engine

15. Install the valve covers.

1989-90 VIN Code 6 Engine 1991-92 VIN Code 5 Engine 1993 VIN Code 6 & 8 Engines

▶ **See Figures 126, 127, 128, 129, 130, 131 and 132**

1. Remove the valve cover.
2. Remove the timing belt covers.
3. Remove the timing belt and idler pulley following procedures outlined previously in this section.
4. Hold the exhaust camshaft with an adjustable wrench and remove the camshaft timing belt gear. Be careful not to damage the head or the camshaft during this work.
5. Gently turn the camshafts with an adjustable wrench until the service bolt hole in the intake camshaft end gear is straight up or in the '12 o'clock' position.

Fig. 126 Correct position of the service bolt hole before removal of the intake camshaft — 1989-90 VIN Code 6 engine, 1991-92 VIN Code 5 engine and all 1993 engines

Fig. 127 Alternately loosen the bolts for the No. 1 bearing cap on both the intake and exhaust camshafts — 1989-90 VIN Code 6 engine, 1991-92 VIN Code 5 engine and all 1993 engines

6. Alternately loosen the bearing cap bolts in the number 1 (closest to the pulleys) intake and exhaust bearing caps.
7. Attach the intake camshaft end gear to the sub gear with a service bolt. The service bolt should match the following specifications:
   • Thread diameter: 6.0mm
   • Thread pitch: 1.0mm
   • Bolt length: 16-20mm
8. Uniformly loosen each intake camshaft bearing cap bolt a little at a time and in the correct sequence.

✳✳WARNING

The camshaft must be held level while it is being removed. If the camshaft is not kept level, the portion of the cylinder head receiving the thrust may crack or become damaged. This in turn could cause the camshaft to bind or break. Before removing the intake camshaft, make sure the rotational force has been removed from the sub gear; that is, the gear should be in a neutral or 'unloaded' state.

9. Remove the bearing caps and remove the intake camshaft.

➡ **If the camshaft cannot be removed straight and level, retighten the No. 3 bearing cap. Alternately loosen the bolts on the bearing cap a little at a time while pulling upwards on the camshaft gear. DO NOT attempt to pry or force the cam loose with tools.**

10. With the intake camshaft removed, turn the exhaust camshaft approximately 105°, so that the guide pin in the end

Fig. 128 Always install a service bolt to lock the intake cam gears together — 1989-90 VIN Code 6 engine, 1991-92 VIN Code 5 engine and all 1993 engines

Fig. 129 Remove the camshaft bearing caps in this order. Intake cam shown, exhaust cam uses identical order — 1989-90 VIN Code 6 engine, 1991-92 VIN Code 5 engine and all 1993 engines

Fig. 131 Examples of bearing cap markings and position. Exhaust cam shown — 1989-90 VIN Code 6 engine, 1990 VIN Code 5 engine, 1991-92 VIN Code 5 engine and all 1993 engines

Fig. 132 Tighten the camshaft bearing cap bolts in this order. Exhaust cam shown, intake uses identical order — 1989-90 VIN Code 6 engine, 1991-92 VIN Code 5 engine and all 1993 engines

is just past the '5 o'clock' position. This puts equal loadings on the camshaft, allowing easier and safer removal.

11. Loosen the exhaust camshaft bearing cap bolts a little at a time and in the correct sequence.

12. Remove the bearing caps and remove the exhaust camshaft.

➡ If the camshaft cannot be removed straight and level, retighten the No. 3 bearing cap. Alternately loosen the bolts on the bearing cap a little at a time while pulling upwards on the camshaft gear. DO NOT attempt to pry or force the cam loose with tools.

To install:

13. When reinstalling, remember that the camshafts must be handled carefully and kept straight and level to avoid damage.

14. Place the exhaust camshaft on the cylinder head so that the cam lobes press evenly on the lifters for cylinders Nos. 1 and 3. This will put the guide pin in the 'just past 5 o'clock' position.

15. Place the bearing caps in position according to the number cast into the cap. The arrow should point towards the pulley end of the motor.

16. Tighten the bearing cap bolts gradually and in the proper sequence to 9.5 ft. lbs. (115 inch lbs.)

17. Apply multi-purpose grease, such as GM 1051344 or similar, to a new exhaust camshaft oil seal.

18. Install the exhaust camshaft oil seal using tool J 35403 or similar. Be very careful not to install the seal on a slant or allow it to tilt during installation.

19. Turn the exhaust cam until the cam lobes of No.4 cylinder press down on their lifters.

Fig. 130 Setting the exhaust cam guide pin to the 'just past 5'O'clock' position — 1989-90 VIN Code 6 engine, 1991-92 VIN Code 5 engine and all 1993 engines

20. Hold the intake camshaft next to the exhaust camshaft and engage the gears by matching the alignment marks on each gear.

21. Keeping the gears engaged, roll the intake camshaft down and into its bearing journals. This is tricky, but not hard to do. Take your time and pay close attention.

22. Place the bearing caps for Nos. 2, 3, 4 and 5 in position. Observe the numbers on each cap and make certain the arrows point to the pulley end of the motor.

23. Gradually tighten each bearing cap bolt in the same order as the exhaust camshaft bolts. Tighten each bolt to 9.5 ft. lbs. (115 inch lbs.)

24. Remove any retaining pins or bolts in the intake camshaft gears.

25. Install the number 1 bearing cap for the intake camshaft.

➡ If the No. 1 bearing cap does not fit properly, gently push the cam gear towards the rear of the engine by levering between the gear and the head.

26. Turn the exhaust camshaft 1 full revolution from TDC/compression on No.1 cylinder to the same position. Check that the mark on the exhaust camshaft gear matches exactly with the mark on the intake camshaft gear.

27. Counterhold the exhaust camshaft and install the timing belt pulley. Tighten the bolt to 43 ft. lbs.

28. Double check both the crankshaft and camshaft positions, insuring that they are both set to TDC/compression for No. 1 cylinder.

29. Install the timing belt following procedures outlined previously in this section.

30. Install the timing belt covers and the valve cover.

INSPECTION AND MEASUREMENT

▶ See Figures 133, 134, 135 and 136

The end-play or thrust clearance of the camshaft(s) must be measured with the camshaft installed in the head. It may be checked before removal or after reinstallation. To check the end-play, mount a dial indicator accurate to ten one-thousandths (4 decimal places) on the end of the block, so that the tip bears on the end of the camshaft. (The timing belt must be removed. On some motors, it will be necessary to remove the pulleys for unobstructed access to the camshaft.) Set the scale on the dial indicator to zero. Using a screwdriver or similar tool, gently lever the camshaft fore-and-aft in its mounts. Record the amount of deflection shown on the gauge and compare this number to the Camshaft Specifications Chart at the beginning of this section.

Excessive end-play may indicate either a worn camshaft or a worn head; the worn cam is most likely and much cheaper to replace. Chances are good that if the cam is worn in this dimension (axial), substantial wear will show up in other measurements.

Mount the cam in V-blocks and set the dial indicator up on the round center journal. Zero the dial and rotate the camshaft. The circular runout should not exceed 0.06mm on the 1985-88 VIN Code 4 engine or 0.04mm on all others. Excess runout means the cam must be replaced.

Using a micrometer or Vernier caliper, measure the diameter of all the journals and the height of all the lobes. Record the readings and compare them to the Camshaft Specifications Chart in the beginning of this section. Any measurement beyond the stated limits indicates wear and the camshaft must be replaced.

Lobe wear is generally accompanied by scoring or visible metal damage on the lobes. Overhead camshaft engines are very sensitive to proper lubrication with clean, fresh oil. A worn cam may be your report card for poor maintenance intervals and late oil changes.

If a new cam is required on the 1985-88 VIN Code 4 engine, order new rockers to accompany it so that there are 2 new surfaces in contact. On the twin-cam motors, a new cam will require readjusting the valves, so new shims are in order. If, by coincidence, one valve measures out the same as before, replace the present shim with a new one to get 2 new surfaces in contact.

The clearance between the camshaft and its journals (bearings) must also be measured. Clean the camshaft, the

Fig. 133 Checking camshaft end play. GM tool number shown

Fig. 134 Use a dial indicator to check the run-out (eccentricity of the center camshaft bearing

Fig. 135 Use a micrometer to check the camshaft journal diameter

Fig. 136 Measure the height of each camshaft lobe. Wear may be caused by infrequent oil changes

journals and the bearing caps of any remaining oil and place the camshaft in position on the head. Lay a piece of compressible gauging material (Plastigage® or similar) on top of each journal on the cam.

Install the bearing caps in their correct order with the arrows pointing towards the front (pulley end) of the motor. Install the bearing cap bolts and tighten them in 3 passes to the correct tightness of 9 ft. lbs.

✳✳WARNING

Do not turn the camshaft with the gauging material installed.

Remove the bearing caps (in the correct order) and measure the gauging material at its widest point by comparing it to the scale provided with the package. Compare these measurements to the Camshaft Specifications Chart at the beginning of this section. Any measurement beyond specifications indicates wear. If you have already measured the cam (or replaced it) and determined it to be usable, excess bearing clearance indicates the need for a new head due to wear of the journals.

Remove the camshaft from the head and remove all traces of the gauging material. Check carefully for any small pieces clinging to contact faces.

Pistons and Connecting Rods

REMOVAL & INSTALLATION

All Engines

▶ **See Figures 137, 138, 139, 140, 141, 142 and 143**

➡**These procedures may be performed with the engine in the car. If additional overhaul work is to be performed, it will be easier if the engine is removed and mounted on an engine stand. Most stands allow the block to be rotated, giving easy access to both the top and bottom. These procedures require certain hand tools which may not be in your tool box. A cylinder ridge reamer, a numbered punch set, piston ring expander, snap-ring tools and piston installation tool (ring compressor) are all necessary for correct piston and rod repair. These tools are commonly available from retail tool suppliers; you may be able to rent them from larger automotive supply houses.**

1. Remove the cylinder head.
2. Elevate and safely support the vehicle on jackstands.
3. Drain the engine oil

❋❋CAUTION

Used motor oil may cause skin cancer if repeatedly left in contact with the skin for prolonged periods. Although this is unlikely unless you handle oil on a daily basis, it is wise to thoroughly wash your hands with soap and water immediately after handling used motor oil.

4. Remove any splash shield or rock guards which are in the way and remove the oil pan.
5. Using a numbered punch set, mark the cylinder number on each piston rod and bearing cap. Do this BEFORE loosening any bolts.
6. Loosen and remove the rod cap nuts and the rod caps. It will probably be necessary to tap the caps loose; do so with a small plastic mallet or other soft-faced tool. Keep the bearing insert with the cap when it is removed.
7. Use short pieces of hose to cover the bolt threads; this protects the bolt, the crankshaft and the cylinder walls during removal.
8. One piston will be at the lowest point in its cylinder. Cover the top of this piston with a rag. Examine the top area of the cylinder with your fingers, looking for a noticeable ridge around the cylinder. If any ridge is felt, it must be carefully

removed by using the ridge reamer. Work with extreme care to avoid cutting too deeply. When the ridge is removed, carefully remove the rag and ALL the shavings from the cylinder. No metal cuttings may remain in the cylinder or the wall will be damaged when the piston is removed. A small magnet can be helpful in removing the fine shavings.

9. After the cylinder is de-ridged, squirt a liberal coating of engine oil onto the cylinder walls until evenly coated. Carefully push the piston and rod assembly upwards from the bottom by using a wooden hammer handle on the bottom of the connecting rod.

10. The next lowest piston should be gently pushed downwards from above. This will cause the crankshaft to turn and relocate the other pistons as well. When the piston is in its lowest position, repeat Steps 8 and 9. Repeat the procedure for each of the remaining pistons.

11. When all the pistons are removed, clean the block and cylinder walls thoroughly with solvent. This makes a tremendous mess under the engine — use a large drain pan to collect the drippings.

12. When ready for reassembly, remember that all the pistons, rods and caps must be reinstalled in the correct cylinder. Make certain that all labels and stamped numbers are present and legible. Double check the piston rings; make certain that the ring gaps DO NOT line up, but are evenly spaced around the piston at about 120° intervals. Double check the bearing insert at the bottom of the rod for proper mounting. Reinstall the protective rubber hose pieces on the bolts.

13. Liberally coat the cylinder walls and the crankshaft journals with clean, fresh engine oil. Also apply oil to the bearing surfaces on the connecting rod and the cap.

14. Identify the 'Front' mark on each piston and rod and position the piston loosely in its cylinder with the marks facing the front (pulley end) of the motor.

❋❋WARNING

Failure to observe the 'Front' marking and its correct placement can lead to sudden and catastrophic engine failure.

15. Install the ring compressor (piston installation tool) around one piston and tighten it gently until the rings are compressed almost completely.

16. Gently push down on the piston top with a wooden hammer handle or similar soft-faced tool and drive the piston into the cylinder bore. Once all 3 rings are within the bore, the piston will move with some ease.

❋❋WARNING

If any resistance or binding is encountered during the installation, DO NOT apply force. Tighten or adjust the ring compressor and/or reposition the piston. Brute force will break the ring(s) or damage the piston.

17. From underneath, pull the connecting rod into place on the crankshaft. Remove the rubber hoses from the bolts. Check the rod cap to confirm that the bearing is present and correctly mounted, then install the rod cap (observing the correct number and position) and its nuts. Leaving the nuts

1. Cylinder block
2. Connecting rod and piston
3. Piston ring
4. Rear oil seal retainer and gasket
5. Rear end plate
6. Rear oil seal
7. Connecting rod bearing
8. Crankshaft
9. Crankshaft bearing cap
10. Crankshaft thrust bearing
11. Crankshaft main bearing
12. Flywheel

Fig. 137 Component detail of the cylinder block assembly — 1985-88 VIN Code 4 engine

finger tight will make installation of the remaining pistons and rods easier.

18. Assemble the remaining pistons in the same fashion, as listed above.

19. With all the pistons installed and the bearing caps secured finger tight, the retaining nuts may be tightened to their final setting. For each pair of nuts, make 3 passes alternating between the 2 nuts on any given rod cap. The 3 tightening steps should be to 12, 24 and 36 ft. lbs. The intent is to draw each cap up to the crank straight and under even pressure at the nuts.

20. Turn the crankshaft through several clockwise rotations, making sure everything moves smoothly and there is no binding. With the piston rods connected, the crank may be stiff to turn — try to turn it in a smooth continuous motion so that any binding or stiff spots may be felt.

21. Reinstall the oil pan. Even if the engine is to remain apart for other repairs, install the oil pan to protect the bottom end and tighten the bolts to the correct specification — this eliminates one easily overlooked mistake during future reassembly.

22. If the engine is to remain apart for other repairs, pack the cylinders with crumpled newspaper or clean rags (to keep out dust and grit) and cover the top of the motor with a large rag. If the engine is on a stand, the whole block can be protected with a large plastic trash bag.

23. If no further work is to be performed, continue reassembly by installing the head, timing belt, etc.

24. When the engine is restarted after reassembly, the exhaust will be very smoky as the oil within the cylinders burns off. This is normal; the smoke should clear quickly during warm up. Depending on the condition of the spark

1. Piston rings
2. Piston
3. Piston pin
4. Snapring
5. Bushing
6. Connecting rod
7. Rod cap
8. Gasket
9. Rear oil seal retainer
10. Rear oil seal
11. Rear end plate
12. Flywheel
13. Connecting rod bearing
14. Crankshaft bearing
15. Crankshaft thrust washer
16. Crankshaft bearing cap
17. Crankshaft
18. Cylinder block

Fig. 138 Component detail of the block assembly — 1988 VIN Code 5 engine, 1990 VIN Code 5 Engine and 1991-92 VIN Code 6 engine

Fig. 139 Use a numbered punch to identify both parts of each connecting rod with its cylinder number

Fig. 140 Use lengths of vacuum hose or rubber tubing to protect the crankshaft journals and cylinder walls during piston installation

Fig. 141 Cylinder ridge

Fig. 142 Push the piston out with a hammer handle

Fig. 143 Install the piston using a ring compressor

plugs, it may be wise to check for any oil fouling after the engine is shut off.

CLEANING AND INSPECTION

▶ See Figures 144, 145, 146, 147, 148, 149 and 150

Pistons

With the pistons removed from the engine, use a ring removing tool (ring expander) to remove the rings. Keep the rings labeled and stored by piston number. Clearly label the pistons by number so that they do not get interchanged.

Fig. 144 Removing the piston rings with a ring expander

Clean the carbon from the piston top and sides with a stiff bristle brush and cleaning solvent. Do not use a wire brush for cleaning.

❊❊CAUTION

Wear goggles during this cleaning; the solvent is very strong and can cause eye damage.

Clean the ring grooves (lands) either with a specially designed tool or with a piece of a broken piston ring. Remove all the carbon from the grooves and make sure that the groove shape (profile) is square all the way around the piston. When all the lands have been cleaned, again bathe the piston in solvent and clean the lands with the bristle brush.

Before any measurements are begun, visually examine the piston (a magnifying glass can be handy) for any signs of cracks — particularly in the skirt area — or scratches in the metal. Anything other than light surface scoring disqualifies the piston from further use. The metal will become unevenly heated and the piston may break apart during use.

Hold the piston and rod upright and attempt to move the piston back and forth along the piston pin (wrist pin). There should be NO motion in this axis. If there is, replace the piston and wrist pin.

Accurately measure the cylinder bore diameter in 2 dimensions (thrust and axial, or if you prefer, left-right and fore-aft) and in 3 locations (upper, middle and bottom) within the cylinder. That's 6 measurements in each bore; record them in order. Normal measurements for all Nova and Prizm engines are:
- New: 81.0-81.03mm
- Max Wear limit: 81.23mm

Having recorded the bore measurements, now measure the piston diameter. Do this with a micrometer at right angles to the piston pin. The location at which the piston is measured varies by engine type:
- 1985-88 VIN Code 4 engine: Measure at a point 5mm from lower edge of the oil ring groove.
- 1988 VIN Code 5, 1990 VIN Code 5 and 1991- VIN Code 6 engine: Measure at a point 42mm from the longest part of the piston skirt.

Fig. 145 The ring grooves can be cleaned and decarboned with a special tool

Fig. 147 Checking the cylinder bore requires six measurements - 3 locations and two dimensions-in each cylinder

Fig. 146 A piece of broken ring serves well to clean piston grooves

Fig. 148 Measuring the piston diameter — 1985-88 VIN Code 4 engine

Fig. 149 Measuring the piston diameter. 42mm=1.65 in. — 1988 VIN Code 5, 1990 VIN Code 5 and 1991-92 VIN Code 6 engine

A. 38.5 mm (1.5")
1. Micrometer
2. Piston hole center line

Fig. 150 Measuring the piston diameter — 1989-90 VIN Code 6 engine and 1991-92 VIN Code 5 engine

• 1989-90 VIN Code engine and 1991- VIN Code 5 engine: Measure at a point 38.5mm from the longest part of the piston skirt.Record each measurement for each piston.

• 1993 VIN Code 6 and 8 engine: Measure at a the piston grading level with and perpendicular with the piston pin. The measurement should be 0.925 in. (23 mm) from top

The piston-to-cylinder wall clearance (sometimes called oil clearance) is determined by subtracting the piston diameter from the measured diameter of its respective cylinder. The difference will be in thousandths or ten-thousandths of an inch. Compare this number to the Piston and Ring Specifications Chart at the beginning of this section. Excess clearance may indicate the need for either new pistons or block reboring.

Connecting Rods

The connecting rods must be free from wear, cracking and bending. Visually examine the rod, particularly at its upper and lower ends. Look for any sign of metal stretching or wear. The piston pin should fit cleanly and tightly through the upper end, allowing no side-play or wobble. The bottom end should also be an exact ½ circle, with no deformity of shape. The bolts must be firmly mounted and parallel.

The rods may be taken to a machine shop for exact measurement of twist or bend. This is generally easier and cheaper than purchasing a seldom used rod-alignment tool.

Piston Pin (Wrist Pin)

REPLACEMENT

▶ See Figures 151, 152 and 153

➡The piston and pin are a matched set and must be kept together. Label everything and store parts in identified containers.

1. Remove the pistons from the engine and remove the rings from the pistons.
2. Remove the snapring at the ends of the piston pin. This may be done with either snapring pliers or needle-nosed pliers; don't try to lever it out with a screwdriver.
3. Support the piston and rod on its side in a press. Make certain the piston is square to the motion of the press and that the rod is completely supported with blocks. Leave open space below the piston for the pin to emerge.
4. Line up the press and insert a brass rod of the same or slightly smaller diameter as the piston pin. It is important that the rod press evenly on the entire face of the pin, but not on the piston itself.
5. Using smooth and controlled motion, press the pin free of the piston. Do not use sudden or jerky motions; the piston may crack.
6. When reassembling, identify the front of the piston by its small dot or cavity on the top. Identify the front of the piston rod by the small mark cast into one face of the rod. Make sure the marks on the piston and rod are both facing the same direction. Also insure that the correct piston pin is to be reinstalled — they are not interchangeable.
7. For the all engines except 1988 VIN Code 5 engine, install 1 snapring in the piston and insert the piston under the press with the snap-ring down. Position the rod and support it. Coat the piston pin with clean oil and press it into place, using the same press set-up as removal. The piston pin will bottom onto the snap-ring; don't force it beyond the stopping point. Install the other snapring to lock the pin in place.
8. For the 1988 VIN Code 5 engine, install 1 snapring. Place the piston in water and gradually heat the water to the boiling point. DO NOT drop the piston into already hot water. The minimum required temperature is 176°F (80°C); a little hotter makes it a little easier. This will expand the piston so that the pin will fit smoothly. While the water is heating, apply

Fig. 151 Remove the circlip

Fig. 152 Align the piston and connecting rod 'front' marks before reassembly

a coat of clean oil to the piston pin and have the pin at hand when the piston is removed from the water.

✳✳CAUTION

You are dealing with hot metal and boiling water. Tongs, thick heat-resistant gloves and towels are required.

Remove the piston from the boiling water (carefully!) and hold it with gloves or several towels. Making sure the front marks align on the piston and connecting rod, hold the rod in position and press the piston pin into place with your thumb. The pin will bottom against the snapring. Allow the piston to air cool and when it is cool to the touch, install the other snapring. Check that the piston rocks freely on its pin without binding.

PISTON RING REPLACEMENT

▶ See Figures 154, 155 and 156

➡Although a piston ring can be reused if in good condition and carefully removed, it is recommended that the rings be replaced with new ones any time they are removed from the pistons.

A piston ring expander is necessary for removing piston rings without damaging them; any other method (screwdriver blades, pliers, etc.) usually results in the rings becoming bent, scratched or broken. When the rings are removed, clean the grooves thoroughly with a bristle brush and solvent. Make sure that all traces of carbon and varnish are removed.

✳✳WARNING

Wear goggles during this cleaning; the solvent is very strong and can cause eye damage. Do not use a wire brush or a caustic solvent on the pistons.

Check the piston condition and diameter following procedures outlined earlier in this section. Piston ring end gap should be checked when the rings are removed from the pistons. Incorrect end gap indicates that the wrong size rings are being used; ring breakage could occur.

Squirt some clean oil into the cylinder so that the top 2 or 3 inches of the wall is covered. Gently compress one of the rings to be used and insert it into the cylinder. Use and upside-down piston and push the ring down about an inch below the top of the cylinder. Using the piston to push the ring keeps the ring square in the cylinder; if it gets crooked, the next measurement may be inaccurate.

Using a feeler gauge, measure the end gap in the ring and compare it to the Piston and Ring Specifications chart at the beginning of this section. If the gap is excessive, either the ring is incorrect or the cylinder walls are worn beyond acceptable limits. If the measurement is too tight, the ends of the ring may be filed to enlarge the gap after the ring is removed form the cylinder. If filing is needed, make certain that the ends are kept square and that a fine file is used.

Check the pistons to see that the ring grooves and oil return holes have been properly cleaned. Slide each piston ring into its groove and check the side clearance with a feeler gauge. Make sure you insert the feeler gauge between the ring and its lower edge; any wear that develops forms a step at the inner portion of the lower land. If the piston grooves have worn to the extent that fairly high steps exist on the lower land, the piston must be replaced. Rings are not sold in oversize thicknesses to compensate for ring groove wear.

Using the ring expander, install the rings on the piston, **lowest ring first**. There is a high risk of ring breakage or piston damage if the rings are installed by hand or without the expander. The correct spacing of the ring end gaps is critical to oil control. No 2 gaps should align, they should be evenly spaced around the piston with the gap in the oil ring expander facing the front of the piston (aligned with the mark on the top of the piston). Once the rings are installed, the pistons must be handled carefully and protected from dirt and impact.

Fig. 153 The piston must be heated to install the piston pin. At 176 degrees F, the pin should push in with thumb pressure — 1988 VIN Code 5 engine

Fig. 154 Checking the piston ring end gap

Fig. 155 Checking the piston ring side clearance

Fig. 156 Piston ring positioning

CONNECTING ROD BEARING REPLACEMENT

▶ **See Figures 157, 158, 159 and 160**

Connecting rod bearings on all Nova and Prizm engines consist of 2 halves or shells which are not interchangeable in the rod and cap. When the shells are in position, the ends extend slightly beyond the rod and cap surfaces so that when the bolts are tightened, the shells will be clamped tightly in place. This insures a positive seating and prevents turning. A small tang holds the shells in place within the cap and rod housings.

➡**The ends of the bearing shells must never be filed flush with the mating surface of the rod or cap.**

Fig. 157 Examples of upper and lower bearing shells. Note the position of the oil hole

If a rod becomes noisy or is worn so that its clearance on the crankshaft is sloppy, a new bearing of the correct undersize must be selected and installed. There is no provision for adjustment. Under no circumstances should the rod end or cap be filed to compensate for wear, nor should shims of any type be used.

Inspect the rod bearings while the rods are out of the engine. If the shells are scored or show flaking they should be replaced. ANY scoring or ridge on the crankshaft means the crankshaft must be replaced. Because of the metallurgy in the crankshaft, welding and/or regrinding the crankshaft is not recommended. The bearing faces of the crank may not be restored to their original condition causing premature bearing wear and possible failure.

Replacement bearings are available in 3 standard sizes marked either '1', '2' or '3' on the bearing shell and possibly on the rod cap. Do not confuse the mark on the bearing cap with the cylinder number. It is quite possible that No. 3 piston rod contains a number 1 size bearing. The rod cap may have a '1' marked on it. (You should have stamped a 3 or other identifying code on both halves of the rod before disassembly.)

Measuring the clearance between the connecting rod bearings and the crankshaft (oil clearance) is done with a plastic measuring material such as Plastigage® or similar product.

1. Remove the rod cap with the bearing shell. Completely clean the cap, bearing shells and the journal on the crankshaft. Blow any oil from the oil hole in the crank. The plastic measuring material is soluble in oil and will begin to dissolve if the area is not totally free of oil.

Fig. 158 Look for the manufacturer's codes to identify standard bearing sizes. Don't confuse the number on the rod end cap with its position (cylinder) number

2. Place a piece of the measuring material lengthwise along the bottom center of the lower bearing shell. Install the cap and shell and tighten the bolts in 3 passes to 36 ft. lbs.

➡**Do not turn the crankshaft with the measuring material installed.**

3. Remove the bearing cap with the shell. The flattened plastic material will be found sticking to either the bearing shell or the crank journal. DO NOT remove it yet.

4. Use the scale printed on the packaging for the measuring material to measure the flattened plastic at its widest point. The number within the scale which is closest to the width of the plastic indicates the bearing clearance in thousandths of an inch.

5. Check the specifications chart in the beginning of this section for the proper clearance. If there is any measurement is approaching the maximum acceptable value, replace the bearing.

6. When the correct bearing is determined, clean off the gauging material, oil the bearing thoroughly on its working face and install it in the cap. Install the other half of the bearing into the rod end and attach the cap to the rod. Tighten the nuts evenly, in 3 passes to 36 ft. lbs.

7. With the proper bearing installed and the nuts properly tightened, it should be possible to move the connecting rod back and forth a bit on the crankshaft. If the rod cannot be moved, either the bearing is too small or the rod is misaligned.

Fig. 159 Plastic measuring material installed on the lower bearing shell

Fig. 160 Measure the compressed plastic to determine the bearing clearance

Rear Main Seal

REMOVAL & INSTALLATION

All Models
▶ **See Figures 161, 162 and 163**

1. Remove the transaxle from the vehicle. Follow procedures outlined in Section 7.

2. If equipped with a manual transaxle, perform the following procedures:

  a. Matchmark the pressure plate and flywheel.

  b. Remove the pressure plate-to-flywheel bolts and the clutch assembly from the vehicle.

  c. Remove the flywheel-to-crankshaft bolts and the flywheel. The flywheel is a moderately heavy component. Handle it carefully and protect it on the workbench.

3. If equipped with an automatic transaxle, perform the following procedures:

  a. Matchmark the flywheel (flexplate or driveplate) and crankshaft.

  b. Remove the torque converter drive plate-to-crankshaft bolts and the torque converter drive plate.

4. Remove the bolts holding the rear end plate to the engine and the remove the rear end plate.

5. Remove the rear oil seal retainer-to-engine bolts, rear oil seal retainer to oil pan bolts and the rear oil seal retainer.

6. Using a small pry bar, pry the rear oil seal retainer from the mating surfaces.

7. Using a drive punch or a hammer and small screwdriver, drive the oil seal from the rear bearing retainer.

8. Using a putty knife, clean the gasket mounting surfaces. Make certain that the contact surfaces are completely free of oil and foreign matter.

➡**When removing the rear oil seal, be careful not to damage the seal mounting surface.**

9. Clean the oil seal mounting surface.

10. Using multi-purpose grease, lubricate the new seal lips.

11. Using a seal installation tool such as J-35388 or similar, tap the seal straight into the bore of the retainer.

12. Position a new gasket on the retainer and coat it lightly with gasket sealer. Fit the seal retainer into place on the motor; be careful when installing the oil seal over the crankshaft.

Fig. 161 Removing the rear oil seal retainer

1. Hammer
2. Screwdriver
3. Rear main oil seal

Fig. 162 Removing the rear main oil seal from the retainer. Note the supports under the housing

J 35388

Fig. 163 Installing the new rear main seal using GM tool

Fig. 164 Use a dial indicator to measure crankshaft end play

Fig. 165 Remove the main bearing cap bolts in this order

Fig. 166 Keep all the pieces in numbered order. Exact reassembly is required

13. Install the 6 retaining bolts and tighten them to 84 inch lbs. (9.5 Nm) for 1985-90 models and 89 inch lbs. (10 Nm) for 1991-93 models.

14. Install the rear end plate. Tighten its bolts to 89 inch lbs.(10 Nm).

15. Reinstall either the flexplate (automatic) or the flywheel (manual), carefully observing the matchmarks made earlier. Tighten the flexplate bolts to 47 ft. lbs. or the flywheel bolts to 58 ft. lbs.

16. Install either the torque converter (automatic) or the clutch disc and pressure plate (manual).

17. Reinstall the transaxle, following procedures outlined in Section 7.

Crankshaft and Main Bearings

REMOVAL & INSTALLATION

▶ **See Figures 164, 165, 166, 167 and 168**

1. Remove the engine assembly from the car, following procedures outlined earlier in this section. Mount the engine securely on a stand which allows it to be rotated.

2. Remove the timing belt and tensioner assemblies.

3. Turn the engine upside down on the stand. Remove the oil pan and the oil strainer.

4. Remove the oil pump.

5. Remove either the clutch and pressure plate (manual transmission).

6. Remove either the flywheel (manual) or the drive plate (automatic).

7. Remove the rear end plate.

8. Remove the rear oil seal retainer.

9. Using a numbered punch set, mark each connecting rod cap with its correct cylinder number. Remove the rod caps and their bearings; keep the bearings with their respective caps.

10. Measure the crankshaft end-play (thrust clearance) before removing the crank. Attach a dial indicator, such as J 8001 or similar, to the end of the block and set the tip to bear on the front end of the crankshaft. With a screw driver, gently move the crankshaft back and forth and record the reading shown on the dial.
   - Standard end-play, NEW: 0.02mm
   - Acceptable end-play: 1985-88 VIN Code 4: 0.020-0.185mm, All others: 0.02-0.22mm
   - Maximum allowable: 0.3mm

If the end-play is excessive, the thrust washers will need to be replaced as a set.

11. Gradually loosen and remove the main bearing cap bolts in 3 passes and in the correct order. Remove just the bolts, leaving the caps in place.

12. When all the bolts are removed, use 2 bolts placed in the No. 3 bearing cap to wiggle the cap back and forth. This will loosen the cap and allow it and the thrust washers to be removed. Note and/or label the thrust washers as to their placement and position. If they are to be reused, they must be reinstalled exactly as they were.

13. Remove the remaining caps. Keep the caps in order and keep the bearing shell with its respective cap.

14. Lift the crankshaft out of the block. The crankshaft is a moderately heavy component.

15. Remove the upper bearing shells from the block and place them in order with the corresponding bearing caps.

16. Check and measure the crankshaft and bearings according to the procedures give in 'Cleaning and Inspection' later in this section.

17. When reassembling, clean the bearing caps and journals in the block thoroughly. Coat the bearings with a liberal application of clean motor oil.

18. Fit the upper bearings halves into the block and position the lower bearing halves in the bearing caps.

19. Place the crankshaft into the engine block, making sure it fits exactly into its mounts.

20. Install the upper thrust washers on the center main bearing with the oil grooves facing outward.

21. Install the main bearing caps and the lower thrust washers in the proper sequence. Make sure the arrows on the caps point towards the front (pulley end) of the motor.

22. Tighten the cap bolts in 3 passes and in the correct sequence to 44 ft. lbs.

23. Double check the end-play of the crank by repeating Step 10 of this procedure.

24. Turn the crankshaft through 1 or 2 full clockwise rotations, making sure that it turns smoothly and evenly with no binding.

25. Attach the piston rods, following procedures given earlier in this section. Remember that the rod caps must be reinstalled in their original positions.

26. Install a new rear main oil seal into the retainer and install the retainer onto the block. Tighten the bolts to 7.0 ft. lbs. (84 inch lbs.).

27. Install the rear end plate on the engine.

28. Install either the driveplate (automatic) or the flywheel (manual), observing the matchmarks made during removal.

29. If equipped with a manual transmission, reinstall the clutch disc and pressure plate.

30. Install the oil pump.

31. Install the oil strainer and oil pan, using new gaskets.

32. Rotate the engine into its upright position and continue reassembly of the timing belt, idler pulley and covers.

33. Reinstall the engine in the car, following procedures outlined earlier in this section.

Fig. 167 Correct position of the upper thrust washer when reinstalling

Fig. 168 Install and tighten the main bearing cap bolts in this order

CLEANING AND INSPECTION

▶ **See Figures 169, 170, 171, 172 and 173**

With the crankshaft removed from the engine, clean the crank, bearings and block areas thoroughly. Visually inspect each crankshaft section for any sign of wear or damage, paying close attention to the main bearing journals. ANY scoring or ridge on the crankshaft means the crankshaft must be replaced. Because of the metallurgy in the crankshaft, welding and/or regrinding the crankshaft is not recommended. The bearing faces of the crank may not be restored to their original condition causing premature bearing wear and possible failure.

Mount the crankshaft on V-blocks and set a dial indicator to bear on the center main journal. Slowly rotate the crank and record the circular runout as shown on the dial. Runout in excess of 0.06mm disqualifies the crankshaft from further use. It must be replaced.

Using a micrometer, measure the diameter of each journal on the crankshaft and record the measurements. The acceptable specifications for both connecting rod and main journals are found in the Crankshaft and Connecting Rod specifications chart at the beginning of this section. If ANY journal is beyond the acceptable range, the crank must be replaced.

Additionally, each journal must be measured at both outer edges. When one measurement is subtracted from the other, the difference is the measurement of journal taper. Any taper beyond 0.2mm is a sign of excess wear on the journal; the crankshaft must be replaced.

BEARING REPLACEMENT

1. With the engine out of the car and inverted on a stand, remove the main bearing caps in the correct sequence, following procedures given earlier in this section.

2. Once the bearing caps are removed, the lower bearing shell may be inspected. Check closely for scoring or abrasion of the bearing surface. If this lower bearing is worn or damaged, both the upper and lower half should be replaced.

➡**Always replace bearing shells in complete pairs.**

3. If the lower bearing half is in good condition, the upper shell may also be considered usable.

Fig. 169 Measuring crankshaft run-out

4. The bearing shells, the crank throws and the flat surface of the engine block (on the oil pan face) are stamped with numbers (1 through 5) indicating the standard bearing size. This size is determined during the initial manufacturing and assembly process; replacement bearings must be of the same code (thickness) if the correct clearances are to be maintained. If the code on the bearing shell is unreadable, use the number on the block and the number on the crank throw to determine the bearing code. Refer to the proper selection chart to find the correct bearing for that position.

5. Lift the crankshaft from the engine block and remove the upper bearing shells. Clean the area thoroughly, allow the surfaces to air dry and coat all the journals with a liberal coating of clean engine oil.

Fig. 170 Measure each journal at its outer points to determine taper

Fig. 171 Location of main bearing codes

Cylinder Block No.	1	2	3	1	2	3	1	2	3
Crankshaft No.	0	0	0	1	1	1	2	2	2
Bearing No.	1	2	3	2	3	4	3	4	5

Example: Block mark
"2", crankshaft mark
"1" = bearing "3"

Fig. 172 Main bearing selection table — 1985-88 VIN Code 4 and 1988 VIN Code 5 engine

Crankshaft Block Mark	1	2	3	1	2	3	1	2	3
Crankshaft Mark	0	0	0	1	1	1	2	2	2
Bearing Mark	1	2	3	3	2	4	3	4	5

Fig. 173 Main bearing selection table — 1989-90 VIN Code 6 engine

6. Coat the new bearings to be installed with clean engine oil and install them in the block. Carefully place the crankshaft in position.

7. Do not oil the lower bearing shells or the caps at this time. Install the bearing shells into the clean, dry caps.

8. Place a piece of plastic gauging material (such as Plastigage® or similar) lengthwise (fore-and-aft) across the full width of each of the 5 crankshaft main bearing journals. Remember that the measuring material is dissolved by oil. Keep the exposed part of the crank clean and dry.

9. Install the bearing caps with their bearing shells in their correct location and with the arrows pointing towards the front of the motor.

10. Install the bearing cap bolts and tighten them in 3 passes and in the correct sequence to 44 ft. lbs.

❊❊WARNING

Do not rotate the crankshaft with the measuring plastic installed.

11. Observing the correct removal sequence, gradually loosen and remove the bearing cap bolts. Carefully remove the bearing caps; the measuring media will be stuck to either the inside of the bearing shell or the face of the crankshaft.

12. Using the scale provided with the package of the measuring media, measure the gauging material at its widest point. This measurement represents the main bearing oil clearance and should be checked against the Crankshaft and Connecting Rod Specifications chart at the beginning of this section.

13. Remove every piece of the plastic gauging material from the crank and bearing caps. Coat the lower bearings (in the caps) with clean motor oil.

14. Install the main bearing caps and the lower thrust washers in the proper sequence. Make sure the arrows on the caps point towards the front (pulley end) of the motor.

15. Tighten the cap bolts in 3 passes and in the correct sequence to 44 ft. lbs.

16. Double check the end-play of the crank by repeating step 10 of this procedure.

17. Turn the crankshaft through 1 or 2 full clockwise rotations, making sure that it turns smoothly and evenly with no binding.

Cylinder Block

▶ See Figure 174

Most inspection and service work on the cylinder block should be handled by a machinist or professional engine rebuilding shop. Included in this work are bearing alignment checks, line boring, deck resurfacing, hot-tanking and cylinder block boring. Any or all of this work requires that the block be completely stripped of all components and transported to the shop. A block that has been checked and properly serviced will last much longer than one whose owner cut corners during a repair.

Cylinder de-glazing (honing) can be performed by the owner/mechanic who is careful and takes time to be accurate. The cylinder bores become glazed during normal operation of the engine as the rings ride up and down constantly. This shiny glaze must be removed in order for a new set of piston rings to seat properly.

Cylinder hones are available at most auto tool stores and parts jobbers. With the piston and rod assemblies removed from the block, cover the crankshaft completely with a rag to keep grit from collecting on it. Install the hone into the chuck of a variable speed drill (preferred in place of a constant speed drill) and insert the hone into the cylinder.

➡Make sure the drill and hone are kept square to the cylinder bore during the entire honing procedure.

Start the hone and move it up and down in the cylinder at a rate which will produce approximately a 60° crosshatch pattern. DO NOT extend the hone below the bottom of the cylinder bore. After the crosshatched pattern is established, remove the hone and check the piston fit.

Remove the piston and wash the cylinder with a solution of detergent and water to remove the honing and cylinder grit. Wipe the bores out several times with a clean rag soaked in fresh engine oil. Remove the cover from the crankshaft and check closely to see that NO grit has found its way onto the crankshaft.

Flywheel and Ring Gear

REMOVAL & INSTALLATION

➡This procedure may be performed with the engine in the car, however, access will be cramped.

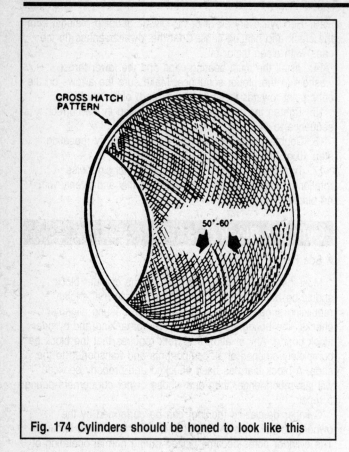

CROSS HATCH PATTERN

50°-60°

Fig. 174 Cylinders should be honed to look like this

1. Remove the transaxle, following procedures outlined in Section Seven.

2. For cars equipped with automatic transmissions:

a. Matchmark the torque converter and the driveplate. Correct positioning will be required during reassembly.

b. Remove the bolts holding the torque converter to the driveplate and remove the torque converter. DON'T drop it.

c. Matchmark the driveplate and the crankshaft.

d. Loosen the retaining bolts a little at a time and in a crisscross pattern. Support the driveplate as the last bolts are removed and then lift the driveplate away from the engine.

3. For manual transmission cars:

a. Matchmark the pressure plate assembly and the flywheel.

b. Loosen the pressure plate retaining bolts a little at a time and in a crisscross pattern. Support the pressure plate and clutch assembly as the last bolt is removed and lift them away from the flywheel.

✳✳CAUTION

The clutch disc contains asbestos, which has been determined to be a cancer causing agent. Never clean the clutch assembly with compressed air! Avoid inhaling dust from the clutch during disassembly. When cleaning components, use commercially available brake cleaning fluids.

c. Matchmark the flywheel and crankshaft. Loosen the retaining bolts evenly and in a crisscross pattern. Support the flywheel during removal of the last bolts and remove the flywheel.

4. Carefully inspect the teeth on the flywheel or driveplate for any signs of wearing or chipping. If anything beyond minimal contact wear is found, replace the unit.

➡Since the flywheel is driven by the starter gear, you would be wise to inspect the starter drive if any wear is found on the flywheel teeth. A worn starter can cause damage to the flywheel.

5. When reassembling, place the flywheel or driveplate in position on the crankshaft and make sure the matchmarks align. Install the retaining bolts finger tight.

6. Tighten the bolts in a diagonal pattern and in 3 passes. Tighten the flywheel bolts (manual transmission) to 58 ft. lbs. or the driveplate bolts (automatic transmission) to 47 ft. lbs.

7. Install either the clutch cover mounting bolts to 14 ft. lbs. or the torque converter, tightening its mounting bolts to 20 ft. lbs. on Nova models and 31 ft. lbs. on Prizm models.

➡If the clutch appears worn or cracked in any way, replace it with a new disc, pressure plate and release bearing. The slight extra cost of the parts will prevent having to remove the transaxle again later.

8. Reinstall the transaxle assembly.

RING GEAR REPLACEMENT

If the ring gear teeth on the driveplate or flywheel are damaged, the unit must be replaced. The ring gear cannot be separated or reinstalled individually.

If a flywheel is replaced on a manual transmission car, the installation of a new clutch disc, pressure plate and release bearing is highly recommended.

EXHAUST SYSTEM

Safety Precautions

For a number of reasons, exhaust system work can be the most dangerous type of work you can do on your car. Always observe the following precautions:

• Support the car extra securely. Not only will you often be working directly under it, but you'll frequently be using a lot of force, say, heavy hammer blows, to dislodge rusted parts. This can cause a car that's improperly supported to shift and possibly fall.

• Wear goggles. Exhaust system parts are always rusty. Metal chips can be dislodged, even when you're only turning rusted bolts. Attempting to pry pipes apart with a chisel makes the chips fly even more frequently.

• If you're using a cutting torch, keep it a great distance from either the fuel tank or lines. Stop what you're doing and feel the temperature of the fuel bearing pipes on the tank frequently. Even slight heat can expand and/or vaporize fuel, resulting in accumulated vapor, or even a liquid leak, near your torch.

• Watch where your hammer blows fall and make sure you hit squarely. You could easily tap a brake or fuel line when you hit an exhaust system part with a glancing blow. Inspect all lines and hoses in the area where you've been working.

✳✳CAUTION

Be very careful when working on or near the catalytic converter. External temperatures can reach 1,500°F (816°C) and more, causing severe burns. Removal or installation should be performed only on a cold exhaust system.

Special Tools

A number of special exhaust system tools can be rented from auto supply houses or local stores that rent special equipment. A common one is a tail pipe expander, designed to enable you to join pipes of identical diameter.

It may also be quite helpful to use solvents designed to loosen rusted bolts or flanges. Soaking rusted parts the night before you do the job can speed the work of freeing rusted parts considerably. Remember that these solvents are often flammable. Apply only to parts after they are cool!

The exhaust system of the Nova and Prizm consists of 4 pieces. At the front of the car, the first section of pipe connects the exhaust manifold to the catalytic converter. On Prizm models, this pipe contains a section of flexible, braided pipe. The catalytic converter is a sealed, non-serviceable unit which can be easily unbolted from the system and replaced if necessary.

An intermediate or center pipe containing a built-in resonator (pre-muffler) runs from the catalytic converter to the muffler at the rear of the car. Should the resonator fail, the entire pipe must be replaced. The muffler and tailpipe at the rear should always be replaced as a unit.

The exhaust system is attached to the body by several welded hooks and flexible rubber hangers; these hangers absorb exhaust vibrations and isolate the system from the body of the car. A series of metal heat shields runs along the exhaust piping, protecting the underbody from excess heat.

When inspecting or replacing exhaust system parts, make sure there is adequate clearance from all points on the body to avoid possible overheating to the floorpan. Check the complete system for broken damaged, missing or poorly positioned parts. Rattles and vibrations in the exhaust system are usually caused by misalignment of parts. When aligning the system, leave all the nuts and bolts loose until everything is in its proper place, then tighten the hardware working from the front to the rear. Remember that what appears to be proper clearance during repair may change as the car moves down the road. The motion of the engine, body and suspension must be considered when replacing parts.

COMPONENT REMOVAL & INSTALLATION

▶ See Figure 175

✳✳CAUTION

DO NOT perform exhaust repairs with the engine or exhaust hot. Allow the system to cool completely before attempting any work. Also, exhaust systems are noted for sharp edges, flaking metal and rusted bolts. Gloves and eye protection are required. A healthy supply of penetrating oil and rags is highly recommended.

➡ALWAYS use a new gasket at each pipe joint whenever the joint is disassembled. Use new nuts and bolts to hold the joint properly. These two low-cost items will serve to prevent future leaks as the system ages.

Front Pipe

1. Elevate and safely support the vehicle on jackstands.
2. Disconnect the oxygen sensor.
3. Remove the 2 bolts holding the pipe to the exhaust manifold.
4. Remove the 2 bolts holding the pipe to the catalytic converter.
5. Remove the bolts from the crossmember bracket and remove the pipe from under the car.
6. Attach the new pipe to the crossmember bracket. Install the bolts at both the manifold and the catalyst ends, leaving them finger tight until the pipe is correctly positioned. Make certain the gaskets are in place and straight.
7. Tighten the pipe-to-manifold bolts to 46 ft. lbs.
8. Tighten the bolts at the converter to 32 ft. lbs.
9. Reconnect the oxygen sensor.
10. Lower the vehicle to the ground, start the system and check for leaks. Small exhaust leaks will be most easily heard when the system is cold.

Catalytic Converter

With the car safely supported on jackstands, the converter is removed simply by removing the 2 bolts at either end. The Nova models have an air suction pipe attached to the converter which must be disconnected (2 bolts) before

Fig. 175 Nova exhaust system

1. Front exhaust pipe
2. Catalytic converter
3. Center exhaust pipe
4. Rear exhaust pipe
5. Gasket
6. Hanger bracket
7. Air suction pipe

removal. When reinstalling the converter, install it with new gaskets and tighten the end bolts to 32 ft. lbs. Reconnect the air suction pipe (Nova) and lower the car to the ground.

Intermediate Pipe (Resonator Pipe)

1. Elevate and safely support the vehicle on jackstands.
2. Remove the 2 bolts holding the pipe to the catalytic converter.
3. Remove the bolts holding the intermediate pipe to the muffler inlet pipe.
4. Disconnect the rubber hangers and remove the pipe.
5. Install the new pipe by suspending it in place on the rubber hangers. Install the gaskets at each end and install the bolts finger tight.

6. Double check the placement of the pipe and insure proper clearance to all body and suspension components.
7. Tighten the bolts holding the pipe to the catalytic converter to 32 ft. lbs., then tighten the bolts to the muffler inlet pipe to 32 ft. lbs.
8. Lower the car to the ground. Start the engine and check for leaks.

Muffler and Tailpipe Assembly

1. Elevate and safely support the vehicle on jackstands.
2. Remove the 2 bolts holding the muffler inlet pipe to the intermediate pipe.
3. Disconnect the forward bracket on the muffler.
4. Disconnect the rear muffler bracket (3 bolts) and remove the muffler from under the car.
5. When reinstalling, suspend the muffler from its front and rear hangers and check it for correct positioning under the body. If the old muffler had been rattling or hitting the body it is possible that the hangers and brackets have become bent from a light impact.
6. Attach the inlet pipe to the intermediate pipe and tighten the bolts to 32 ft. lbs.
7. Lower the vehicle to the ground, start the engine and check for leaks.

Complete System

If the entire exhaust system is to be replaced, it is much easier to remove the system as a unit than remove each individual piece. Disconnect the first pipe at the manifold joint and work towards the rear removing brackets and hangers as you go. Don't forget to disconnect the air suction pipe on the Nova catalytic converter. Remove the rear muffler bracket and slide the entire exhaust system out form under the car. The new system can then be bolted up on the workbench and easily checked for proper tightness and gasket integrity.

When installing the new assembly, suspend it from the flexible hangers first, then attach the fixed (solid) brackets. Check the clearance to the body and suspension and install the manifold joint bolts, tightening them to 46 ft. lbs.

ENGINE MECHANICAL SPECIFICATIONS

Component	U.S.	Metric
Camshaft:		
Journal diameter;		
1985–88 VIN Code 4 engine	1.1015–1.1022 in.	27.979–27.995 mm
1988 VIN Code 5 engine	1.0610–1.0616 in.	26.949–26.965 mm
1990 VIN Code 5 engine	1.0610–1.0616 in.	26.949–26.965 mm
1989–90 VIN Code 6 engine;		
No. 1	0.9822 in.	24.95 mm
All others	0.9035 in.	22.95 mm
1991–92 VIN Code 5 engine;		
No. 1	0.9822 in.	24.95 mm
All others	0.9035 in.	22.95 mm
1991–92 VIN Code 6 engine	1.0610–1.0616 in.	26.949–26.965 mm
1993 VIN Code 6 engine	0.9035–0.9041 in.	22.949–22.965 mm
1993 VIN Code 8 engine	0.9035–0.9041 in.	22.949–22.965 mm
Lobe lift;		
1985–88 VIN Code 4 engine	1.5409 in.	39.14 mm
1988 VIN Code 5 engine	1.3998–1.4002 in.	35.555–35.565 mm
1990 VIN Code engine	1.3941–1.3980 in.	35.410–35.510 mm
1989–90 VIN Code 6 engine;		
Intake	1.370 in.	38.41 mm
Exhaust	1.359 in.	38.51 Nm
1991–92 VIN Code 5 engine;		
Intake	1.370 in.	38.41 mm
Exhaust	1.359 in.	38.51 Nm
1991–92 VIN Code 6 engine	1.3941–1.3980 in.	35.410–35.510 mm
1993 VIN Code 6 engine;		
Intake	1.6500–1.6539 in.	41.910–42.010 mm
Exhaust	1.6520–1.6560 in.	41.960–42.060 mm
1993 VIN Code 8 engine;		
Intake	1.6500–1.6539 in.	41.910–42.010 mm
Exhaust	1.6520–1.6560 in.	41.960–42.060 mm
Connecting Rod:		
Rod bearing journal diameter;		
1985–88 VIN Code 4	1.5742–1.5748 in.	39.985–40.000 mm
1988 VIN Code 5 engine	1.6529–1.6535 in.	41.989–42.000 mm
1990 VIN Code 5 engine	1.6529–1.6535 in.	41.989–42.000 mm
1989–90 VIN Code 6 engine	1.5742–1.5748 in.	39.985–40.000 mm
1991–92 VIN Code 5 engine	1.6529–1.6535 in.	41.989–42.000 mm
1991–92 VIN Code 6 engine	1.5742–1.5748 in.	39.985–40.000 mm
1993 VIN Code 6 engine	1.5742–1.5748 in.	39.985–40.000 mm
1993 VIN Code 8 engine	N.A.	N.A.
Oil clearance;		
1985–92 All engine	0.0008–0.0020 in.	0.020–0.051 mm
1993 VIN Code 6 engine	0.0008–0.0020 in.	0.020–0.051 mm
1993 VIN Code 8 engine	0.0008–0.0020 in.	0.020–0.051 mm
Side clearance;		
1985–92 All engines	0.0059–0.0098 in.	0.15–0.25 mm
1993 VIN Code 6 engine	N.A.	N.A.
1993 VIN Code 8 engine	N.A.	N.A.
Crankshaft;		
Main bearing journal diameter;		
1985–88 VIN Code 4	1.8992–1.8898 in.	47.985–48.000 mm
1988 VIN Code 5 engine;		
Marked 0	1.8995–1.8898 in.	47.994–48.000 mm
Marked 1	1.8993–1.8895 in.	47.998–47.994 mm
Marked 2	1.8991–1.8893 in.	47.982–47.998 mm
1989–90 VIN Code 6 engine	1.8991–1.8898 in.	47.982–48.000 mm
1990 VIN Code 5 engine	1.8991–1.8898 in.	47.982–48.000 mm
1991–92 VIN Code 5 engine	1.8992–1.8898 in.	47.982–48.000 mm
1991–92 VIN Code 6 engine	1.8992–1.8898 in.	47.982–48.000 mm

ENGINE MECHANICAL SPECIFICATIONS

Component	U.S.	Metric
Crankshaft;		
1993 VIN Code 6 engine;		
Marked 0	1.8995–1.8898 in.	47.994–48.000 mm
Marked 1	1.8993–1.8895 in.	47.998–47.994 mm
Marked 2	1.8991–1.8893 in.	47.982–47.998 mm
1993 VIN Code 8 engine;		
Marked 0	1.8995–1.8898 in.	47.994–48.000 mm
Marked 1	1.8993–1.8895 in.	47.998–47.994 mm
Marked 2	1.8991–1.8893 in.	47.982–47.998 mm
Main bearing oil clearance:		
1985–88 VIN Code 4 engine	0.0008–0.0020 in.	0.020–0.051 mm
1988 VIN Code 5 engine	0.0006–0.0013 in.	0.015–0.33 mm
1989–92 All engines	0.0006–0.0013 in.	0.015–0.33 mm
1993 VIN Code 6 engine	0.0006–0.0013 in.	0.015–0.33 mm
1993 VIN Code 8 engine	0.0006–0.0013 in.	0.015–0.33 mm
End play:		
1985–88 VIN Code 4 engine	0.0008–0.0073 in.	0.02–0.185 mm
1988 VIN Code 5 engine	0.0008–0.0087 in.	0.020–0.051 mm
1989–92 All engines	0.0008–0.0087 in.	0.020–0.051 mm
1993 VIN Code 6 engine	0.0008–0.0087 in.	0.020–0.051 mm
1993 VIN Code 8 engine	0.0008–0.0087 in.	0.020–0.051 mm
Cylinder block:		
Cylinder bore diameter;		
1985–92 All engines	3.1890–3.1902 in.	81.00–81.03 mm
1993 VIN Code 6 engine;		
Mark No. 1	31890–31894 in.	81.000–81.010 mm
Mark No. 2	31894–31898 in.	81.010–81.020 mm
Mark No. 3	31898–31902 in.	81.020–81.030 mm
1993 VIN Code 8 engine;		
Mark No. 1	31890–31894 in.	81.000–81.010 mm
Mark No. 2	31894–31898 in.	81.010–81.020 mm
Mark No. 3	31898–31902 in.	81.020–81.030 mm
Cylinder head:		
Maximum surface warpage;		
Cylinder block side:		
1985–88 VIN Code 4 engine	0.0020 in.	0.05 mm
1988 VIN Code 5 engine	0.0020 in.	0.05 mm
1989–90 All engines	0.0020 in.	0.05 mm
1991–92 VIN Code 5 engine	0.0020 in.	0.05 mm
1993 VIN Code 6 engine	0.0020 in.	0.05 mm
1993 VIN Code 8 engine	0.0020 in.	0.05 mm
Either manifold side:	0.0020 in.	0.05 mm
1985–88 VIN Code 4 engine	0.0039 in.	0.10 mm
1988 VIN Code 5 engine	0.0039 in.	0.10 mm
1989–93 All engines	0.0039 in.	0.10 mm
Pistons:		
Piston standard diameter;		
1985–88 VIN Code 4 engine	3.1846–3.1858 in.	80.89–80.92 mm
1988 VIN Code 5 engine	3.1846–3.1858 in.	80.89–80.92 mm
1989–90 All engines;		
Standard size 1	3.1862–3.1866 in.	80.93–80.94 mm
Standard size 2	3.1866–3.1870 in.	80.94–80.95 mm
Standard size 3	3.1870–3.1874 in.	80.95–80.96 mm
1991–92 VIN Code 5 engine;		
Standard size 1	3.1862–3.1866 in.	80.93–80.94 mm
Standard size 2	3.1866–3.1870 in.	80.94–80.95 mm
Standard size 3	3.1870–3.1874 in.	80.95–80.96 mm

ENGINE MECHANICAL SPECIFICATIONS

Component	U.S.	Metric
Pistons:		
1990 VIN Code 5 engine;		
1991–92 VIN Code 6 engine;		
Standard size 1	3.1846–3.1850 in.	80.89–80.90 mm
Standard size 2	3.1850–3.1854 in.	80.90–80.91 mm
Standard size 3	3.1854–3.1858 in.	80.91–80.92 mm
1993 VIN Code 6 engine;		
Standard size 1	3.1852–3.1856 in.	80.905–80.915 mm
Standard size 2	3.1856–3.1860 in.	80.915–80.925 mm
Standard size 3	3.1860–3.1864 in.	80.925–80.935 mm
1993 VIN Code 8 engine;		
Standard size 1	3.1852–3.1856 in.	80.905–80.915 mm
Standard size 2	3.1856–3.1860 in.	80.915–80.925 mm
Standard size 3	3.1860–3.1864 in.	80.925–80.935 mm
Piston to-bore-clearance;		
1985–88 VIN Code 4 engine	0.0035–0.0043 in.	0.09–0.11 mm
1988 VIN Code 5 engine	0.0039–0.0047 in.	0.10–0.12 mm
1989–90 VIN Code 6 engine	0.0024–0.0031 in.	0.06–0.08 mm
1990 VIN Code 5 engine	0.0039–0.0047 in.	0.10–0.12 mm
1991–92 VIN Code 5 engine	0.0024–0.0031 in.	0.06–0.08 mm
1991–92 VIN Code 6 engine	0.0039–0.0047 in.	0.10–0.12 mm
1993 VIN Code 6 engine	0.0008–.0015 in.	0.02–0.04 mm
1993 VIN Code 8 engine	0.0008–.0015 in.	0.02–0.04 mm
Ring gap;		
1985–88 VIN Code 4 engine;		
No. 1	0.0098–0.0185 in.	0.25–0.47 mm
No. 2	0.0059–0.0165 in.	0.15–0.42 mm
No. Oil	0.0118–0.0402 in.	0.30–0.0165 mm
1988 VIN Code 5 engine;		
No. 1	0.0098–0.0138 in.	0.25–0.35 mm
No. 2	0.0078–0.0118 in.	0.20–0.30 mm
No. Oil	0.0059–0.0157 in.	0.15–0.040 mm
1989–90 VIN Code 6 engine;		
No. 1	0.0098–0.0138 in.	0.25–0.35 mm
No. 2	0.0059–0.0118 in.	0.15–0.30 mm
No. Oil	0.0039–0.0236 in.	0.10–0.060 mm
1991–92 VIN Code 5 engine;		
No. 1	0.0098–0.0138 in.	0.25–0.35 mm
No. 2	0.0059–0.0118 in.	0.15–0.30 mm
No. Oil	0.0039–0.0236 in.	0.10–0.060 mm
1990 VIN Code 5 engine;		
1991–92 VIN Code 6 engine;		
No. 1	0.0098–0.0185 in.	0.25–0.47 mm
No. 2	0.0079–0.0165 in.	0.20–0.47 mm
No. Oil	0.0059–0.0205 in.	0.15–0.052 mm
1993 VIN Code 6 engine;		
No. 1	0.0098–0.0138 in.	0.25–0.035 mm
No. 2	0.0138–0.0234 in.	0.035–0.60 mm
No. Oil	0.0039–0.0177 in.	0.10–0.45 mm
1993 VIN Code 8 engine;		
No. 1	0.0098–0.0138 in.	0.25–0.035 mm
No. 2	0.0138–0.0234 in.	0.035–0.60 mm
No. Oil	0.0039–0.0177 in.	0.10–0.45 mm
Ring side clearance;		
1985–88 VIN Code 4 engine;		
No. 1	0.0016–0.0031 in.	0.04–0.08 mm
No. 2	0.0012–0.0028 in.	0.03–0.07 mm
1988 VIN Code 5 engine;		
No. 1	0.0016–0.0031 in.	0.04–0.08 mm
No. 2	0.0012–0.0028 in.	0.03–0.07 mm

ENGINE MECHANICAL SPECIFICATIONS

Component	U.S.	Metric
Pistons:		
1989–90 VIN Code 6 engine;		
No. 1	0.0016–0.0031 in.	0.04–0.08 mm
No. 2	0.0012–0.0028 in.	0.03–0.07 mm
1991–92 VIN Code 5 engine;		
No. 1	0.0016–0.0031 in.	0.04–0.08 mm
No. 2	0.0012–0.0028 in.	0.03–0.07 mm
1990 VIN Code 5 engine;		
1991–92 VIN Code 6 engine;		
No. 2	0.0012–0.0028 in.	0.03–0.07 mm
No. 2	0.0012–0.0028 in.	0.03–0.07 mm
1993 VIN Code 6 engine;		
No. 1	0.0018–0.0035 in.	0.045–0.090 mm
No. 2	0.0012–0.0028 in.	0.030–0.070 mm
1993 VIN Code 8 engine;		
No. 1	0.0018–0.0035 in.	0.045–0.090 mm
No. 2	0.0012–0.0028 in.	0.030–0.070 mm
Valves:		
Face angle;		
1985–88 VIN Code 4 engine	44.5°	
1988 VIN Code 5 engine	44.5°	
1989–90 VIN Code 6 engine	45.5°	
1991–92 VIN Code 5 engine	45.5°	
1990 VIN Code 5 engine	N.A.	
1991–92 VIN Code 6 engine	N.A.	
1993 VIN Code 6 engine	N.A.	
1993 VIN Code 8 engine	N.A.	
Seat angle;		
1985–88 VIN Code 4 engine	45°	
1988 VIN Code 5 engine	45°	
1989–90 VIN Code 6 engine	45°	
1991–92 VIN Code 5 engine	N.A.	
1990 VIN Code 5 engine	N.A.	
1991–92 VIN Code 6 engine	N.A.	
1993 VIN Code 6	45°	
1993 VIN Code 8	45°	
Stem diameter;		
1985–88 VIN Code 4 engine		
Intake	0.2744–0.2750 in.	6.969–6.995
Exhaust	0.2742–0.2748 in.	6.974–6.990
1988 VIN Code 5 engine;		
Intake	0.2350–0.2356 in.	5.970–5.985 mm
Exhaust	0.2748–0.2354 in.	5.965–5.980 mm
1989–92 All engines;		
Intake	0.2350–0.2356 in.	5.970–5.985 mm
Exhaust	0.2748–0.2354 in.	5.965–5.980 mm
1993 VIN Code 6 engine;		
Intake	0.2350–0.2356 in.	5.970–5.985 mm
Exhaust	0.2748–0.2354 in.	5.965–5.980 mm
1993 VIN Code 8 engine;		
Intake	0.2350–0.2356 in.	5.970–5.985 mm
Exhaust	0.2748–0.2354 in.	5.965–5.980 mm
Stem-to-guide-clearance		
1985–88 VIN Code 4 engine;		
Intake	0.0031 in.	0.08 mm
Exhaust	0.0039 in.	0.10 mm
1988 VIN Code 5 engine;		
Intake	0.0031 in.	0.08 mm
Exhaust	0.0039 in.	0.10 mm

ENGINE MECHANICAL SPECIFICATIONS

Component	U.S.	Metric
Valves:		
1989–90 VIN Code 6 engine;		
Intake	0.0031 in.	0.08 mm
Exhaust	0.0039 in.	0.10 mm
1991–92 VIN Code 5 engine;		
Intake	0.0031 in.	0.08 mm
Exhaust	0.0039 in.	0.10 mm
1990 VIN Code 5 engine;		
1991–92 VIN Code 6 engine;		
Intake	0.0010–0.0024 in.	0.025–0.060 mm
Exhaust	0.0012–0.0026 in.	0.030–0.0065 mm
1993 VIN Code 6 engine;		
Intake	0.0010–0.0024 in.	0.025–0.060 mm
Exhaust	0.0012–0.0026 in.	0.030–0.0065 mm
1993 VIN Code 8 engine;		
Intake	0.0010–0.0024 in.	0.025–0.060 mm
Exhaust	0.0012–0.0026 in.	0.030–0.0065 mm
Spring:		
Free height		
1985–88 VIN Code 4 engine	1.756 in.	44.6 mm
1988 VIN Code 5 engine	1.6177 in.	41.09 mm
1989–90 VIN Code 6 engine	1.724 in.	43.8 mm
1990 VIN Code 5 engine	N.A.	N.A.
1991–92 VIN Code 5 engine	1.724 in.	43.8 mm
1991–92 VIN Code 6 engine	N.A.	N.A.
1993 VIN Code 6 engine	1.542 in.	38.57 mm
1993 VIN Code 8 engine	1.542 in.	38.57 mm
Installed tension (minimum);		
1985–88 VIN Code 4 engine	46.3 lbs.	206 N
1988 VIN Code 5 engine	32.2 lbs.	143 N
1990 VIN Code 5 engine	N.A.	
1989–90 VIN Code 6 engine	32.2 lbs.	143 N
1991–92 VIN Code 5 engine	32.2 lbs.	143 N
1991–92 VIN Code 6 engine	N.A.	
1993 VIN Code 6 engine		
Preload	37.3 lbs. @ 1.248 in.	16.9 kg. @ 31.7 mm
1993 VIN Code 8 engine		
Preload	37.3 lbs. @ 1.248 in.	16.9 kg. @ 31.7 mm

TORQUE SPECIFICATIONS

Component	U.S.	Metric
Camshaft		
Bearing cap bolts;		
1985–93 engines:	115 inch lbs.	13 Nm
Camshaft timing gear(s) bolt;		
1985–88 VIN Code 4 engine:	34 ft. lbs.	47 Nm
1988 VIN Code 5 engine:	34 ft. lbs.	47 Nm
1989–90 VIN Code 6 engine:	43 ft. lbs.	59 Nm
1990 VIN Code 5 engine:	43 ft. lbs.	59 Nm
1991–92 VIN Code 5 engine:	43 ft. lbs.	59 Nm
1991–92 VIN Code 6 engine:	34 ft. lbs.	47 Nm
1993 VIN Code 6 engine:	43 ft. lbs.	59 Nm
1993 VIN Code 8 engine:	43 ft. lbs.	59 Nm
Crankshaft main bearing cap bolts;		
1985–93 engines:	44 ft. lbs.	60 Nm
Cylinder head retaining bolts;		
1985–88 VIN Code 4 engine:	43 ft. lbs.	59 Nm
1988 VIN Code 5 engine:		
Step 1:	22 ft. lbs.	29 Nm
Step 2:	+ 90 degrees	+ 90 degrees
Step 3:	+ 90 degrees	+ 90 degrees
1989–92 all engines:	44 ft. lbs.	60 Nm
1993 all engines:		
Step 1:	22 ft. lbs.	29 Nm
Step 2:	+ 90 degrees	+ 90 degrees
Step 3:	+ 90 degrees	+ 90 degrees
Coolant pump retaing bolts;		
1985–92 all engines:	11 ft. lbs.	15 Nm
1993 all engines:	124 inch lbs.	14 Nm
Connecting rod bearing cap nuts;		
1985–88 VIN Code 4 engine:	29 ft. lbs.	39 Nm
1988 VIN Code 5 engine:	36 ft. lbs.	49 Nm
1989–92 all engines:	36 ft. lbs.	49 Nm
1993 all engines;		
Step 1:	22 ft. lbs.	29 Nm
Step 2:	+ 90°	+ 90°
Crankshaft pulley bolt;		
1985–88 VIN Code 4:	87 ft. lbs.	118 Nm
1988 VIN Code 5:	101 ft. lbs.	137 Nm
1989–93 all engines:	87 ft. lbs.	118 Nm
Engine mounting bolts and nuts;		
1988 VIN Code 5;		
Engine mounting center mounting bolts:	29 ft. lbs.	39 Nm
Engine mounts to center member bolts:	38 ft. lbs.	48 Nm
Front mount through bolt:	58 ft. lbs.	78 Nm
1989–90 VIN Code 6 engine;		
1990 VIN Code 5 engine;		
Right mount through bolt:	64 ft. lbs.	87 Nm
Engine mount to engine bracket bolt:	45 ft. lbs.	61 Nm
Engine mount to engine bracket nuts:	45 ft. lbs.	61 Nm
Right mount support bolts:	35 ft. lbs.	47 Nm
Rear transaxle mount-to-main cross-member nuts:	45 ft. lbs.	61 Nm
Center transaxle mount-to-center crossmember nuts:	45 ft. lbs.	61 Nm

TORQUE SPECIFICATIONS

Component	U.S.	Metric
Engine mounting bolts and nuts;		
1991–92 VIN Code 5 & 6 engines;		
Right mount through bolt:	64 ft. lbs.	87 Nm
Engine mount to engine bracket bolt:	45 ft. lbs.	61 Nm
Engine mount to engine bracket nuts:	45 ft. lbs.	61 Nm
Right mount support bolts:	35 ft. lbs.	47 Nm
Rear transaxle mount-to-main cross-member nuts:	45 ft. lbs.	61 Nm
Center transaxle mount-to-center crossmember nuts:	45 ft. lbs.	61 Nm
1993 VIN Code 6 & 8 engines;		
Engine mount-to-body bolts:	19 ft. lbs.	25 Nm
Engine mount through bolt and nut:	47 ft. lbs.	64 Nm
Engine mount-to-cylinder block brace bolts:	38 ft. lbs.	51 Nm
Engine mount-to-engine mount bracket "A" bolts:	19 ft. lbs.	25 Nm
Engine mount-to-engine mount bracket "B" bolts:	47 ft. lbs.	64 Nm
Engine mount-to-engine mount bracket "C" bolts:	47 ft. lbs.	64 Nm
Engine mount bracket-to-engine mount block brace nuts:	38 ft. lbs.	52 Nm
Engine mounting bracket nuts:	38 ft. lbs.	52 Nm
Intake manifold bolts and nuts;		
1985–88 VIN Code 4:	20 ft. lbs.	27 Nm
1988 VIN Code 5:	20 ft. lbs.	27 Nm
1989–90 VIN Code 6 engine:	14 ft. lbs.	19 Nm
1991–92 VIN Code 5:	14 ft. lbs.	19 Nm
1990 VIN Code 5:	20 ft. lbs.	27 Nm
1991–92 VIN Code 6:	20 ft. lbs.	27 Nm
1993 all engines:	14 ft. lbs.	19 Nm
Exhaust manifold bolts and nuts;		
1985–92 all engines:	18 ft. lbs.	25 Nm
1993 all engines:	25 ft. lbs.	34 Nm
Flywheel bolts;		
1985–88 all engines:	58 ft. lbs.	78 Nm
1989–93 engines;		
Manual:	58 ft. lbs.	78 Nm
Automatic:	47 ft. lbs.	64 Nm
Oil pump bolts;		
1985–88 all engines:	89 inch lbs.	10 Nm
1989–90 VIN Code 6:	16 ft. lbs.	21 Nm
1991–92 VIN Code 5:	16 ft. lbs.	21 Nm
1990 VIN Code 5:	89 inch lbs.	10 Nm
1991–92 VIN Code 6:	89 inch lbs.	10 Nm
1993 VIN Code 6 engine:	16 ft. lbs.	21 Nm
1993 VIN Code 8 engine:	16 ft. lbs.	21 Nm
Oil pan bolts;		
1985–88 all engines:	48 inch lbs.	5.4 Nm
1989–90 VIN Code 6:	44 inch lbs.	5.0 Nm
1990 VIN Code 5:	53 inch lbs.	6.0 Nm
1991–92 VIN Code 5:	44 inch lbs.	5.0 Nm
1991–92 VIN Code 6:	53 inch lbs.	6.0 Nm
1993 all engines:	44 inch lbs.	5.0 Nm

TORQUE SPECIFICATIONS

Component	U.S.	Metric
Starter bolts;		
1985–93 all engines:	29 ft. lbs.	39 Nm
Spark plug;		
1985–88 VIN Code 4 engine	13 ft. lbs.	18Nm
1988 VIN Code 5 engine	13 ft. lbs.	18 Nm
1990 VIN Code 5 engine	13 ft. lbs.	18 Nm
1989–90	21 ft. lbs.	28 Nm
1991–92		
VIN Code 5 engine	21 ft. lbs.	28 Nm
VIN Code 6 engine	13 ft. lbs.	18 Nm
1993	13 ft. lbs.	18 Nm

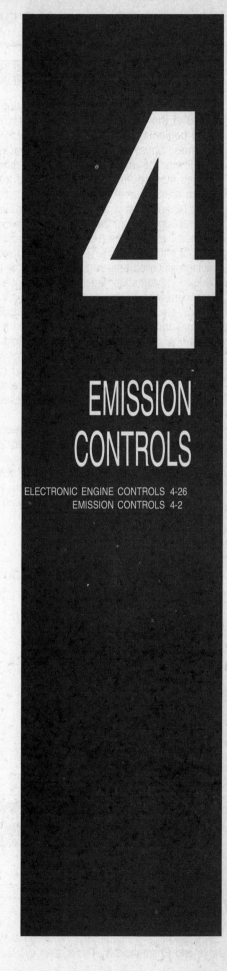

4

EMISSION CONTROLS

EMISSION CONTROLS

Component location and vacuum routing diagrams are located at the end of this Section. Please refer to them before beginning any disassembly or testing. Refer to your underhood emission control label for vacuum diagrams not shown. The underhood label often reflects the latest changes made during the production of a vehicle.

There are 3 sources of automotive pollutants; crankcase fumes, exhaust gases, and gasoline evaporation. The pollutants formed from these substances fall into 3 categories: unburned hydrocarbons (HC), carbon monoxide (CO), and oxides of nitrogen (NOx). The equipment used to limit these pollutants is called emission control equipment.

Due to varying state, federal, and provincial regulations, specific emission control equipment may vary by area of sale. The U.S. emission equipment is divided into 2 categories: California and 49 State. In this section, the term 'California" applies only to cars originally built to be sold in California. Some California emissions equipment is not shared with equipment installed on cars built to be sold in the other 49 states. Models built to be sold in Canada also have specific emissions equipment, although in many cases the 49 State and Canadian equipment is the same.

Both carbureted and fuel injected cars require an assortment of systems and devices to control emissions. Newer cars rely more heavily on computer (ECM) management of many of the engine controls. This eliminates the many of the vacuum hoses and linkages around the engine. In the lists that follow, remember that not every component is found on every car.

ECM CONTROLLED SYSTEMS
- Fuel Evaporative Control (EVAP)
- Carburetor Feedback System
- Deceleration Fuel Cutoff
- Three-Way Oxidation Catalyst (TWC-OC or TWC)
- Cold Mixture Heater (CMH)

NON-ECM CONTROLLED SYSTEMS
- Positive Crankcase Ventilation (PCV)
- Throttle Positioner (TP)
- Exhaust Gas Recirculation (EGR)
- Air Suction (AS)
- High Altitude Compensation (HAC)
- Automatic Hot Air Intake (HAI)
- Hot Idle Compensation (HIC)
- Automatic Choke
- Choke Breaker (CB)
- Choker Opener
- Auxiliary Accelerator Pump (AAP)
- Heat Control Valve

Positive Crankcase Ventilation (PCV) System

SYSTEM OPERATION

▶ See Figures 1, 2, 3, 4 and 5

A closed positive crankcase ventilation system is used on all Nova and Prizm models. This system cycles incompletely

burned fuel which works its way past the piston rings back into the intake manifold for reburning with the fuel/air mixture. The oil filler cap is sealed and the air is drawn from the top of the crankcase into the intake manifold through a valve with a variable orifice.

This valve (commonly known as the PCV valve) regulates the flow of air into the manifold according to the amount of manifold vacuum. When the throttle plates are open fairly wide, the valve fully. However, at idle speed, when the manifold vacuum is at maximum, the PCV valve reduces the flow in order not to unnecessarily affect the small volume of mixture passing into the engine.

During most driving conditions, manifold vacuum is high and all of the vapor from the crankcase, plus a small amount of excess air, is drawn into the manifold via the PCV valve. At full throttle, the increase in the volume of blow-by and the decrease in manifold vacuum make the flow via the PCV valve inadequate. Under these conditions, excess vapors are drawn into the air cleaner and pass into the engine along with the fresh air.

A plugged valve or hose may cause a rough idle, stalling or low idle speed, oil leaks in the engine and/or sludging and oil deposits within the engine and air cleaner. A leaking valve or hose could cause an erratic idle or stalling.

Fig. 1 Positive crankcase ventilation system — 1985-88 VIN code 4 engine

Fig. 2 Positive crankcase ventilation system — 1988 and 1990-91 VIN code 5 engine

Fig. 4 Positive crankcase ventilation system — 1991 VIN code 6 and 1992 VIN code 5 and 6 engines

Fig. 3 Positive crankcase ventilation system — 1989-90

Fig. 5 Positive crankcase ventilation system — 1993

TESTING AND TROUBLESHOOTING

▶ **See Figure 6**

The PCV is easily checked with the engine running at normal idle speed (warmed up). Remove the PCV valve from the valve cover or intake manifold, but leave it connected to its hose. Place your thumb over the end of the valve to check for vacuum. If there is no vacuum, check for plugged hoses or ports. If these are open, the valve is faulty. With the engine off, remove the PCV valve completely. Shake it end to end, listening for the rattle of the needle inside the valve. If no rattle is heard, the needle is jammed (probably with oil sludge) and the valve should be replaced.

An engine which is operated without crankcase ventilation can be damaged very quickly. It is important to check and change the PCV valve at regular maintenance intervals.

REMOVAL & INSTALLATION

Remove the PCV valve from the cylinder head cover or intake manifold. Remove the hose from the valve. Take note of which end of the valve was in the manifold. This 1-way valve must be reinstalled correctly or it will not function. While the valve is removed, the hoses should be checked for splits, kinks and blockages. Check the vacuum port (that the hoses connect to) for any clogging.

Remember that the correct function of the PCV system is based on a sealed engine — an air leak at the oil filler cap and/or around the oil pan can defeat the design of the system.

Evaporative Emission Control System (EVAP or EECS)

OPERATION

The basic evaporative emission control system used on all vehicles is the charcoal canister storage method. This method transfers fuel vapor from the fuel tank to an activated carbon (charcoal) storage device (canister) to hold the vapors when the vehicle is not operating. When the engine is running, the fuel vapor is purged from the carbon element by intake airflow and consumed in the normal combustion process.

TESTING AND CHECKING

Before embarking on component removal or extensive diagnosis, perform a complete visual check of the system. Every vacuum line and vapor line (including the lines running to the tank) should be inspected for cracking, loose clamps, kinks and obstructions. Additionally, check the tank for any signs of deformation or crushing. Each vacuum port on the engine or manifold should be checked for restriction by dirt or sludge.

The evaporative control system is generally not prone to component failure in normal circumstances; most problems can be tracked to the causes listed above.

Fuel Filler Cap

Check that the filler cap seals effectively. Remove the filler cap and pull the safety valve outward to check for smooth operation. Replace the filler cap if the seal is defective or if it is not operating properly.

Charcoal Canister

▶ **See Figures 7 and 8**

1. Label and disconnect the lines running to the canister. Remove the charcoal canister from the vehicle.
2. Visually check the charcoal canister for cracks or damage.
3. Check for a clogged filter and stuck check valve. Using low pressure compressed air, blow into the tank pipe and check that the air flows without resistance from the other pipes. If this does not test positive replace the canister.
4. Clean the filter in the canister by blowing no more than 43 psi of compressed air into the pipe to the outer vent control valve while holding the other upper canister pipes closed.

➡ **Do not attempt to wash the charcoal canister. Also be sure that no activated carbon comes out of the canister during the cleaning process.**

5. Replace or reinstall the canister as needed.

Outer Vent Control Valve

NOVA WITH VIN CODE 4 ENGINE

▶ **See Figure 9**

1. Label and disconnect the hoses from the control valve but leave the wiring for the valve connected.

1 CHECK VALVE

Fig. 6 Cross section of typical PCV valve. The valve should rattle when shaken

1. TANK PIPE
2. PURGE PIPE

Fig. 7 Example of checking a charcoal canister

Fig. 8 Example of cleaning a charcoal canister

2. Check that the valve is open by blowing air through it when the ignition switch is in the OFF position.

3. Check that the valve is closed when the ignition switch is in the ON position.

4. Reconnect the hoses to the proper locations. If the valve doesn't operate correctly, double check the fuse and wiring before replacing the valve.

Thermo Switch

NOVA WITH VIN CODE 4 ENGINE

▶ **See Figure 10**

1. Drain the coolant from the radiator into a clean container.

❋❋CAUTION

When draining the coolant, keep in mind that cats and dogs are attracted by the ethylene glycol antifreeze, and are quite likely to drink any that is left in an uncovered container or in puddles on the ground. This will prove fatal in sufficient quantity. Always drain the coolant into a sealable container. Coolant should be reused unless it is contaminated or several years old.

2. Remove the thermoswitch from the intake manifold. The switch is located behind the TVSV (Thermo Vacuum Switching Valve).

3. Cool the thermo switch off until the temperature is below 109°F (43°C). Check that there is continuity through the switch by the use of an ohmmeter.

Fig. 9 Check the outer vent control valve with the ignition OFF and ON. Note that there should be no flow with the ignition on

Fig. 10 The thermoswitch should have continuity if cooled below 109 degrees F

4. Using hot water, bring the temperature of the switch to above 131°F (55°C). Check that there is no continuity when the switch is in water above this temperature.

5. Apply sealer to the threads of the switch and reinstall it in the manifold.

6. Refill the radiator with coolant.

REMOVAL & INSTALLATION

Removal and installation of the various evaporative emission control system components consists of labeling and unfastening hoses, loosening retaining screws, and removing the part which is to be replaced from its mounting point.

➡ **When replacing any EVAP system hoses, always use hoses that are fuel-resistant or are marked EVAP. Use of hose which is not fuel-resistant will lead to premature hose failure.**

Exhaust Gas Recirculation (EGR) System

OPERATION

The EGR system reduces oxides of nitrogen. This is accomplished by recirculating some of the exhaust gases through the EGR valve to the intake manifold, lowering peak combustion temperatures.

Whenever the engine coolant is below 122°F (50°C), the thermostatic vacuum switching valve (TVSV) connects manifold vacuum to the EGR vacuum modulator and at the same time to the EGR valve.

The EGR vacuum modulator controls the EGR valve by modulating the vacuum signal with an atmospheric bleed. This bleed is controlled by the amount of exhaust pressure acting on the bottom of the EGR vacuum modulator (diaphragm).

Since recirculation of exhaust gas is undesirable at low rpm or idle, the system limits itself by sensing the exhaust flow. Under low load conditions, such as low speed driving, the exhaust pressure is low. In this state, the diaphragm in the modulator is pushed down by spring force and the modulator valve opens to allow outside air into the vacuum passage. The vacuum in the line is reduced, the EGR valve does not open as far, and the amount of recirculation is reduced.

Under high load conditions or high rpm driving, the exhaust pressure is increased. This pushes the modulator diaphragm upwards and closes the bleed valve. A full vacuum signal is transmitted to the EGR valve; it opens completely and allows full recirculation. The slight reduction in combustion temperature (and therefore power) is not noticed at highway speeds or under hard acceleration.

Prizm vehicles also control the EGR with a vacuum solenoid valve (VSV), 1989-92 or exhaust gas recirculation solenoid valve (EGR SV), 1993. These devices allow the ECM to further control the EGR under certain conditions. The ECM will electrically close the VSV or EGR SV if the engine is not warmed up, the throttle valve is in the idle position or if the engine is under very hard acceleration. Aside from these conditions, the Prizm EGR operates in accordance with the normal vacuum modulator function.

TESTING AND SERVICING VIN CODE 4 (CARB.) ENGINE

EGR System Operation
▶ See Figures 11 and 12

1. Check and clean the filter in the EGR vacuum modulator. Use compressed air (if possible) to blow the dirt out of the filters and check the filters for contamination or damage.
2. Using a tee (3-way connector), connect a vacuum gauge to the hose between the EGR valve and the vacuum pipe.
3. Check the seating of the EGR valve by starting the engine and seeing that it runs at a smooth idle. If the valve is not completely closed, the idle will be rough.

4. With the engine coolant temperature below 122°F (50°C), the vacuum gauge should read zero at 2000 rpm. This indicates that the thermostatic vacuum control valve (TVCV) is functioning correctly at this temperature range.
5. Warm the engine to normal operating temperature. Check the vacuum gauge and confirm low vacuum at 2000 rpm. This indicates the TVSV and the EGR vacuum modulator are working correctly in this temperature range.
6. Disconnect the vacuum hose from the **R** port on the EGR vacuum modulator and, using another piece of hose, connect the **R** port directly to the intake manifold. Check that the vacuum gauge indicates high vacuum at 2,000 rpm.

➡**As a large amount of exhaust gas enters, the engine will misfire slightly at this time.**

Fig. 12 EGR vacuum modulator filter

1. E.G.R. valve
2. E.G.R. vacuum modulator
3. Check valve
4. E.G.R. port
5. E.G.R. "R" port
6. Pressure chamber
7. Thermostatic vacuum switching valve

Fig. 11 EGR system components — 1985-88 VIN code 4 engine

7. Disconnect the vacuum gauge and reconnect the vacuum hoses to their proper locations.

8. Check the EGR valve by applying vacuum directly to the valve with the engine at idle. (This may be accomplished by bridging vacuum directly from the intake manifold or by using a hand-held vacuum pump.) The engine should falter and/or stall as the full load of recirculated gasses enters the engine.

9. If no problem is found with this inspection, the system is OK; otherwise inspect each part.

Thermostatic Vacuum Switching Valve

▶ See Figure 13

1. Drain the cooling system.

✳✳CAUTION

When draining the coolant, keep in mind that cats and dogs are attracted by the ethylene glycol antifreeze, and are quite likely to drink any that is left in an uncovered container or in puddles on the ground. This will prove fatal in sufficient quantity. Always drain the coolant into a sealable container. Coolant should be reused unless it is contaminated or several years old.

2. Remove the thermostatic vacuum switching valve.

3. Cool the thermostatic vacuum switching valve to below 45°F (7°C).

4. Check that air flows from pipe **J** to pipes **M** and **L**, and flows from pipe **K** to pipe **N**.

5. Heat the thermostatic vacuum switching valve to 63-122°F (17-50°C) generally room temperature).

6. Check that air flows from pipe **K** to pipes **N** and **L** and flows from pipe **J** to pipe **M**.

7. Heat the TVSV to above 154°F (68°C).

8. Check that air flows from the pipe **K** to pipes **M** and **L**, and does **NOT** flow from pipe **J** to any other pipes.

9. Apply liquid sealer to the threads of the TVSV and reinstall.

10. Refill the cooling system.

11. If a problem is found with any of the above procedures, replace the valve

EGR Valve

1. Remove the EGR valve.

2. Check the valve for sticking and heavy carbon deposits. If a problem is found, replace the valve.

Fig. 13 Port identification for testing the TVSV. Make sure you label each hose during disassembly

3. Reinstall the EGR valve with a new gasket.

EGR Vacuum Modulator

▶ See Figure 11

1. Label and disconnect the vacuum hoses from ports **P**, **Q**, and **R** of the EGR vacuum modulator.

2. Plug the **Q** and **R** ports with your fingers.

3. Blow air into port **P**. Check that the air passes freely through the sides of the air filter side.

4. Start the engine and maintain 2,000 rpm.

5. Repeat the test above. Check that there is a strong resistance to air flow.

6. Reconnect the vacuum hoses to the proper locations.

Check Valve

▶ See Figure 11

Inspect the check valve (1-way valve) by gently blowing air into each end of the valve or hose. Air should flow from the orange pipe to the black pipe but SHOULD NOT flow from the black pipe to the orange pipe.

TESTING AND SERVICING 1988 & 1990 VIN CODE 5 ENGINES 1989-93 ALL ENGINES

EGR System Check

1988 VIN CODE 5 ENGINE

▶ See Figures 12, 14 and 15

1. Check and clean the filter in the EGR vacuum modulator. Use compressed air (if possible) to blow the dirt out of the filters and check the filters for contamination or damage.

2. Using a tee (3-way connector), connect a vacuum gauge to the hose between the EGR valve and the vacuum pipe.

3. Check the seating of the EGR valve by starting the engine and seeing that it runs at a smooth idle. If the valve is not completely closed, the idle will be rough.

4. With the engine coolant temperature below 95°F (35°C), the vacuum gauge should read zero at 3500 rpm. This indicates that the bimetal vacuum switching valve (BVSV) is functioning correctly at this temperature range.

5. Warm the engine to normal operating temperature. Check the vacuum gauge and confirm low vacuum at 3500 rpm. This indicates the BVSV and the EGR vacuum modulator are working correctly in this temperature range.

6. Disconnect the vacuum hose from the **R** port on the EGR vacuum modulator and, using another piece of hose, connect the **R** port directly to the intake manifold. Check that the vacuum gauge indicates high vacuum at 3500 rpm.

➡As a large amount of exhaust gas enters, the engine will misfire slightly at this time.

7. Disconnect the vacuum gauge and reconnect the vacuum hoses to their proper locations.

8. Check the EGR valve by applying vacuum directly to the valve with the engine at idle. (This may be accomplished by bridging vacuum directly from the intake manifold or by using a hand-held vacuum pump.) The engine should falter and/or stall as the full load of recirculated gasses enters the engine.

9. If no problem is found with this inspection, the system is OK; otherwise inspect each part.

EGR Valve

1988 VIN CODE 5 ENGINE

1. Remove the EGR valve.
2. Check the valve for sticking and heavy carbon deposits. If a problem is found, replace the valve.
3. Reinstall the EGR valve with a new gasket.

1989-93 ALL ENGINES

1. Start the engine and allow it to warm up completely. The coolant temperature must be above 120°F (49°C). The following tests are performed with the engine running.
2. Place a finger on the EGR valve diaphragm. Accelerate the engine slightly; the diaphragm should be felt to move.
3. Disconnect a vacuum hose from the EGR valve and connect a hand held vacuum pump.
4. Apply 10 inches of vacuum to the valve. The diaphragm should move (check again with your finger) and the engine may momentarily run rough or stall.
5. An EGR valve failing either of these quick tests should be replaced. The valves cannot be cleaned or adjusted.

EGR VACUUM MODULATOR

1988 VIN CODE 5 ENGINE

▶ See Figure 16

1. Label and disconnect the vacuum hoses from ports **P**, **Q**, and **R** of the EGR vacuum modulator.

2. Plug the **P** and **R** ports with your fingers.
3. Blow air into port **Q**. Check that the air passes freely through the sides of the air filter.
4. Start the engine and maintain 3500 rpm.
5. Repeat the test above. Check that there is a strong resistance to air flow.
6. Reconnect the vacuum hoses to the proper locations.

1989-93 ALL ENGINES

▶ See Figures 17 and 18

1. Label and remove the 3 hoses from the modulator.
2. Place your fingers over ports **P** and **R**; blow into port **Q**. Air should flow freely from the sides of the air filter on the modulator.
3. Connect a vacuum pump to port **S** (on the bottom of the unit) and plug tubes **P** and **R** with your fingers. Blow air into tube **Q** and attempt to draw a vacuum with the pump. You SHOULD NOT be able to develop a vacuum within the system.
4. If the modulator fails any of these tests, it must be replaced.

Fig. 14 EGR system inspection, preparation — 1988 VIN code 5 engine

A. Restricted airflow
R. R port
P. P port
Q. Q port
1. EGR vacuum modulatror

Fig. 16 EGR vacuum modulator test — 1988 VIN code 5 engine

A.. Vacuum gauge
B. Intake manifold
R. R port

1. EGR vacuum modulator
2. EGR valve

Fig. 15 R port connected to the intake manifold — 1988 VIN code 5 engine

P. P port
R. R port
S. S port

Fig. 17 EGR vacuum modulator test — 1989-93

Fig. 18 EGR vacuum modulator and EGR solenoid valve location — 1993

positive terminal and the VSV body. If there is continuity, replace the VSV.

3. Check for an open circuit. Using an ohmmeter, measure the resistance (ohms) between the 2 terminals of the valve. The resistance should be 33-39ω at 68°F (20°C). If the resistance is not within specifications, replace the VSV.

➡️ **The resistance — ohmmage — will vary slightly with temperature. It will decrease in cooler temperatures and increase with heat. Use common sense; slight variations due to temperature range are not necessarily a sign of a failed valve.**

1989-92 ALL ENGINES

▶ **See Figure 21**

1. Label and disconnect the 2 hoses from the VSV.
2. With the ignition OFF, disconnect the connector at the VSV.
3. Check the resistance between the 2 terminals on the VSV. Look for 33-39ω resistance. If the resistance is incorrect, replace the unit. If the resistance is proper, proceed with the next step.
4. Gently blow air into port **A**. Air should come out through the filter but SHOULD NOT come out through port **B**.
5. Reconnect the electrical connector.
6. Turn the ignition switch ON (but don't start the motor) and ground the Diagnosis Switch Terminal. This is found in the diagnostic connector near the air cleaner assembly and is

Vacuum Switching Valve (VSV)

1988 VIN CODE 5 ENGINE

▶ **See Figures 19 and 20**

1. The vacuum switching valve is located on the left strut tower. The vacuum switching circuit is checked by blowing air into the pipe under the following conditions:

   a. Connect the vacuum switching valve terminals to the battery.

   b. Blow into the tube and check that the VSV switch is open.

   c. Disconnect the positive battery terminal.

   d. Blow into the tube and check that the VSV switch is closed (no flow).

2. Check for a short circuit within the valve. Using an ohmmeter, check that there is no continuity between the

Fig. 20 Vacuum switching valve short circuit check — 1988 VIN code 5 engine

Fig. 19 Vacuum switching valve battery connected — 1988 VIN code 5 engine

Legend:
1 TUBE "A"
2 TUBE "B"
3 FILTER
4 VSV

Fig. 21 Vacuum switching valve — 1989-93 VIN code 5 engine

labeled as terminal **T**. Use a jumper wire with clips to ground the terminal.

✳✳WARNING

Be careful not to ground other terminals in the connector (even accidentally) — severe electrical damage may result!

7. Blow air into port **A**; the air should exit through port **B**.
8. If the VSV fails either of the air flow tests, it should be replaced.

EGR Solenoid Vacuum Valve (EGR SV)

1993 ALL ENGINES

▶ See Figure 18

1. Label and disconnect the 2 hoses from the EGR SV.
2. With the ignition OFF, disconnect the connector at the EGR SV.
3. Check the resistance between the 2 terminals on the EGR SV. Look for 33-39ω resistance. If the resistance is incorrect, replace the unit. If the resistance is proper, proceed with the next step.
4. Gently blow air into port **A**. Air should come out through the filter but SHOULD NOT come out through port **B**.
5. Reconnect the electrical connector.
6. Turn the ignition switch ON (but don't start the motor).
7. Blow air into port **A**; the air should exit through port **B**.
8. If the EGR SV fails either of the air flow tests, it should be replaced.

Bi-metal Vacuum Switching Valve (BVSV)

1988 VIN CODE 5 ENGINE 1989-90 VIN CODE 6 ENGINES

▶ See Figure 22

This valve does nothing more than allow vacuum to flow through the system depending on engine coolant temperature. The bimetallic element within the switch reacts to temperature changes, opening or closing the valve at a pre-determined level. To test the valve:

1. Drain the coolant from the radiator into a suitable container.

✳✳CAUTION

When draining the coolant, keep in mind that cats and dogs are attracted by the ethylene glycol antifreeze, and are quite likely to drink any that is left in an uncovered container or in puddles on the ground. This will prove fatal in sufficient quantity. Always drain the coolant into a sealable container. Coolant should be reused unless it is contaminated or several years old.

2. Label and disconnect the hoses from the BVSV.
3. Remove the valve from the intake manifold.
4. Using cool water, cool the threaded part of the valve to below 95°F (35°C). Blow air into the upper (center) port; there should be NO air passage through the valve. It does not allow vacuum to pass until the engine warms up.
5. Using warm water, heat the threaded part of the valve to above 122°F (50°C) and blow into the port again. The valve should allow the air to pass through.

Fig. 22 Testing the BVSV for correct function

6. If a problem is found with either the 'ON" or 'OFF" functions of the valve, replace it with a new one.
7 .
Using an ohmmeter, measure the resistance between the terminal on the VSV. Resistance should be 33-39ω at 68°F (20°C).
7. Apply liquid sealer to the threads of the BVSV and reinstall it. Connect the vacuum lines.
8. Refill the radiator with coolant.

COMPONENT REMOVAL & INSTALLATION

Exhaust emission control equipment is generally simple to work on and easy to get to on the motor. The air cleaner assembly will need to be removed. Always label each vacuum hose before removing it — they must be replaced in the correct position.

Most of the valves and solenoids are made of plastic, particularly at the vacuum ports. Be very careful during removal not to break or crack the ports; you have almost no chance of regluing a broken fitting. Remember that the plastic has been in a hostile environment (heat and vibration); the fittings become brittle and less resistant to abuse or accidental impact.

EGR valves are generally held in place by 2 bolts. The bolts can be difficult to remove due to corrosion. Once the EGR is off the engine, clean the bolts and the bolt holes of any rust or debris. Always replace the gasket any time the EGR valve is removed.

Oxygen Sensor

The oxygen (O$_2$) sensor is located on the exhaust manifold to detect the concentration of oxygen in the exhaust gas. Using highly refined metals (zirconia and platinum), the sensor uses changes in the oxygen content to generate an electrical signal which is transmitted to the ECM. The computer in turn reacts to the signal by adjusting the fuel metering at the injectors or at the carburetor. More or less fuel is delivered into the cylinders and the correct oxygen level is maintained.

TESTING

1985-88 VIN Code 4 Engine

▶ See Figure 23

1. Warm up the engine to normal operating temperature.
2. Connect the voltmeter to the service connector. This round, green connector is located behind the right shock tower. Connect the positive probe to the OX terminal and the negative probe to the E terminal.
3. Run the engine at 2500 rpm for 90 seconds or more. This allows the sensor to achieve a stable temperature and the exhaust flow to stabilize.
4. Maintain the engine at 2500 rpm and check the meter. The meter needle should fluctuate at least 8 times in 10 seconds in the 0-6 volt range. This indicates that the sensor is working properly.
5. If the sensor fails the test, perform a careful inspection of all the wiring and connectors in the system. A loose connection can cause the sensor to fail this test. Repeat the voltage test after the inspection.

1988 VIN Code 5 Engine

▶ See Figure 24

1. Warm up the engine to normal operating temperature.
2. Connect the voltmeter to the check connector. Hook the negative probe to terminal VF and the positive probe to terminal E1.
3. Run the engine at 2500 rpm for at least 90 seconds.
4. With the engine speed being maintained at 2500 rpm, use a jumper wire to connect terminals T and E1 at the check connector.

Fig. 23 Testing hook-up for the oxygen sensor — 1985-88 VIN code 4 engine

Fig. 24 Testing hook-up for the oxygen sensor — 1988 VIN code 5 engine

5. Watch the voltmeter and note the number of times the needle fluctuates in 10 seconds. If it moves 8 times or more, the sensor is working properly.

a. If the needle moves less than 8 times but more than zero, disconnect the terminal T-to-E1 jumper. Still maintaining 2500 rpm, measure the voltage between terminals E1 and VF. If the voltage is above zero, replace the oxygen sensor. If the voltage is zero, read and record the diagnostic codes (refer to 'Check Engine Light and Diagnostic Codes" later in this Section) and repair the necessary items.

b. If the needle does not move at all (zero), read and record the trouble codes and repair the affected system.

➡ Perform a careful inspection of all the wiring and connectors in the system. A loose connection can cause the sensor to fail these tests. Repeat the voltage test after the inspection. (Refer to 'Check Engine Light and Diagnostic Codes" later in this Section.)

1989-93 Engines

For oxygen sensor diagnostic testing on these engines, please refer the appropriate code charts at the end of this Section.

REMOVAL & INSTALLATION

❊❊WARNING

Care should be used during the removal of the oxygen sensor. Both the sensor and its wire can be easily damaged.

1. The best condition in which to remove the sensor is with the engine in a 'mid-warm" state. This is generally achieved after 2 to 5 minutes (depending on outside temperature) of running after a cold start. The exhaust manifold has developed enough heat to expand and make the removal easier but is not so hot that it has become untouchable. Wearing heat resistant gloves is highly recommended during this repair.
2. With the ignition OFF, disconnect the wiring for the sensor.

3. Unscrew the oxygen sensor from the manifold.

➡**Special wrenches, either socket or open-end, are available from reputable retail outlets for removing the oxygen sensor. These tools make the job much easier and often prevent unnecessary damage.**

4. During and after the removal, use great care to protect the tip of the sensor if it is to be reused. Do not allow it to come in contact with fluids or dirt. Do not attempt to clean it or wash it.

5. When re-installing, apply a coat of anti-seize compound to the threads but DO NOT allow any to get on the tip of the sensor. This includes any accidental or momentary contact from rags, etc..

➡**Most replacement sensors come with the compound already on the threads. Do not remove it or try to clean it. On these sensors, application of anti-seize compound is not necessary.**

6. Install the sensor in the manifold. Tighten it to 30 ft. lbs.
7. Reconnect the electrical connector and insure a clean, tight connection.

3-Way and Oxidation Catalyst (TWC-OC) System

OPERATION

The catalytic converter is a muffler-like container built into the exhaust system to aid in the reduction of HC, CO and NOx emissions by changing them into nitrogen, carbon dioxide and water vapor through the action of the catalyst upon the exhaust gas.

The 3-way catalytic convertor is the best type to use since it can change all 3 types of emissions into non-polluting gases. In this type of converter nitrous oxides are chemically reduced by the catalyst and reformed into the molecules of oxygen and nitrogen. The oxygen formed by the reduction reaction is then used to oxidize carbon monoxide and the hydrocarbons, forming carbon dioxide and water vapor.

For the catalytic converter to work most efficiently, the following conditions must be met:
- Operating temperature must be over 500°F (260°C).
- Air/fuel ratio must be held closely at 14.7:1.

PRECAUTIONS

- Use only unleaded fuel.
- Avoid prolonged idling; the engine should run no longer than 20 minutes at curb idle, nor longer than 10 minutes at fast idle.
- Reduce the fast idle speed, by quickly depressing and releasing the accelerator pedal, as soon as the coolant temperature reaches 120°F (49°C).
- DO NOT disconnect any spark plug leads while the engine is running.

- Always make engine compression checks as quickly as possible. Excess fuel can be pumped through the motor and build up in the converter.
- DO NOT dispose of the catalyst in a place where anything coated with grease, gas, or oil is present; spontaneous combustion could result.
- Since the inside of the catalyst must reach 500°F (260°C) to work efficiently, the outside of the converter will also become very hot. Always be aware of what may be under the car when you park. Parking a hot exhaust system over dry grass, leaves or other flammable items may lead to a fire.

Feedback Carburetor System

OPERATION

1985-88 VIN code 4 engines
▶ **See Figures 25, 26 and 27**

The Carburetor Feedback system is designed to keep the air/fuel ratio at an optimum 14.7:1 during normal operation; excluding warm-up and acceleration.

This is a rather simple system. The carburetor is designed to run richer than it normally should. This sets up a rich limit of system operation. When a leaner operation is desired, the computer (ECM) commands air to bleed into the carburetor's main metering system and into the carburetor's primary bore. A lean operating condition is therefore easy to obtain.

The computer (ECM) receives information from the oxygen sensor, 2 vacuum switches and the distributor.

The output of the computer is a signal to the electric air bleed control valve (EBCV). When the EBCV is energized, it bleeds air into the main air bleed circuit and into the slow air bleed port of the carburetor. This additional air leans the fuel mixture. When the EBCV is not energized, the air/fuel ratio moves towards the rich limit.

With the engine running and the coolant temperature below 45°F (7°C), the thermostatic vacuum switch valve (TVSV) applies atmospheric pressure to vacuum switch **B** by connecting ports **J** to **L** (of the TVSV). With these conditions, vacuum switch **B** is de-energized, the electric bleed control valve (EBCV) is off (de-energized) and both air bleeds are off. The carburetor is therefore operating toward its rich limits, desirable on a cold motor. The computer will not be controlling or influencing air/fuel ratio while the engine is cold.

When the coolant temperature rises above 60°F (16°C), with the engine operating between 1500 and 4200 rpm, the thermostatic vacuum switching valve (TVSV) applies vacuum to vacuum switch **B** by connecting ports **K** to **L** of the TVSV.

Vacuum switch **B** closes, signaling the ECM. Vacuum switch **A** is closed (opens at high vacuum) also signaling the ECM. With these 2 switches closed, if the oxygen sensor senses a rich condition in the exhaust (high voltage-1.0v), the ECM commands the electric bleed control valve to be energized, bleeding air into the main metering system of the carburetor and the intake manifold. This action results in the air/fuel ratio becoming leaner.

Once the air/fuel ratio is detected as being too lean by the oxygen sensor (low voltage-0.1v), the ECM will de-energize the EBCV and close both bleed ports. By shutting off the air, the mixture begins moving back towards the rich limit. The system is operating in the 'closed loop'' mode, during which it will adjust itself and then react to the adjustments. It should be noted that to energize the electric bleed control valve (EBCV) the ECM completes its electrical circuit on its ground side.

TESTING

Carburetor Feedback System
▶ **See Figures 25, 26, 27, 28 and 29**

1. Check the TVSV with the engine cold. The coolant temperature must be below 45°F (7°C).

1. Electronic air bleed control valve (EBCV)
2. Vacuum switch "A"
3. Vacuum switch "B"
4. Thermostatic vacuum switching valve
5. Main air bleed port
6. Slow air bleed port
7. Throttle positioner port

Fig. 25 Feedback carburetor component location

2. Disconnect the vacuum hose from the vacuum switch **B**. Start the engine and check no vacuum is felt in the disconnected vacuum hose.

3. Reconnect the vacuum hose and check the EBCV with the engine warmed up to normal operating temperature.

4. Disconnect the EBCV connector. Maintain an engine speed of approximately 2,500 rpm.

5. Reconnect the connector and check that the engine speed drops by about 300 rpm momentarily.

6. With the engine at idle, repeat the disconnect/reconnect test on the EBCV connector. Check that the engine speed does NOT change.

7. Disconnect the hose from the vacuum switch **B**. Repeat Steps 4 and 5 above. Check that the engine speed does not change.

8. If no problems are found with this inspection, the system is operating properly; otherwise inspect each component part.

Air Bleed Control Valve (EBCV)

1. Check for a short circuit. Using an ohmmeter, check that there is no continuity between the positive (+) terminal (the terminal closest to the lock tab) and the EBCV body. If there is continuity, replace the EBCV.

2. Check for an open circuit. Using an ohmmeter, measure the resistance between the positive (+) terminal and the other terminal. The resistance should be between 11-13ω at 68°F (20°C). If the resistance is not within specification, replace the EBCV. Remember that the resistance will vary slightly with temperature. Resistance (ohms) will decrease as the temperature drops. Use common sense here — a reading of 16 ohms on a hot day does not necessarily indicate a failed valve.

1. Vacuum switch "A"
2. Vacuum switch "B"
3. Thermostatic vacuum switching valve
4. Electronic air bleed control valve
5. Distributor
6. Oxygen sensor
7. Main air bleed port
8. Slow air bleed port

Fig. 26 Feedback carburetor system operation

By means of a signal from the Ox sensor, carburetor primary side main air bleed and slow air bleed volume are controlled to maintain optimum air-fuel mixture in accordance with existing driving conditions, thereby cleaning HC, CO and NOx. In addition, driveability and fuel economy are improved.

Coolant Temp.	TVSV	Condition	Engine rpm	Vacuum S/W		Air Fuel Ratio in the Exhaust Manifold	Ox Sensor Signal	Computer	EBCV	Air Bleed
				A	B					
Below 7°C (45°F)	OPEN (J·L)	—	—	—	OFF	—	—	OFF	CLOSED	OFF
Above 17°C (63°F)	OPEN (K·L)	Idling	Below 1,300 rpm	—	—	—	—	OFF	CLOSED	OFF
		Cruising	Between 1,500 and 4,200	ON	ON	RICH	RICH	ON	OPEN	Feedback air bleed
						LEAN	LEAN	OFF	CLOSED	
			Above 4,400 rpm	—	—	—	—	OFF	CLOSED	OFF
		Heavy loads*	—	ON	OFF	—	—	OFF	CLOSED	OFF
		Deceleration	Above 1,500 rpm	OFF	ON	—	—	ON	OPEN	ON

Remark: *Intake vacuum: below 85 mmHg (3.35 in.Hg, 11.3 kPa)

Fig. 27 Feedback carburetor system operation

Fig. 28 EBCV and Vacuum switch

Fig. 29 Vacuum switch 'A'

Vacuum Switch A

1. Using an ohmmeter, check that there is continuity between the switch terminal and the switch body.
2. Start the engine and run it until normal operating temperature is reached.
3. Using an ohmmeter, check that there is NO continuity between the switch terminal and the switch body.
4. If either test is failed, replace the switch.

Vacuum Switch B

1. Using an ohmmeter, check that there is NO continuity between the switch terminal and the switch body.
2. Start the engine and run until normal operating temperature is reached.

3. Using an ohmmeter, check that there is continuity between the switch terminal and the body.
4. If either test is failed, replace the switch.

Deceleration Fuel Cut-Off System

OPERATION

▶ See Figures 30 and 31

This system cuts off part of the fuel flow to the idle (or slow) circuit of the carburetor to prevent overheating and afterburning in the exhaust system. The first fuel cut solenoid is kept energized by the ECM whenever the engine is running. The only exception is if the vacuum signal is above 8.46 in.Hg with the rpm above 2290. (This combination will be sensed by the ECM when the vacuum switch A de-energizes with a vacuum signal above its calibrated value.) With the first fuel cut-off solenoid valve de-energized, the carburetor's slow (or idle) circuit fuel is cut off. This will occur whenever the vehicle is decelerated from an engine rpm higher than 2290.

TESTING

Fuel Cut-Off System Operation

→**Perform this test quickly to avoid overheating the catalytic converter.**

1. Connect a tachometer to the engine.
2. Start the engine.
3. Check that the engine runs normally.
4. Disconnect the vacuum switch **A** connector.
5. Slowly increase the engine speed to 2,300 rpm, and check that the engine speed is fluctuating.
6. Reconnect the vacuum switch connector. Again slowly increase the engine speed to 2,300 rpm and check that the engine operation returns to normal.
7. If no problem is found with this test, the system is working properly. If any problem is found, inspect each component part.

1. Primary fuel cut solenoid
2. Vacuum switch "A"
3. ECM
4. Engine speed input
5. Ignition switch
6. TP port

Fig. 30 Deceleration fuel cut-off components

First Fuel Cut-Off Solenoid Valve

1. Remove the 2-wire solenoid valve from the carburetor.

✳✳CAUTION

Gasoline may run from the carburetor. Observe no smoking/no open flame precautions. Have a dry powder (Type B-C) fire extinguisher within reach at all times.

2. Apply 12v to one of the solenoid wires while grounding the other.
3. You should be able to feel a distinct click within the solenoid as the circuit is completed and released. This shows that the solenoid is engaging and disengaging properly.
4. Check the O-ring for damage.
5. Reinstall the valve and connect the wiring connector.

Cold Mixture Heater (CMH)

OPERATION

▶ **See Figures 32 and 33**

The cold-mixture heater (CMH) system reduces cold engine emissions and improves driveability during engine warm-up. The intake manifold is heated during cold engine warm-up to accelerate vaporization of the liquid fuel.

The computer looks at alternator terminal **L** to determine if the engine is running and also watches the engine's coolant temperature. If the engine is running and the coolant temperature is below 109°F (43°C), the computer energizes the cold mixture heater relay, which in turn applies battery voltage to the cold mixture heater. The CMH is a multi-element heater ring that is mounted between the carburetor base and the intake manifold. Once the coolant temperature exceeds 131°F (55°C) the CMH relay is de-energized and the heater elements turn off.

TESTING

Cold Mixture System Operation

1. Start the engine. The coolant temperature must be below 109°F (43°C).

This system cuts off part of the fuel in the slow circuit of the carburetor to prevent overheating and afterburning in the exhaust system.

Engine RPM	Vacuum in the Vacuum S/W	Vacuum S/W (A)	Computer	1st Fuel Cut Solenoid Valve	Slow Circuit in Carburetor
Below 1,900 rpm	—	—	ON	ON	OPEN
Above 2,290 rpm	Below 180 mm Hg 7.09 in. Hg 24.0 kPa	ON	ON	ON	OPEN
	Above 215 mm Hg 8.46 in. Hg 28.7 kPa	OFF	OFF	OFF	CLOSED

Fig. 31 Deceleration fuel cut-off system operation

1. Cold mixture heater
2. Cold mixture heater relay
3. Thermoswitch
4. ECM
5. Ignition switch
6. Alternator terminal "L"

Fig. 32 Cold mixture heater system

To reduce cold engine emission and improve driveability, the intake manifold is heated during cold engine operation to accelerate vaporization of the liquid fuel.

IG S/W	Engine	Coolant Temp.	Thermo S/W	ECM	CMH Relay	CMH
OFF	Not running	—	—	—	OFF	OFF
ON	Not running	—	—	OFF	OFF	OFF
	Running	Below 43°C (109°F)	ON	ON	ON	ON (Heated)
		Above 55°C (131°F)	OFF	OFF	OFF	OFF

Fig. 33 Cold mixture heater operation chart

2. Using a voltmeter, check that there is voltage between the positive (+) terminal (white/red wire) and the ground.

✳✳WARNING

The voltmeter probe should be inserted from the rear side of the connector.

3. Allow the engine to warm up and check the OHM with the engine warm. The coolant temperature should be above 131°F (55°C).
4. Using a voltmeter, check that there is NO voltage. If no problem is found with this inspection, the system is working properly.

Mixture Heater

1. Unplug the wiring connector.
2. Using an ohmmeter, check the resistance between the heater terminals. The resistance should be 0.5-2.0 ω. Readings outside this range require replacement of the heater element.
3. Replug the wiring connector.

Cold Mixture Heater Relay

1. Check that there is continuity between the No. 1 and 2 terminals. Check that there is NO continuity between the No. 3 and 4 terminals.

➡**The relay is located under the air intake hose behind the battery.**

2. Apply battery voltage to terminal No. 1 and ground terminal No. 2. Use the ohmmeter to check for continuity between terminals 3 and 4.

Throttle Positioner System

OPERATION

▶ **See Figures 34, 35, 36 and 37**

To reduce HC and CO emissions, the throttle positioner (TP) opens the throttle valve to slightly more than the idle position when decelerating. This keeps the air/ fuel ratio from becoming excessively rich when the throttle valve is quickly closed. In addition, the TP is used to increase idle rpm when power steering fluid pressure exceeds a calibrated value and/or when a large electrical load is placed on the electrical system (headlights, rear defogger etc.).

With the engine idling and an electrical load energized, the vacuum switching valve (VSV) is energized. This directs atmospheric pressure through the VSV to the rear TP diaphragm (A). The action of the spring on the diaphragm is transmitted to the push rod. This causes the throttle valve to open slightly and increase engine rpm. If all of the heavy electrical loads are off, the VSV is off, maintaining vacuum on the diaphragm and preventing the push rod from moving.

Vacuum from the **TP** port of the carburetor acts on a second diaphragm (B), closing the throttle valve. With the vehicle cruising, the vacuum signal in both chambers is low which maintains the **TP** in its high speed (open) position. However,

1. Throttle positioner diaphragm
2. Throttle positioner port
3. Vacuum delay valve
4. Vacuum switching valve

Fig. 34 Throttle positioner component location

when the vehicle is decelerated, vacuum on diaphragm A increases quickly which closes the throttle valve somewhat.

The delay action of the vacuum transmitting valve makes the vacuum increase on diaphragm **B** occur slowly which allows the throttle valve to close at a controlled rate. This slow closing prevents the radical change in emissions caused by the throttle valve slamming shut as the driver suddenly lifts completely off the accelerator, such as when going down a steep hill or preparing to use the brakes.

In the event that power steering pressure exceeds a calibrated value, (such as in a full-lock turn while parking) atmospheric pressure is pulled into chamber A causing diaphragm A to move, increasing rpm. This compensates for the power steering system dragging down the idle speed as it delivers needed fluid pressure.

TESTING

Throttle Positioner System Operation

1. Start the engine and warm up to normal operating temperature.
2. Check the idle speed and adjust if necessary.
3. Disconnect the hose from the TVSV **M** port and plug the **M** port. This will shut off the choke opener and EGR system.
4. Disconnect the vacuum hose from **TP** diaphragm **A**. Check that the **TP** is set at the first step (electrical load idle up). Throttle Positioner at the first setting speed:
   - Manual Trans: 800 rpm
   - Auto. Trans: 900 rpm

If not at the specified speed, adjust the speed with the adjusting screw.

➡ **The adjustment should be made with the cooling fan (at the radiator) OFF.**

5. Disconnect the vacuum hose from the throttle positioner diaphragm **B** and plug the end of the hose.
6. Check that the throttle positioner is set at the second step. The setting speed with the throttle positioner on the second step should be as follows:
   - Manual Trans: 1,300 ± 200 rpm
   - Auto. Trans: 1,400 ± 200 rpm
7. Reconnect the vacuum hose to the throttle positioner diaphragm **B** and check that the engine returns to the first step setting speed within 2-6 seconds.
8. Reconnect the vacuum hose to diaphragm **A**.

9. Reconnect the hose to the TVSV **M** port.

Vacuum Delay Valve

1. Check that air flows without resistance from **B** to **A**.
2. Check that air flows with difficulty from **A** to **B**.
3. If a problem is found, replace the vacuum delay valve.

➡ **When replacing the vacuum delay valve, side A should face the throttle positioner.**

Vacuum Switching Valve

With the engine at idling at normal operating temperature, turn on the high beam headlights. The throttle positioner should move to the first step positions and the idle should increase slightly.

Power Steering Idle-Up Switch

With the engine at idling at normal operating temperature, turn the steering wheel until the wheels are against their stops. Hold the wheels against the stops and check that the throttle positioner moves to the first position. The idle should increase slightly.

High Altitude Compensation (HAC) System

OPERATION

▶ **See Figures 38, 39, 40 and 41**

As altitude increases, air density decreases so that the air/fuel mixture becomes richer. (The same amount of fuel is mixing with less air so the percentage of fuel is higher.) The high altitude compensation (HAC) system insures a proper air/fuel mixture by supplying additional air to the primary low and high speed circuits of the carburetor and advancing the ignition timing to improve driveability at altitudes above 3930 feet. Above 3930 feet, the bellows in the high altitude compensation valve is expanded which closes Port **A**.

With Port **A** closed, the manifold vacuum is allowed to act on the HAC diaphragm. The diaphragm opens Port **B** to the atmosphere (through the HAC valve), allowing air to enter the carburetor's primary low and high speed fuel circuits. This same vacuum signal acts on the distributor sub-diaphragm adding 8 degrees of timing advance.

At altitudes below 2,570 feet, the HAC bellows are contracted opening Port **A**. This vacuum signal with air reduces the vacuum to the distributor's sub-diaphragm (no timing advance). With vacuum strength reduced, port **B** is closed allowing no air bleed into the carburetor's low and high speed circuits.

TESTING

High Altitude Compensation System Operation

1. Check the HAC valve as follows:
   a. Visually check and clean the air filter in the HAC valve.

1. Vacuum switching valve
2. Vacuum delay valve
3. Diaphragm A
4. Diaphragm B
5. Throttle positioner port

Fig. 35 Throttle positioner operation

Fig. 36 Checking the vacuum delay valve

b. At high altitude (above 3930 ft), blow into any 1 of the 2 ports on top of the HAC valve with the engine idling and check that the HAC valve is open to the atmosphere.

c. At low altitude (below 2570 ft), blow into any 1 of the 2 ports on top of the HAC valve with the engine idling and check that the HAC valve is closed.

2. Check the ignition timing as follows:

a. Disconnect the vacuum hose with the check valve from the distributor sub-diaphragm and plug the end of the hose.

b. Check the ignition timing. It should be a maximum of 5° BTDC at 950 rpm.

c. Reconnect the hose to the distributor sub-diaphragm.

d. Check the ignition timing. It should be about 13° BTDC at 950 rpm.

3. Disconnect the vacuum hose from the check valve at the back side and plug the end of the hose. Check that the ignition timing remains stable for more than 1 minute.

To reduce HC and CO emissions, the throttle positioner opens the throttle valve slightly more than at idle when decelerating. This causes the air-fuel mixture to burn completely.

Condition	VSV for electrical load	TP Port Vacuum	Diaphragm A	Diaphragm B	Throttle Valve
Idling	ON	—	Pushed out by diaphragm spring	—	slightly opens (Idle up)
	OFF	Intake manifold vacuum	—	Pulled by intake manifold vacuum	Idle speed position
Cruising	—	Nearly atmospheric pressure	—	Pushed out by diaphragm spring	High speed position
Deceleration	—	Intake manifold vacuum	—	*Pulled by intake manifold vacuum	Slightly opens and *slowly closes to the idling position

Remarks: *This action is delayed by the VTV.

Fig. 37 Throttle positioner operation chart

1. Air filter
2. Cover

Fig. 38 High altitude compensation valve

4. Stop the engine and reconnect the hoses to their proper locations.

5. Disconnect the 2 hoses on the top of the HAC valve. Blow air into each hose and check that the air flows into the carburetor.

6. Reconnect the hoses to their proper locations.

7. Any component not opening or closing properly should be replaced.

Check Valve

1. Check the valve by blowing air into each pipe:

2. Check that air flows from the orange pipe to the black pipe.

3. Check that air does not flow from the black pipe to the orange pipe.

Distributor Vacuum Advance

Remove the distributor cap and rotor. Plug 1 port of the sub-diaphragm. Using a hand-held vacuum pump, apply vacuum to the diaphragm, checking that the vacuum advance moves when the vacuum is applied. Reinstall the rotor and distributor cap.

Hot Air Intake (HAI) System

OPERATION

▶ **See Figures 42 and 43**

This system directs hot air to the carburetor in cold weather to improve driveability and to prevent carburetor icing. With the air temperature in the air cleaner below 72°F (22°C), the atmospheric port in the hot idle compensation valve is closed, sending the full manifold vacuum signal to the hot air intake (HAI) diaphragm. The HAI diaphragm moves, opening the air control valve which directs the heated air (from the exhaust manifold) into the air cleaner.

Once the air cleaner temperature exceeds 84°F (29°C), the HIC atmospheric port is open allowing atmospheric pressure to act on the hot air intake diaphragm. This keeps the air control valve closed, allowing the intake air to come directly down the air cleaner's snorkel from outside the car. This air is always cooler than the air from around the exhaust manifold.

TESTING

1. Remove the air cleaner cover and cool the HIC valve by blowing compressed air on it.

2. Check that the air control valve closes the cool air passages at idle.

3. Reinstall the air cleaner cover and warm up the engine.

4. Check that the air control valve opens the cool air passage at idle.

5. Visually check the hoses and connections for cracks, leaks or damage.

Hot Idle Compensation (HIC) System

OPERATION

▶ **See Figures 44, 45 and 46**

The Hot Idle Compensation (HIC) System allows the air controlled by the HIC valve to enter the intake manifold, maintaining proper air/fuel mixture during idle at high temperatures. When the air cleaner temperature is below 72°F (22°C), the HIC valve's atmospheric port is closed. This allows supplies intake manifold vacuum to the hot air intake (HAI) valve, allowing heated air to enter the air cleaner.

As the temperature in the air cleaner rises, the HIC valve will increase its opening to the atmosphere which, in turn, increases pressure on the diaphragm. As the pressure increases the HAC valve will close more, pulling cooler (more dense) air into the carburetor.

When air cleaner temperatures are between 84°F (29°C) and 126°F (52°C), the HIC valve's atmospheric port opens slightly. This begins to increase the pressure on the HAI diaphragm and its air control valve begins to close.

When intake air temperatures reach 138°F (59°C), both the atmospheric port and the vacuum port of the HIC valve open further. This action steadily increases the pressure on HAI

1. High altitude compensation valve
2. Main air bleed port
3. Slow air bleed port
4. Check valve
5. Electronic air bleed control valve
6. Distributor sub-diaphragm
7. Port "A" (closed)
8. Port "B" (open)

Fig. 39 High altitude compensation system components

diaphragm and continues to close the air control valve, pulling more cool air into the carburetor. At the same time, the opening of the vacuum port allows outside air to bleed into the intake manifold to maintain the proper air/fuel mixture during high temperature at idle.

Finally at temperatures above 192°F (89°C), the HIC valve's atmospheric and vacuum ports open fully, applying maximum pressure to the HAI diaphragm and closing the air control valve completely. This allows the coolest possible air to enter the carburetor.

TESTING

1. Check that air flows from the HAI diaphragm side to the carburetor side while closing the atmospheric port.

2. Check that air does not flow from the carburetor side to the HAI diaphragm side.

3. Below 72°F (22°C), check that air does NOT flow from the HAI diaphragm side to the atmosphere port while closing the intake manifold side.

4. Heat the HIC valve to above 84°F (29°C).

5. Check that air flows from the HAI diaphragm side to the atmospheric port while closing the carburetor side.

As altitude increases, the air-fuel mixture becomes richer. This system insures proper air-fuel mixture by supplying additional air to the primary low and high speed circuit of the carburetor and advances the ignition timing to improve driveability at high altitude above 1,198 m (3,930 ft).

Altitude	Bellows in HAC Valve	Port A in HAC Valve	Port B in HAC Valve	Distributor Sub-diaphragm	Air from HAC Valve	Vacuum Ignition Timing
High Above 1,198 m (3,930 ft.)	Expanded	CLOSED	OPEN	Pulled (Always)	Led into primary low and high speed circuit	Advanced (+8°) (Always)
Low Below 783 m (2,570 ft)	Contracted	OPEN	CLOSED	*Not pulled	Stopped	*Not advanced

Remarks: * However, because of an orifice in the distributor sub-diaphragm pipe leading to the HAC valve, the sub-diaphragm is pulled only during high vacuum such as when idling.

Fig. 40 High altitude compensation (HAC) system operation

Fig. 41 Distributor vacuum advance

Automatic Choke

OPERATION

▶ **See Figures 47 and 48**

The automatic choke system temporarily supplies a rich air/fuel mixture to the engine by closing the choke valve (plate) when the engine is cold. At cold temperatures with the ignition switch ON but the engine not running, there is no voltage supplied from the alternator's **L** terminal at the choke heater. The bimetal choke spring is contracted, closing the choke valve.

As soon as the engine is running, the **L** terminal supplies voltage to the choke heater. The heat generated is transferred

COLD   HOT

COOL AIR

HOT AIR

1. Hot idle compensator valve
2. Atmospheric port
3. Check valve
4. Hot air intake diaphragm
5. Air control valve

Fig. 42 Hot air intake system components

This system leads a hot air supply to the carburetor in cold weather to improve driveability and to prevent the carburetor from icing in extremely cold weather.

Temperature in Air Cleaner	HIC Valve	Air Control Valve	Intake Air
Cold Below 22°C (72°F)	Atmospheric port is CLOSED	Hot air passage OPEN	HOT
Hot Above 29°C (84°F)	Atmospheric port is OPEN	Cool air passage OPEN	COOL

Fig. 43 Hot air intake system operation chart

1. To carburetor
2. To hot air intake diaphragm
3. Atmospheric port

Fig. 44 HIC valve

to the bimetal spring causing it to unwind-opening the choke valve. This helps provide a relatively quick transition between the rich (cold) setting to the normally open position when the engine no longer requires the rich air/fuel mixture.

TESTING

Automatic Choke

1. Allow the choke valve to close.
2. Start the engine.
3. Check that the choke valve begins to open and the choke housing is heated.

Heating Coil

1. Unplug the wire connector.
2. Measure the resistance with an ohmmeter. The resistance should read: 19-24 ohms 68°F (20°C). Allow for slight variations due to temperature differences.

Choke Opener System

OPERATION

▶ **See Figures 49 and 50**

The choke opener system, after warm-up, forcibly holds the choke valve open to prevent an over-rich mixture and releases

the fast idle cam to the 3rd (lowest) step to lower the engine rpm.

When engine coolant temperature is below 122°F (50°C), the thermostatic vacuum switching valve connects port **J** to port **M** which places atmospheric pressure on the choke valve. Through the choke opener linkage, the fast idle cam is set at the first (high idle) or second step.

When the coolant temperature exceeds 154°F (68°C), the TVSV connects Port **K** to Port **M** which now applies manifold vacuum to the choke opener diaphragm. This action opens the choke valve further and releases the fast idle cam to the third step and idle speed decreases.

TESTING

Choke Opener System Operation

1. Disconnect the vacuum hose from the choke opener diaphragm. With the coolant temperature below 122°F (50°C), step down on the accelerator pedal and release it.
2. Start the engine.
3. Reconnect the vacuum hose and check that the choke linkage does not move.
4. Warm the engine to normal operating temperature and shut it off.
5. Disconnect the vacuum hose from the choke opener diaphragm.
6. Set the fast idle cam. While holding the throttle slightly open, push the choke plate closed and hold it closed as you release the throttle.
7. Turn the key and start the motor but DO NOT touch the accelerator pedal.
8. Reconnect the vacuum hose. The choke linkage should move and the fast idle cam should release to the third step (lowest rpm).

TVSV

For testing procedures for the TVSV please refer to the EGR system testing procedures earlier in this Section.

Choke Diaphragm

Check that the choke linkage moves in accordance with the amount of vacuum applied. If a problem is found, replace the diaphragm.

COLD

1 (CLOSED)

4 → ← 2
5 ← ← 3

HOT (1)

1 (OPEN)

2

2

HOT (2)

2

2

HOT (3)

2

2

1. Atmospheric port
2. Vacuum port
3. Check valve

4. From hai diaphragm
5. To carburetor

Fig. 45 HIC system operation

This system allows the air controlled by the HIC valve to enter the intake manifold to maintain proper air-fuel mixture during high temperatures at idle.

Temperature in Air Cleaner	HIC Valve Atmospheric Port	HIC Valve Vacuum Port Opening	HIC System
HOT (1) Between 29°C (84°F) and 52°C (126°F)	OPEN	MINIMUM	OFF
HOT (2) Between 59°C (138°F) and 82°C (180°F)	OPEN	PARTIAL	ON Air volume is controlled by HIC valve
HOT (3) Above 89°C (192°F)	OPEN	MAXIMUM	ON

Fig. 46 HIC system operation chart

3

Cool Hot

Electric Current

1

2

1. Bi-metal
2. Ceramic heater
3. Choke valve

Fig. 47 Choke system components

This system temporarily supplies a rich mixture to the engine by closing the choke valve when the engine is cold

IG S/W	Engine	Current from L Terminal to Heater	Bimetal	Choke Valve
OFF	Not running	Not flowing	Expanded	CLOSED
ON	Not running	*Not flowing	Expanded	CLOSED
	Running	Flowing	Heated and contracted	OPEN

Remarks: *On alternators with IC regulator, slight voltage will occur when the ignition switch is turned ON, but not sufficient current to warm up the heater.

Fig. 48 Choke system operation chart

1. Thermostatic vacuum switching valve
2. Choke opener diaphragm

Fig. 49 Choke opener system operation

After warm up, this system forcibly holds the choke valve open to prevent an over-rich mixture and releases the fast idle to the 3rd step to lower engine rpm.

Coolant Temp.	TVSV	Diaphragm	Choke Valve	Fast Idle Cam	Engine RPM
Below 50°C (122°F)	OPEN (J-M)	Released by spring tension	Closed by automatic choke	Set at 1st or 2nd step	HIGH
Above 68°C (154°F)	OPEN (K-M)	Pulled by manifold vacuum	OPEN	Released to 3rd step	LOW

Fig. 50 Choke opener system operation

Auxiliary Acceleration Pump (AAP)

OPERATION

▶ **See Figures 51 and 52**

When accelerating with a cold engine, the main acceleration pump's capacity is insufficient to provide enough fuel for good acceleration. The auxiliary acceleration pump system compensates for this by forcing more fuel into the acceleration nozzle to obtain better cold engine performance.

When engine coolant temperature is below 122°F (50°C), the thermostatic vacuum switching valve connects port **K** to

1. Accelerator nozzle
2. Diaphragm
3. Thermostatic vacuum switching valve
4. Intake manifold

Fig. 51 Auxiliary acceleration pump system components

port **N** which connects manifold vacuum to the AAP diaphragm. When engine rpm is relatively steady, the diaphragm moves against its spring causing its fuel chamber to fill. Whenever the engine is accelerated, the vacuum signal to the AAP diaphragm diminishes quickly. The diaphragm is pushed by its spring, forcing its fuel into the main acceleration circuit and out its nozzle.

After coolant temperature exceeds 154°F (68°C), the TVSV blocks Port **K** and Port **N** stopping the operation of the auxiliary acceleration pump system. The additional fuel requirement for warm engine acceleration is adequately handled by the main acceleration pump (carburetor) circuit.

TESTING

Auxiliary Acceleration Pump System

1. Check that the coolant temperature is below 122°F (50°C). Remove the cover from the air cleaner and start the engine.
2. Pinch the AAP hose, and shut off the engine.
3. Release the hose. Check that gasoline spurts out from the accelerator nozzle in the carburetor. Don't perform this test too often — you may flood the motor.
4. Restart the engine and warm it to normal operating temperature. Repeat steps 2 and 3 above. Check that gasoline DOES NOT spurt out from the accelerator nozzle.
5. Reinstall the air cleaner cover.

Auxiliary Acceleration Pump Diaphragm

1. Start the engine.
2. Disconnect the hose from the AAP diaphragm.
3. Apply vacuum directly to the AAP diaphragm (at idle) with a hand held vacuum pump.

4. Check that the engine rpm changes as the vacuum is released from the system.
5. Reconnect the AAP hose.

Heat Control Valve

OPERATION

▶ **See Figures 53 and 54**

When the engine is cold, the heat control valve improves fuel vaporization for better driveability by quickly heating the intake manifold. Once the engine has warmed up, it helps keep the intake manifold at proper temperature.

With the engine cold, the bimetal spring positions the heat control valve to direct some of the engine's hot exhaust gases under the intake manifold which quickly bring it to the proper operating temperature.

When the engine is hot, the bimetal spring contracts, moving the position of the heat control valve to direct most of the exhaust under the valve and away from direct contact with the intake manifold.

TESTING

The valve within the exhaust system has a counterweight on the outside of the pipe. This counterweight is viewed most easily from under the car. With the engine cold, check that the counterweight is in the upper position. After the engine has been warmed up, check that the weight has moved to the lower position.

When accelerating with a cold engine, the main acceleration pump capacity is insufficient to provide good acceleration. The AAP system compensates for this by forcing more fuel into the acceleration nozzle to obtain better cold engine performance.

Coolant Temp	TVSV	Engine	Intake Vacuum	Diaphragm in AAP	Fuel
Below 50°C (122°F)	OPEN (K-N)	Constant RPM	HIGH	Pulled by vacuum	Drawn into AAP chamber
		Acceleration	LOW	Returned by spring tension	Forced into acceleration nozzle
Above 68°C (154°F)	CLOSED (K-N)	—	—	No operation	—

Fig. 52 Auxiliary acceleration pump system chart

COLD ENGINE   HOT ENGINE

INTAKE MANIFOLD

FROM EXHAUST PORTS

TO EXHAUST MANIFOLD

1 Heat control valve
2 Bi-metal

Fig. 53 Heat control valve operation

When cold, this device improves fuel vaporization for better driveability by quickly heating the intake manifold. After warm-up, it keeps the intake manifold at the proper temperature.

Engine	Bimetal	Exhaust Gas Passage	Intake Manifold
COLD	EXPANDED	Above the heat control valve	Heated quickly
HOT	CONTRACTED	Under the heat control valve	Heated to a suitable temperature

Fig. 54 Heat control valve operation chart

ELECTRONIC ENGINE CONTROLS

BASIC KNOWLEDGE AND TOOLS REQUIRED

To use this manual most effectively, a general understanding of basic electrical circuits and circuit testing tools is required. You should be familiar with wiring diagrams, the meaning of voltage, ohms, amps, the basic theories of electricity, and understand what happens in an open or shorted wire.

To perform system diagnosis, the use of a tachometer, test light, ohmmeter, digital voltmeter with 10 megohms impedance, vacuum gauge and jumper wires are also required. Please become acquainted with the tools and their use before attempting to diagnose a vehicle.

Diagnostic System 1988 VIN Code 5 Engine

Operation

The **Check Engine** light is the device providing communication between the Electronic Control Module (ECM) and the driver. The ECM controls the electronic fuel injection, the electronic spark control, the diagnostic function and the fail-safe or default function.

The ECM receives signals from various sensors indicating changing engine operating conditions. These signals are utilized by the ECM to determine the injection duration (amount of time each injector stays open) to maintain the optimum air/fuel ratio under all conditions. The conditions affecting the injector duration are:
- Exhaust gas oxygen content
- Intake air mass
- Intake air temperature
- Coolant temperature
- Engine rpm
- Acceleration/deceleration
- Electrical load
- Air conditioning on/off

The ECM is programmed with data for optimum ignition timing under any and all operating conditions. Using data provide by the sensors, the ECM triggers the spark within each cylinder at precisely the right instant for the existing conditions.

The ECM detects any malfunctions or abnormalities in the sensor network and lights the **Check Engine** light on the dash panel. At the same time the trouble is identified by circuit and a diagnostic code is recorded within the ECM. This diagnostic code can be read by the number of blinks of the instrument light when both check engine terminals are shorted under the hood. For the VIN code 5 engine in 49-state trim, there are 13 different codes; California cars produce 14 codes.

In the event of an internal computer malfunction, the ECM is programmed with back-up or default values. This allows the car to run on a fixed set of 'rules" for engine operation. Driveability may suffer since the driving conditions cannot be dealt with by the faulty computer. This back-up programming allows the computer to fail with out stranding the car, hence the nickname fail-safe. No computer is safe from failure, but a back-up system helps make the best of the situation.

With the exception of the oxygen sensor (discussed earlier in this Section) the testing and replacement of the various sensors is discussed in Section 5.

Fault Codes

▶ **See Figures 55, 56, 57 and 58**

READING

To read the code(s) from the ECM:
1. The following initial conditions must be met or the code will not be transmitted from the ECM:
    a. Battery voltage above 11 volts
    b. Throttle plate fully closed — keep your foot off the accelerator
    c. Transmission selector in neutral
    d. All accessory switches off
2. Turn the ignition switch ON, but DO NOT start the engine.
3. Use a service (jumper) wire to short both terminals of the engine check connector, located under the hood near the wiper motor.
4. The diagnosis code(s) will be indicated by the number of flashes of the **Check Engine** light. If the system is normal, the light will blink repeatedly every ½ second. This indication is displayed when no codes are stored in the ECM. It serves as a confirmation the the ECM has nothing to tell you — all is well. If a fault code is stored, its 2 digit code will be indicated in the pattern of the flashing. For example, code 21 would be indicated by 2 flashes, a pause, and 1 flash. There will be a 1½ second pause between the first and second digit of a code. If more than 1 code is stored, the next will be transmitted after a 2½ second pause. Once all the codes have been flashed, the system will wait 4½ seconds and repeat the entire series. It will continue sending the fault codes as long as the initial conditions are met and the engine check connector is shorted across terminal **T** and **E1**.

➡**If more than 1 code is stored, they will be delivered in numerical order from the lowest to the highest, regardless of which code occurred first. The order of the codes DOES NOT indicate the order of occurrence.**

5. After the code(s) have been read and recorded, turn the ignition switch to OFF and disconnect the jumper wire.

❋❋WARNING

Disconnecting the wire with the ignition ON may cause severe damage to the ECM.

Resetting The Check Engine Light

▶ **See Figures 59, 60, 61, 62, 63, 64, 65, 66, 67, 68, 69, 70, 71, 72, 73, 74, 75 and 76**

Once the codes have been read and recorded, the memory on the ECM may be cleared of any stored codes by removing the power to the ECM for at least 20 seconds. This is most easily done by removing the STOP fuse from the fusebox for the necessary period of time.

❋❋WARNING

The ignition MUST be OFF when the fuse is removed and reinstalled. Serious and disabling damage may occur if this precaution is not followed.

Remember that the codes are there to indicate a problem area. Don't clear the code just to get the dashboard light off — find the problem and fix it for keeps. If you erase the code and ignore the problem, the code will reset (when the engine is restarted) if the problem is still present.

The necessary time to clear the computer increases as the temperature drops. To be safe, remove the fuse for a full minute under all conditions. The system can also be cleared by disconnecting the negative battery cable, but this will require resetting other memory devices such as the clock and/or radio. If for any reason the memory does not clear, any stored codes will be retained. Any time the ECM is cleared,

Fig. 55 Location of the check engine connector — 1988 VIN code 5 engine

CODE NO. 13   CODE NO. 21   CODE NO. 13

1.5   2.5   4.5   (SECONDS)

Fig. 56 Examples of a multiple code display — 1988 VIN code 5

Code No.	Number of CHECK ENGINE blinks	System	Trouble area
–	⎍⎍⎍⎍⎍⎍⎍ ON OFF	Normal	–
12	⎍⎍⎍	RPM signal	1. Distributor circuit 2. Distributor 3. Igniter circuit 4. Igniter 5. Starter signal circuit 6. ECM
13	⎍⎍⎍⎍	RPM signal	1. Distributor circuit 2. Distributor 3. ECM
14	⎍⎍⎍⎍⎍	Ignition signal	1. Igniter and ignition coil circuit 2 Igniter and ignition coil 3. ECM
21	⎍⎍⎍	Exhaust oxygen sensor signal	1. Exhaust oxygen sensor circuit 2. Exhaust oxygen sensor 3. ECM
		Exhaust oxygen sensor heater	1. Exhaust oxygen sensor heater circuit 2. Exhaust oxygen sensor heater 3. ECM
22	⎍⎍⎍⎍	Coolant temp. sensor signal	1. Coolant temp. sensor circuit 2. Coolant temp. sensor 3. ECM
24	⎍⎍⎍⎍⎍	Manifold air temp. sensor signal	1. Manifold air temp. sensor circuit 2. Manifold air temp. sensor 3. ECM
25	⎍⎍⎍⎍⎍⎍	Air-fuel ratio lean malfunc-tion	1. Injector circuit 2. Injector 3. Fuel line pressure 4. Ignition system 5. Mass air flow sensor 6. Exhaust oxygen sensor circuit 7. Exhaust oxygen sensor 8. ECM 9. Air intake system

Fig. 57 Trouble codes for ECM — 1988 VIN code 5 engine

Code No.	Number of CHECK ENGINE blinks	System	Trouble area
26		Air-fuel ratio Rich malfunction	1. Injector circuit 2. Injector 3. Fuel line pressure 4. Cold start injector 5. Mass air flow sensor 6. ECM 7. Exhaust oxygen sensor circuit 8. Exhaust oxygen sensor
31		Mass air flow sensor signal	1. Mass air flow sensor circuit 2. Air flow meter 3. ECM
41		Throttle position sensor signal	1. Throttle position sensor circuit 2. Throttle position sensor 3. ECM
42		Vehicle speed sensor signal	1. Vehicle speed sensor circuit 2. Vehicle speed sensor 3. ECM
43		Starter signal	1. Starter relay circuit 2. IG switch, main relay circuit 3. ECM
51		Switch signal	1. A/C switch 2. Throttle position sensor circuit 3. Throttle position sensor 4. ECM 5. A/C switch circuit 6. A/C switch amplifier
71		EGR system malfunction	1. EGR system (EGR vale, EGR hose, etc.) 2. EGR gas temp. sensor circuit 3. EGR gas temp. sensor 4. VSV for EGR 5. VSV for EGR circuit 6. ECM

* For California

Fig. 58 Trouble codes for ECM — 1988 VIN code 5 engine

the car should be driven and then re-checked to confirm a 'normal" signal from the ECM.

➡ **In the event of any mechanical work requiring the disconnection of the negative battery cable, the ECM should be interrogated for stored codes before removing the cable. Once the cable is removed, the codes will be lost almost immediately. Always check for stored codes before beginning any other diagnostic work.**

Diagnostic System 1989-93

Diagnostic Information

The diagnostic 'tree" charts and functional checks in this manual are designed to locate a faulty circuit or component through logic based on the process of elimination.

Service Engine Soon Light

This light is on the instrument panel and has the following functions.
- It informs the driver that a problem has occurred and that the vehicle should be taken for service as soon as reasonably possible.
- It displays 'Codes" stored by the ECM which help the technician diagnose system problems.

As a bulb and system check, the light will come 'ON" with the key 'ON" and the engine not running. When the engine is started, the light will turn 'OFF". If the light remains 'ON', the self-diagnostic system has detected a problem. If the problem goes away, the light will go out in most cases after 10 seconds, but a Code will remain stored in the ECM with the following exceptions:
- On 1992 models, any memory of code 51 or 53 is erased as soon as the ignition switch is turned to the **OFF** position. In order to detect an active code 51 or 53 the ignition switch must be in the **ON** position (engine not running) with the diagnostic request terminal (TE1) and the diagnosis check connector grounded. If the ignition switch is turned to the **OFF** position at any time during this procedure, a present code 51 or 53 will be lost.
- On 1993 models, the Diagnostic Trouble Codes (DTC's) 16, 42, 43 and 51 are not stored in the memory of the Engine Control Module (ECM) or the Powertrain Control Module (PCM), once the problem has gone away.

When the light remains 'ON" while the engine is running, or when a malfunction is suspected due to a driveability or emissions problem, a 'Diagnostic Circuit Check" must be performed. These checks will expose malfunctions which may not be detected if other diagnostics are performed prematurely.

Intermittent 'Service Engine Soon" Light

In the case of an 'intermittent problem, the 'Service Engine Soon" light will light for ten (10) seconds and then will go out. However, the corresponding code will be stored in the memory of the ECM until the battery voltage to the ECM has been removed, with the exceptions noted under the explanation of 'Service Engine Soon Light" above.

When unexpected codes appear during the code reading process, one can assume that these codes were set by an intermittent malfunction and could be helpful in diagnosing the system.

An intermittent code may or may not re-set. If it is an intermittent failure, a Diagnostic Code Chart is not used. A physical inspection of the applicable sub-system most often will resolve the problem.

Reading Codes

1989-91 MODELS

▶ **See Figures 77, 78 and 79**

To read the codes from the ECM:
1. With the ignition OFF, use a service (jumper) wire to ground the diagnostic switch in the connector under the hood.
2. Without touching the accelerator pedal, turn the ignition to ON but DO NOT start the motor.
3. The codes will be displayed through the flashing of the **Check Engine** light. Count the number of flashes to determine the numerical code.   If the system is normal and has no codes stored, the lamp will flash on and off several times rhythmically.   If this signal is received, no further codes will be transmitted from the ECM.   Stored fault codes will be displayed in numerical order from lowest to highest without regard to which code occurred first. All codes are 2 digit and will be displayed with a 1 second pause between digits. (Example: Code 21 will show 2 flashes, a 1 second pause and then 1 flash.) Each code will be displayed 3 times in a row with a 3 second pause between each code. After any 1 code has been flashed 3 times, the next stored code will be displayed 3 times .
4. After the code(s) have been read and recorded, turn the ignition switch to OFF and disconnect the jumper wire.

❊❊WARNING

Disconnecting the wire with the ignition ON may cause severe damage to the ECM.

1992 MODELS

▶ **See Figure 80**

The provision for communicating with the ECM is the diagnostic request terminal (TE1) in the diagnosis check connector. The diagnosis check connector is located in the left rear engine compartment on the strut tower. Codes stored in the ECM's memory can be read by counting the number of flashes of the 'CHECK ENGINE" indicator with the ignition switch in the 'ON" position and the diagnostic request terminal (TE1) grounded. When this terminal is grounded, the ECM enters its diagnostic mode and outputs codes to the 'CHECK ENGINE" indicator.

To ground the diagnostic request terminal, connect a jumper between diagnosis check connector terminals 'TE1" and 'E1". At this point, the 'CHECK ENGINE" indicator should either flash 'ON" and 'OFF" continuously or flash Code 51 once and then flash 'ON" and 'OFF" continuously. This would be the following flash sequence: 'flash, pause, flash, pause, flash, pause," etc.., or 'flash-flash-flash-flash-flash, pause, flash, long pause, flash, pause, flash, pause, flash, pause,'etc.. Code 51 indicates the ECM's diagnostic system, the idle switch, the A/C switch and the park/neutral circuits are all functioning correctly. If Code 51 is not indicated and the 'CHECK ENGINE"

1. DISTRIBUTOR
2. CHECK VALVE
3. THERMO SWITCH
4. THERMOSTATIC VACUUM SWITCHING VALVE
5. JET
6. CHOKE BREAKER
7. HOT AIR INTAKE DIAPHRAGM
8. VACUUM SWITCHING VALVE
9. CHARCOAL CANISTER
10. OUTER VENT CONTROL VALVE
11. EGR VALVE
12. EGR VACUUM MODULATOR

13. AUXILIARY ACCELERATION PUMP
14. AIR SUCTION VALVE
15. CHECK VALVE
16. DELAY VALVE
17. ELECTRIC AIR BLEED CONTROL VALVE
18. HIGH ALTITUDE COMPENSATION VALVE
19. VACUUM SWITCH (A)
20. VACUUM SWITCH (B)
21. VACUUM SWITCHING VALVE
22. THROTTLE POSITIONER
23. CHOKE OPENER
24. HOT IDLE COMPENSATOR

Fig. 59 Component location — 1985-88 VIN code 4 engine (49 state and Canada)

1. DISTRIBUTOR
2. THERMO SWITCH
3. THERMOSTATIC VACUUM SWITCHING VALVE
4. JET
5. CHOKE BREAKER
6. HOT AIR INTAKE DIAPHRAGM
7. VACUUM SWITCHING VALVE
8. CHARCOAL CANISTER
9. OUTER VENT CONTROL VALVE
10. EGR VALVE
11. EGR VACUUM MODULATOR
12. AUXILIARY ACCELERATION PUMP
13. AIR SUCTION VALVE (REED VALVE)
14. AIR SUCTION VALVE (SHUT OFF VALVE)
15. CHECK VALVE
16. DELAY VALVE
17. ELECTRIC AIR BLEED CONTROL VALVE
18. VACUUM SWITCH (A)
19. VACUUM SWITCH (B)
20. VACUUM SWITCHING VALVE
21. THROTTLE POSITIONER
22. CHOKE OPENER
23. HOT IDLE COMPENSATOR

Fig. 60 Component location — 1985-88 VIN code 4 engine (California)

indicator is just flashing 'ON'' and 'OFF'' continuously, a problem may be present in either the idle switch, the A/C switch or the park/neutral circuits, and should be addressed by consulting Code 51's diagnostic chart in this section.

If any code exists indicating a problem, that code will be flashed instead of Code 51. If more than one code is stored in the ECM's memory, the codes will be repeatedly output from the lowest to the highest, with each code being displayed 3 times.

1993 Models

▶ **See Figure 81**

The provision for communicating with the Engine Control Module (ECM) and the Powertrain Control Module (PCM) is a set of diagnostic terminals (TE1) and (TE2) in the data link connector (DLC). The DLC is located in the left rear engine compartment on the strut tower. Diagnostic trouble codes

(DTC's) stored in the ECM's/PCM's memory can be read by counting the number of flashes of the malfunction indicator lamp (MIL) with the ignition switch in the 'ON'' position with diagnostic request terminal 'TE1'' grounded. The ECM/PCM has two different diagnostic modes - normal and test. When 'TE1'' is grounded, the ECM/PCM enters its normal diagnostic mode and emits DTC's that have been detected one time within the last two ignition cycles. When 'TE2'' is grounded, the ECM/PCM enters its test diagnostic mode and lowers the threshold at which DTC's can be stored in the ECM's/PCM's memory. This function is helpful when diagnosing intermittent problems. With 'TE1'' and 'TE2'' grounded, DTCs that cannot be read in the normal diagnostic mode can be read.

To ground diagnostic request terminal 'TE1'', connect a fused jumper between DLC terminals 'TE1'' and 'E1'' and turn the ignition switch to 'ON''. At this point, the MIL should flash 'ON'' and 'OFF'' continuously. This would be the following flash

1. THERMO SWITCH
2. CHARCOAL CANISTER
3. OUTER VENT CONTROL VALVE
4. PRIMARY FUEL CUT SOLENOID
5. SECONDARY FUEL CUT SOLENOID
6. VACUUM SWITCHING VALVE
7. COLD MIXTURE HEATER RELAY
8. HIGH ALTITUDE COMPENSATOR VALVE
9. AIR SUCTION VALVE
10. ELECTRIC AIR BLEED CONTROL VALVE
11. CHECK VALVE
12. EGR VACUUM MODULATOR
13. EGR VALVE
14. HOT AIR INTAKE DIAPHRAGM
15. HOT IDLE COMPENSATOR VALVE
16. CHOKE OPENER

17. AUXILIARY ACCELERATOR PUMP
18. CHOKE BREAKER
19. JET
20. THROTTLE POSITIONER
21. DELAY VALVE
22. THERMOSTATIC VACUUM SWITCHING VALVE
23. VACUUM SWITCH (A)
24. VACUUM SWITCH (B)
25. COLD MIXTURE HEATER
26. OXYGEN SENSOR
27. HEAT CONTROL VALVE
28. DISTRIBUTOR
29. CHECK VALVE
30. VACUUM SWITCHING VALVE

Fig. 61 Vacuum and wiring diagram — 1985-88 VIN code 4 engine (49 state and Canada)

1. THERMO SWITCH
2. CHARCOAL CANISTER
3. OUTER VENT CONTROL VALVE
4. PRIMARY FUEL CUT SOLENOID
5. SECONDARY FUEL CUT SOLENOID
6. VACUUM SWITCHING VALVE
7. COLD MIXTURE HEATER RELAY
8. AIR SUCTION VALVE (SHUT OFF VALVE)
9. AIR SUCTION VALVE (REED VALVE)
10. ELECTRIC AIR BLEED CONTROL VALVE
11. CHECK VALVE
12. EGR VACUUM MODULATOR
13. EGR VALVE
14. HOT AIR INTAKE DIAPHRAGM
15. HOT IDLE COMPENSATOR VALVE
16. CHOKE OPENER

17. AUXILIARY ACCELERATOR PUMP
18. CHOKE BREAKER
19. JET
20. THROTTLE POSITIONER
21. DELAY VALVE
22. THERMOSTATIC VACUUM SWITCHING VALVE
23. VACUUM SWITCH (A)
24. VACUUM SWITCH (B)
25. COLD MIXTURE HEATER
26. OXYGEN SENSOR
27. HEAT CONTROL VALVE
28. DISTRIBUTOR
29. VACUUM SWITCHING VALVE

Fig. 62 Vacuum and wiring diagram — 1985-88 VIN code 4 engine (California)

Fig. 63 Component location — 1987 VIN code 4 engine (California)

1. DISTRIBUTOR
2. THERMO SWITCH
3. THERMOSTATIC VACUUM SWITCHING VALVE
4. JET
5. CHOKE BREAKER
6. HOT AIR INTAKE DIAPHRAGM
7. VACUUM SWITCHING VALVE
8. CHARCOAL CANISTER
9. OUTER VENT CONTROL VALVE
10. EGR VALVE
11. EGR VACUUM MODULATOR
12. AUXILIARY ACCELERATION PUMP
13. AIR SUCTION VALVE (REED VALVE)
14. AIR SUCTION VALVE (SHUT OFF VALVE)
15. CHECK VALVE
16. DELAY VALVE
17. ELECTRIC AIR BLEED CONTROL VALVE
18. THROTTLE POSITION SWITCH
19. VACUUM SWITCH
20. VACUUM SWITCHING VALVE
21. THROTTLE POSITIONER
22. CHOKE OPENER
23. HOT IDLE COMPENSATOR
24. JET

1. DISTRIBUTOR
2. CHECK VALVE
3. THERMO SWITCH
4. THERMOSTATIC VACUUM SWITCHING VALVE
5. JET
6. CHOKE BREAKER
7. HOT AIR INTAKE DIAPHRAGM
8. VACUUM SWITCHING VALVE
9. CHARCOAL CANISTER
10. OUTER VENT CONTROL VALVE
11. EGR VALVE
12. EGR VACUUM MODULATOR
13. AUXILIARY ACCELERATION PUMP
14. AIR SUCTION VALVE
15. CHECK VALVE
16. DELAY VALVE
17. ELECTRIC AIR BLEED CONROL VALVE
18. HIGH ALTITUDE COMPENSATION VALVE
19. THROTTLE POSITION SWITCH
20. VACUUM SWITCH
21. VACUUM SWITCHING VALVE
22. THROTTLE POSITIONER
23. CHOKE OPENER
24. HOT IDLE COMPENSATOR
25. JET

Fig. 64 Component location — 1987 VIN code 4 engine (49 state and Canada)

1. THERMO SWITCH
2. CHARCOAL CANISTER
3. OUTER VENT CONTROL VALVE
4. PRIMARY FUEL CUT SOLENOID
5. SECONDARY FUEL CUT SOLENOID
6. VACUUM SWITCHING VALVE
7. COLD MIXTURE HEATER RELAY
8. AIR SUCTION VALVE (SHUT OFF VALVE)
9. AIR SUCTION VALVE (REED VALVE)
10. ELECTRIC AIR BLEED CONTROL VALVE
11. CHECK VALVE
12. EGR VACUUM MODULATOR
13. EGR VALVE
14. HOT AIR INTAKE DIAPHRAGM
15. HOT IDLE COMPENSATOR VALVE
16. CHOKE OPENER
17. AUXILIARY ACCELERATOR PUMP
18. CHOKE BREAKER
19. JET
20. THROTTLE POSITIONER
21. DELAY VALVE
22. THERMOSTATIC VACUUM SWITCHING VALVE
23. THROTTLE POSITION SWITCH
24. VACUUM SWITCH
25. COLD MIXTURE HEATER
26. OXYGEN SENSOR
27. HEAT CONTROL VALVE
28. DISTRIBUTOR
29. VACUUM SWITCHING VALVE
30. JET

Fig. 65 Vacuum and wiring diagram — 1987 VIN code 4 engine (California)

1. THERMO SWITCH
2. CHARCOAL CANISTER
3. OUTER VENT CONTROL VALVE
4. PRIMARY FUEL CUT SOLENOID
5. SECONDARY FUEL CUT SOLENOID
6. VACUUM SWITCHING VALVE
7. COLD MIXTURE HEATER RELAY
8. HIGH ALTITUDE COMPENSATOR VALVE
9. AIR SUCTION VALVE
10. ELECTRIC AIR BLEED CONTROL VALVE
11. CHECK VALVE
12. EGR VACUUM MODULATOR
13. EGR VALVE
14. HOT AIR INTAKE DIAPHRAGM
15. HOT IDLE COMPENSATOR VALVE

16. CHOKE OPENER
17. AUXILIARY ACCELERATOR PUMP
18. CHOKE BREAKER
19. JET
20. THROTTLE POSITIONER
21. DELAY VALVE
22. THERMOSTATIC VACUUM SWITCHING VALVE
23. THROTTLE POSITION SWITCH
24. VACUUM SWITCH
25. COLD MIXTURE HEATER
26. OXYGEN SENSOR
27. HEAT CONTROL VALVE
28. DISTRIBUTOR
29. CHECK VALVE
30. VACUUM SWITCHING VALVE
31. JET

Fig. 66 Vacuum and wiring diagram — 1987 VIN code 4 engine (49 state and Canada)

1   DISTRIBUTOR
2   THERMO SWITCH
3   THERMOSTATIC VACUUM SWITCHING VALVE
4   JET
5   CHOKE BREAKER
6   HOT AIR INTAKE DIAPHRAGM
7   VACUUM SWITCHING VALVE
8   FUEL VAPOR CANISTER
9   OUTER VENT CONTROL VALVE
10 EGR VALVE
11 EGR VACUUM MODULATOR
12 AUXILIARY ACCELERATION PUMP

13 AIR SUCTION VALVE (REED VALVE)
14 AIR SUCTION VALVE (SHUT OFF VALVE)
15 CHECK VALVE
16 DELAY VALVE
17 ELECTRIC AIR BLEED CONTROL VALVE
18 THROTTLE POSITION SWITCH
19 VACUUM SWITCH
20 VACUUM SWITCHING VALVE
21 THROTTLE POSITIONER
22 CHOKE OPENER
23 HOT IDLE COMPENSATOR
24 JET

Fig. 67 Component location — 1988 VIN code 4 engine (California with man. trans.)

1. DISTRIBUTOR
2. CHECK VALVE
3. THERMO SWITCH
4. THERMOSTATIC VACUUM SWITCHING VALVE
5. JET
6. CHOKE BREAKER
7. HOT AIR INTAKE DIAPHRAGM
8. VACUUM SWITCHING VALVE
9. CHARCOAL CANISTER
10. OUTER VENT CONTROL VALVE
11. EGR VALVE
12. EGR VACUUM MODULATOR
13. AUXILIARY ACCELERATION PUMP
14. AIR SUCTION VALVE
15. CHECK VALVE
16. DELAY VALVE
17. ELECTRIC AIR BLEED CONTROL VALVE
18. HIGH ALTITUDE COMPENSATION VALVE
19. VACUUM SWITCH (A)
20. VACUUM SWITCH (B)
21. VACUUM SWITCHING VALVE
22. THROTTLE POSITIONER
23. CHOKE OPENER
24. HOT IDLE COMPENSATOR

Fig. 68 Component location — 1988 VIN code 4 engine (49 state and Canada with man. trans.)

1	TVSV	14	AS SHUT-OFF VALVE
2	CHECK VALVE	15	AS READ VALVE
3	DISTRIBUTOR	16	EGR VACUUM MODULATOR
4	HIC VALVE	17	EGR VALVE
5	VSV	18	JET
6	CHOKE OPENER	19	OUTER VENT CONTROL VALVE
7	TP	20	FUEL VAPOR CANISTER
8	VTV	21	VSV
9	VSV	22	HAI DIAPHRAGM
10	VACUUM SWITCH	23	CB
11	THROTTLE POSITION SWITCH	24	AAP
12	EBCV	25	JET
13	CHECK VALVE	26	THERMO SWITCH

Fig. 69 Component location — 1988 VIN code 4 engine (California with auto. trans.)

Fig. 70 Component location — 1988 VIN code 4 engine (49 state and Canada with auto. trans.)

1 DISTRIBUTOR	14 CHECK VALVE
2 CB	15 AS READ VALVE
3 CHECK VALVE	16 EGR VACUUM MODULATOR
4 HIC VALVE	17 EGR VALVE
5 CHOKE OPENER	18 OUTER VENT CONTROL VALVE
6 VSV	19 JET
7 TP	20 FUEL VAPOR CANISTER
8 VTV	21 VSV
9 VSV	22 HAI DIAPHRAGM
10 VACUUM SWITCH	23 AAP
11 HAC VALVE	24 JET
12 EBCV	25 TVSV
13 THROTTLE POSITION SWITCH	26 THERMO SWITCH

1. THERMO SWITCH
2. CHARCOAL CANISTER
3. OUTER VENT CONTROL VALVE
4. PRIMARY FUEL CUT SOLENOID
5. SECONDARY FUEL CUT SOLENOID
6. VACUUM SWITCHING VALVE
7. COLD MIXTURE HEATER RELAY
8. HIGH ALTITUDE COMPENSATOR VALVE
9. AIR SUCTION VALVE
10. ELECTRIC AIR BLEED CONTROL VALVE
11. CHECK VALVE
12. EGR VACUUM MODULATOR
13. EGR VALVE
14. HOT AIR INTAKE DIAPHRAGM
15. HOT IDLE COMPENSATOR VALVE
16. CHOKE OPENER

17. AUXILIARY ACCELERATOR PUMP
18. CHOKE BREAKER
19. JET
20. THROTTLE POSITIONER
21. DELAY VALVE
22. THERMOSTATIC VACUUM SWITCHING VALVE
23. VACUUM SWITCH (A)
24. VACUUM SWITCH (B)
25. COLD MIXTURE HEATER
26. OXYGEN SENSOR
27. HEAT CONTROL VALVE
28. DISTRIBUTOR
29. CHECK VALVE
30. VACUUM SWITCHING VALVE

Fig. 71 Vacuum and wiring diagrams — 1988 VIN code 4 engine (49 state and Canada with man. trans.)

1. THERMO SWITCH
2. CHARCOAL CANISTER
3. OUTER VENT CONTROL VALVE
4. PRIMARY FUEL CUT SOLENOID
5. SECONDARY FUEL CUT SOLENOID
6. VACUUM SWITCHING VALVE
7. COLD MIXTURE HEATER RELAY
8. AIR SUCTION VALVE (SHUT OFF VALVE)
9. AIR SUCTION VALVE (REED VALVE)
10. ELECTRIC AIR BLEED CONTROL VALVE
11. CHECK VALVE
12. EGR VACUUM MODULATOR
13. EGR VALVE
14. HOT AIR INTAKE DIAPHRAGM
15. HOT IDLE COMPENSATOR VALVE
16. CHOKE OPENER
17. AUXILIARY ACCELERATOR PUMP
18. CHOKE BREAKER
19. JET
20. THROTTLE POSITIONER
21. DELAY VALVE
22. THERMOSTATIC VACUUM SWITCHING VALVE
23. THROTTLE POSITION SWITCH
24. VACUUM SWITCH
25. COLD MIXTURE HEATER
26. OXYGEN SENSOR
27. HEAT CONTROL VALVE
28. DISTRIBUTOR
29. VACUUM SWITCHING VALVE
30. JET

Fig. 72 Vacuum and wiring diagrams — 1988 VIN code 4 engine (California with man. trans.)

Fig. 73 Vacuum and wiring diagrams — 1988 VIN code 4 engine (California with auto. trans.)

1 TVSV	17 EGR VALVE
2 CHECK VALVE	18 JET
3 DISTRIBUTOR	19 OUTER VENT CONTROL VALVE
4 HIC VALVE	20 FUEL VAPOR CANISTER
5 VSV	21 VSV
6 CHOKE OPENER	22 HAI DIAPHRAGM
7 TP	23 CB
8 VTV	24 AAP
9 VSV	25 JET
10 VACUUM SWITCH	26 THERMO SWITCH
11 THROTTLE POSITION SWITCH	27 TWC
12 EBCV	28 SOLENOID VALVE
13 CHECK VALVE	29 CHC RELAY
14 AS SHUT-OFF VALVE	30 HEAT CONTROL VALVE
15 AS READ VALVE	31 DSD
16 EGR VACUUM MODULATOR	32 CMH
	33 CMH RELAY

Fig. 74 Vacuum and wiring diagrams — 1988 VIN code 4 engine (49 state and Canada with auto. trans.)

1	DISTRIBUTOR	17	EGR VALVE
2	CB	18	OUTER VENT CONTROL VALVE
3	CHECK VALVE	19	JET
4	HIC VALVE	20	FUEL VAPOR CANISTER
5	CHOKE OPENER	21	VSV
6	VSV	22	HAI DIAPHRAGM
7	TP	23	AAP
8	VTV	24	JET
9	VSV	25	TVSV
10	VACUUM SWITCH	26	THERMO SWITCH
11	HAC VALVE	27	OXYGEN SENSOR
12	EBCV	28	HEAT CONTROL VALVE
13	THROTTLE POSITION SWITCH	29	TWC
14	CHECK VALVE	30	OC
15	AS READ VALVE	31	SOLENOID VALVE
16	EGR VACUUM MODULATOR	32	CMH
		33	CMH RELAY

1. EGR vacuum modulator
2. Diaphragm (for T-Vis)
3. VSV
4. Vacuum tank
5. Exhaust oxygen sensor
6. Check valve
7. DP (with VTV)
8. Fuel vapor canister
9. BVSV (for EGR)
10. EGR valve
11. BVSV (for evaporator)
12. EGR temperature switch
    (for California)

Fig. 75 Component location — 1988 VIN code 5 engine

sequence: 'flash, pause, flash, pause, flash, pause," etc..If any DTC's exits indicating a problem, that DTC will be flashed. If more than one DTC is stored in the ECM's/PCM's memory, the DTC's will be output from the lowest to the highest. If no

1. EGR vacuum modulator
2. VSV
3. Vacuum tank
4. Exhaust oxygen sensor
5. Check valve
6. Fuel vapor canister
7. BVSV (for EGR)
8. EGR valve
9. BVSV (for evaporator)
10. TWC

Fig. 76 Vacuum routing — 1988 VIN code 5 engine

Fig. 77 Diagnostic monitor connector — 1989-90 VIN code 6 engine

Fig. 78 Diagnostic monitor connector — 1990 VIN code 5 engine

Fig. 80 Diagnostic monitor connector — 1992

Fig. 79 Diagnostic monitor connector — 1991

Fig. 81 Diagnostic monitor connector — 1993

DTC's were flashed, the test diagnostic mode must be initiated and performed. In order to initiate the test diagnostic mode the following procedure must be performed:

1. Remove the fused jumper from terminal 'TE1".

2. Turn the ignition switch to 'LOCK".

3. Connect a fused jumper from DLC terminals 'TE2" to 'E1".

4. Turn the ignition switch to 'ON". At this point, the MIL should be flashing ON and OFF rapidly.

5. Start and run engine until normal operating temperature is attained.

6. Test drive the vehicle at the condition at which the original problem occurred.

7. Connect a fused jumper from terminal 'TE1" to 'E1" and note any DTC's.

At this point, if any DTC's are present, they will be flashed. If no DTC's are present, the trouble does not lie within the ECM/PCM or its wiring.

Clearing Codes

▶ See Figures 82, 83

To clear the codes from the memory of the ECM, either to determine if the malfunction will occur again or because repair has been completed, the ECM power feed must be disconnected for at least thirty (30) seconds, 10 seconds on 1993 models. Ohm 1989-92 models power can be disconnected from the ECM by removing the STOP fuse from the fuse block. On 1993 models, remove power from the ECM/PCM by removing the EFI F-HTR fuse, located in fuse and relay box in the engine compartment. The negative battery terminal may be disconnected, but other on-board memory data, such as preset radio tuning, will also be lost.

✳✳CAUTION

WARNING: To prevent ECM damage, the key must be OFF when disconnecting or reconnecting ECM power.

Fig. 82 Vacuum and wiring diagrams — 1989-90 VIN code 6 engine (49 state and Canada)

1	BATTERY	**11**	MANIFOLD ABSOLUTE PRESSURE (MAP) SENSOR
2	CHECK ENGINE WARNING LIGHT	**12**	MANIFOLD AIR TEMPERATURE (MAT) SENSOR
3	STARTER MOTOR	**13**	AIR CONDITIONING/VACUUM SWITCHING VALVE (A/C VSV) (IF EQUIPPED)
4	ELECTRONIC CONTROL MODULE (ECM)	**14**	COLD START INJECTOR VALVE
5	A/C INPUT	**15**	COLD START INJECTOR VALVE SWITCH
6	PARK/NEUTRAL (P/N) INPUT	**16**	BIMETAL VACUUM SWITCHING VALVE (BVSV)
7	VEHICLE SPEED SENSOR (VSS) INPUT	**17**	COOLANT TEMPERATURE SENSOR (CTS)
8	CIRCUIT OPENING RELAY	**18**	IGNITER
9	FUEL PUMP	**19**	FUEL INJECTOR
10	FUEL VAPOR CANISTER	**20**	OXYGEN (O₂) SENSOR

1	BATTERY	12	VSV (EGR)
2	CHECK ENGINE WARNING LIGHT	13	EGR VACUUM MODULATOR
3	STARTER MOTOR	14	MANIFOLD AIR TEMPERATURE (MAT) SENSOR
4	ELECTRONIC CONTROL MODULE (ECM)	15	AIR CONDITIONING VACUUM SWITCHING VALVE (A/C VSV) (IF EQUIPPED)
5	A/C INPUT	16	EXHUAST GAS RECIRCULATION (EGR) VALVE
6	PARK/NEUTRAL (P/N) SWITCH INPUT	17	COLD START INJECTOR
7	VEHICLE SPEED SENSOR (VSS) INPUT	18	COOLANT TEMPERATURE SENSOR (CTS)
8	CIRCUIT OPENING RELAY	19	BIMETAL VACUUM SWITCHING VALVE (BVSV)
9	FUEL PUMP	20	FUEL INJECTOR
10	FUEL VAPER CANISTER	21	OXYGEN (O₂) SENSOR
11	MANIFOLD ABSOLUTE PRESSURE (MAP) SENSOR	22	IGNITER

Fig. 83 Vacuum and wiring diagrams — 1989-90 VIN code 6 engine (California)

COMPUTER HARNESS

- **C1** Electronic Control Module (ECM)
- **C2** Check Connector
- **C3** "Check Engine" Light
- **C4** Circuit Opening Relay
- **C5** ECM Harness Grounds
- **C6** Fuse Panel
- **C8** Fuel Pump Test Connector (Part of C2)

NOT ECM CONNECTED

- **N1** Crankcase Vent Valve (PCV)
- **N9** Fuel Pressure Regulator Valve
- **N10** Cold Start Injector
- **N11** Cold Start Injector Valve Switch
- **N17** Fuel Vapor Canister
- **N18** A/C Fan Relay #1
- **N19** A/C Fan Relay #2
- **N20** A/C Compressor Relay

 Exhaust Gas Recirculation (EGR) Valve

CONTROLLED DEVICES

- **1** Fuel Injectors
- **2** Idle Vacuum Switching Valve (VSV)
- **4** EFI Main Relay
- **7** *EGR Vacuum Switching Valve (VSV)
- **8** Cooling Fan Relay
- **17** Throttle Body

INFORMATION SENSORS

- **A** Manifold Absolute Pressure (MAP) Sensor
- **B** Oxygen (O_2) Sensor
- **C** Throttle Switch (TS)
- **D** Coolant Temperature Sensor (CTS)
- **F** Vehicle Speed Sensor (VSS)
- **M** Park/Neutral (P/N) Switch
- **T** Manifold Air Temperature (MAT) Sensor

Fig. 84 1989-90 VIN code 6 engine

EXAMPLE: OXYGEN SENSOR SIGNAL (CODE 21)

DIAGNOSTIC CODE		DIAGNOSTIC AREA
NO.	**MODE**	
--	ON / OFF	NORMAL
12		RPM SIGNAL
13		RPM SIGNAL
14		IGNITION SIGNAL
21		OXYGEN SENSOR
22		COOLANT TEMPERATURE SENSOR
24		MANIFOLD AIR TEMPERATURE SENSOR
25		LEAN AIR/FUEL RATIO
26		RICH AIR/FUEL RATIO
31		MANIFOLD ABSOLUTE PRESSURE SENSOR
41		THROTTLE POSITION SENSOR
42		VEHICLE SPEED SENSOR
43		STARTER SIGNAL
51		SWITCH SIGNAL
71		EGR MALFUNCTION

Fig. 85 1989-90 VIN code 6 engine

"S" CARLINE   RPO: LWO   VIN CODE: 5   1.6L L4 PFI

Distributor

☐ COMPUTER HARNESS
- **C1** Electronic Control Module (ECM)
- **C2** Check Connector
- **C3** "Check Engine" Light
- **C4** Circuit Opening Relay
- **C5** ECM Harness Grounds
- **C6** Fuse Panel
- **C8** Fuel Pump Test Connector (Part of C2)
- **C9** Electronic Controlled Transaxle (ECT)

NOT ECM CONNECTED
- **N1** Crankcase Vent Valve (PCV)
- **N9** Fuel Pressure Regulator Valve
- **N10** Cold Start Injector
- **N11** Cold Start Injector Valve Switch
- **N17** Fuel Vapor Canister
- **N18** A/C Fan Relay #1
- **N19** A/C Fan Relay #2
- **N20** A/C Compressor Relay
- **N21** A/C Actuator
- **N22** Cooling Fan Relay

☐ CONTROLLED DEVICES
- **1** Fuel Injectors
- **2** Idle Up (VSV)
- **4** EFI Main Relay
- **7** EGR Vacuum Switching Valve (VSV)
- **17** Throttle Body
- **18** Fuel Pressure Regulator (VSV)
- **19** Distributor Igniter

Exhaust Gas Recirculation (EGR) Valve

○ INFORMATION SENSORS
- **A** Mass Air Flow Sensor (MAF)
- • **B** Oxygen (O₂) Sensor Heated
- **C** Throttle Position Sensor
- **D** Coolant Temperature Sensor (CTS)
- **E** Intake Air Temperature (IAT) Part of (MAF)
- **F** Vehicle Speed Sensor (VSS)
- **M** Park/Neutral (P/N) Switch
- **T** *Sub Oxygen Sensor (After Exhaust Converter)
- **U** *EGR Temperature Sensor
- **W** Knock Sensor

• Located in exhaust pipe after exhaust manifold.
* California Only

Fig. 86 1990-91 VIN code 5 engine

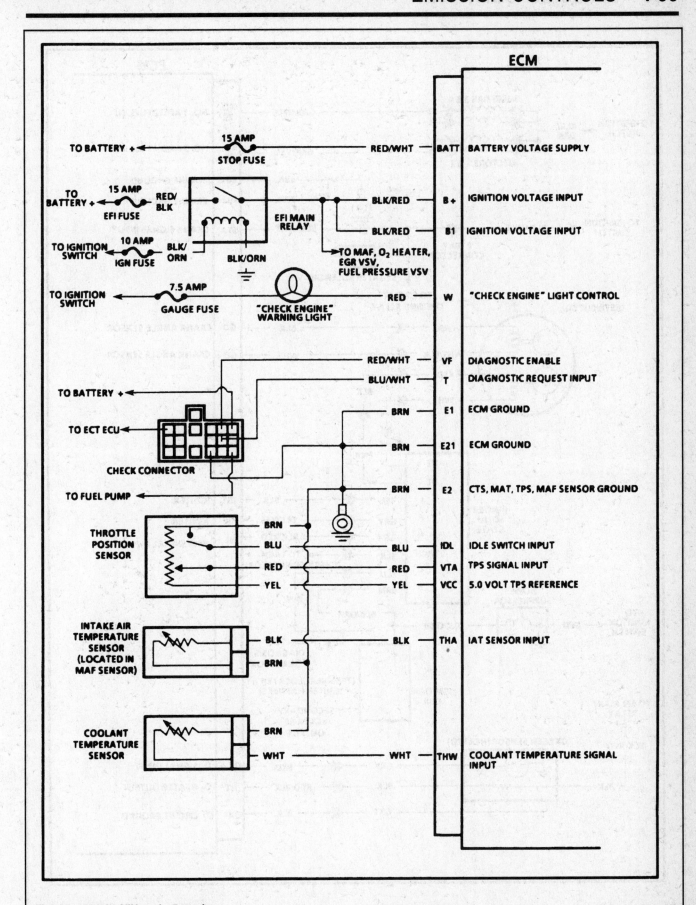

Fig. 87 1990-91 VIN code 5 engine

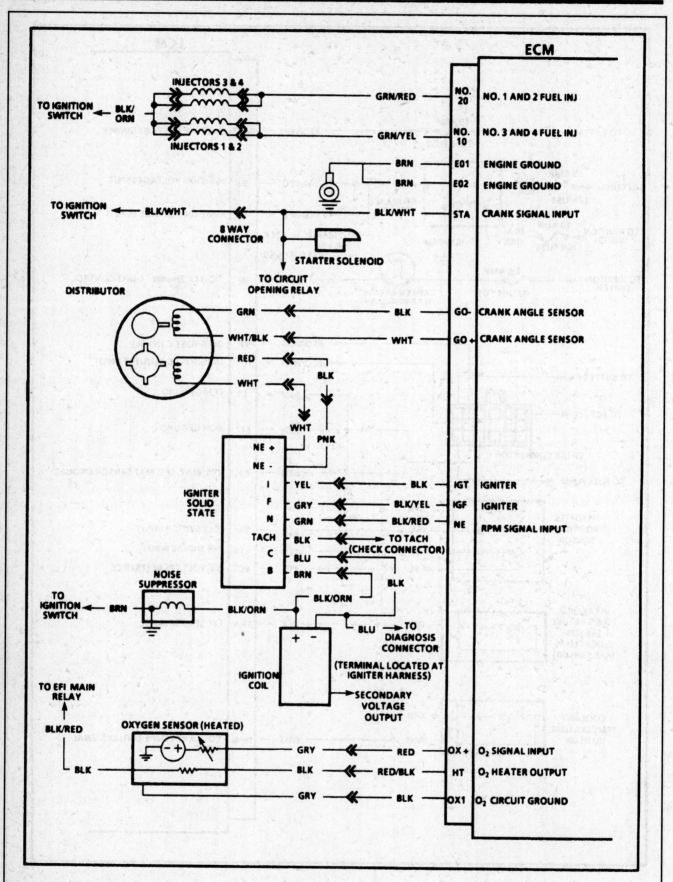

Fig. 88 1990-91 VIN code 5 engine

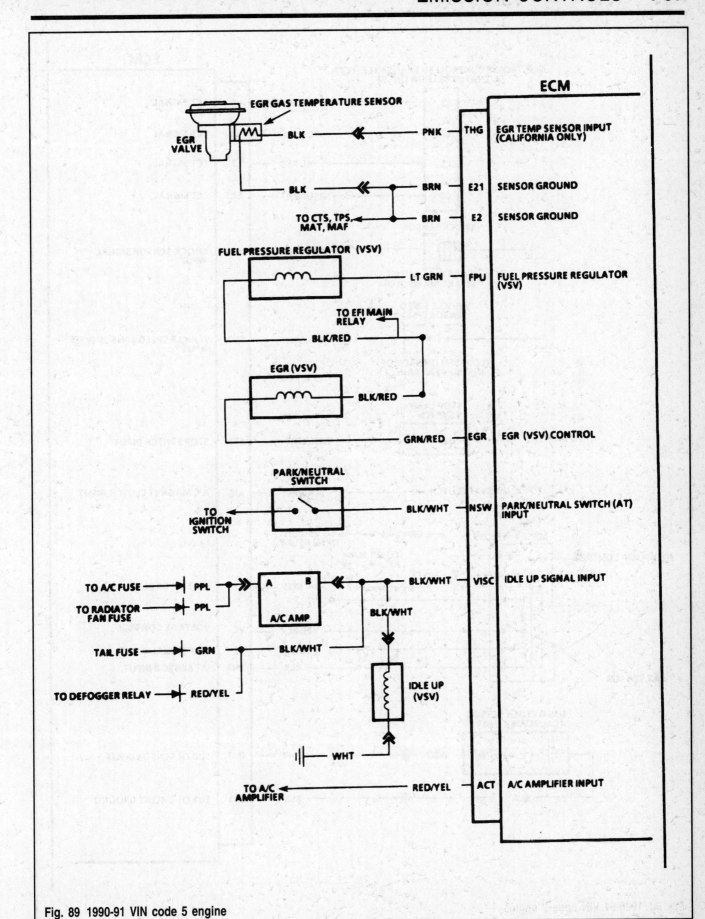

Fig. 89 1990-91 VIN code 5 engine

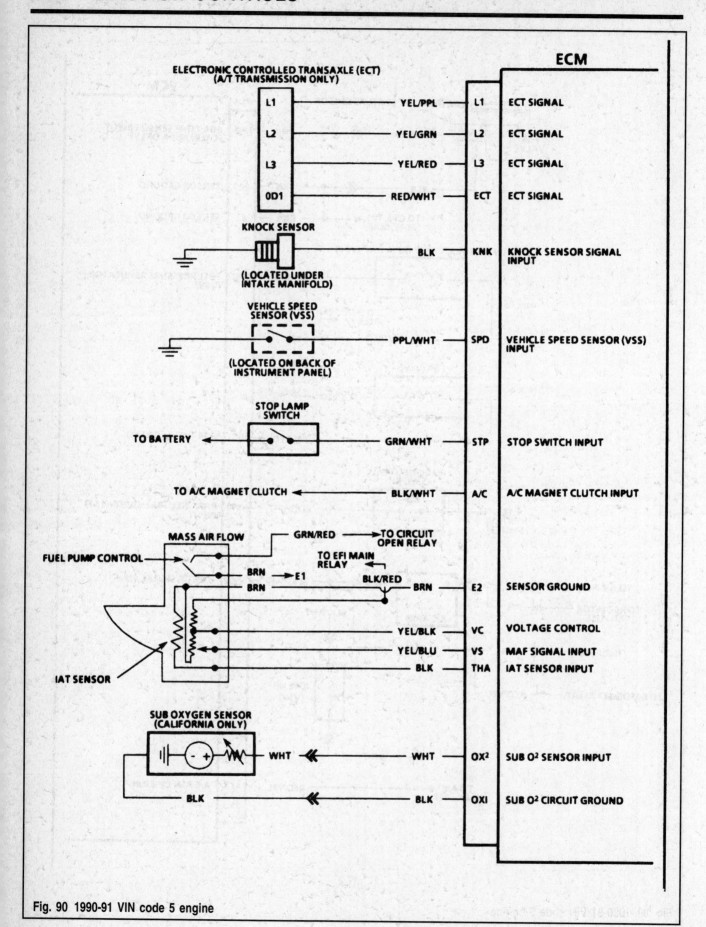

Fig. 90 1990-91 VIN code 5 engine

26 PIN CONNECTOR

EO1	NO10	X	X	V-ISC	ECT	X	X	GO+	NE	1GF	STA	FPU
EO2	NO20	E1	X	IGT	L1	L2	L3	X	GO-	EGR	NSW	HT

16 PIN CONNECTOR

VF	OX+	OX1	OX2	THW	THA	VS	VC
E21	T	KNK	THG	IDL	VCC	VTA	E2

12 PIN CONNECTOR

ACT	STP	X	X	BATT	B1
X	SPD	A/C	X	W	B+

12 PIN

VOLTAGE KEY ON	ENG ON	CIRCUIT	PIN	WIRE COLOR
0	0	A/C AMPLIFIER INPUT	ACT	RED/WHT
0	0	STOP SWITCH INPUT ①	STP	GRN/WHT
--	--	NOT USED	--	---
--	--	NOT USED	--	---
B+	B+	B+ SUPPLY	BATT	RED/WHT
B+	B+	IGNITION VOLTAGE INPUT	B1	BLK/RED
--	--	NOT USED	--	---
0-B+	0-B+	VSS ②	SPD	PPL/WHT
0	0	A/C MAGNET CLUTCH INPUT ⑦	A/C	BLK/WHT
--	--	NOT USED	--	---
1-2 V	B+	CHECK ENGINE LIGHT CONTROL	W	RED
B+	B+	IGNITION VOLTAGE INPUT	B+	BLK/RED

16 PIN

VOLTAGE KEY ON	ENG ON	CIRCUIT	PIN	WIRE COLOR
0	0-1V	DIAGNOSTIC ENABLE	VF	RED/WHT
0	.1-.9 V	O₂ SIGNAL INPUT ●	OX+	RED
0	0	O₂ CIRCUIT GROUND	OX1	BLK
0	.1-to .9	SUB O₂ SENSOR INPUT +	OX2	WHT
③ 5	③ .4	CTS	THW	WHT
③ 2.0	③ 2.0	IAT SENSOR	THA	BLK
2.0	L-9V ④	MAF SIGNAL INPUT	VS	YEL/BLU
8.0	8-9V	MAF VOLTAGE CONTROL	VC	YEL BLK
0	0	ECM GROUND	E21	BRN
B+	B+	DIAGNOSTIC REQUEST INPUT	T	BLU/WHT
0	0	KNOCK SENSOR	KNK	BLK
.5	③ .69	EGR TEMP SENSOR	THG	RED/GRN
0	0	IDLE SWITCH INPUT ⑤	IDL	BLU
5.0	5.0	5V TPS REFERENCE	VCC	YEL
.60	.6 to 4.5	TPS SIGNAL INPUT	VTA	RED
0	0	SENSOR GROUND	E2	BRN

26 PIN

VOLTAGE KEY ON	ENG ON	CIRCUIT	PIN	WIRE COLOR
0	0	ENGINE GROUND	EO1	BRN
B+	B+	INJECTOR 3 & 4	#10	GRN/RED
--	--	NOT USED	--	---
--	--	NOT USED	--	---
B+	B+	IDLE UP SIGNAL INPUT	VISC	BLK/WHT
0	0	ECT *	ECT	YEL/BLK
--	--	NOT USED	--	---
--	--	NOT USED	--	---
.60	.60	CRANK ANGLE SENSOR	GO+	BLK
B+	B+	RPM SIGNAL INPUT	NE	BLK/RED
.8	6-.8	IGNITER	IGF	BLK/YEL
0	0	CRANK SIGNAL INPUT	STA	BLK/WHT
B+	B+	FUEL PRESSURE REGULATOR (VSV)	FPU	LT GRN
0	0	GROUND	EO2	BRN
B+	B+	INJECTOR 1 & 2	#20	GRN/YEL
0	0	ECM GROUND	E1	BRN
--	--	NOT USED	--	---
0	6	IGNITER	IGT	BLK
B+	B+	ECT *	L1	YEL/BLU
B+	B+	ECT *	L2	YEL/GRN
B+	B+	ECT *	L3	YEL/RED
--	--	NOT USED	--	---
.60	.60	CRANK ANGLE	GO-	WHT
B+	B+	EGR (VSV)	EGR	GRN/RED
B+	B+	PARK/NEUTRAL INPUT *	NSW	BLK/WHT
B+	1.0 to B+	O₂ HEATER OUTPUT	HT	BLK/WHT

* AUTOMATIC TRANSAXLE
● FEDERAL & CANADA ONLY
+ CALIFORNIA ONLY
① B+ WITH BRAKE PEDAL DEPRESSED
② VARYING VOLTAGE WITH WHEELS ROTATING
③ VARIES WITH TEMPERATURE
④ INCREASE WITH RPM
⑤ B+ "OFF" IDLE
⑥ B+ IN CRANK MODE
⑦ B+ WITH A/C "ON"
━ DIVIDES UPPER/LOWER ECM CONNECTOR

Fig. 91 1990-91 VIN code 5 engine

DIAGNOSTIC CODE TABLE

EXAMPLE: OXYGEN SENSOR SIGNAL (CODE 21)

DIAGNOSTIC CODE		DIAGNOSTIC AREA	DIAGNOSIS
NO.	MODE		
–	ON ⎍⎍⎍⎍⎍⎍⎍ OFF	NORMAL	APPEARS WHEN NO OTHER CODES ARE PRESENT
12	⎍⎍⎍	RPM SIGNAL	
13	⎍ ⎍⎍⎍	RPM SIGNAL	
14	⎍ ⎍⎍⎍⎍	IGNITION SIGNAL	
21	⎍ ⎍⎍⎍	OXYGEN SENSOR HEATED	
22	⎍⎍ ⎍⎍	COOLANT TEMPERATURE SENSOR	DIAGNOSE TROUBLE ACCORDING TO THE "DIAGNOSTIC FLOW CHART" CORRESPONDING TO EACH CODE NO.
24	⎍⎍ ⎍⎍⎍⎍	INTAKE AIR TEMPERATURE SENSOR	
25	⎍⎍⎍⎍⎍	LEAN AIR/FUEL RATIO	
26	⎍ ⎍⎍⎍⎍⎍⎍	RICH AIR/FUEL RATIO	
27	⎍ ⎍⎍⎍⎍⎍⎍⎍	SUB OXYGEN SENSOR (CALIFORNIA ONLY)	
31	⎍⎍⎍⎍	MASS AIR FLOW	
41	⎍ ⎍⎍⎍⎍	THROTTLE POSITION SENSOR	
42	⎍ ⎍⎍⎍⎍⎍	VEHICLE SPEED SENSOR	
43	⎍⎍⎍⎍⎍ ⎍	STARTER SIGNAL	
51	⎍⎍⎍⎍⎍ ⎍	SWITCH SIGNAL A/C	
52	⎍⎍⎍⎍⎍ ⎍ ⎍	KNOCK SENSOR SIGNAL	
53	⎍⎍⎍⎍⎍⎍ ⎍ ⎍ ⎍	KNOCK CONTROL SIGNAL	
71	⎍ ⎍⎍⎍⎍⎍⎍⎍ ⎍	EGR MALFUNCTION GAS TEMPERATURE SENSOR (CALIFORNIA ONLY)	

Fig. 92 1990-91 VIN code 5 engine

"S" CARLINE   RPO: **LO1**   VIN CODE: **6**   **1.6L L4** PFI

▢ COMPUTER HARNESS

- **C1** Electronic Control Module (ECM)
- **C2** Check Connector
- **C3** "Check Engine" Light
- **C4** Circuit Opening Relay
- **C5** ECM Harness Grounds
- **C6** Fuse Panel
- **C8** Fuel Pump Test Connector (Part of C2)

▢ NOT ECM CONNECTED

- **N1** Crankcase Vent Valve (PCV)
- **N9** Fuel Pressure Regulator Valve
- **N10** Cold Start Injector
- **N11** Cold Start Injector Valve Switch
- **N17** Fuel Vapor Canister
- **N18** A/C Fan Relay #1
- **N19** A/C Fan Relay #2
- **N20** A/C Compressor Relay

◯ Exhaust Gas Recirculation (EGR) Valve

▢ CONTROLLED DEVICES

- **1** Fuel Injectors
- **2** Idle Vacuum Switching Valve (VSV)
- **4** EFI Main Relay
- **7** *EGR Vacuum Switching Valve (VSV)
- **8** Cooling Fan Relay
- **17** Throttle Body
- **18** Distributor (Ignition Coil and Igniter located in Distributor.)

◯ INFORMATION SENSORS

- **A** Manifold Absolute Pressure (MAP) Sensor
- **B** Oxygen (O_2) Sensor
- **C** Throttle Switch (TS)
- **D** Coolant Temperature Sensor (CTS)
- **F** Vehicle Speed Sensor (VSS)
- **M** Park/Neutral (P/N) Switch
- **T** Intake Air Temperature (IAT) Sensor
- **U** *EGR Temperature Sensor

* California Only

Fig. 93 1991 VIN code 6 engine

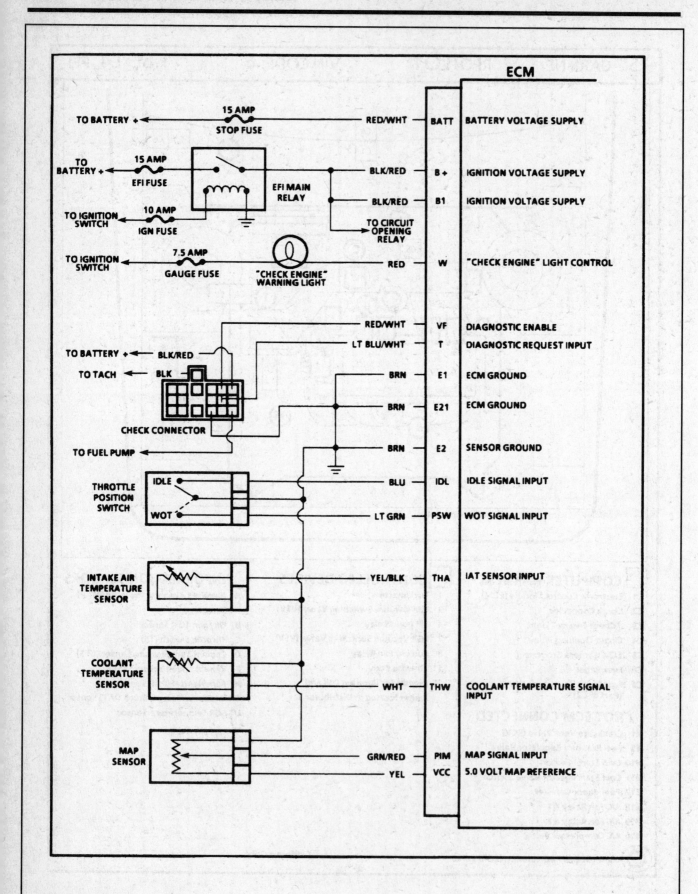

Fig. 94 1991 VIN code 6 engine

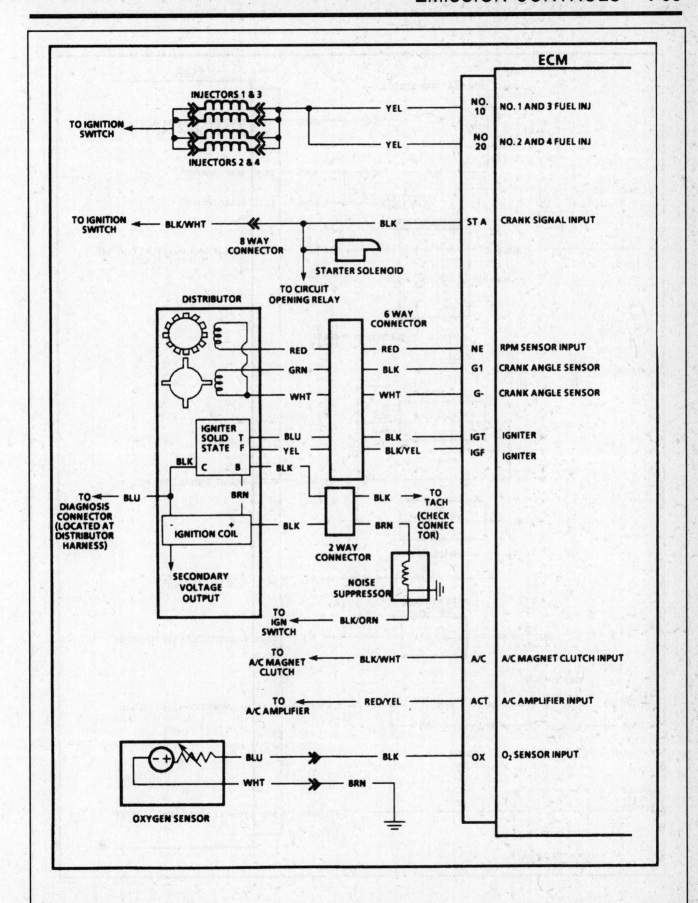

Fig. 95 1991 VIN code 6 engine

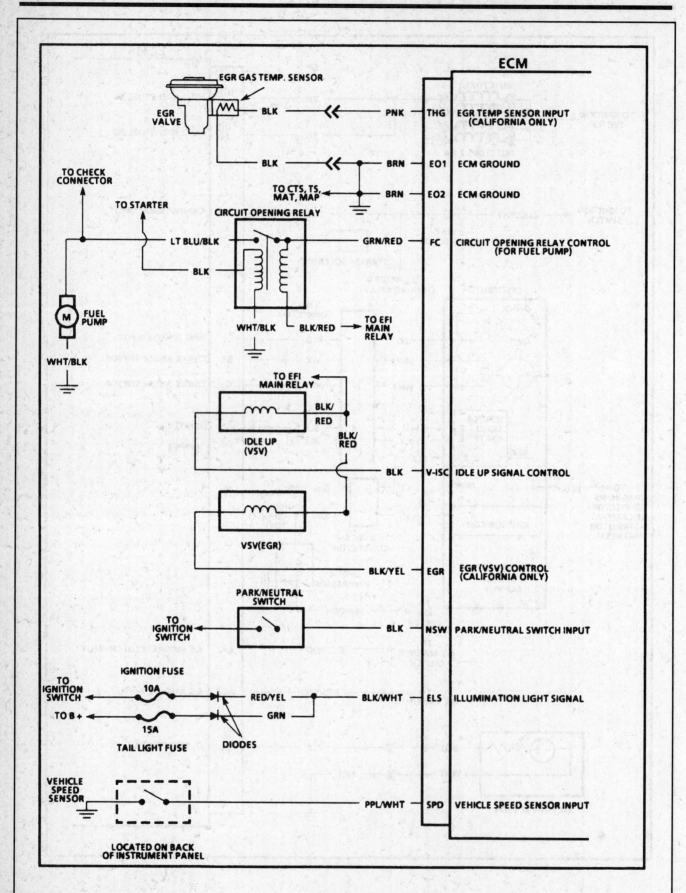

Fig. 96 1991 VIN code 6 engine

Connector pinout:

EO1	#10	STA	OX	G-		G1	IGF	IGT	THA	PIM	THW	NSW	✕		T	ACT	✕	ELS	FC	✕		BATT	B1
EO2	#20	E1	✕		E21	NE	THG	IDL	VCC	PSW	E2	O/D	VISC		VF	✕	✕		VSS	A/C			W	B+

VOLTAGE		26 PIN CIRCUIT	PIN	WIRE COLOR
KEY ON	ENG ON			
0	0	ECM GROUND	E01	BRN
B+	B+	NO. 1 AND 3 FUEL INJECTOR	#10	YEL
⑥	⑥	CRANK SIGNAL INPUT	STA	BLK
0	④	O₂ SENSOR INPUT	OX	BLK
.69	.67	CRANK ANGLE SENSOR	G-	WHT
.69	.67	CRANK ANGLE SENSOR	G1	BLK
.93	1.0	IGNITER	IGF	BLK/YEL
*	.69	IGNITER	IGT	BLK
③2.3	③2.3	IAT SENSOR INPUT	THA	YEL/BLK
3.5	1.82	MAP SIGNAL INPUT	PIM	GRN/RED
③5	③.44	CTS	THW	WHT
• B+	B+	PARK/NEUTRAL INPUT	NSW	BLK/WHT
+ B+	B+	EGR (VSV) CONTROL	EGR	BLK/YEL
0	0	GROUND	E02	BRN
B+	B+	NO. 2 AND 4 FUEL INJECTORS	#20	YEL
0	0	ECM GROUND	E1	BRN
0	0	ECM GROUND	E21	BRN
.69	.67	RPM SENSOR INPUT	NE	RED
+ ③5	③.69	EGR TEMP SENSOR INPUT	THG	PNK
*②	*②	IDLE SIGNAL INPUT	IDL	BLU
5.0	5.0	5.0 VOLT MAP REFERENCE	VCC	YEL
①B+	①B+	WOT SIGNAL INPUT	PSW	LT GRN
0	0	SENSOR GROUND	E2	BRN
• 0	0	CRUISE CONTROL INPUT	O/D	RED
1.4	B+	IDLE UP SIGNAL CONTROL	VISC	BLK

VOLTAGE		16 PIN CIRCUIT	PIN	WIRE COLOR
KEY ON	ENG ON			
B+	B+	DIAGNOSTIC REQUEST INPUT	T	BLU/WHT
0	*	A/C AMPLIFIER INPUT	ACT	RED/YEL
-	-	-	-	-
⑦	⑦	ILLUMINATION LIGHT SIGNAL	ELS	BLK
B+	*	CIRCUIT OPENING RELAY CONTROL	FC	GRN/RED
-	-	-	-	-
B+	B+	BATTERY VOLTAGE SUPPLY	BATT	RED/WHT
B+	B+	IGNITION VOLTAGE SUPPLY	B1	BLK/RED
2.23	2.23	DIAGNOSTIC ENABLE	VF	RED/WHT
-	-	-	-	-
-	-	-	-	-
⑤	⑤	VSS	SPD	PPL/WHT
⑧	⑧	A/C MAGNET CLUTCH INPUT	AC	BLK/WHT
-	-	-	-	-
.93	B+	CHECK ENGINE LIGHT CONTROL	W	RED
B+	B+	IGNITION VOLTAGE SUPPLY	B+	BLK/RED

- •   AUTOMATIC TRANSAXLE
- +   CALIFORNIA ONLY
- *   LESS THAN .5 VOLT
- ①   0 VOLTS AT W.O.T.
- ②   B+ OFF IDLE
- ③   VARIES WITH TEMPERATURE
- ④   VARIES BETWEEN 100MV AND 900MV
- ⑤   VARIES BETWEEN 0 AND B+ WITH WHEELS ROTATING
- ⑥   B+ IN CRANK MODE
- ⑦   B+ WITH HEADLIGHT ON
- ⑧   B+ WITH A/C "ON" 0 VOLT WITH A/C "OFF"
- ■   DIVIDES UPPER/LOWER ECM CONNECTOR

Fig. 97 1991 VIN code 6 engine

Fig. 98 1991 VIN code 6 engine

"S" CARLINE   RPO: LWO   VIN CODE: 5   1.6L L4 PFI

COMPUTER HARNESS

C1	Engine Control Module (ECM)
C2	Diagnosis Check Connector
C3	"CHECK ENGINE" Light
C4	Circuit Opening Relay
C5	ECM Harness Grounds
C6	Junction Block 1
C8	Fuel Pump Test Connector (Part of C2)
C9	Automatic Transaxle Control Module

RELATED COMPONENTS

N1	Crankcase Vent Valve (PCV)
N9	Fuel Pressure Regulator Valve
N10	Cold Start Fuel Injector
N11	Cold Start Injector Timer
N17	Fuel Vapor Canister
N18	A/C Fan Relay No. 2
N19	A/C Fan Relay No. 3
N20	Fan Relay No. 1
N21	A/C Idle-Up VSV
N22	A/C Clutch Relay

CONTROLLED DEVICES

1	Fuel Injectors
2	Idle-Up (VSV)
4	EFI F-HTR Relay
7	EGR Vacuum Switching Valve (VSV)
17	Throttle Body
18	Fuel Pressure Regulator (VSV)
19	Igniter

Exhaust Gas Recirculation (EGR) Valve

INFORMATION SENSORS

A	Mass Airflow Sensor (MAF)
• B	Oxygen (O_2) Sensor Heated
C	Throttle Position Sensor
D	Coolant Temperature Sensor
E	Intake Air Temperature (IAT) Part of (MAF)
F	Vehicle Speed Sensor (VSS)
M	Neutral Start Switch
T	*Sub Oxygen Sensor (After Exhaust Converter)
U	*EGR Temperature Sensor
W	Knock Sensor

• Located in exhaust pipe after exhaust manifold.

* California Only

Fig. 99 1992 VIN code 5 engine

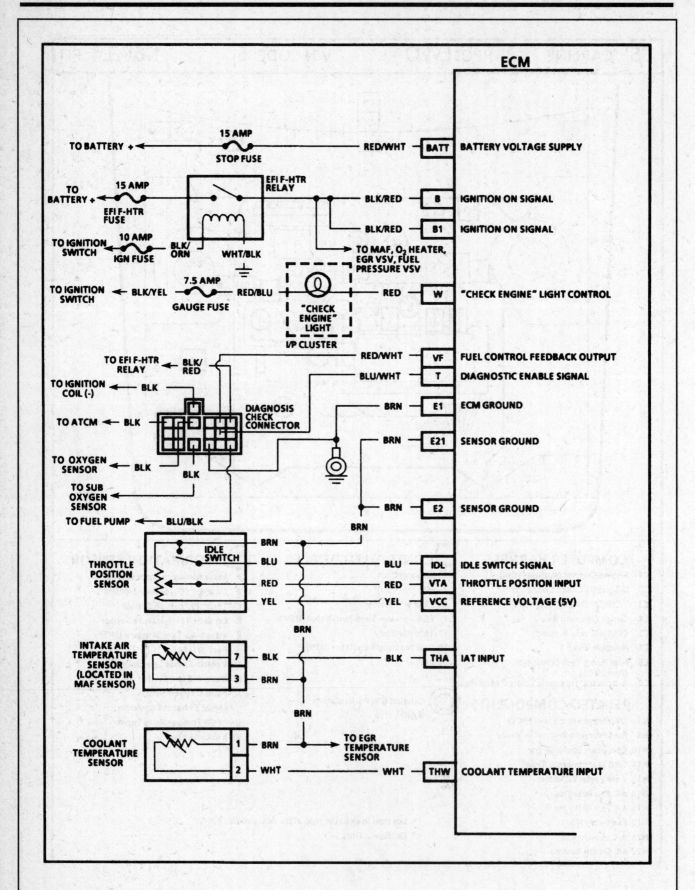

Fig. 100 1992 VIN code 5 engine

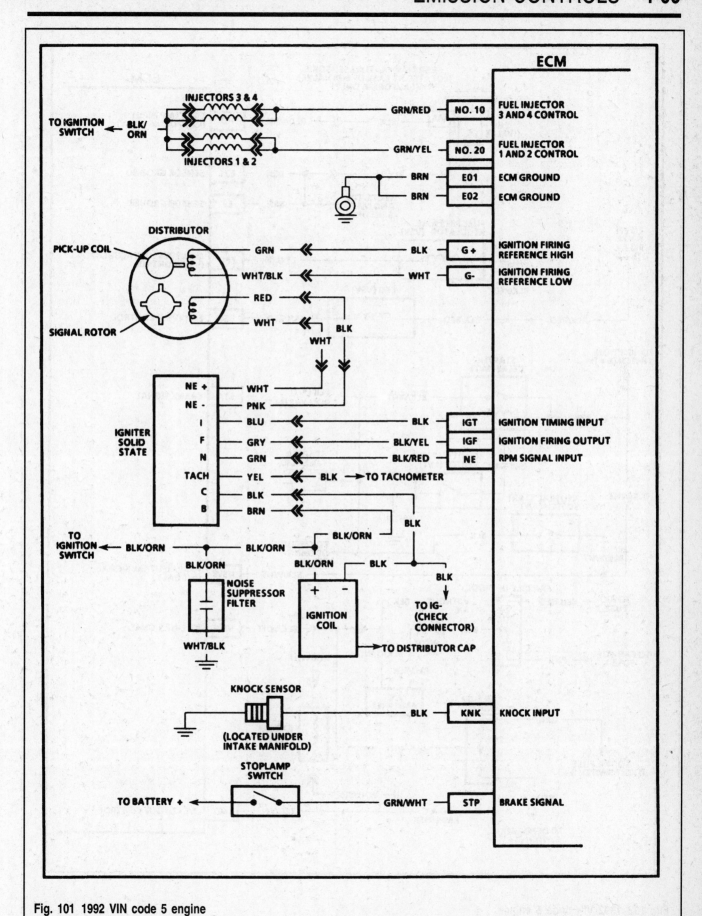

Fig. 101 1992 VIN code 5 engine

ECM

EGR TEMPERATURE SENSOR
(LOCATED AT BASE OF EGR VALVE)
(CALIFORNIA ONLY)

EGR VALVE

BLK ◄◄ RED/GRN — THG — EGR TEMP INPUT (CALIFORNIA ONLY)

BLK ◄◄ BRN — E21 — SENSOR GROUND

TO CTS, TPS AND MAF SENSORS — BRN — E2 — SENSOR GROUND

TO EFI F-HTR RELAY (B+)

FUEL PRESSURE REGULATOR (VSV)

LT GRN — FPU — FUEL PRESSURE REGULATOR (VSV) CONTROL

BLK/RED

EGR (VSV)

BLK/RED — BLK/RED — GRN/RED — EGR — EGR (VSV) CONTROL

TO IGNITION SWITCH (B+)

STARTER RELAY (M/T)

BLK/WHT

BLK/WHT — BLK (A/T) BLK/WHT (M/T) — STA — CRANK SIGNAL

GRY/GRN

CLUTCH START SWITCH (M/T)

STARTER SOLENOID

NEUTRAL START SWITCH (A/T)

BLK/WHT

BLK — WHT/BLK

TO CIRCUIT OPENING RELAY

BLK/WHT

BLK/WHT — NSW — PARK/NEUTRAL SIGNAL (A/T ONLY)

FAN IDLE-UP DIODE

TO A/C FUSE ← BLU/RED

BLU ►► — WITHOUT A/C — BLK

WITH A/C — BLK/ORN

TO FAN-I/UP FUSE ← PNK

BLU/BLK

A/C AMPLIFIER

BLK/WHT — BLK/WHT ◄◄ — BLK/WHT — VISC — IDLE-UP SIGNAL

IDLE-UP DIODE

GRN

BLK/WHT

IDLE-UP (VSV)

TO TAIL FUSE (LIGHT SWITCH B+)

RED/YEL

WHT/BLK

TO A/C AMPLIFIER ← RED/YEL — ACT — A/C CUTOUT CONTROL

TO DEFOGGER SWITCH (B+)

Fig. 102 1992 VIN code 5 engine

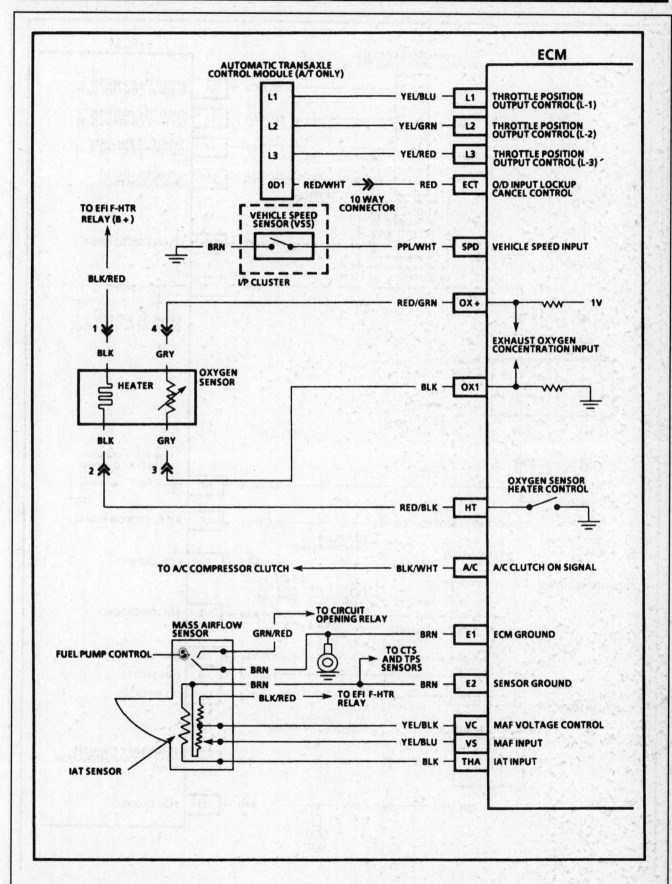

Fig. 103 1992 VIN code 5 engine

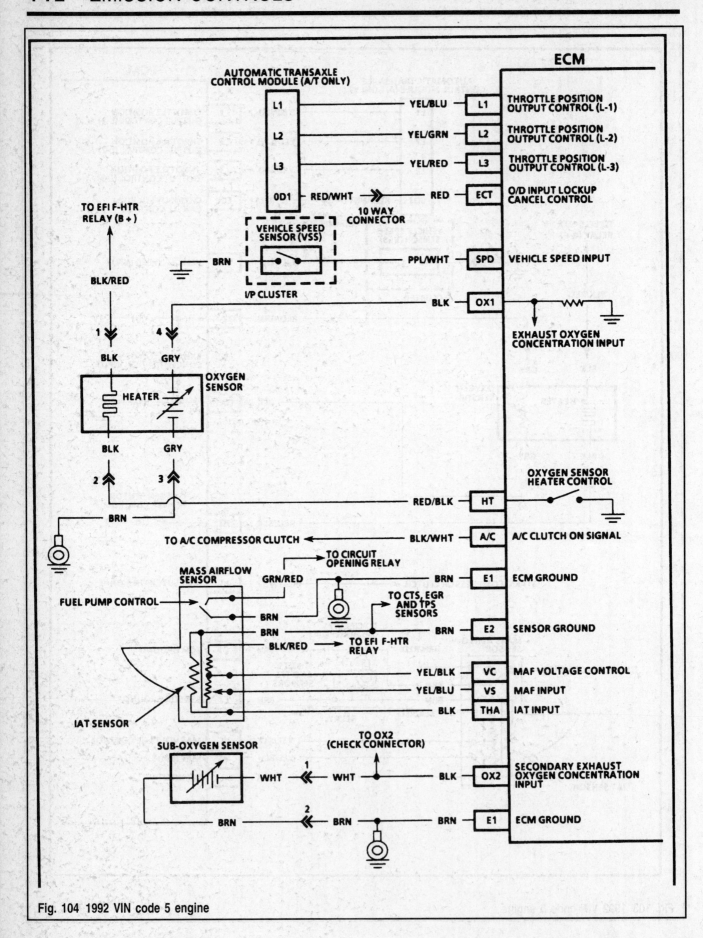

Fig. 104 1992 VIN code 5 engine

FUEL INJECTION ECM CONNECTOR IDENTIFICATION

The following ECM voltage charts are for use with a digital-voltmeter to further aid in diagnosis. The voltages you get may vary due to low battery charge or other reasons, but they should be very close.

THE FOLLOWING CONDITIONS MUST BE MET BEFORE TESTING:

- Engine at operating temperature ● Engine idling (for "Engine Run" column)
- Diagnostic Enable Terminal not grounded
- All voltages shown "B + " indicate battery or charging voltage

ACT	STP	✕	✕	BATT	B1
✕	SPD	A/C	✕	W	B

E01	NO. 10	(★) HT	✕	VISC	ECT	✕	✕	G +	NE	IGF	STA	FPU
E02	NO. 20	E1	IGT	L1	L2	L3	✕	G-	EGR	NSW	(●) HT

BACKVIEW OF ECM CONNECTOR C1   **BACKVIEW OF ECM CONNECTOR C2**

CAVITY/ PIN	WIRE COLOR	CIRCUIT	KEY "ON"	ENG. RUN
1/B1	BLK/RED	IGNITION ON SIGNAL	B +	B +
2/BATT	RED/WHT	BATTERY VOLTAGE SUPPLY	B +	B +
3/–	–	NOT USED	–	–
4/–	–	NOT USED	–	–
5/STP	GRN/WHT	BRAKE SIGNAL	0* (1)	0* (1)
6/ACT	RED/YEL	A/C CUTOUT CONTROL	0*	B + (2)
7/B	BLK/RED	IGNITION ON SIGNAL	B +	B +
8/W	RED	"CHECK ENGINE" LIGHT CONTROL	1-2V	B +
9/–	–	NOT USED	–	–
10/A/C	BLK/WHT	A/C CLUTCH ON SIGNAL	0* (3)	0* (3)
11/SPD	PPL/WHT	VEHICLE SPEED INPUT	0 - B + (4)	0 - B + (4)
12/–	–	NOT USED	–	–

CAVITY/ PIN	WIRE COLOR	CIRCUIT	KEY "ON"	ENG. RUN
1/FPU	LT GRN	FUEL PRESSURE REGULATOR VSV CONTROL	B +	B +
2/STA	BLK (X) BLK/WHT	CRANK SIGNAL	0* (5)	0* (5)
3/IGF	BLK/YEL	IGNITION FIRING OUTPUT	.25V	.6 - .8V
4/NE	BLK/RED	RPM SIGNAL INPUT	B +	10V
5/G +	BLK	IGNITION FIRING REFERENCE HIGH	.60V	.60V
6/–	–	NOT USED	–	–
7/–	–	NOT USED	–	–
8/ECT (X)	RED	OVERDRIVE INPUT LOCKUP CANCEL CONTROL	0*	B + (6)
9/VISC	BLK/WHT	IDLE-UP SIGNAL	0* (7)	0* (7)
10/–	–	NOT USED	–	–
11/HT (★)	RED/BLK	OXYGEN SENSOR HEATER CONTROL	0*	0* (8)
12/NO.10	GRN/RED	FUEL INJECTOR 3 & 4 CONTROL	B +	B +
13/E01	BRN	ECM GROUND	0*	0*
14/HT (●)	RED/BLK	OXYGEN SENSOR HEATER CONTROL	B +	.1 - 3V
15/NSW (X)	BLK/WHT	PARK/NEUTRAL SIGNAL	0* (9)	0* (9)
16/EGR	GRN/RED	EGR VSV CONTROL	B +	B +
17/G-	WHT	IGNITION FIRING REFERENCE LOW	.60V	.60V
18/–	–	NOT USED	–	–
19/L3 (X)	YEL RED	L3 THROTTLE POSITION OUTPUT CONTROL	9V	10V
20/L2 (X)	YEL/GRN	L2 THROTTLE POSITION OUTPUT CONTROL	9V	10V
21/L1 (X)	YEL/BLU	L1 THROTTLE POSITION OUTPUT CONTROL	9V	10V
22/IGT	BLK	IGNITION TIMING INPUT	0*	.76V
23/–	–	NOT USED	–	–
24/E1	BRN	ECM GROUND	0*	0*
25/NO. 20	GRN/YEL	FUEL INJECTOR 1 & 2 CONTROL	B +	B +
26/E02	BRN	ECM GROUND	0*	0*

0*   LESS THAN 0.50 VOLTS
(1)   B + WITH BRAKE PEDAL DEPRESSED
(2)   0V WITH A/C "ON"
(3)   B + WITH A/C "ON"
(4)   VARIES AS FRONT WHEELS ROTATE
(5)   B + WITH IGNITION SWITCH IN "START"
(6)   0V IN OVERDRIVE
(7)   B + WITH RADIATOR FAN, BLOWER MOTOR, HEADLIGHTS OR DEFOGGER "ON"
(8)   0V BELOW 4000 RPM, B + ABOVE 4000 RPM
(9)   B + WITH MANUAL SELECTOR IN "R," "D," "2" OR "L"
(10) INCREASES WITH RPM
(11) VARIES WITH TEMPERATURE
(12) VARIES WITH THROTTLE POSITION
(13) B + WHEN "OFF" IDLE

(★) CALIFORNIA ONLY
(●) FEDERAL AND CANADA ONLY
(X) AUTOMATIC TRANSAXLE ONLY

Fig. 105 1992 VIN code 5 engine

FUEL INJECTION ECM CONNECTOR IDENTIFICATION

The following ECM voltage charts are for use with a digital-voltmeter to further aid in diagnosis. The voltages you get may vary due to low battery charge or other reasons, but they should be very close.

THE FOLLOWING CONDITIONS MUST BE MET BEFORE TESTING:

- Engine at operating temperature • Engine idling (for "Engine Run" column)
- Diagnostic Enable Terminal not grounded
- All voltages shown "B +" indicate battery or charging voltage

VF	OX+	OX1	OX2	THW	THA	VS	VC
E21	T	KNK	THG	IDL	VCC	VTA	E2

BACKVIEW OF ECM CONNECTOR C3

CAVITY/ PIN	WIRE COLOR	CIRCUIT	VOLTAGE	
			KEY "ON"	ENG. RUN
1/VC	YEL/BLK	MAF VOLTAGE CONTROL	8V	8 - 9V
2/VS	YEL/BLU	MAF INPUT	2V	1 - 9V (10)
3/THA	BLK	IAT INPUT	2V (11)	2V (11)
4/THW	WHT	COOLANT TEMPERATURE INPUT	5V (11)	1 - 4V (11)
5/OX2 (★)	BLK	SECONDARY EXHAUST OXYGEN CONCENTRATION INPUT	0*	.1 - .9V VARIES
6/OX1	BLK	EXHAUST OXYGEN CONCENTRATION INPUT	.1 - .9V	.1 - .9V VARIES
7/OX + (●)	RED/GRN	EXHAUST OXYGEN CONCENTRATION INPUT	1V	1V
8/VF	RED/WHT	FUEL CONTROL FEEDBACK OUTPUT	0*	0 - 2.5V
9/E2	BRN	SENSOR GROUND	0*	0*
10/VTA	RED	THROTTLE POSITION INPUT	.60V	.6 - 4V (12)
11/VCC	YEL	REFERENCE VOLTAGE (5V)	5V	5V
12/IDL	BLU	IDLE SWITCH SIGNAL	0* (13)	0* (13)
13/THG (★)	RED/GRN	EGR TEMPERATURE INPUT	4.5V	.69V (11)
14/KNK	BLK	KNOCK INPUT	0*	0*
15/T	BLU/WHT	DIAGNOSTIC ENABLE SIGNAL	B +	B +
16/E21	BRN	SENSOR GROUND	0*	0*

0* LESS THAN 0.50 VOLTS
(1) B + WITH BRAKE PEDAL DEPRESSED
(2) 0V WITH A/C "ON"
(3) B + WITH A/C "ON"
(4) VARIES AS FRONT WHEELS ROTATE
(5) B + WITH IGNITION SWITCH IN "START"
(6) 0V IN OVERDRIVE
(7) B + WITH RADIATOR FAN, BLOWER MOTOR, HEADLIGHTS OR DEFOGGER "ON"
(8) 0V BELOW 4000 RPM, B + ABOVE 4000 RPM

(9) B + WITH MANUAL SELECTOR IN "R," "D," "2" OR "L"
(10) INCREASES WITH RPM
(11) VARIES WITH TEMPERATURE
(12) VARIES WITH THROTTLE POSITION
(13) B + WHEN "OFF" IDLE

(★) CALIFORNIA ONLY
(●) FEDERAL AND CANADA ONLY
(X) AUTOMATIC TRANSAXLE ONLY

Fig. 106 1992 VIN code 5 engine

"S" CARLINE   RPO: LO1   VIN CODE: 6   1.6L L4 PFI

COMPUTER HARNESS
- **C1** Engine Control Module (ECM)
- **C2** Diagnosis Check Connector
- **C3** "CHECK ENGINE" Light
- **C4** Circuit Opening Relay
- **C5** ECM Harness Grounds
- **C6** Junction Block 1
- **C8** Fuel Pump Test Connector (Part of C2)

RELATED COMPONENTS
- **N1** Crankcase Vent Valve (PCV)
- **N9** Fuel Pressure Regulator Valve
- **N10** Cold Start Fuel Injector
- **N11** Cold Start Fuel Injector Timer
- **N17** Fuel Vapor Canister
- **N18** A/C Fan Relay No. 3
- **N19** A/C Fan Relay No. 2
- **N20** A/C Clutch Relay

Exhaust Gas Recirculation (EGR) Valve

CONTROLLED DEVICES
- **1** Fuel Injectors
- **2** Idle Vacuum Switching Valve (VSV)
- **4** EFI F-HTR Relay
- **7** *EGR Vacuum Switching Valve (VSV)
- **8** Fan Relay No. 1
- **17** Throttle Body
- **18** Distributor (Ignition Coil and Igniter located in Distributor.)

INFORMATION SENSORS
- **A** Manifold Absolute Pressure (MAP) Sensor
- **B** Oxygen (O_2) Sensor
- **C** Throttle Switch (TS)
- **D** Coolant Temperature Sensor
- **F** Vehicle Speed Sensor (VSS)
- **M** Neutral Start Switch
- **T** Intake Air Temperature (IAT) Sensor
- **U** *EGR Temperature Sensor

* California Only

Fig. 107 1992 VIN code 6 engine

Fig. 108 1992 VIN code 6 engine

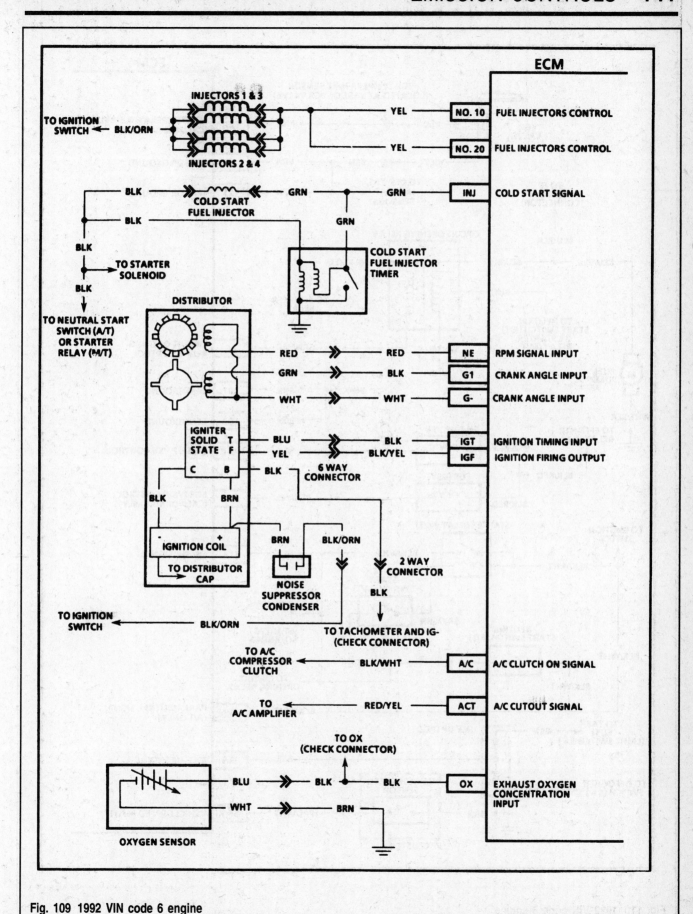

Fig. 109 1992 VIN code 6 engine

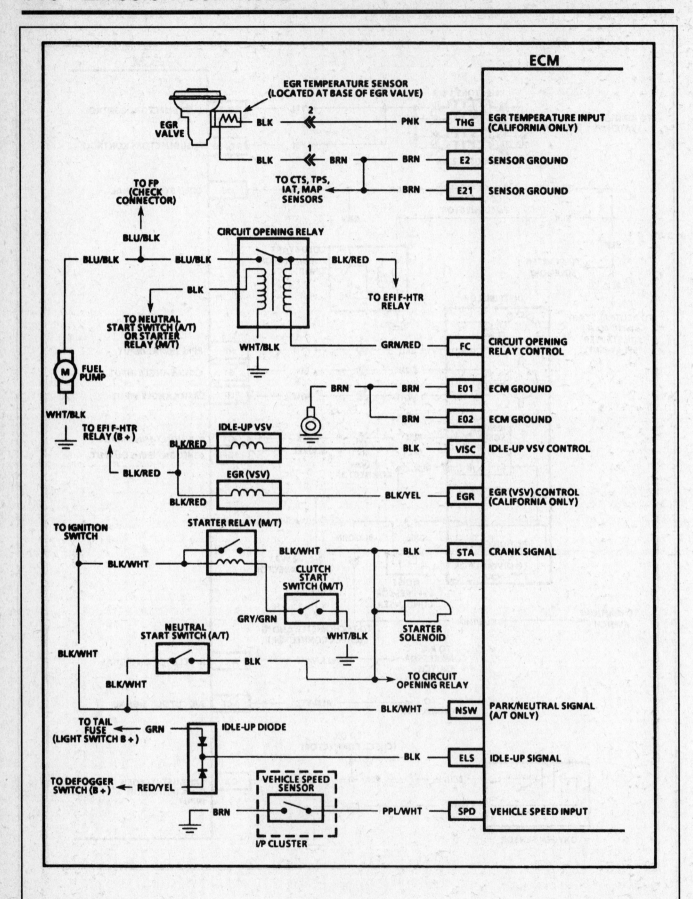

Fig. 110 1992 VIN code 6 engine

FUEL INJECTION ECM CONNECTOR IDENTIFICATION

The following ECM voltage charts are for use with a digital voltmeter to further aid in diagnosis. The voltages you get may vary due to low battery charge or other reasons, but they should be very close.

THE FOLLOWING CONDITIONS JUST BE MET BEFORE TESTING:

- Engine at operating temperature
- Engine idling (for "Engine Run" column)
- Diagnostic enable terminal not grounded
- All voltages shown "B + " indicate battery or charging voltage

BACKVIEW OF ECM CONNECTOR C1

CAVITY/ PIN	WIRE COLOR	CIRCUIT	VOLTAGE KEY "ON"	VOLTAGE ENG. RUN
1/B1	BLK/RED	IGNITION ON SIGNAL	B +	B +
2/BATT	RED/WHT	BATTERY VOLTAGE SUPPLY	B +	B +
3/–	–	NOT USED	–	–
4/FC	GRN/RED	CIRCUIT OPENING RELAY CONTROL	B +	0*
5/ELS	BLK	IDLE-UP SIGNAL	0* (1)	0* (1)
6/INJ	GRN	COLD START SIGNAL	0*	0* (2)
7/ACT	RED/YEL	A/C CUTOUT CONTROL	0*	B + (3)
8/T	BLU/WHT	DIAGNOSTIC ENABLE SIGNAL	B +	B +
9/B	BLK/RED	IGNITION ON SIGNAL	B +	B +
10/WRN	RED	"CHECK ENGINE" LIGHT CONTROL	.8-1.5V	B +
11/-	–	NOT USED	–	–
12/A/C	BLK/WHT	A/C CLUTCH ON SIGNAL	0* (3)	0* (3)
13/SPD	PPL/WHT	VEHICLE SPEED INPUT	0-B + (4)	0-B + (4)
14/-	–	NOT USED	–	–
15/-	–	NOT USED	–	–
16/VF	RED/WHT	FUEL CONTROL FEEDBACK OUTPUT	0*	0-2.5V

0*   LESS THAN 0.50 VOLTS
(1)   B + WITH HEADLIGHTS OR DEFOGGER "ON"
(2)   B + WITH COOLANT TEMPERATURE BELOW 35°C (95°F)
(3)   B + WITH A/C "ON," 0V WITH A/C "OFF"
(4)   VARIES AS FRONT WHEELS ROTATE
(5)   VARIES WITH TEMPERATURE
(6)   VARIES WITH ENGINE LOAD
(7)   B + WITH IGNITION SWITCH IN "START"
(8)   VARIES WITH THROTTLE POSITION
(9)   0V AT WIDE OPEN THROTTLE
(10)   B + OFF IDLE

(★)   CALIFORNIA ONLY
(X)   AUTOMATIC TRANSAXLE ONLY

Fig. 111 1992 VIN code 6 engine

FUEL INJECTION ECM CONNECTOR IDENTIFICATION

The following ECM voltage charts are for use with a digital voltmeter to further aid in diagnosis. The voltages you get may vary due to low battery charge or other reasons, but they should be very close.

THE FOLLOWING CONDITIONS JUST BE MET BEFORE TESTING:

- Engine at operating temperature
- Engine idling (for "Engine Run" column)
- Diagnostic enable terminal not grounded
- All voltages shown "B + " indicate battery or charging voltage

E01	NO. 10	STA	OX	G-	G1	IGF	IGT	THA	PIM	THW	NSW	EGR
E02	NO. 20	E1	✕	E21	NE	THG	IDL	VCC	PSW	E2	O/D	VISC

BACKVIEW OF ECM CONNECTOR C2

CAVITY/ PIN	WIRE COLOR	CIRCUIT	VOLTAGE	
			KEY "ON"	ENG. RUN
1/EGR (★)	BLK/YEL	EGR VSV CONTROL	B +	B +
2/NSW (X)	BLK/WHT	PARK/NEUTRAL SIGNAL	B +	B +
3/THW	WHT	COOLANT TEMPERATURE INPUT	5V	1-4V (5)
4/PIM	LT GRN/ RED	MAP INPUT	3.5V	1-3V (6)
5/THA	YEL/BLK	IAT INPUT	1-3V (5)	1-3V (5)
6/IGT	BLK	IGNITION TIMING INPUT	0*	.69V
7/IGF	BLK/YEL	IGNITION FIRING OUTPUT	.5-1V	1V
8/G1	BLK	CRANK ANGLE INPUT	.69V	.67V
9/G-	WHT	CRANK ANGLE INPUT	.69V	.67V
10/OX	BLK	EXHAUST OXYGEN CONCENTRATION INPUT	0*	.1-.9V VARIES
11/STA	BLK	CRANK SIGNAL	0*	0* (7)
12/NO. 10	YEL	FUEL INJECTORS CONTROL	B +	B +
13E01	BRN	ECM GROUND	0*	0*

CAVITY/ PIN	WIRE COLOR	CIRCUIT	VOLTAGE	
			KEY "ON"	ENG. RUN
14/VISC	BLK	IDLE-UP VSV CONTROL	1.4V	B + (8)
15/O/D	RED/WHT	NOT USED	–	–
16/E2	BRN	SENSOR GROUND	0*	0*
17/PSW	LT GRN	WIDE OPEN THROTTLE SIGNAL	B + (9)	B + (9)
18/VCC	YEL	REFERENCE VOLTAGE (5V)	5V	5V
19/IDL	BLU	IDLE THROTTLE SIGNAL	0* (10)	0* (10)
20/THG (★)	PNK	EGR TEMPERATURE INPUT	5V (5)	.69V (5)
21/NE	RED	RPM INPUT	.69V	.67V
22/E21	BRN	SENSOR GROUND	0*	0*
23/–	–	NOT USED	–	–
24/E1	BRN	ECM GROUND	0*	0*
25/NO. 20	YEL	FUEL INJECTORS CONTROL	B +	B +
26/E02	BRN	ECM GROUND	0*	0*

- 0* LESS THAN 0.50 VOLTS
- (1) B + WITH HEADLIGHTS OR DEFOGGER "ON"
- (2) B + WITH COOLANT TEMPERATURE BELOW 35°C (95°F)
- (3) B + WITH A/C "ON," 0V WITH A/C "OFF"
- (4) VARIES AS FRONT WHEELS ROTATE
- (5) VARIES WITH TEMPERATURE
- (6) VARIES WITH ENGINE LOAD
- (7) B + WITH IGNITION SWITCH IN "START"
- (8) VARIES WITH THROTTLE POSITION
- (9) 0V AT WIDE OPEN THROTTLE
- (10) B + OFF IDLE
- (★) CALIFORNIA ONLY
- (X) AUTOMATIC TRANSAXLE ONLY

Fig. 112 1992 VIN code 6 engine

1.6L (VIN 6) "S" CARLINE

	CONTROLLED DEVICES		INFORMATION SENSORS		RELATED COMPONENTS
1	CIRCUIT OPENING RELAY	1	MAP SENSOR	1	A/C SV VALVE
2	FUEL INJECTORS	2	SUB-02S (CALIFORNIA EMISSIONS)	2	EVAP CANISTER
3	IAC VALVE	3	EGR TEMPERATURE SENSOR (CALIFORNIA EMISSIONS)	3	DLC
4	EGR SV VALVE (CALIFORNIA EMISSIONS)			4	JUNCTION BLOCK 1
5	MIL	4	TP SENSOR	5	EVAP TVV
		5	IAT SENSOR	6	FUSE AND RELAY BOX
		6	VSS	7	A/C FUSE AND RELAY BOX
		7	02S (CALIFORNIA EMISSIONS)	8	FUEL PRESSURE REGULATOR
		8	02S (FEDERAL EMISSIONS)	9	ECM
		9	DISTRIBUTOR		
		10	ECT SENSOR		

Fig. 113 1993 VIN code 6 engine

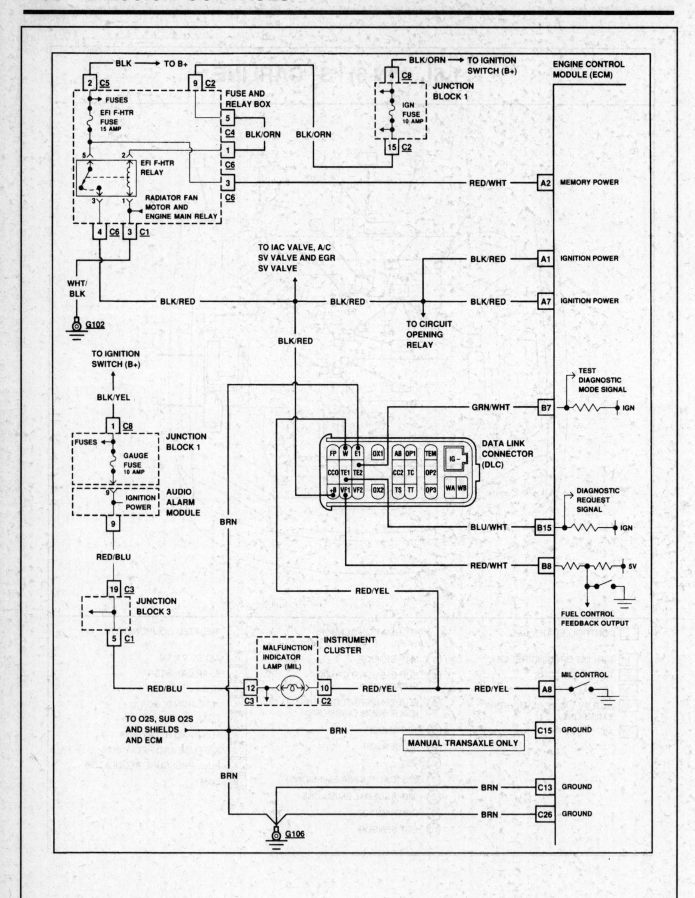

Fig. 114 1993 VIN code 6 engine

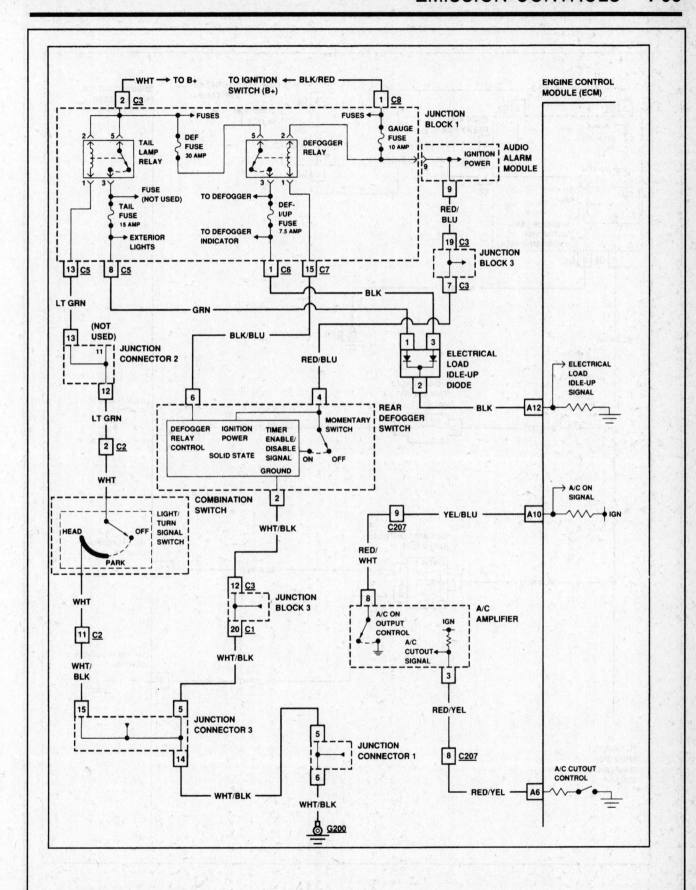

Fig. 115 1993 VIN code 6 engine

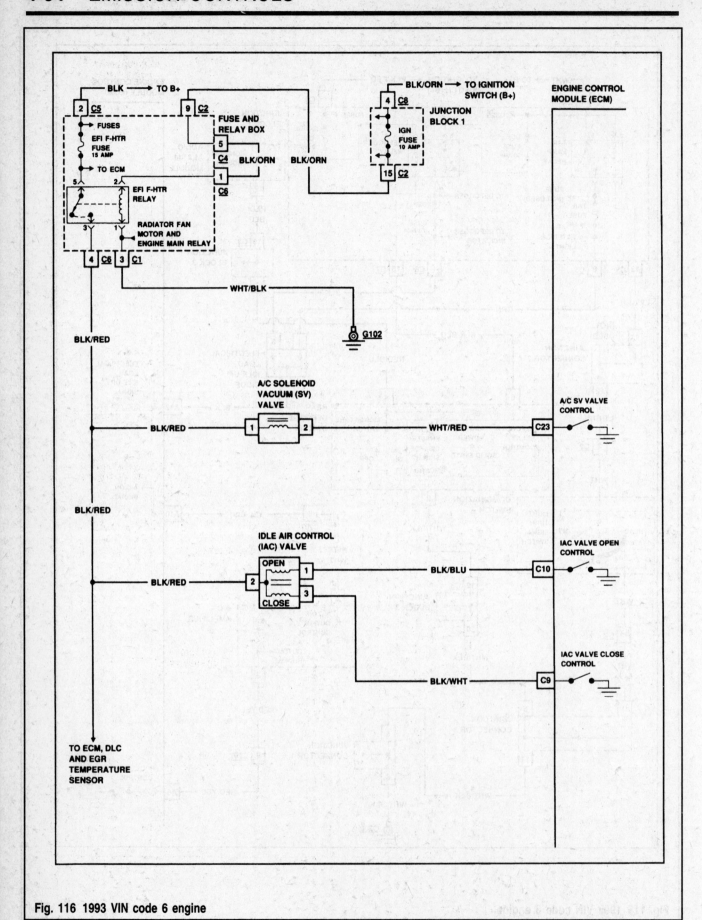

Fig. 116 1993 VIN code 6 engine

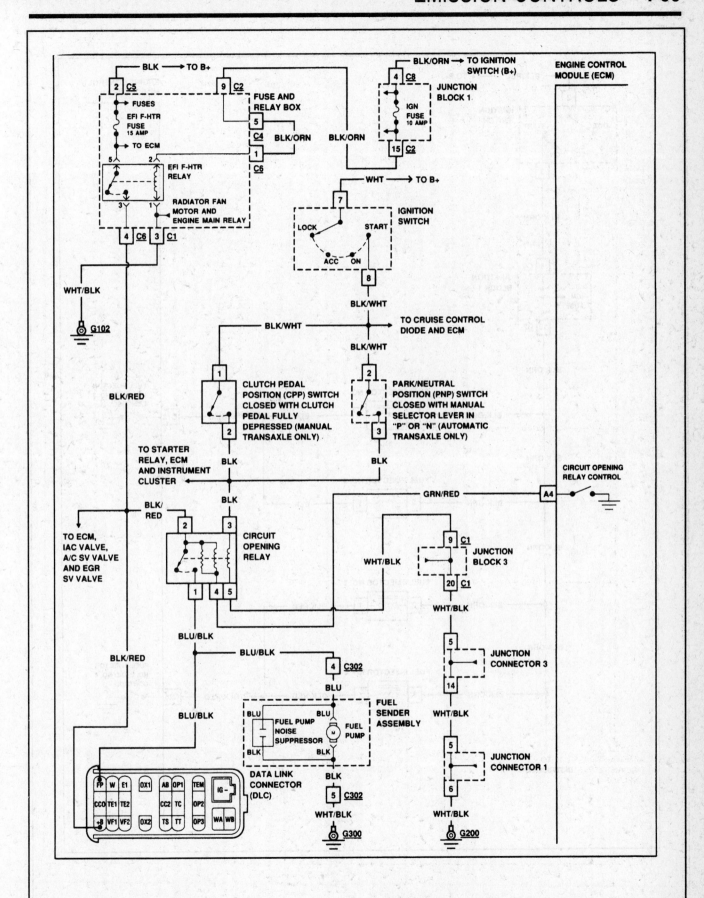

Fig. 117 1993 VIN code 6 engine

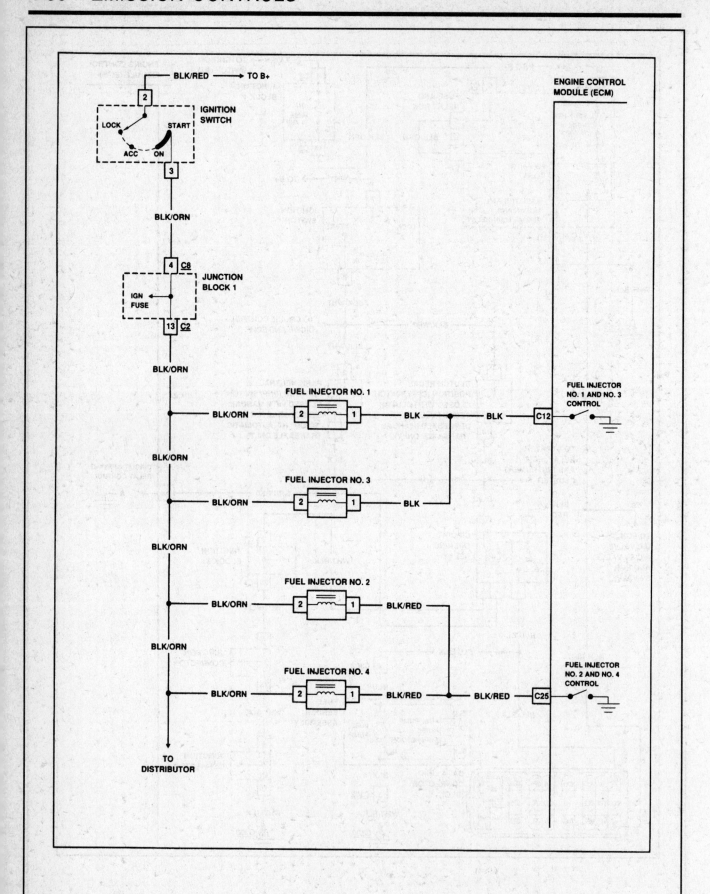

Fig. 118 1993 VIN code 6 engine

Fig. 119 1993 VIN code 6 engine

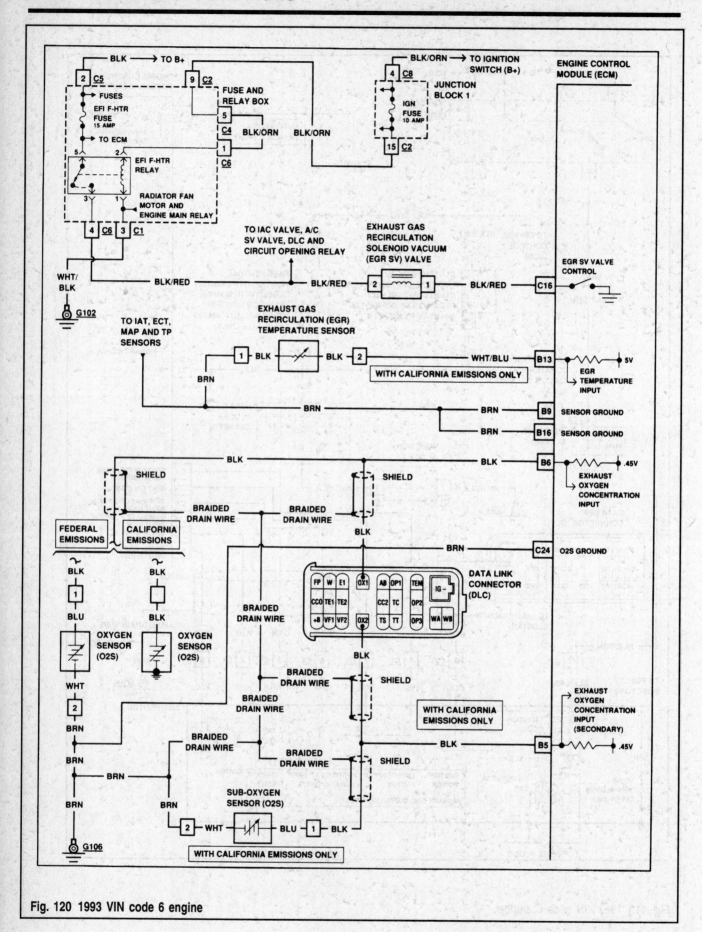

Fig. 120 1993 VIN code 6 engine

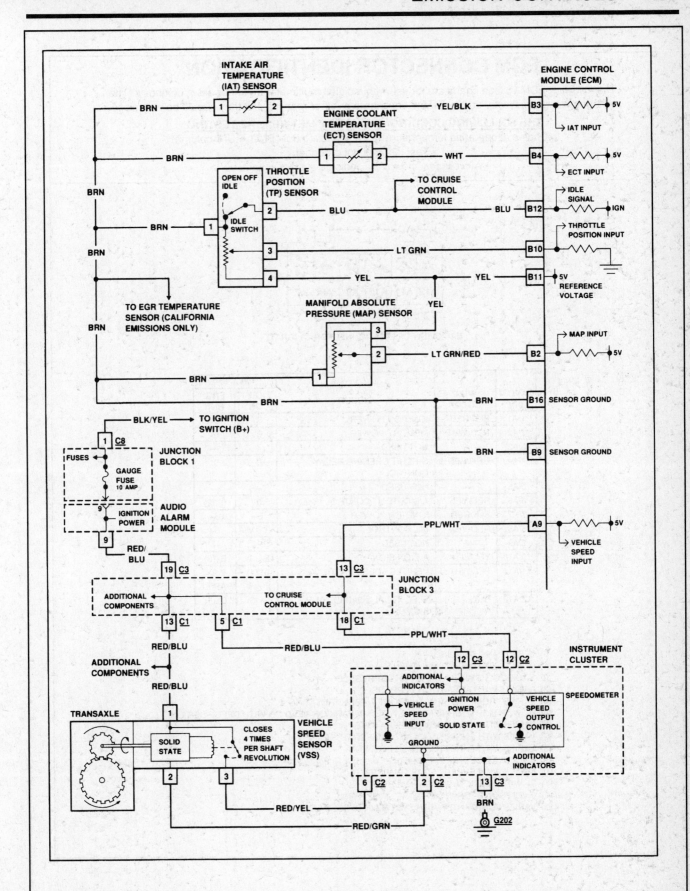

Fig. 121 1993 VIN code 6 engine

ECM CONNECTOR IDENTIFICATION

The following ECM voltage charts are for use with a digital multimeter to further aid in diagnosis. The voltages you get may vary due to low battery charge or other reasons, but they should be very close.

THE FOLLOWING CONDITIONS MUST BE MET BEFORE TESTING:

- Engine at operating temperature • Engine idling (for "ENG. RUN" column)
- Test terminal not grounded
- All voltages shown "B+" indicate system voltage

| A6 | A5 | A4 | A3 | A2 | A1 |
| A12 | A11 | A10 | A9 | A8 | A7 |

BACK VIEW OF ECM CONNECTOR C1 (GRAY)

CAVITY/ PIN	WIRE COLOR	CIRCUIT	VOLTAGE	
			KEY "ON"	ENG. RUN
1/A1	BLK/RED	IGNITION POWER	B+	B+
2/A2	RED/WHT	MEMORY POWER	B+	B+
3/A3	—	NOT USED	—	—
4/A4	GRN/RED	CIRCUIT OPENING RELAY CONTROL	(1)	0*
5/A5	—	NOT USED	—	—
6/A6	RED/YEL	A/C CUTOUT CONTROL	0*	0* (2)
7/A7	BLK/RED	IGNITION POWER	B+	B+
8/A8	RED/YEL	MIL CONTROL	0-1V	B+
9/A9	—	NOT USED	—	—
10/A10	YEL/BLU	A/C ON SIGNAL	B+(3)	B+(3)
11/A11	PPL/WHT	VEHICLE SPEED INPUT	0* (4)	2-3V VARIES
12/A12	BLK	ELECTRICAL LOAD IDLE-UP SIGNAL	0* (5)	0* (5)

0* LESS THAN 0.50 VOLTS
(1) 0 VOLTS FOR 3 SECONDS, THEN B+
(2) 5 TO 6 VOLTS WITH A/C SWITCH DEPRESSED
(3) 0 VOLTS WITH A/C SWITCH DEPRESSED
(4) VARIES FROM 0 TO 5V WITH FRONT WHEELS ROTATING
(5) B+ WITH LIGHT/TURN SIGNAL SWITCH IN PARK OR HEAD OR WITH DEFOGGER ON
(6) VARIES WITH INTAKE AIR TEMPERATURE
(7) VARIES WITH ENGINE COOLANT TEMPERATURE
(8) VARIES WITH THROTTLE LEVER POSITION
(9) 0 VOLTS AT IDLE; B+ OFF IDLE
(10) VARIES WITH EXHAUST GAS TEMPERATURE
(11) B+ WITH IGNITION SWITCH IN "START"
(12) 0 VOLTS IN "P" OR "N"; B+ IN "R", "D", "2" OR "L"
(13) VARIES CONSTANTLY WITH SYSTEM IN CLOSED LOOP

Fig. 122 1993 VIN code 6 engine

ECM CONNECTOR IDENTIFICATION

The following ECM voltage charts are for use with a digital multimeter to further aid in diagnosis. The voltages you get may vary due to low battery charge or other reasons, but they should be very close.

THE FOLLOWING CONDITIONS MUST BE MET BEFORE TESTING:

- Engine at operating temperature • Engine idling (for "ENG. RUN" column)
- Test terminal not grounded
- All voltages shown "B+" indicate system voltage

BACK VIEW OF ECM CONNECTOR C2 (GRAY)

CAVITY/ PIN	WIRE COLOR	CIRCUIT	VOLTAGE KEY "ON"	VOLTAGE ENG. RUN
1/B1	—	NOT USED	—	—
2/B2	LT GRN/RED	MAP INPUT	3-4V	1.1-1.8V
3/B3	YEL/BLK	IAT INPUT	1-3.5V (6)	1.5-2.5V (6)
4/B4	WHT	ECT INPUT	.5-3.5V (7)	1-2V (7)
5/B5	BLK	SECONDARY) (CALIFORNIA ONLY) EXHAUST OXYGEN CONCENTRATION INPUT	0*	0-1V (13)
6/B6	BLK	TEST DIAGNOSTIC MODE SIGNAL	0*	0-1V (13)
7/B7	GRN/WHT	FUEL CONTROL FEEDBACK OUTPUT	B+	B+
8/B8	RED/WHT	SENSOR GROUND	0*	1.5-3.5V
9/B9	BRN	THROTTLE POSITION INPUT	0*	0*
10/B10	LT GRN	REFERENCE VOLTAGE (5V)	.5-4.5V (8)	.5-4.5V (8)
11/B11	YEL	IDLE SIGNAL	5V	5V
12/B12	BLU	EGR TEMPERATURE INPUT (CALIFORNIA ONLY)	(9)	(9)
13/B13	WHT/BLU	NOT USED	1-3.5V (10)	1.5-2.5V(10)
14/B14	—	DIAGNOSTIC REQUEST SIGNAL	—	—
15/B15	BLU/WHT	SENSOR GROUND	B+	B+
16/B16	BRN		0*	0*

0* LESS THAN 0.50 VOLTS
(1) 0 VOLTS FOR 3 SECONDS, THEN B+
(2) 5 TO 6 VOLTS WITH A/C SWITCH DEPRESSED
(3) 0 VOLTS WITH A/C SWITCH DEPRESSED
(4) VARIES FROM 0 TO 5V WITH FRONT WHEELS ROTATING
(5) B+ WITH LIGHT/TURN SIGNAL SWITCH IN PARK OR HEAD OR WITH DEFOGGER ON
(6) VARIES WITH INTAKE AIR TEMPERATURE
(7) VARIES WITH ENGINE COOLANT TEMPERATURE
(8) VARIES WITH THROTTLE LEVER POSITION
(9) 0 VOLTS AT IDLE; B+ OFF IDLE
(10) VARIES WITH EXHAUST GAS TEMPERATURE
(11) B+ WITH IGNITION SWITCH IN "START"
(12) 0 VOLTS IN "P" OR "N"; B+ IN "R", "D", "2" OR "L"
(13) VARIES CONSTANTLY WITH SYSTEM IN CLOSED LOOP

Fig. 123 1993 VIN code 6 engine

ECM CONNECTOR IDENTIFICATION

The following ECM voltage charts are for use with a digital multimeter to further aid in diagnosis. The voltages you get may vary due to low battery charge or other reasons, but they should be very close.

THE FOLLOWING CONDITIONS MUST BE MET BEFORE TESTING:

- Engine at operating temperature • Engine idling (for "ENG. RUN" column)
- Test terminal not grounded
- All voltages shown "B+" indicate system voltage

BACK VIEW OF ECM CONNECTOR C3 (GRAY)

CAVITY/ PIN	WIRE COLOR	CIRCUIT	VOLTAGE KEY "ON"	VOLTAGE ENG. RUN
1/C1	—	NOT USED	—	—
2/C2	BLK	CRANK SIGNAL	0* (11)	0* (11)
3/C3	BLK/YEL	IGNITION FAIL-SAFE SIGNAL INPUT	.56V	1.5V
4/C4	BLK	CRANK ANGLE INPUT HIGH	.69V	.69V
5/C5	RED	CAMSHAFT POSITION INPUT HIGH	.69V	.69V
6/C6	—	NOT USED	—	—
7/C7	—	NOT USED	—	—
8/C8	—	NOT USED	—	—
9/C9	BLK/WHT	IAC VALVE CLOSE CONTROL	.3-.7V	5-7V
10/C10	BLK/BLU	IAC VALVE OPEN CONTROL	B+	8-10V
11/C11	—	NOT USED	—	—
12/C12	BLK	FUEL INJECTOR NO. 1 AND NO. 3 CONTROL	B+	B+
13/C13	BRN	GROUND	0*	0*
14/C14	—	NOT USED	—	—
15/C15	BRN (M/T)	GROUND (M/T ONLY)	0*	0*
	BLK/WHT (A/T)	PARK/NEUTRAL POSITION SIGNAL (A/T ONLY)	(12)	(12)
16/C16	BLK/RED	EGR SV VALVE CONTROL (CALIFORNIA ONLY)	B+	B+
17/C17	WHT	CRANK ANGLE INPUT LOW	.69V	.69V
18/C18	GRN	CAMSHAFT POSITION INPUT LOW	.69V	.69V
19/C19	—	NOT USED	—	—
20/C20	—	NOT USED	—	—
21/C21	—	NOT USED	—	—
22/C22	BLK	IGNITION SIGNAL	0*	0-2V (8)
23/C23	WHT/RED	A/C SV VALVE CONTROL	B+	B+ (3)
24/C24	BRN	O2S GROUND	0*	0*
25/C25	BLK/RED	FUEL INJECTOR NO. 2 AND NO. 4 CONTROL	B+	B+
26/C26	BRN	GROUND	0*	0*

0* LESS THAN 0.50 VOLTS
(1) 0 VOLTS FOR 3 SECONDS, THEN B+
(2) 5 TO 6 VOLTS WITH A/C SWITCH DEPRESSED
(3) 0 VOLTS WITH A/C SWITCH DEPRESSED
(4) VARIES FROM 0 TO 5V WITH FRONT WHEELS ROTATING
(5) B+ WITH LIGHT/TURN SIGNAL SWITCH IN PARK
    OR HEAD OR WITH DEFOGGER ON

(6) VARIES WITH INTAKE AIR TEMPERATURE
(7) VARIES WITH ENGINE COOLANT TEMPERATURE
(8) VARIES WITH THROTTLE LEVER POSITION
(9) 0 VOLTS AT IDLE; B+ OFF IDLE
(10) VARIES WITH EXHAUST GAS TEMPERATURE
(11) B+ WITH IGNITION SWITCH IN "START"
(12) 0 VOLTS IN "P" OR "N"; B+ IN "R", "D", "2" OR "L"
(13) VARIES CONSTANTLY WITH SYSTEM IN CLOSED LOOP

Fig. 124 1993 VIN code 6 engine

DIAGNOSTIC TROUBLE CODE (DTC) TABLE
1.6L (VIN 6) "S" CARLINE
(PAGE 1 OF 2)

EXAMPLE: RPM SIGNAL DTC 13 AND MANIFOLD ABSOLUTE PRESSURE (MAP) SENSOR INPUT DTC 31

DIAGNOSTIC TROUBLE CODE (DTC)		SYSTEM	CONDITIONS THAT MUST BE MET BEFORE DTC WILL SET
NO.	MODE		
—	⎍⎍⎍⎍⎍⎍⎍	NORMAL	• INDICATES THAT ELECTRONIC ENGINE CONTROL SYSTEM IS FUNCTIONING NORMALLY.
12	⎍⎍⎍	RPM SIGNAL	(1) NO CRANK ANGLE INPUT DETECTED AT ECM FOR 2 SECONDS OR MORE WHILE CRANKING ENGINE. (2) NO CAMSHAFT POSITION INPUT DETECTED AT ECM FOR 3 SECONDS OR MORE WITH ENGINE SPEED BETWEEN 600 AND 4,000 RPM. • THIS DTC CAN ONLY BE ACCESSED WHEN IN THE NORMAL DIAGNOSTIC MODE.
13	⎍⎍⎍⎍	RPM SIGNAL	• NO CRANK ANGLE INPUT DETECTED AT ECM FOR 0.30 SECONDS OR MORE WITH ENGINE SPEED ABOVE 1,500 RPM.
14	⎍⎍⎍⎍	IGNITION SIGNAL	• NO IGNITION FAIL-SAFE SIGNAL INPUT DETECTED AT ECM FOR 4 CONSECUTIVE IGNITION CYCLES. • THIS DTC CAN ONLY BE ACCESSED WHEN IN THE NORMAL DIAGNOSTIC MODE.
21	⎍⎍⎍⎍	OXYGEN SENSOR (O2S) INPUT	• OXYGEN SENSOR VOLTAGE INPUT AT ECM CONSTANT BETWEEN 0.35 AND 0.70 VOLTS FOR 60 SECONDS OR MORE WITH ENGINE SPEED ABOVE 1,500 RPM.
22	⎍⎍⎍⎍	ENGINE COOLANT TEMPERATURE (ECT) SENSOR	• ECT INPUT AT ECM OPEN OR SHORTED FOR 0.50 SECONDS OR MORE.
24	⎍⎍⎍⎍⎍	INTAKE AIR TEMPERATURE (IAT) SENSOR	• IAT INPUT AT ECM OPEN OR SHORTED FOR 0.50 SECONDS OR MORE.

Fig. 125 1993 VIN code 6 engine

DIAGNOSTIC TROUBLE CODE (DTC) TABLE
1.6L (VIN 6) "S" CARLINE
(PAGE 2 OF 2)

DIAGNOSTIC TROUBLE CODE (DTC)		SYSTEM	CONDITIONS THAT MUST BE MET BEFORE DTC WILL SET
NO.	MODE		
25		AIR/FUEL RATIO LEAN	(1) OXYGEN SENSOR INPUT AT ECM IS LESS THAN 0.45 VOLTS FOR 90 SECONDS OR MORE WITH OXYGEN SENSOR WARM AND ENGINE SPEED ABOVE 1,500 RPM. (2) WHEN ENGINE SPEED VARIES BY MORE THAN 50 RPM OVER THE PRECEDING CRANK ANGLE PERIOD DURING A PERIOD OF 50 SECONDS WHILE IDLING WITH THE ECT ABOVE 50°C (122°F). • EITHER CONDITION MUST BE DETECTED DURING 2 CONSECUTIVE IGNITION CYCLES FOR DTC TO BE STORED IN ECM MEMORY.
26		AIR/FUEL RATIO RICH	• WHEN ENGINE SPEED VARIES BY MORE THAN 50 RPM OVER THE PRECEDING CRANK ANGLE PERIOD DURING A PERIOD OF 50 SECONDS WHILE IDLING WITH THE ECT ABOVE 50°C (122°F). • CONDITION MUST BE DETECTED DURING 2 CONSECUTIVE IGNITION CYCLES FOR DTC TO BE STORED IN ECM MEMORY.
27		SUB-OXYGEN SENSOR (O2S) INPUT	• WHEN SUB-OXYGEN SENSOR IS WARMED UP AND ENGINE IS OFF IDLE FOR 2 SECONDS OR MORE AND OXYGEN SENSOR INPUT AT PCM IS 0.45 VOLTS OR MORE AND SUB-OXYGEN SENSOR INPUT AT ECM IS 0.45 VOLTS OR LESS. • CONDITION MUST BE DETECTED DURING 2 CONSECUTIVE IGNITION CYCLES FOR DTC TO BE STORED IN ECM MEMORY.
31		MANIFOLD ABSOLUTE PRESSURE (MAP) SENSOR INPUT	• MAP INPUT AT ECM OPEN OR SHORTED FOR 0.50 SECONDS OR MORE.
41		THROTTLE POSITION (TP) SENSOR INPUT	• THROTTLE POSITION INPUT AT ECM OPEN OR SHORTED FOR 0.50 SECONDS OR MORE.
42		VEHICLE SPEED INPUT	• VEHICLE SPEED INPUT NOT DETECTED AT ECM FOR 8 SECONDS OR MORE WITH ENGINE SPEED BETWEEN 3,000 AND 5,000 RPM AND TRANSAXLE IN GEAR.
43		CRANK SIGNAL	• CRANK SIGNAL NOT DETECTED AT ECM DURING IGNITION. • THIS DTC CAN ONLY BE DETECTED WHEN IN THE TEST DIAGNOSTIC MODE.
51		SWITCH CONDITION SIGNAL	• DISPLAYED WHEN A/C IS ON, ACCELERATOR PEDAL IS DEPRESSED OR WHEN MANUAL SELECTOR IS IN "R", "D", "2" OR "L" POSITION WITH DLC TERMINAL "TE1" AND "E1" CONNECTED. • THIS DTC CAN ONLY BE ACCESSED WHEN IN THE TEST DIAGNOSTIC MODE AND INDICATES THE ABOVE MENTIONED SYSTEMS ARE FUNCTIONING NORMALLY. IF DTC 51 IS NOT INDICATED WHEN THE CONDITIONS ARE MET, A FAULT IS PRESENT, AND DTC 51's DIAGNOSTIC CHART MUST BE USED.
71		EGR SYSTEM	• WITH ECT ABOVE 60°C (140°F) 50 SECONDS FROM START OF EGR OPERATION. THE EGR TEMPERATURE IS LESS THAN 80°C (176°F) AND THE EGR TEMPERATURE HAS RISEN LESS THAN 10°C (18°F) DURING THE 50 SECONDS. • CONDITION MUST BE DETECTED DURING 2 CONSECUTIVE IGNITION CYCLES FOR DTC TO BE STORED IN ECM MEMORY.

Fig. 126 1993 VIN code 6 engine

1.8L (VIN 8) "S" CARLINE

CONTROLLED DEVICES

1 CIRCUIT OPENING RELAY
2 FUEL INJECTORS
3 IAC VALVE
4 EGR SV VALVE (CALIFORNIA EMISSIONS)
5 MIL

INFORMATION SENSORS

1 MAP SENSOR
2 SUB-02S (CALIFORNIA EMISSIONS)
3 EGR TEMPERATURE SENSOR (CALIFORNIA EMISSIONS)
4 TP SENSOR
5 IAT SENSOR
6 VSS
7 02S (CALIFORNIA EMISSIONS)
8 02S (FEDERAL EMISSIONS)
9 DISTRIBUTOR
10 ECT SENSOR

RELATED COMPONENTS

1 A/C SV VALVE
2 EVAP CANISTER
3 DLC
4 JUNCTION BLOCK 1
5 EVAP TVV
6 FUSE AND RELAY BOX
7 A/C FUSE AND RELAY BOX
8 FUEL PRESSURE REGULATOR
9 PCM

Fig. 127 1993 VIN code 8 engine

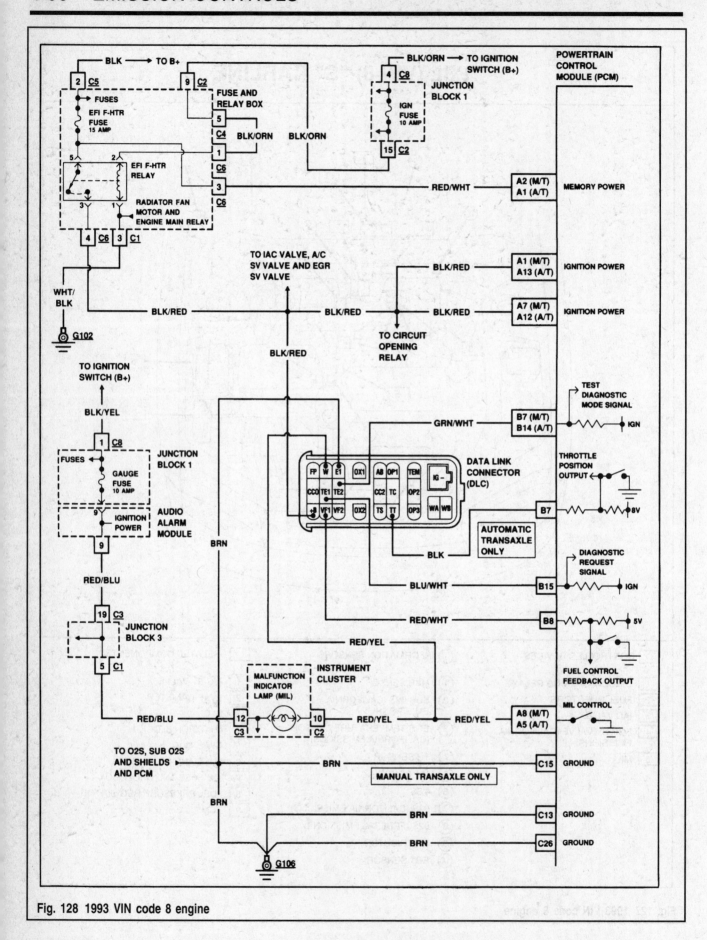

Fig. 128 1993 VIN code 8 engine

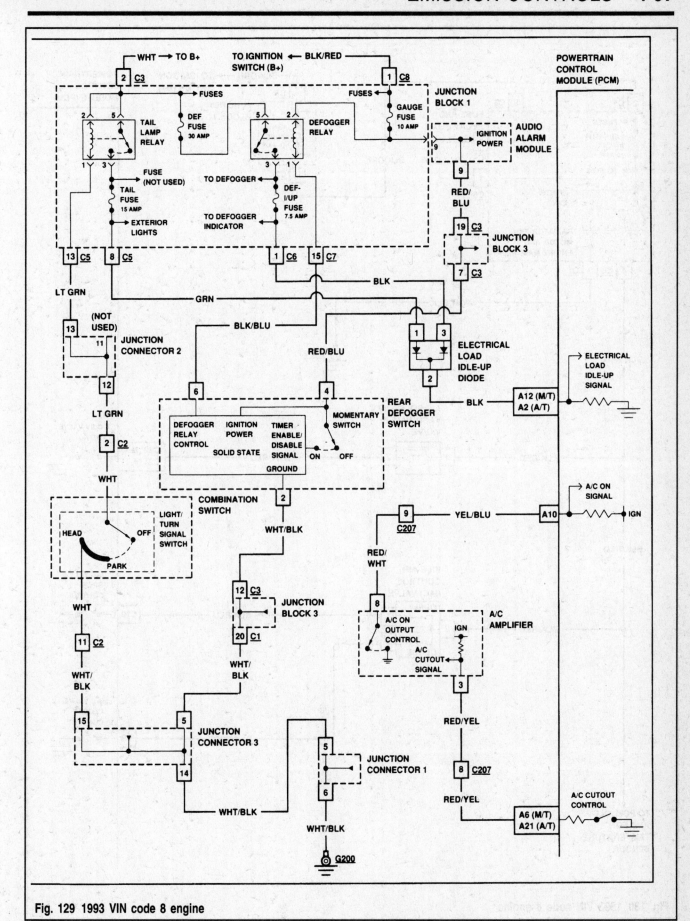

Fig. 129 1993 VIN code 8 engine

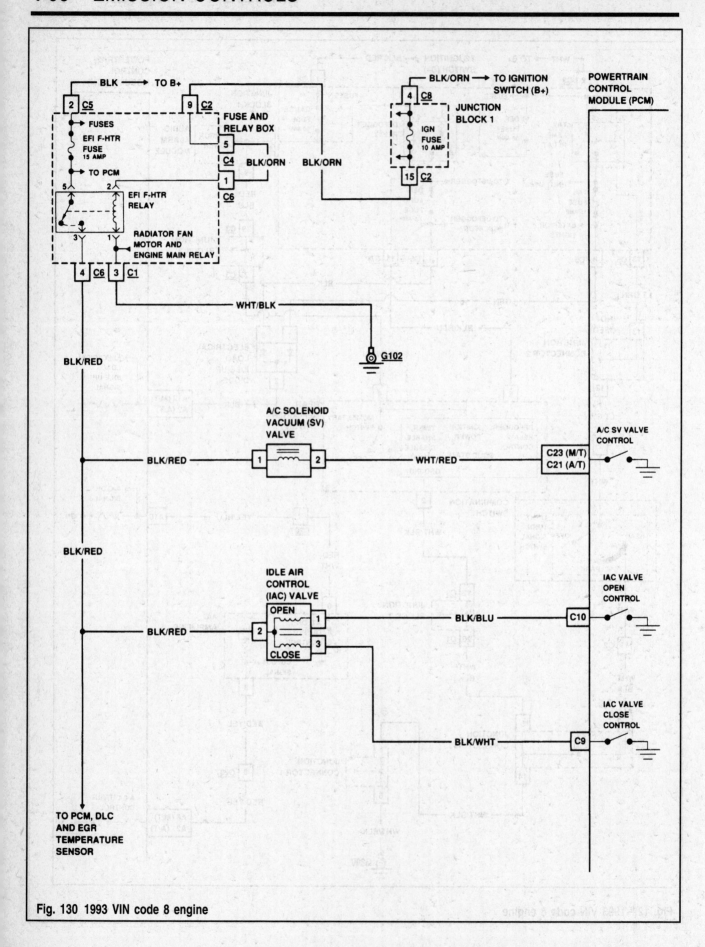

Fig. 130 1993 VIN code 8 engine

Fig. 131 1993 VIN code 8 engine

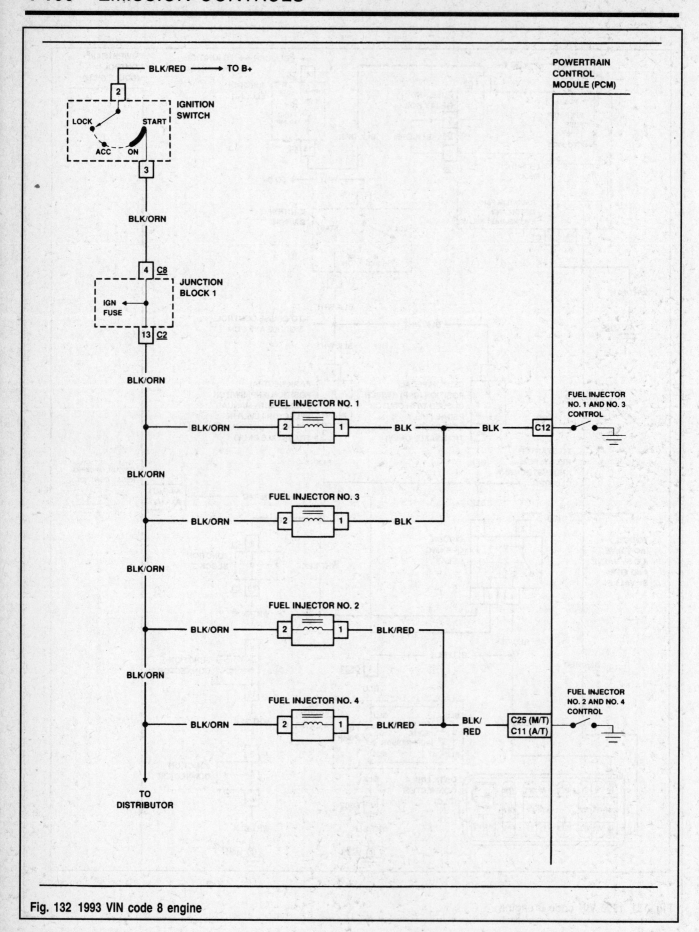

Fig. 132 1993 VIN code 8 engine

Fig. 133 1993 VIN code 8 engine

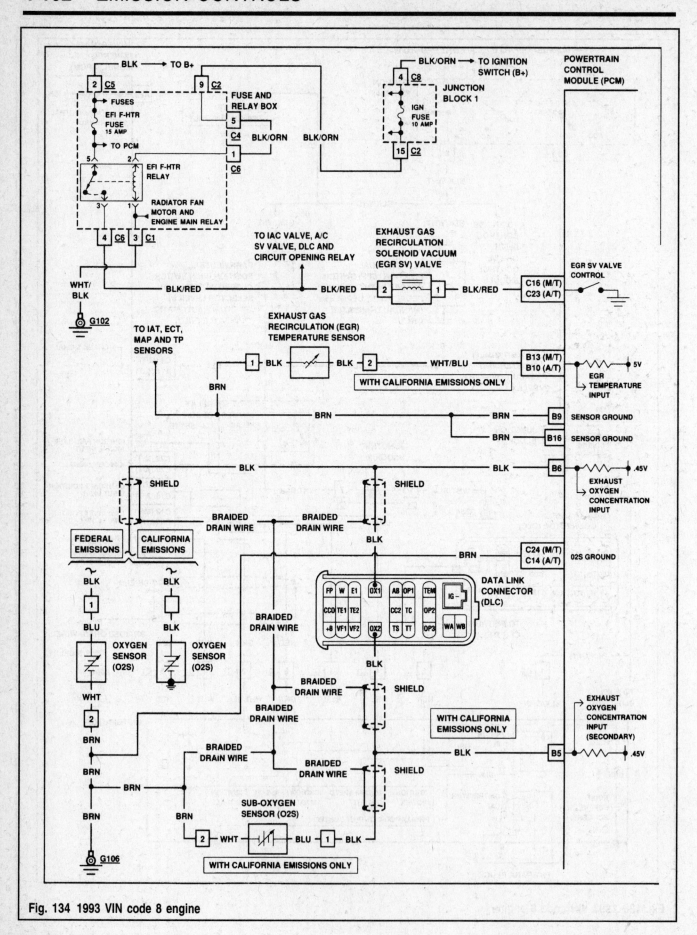

Fig. 134 1993 VIN code 8 engine

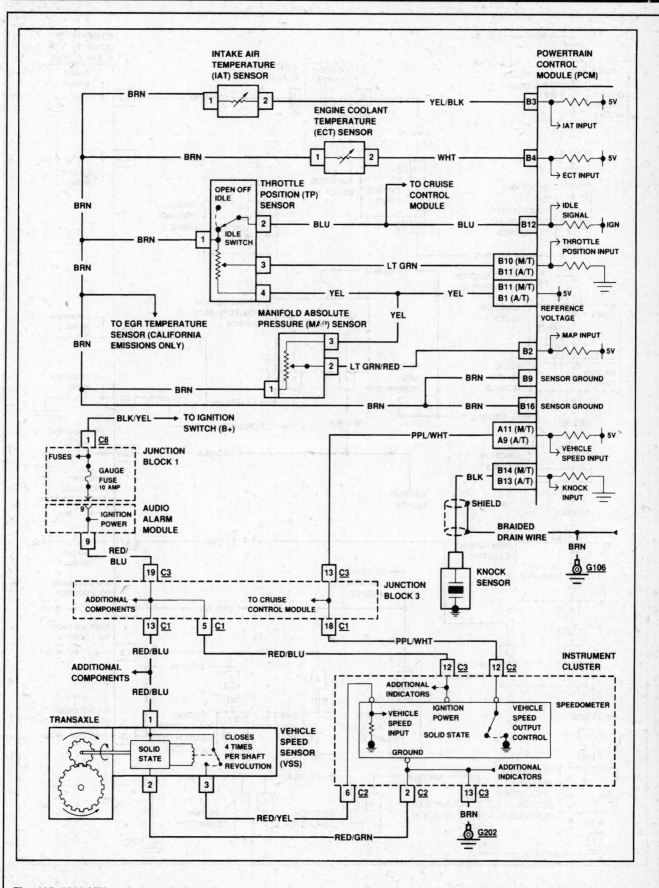

Fig. 135 1993 VIN code 8 engine

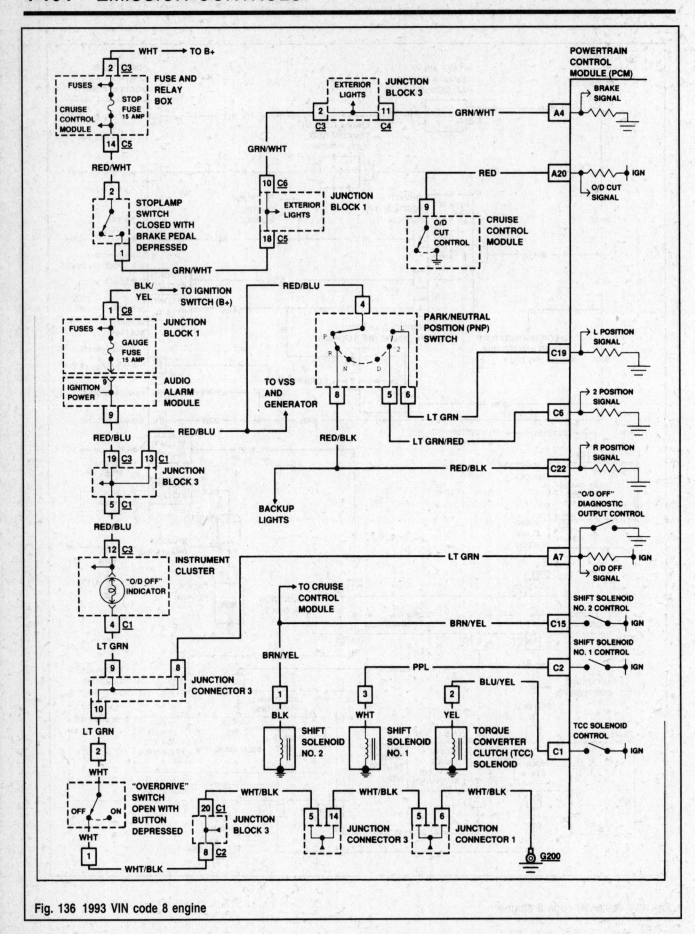

Fig. 136 1993 VIN code 8 engine

PCM CONNECTOR IDENTIFICATION

The following PCM voltage charts are for use with a digital multimeter to further aid in diagnosis. The voltages you get may vary due to low battery charge or other reasons, but they should be very close.

THE FOLLOWING CONDITIONS MUST BE MET BEFORE TESTING:
- Engine at operating temperature • Engine idling (for "ENG. RUN" column)
- Test terminal not grounded
- All voltages shown "B+" indicate system voltage

BACK VIEW OF PCM CONNECTOR C1 (MANUAL TRANSAXLE) (GRAY)

CAVITY/ PIN	WIRE COLOR	CIRCUIT	VOLTAGE	
			KEY "ON"	ENG. RUN
1/A1	BLK/RED	IGNITION POWER	B+	B+
2/A2	RED/WHT	MEMORY POWER	B+	B+
3/A3	—	NOT USED	—	—
4/A4	GRN/RED	CIRCUIT OPENING RELAY CONTROL	(7)	0*
5/A5	—	NOT USED	—	—
6/A6	RED/YEL	A/C CUTOUT CONTROL	0*	0* (8)
7/A7	BLK/RED	IGNITION POWER	B+	B+
8/A8	RED/YEL	MIL CONTROL	0-1V	B+
9/A9	—	NOT USED	—	—
10/A10	YEL/BLU	A/C ON SIGNAL	B+(5)	B+(5)
11/A11	PPL/WHT	VEHICLE SPEED INPUT	0* (4)	2-3V VARIES
12/A12	BLK	ELECTRICAL LOAD IDLE-UP SIGNAL	0* (1)	0* (1)

0* LESS THAN 0.50 VOLTS
(1) B+ WITH LIGHT/TURN SIGNAL SWITCH IN PARK OR HEAD OR WITH DEFOGGER ON
(2) B+ WITH BRAKE PEDAL DEPRESSED
(3) 0 VOLTS WITH OVERDRIVE SWITCH RELEASED; B+ WITH OVERDRIVE SWITCH DEPRESSED
(4) VARIES FROM 0 TO 5V WITH FRONT WHEELS ROTATING
(5) 0 VOLTS WITH A/C SWITCH DEPRESSED
(6) B+ WITH IGNITION SWITCH IN "START"
(7) 0 VOLTS FOR 3 SECONDS, THEN B+
(8) 5 TO 6 VOLTS WITH A/C SWITCH DEPRESSED
(9) 0 VOLTS IN "P" OR "N"; B+ IN "R", "D", "2" OR "L"

(10) VARIES WITH INTAKE AIR TEMPERATURE
(11) VARIES WITH ENGINE COOLANT TEMPERATURE
(12) VARIES WITH EXHAUST GAS TEMPERATURE
(13) VARIES WITH THROTTLE LEVER POSITION
(14) 0 VOLTS AT IDLE; B+ OFF IDLE
(15) B+ WITH MANUAL SELECTOR LEVER IN "2"
(16) B+ WITH MANUAL SELECTOR LEVER IN "L"
(17) B+ WITH MANUAL SELECTOR LEVER IN "R"
(18) VARIES CONSTANTLY WITH SYSTEM IN CLOSED LOOP
(19) B+ WITH VEHICLE IN TCC LOCKUP CONDITION
(20) B+ WITH TRANSAXLE IN 1st OR 2nd GEAR
(21) B+ WITH TRANSAXLE IN 2nd OR 3rd GEAR

Fig. 137 1993 VIN code 8 engine

PCM CONNECTOR IDENTIFICATION

The following PCM voltage charts are for use with a digital multimeter to further aid in diagnosis. The voltages you get may vary due to low battery charge or other reasons, but they should be very close.

THE FOLLOWING CONDITIONS MUST BE MET BEFORE TESTING:
• Engine at operating temperature   • Engine idling (for "ENG. RUN" column)
• Test terminal not grounded
• All voltages shown "B+" indicate system voltage

A11	A10	A9	A8	A7	A6	A5	A4	A3	A2	A1
A22	A21	A20	A19	A18	A17	A16	A15	A14	A13	A12

BACK VIEW OF PCM CONNECTOR C1 (AUTOMATIC TRANSAXLE) (GRAY)

CAVITY/ PIN	WIRE COLOR	CIRCUIT	VOLTAGE KEY "ON"	VOLTAGE ENG. RUN
1/A1	RED/WHT	MEMORY POWER	B+	B+
2/A2	BLK	ELECTRICAL LOAD IDLE-UP SIGNAL	0* (1)	0* (1)
3/A3	—	NOT USED	—	—
4/A4	GRN/WHT	BRAKE SIGNAL	0* (2)	0* (2)
5/A5	RED/YEL	MIL CONTROL	0-1V	B+
6/A6	—	NOT USED	—	—
7/A7	LT GRN	O/D ON/OFF SIGNAL/"O/D OFF" DIAGNOSTIC OUTPUT CONTROL	(3)	(3)
8/A8	—	NOT USED	—	—
9/A9	PPL/WHT	VEHICLE SPEED INPUT	0* (4)	2-3V VARIES
10/A10	YEL/BLU	A/C ON SIGNAL	B+ (5)	B+ (5)
11/A11	BLK	CRANK SIGNAL	0* (6)	0* (6)
12/A12	BLK/RED	IGNITION POWER	B+	B+
13/A13	BLK/RED	IGNITION POWER	B+	B+
14/A14	GRN/RED	CIRCUIT OPENING RELAY CONTROL	(7)	0*
15/A15	—	NOT USED	—	—
16/A16	—	NOT USED	—	—
17/A17	—	NOT USED	—	—
18/A18	—	NOT USED	—	—
19/A19	—	NOT USED	—	—
20/A20	RED	O/D CUT SIGNAL	B+	B+
21/A21	RED/YEL	A/C CUTOUT CONTROL	0*	0* (8)
22/A22	BLK/YEL	PARK/NEUTRAL POSITION SIGNAL	(9)	(9)

0* LESS THAN 0.50 VOLTS
(1) B+ WITH LIGHT/TURN SIGNAL SWITCH IN PARK OR HEAD OR WITH DEFOGGER ON
(2) B+ WITH BRAKE PEDAL DEPRESSED
(3) 0 VOLTS WITH OVERDRIVE SWITCH RELEASED; B+ WITH OVERDRIVE SWITCH DEPRESSED
(4) VARIES FROM 0 TO 5V WITH FRONT WHEELS ROTATING
(5) 0 VOLTS WITH A/C SWITCH DEPRESSED
(6) B+ WITH IGNITION SWITCH IN "START"
(7) 0 VOLTS FOR 3 SECONDS, THEN B+
(8) 5 TO 6 VOLTS WITH A/C SWITCH DEPRESSED
(9) 0 VOLTS IN "P" OR "N"; B+ IN "R", "D", "2" OR "L"
(10) VARIES WITH INTAKE AIR TEMPERATURE
(11) VARIES WITH ENGINE COOLANT TEMPERATURE
(12) VARIES WITH EXHAUST GAS TEMPERATURE
(13) VARIES WITH THROTTLE LEVER POSITION
(14) 0 VOLTS AT IDLE; B+ OFF IDLE
(15) B+ WITH MANUAL SELECTOR LEVER IN "2"
(16) B+ WITH MANUAL SELECTOR LEVER IN "L"
(17) B+ WITH MANUAL SELECTOR LEVER IN "R"
(18) VARIES CONSTANTLY WITH SYSTEM IN CLOSED LOOP
(19) B+ WITH VEHICLE IN TCC LOCKUP CONDITION
(20) B+ WITH TRANSAXLE IN 1st OR 2nd GEAR
(21) B+ WITH TRANSAXLE IN 2nd OR 3rd GEAR

Fig. 138 1993 VIN code 8 engine

PCM CONNECTOR IDENTIFICATION

The following PCM voltage charts are for use with a digital multimeter to further aid in diagnosis. The voltages you get may vary due to low battery charge or other reasons, but they should be very close.

THE FOLLOWING CONDITIONS MUST BE MET BEFORE TESTING:
- Engine at operating temperature   • Engine idling (for "ENG. RUN" column)
- Test terminal not grounded
- All voltages shown "B+" indicate system voltage

BACK VIEW OF PCM CONNECTOR C2 (GRAY)

CAVITY/PIN	WIRE COLOR	CIRCUIT	VOLTAGE KEY "ON"	VOLTAGE ENG. RUN
1/B1	YEL	REFERENCE VOLTAGE (5V) (A/T ONLY)	4-6V	4-6V
2/B2	LT GRN/RED	MAP INPUT	3-4V	1.1-1.8V
3/B3	YEL/BLK	IAT INPUT	1-3.5V (10)	1.5-2.5V (10)
4/B4	WHT	ECT INPUT	.5-3.5V (11)	1-2V (11)
5/B5	BLK	EXHAUST OXYGEN CONCENTRATION INPUT (SECONDARY) (CALIFORNIA ONLY)	0*	0-1V (18)
6/B6	BLK	EXHAUST OXYGEN CONCENTRATION INPUT	0*	0-1V (18)
7/B7	GRN/WHT (M/T)	TEST DIAGNOSTIC MODE SIGNAL (M/T ONLY)	B+	B+
	BLK (A/T)	THROTTLE POSITION OUTPUT (A/T ONLY)	0*	(13)
8/B8	RED/WHT	FUEL CONTROL FEEDBACK OUTPUT	0*	1.5-3.5V
9/B9	BRN	SENSOR GROUND	0*	0*
10/B10	LT GRN (M/T)	THROTTLE POSITION INPUT (M/T ONLY)	.5-4.5V (13)	.5-4.5V (13)
	WHT/BLU (A/T)	EGR TEMPERATURE INPUT (CALIFORNIA A/T ONLY)	1-3.5V (12)	1.5-2.5V (12)
11/B11	YEL (M/T)	REFERENCE VOLTAGE (5V) (M/T ONLY)	4-6V	4-6V
	LT GRN (A/T)	THROTTLE POSITION INPUT (A/T ONLY)	.5-4.5V (13)	.5-4.5V (13)
12/B12	BLU	IDLE SIGNAL	(14)	(14)
13/B13	WHT/BLU (M/T)	EGR TEMPERATURE INPUT (CALIFORNIA M/T ONLY)	1-3.5V (12)	1.5-2.5V (12)
	BLK (A/T)	KNOCK INPUT	0*	0-.2V
14/B14	BLK (M/T)	KNOCK INPUT	0*	0-.2V
	GRN/WHT (A/T)	TEST DIAGNOSTIC MODE SIGNAL (A/T ONLY)	B+	B+
15/B15	BLU/WHT	DIAGNOSTIC REQUEST SIGNAL	B+	B+
16/B16	BRN	SENSOR GROUND	0*	0*

0* LESS THAN 0.50 VOLTS
(1) B+ WITH LIGHT/TURN SIGNAL SWITCH IN PARK OR HEAD OR WITH DEFOGGER ON
(2) B+ WITH BRAKE PEDAL DEPRESSED
(3) 0 VOLTS WITH OVERDRIVE SWITCH RELEASED; B+ WITH OVERDRIVE SWITCH DEPRESSED
(4) VARIES FROM 0 TO 5V WITH FRONT WHEELS ROTATING
(5) 0 VOLTS WITH A/C SWITCH DEPRESSED
(6) B+ WITH IGNITION SWITCH IN "START"
(7) 0 VOLTS FOR 3 SECONDS, THEN B+
(8) 5 TO 6 VOLTS WITH A/C SWITCH DEPRESSED
(9) 0 VOLTS IN "P" OR "N"; B+ IN "R", "D", "2" OR "L"

(10) VARIES WITH INTAKE AIR TEMPERATURE
(11) VARIES WITH ENGINE COOLANT TEMPERATURE
(12) VARIES WITH EXHAUST GAS TEMPERATURE
(13) VARIES WITH THROTTLE LEVER POSITION
(14) 0 VOLTS AT IDLE; B+ OFF IDLE
(15) B+ WITH MANUAL SELECTOR LEVER IN "2"
(16) B+ WITH MANUAL SELECTOR LEVER IN "L"
(17) B+ WITH MANUAL SELECTOR LEVER IN "R"
(18) VARIES CONSTANTLY WITH SYSTEM IN CLOSED LOOP
(19) B+ WITH VEHICLE IN TCC LOCKUP CONDITION
(20) B+ WITH TRANSAXLE IN 1st OR 2nd GEAR
(21) B+ WITH TRANSAXLE IN 2nd OR 3rd GEAR

Fig. 139 1993 VIN code 8 engine

PCM CONNECTOR IDENTIFICATION

The following PCM voltage charts are for use with a digital multimeter to further aid in diagnosis. The voltages you get may vary due to low battery charge or other reasons, but they should be very close.

THE FOLLOWING CONDITIONS MUST BE MET BEFORE TESTING:
• Engine at operating temperature   • Engine idling (for "ENG. RUN" column)
• Test terminal not grounded
• All voltages shown "B+" indicate system voltage

| C13 | C12 | C11 | C10 | C9 | C8 | C7 | C6 | C5 | C4 | C3 | C2 | C1 |
| C26 | C25 | C24 | C23 | C22 | C21 | C20 | C19 | C18 | C17 | C16 | C15 | C14 |

BACK VIEW OF PCM CONNECTOR C3 (GRAY)

CAVITY/ PIN	WIRE COLOR	CIRCUIT	VOLTAGE KEY "ON"	VOLTAGE ENG. RUN
1/C1	BLU/YEL	TCC SOLENOID CONTROL (A/T ONLY)	0*	0* (19)
2/C2	BLK (M/T)	CRANK SIGNAL (M/T ONLY)	0* (6)	0* (6)
	PPL (A/T)	SHIFT SOLENOID NO. 1 CONTROL (A/T ONLY)	0*	B+ (20)
3/C3	BLK/YEL	IGNITION FAIL-SAFE SIGNAL INPUT	.56V	1.5V
4/C4	BLK	CRANK ANGLE INPUT HIGH	.69V	.69V
5/C5	RED (M/T)	CAMSHAFT POSITION INPUT HIGH (M/T ONLY)	.69V	.69V
	GRN (A/T)	CAMSHAFT POSITION INPUT LOW (A/T ONLY)	.69V	.69V
6/C6	LT GRN/RED	2 POSITION SIGNAL (A/T ONLY)	0* (15)	0* (15)
7/C7	—	NOT USED	—	—
8/C8	—	NOT USED	—	—
9/C9	BLK/WHT	IAC VALVE CLOSE CONTROL	.3-.7V	5-7V
10/C10	BLK/BLU	IAC VALVE OPEN CONTROL	B+	8-10V
11/C11	BLK/RED	FUEL INJECTOR NO. 2 AND NO. 4 CONTROL (A/T ONLY)	B+	B+
12/C12	BLK	FUEL INJECTOR NO. 1 AND NO. 3 CONTROL	B+	B+
13/C13	BRN	GROUND	0*	0*
14/C14	BRN	O2S GROUND (A/T ONLY)	0*	0*
15/C15	BRN (M/T)	GROUND (M/T ONLY)	0*	0*
	BRN/YEL (A/T)	SHIFT SOLENOID NO. 2 CONTROL (A/T ONLY)	0*	0* (21)
16/C16	BLK/RED	EGR SV VALVE CONTROL (CALIFORNIA M/T ONLY)	B+	B+
17/C17	WHT	CRANK ANGLE INPUT LOW	.69V	.69V
18/C18	GRN (M/T)	CAMSHAFT POSITION INPUT LOW (M/T ONLY)	.69V	.69V
	RED (A/T)	CAMSHAFT POSITION INPUT HIGH (A/T ONLY)	.69V	.69V
19/C19	LT GRN	L POSITION SIGNAL (A/T ONLY)	0* (16)	0* (16)
20/C20	BLK	IGNITION SIGNAL (A/T ONLY)	0*	0-2V (13)
21/C21	WHT/RED	A/C SV VALVE CONTROL (A/T ONLY)	B+	B+ (5)
22/C22	BLK (M/T)	IGNITION SIGNAL (M/T ONLY)	0*	0-2V (13)
	RED/BLK (A/T)	R POSITION SIGNAL (A/T ONLY)	0* (17)	0* (17)
23/C23	WHT/RED (M/T)	A/C SV VALVE CONTROL (M/T ONLY)	B+	B+(5)
	BLK/RED (A/T)	EGR SV VALVE CONTROL (CALIFORNIA A/T ONLY)	B+	B+
24/C24	BRN	O2S GROUND (M/T ONLY)	0*	0*
25/C25	BLK/RED	FUEL INJECTOR NO. 2 AND NO. 4 CONTROL (M/T ONLY)	B+	B+
26/C26	BRN	GROUND	0*	0*

0* LESS THAN 0.50 VOLTS
(1) B+ WITH LIGHT/TURN SIGNAL SWITCH IN PARK OR HEAD OR WITH DEFOGGER ON
(2) B+ WITH BRAKE PEDAL DEPRESSED
(3) 0 VOLTS WITH OVERDRIVE SWITCH RELEASED: B+ WITH OVERDRIVE SWITCH DEPRESSED
(4) VARIES FROM 0 TO 5V WITH FRONT WHEELS ROTATING
(5) 0 VOLTS WITH A/C SWITCH DEPRESSED

(6) B+ WITH IGNITION SWITCH IN "START"
(7) 0 VOLTS FOR 3 SECONDS, THEN B+
(8) 5 TO 6 VOLTS WITH A/C SWITCH DEPRESSED
(9) 0 VOLTS IN "P" OR "N"; B+ IN "R", "D", "2" OR "L"
(10) VARIES WITH INTAKE AIR TEMPERATURE
(11) VARIES WITH ENGINE COOLANT TEMPERATURE
(12) VARIES WITH EXHAUST GAS TEMPERATURE
(13) VARIES WITH THROTTLE LEVER POSITION
(14) 0 VOLTS AT IDLE; B+ OFF IDLE

(15) B+ WITH MANUAL SELECTOR LEVER IN "2"
(16) B+ WITH MANUAL SELECTOR LEVER IN "L"
(17) B+ WITH MANUAL SELECTOR LEVER IN "R"
(18) VARIES CONSTANTLY WITH SYSTEM IN CLOSED LOOP
(19) B+ WITH VEHICLE IN TCC LOCKUP CONDITION
(20) B+ WITH TRANSAXLE IN 1st OR 2nd GEAR
(21) B+ WITH TRANSAXLE IN 2nd OR 3rd GEAR

Fig. 140 1993 VIN code 8 engine

DIAGNOSTIC TROUBLE CODE (DTC) TABLE
1.8L (VIN 8) "S" CARLINE
(PAGE 1 OF 2)

EXAMPLE: RPM SIGNAL DTC 13 AND MANIFOLD ABSOLUTE PRESSURE (MAP) SENSOR INPUT DTC 31

DIAGNOSTIC TROUBLE CODE (DTC)		SYSTEM	CONDITIONS THAT MUST BE MET BEFORE DTC WILL SET
NO.	MODE		
—		NORMAL	• INDICATES THAT THE ELECTRONIC ENGINE CONTROL SYSTEM IS FUNCTIONING NORMALLY.
12		RPM SIGNAL	(1) NO CRANK ANGLE INPUT DETECTED AT PCM FOR 2 SECONDS OR MORE WHILE CRANKING ENGINE. (2) NO CAMSHAFT POSITION INPUT DETECTED AT PCM FOR 3 SECONDS OR MORE WITH ENGINE SPEED BETWEEN 600 AND 4,000 RPM. • THIS DTC CAN ONLY BE ACCESSED WHEN IN THE NORMAL DIAGNOSTIC MODE.
13		RPM SIGNAL	• NO CRANK ANGLE INPUT DETECTED AT PCM FOR 0.30 SECONDS OR MORE WITH ENGINE SPEED ABOVE 1,500 RPM.
14		IGNITION SIGNAL	• NO IGNITION FAIL-SAFE SIGNAL INPUT DETECTED AT PCM FOR 4 CONSECUTIVE IGNITION CYCLES. • THIS DTC CAN ONLY BE ACCESSED WHEN IN THE NORMAL DIAGNOSTIC MODE.
16		PCM CONTROL SIGNAL	• COMMUNICATION FAILURE BETWEEN PCM'S ELECTRONIC ENGINE AND ELECTRONIC TRANSAXLE CIRCUITRY. • THIS DTC CAN ONLY BE ACCESSED WHEN IN THE NORMAL DIAGNOSTIC MODE.
21		OXYGEN SENSOR (O2S) INPUT	• OXYGEN SENSOR VOLTAGE INPUT AT PCM CONSTANT BETWEEN 0.35 AND 0.70 VOLTS FOR 60 SECONDS OR MORE WITH ENGINE SPEED ABOVE 1,500 RPM.
22		ENGINE COOLANT TEMPERATURE (ECT) SENSOR	• ECT INPUT AT PCM OPEN OR SHORTED FOR 0.50 SECONDS OR MORE.
24		INTAKE AIR TEMPERATURE (IAT) SENSOR	• IAT INPUT AT PCM OPEN OR SHORTED FOR 0.50 SECONDS OR MORE.
25		AIR/FUEL RATIO LEAN	(1) OXYGEN SENSOR INPUT AT PCM IS LESS THAN 0.45 VOLTS FOR 90 SECONDS OR MORE WITH OXYGEN SENSOR WARM AND ENGINE SPEED ABOVE 1,500 RPM. (2) WHEN ENGINE SPEED VARIES BY MORE THAN 50 RPM OVER THE PRECEDING CRANK ANGLE PERIOD DURING A PERIOD OF 50 SECONDS WHILE IDLING WITH THE ECT ABOVE 50°C (122°F). • EITHER CONDITION MUST BE DETECTED DURING 2 CONSECUTIVE IGNITION CYCLES FOR DTC TO BE STORED IN PCM MEMORY.

Fig. 141 1993 VIN code 8 engine

DIAGNOSTIC TROUBLE CODE (DTC) TABLE
1.8L (VIN 8) "S" CARLINE
(PAGE 2 OF 2)

DIAGNOSTIC TROUBLE CODE (DTC)		SYSTEM	CONDITIONS THAT MUST BE MET BEFORE DTC WILL SET
NO.	MODE		
26	⊓⊔⊓⊔⊓⊔⊓⊔	AIR/FUEL RATIO RICH	• WHEN ENGINE SPEED VARIES BY MORE THAN 50 RPM OVER THE PRECEDING CRANK ANGLE PERIOD DURING A PERIOD OF 50 SECONDS WHILE IDLING WITH THE ECT ABOVE 50°C (122°F). • CONDITION MUST BE DETECTED DURING 2 CONSECUTIVE IGNITION CYCLES FOR DTC TO BE STORED IN PCM MEMORY.
27	⊓⊔⊓⊔⊓⊔⊓⊔	SUB-OXYGEN SENSOR (O2S) INPUT	• WHEN SUB-OXYGEN SENSOR IS WARMED UP AND ENGINE IS OFF IDLE FOR 2 SECONDS OR MORE AND OXYGEN SENSOR INPUT AT PCM IS 0.45 VOLTS OR MORE AND SUB-OXYGEN SENSOR INPUT AT PCM IS 0.45 VOLTS OR LESS. • CONDITION MUST BE DETECTED DURING 2 CONSECUTIVE IGNITION CYCLES FOR DTC TO BE STORED IN PCM MEMORY.
31	⊓⊔⊓⊔	MANIFOLD ABSOLUTE PRESSURE (MAP) SENSOR INPUT	• MAP INPUT AT PCM OPEN OR SHORTED FOR 0.50 SECONDS OR MORE.
41	⊓⊔⊓⊔⊓	THROTTLE POSITION (TP) SENSOR INPUT	• THROTTLE POSITION INPUT AT PCM OPEN OR SHORTED FOR 0.50 SECONDS OR MORE.
42	⊓⊔⊓⊔⊓	VEHICLE SPEED INPUT	• VEHICLE SPEED INPUT NOT DETECTED AT PCM FOR 8 SECONDS OR MORE WITH ENGINE SPEED BETWEEN 3,000 AND 5,000 RPM AND TRANSAXLE IN GEAR.
43	⊓⊔⊓⊔⊓	CRANK SIGNAL	• CRANK SIGNAL NOT DETECTED AT PCM DURING IGNITION. • THIS DTC CAN ONLY BE DETECTED WHEN IN THE TEST DIAGNOSTIC MODE.
51	⊓⊔⊓⊔⊓	SWITCH CONDITION SIGNAL	• DISPLAYED WHEN A/C IS ON, ACCELERATOR PEDAL IS DEPRESSED OR WHEN MANUAL SELECTOR IS IN "R", "D", "2" OR "L" POSITION WITH DLC TERMINAL "TE1" AND "E1" CONNECTED. • THIS DTC CAN ONLY BE ACCESSED WHEN IN THE TEST DIAGNOSTIC MODE AND INDICATES THE ABOVE MENTIONED SYSTEMS ARE FUNCTIONING NORMALLY. IF DTC 51 IS NOT INDICATED WHEN THE CONDITIONS ARE MET, A FAULT IS PRESENT, AND DTC 51's DIAGNOSTIC CHART MUST BE USED.
52	⊓⊔⊓⊔⊓	KNOCK SENSOR (KS) INPUT	• KNOCK SENSOR INPUT AT PCM OPEN OR SHORTED WITH ENGINE SPEED BETWEEN 1,200 RPM AND 6,000 RPM. • THIS DTC CAN ONLY BE DETECTED WHEN IN THE NORMAL DIAGNOSTIC MODE.
71	⊓⊔⊓⊔⊓⊔⊓	EGR SYSTEM	• WITH ECT ABOVE 60°C (140°F) 50 SECONDS FROM START OF EGR OPERATION. THE EGR TEMPERATURE IS LESS THAN 80°C (176°F) AND THE EGR TEMPERATURE HAS RISEN LESS THAN 10°C (18°F) DURING THE 50 SECONDS. • CONDITION MUST BE DETECTED DURING 2 CONSECUTIVE IGNITION CYCLES FOR DTC TO BE STORED IN PCM MEMORY.

Fig. 142 1993 VIN code 8 engine

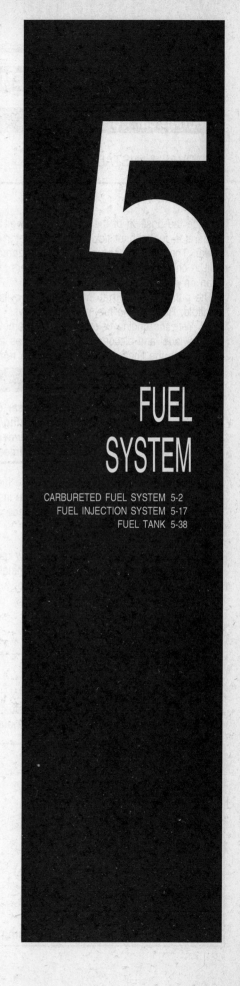

5

FUEL
SYSTEM

CARBURETED FUEL SYSTEM

Mechanical Fuel Pump

REMOVAL & INSTALLATION

▶ **See Figure 1**

Since the position of the fuel tank is lower than the carburetor, fuel cannot flow to the carburetor under its own power. The mechanical fuel pump is a diaphragm type with built in check valves in the pump chambers. These valves open only in the direction of fuel flow.

The pump is located at the side of the cylinder head intake manifold. Remove the fuel pump as follows:

1. With the engine cold and the key removed from the ignition, label and disconnect the fuel hoses from the fuel pump. Plug the lines as soon as they are removed.

✳✳CAUTION

The fuel system contains gasoline. Wear eye protection and contain spillage. Observe no smoking/no open flame precautions. Have a Class B-C (dry powder) fire extinguisher within arm's reach at all times.

2. Remove the mounting bolts from the fuel pump.
3. Remove the fuel pump and the heat insulator assembly.
4. Cover the fuel pump mounting surface on the cylinder head to prevent oil leakage.

To install:

5. When reinstalling, always use a new gasket. Place the pump and heat insulator in position and install the 2 bolts.
6. Connect the hoses to the fuel pump.
7. Start the engine and check for leaks.

TESTING

▶ **See Figures 2, 3, 4, 5 and 6**

Before performing any checks on the fuel pump, two conditions must be met. First, the pump must be internally 'wet'. Run a small amount of fuel into the pump so that the check valves will seal properly when tested. Dry valves may not seal and will yield false test results.

Hold the pump without blocking either pipe and operate the pump lever, noting the amount of force needed to move it. This is the reference point for all the tests. Do not apply more than this amount of force to the lever during the testing. Excessive force can damage an otherwise usable pump.

1. To check the inlet valve, block off the outlet and return pipes with your fingers. Operate the lever. There should be an increase in the free-play and the arm should move freely.
2. Check the outlet valve by blocking the inlet port with your finger and operating the lever. The arm should lock when the normal amount of force is applied.
3. The diaphragm is checked by blocking the inlet and outlet pipes. When normal force is applied to the lever, the lever should lock and not move. Any lever motion indicates a ruptured diaphragm. This is a common cause of poor fuel mileage and poor acceleration since the correct amount of fuel is not being delivered to the carburetor.

➡**The fuel pump must pass all three of these tests to be considered usable. If the pump fails 1 or more tests, it must be replaced.**

4. Check the oil seal within the pump. Block off the vent hole in the lower part of the pump housing. The lever arm should lock when normal force is applied.

1. Diaphragm
2. Inlet valve
3. Outlet valve
4. Oil seal

Fig. 2 Fuel pump components

Fig. 1 Location of mechanical fuel pump on engine

Fig. 3 Checking the inlet valve

Fig. 4 Checking the outlet valve

Fig. 5 Checking the fuel pump diaphragm

Fig. 6 Checking the fuel pump oil seal

Carburetor

The carburetor is the most complex part of the fuel system. Carburetors vary greatly in construction, but they all operate the same way; their job is to supply the correct mixture of fuel and air to the engine in response to varying conditions.

Despite their complexity, carburetors function on a simple physical principle known as the venturi principle. Air is drawn into the engine by the pumping action of the pistons. As the air enters the top of the carburetor, it passes through a venturi or restriction in the throttle bore. The air speeds up as it passes through the venturi, causing a slight drop in pressure. This pressure drop pulls fuel from the float bowl through a nozzle in the throttle bore. The air and fuel mix to form a fine mist, which is distributed to the cylinders through the intake manifold.

There are 6 different systems (fuel/air circuits) in a carburetor that make it work; the Float system, Main Metering system, Idle and Low Speed system, Accelerator Pump system, Power system, and the Choke System. The way these systems are arranged in the carburetor determines the carburetor's size and shape.

It's important to remember that carburetors seldom give trouble during normal operation. Other than changing the fuel and air filters and making sure the idle speed and mixture are proper at every tune-up, there's not much maintenance you can perform on the average carburetor.

The carburetor used on the Nova model, 1985-88 VIN Code 4 engine, is a conventional 2-barrel, downdraft type similar to domestic carburetors. The main circuits are: primary, for normal operational requirements; secondary, to supply high speed fuel needs; float, to supply fuel to the primary and secondary circuits; accelerator, to supply fuel for quick and safe acceleration; choke, for reliable starting in cold weather; and power valve, for fuel economy.

ADJUSTMENTS

▶ **See Figures 7, 8, 9 and 10**

Before making any adjustments to the carburetor, ALL of the following conditions must be met:
- All accessories switched off
- Ignition timing correctly set
- Transmission in neutral, parking brake set, wheels blocked front and rear.
- Fuel level (float level) correctly set; view the fuel level in the small window on the right side of the carburetor.
- Tachometer correctly connected. Please refer to Chapter 2 for detailed instructions.

When adjusting the carburetor, please resist the temptation to randomly turn screws hoping for the best. The many adjustments on a carburetor interrelate; if you change 1 setting you may affect three other things. A detailed, reasoned approach to driveability problems will yield much better (and quicker) results than guessing and groping.

Curb Idle (Warm Idle)
▶ **See Figures 8 and 9**

The curb idle is adjusted by turning the idle adjusting screw located on the rear of the carburetor. The knob has a knurled plastic head to make grasping easier. Turn it clockwise to increase idle speed. Correct idle speed for the carbureted Nova is 650 rpm w/manual transmission and 750 rpm w/automatic transmission.

Fast Idle
▶ **See Figures 8, 11 and 12**

1. Stop the engine and remove the air cleaner housing.
2. Disconnect and plug the hot idle compensator hose to prevent rough idling.
3. Disconnect the hose from the Thermovacuum Switching Valve (TVSV) port M and plug the port. This will shut off the choke opener and EGR systems.

1. Atmosphere port to port J of TVSV
2. Choke breaker
3. To port L of TVSV
4. TP port to throttle positioner
5. Fuel inlet line
6. Vacuum delay valve
7. Secondary throttle vacuum actuator
8. Manifold vacuum to choke breaker
9. Manifold vacuum to HIC valve at the air cleaner
10. No. 2 secondary fuel cut relay
11. To VSV
12. Manifold vacuum (on intake manifold)
13. To M port of TVSV
14. Choke opener
15. Secondary air bleed port to high altitude compensator (HAC)

Fig. 7 Front view of the Nova carburetor

1. Main acceleration pump lever arm
2. Main air bleed port to EBCV
3. Fuel inlet union
4. Bowl vent to charcoal canister
5. Aux.accelerator pump-- vacuum from TVSV
6. Idle mixture adjustment screw plug
7. EGR port to port P of EGR vacuum modulator
8. Charcoal canister purge port from VSV
9. Fast idle adjusting screw
10. No.1 slow cut fuel solenoid
11. Idle speed adjustment screw
12. EGR R port to R port of EGR vacuum modulator
13. Slow air bleed port to EBCV

Fig. 8 Rear view of the Nova carburetor

1. Choke breaker
2. Electric choke
3. Accelerator pump lever arm
4. Idle speed adjustment screw
5. Primary throttle lever
6. Throttle return spring
7. Secondary throttle vacuum actuator
8. Manifold vacuum
9. Fuel inlet line
10. From port L of TVSV

Fig. 9 Left side view of the Nova carburetor

1. Vacuum signal from TVSV to aux. acceleration pump
2. Main air bleed from EBCV
3. Union--fuel line
4. Float bowl window
5. Bowl vent to charcoal canister
6. Choke opener
7. Ported vacuum signal from throttle port
8. Manifold vacuum to VSV
9. Throttle positioner diaphragm
10. Manifold vacuum to HIC valve at the air cleaner
11. Throttle positioner adjustment screw
12. Connector for electric choke and fuel cut solenoids 1 and 2

Fig. 10 Right side view of the Nova carburetor

Fig. 11 Adjusting the fast idle screw

Fig. 12 'M" port on the TVSV

4. Hold the throttle slightly open by either moving the linkage on the carburetor or pull lightly on the throttle cable. Push the choke plate closed and hold it closed as you release the throttle. The carburetor is now 'fooled" into thinking it is performing a cold start — the choke is set and the various external controls are not functioning. These conditions duplicate cold start conditions.

5. Start the engine but DO NOT touch the accelerator pedal or cable. (If you do, the choke will release and Step 4 will be needed again.)

✳✳CAUTION

The engine will be running; be careful of moving parts and belts! Keep loose fitting clothes and long hair well away from the engine area!

6. The correct fast idle speed is 3000 rpm. If adjustment is necessary, turn the fast idle adjusting screw at the lower rear of the carburetor.

✳✳WARNING

Do not allow the engine to run on fast idle any longer than necessary. Once the correct fast idle is achieved, release the fast idle by depressing the accelerator and releasing it. Allow the engine to run at curb idle for about 30 seconds and switch the engine off.

7. Remove the plug and reconnect the hose to the M port of the TVSV.

Throttle Positioner
▶ **See Figures 10, 13, 14 and 15**

1. Disconnect the hose from the Thermovacuum Switching Valve (TVSV) port **M** and plug the port. Disconnect the vacuum hose from throttle positioner (TP) diaphragm **A**.

2. Check that the TP is set at the first step; correct engine speed is:
- Manual transmission: 800 rpm
- Automatic transmission: 900 rpm If necessary, adjust the speed with the adjusting screw.

➡**Make the adjustment with the cooling (radiator) fan OFF.**

3. Reconnect the vacuum hose to diaphragm **A**.

4. Disconnect the hose from diaphragm **B** and plug the hose end.

5. Check that the TP is set at the second step. The correct engine speed in this position is:
- Manual transmission: 1400 ± 200 rpm
- Automatic transmission: 1500 ± 200 rpm

6. Reconnect the vacuum hose to diaphragm **B** and check that the engine returns to normal idle within 2-6 seconds.

7. Remove the plug and reconnect the vacuum hose to TVSV port **M**.

Float and Fuel Level
▶ **See Figures 16, 17, 18, 19 and 20**

The float level is not externally adjustable. Removal of the air horn assembly or top of the carburetor is required. The

Fig. 13 Vacuum hose at diaphragm 'A"

Fig. 14 Throttle positioner adjusting screw

Fig. 15 Vacuum hose at diaphragm 'B''

engine should be cold during this procedure. All work is performed with the engine off.

The float in the carburetor controls the entry of fuel into the bowl of the carburetor. (The bowl is simply a reservoir which keeps fuel available at all times.) The function of the float is to react to the level of fuel in the bowl and open or close a valve, thus maintaining the correct amount of fuel. The principle is identical to the float in a toilet tank; when the correct level is reached, the flow is shut off.

The position of the float (and therefore the amount of fuel available) is critical to the proper operation of the engine. If too little fuel is in the bowl, the engine may starve on sharp corners or on hills; too much fuel can literally lead to overflowing and flooding of the engine. To adjust the float level:

1. Remove the air cleaner assembly and disconnect the choke linkage.
2. Disconnect the accelerator pump connecting rod.
3. Remove the pump arm pivot screw and the pump arm.
4. Remove the fuel hose and union.
5. Remove the 8 air horn screws. Be careful to identify and collect the external parts attached to the screws, such as wire clamps, brackets and the steel number plate.
6. Disconnect the choke link.
7. Lift the air horn with its gasket from the body of the carburetor.
8. Disconnect the wires at the connector.
9. Remove the gasket from the air horn assembly. Invert the air horn so that the float hangs down by its own weight. Check the clearance between the float tip and the air horn. The correct clearance is 7.0mm. If necessary, adjust the float lip by bending it gently into position.

Fig. 16 No float level adjustment is necessary when the fuel level falls between the line on the carburetor sight glass

Fig. 17 Checking the float level with the float in resting on the needle valve

10. Lift up the float and check the clearance between the needle valve plunger and the float lip. Correct clearance is 1.6-2.0mm. If necessary, adjust the clearance by bending the outer part of the float lip.

➡ **If the float has become misadjusted, it may be due to the float filling with gasoline. Give the float a gentle shake and listen for any liquid within. If fuel is inside the float, replace the float and reset the levels.**

11. Install a new gasket onto the air horn.
12. Place the air horn in position on the carburetor body and install the choke link.
13. Install the 8 screws. Make certain the brackets, clips and steel tag are reinstalled as well.
14. Connect the fuel hose and union.
15. Install the pump arm pivot screw and pump arm.

Fig. 18 Float adjustment at point (A) while in the resting position

Fig. 19 Measuring the float in the raised position

Fig. 20 Float adjustment at point (B) while in the raised position

16. Connect the pump arm connecting rod.
17. Attach the choke linkage.
18. Install the air cleaner. Start the engine and check carefully for fuel and/or vacuum leaks. The engine may be difficult to start; once it is running smoothly, recheck the fuel level in the sight glass.

Carburetor

REMOVAL & INSTALLATION

▶ See Figure 21

➡Each fuel and vacuum line must be tagged or labeled individually during disassembly.

1. Remove the air cleaner assembly.
2. Disconnect the accelerator cable from the carburetor.
3. If equipped with automatic transmission, disconnect the throttle position cable.
4. Unplug the wiring connector.
5. Label and disconnect the:
   a. carburetor vacuum hoses
   b. fuel inlet hoses
   c. charcoal canister hose

✳✳CAUTION

The carburetor contains gasoline. Wear eye protection and contain spillage. Observe no smoking/no open flame precautions. Have a Class B-C (dry powder) fire extinguisher within arm's reach at all times.

6. Remove the carburetor mounting nuts.
7. Remove the cold mixture heater wire clamp and lift out the EGR vacuum modulator bracket.
8. Lift the carburetor off the engine and place it on a clean cloth on the workbench. If desired, the insulator (base gasket) may also be removed.
9. Cover the inlet area of the manifold with clean rags. This will prevent the entry of dust, dirt and loose parts.

To install:
10. Place the insulator on the manifold, making sure it is correctly positioned.
11. Install the carburetor onto the manifold.
12. Install the EGR vacuum modulator bracket. Clamp the cold mixture heater wire into place.
13. Tighten the carburetor mounting nuts.
14. Reconnect the fuel inlet hose, the charcoal canister hose and the vacuum hoses.
15. Connect the wiring connector.
16. Connect the accelerator cable; connect the throttle position cable if equipped with automatic transmission.
17. Reinstall the air cleaner.

CARBURETOR OVERHAUL

▶ See Figures 22, 23, 24, 25, 26, 27, 28, 29, 30, 31, 32, 33, 34, 35, 36, 37, 38, 39, 40, 41, 42 and 43

Efficient carburetion depends greatly on careful cleaning and inspection during overhaul since dirt, gum, water, or varnish in or on the carburetor parts are often responsible for poor performance.

Overhaul your carburetor in a clean, dust free area. Carefully disassemble the carburetor, referring often to the exploded views. Keep all similar and look-alike parts segregated during disassembly and cleaning to avoid accidental interchange during assembly. Make a note of all jet sizes.

When the carburetor is disassembled, wash all parts (except diaphragms, electric choke units, pump plunger, and any other plastic, leather, fiber, or rubber parts) in clean carburetor solvent. Do not leave parts in the solvent any longer than necessary to sufficiently loosen the deposits. Excessive cleaning may remove the special finish from the float bowl and check valve bodies leaving these parts unfit for service. Rinse all parts in clean solvent and blow them dry with compressed air or allow them to air dry. Wipe clean all cork, plastic, and fiber parts with clean, lint-free cloth.

Blow out all passages and jets with compressed air and be sure that there are no restrictions or blockages. Never use wire or similar tools to clean jets, fuel passages, or air bleeds. Clean all jets and valves separately to avoid accidental interchange.

Fig. 21 Tag and label every hose during disassembly

Check all parts for wear or damage. If wear or damage is found, replace the defective parts. Pay special attention to the following areas:

1. Check the float needle and seat for wear. If wear is found, replace the complete assembly.

2. Check the float hinge pin for wear and the float(s) for dents or distortion. Replace the float if fuel has leaked into it.

3. Check the throttle and choke shaft bores for wear or an out-of-round condition. Damage or wear to the throttle arm, shaft or shaft bore will often require the replacement of the throttle body. These parts require a close tolerance of fit; wear may allow air leakage, which could affect starting and idling.

➡**Throttle shafts and bushings are not included in overhaul kits. They may be available separately.**

4. Inspect the idle mixture adjusting needles for burrs or grooves. Any such condition requires replacement of the needle, since you will not be able to obtain a satisfactory idle.

5. Test the accelerator pump check valves. They should pass air 1 way but not the other. Replace the valve if necessary. If the valve is satisfactory, wash the valve again to remove breath moisture.

6. Check the bowl cover for warped surfaces with a straightedge.

7. Closely inspect the valves and seats for wear and damage, replacing as necessary.

8. After the carburetor is assembled, check the choke valve (plate) for freedom of operation.

Carburetor overhaul kits are recommended for each overhaul. These kits contain all the gaskets and new parts to replace those that deteriorate most rapidly. Failure to replace all parts supplied with the kit (especially gaskets) can result in poor performance later.

Some carburetor manufacturers supply overhaul kits of 3 basic types: minor repair; major repair; and gasket kits. Generally, they contain the following:

Minor Repair
- All gaskets
- Float needle valve
- Volume control screw
- All diaphragms
- Spring for the pump diaphragm
- All gaskets

Major Repair Kits:
- All jets and gaskets
- All diaphragms
- Float needle valve
- Volume control screw
- Pump ball valve
- Float(s)
- All gaskets

Gasket Kits:
- All gaskets

After cleaning and checking all components, reassemble the carburetor, using new parts and referring to the exploded view. When reassembling, make sure that all screws and jets are tight in their seats, but do not overtighten, as the tips will be distorted. Tighten all screws gradually, in rotation. Do not tighten the needle valve(s) into their seats; uneven jetting will

result. Always use new gaskets. Be sure to adjust the float level when reassembling.

➡**The following instructions are organized so that only 1 component group is being worked on at a time. This helps avoid confusion and interchange of parts. To make reassembly easier, always arrange disassembled parts in order on the workbench. Be very careful not to mix up or lose small pieces such as balls, clips or springs.   Reassembly and adjustment of the carburetor requires accurate measuring equipment capable of checking clearances to the 1/10 mm. These specialized carburetor clearance gauges are available at reputable tool retailers but may be difficult to find.**

9. Remove the carburetor as outlined previously.

10. To remove the AIR HORN assembly, disconnect the choke link and the pump connecting rod.

11. Remove the pump arm pivot screw and the pump arm.

12. Remove the fuel hose and union.

13. Remove the 8 air horn screws. Be careful to identify and collect the external parts attached to the screws, such as wire clamps, brackets and the steel number plate.

14. Disconnect the choke link.

15. Lift the air horn with its gasket from the body of the carburetor.

16. Disconnect the wires at the connector.

17. Remove the first and second solenoids from the carburetor body.

18. Remove the float pivot pin, float and needle valve assembly.

19. Remove the air horn gasket.

20. Remove the needle valve seat and gasket.

21. Remove the power piston retainer, power piston and spring.

22. Pull out the pump plunger and remove the boot.

23. Begin disassembly of the BODY by removing the throttle positioner. Disconnect the link and remove the 2 bolts.

24. Remove the stopper gasket, the pump discharge weight, the long spring and the large discharge ball.

25. Using a pair of tweezers, remove the plunger retainer and the small ball.

26. Remove the slow jet from the body.

27. Remove the power valve with the jet.

28. Disassemble the power valve and jet.

29. Remove the throttle positioner levers. Remove the primary main passage plug, primary main jet and the gasket.

30. Remove the auxiliary accelerator pump (AAP) housing, spring and diaphragm.

31. Remove the inlet plug and the small ball for the AAP.

32. Remove the outlet plug, short spring and the small ball.

33. Remove the primary and secondary ventures.

34. Remove the sight glass retainer, the glass and its O-ring.

35. Remove the throttle return spring and the throttle back spring.

36. Remove the nut and the throttle lever.

37. Remove the bolt and the fast idle cam.

38. Remove the secondary throttle valve diaphragm by disconnecting the linkage and removing the assembly with its gasket.

39. Remove the 3 bolts and the vacuum passage bolt. Separate the carburetor body from the carburetor flange.

1. Choke coil
2. Choke breaker
3. Fuel pipe
4. Union
5. Air horn
6. Accelerator pump arm
7. Secondary solenoid valve
8. Needle valve and seat
9. Float

Fig. 22 Nova carburetor, exploded detail

40. Clean all the disassembled parts before inspecting them. Wash and clean the cast metal parts with a soft brush in carburetor cleaner. Clean off the carbon around the throttle plates. Wash the other parts thoroughly in cleaner. Blow all dirt and other foreign matter from the jets, fuel passages and restrictions within the body.

41. Inspect the float and needle valve. Check the pivot pin for scratches and excessive wear. Inspect the float for breaks in the lip and wear in the pivot pin holes. Check the needle valve plunger for wear or damage and the spring for deformation. The strainer should be checked for rust or breaks.

42. Make certain the power piston moves smoothly within its bore.

43. Check the power valve for proper air flow. In its normal (expanded) condition, no air should pass through it. When compressed at 1 end, air should enter the end and exit through the side vent.

44. Inspect the fuel cut solenoids. Connect the solenoid leads to the battery terminals (the solenoid with only 1 lead requires a jumper between the case and the battery) and check that the solenoid clicks as the last connection is made. The solenoid should click each time the battery is connected or disconnected. If a solenoid is not operating correctly, replace it.

45. Install new O-rings on the solenoids.

46. Inspect the choke heater by using an ohmmeter to measure its resistance. Correct resistance is 18 ohms. If a problem is found, the air horn assembly must be replaced.

47. Reassembly begins by placing a new gasket and the carburetor body onto the flange.

48. Install the vacuum passage bolt, then install the 3 retaining bolts.

49. Assemble the secondary throttle diaphragm, position the gasket and install the assembly. Connect the linkage.

1. Power piston spring
2. Power piston
3. Power valve
4. Power jet
5. Pump discharge weight
6. Spring
7. Steel ball
8. Slow jet (idle jet)
9. Secondary small venturi
10. Primary small venturi
11. Secondary throttle valve actuator assembly
12. Primary solenoid valve
13. Fast idle adjusting screw
14. Idle mixture adjusting screw
15. Idle speed adjusting screw
16. Throttle positioner lever
17. Aux. accelerator pump
18. Primary main jet
19. Secondary main jet
20. Sight glass retainer
21. Choke breaker and throttle positioner diaphragm
22. Steel ball
23. Spring
24. Steel ball
25. Steel ball
26. Check ball retainer
27. Pump damping spring
28. Pump plunger

Fig. 23 Exploded view of the Nova carburetor

1. PUMP ARM PIVOT
2. CHOKE LINK
3. PUMP ROD

Fig. 24 Carburetor pump linkage

1. STOPPER GASKET
2. PUMP DISCHARGE WEIGHT
3. SPRING
4. DISCHARGE BALL (LARGE)
5. PLUNGER RETAINER
6. CHECK BALL (SMALL)

Fig. 28 Accelerator pump check balls and components

1. NEEDLE VALVE
2. SEAT

Fig. 25 Needle valve removal

Fig. 29 Removing the power valve

1. POWER PISTON
2. POWER PISTON RETAINER
3. PUMP PLUNGER

Fig. 26 Removing the power piston

1. PRIMARY JET
2. SECONDARY JET

Fig. 30 Removing the main jets

1. PUMP ARM PIVOT
2. CHOKE LINK
3. PUMP ROD

Fig. 27 Float and needle valve components

Fig. 31 Removing the auxiliary accelerator pump

Fig. 32 Removing the auxiliary accelerator pump check ball plugs

Fig. 33 Body and linkage retaining screws. Note that one screw contains a vacuum passage

Fig. 34 Inspecting the power piston

Fig. 35 Testing the primary (left) and secondary fuel cut solenoids

Fig. 36 Checking the resistance of the choke heater

Fig. 37 Installing the secondary throttle valve diaphragm

Fig. 38 Install the pin clip after the float is adjusted

50. Install the fast idle cam with the bolt.
51. Install the throttle lever with its nut.
52. Install the throttle back spring and the throttle return spring.
53. Install the sight glass with its O-ring and retainer.
54. Install the primary and secondary small ventures over new gaskets. Install the O-ring on the primary small ventures.
55. Install the auxiliary accelerator pump by first installing the outer plug, the short spring and the small ball. Install the inlet plug and the small ball, followed by the AAP housing, spring and diaphragm.
56. Install the primary main jet and passage plug with a new gasket.
57. Install the secondary main jet and passage plug with a new gasket.

58. Install the throttle lever.
59. Install the slow jet.
60. Assemble the power valve and jet and install them in position.
61. Install the discharge large ball, the long spring, the pump discharge weight and the stopper gasket.
62. Use tweezers to insert the plunger small ball and the retainer.
63. Reinstall the throttle positioner and connect its linkage.
64. On the air horn, install the valve seat over the gasket into the fuel inlet.
65. Install the needle valve, spring, and plunger onto the seat.
66. Install the float and pivot pin.
67. Measure and adjust the float clearances (level) by following procedures and specifications outlined earlier in this chapter.
68. After adjusting the float level, remove the float, plunger, spring and needle valve. Assemble the pin clip onto the needle valve.
69. Install the power piston spring and piston into its bore and install the retainer.
70. Install the acceleration pump plunger and its boot.
71. Place a new gasket onto the air horn.
72. Install the needle valve assembly, the float and the pivot pin. Insert the float lip between the plunger and the clip when installing the float.
73. Install the solenoid valves into the body of the carburetor.
74. Assemble the air horn and body. Install the 8 screws, paying particular attention to the various brackets, wire clamps and steel number plate.
75. Install the accelerator pump arm. Install the pump arm to the air horn with the pump plunger hole and lever aligned.
76. Connect the choke link and the pump connecting link.
77. Install the fuel pipe and union.
78. With the carburetor still on the bench, move the various linkages by hand, checking for smooth operation.
79. Check the throttle plate for full opening. It should move 90° from horizontal. If needed, adjust its travel by bending the first throttle lever stopper.

80. Check the clearance of the secondary throttle plate. When wide open, the secondary throttle plate should have 13mm clearance to the body of the bore. Adjust this clearance by bending the secondary throttle lever stopper.
81. Check the clearance for the secondary touch. This is the point at which the secondary throttle begins to open under acceleration. Move the primary throttle plate open, watching for the point at which the first kick lever just touches the second kick lever. At this point, the primary throttle plate should have 0.230 in. clearance.
82. Set the throttle lever to the first step of the fast idle cam. With the choke plate fully closed, check the clearance of the primary throttle plate. The correct clearance is 1.15mm; the clearance may be adjusted by turning the fast idle adjusting screw.
83. The choke unloader is adjusted by bending the fast idle lever as necessary. Open the primary throttle plate fully (with the choke plate closed, from the previous Step) and check that the choke plate has 3mm of clearance.
84. Check the choke breaker. Hold the throttle slightly open, push the choke closed and hold it closed as your release the throttle. Apply vacuum to the choke breaker 1st diaphragm. The choke plate should have 2.5mm of clearance. The clearance is adjusted by bending the relief lever.
85. Now apply vacuum to both the first and second diaphragms. Clearance at the choke plate should become 6mm. Adjustment is by turning the diaphragm adjustment screw.
86. Release the choke and throttle settings. With the choke plate fully open, measure the length of the pump stroke. Correct stroke is 2mm; it may be adjusted by bending the connecting link.
87. Reinstall the carburetor on the intake manifold, following directions outlined earlier.
88. Start the engine and allow it to warm up normally. During this time, pay careful attention to the high idle speed, the operation of the choke and its controls and the idle quality. If you worked carefully and accurately, and performed the bench set-up properly, the carburetor should need very little fussing after it's reinstalled.

MEASURING THE ANGLE

ADJUSTING

Fig. 39 Adjusting the primary throttle plate

MEASURING THE CLEARANCE

ADJUSTING

Fig. 40 Adjusting the secondary throttle plate clearance

MEASURING THE CLEARANCE

1. PRIMARY KICK LEVER
2. SECONDARY KICK LEVER

ADJUSTING

Fig. 41 Measuring and adjusting the secondary touch

1. FAST IDLE CAM
2. STOP

SETTING FAST IDLE
CAM ON 1ST STEP

ADJUSTING

Fig. 42 Adjusting the fast idle setting

MEASURING THE CLEARANCE

ADJUSTING

Fig. 43 Adjusting the choke unloader

FUEL INJECTION SYSTEM

Relieving Fuel System Pressure

✳✳CAUTION

To reduce the risk of fire and personal injury, it is necessary to release the fuel system pressure before servicing any fuel system components.

1988-92

1. Remove the fuel cap to remove fuel tank pressure.
2. Disconnect the circuit opening relay located under the dash near the ECM.
3. Crank the engine and allow it to run until it stalls, then crank for an additional 30 seconds.
4. Disconnect the negative battery cable to prevent accidental cranking of the engine.
5. Use a shop towel to catch any fuel and slowly loosen and remove the cold start injector valve line bolt at the fuel rail.

1993

▶ See Figure 44

1. Remove the fuel cap to remove fuel tank pressure.

2. Disconnect the circuit opening relay as follows:
  a. Remove the radio as outlined in Section 6.
  b. Disconnect the circuit opening relay electrical connector from the center console.
3. Crank the engine and allow it to run until it stalls, then crank for an additional 3 seconds.
4. Disconnect the negative battery cable to prevent accidental cranking of the engine and a discharge of fuel.
5. Reconnect the circuit opening relay.
6. Install the radio.
7. Install the fuel filler cap.

Fig. 44 Circuit opening relay — 1993

Electric Fuel Pump

REMOVAL & INSTALLATION

The electric fuel pump used on fuel injected Nova and Prizm cars is contained within the fuel tank. On 1988-92 models it cannot be removed without removing the tank from the car.

➡Before removing fuel system parts, clean them with a spray-type engine cleaner. Follow the instructions on the cleaner. Do not soak fuel system parts in liquid cleaning solvent.

❊❊CAUTION

The fuel injection system is under pressure. Refer to the procedure above and release pressure slowly and contain spillage. Observe no smoking/no open flame precautions. Have a Class B-C (dry powder) fire extinguisher within arm's reach at all times.

1988-92

▶ **See Figures 45 and 46**

1. Release the fuel system pressure as outlined earlier.
2. Using a siphon or pump, drain the fuel from the tank and store it in a proper metal container with a tight cap.
3. Remove the rear seat cushion to gain access to the electrical wiring.
4. Disconnect the fuel pump and sending unit wiring at the connector.
5. Raise the vehicle and safely support it on jackstands.
6. Loosen the clamp and remove the filler neck and overflow pipe from the tank.
7. Remove the supply hose from the tank. Wrap a rag around the fitting to collect escaping fuel. Disconnect the breather hose from the tank, again using a rag to control spillage.
8. Cover or plug the end of each disconnected line to keep dirt out and fuel in.
9. Support the fuel tank with a floor jack or transmission jack. Use a broad piece of wood to distribute the load. Be careful not to deform the bottom of the tank.
10. Remove the fuel tank support strap bolts.
11. Swing the straps away from the tank and lower the jack. Balance the tank with your other hand or have a helper assist you. The tank is bulky and may have some fuel left in it. If its balance changes suddenly, the tank may fall.
12. Remove the fuel filler pipe extension, the breather pipe assembly and the sending unit assembly. Keep these items in a clean, protected area away from the car.
13. To remove the electric fuel pump:
    a. Disconnect the 2 pump-to-harness wires.
    b. Loosen the pump outlet hose clamp at the bracket pipe.
    c. Remove the pump from the bracket and the outlet hose from the bracket pipe.
    d. Separate the outlet hose and the filter from the pump.
14. While the tank is out and disassembled, inspect it for any signs of rust, leakage or metal damage. If any problem is found, replace the tank. Clean the inside of the tank with water and a light detergent and rinse the tank thoroughly several times.
15. Inspect all of the lines, hoses and fittings for any sign of corrosion, wear or damage to the surfaces. Check the pump outlet hose and the filter for restrictions.

To install:

16. When reassembling, ALWAYS replace the sealing gaskets with new ones. Also replace any rubber parts showing any sign of deterioration.
17. Assemble the outlet hose and filter onto the pump; then attach the pump to the bracket.
18. Connect the outlet hose clamp to the bracket pipe and connect the pump wiring to the harness wire.
19. Install the fuel pump and bracket assembly onto the tank.
20. Install the sending unit assembly.
21. Connect the breather pipe assembly and the filler pipe extension.

➡Tighten the breather pipe screw to 17 inch lbs. and all other attaching screws to 30 inch lbs.

22. Place the fuel tank on the jack and elevate it into place within the car. Attach the straps and install the strap bolts, tightening them to 29 ft. lbs.
23. Connect the breather hose to the tank pipe, the return hose to the tank pipe and the supply hose to its tank pipe. tighten the supply hose fitting to 21 ft. lbs.
24. Connect the filler neck and overflow pipe to the tank. Make sure the clamps are properly seated and secure.
25. Lower the vehicle to the ground.
26. Connect the pump and sending unit electrical connectors to the harness.
27. Install the rear seat cushion.
28. Using a funnel, pour the fuel that was drained from its container into the fuel filler.
29. Install the fuel filler cap.
30. Start the engine and check carefully for any sign of leakage around the tank and lines.

1993

▶ **See Figures 47, 48 and 49**

1. Release the fuel system pressure as outlined earlier.
2. Using a siphon or pump, drain the fuel from the tank and store it in a proper metal container with a tight cap.
3. Remove the rear seat cushion as outlined in Section 10 to gain access to the service hole.
4. Remove the 4 screws and remove the service hole cover.
5. Disconnect the fuel pump and sending unit wiring at the connector.
6. Remove the 1 nut and disconnect the fuel feed hose from the sender assembly.
7. Remove the 1 clamp and disconnect the fuel return hose from the sender assembly.
8. Remove the 8 bolts and remove the fuel sender assembly from the fuel tank.
9. Remove the fuel pump from the fuel pump bracket by pulling off the lower side of the fuel pump from the bracket.
10. Disconnect the fuel pump electrical connector.
11. Remove the rubber cushion from the fuel pump.

1. Fuel pump
2. Fuel tank
3. Fuel sender gauge
4. Protector
5. Inlet pipe
6. Rubber protectors

Fig. 45 Fuel tank components — 1988 VIN Code 5 engine (Nova)

1. Fuel tank breather pipe
2. Fuel cutoff valve
3. Fuel tank sending unit
4. Fuel pump
5. Overflow pipe
6. Fuel filler neck bezel
7. Fuel filler neck
8. Bezel
9. Gasket
10. Fuel tank mounting straps

Fig. 46 Fuel tank components — 1989-92

12. Remove the 1 clamp and disconnect the fuel pump strainer from the pump.

To install:

13. Install the 1 clamp and connect the fuel pump strainer to the pump.

14. Install the rubber cushion to the fuel pump.

15. Connect the fuel pump electrical connector.

16. Install the fuel pump to the fuel pump bracket.

17. Install the 8 bolts and install the fuel sender assembly to the fuel tank. Tighten the bolts to 89 inch lbs. (10 Nm).

18. Install the 1 clamp and connect the fuel return hose to the sender assembly.

19. Install the 1 nut and connect the fuel feed hose to the sender assembly. Tighten the nut to 15 ft. lbs. (20 Nm).

20. Connect the fuel pump electrical connector.

21. Install the 4 screws and install the service hole cover.

22. Install the rear seat cushion as outlined in Section 10.

23. Refill the tank.

24. Connect the negative battery cable.

TESTING

1988

▶ See Figure 50

Since the fuel pump is concealed within the tank, it is difficult to test directly at the pump. It is possible to test the pump from under the hood, listening for pump function and feeling the fuel delivery lines for the build-up of pressure.

1. Turn the ignition switch ON, but do not start the motor.

2. Using a jumper wire, short both terminals of the fuel pump check connector. The check connector is located under the hood near the wiper motor. Connect the terminals labeled **FP** and **+B**.

3. Check that there is pressure in the hose running to the delivery pipe. You should hear fuel pressure noise and possibly hear the pump at the rear of the car.

4. Remove the jumper wire.

5. Turn the ignition to OFF. If the fuel pump failed to function, it may indicate a faulty pump, but before removing the tank and pump, check the following items within the pump system:

  a. the fusible link

  b. fuses (EFI/15 amp and IGN/7.5 amp)

  c. fuel injection main relay

  d. fuel pump circuit opening relay

  e. all wiring connections and grounds.

1. Rear seat cushion
2. Fuel tank
3. Fuel tank filler
4. Exhaust heat shield
5. Resonator intermediate
   pipe assembly
6. Fuel return hose
7. Fuel feed pipe

Fig. 47 Fuel tank components — 1993

1. Floor service hole cover
2. Floor service hole cover screw

Fig. 48 Removing the floor service hole cover — 1993

1. Fuel pump
2. Fuel pumpstrainer

Fig. 49 Removing the fuel pump and strainer — 1993

1989-93

For fuel pump electrical and pressure test on 1989-93 models, please refer to the Fuel System Diagnostic Charts at the end of this section.

Fuel injectors

The injectors — electrically triggered valves — deliver a measured quantity of fuel into the intake manifold according to signals from the ECM. As driving conditions change, the computer signals each injector to stay open a longer or shorter period of time, thus controlling the amount of fuel introduced into the engine. An injector, being an electric component, is either on or off (open or closed); there is no variable control for an injector other than duration.

1. FP terminal
2. Battery positive (+) terminal
3. Jumper wire

Fig. 50 Checking the electric fuel pump at the check connector

Cleanliness equals success when working on a fuel injected system. Every component must be treated with the greatest care and be protected from dust, grime and impact damage. The miniaturized and solid state circuitry is easily damaged by a jolt. Additionally, care must be used in dealing with electrical connectors. Look for and release any locking mechanisms on the connector before separating the connectors. When reattaching, make sure each pin is properly lined up and seated before pushing the connector closed.

REMOVAL & INSTALLATION

1988 VIN Code 5 Engine
▶ **See Figures 52, 53 and 54**

✳✳CAUTION

The fuel system is under pressure. Release pressure slowly and contain spillage. Observe no smoking/no open flame precautions. Have a Class B-C (dry powder) fire extinguisher within arm's reach at all times.

1. Release the fuel system pressure as outlined earlier in this section and disconnect the negative battery cable.

➡**If you are diagnosing a driveability problem, check the ECM for any stored trouble codes BEFORE disconnecting the cable. The codes will be lost after the battery is disconnected.**

2. Disconnect the PCV hose from the valve cover.

Fig. 51 Cross section of a fuel injector

3. Remove the vacuum sensing hose from the pressure regulator.

4. Disconnect the fuel return hose from the pressure regulator.

5. Place a towel or container under the cold start injector pipe. Loosen the 2 union bolts at the fuel line and remove the pipe with its gaskets.

6. Remove the fuel inlet pipe mounting bolt and disconnect the fuel inlet hose by removing the fuel union bolt, the 2 gaskets and the hose.

7. Disconnect the injector electrical connections.

8. At the fuel delivery pipe (rail), remove the 3 bolts. Lift the delivery pipe and the injectors free of the engine. DON'T drop the injectors!

9. Remove the 4 insulators and 3 collars from the cylinder head.

10. Pull the injectors free of the delivery pipe.

To install:

11. Before installing the injectors back into the fuel rail, install a NEW O-ring on each injector.

12. Coat each O-ring with a light coat of gasoline (NEVER use oil of any sort)and install the injectors into the delivery pipe. Make certain each injector can be smoothly rotated. If they do not rotate smoothly, the O-ring is not in its correct position.

13. Install the insulators into each injector hole. Place the 3 spacers on the delivery pipe mounting holes in the cylinder head.

14. Place the delivery pipe and injectors on the cylinder head and again check that the injectors rotate smoothly. Install the 3 bolts and tighten them to 13 ft. lbs.

Fig. 52 Removing fuel delivery pipe hose

1. O-ring
2. Grommet

Fig. 53 Injector with seals

Fig. 54 Make certain the injector can be rotated in place after installation

15. Connect the electrical connectors to each injector.

16. Install 2 new gaskets and attach the inlet pipe and fuel union bolt. Tighten the bolt to 22 ft. lbs. Install the mounting bolt.

17. Install new gaskets and connect the cold start injector pipe to the delivery pipe and cold start injector. Install the fuel line union bolts and tighten them to 13 ft. lbs.

18. Connect the fuel return hose and the vacuum sensing hose to the pressure regulator. Attach the PCV hose to the valve cover.

19. Connect the battery cable to the negative battery terminal. Start the engine and check for leaks.

✳✳CAUTION

If there is a leak at any fitting, the line will be under pressure and the fuel may spray in a fine mist. This mist is extremely explosive. Shut the engine off immediately if any leakage is detected. Use rags to wrap the leaking fitting until the pressure diminishes and wipe up any fuel from the engine area.

1989-90

▶ See Figures 55, 56, 57 and 58

✳✳CAUTION

The fuel system is under pressure. Release pressure slowly and contain spillage. Observe no smoking/no open flame precautions. Have a Class B-C (dry powder) fire extinguisher within arm's reach at all times.

1. Release the fuel system pressure as outlined earlier in this section and disconnect the negative battery cable.
2. Disconnect the PCV hoses from the valve cover and the vacuum sensing hose from the fuel pressure regulator.
3. Disconnect the fuel return hose from the fuel pressure regulator.
4. Remove the wiring connectors from the injectors.
5. Remove the pressure regulator by loosening the 2 bolts and pulling the regulator from the delivery pipe.

6. Label and remove the 4 vacuum hoses running to the EGR vacuum modulator. Remove the nut and bracket with the modulator.
7. Disconnect the fuel union bolt at the inlet pipe. Remove the pipe and the 2 gaskets.
8. Remove the 2 bolts holding the delivery pipe and then remove the delivery pipe and the injectors. Don't drop the injectors!
9. Remove the 2 spacers and the 4 insulators from the cylinder head.
10. Pull the injectors free of the delivery pipe.
To install:
11. Before installing the injectors back into the fuel rail, install a NEW O-ring on each injector.
12. Coat each O-ring with a light coat of gasoline (NEVER use oil of any sort)and install the injectors into the delivery pipe. Make certain each injector can be smoothly rotated. If they do not rotate smoothly, the O-ring is not in its correct position.
13. Install the 4 insulators and 2 spacers in place.
14. Place the delivery pipe and injectors on the cylinder head and again check that the injectors rotate smoothly. Install the 2 bolts and tighten them to 11 ft. lbs.
15. Install 2 new gaskets and attach the inlet pipe and fuel union bolt. Tighten the bolt to 22 ft. lbs.
16. Install the EGR vacuum modulator with its bracket and nut. Connect the 4 vacuum hoses to their proper ports.
17. Install new gaskets and connect the cold start injector pipe to the delivery pipe and cold start injector. Install the fuel line union bolts and tighten them to 13 ft. lbs.

1. Vacuum sensing hose
2. Fuel return hose

Fig. 55 Pressure regulator hoses

Fig. 57 Removing the fuel delivery pipe. Prizm shown, Nova similar, but with three retaining bolts

Fig. 56 Removing the regulator mounting bolts

Fig. 58 Placement of injector insulators

18. Install a new O-ring on the pressure regulator. Push the regulator into the delivery pipe and install the 2 bolts. Tighten the bolts to 5.5 ft. lbs. (65 inch lbs.)

19. Connect the injector wiring connectors.

20. Connect the fuel return hose and the vacuum sensing hose to the pressure regulator. Attach the PCV hoses to the valve cover.

21. Connect the battery cable to the negative battery terminal. Start the engine and check for leaks.

❊❊CAUTION

If there is a leak at any fitting, the line will be under pressure and the fuel may spray in a fine mist. This mist is extremely explosive. Shut the engine off immediately if any leakage is detected. Use rags to wrap the leaking fitting until the pressure diminishes and wipe up any fuel from the engine area.

1991-92
▶ See Figure 59

❊❊CAUTION

The fuel system is under pressure. Release pressure slowly and contain spillage. Observe no smoking/no open flame precautions. Have a Class B-C (dry powder) fire extinguisher within arm's reach at all times.

1. Release the fuel system pressure as outlined earlier in this section and disconnect the negative battery cable.

2. Disconnect the PCV hose from the valve cover.

3. Disconnect the vacuum hose from the fuel pressure regulator.

4. Use a shop towel to catch any leftover fuel that might be in the fuel rail and disconnect the fuel pressure line from the rail.

5. Disconnect the return line from the pressure regulator.

6. Disconnect the injector electrical connectors.

7. Disconnect the cold start injection feed line.

8. Remove the 2 fasteners holding the fuel rail and remove the fuel rail from the head.

To install:

9. Before installing the injectors back into the fuel rail, install a NEW O-ring on each injector.

10. Install the fuel rail to the head and tighten the fasteners to 11 ft. lbs. (15 Nm).

11. Connect the cold start injection feed line.

12. Connect the return line to the pressure regulator.

13. Connect the fuel pressure line to the rail.

14. Connect the injector electrical connectors.

15. Connect the vacuum hose to the fuel pressure regulator.

16. Connect the PCV hose to the valve cover.

17. Connect the battery cable to the negative battery terminal. Start the engine and check for leaks.

❊❊CAUTION

If there is a leak at any fitting, the line will be under pressure and the fuel may spray in a fine mist. This mist is extremely explosive. Shut the engine off immediately if

any leakage is detected. Use rags to wrap the leaking fitting until the pressure diminishes and wipe up any fuel from the engine area.

1993
▶ See Figures 60, 61, 62, 63, 64 and 65

❊❊CAUTION

The fuel system is under pressure. Release pressure slowly and contain spillage. Observe no smoking/no open flame precautions. Have a Class B-C (dry powder) fire extinguisher within arm's reach at all times.

➡The following procedure also includes removal of the fuel rail, if necessary:

1. Relieve the fuel system pressure as outlined in this section.

2. Disconnect the negative battery cable.

3. Disconnect the accelerator cable and cruise control cable, if equipped, from the air cleaner clip.

4. Disconnect and tag the Intake Air Temperature sensor (IAT) electrical connector.

5. Disconnect the 4 air cleaner cap clips.

6. Remove the air cleaner hose from the throttle body and cap.

7. Disconnect the accelerator cable from the throttle body.

8. Remove the 2 nuts and disconnect the TV cable from the throttle body, if equipped with automatic transaxle.

9. Disconnect the 2 EGR vacuum hoses, on California specification vehicles only.

1. Fuel injector
2. Fuel pressure line connector
3. Cold start fuel injector valve
4. Fuel rail
5. Fuel pressure regulator
6. Fuel return line connection

Fig. 59 Fuel rail and injectors — 1991-92

10. Disconnect the 1 evaporative (EVAP) emissions hose.

11. Disconnect the throttle position sensor and idle air control valve electrical connectors.

12. Remove the 2 bolts and 2 nuts and remove the throttle body and gasket from the intake manifold.

13. Remove the 1 bolt and disconnect the delivery air pipe.

14. Disconnect the fuel feed inlet hose.

15. Disconnect the EGR valve hose from the EGR valve, on California specification vehicles only.

16. Remove the engine hanger and air intake chamber stay and EGR vacuum modulator, on California specification vehicles.

17. Disconnect the EGR gas sensor electrical connector, California only.

18. Remove the 4 nuts and remove the EGR valve and pipe, if so equipped.

19. Disconnect the vacuum hose from the fuel pressure regulator.

20. Disconnect the PCV valve hose from the PCV valve.

21. Disconnect the PCV valve hose from the air intake chamber.

22. Remove the 2 nuts and the 3 Allen® head screws and remove the air intake chamber cover and gasket.

23. Disconnect the injector electrical connectors.

24. Disconnect the fuel inlet hose from the fuel rail.

25. Disconnect the fuel return hose from the fuel pressure regulator.

26. At the fuel delivery pipe (rail), remove the 2 bolts. Lift the fuel rail and the injectors free of the engine. DON'T drop the injectors.

27. Remove the 4 insulators and 2 spacers from the intake manifold.

28. Pull the 4 injectors free of the fuel rail.

29. Remove the O-rings and grommet from each injector.

30. Remove the 2 bolts and remove the pressure regulator from the fuel rail as necessary.

To install:

31. Install the pressure regulator to the fuel rail and tighten the 2 bolts to 82 inch lbs. (9.3 Nm).

32. Before installing the injectors back into the fuel rail, install a NEW O-ring on each injector.

33. Coat each O-ring with a light coat of gasoline (NEVER use oil of any sort) and install the injectors into the delivery pipe. Make certain each injector can be smoothly rotated. If they do not rotate smoothly, the O-ring is not in its correct position.

34. Install the insulators into each injector hole. Place the 2 spacers on the delivery pipe mounting holes in the intake manifold.

35. Place the fuel rail and injectors on the intake manifold and again check that the injectors rotate smoothly. Position the injector connector upward. Install the 2 bolts and tighten them to 11 ft. lbs. (15 Nm).

36. Install the fuel feed inlet hose to the fuel rail. Tighten the bolt to 22 ft. lbs. (29 Nm).

37. Connect the fuel return hose to the fuel pressure regulator.

38. Connect the electrical connectors to each injector.

39. Install the air intake chamber cover with a NEW gasket. Torque the retaining bolts in steps to 14 ft. lbs.

40. Install all necessary hoses and electrical connections.

41. Install the EGR valve and pipe and tighten the retaining bolts to 115 inch lbs. (13 Nm).

42. Install the engine hanger and air intake chamber stay and EGR vacuum modulator, if so equipped, and tighten the modulator bolts to 21 ft. lbs. 28 Nm).

43. Install a new gasket on the air intake chamber stay, facing the protrusion downward. Install the throttle body and torque the bolts evenly (in a X-pattern) to 16 ft. lbs. (22 Nm).

44. Connect the throttle position sensor and idle air control valve electrical connectors.

45. Connect the 1 evaporative (EVAP) emissions hose.

46. Connect the 2 EGR vacuum hoses, on California specification vehicles only.

47. Connect the TV cable to the throttle body, if equipped with automatic transaxle. Adjust as necessary. Refer to Section 7 for TV cable adjustment.

48. Install the air cleaner hose and cap to the throttle body.

49. Connect the 4 air cleaner cap clips.

50. Connect the Intake Air Temperature sensor (IAT) electrical connector.

51. Connect the accelerator cable and cruise control cable, if equipped, to the air cleaner clip.

52. Connect the negative battery cable.

TESTING

▶ **See Figure 66**

The simplest way to test the injectors is simply to listen to them with the engine running. Use either a stethoscope-type

1. Fuel feed inlet hose
2. Fuel rail

Fig. 60 Removing the fuel feed hose from the fuel rail — 1993

1. Fuel rail

Fig. 61 Removing the fuel rail — 1993

**Fig. 62 Fuel injector O-ring and grommet installation —
1993**

1. Fuel injector o-ring
2. Fuel injector
3. Fuel injector grommet

1. Fuel rail
2. Fuel injector o-ring
3. Fuel injector
4. Fuel injector

Fig. 63 Fuel injector installation — 1993

FUEL INJECTOR ELECTRICAL CONNECTOR

FUEL INJECTOR ELECTRICAL CONNECTOR

Fig. 64 Fuel injector electrical connectors — 1993

AIR INTAKE CHAMBER COVER

Fig. 65 Air intake chamber cover — 1993

Ohmmeter

Fig. 66 Testing injector resistance

tool or the blade of a long screw driver to touch each injector while the engine is idling. You should hear a distinct clicking as each injector opens and closes.

Additionally, the resistance of the injector can be easily checked. Disconnect the negative battery cable and remove the electrical connector from the injector to be tested. Use an ohmmeter to check the resistance across the terminals of the injector. Correct resistance is approximately 12-15 ohms at 68°F; slight variations are acceptable due to temperature conditions.

Bench testing of the injectors can only be done using expensive special equipment. Generally this equipment can be found at a dealership and sometimes at a well-equipped machine shop or performance shop. There is no provision for field testing the injectors by the owner/mechanic. DO NOT attempt to test the injector by removing it from the engine and making it spray into a jar.

Never attempt to check a removed injector by hooking it directly to the battery. The injector runs on a much smaller voltage and the 12 volts from the battery will destroy it internally. Since this happens at the speed of electricity, you don't get a second chance.

Fuel Injection Sensors and Controls

❄❄CAUTION

The fuel system is under pressure. Before disconnecting any fuel lines or components release the fuel system pressure as outlined earlier in this section. Observe no smoking/no open flame precautions. Have a Class B-C (dry powder) fire extinguisher within arm's reach at all times.

REMOVAL & INSTALLATION

1988 VIN Code 5 Engines

COLD START INJECTOR

▶ **See Figure 67**

1. Test the resistance of the cold start injector before removing it. Disconnect its electrical lead and use an ohmmeter to measure resistance between the terminals. Correct resistance is 3-5 ohms allow for slight variations due to temperature.

2. If the injector must be replaced, release the fuel system pressure and disconnect the negative battery cable.

3. Remove the wiring connector at the injector if not already done for testing purposes.

❈❈CAUTION

The fuel system is under pressure. Release pressure slowly and contain spillage. Observe no smoking/no open flame precautions. Have a Class B-C (dry powder) fire extinguisher within arm's reach at all times.

4. Wrap the fuel pipe connection in a rag or towel. Remove the 2 union bolts and the cold start injector pipe with its gaskets. Loosen the union bolts at the other end as necessary.

5. Remove the 2 retaining bolts and remove the cold start injector with its gaskets.

6. When reinstalling, always use a new gasket for the injector. Install it with the injector and tighten the 2 mounting bolts to 7 ft. lbs. (84 inch lbs.).

7. Again using new gaskets, connect the cold start injector pipe to the delivery pipe (fuel rail) and to the cold start injector. Tighten the bolts to 13 ft. lbs.

8. Install the wiring to the cold start injector.

9. Connect the negative battery cable.

10. Start the engine and check for leaks.

FUEL PRESSURE REGULATOR

▶ See Figure 68

1. Release the fuel system pressure and disconnect the negative battery cable.

2. Remove the vacuum sensing hose from the fuel pressure regulator.

❈❈CAUTION

The fuel system is under pressure. Release pressure slowly and contain spillage. Observe no smoking/no open flame precautions. Have a Class B-C (dry powder) fire extinguisher within arm's reach at all times.

3. Remove the fuel hose from the regulator.

Fig. 67 Cold start injector electrical schematic

Fig. 68 Location of fuel pressure regulator

4. Remove the 2 retaining bolts and pull the regulator out of the fuel rail.

5. When reinstalling, the 2 retaining bolts are tightened to 5.5 ft. lbs. (65 inch lbs) Connect the 2 hoses (fuel and vacuum).

6. Start the engine and check carefully for leaks.

MASS AIR FLOW SENSOR

▶ See Figures 69, 70 and 71

The mass air flow sensor communicates with the ECM about the amount of air being taken into the engine. The intake air flow moves a trap door which is connected to a potentiometer. This variable load switch controls the amount of electricity sent to the ECM. Depending on the signal received, the ECM governs the fuel injectors to deliver the proportionally correct amount of fuel into the engine. The air box must be handled carefully during testing and/or replacement.

1. Unplug the wiring connector at the mass air flow sensor.

2. Using an ohmmeter and the chart, measure the resistance between the terminals as indicated. The sensor must pass ALL tests; if any one is failed, the air sensor must be replaced. Note that the temperature related reading is measured in kilo-ohms. Don't forget to reset the meter to a higher scale.

3. If replacement is needed, label and disconnect the vacuum lines running to the sensor.

4. Remove the air cleaner hose.

5. Disconnect the wiring connector if not already done for testing purposes.

6. Remove the 4 nuts and the mass air flow sensor and its gasket.

7. When reinstalling, make absolutely sure that the air sensor and its gasket are correctly positioned. No air leaks are acceptable. Install and tighten the 4 nuts.

8. Install the wiring connector, the air cleaner hose and the vacuum hoses.

THROTTLE BODY

▶ See Figures 72, 73, 74 and 75

1. Release the fuel system pressure and disconnect the negative battery cable. Either drain the coolant from the throttle

Between terminals	Resistance	Temperature
$V_s - E_2$	$20 - 3,000 \ \Omega$	–
$V_c - E_2$	$100 - 300 \ \Omega$	–
$V_B - E_2$	$200 - 400 \ \Omega$	–
$THA - E_2$	$10 - 20 \ k\Omega$	$-20°C \ (-4°F)$
	$4 - 7 \ k\Omega$	$0°C \ (32°F)$
	$2 - 3 \ k\Omega$	$20°C \ (68°F)$
	$0.9 - 1.3 \ k\Omega$	$40°C \ (104°F)$
	$0.4 - 0.7 \ k\Omega$	$60°C \ (204°F)$
$F_c - E_1$	Infinity	–

Fig. 69 Resistance chart for testing the mass air flow sensor

Fig. 70 Mass air flow sensor schematic (above) and terminal identification

Fig. 71 Removing the mass air flow sensor (A)

Fig. 72 Throttle body assembly. Arrow indicates throttle position sensor

A THROTTLE LEVER
B NO CLEARANCE
C THROTTLE STOP SCREW

Fig. 73 Checking the throttle valve

Fig. 74 Adjusting the throttle position sensor

body by disconnecting a coolant hose or open the engine draincock until the fluid level is reduced.

✳✳WARNING

Housepets and small animals are attracted to the odor and taste of engine coolant (antifreeze). It is a highly poisonous mixture of chemicals; special care must be taken to protect open containers and spillage.

2. Disconnect the throttle return spring.
3. Disconnect the throttle cable.
4. Label and disconnect the vacuum hoses.
5. Carefully remove the throttle potion sensor wiring connector.

6. Remove the air cleaner hose.

7. Remove the water hoses from the air valve.

8. Remove the 2 bolts and 2 nuts and the throttle body with its gasket.

9. Wash and clean the cast metal parts with a soft brush and carburetor cleaner. Use compressed air to blow through all the passages and openings.

10. Check the throttle valve to see that there is NO clearance between the stop screw and the throttle lever when the throttle plate is fully closed.

11. Check the throttle position sensor (TPS). Insert a 0.47mm feeler gauge between the throttle stop screw and the lever. Connect an ohmmeter between terminal **IDL** and E_2. Loosen the 2 screws holding the TPS and gradually turn the TPS clockwise until the ohmmeter deflects, but no more. Secure the TPS screws at this point. Double check the clearance at the lever and stop screw.   Additional resistance tests may be made on the TPS using the chart.

To install:

12. Place a new gasket in position and install the throttle body with its 2 nuts and 2 bolts. Make certain everything is properly positioned before securing the unit. Tighten the bolts to 16 ft. lbs.

13. Connect the water hoses to the air valve.

14. Install the air cleaner hose and the vacuum hoses.

15. Connect the wiring to the throttle position sensor.

16. Connect the accelerator cable and its return spring.

17. Refill the coolant to the proper level.

ELECTRONIC FUEL INJECTION (EFI) MAIN RELAY

▶ **See Figure 76**

1. The relay is located under the hood, behind the left headlight area. Turn the ignition ON without starting the engine and listen for a noise from the relay.

2. Turn the ignition off and remove the connector from the relay. Using the ohmmeter, check for continuity between terminals **1** and **3**.

3. Check that there is NO continuity between terminals **2** and **4**.

4. Check that there is NO continuity between terminals **3** and **4**.

5. If the relay fails ANY of these tests, replace it.

Fig. 76 Testing the EFI main relay

CIRCUIT OPENING RELAY

▶ **See Figure 77**

1. The relay is located behind the lower center of the dashboard, adjacent to the ECM. With the ignition off, unplug the connector and use an ohmmeter to check for continuity between terminals **STA** and **E**.

2. Check that there is continuity between terminals **B** and **Fc**.

3. Check that there is NO continuity between terminals **B** and **Fp**.

4. If the relay fails any test, it must be replaced.

START INJECTOR TIME SWITCH

▶ **See Figure 78**

1. Remove the connector at the switch.

2. Use an ohmmeter to measure the resistance between terminals **STA** and **STJ**. Refer to the chart for the proper values.

3. If the time switch is to be replaced, drain the coolant from the system.

❋❋WARNING

Housepets and small animals are attracted to the odor and taste of engine coolant (antifreeze). It is a highly poisonous mixture of chemicals; special care must be taken to protect open containers and spillage.

4. Remove the switch and its gasket.

5. Install the new switch with a new gasket and tighten it to 25 ft. lbs.

Clearance between lever and stop screw	Between terminals	Resistance
0 mm (0 in.)	VTA – E_2	0.2 – 0.8 kΩ
0.35 mm (0.0138 in.)	IDL – E_2	Less than 2.3 kΩ
0.59 mm (0.0232 in.)	IDL – E_2	Infinity
Throttle valve fully opened position	VTA – E_2	3.3 – 10 kΩ
–	Vcc – E_2	3 – 7 kΩ

Fig. 75 Throttle position sensor resistance check

Fig. 77 Checking continuity on the circuit opening relay

Between terminals	Resistance (Ω)	Coolant temp.
STA – STJ	20 – 40	Below 30°C (95°F)
	40 – 60	Above 40°C (95°F)
STA – Ground	20 – 80	—

Fig. 78 Resistance chart for checking the start injector time switch sensor

6. Refill the coolant and attach the wiring connector to the switch.

COOLANT TEMPERATURE SENSOR

▶ See Figure 79

1. Disconnect the wiring to the sensor.
2. Using an ohmmeter, measure the resistance across the terminals of the sensor. Refer to the chart for the correct resistance values. Note that the resistance will change as a function of the coolant temperature, not the air temperature.

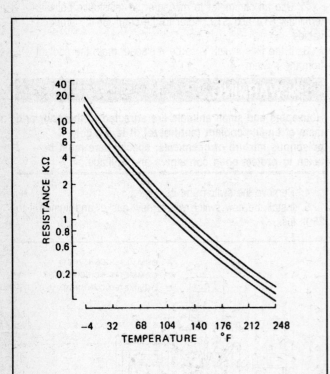

Fig. 79 Resistance chart for testing the water temperature sensor

3. If the sensor must be changed, the coolant must be drained. Do this only with the engine cold.

✳✳WARNING

Housepets and small animals are attracted to the odor and taste of engine coolant (antifreeze). It is a highly poisonous mixture of chemicals; special care must be taken to protect open containers and spillage.

4. Using the correct size wrench, remove the sensor by unscrewing it. Install the new sensor and tighten it.
5. Refill the coolant to the proper level.
6. Connect the wiring to the sensor.

1989-90 VIN Code 6 Engines

COLD START INJECTOR

▶ See Figure 80

1. Release the fuel system pressure and disconnect the negative battery cable.
2. Disconnect the wiring at the injector.
3. Loosen and remove the fuel line at the injector.

✳✳WARNING

The fuel system is under pressure. Release pressure slowly and contain spillage. Observe no smoking/no open flame precautions. Have a Class B-C (dry powder) fire extinguisher within arm's reach at all times.

4. Remove the 2 retaining bolts and remove the injector.
5. When reinstalling, position the new injector in the intake manifold, install the retaining bolts and tighten them to 7 ft. lbs. (84 inch lbs.)
6. Connect the fuel line, then connect the wiring harness to the injector.
7. Connect the negative battery cable.

FUEL PRESSURE REGULATOR

▶ See Figures 80 and 81

1. Release the fuel system pressure and disconnect the negative battery cable.
2. Disconnect the vacuum hose from the regulator.
3. Disconnect the fuel return line from the regulator.

✳✳CAUTION

The fuel system is under pressure. Release pressure slowly and contain spillage. Observe no smoking/no open flame precautions. Have a Class B-C (dry powder) fire extinguisher within arm's reach at all times.

4. Remove the 2 retaining bolts and remove the fuel pressure regulator.
5. When reinstalling, place the new regulator on the fuel rail, install the bolts and tighten them to 7 ft. lbs. (84 inch lbs.).
6. Connect the fuel return line, making sure the clamp is properly placed and secure.
7. Connect the vacuum hose, then connect the negative battery cable.

COMPUTER HARNESS

C1 Electronic Control Module (ECM)
C2 Check Connector
C3 "Check Engine" Light
C4 Circuit Opening Relay
C5 ECM Harness Grounds
C6 Fuse Panel
C8 Fuel Pump Test Connector (Part of C2)

NOT ECM CONNECTED

N1 Crankcase Vent Valve (PCV)
N9 Fuel Pressure Regulator Valve
N10 Cold Start Injector
N11 Cold Start Injector Valve Switch
N17 Fuel Vapor Canister
N18 A/C Fan Relay #1
N19 A/C Fan Relay #2
N20 A/C Compressor Relay

◎ Exhaust Gas Recirculation (EGR) Valve

CONTROLLED DEVICES

1 Fuel Injectors
2 Idle Vacuum Switching Valve (VSV)
4 EFI Main Relay
7 *EGR Vacuum Switching Valve (VSV)
8 Cooling Fan Relay
17 Throttle Body

INFORMATION SENSORS

A Manifold Absolute Pressure (MAP) Sensor
B Oxygen (O_2) Sensor
C Throttle Switch (TS)
D Coolant Temperature Sensor (CTS)
F Vehicle Speed Sensor (VSS)
M Park/Neutral (P/N) Switch
T Manifold Air Temperature (MAT) Sensor

* California Only

Fig. 80 Location of electronic components — 1989-90 VIN Code 6 engine

Fig. 81 Fuel pressure regulator

MANIFOLD VACUUM

THROTTLE BODY

▶ **See Figures 80 and 82**

1. Release the fuel system pressure and disconnect the negative battery cable.
2. Remove the air cleaner and intake duct assembly.
3. Disconnect the electrical wiring from the throttle switch.
4. Remove the 2 bolts holding the throttle cable bracket.
5. If so equipped, remove the transaxle shift cable (automatic transmission) and/or the cruise control cable.
6. Label and remove the vacuum hoses to the throttle body.
7. Remove the vacuum hose to the air valve.
8. Remove the 4 bolts holding the throttle body and carefully remove the throttle body.
9. When reinstalling, always use a new gasket between the throttle body and the intake. Do not use sealants of any kind

on the gasket. Place the throttle body in position, install the 4 bolts and tighten them to 16 ft. lbs. Make very certain that the throttle body is properly placed before tightening the bolts; no air leaks are acceptable.

10. Install the throttle cable and its bracket.

11. If so equipped, reattach the transaxle cable and/or the cruise control cable.

12. Connect the vacuum hose to the air valve.

13. Connect the vacuum hoses to the throttle body.

14. Connect the electrical connector to the throttle switch and install the air cleaner and duct assembly.

15. Connect the negative battery cable.

THROTTLE SWITCH ADJUSTMENT

▶ See Figures 82 and 83

➡ This procedure may be performed on the car; removal of the throttle body is not required.

1. With the ignition **OFF**, remove the electrical connector from the throttle switch.

2. Loosen the 2 small bolts holding the switch to the throttle body. Loosen them just enough to allow the switch to be moved if necessary, but no more.

3. Insert a 0.0276 in (0.70mm) feeler gauge between the throttle stop screw and the throttle lever. Connect an ohmmeter between terminals **IDL** and **E2** on the switch.

4. Gradually turn the switch clockwise until the meter deflects, showing continuity; secure the sensor with the 2 screws.

5. Remove the feeler gauge and insert another of 0.80mm. The ohmmeter should show NO continuity with the larger gauge inserted.

Fig. 83 Adjusting the throttle switch

6. Adjust the switch as necessary to gain the correct function for each feeler gauge. Tighten the screws when the correct position is achieved.

7. Connect the wiring harness to the throttle switch

MANIFOLD ABSOLUTE PRESSURE (MAP) SENSOR

▶ See Figure 84

Located on the firewall, this sensor advises the ECM of pressure changes in the intake manifold. It consists of a semi-conductor pressure converting element which converts a pressure change into an electrical signal. The ECM sends a 5 volt reference signal to the MAP sensor; the change in air pressure changes the resistance within the sensor. The ECM reads the change from its reference voltage and signals the injectors to react accordingly.

Replacing the MAP sensor simply requires disconnecting the vacuum hose and the electrical connector, and unbolting the

Fig. 82 Throttle body assembly with throttle switch

Fig. 84 Cross section of MAP sensor

sensor from the firewall. Inspect the vacuum hose over its entire length for any signs of cracking or splitting. The slightest leak can cause false messages to be send to the ECM.

MANIFOLD AIR TEMPERATURE (MAT) SENSOR

▶ See Figure 80

The MAT sensor advises the ECM of changes in intake air temperature (and therefore air density). As air temperature of the intake varies, the ECM, by monitoring the voltage change, adjusts the amount of fuel injection according to the air temperature.

To replace the MAT sensor:

1. Remove the air cleaner cover.
2. With the ignition OFF, disconnect the electrical connector.
3. Push the MAT sensor out from inside the air cleaner housing.
4. Install the new sensor, making sure it is properly placed and secure.
5. Connect the wiring harness, and replace the air cleaner cover.

COOLANT TEMPERATURE SENSOR

▶ See Figure 85

The coolant temperature sensor is located under the air cleaner assembly and behind the distributor. Its function is to advise the ECM of changes in engine temperature by monitoring the changes in coolant temperature. The sensor must be handled carefully during removal. It can be damaged (thereby affecting engine performance) by impact.

The sensor may be tested following the procedures listed previously for the 1988 VIN Code 5 engine. The temperature and resistance chart is the same. If the sensor must be replaced:

❊❊WARNING

Perform this procedure only on a cold engine.

1. Relieve the pressure within the cooling system. It may be helpful to partially drain the block to lower the coolant level.

❊❊WARNING

Housepets and small animals are attracted to the odor and taste of engine coolant (antifreeze). It is a highly poisonous mixture of chemicals; special care must be taken to protect open containers and spillage.

2. Remove the air cleaner assembly.
3. With the ignition OFF, disconnect the electrical connector to the coolant temperature sensor.
4. Using the proper sized wrench, carefully unscrew the sensor from the engine.
5. Before reinstalling, coat the threads of the sensor with a sealant. Install the sensor and tighten it to 18 ft. lbs.
6. Reconnect the electrical connector. Install the air cleaner assembly.
7. Refill the coolant to the proper level.

ELECTRONIC FUEL INJECTION (EFI) MAIN RELAY

▶ See Figures 86 and 87

1. The EFI relay is located on the fuse block (junction block) under the hood behind the left headlight. Test the function of the relay by turning the ignition ON and listening or feeling the relay. An operation noise should be heard (or felt) from the relay.
2. Turn the ignition OFF. Disconnect the connector from the relay and use an ohmmeter to check for continuity between relay terminals 3 and 4.

Fig. 86 Continuity check, EFI relay

Fig. 85 Coolant temperature sensor. Remember to coat the threads with sealant before reassembly

Fig. 87 Function check, EFI relay

3. There should be NO continuity between terminals 1 and 2. If the relay fails either of these tests, replace it.

4. Using jumper wires, connect battery voltage across terminals 3 and 4 (Connect the battery positive (+) to terminal 4) and check terminals 1 and 2 for continuity. With 12 volts applied, continuity should be present.

5. Reinstall the relay in place.

CIRCUIT OPENING RELAY

▶ **See Figures 88 and 89**

1. Remove the ECM cover under the center console. Remove the circuit opening relay and its wiring.

2. With the ignition **OFF**, disconnect the relay.

3. Using an ohmmeter, check that there is continuity between terminals **STA** and **E1**.

4. Check that there is continuity between terminals **B** and **FC**.

5. Check that there is NO continuity between terminals **B** and **FP**. If the relay fails any of these checks, it must be replaced.

6. Using jumper wires, connect the battery positive (+) terminal to terminal **STA** and the battery negative terminal to terminal **E1**. Use the ohmmeter to check that there is now continuity between terminals **B** and **FP**.

7. Change the jumper wires so that the positive terminal connects to terminal **B** and the negative connects to terminal **FC**. Check that there is now continuity between terminals **B** and **FP**.

8. If the relay fails either of these functional tests, it must be replaced.

1990-92 VIN Code 5 & 6 Engine

COLD START INJECTOR

▶ **See Figure 59**

1. Release the fuel system pressure and disconnect the negative battery cable.

2. Disconnect the wiring at the injector.

3. Loosen and remove the fuel line at the injector.

✳✳WARNING

The fuel system is under pressure. Release pressure slowly and contain spillage. Observe no smoking/no open flame precautions. Have a Class B-C (dry powder) fire extinguisher within arm's reach at all times.

Fig. 88 Checking continuity of the circuit opening relay

Fig. 89 Checking the function of the circuit opening relay

4. Remove the 2 retaining bolts and remove the injector.

5. When reinstalling, position the new injector in the intake manifold, install the retaining bolts and tighten them to 82 inch lbs. (9.3 Nm).

6. Connect the fuel line, then connect the wiring harness to the injector.

7. Connect the negative battery cable.

FUEL PRESSURE REGULATOR

▶ **See Figure 59**

1. Release the fuel system pressure and disconnect the negative battery cable.

2. Disconnect the vacuum hose from the regulator.

3. Disconnect the fuel return line from the regulator.

✳✳CAUTION

The fuel system is under pressure. Release pressure slowly and contain spillage. Observe no smoking/no open flame precautions. Have a Class B-C (dry powder) fire extinguisher within arm's reach at all times.

4. Remove the 2 retaining bolts and remove the fuel pressure regulator.

5. When reinstalling, place the new regulator on the fuel rail, install the bolts and tighten them to 82 inch lbs. (9.3 ft. lbs.).

6. Connect the fuel return line, making sure the clamp is properly placed and secure.

7. Connect the vacuum hose, then connect the negative battery cable.

THROTTLE BODY

▶ **See Figures 90 and 91**

1. Release the fuel system pressure and disconnect the negative battery cable.

2. Remove the air cleaner and intake duct assembly.

3. Disconnect the electrical wiring from the throttle switch.

4. Remove the 2 bolts holding the throttle cable bracket.

5. If so equipped, remove the transaxle shift cable (automatic transmission) and/or the cruise control cable.

6. Label and remove the vacuum hoses to the throttle body.

7. Remove the vacuum hose to the air valve.

8. Remove the 4 bolts holding the throttle body and carefully remove the throttle body.

9. When reinstalling, always use a new gasket between the throttle body and the intake. Do not use sealants of any kind on the gasket. Place the throttle body in position, install the 4 bolts and tighten them to 16 ft. lbs. (22 Nm). Make very certain that the throttle body is properly placed before tightening the bolts; no air leaks are acceptable.

10. Install the throttle cable and its bracket.

11. If so equipped, reattach the transaxle cable and/or cruise control cable.

12. Connect the vacuum hose to the air valve.

13. Connect the vacuum hoses to the throttle body.

14. Connect the electrical connector to the throttle switch and install the air cleaner and duct assembly.

15. Connect the negative battery cable.

Fig. 91 Throttle body assembly — VIN Code 6 engine

THROTTLE POSITION SENSOR (TPS)

▶ **See Figure 92**

VIN Code 5 Engine

1. Disconnect the negative battery cable.

2. Disconnect the electrical connection for sensor.

3. Remove the 2 screws and remove the sensor.

To install:

4. Check that the throttle valve is fully closed.

5. Place the sensor on the throttle body. Turn the sensor clockwise and install the 2 screws loosely.

6. Adjust the throttle position sensor. Insert a 0.35mm or 0.0138 inch feeler gauge between the throttle stop screw and the lever. Connect an ohmmeter between terminals **IDL** and **E₂**. There should be continuity.

7. Insert a 0.39 mm (0.0232 inch) feeler gauge. There should be no continuity. Rotate the TPS as necessary, to adjust. Secure the TPS screws at this point.

8. Reconnect electrical connector. Start engine and check for proper operation.

THROTTLE SWITCH (TS)

▶ **See Figures 93 and 94**

VIN Code 6 Engine

1. Disconnect the negative battery cable.

2. Disconnect switch connector.

3. Hold the throttle valve opening angle at 45 degrees. Remove the 2 screws and remove the switch.

To install:

4. Place the throttle switch over the throttle valve shaft in correct alignment.

1. Throttle body
2. Throttle position sensor
3. Auxiliary air valve
4. Dash-pot

Fig. 90 Throttle body assembly — VIN Code 5 engine

Fig. 92 Throttle position sensor adjustment — VIN Code 5 engine

5. Install the 2 screws. Adjust the throttle switch. Insert a 0.70mm or 0.0276 in. feeler gauge between the throttle stop screw and the lever. Connect an ohmmeter between terminal **IDL** and **E₂**. There should be continuity.

6. Insert a 0.80 mm (0.0315 inch) feeler gauge. There should be no continuity. Rotate the switch as necessary to adjust. Secure the switch screws at this point.

7. Reconnect electrical connector. Start engine and check for proper operation.

AUXILIARY AIR VALVE

VIN Code 5 Engine

1. Remove the throttle body.
2. Remove the retaining screws and remove the air valve. Remove the O-ring and gasket.

3. Use a new O-ring and/or gasket; install the air valve to the throttle body.
4. Reinstall the throttle body.

AIR VALVE

▶ **See Figure 95**

VIN Code 6 Engine

1. Remove the throttle body as outlined earlier in this section.
2. Remove the retaining screws and remove the air valve. Remove the O-ring and gasket.
3. Use a new O-ring and/or gasket; install the air valve to the throttle body.
4. Reinstall the throttle body.

DASH POT REPLACEMENT

▶ **See Figure 96**

1. Remove the 2 retaining screws and remove the dashpot from the throttle body.
2. Installation is the reverse of removal.
3. Adjust the dashpot may be adjusted

DASH POT ADJUSTMENT

▶ **See Figure 97**

1. Run engine to normal operating temperature.
2. Check engine idle speed and adjust if necessary. Idle speed adjustment is 800 rpm (VIN 5), 700 rpm (VIN 6) in **NEUTRAL**, manual transaxle, and 800 rpm (VIN 5), 700 rpm (VIN 6) in **DRIVE**, automatic transaxle.

Fig. 93 Throttle switch — VIN Code 6 engine

Fig. 95 Air valve — VIN Code 6 engine

Fig. 94 Throttle switch adjustment — VIN Code 6 engine

Fig. 96 Dash pot location

3. Connect a tachometer to **IG** terminal of the check connector.

4. Jumper terminal **TE1** to **E1** (VIN 6) of the check connector.

5. Disconnect the EGR VSV connector (VIN 6) (California Only).

6. Remove dash pot cap and filter and separator.

7. Maintain engine speed at 2,500 rpm (VIN 5), 3,000 rpm (VIN 6), and plug the VTV hole in dash pot.

8. Release the throttle valve and check dash pot rpm setting. Dash pot setting speed is 1,800 rpm (VIN 5), 1,500 rpm (VIN 6). If not within specifications, adjust the stop screw on the throttle shaft.

9. With dash pot rpm set, remove plug from VTV hole and check that the engine speed returns to idle in about 1 second. If longer than 2 seconds or less that 1 second, replace dash pot.

1993 VIN Code 6 & 8 Engines

THROTTLE BODY

1. Relieve the fuel system pressure as outlined in this section.

2. Disconnect the negative battery cable.

3. Disconnect the accelerator cable and cruise control cable, if equipped, from the air cleaner clip.

4. Disconnect and tag the Intake Air Temperature sensor (IAT) electrical connector.

5. Disconnect the 4 air cleaner cap clips.

6. Remove the air cleaner hose and cap from the throttle body.

7. Disconnect the accelerator cable from the throttle body.

8. Remove the 2 nuts and disconnect the TV cable from the throttle body, if equipped with automatic transaxle.

9. Disconnect the 2 EGR vacuum hoses, on California specification vehicles only.

10. Disconnect the 1 evaporative (EVAP) emissions hose.

11. Disconnect the throttle position sensor and idle air control valve electrical connectors.

12. Remove the 2 bolts and 2 nuts and remove the throttle body and gasket from the intake manifold.

To install:

13. Install a new gasket, then throttle body and torque the bolts evenly (in a X-pattern) to 16 ft. lbs. (22 Nm).

14. Connect the throttle position sensor and idle air control valve electrical connectors.

15. Connect the 1 evaporative (EVAP) emissions hose.

16. Connect the 2 EGR vacuum hoses, on California specification vehicles only.

17. Connect the TV cable to the throttle body, if equipped with automatic transaxle. Adjust as necessary. Refer to Section 7 for TV cable adjustment.

18. Install the air cleaner hose and cap to the throttle body.

19. Connect the 4 air cleaner cap clips.

20. Connect the Intake Air Temperature sensor (IAT) electrical connector.

21. Connect the accelerator cable and cruise control cable, if equipped, to the air cleaner clip.

22. Connect the negative battery cable.

FUEL PRESSURE REGULATOR

▶ See Figure 98

1. Release the fuel system pressure and disconnect the negative battery cable.

2. Disconnect the vacuum hose from the regulator.

3. Disconnect the fuel return line from the regulator.

✳✳CAUTION

The fuel system is under pressure. Release pressure slowly and contain spillage. Observe no smoking/no open flame precautions. Have a Class B-C (dry powder) fire extinguisher within arm's reach at all times.

4. Remove the 2 retaining bolts and remove the fuel pressure regulator.

5. When reinstalling, place the new regulator on the fuel rail, install the bolts and tighten them to 82 inch lbs. (9.3 ft. lbs.).

6. Connect the fuel return line, making sure the clamp is properly placed and secure.

7. Connect the vacuum hose, then connect the negative battery cable.

IDLE AIR CONTROL VALVE

▶ See Figure 99

1. Remove the throttle body.

2. Remove the retaining screws and remove the air valve. Remove the gasket.

3. Use a new gasket and install the air valve to the throttle body.

4. Reinstall the throttle body.

Fig. 97 Dash pot

Fig. 98 Removing the fuel pressure regulator

Fig. 99 Removing the Idle Air Control (IAC) valve

THROTTLE POSITION SENSOR (TPS)

▶ See Figure 100

VIN Code 5 Engine
1. Disconnect the negative battery cable.
2. Disconnect the electrical connection for sensor.
3. Remove the 2 screws and remove the sensor.

To install:
4. Check that the throttle valve is fully closed.
5. Place the sensor on the throttle body. Turn the sensor clockwise and install the 2 screws loosely.

6. Adjust the throttle position sensor. Insert a 0.35mm or 0.0138 inch feeler gauge between the throttle stop screw and the lever. Connect an ohmmeter between terminals **IDL** and **E₂**. There should be continuity.
7. Insert a 0.59 mm (0.0232 inch) feeler gauge. There should be no continuity. Rotate the TPS , necessary to adjust. Secure the TPS screws at this point.
8. Reconnect electrical connector. Start engine and check for proper operation.

Fig. 100 Throttle position sensor

FUEL TANK

REMOVAL & INSTALLATION

1985-92

➡Before removing fuel system parts, clean them with a spray-type engine cleaner. Follow the instructions on the cleaner. Do not soak fuel system parts in liquid cleaning solvent.

✳✳CAUTION

The fuel injection system is under pressure. Release pressure slowly and contain spillage. Observe no smoking/no open flame precautions. Have a Class B-C (dry powder) fire extinguisher within arm's reach at all times.

1. Remove the filler cap.
2. Using a siphon or pump, drain the fuel from the tank and store it in a proper metal container with a tight cap.
3. Remove the rear seat cushion to gain access to the electrical wiring.
4. Disconnect the fuel pump and sending unit wiring at the connector.
5. Raise the vehicle and safely support it on jackstands.
6. Loosen the clamp and remove the filler neck and overflow pipe from the tank.
7. Remove the supply hose from the tank. Wrap a rag around the fitting to collect escaping fuel. Disconnect the breather hose from the tank, again using a rag to control spillage.
8. Cover or plug the end of each disconnected line to keep dirt out and fuel in.

9. Support the fuel tank with a floor jack or transmission jack. Use a broad piece of wood to distribute the load. Be careful not to deform the bottom of the tank.
10. Remove the fuel tank support strap bolts.
11. Swing the straps away from the tank and lower the jack. Balance the tank with your other hand or have a helper assist you. The tank is bulky and may have some fuel left in it. If its balance changes suddenly, the tank may fall.
12. Remove the fuel filler pipe extension, the breather pipe assembly and the sending unit assembly. Keep these items in a clean, protected area away from the car.
13. While the tank is out and disassembled, inspect it for any signs of rust, leakage or metal damage. If any problem is found, replace the tank. Clean the inside of the tank with water and a light detergent and rinse the tank thoroughly several times.
14. Inspect all of the lines, hoses and fittings for any sign of corrosion, wear or damage to the surfaces. Check the pump outlet hose and the filter for restrictions.

To install:
15. When reassembling, ALWAYS replace the sealing gaskets with new ones. Also replace any rubber parts showing any sign of deterioration.
16. Connect the breather pipe assembly and the filler pipe extension.

➡Tighten the breather pipe screw to 17 inch lbs. and all other attaching screws to 30 inch lbs.

17. Place the fuel tank on the jack and elevate it into place within the car. Attach the straps and install the strap bolts, tightening them to 29 ft. lbs.

18. Connect the breather hose to the tank pipe, the return hose to the tank pipe and the supply hose to its tank pipe. Tighten the supply hose fitting to 21 ft. lbs.

19. Connect the filler neck and overflow pipe to the tank. Make sure the clamps are properly seated and secure.

20. Lower the vehicle to the ground.

21. Connect the pump and sending unit electrical connectors to the harness.

22. Install the rear seat cushion.

23. Using a funnel, pour the fuel that was drained from its container into the fuel filler.

24. Install the fuel filler cap.

25. Start the engine and check carefully for any sign of leakage around the tank and lines.

1993

1. Relieve the fuel system pressure as outlined earlier in this section.

2. Drain the fuel tank.

3. Remove the rear seat cushion, as outlined in Section 10.

4. Remove the 4 screws and service hole cover.

5. Remove the fuel sender assembly electrical connector. Raise and suitably support the vehicle.

6. Remove the 2 bolts, the 2 nuts and resonator intermediate pipe assembly from the 3 way catalytic converter (TWC).

7. Remove the 2 bolts and resonator intermediate pipe assembly from the muffler assembly.

8. Remove the 3 bolts and exhaust heat shield from underbody.

9. Remove the 2 bolts and the parking brake cables from underbody.

10. Remove 1 bolt, 1 clamp and fuel filler hose from fuel tank.

11. Remove 1 bolt, 1 clamp and fuel breather hose from fuel tank.

12. Remove 1 nut and fuel feed hose from fuel feed pipe.

13. Remove 1 clamp and fuel return hose from the fuel return pipe at fuel tank.

14. Remove 1 clamp and fuel vapor hose from the fuel vapor pipe at fuel tank.

15. Remove 4 bolts and fuel tank from vehicle.

16. Disassemble 8 bolts and fuel sender assembly from the fuel tank.

17. Disassemble 1 clamp, fuel vapor hose and fuel tank vent valve from fuel tank.

To install:

18. Assemble 1 clamp, fuel vapor hose and fuel tank vent valve to the fuel tank.

19. Install the fuel sender assembly to the fuel tank and tighten the 8 bolts to 89 inch lbs. (10 Nm).

20. Install the fuel tank to the vehicle and tighten the 4 bolts to 22 ft. lbs. (30 Nm).

21. Install the 1 clamp and the fuel vapor hose to the fuel vapor pipe at fuel tank.

22. Install the 1 clamp and the fuel return hose to the fuel return pipe at fuel tank.

23. Install the fuel feed hose to fuel feed pipe and tighten the 1 nut to 15 ft. lbs. (20 Nm).

24. Install the fuel breather hose to the fuel tank and install the clamp. Tighten the bolt to 15 ft. lbs. (20 Nm).

25. Install the fuel filler hose to the fuel tank and install the clamp. Tighten the bolt to 15 ft. lbs. (20 Nm).

26. Install the parking brake cables to the underbody and tighten the 2 bolts to 22 ft. lbs. (30 Nm).

27. Install the exhaust heat shield to the underbody and tighten the 3 bolts to 48 inch lbs. (5.4 Nm).

28. Install the bolts and resonator intermediate pipe assembly to the muffler assembly and tighten the 2 bolts to 14 f. ft. lbs. (19 Nm).

29. Install the resonator intermediate pipe assembly to the 3 way catalytic converter (TWC) and tighten the 2 bolts and 2 nuts to 32 ft. lbs. (43 Nm).

30. Lower the vehicle.

TORQUE SPECIFICATIONS

Component	U.S.	Metric
Cold start injector bolts:	82 inch lbs.	9.3 Nm
Fuel Filter		
Fuel feed inlet pipe connecting bolt		
1989–93:	22 ft.lbs.	30 Nm
Fuel feed outlet pipe connecting bolt		
1989–93:	21 ft.lbs.	29 Nm
Fuel rail to intake manifold:	11 ft. lbs.	15 Nm
Fuel tank strap retaining bolts:	29 ft. lbs.	39 Nm
Fuel pump bracket bolts:	30 inch lbs.	3.4 Nm
Pressure regulator retaining bolts		
1988:	65 inch lbs.	7.4 Nm
1989–93:	82 inch lbs.	9.3 Nm
Sending unit to tank screws		
1985–88:	35 inch lbs.	3.9 Nm
1989–92:	30 inch lbs.	3.4 Nm
1993:	89 inch lbs.	10 Nm
Throttle body retaining bolts and nuts:	16 ft. lbs.	22 Nm

CHART A-5

ENGINE CRANKS BUT WILL NOT RUN
(FUEL SYSTEM ELECTRICAL TEST)
1.6L (VIN 6) "S" CARLINE (PORT)

Circuit Description:

When the engine is cranked the ECM will turn "ON" the circuit opening relay to operate the fuel pump. If the ECM receives ignition reference pulses the fuel pump will continue to run. If the ECM receives no reference pulses from the ignition circuit it will shut "OFF" the fuel pump.

Test Description: Numbers below refer to circled numbers on the diagnostic chart.

1. Fuel pump should run when ignition is cranked.
2. Test for an open between fuel pump and ground circuit opening relay.
3. Checks for crank signal to circuit opening relay.
4. Checks for proper EFI relay operation.
5. This will determine if ECM fuel pump driver circuit inside ECM is faulty.

Diagnostic Aids:

Visual inspection of wiring and connectors should be made if an intermittent problem exists.

Fig. 101 Fuel system diagnosis — 1989-90 VIN code 6 engine

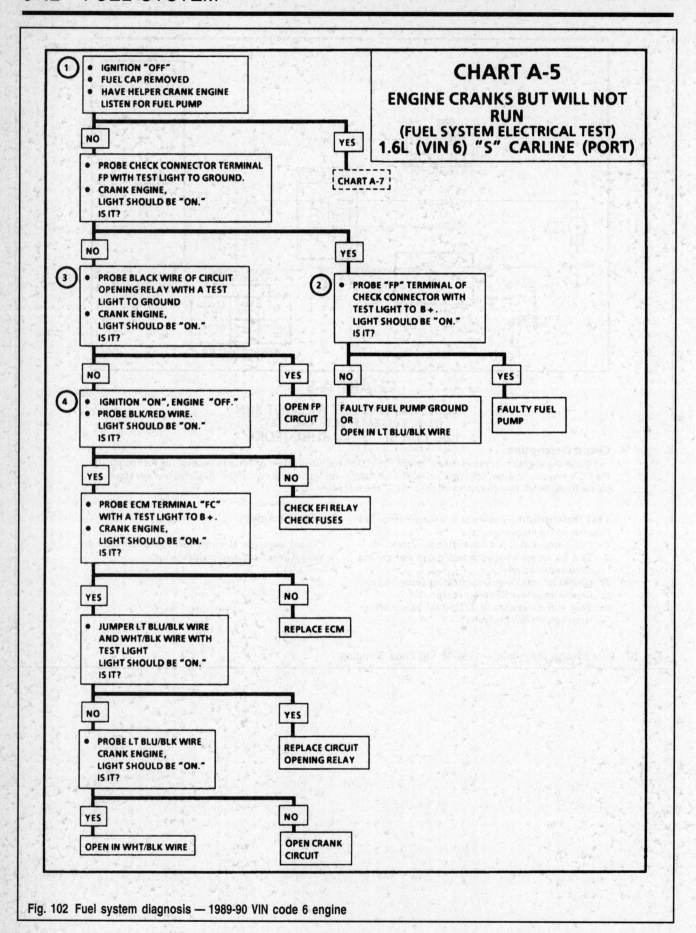

CHART A-5
ENGINE CRANKS BUT WILL NOT RUN
(FUEL SYSTEM ELECTRICAL TEST)
1.6L (VIN 6) "S" CARLINE (PORT)

1
- IGNITION "OFF"
- FUEL CAP REMOVED
- HAVE HELPER CRANK ENGINE LISTEN FOR FUEL PUMP

NO

YES → CHART A-7

- PROBE CHECK CONNECTOR TERMINAL FP WITH TEST LIGHT TO GROUND.
- CRANK ENGINE, LIGHT SHOULD BE "ON." IS IT?

NO

YES

3
- PROBE BLACK WIRE OF CIRCUIT OPENING RELAY WITH A TEST LIGHT TO GROUND
- CRANK ENGINE, LIGHT SHOULD BE "ON." IS IT?

2
- PROBE "FP" TERMINAL OF CHECK CONNECTOR WITH TEST LIGHT TO B+. LIGHT SHOULD BE "ON." IS IT?

NO

YES → OPEN FP CIRCUIT

NO → FAULTY FUEL PUMP GROUND OR OPEN IN LT BLU/BLK WIRE

YES → FAULTY FUEL PUMP

4
- IGNITION "ON", ENGINE "OFF."
- PROBE BLK/RED WIRE. LIGHT SHOULD BE "ON." IS IT?

YES

NO → CHECK EFI RELAY CHECK FUSES

- PROBE ECM TERMINAL "FC" WITH A TEST LIGHT TO B+.
- CRANK ENGINE, LIGHT SHOULD BE "ON." IS IT?

YES

NO → REPLACE ECM

- JUMPER LT BLU/BLK WIRE AND WHT/BLK WIRE WITH TEST LIGHT LIGHT SHOULD BE "ON." IS IT?

NO

YES → REPLACE CIRCUIT OPENING RELAY

- PROBE LT BLU/BLK WIRE CRANK ENGINE, LIGHT SHOULD BE "ON." IS IT?

YES → OPEN IN WHT/BLK WIRE

NO → OPEN CRANK CIRCUIT

Fig. 102 Fuel system diagnosis — 1989-90 VIN code 6 engine

CHART A-7

(Page 1 of 3)
FUEL SYSTEM PRESSURE TEST
1.6L (VIN 6) "S" CARLINE (PORT)

Circuit Description:

The fuel pump delivers fuel to the fuel rail and injectors, where the system pressure is controlled from 262 to 303 kPa (35 to 38 psi) by the pressure regulator. Excess fuel is returned to the fuel tank. When the engine is stopped, the pump can be energized by applying battery voltage to the test terminal located in the engine compartment.

Test Description: Numbers below refer to circled numbers on the diagnostic chart.

1. Use pressure gage J 34730-1. Wrap a shop towel around the fuel pressure tap to absorb any small amount of fuel leakage that may occur when installing the gage. (The pressure will not leak down after the fuel pump is stopped on a correctly functioning system.)

2. While the engine is idling, manifold pressure is low (vacuum). When applied to the fuel regulator diaphragm, the pressure will result in a lower fuel pressure of about 207-241 kPa (30-35 psi).

3. The application of vacuum to the pressure regulator should result in a fuel pressure drop.

4. Pressure leak-down may be caused by one of the following:
   - In-tank fuel pump check valve not holding
   - Pump coupling hose leaking
   - Fuel pressure regulator valve leaking
   - Injector sticking open

Diagnostic Aids:

Improper fuel system pressure may contribute to one or all of the following symptoms
- Cranks but won't run
- Cutting out (May feel like ignition problem)
- Hesitation, loss of power or poor fuel economy

Fig. 103 Fuel system diagnosis — 1989-90 VIN code 6 engine

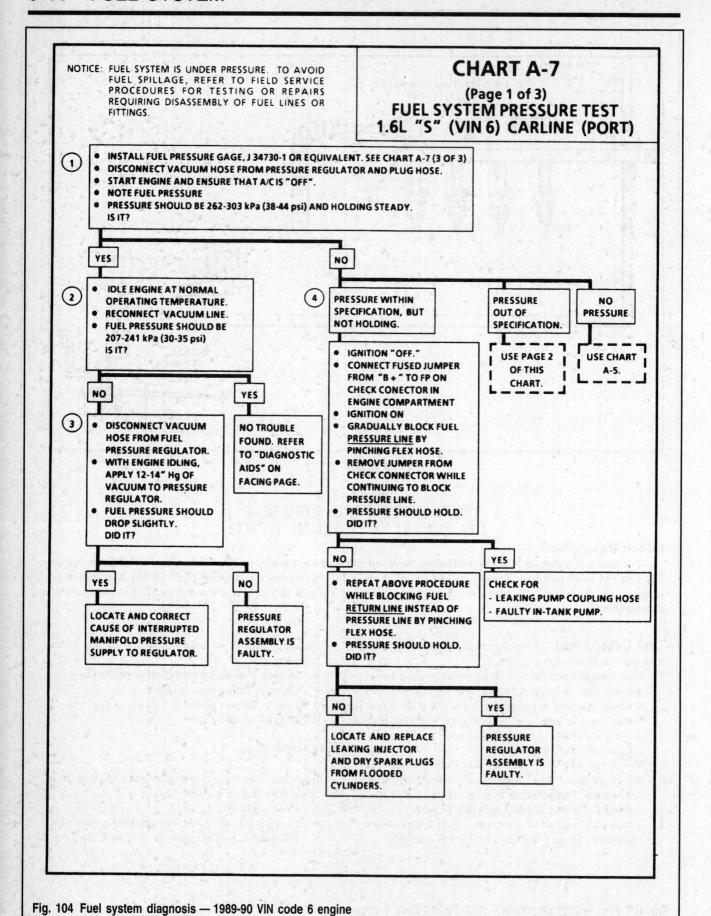

NOTICE: FUEL SYSTEM IS UNDER PRESSURE. TO AVOID FUEL SPILLAGE, REFER TO FIELD SERVICE PROCEDURES FOR TESTING OR REPAIRS REQUIRING DISASSEMBLY OF FUEL LINES OR FITTINGS.

CHART A-7

(Page 1 of 3)
FUEL SYSTEM PRESSURE TEST
1.6L "S" (VIN 6) CARLINE (PORT)

1
- INSTALL FUEL PRESSURE GAGE, J 34730-1 OR EQUIVALENT. SEE CHART A-7 (3 OF 3)
- DISCONNECT VACUUM HOSE FROM PRESSURE REGULATOR AND PLUG HOSE.
- START ENGINE AND ENSURE THAT A/C IS "OFF".
- NOTE FUEL PRESSURE
- PRESSURE SHOULD BE 262-303 kPa (38-44 psi) AND HOLDING STEADY. IS IT?

YES

NO

2
- IDLE ENGINE AT NORMAL OPERATING TEMPERATURE.
- RECONNECT VACUUM LINE.
- FUEL PRESSURE SHOULD BE 207-241 kPa (30-35 psi) IS IT?

4
PRESSURE WITHIN SPECIFICATION, BUT NOT HOLDING.

PRESSURE OUT OF SPECIFICATION.

NO PRESSURE

USE PAGE 2 OF THIS CHART.

USE CHART A-5.

NO

YES

3
- DISCONNECT VACUUM HOSE FROM FUEL PRESSURE REGULATOR.
- WITH ENGINE IDLING, APPLY 12-14" Hg OF VACUUM TO PRESSURE REGULATOR.
- FUEL PRESSURE SHOULD DROP SLIGHTLY. DID IT?

NO TROUBLE FOUND. REFER TO "DIAGNOSTIC AIDS" ON FACING PAGE.

- IGNITION "OFF."
- CONNECT FUSED JUMPER FROM "B +" TO FP ON CHECK CONECTOR IN ENGINE COMPARTMENT
- IGNITION ON
- GRADUALLY BLOCK FUEL PRESSURE LINE BY PINCHING FLEX HOSE.
- REMOVE JUMPER FROM CHECK CONNECTOR WHILE CONTINUING TO BLOCK PRESSURE LINE.
- PRESSURE SHOULD HOLD. DID IT?

YES

NO

LOCATE AND CORRECT CAUSE OF INTERRUPTED MANIFOLD PRESSURE SUPPLY TO REGULATOR.

PRESSURE REGULATOR ASSEMBLY IS FAULTY.

NO

YES

- REPEAT ABOVE PROCEDURE WHILE BLOCKING FUEL RETURN LINE INSTEAD OF PRESSURE LINE BY PINCHING FLEX HOSE.
- PRESSURE SHOULD HOLD. DID IT?

CHECK FOR
- LEAKING PUMP COUPLING HOSE
- FAULTY IN-TANK PUMP.

NO

YES

LOCATE AND REPLACE LEAKING INJECTOR AND DRY SPARK PLUGS FROM FLOODED CYLINDERS.

PRESSURE REGULATOR ASSEMBLY IS FAULTY.

Fig. 104 Fuel system diagnosis — 1989-90 VIN code 6 engine

CHART A-7

(Page 2 of 3)
FUEL SYSTEM PRESSURE TEST
1.6L (VIN 6) "S" CARLINE (PORT)

Circuit Description:

The fuel pump delivers fuel to the fuel rail and injectors, where the system pressure is controlled from 262 to 303 kPa (38 to 44 psi) by the pressure regulator. Excess fuel is returned to the fuel tank. When the engine is stopped, the pump can be energized by applying battery voltage to the test terminal located in the engine compartment.

Test Description: Numbers below refer to circled numbers on the diagnostic chart.

5. Pressure less than 262 kPa (38 psi) may be caused by one of two problems.
   - The regulated fuel pressure is too low. The system will be running lean and may set Code 25. Also, hard cold starting and overall poor performance is possible.
   - Restricted flow is causing a pressure drop. Normally, a vehicle with a fuel pressure loss at idle will not be driveable. However, if the pressure drop occurs only while driving, the engine will surge and then stop as pressure begins to drop rapidly.

6. Restricting the fuel return line allows the fuel pump to build above regulated pressure. When battery voltage is applied to "Fp" on the check connector, pressure should be above 450 kPa (65 psi).

7. This test determines if the high fuel pressure is due to a restricted fuel return line or a pressure regulator problem.

Fig. 105 Fuel system diagnosis — 1989-90 VIN code 6 engine

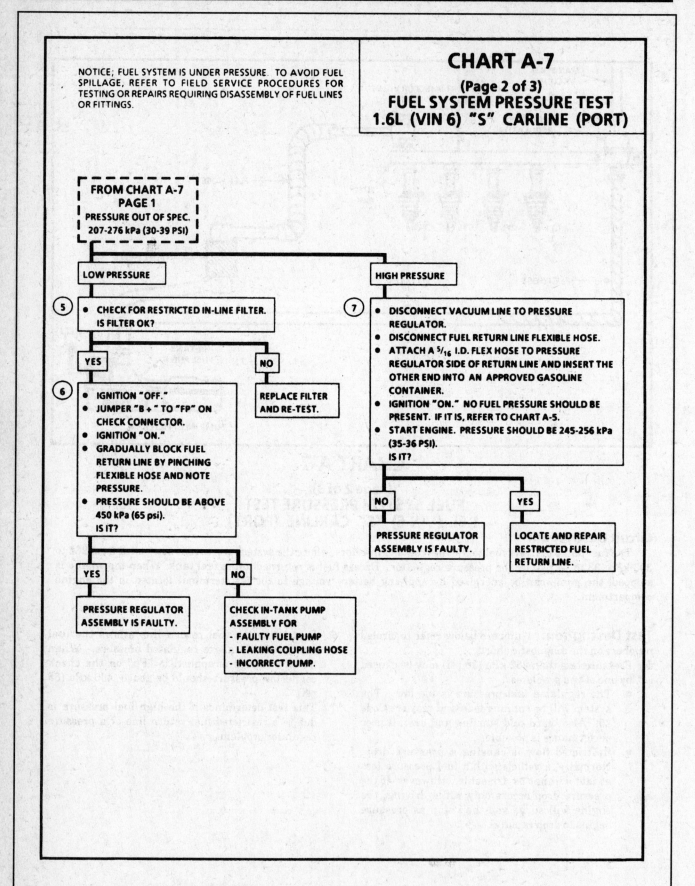

CHART A-7
(Page 2 of 3)
FUEL SYSTEM PRESSURE TEST
1.6L (VIN 6) "S" CARLINE (PORT)

NOTICE; FUEL SYSTEM IS UNDER PRESSURE. TO AVOID FUEL SPILLAGE, REFER TO FIELD SERVICE PROCEDURES FOR TESTING OR REPAIRS REQUIRING DISASSEMBLY OF FUEL LINES OR FITTINGS.

FROM CHART A-7
PAGE 1
PRESSURE OUT OF SPEC.
207-276 kPa (30-39 PSI)

LOW PRESSURE

5 • CHECK FOR RESTRICTED IN-LINE FILTER. IS FILTER OK?

YES

NO

6 • IGNITION "OFF."
• JUMPER "B +" TO "FP" ON CHECK CONNECTOR.
• IGNITION "ON."
• GRADUALLY BLOCK FUEL RETURN LINE BY PINCHING FLEXIBLE HOSE AND NOTE PRESSURE.
• PRESSURE SHOULD BE ABOVE 450 kPa (65 psi). IS IT?

REPLACE FILTER AND RE-TEST.

YES

NO

PRESSURE REGULATOR ASSEMBLY IS FAULTY.

CHECK IN-TANK PUMP ASSEMBLY FOR
- FAULTY FUEL PUMP
- LEAKING COUPLING HOSE
- INCORRECT PUMP.

HIGH PRESSURE

7 • DISCONNECT VACUUM LINE TO PRESSURE REGULATOR.
• DISCONNECT FUEL RETURN LINE FLEXIBLE HOSE.
• ATTACH A 5/16 I.D. FLEX HOSE TO PRESSURE REGULATOR SIDE OF RETURN LINE AND INSERT THE OTHER END INTO AN APPROVED GASOLINE CONTAINER.
• IGNITION "ON." NO FUEL PRESSURE SHOULD BE PRESENT. IF IT IS, REFER TO CHART A-5.
• START ENGINE. PRESSURE SHOULD BE 245-256 kPa (35-36 PSI). IS IT?

NO

YES

PRESSURE REGULATOR ASSEMBLY IS FAULTY.

LOCATE AND REPAIR RESTRICTED FUEL RETURN LINE.

Fig. 106 Fuel system diagnosis — 1989-90 VIN code 6 engine

CHART A-7

(3 of 3)
FUEL SYSTEM PRESSURE TEST
1.6L (VIN 6) "S" CARLINE (PORT)

The follow procedure outlines the installation a removal of the Fuel Pressure Gage Assembly. Make certain to observe all "Cautions" while performing this procedure.

Required Tools:

Port Fuel Pressure Gage   J 34730-1
Fuel Rail Adaptor   J 38347

Fig. 107 Fuel system diagnosis — 1989-90 VIN code 6 engine

CAUTION: TO REDUCE THE RISK OF FIRE AND PERSONAL INJURY, RELIEVE FUEL SYSTEM PRESSURE BEFORE DISCONNECTING FUEL LINES.

- LOOSEN FUEL FILLER CAP TO RELIEVE TANK PRESSURE.
- REMOVE CIRCUIT OPENING RELAY, LOCATED UNDER CONSOLE IN FRONT OF SHIFT LEVER.
- CRANK ENGINE AND ALLOW TO RUN UNTIL IT STALLS.
- ENGAGE STARTER FOR 30 SECONDS.
- USE SHOP TOWEL TO COLLECT FUEL DURING FUEL LINE DISCONNECT, PLACE TOWEL IN APPROVED CONTAINER.

CHART A-7
(3 OF 3)
FUEL SYSTEM PRESSURE TEST
1.6L (VIN 6) "S" CARLINE (PORT)

FUEL PRESSURE GAGE INSTALLATION

1. IGNITION "OFF". DISCONNECT NEGATIVE BATTERY CABLE.
2. CAREFULLY, REMOVE COLD START INJECTOR VALVE FUEL LINE HOLD DOWN BOLT AT THE FUEL RAIL.
3. INSTALL ADAPTER J 38347 AND TIGHTEN SECURELY.
4. INSTALL FUEL PRESSURE GAGE J 34370-1 AND TIGHTEN SECURELY.
5. RECONNECT NEGATIVE BATTERY CABLE.
6. REINSTALL CIRCUIT OPENING RELAY.
7. START ENGINE AND CHECK FOR LEAKS.
8. PURGE AIR FROM FUEL PRESSURE GAGE INTO AN APPROVED CONTAINER.
9. PROCEED TO FUEL SYSTEM PRESSURE TEST CHART A-7 (1 OF 3).

FUEL PRESSURE GAGE REMOVAL

1. REMOVE NEGATIVE BATTERY CABLE.
2. PURGE FUEL PRESSURE FROM FUEL PRESSURE GAGE INTO AN APPROVED CONTAINER.
3. CAREFULLY DISCONNECT FUEL PRESSURE GAGE.
4. REMOVE ADAPTER.
5. REINSTALL FUEL LINE HOLD DOWN BOLT. TIGHTEN TO SPECIFICATION.
6. RECONNECT NEGATIVE BATTERY CABLE.
7. START ENGINE AND CHECK FOR FUEL LEAKS.

Fig. 108 Fuel system diagnosis — 1989-90 VIN code 6 engine

CHART A-9

COLD START INJECTOR VALVE
1.6L (VIN 6) "S" CARLINE (PORT)

Circuit Description:

The cold start injector valve is used to provide additional fuel during the crank mode to improve cold start-ups. This circuit is important when engine coolant temperature is low because the other injectors are not pulsed "ON" long enough to provide the needed amount of fuel to start.

The circuit is activated only in the crank mode. The power is supplied directly from the starter solenoid and is protected by a fuse. The system is controlled by a cold start fuel injection switch which provides a ground path for the valve during cranking when engine coolant is below 35°C (95°F).

The switch contains a bimetal material which opens at a specified coolant temperature. This bimetal is also heated by the winding in the thermal switch which allows the valve to stay "ON" for 8 seconds at -20°C (-5°F) coolant. The time the switch will stay closed varies inversely with coolant temperature. In other words, as the coolant temperature goes up, the cold start injector valve "ON" time goes down.

Test Description: Numbers below refer to circled numbers on the diagnostic chart.

1. Disconnecting the distributor 4-way connector will disable the other injectors. The amount of pressure drop depends on the temperature of the engine.

2. This test will determine the continuity through the switch to ground.

Fig. 109 Fuel system diagnosis — 1989-90 VIN code 6 engine

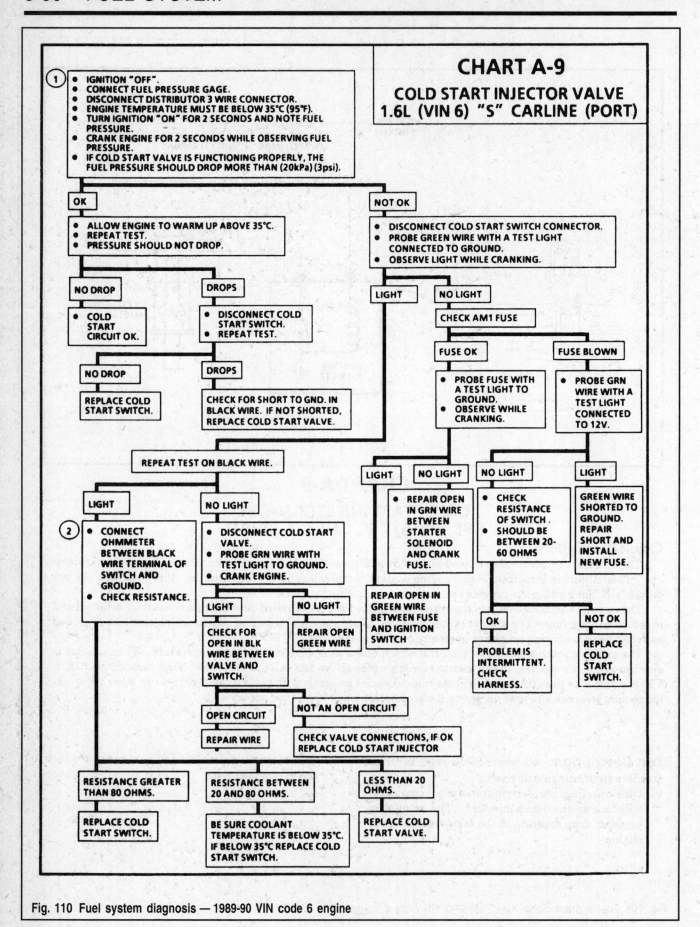

CHART A-9
COLD START INJECTOR VALVE
1.6L (VIN 6) "S" CARLINE (PORT)

1
- IGNITION "OFF".
- CONNECT FUEL PRESSURE GAGE.
- DISCONNECT DISTRIBUTOR 3 WIRE CONNECTOR.
- ENGINE TEMPERATURE MUST BE BELOW 35°C (95°F).
- TURN IGNITION "ON" FOR 2 SECONDS AND NOTE FUEL PRESSURE.
- CRANK ENGINE FOR 2 SECONDS WHILE OBSERVING FUEL PRESSURE.
- IF COLD START VALVE IS FUNCTIONING PROPERLY, THE FUEL PRESSURE SHOULD DROP MORE THAN (20kPa) (3psi).

OK
- ALLOW ENGINE TO WARM UP ABOVE 35°C.
- REPEAT TEST.
- PRESSURE SHOULD NOT DROP.

NO DROP
- COLD START CIRCUIT OK.

DROPS
- DISCONNECT COLD START SWITCH.
- REPEAT TEST.

NO DROP
- REPLACE COLD START SWITCH.

DROPS
CHECK FOR SHORT TO GND. IN BLACK WIRE. IF NOT SHORTED, REPLACE COLD START VALVE.

REPEAT TEST ON BLACK WIRE.

LIGHT

2
- CONNECT OHMMETER BETWEEN BLACK WIRE TERMINAL OF SWITCH AND GROUND.
- CHECK RESISTANCE.

NO LIGHT
- DISCONNECT COLD START VALVE.
- PROBE GRN WIRE WITH TEST LIGHT TO GROUND.
- CRANK ENGINE.

LIGHT
CHECK FOR OPEN IN BLK WIRE BETWEEN VALVE AND SWITCH.

NO LIGHT
REPAIR OPEN GREEN WIRE

OPEN CIRCUIT
REPAIR WIRE

NOT AN OPEN CIRCUIT
CHECK VALVE CONNECTIONS, IF OK REPLACE COLD START INJECTOR

RESISTANCE GREATER THAN 80 OHMS.
REPLACE COLD START SWITCH.

RESISTANCE BETWEEN 20 AND 80 OHMS.
BE SURE COOLANT TEMPERATURE IS BELOW 35°C. IF BELOW 35°C REPLACE COLD START SWITCH.

LESS THAN 20 OHMS.
REPLACE COLD START VALVE.

NOT OK
- DISCONNECT COLD START SWITCH CONNECTOR.
- PROBE GREEN WIRE WITH A TEST LIGHT CONNECTED TO GROUND.
- OBSERVE LIGHT WHILE CRANKING.

LIGHT

NO LIGHT
CHECK AM1 FUSE

FUSE OK
- PROBE FUSE WITH A TEST LIGHT TO GROUND.
- OBSERVE WHILE CRANKING.

FUSE BLOWN
- PROBE GRN WIRE WITH A TEST LIGHT CONNECTED TO 12V.

LIGHT
REPAIR OPEN IN GRN WIRE BETWEEN STARTER SOLENOID AND CRANK FUSE.

NO LIGHT
REPAIR OPEN IN GREEN WIRE BETWEEN FUSE AND IGNITION SWITCH

NO LIGHT
- CHECK RESISTANCE OF SWITCH. SHOULD BE BETWEEN 20-60 OHMS

LIGHT
GREEN WIRE SHORTED TO GROUND. REPAIR SHORT AND INSTALL NEW FUSE.

OK
PROBLEM IS INTERMITTENT. CHECK HARNESS.

NOT OK
REPLACE COLD START SWITCH.

Fig. 110 Fuel system diagnosis — 1989-90 VIN code 6 engine

CHART A-5

ENGINE CRANKS BUT WILL NOT RUN
(FUEL SYSTEM ELECTRICAL TEST)
1.6L (VIN 5) "S" CARLINE (PORT)

Circuit Description:

When the engine is cranked the signal from starter will turn "ON" the circuit opening relay to operate the fuel pump. Once the engine has started, the starter signal is removed from circuit opening relay and the fuel control switch in MAF sensor continues to run fuel pump. If the fuel control switch in the MAF sensor is non-functional, the engine will start but will not stay running.

Test Description: Numbers below refer to circled numbers on the diagnostic chart.

1. Fuel pump should run when ignition is cranked.
2. Test for an open between fuel pump and ground circuit opening relay.
3. Checks for B+ signal to circuit opening relay.
4. Checks for proper MAF fuel pump switch.

Diagnostic Aids:

Visual inspection of wiring and connectors should be made if an intermittent problem exists.

Fig. 111 Fuel system diagnosis — 1990 VIN code 5 engine

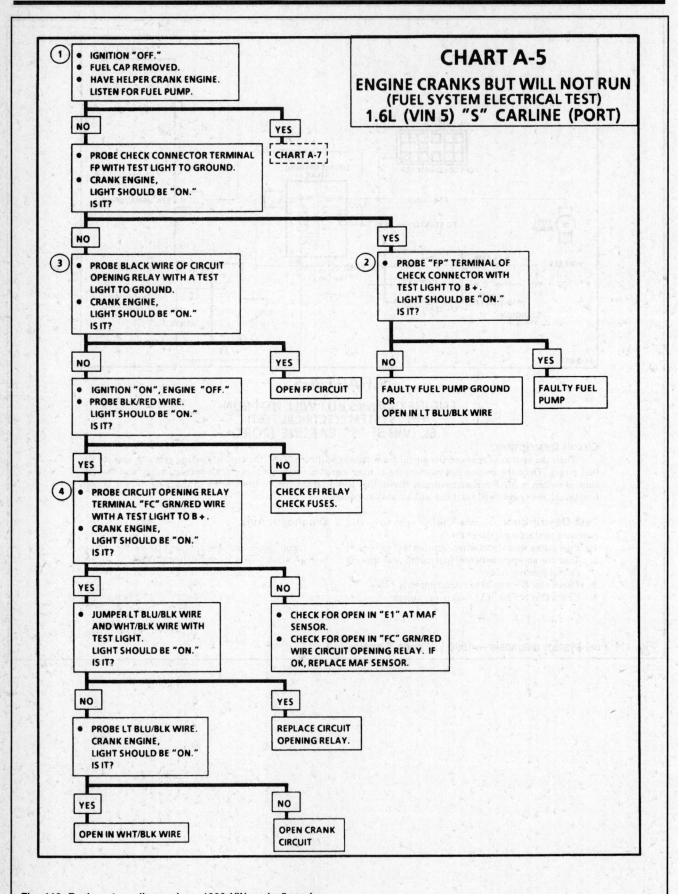

CHART A-5

ENGINE CRANKS BUT WILL NOT RUN
(FUEL SYSTEM ELECTRICAL TEST)
1.6L (VIN 5) "S" CARLINE (PORT)

1.
- IGNITION "OFF."
- FUEL CAP REMOVED.
- HAVE HELPER CRANK ENGINE.
  LISTEN FOR FUEL PUMP.

NO

YES → CHART A-7

- PROBE CHECK CONNECTOR TERMINAL FP WITH TEST LIGHT TO GROUND.
- CRANK ENGINE, LIGHT SHOULD BE "ON." IS IT?

NO

YES

3.
- PROBE BLACK WIRE OF CIRCUIT OPENING RELAY WITH A TEST LIGHT TO GROUND.
- CRANK ENGINE, LIGHT SHOULD BE "ON." IS IT?

2.
- PROBE "FP" TERMINAL OF CHECK CONNECTOR WITH TEST LIGHT TO B +. LIGHT SHOULD BE "ON." IS IT?

NO

YES → OPEN FP CIRCUIT

NO → FAULTY FUEL PUMP GROUND OR OPEN IN LT BLU/BLK WIRE

YES → FAULTY FUEL PUMP

- IGNITION "ON", ENGINE "OFF."
- PROBE BLK/RED WIRE. LIGHT SHOULD BE "ON." IS IT?

YES

NO → CHECK EFI RELAY CHECK FUSES.

4.
- PROBE CIRCUIT OPENING RELAY TERMINAL "FC" GRN/RED WIRE WITH A TEST LIGHT TO B +.
- CRANK ENGINE, LIGHT SHOULD BE "ON." IS IT?

YES

NO
- CHECK FOR OPEN IN "E1" AT MAF SENSOR.
- CHECK FOR OPEN IN "FC" GRN/RED WIRE CIRCUIT OPENING RELAY. IF OK, REPLACE MAF SENSOR.

- JUMPER LT BLU/BLK WIRE AND WHT/BLK WIRE WITH TEST LIGHT. LIGHT SHOULD BE "ON." IS IT?

NO

YES → REPLACE CIRCUIT OPENING RELAY.

- PROBE LT BLU/BLK WIRE. CRANK ENGINE, LIGHT SHOULD BE "ON." IS IT?

YES → OPEN IN WHT/BLK WIRE

NO → OPEN CRANK CIRCUIT

Fig. 112 Fuel system diagnosis — 1990 VIN code 5 engine

CHART A-7

(Page 1 of 3)
FUEL SYSTEM PRESSURE TEST
1.6L (VIN 5) "S" CARLINE (PORT)

Circuit Description:

The fuel pump delivers fuel to the fuel rail and injectors, where the system pressure is controlled from 265 to 304 kPa (38 to 44 psi) by the pressure regulator. Excess fuel is returned to the fuel tank. When the engine is stopped, the pump can be energized by applying battery voltage to the test terminal located in the engine compartment. With engine turned "OFF," fuel pressure should remain above 147 kPa (21 psi) for five minutes.

Test Description: Numbers below refer to circled numbers on the diagnostic chart.

1. Use pressure gage J 34730-1. Wrap a shop towel around the fuel pressure tap to absorb any small amount of fuel leakage that may occur when installing the gage. (The pressure will not leak down after the fuel pump is stopped on a correctly functioning system.)
2. While the engine is idling, manifold pressure is low (vacuum). When applied to the fuel regulator diaphragm, the pressure will result in a lower fuel pressure of about 207-241 kPa (30-35 psi).
3. The application of vacuum to the pressure regulator should result in a fuel pressure drop.

4. Pressure leak-down may be caused by one of the following:
   - In-tank fuel pump check valve not holding
   - Pump coupling hose leaking
   - Fuel pressure regulator valve leaking
   - Injector sticking open

Diagnostic Aids:

Improper fuel system pressure may contribute to one or all of the following symptoms:
- Cranks but won't run.
- Cutting out (May feel like ignition problem).
- Hesitation, loss of power or poor fuel economy.

Fig. 113 Fuel system diagnosis — 1990 VIN code 5 engine

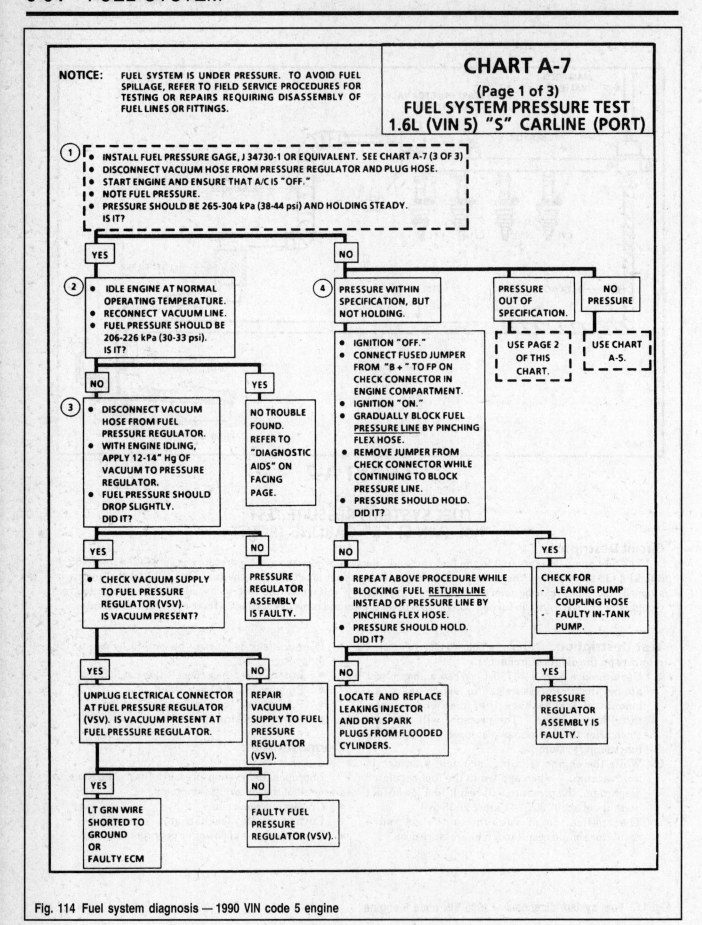

NOTICE: FUEL SYSTEM IS UNDER PRESSURE. TO AVOID FUEL SPILLAGE, REFER TO FIELD SERVICE PROCEDURES FOR TESTING OR REPAIRS REQUIRING DISASSEMBLY OF FUEL LINES OR FITTINGS.

CHART A-7
(Page 1 of 3)
FUEL SYSTEM PRESSURE TEST
1.6L (VIN 5) "S" CARLINE (PORT)

1
- INSTALL FUEL PRESSURE GAGE, J 34730-1 OR EQUIVALENT. SEE CHART A-7 (3 OF 3)
- DISCONNECT VACUUM HOSE FROM PRESSURE REGULATOR AND PLUG HOSE.
- START ENGINE AND ENSURE THAT A/C IS "OFF."
- NOTE FUEL PRESSURE.
- PRESSURE SHOULD BE 265-304 kPa (38-44 psi) AND HOLDING STEADY. IS IT?

YES

NO

2
- IDLE ENGINE AT NORMAL OPERATING TEMPERATURE.
- RECONNECT VACUUM LINE.
- FUEL PRESSURE SHOULD BE 206-226 kPa (30-33 psi). IS IT?

4 PRESSURE WITHIN SPECIFICATION, BUT NOT HOLDING.

PRESSURE OUT OF SPECIFICATION.

NO PRESSURE

USE PAGE 2 OF THIS CHART.

USE CHART A-5.

NO

YES

- IGNITION "OFF."
- CONNECT FUSED JUMPER FROM "B +" TO FP ON CHECK CONNECTOR IN ENGINE COMPARTMENT.
- IGNITION "ON."
- GRADUALLY BLOCK FUEL PRESSURE LINE BY PINCHING FLEX HOSE.
- REMOVE JUMPER FROM CHECK CONNECTOR WHILE CONTINUING TO BLOCK PRESSURE LINE.
- PRESSURE SHOULD HOLD. DID IT?

3
- DISCONNECT VACUUM HOSE FROM FUEL PRESSURE REGULATOR.
- WITH ENGINE IDLING, APPLY 12-14" Hg OF VACUUM TO PRESSURE REGULATOR.
- FUEL PRESSURE SHOULD DROP SLIGHTLY. DID IT?

NO TROUBLE FOUND. REFER TO "DIAGNOSTIC AIDS" ON FACING PAGE.

YES

NO

NO

YES

- CHECK VACUUM SUPPLY TO FUEL PRESSURE REGULATOR (VSV). IS VACUUM PRESENT?

PRESSURE REGULATOR ASSEMBLY IS FAULTY.

- REPEAT ABOVE PROCEDURE WHILE BLOCKING FUEL RETURN LINE INSTEAD OF PRESSURE LINE BY PINCHING FLEX HOSE.
- PRESSURE SHOULD HOLD. DID IT?

CHECK FOR
- LEAKING PUMP COUPLING HOSE
- FAULTY IN-TANK PUMP.

YES

NO

NO

YES

UNPLUG ELECTRICAL CONNECTOR AT FUEL PRESSURE REGULATOR (VSV). IS VACUUM PRESENT AT FUEL PRESSURE REGULATOR.

REPAIR VACUUM SUPPLY TO FUEL PRESSURE REGULATOR (VSV).

LOCATE AND REPLACE LEAKING INJECTOR AND DRY SPARK PLUGS FROM FLOODED CYLINDERS.

PRESSURE REGULATOR ASSEMBLY IS FAULTY.

YES

NO

LT GRN WIRE SHORTED TO GROUND OR FAULTY ECM

FAULTY FUEL PRESSURE REGULATOR (VSV).

Fig. 114 Fuel system diagnosis — 1990 VIN code 5 engine

CHART A-7

(Page 2 of 3)
FUEL SYSTEM PRESSURE TEST
1.6L (VIN 5) "S" CARLINE (PORT)

Circuit Description:

The fuel pump delivers fuel to the fuel rail and injectors, where the system pressure is controlled from 265 to 304 kPa (38 to 44 psi) by the pressure regulator. Excess fuel is returned to the fuel tank. When the engine is stopped, the pump can be energized by applying battery voltage to the test terminal located in the engine compartment. With engine turned "OFF," fuel pressure should remain above 21 psi (147 kPa) for five minutes.

Test Description: Numbers below refer to circled numbers on the diagnostic chart.

5. Pressure less than 265 kPa (38 psi) may be caused by one of two problems.
   - The regulated fuel pressure is too low. The system will be running lean and may set Code 25. Also, hard cold starting and overall poor performance is possible.
   - Restricted flow is causing a pressure drop. Normally, a vehicle with a fuel pressure loss at idle will not be driveable. However, if the pressure drop occurs only while driving, the engine will surge and then stop as pressure begins to drop rapidly.

6. Restricting the fuel return line allows the fuel pump to build above regulated pressure. When battery voltage is applied to "Fp" on the check connector, pressure should be above 450 kPa (65 psi).
7. This test determines if the high fuel pressure is due to a restricted fuel return line or a pressure regulator problem.

Fig. 115 Fuel system diagnosis — 1990 VIN code 5 engine

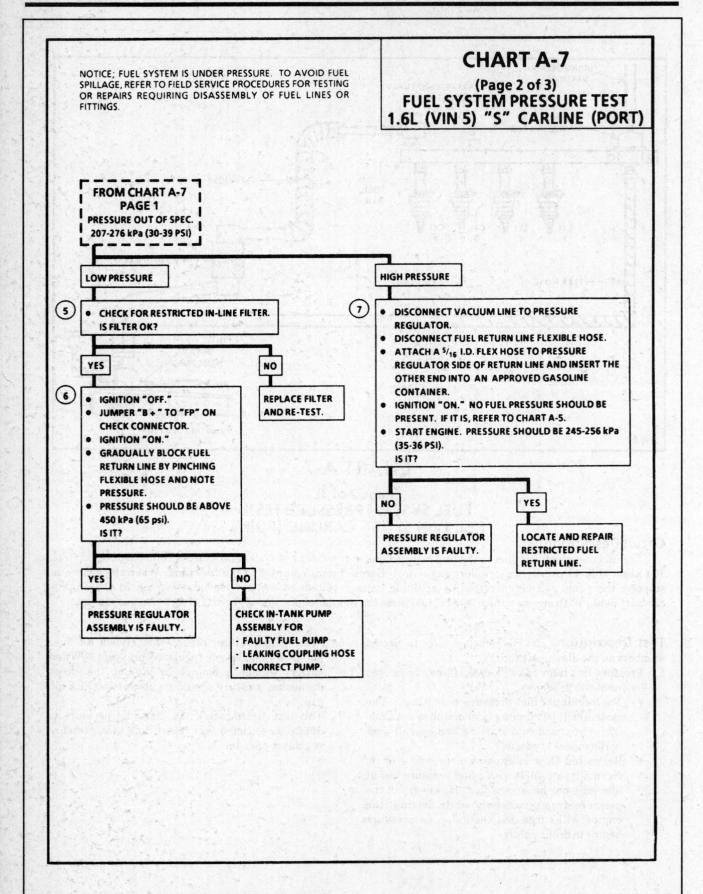

NOTICE; FUEL SYSTEM IS UNDER PRESSURE. TO AVOID FUEL SPILLAGE, REFER TO FIELD SERVICE PROCEDURES FOR TESTING OR REPAIRS REQUIRING DISASSEMBLY OF FUEL LINES OR FITTINGS.

CHART A-7
(Page 2 of 3)
FUEL SYSTEM PRESSURE TEST
1.6L (VIN 5) "S" CARLINE (PORT)

FROM CHART A-7
PAGE 1
PRESSURE OUT OF SPEC.
207-276 kPa (30-39 PSI)

LOW PRESSURE

5 • CHECK FOR RESTRICTED IN-LINE FILTER.
IS FILTER OK?

YES

NO

REPLACE FILTER AND RE-TEST.

6 • IGNITION "OFF."
• JUMPER "B + " TO "FP" ON CHECK CONNECTOR.
• IGNITION "ON."
• GRADUALLY BLOCK FUEL RETURN LINE BY PINCHING FLEXIBLE HOSE AND NOTE PRESSURE.
• PRESSURE SHOULD BE ABOVE 450 kPa (65 psi).
IS IT?

YES

NO

PRESSURE REGULATOR ASSEMBLY IS FAULTY.

CHECK IN-TANK PUMP ASSEMBLY FOR
- FAULTY FUEL PUMP
- LEAKING COUPLING HOSE
- INCORRECT PUMP.

HIGH PRESSURE

7 • DISCONNECT VACUUM LINE TO PRESSURE REGULATOR.
• DISCONNECT FUEL RETURN LINE FLEXIBLE HOSE.
• ATTACH A 5/16 I.D. FLEX HOSE TO PRESSURE REGULATOR SIDE OF RETURN LINE AND INSERT THE OTHER END INTO AN APPROVED GASOLINE CONTAINER.
• IGNITION "ON." NO FUEL PRESSURE SHOULD BE PRESENT. IF IT IS, REFER TO CHART A-5.
• START ENGINE. PRESSURE SHOULD BE 245-256 kPa (35-36 PSI).
IS IT?

NO

YES

PRESSURE REGULATOR ASSEMBLY IS FAULTY.

LOCATE AND REPAIR RESTRICTED FUEL RETURN LINE.

Fig. 116 Fuel system diagnosis — 1990 VIN code 5 engine

CHART A-7

(Page 3 of 3)
FUEL SYSTEM PRESSURE TEST
1.6L (VIN 5) "S" CARLINE (PORT)

The following procedure outlines the installation a removal of the fuel pressure gage assembly. Make certain to observe all "Cautions" while performing this procedure.

Required Tools:

Port Fuel Pressure Gage	J 34730-1
Fuel Rail Adaptor	J 38347

Fig. 117 Fuel system diagnosis — 1990 VIN code 5 engine

CAUTION: TO REDUCE THE RISK OF FIRE AND PERSONAL INJURY, RELIEVE FUEL SYSTEM PRESSURE BEFORE DISCONNECTING FUEL LINES.

- LOOSEN FUEL FILLER CAP TO RELIEVE TANK PRESSURE.
- REMOVE CIRCUIT OPENING RELAY, LOCATED UNDER CONSOLE IN FRONT OF SHIFT LEVER.
- CRANK ENGINE AND ALLOW TO RUN UNTIL IT STALLS.
- ENGAGE STARTER FOR 30 SECONDS.
- USE SHOP TOWEL TO COLLECT FUEL DURING FUEL LINE DISCONNECT, PLACE TOWEL IN APPROVED CONTAINER.

FUEL PRESSURE GAGE INSTALLATION

1. IGNITION "OFF". DISCONNECT NEGATIVE BATTERY CABLE.
2. CAREFULLY, REMOVE COLD START INJECTOR VALVE FUEL LINE HOLD DOWN BOLT <u>AT THE FUEL RAIL</u>.
3. INSTALL ADAPTER J 38347 AND TIGHTEN SECURELY.
4. INSTALL FUEL PRESSURE GAGE J 34370-1 AND TIGHTEN SECURELY.
5. RECONNECT NEGATIVE BATTERY CABLE.
6. REINSTALL CIRCUIT OPENING RELAY.
7. START ENGINE AND CHECK FOR LEAKS.
8. PURGE AIR FROM FUEL PRESSURE GAGE INTO AN APPROVED CONTAINER.
9. PROCEED TO FUEL SYSTEM PRESSURE TEST CHART A-7 (1 OF 3).

FUEL PRESSURE GAGE REMOVAL

1. REMOVE NEGATIVE BATTERY CABLE.
2. PURGE FUEL PRESSURE FROM FUEL PRESSURE GAGE INTO AN APPROVED CONTAINER.
3. CAREFULLY DISCONNECT FUEL PRESSURE GAGE.
4. REMOVE ADAPTER.
5. REINSTALL FUEL LINE HOLD DOWN BOLT. TIGHTEN TO SPECIFICATION.
6. RECONNECT NEGATIVE BATTERY CABLE.
7. START ENGINE AND CHECK FOR FUEL LEAKS.

Fig. 118 Fuel system diagnosis — 1990 VIN code 5 engine

CHART A-9

COLD START INJECTOR VALVE
1.6L (VIN 5) "S" CARLINE (PORT)

Circuit Description:

The cold start injector valve is used to provide additional fuel during the crank mode to improve cold start-ups. This circuit is important when engine coolant temperature is low because the other injectors are not pulsed "ON" long enough to provide the needed amount of fuel to start.

The circuit is activated only in the crank mode. The power is supplied directly from the starter solenoid and is protected by a fuse. The system is controlled by a cold start fuel injection switch which provides a ground path for the valve during cranking when engine coolant is below 35°C (95°F).

The switch contains a bimetal material which opens at a specified coolant temperature. This bimetal is also heated by the winding in the thermal switch which allows the valve to stay "ON" for 8 seconds at -20°C (-5°F) coolant. The time the switch will stay closed varies inversely with coolant temperature. In other words, as the coolant temperature goes up, the cold start injector valve "ON" time goes down.

Test Description: Numbers below refer to circled numbers on the diagnostic chart.

1. Disconnecting the distributor 2-way connector will disable the other injectors. The amount of pressure drop depends on the temperature of the engine.

2. This test will determine the continuity through the switch to ground.

Fig. 119 Fuel system diagnosis — 1990 VIN code 5 engine

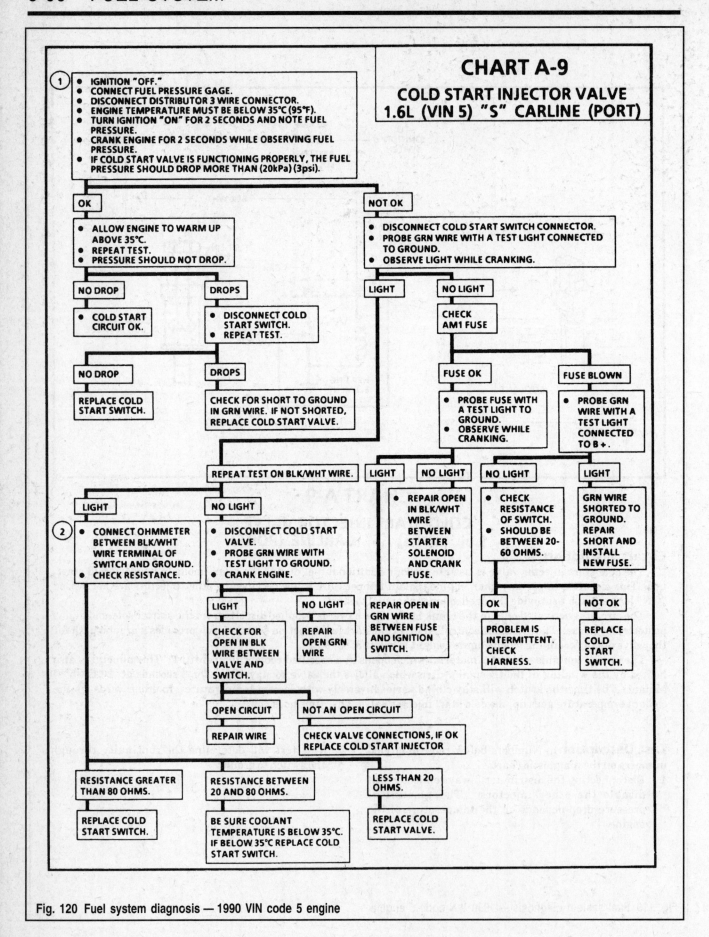

CHART A-9
COLD START INJECTOR VALVE
1.6L (VIN 5) "S" CARLINE (PORT)

1
- IGNITION "OFF."
- CONNECT FUEL PRESSURE GAGE.
- DISCONNECT DISTRIBUTOR 3 WIRE CONNECTOR.
- ENGINE TEMPERATURE MUST BE BELOW 35°C (95°F).
- TURN IGNITION "ON" FOR 2 SECONDS AND NOTE FUEL PRESSURE.
- CRANK ENGINE FOR 2 SECONDS WHILE OBSERVING FUEL PRESSURE.
- IF COLD START VALVE IS FUNCTIONING PROPERLY, THE FUEL PRESSURE SHOULD DROP MORE THAN (20kPa) (3psi).

OK
- ALLOW ENGINE TO WARM UP ABOVE 35°C.
- REPEAT TEST.
- PRESSURE SHOULD NOT DROP.

NO DROP
- COLD START CIRCUIT OK.

DROPS
- DISCONNECT COLD START SWITCH.
- REPEAT TEST.

NO DROP
REPLACE COLD START SWITCH.

DROPS
CHECK FOR SHORT TO GROUND IN GRN WIRE. IF NOT SHORTED, REPLACE COLD START VALVE.

NOT OK
- DISCONNECT COLD START SWITCH CONNECTOR.
- PROBE GRN WIRE WITH A TEST LIGHT CONNECTED TO GROUND.
- OBSERVE LIGHT WHILE CRANKING.

LIGHT

NO LIGHT
CHECK AM1 FUSE

FUSE OK
- PROBE FUSE WITH A TEST LIGHT TO GROUND.
- OBSERVE WHILE CRANKING.

FUSE BLOWN
- PROBE GRN WIRE WITH A TEST LIGHT CONNECTED TO B + .

LIGHT
- REPAIR OPEN IN BLK/WHT WIRE BETWEEN STARTER SOLENOID AND CRANK FUSE.

NO LIGHT

NO LIGHT
- CHECK RESISTANCE OF SWITCH.
- SHOULD BE BETWEEN 20-60 OHMS.

LIGHT
GRN WIRE SHORTED TO GROUND. REPAIR SHORT AND INSTALL NEW FUSE.

REPEAT TEST ON BLK/WHT WIRE.

LIGHT

2
- CONNECT OHMMETER BETWEEN BLK/WHT WIRE TERMINAL OF SWITCH AND GROUND.
- CHECK RESISTANCE.

NO LIGHT
- DISCONNECT COLD START VALVE.
- PROBE GRN WIRE WITH TEST LIGHT TO GROUND.
- CRANK ENGINE.

LIGHT
CHECK FOR OPEN IN BLK WIRE BETWEEN VALVE AND SWITCH.

NO LIGHT
REPAIR OPEN GRN WIRE

REPAIR OPEN IN GRN WIRE BETWEEN FUSE AND IGNITION SWITCH.

OK
PROBLEM IS INTERMITTENT. CHECK HARNESS.

NOT OK
REPLACE COLD START SWITCH.

OPEN CIRCUIT
REPAIR WIRE

NOT AN OPEN CIRCUIT
CHECK VALVE CONNECTIONS, IF OK REPLACE COLD START INJECTOR

RESISTANCE GREATER THAN 80 OHMS.
REPLACE COLD START SWITCH.

RESISTANCE BETWEEN 20 AND 80 OHMS.
BE SURE COOLANT TEMPERATURE IS BELOW 35°C. IF BELOW 35°C REPLACE COLD START SWITCH.

LESS THAN 20 OHMS.
REPLACE COLD START VALVE.

Fig. 120 Fuel system diagnosis — 1990 VIN code 5 engine

CHART A-5

ENGINE CRANKS BUT WILL NOT RUN
(FUEL SYSTEM ELECTRICAL TEST)
1.6L (VIN 5) "S" CARLINE (PORT)

Circuit Description:

    When the engine is cranked the signal from starter will turn "ON" the circuit opening relay to operate the fuel pump. Once the engine has started, the starter signal is removed from circuit opening relay and the fuel control switch in MAF sensor continues to run fuel pump. If the fuel control switch in the MAF sensor is nonfunctional, the engine will start but will not stay running.

Test Description: Number(s) below refer to circled number(s) on the diagnostic chart.

1. Fuel pump should run when ignition is cranked.
2. Test for B+ from circuit opening relay to fuel pump.
3. Checks for B+ signal to circuit opening relay.
4. Checks for proper MAF fuel pump switch.

Diagnostic Aids:

    Visual inspection of wiring and connectors should be made if an intermittent problem exists.

Fig. 121 Fuel system diagnosis — 1991 VIN code 5 engine

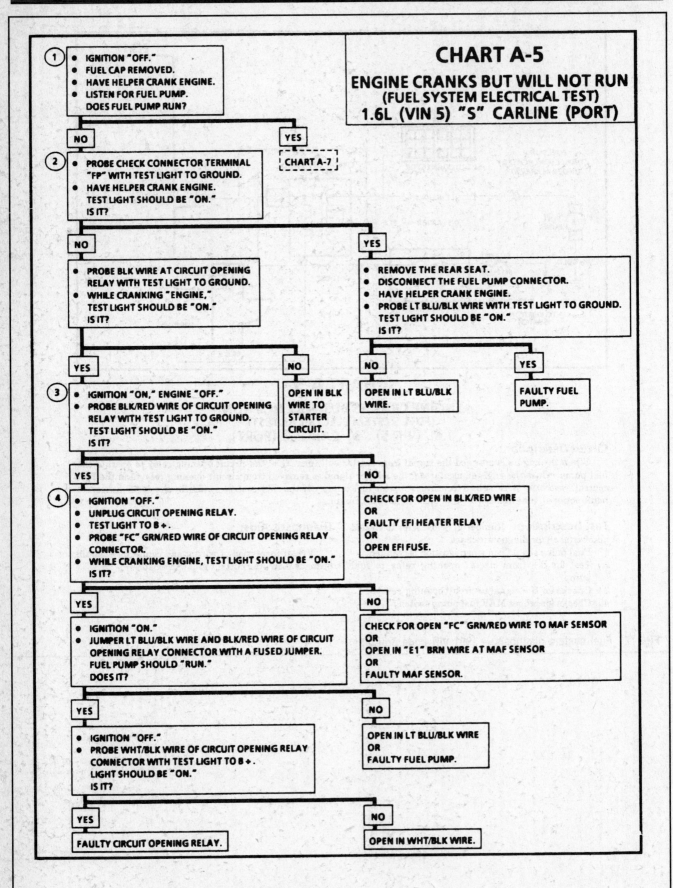

Fig. 122 Fuel system diagnosis — 1991 VIN code 5 engine

CHART A-7

(Page 1 of 3)
FUEL SYSTEM PRESSURE TEST
1.6L (VIN 5) "S" CARLINE (PORT)

Circuit Description:

The fuel pump delivers fuel to the fuel rail and injectors, where the system pressure is controlled from 265 to 304 kPa (38 to 44 psi) by the pressure regulator. Excess fuel is returned to the fuel tank. When the engine is stopped, the pump can be energized by applying battery voltage to the test terminal located in the engine compartment. With engine turned "OFF," fuel pressure should remain above 147 kPa (21 psi) for five minutes.

Test Description: Number(s) below refer to circled number(s) on the diagnostic chart.

1. Use pressure gage J 34730-1. Wrap a shop towel around the fuel pressure tap to absorb any small amount of fuel leakage that may occur when installing the gage. (The pressure will not leak down after the fuel pump is stopped on a correctly functioning system.)

2. While the engine is idling, manifold pressure is low (vacuum). When applied to the fuel regulator diaphragm, the pressure will result in a lower fuel pressure of about 207-241 kPa (30-35 psi).

3. The application of vacuum to the pressure regulator should result in a fuel pressure drop.

4. Pressure leak-down may be caused by one of the following:
   - In-tank fuel pump check valve not holding.
   - Pump coupling hose leaking.

   - Fuel pressure regulator valve leaking.
   - Injector sticking open.

4A.
   - Check for basic engine problem.
   - Check for water in fuel.

Diagnostic Aids:

Improper fuel system pressure may contribute to one or all of the following symptoms:
- Cranks but won't run.
- Cutting out (may feel like ignition problem).
- Hesitation, loss of power or poor fuel economy.

Fig. 123 Fuel system diagnosis — 1991 VIN code 5 engine

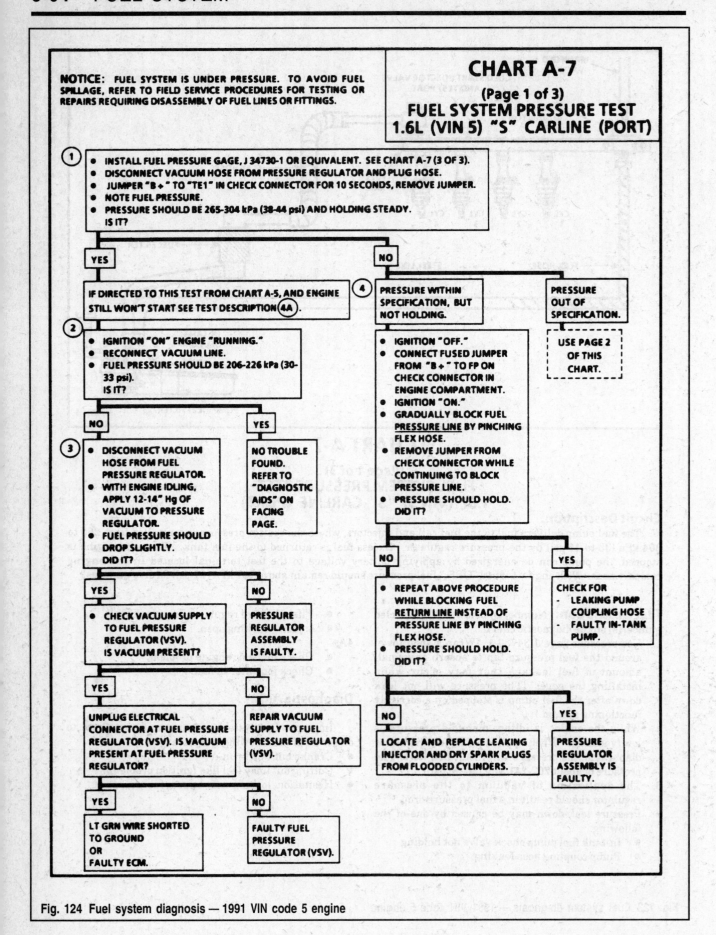

NOTICE: FUEL SYSTEM IS UNDER PRESSURE. TO AVOID FUEL SPILLAGE, REFER TO FIELD SERVICE PROCEDURES FOR TESTING OR REPAIRS REQUIRING DISASSEMBLY OF FUEL LINES OR FITTINGS.

CHART A-7
(Page 1 of 3)
FUEL SYSTEM PRESSURE TEST
1.6L (VIN 5) "S" CARLINE (PORT)

①
- INSTALL FUEL PRESSURE GAGE, J 34730-1 OR EQUIVALENT. SEE CHART A-7 (3 OF 3).
- DISCONNECT VACUUM HOSE FROM PRESSURE REGULATOR AND PLUG HOSE.
- JUMPER "B+" TO "TE1" IN CHECK CONNECTOR FOR 10 SECONDS, REMOVE JUMPER.
- NOTE FUEL PRESSURE.
- PRESSURE SHOULD BE 265-304 kPa (38-44 psi) AND HOLDING STEADY. IS IT?

YES

NO

IF DIRECTED TO THIS TEST FROM CHART A-5, AND ENGINE STILL WON'T START SEE TEST DESCRIPTION **④A**.

④ PRESSURE WITHIN SPECIFICATION, BUT NOT HOLDING.

PRESSURE OUT OF SPECIFICATION.

②
- IGNITION "ON" ENGINE "RUNNING."
- RECONNECT VACUUM LINE.
- FUEL PRESSURE SHOULD BE 206-226 kPa (30-33 psi). IS IT?

USE PAGE 2 OF THIS CHART.

- IGNITION "OFF."
- CONNECT FUSED JUMPER FROM "B+" TO FP ON CHECK CONNECTOR IN ENGINE COMPARTMENT.
- IGNITION "ON."
- GRADUALLY BLOCK FUEL PRESSURE LINE BY PINCHING FLEX HOSE.
- REMOVE JUMPER FROM CHECK CONNECTOR WHILE CONTINUING TO BLOCK PRESSURE LINE.
- PRESSURE SHOULD HOLD. DID IT?

NO

YES

③
- DISCONNECT VACUUM HOSE FROM FUEL PRESSURE REGULATOR.
- WITH ENGINE IDLING, APPLY 12-14" Hg OF VACUUM TO PRESSURE REGULATOR.
- FUEL PRESSURE SHOULD DROP SLIGHTLY. DID IT?

NO TROUBLE FOUND. REFER TO "DIAGNOSTIC AIDS" ON FACING PAGE.

NO

YES

- REPEAT ABOVE PROCEDURE WHILE BLOCKING FUEL RETURN LINE INSTEAD OF PRESSURE LINE BY PINCHING FLEX HOSE.
- PRESSURE SHOULD HOLD. DID IT?

CHECK FOR
- LEAKING PUMP COUPLING HOSE
- FAULTY IN-TANK PUMP.

YES

NO

- CHECK VACUUM SUPPLY TO FUEL PRESSURE REGULATOR (VSV). IS VACUUM PRESENT?

PRESSURE REGULATOR ASSEMBLY IS FAULTY.

NO

YES

LOCATE AND REPLACE LEAKING INJECTOR AND DRY SPARK PLUGS FROM FLOODED CYLINDERS.

PRESSURE REGULATOR ASSEMBLY IS FAULTY.

YES

NO

UNPLUG ELECTRICAL CONNECTOR AT FUEL PRESSURE REGULATOR (VSV). IS VACUUM PRESENT AT FUEL PRESSURE REGULATOR?

REPAIR VACUUM SUPPLY TO FUEL PRESSURE REGULATOR (VSV).

YES

NO

LT GRN WIRE SHORTED TO GROUND OR FAULTY ECM.

FAULTY FUEL PRESSURE REGULATOR (VSV).

Fig. 124 Fuel system diagnosis — 1991 VIN code 5 engine

CHART A-7

(Page 2 of 3)
FUEL SYSTEM PRESSURE TEST
1.6L (VIN 5) "S" CARLINE (PORT)

Circuit Description:

The fuel pump delivers fuel to the fuel rail and injectors, where the system pressure is controlled from 265 to 304 kPa (38 to 44 psi) by the pressure regulator. Excess fuel is returned to the fuel tank. When the engine is stopped, the pump can be energized by applying battery voltage to the test terminal located in the engine compartment. With engine turned "OFF," fuel pressure should remain above 21 psi (147 kPa) for five minutes.

Test Description: Number(s) below refer to circled number(s) on the diagnostic chart.

5. Pressure less than 265 kPa (38 psi) may be caused by one of two problems:
   - The regulated fuel pressure is too low. The system will be running lean and may set Code 25. Also, hard cold starting and overall poor performance is possible.
   - Restricted flow is causing a pressure drop. Normally, a vehicle with a fuel pressure loss at idle will not be drivable. However, if the pressure drop occurs only while driving, the engine will surge and then stop as pressure begins to drop rapidly.

6. Restricting the fuel return line allows the fuel pump to build above regulated pressure. When battery voltage is applied to "Fp" on the check connector, pressure should be above 450 kPa (65 psi).

7. This test determines if the high fuel pressure is due to a restricted fuel return line or a pressure regulator problem.

Fig. 125 Fuel system diagnosis — 1991 VIN code 5 engine

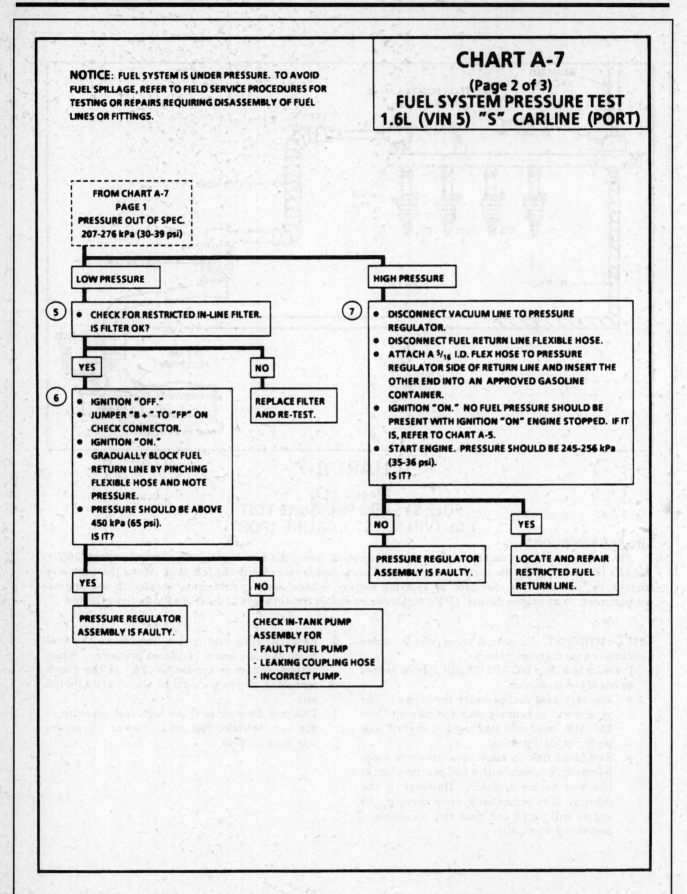

NOTICE: FUEL SYSTEM IS UNDER PRESSURE. TO AVOID FUEL SPILLAGE, REFER TO FIELD SERVICE PROCEDURES FOR TESTING OR REPAIRS REQUIRING DISASSEMBLY OF FUEL LINES OR FITTINGS.

CHART A-7
(Page 2 of 3)
FUEL SYSTEM PRESSURE TEST
1.6L (VIN 5) "S" CARLINE (PORT)

FROM CHART A-7
PAGE 1
PRESSURE OUT OF SPEC.
207-276 kPa (30-39 psi)

LOW PRESSURE

5 • CHECK FOR RESTRICTED IN-LINE FILTER. IS FILTER OK?

YES

NO

REPLACE FILTER AND RE-TEST.

6 • IGNITION "OFF."
• JUMPER "B +" TO "FP" ON CHECK CONNECTOR.
• IGNITION "ON."
• GRADUALLY BLOCK FUEL RETURN LINE BY PINCHING FLEXIBLE HOSE AND NOTE PRESSURE.
• PRESSURE SHOULD BE ABOVE 450 kPa (65 psi). IS IT?

YES

PRESSURE REGULATOR ASSEMBLY IS FAULTY.

NO

CHECK IN-TANK PUMP ASSEMBLY FOR
- FAULTY FUEL PUMP
- LEAKING COUPLING HOSE
- INCORRECT PUMP.

HIGH PRESSURE

7 • DISCONNECT VACUUM LINE TO PRESSURE REGULATOR.
• DISCONNECT FUEL RETURN LINE FLEXIBLE HOSE.
• ATTACH A $^5/_{16}$ I.D. FLEX HOSE TO PRESSURE REGULATOR SIDE OF RETURN LINE AND INSERT THE OTHER END INTO AN APPROVED GASOLINE CONTAINER.
• IGNITION "ON." NO FUEL PRESSURE SHOULD BE PRESENT WITH IGNITION "ON" ENGINE STOPPED. IF IT IS, REFER TO CHART A-5.
• START ENGINE. PRESSURE SHOULD BE 245-256 kPa (35-36 psi). IS IT?

NO

PRESSURE REGULATOR ASSEMBLY IS FAULTY.

YES

LOCATE AND REPAIR RESTRICTED FUEL RETURN LINE.

Fig. 126 Fuel system diagnosis — 1991 VIN code 5 engine

CHART A-7

(Page 3 of 3)
FUEL SYSTEM PRESSURE TEST
1.6L (VIN 5) "S" CARLINE (PORT)

The following procedure outlines the installation and removal of the fuel pressure gage assembly. Make certain to observe all "Cautions" while performing this procedure.

Required Tools:

Port Fuel Pressure Gage	J 34730-1
Fuel Rail Adaptor	J 38347

Fig. 127 Fuel system diagnosis — 1991 VIN code 5 engine

CAUTION: TO REDUCE THE RISK OF FIRE AND PERSONAL INJURY, RELIEVE FUEL SYSTEM PRESSURE BEFORE DISCONNECTING FUEL LINES.

- LOOSEN FUEL FILLER CAP TO RELIEVE TANK PRESSURE.
- REMOVE CIRCUIT OPENING RELAY, LOCATED UNDER CONSOLE IN FRONT OF SHIFT LEVER.
- CRANK ENGINE AND ALLOW TO RUN UNTIL IT STALLS.
- ENGAGE STARTER FOR 30 SECONDS.
- USE SHOP TOWEL TO COLLECT FUEL DURING FUEL LINE DISCONNECT, PLACE TOWEL IN APPROVED CONTAINER.

CHART A-7

(Page 3 of 3)
FUEL SYSTEM PRESSURE TEST
1.6L (VIN 5) "S" CARLINE (PORT)

FUEL PRESSURE GAGE INSTALLATION

1. IGNITION "OFF". DISCONNECT NEGATIVE BATTERY CABLE.
2. CAREFULLY, REMOVE COLD START INJECTOR VALVE FUEL LINE HOLD DOWN BOLT AT THE FUEL RAIL.
3. INSTALL ADAPTER J 38347 AND TIGHTEN SECURELY.
4. INSTALL FUEL PRESSURE GAGE J 34370-1 AND TIGHTEN SECURELY.
5. RECONNECT NEGATIVE BATTERY CABLE.
6. REINSTALL CIRCUIT OPENING RELAY.
7. START ENGINE AND CHECK FOR LEAKS.
8. PURGE AIR FROM FUEL PRESSURE GAGE INTO AN APPROVED CONTAINER.
9. PROCEED TO FUEL SYSTEM PRESSURE TEST CHART A-7 (1 OF 3).

FUEL PRESSURE GAGE REMOVAL

1. REMOVE NEGATIVE BATTERY CABLE.
2. PURGE FUEL PRESSURE FROM FUEL PRESSURE GAGE INTO AN APPROVED CONTAINER.
3. CAREFULLY DISCONNECT FUEL PRESSURE GAGE.
4. REMOVE ADAPTER.
5. REINSTALL FUEL LINE HOLD DOWN BOLT. TIGHTEN TO SPECIFICATION.
6. RECONNECT NEGATIVE BATTERY CABLE.
7. START ENGINE AND CHECK FOR FUEL LEAKS.

Fig. 128 Fuel system diagnosis — 1991 VIN code 5 engine

CHART A-9

COLD START INJECTOR VALVE
1.6L (VIN 5) "S" CARLINE (PORT)

Circuit Description:

The cold start injector valve is used to provide additional fuel during the crank mode to improve cold start-ups. This circuit is important when engine coolant temperature is low because the other injectors are not pulsed "ON" long enough to provide the needed amount of fuel to start.

The circuit is activated only in the crank mode. The power is supplied directly from the starter solenoid and is protected by a fuse. The system is controlled by a cold start fuel injection switch which provides a ground path for the valve during cranking when engine coolant is below 35°C (95°F).

The switch contains a bimetal material which opens at a specified coolant temperature. This bimetal is also heated by the winding in the thermal switch which allows the valve to stay "ON" for 8 seconds at -20°C (-5°F) coolant. The time the switch will stay closed varies inversely with coolant temperature. In other words, as the coolant temperature goes up, the cold start injector valve "ON" time goes down.

Test Description: Number(s) below refer to circled number(s) on the diagnostic chart.

1. Disconnecting the two distributor connectors will disable the other injectors. The amount of pressure drop depends on the temperature of the engine.

2. This test will determine the continuity through the switch to ground.

Fig. 129 Fuel system diagnosis — 1991 VIN code 5 engine

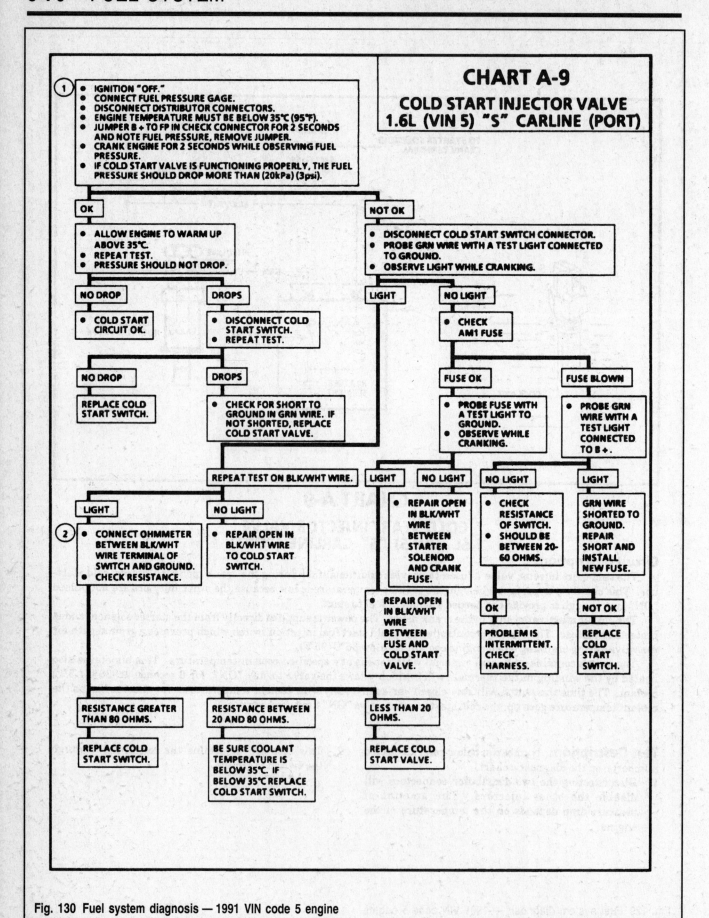

CHART A-9
COLD START INJECTOR VALVE
1.6L (VIN 5) "S" CARLINE (PORT)

1
- IGNITION "OFF."
- CONNECT FUEL PRESSURE GAGE.
- DISCONNECT DISTRIBUTOR CONNECTORS.
- ENGINE TEMPERATURE MUST BE BELOW 35°C (95°F).
- JUMPER B + TO FP IN CHECK CONNECTOR FOR 2 SECONDS AND NOTE FUEL PRESSURE, REMOVE JUMPER.
- CRANK ENGINE FOR 2 SECONDS WHILE OBSERVING FUEL PRESSURE.
- IF COLD START VALVE IS FUNCTIONING PROPERLY, THE FUEL PRESSURE SHOULD DROP MORE THAN (20kPa) (3psi).

OK
- ALLOW ENGINE TO WARM UP ABOVE 35°C.
- REPEAT TEST.
- PRESSURE SHOULD NOT DROP.

NOT OK
- DISCONNECT COLD START SWITCH CONNECTOR.
- PROBE GRN WIRE WITH A TEST LIGHT CONNECTED TO GROUND.
- OBSERVE LIGHT WHILE CRANKING.

NO DROP
- COLD START CIRCUIT OK.

DROPS
- DISCONNECT COLD START SWITCH.
- REPEAT TEST.

LIGHT

NO LIGHT
- CHECK AM1 FUSE

NO DROP
- REPLACE COLD START SWITCH.

DROPS
- CHECK FOR SHORT TO GROUND IN GRN WIRE. IF NOT SHORTED, REPLACE COLD START VALVE.

FUSE OK
- PROBE FUSE WITH A TEST LIGHT TO GROUND.
- OBSERVE WHILE CRANKING.

FUSE BLOWN
- PROBE GRN WIRE WITH A TEST LIGHT CONNECTED TO B +.

REPEAT TEST ON BLK/WHT WIRE.

LIGHT

NO LIGHT

NO LIGHT

LIGHT

LIGHT
2
- CONNECT OHMMETER BETWEEN BLK/WHT WIRE TERMINAL OF SWITCH AND GROUND.
- CHECK RESISTANCE.

NO LIGHT
- REPAIR OPEN IN BLK/WHT WIRE TO COLD START SWITCH.

- REPAIR OPEN IN BLK/WHT WIRE BETWEEN STARTER SOLENOID AND CRANK FUSE.

- REPAIR OPEN IN BLK/WHT WIRE BETWEEN FUSE AND COLD START VALVE.

- CHECK RESISTANCE OF SWITCH.
- SHOULD BE BETWEEN 20-60 OHMS.

- GRN WIRE SHORTED TO GROUND. REPAIR SHORT AND INSTALL NEW FUSE.

OK
PROBLEM IS INTERMITTENT. CHECK HARNESS.

NOT OK
REPLACE COLD START SWITCH.

RESISTANCE GREATER THAN 80 OHMS.
REPLACE COLD START SWITCH.

RESISTANCE BETWEEN 20 AND 80 OHMS.
BE SURE COOLANT TEMPERATURE IS BELOW 35°C. IF BELOW 35°C REPLACE COLD START SWITCH.

LESS THAN 20 OHMS.
REPLACE COLD START VALVE.

Fig. 130 Fuel system diagnosis — 1991 VIN code 5 engine

CHART A-5

ENGINE CRANKS BUT WILL NOT RUN
(FUEL SYSTEM ELECTRICAL TEST)
1.6L (VIN 6) "S" CARLINE (PORT)

Circuit Description:
When the engine is cranked the ECM will turn "ON" the circuit opening relay to operate the fuel pump. If the ECM receives ignition reference pulses the fuel pump will continue to run. If the ECM receives no reference pulses from the ignition circuit it will shut "OFF" the fuel pump.

Test Description: Number(s) below refer to circled number(s) on the diagnostic chart.
1. Fuel pump should run when ignition is cranked.
2. Test for an open between fuel pump and circuit opening relay.
3. Checks for crank signal to circuit opening relay.
4. Checks for proper EFI relay operation.
5. This will determine if ECM fuel pump driver circuit inside ECM is faulty.

Diagnostic Aids:

Visual inspection of wiring and connectors should be made if an intermittent problem exists.

Fig. 131 Fuel system diagnosis — 1991 VIN code 6 engine

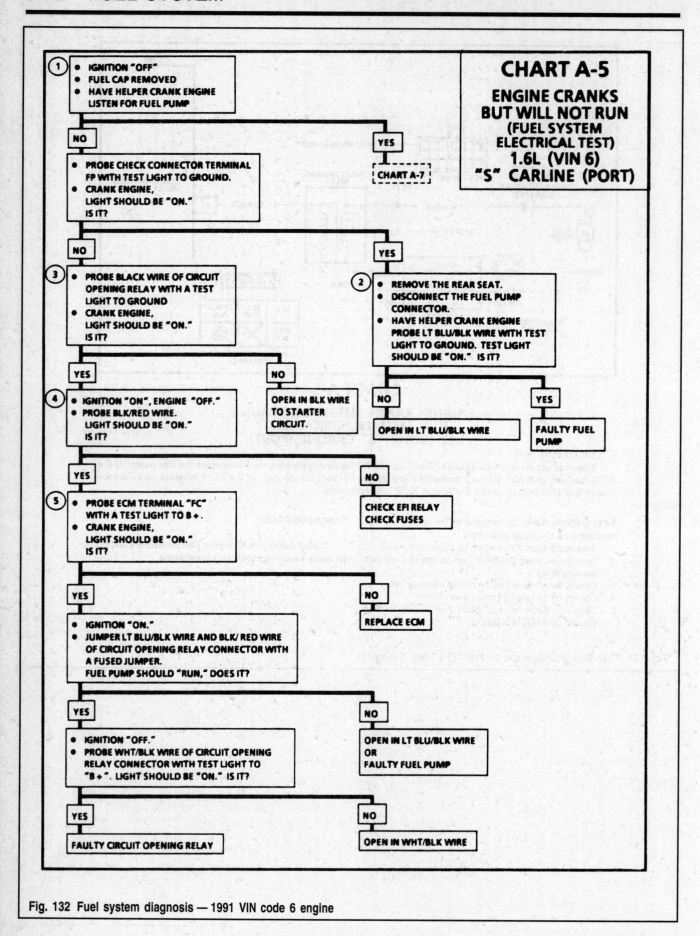

CHART A-5
ENGINE CRANKS BUT WILL NOT RUN
(FUEL SYSTEM ELECTRICAL TEST)
1.6L (VIN 6)
"S" CARLINE (PORT)

1
- IGNITION "OFF"
- FUEL CAP REMOVED
- HAVE HELPER CRANK ENGINE LISTEN FOR FUEL PUMP

NO

YES → CHART A-7

- PROBE CHECK CONNECTOR TERMINAL FP WITH TEST LIGHT TO GROUND.
- CRANK ENGINE, LIGHT SHOULD BE "ON." IS IT?

NO

YES

3
- PROBE BLACK WIRE OF CIRCUIT OPENING RELAY WITH A TEST LIGHT TO GROUND
- CRANK ENGINE, LIGHT SHOULD BE "ON." IS IT?

2
- REMOVE THE REAR SEAT.
- DISCONNECT THE FUEL PUMP CONNECTOR.
- HAVE HELPER CRANK ENGINE PROBE LT BLU/BLK WIRE WITH TEST LIGHT TO GROUND. TEST LIGHT SHOULD BE "ON." IS IT?

YES

NO
OPEN IN BLK WIRE TO STARTER CIRCUIT.

NO
OPEN IN LT BLU/BLK WIRE

YES
FAULTY FUEL PUMP

4
- IGNITION "ON", ENGINE "OFF."
- PROBE BLK/RED WIRE. LIGHT SHOULD BE "ON." IS IT?

YES

NO
CHECK EFI RELAY
CHECK FUSES

5
- PROBE ECM TERMINAL "FC" WITH A TEST LIGHT TO B+.
- CRANK ENGINE, LIGHT SHOULD BE "ON." IS IT?

YES

NO
REPLACE ECM

- IGNITION "ON."
- JUMPER LT BLU/BLK WIRE AND BLK/RED WIRE OF CIRCUIT OPENING RELAY CONNECTOR WITH A FUSED JUMPER. FUEL PUMP SHOULD "RUN," DOES IT?

YES

NO
OPEN IN LT BLU/BLK WIRE
OR
FAULTY FUEL PUMP

- IGNITION "OFF."
- PROBE WHT/BLK WIRE OF CIRCUIT OPENING RELAY CONNECTOR WITH TEST LIGHT TO "B+". LIGHT SHOULD BE "ON." IS IT?

YES
FAULTY CIRCUIT OPENING RELAY

NO
OPEN IN WHT/BLK WIRE

Fig. 132 Fuel system diagnosis — 1991 VIN code 6 engine

CHART A-7

(Page 1 of 3)
FUEL SYSTEM PRESSURE TEST
1.6L (VIN 6) "S" CARLINE (PORT)

Circuit Description:

The fuel pump delivers fuel to the fuel rail and injectors, where the system pressure is controlled from 262 to 303 kPa (35 to 38 psi) by the pressure regulator. Excess fuel is returned to the fuel tank. When the engine is stopped, the pump can be energized by applying battery voltage to the test terminal located in the engine compartment.

Test Description: Number(s) below refer to circled number(s) on the diagnostic chart.

1. Use pressure gage J 34730-1. Wrap a shop towel around the fuel pressure tap to absorb any small amount of fuel leakage that may occur when installing the gage. (The pressure will not leak down after the fuel pump is stopped on a correctly functioning system.)

2. While the engine is idling, manifold pressure is low (vacuum). When applied to the fuel regulator diaphragm, the pressure will result in a lower fuel pressure of about 207-241 kPa (30-35 psi).

3. The application of vacuum to the pressure regulator should result in a fuel pressure drop.

4. Pressure leak-down may be caused by one of the following:
   - In-tank fuel pump check valve not holding.
   - Pump coupling hose leaking.
   - Fuel pressure regulator valve leaking.
   - Injector sticking open.

4A.
   - Check for basic engine problem.
   - Check for water in fuel.

Diagnostic Aids:

Improper fuel system pressure may contribute to one or all of the following symptoms:
- Cranks but won't run.
- Cutting out (may feel like ignition problem).
- Hesitation, loss of power or poor fuel economy.

Fig. 133 Fuel system diagnosis — 1991 VIN code 6 engine

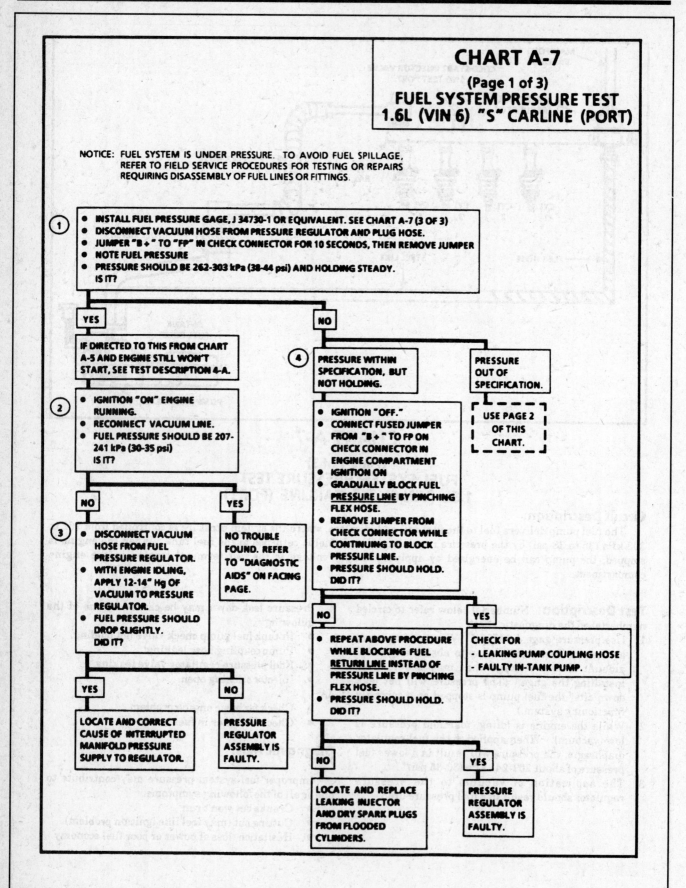

CHART A-7
(Page 1 of 3)
FUEL SYSTEM PRESSURE TEST
1.6L (VIN 6) "S" CARLINE (PORT)

NOTICE: FUEL SYSTEM IS UNDER PRESSURE. TO AVOID FUEL SPILLAGE, REFER TO FIELD SERVICE PROCEDURES FOR TESTING OR REPAIRS REQUIRING DISASSEMBLY OF FUEL LINES OR FITTINGS.

1
- INSTALL FUEL PRESSURE GAGE, J 34730-1 OR EQUIVALENT. SEE CHART A-7 (3 OF 3)
- DISCONNECT VACUUM HOSE FROM PRESSURE REGULATOR AND PLUG HOSE.
- JUMPER "B +" TO "FP" IN CHECK CONNECTOR FOR 10 SECONDS, THEN REMOVE JUMPER
- NOTE FUEL PRESSURE
- PRESSURE SHOULD BE 262-303 kPa (38-44 psi) AND HOLDING STEADY. IS IT?

YES

IF DIRECTED TO THIS FROM CHART A-5 AND ENGINE STILL WON'T START, SEE TEST DESCRIPTION 4-A.

2
- IGNITION "ON" ENGINE RUNNING.
- RECONNECT VACUUM LINE.
- FUEL PRESSURE SHOULD BE 207-241 kPa (30-35 psi) IS IT?

NO

3
- DISCONNECT VACUUM HOSE FROM FUEL PRESSURE REGULATOR.
- WITH ENGINE IDLING, APPLY 12-14" Hg OF VACUUM TO PRESSURE REGULATOR.
- FUEL PRESSURE SHOULD DROP SLIGHTLY. DID IT?

YES

LOCATE AND CORRECT CAUSE OF INTERRUPTED MANIFOLD PRESSURE SUPPLY TO REGULATOR.

NO

PRESSURE REGULATOR ASSEMBLY IS FAULTY.

YES

NO TROUBLE FOUND. REFER TO "DIAGNOSTIC AIDS" ON FACING PAGE.

NO

4 PRESSURE WITHIN SPECIFICATION, BUT NOT HOLDING.

PRESSURE OUT OF SPECIFICATION.

USE PAGE 2 OF THIS CHART.

- IGNITION "OFF."
- CONNECT FUSED JUMPER FROM "B +" TO FP ON CHECK CONNECTOR IN ENGINE COMPARTMENT
- IGNITION ON
- GRADUALLY BLOCK FUEL PRESSURE LINE BY PINCHING FLEX HOSE.
- REMOVE JUMPER FROM CHECK CONNECTOR WHILE CONTINUING TO BLOCK PRESSURE LINE.
- PRESSURE SHOULD HOLD. DID IT?

NO

- REPEAT ABOVE PROCEDURE WHILE BLOCKING FUEL RETURN LINE INSTEAD OF PRESSURE LINE BY PINCHING FLEX HOSE.
- PRESSURE SHOULD HOLD. DID IT?

YES

CHECK FOR
- LEAKING PUMP COUPLING HOSE
- FAULTY IN-TANK PUMP.

NO

LOCATE AND REPLACE LEAKING INJECTOR AND DRY SPARK PLUGS FROM FLOODED CYLINDERS.

YES

PRESSURE REGULATOR ASSEMBLY IS FAULTY.

Fig. 134 Fuel system diagnosis — 1991 VIN code 6 engine

CHART A-7

(Page 2 of 3)
FUEL SYSTEM PRESSURE TEST
1.6L (VIN 6) "S" CARLINE (PORT)

Circuit Description:

The fuel pump delivers fuel to the fuel rail and injectors, where the system pressure is controlled from 262 to 303 kPa (38 to 44 psi) by the pressure regulator. Excess fuel is returned to the fuel tank. When the engine is stopped, the pump can be energized by applying battery voltage to the test terminal located in the engine compartment.

Test Description: Number(s) below refer to circled number(s) on the diagnostic chart.

5. Pressure less than 262 kPa (38 psi) may be caused by one of two problems:
   - The regulated fuel pressure is too low. The system will be running lean and may set Code 25. Also, hard cold starting and overall poor performance is possible.
   - Restricted flow is causing a pressure drop. Normally, a vehicle with a fuel pressure loss at idle will not be drivable. However, if the pressure drop occurs only while driving, the engine will surge and then stop as pressure begins to drop rapidly.

6. Restricting the fuel return line allows the fuel pump to build above regulated pressure. When battery voltage is applied to "Fp" on the check connector, pressure should be above 450 kPa (65 psi).

7. This test determines if the high fuel pressure is due to a restricted fuel return line or a pressure regulator problem.

Fig. 135 Fuel system diagnosis — 1991 VIN code 6 engine

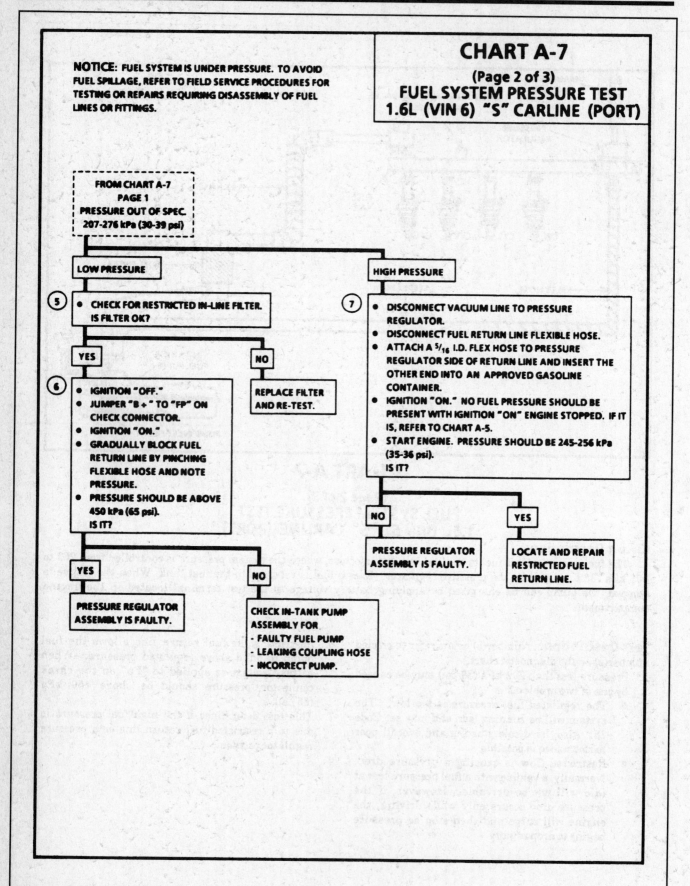

NOTICE: FUEL SYSTEM IS UNDER PRESSURE. TO AVOID FUEL SPILLAGE, REFER TO FIELD SERVICE PROCEDURES FOR TESTING OR REPAIRS REQUIRING DISASSEMBLY OF FUEL LINES OR FITTINGS.

CHART A-7
(Page 2 of 3)
FUEL SYSTEM PRESSURE TEST
1.6L (VIN 6) "S" CARLINE (PORT)

FROM CHART A-7
PAGE 1
PRESSURE OUT OF SPEC.
207-276 kPa (30-39 psi)

LOW PRESSURE

5 • CHECK FOR RESTRICTED IN-LINE FILTER. IS FILTER OK?

YES

NO

6 • IGNITION "OFF."
• JUMPER "B +" TO "FP" ON CHECK CONNECTOR.
• IGNITION "ON."
• GRADUALLY BLOCK FUEL RETURN LINE BY PINCHING FLEXIBLE HOSE AND NOTE PRESSURE.
• PRESSURE SHOULD BE ABOVE 450 kPa (65 psi). IS IT?

REPLACE FILTER AND RE-TEST.

YES

NO

PRESSURE REGULATOR ASSEMBLY IS FAULTY.

CHECK IN-TANK PUMP ASSEMBLY FOR
- FAULTY FUEL PUMP
- LEAKING COUPLING HOSE
- INCORRECT PUMP.

HIGH PRESSURE

7 • DISCONNECT VACUUM LINE TO PRESSURE REGULATOR.
• DISCONNECT FUEL RETURN LINE FLEXIBLE HOSE.
• ATTACH A 5/16 I.D. FLEX HOSE TO PRESSURE REGULATOR SIDE OF RETURN LINE AND INSERT THE OTHER END INTO AN APPROVED GASOLINE CONTAINER.
• IGNITION "ON." NO FUEL PRESSURE SHOULD BE PRESENT WITH IGNITION "ON" ENGINE STOPPED. IF IT IS, REFER TO CHART A-5.
• START ENGINE. PRESSURE SHOULD BE 245-256 kPa (35-36 psi). IS IT?

NO

YES

PRESSURE REGULATOR ASSEMBLY IS FAULTY.

LOCATE AND REPAIR RESTRICTED FUEL RETURN LINE.

Fig. 136 Fuel system diagnosis — 1991 VIN code 6 engine

CHART A-7

(Page 3 of 3)
FUEL SYSTEM PRESSURE TEST
1.6L (VIN 6) "S" CARLINE (PORT)

The following procedure outlines the installation and removal of the Fuel Pressure Gage Assembly. Make certain to observe <u>all</u> "Cautions" while performing this procedure.

Required Tools:

Port Fuel Pressure Gage	J 34730-1
Fuel Rail Adaptor	J 38347

Fig. 137 Fuel system diagnosis — 1991 VIN code 6 engine

CAUTION: TO REDUCE THE RISK OF FIRE AND PERSONAL INJURY, RELIEVE FUEL SYSTEM PRESSURE BEFORE DISCONNECTING FUEL LINES.

- LOOSEN FUEL FILLER CAP TO RELIEVE TANK PRESSURE.
- REMOVE CIRCUIT OPENING RELAY, LOCATED UNDER CONSOLE IN FRONT OF SHIFT LEVER.
- CRANK ENGINE AND ALLOW TO RUN UNTIL IT STALLS.
- ENGAGE STARTER FOR 30 SECONDS.
- USE SHOP TOWEL TO COLLECT FUEL DURING FUEL LINE DISCONNECT, PLACE TOWEL IN APPROVED CONTAINER.

FUEL PRESSURE GAGE INSTALLATION

1. IGNITION "OFF". DISCONNECT NEGATIVE BATTERY CABLE.
2. CAREFULLY, REMOVE COLD START INJECTOR VALVE FUEL LINE HOLD DOWN BOLT AT THE FUEL RAIL.
3. INSTALL ADAPTER J 38347 AND TIGHTEN SECURELY.
4. INSTALL FUEL PRESSURE GAGE J 34370-1 AND TIGHTEN SECURELY.
5. RECONNECT NEGATIVE BATTERY CABLE.
6. REINSTALL CIRCUIT OPENING RELAY.
7. START ENGINE AND CHECK FOR LEAKS.
8. PURGE AIR FROM FUEL PRESSURE GAGE INTO AN APPROVED CONTAINER.
9. PROCEED TO FUEL SYSTEM PRESSURE TEST CHART A-7 (1 OF 3).

FUEL PRESSURE GAGE REMOVAL

1. REMOVE NEGATIVE BATTERY CABLE.
2. PURGE FUEL PRESSURE FROM FUEL PRESSURE GAGE INTO AN APPROVED CONTAINER.
3. CAREFULLY DISCONNECT FUEL PRESSURE GAGE.
4. REMOVE ADAPTER.
5. REINSTALL FUEL LINE HOLD DOWN BOLT. TIGHTEN TO SPECIFICATION.
6. RECONNECT NEGATIVE BATTERY CABLE.
7. START ENGINE AND CHECK FOR FUEL LEAKS.

Fig. 138 Fuel system diagnosis — 1991 VIN code 6 engine

CHART A-9
COLD START INJECTOR VALVE
1.6L (VIN 6) "S" CARLINE (PORT)

Circuit Description:

The cold start injector valve is used to provide additional fuel during the crank mode to improve cold start-ups. This circuit is important when engine coolant temperature is low because the other injectors are not pulsed "ON" long enough to provide the needed amount of fuel to start.

The circuit is activated only in the crank mode. The power is supplied directly from the starter solenoid and is protected by a fuse. The system is controlled by a cold start fuel injection switch which provides a ground path for the valve during cranking when engine coolant is below 35°C (95°F).

The switch contains a bimetal material which opens at a specified coolant temperature. This bimetal is also heated by the winding in the thermal switch which allows the valve to stay "ON" for 8 seconds at -20°C (-5°F) coolant. The time the switch will stay closed varies inversely with coolant temperature. In other words, as the coolant temperature goes up, the cold start injector valve "ON" time goes down.

Test Description: Number(s) below refer to circled number(s) on the diagnostic chart.

1. Disconnecting the distributor 4-way connector will disable the other injectors. The amount of pressure drop depends on the temperature of the engine.

2. This test will determine the continuity through the switch to ground.

Fig. 139 Fuel system diagnosis — 1991 VIN code 6 engine

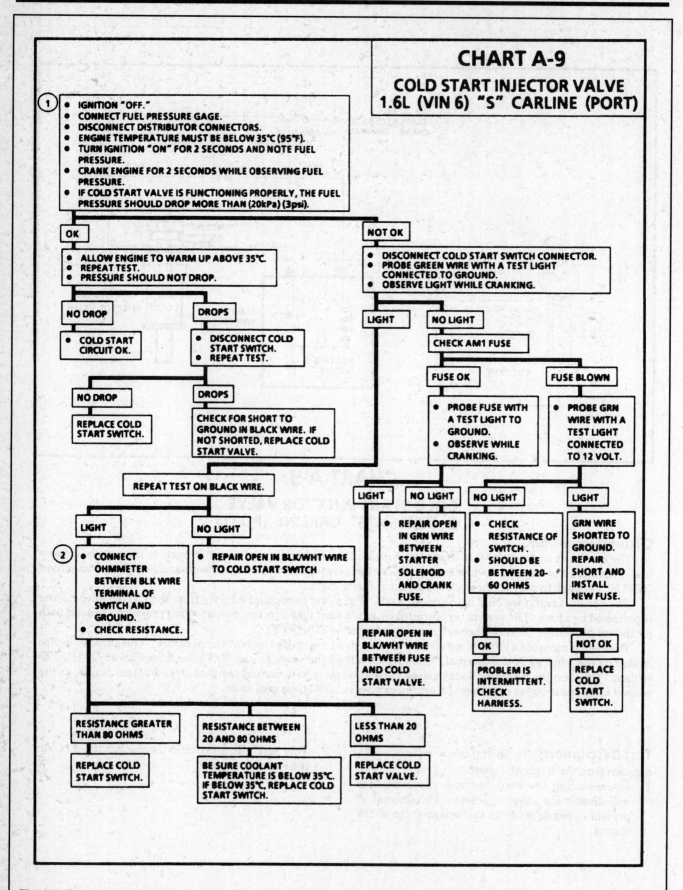

CHART A-9

COLD START INJECTOR VALVE
1.6L (VIN 6) "S" CARLINE (PORT)

1
- IGNITION "OFF."
- CONNECT FUEL PRESSURE GAGE.
- DISCONNECT DISTRIBUTOR CONNECTORS.
- ENGINE TEMPERATURE MUST BE BELOW 35°C (95°F).
- TURN IGNITION "ON" FOR 2 SECONDS AND NOTE FUEL PRESSURE.
- CRANK ENGINE FOR 2 SECONDS WHILE OBSERVING FUEL PRESSURE.
- IF COLD START VALVE IS FUNCTIONING PROPERLY, THE FUEL PRESSURE SHOULD DROP MORE THAN (20kPa) (3psi).

OK

- ALLOW ENGINE TO WARM UP ABOVE 35°C.
- REPEAT TEST.
- PRESSURE SHOULD NOT DROP.

NOT OK

- DISCONNECT COLD START SWITCH CONNECTOR.
- PROBE GREEN WIRE WITH A TEST LIGHT CONNECTED TO GROUND.
- OBSERVE LIGHT WHILE CRANKING.

NO DROP

- COLD START CIRCUIT OK.

DROPS

- DISCONNECT COLD START SWITCH.
- REPEAT TEST.

LIGHT

NO LIGHT

CHECK AM1 FUSE

FUSE OK

- PROBE FUSE WITH A TEST LIGHT TO GROUND.
- OBSERVE WHILE CRANKING.

FUSE BLOWN

- PROBE GRN WIRE WITH A TEST LIGHT CONNECTED TO 12 VOLT.

NO DROP

REPLACE COLD START SWITCH.

DROPS

CHECK FOR SHORT TO GROUND IN BLACK WIRE. IF NOT SHORTED, REPLACE COLD START VALVE.

REPEAT TEST ON BLACK WIRE.

LIGHT

2
- CONNECT OHMMETER BETWEEN BLK WIRE TERMINAL OF SWITCH AND GROUND.
- CHECK RESISTANCE.

NO LIGHT

- REPAIR OPEN IN BLK/WHT WIRE TO COLD START SWITCH

LIGHT

- REPAIR OPEN IN GRN WIRE BETWEEN STARTER SOLENOID AND CRANK FUSE.

NO LIGHT

REPAIR OPEN IN BLK/WHT WIRE BETWEEN FUSE AND COLD START VALVE.

NO LIGHT

- CHECK RESISTANCE OF SWITCH.
- SHOULD BE BETWEEN 20-60 OHMS

LIGHT

GRN WIRE SHORTED TO GROUND. REPAIR SHORT AND INSTALL NEW FUSE.

OK

PROBLEM IS INTERMITTENT. CHECK HARNESS.

NOT OK

REPLACE COLD START SWITCH.

RESISTANCE GREATER THAN 80 OHMS

REPLACE COLD START SWITCH.

RESISTANCE BETWEEN 20 AND 80 OHMS

BE SURE COOLANT TEMPERATURE IS BELOW 35°C. IF BELOW 35°C, REPLACE COLD START SWITCH.

LESS THAN 20 OHMS

REPLACE COLD START VALVE.

Fig. 140 Fuel system diagnosis — 1991 VIN code 6 engine

CHART A-5

ENGINE CRANKS BUT WILL NOT RUN
(FUEL SYSTEM ELECTRICAL TEST)
1.6L (VIN 5) "S" CARLINE (PORT)

Circuit Description:

When the engine is cranked the signal from starter relay (M/T) or neutral start switch (A/T) will turn "ON" the circuit opening relay to operate the fuel pump. Once the engine has started, the starter signal is removed from circuit opening relay and the fuel control switch in MAF sensor continues to run fuel pump. If the fuel control switch in the MAF sensor is nonfunctional, the engine will start but will not stay running.

Test Description: Number(s) below refer to circled number(s) on the diagnostic chart.

1. Fuel pump should run when ignition is cranked.
2. Test for B+ from circuit opening relay to fuel pump.
3. Checks for B+ signal to circuit opening relay.
4. Checks for proper MAF fuel pump switch operation.

Diagnostic Aids:

Visual inspection of wiring and connectors should be made if an intermittent problem exists.

Fig. 141 Fuel system diagnosis — 1992 VIN code 5 engine

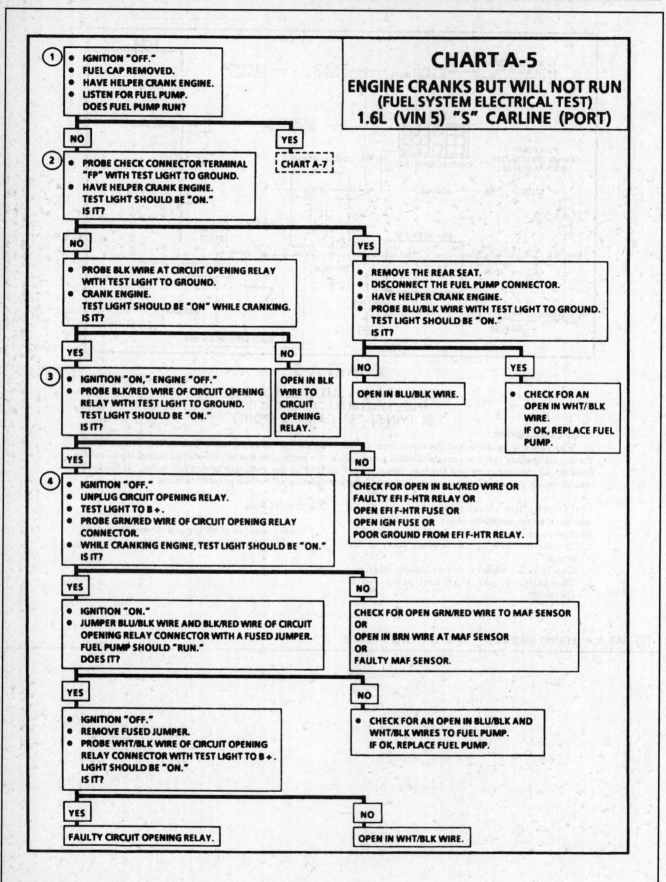

CHART A-5
ENGINE CRANKS BUT WILL NOT RUN
(FUEL SYSTEM ELECTRICAL TEST)
1.6L (VIN 5) "S" CARLINE (PORT)

1
- IGNITION "OFF."
- FUEL CAP REMOVED.
- HAVE HELPER CRANK ENGINE.
- LISTEN FOR FUEL PUMP.
  DOES FUEL PUMP RUN?

NO / **YES**

CHART A-7

2
- PROBE CHECK CONNECTOR TERMINAL "FP" WITH TEST LIGHT TO GROUND.
- HAVE HELPER CRANK ENGINE.
  TEST LIGHT SHOULD BE "ON."
  IS IT?

NO

- PROBE BLK WIRE AT CIRCUIT OPENING RELAY WITH TEST LIGHT TO GROUND.
- CRANK ENGINE.
  TEST LIGHT SHOULD BE "ON" WHILE CRANKING.
  IS IT?

YES

- REMOVE THE REAR SEAT.
- DISCONNECT THE FUEL PUMP CONNECTOR.
- HAVE HELPER CRANK ENGINE.
- PROBE BLU/BLK WIRE WITH TEST LIGHT TO GROUND.
  TEST LIGHT SHOULD BE "ON."
  IS IT?

YES / **NO**

3
- IGNITION "ON," ENGINE "OFF."
- PROBE BLK/RED WIRE OF CIRCUIT OPENING RELAY WITH TEST LIGHT TO GROUND.
  TEST LIGHT SHOULD BE "ON."
  IS IT?

OPEN IN BLK WIRE TO CIRCUIT OPENING RELAY.

NO

OPEN IN BLU/BLK WIRE.

YES

- CHECK FOR AN OPEN IN WHT/BLK WIRE.
  IF OK, REPLACE FUEL PUMP.

YES / **NO**

4
- IGNITION "OFF."
- UNPLUG CIRCUIT OPENING RELAY.
- TEST LIGHT TO B+.
- PROBE GRN/RED WIRE OF CIRCUIT OPENING RELAY CONNECTOR.
- WHILE CRANKING ENGINE, TEST LIGHT SHOULD BE "ON."
  IS IT?

CHECK FOR OPEN IN BLK/RED WIRE OR
FAULTY EFI F-HTR RELAY OR
OPEN EFI F-HTR FUSE OR
OPEN IGN FUSE OR
POOR GROUND FROM EFI F-HTR RELAY.

YES / **NO**

- IGNITION "ON."
- JUMPER BLU/BLK WIRE AND BLK/RED WIRE OF CIRCUIT OPENING RELAY CONNECTOR WITH A FUSED JUMPER.
  FUEL PUMP SHOULD "RUN."
  DOES IT?

CHECK FOR OPEN GRN/RED WIRE TO MAF SENSOR
OR
OPEN IN BRN WIRE AT MAF SENSOR
OR
FAULTY MAF SENSOR.

YES / **NO**

- IGNITION "OFF."
- REMOVE FUSED JUMPER.
- PROBE WHT/BLK WIRE OF CIRCUIT OPENING RELAY CONNECTOR WITH TEST LIGHT TO B+.
  LIGHT SHOULD BE "ON."
  IS IT?

- CHECK FOR AN OPEN IN BLU/BLK AND WHT/BLK WIRES TO FUEL PUMP.
  IF OK, REPLACE FUEL PUMP.

YES / **NO**

FAULTY CIRCUIT OPENING RELAY.

OPEN IN WHT/BLK WIRE.

Fig. 142 Fuel system diagnosis — 1992 VIN code 5 engine

CHART A-7

(Page 1 of 3)
FUEL SYSTEM PRESSURE TEST
1.6L (VIN 5) "S" CARLINE (PORT)

Circuit Description:

The fuel pump delivers fuel to the fuel rail and injectors, where the system pressure is controlled from 265 to 304 kPa (38 to 44 psi) by the pressure regulator. Excess fuel is returned to the fuel tank. When the engine is stopped, the pump can be energized by applying battery voltage to the test terminal located in the engine compartment. With engine turned "OFF," fuel pressure should remain above 147 kPa (21 psi) for five minutes.

Test Description: Number(s) below refer to circled number(s) on the diagnostic chart.

1. Use pressure gage J 34730-1. Wrap a shop towel around the fuel pressure tap to absorb any small amount of fuel leakage that may occur when installing the gage. (The pressure will not leak down after the fuel pump is stopped on a correctly functioning system.)

2. While the engine is idling, manifold pressure is low (vacuum). When applied to the fuel regulator diaphragm, the pressure will result in a lower fuel pressure of about 207-241 kPa (30-35 psi).

3. The application of vacuum to the pressure regulator should result in a fuel pressure drop.

4. Pressure leak-down may be caused by one of the following:
   - In-tank fuel pump check valve not holding.
   - Pump coupling hose leaking.

- Fuel pressure regulator valve leaking.
- Injector sticking open.

Diagnostic Aids:

Improper fuel system pressure may contribute to one or all of the following symptoms:
- Cranks but won't run.
- Cutting out (may feel like ignition problem).
- Hesitation, loss of power or poor fuel economy.

- Check for basic engine problem.
- Check for water in fuel.

Fig. 143 Fuel system diagnosis — 1992 VIN code 5 engine

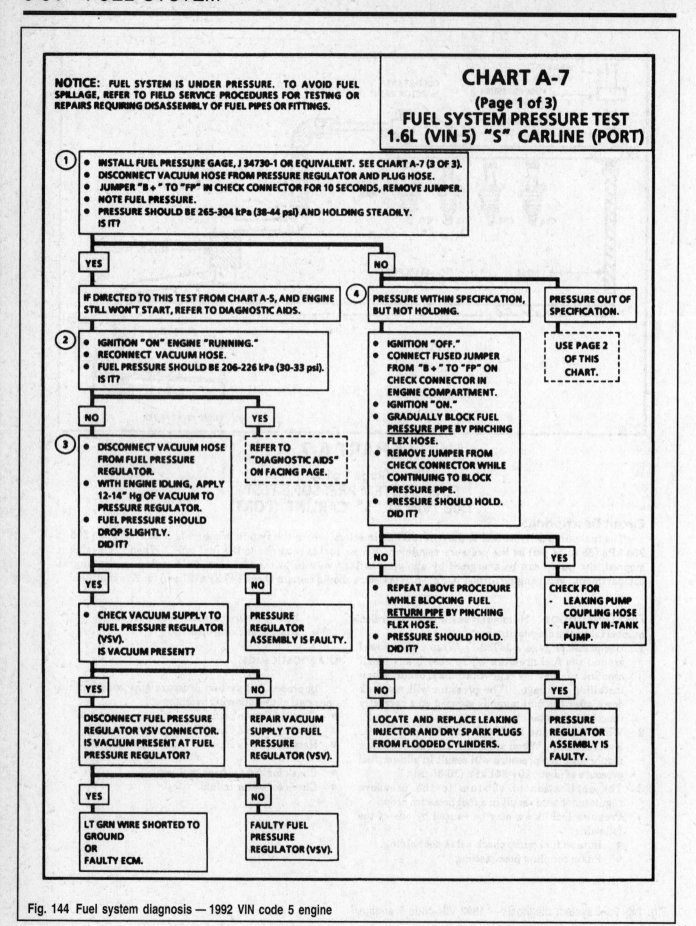

NOTICE: FUEL SYSTEM IS UNDER PRESSURE. TO AVOID FUEL SPILLAGE, REFER TO FIELD SERVICE PROCEDURES FOR TESTING OR REPAIRS REQUIRING DISASSEMBLY OF FUEL PIPES OR FITTINGS.

CHART A-7
(Page 1 of 3)
FUEL SYSTEM PRESSURE TEST
1.6L (VIN 5) "S" CARLINE (PORT)

1
- INSTALL FUEL PRESSURE GAGE, J 34730-1 OR EQUIVALENT. SEE CHART A-7 (3 OF 3).
- DISCONNECT VACUUM HOSE FROM PRESSURE REGULATOR AND PLUG HOSE.
- JUMPER "B+" TO "FP" IN CHECK CONNECTOR FOR 10 SECONDS, REMOVE JUMPER.
- NOTE FUEL PRESSURE.
- PRESSURE SHOULD BE 265-304 kPa (38-44 psi) AND HOLDING STEADILY. IS IT?

YES

IF DIRECTED TO THIS TEST FROM CHART A-5, AND ENGINE STILL WON'T START, REFER TO DIAGNOSTIC AIDS.

2
- IGNITION "ON" ENGINE "RUNNING."
- RECONNECT VACUUM HOSE.
- FUEL PRESSURE SHOULD BE 206-226 kPa (30-33 psi). IS IT?

NO   **YES**

3
- DISCONNECT VACUUM HOSE FROM FUEL PRESSURE REGULATOR.
- WITH ENGINE IDLING, APPLY 12-14" Hg OF VACUUM TO PRESSURE REGULATOR.
- FUEL PRESSURE SHOULD DROP SLIGHTLY. DID IT?

REFER TO "DIAGNOSTIC AIDS" ON FACING PAGE.

YES   **NO**

- CHECK VACUUM SUPPLY TO FUEL PRESSURE REGULATOR (VSV). IS VACUUM PRESENT?

PRESSURE REGULATOR ASSEMBLY IS FAULTY.

YES   **NO**

DISCONNECT FUEL PRESSURE REGULATOR VSV CONNECTOR. IS VACUUM PRESENT AT FUEL PRESSURE REGULATOR?

REPAIR VACUUM SUPPLY TO FUEL PRESSURE REGULATOR (VSV).

YES   **NO**

LT GRN WIRE SHORTED TO GROUND OR FAULTY ECM.

FAULTY FUEL PRESSURE REGULATOR (VSV).

NO

4 PRESSURE WITHIN SPECIFICATION, BUT NOT HOLDING.

PRESSURE OUT OF SPECIFICATION.

USE PAGE 2 OF THIS CHART.

- IGNITION "OFF."
- CONNECT FUSED JUMPER FROM "B+" TO "FP" ON CHECK CONNECTOR IN ENGINE COMPARTMENT.
- IGNITION "ON."
- GRADUALLY BLOCK FUEL PRESSURE PIPE BY PINCHING FLEX HOSE.
- REMOVE JUMPER FROM CHECK CONNECTOR WHILE CONTINUING TO BLOCK PRESSURE PIPE.
- PRESSURE SHOULD HOLD. DID IT?

NO   **YES**

- REPEAT ABOVE PROCEDURE WHILE BLOCKING FUEL RETURN PIPE BY PINCHING FLEX HOSE.
- PRESSURE SHOULD HOLD. DID IT?

CHECK FOR
- LEAKING PUMP COUPLING HOSE
- FAULTY IN-TANK PUMP.

NO   **YES**

LOCATE AND REPLACE LEAKING INJECTOR AND DRY SPARK PLUGS FROM FLOODED CYLINDERS.

PRESSURE REGULATOR ASSEMBLY IS FAULTY.

Fig. 144 Fuel system diagnosis — 1992 VIN code 5 engine

CHART A-7

(Page 2 of 3)
FUEL SYSTEM PRESSURE TEST
1.6L (VIN 5) "S" CARLINE (PORT)

Circuit Description:

The fuel pump delivers fuel to the fuel rail and injectors, where the system pressure is controlled from 265 to 304 kPa (38 to 44 psi) by the pressure regulator. Excess fuel is returned to the fuel tank. When the engine is stopped, the pump can be energized by applying battery voltage to the test terminal located in the engine compartment. With engine turned "OFF," fuel pressure should remain above 21 psi (147 kPa) for five minutes.

Test Description: Number(s) below refer to circled number(s) on the diagnostic chart.

5. Pressure less than 265 kPa (38 psi) may be caused by one of two problems:
   - The regulated fuel pressure is too low. The system will be running lean and may set Code 25. Also, hard cold starting and overall poor performance is possible.
   - Restricted flow is causing a pressure drop. Normally, a vehicle with a fuel pressure loss at idle will not be drivable. However, if the pressure drop occurs only while driving, the engine will surge and then stop as pressure begins to drop rapidly.

6. Restricting the fuel return line allows the fuel pump to build above regulated pressure. When battery voltage is applied to "FP" on the check connector, pressure should be above 450 kPa (65 psi).

7. This test determines if the high fuel pressure is due to a restricted fuel return pipe or a pressure regulator problem.

Fig. 145 Fuel system diagnosis — 1992 VIN code 5 engine

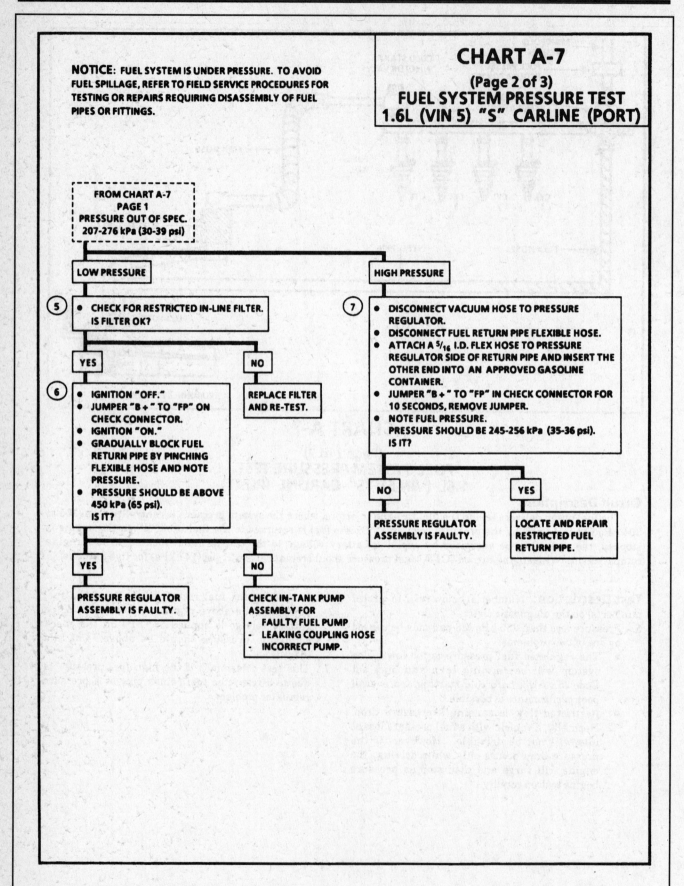

CHART A-7
(Page 2 of 3)
FUEL SYSTEM PRESSURE TEST
1.6L (VIN 5) "S" CARLINE (PORT)

NOTICE: FUEL SYSTEM IS UNDER PRESSURE. TO AVOID FUEL SPILLAGE, REFER TO FIELD SERVICE PROCEDURES FOR TESTING OR REPAIRS REQUIRING DISASSEMBLY OF FUEL PIPES OR FITTINGS.

FROM CHART A-7
PAGE 1
PRESSURE OUT OF SPEC.
207-276 kPa (30-39 psi)

LOW PRESSURE

HIGH PRESSURE

5. • CHECK FOR RESTRICTED IN-LINE FILTER. IS FILTER OK?

YES

NO

6. • IGNITION "OFF."
• JUMPER "B +" TO "FP" ON CHECK CONNECTOR.
• IGNITION "ON."
• GRADUALLY BLOCK FUEL RETURN PIPE BY PINCHING FLEXIBLE HOSE AND NOTE PRESSURE.
• PRESSURE SHOULD BE ABOVE 450 kPa (65 psi). IS IT?

REPLACE FILTER AND RE-TEST.

7. • DISCONNECT VACUUM HOSE TO PRESSURE REGULATOR.
• DISCONNECT FUEL RETURN PIPE FLEXIBLE HOSE.
• ATTACH A 5/16 I.D. FLEX HOSE TO PRESSURE REGULATOR SIDE OF RETURN PIPE AND INSERT THE OTHER END INTO AN APPROVED GASOLINE CONTAINER.
• JUMPER "B +" TO "FP" IN CHECK CONNECTOR FOR 10 SECONDS, REMOVE JUMPER.
• NOTE FUEL PRESSURE. PRESSURE SHOULD BE 245-256 kPa (35-36 psi). IS IT?

NO

YES

PRESSURE REGULATOR ASSEMBLY IS FAULTY.

LOCATE AND REPAIR RESTRICTED FUEL RETURN PIPE.

YES

NO

PRESSURE REGULATOR ASSEMBLY IS FAULTY.

CHECK IN-TANK PUMP ASSEMBLY FOR
- FAULTY FUEL PUMP
- LEAKING COUPLING HOSE
- INCORRECT PUMP.

Fig. 146 Fuel system diagnosis — 1992 VIN code 5 engine

CHART A-7

(Page 3 of 3)
FUEL SYSTEM PRESSURE TEST
1.6L (VIN 5) "S" CARLINE (PORT)

The following procedure outlines the installation and removal of the fuel pressure gage assembly. Make certain to observe all "Cautions" while performing this procedure.

Required Tools:

Fuel Pressure Gage	J 34730-1
Fuel Pressure Gage Adapter	J 38347

Fig. 147 Fuel system diagnosis — 1992 VIN code 5 engine

CAUTION: TO REDUCE THE RISK OF FIRE AND PERSONAL INJURY, RELIEVE FUEL SYSTEM PRESSURE BEFORE DISCONNECTING FUEL PIPES.

- LOOSEN FUEL FILLER CAP TO RELIEVE TANK PRESSURE.
- REMOVE CIRCUIT OPENING RELAY, LOCATED UNDER CONSOLE BELOW RADIO.
- CRANK ENGINE AND ALLOW TO RUN UNTIL IT STALLS.
- CRANK ENGINE FOR AN ADDITIONAL 3 SECONDS.
- USE SHOP TOWEL TO COLLECT FUEL DURING FUEL PIPE DISCONNECT, PLACE TOWEL IN APPROVED CONTAINER.

FUEL PRESSURE GAGE INSTALLATION

1.   IGNITION "OFF." DISCONNECT NEGATIVE BATTERY CABLE.
2.   CAREFULLY, REMOVE COLD START INJECTOR VALVE FUEL PIPE HOLD DOWN BOLT <u>AT THE FUEL RAIL</u>.
3.   INSTALL ADAPTER J 38347 AND TIGHTEN SECURELY.
4.   INSTALL FUEL PRESSURE GAGE J 34730-1 AND TIGHTEN SECURELY.
5.   RECONNECT NEGATIVE BATTERY CABLE.
6.   REINSTALL CIRCUIT OPENING RELAY.
7.   START ENGINE *AND CHECK FOR LEAKS.
8.   PURGE AIR FROM FUEL PRESSURE GAGE INTO AN APPROVED CONTAINER.
9.   PROCEED TO FUEL SYSTEM PRESSURE TEST CHART A-7 (1 OF 3).

FUEL PRESSURE GAGE REMOVAL

1.   REMOVE NEGATIVE BATTERY CABLE.
2.   PURGE FUEL PRESSURE FROM FUEL PRESSURE GAGE INTO AN APPROVED CONTAINER.
3.   CAREFULLY DISCONNECT FUEL PRESSURE GAGE.
4.   REMOVE ADAPTER.
5.   REINSTALL FUEL PIPE HOLD DOWN BOLT. TIGHTEN TO 15 N·m (11 LB. FT.).
6.   RECONNECT NEGATIVE BATTERY CABLE.
7.   START ENGINE *AND CHECK FOR FUEL LEAKS.

* IF ENGINE WILL NOT START, JUMPER B + TO "FP" ON CHECK CONNECTOR.

Fig. 148 Fuel system diagnosis — 1992 VIN code 5 engine

CHART A-9
COLD START FUEL INJECTOR
1.6L (VIN 5) "S" CARLINE (PORT)

Circuit Description:

The cold start fuel injector is used to provide additional fuel during the crank mode to improve cold start-ups. This circuit is important when engine coolant temperature is low because the other injectors are not pulsed "ON" long enough to provide the needed amount of fuel to start.

The circuit is activated only in the crank mode. The power is supplied directly from the starter solenoid circuit and is protected by a fuse. The system is controlled by a cold start fuel injector timer which provides a ground path for the injector during cranking when engine coolant is below 35°C (95°F).

The timer contains a bimetal material which opens at a specified coolant temperature. This bimetal is also heated by the winding in the thermal switch which allows the valve to stay "ON" for 8 seconds at -20°C (-5°F) coolant. The time the switch will stay closed varies inversely with coolant temperature. In other words, as the coolant temperature goes up, the cold start fuel injector "ON" time goes down.

Test Description: Number(s) below refer to circled number(s) on the diagnostic chart.

1. Disconnecting the two distributor connectors will disable the other injectors. The amount of pressure drop depends on the temperature of the engine.

2. This checks for power at the cold start fuel injector.
3. This checks for ground source at the cold start fuel injector.
4. This checks for power at the cold start fuel injector timer.

Fig. 149 Fuel system diagnosis — 1992 VIN code 5 engine

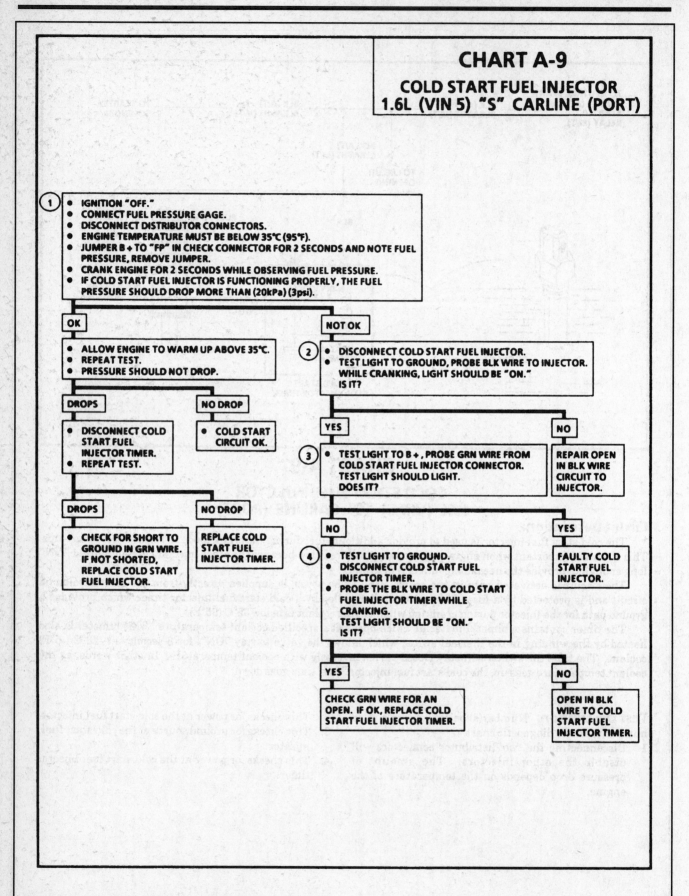

CHART A-9
COLD START FUEL INJECTOR
1.6L (VIN 5) "S" CARLINE (PORT)

①
- IGNITION "OFF."
- CONNECT FUEL PRESSURE GAGE.
- DISCONNECT DISTRIBUTOR CONNECTORS.
- ENGINE TEMPERATURE MUST BE BELOW 35°C (95°F).
- JUMPER B + TO "FP" IN CHECK CONNECTOR FOR 2 SECONDS AND NOTE FUEL PRESSURE, REMOVE JUMPER.
- CRANK ENGINE FOR 2 SECONDS WHILE OBSERVING FUEL PRESSURE.
- IF COLD START FUEL INJECTOR IS FUNCTIONING PROPERLY, THE FUEL PRESSURE SHOULD DROP MORE THAN (20kPa) (3psi).

OK

- ALLOW ENGINE TO WARM UP ABOVE 35°C.
- REPEAT TEST.
- PRESSURE SHOULD NOT DROP.

NOT OK

②
- DISCONNECT COLD START FUEL INJECTOR.
- TEST LIGHT TO GROUND, PROBE BLK WIRE TO INJECTOR. WHILE CRANKING, LIGHT SHOULD BE "ON." IS IT?

DROPS

- DISCONNECT COLD START FUEL INJECTOR TIMER.
- REPEAT TEST.

NO DROP

- COLD START CIRCUIT OK.

YES

③
- TEST LIGHT TO B + , PROBE GRN WIRE FROM COLD START FUEL INJECTOR CONNECTOR. TEST LIGHT SHOULD LIGHT. DOES IT?

NO

- REPAIR OPEN IN BLK WIRE CIRCUIT TO INJECTOR.

DROPS

- CHECK FOR SHORT TO GROUND IN GRN WIRE. IF NOT SHORTED, REPLACE COLD START FUEL INJECTOR.

NO DROP

- REPLACE COLD START FUEL INJECTOR TIMER.

NO

④
- TEST LIGHT TO GROUND.
- DISCONNECT COLD START FUEL INJECTOR TIMER.
- PROBE THE BLK WIRE TO COLD START FUEL INJECTOR TIMER WHILE CRANKING. TEST LIGHT SHOULD BE "ON." IS IT?

YES

- FAULTY COLD START FUEL INJECTOR.

YES

- CHECK GRN WIRE FOR AN OPEN. IF OK, REPLACE COLD START FUEL INJECTOR TIMER.

NO

- OPEN IN BLK WIRE TO COLD START FUEL INJECTOR TIMER.

Fig. 150 Fuel system diagnosis — 1992 VIN code 5 engine

CHART A-5

ENGINE CRANKS BUT WILL NOT RUN
(FUEL SYSTEM ELECTRICAL TEST)
1.6L (VIN 6) "S" CARLINE (PORT)

Circuit Description:
   When the engine is cranked the ECM will turn "ON" the circuit opening relay to operate the fuel pump. If the ECM receives ignition reference pulses the fuel pump will continue to run. If the ECM receives no reference pulses from the ignition circuit it will shut "OFF" the fuel pump.

Test Description: Number(s) below refer to circled number(s) on the diagnostic chart.

1. Fuel pump should run when ignition is cranked.
2. Test for B+ from circuit opening relay to fuel pump.
3. Checks for crank signal to circuit opening relay.
4. This will determine if ECM fuel pump driver circuit inside ECM is faulty.

Diagnostic Aids:

   Visual inspection of wiring and connectors should be made if an intermittent problem exists.

Fig. 151 Fuel system diagnosis — 1992 VIN code 6 engine

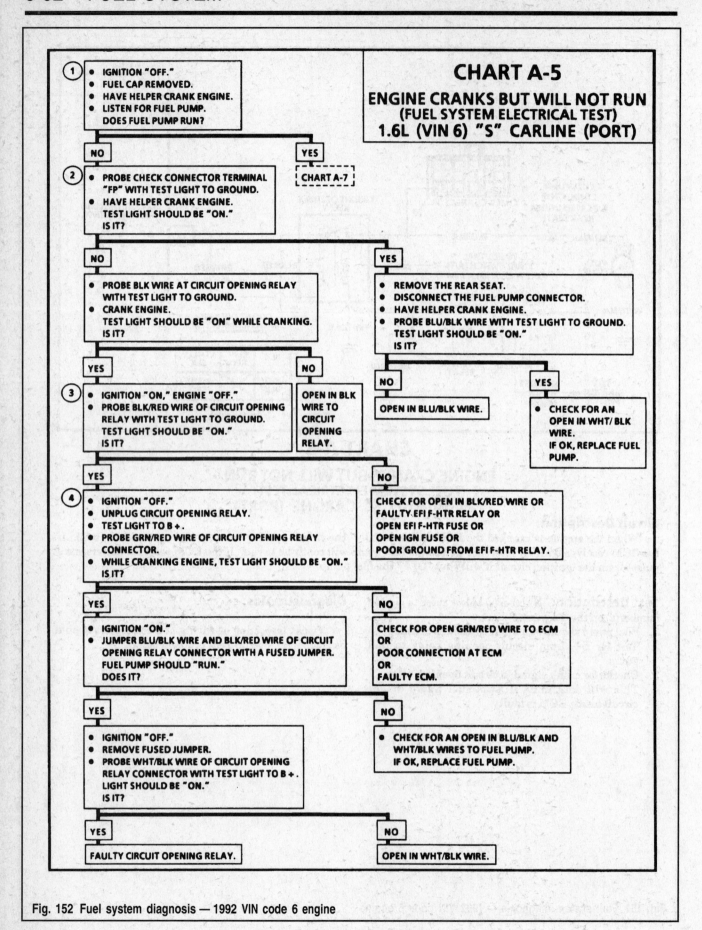

CHART A-5

ENGINE CRANKS BUT WILL NOT RUN
(FUEL SYSTEM ELECTRICAL TEST)
1.6L (VIN 6) "S" CARLINE (PORT)

① • IGNITION "OFF."
• FUEL CAP REMOVED.
• HAVE HELPER CRANK ENGINE.
• LISTEN FOR FUEL PUMP.
DOES FUEL PUMP RUN?

NO → YES

CHART A-7

② • PROBE CHECK CONNECTOR TERMINAL "FP" WITH TEST LIGHT TO GROUND.
• HAVE HELPER CRANK ENGINE.
TEST LIGHT SHOULD BE "ON."
IS IT?

NO → YES

• PROBE BLK WIRE AT CIRCUIT OPENING RELAY WITH TEST LIGHT TO GROUND.
• CRANK ENGINE.
TEST LIGHT SHOULD BE "ON" WHILE CRANKING.
IS IT?

• REMOVE THE REAR SEAT.
• DISCONNECT THE FUEL PUMP CONNECTOR.
• HAVE HELPER CRANK ENGINE.
• PROBE BLU/BLK WIRE WITH TEST LIGHT TO GROUND.
TEST LIGHT SHOULD BE "ON."
IS IT?

YES → NO

NO → YES

③ • IGNITION "ON," ENGINE "OFF."
• PROBE BLK/RED WIRE OF CIRCUIT OPENING RELAY WITH TEST LIGHT TO GROUND.
TEST LIGHT SHOULD BE "ON."
IS IT?

OPEN IN BLK WIRE TO CIRCUIT OPENING RELAY.

OPEN IN BLU/BLK WIRE.

• CHECK FOR AN OPEN IN WHT/BLK WIRE.
IF OK, REPLACE FUEL PUMP.

YES → NO

④ • IGNITION "OFF."
• UNPLUG CIRCUIT OPENING RELAY.
• TEST LIGHT TO B + .
• PROBE GRN/RED WIRE OF CIRCUIT OPENING RELAY CONNECTOR.
• WHILE CRANKING ENGINE, TEST LIGHT SHOULD BE "ON."
IS IT?

CHECK FOR OPEN IN BLK/RED WIRE OR
FAULTY EFI F-HTR RELAY OR
OPEN EFI F-HTR FUSE OR
OPEN IGN FUSE OR
POOR GROUND FROM EFI F-HTR RELAY.

YES → NO

• IGNITION "ON."
• JUMPER BLU/BLK WIRE AND BLK/RED WIRE OF CIRCUIT OPENING RELAY CONNECTOR WITH A FUSED JUMPER.
FUEL PUMP SHOULD "RUN."
DOES IT?

CHECK FOR OPEN GRN/RED WIRE TO ECM
OR
POOR CONNECTION AT ECM
OR
FAULTY ECM.

YES → NO

• IGNITION "OFF."
• REMOVE FUSED JUMPER.
• PROBE WHT/BLK WIRE OF CIRCUIT OPENING RELAY CONNECTOR WITH TEST LIGHT TO B + .
LIGHT SHOULD BE "ON."
IS IT?

• CHECK FOR AN OPEN IN BLU/BLK AND WHT/BLK WIRES TO FUEL PUMP.
IF OK, REPLACE FUEL PUMP.

YES → NO

FAULTY CIRCUIT OPENING RELAY.

OPEN IN WHT/BLK WIRE.

Fig. 152 Fuel system diagnosis — 1992 VIN code 6 engine

CHART A-7

(Page 1 of 3)
FUEL SYSTEM PRESSURE TEST
1.6L (VIN 6) "S" CARLINE (PORT)

Circuit Description:

The fuel pump delivers fuel to the fuel rail and injectors, where the system pressure is controlled from 262 to 303 kPa (35 to 38 psi) by the pressure regulator. Excess fuel is returned to the fuel tank. When the engine is stopped, the pump can be energized by applying battery voltage to the test terminal located in the engine compartment.

Test Description: Number(s) below refer to circled number(s) on the diagnostic chart.

1. Use pressure gage J 34730-1. Wrap a shop towel around the fuel pressure tap to absorb any small amount of fuel leakage that may occur when installing the gage. (The pressure will not leak down after the fuel pump is stopped on a correctly functioning system.)
2. While the engine is idling, manifold pressure is low (vacuum). When applied to the fuel regulator diaphragm, the pressure will result in a lower fuel pressure of about 207-241 kPa (30-35 psi).
3. The application of vacuum to the pressure regulator should result in a fuel pressure drop.
4. Pressure leak-down may be caused by one of the following:
   - In-tank fuel pump check valve not holding.
   - Pump coupling hose leaking.
   - Fuel pressure regulator valve leaking.
   - Injector sticking open.

Diagnostic Aids:

Improper fuel system pressure may contribute to one or all of the following symptoms:
- Cranks but won't run.
- Cutting out (may feel like ignition problem).
- Hesitation, loss of power or poor fuel economy.

- Check for basic engine problem.
- Check for water in fuel.

Fig. 153 Fuel system diagnosis — 1992 VIN code 6 engine

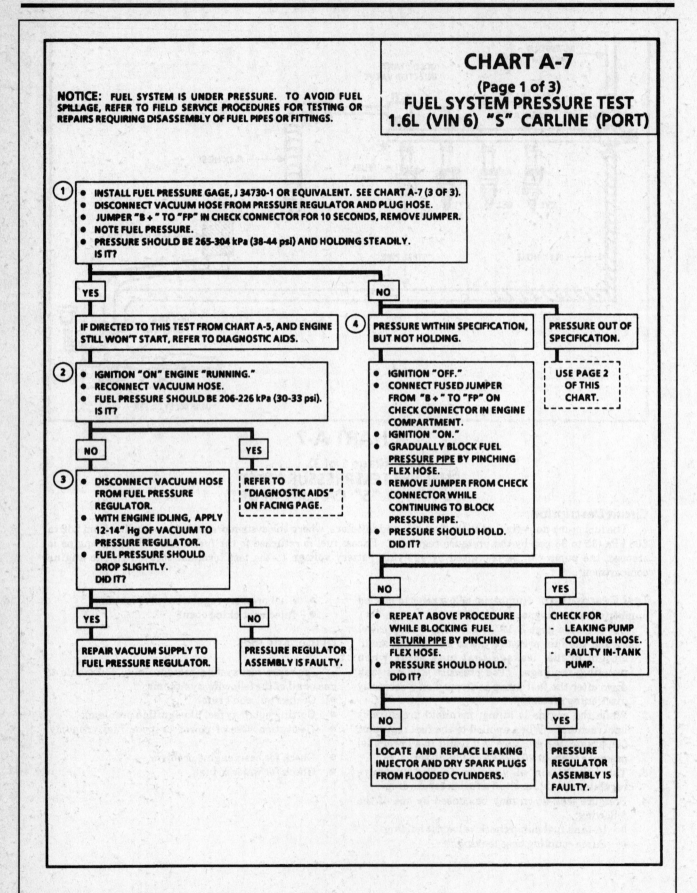

CHART A-7
(Page 1 of 3)
FUEL SYSTEM PRESSURE TEST
1.6L (VIN 6) "S" CARLINE (PORT)

NOTICE: FUEL SYSTEM IS UNDER PRESSURE. TO AVOID FUEL SPILLAGE, REFER TO FIELD SERVICE PROCEDURES FOR TESTING OR REPAIRS REQUIRING DISASSEMBLY OF FUEL PIPES OR FITTINGS.

1
- INSTALL FUEL PRESSURE GAGE, J 34730-1 OR EQUIVALENT. SEE CHART A-7 (3 OF 3).
- DISCONNECT VACUUM HOSE FROM PRESSURE REGULATOR AND PLUG HOSE.
- JUMPER "B +" TO "FP" IN CHECK CONNECTOR FOR 10 SECONDS, REMOVE JUMPER.
- NOTE FUEL PRESSURE.
- PRESSURE SHOULD BE 265-304 kPa (38-44 psi) AND HOLDING STEADILY.
  IS IT?

YES

IF DIRECTED TO THIS TEST FROM CHART A-5, AND ENGINE STILL WON'T START, REFER TO DIAGNOSTIC AIDS.

2
- IGNITION "ON" ENGINE "RUNNING."
- RECONNECT VACUUM HOSE.
- FUEL PRESSURE SHOULD BE 206-226 kPa (30-33 psi).
  IS IT?

NO

3
- DISCONNECT VACUUM HOSE FROM FUEL PRESSURE REGULATOR.
- WITH ENGINE IDLING, APPLY 12-14" Hg OF VACUUM TO PRESSURE REGULATOR.
- FUEL PRESSURE SHOULD DROP SLIGHTLY.
  DID IT?

YES

REFER TO "DIAGNOSTIC AIDS" ON FACING PAGE.

YES

REPAIR VACUUM SUPPLY TO FUEL PRESSURE REGULATOR.

NO

PRESSURE REGULATOR ASSEMBLY IS FAULTY.

NO

4 PRESSURE WITHIN SPECIFICATION, BUT NOT HOLDING.

PRESSURE OUT OF SPECIFICATION.

- IGNITION "OFF."
- CONNECT FUSED JUMPER FROM "B +" TO "FP" ON CHECK CONNECTOR IN ENGINE COMPARTMENT.
- IGNITION "ON."
- GRADUALLY BLOCK FUEL PRESSURE PIPE BY PINCHING FLEX HOSE.
- REMOVE JUMPER FROM CHECK CONNECTOR WHILE CONTINUING TO BLOCK PRESSURE PIPE.
- PRESSURE SHOULD HOLD.
  DID IT?

USE PAGE 2 OF THIS CHART.

NO

- REPEAT ABOVE PROCEDURE WHILE BLOCKING FUEL RETURN PIPE BY PINCHING FLEX HOSE.
- PRESSURE SHOULD HOLD.
  DID IT?

YES

CHECK FOR
- LEAKING PUMP COUPLING HOSE.
- FAULTY IN-TANK PUMP.

NO

LOCATE AND REPLACE LEAKING INJECTOR AND DRY SPARK PLUGS FROM FLOODED CYLINDERS.

YES

PRESSURE REGULATOR ASSEMBLY IS FAULTY.

Fig. 154 Fuel system diagnosis — 1992 VIN code 6 engine

CHART A-7

(Page 2 of 3)

FUEL SYSTEM PRESSURE TEST
1.6L (VIN 6) "S" CARLINE (PORT)

Circuit Description:

The fuel pump delivers fuel to the fuel rail and injectors, where the system pressure is controlled from 262 to 303 kPa (38 to 44 psi) by the pressure regulator. Excess fuel is returned to the fuel tank. When the engine is stopped, the pump can be energized by applying battery voltage to the test terminal located in the engine compartment.

Test Description: Number(s) below refer to circled number(s) on the diagnostic chart.

5. Pressure less than 262 kPa (38 psi) may be caused by one of two problems:
   - The regulated fuel pressure is too low. The system will be running lean and may set Code 25. Also, hard cold starting and overall poor performance is possible.
   - Restricted flow is causing a pressure drop. Normally, a vehicle with a fuel pressure loss at idle will not be drivable. However, if the pressure drop occurs only while driving, the engine will surge and then stop as pressure begins to drop rapidly.

6. Restricting the fuel return line allows the fuel pump to build above regulated pressure. When battery voltage is applied to "FP" on the check connector, pressure should be above 450 kPa (65 psi).

7. This test determines if the high fuel pressure is due to a restricted fuel return pipe or a pressure regulator problem.

Fig. 155 Fuel system diagnosis — 1992 VIN code 6 engine

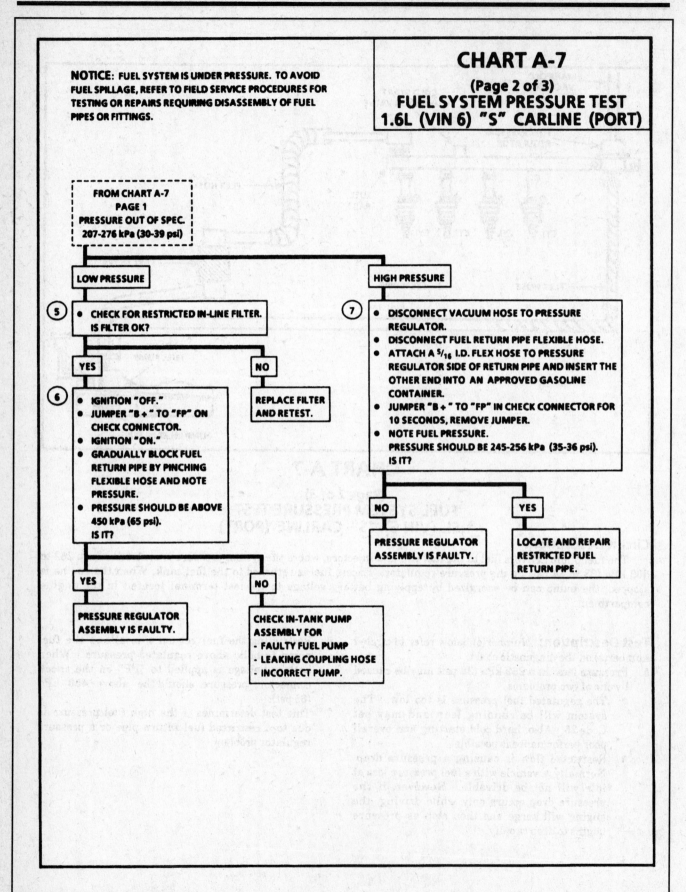

NOTICE: FUEL SYSTEM IS UNDER PRESSURE. TO AVOID FUEL SPILLAGE, REFER TO FIELD SERVICE PROCEDURES FOR TESTING OR REPAIRS REQUIRING DISASSEMBLY OF FUEL PIPES OR FITTINGS.

CHART A-7
(Page 2 of 3)
FUEL SYSTEM PRESSURE TEST
1.6L (VIN 6) "S" CARLINE (PORT)

FROM CHART A-7
PAGE 1
PRESSURE OUT OF SPEC.
207-276 kPa (30-39 psi)

LOW PRESSURE

HIGH PRESSURE

(5)
- CHECK FOR RESTRICTED IN-LINE FILTER. IS FILTER OK?

(7)
- DISCONNECT VACUUM HOSE TO PRESSURE REGULATOR.
- DISCONNECT FUEL RETURN PIPE FLEXIBLE HOSE.
- ATTACH A 5/16 I.D. FLEX HOSE TO PRESSURE REGULATOR SIDE OF RETURN PIPE AND INSERT THE OTHER END INTO AN APPROVED GASOLINE CONTAINER.
- JUMPER "B+" TO "FP" IN CHECK CONNECTOR FOR 10 SECONDS, REMOVE JUMPER.
- NOTE FUEL PRESSURE. PRESSURE SHOULD BE 245-256 kPa (35-36 psi). IS IT?

YES

NO

REPLACE FILTER AND RETEST.

(6)
- IGNITION "OFF."
- JUMPER "B+" TO "FP" ON CHECK CONNECTOR.
- IGNITION "ON."
- GRADUALLY BLOCK FUEL RETURN PIPE BY PINCHING FLEXIBLE HOSE AND NOTE PRESSURE.
- PRESSURE SHOULD BE ABOVE 450 kPa (65 psi). IS IT?

NO

YES

PRESSURE REGULATOR ASSEMBLY IS FAULTY.

LOCATE AND REPAIR RESTRICTED FUEL RETURN PIPE.

YES

NO

PRESSURE REGULATOR ASSEMBLY IS FAULTY.

CHECK IN-TANK PUMP ASSEMBLY FOR
- FAULTY FUEL PUMP
- LEAKING COUPLING HOSE
- INCORRECT PUMP.

Fig. 156 Fuel system diagnosis — 1992 VIN code 6 engine

CHART A-7

(Page 3 of 3)
FUEL SYSTEM PRESSURE TEST
1.6L (VIN 6) "S" CARLINE (PORT)

The following procedure outlines the installation and removal of the Fuel Pressure Gage Assembly. Make certain to observe all "Cautions" while performing this procedure.

Required Tools:

Fuel Pressure Gage	J 34730-1
Fuel Pressure Gage Adapter	J 38347

Fig. 157 Fuel system diagnosis — 1992 VIN code 6 engine

CAUTION: TO REDUCE THE RISK OF FIRE AND PERSONAL INJURY, RELIEVE FUEL SYSTEM PRESSURE BEFORE DISCONNECTING FUEL PIPES.

- LOOSEN FUEL FILLER CAP TO RELIEVE TANK PRESSURE.
- REMOVE CIRCUIT OPENING RELAY, LOCATED UNDER CONSOLE BELOW RADIO.
- CRANK ENGINE AND ALLOW TO RUN UNTIL IT STALLS.
- CRANK ENGINE FOR AN ADDITIONAL 3 SECONDS.
- USE SHOP TOWEL TO COLLECT FUEL DURING FUEL PIPE DISCONNECT, PLACE TOWEL IN APPROVED CONTAINER.

FUEL PRESSURE GAGE INSTALLATION

1. IGNITION "OFF." DISCONNECT NEGATIVE BATTERY CABLE.
2. CAREFULLY, REMOVE COLD START INJECTOR VALVE FUEL PIPE HOLD DOWN BOLT <u>AT THE FUEL RAIL</u>.
3. INSTALL ADAPTER J 38347 AND TIGHTEN SECURELY.
4. INSTALL FUEL PRESSURE GAGE J 34730-1 AND TIGHTEN SECURELY.
5. RECONNECT NEGATIVE BATTERY CABLE.
6. REINSTALL CIRCUIT OPENING RELAY.
7. START ENGINE *AND CHECK FOR LEAKS.
8. PURGE AIR FROM FUEL PRESSURE GAGE INTO AN APPROVED CONTAINER.
9. PROCEED TO FUEL SYSTEM PRESSURE TEST CHART A-7 (1 OF 3).

FUEL PRESSURE GAGE REMOVAL

1. REMOVE NEGATIVE BATTERY CABLE.
2. PURGE FUEL PRESSURE FROM FUEL PRESSURE GAGE INTO AN APPROVED CONTAINER.
3. CAREFULLY DISCONNECT FUEL PRESSURE GAGE.
4. REMOVE ADAPTER.
5. REINSTALL FUEL PIPE HOLD DOWN BOLT. TIGHTEN TO 15 N·m (11 LB. FT.).
6. RECONNECT NEGATIVE BATTERY CABLE.
7. START ENGINE *AND CHECK FOR FUEL LEAKS.

* IF ENGINE WILL NOT START, JUMPER B + TO "FP" ON CHECK CONNECTOR.

Fig. 158 Fuel system diagnosis — 1992 VIN code 6 engine

CHART A-9
COLD START FUEL INJECTOR
1.6L (VIN 6) "S" CARLINE (PORT)

Circuit Description:

The cold start fuel injector is used to provide additional fuel during the crank mode to improve cold start-ups. This circuit is important when engine coolant temperature is low because the other injectors are not pulsed "ON" long enough to provide the needed amount of fuel to start.

The circuit is activated only in the crank mode. The power is supplied directly from the starter solenoid circuit and is protected by a fuse. The system is controlled by a cold start fuel injector timer which provides a ground path for the injector during cranking when engine coolant is below 35°C (95°F).

The timer contains a bimetal material which opens at a specified coolant temperature. This bimetal is also heated by the winding in the thermal switch which allows the valve to stay "ON" for 8 seconds at -20°C (-5°F) coolant. The time the switch will stay closed varies inversely with coolant temperature. In other words, as the coolant temperature goes up, the cold start fuel injector "ON" time goes down. The ECM receives a signal when the cold start fuel injector timer switch is closed. The ECM uses this information to control the "ON" time of the other fuel injectors.

Test Description: Number(s) below refer to circled number(s) on the diagnostic chart.

1. Disconnecting the distributor connectors will disable the other injectors. The amount of pressure drop depends on the temperature of the engine.

2. This checks for power at the cold start fuel injector.

3. This checks for ground source at the cold start fuel injector.

4. This checks for power at the cold start fuel injector timer.

Fig. 159 Fuel system diagnosis — 1992 VIN code 6 engine

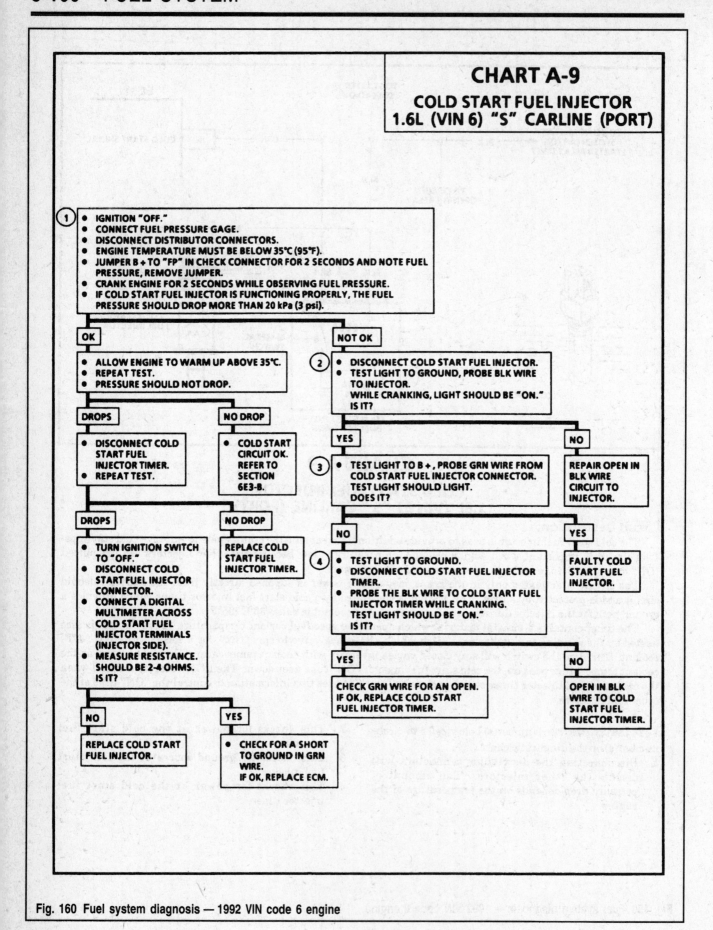

CHART A-9
COLD START FUEL INJECTOR
1.6L (VIN 6) "S" CARLINE (PORT)

1
- IGNITION "OFF."
- CONNECT FUEL PRESSURE GAGE.
- DISCONNECT DISTRIBUTOR CONNECTORS.
- ENGINE TEMPERATURE MUST BE BELOW 35°C (95°F).
- JUMPER B+ TO "FP" IN CHECK CONNECTOR FOR 2 SECONDS AND NOTE FUEL PRESSURE, REMOVE JUMPER.
- CRANK ENGINE FOR 2 SECONDS WHILE OBSERVING FUEL PRESSURE.
- IF COLD START FUEL INJECTOR IS FUNCTIONING PROPERLY, THE FUEL PRESSURE SHOULD DROP MORE THAN 20 kPa (3 psi).

OK

- ALLOW ENGINE TO WARM UP ABOVE 35°C.
- REPEAT TEST.
- PRESSURE SHOULD NOT DROP.

DROPS

- DISCONNECT COLD START FUEL INJECTOR TIMER.
- REPEAT TEST.

NO DROP

- COLD START CIRCUIT OK. REFER TO SECTION 6E3-B.

DROPS

- TURN IGNITION SWITCH TO "OFF."
- DISCONNECT COLD START FUEL INJECTOR CONNECTOR.
- CONNECT A DIGITAL MULTIMETER ACROSS COLD START FUEL INJECTOR TERMINALS (INJECTOR SIDE).
- MEASURE RESISTANCE. SHOULD BE 2-4 OHMS. IS IT?

NO DROP

- REPLACE COLD START FUEL INJECTOR TIMER.

NO

- REPLACE COLD START FUEL INJECTOR.

YES

- CHECK FOR A SHORT TO GROUND IN GRN WIRE. IF OK, REPLACE ECM.

NOT OK

2
- DISCONNECT COLD START FUEL INJECTOR.
- TEST LIGHT TO GROUND, PROBE BLK WIRE TO INJECTOR. WHILE CRANKING, LIGHT SHOULD BE "ON." IS IT?

YES

3
- TEST LIGHT TO B+, PROBE GRN WIRE FROM COLD START FUEL INJECTOR CONNECTOR. TEST LIGHT SHOULD LIGHT. DOES IT?

NO

4
- TEST LIGHT TO GROUND.
- DISCONNECT COLD START FUEL INJECTOR TIMER.
- PROBE THE BLK WIRE TO COLD START FUEL INJECTOR TIMER WHILE CRANKING. TEST LIGHT SHOULD BE "ON." IS IT?

YES

CHECK GRN WIRE FOR AN OPEN. IF OK, REPLACE COLD START FUEL INJECTOR TIMER.

NO

REPAIR OPEN IN BLK WIRE CIRCUIT TO INJECTOR.

YES

FAULTY COLD START FUEL INJECTOR.

NO

OPEN IN BLK WIRE TO COLD START FUEL INJECTOR TIMER.

Fig. 160 Fuel system diagnosis — 1992 VIN code 6 engine

CHART A1-5
FUEL INJECTOR CIRCUIT CHECK (ENGINE NO-START)
1.6L (VIN 6) "S" CARLINE

Circuit Description:

When the ignition switch is turned to the "ON" or "START" position (engine running), the engine control module (ECM) will energize/de-energize the fuel injectors solenoid coil. With this coil energized, a plunger is activated, allowing pressurized fuel to be sprayed through the fuel injectors into the combustion chamber where it is mixed with air from the intake manifold; thus creating the proper air/fuel mixture needed for combustion.

Test Description: Number(s) below refer to circled number(s) on the diagnostic chart.

1. This checks to see if the ECM is controlling the ground path to the fuel injectors.
2. This checks the resistance of the fuel injectors.
3. This checks for an open or short to ground in the BLK or BLK/RED wires between the fuel injectors and the ECM, or for faulty fuel injectors or faulty ECM.

Diagnostic Aids:

There may be fuel spray at the fuel injectors, but it may not be enough to start the engine. If the fuel injectors and their circuits are OK, and fuel spray is detected, the fuel injector nozzle may be partly blocked or restricted, refer to Chart A1-7A for circuit opening relay circuit test.

An intermittent may be caused by a poor connection, rubbed through wire insulation, or a wire broken inside the insulation. Inspect harness connectors for backed out terminals, improper mating, broken locks, improperly formed or damaged terminals and poor terminal-to-wire connections before component replacement.

Fig. 161 Fuel system diagnosis — 1993 VIN code 6 engine

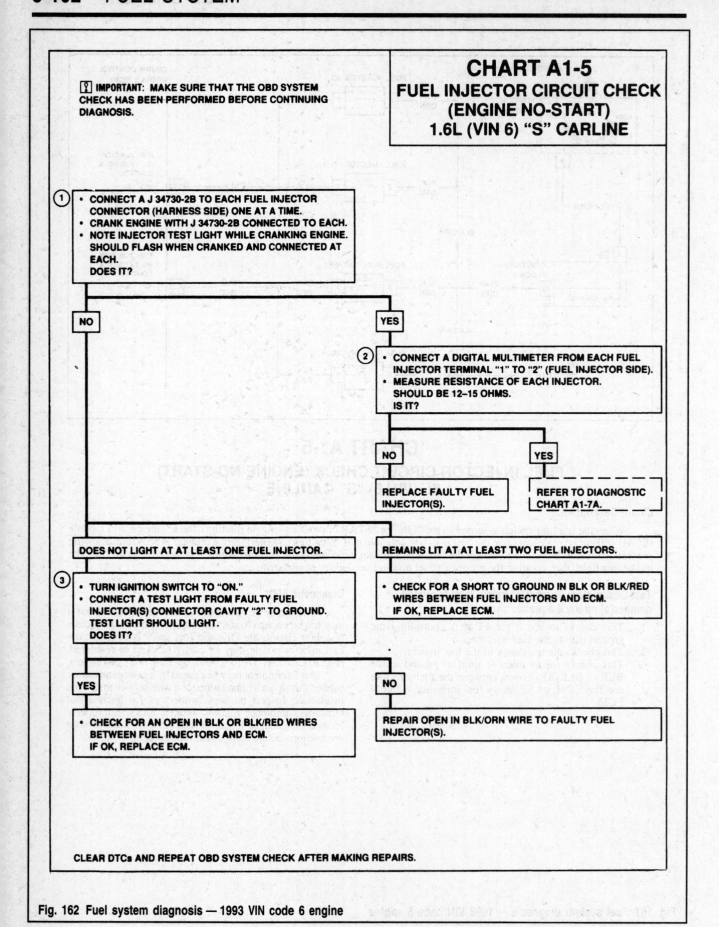

CHART A1-5
FUEL INJECTOR CIRCUIT CHECK
(ENGINE NO-START)
1.6L (VIN 6) "S" CARLINE

▢ IMPORTANT: MAKE SURE THAT THE OBD SYSTEM CHECK HAS BEEN PERFORMED BEFORE CONTINUING DIAGNOSIS.

①
- CONNECT A J 34730-2B TO EACH FUEL INJECTOR CONNECTOR (HARNESS SIDE) ONE AT A TIME.
- CRANK ENGINE WITH J 34730-2B CONNECTED TO EACH.
- NOTE INJECTOR TEST LIGHT WHILE CRANKING ENGINE. SHOULD FLASH WHEN CRANKED AND CONNECTED AT EACH.
  DOES IT?

NO

YES

②
- CONNECT A DIGITAL MULTIMETER FROM EACH FUEL INJECTOR TERMINAL "1" TO "2" (FUEL INJECTOR SIDE).
- MEASURE RESISTANCE OF EACH INJECTOR. SHOULD BE 12–15 OHMS.
  IS IT?

NO

YES

REPLACE FAULTY FUEL INJECTOR(S).

REFER TO DIAGNOSTIC CHART A1-7A.

DOES NOT LIGHT AT AT LEAST ONE FUEL INJECTOR.

REMAINS LIT AT AT LEAST TWO FUEL INJECTORS.

③
- TURN IGNITION SWITCH TO "ON."
- CONNECT A TEST LIGHT FROM FAULTY FUEL INJECTOR(S) CONNECTOR CAVITY "2" TO GROUND. TEST LIGHT SHOULD LIGHT.
  DOES IT?

- CHECK FOR A SHORT TO GROUND IN BLK OR BLK/RED WIRES BETWEEN FUEL INJECTORS AND ECM.
  IF OK, REPLACE ECM.

YES

NO

- CHECK FOR AN OPEN IN BLK OR BLK/RED WIRES BETWEEN FUEL INJECTORS AND ECM.
  IF OK, REPLACE ECM.

REPAIR OPEN IN BLK/ORN WIRE TO FAULTY FUEL INJECTOR(S).

CLEAR DTCs AND REPEAT OBD SYSTEM CHECK AFTER MAKING REPAIRS.

Fig. 162 Fuel system diagnosis — 1993 VIN code 6 engine

CHART A1-7A

(Page 1 of 2)
FUEL SYSTEM DIAGNOSIS (CIRCUIT OPENING RELAY CHECK)
1.6L (VIN 6) "S" CARLINE

Circuit Description:

When the ignition switch is turned to the "START" position, the circuit opening relay will be energized to allow the fuel pump to operate to pressurize the system. The fuel pump will continue to operate if the engine control module (ECM) receives an ignition signal when the engine is started. The fuel pump operates as long as the circuit opening relay is energized by the ECM. When the circuit opening relay is de-energized, the fuel pump will stop operating.

Test Description: Number(s) below refer to circled number(s) on the diagnostic chart.

1. This checks for normal fuel pump operation.
2. This checks to see if the fuel pump will run when DLC terminals "+B" and "FP" are jumpered together.
3. This checks fuel pump operation while the ignition signal is present at the ECM.
4. This checks for an open in BLK/RED wire to circuit opening relay.
5. This checks for an open in BLK/RED wire to DLC.

Diagnostic Aids:

A restricted or leaking fuel feed pipe or hose will cause an "Engine Cranks But Will Not Run" condition. Check fuel sender assembly connections inside of fuel tank for poor connections. Refer to Chart A1-7B for fuel pressure test.

An intermittent may be caused by a poor connection, rubbed through wire insulation, or a wire broken inside the insulation. Inspect harness connectors for backed out terminals, improper mating, broken locks, improperly formed or damaged terminals and poor terminal-to-wire connections before component replacement.

Fig. 163 Fuel system diagnosis — 1993 VIN code 6 engine

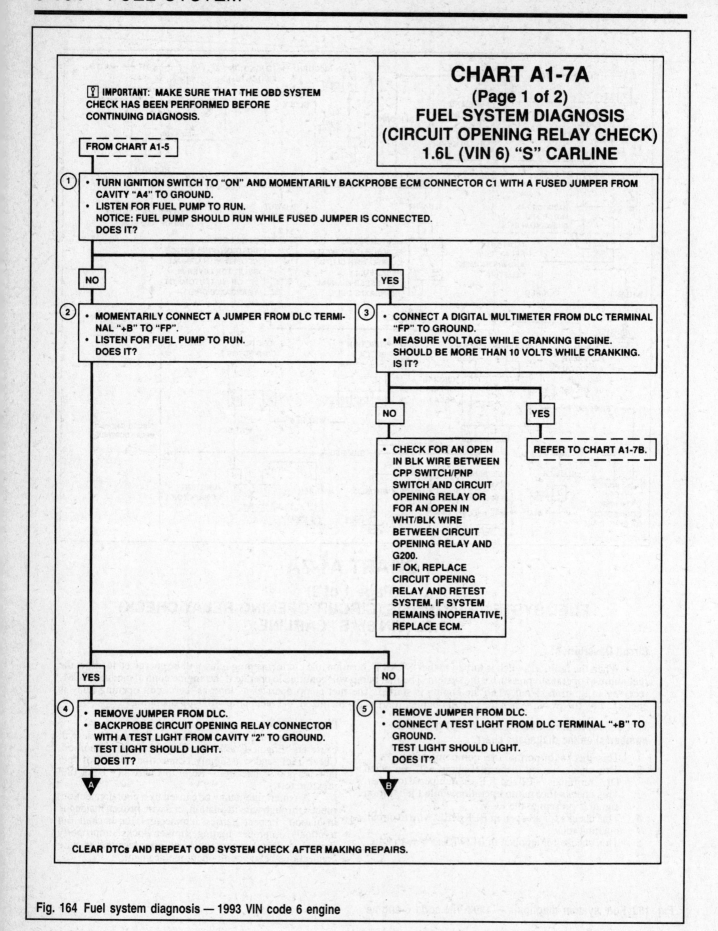

Fig. 164 Fuel system diagnosis — 1993 VIN code 6 engine

CHART A1-7A

(Page 2 of 2)
FUEL SYSTEM DIAGNOSIS (CIRCUIT OPENING RELAY CHECK)
1.6L (VIN 6) "S" CARLINE

Circuit Description:

When the ignition switch is turned to the "START" position, the circuit opening relay will be energized to allow the fuel pump to operate to pressurize the system. The fuel pump will continue to operate if the engine control module (ECM) receives an ignition signal when the engine is started. The fuel pump operates as long as the circuit opening relay is energized by the ECM. When the circuit opening relay is de-energized, the fuel pump will stop operating.

Test Description: Number(s) below refer to circled number(s) on the diagnostic chart.

6. This checks for an open BLU/BLK or GRN/RED wire, a faulty ECM or for a faulty circuit opening relay.

7. This checks for an open WHT/BLK or BLU/BLK wire, or for a faulty fuel pump.

Diagnostic Aids:

A restricted fuel feed pipe or hose will cause an "Engine Cranks But Will Not Run" condition. Check fuel sender assembly connections inside of fuel tank for poor connections.

An intermittent may be caused by a poor connection, rubbed through wire insulation, or a wire broken inside the insulation. Inspect harness connectors for backed out terminals, improper mating, broken locks, improperly formed or damaged terminals and poor terminal-to-wire connections before component replacement.

Fig. 165 Fuel system diagnosis — 1993 VIN code 6 engine

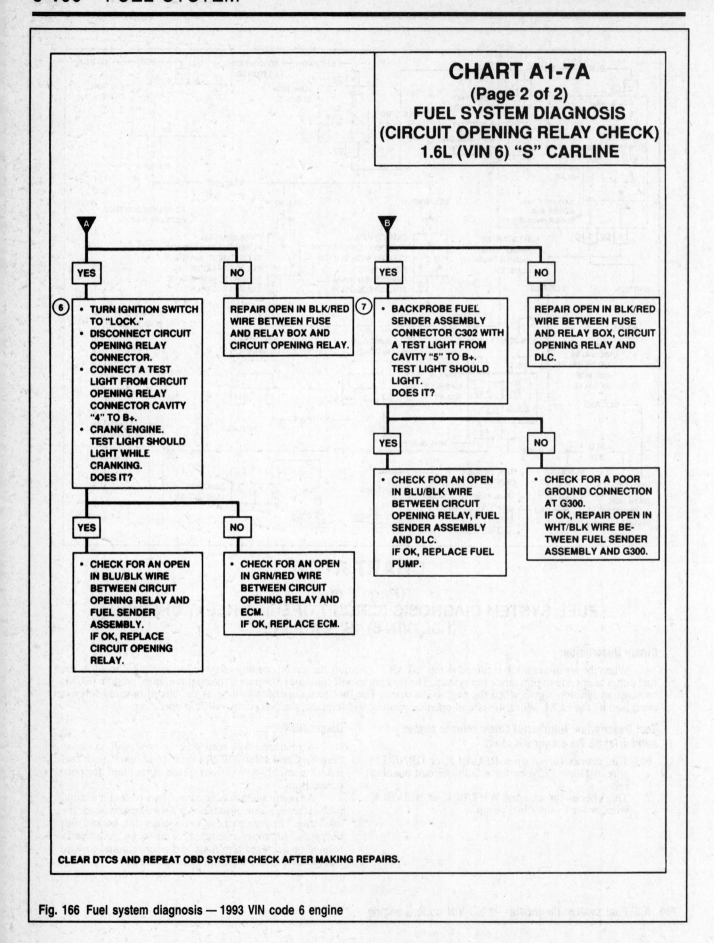

CHART A1-7A
(Page 2 of 2)
FUEL SYSTEM DIAGNOSIS
(CIRCUIT OPENING RELAY CHECK)
1.6L (VIN 6) "S" CARLINE

A

YES

NO

⑥
- TURN IGNITION SWITCH TO "LOCK."
- DISCONNECT CIRCUIT OPENING RELAY CONNECTOR.
- CONNECT A TEST LIGHT FROM CIRCUIT OPENING RELAY CONNECTOR CAVITY "4" TO B+.
- CRANK ENGINE. TEST LIGHT SHOULD LIGHT WHILE CRANKING. DOES IT?

REPAIR OPEN IN BLK/RED WIRE BETWEEN FUSE AND RELAY BOX AND CIRCUIT OPENING RELAY.

YES

NO

- CHECK FOR AN OPEN IN BLU/BLK WIRE BETWEEN CIRCUIT OPENING RELAY AND FUEL SENDER ASSEMBLY. IF OK, REPLACE CIRCUIT OPENING RELAY.

- CHECK FOR AN OPEN IN GRN/RED WIRE BETWEEN CIRCUIT OPENING RELAY AND ECM. IF OK, REPLACE ECM.

B

YES

NO

⑦
- BACKPROBE FUEL SENDER ASSEMBLY CONNECTOR C302 WITH A TEST LIGHT FROM CAVITY "5" TO B+. TEST LIGHT SHOULD LIGHT. DOES IT?

REPAIR OPEN IN BLK/RED WIRE BETWEEN FUSE AND RELAY BOX, CIRCUIT OPENING RELAY AND DLC.

YES

NO

- CHECK FOR AN OPEN IN BLU/BLK WIRE BETWEEN CIRCUIT OPENING RELAY, FUEL SENDER ASSEMBLY AND DLC. IF OK, REPLACE FUEL PUMP.

- CHECK FOR A POOR GROUND CONNECTION AT G300. IF OK, REPAIR OPEN IN WHT/BLK WIRE BETWEEN FUEL SENDER ASSEMBLY AND G300.

CLEAR DTCS AND REPEAT OBD SYSTEM CHECK AFTER MAKING REPAIRS.

Fig. 166 Fuel system diagnosis — 1993 VIN code 6 engine

CHART A1-7B

(Page 1 of 2)
FUEL SYSTEM DIAGNOSIS (FUEL PRESSURE CHECK)
1.6L (VIN 6) "S" CARLINE

Circuit Description:

When the ignition switch is turned to the "START" position, the circuit opening relay will be energized to allow the fuel pump to operate to pressurize the system. The fuel pump will continue to operate if the engine control module (ECM) receives an ignition signal when the engine is started. The fuel pump operates as long as the circuit opening relay is energized by the ECM. When the circuit opening relay is de-energized, the fuel pump will stop operating. The fuel pump delivers fuel to the fuel rail where the pressure is maintained by the fuel pressure regulator at 284 kPa (41 psi) higher than the pressure inside the intake manifold. Excess fuel is returned to the fuel tank through a return pipe and hoses.

Test Description: Number(s) below refer to the circled number(s) on the diagnostic chart.

1. This measures the fuel pressure with the ignition switch in "ON."
2. This determines if the fuel pressure is normal.
3. This checks for a leaking fuel pressure regulator.
4. This checks for plugged fuel injectors.
5. This checks for leaking fuel injectors or a leaking fuel pump.

Diagnostic Aids:

Check for leakage around all fuel hose/pipe connections.

A plugged fuel injector could be the cause of a hard/no-start condition or loss of power/poor fuel economy.

Fig. 167 Fuel system diagnosis — 1993 VIN code 6 engine

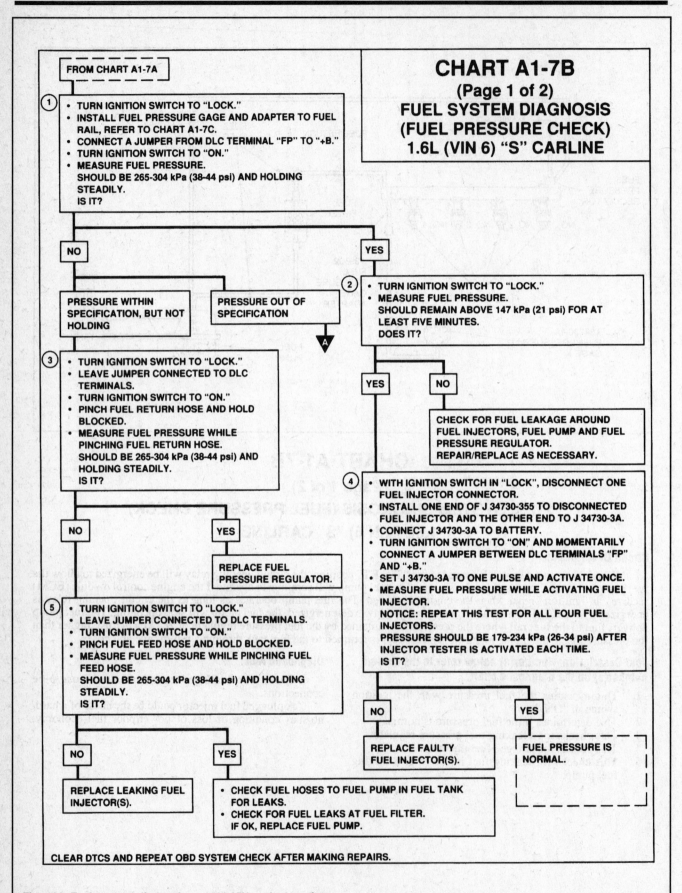

FROM CHART A1-7A

CHART A1-7B
(Page 1 of 2)
FUEL SYSTEM DIAGNOSIS
(FUEL PRESSURE CHECK)
1.6L (VIN 6) "S" CARLINE

1
- TURN IGNITION SWITCH TO "LOCK."
- INSTALL FUEL PRESSURE GAGE AND ADAPTER TO FUEL RAIL, REFER TO CHART A1-7C.
- CONNECT A JUMPER FROM DLC TERMINAL "FP" TO "+B."
- TURN IGNITION SWITCH TO "ON."
- MEASURE FUEL PRESSURE.
  SHOULD BE 265-304 kPa (38-44 psi) AND HOLDING STEADILY.
  IS IT?

NO

YES

PRESSURE WITHIN SPECIFICATION, BUT NOT HOLDING

PRESSURE OUT OF SPECIFICATION

A

2
- TURN IGNITION SWITCH TO "LOCK."
- MEASURE FUEL PRESSURE.
  SHOULD REMAIN ABOVE 147 kPa (21 psi) FOR AT LEAST FIVE MINUTES.
  DOES IT?

YES

NO

CHECK FOR FUEL LEAKAGE AROUND FUEL INJECTORS, FUEL PUMP AND FUEL PRESSURE REGULATOR.
REPAIR/REPLACE AS NECESSARY.

3
- TURN IGNITION SWITCH TO "LOCK."
- LEAVE JUMPER CONNECTED TO DLC TERMINALS.
- TURN IGNITION SWITCH TO "ON."
- PINCH FUEL RETURN HOSE AND HOLD BLOCKED.
- MEASURE FUEL PRESSURE WHILE PINCHING FUEL RETURN HOSE.
  SHOULD BE 265-304 kPa (38-44 psi) AND HOLDING STEADILY.
  IS IT?

4
- WITH IGNITION SWITCH IN "LOCK", DISCONNECT ONE FUEL INJECTOR CONNECTOR.
- INSTALL ONE END OF J 34730-355 TO DISCONNECTED FUEL INJECTOR AND THE OTHER END TO J 34730-3A.
- CONNECT J 34730-3A TO BATTERY.
- TURN IGNITION SWITCH TO "ON" AND MOMENTARILY CONNECT A JUMPER BETWEEN DLC TERMINALS "FP" AND "+B."
- SET J 34730-3A TO ONE PULSE AND ACTIVATE ONCE.
- MEASURE FUEL PRESSURE WHILE ACTIVATING FUEL INJECTOR.
  NOTICE: REPEAT THIS TEST FOR ALL FOUR FUEL INJECTORS.
  PRESSURE SHOULD BE 179-234 kPa (26-34 psi) AFTER INJECTOR TESTER IS ACTIVATED EACH TIME.
  IS IT?

NO

YES

REPLACE FUEL PRESSURE REGULATOR.

5
- TURN IGNITION SWITCH TO "LOCK."
- LEAVE JUMPER CONNECTED TO DLC TERMINALS.
- TURN IGNITION SWITCH TO "ON."
- PINCH FUEL FEED HOSE AND HOLD BLOCKED.
- MEASURE FUEL PRESSURE WHILE PINCHING FUEL FEED HOSE.
  SHOULD BE 265-304 kPa (38-44 psi) AND HOLDING STEADILY.
  IS IT?

NO

YES

REPLACE LEAKING FUEL INJECTOR(S).

- CHECK FUEL HOSES TO FUEL PUMP IN FUEL TANK FOR LEAKS.
- CHECK FOR FUEL LEAKS AT FUEL FILTER.
  IF OK, REPLACE FUEL PUMP.

NO

YES

REPLACE FAULTY FUEL INJECTOR(S).

FUEL PRESSURE IS NORMAL.

CLEAR DTCS AND REPEAT OBD SYSTEM CHECK AFTER MAKING REPAIRS.

Fig. 168 Fuel system diagnosis — 1993 VIN code 6 engine

CHART A1-7B

(Page 2 of 2)
FUEL SYSTEM DIAGNOSIS (FUEL PRESSURE CHECK)
1.6L (VIN 6) "S" CARLINE

Circuit Description:

When the ignition switch is turned to the "START" position, the circuit opening relay will be energized to allow the fuel pump to operate to pressurize the system. The fuel pump will continue to operate if the engine control module (ECM) receives an ignition signal when the engine is started. The fuel pump operates as long as the circuit opening relay is energized by the ECM. When the circuit opening relay is de-energized, the fuel pump will stop operating. The fuel pump delivers fuel to the fuel rail where the pressure is maintained by the fuel pressure regulator at 284 kPa (41 psi) higher than the pressure inside the intake manifold. Excess fuel is returned to the fuel tank through a return pipe and hoses.

Test Description: Number(s) below refer to the circled number(s) on the diagnostic chart.

6. This checks for a leaking fuel pressure regulator or fuel pump.

Diagnostic Aids:

Check for leakage around all fuel hose/pipe connections.

A plugged fuel injector could be the cause of a hard/no-start condition or loss of power/poor fuel economy.

Fig. 169 Fuel system diagnosis — 1993 VIN code 6 engine

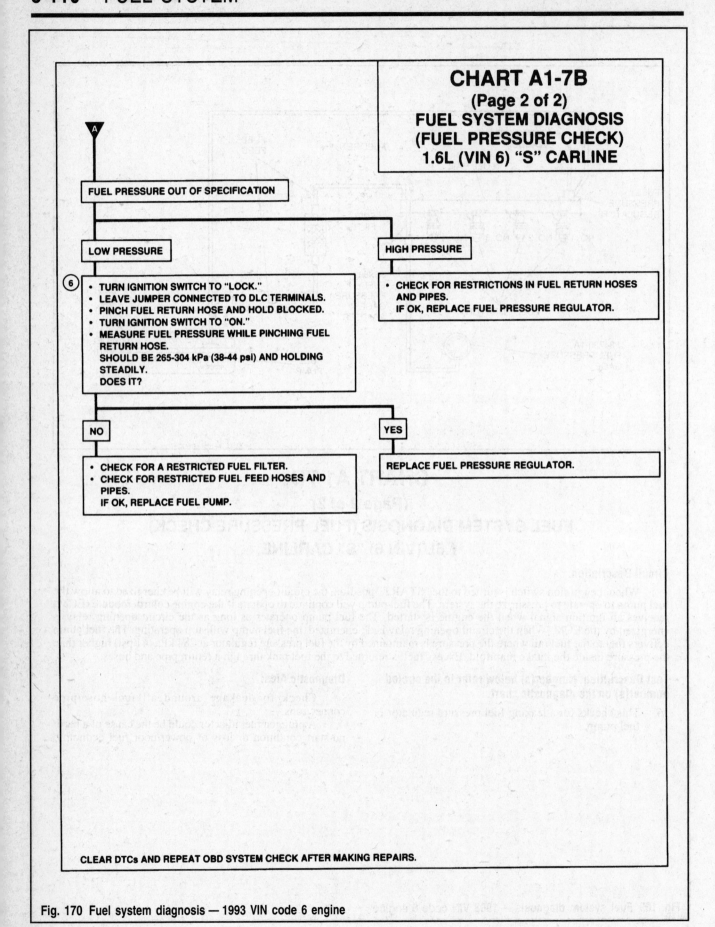

CHART A1-7B
(Page 2 of 2)
FUEL SYSTEM DIAGNOSIS
(FUEL PRESSURE CHECK)
1.6L (VIN 6) "S" CARLINE

A

FUEL PRESSURE OUT OF SPECIFICATION

LOW PRESSURE

6 • TURN IGNITION SWITCH TO "LOCK."
• LEAVE JUMPER CONNECTED TO DLC TERMINALS.
• PINCH FUEL RETURN HOSE AND HOLD BLOCKED.
• TURN IGNITION SWITCH TO "ON."
• MEASURE FUEL PRESSURE WHILE PINCHING FUEL
RETURN HOSE.
SHOULD BE 265-304 kPa (38-44 psi) AND HOLDING
STEADILY.
DOES IT?

HIGH PRESSURE

• CHECK FOR RESTRICTIONS IN FUEL RETURN HOSES
AND PIPES.
IF OK, REPLACE FUEL PRESSURE REGULATOR.

NO

• CHECK FOR A RESTRICTED FUEL FILTER.
• CHECK FOR RESTRICTED FUEL FEED HOSES AND
PIPES.
IF OK, REPLACE FUEL PUMP.

YES

REPLACE FUEL PRESSURE REGULATOR.

CLEAR DTCs AND REPEAT OBD SYSTEM CHECK AFTER MAKING REPAIRS.

Fig. 170 Fuel system diagnosis — 1993 VIN code 6 engine

CHART A1-7C
FUEL SYSTEM DIAGNOSIS (FUEL PRESSURE GAGE)
1.6L (VIN 6) "S" CARLINE

Circuit Description:

The procedure on the facing page must be followed in order to install/remove the fuel pressure gage and adapter correctly. Make sure to observe all CAUTIONS while performing this procedure.

Fig. 171 Fuel system diagnosis — 1993 VIN code 6 engine

CHART A1-7C
FUEL SYSTEM DIAGNOSIS (FUEL PRESSURE GAGE) 1.6L (VIN 6) "S" CARLINE

Tools Required:
J 34730-1A Fuel Pressure Gage
J 39802 Fuel Pressure Gage Adapter

CAUTION

- To reduce the risk of fire and personal injury, it is necessary to relieve the fuel system pressure before servicing the fuel system.
- After relieving fuel system pressure, a small amount of fuel may be released when servicing fuel pipe or hose connections. To reduce the chance of personal injury and to catch any fuel that may leak out, cover fuel pipe fittings with a shop towel before disconnecting them. Place the shop towel in an approved container when disconnect is completed.

FUEL PRESSURE GAGE INSTALLATION:

1. Relieve fuel system pressure.
   A. Loosen fuel filler cap to relieve tank pressure.
   B. Remove center trim bezel from center console by gently prying around edges to disconnect clips.
   C. Remove four screws and radio from center console (if equipped).
   D. Disconnect circuit opening relay electrical connector.
   E. Crank engine and allow to stall. Crank engine for an additional 3 seconds to assure relief of any remaining fuel pressure.
   F. Remove negative (-) battery cable.
   G. Reconnect circuit opening relay electrical connector.
   H. Tighten fuel filler cap.
2. Remove one bolt and fuel feed hose bracket from bottom on intake manifold.
3. Remove one bolt and fuel feed hose from fuel rail.
4. Install J 39802 with two gaskets and fuel feed hose to fuel rail.

   Tighten
   - J 39802 bolt to 29 N·m (22 lb.ft.).

5. Connect J 34730-1A to J 39802.
6. Reconnect negative (-) battery cable.

   Tighten
   - Negative (-) battery cable-to-negative (-) battery cable retainer to 15 N·m (11 lb.ft.).

FUEL PRESSURE GAGE REMOVAL

1. Relieve fuel system pressure.
   A. Loosen fuel filler cap to relieve tank pressure.
   B. Disconnect circuit opening relay electrical connector.
   C. Crank engine and allow to stall. Crank engine for an additional 3 seconds to assure relief of any remaining fuel pressure.
   D. Remove negative (-) battery cable.
   E. Reconnect circuit opening relay electrical connector.
   F. Install radio into center console (if equipped); secure with four screws.
   G. Install center trim bezel to center console, pushing in until clips engage.
   H. Tighten fuel filler cap.
2. Remove J 34730-1A from J 39802 and J 39802 from fuel rail.
3. Connect fuel feed hose with new gaskets to fuel rail.

   Tighten
   - Fuel feed hose bolt to 29 N·m (22 lb.ft.).

4. Connect fuel feed hose bracket to bottom of intake manifold, secure with one bolt.

   Tighten
   - Fuel feed hose bracket bolt to 10 N·m (89 lb. in.)

5. Reconnect negative (-) battery cable.

   Tighten
   - Negative (-) battery cable-to-negative (-) battery cable retainer to 15 N·m (11 lb.ft.).

6. Turn ignition switch to "ON" and momentarily connect a jumper between DLC terminals "+B" and "Fp" to pressurize the fuel system. Check for fuel leaks.

Fig. 172 Fuel system diagnosis — 1993 VIN code 6 engine

CHART A2-5

FUEL INJECTOR CIRCUIT CHECK (ENGINE NO-START)
1.8L (VIN 8) "S" CARLINE

Circuit Description:

When the ignition switch is turned to the "ON" or "START" position (engine running), the powertrain control module (PCM) will energize/de-energize the fuel injectors solenoid coil. With this coil energized, a plunger is activated, allowing pressurized fuel to be sprayed through the fuel injectors into the combustion chamber where it is mixed with air from the intake manifold; thus creating the proper air/fuel mixture needed for combustion.

Test Description: Number(s) below refer to circled number(s) on the diagnostic chart.

1. This checks to see if the PCM is controlling the ground path to the fuel injectors.
2. This checks the resistance of the fuel injectors.
3. This checks for an open or short to ground in the BLK or BLK/RED wires between the fuel injectors and the PCM, or for faulty fuel injectors or faulty PCM.

Diagnostic Aids:

There may be fuel spray at the fuel injectors, but it may not be enough to start the engine. If the fuel injectors and their circuit are OK, and fuel spray is detected, the fuel injector nozzle may be partly blocked or restricted. Refer to Chart A2-7A for circuit opening relay circuit test.

An intermittent may be caused by a poor connection, rubbed through wire insulation, or a wire broken inside the insulation. Inspect harness connectors for backed out terminals, improper mating, broken locks, improperly formed or damaged terminals and poor terminal-to-wire connections before component replacement.

Fig. 173 Fuel system diagnosis — 1993 VIN code 8 engine

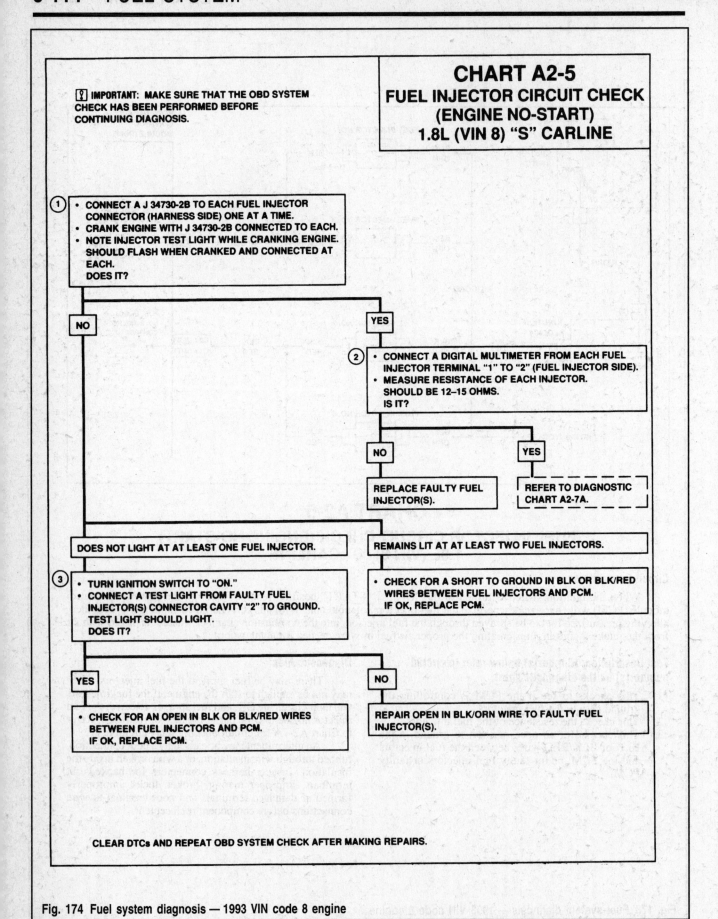

① • CONNECT A J 34730-2B TO EACH FUEL INJECTOR
  CONNECTOR (HARNESS SIDE) ONE AT A TIME.
 • CRANK ENGINE WITH J 34730-2B CONNECTED TO EACH.
 • NOTE INJECTOR TEST LIGHT WHILE CRANKING ENGINE.
  SHOULD FLASH WHEN CRANKED AND CONNECTED AT
  EACH.
  DOES IT?

CHART A2-5
FUEL INJECTOR CIRCUIT CHECK
(ENGINE NO-START)
1.8L (VIN 8) "S" CARLINE

⚷ IMPORTANT: MAKE SURE THAT THE OBD SYSTEM
CHECK HAS BEEN PERFORMED BEFORE
CONTINUING DIAGNOSIS.

NO

YES

② • CONNECT A DIGITAL MULTIMETER FROM EACH FUEL
  INJECTOR TERMINAL "1" TO "2" (FUEL INJECTOR SIDE).
 • MEASURE RESISTANCE OF EACH INJECTOR.
  SHOULD BE 12–15 OHMS.
  IS IT?

NO

YES

REPLACE FAULTY FUEL
INJECTOR(S).

REFER TO DIAGNOSTIC
CHART A2-7A.

DOES NOT LIGHT AT AT LEAST ONE FUEL INJECTOR.

REMAINS LIT AT AT LEAST TWO FUEL INJECTORS.

③ • TURN IGNITION SWITCH TO "ON."
 • CONNECT A TEST LIGHT FROM FAULTY FUEL
  INJECTOR(S) CONNECTOR CAVITY "2" TO GROUND.
  TEST LIGHT SHOULD LIGHT.
  DOES IT?

• CHECK FOR A SHORT TO GROUND IN BLK OR BLK/RED
 WIRES BETWEEN FUEL INJECTORS AND PCM.
 IF OK, REPLACE PCM.

YES

NO

• CHECK FOR AN OPEN IN BLK OR BLK/RED WIRES
 BETWEEN FUEL INJECTORS AND PCM.
 IF OK, REPLACE PCM.

REPAIR OPEN IN BLK/ORN WIRE TO FAULTY FUEL
INJECTOR(S).

CLEAR DTCs AND REPEAT OBD SYSTEM CHECK AFTER MAKING REPAIRS.

Fig. 174 Fuel system diagnosis — 1993 VIN code 8 engine

CHART A2-7A
(Page 1 of 2)
FUEL SYSTEM DIAGNOSIS (CIRCUIT OPENING RELAY CHECK)
1.8L (VIN 8) "S" CARLINE

Circuit Description:

When the ignition switch is turned to the "START" position, the circuit opening relay will be energized to allow the fuel pump to operate to pressurize the system. The fuel pump will continue to operate if the powertrain control module (PCM) receives an ignition signal when the engine is started. The fuel pump operates as long as the circuit opening relay is energized by the PCM. When the circuit opening relay is de-energized, the fuel pump will stop operating.

Test Description: Number(s) below refer to circled number(s) on the diagnostic chart.

1. This checks for normal fuel pump operation.
2. This checks to see if the fuel pump will run when DLC terminals "+B" and "FP" are jumpered together.
3. This checks fuel pump operation while the ignition signal is present at the PCM.
4. This checks for an open in BLK/RED wire to circuit opening relay.
5. This checks for an open in BLK/RED wire to DLC.

Diagnostic Aids:

A restricted or leaking fuel feed pipe or hose will cause an "Engine Cranks But Will Not Run" condition. Check fuel sender assembly connections inside of fuel tank for poor connections. Refer to Chart A2-7B for fuel pressure test.

An intermittent may be caused by a poor connection, rubbed through wire insulation, or a wire broken inside the insulation. Inspect harness connectors for backed out terminals, improper mating, broken locks, improperly formed or damaged terminals and poor terminal-to-wire connections before component replacement.

Fig. 175 Fuel system diagnosis — 1993 VIN code 8 engine

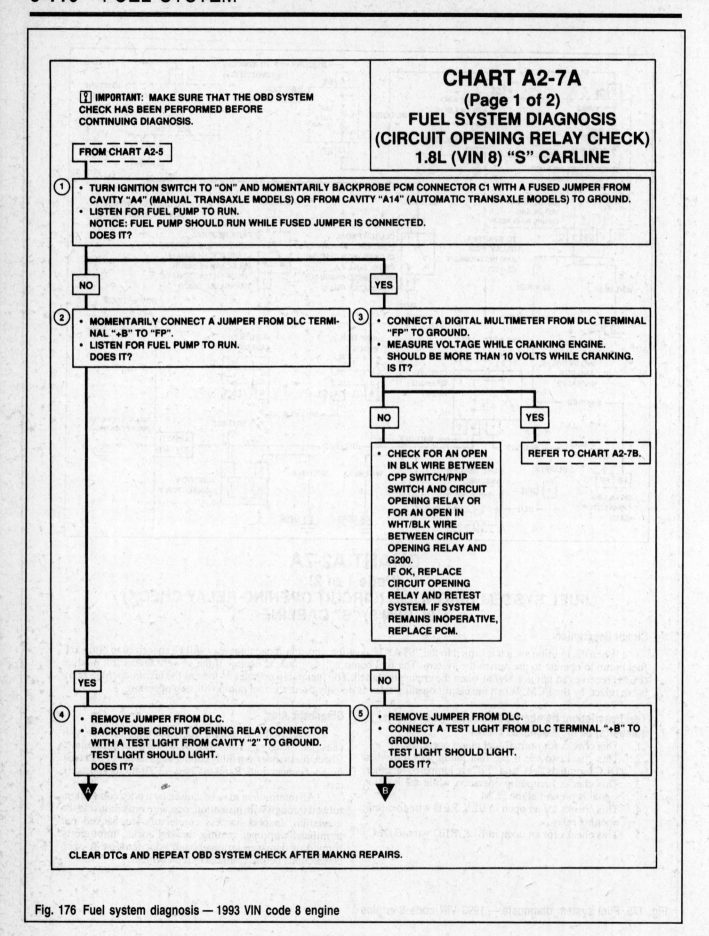

CHART A2-7A
(Page 1 of 2)
FUEL SYSTEM DIAGNOSIS
(CIRCUIT OPENING RELAY CHECK)
1.8L (VIN 8) "S" CARLINE

⚠ IMPORTANT: MAKE SURE THAT THE OBD SYSTEM CHECK HAS BEEN PERFORMED BEFORE CONTINUING DIAGNOSIS.

FROM CHART A2-5

① • TURN IGNITION SWITCH TO "ON" AND MOMENTARILY BACKPROBE PCM CONNECTOR C1 WITH A FUSED JUMPER FROM CAVITY "A4" (MANUAL TRANSAXLE MODELS) OR FROM CAVITY "A14" (AUTOMATIC TRANSAXLE MODELS) TO GROUND.
• LISTEN FOR FUEL PUMP TO RUN.
NOTICE: FUEL PUMP SHOULD RUN WHILE FUSED JUMPER IS CONNECTED.
DOES IT?

NO

YES

② • MOMENTARILY CONNECT A JUMPER FROM DLC TERMINAL "+B" TO "FP".
• LISTEN FOR FUEL PUMP TO RUN.
DOES IT?

③ • CONNECT A DIGITAL MULTIMETER FROM DLC TERMINAL "FP" TO GROUND.
• MEASURE VOLTAGE WHILE CRANKING ENGINE. SHOULD BE MORE THAN 10 VOLTS WHILE CRANKING.
IS IT?

NO

YES

• CHECK FOR AN OPEN IN BLK WIRE BETWEEN CPP SWITCH/PNP SWITCH AND CIRCUIT OPENING RELAY OR FOR AN OPEN IN WHT/BLK WIRE BETWEEN CIRCUIT OPENING RELAY AND G200.
IF OK, REPLACE CIRCUIT OPENING RELAY AND RETEST SYSTEM. IF SYSTEM REMAINS INOPERATIVE, REPLACE PCM.

REFER TO CHART A2-7B.

YES

NO

④ • REMOVE JUMPER FROM DLC.
• BACKPROBE CIRCUIT OPENING RELAY CONNECTOR WITH A TEST LIGHT FROM CAVITY "2" TO GROUND.
TEST LIGHT SHOULD LIGHT.
DOES IT?

⑤ • REMOVE JUMPER FROM DLC.
• CONNECT A TEST LIGHT FROM DLC TERMINAL "+B" TO GROUND.
TEST LIGHT SHOULD LIGHT.
DOES IT?

Ⓐ

Ⓑ

CLEAR DTCs AND REPEAT OBD SYSTEM CHECK AFTER MAKING REPAIRS.

Fig. 176 Fuel system diagnosis — 1993 VIN code 8 engine

CHART A2-7A
(Page 2 of 2)
FUEL SYSTEM DIAGNOSIS (CIRCUIT OPENING RELAY CHECK)
1.8L (VIN 8) "S" CARLINE

Circuit Description:

When the ignition switch is turned to the "START" position, the circuit opening relay will be energized to allow the fuel pump to operate to pressurize the system. The fuel pump will continue to operate if the powertrain control module (PCM) receives an ignition signal when the engine is started. The fuel pump operates as long as the circuit opening relay is energized by the PCM. When the circuit opening relay is de-energized, the fuel pump will stop operating.

Test Description: Number(s) below refer to the circled number(s) on the diagnostic charts.

6. This checks for an open BLU/BLK or GRN/RED wire, a faulty PCM or for a faulty circuit opening relay.
7. This checks for an open WHT/BLK or BLU/BLK wire, or for a faulty fuel pump.

Diagnostic Aids:

A restricted or leaking fuel feed pipe or hose will cause an "Engine Cranks But Will Not Run" condition. Check fuel sender assembly connections inside of fuel tank for poor connections. Refer to Chart A2-7B for fuel pressure test.

An intermittent may be caused by a poor connection, rubbed through wire insulation, or a wire broken inside the insulation. Inspect harness connectors for backed out terminals, improper mating, broken locks, improperly formed or damaged terminals and poor terminal-to-wire connections before component replacement.

Fig. 177 Fuel system diagnosis — 1993 VIN code 8 engine

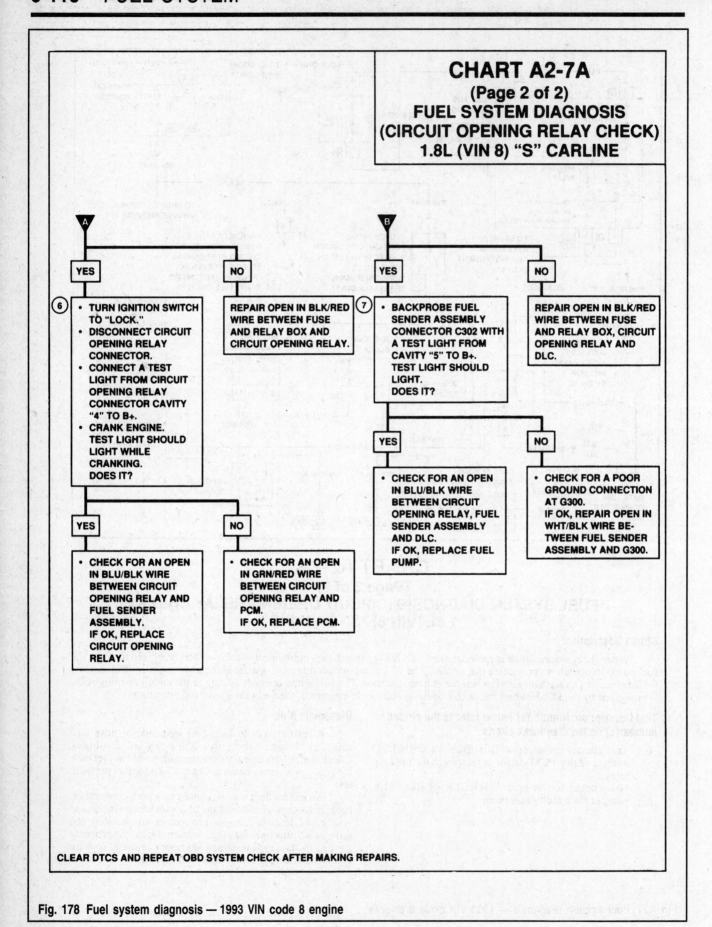

CHART A2-7A
(Page 2 of 2)
FUEL SYSTEM DIAGNOSIS
(CIRCUIT OPENING RELAY CHECK)
1.8L (VIN 8) "S" CARLINE

A

YES

NO

6 • TURN IGNITION SWITCH TO "LOCK."
• DISCONNECT CIRCUIT OPENING RELAY CONNECTOR.
• CONNECT A TEST LIGHT FROM CIRCUIT OPENING RELAY CONNECTOR CAVITY "4" TO B+.
• CRANK ENGINE. TEST LIGHT SHOULD LIGHT WHILE CRANKING. DOES IT?

REPAIR OPEN IN BLK/RED WIRE BETWEEN FUSE AND RELAY BOX AND CIRCUIT OPENING RELAY.

YES

NO

• CHECK FOR AN OPEN IN BLU/BLK WIRE BETWEEN CIRCUIT OPENING RELAY AND FUEL SENDER ASSEMBLY. IF OK, REPLACE CIRCUIT OPENING RELAY.

• CHECK FOR AN OPEN IN GRN/RED WIRE BETWEEN CIRCUIT OPENING RELAY AND PCM. IF OK, REPLACE PCM.

B

YES

NO

7 • BACKPROBE FUEL SENDER ASSEMBLY CONNECTOR C302 WITH A TEST LIGHT FROM CAVITY "5" TO B+. TEST LIGHT SHOULD LIGHT. DOES IT?

REPAIR OPEN IN BLK/RED WIRE BETWEEN FUSE AND RELAY BOX, CIRCUIT OPENING RELAY AND DLC.

YES

NO

• CHECK FOR AN OPEN IN BLU/BLK WIRE BETWEEN CIRCUIT OPENING RELAY, FUEL SENDER ASSEMBLY AND DLC. IF OK, REPLACE FUEL PUMP.

• CHECK FOR A POOR GROUND CONNECTION AT G300. IF OK, REPAIR OPEN IN WHT/BLK WIRE BETWEEN FUEL SENDER ASSEMBLY AND G300.

CLEAR DTCS AND REPEAT OBD SYSTEM CHECK AFTER MAKING REPAIRS.

Fig. 178 Fuel system diagnosis — 1993 VIN code 8 engine

CHART A2-7B
(Page 1 of 2)
FUEL SYSTEM DIAGNOSIS (FUEL PRESSURE CHECK)
1.8L (VIN 8) "S" CARLINE

Circuit Description:

When the ignition switch is turned to the "START" position, the circuit opening relay will be energized to allow the fuel pump to operate to pressurize the system. The fuel pump will continue to operate if the powertrain control module (PCM) receives an ignition signal when the engine is started. The fuel pump operates as long as the circuit opening relay is energized by the PCM. When the circuit opening relay is de-energized, the fuel pump will stop operating. The fuel pump delivers fuel to the fuel rail where the pressure is maintained by the fuel pressure regulator at 284 kPa (41 psi) higher than the pressure inside the intake manifold. Excess fuel is returned to the fuel tank through a return pipe and hoses.

Test Description: Number(s) below refer to the circled number(s) on the diagnostic chart.

1. This measures the fuel pressure with the ignition switch in "ON."
2. This determines if the fuel pressure is normal.
3. This checks for a leaking fuel pressure regulator.
4. This checks for plugged fuel injectors.
5. This checks for leaking fuel injectors or a leaking fuel pump.

Diagnostic Aids:

Check for leakage around all fuel hose/pipe connections.

A plugged fuel injector could be the cause of a hard/no-start condition or loss of power/poor fuel economy.

Fig. 179 Fuel system diagnosis — 1993 VIN code 8 engine

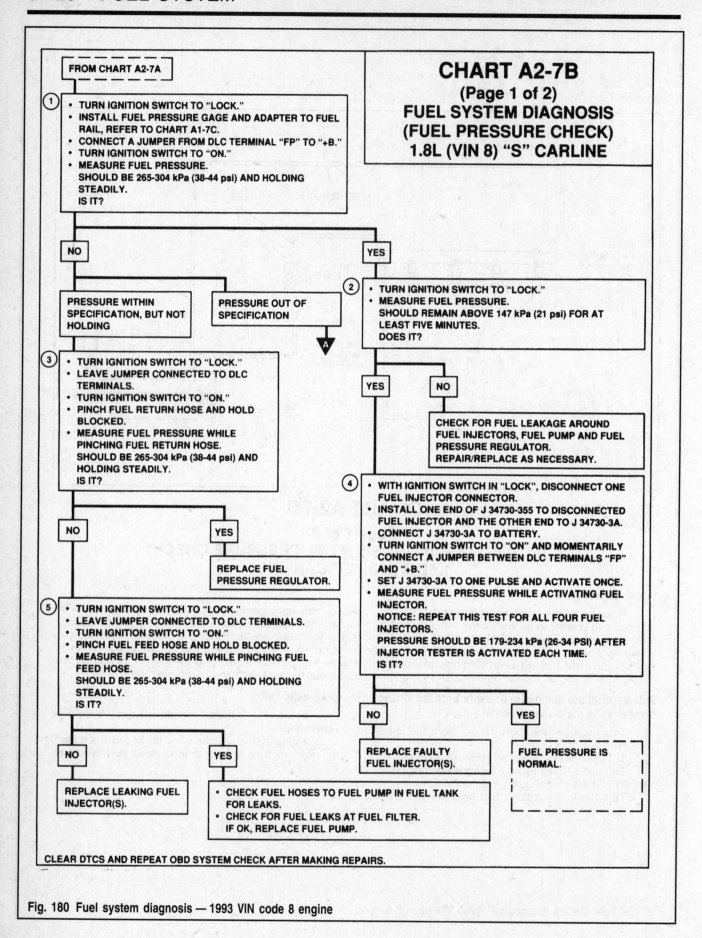

FROM CHART A2-7A

CHART A2-7B
(Page 1 of 2)
FUEL SYSTEM DIAGNOSIS
(FUEL PRESSURE CHECK)
1.8L (VIN 8) "S" CARLINE

1
- TURN IGNITION SWITCH TO "LOCK."
- INSTALL FUEL PRESSURE GAGE AND ADAPTER TO FUEL RAIL, REFER TO CHART A1-7C.
- CONNECT A JUMPER FROM DLC TERMINAL "FP" TO "+B."
- TURN IGNITION SWITCH TO "ON."
- MEASURE FUEL PRESSURE.
  SHOULD BE 265-304 kPa (38-44 psi) AND HOLDING STEADILY.
  IS IT?

NO

YES

PRESSURE WITHIN SPECIFICATION, BUT NOT HOLDING

PRESSURE OUT OF SPECIFICATION

A

2
- TURN IGNITION SWITCH TO "LOCK."
- MEASURE FUEL PRESSURE.
  SHOULD REMAIN ABOVE 147 kPa (21 psi) FOR AT LEAST FIVE MINUTES.
  DOES IT?

3
- TURN IGNITION SWITCH TO "LOCK."
- LEAVE JUMPER CONNECTED TO DLC TERMINALS.
- TURN IGNITION SWITCH TO "ON."
- PINCH FUEL RETURN HOSE AND HOLD BLOCKED.
- MEASURE FUEL PRESSURE WHILE PINCHING FUEL RETURN HOSE.
  SHOULD BE 265-304 kPa (38-44 psi) AND HOLDING STEADILY.
  IS IT?

YES

NO

CHECK FOR FUEL LEAKAGE AROUND FUEL INJECTORS, FUEL PUMP AND FUEL PRESSURE REGULATOR.
REPAIR/REPLACE AS NECESSARY.

NO

YES

REPLACE FUEL PRESSURE REGULATOR.

4
- WITH IGNITION SWITCH IN "LOCK", DISCONNECT ONE FUEL INJECTOR CONNECTOR.
- INSTALL ONE END OF J 34730-355 TO DISCONNECTED FUEL INJECTOR AND THE OTHER END TO J 34730-3A.
- CONNECT J 34730-3A TO BATTERY.
- TURN IGNITION SWITCH TO "ON" AND MOMENTARILY CONNECT A JUMPER BETWEEN DLC TERMINALS "FP" AND "+B."
- SET J 34730-3A TO ONE PULSE AND ACTIVATE ONCE.
- MEASURE FUEL PRESSURE WHILE ACTIVATING FUEL INJECTOR.
  NOTICE: REPEAT THIS TEST FOR ALL FOUR FUEL INJECTORS.
  PRESSURE SHOULD BE 179-234 kPa (26-34 PSI) AFTER INJECTOR TESTER IS ACTIVATED EACH TIME.
  IS IT?

5
- TURN IGNITION SWITCH TO "LOCK."
- LEAVE JUMPER CONNECTED TO DLC TERMINALS.
- TURN IGNITION SWITCH TO "ON."
- PINCH FUEL FEED HOSE AND HOLD BLOCKED.
- MEASURE FUEL PRESSURE WHILE PINCHING FUEL FEED HOSE.
  SHOULD BE 265-304 kPa (38-44 psi) AND HOLDING STEADILY.
  IS IT?

NO

YES

NO

YES

REPLACE FAULTY FUEL INJECTOR(S).

FUEL PRESSURE IS NORMAL.

REPLACE LEAKING FUEL INJECTOR(S).

- CHECK FUEL HOSES TO FUEL PUMP IN FUEL TANK FOR LEAKS.
- CHECK FOR FUEL LEAKS AT FUEL FILTER.
  IF OK, REPLACE FUEL PUMP.

CLEAR DTCS AND REPEAT OBD SYSTEM CHECK AFTER MAKING REPAIRS.

Fig. 180 Fuel system diagnosis — 1993 VIN code 8 engine

CHART A2-7B
(Page 2 of 2)
FUEL SYSTEM DIAGNOSIS (FUEL PRESSURE CHECK)
1.8L (VIN 8) "S" CARLINE

Circuit Description:

When the ignition switch is turned to the "START" position, the circuit opening relay will be energized to allow the fuel pump to operate to pressurize the system. The fuel pump will continue to operate if the powertrain control module (PCM) receives an ignition signal when the engine is started. The fuel pump operates as long as the circuit opening relay is energized by the PCM. When the circuit opening relay is de-energized, the fuel pump will stop operating. The fuel pump delivers fuel to the fuel rail where the pressure is maintained by the fuel pressure regulator at 284 kPa (41 psi) higher than the pressure inside the intake manifold. Excess fuel is returned to the fuel tank through a return pipe and hoses.

Test Description: Number(s) below refer to the circled number(s) on the diagnostic chart.

6. This checks for a leaking fuel pressure regulator or fuel pump.

Diagnostic Aids:

Check for leakage around all fuel hose/pipe connections.

A plugged fuel injector could be the cause of a hard/no-start condition or loss of power/poor fuel economy

Fig. 181 Fuel system diagnosis — 1993 VIN code 8 engine

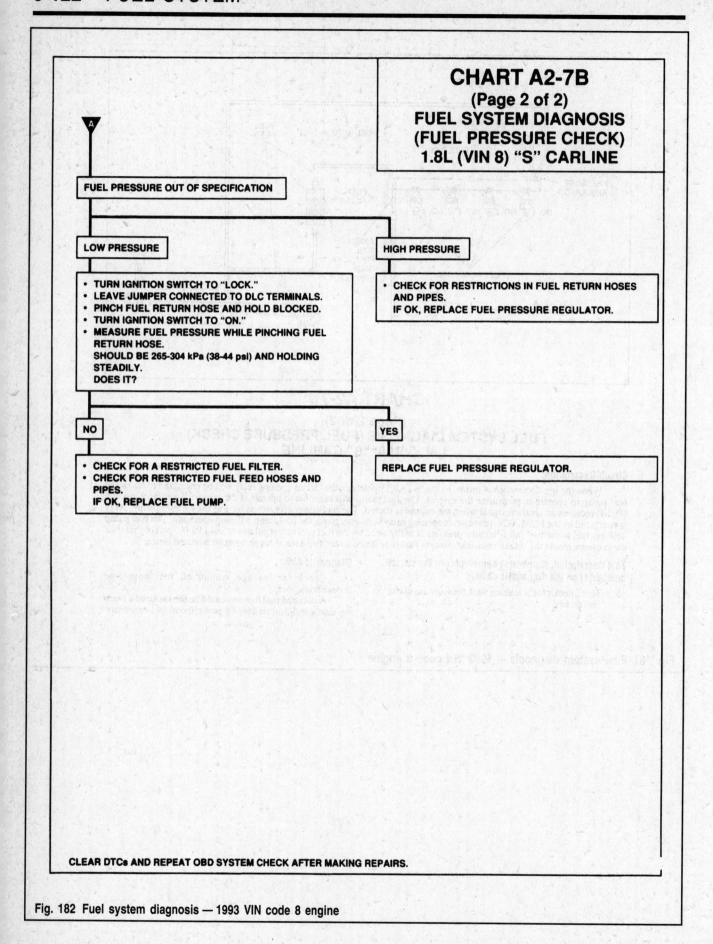

CHART A2-7B
(Page 2 of 2)
FUEL SYSTEM DIAGNOSIS
(FUEL PRESSURE CHECK)
1.8L (VIN 8) "S" CARLINE

A

FUEL PRESSURE OUT OF SPECIFICATION

LOW PRESSURE

HIGH PRESSURE

- TURN IGNITION SWITCH TO "LOCK."
- LEAVE JUMPER CONNECTED TO DLC TERMINALS.
- PINCH FUEL RETURN HOSE AND HOLD BLOCKED.
- TURN IGNITION SWITCH TO "ON."
- MEASURE FUEL PRESSURE WHILE PINCHING FUEL RETURN HOSE.
  SHOULD BE 265-304 kPa (38-44 psi) AND HOLDING STEADILY.
  DOES IT?

- CHECK FOR RESTRICTIONS IN FUEL RETURN HOSES AND PIPES.
  IF OK, REPLACE FUEL PRESSURE REGULATOR.

NO

YES

- CHECK FOR A RESTRICTED FUEL FILTER.
- CHECK FOR RESTRICTED FUEL FEED HOSES AND PIPES.
  IF OK, REPLACE FUEL PUMP.

REPLACE FUEL PRESSURE REGULATOR.

CLEAR DTCs AND REPEAT OBD SYSTEM CHECK AFTER MAKING REPAIRS.

Fig. 182 Fuel system diagnosis — 1993 VIN code 8 engine

CHART A2-7C
FUEL SYSTEM DIAGNOSIS
(FUEL PRESSURE GAGE)
1.8L (VIN 8) "S" CARLINE

Circuit Description:

The procedure on the facing page must be followed in order to install/remove the fuel pressure gage and adapter correctly. Make sure to observe all CAUTIONS while performing this procedure.

Fig. 183 Fuel system diagnosis — 1993 VIN code 8 engine

Tools Required:
J 34730-1A Fuel Pressure Gage
J 39802 Fuel Pressure Gage Adapter

CHART A2-7C
FUEL SYSTEM DIAGNOSIS
(FUEL PRESSURE GAGE)
1.8L (VIN 8) "S" CARLINE

CAUTION

- To reduce the risk of fire and personal injury, it is necessary to relieve the fuel system pressure before servicing the fuel system.
- After relieving fuel system pressure, a small amount of fuel may be released when servicing fuel pipe or hose connections. To reduce the chance of personal injury and to catch any fuel that may leak out, cover fuel pipe fittings with a shop towel before disconnecting them. Place the shop towel in an approved container when disconnect is completed.

FUEL PRESSURE GAGE INSTALLATION:

1. Relieve fuel system pressure.
   A. Loosen fuel filler cap to relieve tank pressure.
   B. Remove center trim bezel from center console by gently prying around edges to disconnect clips.
   C. Remove four screws and radio from center console (if equipped).
   D. Disconnect circuit opening relay electrical connector.
   E. Crank engine and allow to stall. Crank engine for an additional 3 seconds to assure relief of any remaining fuel pressure.
   F. Remove negative (-) battery cable.
   G. Reconnect circuit opening relay electrical connector.
   H. Tighten fuel filler cap.
2. Remove one bolt and fuel feed hose bracket from bottom on intake manifold.
3. Remove one bolt and fuel feed hose from fuel rail.
4. Install J 39802 with two gaskets and fuel feed hose to fuel rail.

   🔧 **Tighten**
   - J 39802 bolt to 29 N·m (22 lb.ft.).

5. Connect J 34730-1A to J 39802.
6. Reconnect negative (-) battery cable.

   🔧 **Tighten**
   - Negative (-) battery cable-to-negative (-) battery cable retainer to 15 N·m (11 lb.ft.).

FUEL PRESSURE GAGE REMOVAL

1. Relieve fuel system pressure.
   A. Loosen fuel filler cap to relieve tank pressure.
   B. Disconnect circuit opening relay electrical connector.
   C. Crank engine and allow to stall. Crank engine for an additional 3 seconds to assure relief of any remaining fuel pressure.
   D. Remove negative (-) battery cable.
   E. Reconnect circuit opening relay electrical connector.
   F. Install radio into center console (if equipped); secure with four screws.
   G. Install center trim bezel to center console, pushing in until clips engage.
   H. Tighten fuel filler cap.
2. Remove J 34730-1A from J 39802 and J 39802 from fuel rail.
3. Connect fuel feed hose with new gaskets to fuel rail.

   🔧 **Tighten**
   - Fuel feed hose bolt to 29 N·m (22 lb.ft.).

4. Connect fuel feed hose bracket to bottom of intake manifold, secure with one bolt.

   🔧 **Tighten**
   - Fuel feed hose bracket bolt to 10 N·m (89 lb. in.).

5. Reconnect negative (-) battery cable.

   🔧 **Tighten**
   - Negative (-) battery cable-to-negative (-) battery cable retainer to 15 N·m (11 lb.ft.).

6. Turn ignition switch to "ON" and momentarily connect a jumper between DLC terminals "+B" and "Fp" to pressurize the fuel system. Check for fuel leaks.

Fig. 184 Fuel system diagnosis — 1993 VIN code 8 engine

6

CHASSIS ELECTRICAL

UNDERSTANDING AND TROUBLESHOOTING ELECTRICAL SYSTEMS

At the rate which both import and domestic manufacturers are incorporating electronic control systems into their production lines, it won't be long before every new vehicle is equipped with one or more on-board computer. These electronic components (with no moving parts) should theoretically last the life of the vehicle, provided nothing external happens to damage the circuits or memory chips.

While it is true that electronic components should never wear out, in the real world malfunctions do occur. It is also true that any computer-based system is extremely sensitive to electrical voltages and cannot tolerate careless or haphazard testing or service procedures. An inexperienced individual can literally do major damage looking for a minor problem by using the wrong kind of test equipment or connecting test leads or connectors with the ignition switch ON. When selecting test equipment, make sure the manufacturers instructions state that the tester is compatible with whatever type of electronic control system is being serviced. Read all instructions carefully and double check all test points before installing probes or making any test connections.

The following section outlines basic diagnosis techniques for dealing with computerized automotive control systems. Along with a general explanation of the various types of test equipment available to aid in servicing modern electronic automotive systems, basic repair techniques for wiring harnesses and connectors is given. Read the basic information before attempting any repairs or testing on any computerized system, to provide the background of information necessary to avoid the most common and obvious mistakes that can cost both time and money. Although the replacement and testing procedures are simple in themselves, the systems are not, and unless one has a thorough understanding of all components and their function within a particular computerized control system, the logical test sequence that these systems demand cannot be followed. Minor malfunctions can make a big difference, so it is important to know how each component affects the operation of the overall electronic system to find the ultimate cause of a problem without replacing good components unnecessarily. It is not enough to use the correct test equipment; the test equipment must be used correctly.

Safety Precautions

❊❊CAUTION

Whenever working on or around any computer based microprocessor control system, always observe these general precautions to prevent the possibility of personal injury or damage to electronic components.

• Never install or remove battery cables with the key ON or the engine running. Jumper cables should be connected with the key OFF to avoid power surges that can damage electronic control units. Engines equipped with computer controlled systems should avoid both giving and getting jump starts due to the possibility of serious damage to components from arcing in the engine compartment when connections are made with the ignition ON.

• Always remove the battery cables before charging the battery. Never use a high output charger on an installed battery or attempt to use any type of 'hot shot' (24 volt) starting aid.

• Exercise care when inserting test probes into connectors to insure good connections without damaging the connector or spreading the pins. Always probe connectors from the rear (wire) side, NOT the pin side, to avoid accidental shorting of terminals during test procedures.

• Never remove or attach wiring harness connectors with the ignition switch ON, especially to an electronic control unit.

• Do not drop any components during service procedures and never apply 12 volts directly to any component (like a solenoid or relay) unless instructed specifically to do so. Some component electrical windings are designed to safely handle only 4 or 5 volts and can be destroyed in seconds if 12 volts are applied directly to the connector.

• Remove the electronic control unit if the vehicle is to be placed in an environment where temperatures exceed approximately 176°F (80°C), such as a paint spray booth or when arc or gas welding near the control unit location in the car.

ORGANIZED TROUBLESHOOTING

When diagnosing a specific problem, organized troubleshooting is a must. The complexity of a modern automobile demands that you approach any problem in a logical, organized manner. There are certain troubleshooting techniques that are standard:

1. Establish when the problem occurs. Does the problem appear only under certain conditions? Were there any noises, odors, or other unusual symptoms?

2. Isolate the problem area. To do this, make some simple tests and observations; then eliminate the systems that are working properly. Check for obvious problems such as broken wires, dirty connections or split or disconnected vacuum hoses. Always check the obvious before assuming something complicated is the cause.

3. Test for problems systematically to determine the cause once the problem area is isolated. Are all the components functioning properly? Is there power going to electrical switches and motors? Is there vacuum at vacuum switches and/or actuators? Is there a mechanical problem such as bent linkage or loose mounting screws? Doing careful, systematic checks will often turn up most causes on the first inspection without wasting time checking components that have little or no relationship to the problem.

4. Test all repairs after the work is done to make sure that the problem is fixed. Some causes can be traced to more than one component, so a careful verification of repair work is important to pick up additional malfunctions that may cause a problem to reappear or a different problem to arise. A blown fuse, for example, is a simple problem that may require more than another fuse to repair. If you don't look for a problem that caused a fuse to blow, for example, a shorted wire may go undetected.

Experience has shown that most problems tend to be the result of a fairly simple and obvious cause, such as loose or corroded connectors or air leaks in the intake system; making careful inspection of components during testing essential to quick and accurate troubleshooting. Special, hand held computerized testers designed specifically for diagnosing a system are available from a variety of aftermarket sources, as well as from the vehicle manufacturer, but care should be taken that any test equipment being used is designed to diagnose that particular computer controlled system accurately without damaging the control unit (ECU) or components being tested.

➡**Pinpointing the exact cause of trouble in an electrical system can sometimes only be accomplished by the use of special test equipment. The following describes commonly used test equipment and explains how to put it to best use in diagnosis. In addition to the information covered below, the manufacturer's instructions booklet provided with the tester should be read and clearly understood before attempting any test procedures.**

TEST EQUIPMENT

Jumper Wires

Jumper wires are simple, yet extremely valuable, pieces of test equipment. Jumper wires are merely wires that are used to bypass sections of a circuit. The simplest type of jumper wire is merely a length of multi-strand wire with an alligator clip at each end. Jumper wires are usually fabricated from lengths of standard automotive wire and whatever type of connector (alligator clip, spade connector or pin connector) that is required for the particular vehicle being tested. The well equipped tool box will have several different styles of jumper wires in several different lengths. Some jumper wires are made with three or more terminals coming from a common splice for special purpose testing. In cramped, hard-to-reach areas it is advisable to have insulated boots over the jumper wire terminals in order to prevent accidental grounding, sparks, and possible fire, especially when testing fuel system components.

Jumper wires are used primarily to locate open electrical circuits, on either the ground (-) side of the circuit or on the hot (+) side. If an electrical component fails to operate, connect the jumper wire between the component and a good ground. If the component operates only with the jumper installed, the ground circuit is open. If the ground circuit is good, but the component does not operate, the circuit between the power feed and component is open. You can sometimes connect the jumper wire directly from the battery to the hot terminal of the component, but first make sure the component uses 12 volts in operation. Some electrical components, such as fuel injectors, are designed to operate on about 4 volts and running 12 volts directly to the injector terminals can burn out the wiring. By inserting an inline fuseholder between a set of test leads, a fused jumper wire can be used for bypassing open circuits. Use a 5 amp fuse to provide protection against voltage spikes. When in doubt, use a voltmeter to check the voltage input to the component and measure how much voltage is being applied normally. By moving the jumper wire

successively back from the lamp toward the power source, you can isolate the area of the circuit where the open is located. When the component stops functioning, or the power is cut off, the open is in the segment of wire between the jumper and the point previously tested.

✳✳CAUTION

Never use jumpers made from wire that is of lighter gauge than used in the circuit under test. If the jumper wire is of too small gauge, it may overheat and possibly melt. Never use jumpers to bypass high resistance loads (such as motors) in a circuit. Bypassing resistances, in effect, creates a short circuit which may, in turn, cause damage and fire. Never use a jumper for anything other than temporary bypassing of components in a circuit.

12 Volt Test Light

The 12 volt test light is used to check circuits and components while electrical current is flowing through them. It is used for voltage and ground tests. 12 volt test lights come in different styles but all have three main parts; a ground clip, a probe and a light. The most commonly used 12 volt test lights have pick-type probes. To use a 12 volt test light, connect the ground clip to a good ground and probe wherever necessary with the pick. The pick should be sharp so that it can penetrate wire insulation to make contact with the wire, without making a large hole in the insulation. The wrap-around light is handy in hard to reach areas or where it is difficult to support a wire to push a probe pick into it. To use the wrap around light, hook the wire to probed with the hook and pull the trigger. A small pick will be forced through the wire insulation into the wire core.

✳✳CAUTION

Do not use a test light to probe electronic ignition spark plug or coil wires. Never use a pick-type test light to probe wiring on computer controlled systems unless specifically instructed to do so. Any wire insulation that is pierced by the test light probe should be taped and sealed with silicone after testing.

Like the jumper wire, the 12 volt test light is used to isolate opens in circuits. But, whereas the jumper wire is used to bypass the open to operate the load, the 12 volt test light is used to locate the presence of voltage in a circuit. If the test light glows, you know that there is power up to that point; if the 12 volt test light does not glow when its probe is inserted into the wire or connector, you know that there is an open circuit (no power). Move the test light in successive steps back toward the power source until the light in the handle does glow. When it does glow, the open is between the probe and point previously probed.

➡**The test light does not detect that 12 volts (or any particular amount of voltage) is present; it only detects that some voltage is present. It is advisable before using the test light to touch its terminals across the battery posts to make sure the light is operating properly.**

Self-Powered Test Light

The self-powered test light usually contains a 1.5 volt penlight battery. One type of self-powered test light is similar in design to the 12 volt test light. This type has both the battery and the light in the handle and pick-type probe tip. The second type has the light toward the open tip, so that the light illuminates the contact point. The self-powered test light is dual purpose piece of test equipment. It can be used to test for either open or short circuits when power is isolated from the circuit (continuity test). A powered test light should not be used on any computer controlled system or component unless specifically instructed to do so. Many engine sensors can be destroyed by even this small amount of voltage applied directly to the terminals.

Open Circuit Testing

To use the self-powered test light to check for open circuits, first isolate the circuit from the vehicle's 12 volt power source by disconnecting the battery or wiring harness connector. Connect the test light ground clip to a good ground and probe sections of the circuit sequentially with the test light. (start from either end of the circuit). If the light is out, the open is between the probe and the circuit ground. If the light is on, the open is between the probe and end of the circuit toward the power source.

Short Circuit Testing

By isolating the circuit both from power and from ground, and using a self-powered test light, you can check for shorts to ground in the circuit. Isolate the circuit from power and ground. Connect the test light ground clip to a good ground and probe any easy-to-reach test point in the circuit. If the light comes on, there is a short somewhere in the circuit. To isolate the short, probe a test point at either end of the isolated circuit (the light should be on). Leave the test light probe connected and open connectors, switches, remove parts, etc., sequentially, until the light goes out. When the light goes out, the short is between the last circuit component opened and the previous circuit opened.

➡The 1.5 volt battery in the test light does not provide much current. A weak battery may not provide enough power to illuminate the test light even when a complete circuit is made (especially if there are high resistances in the circuit). Always make sure that the test battery is strong. To check the battery, briefly touch the ground clip to the probe; if the light glows brightly the battery is strong enough for testing. Never use a self-powered test light to perform checks for opens or shorts when power is applied to the electrical system under test. The 12 volt vehicle power will quickly burn out the 1.5 volt light bulb in the test light.

Voltmeter

A voltmeter is used to measure voltage at any point in a circuit, or to measure the voltage drop across any part of a circuit. It can also be used to check continuity in a wire or circuit by indicating current flow from one end to the other. Voltmeters usually have various scales on the meter dial and a selector switch to allow the selection of different voltages. The voltmeter has a positive and a negative lead. To avoid damage to the meter, always connect the negative lead to the negative (-) side of the circuit (to ground or nearest the ground side of the circuit) and connect the positive lead to the positive (+) side of the circuit (to the power source or the nearest power source). Note that the negative voltmeter lead will always be black and that the positive voltmeter will always be some color other than black (usually red). Depending on how the voltmeter is connected into the circuit, it has several uses.

A voltmeter can be connected either in parallel or in series with a circuit and it has a very high resistance to current flow. When connected in parallel, only a small amount of current will flow through the voltmeter current path; the rest will flow through the normal circuit current path and the circuit will work normally. When the voltmeter is connected in series with a circuit, only a small amount of current can flow through the circuit. The circuit will not work properly, but the voltmeter reading will show if the circuit is complete or not.

Available Voltage Measurement

Set the voltmeter selector switch to the 20V position and connect the meter negative lead to the negative (-) post of the battery. Connect the positive meter lead to the positive (+) post of the battery and turn the ignition switch ON to provide a load. Read the voltage on the meter or digital display. A well charged battery should register over 12 volts. If the meter reads below 11.5 volts, the battery power may be insufficient to operate the electrical system properly. This test determines voltage available from the battery and should be the first step in any electrical trouble diagnosis procedure. Many electrical problems, especially on computer controlled systems, can be caused by a low state of charge in the battery. Excessive corrosion at the battery cable terminals can cause a poor contact that will prevent proper charging and full battery current flow.

Normal battery voltage is 12 volts when fully charged. When the battery is supplying current to one or more circuits it is said to be 'under load'. When everything is off the electrical system is under a 'no-load' condition. A fully charged battery may show about 12.5 volts at no load; will drop to 12 volts under medium load; and will drop even lower under heavy load. If the battery is partially discharged the voltage decrease under heavy load may be excessive, even though the battery shows 12 volts or more at no load. When allowed to discharge further, the battery's available voltage under load will decrease more severely. For this reason, it is important that the battery be fully charged during all testing procedures to avoid errors in diagnosis and incorrect test results.

Voltage Drop

When current flows through a resistance, the voltage beyond the resistance is reduced (the larger the current, the greater the reduction in voltage). When no current is flowing, there is no voltage drop because there is no current flow. All points in the circuit which are connected to the power source are at the same voltage as the power source. The total voltage drop always equals the total source voltage. In a long circuit with many connectors, a series of small, unwanted voltage drops due to corrosion at the connectors can add up to a total loss of voltage which impairs the operation of the normal loads in the circuit.

INDIRECT COMPUTATION OF VOLTAGE DROPS

1. Set the voltmeter selector switch to the 20 volt position.
2. Connect the meter negative lead to a good ground.
3. Probe all resistances in the circuit with the positive meter lead.
4. Operate the circuit in all modes and observe the voltage readings.

DIRECT MEASUREMENT OF VOLTAGE DROPS

1. Set the voltmeter switch to the 20 volt position.
2. Connect the voltmeter negative lead to the ground side of the resistance load to be measured.
3. Connect the positive lead to the positive side of the resistance or load to be measured.
4. Read the voltage drop directly on the 20 volt scale.

Too high a voltage indicates too high a resistance. If, for example, a blower motor runs too slowly, you can determine if there is too high a resistance in the resistor pack. By taking voltage drop readings in all parts of the circuit, you can isolate the problem. Too low a voltage drop indicates too low a resistance. If, for example, a blower motor runs too fast in the MED and/or LOW position, the problem can be isolated in the resistor pack by taking voltage drop readings in all parts of the circuit to locate a possibly shorted resistor. The maximum allowable voltage drop under load is critical, especially if there is more than one high resistance problem in a circuit because all voltage drops are cumulative. A small drop is normal due to the resistance of the conductors.

HIGH RESISTANCE TESTING

1. Set the voltmeter selector switch to the 4 volt position.
2. Connect the voltmeter positive lead to the positive (+) post of the battery.
3. Turn on the headlights and heater blower to provide a load.
4. Probe various points in the circuit with the negative voltmeter lead.
5. Read the voltage drop on the 4 volt scale. Some average maximum allowable voltage drops are:

FUSE PANEL — 7 volts
IGNITION SWITCH — 5 volts
HEADLIGHT SWITCH — 7 volts
IGNITION COIL (+) — 5 volts
ANY OTHER LOAD — 1.3 volts

➡**Voltage drops are all measured while a load is operating; without current flow, there will be no voltage drop.**

Ohmmeter

The ohmmeter is designed to read resistance (ohms) in a circuit or component. Although there are several different styles of ohmmeters, all will usually have a selector switch which permits the measurement of different ranges of resistance (usually the selector switch allows the multiplication of the meter reading by 10, 100, 1000, and 10,000). A calibration knob allows the meter to be set at zero for accurate measurement. Since all ohmmeters are powered by an internal battery (usually 9 volts), the ohmmeter can be used as a self-powered test light. When the ohmmeter is connected, current from the ohmmeter flows through the circuit or component being tested. Since the ohmmeter's internal resistance and voltage are known values, the amount of current flow through the meter depends on the resistance of the circuit or component being tested.

The ohmmeter can be used to perform continuity test for opens or shorts (either by observation of the meter needle or as a self-powered test light), and to read actual resistance in a circuit. It should be noted that the ohmmeter is used to check the resistance of a component or wire while there is no voltage applied to the circuit. Current flow from an outside voltage source (such as the vehicle battery) can damage the ohmmeter, so the circuit or component should be isolated from the vehicle electrical system before any testing is done. Since the ohmmeter uses its own voltage source, either lead can be connected to any test point.

➡**When checking diodes or other solid state components, the ohmmeter leads can only be connected one way in order to measure current flow in a single direction. Make sure the positive (+) and negative (-) terminal connections are as described in the test procedures to verify the one-way diode operation.**

In using the meter for making continuity checks, do not be concerned with the actual resistance readings. Zero resistance, or any resistance readings, indicate continuity in the circuit. Infinite resistance indicates an open in the circuit. A high resistance reading where there should be none indicates a problem in the circuit. Checks for short circuits are made in the same manner as checks for open circuits except that the circuit must be isolated from both power and normal ground. Infinite resistance indicates no continuity to ground, while zero resistance indicates a dead short to ground.

RESISTANCE MEASUREMENT

The batteries in an ohmmeter will weaken with age and temperature, so the ohmmeter must be calibrated or 'zeroed' before taking measurements. To zero the meter, place the selector switch in its lowest range and touch the two ohmmeter leads together. Turn the calibration knob until the meter needle is exactly on zero.

➡**All analog (needle) type ohmmeters must be zeroed before use, but some digital ohmmeter models are automatically calibrated when the switch is turned on. Self-calibrating digital ohmmeters do not have an adjusting knob, but its a good idea to check for a zero readout before use by touching the leads together. All computer controlled systems require the use of a digital ohmmeter with at least 10 megohms impedance for testing. Before any test procedures are attempted, make sure the ohmmeter used is compatible with the electrical system or damage to the on-board computer could result.**

To measure resistance, first isolate the circuit from the vehicle power source by disconnecting the battery cables or the harness connector. Make sure the key is OFF when disconnecting any components or the battery. Where necessary, also isolate at least one side of the circuit to be checked to avoid reading parallel resistances. Parallel circuit resistances will always give a lower reading than the actual resistance of either of the branches. When measuring the resistance of parallel circuits, the total resistance will always be lower than the smallest resistance in the circuit. Connect the meter leads to both sides of the circuit (wire or component) and read the actual measured ohms on the meter scale. Make sure the selector switch is set to the proper ohm scale for the circuit being tested to avoid misreading the ohmmeter test value.

✳✳CAUTION

Never use an ohmmeter with power applied to the circuit. Like the self-powered test light, the ohmmeter is designed to operate on its own power supply. The normal 12 volt automotive electrical system current could damage the meter.

Ammeters

An ammeter measures the amount of current flowing through a circuit in units called amperes or amps. Amperes are units of electron flow which indicate how fast the electrons are flowing through the circuit. Since Ohms Law dictates that current flow in a circuit is equal to the circuit voltage divided by the total circuit resistance, increasing voltage also increases the current level (amps). Likewise, any decrease in resistance will increase the amount of amps in a circuit. At normal operating voltage, most circuits have a characteristic amount of amperes, called 'current draw' which can be measured using an ammeter. By referring to a specified current draw rating, measuring the amperes, and comparing the two values, one can determine what is happening within the circuit to aid in diagnosis. An open circuit, for example, will not allow any current to flow so the ammeter reading will be zero. More current flows through a heavily loaded circuit or when the charging system is operating.

An ammeter is always connected in series with the circuit being tested. All of the current that normally flows through the circuit must also flow through the ammeter; if there is any other path for the current to follow, the ammeter reading will not be accurate. The ammeter itself has very little resistance to current flow and therefore will not affect the circuit, but it will measure current draw only when the circuit is closed and electricity is flowing. Excessive current draw can blow fuses and drain the battery, while a reduced current draw can cause motors to run slowly, lights to dim and other components to not operate properly. The ammeter can help diagnose these conditions by locating the cause of the high or low reading.

Multimeters

Different combinations of test meters can be built into a single unit designed for specific tests. Some of the more common combination test devices are known as Volt/Amp testers, Tach/Dwell meters, or Digital Multimeters. The Volt/Amp tester is used for charging system, starting system or battery tests and consists of a voltmeter, an ammeter and a variable resistance carbon pile. The voltmeter will usually have at least two ranges for use with 6, 12 and 24 volt systems. The ammeter also has more than one range for testing various levels of battery loads and starter current draw and the carbon pile can be adjusted to offer different amounts of resistance. The Volt/Amp tester has heavy leads to carry large amounts of current and many later models have an inductive ammeter pickup that clamps around the wire to simplify test

connections. On some models, the ammeter also has a zero-center scale to allow testing of charging and starting systems without switching leads or polarity. A digital multimeter i s a voltmeter, ammeter and ohmmeter combined in an instrument which gives a digital readout. These are often used when testing solid state circuits because of their high input impedance (usually 10 megohms or more).

The tach/dwell meter combines a tachometer and a dwell (cam angle) meter and is a specialized kind of voltmeter. The tachometer scale is marked to show engine speed in rpm and the dwell scale is marked to show degrees of distributor shaft rotation. In most electronic ignition systems, dwell is determined by the control unit, but the dwell meter can also be used to check the duty cycle (operation) of some electronic engine control systems. Some tach/dwell meters are powered by an internal battery, while others take their power from the car battery in use. The battery powered testers usually require calibration much like an ohmmeter before testing.

Special Test Equipment

A variety of diagnostic tools are available to help troubleshoot and repair computerized engine control systems. The most sophisticated of these devices are the console type engine analyzers that usually occupy a garage service bay, but there are several types of aftermarket electronic testers available that will allow quick circuit tests of the engine control system by plugging directly into a special connector located in the engine compartment or under the dashboard. Several tool and equipment manufacturers offer simple, hand held testers that measure various circuit voltage levels on command to check all system components for proper operation. Although these testers usually cost about $300-500, consider that the average computer control unit (or ECM) can cost just as much and the money saved by not replacing perfectly good sensors or components in an attempt to correct a problem could justify the purchase price of a special diagnostic tester the first time it's used.

These computerized testers can allow quick and easy test measurements while the engine is operating or while the car is being driven. In addition, the on-board computer memory can be read to access any stored trouble codes; in effect allowing the computer to tell you where it hurts and aid trouble diagnosis by pinpointing exactly which circuit or component is malfunctioning. In the same manner, repairs can be tested to make sure the problem has been corrected. The biggest advantage these special testers have is their relatively easy hookups that minimize or eliminate the chances of making the wrong connections and getting false voltage readings or damaging the computer accidentally.

➡**It should be remembered that these testers check voltage levels in circuits; they don't detect mechanical problems or failed components if the circuit voltage falls within the preprogrammed limits stored in the tester PROM unit. Also, most of the hand held testes are designed to work only on one or two systems made by a specific manufacturer.**

A variety of aftermarket testers are available to help diagnose different computerized control systems. Owatonna Tool Company (OTC), for example, markets a device called the OTC Monitor which plugs directly into the assembly line diagnostic link (ALDL). The OTC tester makes diagnosis a simple matter of pressing the correct buttons and, by changing the internal PROM or inserting a different diagnosis cartridge, it will work on any model from full size to subcompact, over a wide range of years. An adapter is supplied with the tester to allow connection to all types of ALDL links, regardless of the number of pin terminals used. By inserting an updated PROM into the OTC tester, it can be easily updated to diagnose any new modifications of computerized control systems.

Wiring Harnesses

The average automobile contains about 1/2 mile of wiring, with hundreds of individual connections. To protect the many wires from damage and to keep them from becoming a confusing tangle, they are organized into bundles, enclosed in plastic or taped together and called wire harnesses. Different wiring harnesses serve different parts of the vehicle. Individual wires are color coded to help trace them through a harness where sections are hidden from view.

A loose or corroded connection or a replacement wire that is too small for the circuit will add extra resistance and an additional voltage drop to the circuit. A ten percent voltage drop can result in slow or erratic motor operation, for example, even though the circuit is complete. Automotive wiring or circuit conductors can be in any one of three forms:
1. Single strand wire
2. Multi-strand wire
3. Printed circuitry

Single strand wire has a solid metal core and is usually used inside such components as alternators, motors, relays and other devices. Multi-strand wire has a core made of many small strands of wire twisted together into a single conductor. Most of the wiring in an automotive electrical system is made up of multi-strand wire, either as a single conductor or grouped together in a harness. All wiring is color coded on the insulator, either as a solid color or as a colored wire with an identification stripe. A printed circuit is a thin film of copper or other conductor that is printed on an insulator backing. Occasionally, a printed circuit is sandwiched between two sheets of plastic for more protection and flexibility. A complete printed circuit, consisting of conductors, insulating material and connectors for lamps or other components is called a printed circuit board. Printed circuitry is used in place of individual wires or harnesses in places where space is limited, such as behind instrument panels.

Wire Gauge

Since computer controlled automotive electrical systems are very sensitive to changes in resistance, the selection of properly sized wires is critical when systems are repaired. The wire gauge number is an expression of the cross section area of the conductor. The most common system for expressing wire size is the American Wire Gauge (AWG) system.

Wire cross section area is measured in circular mils. A mil is 1/1000 in. (0.001 in.); a circular mil is the area of a circle one mil in diameter. For example, a conductor 1/4 inch in diameter is 0.250 inch or 250 mils. The circular mil cross section area of the wire is 250 squared (250^2) or 62,500 circular mils. Imported car models usually use metric wire gauge

designations, which is simply the cross section area of the conductor in square millimeters (mm^2).

Gauge numbers are assigned to conductors of various cross section areas. As gauge number increases, area decreases and the conductor becomes smaller. A 5 gauge conductor is smaller than a 1 gauge conductor and a 10 gauge is smaller than a 5 gauge. As the cross section area of a conductor decreases, resistance increases and so does the gauge number. A conductor with a higher gauge number will carry less current than a conductor with a lower gauge number.

➡**Gauge wire size refers to the size of the conductor, not the size of the complete wire. It is possible to have two wires of the same gauge with different diameters because one may have thicker insulation than the other.**

12 volt automotive electrical systems generally use 10, 12, 14, 16 and 18 gauge wire. Main power distribution circuits and larger accessories usually use 10 and 12 gauge wire. Battery cables are usually 4 or 6 gauge, although 1 and 2 gauge wires are occasionally used. Wire length must also be considered when making repairs to a circuit. As conductor length increases, so does resistance. An 18 gauge wire, for example, can carry a 10 amp load for 10 feet without excessive voltage drop; however if a 15 foot wire is required for the same 10 amp load, it must be a 16 gauge wire.

An electrical schematic shows the electrical current paths when a circuit is operating properly. It is essential to understand how a circuit works before trying to figure out why it doesn't. Schematics break the entire electrical system down into individual circuits and show only one particular circuit. In a schematic, no attempt is made to represent wiring and components as they physically appear on the vehicle; switches and other components are shown as simply as possible. Face views of harness connectors show the cavity or terminal locations in all multi-pin connectors to help locate test points.

If you need to backprobe a connector while it is on the component, the order of the terminals must be mentally reversed. The wire color code can help in this situation, as well as a keyway, lock tab or other reference mark.

WIRING REPAIR

Soldering is a quick, efficient method of joining metals permanently. Everyone who has the occasion to make wiring repairs should know how to solder. Electrical connections that are soldered are far less likely to come apart and will conduct electricity much better than connections that are only 'pig-tailed' together. The most popular (and preferred) method of soldering is with an electrical soldering gun. Soldering irons are available in many sizes and wattage ratings. Irons with higher wattage ratings deliver higher temperatures and recover lost heat faster. A small soldering iron rated for no more than 50 watts is recommended, especially on electrical systems where excess heat can damage the components being soldered.

There are three ingredients necessary for successful soldering; proper flux, good solder and sufficient heat. A soldering flux is necessary to clean the metal of tarnish, prepare it for soldering and to enable the solder to spread into tiny crevices. When soldering, always use a resin flux or resin core solder which is non-corrosive and will not attract moisture once the job is finished. Other types of flux (acid core) will leave a residue that will attract moisture and cause the wires to corrode. Tin is a unique metal with a low melting point. In a molten state, it dissolves and alloys easily with many metals. Solder is made by mixing tin with lead. The most common proportions are 40/60, 50/50 and 60/40, with the percentage of tin listed first. Low priced solders usually contain less tin, making them very difficult for a beginner to use because more heat is required to melt the solder. A common solder is 40/60 which is well suited for all-around general use, but 60/40 melts easier, has more tin f or a better joint and is preferred for electrical work.

Soldering Techniques

Successful soldering requires that the metals to be joined be heated to a temperature that will melt the solder — usually 360-460°F (182-238°C). Contrary to popular belief, the purpose of the soldering iron is not to melt the solder itself, but to heat the parts being soldered to a temperature high enough to melt the solder when it is touched to the work. Melting flux-cored solder on the soldering iron will usually destroy the effectiveness of the flux.

➡**Soldering tips are made of copper for good heat conductivity, but must be 'tinned' regularly for quick transference of heat to the project and to prevent the solder from sticking to the iron. To 'tin' the iron, simply heat it and touch the flux-cored solder to the tip; the solder will flow over the hot tip. Wipe the excess off with a clean rag, but be careful as the iron will be hot.**

After some use, the tip may become pitted. If so, simply dress the tip smooth with a smooth file and 'tin' the tip again. An old saying holds that 'metals well cleaned are half soldered.' Flux-cored solder will remove oxides, but rust, bits of insulation and oil or grease must be removed with a wire brush or emery cloth. For maximum strength in soldered parts, the joint must start off clean and tight. Weak joints will result in gaps too wide for the solder to bridge.

If a separate soldering flux is used, it should be brushed or swabbed on only those areas that are to be soldered. Most solders contain a core of flux and separate fluxing is unnecessary. Hold the work to be soldered firmly. It is best to solder on a wooden board, because a metal vise will only rob the piece to be soldered of heat and make it difficult to melt the solder. Hold the soldering tip with the broadest face against the work to be soldered. Apply solder under the tip close to the work, using enough solder to give a heavy film between the iron and the piece being soldered, while moving slowly and making sure the solder melts properly. Keep the work level or the solder will run to the lowest part and favor the thicker parts, because these require more heat to melt the solder. If the soldering tip overheats (the solder coating on the face of the tip burns up), it should be retinned. Once the soldering is completed, let the soldered joint stand until cool. Tape and seal all soldered wire splices after the repair has cooled.

Wire Harness and Connectors

The on-board computer (ECM) wire harness electrically connects the control unit to the various solenoids, switches and sensors used by the control system. Most connectors in the engine compartment or otherwise exposed to the elements are protected against moisture and dirt which could create oxidation and deposits on the terminals. This protection is important because of the very low voltage and current levels used by the computer and sensors. All connectors have a lock which secures the male and female terminals together, with a secondary lock holding the seal and terminal into the connector. Both terminal locks must be released when disconnecting ECM connectors.

These special connectors are weather-proof and all repairs require the use of a special terminal and the tool required to service it. This tool is used to remove the pin and sleeve terminals. If removal is attempted with an ordinary pick, there is a good chance that the terminal will be bent or deformed. Unlike standard blade type terminals, these terminals cannot be straightened once they are bent. Make certain that the connectors are properly seated and all of the sealing rings in place when connecting leads. On some models, a hinge-type flap provides a backup or secondary locking feature for the terminals. Most secondary locks are used to improve the connector reliability by retaining the terminals if the small terminal lock tangs are not positioned properly.

Molded-on connectors require complete replacement of the connection. This means splicing a new connector assembly into the harness. All splices in on-board computer systems should be soldered to insure proper contact. Use care when probing the connections or replacing terminals in them as it is possible to short between opposite terminals. If this happens to the wrong terminal pair, it is possible to damage certain components. Always use jumper wires between connectors for circuit checking and never probe through weatherproof seals.

Open circuits are often difficult to locate by sight because corrosion or terminal misalignment are hidden by the connectors. Merely wiggling a connector on a sensor or in the wiring harness may correct the open circuit condition. This should always be considered when an open circuit or a failed sensor is indicated. Intermittent problems may also be caused by oxidized or loose connections. When using a circuit tester for diagnosis, always probe connections from the wire side. Be careful not to damage sealed connectors with test probes.

All wiring harnesses should be replaced with identical parts, using the same gauge wire and connectors. When signal wires are spliced into a harness, use wire with high temperature insulation only. With the low voltage and current levels found in the system, it is important that the best possible connection at all wire splices be made by soldering the splices together. It is seldom necessary to replace a complete harness. If replacement is necessary, pay close attention to insure proper harness routing. Secure the harness with suitable plastic wire clamps to prevent vibrations from causing the harness to wear in spots or contact any hot components.

➡**Weatherproof connectors cannot be replaced with standard connectors. Instructions are provided with replacement connector and terminal packages. Some wire harnesses have mounting indicators (usually pieces of colored tape) to mark where the harness is to be secured.**

In making wiring repairs, it's important that you always replace damaged wires with wires that are the same gauge as the wire being replaced. The heavier the wire, the smaller the gauge number. Wires are color-coded to aid in identification and whenever possible the same color coded wire should be used for replacement. A wire stripping and crimping tool is necessary to install solderless terminal connectors. Test all crimps by pulling on the wires; it should not be possible to pull the wires out of a good crimp.

Wires which are open, exposed or otherwise damaged are repaired by simple splicing. Where possible, if the wiring harness is accessible and the damaged place in the wire can be located, it is best to open the harness and check for all possible damage. In an inaccessible harness, the wire must be bypassed with a new insert, usually taped to the outside of the old harness.

When replacing fusible links, be sure to use fusible link wire, NOT ordinary automotive wire. Make sure the fusible segment is of the same gauge and construction as the one being replaced and double the stripped end when crimping the terminal connector for a good contact. The melted (open) fusible link segment of the wiring harness should be cut off as close to the harness as possible, then a new segment spliced in as described. In the case of a damaged fusible link that feeds two harness wires, the harness connections should be replaced with two fusible link wires so that each circuit will have its own separate protection.

➡️**Most of the problems caused in the wiring harness are due to bad ground connections. Always check all vehicle ground connections for corrosion or looseness before performing any power feed checks to eliminate the chance of a bad ground affecting the circuit.**

Repairing Hard Shell Connectors

Unlike molded connectors, the terminal contacts in hard shell connectors can be replaced. Weatherproof hard-shell connectors with the leads molded into the shell have non-replaceable terminal ends. Replacement usually involves the use of a special terminal removal tool that depress the locking tangs (barbs) on the connector terminal and allow the connector to be removed from the rear of the shell. The connector shell should be replaced if it shows any evidence of burning, melting, cracks, or breaks. Replace individual terminals that are burnt, corroded, distorted or loose.

➡️**The insulation crimp must be tight to prevent the insulation from sliding back on the wire when the wire is pulled. The insulation must be visibly compressed under the crimp tabs, and the ends of the crimp should be turned in for a firm grip on the insulation.**

The wire crimp must be made with all wire strands inside the crimp. The terminal must be fully compressed on the wire strands with the ends of the crimp tabs turned in to make a firm grip on the wire. Check all connections with an ohmmeter to insure a good contact. There should be no measurable resistance between the wire and the terminal when connected.

Mechanical Test Equipment

Vacuum Gauge

Most gauges are graduated in inches of mercury (in.Hg), although a device called a manometer reads vacuum in inches of water (in. H_2O). The normal vacuum reading usually varies between 18 and 22 in.Hg at sea level. To test engine vacuum, the vacuum gauge must be connected to a source of manifold vacuum. Many engines have a plug in the intake manifold which can be removed and replaced with an adapter fitting. Connect the vacuum gauge to the fitting with a suitable rubber hose or, if no manifold plug is available, connect the vacuum gauge to any device using manifold vacuum, such as EGR valves, etc. The vacuum gauge can be used to determine if enough vacuum is reaching a component to allow its actuation.

Hand Vacuum Pump

Small, hand-held vacuum pumps come in a variety of designs. Most have a built-in vacuum gauge and allow the component to be tested without removing it from the vehicle. Operate the pump lever or plunger to apply the correct amount of vacuum required for the test specified in the diagnosis routines. The level of vacuum in inches of Mercury (in.Hg) is indicated on the pump gauge. For some testing, an additional vacuum gauge may be necessary.

Intake manifold vacuum is used to operate various systems and devices on late model vehicles. To correctly diagnose and solve problems in vacuum control systems, a vacuum source is necessary for testing. In some cases, vacuum can be taken from the intake manifold when the engine is running, but vacuum is normally provided by a hand vacuum pump. These hand vacuum pumps have a built-in vacuum gauge that allow testing while the device is still attached to the component. For some tests, an additional vacuum gauge may be necessary.

SUPPLEMENTAL RESTRAINT SYSTEM (SRS)

General Description

The Supplemental Restraint System (SRS) helps supplement the protection offered by the driver's seat belt by deploying an air bag from the center of the steering wheel. The air bag deploys when the vehicle is involved in a frontal crash of sufficient force up to 30 degrees off the centerline of the vehicle. To further absorb the crash energy there is a knee bolster located below the steering column for the driver. The steering column continues to be collapsible.

COMPONENT DESCRIPTION

Center Sensor Assembly

➡️**Do not open the center sensor assembly case for any reason. Touching the connector pins or soldered components may cause electrostatic discharge (ESD) damage. Repair of a faulty center sensor assembly is by replacement only.**

The center sensor assembly is designed to perform the following functions in the SRS:

1. **Energy Reserve** — The center sensor assembly maintains a 6 volt reserve power supply to provide deployment energy when the vehicle voltage is low or lost in a frontal crash.

2. **Fault Detection** — The center sensor assembly performs diagnostic monitoring of SRS electrical components.

3. **Fault Recording** — The center sensor assembly provides SRS diagnostic trouble code (DTC) information through the air bag indicator.

4. **Driver Notification** — The center sensor assembly warns the vehicle driver of SRS faults by controlling the air bag indicator.

5. **Safety Circuit** — The center sensor assembly prevents SRS operation by opening the power feed to the arming sensor when an SRS fault is detected.

6. **Arming Sensor** — The arming sensor is contained within the center sensor assembly.

7. **Passenger Compartment Sensor** — The passenger compartment sensor is contained within the center sensor assembly.

The center sensor assembly is connected to the vehicle harness by a 10-cavity connector. This harness connector uses a shorting bar across two terminals **B7** to **B8** in the contact area. This shorting bar shorts the inflator module circuits (D+ and D-) together when the center sensor assembly connector **B** is disconnected. This will prevent accidental deployment of the air bag. The center sensor assembly is also connected to each forward sensor by two 2-cavity connectors.

Air Bag Indicator

Battery voltage is applied to the air bag indicator at all times. The center sensor assembly controls the indicator by providing ground with a lamp driver. The air bag indicator is used in the SRS to do the following:

1. Verify indicator and center sensor assembly operation by illuminating steadily for approximately 6 seconds when the ignition switch is first turned to **ACC** or **ON**.

2. Warn the vehicle driver of SRS electrical system faults which have affected the operation of the SRS. When the center sensor assembly detects an SRS fault, the safety circuit opens the power feed to the arming sensor and prevents SRS operation.

3. Provide diagnostic information by flashing diagnostic trouble codes (DTCs) when the 'Flash Code' diagnostic mode is enabled.

The air bag indicator is the key to driver notification of SRS faults.

Arming Sensor

The arming sensor is a protective switch located on the power feed (high) side of the deployment loop in the center sensor assembly. The arming sensor is calibrated to close at low level velocity changes (lower than the other three sensors). This ensures that the inflator module is connected directly to the 6 volt reserve power supply, ignition voltage or accessory voltage when either the LH forward sensor, RH forward sensor or center sensor closes.

The arming sensor consists of a sensing element and normally open switch contacts. The sensing element closes the switch contacts when the velocity of the vehicle changes at a rate indicating potential need for deployment.

Forward Sensors

There are two forward sensors in the SRS. The LH forward sensor is located inside the left wheelwell and the RH forward sensor is located inside the right wheelwell. The forward sensors are protective switches wired in parallel on the ground (low) side of the deployment loop. These sensors are calibrated to close with velocity changes which are severe enough to warrant deployment.

Each forward sensor consists of a sensing element, normally open switch contact and a diagnostic resistor. The sensing element closes the switch contacts when the vehicle velocity changes are server enough to warrant deployment.

A diagnostic resistor is connected in parallel with the switch contacts and connector within each of the forward sensors. These parallel resistors supply ground path for the current passing through the deployment loop during normal, nondeployment operation. This current flow results in voltage drops across each component within the loop. The center sensor assembly monitors these voltage drops to detect circuit or component faults. In order for the diagnostic resistor to function properly, the forward sensor connectors must be fully engaged to the sensors. There is an electrical check mechanism inside of the connector which completes the diagnostic resistor circuit.

Passenger Compartment Sensor

The passenger compartment sensor is located inside the center sensor assembly, mounted to the floor under the center console. The passenger compartment sensor is a protective switch wired in parallel on the ground (low) side of the deployment loop. This sensor is calibrated to close with velocity changes which are severe enough to warrant deployment. The passenger compartment sensor is a semiconductor (solid state) sensor.

SRS Coil Assembly

The SRS coil assembly consists of current-carrying coils. The SRS coil assembly is combined with the combination switch and mounted together on the steering column, allowing rotation of the steering wheel while maintaining continuous contact of the deployment loop to the inflator module.

There is a shorting bar on the lower steering column connector which connects the SRS coil assembly to the wiring harness. This shorting bar shorts the circuits of the SRS coil assembly and inflator module when the lower steering column connector is disconnected. The circuit to the inflator module is shorted in this way to help prevent unwanted deployment of the air bag when servicing the steering column or other SRS components.

Inflator Module

The inflator module is located in the center of the steering wheel. The inflator module consists of an inflatable bag and an inflator (a canister of gas-generating material and an initiating device). When the vehicle is in a frontal crash of sufficient force to close the arming sensor and at least one of the other three sensors, current flows through the deployment loop. Current passing through the initiator thus ignites the material in the inflator module. The gas produced from this reaction rapidly inflates the air bag.

There is a shorting bag on the inflator module side of the upper steering column connector which connects the SRS coil assembly to the inflator module. The shorting bar shorts across the inflator module circuits when the upper steering column connector is disconnected. The circuit to the inflator module is shorted in this way to prevent unwanted deployment of the air bag when servicing the inflator module or other SRS components.

Steering Column

The steering column is energy absorbing and is designed to compress in a frontal crash to decrease the chance of injury to the driver.

Knee Bolster

The knee bolster is used to absorb energy and control the forward movement of the driver during a frontal crash, by limiting leg movement.

SERVICE PRECAUTIONS

❊❊CAUTION

The procedures in this section must be followed in the order listed to temporarily disable the Supplemental Restraint System (SRS) and prevent false diagnostic trouble codes (DTCs) from setting. Failure to follow procedures could result in possible air bag deployment, personal injury or otherwise unneeded SRS repairs.

The center sensor assembly can maintain sufficient voltage to cause a deployment for up to two minutes after the ignition switch is turned to **LOCK** or the battery is disconnected. Many service procedures require disconnection of the **IGN** fuse, **CIG & RADIO** fuse and the steering column circuit from the deployment loop to avoid an accidental deployment.

DISABLING THE SRS

▶ **See Figures 1 and 2**

1. Turn the steering wheel so that the vehicle's wheels are pointing straight ahead.
2. Turn the ignition switch to **LOCK**.
3. Disconnect **IGN** fuse and **CIG** and **RADIO** fuse from junction block 1.2. Disconnect the connector position assurance (CPA) and disconnect the lower steering column (yellow two cavity) connector at the base of the steering column.

ENABLING THE SRS

1. Turn the ignition switch to **LOCK**.
2. Connect the lower steering column connector and secure with CPA.
3. Connect **IGN** fuse and **CIG** and **RADIO** fuse to junction block 1.

Fig. 2 Lower steering column connector

1. Instrument panel
2. Knee bolster
3. Lower steering column connector

4. Turn the ignition switch to ACC or ON and verify that the air bag indicator illuminates steadily for approximately six seconds and then turns off. If it does not operate as described, 'SRS Diagnostic System Check' will have to be performed by an authorized dealer.

HANDLING/INSTALLATION/DIAGNOSIS

1. Inflator modules should not be stored at temperatures above 150°F (65°C).
2. Forward sensors, inflator modules and center sensor assemblies should not be used if they have been dropped from a height of 91.4 cm (3-feet) or more.
3. When a forward sensor is replaced, it MUST be oriented with the arrow on the sensor pointing toward the front of the vehicle. It is very important for forward sensors and the center

1. Junction Block 1
2. ECU-B fuse
3. Cig and radio fuse
4. Ign fuse

Fig. 1 Junction block 1

sensor assembly to be located flat on the mounting surface, parallel with the vehicle datum line. It is important that the sensor mounting surface is free of any dirt or other foreign material.

4. Do not apply power to the SRS unless all components are connected or a diagnostic chart requests it. Powering up the SRS with components disconnected will set a diagnostic trouble code (DTC).

5. The 'SRS Diagnostic System Check' must be the starting point of any SRS diagnostics. The 'SRS Diagnostic System Check' should be performed by an authorized dealer and will verify proper air bag indicator operation and will lead you to the correct chart to diagnose any SRS faults. Bypassing these procedures may result in extended diagnostic time, incorrect diagnosis and incorrect parts replacement.

HEATING

Blower Motor (Fan Motor)

The blower motor is located under the dashboard on the far right side of the car. It is accessible from under the dashboard without removing the dash. The blower motor turns the fan, which circulates the heated, cooled or fresh air within the car. Aside from common electrical problems, the blower motor may need to be removed to clean out leaves or debris which have been sucked into the casing.

➡The blower motor may be removed without disconnecting heater hoses. If the car is equipped with air conditioning, the air conditioning system must be discharged and the evaporator unit removed. Please refer to 'Evaporator — Removal and Installation' later in this section. Once the unit is removed, the blower motor can be removed following the procedures below.

REMOVAL & INSTALLATION

1985-90
▶ See Figure 3

1. Remove the 3 screws attaching the retainer.
2. Remove the glove box assembly.
3. Remove the air duct between the heater case and blower assembly.
4. Disconnect the blower motor wire connector at the motor case.
5. Disconnect the air source selector control cable at the blower assembly.
6. Loosen the 2 nuts and the bolt attaching the blower assembly, then remove the blower.
7. With the blower removed, check the case for any debris or signs of fan contact. Inspect the fan for wear spots, cracked blades or hub, loose retaining nut or poor alignment.
   To install:
8. Place the blower in position, making sure it is properly aligned within the case. Install the 2 bolts and the nut and tighten them.
9. Connect the selector control cable at the blower assembly.
10. Connect the wire harness to the motor and install the ductwork between the heater case and the blower assembly.
11. Install the glove box assembly and install the retainer with its 3 screws.

1991-92
▶ See Figure 3

1. Disconnect the negative battery cable.
2. Remove the rubber duct running between the heater case and the blower.
3. Disconnect the wiring from the motor.
4. Remove the 3 screws holding the motor and remove the blower motor.
5. With the blower removed, check the case for any debris or signs of fan contact. Inspect the fan for wear spots, cracked blades or hub, loose retaining nut or poor alignment.
   To install:
6. Place the blower in position, making sure it is properly aligned within the case. Install the 3 screws and tighten them.
7. Connect the wiring to the motor.
8. Install the rubber air duct and connect the negative battery cable.

1993
▶ See Figure 4

1. Disconnect the negative battery cable.
2. Remove the 3 bolts and 3 screws and remove the glove box from the vehicle.
3. Disconnect the blower motor electrical connector.
4. Remove the 3 screws and remove the blower motor from the vehicle.
   To install:
5. Place the blower in position, making sure it is properly aligned within the case. Install the 3 screws and tighten them.
6. Connect the blower motor electrical connector.
7. Install the glove box to the vehicle and secure with the 3 bolts and 3 screws.
8. Connect the negative battery cable.

Heater Core

The heater core is simply a small heat exchanger (radiator) within the car. If the driver selects heat on the control panel, a water valve is opened allowing engine coolant to circulate through the heater core. The blower fan circulates air through the fins, picking up the heat from the engine coolant. The heated air is ducted into the car and the coolant is routed back to the engine. Moving the control to a cooler setting reduces the amount of hot water flowing into the core, thus reducing the amount of heat.

1. BLOWER ASSEMBLY
2. DUCT
3. HEATER ASSEMBLY

Fig. 3 Heater assembly — 1985-92

Fig. 4 Blower motor — 1993 models

REMOVAL & INSTALLATION

1985-88

▶ See Figure 3

1. Disconnect the negative battery cable and then drain the cooling system.

✳✳CAUTION

When draining the coolant, keep in mind that cats and dogs are attracted by the ethylene glycol antifreeze, and are quite likely to drink any that is left in an uncovered container or in puddles on the ground. This will prove fatal in sufficient quantity. Always drain the coolant into a sealable container. Coolant should be reused unless it is contaminated or several years old.

2. Disconnect the heater hose from the core in the engine compartment.
3. Remove the 6 clips from the lower part of the heater case, then remove the lower part of the case.
4. Carefully pry open the lower part of the heater case.
5. Remove the core assembly from the heater case. Handle the core carefully and do not allow the fins to be crushed or deformed.
   To install:
6. When reinstalling, position the core properly and install the lower part of the case.
7. Install the 6 clips, making sure each is properly secured.
8. Connect the heater hoses. Check them for any signs of weakness or fraying and use new clamps if necessary.
9. Refill the coolant to the proper level.
10. Connect the negative battery cable.

1989-92

▶ See Figure 3

➡The heater case and core are located directly behind the center console. Access to the heater case requires removal of the entire console as well as most of the dashboard assembly. Please refer to the proper sub-topics for removal procedures. Instrument Cluster and Radio removal are explained later in this section. Instrument Panel and Console removal are found in Section 10. Steering Wheel removal and installation is discussed in Section 8.

1. Disconnect the negative battery cable.
2. Remove the steering wheel.
3. Remove the trim bezel from the instrument cluster.
4. Remove the cup holder from the console.
5. Remove the radio.
6. Remove the instrument panel (dashboard) assembly and the instrument cluster. Label and carefully disconnect all of the dash wiring harnesses. Remember to release the locking mechanism on each connector first.
7. Remove the center console and all the console trim. Work carefully and don't break the plastic pieces.
8. Remove the lower dash trim and the side window air deflectors.
9. Drain the coolant from the cooling system.

✳✳CAUTION

When draining the coolant, keep in mind that cats and dogs are attracted by the ethylene glycol antifreeze, and are quite likely to drink any that is left in an uncovered container or in puddles on the ground. This will prove fatal in sufficient quantity. Always drain the coolant into a sealable container. Coolant should be reused unless it is contaminated or several years old.

10. Disconnect the control cables from the heater case. Don't lose any of the small clips.
11. Disconnect the ductwork from the heater case.
12. Disconnect the blower switch wiring harness and heater control assembly.
13. Remove the 2 center console support braces.
14. Loosen the clamps and remove the heater hoses from the case. Remove the grommet from the cowling.
15. Remove the mounting nuts and bolts holding the heater core and the air distribution case to the firewall.
16. Remove the heater case and air distribution case from the car as a unit.
17. Remove the screws and clips from the case halves and separate the case.
18. Remove the heater core from the case.

To install:

19. Install the heater core into the case, position the case halves and secure the retaining screws and clips.
20. Install the case assembly in the car and secure it with the mounting nuts and bolts.
21. Connect the heater hoses (use new clamps if necessary) and attach the grommet to the cowl.
22. Connect the air ducts to the case and connect the control cables.
23. Install the 2 center console support braces.

24. Install the blower wiring harness and the heater control assembly.
25. Place the dashboard in position within the car. When it is loosely in place, connect the wiring harness connectors, making sure each is firmly seated and the wiring properly secured.
26. Install the center console and its trim pieces.
27. Install the radio.
28. Install the cup holder.
29. Install the trim bezel around the instrument cluster.
30. Install the steering wheel.
31. Refill the coolant to the proper level.
32. Connect the negative battery cable.

1993

▶ See Figures 5, 6, 7, 8, 9, 10, 11 and 12

1. Disconnect the negative battery cable.
2. If equipped with air conditioning, remove the evaporator case.
3. Drain the coolant from the cooling system.

✳✳CAUTION

When draining the coolant, keep in mind that cats and dogs are attracted by the ethylene glycol antifreeze, and are quite likely to drink any that is left in an uncovered container or in puddles on the ground. This will prove fatal in sufficient quantity. Always drain the coolant into a sealable container. Coolant should be reused unless it is contaminated or several years old.

4. Disconnect the heater core inlet and outlet hoses.
5. Remove the heater core grommet from the vehicle.
6. Refer to Section 10 and remove the instrument panel from the vehicle.
7. Remove the left side instrument panel brace from the vehicle by removing the 6 retaining bolts.
8. Remove the right side instrument panel brace from the vehicle by removing the 1 retaining bolt and nut.
9. Remove the center ventilation duct from the vehicle by removing the 2 retaining screws.
10. Disconnect the instrument panel left side ventilation duct.
11. Remove the case from the vehicle by removing the 4 retaining nuts.
12. Disconnect the heater core mounting brackets by removing the 2 retaining screws.
13. Slide the heater core out of the heater case.

To install:

14. Slide the heater core into the heater case and install the 2 retaining screws.
15. Install the case to the vehicle and tighten the 4 retaining nuts to 89 inch lbs. (10 Nm).
16. Connect the instrument panel left side ventilation duct.
17. Install the center ventilation duct to the vehicle and install the 2 retaining screws.
18. Install the right side instrument panel brace to the vehicle and tighten the 1 retaining bolt and nut to 18 ft. lbs. (25 Nm).
19. Install the left side instrument panel brace to the vehicle and tighten the 6 retaining bolts 18 ft. lbs. (25 Nm).
20. Refer to Section 10 and install the instrument panel to the vehicle.

21. Install the heater core grommet to the vehicle.
22. Connect the heater core inlet and outlet hoses.
23. Fill the cooling system.
24. If equipped with air conditioning, install the evaporator case.
25. Connect the negative battery cable.

Fig. 7 Blower motor case — 1993 models

Heater Control Unit Control Cables

REMOVAL & INSTALLATION

Temperature Control Cable (To Heater Case)

1993

▶ **See Figure 13**

1. Disconnect the negative battery cable.
2. Remove the instrument panel from the vehicle.
3. Disconnect the temperature control cable from the heater control unit.
4. Disconnect the temperature control cable from the heater case and remove the cable from the vehicle.

Fig. 6 Instrument panel support beam — 1993 models

Fig. 5 Heater and ventilation system components — 1993 models

1. Center trim bezel
2. Heater control unit
3. Knee bolster outlet
4. Knee bolster
5. Left side ventilation duct
6. Left side outlet trim bezel
7. Left side outlet duct
8. Left side window outlet
9. Left side window outlet duct
10. Center ventilation duct
11. Defroster nozzle duct
12. Defroster nozzle
13. Defroster nozzle outlet
14. Right-side window outlet duct
15. Right-side side ventilation duct
16. Glove box

Fig. 8 Heater and ventilation ducts — 1993 models

CENTER VENTILATION DUCT

Fig. 9 Instrument panel center ventilation duct — 1993 models

HEATER CORE INLET HOSE

HEATER CORE OUTLET HOSE

ENGINE COOLANT CONTROL VALVE

Fig. 10 Heater core hoses — 1993 models

Fig. 11 Heater case — 1993 models

Fig. 12 Heater core — 1993 models

To install:

5. Connect the temperature control cable to the heater case.

6. Connect the temperature control cable to the heater control unit.

7. Install the instrument panel to the vehicle.

8. Connect the negative battery cable.

Temperature Control Cable (To Engine Coolant Valve)

1993

▶ See Figures 13 and 14

1. Disconnect the negative battery cable.

2. Remove the instrument panel from the vehicle.

3. Disconnect the temperature control cable from the heater control unit.

4. Disconnect the temperature control cable from the engine coolant control valve and remove the cable from the vehicle.

To install:

5. Connect the temperature control cable to the engine coolant control valve.

6. Connect the temperature control cable to the heater control unit.

7. Install the instrument panel to the vehicle.

8. Connect the negative battery cable.

Fresh/Recirc Control Lever Cable

1993

▶ See Figures 13 and 15

1. Disconnect the negative battery cable.

2. Remove the instrument panel from the vehicle.

3. Disconnect the fresh/recirc control lever cable from the heater control unit.

4. Disconnect the fresh/recirc control lever cable from the blower motor case and remove the cable from the vehicle.

To install:

5. Connect the fresh/recirc control lever cable to the blower motor case. Connect temperature control cable to the heater cable.

6. Connect the fresh/recirc control lever cable to the heater control unit.

7. Install the instrument panel to the vehicle.

8. Connect the negative battery cable.

Mode Control Cable

1993

▶ See Figures 13 and 16

1. Disconnect the negative battery cable.

2. Remove the instrument panel from the vehicle.

3. Disconnect the mode control lever cable from the heater control unit.

4. Disconnect the mode control lever cable from the heater control case.

To install:

5. Connect the mode control lever cable to the heater control case.

6. Connect the mode control lever cable to the heater control unit.

7. Install the instrument panel to the vehicle.

8. Connect the negative battery cable.

Heater Control Panel (Unit)

REMOVAL & INSTALLATION

1985-92

▶ See Figures 17 and 18

1. Disconnect the negative battery cable.

2. Remove the steering wheel.

3. Remove the 2 screws holding the hood release lever assembly.

4. Remove the 4 screws holding the left lower dashboard panel.

5. Remove the upper and lower steering column covers.

6. Use a small screwdriver or similar tool to gently pry the switches from the lower dash trim panel. Disconnect the wiring and remove the switches.

7. Remove the 2 screws under the panel and pull out the center cluster finish panel. It is also secured by spring clips behind the dash — pull straight out away from the dash so as not to break the plastic.

1. Heater control unit
2. Temperature control cable
   (to engine coolant control
   valve)
3. Temperature control cable
   (to engine coolant control
   valve)
4. Mode control cable
5. Fresh/recirc control lever
   cable

Fig. 13 Heater control unit cable routing — 1993 models

Fig. 14 Temperature control cable to engine coolant control valve — 1993 models

Fig. 16 Mode control cable heater case

Fig. 15 Fresh/recirc control lever Cable to blower motor case

◯: 9-clip

Fig. 17 Location of screws and clips retaining the dash trim panel — 1985-92

8. Remove the 4 screws holding the heater control panel and slide the panel out of the dash.

To install:

9. When reinstalling, place the control panel in the dash, make sure it is straight and install the 4 retaining screws.

10. Place the finish panel in place and push it into the dash so that each spring clip engages. Install the 2 lower screws.

11. Connect the wiring to the switches and press the switches firmly into place.

12. Install the upper and lower steering wheel covers.

13. Install the lower left dash cover and its 4 screws.

14. Install the hood release lever assembly.

15. Install the steering wheel.

16. Connect the negative battery cable.

1993

▶ **See Figures 19 and 20**

1. Disconnect the negative battery cable.

2. Pull the center trim bezel from the instrument panel, disconnecting the cigar lighter and ashtray bulb socket.

3. Remove the 3 screws and pull the heater control unit from the instrument panel.

To install:

4. Install the heater control unit to the instrument panel.

5. Press the center trim bezel to the instrument panel and connect the cigar lighter and ashtray bulb socket.

6. Connect the negative battery cable.

Fig. 18 Heater control unit retaining bolts — 1985-92

Fig. 19 Center trim bezel — 1993

Blower Speed Control Switch

REMOVAL & INSTALLATION

1985-92

1. Disconnect the negative battery cable. Remove the illumination light from the control assembly.

2. Using a tool, pry loose the clip and push out the blower speed control switch to the rear of the control assembly.

3. Installation is the reverse of the removal procedure. Connect the negative battery cable. Check operation of the system.

1993

▶ **See Figures 19 and 20**

1. Disconnect the negative battery cable.

2. Pull the center trim bezel from the instrument panel, disconnecting the cigar lighter and ashtray bulb socket.

3. Remove the 3 screws and pull the heater control unit from the instrument panel.

4. Pull the knob off of the blower speed selector switch.

5. Disconnect the blower speed selector switch electrical connector.

6. Remove the switch by removing the 2 screws retaining it to the control unit.

To install:

7. Position the switch and install the 2 screws retaining it to the control unit.

8. Connect the blower speed selector switch electrical connector.

9. Push the knob on the blower speed selector switch.

10. Install the heater control unit to the instrument panel.

11. Press the center trim bezel to the instrument panel and connect the cigar lighter and ashtray bulb socket.

12. Connect the negative battery cable.

Blower Motor Resistor

REMOVAL AND INSTALLATION

1993

▶ **See Figure 21**

1. Disconnect the negative cable.

2. Remove the 3 bolts and 3 screws and remove the glove box from the vehicle.

3. Disconnect the electrical connector from the blower resistor assembly.

4. Remove the 2 screws and remove the resistor from the vehicle.

5. Installation is the reverse of the removal procedure. Reconnect the negative battery cable. Check the blower motor for proper operation at all speeds after installation.

Fig. 21 Blower motor resistor — 1993

Fig. 20 Heater control unit — 1993

AIR CONDITIONING

Compressor

REMOVAL & INSTALLATION

1985-88

▶ See Figure 22

❋❋CAUTION

Please re-read the air conditioning section in Section One so that the system may be discharged properly. Always wear eye protection and gloves when discharging the system. Observe no smoking/no open flame rules.

1. Disconnect the negative battery cable.
2. Remove the electrical connector to the compressor.
3. Safely discharge the system.
4. Remove the 2 hoses from the compressor fittings. Immediately cap the compressor ports and the hose ends to prevent dirt from entering.
5. Remove the fan shroud.
6. Loosen the compressor drive belt.
7. Remove the compressor mounting bolts and remove the compressor from the engine. You are reminded that the compressor is a heavy component — support it securely when removing the bolts.
   To install:
8. Attach the compressor mounting bolts and tighten them to 20 ft. lbs.
9. Install and tighten the drive belt to the correct tension. Make sure the belt is correctly seated on its pulleys.
10. Install the fan shroud.
11. Connect the hoses to the compressor and connect the electrical leads.
12. Connect the negative battery cable.
13. Evacuate and recharge the air conditioning system as explained in Section One.

4A-GE ENGINE

1. Idle pulley
2. Compressor mounting bracket
3. Compressor
4. Compressor
5. Driven belt
6. Alternator bracket

4A-LC ENGINE

Fig. 22 Compressor mounting — 1985-88

1989-92

▶ See Figure 23

❋❋CAUTION

Please re-read the air conditioning section in Section One so that the system may be discharged properly. Always wear eye protection and gloves when discharging the system. Observe no smoking/no open flame rules.

1. Disconnect the negative battery cable.
2. Remove the electrical connector to the compressor.
3. Safely discharge the system.

4. Remove the 2 hoses from the compressor fittings. Immediately cap the compressor ports and the hose ends to prevent dirt from entering.

5. Loosen or remove the compressor drive belt.

6. Elevate and safely support the vehicle on jackstands. Remove the splash shield under the engine.

7. Remove the compressor mounting bolts and remove the compressor from the engine. You are reminded that the compressor is a heavy component — support it securely when removing the bolts.

To install:

8. Support the compressor in place and install the retaining bolts. Tighten them to 18. ft. lbs.

9. With the vehicle safely supported by jackstands, reinstall the splash shields.

10. Lower the vehicle and install the drive belt. Adjust it to the proper tension.

11. Use new O-rings in the hose ends and connect the hoses to the compressor. tighten both lines only to 18 ft. lbs.

12. Install the wiring to the compressor.

13. Connect the negative battery cable.

14. Evacuate and recharge the air conditioning system as explained in Section One.

1993

▶ **See Figure 24**

1. Run the engine at idle with the air conditioning on for approximately 10 minutes.

2. Stop engine and disconnect the negative battery cable.

3. Remove the washer reserve tank.

4. Disconnect all electrical connections.

5. Recover refrigerant (discharge system) from refrigeration system.

6. Disconnect hoses from the compressor service valves. Cap open fittings immediately.

7. Remove engine undercover, if necessary. Loosen the compressor mounting bolts. Remove the compressor drive belt.

8. Remove the compressor mounting bolts. Remove the compressor from the vehicle.

To install:

9. Install compressor with mounting bolts and torque retaining bolts evenly to 18 ft. lbs. (25 Nm) Install and adjust the drive belt. Install engine undercover, if necessary.

10. Reconnect hoses to the compressor service valves.

11. Reconnect all electrical connections.

12. Install the washer reserve tank.

Fig. 23 Compressor mounting — 1989-92

13. Reconnect the battery cable.

14. Evacuate, charge and test refrigerant system. Check system for leaks.

Condenser

REMOVAL & INSTALLATION

1985-88

▶ **See Figures 25 and 26**

> ✳✳**CAUTION**
>
> **Please re-read the air conditioning section in Section One so that the system may be discharged properly. Always wear eye protection and gloves when discharging the system. Observe no smoking/no open flame rules.**

1. Safely discharge the air conditioning system.

2. Remove the grille and the hood lock brace.

3. Disconnect the flexible discharge hose from the condenser inlet fitting. Use 2 wrenches, one to counterhold the fitting and one to turn. Failure to counterhold the fitting may result in damage to the lines.

4. Disconnect the liquid line from the condenser outlet. Again, use 2 wrenches.

5. Cap the open lines immediately to prevent moisture from entering the system.

6. Remove the 4 bolts holding the condenser and remove the condenser. Take great care not to damage the fins on the condenser during removal.

To install:

7. When reinstalling, make sure the rubber cushions fit on the mounting flange correctly.

8. Install the 4 bolts holding the condenser.

9. Connect the liquid line to the condenser and tighten it to 10 ft. lbs.

10. Connect the flexible discharge hose and tighten it to 16 ft. lbs.

➡ **The lightweight fittings on the lines and hoses are easily damaged. Do not overtighten the threaded fittings.**

11. Install the front grille and hood lock brace.

12. If a different condenser was installed, add 1.4-1.7 oz. of compressor oil to the compressor.

13. Evacuate and recharge the system.

1989-92

▶ **See Figure 27**

> ✳✳**CAUTION**
>
> **Please re-read the air conditioning section in Section One so that the system may be discharged properly. Always wear eye protection and gloves when discharging the system. Observe no smoking/no open flame rules.**

1. Safely discharge the system.

2. Disconnect the negative battery cable.

3. Remove the front grille, the hood lock and its brace.

COMPRESSOR

Fig. 24 Compressor mounting — 1993

Fig. 26 Condenser — 1985-88

4. Remove the front bumper.

5. Disconnect the liquid line and the discharge hose at the condenser. Use 2 wrenches, one to hold the assembly and one to turn the fitting. Failure to counterhold the lines may result in damage to the lines, hoses and fittings. Cap the open lines immediately to prevent moisture from entering the system.

6. Remove the 4 mounting bolts and remove the condenser.

To install:

7. When reinstalling, mount the condenser and install its 4 bolts.

4A-GE ENGINE

4A-LC ENGINE

1. Condenser fan motor	5. Oil cooler
2. Hood lock and center brace	6. Suction tube
3. Horn	7. Suction hose
4. Liquid tube	8. Discharge tube

Fig. 25 Liquid line — 1985-88

8. Connect the liquid tube and the discharge hose to the condenser. Tighten the liquid tube to 10 ft. lbs. and the discharge hose to 18 ft. lbs.

➡**The lightweight fittings on the lines and hoses are easily damaged. Do not overtighten the threaded fittings.**

9. Reinstall the front bumper.
10. Install the hood lock and center brace. Install the grille.
11. If the condenser has been replaced with a different unit, add 1.4-1.7 ounces of compressor oil to the compressor.
12. Connect the negative battery cable.
13. Evacuate and recharge the system.

1993

▶ **See Figure 28**

✳✳CAUTION

Please re-read the air conditioning section in Section 1 so that the system may be discharged properly. Always wear eye protection and gloves when discharging the system. Observe no smoking/no open flame rules.

1. Disconnect the negative battery cable.
2. Recover refrigerant (discharge system) from refrigeration system.
3. Remove the following parts:
   a. radiator grille
   b. horn
   c. hood lock
   d. center brace
   e. battery
   f. radiator reserve tank
4. Remove the condenser fan assembly.
5. Remove the oxygen sensor.
6. Remove all refrigerant system connections. Remove the receiver with bracket. Cap open fittings immediately.
7. Remove the radiator support brackets — remove the condenser mounting bolts lean the radiator back and pull out the condenser.

To install:

8. Install the condenser assembly to the vehicle. Install radiator support brackets. Make sure all rubber cushions fit on the mounting flanges correctly.
9. Reconnect all refrigerant system connections. Install receiver with bracket. Replace O-rings, as required.

10. Install the oxygen sensor, torque the nuts to 15 ft. lbs. Install condenser fan.
11. Install all other remaining components in reverse order of removal procedure.
12. If condenser assembly was replaced, add 1.4-1.7 fl. oz. of compressor oil.
13. Reconnect battery cable. Evacuate, charge and test refrigerant system. Check system for leaks.

Evaporator Unit and Expansion Valve

REMOVAL & INSTALLATION

✳✳CAUTION

Please re-read the air conditioning section in Section 1 so that the system may be discharged properly. Always wear eye protection and gloves when discharging the system. Observe no smoking/no open flame rules.

1985-88

▶ **See Figures 29 and 30**

1. Disconnect the negative battery cable.
2. Safely discharge the air conditioning system.
3. Disconnect the suction tube from the evaporator assembly, then disconnect the liquid line from the assembly. Cap the open fittings immediately to prevent the entry of dirt and moisture.

Fig. 28 Condenser — 1989-92

Fig. 27 Condenser — 1989-92

Fig. 29 Evaporator assembly — 1985-88

4. Remove the grommets from the inlet and outlet fittings.

5. Remove the glove box.

6. Remove the lower cover from under the dashboard.

7. Disconnect the air conditioning switch connector.

8. Disconnect the vehicle wiring harness at the connector.

9. Remove the 4 nuts and 3 bolts securing the cooling assembly and remove the evaporator assembly from the car.

10. Remove the air conditioning amplifier.

11. Remove the air conditioning wiring harness from the case.

12. Remove the 5 clamps and 2 screws and remove the lower casing.

13. Remove the 2 screws holding the upper casing and remove the casing.

14. Remove the heat insulator and clamp from the outlet tube.

15. Disconnect the liquid line tube from the inlet fitting of the expansion valve.

16. Disconnect the expansion valve from the inlet fitting of the evaporator.

17. Remove the pressure switch if necessary.

18. Inspect the evaporator fins for blockage. Check all the fittings for cracks or scratches.

To install:

19. To reassemble, connect the expansion valve to the inlet fitting of the evaporator and tighten the nut to 17 ft. lbs.

20. Connect the liquid line tube to the inlet fitting of the expansion valve.

21. Install the pressure switch, if removed, and tighten it to 10 ft. lbs.

22. Install the clamp and heat insulator to the outlet tube.

23. Assemble the upper and lower cases onto the evaporator unit.

24. Reinstall the thermistor if it was removed.

25. Install the air conditioning wire harness onto the evaporator unit.

26. Install the air conditioning amplifier.

27. Place the assembled unit in place inside the car and install the retaining nuts and bolts.

❋❋WARNING

Be careful not to pinch the wiring harness(es) during installation.

28. Connect the air conditioning switch.

29. Connect the vehicle wiring harness to the connector.

Fig. 30 Separating the evaporator case halves — 1985-88

30. Install the glove box and the under-dash cover.

31. Install the grommets on the inlet and outlet fittings.

32. Connect the liquid line to the evaporator inlet fitting and tighten it to 10 ft. lbs. Make sure the rubber washer (O-ring) is present inside the line and make certain the joint is correctly threaded before tightening it. Do not overtighten the joint.

33. Connect the suction tube to the evaporator unit outlet fitting and tighten it to 24 ft. lbs. Again, make sure the rubber washer (O-ring) is present inside the line and make certain the joint is correctly threaded before tightening it. Do not overtighten the joint.

34. If the evaporator was replaced with a NEW unit, add 1.5 oz. of compressor oil to the compressor. This replaces oil in the system removed with the old evaporator.

35. Connect the negative battery cable.

36. Evacuate and recharge the air conditioning system.

1989-90

▶ **See Figure 31**

1. Disconnect the negative battery cable.

2. Safely discharge the air conditioning system.

3. Disconnect the suction tube from the evaporator assembly, then disconnect the liquid line from the assembly. Cap the open fittings immediately to prevent the entry of dirt and moisture.

4. Remove the grommets from the inlet and outlet fittings.

5. Remove the glove box.

6. Disconnect the wiring harness connectors.

7. Remove the 4 nuts and 4 screws holding the evaporator unit. Remove the unit through the front of the instrument panel.

8. Remove the connectors and the wiring harness from the case.

9. Remove the 4 clips and 4 screws; remove the upper casing and then the lower casing.

10. Disconnect the liquid tube from the inlet fitting of the expansion tube.

11. Remove the packing and the heat sensing tube from the suction tube of the evaporator.

➡**Cap the open lines and fittings immediately to prevent the entry of dirt and moisture.**

12. Remove the expansion valve.

To install:

13. Inspect the evaporator fins for blockage. Check all the fittings for cracks or scratches. Never use water to clean the evaporator.

14. When reinstalling, assemble the expansion valve to the inlet fitting of the evaporator and tighten the nut to 17 ft. lbs.

15. Install the heat sensing tube and its packing to the suction tube of the evaporator.

16. Connect the liquid tube to the inlet fitting of the expansion valve and tighten it to 10 ft. lbs.

17. Assemble the lower casing and the upper casing and secure them with the 4 clips and the 4 screws.

18. Connect the wiring harness connectors.

19. Place the assembled unit in place within the car and secure its 4 mounting bolts and 4 nuts.

20. Install the wiring connectors onto the evaporator case.

21. Install the glove box.

22. Install the grommets on the inlet and outlet fittings.

23. Connect the liquid tube to the inlet fitting. Make sure the O-ring is in place and that the joint is correctly threaded. Tighten the joint to 10 ft. lbs. Do not overtighten.

24. Install the suction tube to the case inlet fitting. Make sure the O-ring is in place and that the joint is correctly threaded. Tighten the joint to 24 ft. lbs. Do not overtighten.

25. If the evaporator was replaced with a NEW unit, add 1.5 oz. of compressor oil to the compressor. This replaces oil in the system removed with the old evaporator.

26. Connect the negative battery cable.

27. Evacuate and recharge the air conditioning system.

1991-92

▶ **See Figure 31**

1. Disconnect the negative battery cable. Discharge and recover the refrigerant from the system as outlined in Section 1.

2. Disconnect the outlet tube from the evaporator assembly, then disconnect the (inlet) liquid line from the assembly. Cap the open fittings immediately to prevent the entry of dirt and moisture.

3. Disconnect the hold-down brackets for both inlet and outlet lines.

4. Remove the right lower instrument panel trim assembly.

5. Disconnect the A/C amplifier electrical connector and remove the amplifier from the vehicle.

6. Remove the evaporator bolts and nuts from the evaporator case.

1. Amplifier
2. Upper unit case
3. Evaporator
4. Expansion valve
5. Lower unit case
6. Drain hose
7. Wire harness
8. Thermistor
9. Clips
10. Screw

Prizm evaporator components

Fig. 31 Evaporator components — 1989-92

7. Disconnect the thermistor electrical connector.

8. Remove the evaporator case from the vehicle.

9. Separate the evaporator case halves.

10. Remove the A/C thermistor from the evaporator.

11. Remove the evaporator from the case.

12. Disconnect the expansion valve inlet pipe from the expansion valve and remove the expansion valve from the vehicle.

To install:

13. Install the expansion valve to the vehicle. Tighten the expansion valve to evaporator fitting to 24 ft. lbs. (32 Nm) and tighten the expansion valve inlet pipe to 17 ft. lbs. (23 Nm).

14. Install the evaporator into the lower evaporator case.

15. Install the A/C thermistor to the evaporator.

16. Combine the evaporator case halves.

17. Install the evaporator case into the vehicle and tighten the evaporator bolts and nuts to 11 ft. lbs. (15 Nm).

18. Install the amplifier to the vehicle and connect the A/C amplifier electrical connector

19. Install the A/C thermistor to the evaporator and connect the connector.

20. Install the right lower instrument panel trim assembly.

21. .Connect the outlet and the (inlet) liquid line to the evaporator and tighten both pipe fittings to 24 ft. lbs. (32 Nm).

22. Connect the hold-down brackets for both inlet and outlet lines.

23. Evacuate and charge the A/C system as outlined in Section 1.

24. If the evaporator was replaced, add 1.4-1.7 oz. of compressor oil to the compressor. Connect the negative battery cable.

25. Operate the A/C system and check for leaks.

1993

▶ See Figure 32

1. Disconnect the negative battery cable. Discharge and recover the refrigerant from the system as outlined in Section 1.

2. Remove the right side kick panel by removing the 1 plastic retaining nut.

3. Remove the glove box by removing the 3 nuts and 3 screws.

4. .Disconnect the outlet tube from the evaporator assembly, then disconnect the (inlet) liquid line from the assembly. Cap the open fittings immediately to prevent the entry of dirt and moisture.

5. Disconnect the hold-down brackets for both inlet and outlet lines.

6. Disconnect the A/C amplifier electrical connector and remove the amplifier from the vehicle.

7. Remove the evaporator bolts and nuts from the evaporator case.

8. Disconnect the thermistor electrical connector.

9. Remove the evaporator case from the vehicle.

10. Separate the evaporator case halves.

11. Remove the A/C thermistor from the evaporator.

12. Remove the evaporator from the case.

13. Disconnect the expansion valve inlet pipe from the expansion valve and remove the expansion valve from the vehicle.

To install:

14. Install the expansion valve to the vehicle. Tighten the expansion valve to evaporator fitting to 48 inch lbs. (5.4 Nm) and tighten the expansion valve inlet pipe to 48 inch lbs. (5.4 Nm).

15. Install the evaporator into the lower evaporator case.

16. Install the A/C thermistor to the evaporator.

17. Combine the evaporator case halves.

18. Install the evaporator case into the vehicle and tighten the evaporator bolts and nuts to 89 inch lbs. (10 Nm).

19. Install the amplifier to the vehicle and connect the A/C amplifier electrical connector

20. Install the A/C thermistor to the evaporator and connect the connector.

21. Connect the inlet line to the evaporator and tighten pipe fitting to 124 inch lbs. (14 Nm).

22. Connect the outlet line to the evaporator and tighten pipe fitting to 24 ft. lbs. (32 Nm).

23. Connect the hold-down brackets for both inlet and outlet lines.

24. Install the glove box and tighten the 3 nuts and 3 screws to 89 inch lbs. (10 Nm).

25. Install the right side kick panel and tighten the 1 plastic retaining nut to 89 inch lbs. (10 Nm).

26. Evacuate and charge the A/C system as outlined in Section 1.

27. If the evaporator was replaced, add 1.4-1.7 oz. of compressor oil to the compressor. Connect the negative battery cable.

28. Operate the A/C system and check for leaks.

Receiver/Drier

REMOVAL & INSTALLATION

▶ See Figures 33, 34, 35 and 36

1. Disconnect the negative battery cable.

2. Discharge system (recover refrigerant) from refrigeration system as outlined in Section 1.

3. Remove the radiator grille and horn.

4. Disconnect lines from the receiver. Cap open fittings immediately.

5. Remove the receiver from the receiver holder assembly.

To install:

6. Install receiver in receiver holder assembly. Reconnect lines to the receiver. Reconnect the negative battery cable.

7. Install horn and radiator grille.

8. If receiver assembly was replaced, add oil as outlined in Section 1.

9. Evacuate, charge and test refrigerant system. Check system for leaks.

1. Air cond. amplifier
2. Evaporator case
   upper half
3. Evaporator
4. Evaporator inlet pipe
5. Evaporator suction
   pipe
6. Expansion valve
7. Evaporator case
   lower half
8. Evaporator thermistor

Fig. 32 Evaporator components — 1993

Refrigerant Lines

REMOVAL AND INSTALLATION

▶ **See Figures 33, 34, 35 and 36**

1. Disconnect the negative battery cable.
2. Recover refrigerant (discharge system) from refrigeration system.
3. Replace faulty line or hose. Always replace O-rings.
4. Connect the negative battery cable. Evacuate, charge and test the refrigeration system, as outlined in Section 1.

Thermistor

REMOVAL AND INSTALLATION

To remove the thermistor, please refer to the Evaporator and Expansion Valve service procedures outlined earlier.

A/C Amplifier

REMOVAL AND INSTALLATION

▶ **See Figures 33, 34, 35 and 36**

1. Disconnect the negative battery cable.
2. Remove the front door scuff plate and glove box assembly.
3. Disconnect the connector. Remove the A/C amplifier.
4. Installation is the reverse of the removal procedure. Connect the negative battery cable. Check operation of the A/C system.

10. Condenser
11. Air cond. switch
12. Thermistor
13. Expansion valve
14. Low pressure switch
15. Amplifier
16. Evaporator
17. High pressure switch
18. Air cond. amplifier

1. Liquid line tube
2. Fan shroud
3. Discharge flexible tube
4. Suction tube
5. Compressor
6. Air cond. tuator
7. Suction flexible hose
8. Receiver
9. Liquid tube

Fig. 33 Air conditioner major components — 1985-88 VIN code 4 engine

1. Insulator
2. Suction tube
3. VSV
4. Liquid tube
5. Pressure switch
6. Receiver
7. Condenser fan motor
8. Discharge tube
9. Discharge hose
10. Compressor
11. Suction hose
12. A/C switch
13. Thermistor
14. Expansion valve
15. Low pressure switch
16. Amplifier
17. Evaporator
18. A/C amplifier

Fig. 34 Air conditioner major components — 1988 VIN code 5 engine

1. Liquid tube
2. Suction tube
3. Magnetic clutch
4. Compressor
5. Dual pressure switch
6. Evaporator
7. Air cond. switch
8. Condenser
9. Receiver & drier
10. Upper case
11. Pressure switch
12. Expansion valve
13. Air cond. amplifier
14. Lower case
15. Evaporator
16. Thermistor
17. Evaporator case
18. Condenser fan

Fig. 35 Air conditioner major components — 1989-90

1. Blower motor case
2. Evaporator case
3. Heater case
4. Receiver & drier
5. Condenser
6. Condenser fan
7. Compressor

Fig. 36 Air conditioner major components — 1993

Cruise Control

Cruise Control Switch

REMOVAL & INSTALLATION

1985-88

▶ **See Figure 37**

1. Disconnect the negative battery cable.
2. Remove the terminals from the connector.
3. Remove the 2 screws from the control switch and remove the switch.
4. Installation is the reverse of removal.

1989-92

▶ **See Figure 38**

1. Disconnect the negative battery cable.
2. Remove the trim bezel.
3. Disconnect the electrical connector.
4. Remove the switch from the dash panel.
5. Installation is the reverse of removal.

1993

The cruise control master switch is part of the combination switch in the steering column. Please refer to the Combination Switch removal and installation procedure outlined in Section 8.

Cruise Control Module

REMOVAL & INSTALLATION

1989-90

1. Disconnect the negative battery cable.
2. Remove the right side cowl trim.
3. Remove the glove box and trim assembly.
4. Remove the cruise control module from the vehicle.
5. Installation is the reverse of removal.

Fig. 37 Control switch installation — 1985-88

1991-92

1. Disconnect the negative battery cable.
2. Remove the right side lower trim panel.
3. Remove the cruise control module from the vehicle.
4. Installation is the reverse of removal.

1993

▶ **See Figure 39**

1. Disable the SRS (Air Bag) system as outlined at the beginning of this Section.
2. Disconnect the negative battery cable.
3. Unclip and set aside the left and right front carpet retainers.
4. Remove the glove box by removing the 4 bolts and 3 screws.
5. Remove the parking brake console by removing the five retaining screws.
6. Disconnect the hood release lever from the knee bolster.
7. Remove the trim caps.
8. Remove the knee bolster from the instrument panel by removing the 4 retaining bolts.
9. Remove the shift lever trim bezel.
10. Remove the package tray.
11. Remove the center trim bezel.
12. Disconnect the electrical connectors from the hazard lights, defogger and cigar lighter.
13. Remove the four screws and remove the radio.
14. Remove the 2 screws and remove the center console.
15. Remove the cruise control module by removing the 2 bolts and clip and disconnecting the module electrical connector.

To install:

16. Reposition the cruise control module, install the 2 bolts and clip and connect the module electrical connector.
17. Install the center console and 2 retaining screws.
18. Connect the radio electrical connector and install the 4 radio retaining screws.
19. Connect the electrical connectors to the hazard lights, defogger and cigar lighter.
20. Install the center trim bezel.
21. Install the package tray.
22. Install the shift lever trim bezel.
23. Install the knee bolster to the instrument panel with the 4 retaining bolts.
24. Install the trim caps.
25. Connect the hood release lever to the knee bolster.
26. Install the parking brake console with the five retaining screws.
27. Install the glove box and the 4 bolts and 3 screws.
28. Position and clip the left and right front carpet retainers.
29. Enable the SRS (Air Bag) system as outlined at the beginning of this Section.
30. Connect the negative battery cable.

1. Electrical connector
2. Rear wiper & washer switch
3. Electrical connector
4. Cruise control & defogger switch
5. Trim bezel

Fig. 38 Control switch installation — 1989-92

1. Clutch pedal position interrupt switch
2. Stoplamp switch
3. Cruise control module
4. Parking brake switch

Fig. 39 Cruise control components — 1993

Actuator

REMOVAL & INSTALLATION

1989-93

▶ **See Figures 39 and 40**

1. Disconnect the negative battery cable.
2. Disconnect the electrical connector.
3. Disconnect the vacuum hose.
4. Remove the actuator cover.
5. Disconnect the control cable.
6. Remove the actuator from the vehicle.
7. Installation is the reverse of removal.

Control Cable

REMOVAL & INSTALLATION

1989-92

▶ **See Figure 40**

1. Remove the actuator cover.
2. Disconnect the control cable from the actuator.
3. Remove the left lower dash trim.
4. Remove the 2 nuts from the cable plate (inside).
5. Remove the attaching bolt from the cable plate (outside).

6. Disconnect the cable from the cable plate and remove the cable from the vehicle.
7. Installation is the reverse of removal.

1993

▶ **See Figure 39**

1. Remove the actuator cover.
2. Loosen the jamb nuts on the control.
3. Remove the cruise control cable from the 3 retaining brackets.
4. Unbolt and remove the control cable from the accelerator.
5. Unclip the accelerator cable from the cruise control cable bracket and remove the cruise control cable from the vehicle.
6. Installation is the reverse of removal.

Engage Switch

REMOVAL & INSTALLATION

1989-92

1. Disconnect the negative battery cable.
2. Remove the steering wheel as outlined in Section 8.
3. Remove the upper and lower steering column covers.
4. Disconnect the engage switch electrical connector.
5. Remove the engage switch from the vehicle.
6. Installation is the reverse of removal.

Fig. 40 Cruise control components — 1989-92

Vacuum Pump

REMOVAL & INSTALLATION

1989-92

▶ **See Figure 40**

1. Disconnect the negative battery cable.

RADIO

REMOVAL & INSTALLATION

1985-88

▶ **See Figure 41**

1. Disconnect the negative battery cable.
2. Remove the steering wheel and then the upper and lower steering column covers.
3. Use a small screwdriver or similar tool to gently pry the switches from the lower dash trim panel. Disconnect the wiring and remove the switches.
4. Remove the 2 screws under the panel and pull out the center cluster finish panel. It is also secured by spring clips behind the dash — pull straight out away from the dash so as not to break the plastic.
5. Remove the 7 screws holding the upper trim panel.

Fig. 41 Radio removal and installation — 1985-88

2. Disconnect the electrical connector.
3. Disconnect the vacuum hose.
4. Remove the vacuum pump from the vehicle.
5. Installation is the reverse of removal.

6. Remove the 8 screws holding the radio and its accessories trim cover.
7. Slide the radio out of the dash. Disconnect the antenna lead and the wiring connector.
   To install:
8. When reinstalling, connect the wiring and antenna leads and place the radio in the dash. Make sure the wiring is not crushed or pinched.
9. Install the 8 screws, making sure the radio is straight and in position.
10. Install the upper trim panel.
11. Route the switch cables through the openings in the center trim panel. Install the center cluster finish panel, making sure all the clips engage properly. Install the 2 screws.
12. Connect the switches to the wiring harnesses and push the switches firmly into place in the trim panel.
13. Install the upper and lower steering column covers and reinstall the steering wheel.
14. Connect the negative battery cable.

1989-92

▶ **See Figure 42**

1. Disconnect the negative battery cable and remove the 7 screws from the steering column covers and remove the covers.
2. Remove the 2 attaching screws from the lower part of the trim panel.
3. Remove the trim panel, being careful of the concealed spring clips behind the panel.
4. Disconnect the wiring from the switches mounted in the trim panel.
5. Remove the 4 mounting screws from the radio.

Fig. 42 Radio removal and installation — 1989-92

6. Remove the radio from the dash until the wiring connectors are exposed.

7. Disconnect the 2 electrical connectors and the antenna cable from the body of the radio and remove the radio from the car.

To install:

8. When reinstalling, connect all the wiring and antenna cable first, then place the radio in position within the dash.

9. Install the 4 attaching screws.

10. Reconnect the wiring harnesses to the switches in the trim panel and make sure the switches are secure in the panel.

11. Install the trim panel (make sure all the spring clips engage) and install the 2 screws.

12. Install the steering column covers and the 7 screws.

13. Install the steering wheel.

1993

1. Disconnect the negative battery cable.

2. Remove the center trim panel by gently prying around the edges to disconnect the clips.

3. Remove the 4 screws and the radio with the cup holder from the center console.

4. Disconnect the electrical and antenna connectors from the radio.

5. Remove the radio from the vehicle.

6. Installation is the reverse of removal.

Front Speakers

REMOVAL & INSTALLATION

1989-90

LEFT

▶ **See Figure 43**

1. Disconnect the negative battery cable.

2. Remove the 2 attaching screws from the hood release lever and remove the lever.

3. Remove the lower left dash trim and 4 retaining screws.

4. Disconnect the electrical connector from the speaker.

5. Remove the 3 speaker attaching screws and remove the speaker from the lower dash trim.

6. Installation is the reverse of removal.

Fig. 43 Removing the left lower dash trim — 1989-90

RIGHT

▶ **See Figure 44**

1. Disconnect the negative battery cable.

2. Remove the right side scuff plate.

3. Remove the right side cowl trim by removing the 1 attaching screw.

4. Remove the 5 attaching screws and pull out the glove box and trim assembly.

5. Disconnect the speaker electrical connector.

6. Remove the 3 speaker attaching screws and remove the speaker from the glove box and trim assembly.

7. Installation is the reverse of removal.

1991-92

1. Disconnect the negative battery cable.

2. Using a flat bladed tool, gently pry the speaker grille from the lower instrument trim panel.

3. Remove the 4 retaining screws, disconnect the electrical connector and remove the speaker from the housing.

4. Installation is the reverse of removal.

1993

▶ **See Figure 45**

1. Disconnect the negative battery cable.

2. Using a flat bladed tool, gently pry the speaker cover from the inner door panel.

3. Remove the 3 retaining bolts, disconnect the electrical connector and remove the speaker from the door.

4. Installation is the reverse of removal. Tighten the 3 retaining bolts to 89 inch lbs. (10 Nm).

Fig. 44 Removing the glove box and trim assembly — 1989-90

Fig. 45 Front speaker removal — 1993

2. Unclip the C-pillar trim panels and set aside.

3. Remove the 2 plastic retaining clips and the center high mounted stoplamp housing from the stoplamp assembly.

4. Remove the 2 bolts, disconnect the electrical connector and remove the center high mounted stoplamp from the vehicle.

5. Unclip the rear seatback to rear window trim panel at 3 places and remove the trim panel from the vehicle.

6. Remove the 5 push nuts from the speaker cover and remove the cover from the trim panel.

7. Remove the 3 retaining bolts, disconnect the electrical connector and remove the speaker from the trim panel.

8. Installation is the reverse of removal. Tighten the 3 speaker retaining bolts to 89 inch lbs. (10 Nm) and the center high mounted stoplamp bolts to 48 inch lbs. (5.4 Nm).

Rear Speakers

REMOVAL & INSTALLATION

1989-92

1. Disconnect the negative battery cable.
2. Remove the rear window shelf.
3. Remove the 3 retaining screws, disconnect the electrical connector and remove the speaker and the base.
4. Installation is the reverse of removal.

1993
▶ See Figure 46

1. Disconnect the negative battery cable.

Fig. 46 Rear speaker mounting — 1993

WINDSHIELD WIPERS AND WASHERS

Blade and Arm

REMOVAL & INSTALLATION

1985-88
▶ See Figure 47

1. To remove the wiper blades lift up on the spring release tab on the wiper blade-to-wiper arm connector.

2. Pull the blade assembly off the wiper arm.

3. Press the old wiper blade insert down, away from the blade assembly, to free it from the retaining clips on the blade ends. Slide the insert out of the blade. Slide the new insert into the blade assembly and bend the insert upward slightly to engage the retaining clips.

4. To replace a wiper arm, unscrew the acorn nut which secures it to the pivot and carefully pull the arm upward and off the pivot. Install the arm by placing it on the pivot and tightening the nut. Remember that the arm must be reinstalled in its exact previous position or it will not cover the correct area during use.

1989-92
▶ See Figure 48

The wiper blade can be removed by detaching the blade tip from the first wiper arm notch, then sliding the blade off the wiper arm. The new blade is installed by sliding the blade groove through the wiper arm notches.

The wiper arm is removed by lifting up the cap at the bottom of the arm, removing the locknut and lifting the arm free of the pivot. When reinstalling, make sure the arm is installed in its exact previous position before tightening the nut.

➡**CHILTON TIP: If one wiper arm does not move when turned on or only moves a little bit, check the retaining nut at the bottom of the arm. The extra effort of moving wet snow or leaves off the glass can cause the nut to come loose — the pivot will turn without moving the arm.**

1993
▶ See Figure 49

1. Raise the wiper arm away from the windshield until it locks in the upright position.

2. Swivel the wiper blade assembly from the wiper arm so the release tab can be accessed behind the assembly.

1. Rubber
2. Rubber
3. Blade
4. Arm
5. Nut
6. Nut
7. Arm
8. Link
9. Motor

Fig. 47 Windshield wiper components — 1985-88

1. Wiper arm cap
2. Wiper linkage cover
3. Attaching nut
4. Wiper arm
5. Wiper linkage
6. Wiper motor

Fig. 48 Windshield wiper components — 1989-92

3. Push the retaining tab and slide the wiper blade assembly toward the vehicle (down on the wiper arm) until it is clear of the hook.

4. Swivel the wiper blade assembly to a 90 ° angle from the wiper arm and slide up and off of the wiper arm.

To install:

5. Slide the wiper blade assembly over the wiper arm to clear the hook.

6. While guiding the retaining tab into the hook, slide the blade up until the tab engages.

7. Lower the wiper arm until the blade contacts the windshield.

Fig. 49 Windshield wiper blade removal — 1993

Windshield Wiper Motor

REMOVAL & INSTALLATION

Front wipers

▶ See Figures 47, 48, 50 and 51

1. Disconnect the negative battery terminal.
2. Disconnect the electrical connector from the wiper motor.
3. Remove the mounting bolts and remove the motor from the firewall.
4. Remove the wiper linkage from the wiper motor assembly.
5. Installation is the reverse of removal.

Fig. 50 Windshield wiper motor removal — 1993

1. Wiper motor
2. Claw
3. Wiper motor crank arm

Fig. 51 Disconnecting the wiper linkage from the wiper motor crank arm — 1993

Rear Wiper

▶ **See Figures 52 and 53**

1. Remove the wiper arm from the pivot and remove the spacer and washer on the pivot.
2. Remove the cover (trim) panel on the inside of the hatch lid.
3. Remove the plastic cover on the wiper motor and disconnect the wiring connector from the motor.
4. Remove the mounting nuts and bolts and remove the wiper motor.

To install:

5. When reinstalling, position the motor and secure it in the hatch lid.
6. Connect the wiring harness and install the plastic cover.
7. Install the inner trim panel on the hatch lid.
8. Install the wiper arm with its washer and spacer, making sure the arm is correctly positioned before tightening the nut.

Front Wiper Linkage

REMOVAL & INSTALLATION

1985-92

▶ **See Figures 47 and 48**

1. Remove the windshield wiper motor as previously outlined.
2. Loosen the wiper arm retaining nuts and remove the arms.
3. Unfasten the large wiper pivot retaining nuts and remove the linkage assembly through the access hole.

To install:

4. Place the linkage through the access hole and line up the pivots in their holes. This can be like trying to put an octopus into a paper bag; keep your temper and take your time.
5. Install the 2 large pivot retaining nuts onto the pivots. Before final tightening, make sure the linkage is aligned in all its holes.
6. Reinstall the wiper motor.

1993

▶ **See Figures 51, 54 and 55**

1. Disconnect the negative battery terminal.

1. Arm
2. Rubber
3. Cover
4. Motor
5. Cover

Fig. 52 Rear wiper components — 1985-88

2. Make sure the wiper arms are in the park position.
3. Remove the plastic nut cover from end of each wiper arm.
4. Remove the 2 nuts and remove the wiper arms from the vehicle.
5. Remove the 10 screws and remove the cowl vent grille from the vehicle.
6. Remove the 6 bolts retaining the wiper linkage to the cowl assembly.
7. Disconnect the wiper motor electrical connector.
8. Remove the 4 bolts and remove the wiper motor from the bulkhead.
9. Connect the claw of the wiper linkage to the bulkhead and gently pry the wiper linkage from the wiper motor.
10. Slide the wiper linkage through the hole at the far left of the cowl.
11. Remove the 1 screw and separate the wiper arm linkage from the intermediate linkage.
12. Remove the 1 screw and separate the wiper motor linkage from the intermediate linkage.

To install:

13. Install the 1 screw and connect the wiper arm linkage to the intermediate linkage.
14. Install the 1 screw and connect the wiper motor linkage to the intermediate linkage.
15. Slide the wiper linkage through the hole at the far left of the cowl.
16. Install the wiper linkage to the motor crank arm.
17. Install the wiper motor to the bulkhead and tighten the 4 retaining bolts to 15 ft. lbs. (20 Nm).
18. Connect the wiper motor electrical connector.

1. Liftback trim
2. Rear wiper arm
3. Rear wiper motor

(12-CLIP)

Fig. 53 Rear wiper components — 1989-90

19. Install the cowl vent grille to the vehicle with the 10 retaining screws.

20. Install the wiper arms to the wiper linkage and tighten the 2 nuts to 15 ft. lbs. (20 Nm).

21. Lower the plastic nut cover over end of each wiper arm.

22. Connect the negative battery terminal.

Washer Pump

REMOVAL & INSTALLATION

1985-92

1. Remove the washer reservoir as outlined in this section.
2. Pry the pump off the reservoir.

WIPER LINKAGE   HOOD

Fig. 54 Removing the wiper linkage from the vehicle — 1993

1. Screw
2. Wiper linkage
3. Intermediate wiper linkage
4. Wiper motor linkage

Fig. 55 Wiper linkage disassembly — 1993

3. Installation is the reverse of removal procedure.

1993

1. Disconnect the negative battery cable.
2. Locate the washer reservoir and disconnect the washer pump electrical connector.
3. Slide the washer pump from the reservoir.
4. Installation is the reverse of removal

Washer Reservoir

REMOVAL & INSTALLATION

1. Remove the washer reservoir attaching bolt.

2. Disconnect the electrical connector.

3. Disconnect the fluid hose and remove the reservoir from the vehicle.

INSTRUMENTS AND SWITCHES

Instrument Cluster

REMOVAL & INSTALLATION

1985-88

▶ **See Figures 56, 57 and 58**

1. Disconnect the negative battery cable.
2. Remove the steering wheel.
3. Remove the left side speaker grille. The grille may be attached with a clip (which must be pulled loose to remove the grille) or with a screw.
4. Remove the lower trim cover from the steering column.
5. Remove the hood release lever.
6. Remove the heater duct assembly.
7. Remove the instrument hood. Remove the air conditioner outlet register, then remove the 4 screws and remove the hood.
8. Remove the 6 screws from the instrument cluster, and disconnect the speedometer cable and the wiring connectors. Remove the meter assembly from the instrument panel.

Fig. 56 Removing the lower steering column cover — 1985-88

Fig. 57 Removing the heater ducts — 1985-88

Fig. 58 Removing the instrument hood — 1985-88

4. Installation is the reverse of removal

To install:

9. Connect the wiring harnesses and the speedometer cable to the cluster. Place the cluster in the dash and secure the 6 screws. Make certain the wiring is properly placed so as not to become pinched or crushed.
10. Install the air conditioning outlet then install the hood and its screws.
11. Install the heater duct assembly.
12. Install the hood release lever and the lower steering column trim.
13. Reinstall the speaker grille.
14. Install the steering wheel and connect the negative battery cable.

1989-92

▶ **See Figures 59, 60 and 61**

➡**Removing the steering wheel is not required, but may make the job easier.**

1. Disconnect the negative battery cable.
2. On 1989-90 models, remove the hood release lever.
3. Remove the 4 screws from the lower left dash trim and pull the trim out.
4. If necessary, disconnect the wiring from the radio speaker.
5. If equipped with air conditioning, remove the ductwork from the lower air outlet.
6. Remove the trim panel from the car.
7. Remove the upper and lower steering column covers.
8. Remove the 2 screws from the trim panel (bezel).
9. Pull the panel out, releasing the spring clips behind the dash. With the panel loose, disconnect the wiring to the dash switches.
10. Remove the switches from the panel.
11. Remove the 2 electrical connectors and the cigarette lighter from the trim bezel and remove the bezel from the car.
12. Remove the 4 screws holding the instrument cluster trim.
13. Disconnect the wiring from the hazard (4-way) flasher and dimmer switches.
14. Remove the cluster trim panel.

1. Electrical connector
2. Rear wiper-washer switch
3. Electrical connector
4. Cruise control/defogger switch
5. Trim bezel

Fig. 59 Removing the lower dash panel bezel — 1989-92

Fig. 60 Removing the lower dash panel bezel — 1989-92

1. Clip locations
2. Instrument panel
3. Instrument cluster trim panel

Fig. 62 Removing the instrument cluster trim panel — 1993

Fig. 61 Removing the instrument cluster — 1989-92

Fig. 63 Combination switch — 1985-92

15. Remove the 4 attaching screws holding the cluster, move it away from the dash and disconnect the wiring harnesses and the speedometer cable.

16. Remove the instrument cluster from the car.

To install:

17. Connect the speedometer and electrical cables to the cluster. Install the cluster and the 4 retaining screws.

18. Attach the wiring connectors for the hazard flasher and the dimmer switches.

19. Install the cluster trim bezel.

20. Place the dash switches in place on the lower trim bezel and connect the wiring to the switches.

21. Install the lower trim bezel, making sure all the clips engage.

22. Install the steering column upper and lower covers.

23. Connect the air conditioning ductwork to the lower air outlet if so equipped.

24. Attach the wiring to the radio speaker.

25. Install the lower left dashboard trim panel and its 4 screws.

26. Install the hood release lever.

27. Connect the negative battery cable.

1993

▶ **See Figure 62**

1. Disconnect the negative battery cable.

2. Remove the 2 screws from the instrument cluster trim panel, disengaging the 2 lower clips.

3. Remove the 4 screws, disconnect the 3 electrical connectors and remove the instrument cluster assembly from the vehicle.

4. Installation is the reverse of removal.

Speedometer Cable

The speedometer cable connects a rotating gear within the transaxle to the dashboard speedometer/odometer assembly. The dashboard unit interprets the number of turns the made by the cable and displays the information as miles per hour and total mileage.

Assuming that the transmission contains the correct gear for the car, the accuracy of the speedometer depends primarily on tire condition and tire diameter. Badly worn tires (too small in diameter) or overinflation (too large in diameter) can affect the speedometer reading. Replacement tires of the incorrect overall diameter (such as oversize snow tires) can also affect the readings.

Generally, manufacturers state that speedometer/odometer error of ±10% is considered normal due to wear and other variables. Stated another way, if you drove the car over a measured 1 mile course and the odometer showed anything between 0.9 and 1.1 miles, the error is considered normal. If you plan to do any checking, always use a measured course such as mileposts on an Interstate highway or turnpike. Never use another car for comparison — the other car's inherent error may further cloud your readings.

The speedometer cable can become dry or develop a kink within its case. As it turns, the ticking or light knocking noise it makes can easily lead an owner to chase engine related problems in error. If such a noise is heard, carefully watch the speedometer needle during the speed range in which the noise is heard. Generally, the needle will jump or deflect each time the cable binds. The needle motion may be very small and hard to notice; a helper in the back seat should look over the driver's shoulder at the speedometer while the driver concentrates on driving.

➡**CHILTON TIP: The slightest bind in the speedometer cable can cause unpredictable behavior in the cruise control system. If the cruise control exhibits intermittent surging or loss of set speed symptoms, check the speedometer cable first.**

To replace the speedometer cable:

1. Follow the appropriate procedure given previously for removal of the instrument cluster. The cluster need not be fully removed, but only loosened to the point of being able to disconnect the speedometer cable.

2. Disconnect the speedometer cable and check that any retaining clamps or clips between the dash and the firewall are released.

3. Safely elevate the car and support it on jackstands.

➡**Depending on the length of your arm, you may be able to reach the cable connection at the transaxle without raising the car, but it's much easier with the car elevated.**

4. Disconnect the cable fitting at the transaxle and lift the cable and case away from the transaxle.

5. Follow the cable back to the firewall, releasing any clips or retainers.

6. From inside the car, work the speedometer cable through the grommet in the firewall into the engine compartment. It may be necessary to pop the grommet out of the firewall and transfer it to the new cable.

7. When reinstalling, track the new cable into position, remembering to attach the grommet to the firewall securely. Make absolutely certain that the cable is not kinked, or routed near hot or moving parts. All curves in the cable should be very gentle and not located near the ends.

8. Attach any retaining clips, brackets or retainers, beginning from the middle of the cable and working towards each end.

9. Attach the cable to the transaxle. Remember that the cable has a formed, square end on it; this shaped end must fit into a matching hole in the transaxle mount. Don't try to force the cable collar (screw fitting) into place if the cable isn't seated properly.

10. Inside the car, hold the other end of the cable with your fingers or a pair of tapered-nose pliers. Gently attempt to turn the cable; if it's properly seated at the other end, the cable will NOT turn more than about ¼ turn. If the cable turns freely, the other end is not correctly seated.

11. Lower the car to the ground.

12. Attach the speedometer cable to the instrument cluster, again paying close attention to the fit of the square-cut end into the square hole. Don't force the cable retainer — you'll break the clips.

13. Reinstall the instrument cluster following procedures outlined previously.

Instrument Panel Gauges

The printed circuit board, and all gauges, including the speedometer, engine coolant, oil pressure etc., are removed from the back of the cluster assembly. Please refer to the appropriate Instrument Cluster removal and installation procedure outlined above and separate the gauge(s) from the back, by removing the retaining screws or clips.

Windshield Wiper Switch

REMOVAL & INSTALLATION

▶ See Figure 63

➡The windshield wiper switch is part of the combination switch. Please refer to the Combination Switch removal and installation procedure in Section 8.

Rear Window Wiper/Washer Switch

REMOVAL & INSTALLATION

1985-88

1. Disconnect the negative battery cable.
2. Remove the hood release lever.
3. Remove the 4 screws from the lower left dash trim and pull the trim out.
4. Disconnect the wiring from the radio speaker.
5. If equipped with air conditioning, remove the ductwork from the lower air outlet and remove the trim panel from the car.

6. Remove the steering wheel.
7. Remove the upper and lower steering column covers.
8. Remove the 2 screws from the trim panel (bezel).
9. Pull the panel out, releasing the spring clips behind the dash. With the panel loose, disconnect the wiring to the dash switches.
10. Remove the switch from the panel.
To install:
11. Press the switch into place in the lower trim bezel and connect the wiring to the switches.
12. Install the lower trim bezel, making sure all the clips engage.
13. Install the steering column upper and lower covers.
14. Connect the air conditioning ductwork to the lower air outlet if so equipped.
15. Attach the wiring to the radio speaker.
16. Install the lower left dashboard trim panel and its 4 screws.
17. Install the hood release lever.
18. Install the steering wheel.
19. Connect the negative battery cable.

1989-93

1. Disconnect the negative battery cable.
2. Remove the trim bezel.
3. Disconnect the electrical connector and remove the switch.
4. Installation is the reverse of removal.

Headlight Switch

➡The headlight switch is part of the combination switch. Please refer to the Combination Switch removal and installation procedure in Section 8.

LIGHTING

Headlights

REMOVAL & INSTALLATION

Sealed beam

1. Remove the headlight bezel (trim) and/or the radiator grille, as necessary.
2. The sealed beam is held in place by a retainer and either 2 or 4 small screws. Identify these screws before applying any tools.

❋❋WARNING

DO NOT confuse the small retaining screws with the larger aiming screws! There will be 2 aiming screws or adjustors for each lamp. (One adjustor controls the up/down motion and the other controls the left/right motion.) Identify the adjustors and avoid them during removal. If they are not disturbed, the new headlamp will be in identical aim to the old one.

3. Using a small screwdriver (preferably magnetic) and a pair of taper-nose pliers if necessary, remove the small screws in the headlamp retainer. DON'T drop the screws; they vanish into unknown locations.

➡CHILTON TIP: A good kitchen or household magnet placed on the shank of the screwdriver will provide enough grip to hold the screw during removal.

4. Remove the retainer and the headlamp may be gently pulled free from its mounts. Detach the connector from the back of the sealed beam unit and remove the unit from the car.

❋❋CAUTION

The retainers can have very sharp edges. Wear gloves.

To install:

5. Place the new headlamp in position and connect the wiring harness. Remember to install the rubber boot on the back of the new lamp — its a water seal. Make sure the headlight is right-side up.

6. Have an assistant turn on the headlights and check the new lamp for proper function, checking both high and low beams before final assembly.

7. Install the retainer and the small screws that hold it.

8. Reinstall the headlight bezel and/or grille.

Replaceable Bulb/Fixed Lens

♦ **See Figures 64 and 65**

➡**This type of light is replace from behind the unit. The lens is not removed or loosened.**

1. Open and support the hood and disconnect the negative battery cable.

2. Remove the wiring connector from the back the lamp. Be careful to release the locking tab completely before removal.

3. Grasp the base of the bulb holder and collar, twist it counterclockwise (as viewed from the engine compartment) and carefully remove the bulb holder and bulb from the housing.

4. Using gloves or a rag, hold the bulb and release the clip on the holder. Remove the bulb.

To install:

5. Install the new bulb in the holder and make sure the clip engages firmly.

❊❊WARNING

Hold the new bulb with a clean cloth or a piece of paper. DO NOT touch or grasp the bulb with your fingers. The oils from your skin will produce a hot spot on the glass envelope, shortening bulb life by up to 50%. If the bulb is touched accidentally, clean it with alcohol and a clean rag before installation.

6. Install the holder and bulb into the housing. Note that the holder has guides which must align with the housing. When the holder is correctly seated, turn the collar clockwise to lock the holder in place.

7. Connect the wiring harness. Turn on the headlights and check the function of the new bulb on both high and low beam.

HEADLIGHT AIMING

♦ **See Figures 65 and 66**

The headlamps should be aimed with a special alignment tool, state regulations may vary this procedure, use this procedure below for temporary adjustments.

1. Inspect and correct all components that could interfere with proper headlamp alignment.

1. Headlamp bulb
2. Headlamp assembly

Fig. 64 Headlamp bulb replacement — 1985-92

1. Right-left adjustment screw
2. Headlamp assembly
3. Up-down adjustment screw

Fig. 65 Adjuster locations for replaceable bulb headlamp assemblies — 1985-92

2. Verify proper tire pressure. Clean headlamp lenses and make sure that there is no heavy loads in the trunk or hatch luggage area. The gas tank should be filled.

3. Position the vehicle on a level surface perpendicular to flat wall 25 feet away.

4. Rock the vehicle side to side and up and down a few times to allow the suspension to stabilize.

5. Turn lights On, adjust the horizontal direction of headlamps to achieve a straight and high intensity pattern. Adjust the vertical direction of headlamps to achieve a straight and high intensity pattern. Refer to the adjustment illustrations.

Signal and Marker Lights

REMOVAL & INSTALLATION

Front Turn Signals

1985-92

▶ See Figures 67 and 68

➡This can be done with the car on the ground. Access is improved if the car is safely supported on jackstands.

1. From behind the bumper, disconnect the electrical connector.
2. Remove the 2 nuts from the housing.
3. Remove the turn signal lamp housing.

➡If only the bulb is to be changed, the lens may be removed from the front.

Fig. 66 Composite headlamp aiming mount. Follow the instructions with the headlamp aiming tool — 1993

4. Reassemble the housing in reverse order of disassembly.

1993

1. Disconnect the negative battery cable.
2. Remove the 1 screw and gently pry the front turn signal housing from the fascia.
3. Disconnect the electrical connector from the turn signal lamp.
4. Remove the turn signal lamp socket from the housing.
5. Remove the turn signal lamp bulb from the socket, as necessary.
6. Installation is the reverse of removal.

1. Front parking/sidemarker lamp housing
2. Front parking lamp

Fig. 67 Front parking lamp assembly — 1989-92

FRONT CLEARANCE LAMP

Fig. 68 Front parking lamp assembly — 1985-88

Side Marker Lights (Parking Lights)

FRONT

1985-92

▶ **See Figures 67 and 68**

1. Remove the retaining screws. On Nova models, the screws are visible at the rear corner of the lens. On the Prizm, the screw is under the hood.
2. Gently remove the lighting assembly from the body of the car.
3. Disconnect the bulb and socket(s) from the housing.
4. Reassemble in reverse order.

REAR

Nova

1. Only the Nova models have separate rear sidemarker lights. The Prizm incorporates the sidelights into the taillight assemblies. For the Nova, remove the 2 screws in the sidemarker lens.
2. Remove the lighting assembly from the bodywork.
3. Disconnect the bulb and socket from the lighting assembly.
4. Reassemble in reverse order.

Rear Turn Signal, Brake and Parking Lights

1985-92

1. Raise the trunk lid and remove or fold back the trunk carpeting.
2. Disconnect the wiring from the bulb holder(s).
3. If a bulb is to be changed, remove the bulb holder from the housing by pressing the tab and lifting out the holder. Replace the bulb and reinsert the housing.
4. Remove the nuts holding the taillight assembly in place. Some may be difficult to reach; a swivel or 'wobble' fitting for your socket set can be a valuable asset for this job.
5. Remove the lens assembly from the outside of the car.

To install:

6. When reinstalling the lens assembly, pay close attention to the placement of the gasket. It must be correctly positioned and evenly crushed to prevent water from entering the trunk. Double check the holes through which the threaded studs pass; caulk them if needed.
7. Install the retaining nuts and tighten them evenly. Do not overtighten them or the lens may crack.
8. Install the electrical connectors. Have a helper operate the lights while you check the function at the rear of the car.
9. Replace the trunk carpet.

1993

▶ **See Figures 69 and 70**

1. Disconnect the negative battery cable.
2. Raise the deck lid.
3. Remove the 2 bolts from the side of the rear combination lamp.
4. In the luggage compartment, remove the 1 nut from the rear combination lamp assembly.
5. Gripping both ends of the rear combination lamp assembly, pull firmly, to release the pin from the clamp and remove the assembly from the vehicle.
6. Installation is the reverse of removal.

Fig. 70 Rear combination lamp assembly — 1993

High Mounted Stoplight

REMOVAL AND INSTALLATION

1985-92

1. Remove the high mounted stoplight cover by pressing the center portion of the clip in while removing it.
2. Remove the bulb from the high mounted stoplight holder.
3. Reassemble in reverse order of the removal procedure. Before installing retaining clips position center of clip correctly before installation.

1993

1. Disconnect the negative battery cable.
2. Raise the deck lid.
3. Disconnect the 2 plastic clips and remove the housing from the assembly.
4. Remove the 2 bolts and remove the lamp from the vehicle.
5. If necessary, remove the socket and bulb from the lamp.
6. Installation is the reverse of removal.

Dome Light

REMOVAL AND INSTALLATION

1. Remove the dome light cover.

Fig. 69 Rear combination lamp assembly bolts — 1993

2. Remove the bulb from holder.

3. Reassemble in reverse order of the removal procedure.

License Plate Lights

REMOVAL AND INSTALLATION

1. Remove the lighting assembly from the bodywork.

2. Disconnect the bulb and socket from the lighting assembly.

3. Remove the bulb from the holder.

4. Reassemble in reverse order of the removal procedure.

TRAILER WIRING

Wiring the car for towing is fairly easy. There are a number of good wiring kits available and these should be used, rather than trying to design your own. All trailers will need brake lights and turn signals as well as tail lights and side marker lights. Most states require extra marker lights for overly wide trailers. Also, most states have recently required back-up lights for trailers, and most trailer manufacturers have been building trailers with back-up lights for several years.

Additionally, some trailers have electric brakes. Others can be fitted with them as an option, depending on the weight to be carried.

Add to this an accessories wire, to operate trailer internal equipment or to charge the trailer's battery, and you can have as many as 7 wires in the harness.

Determine the equipment on your trailer and buy the wiring kit necessary. The kit will contain all the wires needed, plus a plug adapter set which includes the female plug, mounted on the bumper or hitch, and the male plug to be wired into the trailer harness.

When installing the kit, follow the manufacturer's instructions. The color coding of the wires is standard throughout the industry.

One point to note: some domestic vehicles, and most imported vehicles, have separate turn signals at the rear. On most domestic vehicles, the brake lights and rear turn signals operate with the same bulb. For those vehicles with separate turn signals, you can purchase an isolation unit so that the brake lights won't blink whenever the turn signals are operated.

You can also go to your local electronics supply house and buy 4 diodes to wire in series with the brake and turn signal bulbs. Diodes will isolate the brake and turn signals. The choice is yours. The isolation units are simple and quick to install, but far more expensive than the diodes. The diodes, however, require more work to install properly, since they require the cutting of each bulb's wire and soldering the diode into place.

The best wiring kits are those with a spring loaded cover on the vehicle mounted socket. This cover prevents dirt and moisture from corroding the terminals. Never let the vehicle socket hang loosely. Always mount it securely to the bumper or hitch. If you don't get a connector with a cover, at least put a piece of tape over the end of the connector when not in use. Most trailer lighting failures can be traced to corroded connectors and/or poor grounds.

CIRCUIT PROTECTION

1985-90

▶ See Figures 71, 72 and 73

Both the Nova and the Prizm have fuses found in 2 locations. One fuse box is located within the cabin of the car, just under the extreme left side of the dashboard. This fuse box generally contains the fuses for body and cabin electrical circuits such as the wipers, rear defogger, ignition, cigarette lighter, etc. In addition, various relays and circuit breakers for cabin equipment are also mounted on or around this fuse box.

The second fuse block is found under the hood on the forward part of the left wheelhouse. The Nova uses a combination fuse block and relay board while the Prizm has an additional relay board next to the fusebox. The fuses and relays generally control the engine and major electrical systems on the car, such as headlights (separate fuses for left and right), air conditioning, horns, fuel injection, ECM, and fans.

Both the Nova and the Prizm have an additional small panel below the right side dash board containing a fuse (air conditioner) and a relay and circuit breaker for the heater system.

1991-93

▶ See Figures 74, 75 and 76

Vehicle fuses, fusible links and or relays are found in relay or junction blocks. Refer to the illustrated junction blocks the end of this section for identification and locations of fuses and relays. The covers for the relay or junction blocks identify each fuse, fusible link or relay. The junction blocks are located as follows:**1991-92**

- Junction Block No. 1: Lower left side shroud
- Junction Block No. 2: Left side front of engine compartment
- Junction Block No. 3: Contains no fuses
- Junction Block No. 4: Lower right side shroud
- Junction Block No. 5: Engine compartment left of battery**1993**

1. Emission computer
2. Clutch switch (M/T)
3. Circuit breaker (for defogger)
4. Defogger relay
5. Taillight relay
6. Seat belt relay
7. Circuit breaker (for door lock)
8. Cruise computer
9. Clutch start relay (M/T)
10. Heater relay
11. Circuit breaker (for heater)
12. Flasher
13. Circuit breaker (for power window)
14. Power window relay

Fig. 71 Passenger compartment relay location — 1985-88

1. Defogger circuit breaker (30A)
2. Rear window defogger relay
3. Heater main relay
4. Heater circuit breaker (30A)
5. A/C fuse (7.5A)
6. Door lock control relay
7. Turn signal flasher
8. Power window circuit breaker (30A)
9. Power window main relay
10. Number 1 fuse and relay block
11. Integration relay
12. Taillamp control relay

Fig. 72 Passenger compartment relay location — 1989-90

fuses and relays
1. "left head" (10A)
2. "Right head" (10A)
3. "Fan relay #1"
4. "Engine main" relay
5. "EFI" (15A)
6. "Hazard-horn" (15A)
7. "Dome" (10A)
8. Not used
9. "Horn" relay
10. "Fan-l/up" (75A)
11. "Charge" (75A)
12. "Headlight control" relay
13. "EFI" relay
14. "Fan" (30A)

Fig. 73 Underhood fuse block — 1989-90

Fig. 74 Junction block No. 1 — 1993

1. Air cond. fuse (15A)
2. Heater relay
3. HEATER fuse (40A)
4. I/P harness 1 connector (C2)
5. I/P harness 1 connector (C1)
6. Engine compartment harness connector (C3)

Fig. 75 Junction block No. 2 — 1993

1. Horn relay
2. Fan No 1 relay
3. ALT-SF fuse (7.5A)
4. Engine main relay
5. Head relay
6. EFI F-heater relay
7. EFI F-heater fuse (15A)
8. ABS fuse (50A)
9. ALT fuse (100A)
10. AM1(40A)
11. HEAD (LH) fuse (15A)
12. HEAD (RH) fuse (15A)
13. Spare fuse
14. Spare fuse
15. Spare fuse
16. FAN fuse (30A)
17. AM2 fuse (30A)
18. FAN-1/UP fuse (7.5A)
19. HAZ-HORN fuse (20A)
20. DOME fuse (20A)

Fig. 76 Fuse and relay block — 1993

- Junction Block No. 1: Lower left side shroud
- Junction Block No. 2: Lower right side shroud
- Fuse and Relay box: Left side front of engine compartment left of air cleaner

Fuses

▶ **See Figures 77 and 78**

Each fuse location is labeled on the fuseblock identifying its primary circuit, but designations such as 'Engine', 'CDS Fan' or 'ECU-B' may not tell you what you need to know. A fuse can control more than one circuit, so check related fuses. As an example, you'll find the Prizm cruise control drawing its power through the fuse labeled 'ECM-IG'. (This sharing of fuses is

Fig. 77 Use the fuse puller to remove the fuse. Do not twist the fuse when removing.

Fig. 78 A blown fuse (left) compared with an intact fuse. The fuse cannot be inspected without removing it from the fusebox

necessary to conserve space and wiring; if each circuit had its own fuse, the fuse box would be the size of the trunk lid.)

The individual fuses are of the plastic or 'slip-fuse' type. They connect into the fusebox with 2 small blades, similar to a household wall plug. Removing the fuse with the fingers can be difficult; there isn't a lot to grab onto. For this reason, the fusebox contains a small plastic fuse remover which can be clipped over the back of the fuse and used as a handle to pull it free.

Once the fuse is out, view the fusible element through the clear plastic of the fuse case. An intact fuse will show a continuous horseshoe-shaped wire within the plastic. This element simply connects one blade with the other; if it's intact, power can pass. If the fuse is blown, the link inside the fuse will show a break, possibly accompanied by a small black mark. This shows that the link broke when the electrical current exceeded the wires ability to carry it.

It is possible for the link to become weakened (from age or vibration) without breaking. In this case, the fuse will look good but fail to pass the proper amount of current, causing some electrical item to not work.

Once removed, any fuse may be checked for continuity with an ohmmeter. A reliable general rule is to always replace a suspect fuse with a new one. So doing eliminates one variable in the diagnostic path and may cure the problem outright. Remember, however, that a blown fuse is rarely the cause of a problem; the fuse is opening to protect the circuit from some other malfunction either in the wiring or the component itself. Always replace a fuse or other electrical component with one of equal amperage rating; NEVER increase the ampere rating of the circuit. The number on the back of the fuse body (5, 7.5, 10, 15 ,etc.) indicates the rated amperage of the fuse.

Circuit Breakers

▶ **See Figure 79**

REPLACEMENT

The circuit breakers found on the fuse and relay boards mount to the boards with blades similar to the fuses. Before removing a breaker, always disconnect the negative battery cable to prevent potentially damaging electrical 'spikes' within the system. Simply remove the breaker by pulling straight out

Push

Fig. 79 Resetting a circuit breaker

from the relay board. Do not twist the relay; damage may occur to the connectors inside the housing.

➡ Some circuit breakers on the Nova and Prizm do not reset automatically. Once tripped, they must be reset by hand. Use a small screwdriver or similar tool; insert it in the hole in the back of the breaker and push gently. Once the breaker is reset, either check it for continuity with an ohmmeter or reinstall it and check the circuit for function.

Reinstall the circuit breaker by pressing it straight in to its mount. Make certain the blades line up correctly and that the circuit breaker is fully seated. Reconnect the negative battery cable and check the circuit for function.

Turn Signal and Hazard Flasher

The combination turn signal and hazard flasher unit is located under the dash on the left side near the fuse box. The flasher unit is not the classic round 'can' found on many domestic cars; instead, it is a small box-shaped unit easily mistaken for another relay. Depending on the year and model of your Nova or Prizm, the flasher may be plugged directly into the fuse and relay panel or it may be plugged into its own connector and mounted near the fuse panel. The flasher unit emits the familiar ticking sound when the signals are in use and may be identified by touching the case and feeling the 'click' as the system functions.

WIRING DIAGRAMS

The flasher unit simply unplugs from its connector and a replacement may be installed. Assuming that all the bulbs on the exterior of the car are working properly, the correct rate of flash for the turn signals or hazard lights is 60-75 flashes per minute. Very rapid flashing on one side only or no flashing on one side generally indicates a failed bulb rather than a failed flasher.

Communication and 'Add-on' Electrical Equipment

The electrical system in your car is designed to perform under reasonable operating conditions without interference between components. Before any additional electrical equipment is installed, it is recommended that you consult your Chevrolet or Geo dealer or a reputable repair facility familiar with the vehicle and its systems.

If the vehicle is equipped with mobile radio equipment (CB, HAM, Business radio and/or mobile telephone) it may have an effect upon the operation of the ECM. Radio frequency interference (RFI) from the communications system can be picked up by the car's wiring harnesses and conducted into the ECM, giving it the wrong messages at the wrong time. Although well shielded against RFI, the ECM should be further protected through the following steps:

1. Install the antenna as far as possible from the ECM. Since the ECM is located behind the center console, the antenna should be mounted at the rear of the car.

2. Keep the antenna wiring a minimum of 8 inches away from any wiring running to the ECM and from the ECM itself. NEVER wind the antenna wire around any other wiring.

3. Mount the equipment as far from the ECM as possible. Be very careful during installation not to drill through any wires or short a wire harness with a mounting screw.

4. Insure that the electrical feed wire(s) to the equipment are properly and tightly connected. Loose connectors can cause interference.

5. Make certain that the equipment is properly grounded to the car. Poor grounding can damage expensive equipment.

6. Make sure the antenna is 'trimmed' or adjusted for optimum function.

Fig. 80 Wiring schematic — 1985 Nova (Part 1 of 13)

Fig. 81 Wiring schematic — 1985 Nova (Part 2 of 13)

EMISSION CONTROL

Fig. 82 Wiring schematic — 1985 Nova (Part 3 of 13)

COOLING FAN (ENGINE)

AIR CONDITIONER, COOLER & HEATER

Fig. 83 Wiring schematic — 1985 Nova (Part 4 of 13)

Fig. 84 Wiring schematic — 1985 Nova (Part 5 of 13)

HORN

COMBINATION METER

10A HAZ-HORN

7.5A GUAGE

HORN

HORN S/W (COMB S/W)

OIL

FUEL

BRAKE

OIL PRESSURE S/W

FUEL LEVEL SENDER

BRAKE FLUID LEVEL S/W

VACUUM S/W

PARKING BRAKE S/W

Fig. 85 Wiring schematic — 1985 Nova (Part 6 of 13)

BACK-UP LIGHTS   SEAT BELT

FROM 'DOME' FUSE

WATER TEMP

WATER TEMP SENDER

Y-G

FUEL

FUEL LEVEL SENDER

Y-R   W-B

TACH

BR

W-B   W-B

R-L

R-B   R-L

BACK UP LIGHT S/W

R-B

LH   BACK-UP LAMP (RR. COMB LAMP)   RH

W-B

R-G

R-G

UNLOCK WARNING S/W

L-G

W-B

BUCKLE S/W

L-W

3

W-B   W-B

1   4

R-L

R-L

SEAT BELT WARNING (COMB. METER)

R

SEATBELT WARNING RELAY

R-W

TO DOOR COURTESY S/W FL

Fig. 86 Wiring schematic — 1985 Nova (Part 7 of 13)

Fig. 87 Wiring schematic — 1985 Nova (Part 8 of 13)

Fig. 88 Wiring schematic — 1985 Nova (Part 9 of 13)

Fig. 89 Wiring schematic — 1985 Nova (Part 10 of 13)

HEADLIGHT   INTERIOR LIGHT

ON RIGHT FRONT FENDER   b-LOCATED ON ENGINE BLOCK   c-LOCATED

Fig. 90 Wiring schematic — 1985 Nova (Part 11 of 13)

Fig. 91 Wiring schematic — 1985 Nova (Part 12 of 13)

Fig. 92 Wiring schematic — 1985 Nova (Part 13 of 13)

Fig. 93 Wiring schematic — 1986 Nova (Part 1 of 13)

Fig. 94 Wiring schematic — 1986 Nova (Part 2 of 13)

Fig. 95 Wiring schematic — 1986 Nova (Part 3 of 13)

AIR CONDITIONER, COOLER & HEATER

Fig. 96 Wiring schematic — 1986 Nova (Part 4 of 13)

Fig. 97 Wiring schematic — 1986 Nova (Part 5 of 13)

HORN   COMBINATION METER

A
10A
HAZ-HORN

F
7.5A
GUAGE

W   2

3   R-L   1   1   R-L   3

R-L
3

HORN

G-R

OIL   Y-B   OIL PRESSURE S/W

FUEL   Y-L   FUEL LEVEL SENDER   W-B

BRAKE   R-B   3   R-B   R-B   BRAKE FLUID LEVEL S/W   W-B

W-B   HORN S/W (COMB S/W)

R-B

VACUUM S/W
R-B

PARKING BRAKE S/W
R-B

3

W-B   1

Fig. 98 Wiring schematic — 1986 Nova (Part 6 of 13)

BACK-UP LIGHTS   SEAT BELT

FROM 'DOME' FUSE

R-L

WATER TEMP

WATER TEMP SENDER

Y-G

FUEL

FUEL LEVEL SENDER

Y-R   W-B

TACH

BR

R-L

R-L

BACK UP LIGHT S/W

R-B

W-B   W-B   R-B

BACK-UP LAMP
(RR. COMB LAMP)

LH   RH

W-B

R-G

UNLOCK WARNING S/W

R-G

L-G

SEAT BELT WARNING
(COMB. METER)

R-L

R-L

R

SEATBELT
WARNING RELAY

W-B   L-W   R-W

BUCKLE S/W

TO DOOR
COURTESY S/W FL

W-B   W-B

I   4

Fig. 99 Wiring schematic — 1986 Nova (Part 7 of 13)

Fig. 100 Wiring schematic — 1986 Nova (Part 8 of 13)

Fig. 101 Wiring schematic — 1986 Nova (Part 9 of 13)

Fig. 102 Wiring schematic — 1986 Nova (Part 10 of 13)

ON RIGHT FRONT FENDER b-LOCATED ON ENGINE BLOCK

Fig. 103 Wiring schematic — 1986 Nova (Part 11 of 13)

Fig. 104 Wiring schematic — 1986 Nova (Part 12 of 13)

LEFT FRONT PILLAR   •-LOCATED ON CENTER OF PACK PANE

Fig. 105 Wiring schematic — 1986 Nova (Part 13 of 13)

Fig. 106 Wiring schematic — 1987 Nova (Part 1 of 14)

Fig. 107 Wiring schematic — 1987 Nova (Part 2 of 14)

Fig. 108 Wiring schematic — 1987 Nova (Part 3 of 14)

AIR CONDITIONER, COOLER & HEATER

Fig. 109 Wiring schematic — 1987 Nova (Part 4 of 14)

Fig. 110 Wiring schematic — 1987 Nova (Part 5 of 14)

Fig. 111 Wiring schematic — 1987 Nova (Part 6 of 14)

BACK-UP LIGHTS   SEAT BELT

Fig. 112 Wiring schematic — 1987 Nova (Part 7 of 14)

Fig. 113 Wiring schematic — 1987 Nova (Part 8 of 14)

Fig. 114 Wiring schematic — 1987 Nova (Part 9 of 14)

Fig. 115 Wiring schematic — 1987 Nova (Part 10 of 14)

Fig. 116 Wiring schematic — 1987 Nova (Part 11 of 14)

INTERIOR LIGHT

CIG. LIGHTER

D

E

7.5A
DOME

TO UNLOCK WARNING S/W

15A
CIG

R

R-G

R-G

P-L

P-L

P-L

INTERIOR LAMP

DOOR WARNING LAMP
R-G
R-W

LUGGAGE ROOM LAMP
R-G
R-W

P-L

B-W

CIGARETTE LIGHTER

1

3

R-W

3

(L/B)

R-W

W-B

FROM SEAT-BELT WARNING RELAY

R-W R-L

R-W

R-W

W-B

3

R-W

FRONT LH

FRONT RH

REAR RH

REAR LH

LUGGAGE ROOM LAMP S/W

W-B

DOOR COURTESY S/W

1

b-LOCATED ON ENGINE BLOCK   **c**-LOCATED UNDER RIGHT FRONT PILLAR

Fig. 117 Wiring schematic — 1987 Nova (Part 12 of 14)

LEFT FRONT PILLAR   •-LOCATED ON CENTER OF PACK PANE

Fig. 118 Wiring schematic — 1987 Nova (Part 13 of 14)

Fig. 119 Wiring schematic — 1987 Nova (Part 14 of 14)

Fig. 120 Wiring schematic — 1988 Nova (Part 1 of 20)

Fig. 121 Wiring schematic — 1988 Nova (Part 2 of 20)

Fig. 122 Wiring schematic — 1988 Nova (Part 3 of 20)

Fig. 123 Wiring schematic — 1988 Nova (Part 4 of 20)

Fig. 124 Wiring schematic — 1988 Nova (Part 5 of 20)

Fig. 125 Wiring schematic — 1988 Nova (Part 6 of 20)

Fig. 126 Wiring schematic — 1988 Nova (Part 7 of 20)

Fig. 127 Wiring schematic — 1988 Nova (Part 8 of 20)

AIR CONDITIONER (4A-LC) COOLER & HEATER   **TURN SIGNAL & HAZARD**

Fig. 128 Wiring schematic — 1988 Nova (Part 9 of 20)

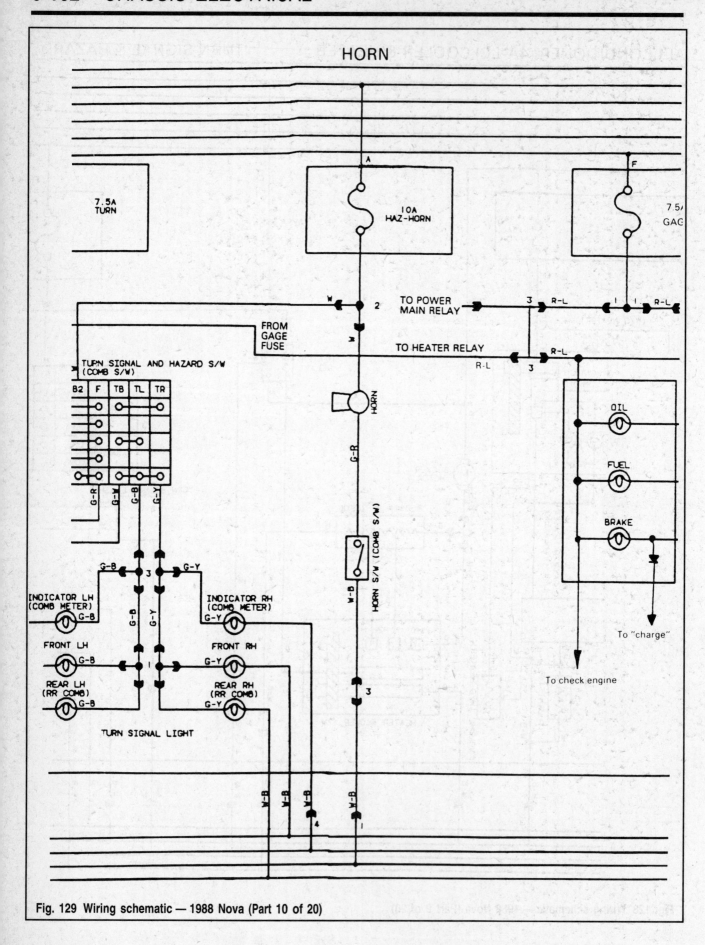

Fig. 129 Wiring schematic — 1988 Nova (Part 10 of 20)

Fig. 130 Wiring schematic — 1988 Nova (Part 11 of 20)

Fig. 131 Wiring schematic — 1988 Nova (Part 12 of 20)

BACK-UP LIGHTS SEAT BELT DEFOGGER

Fig. 132 Wiring schematic — 1988 Nova (Part 13 of 20)

CRUISE CONTROL   **STOP LIGHT**

Fig. 133 Wiring schematic — 1988 Nova (Part 14 of 20)

Fig. 134 Wiring schematic — 1988 Nova (Part 15 of 20)

Fig. 135 Wiring schematic — 1988 Nova (Part 16 of 20)

Fig. 136 Wiring schematic — 1988 Nova (Part 17 of 20)

UNDER RIGHT FRONT PILLAR d-LOCATED UNDER LEFT FRONT PILLAR

Fig. 137 Wiring schematic — 1988 Nova (Part 18 of 20)

Fig. 138 Wiring schematic — 1988 Nova (Part 19 of 20)

Fig. 139 Wiring schematic — 1988 Nova (Part 20 of 20)

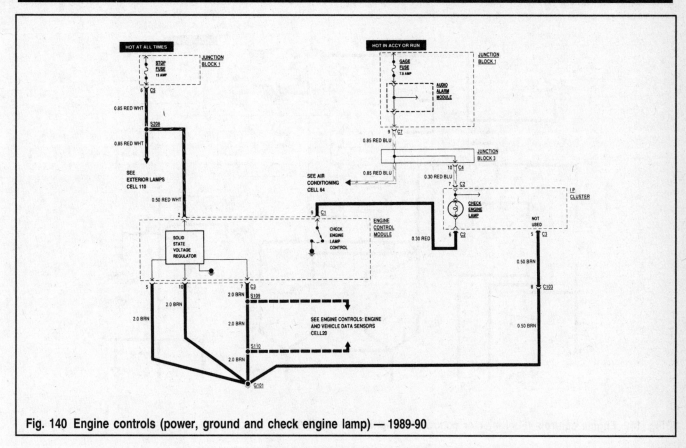

Fig. 140 Engine controls (power, ground and check engine lamp) — 1989-90

Fig. 141 Engine controls (Fuel pump and idle speed controls) — 1989-90

Fig. 142 Engine controls (Fuel injector controls and ignition) — 1989-90

Fig. 143 Engine controls (Fuel injector controls and ignition) — 1989-90

Fig. 144 Engine controls (Engine and vehicle data sensors) — 1989-90

Fig. 145 Engine controls (Engine and vehicle data sensors) — 1989-90

Fig. 146 Starter and charging system — 1989-90

Fig. 147 Starter and charging system — 1989-90

Fig. 148 Coolant fans (with air conditioning) — 1989-90

Fig. 149 Coolant fans (with air conditioning) — 1989-90

Fig. 150 Coolant fans (without air conditioning) — 1989-90

Fig. 151 Cruise control — 1989-90

Fig. 152 Cruise control — 1989-90

Fig. 153 Brake warning system — 1989-90

Fig. 154 Heater — 1989-90

Fig. 155 Air conditioning (compressor clutch controls) — 1989-90

Fig. 156 Air conditioning (compressor clutch controls) — 1989-90

Fig. 157 Air conditioning (blower controls) — 1989-90

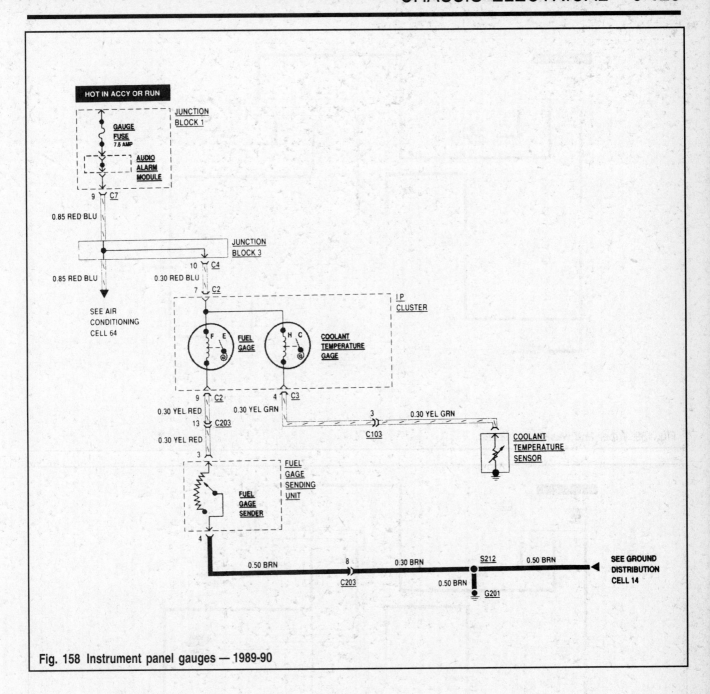

Fig. 158 Instrument panel gauges — 1989-90

Fig. 159 Wiper and washer — 1989-90

Fig. 160 Wiper and washer (pulse) — 1989-90

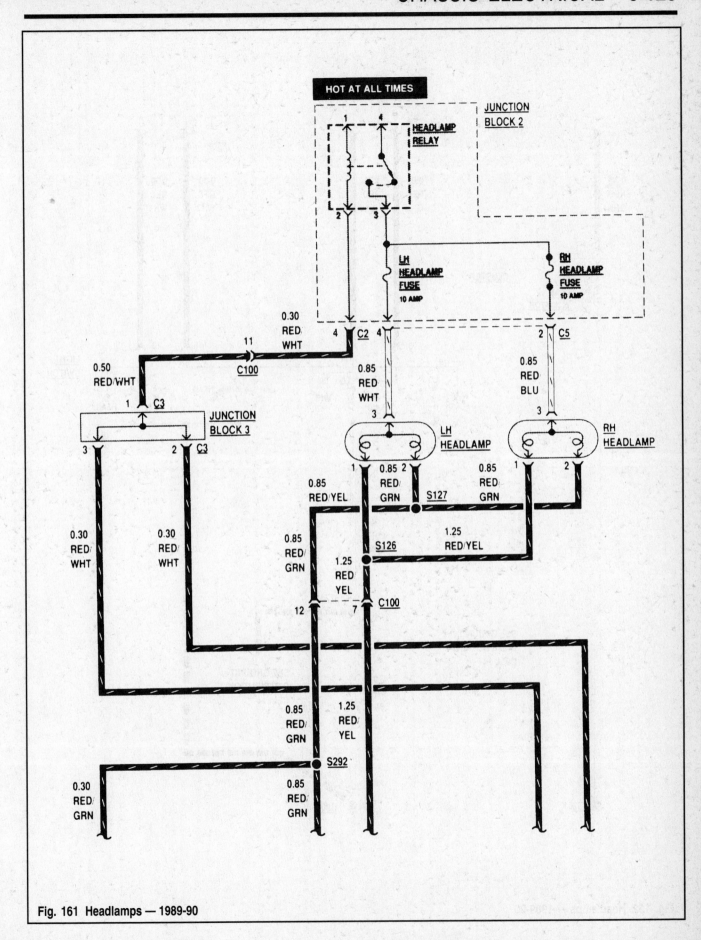

Fig. 161 Headlamps — 1989-90

Fig. 162 Headlamps — 1989-90

Fig. 163 Exterior lamps (park, front marker, tail, rear marker, license) — 1989-90 sedan with VIN 5 engine

Fig. 164 Exterior lamps (park, front marker, tail, rear marker, license) — 1989-90 hatchback with VIN 6 engine

Fig. 165 Exterior lamps (turn and hazard) — 1989-90

Fig. 166 Exterior lamps (turn and hazard) — 1989-90

Fig. 167 Exterior lamps (stop and high level stop) — 1989-90

Fig. 168 Exterior lamps (back up) — 1989-90

Fig. 169 Interior lamps — 1989-90

Fig. 170 Interior lamps — 1989-90

Fig. 171 Power windows — 1989-90

Fig. 172 Power windows — 1989-90

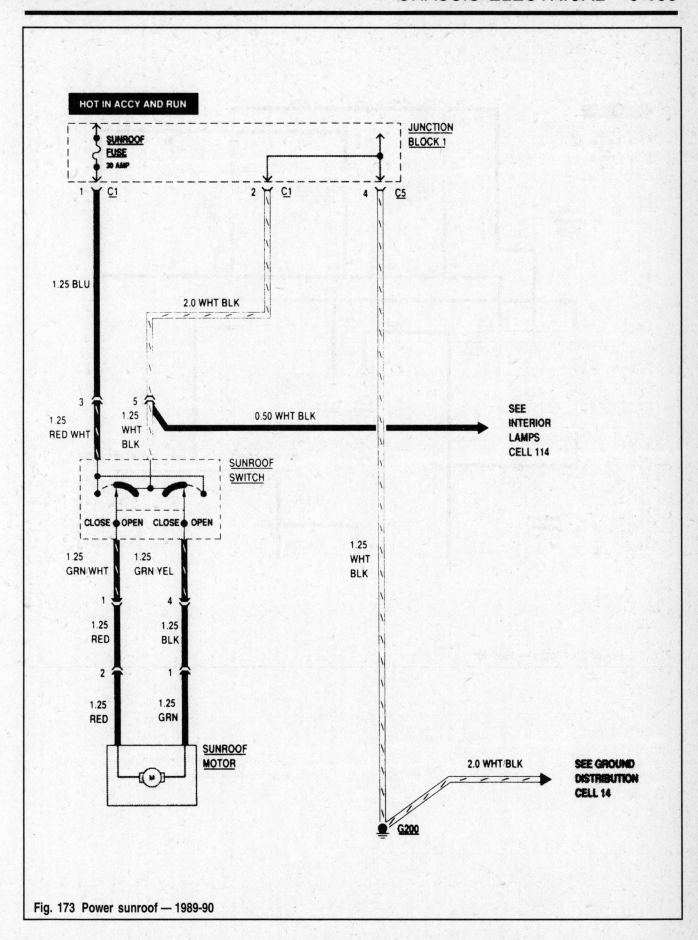

Fig. 173 Power sunroof — 1989-90

Fig. 174 Power door locks — 1989-90

Fig. 175 Power door locks — 1989-90

Fig. 176 Engine controls (power, ground and check engine lamp) — 1991 with VIN code 6 engine

Fig. 177 Engine controls (idle speed controls) — 1991 with VIN code 6 engine

Fig. 178 Engine controls (ignition) — 1991 with VIN code 6 engine

Fig. 179 Engine controls (ignition) — 1991 with VIN code 6 engine

Fig. 180 Engine controls (Fuel injector and fuel pump controls) — 1991 with VIN code 6 engine

Fig. 181 Engine controls (Fuel injector and fuel pump controls) — 1991 with VIN code 6 engine

Fig. 182 Engine controls (Engine and vehicle data sensors) — 1991 with VIN code 6 engine

Fig. 183 Engine controls (Engine and vehicle data sensors) — 1991 with VIN code 6 engine

Fig. 184 Engine controls (power, ground and check engine lamp) — 1991 with VIN code 5 engine

Fig. 185 Engine controls (idle speed controls) — 1991 with VIN code 5 engine

Fig. 186 Engine controls (ignition) — 1991 with VIN code 5 engine

Fig. 187 Engine controls (ignition) — 1991 with VIN code 5 engine

Fig. 188 Engine controls (Fuel injector and fuel pump controls) — 1991 with VIN code 5 engine

Fig. 189 Engine controls (Fuel injector and fuel pump controls) — 1991 with VIN code 5 engine

Fig. 190 Engine controls (Engine and vehicle data sensors) — 1991 with VIN code 5 engine

Fig. 191 Engine controls (Engine and vehicle data sensors) — 1991 with VIN code 5 engine

Fig. 192 Starter and charging system — 1991

Fig. 193 Starter and charging system — 1991

Fig. 194 Starter and charging system — 1991

Fig. 195 Coolant fans (with air conditioning) — 1991

Fig. 196 Coolant fans (with air conditioning) — 1991

Fig. 197 Coolant fans (without air conditioning) — 1991

Fig. 198 Cruise control — 1991

Fig. 199 Cruise control — 1991

Fig. 200 Cruise control — 1991

Fig. 201 Automatic transaxle controls — 1991

Fig. 202 Automatic transaxle controls — 1991

Fig. 203 Brake warning system — 1991

Fig. 204 Heater — 1991

Fig. 205 Air conditioning (compressor controls) — 1991 base, LSi

Fig. 206 Air conditioning (compressor controls) — 1991 base, LSi

Fig. 207 Air conditioning (compressor controls) — 1991 GSi

Fig. 208 Air conditioning (compressor controls) — 1991 GSi

Fig. 209 Instrument panel gauges (with cluster, indicators) — 1991

Fig. 210 Instrument panel gauges (with cluster, gauges) — 1991

Fig. 211 Wiper and washer — 1991

Fig. 212 Wiper and washer (pulse) — 1991

Fig. 213 Headlamps — 1991

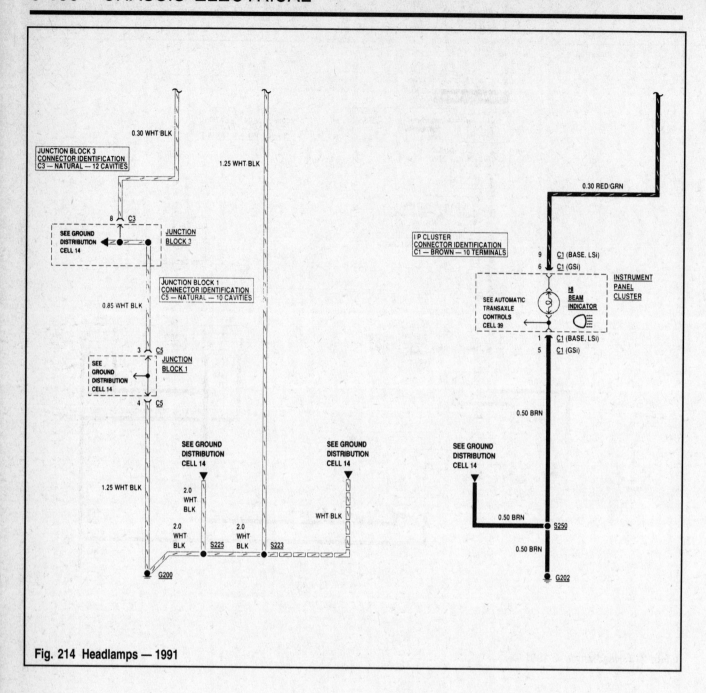

0.30 WHT BLK

JUNCTION BLOCK 3
CONNECTOR IDENTIFICATION
C3 — NATURAL — 12 CAVITIES

1.25 WHT BLK

8   C3

SEE GROUND
DISTRIBUTION
CELL 14

JUNCTION
BLOCK 3

JUNCTION BLOCK 1
CONNECTOR IDENTIFICATION
C5 — NATURAL — 10 CAVITIES

0.85 WHT BLK

3   C5

SEE
GROUND
DISTRIBUTION
CELL 14

JUNCTION
BLOCK 1

4   C5

1.25 WHT BLK

SEE GROUND
DISTRIBUTION
CELL 14

2.0
WHT
BLK

SEE GROUND
DISTRIBUTION
CELL 14

WHT BLK

2.0
WHT
BLK

2.0
WHT
BLK

S225

S223

G200

0.30 RED/GRN

I P CLUSTER
CONNECTOR IDENTIFICATION
C1 — BROWN — 10 TERMINALS

9   C1 (BASE, LSi)
6   C1 (GSi)

SEE AUTOMATIC
TRANSAXLE
CONTROLS
CELL 39

HI
BEAM
INDICATOR

INSTRUMENT
PANEL
CLUSTER

1   C1 (BASE, LSi)
5   C1 (GSi)

0.50 BRN

SEE GROUND
DISTRIBUTION
CELL 14

0.50 BRN

S250

0.50 BRN

G202

Fig. 214 Headlamps — 1991

Fig. 215 Engine controls (power, ground and check engine indicator and diagnostics) — 1992 with VIN code 6 engine

Fig. 216 Engine controls (power, ground and check engine indicator and diagnostics) — 1992 with VIN code 6 engine

Fig. 217 Engine controls (ignition) — 1992 with VIN code 6 engine

Fig. 218 Engine controls (ignition) — 1992 with VIN code 6 engine

Fig. 219 Engine controls (Fuel injector and fuel pump controls) — 1992 with VIN code 6 engine

Fig. 220 Engine controls (Fuel injector and fuel pump controls) — 1992 with VIN code 6 engine

Fig. 221 Engine controls (Engine and vehicle data sensors) — 1992 with VIN code 6 engine

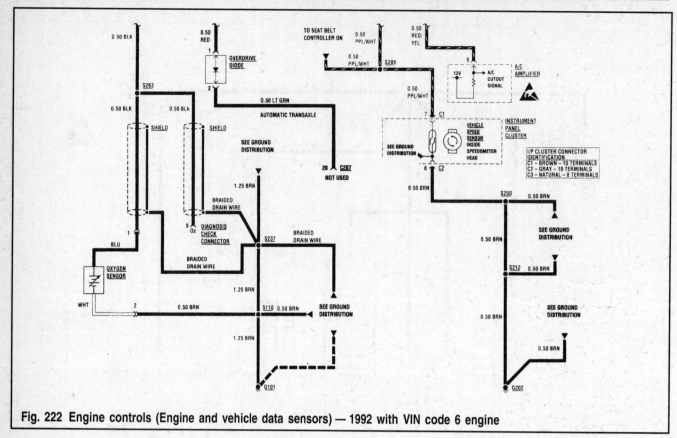

Fig. 222 Engine controls (Engine and vehicle data sensors) — 1992 with VIN code 6 engine

Fig. 223 Engine controls (power, ground and check engine indicator and diagnostics) — 1992 with VIN code 5 engine

Fig. 224 Engine controls (idle speed controls) — 1992 with VIN code 5 engine

Fig. 225 Engine controls (ignition) — 1992 with VIN code 5 engine

Fig. 226 Engine controls (ignition) — 1992 with VIN code 5 engine

Fig. 227 Engine controls (Fuel injector and fuel pump controls) — 1992 with VIN code 5 engine

Fig. 228 Engine controls (Fuel injector and fuel pump controls) — 1992 with VIN code 5 engine

Fig. 229 Engine controls (Federal emissions, engine and vehicle data sensors) — 1992 with VIN code 5 engine

Fig. 230 Engine controls (Federal emissions, engine and vehicle data sensors) — 1992 with VIN code 5 engine

Fig. 231 Engine controls (California emissions, engine and vehicle data sensors) — 1992 with VIN code 5 engine

Fig. 232 Engine controls (California emissions, engine and vehicle data sensors) — 1992 with VIN code 5 engine

Fig. 233 Starter and charging system — 1992

Fig. 234 Starter and charging system — 1992

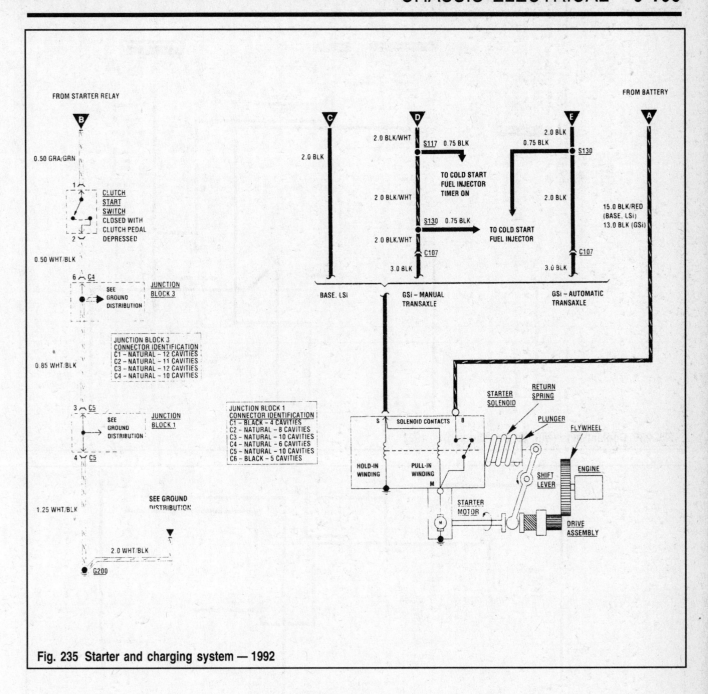

Fig. 235 Starter and charging system — 1992

Fig. 236 Coolant fans (with air conditioning) — 1992

Fig. 237 Coolant fans (with air conditioning) — 1992

Fig. 238 Coolant fans (without air conditioning) — 1992

Fig. 239 Cruise control — 1992

Fig. 240 Cruise control — 1992

Fig. 241 Cruise control — 1992

Fig. 242 Automatic transaxle controls — 1992

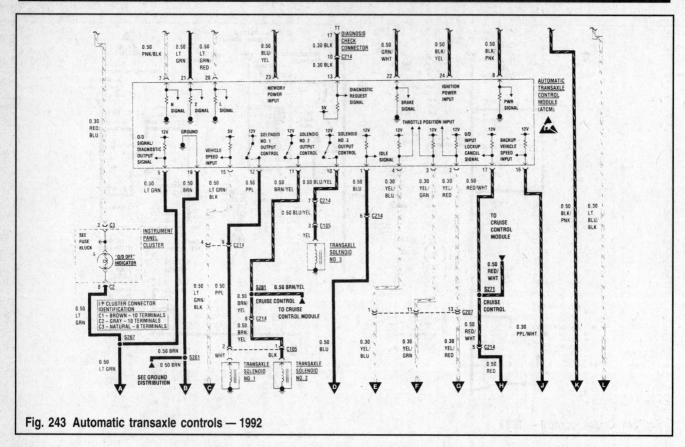

Fig. 243 Automatic transaxle controls — 1992

Fig. 244 Automatic transaxle controls — 1992

Fig. 245 Brake warning system — 1992

Fig. 246 Heater — 1992

Fig. 247 Air conditioning (compressor controls) — 1992 base, LSi

Fig. 248 Air conditioning (compressor controls) — 1992 base, LSi

Fig. 249 Air conditioning (compressor controls) — 1992 GSi

Fig. 250 Air conditioning (compressor controls) — 1992 GSi

Fig. 251 Engine controls (power, ground, and malfunction indicator lamp and diagnostics) — 1993 with VIN code 6 engine

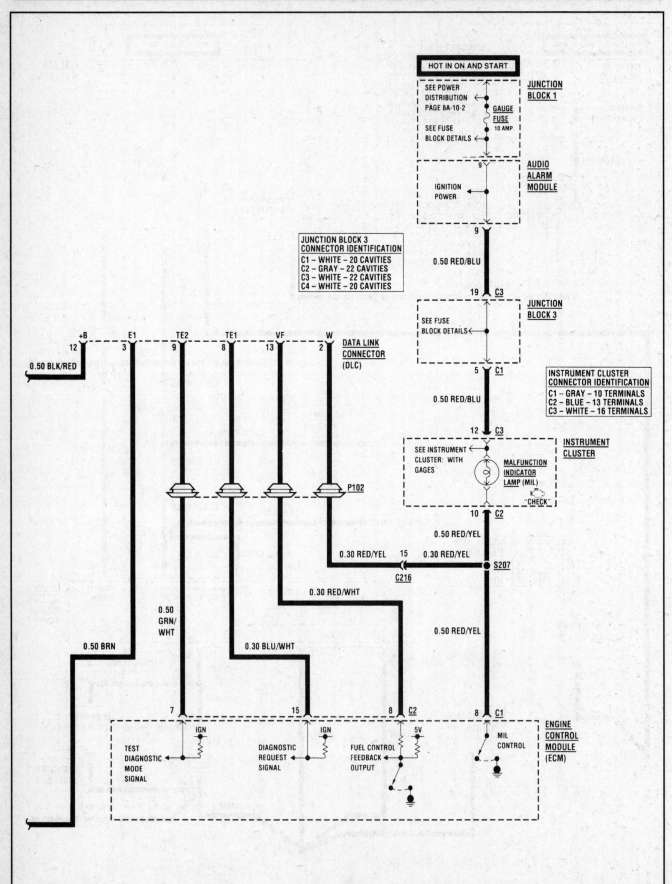

Fig. 252 Engine controls (power, ground, and malfunction indicator lamp and diagnostics) — 1993 with VIN code 6 engine

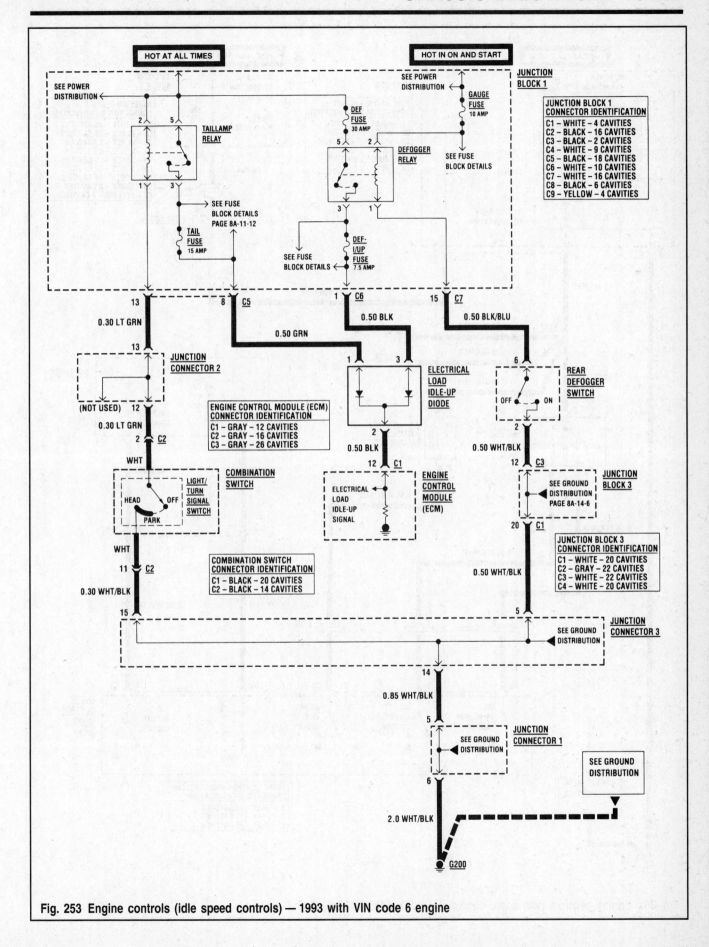

Fig. 253 Engine controls (idle speed controls) — 1993 with VIN code 6 engine

Fig. 254 Engine controls (idle speed controls) — 1993 with VIN code 6 engine

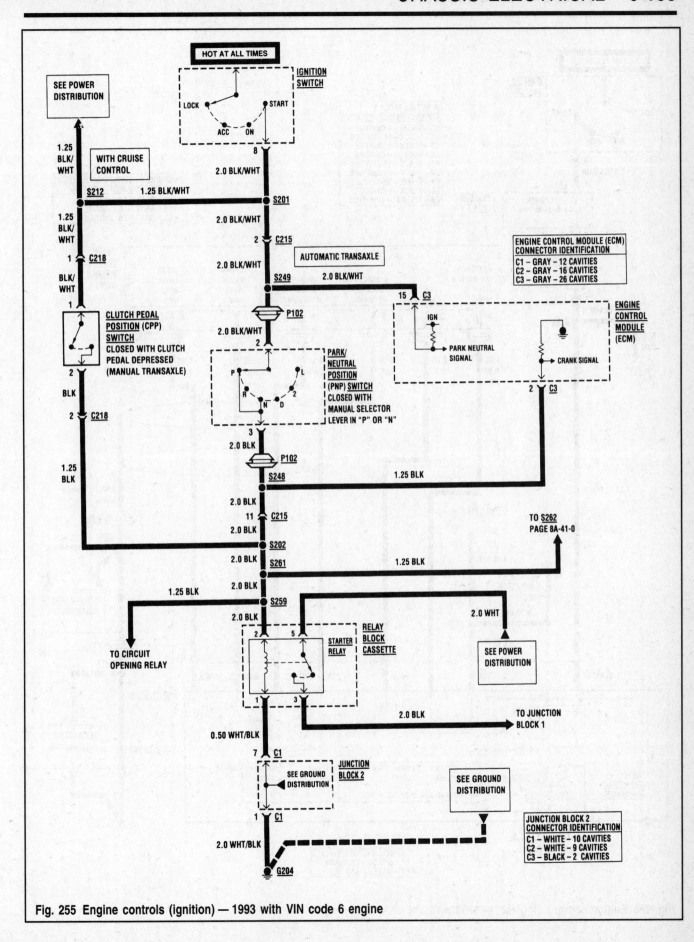

Fig. 255 Engine controls (ignition) — 1993 with VIN code 6 engine

Fig. 256 Engine controls (ignition) — 1993 with VIN code 6 engine

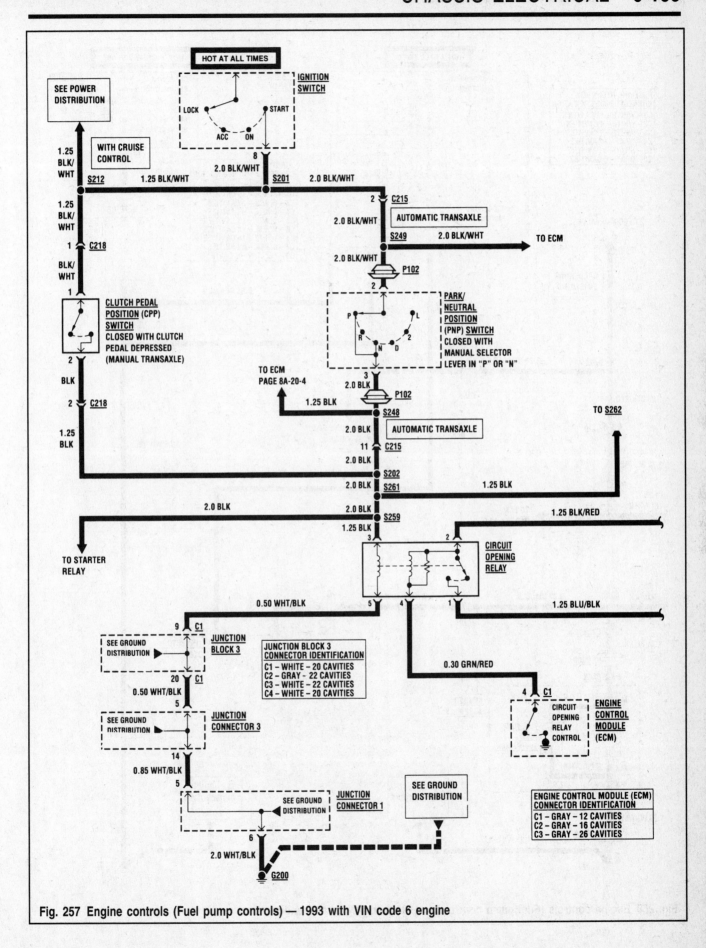

Fig. 257 Engine controls (Fuel pump controls) — 1993 with VIN code 6 engine

Fig. 258 Engine controls (Fuel pump controls) — 1993 with VIN code 6 engine

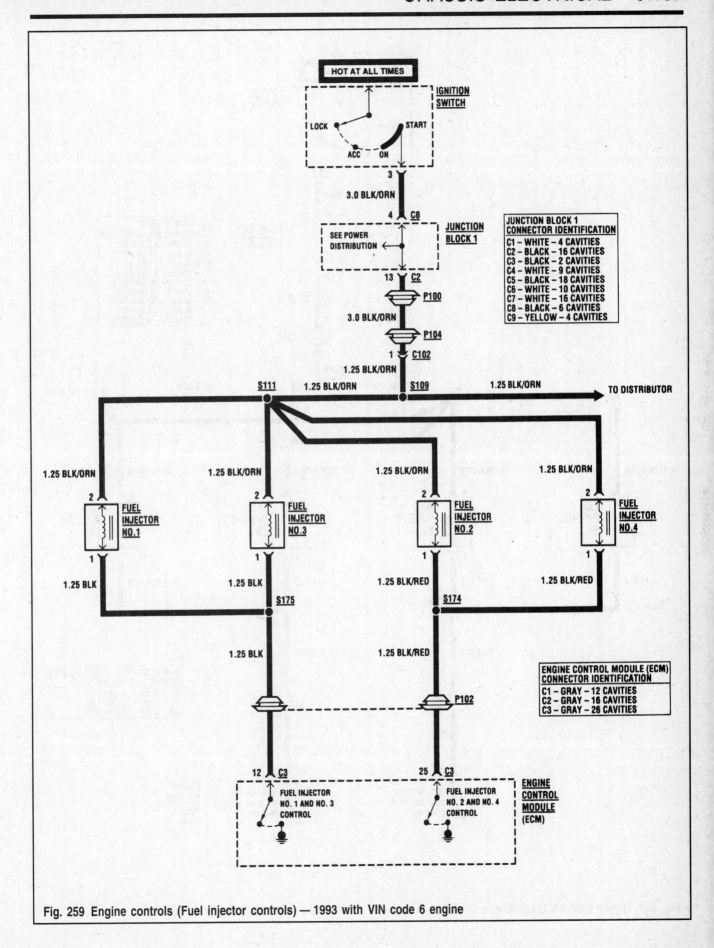

Fig. 259 Engine controls (Fuel injector controls) — 1993 with VIN code 6 engine

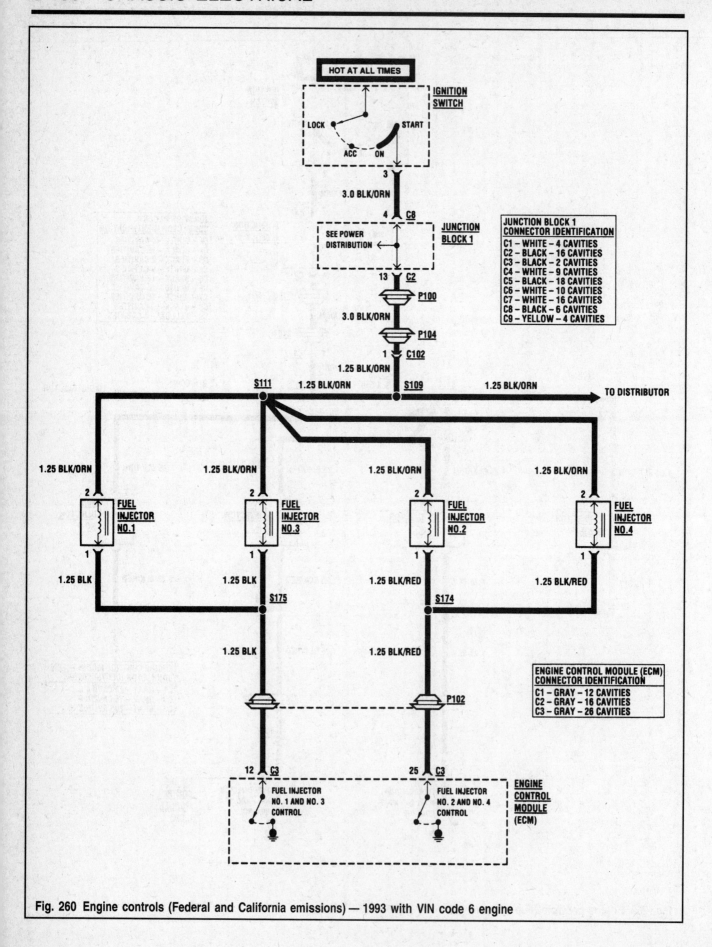

Fig. 260 Engine controls (Federal and California emissions) — 1993 with VIN code 6 engine

Fig. 261 Engine controls (California emissions only) — 1993 with VIN code 6 engine

Fig. 262 Engine controls (Engine sensors) — 1993 with VIN code 6 engine

Fig. 263 Engine controls (Vehicle data sensors) — 1993 with VIN code 6 engine

Fig. 264 Engine controls (power, ground, and malfunction indicator lamp and diagnostics) — 1993 with VIN code 8 engine

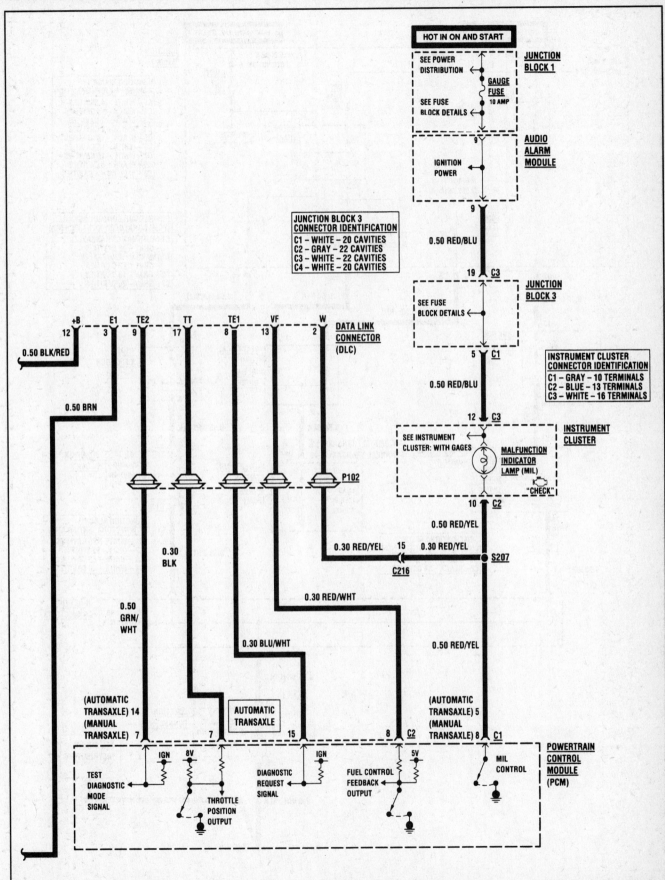

Fig. 265 Engine controls (power, ground, and malfunction indicator lamp and diagnostics) — 1993 with VIN code 8 engine

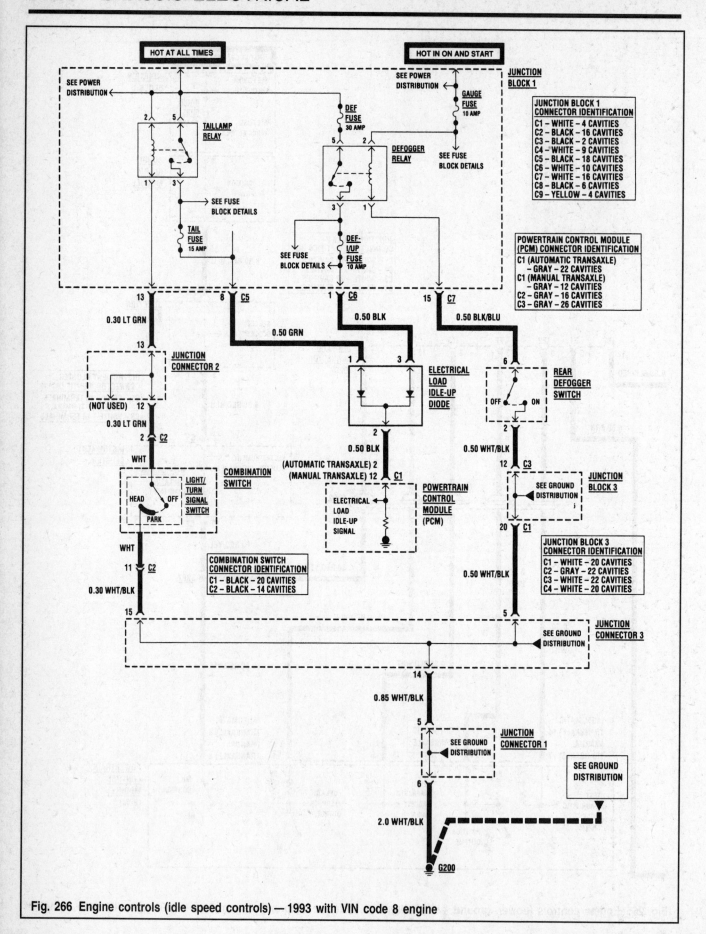

Fig. 266 Engine controls (idle speed controls) — 1993 with VIN code 8 engine

Fig. 267 Engine controls (idle speed controls) — 1993 with VIN code 8 engine

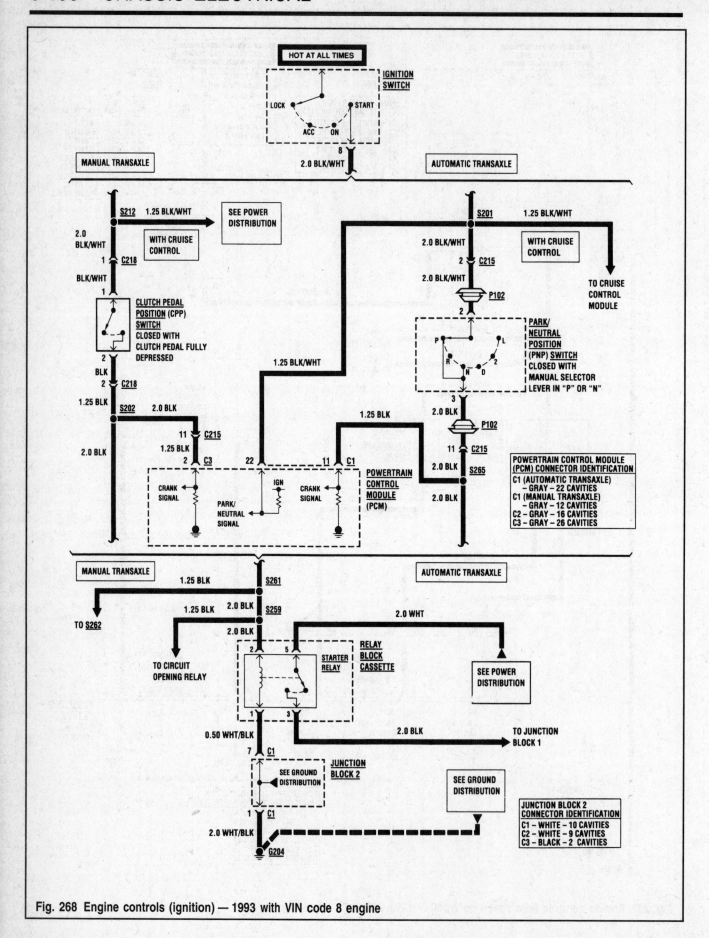

Fig. 268 Engine controls (ignition) — 1993 with VIN code 8 engine

Fig. 269 Engine controls (ignition) — 1993 with VIN code 8 engine

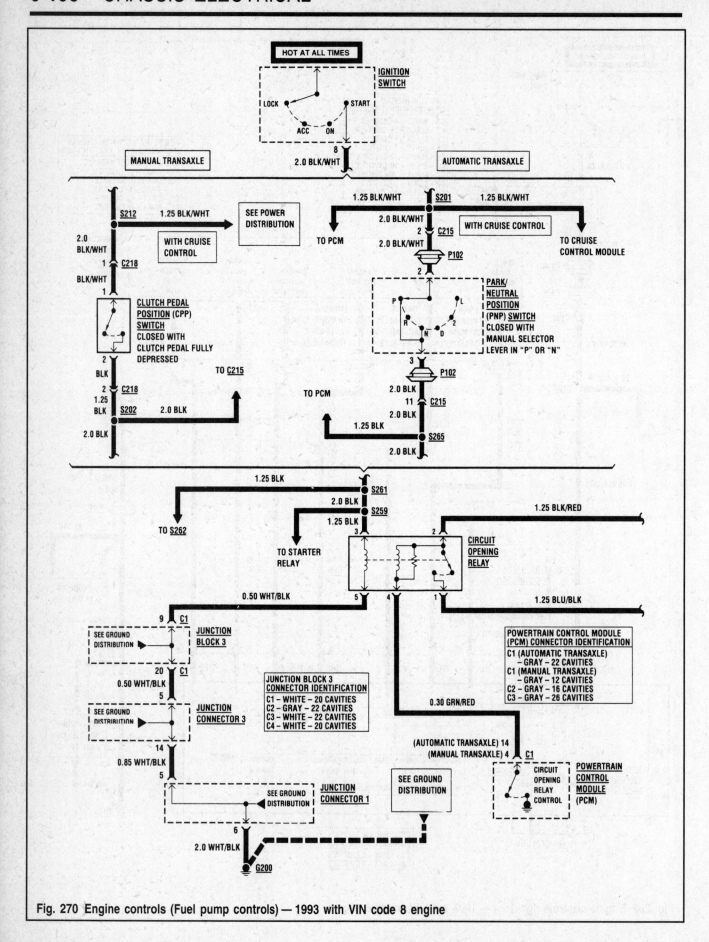

Fig. 270 Engine controls (Fuel pump controls) — 1993 with VIN code 8 engine

Fig. 271 Engine controls (Fuel pump controls) — 1993 with VIN code 8 engine

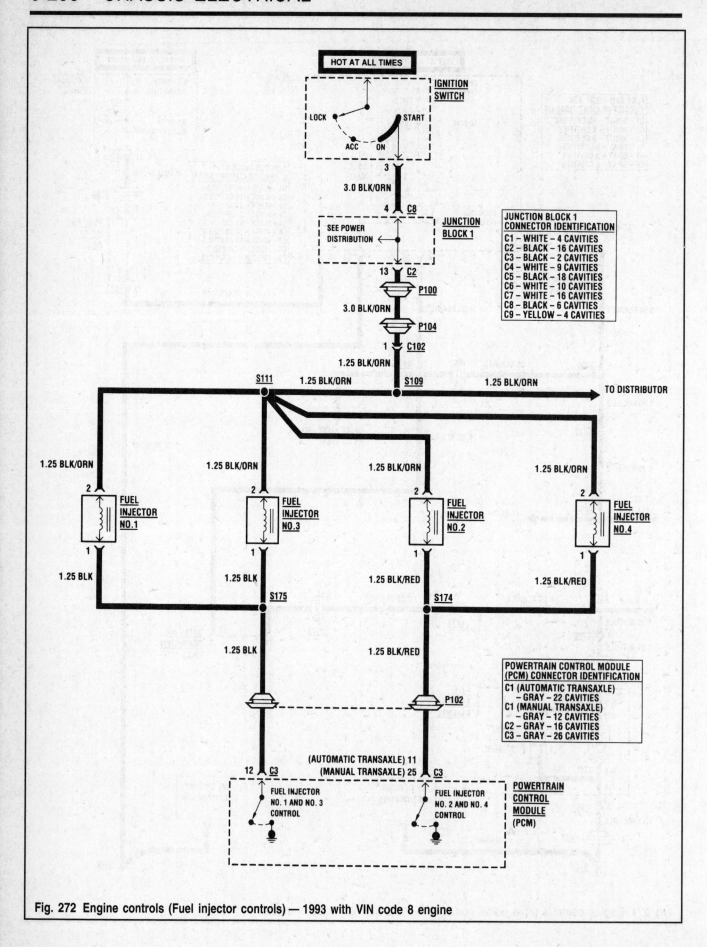

Fig. 272 Engine controls (Fuel injector controls) — 1993 with VIN code 8 engine

Fig. 273 Engine controls (Federal and California emissions) — 1993 with VIN code 8 engine

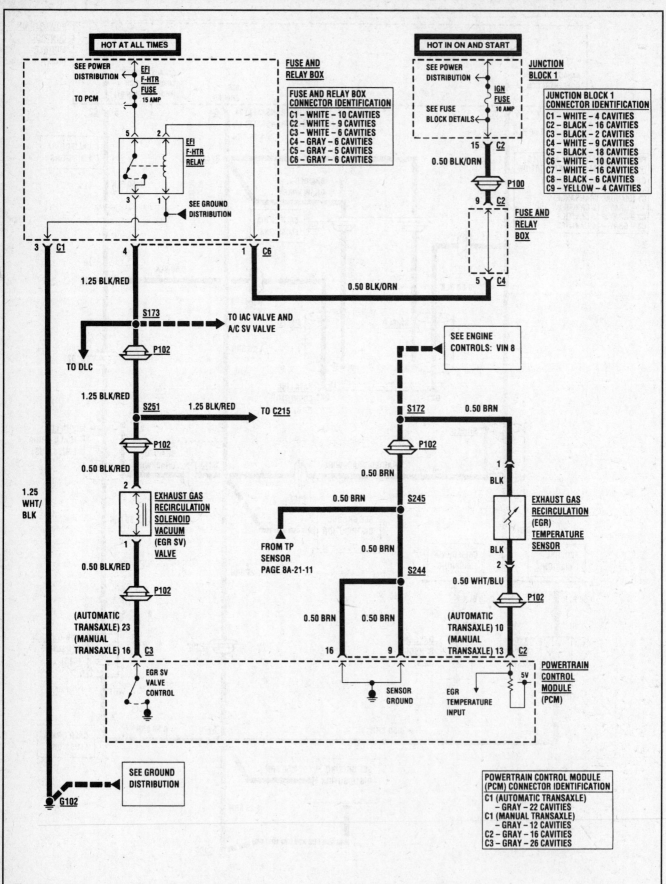

Fig. 274 Engine controls (California emissions only) — 1993 with VIN code 8 engine

Fig. 275 Engine controls (Engine sensors) — 1993 with VIN code 8 engine

Fig. 276 Engine controls (Vehicle data sensors) — 1993 with VIN code 8 engine

Fig. 277 Engine controls (Automatic transaxle controls) — 1993 with VIN code 8 engine

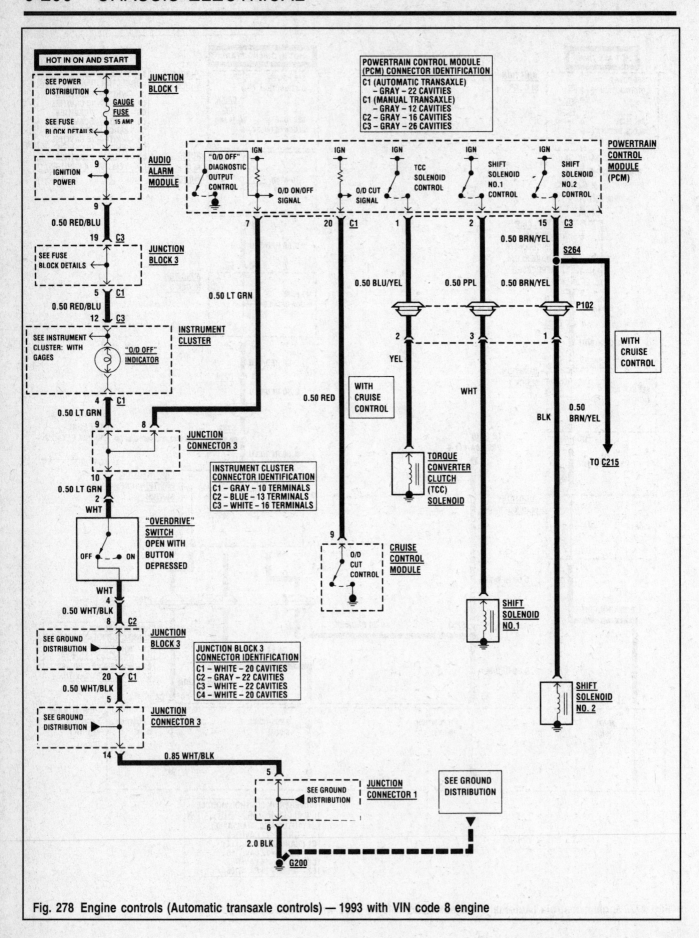

Fig. 278 Engine controls (Automatic transaxle controls) — 1993 with VIN code 8 engine

7

DRIVE
TRAIN

MANUAL TRANSAXLE

Understanding the Manual Transaxle and Clutch

Because of the way an internal combustion engine breathes, it can produce torque, or twisting force, only within a narrow speed range. Most modern engines must turn at about 2,500-3,000 rpm to produce their peak torque. By 4,500 rpm they are producing so little torque that continued increases in engine speed produce no power increases.

The manual transaxle and clutch are employed to vary the relationship between engine speed and the speed of the wheels so that adequate engine power can be produced under all circumstances. The clutch allows engine torque to be applied to the transaxle input shaft gradually, due to mechanical slippage. The car can then be started smoothly from a full stop.

The transaxle changes the ratio between the rotating speeds of the engine and the wheels by the use of gears. 4-speed or 5-speed transaxles are most common. The lower gears allow full engine power to be applied to the rear wheels during acceleration at low speeds.

The clutch drive plate is a thin fiber disc, the center of which is splined to the transaxle input shaft. Both sides of the disc are covered with a layer of material which is similar to brake lining and is capable of allowing slippage without roughness or excessive noise.

The clutch cover or pressure plate is bolted to the engine flywheel and incorporates a diaphragm spring which provides the pressure to engage the clutch. The driven disc is sandwiched between the pressure plate and the smooth surface of the flywheel when the clutch pedal is released, thus forcing it to turn at the same speed as the engine crankshaft.

The mainshaft passes all the way through the transaxle, from the clutch to the driveshaft. This shaft is separated at one point, so that front and rear portions can turn at different speeds.

Power is transmitted by a countershaft in the lower gears and reverse. The gears of the countershaft mesh with gears on the mainshaft, allowing power to be carried from one to the other. All the countershaft gears are integral with that shaft, while several of the mainshaft gears can either rotate independently of the shaft or be locked to it. Shifting from one gear to the next causes one of the gears to be freed from rotating with the shaft and locks another to it. Gears are locked and unlocked by internal dog clutches which slide between the center of the gear and the shaft. The forward gears usually employ synchronizers — friction members which smoothly bring gear and shaft to the same speed before the toothed dog clutches are engaged. The clutch is operating properly if:

1. It will stall the engine when released with the vehicle held stationary.
2. The shift lever can be moved freely between first and reverse gears when the vehicle is stationary and the clutch disengaged and the engine running at normal idle speed.

Clutch pedal free-play adjustment is important. There should be a small but noticeable amount of play in the clutch pedal before it begins to release the clutch. This play or looseness should be easily felt at the top of the pedal travel. (As you begin to push the clutch pedal towards the floor, the first inch or so of travel should have no effect on the clutch engagement). Inadequate free-play wears all parts of the clutch releasing mechanisms and may cause slippage. Excessive free-play may cause inadequate release and hard shifting of gears.

Some clutches use a hydraulic system in place of mechanical linkage. In these systems, moving the clutch pedal develops pressure in a column of fluid rather than pulling on a cable. If the clutch fails to release, fill the clutch master cylinder with fluid to the proper level and pump the clutch pedal to fill the system with fluid. Bleed the system in the same way as a brake system. If leaks are located, tighten loose connections or overhaul the master or slave cylinder as necessary.

Manual transaxles used in Nova/Prizm cars are mated to their engine families. Please refer the manual transaxle application chart in Section One.

Adjustments

SHIFT LEVER FREE-PLAY

1985-88

▶ **See Figures 1 and 2**

The shift lever free-play is adjusted through the use of a replaceable shim installed at the bottom of the lower shift lever seat. Select a shim of a thickness that allows about lb. preload at the top of the lever and install it in the shift lever seat.

SHIFT CABLES

The shift control cables are precisely adjusted at the factory during assembly and cannot be accurately adjusted in the field. Should either of the cables become stretched and therefore out of adjustment, the individual cable must be replaced. Any attempt to adjust the shift cables can cause poor shifting and/or transaxle damage. If the shift cable(s) must be replaced, proceed as follows:

1985-88

▶ **See Figure 2**

1. Disconnect the negative battery cable.
2. Disconnect the shift cable(s) and retaining clips at the transaxle.
3. Remove the center console and shifter boot.
4. Disconnect the shift cable(s) from the shifter assembly.
5. Remove the left front sill plate and lift or pull the carpet back to gain access to the cables.
6. Remove the retaining screws at the floor pan and remove the shift cable(s) from the car.

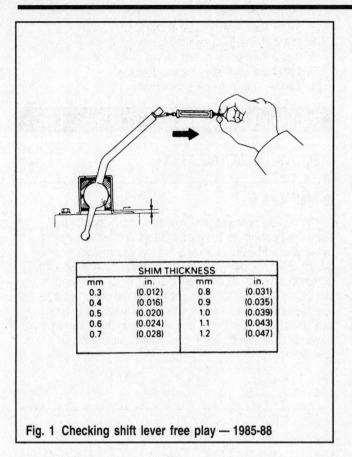

SHIM THICKNESS			
mm	in.	mm	in.
0.3	(0.012)	0.8	(0.031)
0.4	(0.016)	0.9	(0.035)
0.5	(0.020)	1.0	(0.039)
0.6	(0.024)	1.1	(0.043)
0.7	(0.028)	1.2	(0.047)

Fig. 1 Checking shift lever free play — 1985-88

1. Cable retainer
2. Shift control cable
3. Shift select cable
4. Cable end clip
5. Cable end washer

Fig. 3 Shift cables at transaxle — 1989-93

1. Retainer
2. Shift control cable
3. Select control cable
4. Selecting bellcrank
5. Spacer
6. Upper seat
7. Lower seat
8. Adjusting shim
9. Bushing No. 2
10. Bushing No. 1
11. Shift lever
12. Shift lever cover
13. Shift lever cap
14. Washer
15. Bushing
16. Torsion spring
17. Selecting bellcrank
18. Spring holder
19. Shift lever retainer

Fig. 2 Shifter and cable assembly — 1985-88

To install:

7. Position the new cable(s) and install the retaining screws.

8. Reposition the carpet and install the sill plate.

9. Route the cable(s) to the transaxle. This is easier if the car is elevated and safely supported. Lower the car after the cables are in position.

10. Position the cable(s) and install the retaining clips at the transaxle.

11. Connect the cable(s) to the shifter assembly.

12. Install the center console and shifter boot.

13. Connect the negative battery cable.

1989-93
▶ **See Figure 3**

1. Disconnect the negative battery cable.

2. Remove the shift lever knob and the shifter boot.

3. Remove the front and rear center console halves.

4. Remove the center air duct.

5. Remove the ECM mounting nuts and remove the ECM from under the dashboard.

6. Remove the cable hold-down brackets.

7. Remove the 4 shifter assembly mounting bolts.

8. Remove the shift cable retainer and end clips from the shifter assembly.

9. Remove the shifter control assembly.

10. Disconnect the cable retainers at the transaxle.

11. Remove the shift cables by pulling them from the outside of the firewall.

To install:

12. Install the new cables by going through the firewall from the outside.

13. Position the cables in their brackets at the transaxle and install the retaining clips.

14. Connect the cables to their transaxle mounts and install the clips.

15. Connect the cables and install the clips at the shifter assembly.

16. Install the shifter assembly and its 4 bolts. Tighten the bolts to 15 ft. lbs.

17. Install the cable hold-down brackets.

18. Reinstall the ECM and the center air duct.

19. Install the front and rear halves of the console.

20. Install the shift lever boot and knob.

21. Connect the negative battery cable.

Back-up Light Switch

REMOVAL & INSTALLATION

▶ **See Figure 4**

The reverse light switch is mounted on the side of the transaxle housing. Its removal and replacement is easily accomplished by disconnecting the wiring connector from the switch and unscrewing the switch from the case. A specially sized socket such as GM Tool J-35451 or its equivalent is necessary. Because of the placement of the switch, it is extremely difficult to reach the switch with any other type of tool. Install the new switch and tighten it to 30 ft. lbs. for the Nova or 15 ft. lbs. for the Prizm. Reinstall the electrical connector.

J 35451

Fig. 4 Installing reverse light switch; GM tool shown

TRANSAXLE

Before attempting to repair the clutch or transaxle for reasons beyond obvious failure, the problem and probable cause should be identified. A great percentage of manual transaxle and clutch problems are accompanied by shifting difficulties such as gear clash, grinding or refusal to engage gears. When any of these problems occur, a careful analysis should be performed to determine cause.

Driveline noises can become baffling, but don't be too quick to assign fault to the transaxle. The noise may actually be coming from other sources such as tires, road surfaces, wheel bearings, engine or exhaust system. Noises will also vary by vehicle size, engine type and amount of insulation within the body. Remember also that the transaxle, like any mechanical device, is not totally quiet in its operation and will exhibit some normal operating noise.

When checking for driveline noises, follow these guide lines:

1. Select a smooth , level asphalt road to reduce tire and body noises. Check and set the tire pressures before beginning.

2. Drive the vehicle far enough to thoroughly warm up all the lubricants; this may require driving as much as 10 or 12 miles before testing.

3. Note the speed at which the noise occurs and in which gear(s).

4. Check for noises with the vehicle stopped and the engine running.

5. Does the noise change when the clutch pedal is pushed in or released?

6. Determine the throttle condition(s) at which the noise occurs:

   a. Drive (leading throttle) — the engine is under load and the car is accelerating at some rate.

b. Float (neutral throttle) — the engine is maintaining a constant speed at light throttle on a level road.

c. Coast (trailing throttle) — the engine is not driving the car, the throttle is closed with the car in gear and in motion. An example is a long downhill grade.

d. Some combination of the above.

7. Does the noise change as the car corners or changes direction? Is the change in the noise different on left and right turns? Does the noise change as the car rises and falls on its suspension over bumps and dips?

8. Identify the noise by type (whine, click, knock, grinding, buzzing, etc.) and think through possible causes such as loose components, something rubbing, poor lubrication, or worn parts.

9. Check all other causes first. Its much easier to check the wheel bearings and the exhaust system than to remove the transaxle. Modern manual transaxles are extremely reliable and rarely fail if given reasonable maintenance and freedom from outright abuse. Assume that the noise is not in the transaxle until diagnosed otherwise.

REMOVAL & INSTALLATION

1985-88

▶ **See Figures 5, 6, 7 and 8**

1. Disconnect the negative battery terminal.
2. Remove the air cleaner and inlet duct.
3. From the transaxle, disconnect the back-up light switch connector, the speedometer cable, the thermostat housing and the ground wire.
4. Remove the 4 shift cable-to-transaxle clips, the clutch slave cylinder-to-transaxle bolts and the slave cylinder.
5. Remove the (2) upper transaxle-to-engine bolts and the upper transaxle mount bolt.
6. Attach an engine support tool or equivalent, and support the engine. Raise and support the front of the vehicle on jackstands.
7. Remove the left wheel. From under the vehicle, remove the left, right and center splash shields. Remove the center beam-to-chassis bolts and the center beam.
8. Remove the flywheel cover-to-engine bolts and the cover.

Fig. 5 GM engine support apparatus

J 28467-A

9. Disconnect the lower control arms from the steering knuckles.
10. Disconnect both halfshafts from the transaxle.
11. Disconnect the battery cable and ignition switch wire from the starter. Remove the starter-to-engine bolts and the starter.
12. Support the transaxle with a floor jack.
13. Remove the transaxle-to-engine bolts and the lower the transaxle from the vehicle.

To install:

14. Make sure the input shaft splines align with the clutch disc splines. Elevate the transaxle and slide it into position. Do not remove the jack until the retaining bolts are installed; the transaxle may be damaged if left hanging on the input shaft.
15. Install the lower bellhousing bolts and the bolts at the back side of the transaxle. Tighten the 12mm bolts to 47 ft. lbs. and the 10mm bolts to 34 ft. lbs.
16. Install the starter and the starter retaining bolts. The jack may be removed from under the transaxle when these bolts are secured.
17. Connect the driveshafts to the transaxle and tighten the bolts to 27 ft. lbs.
18. Reconnect the left and right control arms at the steering knuckles.
19. Reinstall the flywheel inspection cover.
20. Install the center beam and tighten its bolts to 29 ft. lbs.
21. Install the splash shields and the left front wheel.
22. Lower the vehicle from the stands. Install the 2 upper bellhousing bolts and the transaxle mount upper bolt. The engine support devices may be removed from the engine.
23. Connect the back-up light switch.
24. Reinstall the shift cables and their clips. Install the clutch slave cylinder.
25. Connect the ground wire to the transaxle and attach the wiring to the starter.
26. Connect the thermostat housing and the speedometer cable to the transaxle.
27. Install the air cleaner and intake duct.
28. Connect the negative battery cable.
29. Check the level of the fluid in the transaxle and fill or top off as needed.

1989-93

1. Install an engine support and tension it to support the engine without raising it.
2. Remove the battery hold-down, the battery and tray.
3. Disconnect the electrical connector to the reverse lights and disconnect the ground strap running to the transaxle.
4. Remove the 2 actuator mounting bolts and the actuator line bracket.
5. Remove the shift cable retainers and end clips.
6. Remove the shift cables from their brackets and place the cables out of the way.
7. Remove the cover and brace from the left transaxle mount.
8. Remove the through bolt from the mount.
9. Remove the 2 upper transaxle to engine bolts.
10. Remove the upper starter bolt and remove the speedometer cable.

1. Front transaxle mount
2. Rear transaxle mount
3. Main crossmember
4. Center crossmember
5. Center transaxle mount
6. Mount bolt shields

Fig. 6 Location of mounts and crossmembers. Prizm shown, Nova similar

1. Transaxle mount brace
2. Left transaxle mount

Fig. 8 Detail of left transaxle mount assembly

1. Front transaxle mount
2. Rear transaxle mount
3. Center transaxle mount

Fig. 7 Location of transaxle mounts

11. Raise the vehicle and safely support it.

✳✳CAUTION

The engine hoist is in place and under tension. Use care when repositioning the vehicle and make necessary adjustments to the engine support.

12. Remove the splash shields. Drain the transaxle oil.
13. Disconnect the electrical connections at the starter.
14. Remove the bottom starter bolt and the starter.
15. Remove the drive axles.
16. Remove the 3 bolts holding the center crossmember to the radiator support.
17. Remove the covers from the front and center mount bolts.
18. Remove the 2 front mount bolts, then the center mount bolts and then the 2 rear mount bolts.
19. Remove the 2 bolts holding the center crossmember to the main crossmember.
20. Remove the 3 exhaust hanger bracket nuts and the exhaust hanger.
21. Use a floor jack and a wide piece of wood to support the main crossmember.
22. Remove the 8 bolts holding the main crossmember to the body.

23. Remove the 2 bolts holding the lower control arm brackets to the body.

✳✳CAUTION

The crossmembers are loose and free to fall. Make sure they are properly supported.

24. Slowly lower the main crossmember while holding onto the center crossmember.
25. At the front transaxle mount, remove the through bolt and mount.
26. Remove the front mounting bracket from the transaxle.
27. Remove the center mount from the transaxle with its 2 bolts.
28. Remove the inspection cover bolt.
29. Remove the 2 lower transaxle bracket to transaxle mount bolts.
30. Lower the vehicle to the ground.

✳✳CAUTION

The engine hoist is in place and under tension. Use care when repositioning the vehicle and make necessary adjustments to the engine support.

31. Remove the remaining transaxle mount to transaxle bracket bolt.
32. Slowly lower the engine support device to gain clearance for the removal of the transaxle.
33. Remove the transaxle mount.
34. Safely elevate and support the vehicle on stands.

✳✳CAUTION

The engine hoist is in place and under tension. Use care when repositioning the vehicle and make necessary adjustments to the engine support.

35. Support the transaxle with a floor jack, making sure it is properly placed and balanced.
36. Remove the lower front and rear bolts holding the transaxle to the engine.
37. Remove the transaxle assembly from the engine and lower it slowly on the floor jack.

To install:
38. Elevate the transaxle into position, making sure the input shaft aligns with the clutch splines.
39. Install the lower front and rear bolts holding the transaxle to the engine.
40. Remove the floor jack from under the transaxle.
41. Attach the electrical wiring to the starter.
42. Install the lower starter bolt snugly.
43. Lower the vehicle to the ground

✳✳CAUTION

The engine hoist is in place and under tension. Use care when repositioning the vehicle and make necessary adjustments to the engine support.

44. Install the left transaxle mount upper bolt and 2 lower bolts snugly.

45. Take tension on the engine support device and raise the transaxle. Install the through bolt loosely in the mount.
46. Tighten the through bolt to 69 ft. lbs. Tighten the upper transaxle mount bolt to 45 ft. lbs.
47. Install the mount cover and bracket. Tighten the cover bolts to 45   ft. lbs.
48. Install the 2 upper transaxle to engine bolts and tighten them to 34 ft. lbs.
49. Install the upper starter bolt and tighten it to 29 ft. lbs.
50. Connect the speedometer cable.
51. Position the shift cables into the brackets and connect the cable retainers and end clips.
52. Install the 2 actuator mounting bolts snugly, then install the actuator line bracket and bolt. Tighten the actuator line and mounting bolts to 15 ft. lbs.
53. Connect the ground strap and the electrical connector for the reverse lights.
54. Install the air cleaner assembly.
55. Elevate and safely support the vehicle.

✳✳CAUTION

The engine hoist is in place and under tension. Use care when repositioning the vehicle and make necessary adjustments to the engine support.

56. Tighten the 2 remaining lower transaxle mount bolts to 45 ft. lbs. (These are the bolts installed in step 39.).
57. Tighten the lower starter bolt to 29 ft. lbs.
58. Install the center mount and its 2 bolts and tighten them to 45 ft. lbs. Install the inspection cover bolt and tighten it to 45 ft. lbs.
59. Install the front mount bracket on the transaxle.
60. Install the front mount and through bolt loosely.

➡**When installing the front mount, the weight on the mount must go toward the transaxle for proper mount alignment.**

61. Position the center crossmember over the center and rear transaxle mount studs; start 2 nuts on the center mount.
62. Loosely install the 3 bolts holding the center crossmember to the radiator support.
63. Loosely install the 2 front mount bolts.
64. Raise the main crossmember into position over the rear mount studs and align all underbody bolts. Install the 2 rear mount nuts loosely.
65. Install the 8 main crossmember to underbody bolts loosely.
66. Install the 2 lower control arm bracket bolts loosely.
67. Loosely install the 2 bolts holding the center crossmember to the main crossmember.
68. Install the exhaust hanger bracket and its 3 nuts. The crossmembers, mounts, through bolts and brackets should now all be in place and held loosely by their nuts and bolts. If any repositioning is necessary, do so now.
69. Tighten the components below in the order listed to the correct torque specification:

   a. Main crossmember to underbody bolts: 152 ft. lbs.
   b. Lower control arm bolts: 94 ft. lbs.
   c. Center crossmember to radiator support bolts: 45 ft. lbs.
   d. Front, center and rear mount bolts: 45 ft. lbs.

e. Exhaust hanger bracket nuts: 9.5 ft. lbs. (115 INCH lbs.)

f. Front mount through bolt: 69 ft. lbs.

70. Install the covers on the front and center mount bolts.

71. Reinstall the drive axles.

72. Fill the transaxle with the correct amount of oil.

73. Install the splash shields.

74. Lower the vehicle to the ground. Remove the engine support apparatus.

75. Install the battery tray, battery and hold-down clamp.

Overhaul

▶ **See Figures 9, 10, 11, 12, 13, 14, 15 and 16**

✴✴WARNING

The use of the correct special tools or their equivalent is REQUIRED for this procedure.

Before servicing the transaxle, it is important to insure cleanliness. The outside of the case should be thoroughly cleaned with solvent or spray cleaner. Any dirt entering the unit may damage moving parts. The work area and workbench should be cleaned before the work is begun and maintained in clean condition during the repair. If the repair must be abandoned for more than a few minutes, cover the work area and components with a large cloth or sheet.

All disassembled parts should be cleaned with solvent and dried with compressed air if possible. Do not use solvent on Neoprene seals. Lubricate the seals with clean transaxle oil and use petroleum jelly to hold thrust washers in place during assembly. This eases installation and does not leave harmful residue in the system.

Before installing bolts into aluminum parts, dip the threads in clean oil or coat them with an anti-seize compound to prevent galling or seizing. Always use a torque wrench to avoid overtightening fittings. Aluminum parts are very susceptible to damage and must be handled carefully. Certain internal parts are made of very soft metals and must be protected from impacts which could cause damage or cracks. While a certain amount of force is needed to separate or assemble parts, the force should be applied smoothly and evenly; sharp impact will damage components. Reusing snaprings and circlips is not recommended; they lose their tension during the removal process.

TRANSAXLE DISASSEMBLY

1. Remove the transaxle from the car, following procedures outlined previously. Secure the transaxle to a work stand.

2. Remove the clutch release fork, the clutch release bearing and the speedometer driven gear.

3. Remove the clutch release cylinder-to-transaxle bolts and the release cylinder.

4. Using the back-up light switch socket or equivalent, remove the back-up light switch.

5. Remove the transaxle case cover bolts and the cover.

6. Using a dial indicator, measure the 5th gear thrust clearance. The clearance must be 0.10-0.66mm; if not, the selective snapring will need to be replaced during reassembly.

1. Ground wire bolt
2. Left mount brace
3. Backup switch
4. Shift cable bracket
5. Shift control bellcrank
6. Shift select bellcrank
7. Left mount bracket

Fig. 9 Transaxle assembly removed from vehicle

MARK	THICKNESS
A	2.25 mm (0.0886″)
B	2.31 mm (0.0909″)
C	2.37 mm (0.0933″)
D	2.47 mm (0.0957″)
E	2.49 mm (0.0980″)
F	2.55 mm (0.1004″)
G	2.61 mm (0.1028″)

Fig. 10 Measuring 5th gear thrust clearance with a dial indicator. Use the chart to select a replacement snapring if needed

Fig. 11 Removing 5th gear; GM tool shown

Fig. 12 Removing the set bolt

Fig. 13 The two screwdriver trick for removing snaprings. Note the blades positioned vertically

7. Remove the shift selector bellcrank, the set bolt, the shift and selecting lever.

8. Engage the gears, remove the 5th gear locknut and disengage the gears.

9. Remove the bolt with the lockwasher from the No. 3 shift fork.

10. Using a pair of small prybars or screwdrivers and a hammer, tap the 5th gear snapring from the shaft.

11. Remove the 5th gear hub sleeve and driven gear. Using a gear puller or equivalent, press the 5th drive gear from the shaft.

12. Remove the rear bearing retainer and both bearing snaprings. Remove the reverse idler gear shaft bolt and the No. 2 shift fork shaft snapring.

Fig. 15 Removing the reverse shaft arm bracket and idler

13. Using a No. 40 Torx® bit or equivalent, remove the 3 plug, seal, spring, ball and lockball assemblies. If necessary, use a magnet to remove the seats, springs and balls.

14. Remove the transaxle case-to-bellhousing case bolts and tap the cases apart with a plastic hammer.

15. Remove the reverse shift arm bracket. Remove the reverse idler gear, thrust washer and shaft. Using a pair of prybars and a hammer, tap out the shift shaft snaprings and remove the set bolts.

16. To remove the shift forks and shift fork shafts, perform the following procedures:
   a. Remove the No. 2 fork shaft and shift head.
   b. Using a magnet, remove both balls.
   c. Remove the No. 3 fork shaft and the reverse shift fork.
   d. Pull out the No. 1 fork shaft.
   e. Remove the No. 1 and No. 2 shift forks.

Fig. 14 Removing the plugs and lockbolt assemblies

Fig. 16 Removing the shift forks and shafts

17. Remove both the input and output shafts at the same time.

18. Remove the differential assembly, the magnet and the oil receiver.

Input shaft

▶ **See Figures 17, 18, 19, 20, 21, 22 and 23**

1. Using a feeler gauge, measure the 3rd and 4th thrust clearance. Standard clearances are: 3rd gear, 0.10-0.35mm and 4th gear, 0.10-0.55mm. Maximum allowable clearances: 3rd gear, 0.40mm and 4th gear, 0.60mm. If the 3rd gear clearance is exceeded, 3rd and 4th gears must be replaced. If the 4th gear clearance is exceeded, 4th and 5th gears must be replaced.

2. Using a small pair of prybars and a hammer, tap the snaprings from the input shaft.

3. Using a press and a split plate tool, press the radial ball bearing and 4th gear from the input shaft. Remove the needle roller bearings and the synchronizer ring.

4. Using a pair of snaping pliers, remove the snapring from the input shaft. Use a press and a split plate tool to press the No. 2 sleeve, 3rd gear, the synchronizer ring and the needle roller bearing from the input shaft.

5. Clean all components thoroughly and dry with compressed air if possible. Inspect components as follows:

a. Check the input shaft bearing surfaces for scoring and/or wear; if necessary, replace the shaft.

b. Check the input shaft splines for wear; if necessary, replace the shaft.

c. Inspect the bearings for scoring, wear and/or damage; if necessary, replace them.

d. Check the gears and synchronizer parts for damage and/or excessively worn teeth; if necessary, replace them.

e. Using a dial indicator, check the shaft runout; if runout exceeds 0.50mm, replace the shaft.

f. Using a feeler gauge, measure the clearance between the shift forks and the hub sleeves. If the clearance is less than 0.60mm, replace the synchronizer.

6. Using multi-purpose grease, lubricate the needle roller bearings.

7. Place the synchronizer ring onto the 3rd gear, align the ring slots with the shifting keys. Using a shop press and a split plate tool, press the 3rd gear/No. 2 hub sleeve onto the input shaft.

Fig. 19 Use V-blocks and a dial indicator to measure runout

Fig. 17 Measuring 3rd and 4th gear thrust clearances

Fig. 20 Measuring shift fork clearance to hub sleeve

Fig. 18 Use a split-plate and a press to remove 4th gear, bearing and synchronizer

Fig. 21 3rd gear bearing, synchronizer ring and No. 2 hub

MARK	THICKNESS
0	2.30 mm (0.0906")
1	2.36 mm (0.0929")
2	2.42 mm (0.0953")
3	2.48 mm (0.0976")
4	2.54 mm (0.1000")
5	2.60 mm (0.1034")

Fig. 22 Use the chart to select the correct snapring for 3rd gear and 4th gear retention

8. Select a snapring which will allow minimum axial play and install it onto the input shaft.

9. Using a feeler gauge, measure the 3rd gear thrust clearance; it should be 0.10-0.35mm.

10. Using multi-purpose grease, lubricate the needle roller bearings.

11. Place the synchronizer ring onto the 4th gear and align the ring slots with the shifting keys.

12. Using a shop press, press the radial ball bearing onto the input shaft.

13. Select a snapring which will allow minimum axial play and install it onto the shaft.

14. Using a feeler gauge, measure the 4th gear thrust clearance; it should be 0.10-0.55mm.

Output Shaft
▶ **See Figures 24, 25, 26, 27 and 28**

1. Using a feeler gauge, measure the 1st and 2nd gear thrust clearance on the output shaft. Standard clearances are: 1st gear, 0.10-40mm and 2nd gear, 0.10-0.45mm. Maximum allowable clearances are: 1st gear, 0.45mm and 2nd gear, 0.50mm. If 1st gear clearance is incorrect, 1st and 2nd gears must be replaced. If 2nd gear clearance is incorrect, replace 2nd and 3rd gears.

2. Using a press and a split plate tool, press the radial ball bearing, the 4th driven gear and spacer from the output shaft.

3. Using a shop press and a split plate tool, press the 3rd driven gear, 2nd gear, the needle roller bearing, the spacer and the synchronizer ring from the output shaft. Remove the needle roller bearings and the synchronizer ring.

4. Remove the snapring.

5. Now press the No. 1 hub sleeve, the 1st gear/synchronizer ring, the needle roller bearing, the thrust washer and locking ball from the output shaft. Remove the needle roller bearings and the synchronizer ring.

6. Clean all components thoroughly and dry with compressed air if possible. Inspect components as follows:

  a. Check the input shaft bearing surfaces for scoring and/or wear; if necessary, replace the shaft.

  b. Check the input shaft splines for wear; if necessary, replace the shaft.

  c. Inspect the bearings for scoring, wear and/or damage; if necessary, replace them.

  d. Check the gears and synchronizer parts for damage and/or excessively worn teeth; if necessary, replace them.

  e. Using a dial indicator, check the shaft runout; if runout exceeds 0.50mm, replace the shaft.

  f. Using a feeler gauge, measure the clearance between the shift forks and the hub sleeves.

7. Install the locking ball into the output shaft. Install the thrust washer onto the shaft by positioning it's groove securely over the locking ball.

➡ **If the output shaft was replaced, drive a slotted spring pin into the output shaft to a depth of 6.0mm.**

8. Using multi-purpose grease, lubricate the needle roller bearing.

9. Place the synchronizer ring onto the 1st gear and align the ring slots with the shifting keys.

10. Press the 1st gear/No. 1 hub sleeve assembly onto the output shaft.

11. Select a snapring which will allow minimum axial play and install it onto the shaft.

12. Using a feeler gauge, measure the 1st gear thrust clearance; is should be 0.10-0.40mm.

13. Install the spacer. Position the synchronizer ring onto the gear and align the ring slots with the shifting keys.

14. Using multi-purpose grease, lubricate the needle roller bearings and install the 2nd gear.

15. Using a shop press and a split plate tool, press the 3rd driven gear onto the output shaft.

16. Using a feeler gauge, measure the 2nd gear thrust clearance; is should be 0.10-0.45mm.

17. Install the spacer. Use a press and a split plate to press the 4th driven gear and bearing onto the output shaft.

Synchronizers
▶ **See Figure 29**

The transaxle is equipped with 3 synchronizers: 1st-2nd, 3rd-4th and 5th speeds.

1. From each synchronizer, remove both key springs.

2. Noting the relative positions, separate the hub, sleeve and keys; be sure to scribe the hub-to-sleeve location.

3. Clean, inspect and/or replace any worn or damaged parts.

4. Using a feeler gauge, measure the synchronizer ring back-to-gear spline end clearance; it should be a minimum of 0.6mm.

5. Align the scribe marks and assemble the hub to the sleeve; the extruded hub lip should be directed away from the sleeve's shift fork groove.

1. Thrust washer
2. Needle roller bearing
3. 1st gear
4. No. 1 hub sleeve
5. Output shaft cover
6. Slotted spring pin
7. Output shaft
8. Snapring
9. Spacer
10. Needle roller bearing
11. 2nd gear
12. 3rd driven gear
13. Output gear spacer
14. 4th driven gear
15. Rear bearing
16. Snapring
17. 5th driven gear
18. Lock nut
19. Snapring
20. No. 2 hub sleeve
21. 3rd gear
22. Needle roller bearing
23. Synchronizer rings
24. Snapring
25. No. 3 hub sleeve
26. Synchronizer rings
27. 5th gear
28. Needle roller bearing
29. Spacer
30. Idler gear shaft
31. Reverse idler gear
32. Rear bearing retainer
33. Snapring
34. Rear bearing
35. 4th gear
36. Needle roller bearing
37. Spacer
38. Input shaft
39. Input shaft front bearing
40. Synchronizer rings

Fig. 23 Input and output shaft components

Fig. 24 Measuring 1st and 2nd gear thrust clearances

A 6.0 mm (0.236")

Fig. 25 Slotted spring pin

Fig. 26 Hub sleeve assembly; arrow points to engine side

MARK	THICKNESS
A	2.50 mm (0.0984")
B	2.56 mm (0.1008")
C	2.62 mm (0.1031")
D	2.68 mm (0.1055")
E	2.74 mm (0.1074")
F	2.80 mm (0.1102")

Fig. 27 Chart for selecting 1st gear snaprings

Fig. 28 Second gear and 3rd driven gear assembled on shaft

Fig. 29 Checking synchronizer function and clearance

Fig. 30 Removal (left) and installation of input shaft front bearing. GM tools shown

6. Install a retaining ring. Carefully pry the ring back and insert the keys (1 at a time); be sure to position the ring so it is locked in place by the keys.

7. Install the other retaining ring; be sure the ring's open segment is out of phase with the open segment of the other ring. The open areas should NOT align.

FRONT CASE

▶ See Figures 30, 31 and 32

1. Use an input shaft bearing removal tool (or equivalent) and a slide hammer/puller to press the input shaft's front bearing from the case.

2. Remove the bolt and bearing lockplate. Using an output shaft bearing removal tool or equivalent, and a slide hammer/puller, press the output shaft's front bearing from the case.

3. Using a small prybar, pry the input shaft front oil seal and the right hand differential oil seal from the case.

4. Using the differential side bearing cup removal tool or equivalent, and a hammer, drive the right hand differential outer race from the case.

5. Check and clean the case.

6. Using a scraper or gasket cleaning tool, remove the sealant from the mating surfaces; be careful not to gouge or damage the aluminum surfaces.

7. Use the input shaft seal installation tool, drive the new oil seal into the case until it seats.

8. Drive the input shaft bearing into the case with the correct size bearing driver.

9. Drive the output shaft bearing into the case.

10. Install the right hand differential outer race into the case.

11. Lubricate the new oil seal with multi-purpose grease. Using the differential seal driver and a hammer, drive the new differential oil seal into the case.

DIFFERENTIAL

▶ **See Figures 33, 34, 35, 36, 37, 38 and 39**

1. Using the differential side bearing puller tool (GM J-22888-20) or equivalent, and a differential side bearing puller

Fig. 31 Removing and installing seals

Fig. 32 Removing and installing case bearings. GM tool shown

Fig. 33 Removing the side bearing using GM tools

pilot (GM J-35378) or equivalent, press the side bearings from the differential case.

2. Loosen the staked part of the lockplate. Using a scribing tool, make alignment marks at the ring gear-to-case location.

3. Remove the ring gear-to-case bolts and tap the ring gear from the case.

4. Using a dial micrometer, hold a pinion and side gear toward the case and measure the backlash of the other side gear; it should be 0.05-0.20mm. If the backlash is not within specifications, replace the thrust washer.

5. Using a punch and a hammer, drive the pinion shaft lockpin from the ring gear side of the case. Remove the pinion shaft, both pinions, both side gears and the thrust washers.

6. Clean and inspect the parts for damage and replace parts as necessary.

THRUST WASHER	THICKNESS
0.95 mm	(0.0374")
1.00 mm	(0.0394")
1.05 mm	(0.0413")
1.10 mm	(0.0433")
1.15 mm	(0.0453")
1.20 mm	(0.0472")

Fig. 34 Measuring pinion gear backlash; use the chart to select replacement thrust washers

Fig. 35 Removing the pinion shaft lock pin

Fig. 36 Assembling pinion and side gears

7. Assemble the pinion shaft, both pinions, both side gears and the thrust washers into the case.

8. Using a dial micrometer, hold a pinion and side gear toward the case and measure the backlash of the other side gear; it should be 0.05-0.20mm. If the backlash is not within specifications, replace the thrust washer.

9. Using a punch and a hammer, drive the pinion shaft lockpin into the ring gear side of the case.

10. Align the ring gear with the differential case, install a new locking plate and set bolts. Torque the bolts evenly, in several steps, to 71 ft. lbs.

11. Using a hammer and a punch, stake the locking plates.

➡**Stake a claw flush with the flat surface of the nut. For the claw contacting the protruding portion of the nut, stake only ½ on the tightening side.**

12. Using a press and the differential side bearing installer tool, press the differential side bearings onto the differential case.

SHIFT AND SELECT LEVER

▶ **See Figures 40, 41 and 42**

1. Remove the shift/select lever assembly from the case.
2. Remove the E-ring and compression ring.
3. Using a pin punch and a hammer, drive the slotted spring pins from the No. 1 and No. 2 inner shift levers.
4. Remove the No. 2 shift inner lever, the No. 1 shift inner lever and the shift interlock plate.

Fig. 37 Installing pinion shaft locking pin

5. Using a pin punch and a hammer, drive the slotted spring pins from the select inner lever.

6. Remove the select inner lever, the compression spring and the spring seat.

7. Tap the snapring from the lever shaft and remove the lever shaft and boot.

8. Using a small prybar, pry the out seal and replace it.

9. Clean and inspect the parts for damage; replace the parts, if necessary.

10. Grease the shaft, install the boot and shaft to the control shaft cover.

➡**When installing the boot, be sure to position the boot's air bleed downward.**

11. Install the snapring, the spring seat, the compression spring and the select inner lever.

12. Using a pin punch and a hammer, drive in the slotted spring pin.

13. Align the interlock plate to the No. 1 inner shift lever and install it.

14. Install the No. 2 inner shift lever.

15. Using a pin punch and a hammer, drive in the slotted spring pins.

16. Install the compression spring, seat and E-ring.

TRANSAXLE RE-ASSEMBLY

▶ **See Figures 43, 44, 45, 46 and 47**

1. Install the magnet into the bottom of the case.
2. Install the oil receiver and the differential into the case.
3. To adjust the differential side bearing preload, perform the following procedures:

   a. Install the thinnest side bearing shim into the transaxle case.

   b. Install the differential into the transaxle case.

   c. Install the transaxle case and tighten the bolts to 22 ft. lbs.

   d. Using the differential preload wrench and a torque wrench, measure the bearing preload; the new bearings should be 7-14 INCH lbs. or old bearings should be 4-9 INCH lbs.

➡**The preload will change about 2.6-3.5 inch lbs. with each shim thickness.**

   e. If the preload is not correct, use the differential side bearing cup remover to remove the transaxle case side outer side bearing race. Select and install a different side bearing shim, install the side bearing outer race and the case. Torque the case bolts and check the preload.

   f. After the preload has been adjusted, remove the transaxle case.

4. Install the input and output shaft assemblies.

5. Install the shift forks and shift fork shafts by positioning the No. 1 and No. 2 shift forks into the No. 1 and No. 2 hub sleeve grooves. Insert the No. 1 fork shaft into the No. 1 shift fork hole.

6. Insert both interlock balls into the reverse shift fork hole. Install the No. 3 fork shaft and the reverse shift fork.

7. Install the No. 2 fork shaft, the shift head and the bolts; tighten the bolts to 12 ft. lbs.

1. Thrust washer
2. Side gear
3. Pinion gear
4. Thrust washer
5. Pinion shaft
6. Side gear
7. Thrust washer
8. Pinion gear
9. Thrust washer
10. Differential case
11. Ring gear
12. Side bearing
13. Locking plate
14. Pinion shaft lock pin
15. Speedometer drive gear
16. Side bearing

Fig. 38 Differential assembly

8. Install the snaprings.

9. Place the reverse shift fork pivot into the reverse shift arm and install the reverse shift arm into the transaxle case; the bolts should be tightened to 13 ft. lbs.

10. Install the reverse idler gear and shaft; align the gear mark with the case hole.

11. Apply Loctite® sealant No. 518 or equivalent to the front and main transaxle case mounting surfaces and assemble the cases. Tighten the main case-to-front case bolts to 22 ft. lbs.

12. Install the balls, springs and seats into the lockball assembly holes. Apply sealant to the plugs and lockball assembly. Tighten the plugs to 18 ft. lbs. and the lockball assembly to 29 ft. lbs.

13. Install the reverse idler gear shaft and torque the lockbolt to 18 ft. lbs.

14. Install both bearing snaprings and the No. 2 fork shaft snapring.

Fig. 39 Removing No. 1 and No. 2 shift inner lever

1. Reverse restrict pin
2. Reverse light switch
3. Protector
4. Drive axle seal
5. Transmission case cover
6. Shift and select lever shaft
7. No. 1 shift fork
8. No. 1 shift fork shaft
9. No. 2 shift fork shaft
10. Shift head
11. No. 2 shift fork
12. No. 3 shift fork
13. Ball
14. Spring
15. Seat
16. Plug
17. No. 3 shift fork shaft
18. Reverse shift fork
19. Fork lock balls
20. E-clip
21. No. 2 select spring seat
22. Spring
23. No.2 shift inner lever
24. Slotted spring pin
25. No.1 shift inner lever
26. Select inner lever
27. Spring
28. Select spring seat
29. Gasket
30. Control shaft cover
31. Oil seal
32. Boot
33. Transaxle case

Fig. 40 Shift forks and shaft assemblies

Fig. 41 Removing select inner shaft

Fig. 44 Reverse shaft and idler gear alignment

Fig. 42 Lever shaft and boot assembly

Fig. 45 Apply sealant to mating surface of the front and main cases

J 35405

MARK	THICKNESS
A	2.10 mm (0.00827")
B	2.15 mm (0.0846")
C	2.20 mm (0.0866")
D	2.25 mm (0.0886")
E	2.30 mm (0.0906")
F	2.35 mm (0.0925")
G	2.40 mm (0.0945")
H	2.45 mm (0.0965")
J	2.50 mm (0.0984")
K	2.55 mm (0.1004")
L	2.60 mm (0.1024")
M	2.65 mm (0.1043")
N	2.70 mm (0.1063")
P	2.75 mm (0.1083")
Q	2.80 mm (0.1102")
R	2.85 mm (0.1122")
S	2.90 mm (0.1142")
T	2.95 mm (0.1162")
U	3.00 mm (0.1182")

Fig. 43 Checking the differential preload with GM tool. Use the chart to select the correct adjusting shims

Fig. 46 Installing 5th gear; GM tools shown

15. Install the rear bearing retainer; tighten the bolts to 14 ft. lbs.

16. Use the proper installation tool and a hammer to drive the 5th driven gear onto the shaft.

17. Install the spacer, the needle bearing, the 5th gear and the synchronizer ring.

18. Install the clutch hub, the shifting keys and the key springs onto the hub sleeve

➡ When installing the shifting springs, position them under the shifting keys and position them so their gaps do not align with each other.

19. Using the gear installation tool, drive the No. 3 hub sleeve, with the No. 3 shifting fork, and align the synchronizer ring slots with the shifting keys.

20. Using a dial indicator, measure the 5th gear thrust clearance; it should be 0.10-0.57mm.

21. Select and install a snapring which will allow minimum axial play, onto the output shaft.

22. Engage the 5th gear and install the locknut; tighten it to 87 ft. lbs. After installation, disengage the gear and stake the locknut.

23. Install the shifting fork bolt and tighten it to 12 ft. lbs.

24. Position a new gasket on the control shaft cover, install the shift/select lever and torque the bolts to 14 ft. lbs.

25. Install the bellcrank to the transaxle case and tighten the bolt to 22 ft. lbs.

26. Apply Loctite® No. 518 (or its equivalent) to the transaxle case, install the case cover and tighten the retaining bolts to 13 ft. lbs.

27. Install the front bearing retainer and tighten the bolts to 8 ft. lbs.

28. Apply lithium grease to the inside groove of the release bearing hub, the input shaft spline and the release fork contact surface. Install the release fork and the bearing.

29. Using the proper size socket, install and tighten the back-up light switch to 30 ft. lbs.

30. Install the speedometer driven gear.

31. Shift the transaxle and check it for smooth operation.

Halfshafts

REMOVAL & INSTALLATION

1985-88 Vehicle With VIN Code 4 Engine and 1989-92 Prizm

▶ See Figures 48 and 49

1. Remove the wheel cover.
2. Remove the cotter pin, hub nut cap, hub nut and washer.
3. Loosen the wheel nuts.
4. Elevate and safely support the car.
5. Remove the front wheel.
6. Remove the lower control arm to ball joint attaching nuts and bolts.
7. Use a ball joint separator such as GM J-24319-01 or equivalent to remove the tie rod ball joint from the knuckle.
8. Remove the bolts holding the brake caliper bracket to the steering knuckle. Use stiff wire to suspend the caliper out of the way; do not let the caliper hang by its hose. Remove the brake disc.

9. Using a puller such as GM J-25287 or equivalent, push the axle from the hub.

➡The Prizm axle can be separated from the hub using a brass or plastic hammer. Nova requires the use of the puller.

10. Use a slide hammer and appropriate end fitting (GM J-2619-01 and J 35762 or equivalents) to pull the driveshaft from the transaxle. Remove the shaft from the car.

To install:

11. Install shaft into transaxle. If necessary, use a long brass drift and a hammer to drive the housing ribs onto the inner joint.

12. Install the shaft into the wheel hub.

13. Install the lower control arm to the lower ball joint. Tighten the nuts and bolts to 59 ft. lbs.

14. Install the tie rod end to the steering knuckle and tighten the nut to 36 ft. lbs.

15. Install the brake disc; install the brake caliper and tighten the bolts to 65 ft. lbs.

16. Install the wheel.

17. Install the hub nut and washer.

18. Lower the vehicle to the ground.

19. Tighten the wheel lugs to 76 ft. lbs. Tighten the hub nut to 137 ft. lbs.

20. Install the nut, cap, cotter pin and washer. Install the wheel cover.

MARK	THICKNESS
A	2.25 mm (0.0886")
B	2.31 mm (0.0909")
C	2.37 mm (0.0933")
D	2.43 mm (0.0957")
E	2.49 mm (0.0980")
F	2.55 mm (0.1004")
G	2.61 mm (0.1028")

Fig. 47 Selection chart for 5th gear snaprings

Fig. 48 Using GM tool to remove axle from the hub — 1985-88 VIN Code 4 engine

Fig. 49 Using a slide hammer and adaptor to remove the driveshaft from the transaxle — 1985-88 VIN Code 4 engine

1985-88 Nova With VIN Code 5 Engine

1. Raise the front of the vehicle and support it with jackstands. Remove the tires.
2. Remove the cotter pin and locknut cap.
3. Have an assistant step on the brake pedal and at the same time, loosen and remove the bearing locknut.
4. While the assistant is still depressing the brake pedal, loosen and remove the 6 nuts which connect the halfshaft to the differential side gear shaft.
5. Remove the brake caliper and position it out of the way. Remove the brake disc.
6. Remove the 2 retaining nuts and then disconnect the lower arm from the steering knuckle.
7. Use a 2-armed puller and remove the axle hub from the outer end of the halfshaft.
8. Remove the halfshaft.

To install:

9. Place the outboard side of the shaft into the axle hub and then insert the inner end into the differential. Finger tighten the 6 nuts.

❋❋WARNING

Be careful not to damage the boots during installation.

10. Install the lower arm to the steering knuckle and tighten the bolts to 47 ft. lbs.
11. Install the disc and reinstall the caliper and bracket. tighten the bolts to 65 ft. lbs.
12. While an assistant depresses the brake pedal, tighten the 6 nuts holding the axle to the side gear shaft to 27 ft. lbs.
13. Install the hub nut and washer.
14. Install the wheel.
15. Lower the vehicle to the ground.
16. Tighten the wheel lugs to 76 ft. lbs. Tighten the hub nut to 137 ft. lbs.
17. Install the nut, cap, cotter pin and washer. Install the wheel cover.

1993

▶ **See Figures 50, 51, 52, 53, 54, 55, 56 and 57**

❋❋WARNING

Care must be exercised to prevent the differential-side joint from being over-extended. When either end of the shaft is disconnected, over-extension of the differential-side joint could result in separation of internal components and possible joint failure. If the vehicle is to be lowered to the ground and moved, the front wheel bearings must be supported with a 9/16 inch (14 mm) bolt, one 1 3/4 inch (44.45 mm) washer, one 2 inch (50.8 mm) washer, and a 9/16 inch (14 mm) nut assembled through the shaft opening in the hub; tighten the nut and bolt to 40 ft. lb. (54 Nm). On vehicles equipped with antilock brake systems (ABS), use caution not to damage the ABS speed sensor ring on the wheel-side joint. DO NOT pry against the ABS speed sensor ring with metal tools when removing the wheel-side joint from the steering knuckle. If the serrations on the ABS speed sensor ring appear damaged, replace the wheel-side joint.

1. Disconnect the negative (-) battery cable. Raise and suitably support the vehicle.
2. Remove the 6 bolts and splash shield from the vehicle.
3. Remove the 1 retaining bolt and the ABS speed sensor from the steering knuckle, if equipped, and set aside.
4. Remove the front tire and wheel.
5. Remove the cotter pin and lock cap from the drive axle.
6. Remove the drive axle nut from the drive axle.
7. Remove 1 cotter pin from the tie rod end.
8. Remove 1 nut from the tie rod end.
9. Remove the tie rod end from the steering knuckle using tool J 6627-A or equivalent.
10. Remove 1 bolt, 2 nuts and separate the ball joint and steering knuckle from the control arm.
11. Remove the wheel-side joint from the steering knuckle.
12. Remove the differential-side joint from the transaxle by gently prying the differential-side joint housing away and out of the transaxle.

To install:

13. Inspect the differential-side and wheel-side joint boots for tears or deterioration. Replace as necessary.
14. Inspect the front wheel bearing inner and outer oil seals fro damage or deterioration. Replace as necessary.
15. Inspect the drive axle shaft fluid seal at transaxle for leakage or damage. Replace as necessary.
16. Install the differential-side joint into the transaxle.
17. Install the wheel-side joint into the steering knuckle.
18. Install the ball joint and steering knuckle to the control arm; secure with 2 nuts and 1 bolt. Tighten the ball joint-to-control arm bolt and nuts to 105 ft. lbs. (142 Nm).
19. Install tie rod end to steering knuckle.

1. Washer (2 inch O. D.)
2. Washer (1 3/4 inch O. D.)
3. Washer (9/16 inch O. D.)
4. Lock washer
5. Bolt (9/16 inch)

Fig. 50 Front wheel bearing support

1. Wheel side joint
2. Wheel side boot
3. ABS speed sensor ring

Fig. 51 ABS speed sensor ring

1. Drive axle nut
2. Lock cap
3. Cotter pin

Fig. 53 Cotter pin and lock cap

1. ABS speed sensor
2. ABS speed sensor retaining bolt
3. ABS speed sensor wire

Fig. 52 ABS speed sensor

Fig. 55 Removing the wheel side joint from the steering knuckle

20. Install the 1 nut to tie rod end and tighten the tie rod end nut to 40 ft. lb. (54 Nm).
21. Install new cotter pin into tie rod end.
22. Install drive axle nut onto drive axle shaft. Tighten the drive axle nut to 159 ft. lbs. (216 Nm)
23. Install the lock cap onto the drive axle; secure with new cotter pin.
24. Install the front tire and wheel.
25. Install the ABS speed sensor into steering knuckle, if equipped, and secure with the 1 bolt. Tighten the ABS speed sensor retaining bolt to 71 inch lbs. (8 Nm).
26. Install the splash shield to vehicle and secure with the 6 bolts. Tighten the splash shield bolts to 71 inch lbs. (8 Nm). Lower the vehicle.
27. Connect the negative (-) battery cable.
28. Inspect the toe adjustment and adjust as necessary.

1. Ball joint
2. Ball joint to control arm bolt
3. Ball joint to control arm nut

Fig. 54 Ball joint to control arm bolts and nuts

Fig. 56 Removing the differential side joint from the transaxle

J 6627-A

Fig. 57 Example of tie rod and wheel stud puller tool

CONSTANT VELOCITY (CV) JOINT OVERHAUL

The drive axle assembly is a flexible unit consisting of an inner and outer Constant Velocity (CV) joint joined by an axle shaft. The inner joint, because of its 'tri-pod' design, is completely flexible and allows the joint to flex left/right, up/down and compress/extend while the shaft is turning. This range of motion is necessary to allow the car to accelerate during all possible positions of the front wheels.

Because of the inner joint's flexibility, care must be taken not to over-extend the joint during repairs or handling. When either end of the shaft is disconnected from the car, any over-extension could result in separation of the internal components and possible joint failure.

The outer joint, being fixed into the hub, does not require the extreme flexibility of the inner joint. The outer joint is a Rzeppa design (named for its inventor) and allows left/right motion while the axle is turning.

CV joints are protected by rubber boots or seals, designed to keep the high-temperature grease in and the road grime and water out. The most common cause of joint failure is a ripped boot which allows the lubricant to leave the joint, thus causing heavy wear. The boots are exposed to road hazards all the time and should be inspected frequently. Any time a boot is found to be damaged or slit, it should be replaced immediately. This is another very good example of

maintenance being cheaper than repair; replacement boot kits are far less expensive than replacing a whole new joint.

➡**Whenever the driveshaft is held in a vise, use pieces of wood in the jaws to protect the components from damage or deformation.**

1985-88 Vehicle With VIN Code 4 Engine and 1989-92 Prizm

▶ **See Figures 58, 59 and 60**

1. Remove the axle and mount in a vise so that the outer joint may be worked on.
2. Remove the boot retaining clamps. Slide the boot out of the way, exposing the joint.
3. Use snapring pliers to release the race retaining ring. Pull the shaft from the cage.
4. Using a brass drift, gently tap on the bottom of the cage until it tilts enough to all the first ball to be removed at the top.
5. Continue removing other balls is a similar fashion.
6. Rotate the cage and inner race 90° and remove the cage and inner race.
7. Clean and inspect all parts. The slightest imperfection on either the balls or the race will require replacement of the components. Look for any scratches, cracks or galling of the metal.
8. Position the driveshaft in the vise so that the inner joint may be worked on.
9. Remove the boot clamps. Slide the boot back, exposing the joint.
10. Remove the tri-pot housing from the axle shaft.
11. Remove the spacer ring with snapring pliers.

1. Outer race
2. Ball
3. Inner race
4. Brass drift
5. Case

Fig. 58 Removing ball bearing assembly

PIVOT CAGE AND INNER RACE AT 90°
TO CENTER LINE OF OUTER RACE
WITH CAGE WINDOWS ALIGNED
WITH LANDS OF OUTER RACE,
LIFT OUT CAGE AND INNER RACE.

CAGE

LAND

LAND

OUTER RACE

WINDOWS

Fig. 59 Removing the cage and inner race

12. Use a brass drift and hammer to gently tap the joint assembly towards the center of the axle.

13. Remove the outer driveshaft snapring.

14. Remove the spider assembly from the axle by tapping it off with a brass punch and hammer. Apply force evenly around spider.

➡**The spider assembly and axle should have factory alignment marks showing. Also note the marks on axle shaft and tri-pot housing. If no marks are present, make matchmarks before disassembly.**

15. Remove the boot.

16. Disassemble the spider assembly into its component parts of retainer, ball, needle bearing and spider.

17. Clean all parts thoroughly and inspect for wear, damage or corrosion. Replace any component which is not in virtually perfect condition.

To install:

18. Reassemble the spider assembly

19. Apply molybdenum grease liberally to tri-pot housing and spider.

20. Install the new boot onto the axle shaft and install a new small clamp.

21. Using the brass drift and hammer, install the spider assembly onto the shaft.

22. Install the outboard snapring, then tap the tri-pot assembly down over the snapring.

23. Install the spider assembly and drive axle assembly into the tri-pot housing.

24. Install the boot over the joint and secure the new large clamp.

➡**Boot clamp pliers and installing tools such as GM J-35556 and J-34773-A make this job much easier.**

25. Position the axle shaft so that the outer joint may be worked on.

26. Install the cage into the race with the retaining ring side of the inner race facing the transaxle side of the shaft.

27. Pack the joint liberally with molybdenum grease and install the cage and inner race at 90° into the outer race.

28. Tip the race and install the 6 balls.

29. Install a new boot onto the shaft.

30. Install the race retaining ring on the shaft.

31. Insert the shaft into the inner race and make sure that the retaining ring is properly seated.

32. Fit the boot over the joint and install new boot clamps.

33. Check both joints for freedom of motion and lack of binding.

1988 Nova VIN Code 5 Engine

◆ **See Figures 61, 62, 63 and 64**

1. Remove the boot retaining clamps.

2. Using paint or a scribing tool, place matchmarks on the tri-pod housing and driveshaft. Do not punch the marks into the metal.

3. Remove the tri-pot housing from the driveshaft.

4. Use snapring pliers to remove the shaft retaining ring.

5. Use a punch and hammer to matchmark the driveshaft and spider.

6. Remove the spider assembly from the drive shaft with a brass punch and hammer.

7. Remove the boot from the inner joint.

8. If working on the right axle, remove the driveshaft damper.

9. If working on the right axle, remove the outer joint boot.

10. Check the inside and outside of the seals for damage.

11. Clean all parts thoroughly and inspect for wear, damage or corrosion. Replace any component which is not in virtually perfect condition.

To install:

12. Reassemble the spider assembly.

13. If working on the right axle, temporarily install a new boot and new clamp to the outer joint.

14. If working on the right axle, install the drive shaft damper with a new clamp. Place the clamp in line with the groove of the driveshaft.

15. Temporarily install a new inner joint boot and new clamp to the driveshaft.

➡**The boot and clamp for the inner joint are larger than those for the outer joint.**

16. Position the beveled side of the spider splines toward the outer CV joint. Align the matchmarks made earlier and tap the spider onto the driveshaft with a brass punch and hammer.

17. Install a NEW shaft retaining ring.

18. If working on the right axle, pack the outer joint boot with molybdenum grease. (Capacity is 0.25-0.30 lbs).

19. Install the boot over the joint.

20. Pack the tri-pot joint and boot with molybdenum grease. Correct capacities are: Manual transaxle, 0.35-0.40 lbs. and Automatic transaxle, 0.40-0.50 lbs.

21. Align the matchmarks made earlier and install the tri-pot housing onto the drive shaft.

22. Install the boot over the joint.

23. Be sure each boot in on the shaft groove. Bend each boot clamp into place and secure it.

24. Check both joints for freedom of motion and lack of binding.

25. Check that the boots are not stretched or compressed when the axle is in a normal or 'at rest' position.

SHAFT RETAINING RING
REMOVE FROM AXLE SHAFT
THEN SLIDE SPIDER
ASSEMBLY OFF AXLE SPIDER ASSEMBLY

SNAP RING
PLIERS

SPACER
RING

SPACER RING
SLIDE RING BACK ON
AXLE SHAFT

NOTICE: BE SURE
SPACER RING IS SEATED IN
GROOVE AT REASSEMBLY

Fig. 60 Removing the spider assembly from the shaft

1. Joint, outer CV
2. Shaft, drive (RH)
3. Clamp, outer CV joint seal ret.
4. Seal, outer CV joint
5. Damper, drive shaft
6. Clamp, damper ret.
7. Clamp, tri-pot joint seal ret.
8. Seal, tri-pot joint
9. Spider tri pot joint
10. Ring, shaft ret.
11. Housing, tri pot
12. Shaft, side gear (RH)
13. Shaft, side gear (LH)
14. Nut, axle to side gear shaft
15. Shaft, drive (LH)
16. Seal, side gear shaft oil
17. Ring, oil seal ret

Fig. 61 Driveshaft components — 1988 Nova with VIN Code 5 engine

1993

► **See Figures 65, 66, 67, 68, 69, 70, 71, 72, 73, 74, 75, 76, 77, 78, 79, 80, 81 and 82**

➡ **During differential-side and wheel-side joint service, index marks (reference marks) should be placed on the differential-side joint housing and the drive axle shaft as well as the Tri-Pod joint spider, wheel-side joint and drive axle shaft to ensure that all components are installed in the same position from which they were removed. If this precaution is not observed and the components are installed in a different position, uneven or premature component wear may result.**

1. Remove the large differential-side boot clamp from the differential-side boot by drawing the clamp hooks together using tool J 35566 or equivalent.

2. Remove the small differential-side boot clamp from the differential-side boot. Temporarily slide the differential-side boot toward the center of the drive axle shaft. Place an index mark (reference mark) on the differential-side joint housing and drive axle shaft to ensure correct assembly.

3. Remove the differential-side joint housing from Tri-Pod joint spider. Place an index mark (reference mark) on the Tri-Pod joint spider and drive axle shaft to ensure correct assembly.

4. Remove the 1 snapring and Tri-Pod joint spider from the drive axle shaft.

5. Remove the differential-side boot from the drive axle shaft.

6. Remove the large wheel-side boot clamp from the wheel-side boot.

7. Remove the small wheel-side boot clamp from the wheel-side boot.

Fig. 62 Correct placement of matchmarks before disassembly

Fig. 63 On the right side axle, make certain the damper retaining ring is in the groove — 1988 Nova with VIN Code 5 engine

8. Remove the wheel-side boot from the drive axle shaft. Place an index mark(reference mark) on the wheel-side joint and the drive axle shaft to ensure correct assembly.

9. Remove the wheel-side joint from the drive axle shaft by expanding the wheel-side joint snapring.

➡Do not disassemble the wheel-side joint. If any abnormality is found in the joint, replace it as an assembly. Do not disassemble the Tri-Pod joint spider.If any abnormality is found in the Tri-Pod joint spider, replace it as an assembly.   Do not wash drive axle boots in solvent. Washing drive axle boots in degreaser or other solvents causes deterioration of boots. DO NOT wash the Tri-Pod joint spider in degreaser. Washing the Tri-Pod joint spider in degreaser will remove all lubrication in the Tri-

Fig. 64 Observe the matchmarks when installing the spider onto the shaft

Pod joint spider needle bearings. Clean the Tri-Pod joint spider assembly and drive axle boots with a clean, dry, solvent-free rag.

 To install:
 10. Clean the differential-side and the wheel-side boots with a clean, dry, solvent-free cloth.
 11. Clean the tri-pod joint spider and the wheel-side joint with a clean, dry, solvent-free cloth.
 12. Inspect the differential-side and the wheel-side boots for tears, damage or fatigue. Replace as necessary.
 13. Inspect the Tri-Pod joint spider for excessive wear or damage. If any excessive wear, damage or abnormality is found, replace the Tri-Pod joint spider as an assembly.
 14. Inspect the wheel-side joint for excessive wear or damage. If any excessive wear, damage or abnormality is found, replace the wheel-side joint as an assembly.
 15. Inspect the dynamic dampener on the right drive axle shaft for damage or distortion. Replace the right drive axle shaft as necessary.
 16. Align the reference marks on the wheel-side joint and drive axle shaft made during wheel-side joint removal.
 17. Install the wheel-side joint onto the drive axle shaft by expanding the wheel-side snapring and slide wheel-side joint onto the drive axle shaft. After installing the wheel-side joint onto the drive axle shaft, make sure the wheel-side joint snapring is securely seated into the groove in the drive axle shaft.
 18. Install the wheel-side boot onto the drive axle shaft. Temporarily install the large and small wheel-side boot clamps onto the drive axle shaft. Do not crimp. Pack the wheel-side

joint with approximately 4.6-5.3 oz. (130-150 g) of black grease provided in the wheel-side boot kit.

19. Install the small wheel-side boot clamp onto the wheel-side boot using tool J 22610 or equivalent.

20. Install the large wheel-side boot clamp onto the wheel-side boot using tool J 22610 or equivalent. Temporarily install the large and small differential-side boot clamps onto the drive axle shaft. Do not crimp.

21. Install the differential-side boot onto the drive axle shaft.

➡**When installing the Tri-Pod joint spider onto the drive axle shaft, place the Tri-Pod joint spider onto the drive axle shaft with the short sided splines facing toward the differential-side boot (away from transaxle).**

22. Install the Tri-Pod joint spider onto the drive axle shaft aligning reference marks made during disassembly; secure with Tri-Pod joint spider snapring. Pack the differential-side joint housing with approximately 8.1-8.8 oz. (230-250 g) of the lubricant provided in the differential-side boot kit.

23. Install the differential-side joint housing onto Tri-Pod joint spider aligning reference marks made during disassembly.

24. Install the small differential-side boot clamp onto the differential-side boot using the tool J 22610 or equivalent.

➡**When installing the large differential-side boot clamp, use tool J 35566 or equivalent to draw the closing hooks of the clamp together so that the clamp locks into position.**

25. Install the large differential-side boot clamp onto the differential-side boot using tool J 35566 or equivalent.

26. Inspect both boots for distortion or dents. Correct by pulling outward on the boot in the desired areas until all boot deformation is corrected. Do not pull outward on the differential-side joint housing. If the housing is pulled, the joint may become over-extended and detach from the drive axle.

27. Measure the standard drive axle length to ensure that the boots are not stretched or excessively contracted when the drive axle is at standard length.
   - Right drive axle — 33.756 inches (857.4 mm)
   - Left drive axle — 21.268 inches (540.2 mm)

1. Reference marks
2. Differential side joint housing
3. Drive axle shaft

Fig. 67 Marking the differential side joint housing and drive axle shaft

LARGE DIFFERENTIAL SIDE BOOT CAMP

DIFFERENTIAL SIDE BOOT

Fig. 65 Removing the large differential side boot clamp

DIFFERENTIAL SIDE BOOT

SMALL DIFFERENTIAL SIDE BOOT CLAMP

DRIVE AXLE SHAFT

Fig. 66 Removing the small differential side boot clamp

Fig. 68 Marking the tri-pod joint spider and drive axle shaft

1. Drive axle shaft
2. Tri-pod joint spider
3. Tri-pod joint spider snap ring

Fig. 69 Removing the tri-pod joint spider snap ring

Fig. 70 Removing the tri-pod joint spider

Fig. 71 Removing the differential side boot

Fig. 72 Removing the large wheel side boot clamp

Fig. 73 Removing the small wheel side boot clamp

Fig. 74 Marking the wheel side joint and drive axle shaft

Fig. 75 Removing the wheel side joint

WHEEL SIDE JOINT

REFERENCE MARKS

DRIVE AXLE SHAFT

Fig. 76 Aligning the reference marks for assembly

GREASE (PROVIDED WITH BOOT KIT)

WHEEL SIDE JOINT

WHEEL SIDE BOOT

Fig. 77 Packing the wheel side joint

SMALL WHEEL SIDE BOOT CLAMP

WHEEL SIDE BOOT

Fig. 78 Crimping the small wheel side boot clamp

TOWARD DIFFERENTIAL SIDE BOOT

SHORT SIDED SPLINES

TRI-POD JOINT SPIDER

Fig. 79 Installing the tri-pod joint spider

GREASE (PROVIDED WITH BOOT KIT)

DIFFERENTIAL SIDE JOINT HOUSING

Fig. 80 Packing the differential side joint housing

1. Differential side boot
2. Large differential side boot clamp

Fig. 81 Installing the large differential side boot clamp

857.4 mm
(33.756")

540.2 mm
(21.268")

1. Differential side joint housing
2. Drive axle shaft
3. Wheel side joint
4. Dynamic dampener

Fig. 82 Measuring the drive axle assemblies

CLUTCH

Adjustments

PEDAL HEIGHT AND FREE-PLAY

▶ See Figures 83 and 84

Adjust the pedal height to specification, by rotating the pedal stop.

1. Adjust the clearance between the master cylinder piston and the pushrod to 1-5mm (Nova) or 5-15mm (Prizm). Loosen the pushrod locknut and rotate the pushrod while depressing the clutch pedal lightly with your finger.
2. Tighten the locknut when finished with the adjustment.
3. Adjust the release cylinder free-play by loosening the release cylinder pushrod locknut and rotating the pushrod until the specification is obtained.

Fig. 83 Clutch pedal height and free-play adjustment

Fig. 84 Clutch pedal freeplay

4. Measure the clutch pedal free-play after performing the above adjustments. If it is not within specifications, repeat Steps 1-3 until it is.

Disc and Pressure Plate

REMOVAL & INSTALLATION

▶ See Figure 85

➡Do not allow grease or oil to get on any of the disc, pressure plate, or flywheel surfaces.

1. Remove the transaxle from the car as previously detailed.
2. Remove the clutch cover and disc from the bellhousing.
3. Unfasten the release fork bearing clips. Withdraw the release bearing hub, complete with the release bearing.
4. Remove the tension spring from the clutch linkage.
5. Remove the release fork and support.
6. Punch matchmarks on the clutch cover (pressure plate) and flywheel so that the pressure plate can be returned to its original position during installation.
7. Slowly unfasten the screws which attach the retracting springs. Loosen each screw 1 turn at a time until the tension is released.

8. Separate the pressure plate from the clutch cover/spring assembly.
9. Inspect the parts for wear or deterioration. It is strongly recommended that all 3 components of the clutch system-disc, pressure plate and bearing-be replaced as a unit if any part is worn. The slight additional cost of the parts is more than offset by not having to disassemble it again later on to replace another component.
10. Inspect the flywheel for any signs of cracking, bluing in the steel (a sign of extreme heat) or scoring. Any bluing or cracks which are found require replacement of the flywheel. While the flywheel will not be perfectly smooth, it should be free of all but the slightest ridges and valleys or scores. Any gouging deep enough to catch your fingernail during inspection requires replacement. A scored flywheel will immediately attack a new clutch disc, causing slippage and vibration. If the flywheel must be replaced, please refer to Section Three for further directions.

To install:

11. When reassembling, apply a thin coating of multipurpose grease to the release bearing hub and release fork contact points. Also, pack the groove inside the clutch hub with multipurpose grease and lubricate the pivot points of the release fork.
12. Align the matchmarks on the clutch cover and flywheel which were made during disassembly. Install the clutch and

Fig. 85 Always use a pilot tool when installing the clutch assembly

pressure plate assembly and tighten the retaining bolts just finger tight.

13. Center the clutch disc by using a clutch pilot tool or an old input shaft. (Pilot tools are available at most automotive parts stores.) Insert the pilot into the end of the input shaft front bearing, wiggle it gently to align the clutch disc and pressure plate and tighten the retaining bolts. The bolts should be tightened in 2 or 3 steps, gradually and evenly. Final bolt torque is 14 ft. lbs.

14. Install the release bearing, fork and boot.

15. Reinstall the transaxle as outlined previously in this Section.

Clutch Master Cylinder

➡**CHILTON TIP: When inspecting the clutch hydraulic system for leakage or impaired function, check the inside of the firewall (under the carpet) below the clutch master cylinder. A master cylinder leak may not show up under the cylinder on the engine side of the firewall.**

REMOVAL & INSTALLATION

1985-93

▶ **See Figure 86**

1. Drain or siphon the fluid from the master cylinder.
2. Disconnect the hydraulic line to the clutch from the master cylinder.

✳✳WARNING

Do not spill brake fluid on the painted surfaced of the vehicle.

3. Inside the car, remove the underdash panel and the air duct.
4. Remove the pedal return spring.
5. Remove the spring clip and clevis pin.
6. Unfasten the bolts which secure the master cylinder to the firewall. Withdraw the assembly from the firewall side.
To install:
7. Install the master cylinder with its retaining nuts to the firewall.
8. Connect the line from the clutch to the master cylinder.

9. Connect the clevis and install the clevis pin and spring clip.
10. Install the pedal return spring.
11. Fill the reservoir with clean, fresh brake fluid and bleed the system.
12. Check the cylinder and the hose connection for leaks.
13. Adjust the clutch pedal.
14. Reinstall the air duct and underdash cover panel.

OVERHAUL

▶ **See Figure 86**

1. Clamp the master cylinder body in a vise with protected jaws.
2. Separate the reservoir assembly from the master cylinder.
3. Remove the snapring and remove the pushrod/piston assembly.
4. Inspect the master cylinder bore for scoring, grooving or corrosion. If any of these conditions are observed, replace the cylinder. Inspect piston, spring, push rod and boot for damage or wear replace any parts which are worn or defective.
5. Before reassembly, coat all parts with clean brake fluid.
6. Install the piston assembly in the cylinder bore.
7. Fit the pushrod over the washer and secure them with the snapring.
8. Install the reservoir and tighten the nut.

Clutch Slave Cylinder

REMOVAL & INSTALLATION

✳✳WARNING

Do not spill brake fluid on the painted surface of the vehicle.

1. If access under the hood is limited, it may be easier to reach the actuator from under the vehicle. Raise the front of the car and support it with jackstands. Be sure that is supported securely.
2. If necessary, remove the rear splash shield to gain access to the release cylinder.
3. Remove the clutch fork return spring.
4. Unfasten the hydraulic line from the release cylinder by removing its retaining nut.
5. Remove the release cylinder retaining nuts and remove the cylinder.
To install:
6. Reinstall the cylinder to the clutch housing and tighten the bolts to 106 inch lbs (12 Nm).
7. Connect the hydraulic line and tighten it to 11 ft. lbs. (11 Nm).
8. Install the clutch release spring.
9. Bleed the system and remember to top up the fluid in the master cylinder when finished.
10. Install the splash shield if it was removed.
11. Lower the car to the ground.

1. Reservoir tank bolt
2. Reservoir tank
3. Clutch line
4. Mounting nut
5. Piston
6. Pushrod
7. Clevis pin
8. Spring clip
9. Clevis
10. Boot
11. Snap ring
12. Master cylinder

Fig. 86 Clutch master cylinder components — 1989-91

OVERHAUL

▶ **See Figure 87**

1. Remove the pushrod assembly and the rubber boot.
2. Withdraw the piston, complete with its cup; don't remove the cup unless it is being replaced.
3. Wash all the parts in brake fluid.
4. Replace any worn or damaged parts. Inspect the cylinder bore carefully for any sign of damage, wear or corrosion.
5. Before reassembly, coat all the parts in clean brake fluid. Insert the spring and piston into the cylinder.
6. Install the boot and insert the pushrod.

BLEEDING

▶ **See Figure 88**

1. Fill the master cylinder reservoir with brake fluid.

❋❋WARNING

Do not spill brake fluid on the painted surface of the vehicle!

2. Fit a tube over the bleeder plug and place the other end into a clean jar half-filled with brake fluid.
3. Depress the clutch pedal, loosen the bleeder plug with a wrench, and allow the fluid to flow into the jar.
4. Tighten the plug and then release the clutch pedal.

1. Bleeder screw
2. Cylinder
3. Boot
4. Push rod
5. Piston
6. Spring
7. Mounting bolts
8. Clutch line

Fig. 87 Clutch slave (actuator) cylinder components

Fig. 88 Slave cylinder bleeding

5. Repeat these steps until no air bubbles are visible in the bleeder tube.

AUTOMATIC TRANSAXLE

The Nova/Prizm family is found with 3 automatic transaxles, selected by the manufacturer for the best match of power transaxle characteristics and engine performance. The A131L 3-speed automatic transaxle and two 4-speed automatic transaxles, the A240E and A245E were used. Refer to the Automatic Transaxle Application chart in Section One.

The A131L transaxle is a 3-speed automatic, developed specifically for transversely mounted engines. The wide gear ratios and efficient torque converter combine with the built-in locking clutches to operate quietly and efficiently.

The A240E and A245E, 4-speed transaxles may also be referred to as an ECT type or Electronically Controlled Transaxle. Is is controlled by a microcomputer, allowing the driver to select either the Normal or Power mode. The system function is overseen by an electronic control module (ECM); shift behavior and timing are triggered by the computer rather than by internal oil pressures. Should the system malfunction, the ECM will select a gear which allows the car to be driven, although performance will be greatly reduced.

Troubles occurring with the automatic transaxle can be caused by either the engine, the electronics or the transaxle itself. These areas should be distinctly isolated during troubleshooting. Begin with the simplest of possibilities (low fluid, loose wires, etc.) and eliminate all the external causes before committing to transaxle removal and repair.

Fluid Pan and Filter

REMOVAL & INSTALLATION

1. Raise and safely support the vehicle.
2. Drain the transaxle fluid.
3. Carefully loosen and remove the bolts holding the oil pan. Tap around the pan lightly with a plastic mallet, breaking the gasket tension by vibration. Do not pry the pan down with a screwdriver or similar tool; the pan is lightweight metal and will deform, causing leaks.

6. When there are no more air bubbles, tighten the plug while keeping the clutch pedal fully depressed.
7. Top off the fluid in the master cylinder reservoir.
8. Check the system for leaks.

4. Remove all traces of gasket material from the pan and the transaxle mating faces. Clean then carefully with a plastic or wooden scraper. Do not gouge the metal.
5. Clean the pan thoroughly of all oil and sediment.
6. Remove the bolts holding the screen (filter) and remove it from the car. Note that the bolts holding the filter may be different lengths; they must be replaced in the correct positions at reassembly.

To install:
7. Install the filter and tighten the bolts to 89 inch lbs. (10 Nm).
8. Install a new gasket on the pan and bolt the pan into place. Snug the bolts in a crisscross pattern, working from the center out. Tighten the pan bolts to 44 inch lbs. (5 Nm).

➡**If the mating surfaces of the oil pan and transaxle are clean and straight, there is no need for gasket sealer during reassembly. The use of sealer is generally not recommended on these transaxles.**

9. Lower the vehicle to the ground and refill the automatic transaxle fluid.

Adjustments

THROTTLE VALVE (TV) CABLE

▶ **See Figure 89**

1. With the ignition **OFF**, depress the accelerator pedal all the way. On carbureted vehicles, check that the throttle plates are fully open. If they are not, adjust the throttle linkage.
2. Peel the rubber dust boot back from the throttle valve cable.
3. Loosen the adjustment nuts on the throttle cable bracket (rocker cover) just enough to allow cable housing movement.
4. Have an assistant depress the accelerator pedal fully.
5. Adjust the cable housing so that the distance between its end and the cable stop collar is 0-0.04 inches (0-1.0mm).
6. Tighten the adjustment nuts. Make sure that the adjustment hasn't changed. Install the dust boot.

Fig. 89 Throttle linkage adjustment — 0-0.04 inch (0--1mm)

NEUTRAL SAFETY/BACKUP SWITCH

1985-90

▶ See Figures 90 and 91

1. Locate the neutral safety switch on the side of the transaxle and loosen the switch retaining bolts.

2. Move the gear selector to the **NEUTRAL** position.

3. Disconnect the neutral safety switch connector and connect an ohmmeter between the 2 adjacent terminals on the switch lead.

4. Adjust the switch to the point where there is continuity between the 2 terminals. Tighten the retaining bolts.

5. Move the shift selector to **PARK** and check that continuity is present. Move the selector to any of the other

Fig. 91 Connect an ohmmeter between the terminals as shown — 1985-90

positions and check that there is no continuity when the car is in gear.

6. Reconnect the wiring to the switch.

1991-93

▶ See Figure 92

Adjust the switch by aligning the neutral basic line scribed in the switch with the groove in the switch sleeve.

SHIFT CONTROL CABLE

1985-90

1. Loosen the adjusting nut on the linkage and check the linkage for freedom of movement.

2. Push the manual lever fully toward the right side of the car as far as it will go.

3. Return the lever 2 notches to the **NEUTRAL** position.

4. Set the gear selector to **NEUTRAL**. While holding the selector slightly to the right, have someone tighten the adjusting nut on the manual lever.

1991-92

▶ See Figure 93

1. Loosen the cap nut on the manual lever.

2. Position the manual lever in the **NEUTRAL** range.

3. Set the shift selector to **NEUTRAL**.

4. Tighten the cap nut to 89 inch lbs. (10 Nm)

Fig. 90 Neutral safety switch adjustment — 1985-90

1. Neutral basic line
2. Switch sleeve groove
3. Switch bolts

Fig. 92 Park/neutral position switch adjustment — 1991-93

Fig. 93 Shift control cable adjustment — 1991-92

1993

▶ **See Figure 94**

1. Position the manual lever in the **NEUTRAL** range.
2. Raise and safely support the vehicle.
3. Remove the left splash shield by removing the 6 retaining bolts.
4. Remove the shift select cable nut, lock washer and the shift select cable from the manual lever.
5. Rotate the manual lever counterclockwise until it reaches the **PARK** position.
6. Rotate the manual lever clockwise 2 detent positions until the manual lever is in the neutral position.
7. Install the shift select cable into the manual lever and secure with the shift select cable nut.
8. Pull the shift select cable taut by making sure no deflection exists in the shift select cable. Tighten the shift select cable nut to 115 inch lbs. (13 Nm).
9. Install the splash shield bolts and tighten them to 44 inch lbs. (5 Nm).
10. Lower the vehicle.

➡ **After adjusting the shift select cable, check the following:**

11. With the ignition switch in the **LOCK** position and the manual selector lever in the **P**, park position try to manually push the vehicle. The vehicle should not move.
12. Verify that the vehicle cannot be driven in the **N**, neutral position.
13. Verify that the vehicle can be driven in the **D**, **2** and **L** positions.
14. Verify that the reverse gear does operate in **R**

Fig. 94 Shift select cable nut at the manual lever — 1993

Neutral Safety/Backup Switch

REPLACEMENT

The reverse light function is controlled by the neutral/start switch. When the switch is properly adjusted, the white lamps at the rear will only come on when the car is in reverse. Should it be necessary to replace the switch, simply unplug and unbolt it.

Automatic Transaxle

REMOVAL & INSTALLATION

1985-88 VIN Code 4 Engine With A131L Transaxle

▶ **See Figures 95 and 96**

1. Disconnect the negative battery cable
2. Remove the air intake tube.
3. Disconnect the speedometer cable and neutral start wiring connector at the transaxle. Loosen the lug nuts on the left front wheel.
4. Disconnect the thermostat housing at the transaxle.
5. Disconnect the ground cable at the transaxle.
6. Remove 1 upper mount to bracket bolt.
7. Label and disconnect any interfering wiring in the area of the transaxle case.
8. Disconnect the throttle valve cable at the carburetor.
9. Remove 2 upper bellhousing bolts.
10. Support the engine using either GM tool J-28467-A or equivalent.
11. Raise the vehicle and support it safely on stands.
12. Remove the left front wheel.
13. Remove the splash shields under the car.
14. Remove the center beam.
15. Disconnect the shift cable at the transaxle.
16. Remove the shift cable bracket.
17. Remove the cooler bracket and disconnect the cooler lines at the transaxle. Plug the lines to prevent leakage.
18. Remove the inspection cover on the bell housing and remove the torque converter bolts through the inspection hole.
19. Disconnect the left control arm at the ball joint.
20. Disconnect the right control arm at the ball joint.
21. Remove the right and left axle shafts from the transaxle.
22. Disconnect the starter bolts
23. Remove the 3 rear transaxle bolts.
24. Support the transaxle with a floor jack.
25. Remove the remaining mount bolts and remove the remaining bellhousing bolts.
26. Remove the transaxle from the vehicle. Handle the unit carefully and do not allow it to tip; the torque converter may fall from the unit and become damaged.

To install:

27. Before reinstallation, install the torque converter in the transaxle. If the converter has been drained, refill it with 2.3 US qts. of Dexron®II ATF. Refer to the Capacities Chart in Section 1.

28. Check the torque converter installation. Use a straightedge and calipers to check the distance between the face of the converter and the surface of the transaxle housing. Correct free space is more than 20mm.

29. Apply multi-purpose grease to the contact points of the torque converter and the crankshaft.

30. Place the transaxle on the jack and lift into position. Align the guide pin with 1 of the holes in the driveplate (flywheel) and align the 2 pins on the block with the converter housing holes. Temporarily install 1 bolt to hold everything together.

31. Install all of the transaxle housing bolts and tighten them. The larger bolts (12mm) should be tightened to 47 ft. lbs. and the smaller (10mm) bolts tightened to 34 ft. lbs.

32. Install the left engine mount and tighten the bolts to 38 ft, lbs.

33. Install the 6 torque converter bolts. Remove the guide pin and install the white bolt, then install the 5 yellow bolts. Tighten the bolts evenly and to 13 ft. lbs.

34. Install the inspection plate (engine rear cover plate).

35. Reinstall the starter.

36. Connect the drive shafts to the transaxle.

37. Install the center engine support and tighten the bolts to 29 ft. lbs.

38. Install the front and rear mounts, tightening the 4 bolts to 29 ft. lbs.

39. Connect the left and right control arms to the ball joints.

40. Reinstall the thermostat housing.

41. Connect the oil cooler lines to the transaxle.

42. Connect and adjust the shift control cable.

43. Install the speedometer cable.

44. Install and adjust the throttle valve cable.

45. Connect the neutral start switch connector. Connect or reposition any wiring which was moved to gain access during removal.

46. Install the air cleaner.

47. Fill the transaxle with the correct amount of Dexron®II ATF. If the transaxle has been disassembled and drained, install 5.8 US qts. If the transaxle was not disassembled and still contains fluid, add 2.4 US qts.

48. Double check all installation items, paying particular attention to loose hoses or hanging wires, untightened nuts, poor routing of hoses and wires (too tight or rubbing) and tools left in the engine area.

49. Install the splash shields below the engine. Install the left front wheel and lower the vehicle to the ground.

50. Connect the negative battery cable.

51. Start the engine and allow it to idle. With the wheels blocked front and rear and your foot on the brake, engage each gear and check that the transaxle engages properly. Check that the car will not roll in **PARK**.

52. Allow the engine to idle with the transaxle in **PARK**; check the fluid level on the dipstick. Check all assembly points for any sign of leakage.

1988 VIN Code 5 Engine With A240E Transaxle
▶ **See Figures 95 and 96**

1. Disconnect the negative battery cable.
2. Remove the air cleaner assembly.
3. Disconnect the neutral start switch.
4. Disconnect the solenoid valve wiring connector.
5. Disconnect the speed sensor.
6. Disconnect the speedometer cable.
7. Remove the water inlet assembly.
8. Remove the throttle cable from the throttle linkage.
9. Remove the transaxle dipstick tube.
10. Disconnect the battery ground cable from the transaxle housing.
11. Loosen, but do not remove the lug nuts on the left front wheel. Raise the vehicle and safely support it.
12. Drain the transaxle oil.
13. Remove the splash shields from under the engine.
14. Remove the shift control cable and brackets.
15. Disconnect the oil cooler lines at the transaxle. Plug the lines to prevent leakage.
16. Remove the front and rear engine mount bolts.
17. Remove the center engine mount member.
18. Carefully disconnect the oxygen sensor connector and remove the front exhaust pipe.
19. Disconnect and remove the left and right driveshafts from the transaxle.
20. Remove the left front wheel.
21. Remove the cotter pin, lock nut cap, lock nut and washer.

Fig. 95 Measuring converter to case clearance

Fig. 96 Using tool J-28467 to support the engine. An external hoist may be used but raising and lowering the car becomes difficult

22. Remove the brake caliper assembly and support it with stiff wire out of the way. Do not disconnect the hose. Do not allow the caliper to hang by the hose.

❋❋CAUTION

Brake pads and shoes contain asbestos, which has been determined to be a cancer causing agent. Never clean the brake surfaces with compressed air! Avoid inhaling any dust from brake surfaces! When cleaning brakes, use commercially available brake cleaning fluids.

23. Remove the brake disc.
24. Remove the steering knuckle from the lower control arm.
25. Remove the left driveshaft.
26. Remove the starter motor and the bracket (stiffener plate).
27. Remove the engine rear cover plate (inspection plate).
28. Remove the torque converter mounting bolts.
29. Lower the vehicle to the ground.
30. Support the engine using GM tool J-28467 or equivalent.
31. Remove the 3 bolts from the rear engine mount.
32. Raise and safely support the vehicle. Remember that the engine support is in place; make necessary adjustments during jacking.
33. Support the transaxle with a jack. Remove the transaxle, keeping it level.
34. Remove the torque converter.
To install:
35. Before reinstallation, install the torque converter in the transaxle. If the converter has been drained, refill it with 2.3 US qts. of Dexron®II ATF. Refer to the Capacities Chart in Section one.
36. Check the torque converter installation. Use a straightedge and calipers to check the distance between the face of the converter and the surface of the transaxle housing. Correct free space is more than 20mm.
37. Apply multi-purpose grease to the contact points of the torque converter and the crankshaft.
38. Place the transaxle on the jack and lift into position. Use a guide pin to align the holes in the driveplate (flywheel) and align the 2 pins on the block with the converter housing holes. Temporarily install 1 bolt to hold everything together.
39. Install all of the transaxle housing bolts and tighten them. The larger bolts (12mm) should be tightened to 47 ft. lbs. and the smaller (10mm) bolts tightened to 34 ft. lbs.
40. Install the 3 engine rear mount bolts and tighten them to 38 ft. lbs.
41. Install the 6 torque converter bolts. Remove the guide pin and install the white bolt, then install the 5 yellow bolts. Tighten the bolts evenly and to 20 ft. lbs.
42. Install the inspection plate (engine rear cover plate).
43. Reinstall the stiffener plate and the starter.
44. Install the left driveshaft with its washer, lock nut, lock nut cap and cotter pin.
45. Reconnect the steering knuckle to the lower control arm.
46. Install the brake disc. Install the caliper and tighten the mounting bolts to 18 ft. lbs.
47. Install the left front wheel; tighten the wheel nuts to 76 ft. lbs.
48. Connect both driveshafts to the transaxle.

49. Reinstall the front exhaust pipe using new gaskets. Connect the wiring to the oxygen sensor.
50. Install the engine center mounting member. Tighten the bolts to 29 ft. lbs.
51. Install the bolts for the front and rear engine mounts. Correct torque is 29 ft. lbs. When the mount bolts are secure, the engine support apparatus may be removed.
52. Connect the oil cooler lines to the transaxle.
53. Install the shift control cable and brackets.
54. Replace the splash shields under the engine.
55. Lower the vehicle to the ground.
56. Connect the ground strap to the transaxle housing.
57. Install the transaxle dipstick tube.
58. Install the water inlet assembly.
59. Attach the throttle cable to the linkage and adjust as necessary.
60. Install the speedometer cable and the speed sensor.
61. Connect the wiring to the solenoid valve.
62. Connect the wiring to the neutral start switch.
63. Install the air cleaner.
64. Fill the transaxle with the correct amount of Dexron® II ATF. If the transaxle has been disassembled and drained, install 7.6 US qts. If the transaxle was not disassembled and still contains fluid, add 3.1 US qts. Refer to the Capacities Chart in Section one.
65. Double check all installation items, paying particular attention to loose hoses or hanging wires, untightened nuts, poor routing of hoses and wires (too tight or rubbing) and tools left in the engine area.
66. Connect the negative battery cable.
67. Start the engine and allow it to idle. With the wheels blocked front and rear and your foot on the brake, engage each gear and check that the transaxle engages properly. Check that the car will not roll in **PARK**.
68. Allow the engine to idle with the transaxle in **PARK**; check the fluid level on the dipstick. Check all assembly points for any sign of leakage.

1989-92

▶ **See Figures 95 and 96**

1. Support the engine with GM tool J-28467-A or equivalent.
2. Remove the battery hold-down, battery and tray.
3. Remove the air cleaner assembly
4. Disconnect the connector at the neutral start switch.
5. Disconnect the ground strap from the transaxle case.
6. Remove the throttle cable from the throttle body.
7. Disconnect the cooling lines at the transaxle and plug the lines to prevent leakage.
8. Remove the shift cable retainer and end clip.
9. Remove the shift cable from its brackets and place the cable out of the way.
10. Remove the upper shift cable bracket from the transaxle housing.
11. Remove the left transaxle mount brace.
12. Remove the through bolt in the mount.
13. Remove the 2 upper transaxle-to-engine bolts.
14. Remove the upper starter bolts.
15. Disconnect the speedometer cable.
16. Raise the vehicle and safely support it.
17. Remove the splash shields from below the car.

18. Drain the transaxle oil.

19. Disconnect the electrical connections to the starter. Remove the bottom starter bolt and remove the starter.

20. Remove the driveshafts from the transaxle.

21. Remove the 3 bolts holding the center crossmember to the radiator support.

22. Remove the covers from the front and center mount bolts; remove the 2 front mount bolts, then the 2 center mount bolts.

23. Remove the 2 nuts from the rear mount.

24. Remove the 2 bolts holding the center crossmember to the main crossmember.

25. Remove the 3 nuts holding the exhaust hanger bracket and remove the bracket.

26. Use a floor jack to support the main crossmember. Check its placement carefully so that the crossmember will be balanced during removal.

27. Remove the 8 bolts holding the main crossmember to the underbody.

28. On the left and right sides, remove the 2 bolts holding the control arm bracket to the underbody.

✳✳CAUTION

Lower the main crossmember slowly while holding onto the center crossmember. The center crossmember is free to fall at this point and could cause serious injury or damage.

29. At the front mount, remove the through bolt and the mount.

30. Remove the front mount bracket from the transaxle.

31. Remove the center mount from the transaxle with its 2 bolts.

32. Remove the torque converter bolt shield and remove the bolts holding the torque converter to the flywheel.

33. Remove the 2 bolts holding the lower transaxle mount to the bracket.

34. Lower the vehicle to the ground.

35. Remove the remaining transaxle mount-to-bracket bolt.

36. Adjust the engine support apparatus to lower the transaxle and gain clearance for removal.

37. Disconnect the transaxle mount.

38. Raise and safely support the vehicle.

✳✳WARNING

The engine support apparatus has been repositioned and the crossmembers are removed. Be very careful when raising the car.

39. Use a floor jack to support the transaxle. Make sure it is properly positioned.

40. Remove the front and rear lower bolts holding the transaxle to the engine.

41. Carefully remove the transaxle, keeping it as level as possible. Remove the torque converter.

To install:

42. Before installing the transaxle, make sure that the torque converter is all the way into the pump and bushing. Use a straightedge across the front of the transaxle case and

measure the inset to the converter. Clearance must be at least 20mm.

43. Lightly coat the converter to flywheel contact point with multi-purpose grease.

44. Support the transaxle on the floor jack and move it into place. Install the transaxle and hold it in place with the front and rear lower transaxle-to- engine bolts. Tighten the bolts snugly; they will be final tightened later.

45. Remove the jack from under the transaxle.

46. Install the starter and its lower bolt snugly. Connect the starter wiring.

47. Lower the vehicle to the ground.

✳✳WARNING

The engine support apparatus has been repositioned and the crossmembers are removed. Be very careful when moving the car.

48. Install the left transaxle mount.

49. Install the bolt for the upper mount bracket and the 2 bolts for the lower bracket snugly.

50. Adjust the engine support apparatus to raise the transaxle into position.

51. Install the through bolt for the transaxle mount and tighten it to 64 ft. lbs. Tighten the upper transaxle mounting bracket bolt to 45 ft. lbs.

52. Install the brace at the mount and tighten the bolts to 13 ft. lbs.

53. Install the 2 upper transaxle-to-engine bolts snugly.

54. Install the upper starter bolt snugly.

55. Tighten all the transaxle-to-engine bolts to 34 ft. lbs.

56. Tighten the upper starter bolt to 29 ft. lbs.

57. Install the speedometer cable.

58. Install the upper shift cable bracket, position the shift cable into the bracket and install the cable retainer and end clips.

59. Install the oil cooling lines.

60. Connect the throttle cable at the throttle body.

61. Install the ground strap to the transaxle case.

62. Install the connector to the neutral start switch.

63. Install the air cleaner assembly.

64. Raise and safely support the vehicle.

65. Tighten the 2 lower transaxle mount bolts to 45 ft. lbs.

66. Tighten the lower starter bolt to 29 ft. lbs.

67. Install the torque converter to flywheel bolts and tighten them to 31 ft. lbs.

68. Install the converter bolt shield.

69. Install the center mount with 2 bolts to the transaxle; tighten the bolts to 45 ft. lbs.

70. Install the front mount bracket on the transaxle and tighten the bolts to 13 ft. lbs.

71. Install the front mount. Loosely install the through bolt.

➡As the front mount is installed, the weight on the mount must go towards the transaxle; this allows the mount to align properly.

72. Position the center crossmember over the center and rear transaxle mount studs. Start 2 nuts on the center mount.

73. Loosely install the 3 bolts which hold the center crossmember to the radiator support.

74. Loosely install the 2 front mount bolts.

75. Raise the main crossmember into position over the rear mounting studs.

76. Align all the under body bolts and bolt holes.

77. Install the 2 rear mount nuts loosely.

78. Loosely install the 8 bolts to hold the main crossmember to the underbody.

79. On each side, loosely install the 2 bolts holding control arm brackets to the underbody.

80. Loosely install the 2 bolts holding the center crossmember to the main crossmember.

81. Install the exhaust hanger bracket and its 3 nuts. The crossmembers, mounts, through bolts and brackets should now all be in place and held loosely by their nuts and bolts. If any repositioning is necessary, do so now.

82. Tighten the components below in the order listed to the correct torque specification:

    a. Main crossmember to underbody bolts: 152 ft. lbs.

    b. Lower control arm bolts: 94 ft. lbs.

    c. Center crossmember to radiator support bolts: 45 ft. lbs.

    d. Front, center and rear mount bolts: 45 ft. lbs.

    e. Exhaust hanger bracket nuts: 9.5 ft. lbs. (115 inch lbs.)

    f. Front mount through bolt: 64 ft. lbs.

83. Install the covers on the front and center mount bolts.

84. Reinstall the drive axles.

85. Fill the transaxle with the correct amount of Dexron®II ATF. If the transaxle has been disassembled and drained, install 5.8 US qts. If the transaxle was not disassembled and still contains fluid, add 2.4 US qts. Refer to the Capacities Chart in Section one.

86. Double check all installation items, paying particular attention to loose hoses or hanging wires, untightened nuts, poor routing of hoses and wires (too tight or rubbing) and tools left in the engine area.

87. Install the splash shields below the engine. Install the left front wheel and lower the vehicle to the ground.

88. Remove the engine support apparatus.

89. Install the battery tray, battery and hold-down.

90. Start the engine and allow it to idle. With the wheels blocked front and rear and your foot on the brake, engage each gear and check that the transaxle engages properly. Check that the car will not roll in **PARK**.

91. Allow the engine to idle with the transaxle in **PARK**; check the fluid level on the dipstick. Check all assembly points for any sign of leakage.

1993

◗ **See Figures 95, 96 and 97**

1. Disconnect the negative (-) battery cable.

2. Disconnect the intake air temperature (IAT) sensor electrical connector from the IAT sensor.

3. Remove the air cleaner (ACL) cover and ACL filter from ACL. Loosen the ACL intake tube clamp.

4. Remove the 3 bolts and ACL from the vehicle.

5. Remove the TV cable from the throttle linkage and TV cable bracket.

6. Remove the 2 bolts and the left transaxle mounting bracket reinforcement from the transaxle.

7. Remove the 1 bolt from the left transaxle mounting bracket.

8. Remove 1 bolt and the ground strap from the transaxle.

9. Remove 1 bolt and the throttle cable guide bracket from the transaxle.

10. Disconnect the vehicle speed sensor (VSS) electrical connector from VSS.

11. Remove the 3 upper transaxle-to-engine bolts from the transaxle. Install the tool J 28467-89 along with a J 28467-A or equivalent. Raise and suitably support the vehicle.

12. Remove the 12 bolts and the right and left splash shields from the vehicle. Place a drain pan or suitable container underneath the transaxle fluid pan.

13. Remove the transaxle drain plug from the transaxle fluid pan and drain the transaxle fluid.

14. Remove the differential filler plug from the differential cover at the rear of the transaxle, on vehicles equipped with the A131L transaxle.

15. Remove the differential drain plug from the transaxle and drain the differential fluid, A131L transaxle only.

16. Remove the right and left drive axles from the vehicle.

17. Remove the 2 bolts from the exhaust pipe support.

18. Remove 1 nut and exhaust pipe support from the center crossmember.

19. Disconnect the oxygen sensor O2 electrical connector from O2 at the front exhaust pipe (California specification vehicles).

20. Remove the 2 bolts from the front exhaust pipe-to-three way catalytic converter (TWC) mating flange.

21. Remove the 2 nuts from the front exhaust pipe-to-warm up three way catalytic converter (WU-TWC) mating flange and front exhaust pipe from vehicle (California specification vehicles).

22. Remove the 2 nuts from the front exhaust pipe-to-exhaust manifold mating flange and front exhaust pipe from vehicle.

23. Remove the plastic cover from the front transaxle mounting cavity in center crossmember.

24. Remove the 14 bolts, 3 nuts, and the front suspension crossmember and center crossmember from the vehicle.

25. Remove the starter motor positive (+) terminal nut, positive(+) battery cable and the electrical connector from the starter motor.

26. Remove the 2 bolts and the starter motor from the transaxle.

27. Disconnect the park/neutral position (PNP) switch electrical connector from the PNP switch.

28. Disconnect the solenoid wire harness electrical connector from the solenoid wire harness (A245E).

29. Remove 1 nut, 1 lock washer and the shift select cable from the manual lever.

30. Remove 1 E-clip and the shift select cable from the shift select cable bracket at the transaxle.

➡**Plug the fluid cooler hoses to prevent transaxle fluid cooler leakage.**

31. Remove the 2 fluid cooler hose clamps and the fluid cooler hoses from the fluid cooler pipes at the transaxle.

32. Remove the flywheel cover from the engine rear end plate.

33. Remove 6 flywheel-to-torque converter bolts from the flywheel. Remove the drain pan from underneath the transaxle fluid pan. Support the transaxle with a suitable hydraulic jack.

34. Remove the 2 bolts from the left transaxle mounting bracket.

35. Remove the 5 lower transaxle-to-engine bolts from the transaxle.

36. Remove the transaxle from the engine by carefully moving the transaxle away from the engine toward the left side of the engine compartment and very slowly lowering the hydraulic jack making sure no obstructions exist.

To install:

37. Before installing the transaxle assembly, these steps and precautions must be followed:

　a. Apply grease around the pilot at the center of the torque converter. This will ensure ease of assembly.

　b. Measure the distance between the outside edge of the torque converter housing and the torque converter lug. The distance should be more than 0.906-inch (23 mm). If it is less than 0.906-inch (23 mm), the torque converter is improperly installed. Remove the torque converter and properly seat it on the input shaft.

38. Install the transaxle to the engine by carefully raising the transaxle using a suitable hydraulic jack making sure no obstructions exist.

39. Connect 5 lower transaxle-to-engine bolts into the transaxle. Tighten transaxle-to-engine bolts to 47 ft. lbs. (64 Nm).

40. Install 2 bolts into the left transaxle mounting bracket. Tighten the left transaxle mounting bracket bolts to 17 ft. lbs. (23 Nm). Remove the hydraulic jack from underneath the transaxle.

41. Install 6 flywheel-to-torque converter bolts into the flywheel. Tighten the flywheel-to-torque converter bolts to 14 ft. lbs. (19 Nm).

42. Install the flywheel cover into the engine rear end plate.

43. Connect the fluid cooler hoses to fluid cooler pipes at the transaxle; secure with two fluid cooler hose clamps.

44. Install shift select cable into the shift select cable bracket at the transaxle; secure with one E-clip.

45. Install shift select cable to manual lever and secure with 1 nut and 1 lock washer. Adjust the shift select cable.

46. Install the solenoid wire harness electrical connector to the solenoid wire harness.

47. Install PNP switch electrical connector to the PNP switch.

48. Install the starter motor into the transaxle and secure with 2 bolts. Tighten the starter motor bolts to 29 ft. lbs. (39 Nm).

49. Install the starter motor electrical connector and the positive (+) battery cable to the starter motor; secure with starter motor positive (+) terminal nut. Tighten the starter motor positive (+) terminal nut to 44 inch lbs. (5 Nm).

50. Install the center crossmember and the front suspension crossmember to the vehicle and secure with the 3 nuts and 14 bolts. Tighten the center crossmember and the front suspension crossmember bolts and nuts as shown:

　A bolt: 45 ft. lbs. (61 Nm)
　B bolt: 47 ft. lbs. (64 Nm)
　C bolt: 152 ft. lbs. (206 Nm)
　D bolt: 152 ft. lbs. (206 Nm)
　E nut: 42 ft. lbs. (57 Nm)

A. Bolt
B. Bolt
C. Bolt
D. Bolt
1. Center crossmember
2. Front suspension crossmember
3. Right control arm
4. Left control arm

Fig. 97 Tighten the front suspension crossmember and center crossmember bolts and nuts to the values outlined in the text.

51. Install the plastic cover into the front transaxle mounting cavity in the center crossmember.

52. Install the front exhaust pipe to the vehicle and secure with the 2 nuts at the front exhaust pipe-to-exhaust manifold mating flange. Tighten the front exhaust pipe-to-exhaust manifold nuts to 46 ft. lbs. (62 Nm).

53. Install the front exhaust pipe to the vehicle and secure with the 2 nuts at front exhaust pipe-to-WU-TWC mating flange (California specification vehicles). Tighten the front exhaust pipe-to-WU-TWC mating flange nuts to 46 ft. lbs. (62 Nm).

54. Install the 2 bolts to the front exhaust pipe-to-TWC mating flange. Tighten the front exhaust pipe-to-TWC mating flange bolts to 32 ft. lbs. (43 Nm). (California specification vehicles).

55. Install the O2 electrical connector to the O2 at the front exhaust pipe (California specification vehicles).

56. Install the exhaust pipe support to center crossmember and secure with the 1 nut. Tighten the exhaust pipe support not to 14 ft. lbs. (19 Nm).

57. Install the exhaust pipe support to the front exhaust pipe and secure with the 2 bolts. Tighten the exhaust pipe support bolts to 14 ft. lbs. (19 Nm)

58. Install the right and left drive axles into the vehicle.

59. Install the differential drain plug into the transaxle, on A131L transaxles only. Tighten the differential drain plug to 11 ft. lbs. (15 Nm).

✳✳WARNING

The differential portion of the A131L 3-speed automatic transaxle is separated from the rest of the transaxle and must be drained and refilled separately. The differential portion of the A131L 3-speed automatic transaxle cannot be drained or refilled through the transaxle drain plug or fluid filler tube. If the differential portion is drained and not refilled as outlined in this procedure, damage to the differential due to lack of lubrication will result.

60. Refill differential with approximately 1.5 qts. (1.4 liters) of Dexron®II Automatic Transmission Fluid GM P/N 1051855, or equivalent into the differential filler plug hole. Fluid level should be even with the bottom of the differential filler plug hole (A131L). Install the differential filler plug into the differential cover at the rear of the transaxle (A131L). Tighten the differential filler plug to 11 ft. lbs. (15 Nm).

61. Install the transaxle drain plug into the transaxle fluid pan. Tighten the transaxle drain plug to 13 ft. lbs. (17 Nm).

62. Install the right and left splash shields to the vehicle and secure with the 12 bolts. Tighten the splash shield bolts to 44 inch lbs. (5 Nm). Lower the vehicle. Remove the tool J 28467-A along with tool J 28467-89.

63. Install the 3 upper transaxle-to-engine bolts into the transaxle. Tighten the transaxle-to-engine bolts to 47 ft. lbs. (64 Nm).

64. Install the VSS electrical connector the VSS.

65. Install the TV cable guide bracket onto the transaxle and secure with the 1 bolt. Tighten the TV cable guide bracket bolt to 71 inch lbs. (8 Nm).

66. Install the ground strap to the transaxle and secure with the 1 bolt. Tighten the ground strap bolt to 115 inch lbs. (13 Nm).

67. Install the 1 bolt into the left transaxle mounting bracket. Tighten the left transaxle mounting bracket bolt to 17 ft. lbs. (23 Nm).

68. Install the left transaxle mounting bracket reinforcement onto the transaxle and secure with the 2 bolts. Tighten the left transaxle mounting bracket reinforcement bolts to 17 ft. lbs. (23 Nm).

69. Install the TV cable into TV cable bracket and throttle linkage. Adjust the TV cable as outlined earlier in this Section.

70. Install ACL into the vehicle and secure with the 3 bolts. Tighten the ACL bolts to 44 inch lbs. (5 Nm). Tighten the ACL intake tube clamp.

71. Install the ACL filter and the ACL cover onto the ACL.

72. Install the IAT sensor electrical connector to IAT sensor.

73. Install the negative (-) battery cable. Tighten the negative battery cable-to-negative battery terminal retainer to 11 ft. lbs. (15 Nm).

74. Refill the transaxle as necessary. Please refer to Capacities Chart in Section 1.

TORQUE SPECIFICATIONS

Component	U.S.	Metric
Backup light switch mounting bolts:		
With Manual transaxle		
1988–88:	30 ft. lbs.	40.8 Nm
1989–93:	15 ft. lbs.	20.4 Nm
Manual Transaxle Mounting		
1989–93 Models;		
Front mount bracket bolts:	45 ft. lbs.	61 Nm
Front mount thru bolts:	45 ft. lbs.	61 Nm
Front mount mounting bolts:	45 ft. lbs.	61 Nm
Center mount to transaxle bolts:	45 ft. lbs.	61 Nm
Left mount thru bolts:	64 ft. lbs.	87 Nm
Left mount bracket bolts:	45 ft. lbs.	61 Nm
Rear mount thru bolt:	64 ft. lbs.	87 Nm
Transaxle to engine bolts:	34 ft. lbs.	46 Nm
Center crossmember to main crossmember bolts:	45 ft. lbs.	61 Nm
Center crossmember to radiator support bolts:	45 ft. lbs.	61 Nm
Main crossmember to underbody bolts:	152 ft. lbs.	206 Nm
Lower A frame to underbody bolts:	94 ft. lbs.	127 Nm
Oil drain plug:	97 inch lbs.	11 Nm
Oil fill plug:	97 inch lbs.	11 Nm
Clutch cover bolts:	14 ft. lbs.	19 Nm
Flywheel bolts:	58 ft. lbs.	78 Nm
Master cylinder mounting nuts:	11 ft. lbs.	15 Nm
Automatic Transaxle Mounting		
1985–88 Models;		
12mm bolts:	47 ft. lbs.	64 Nm
10mm bolts:	34 ft. lbs.	46 Nm
Left side engine bolts:	38 ft. lbs.	52 Nm
Converter mounting bolts;		
A131L trans.	13 ft. lbs.	18 Nm
A240E trans.	20 ft. lbs.	27 Nm
Four engine mounting center support bolts:	29 ft. lbs.	39 Nm
Four front and rear mount bolts:	29 ft. lbs.	39 Nm

TORQUE SPECIFICATIONS

Component	U.S.	Metric
Automatic Transaxle Mounting		
1989–92 Models;		
Front mount thru bolts:	64 ft. lbs.	87 Nm
Front mount mounting bolts:	45 ft. lbs.	61 Nm
Center mount mounting nuts:	45 ft. lbs.	61 Nm
Center crossmember to main crossmember bolts:	45 ft. lbs.	61 Nm
Center crossmember to radiator support bolts:	45 ft. lbs.	61 Nm
Main crossmember to underbody bolts:	152 ft. lbs.	206 Nm
Lower A frame to underbody bolts:	94 ft. lbs.	127 Nm
Flywheel to torque converter or flexplate bolts:	31 ft. lbs.	42 Nm
Differential fill and drain plug:	29 ft. lbs.	39 Nm
Differential check fill plug:	29 ft. lbs.	39 Nm
Automatic Transaxle Mounting;		
1993 Models;		
Flywheel to torque converter bolts:	14 ft. lbs.	19 Nm
Differential fill plug (A131L)	11 ft. lbs.	15 Nm
Differential drain plug (A131L):	11 ft. lbs.	15 Nm
Transaxle to engine bolts:	47 ft. lbs.	64 Nm
Transaxle fluid pan bolts:	44 inch lbs.	5 Nm
Fluid filter screen bolts:	89 inch lbs.	10 Nm
Transaxle drain plug:	13 ft. lbs.	17 Nm
Center crossmember and front suspension bolts and nuts;		
A bolt:	45 ft. lbs.	61 Nm
B bolt:	47 ft. lbs.	64 Nm
C bolt:	152 ft. lbs.	206 Nm
D bolt:	152 ft. lbs.	206 Nm
E nut:	42 ft. lbs.	57 Nm

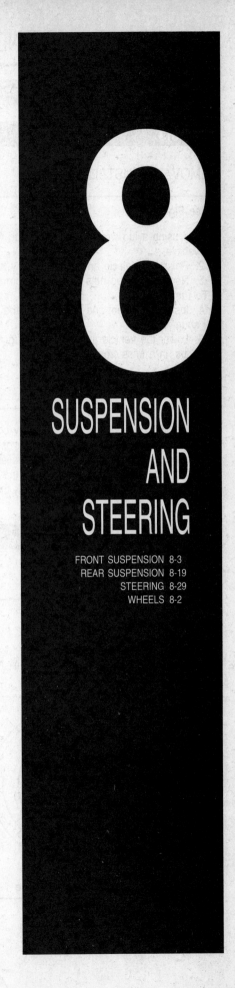

8

SUSPENSION AND STEERING

WHEELS

Wheels

REMOVAL & INSTALLATION

▶ **See Figure 1**

1. If using a lug wrench, loosen the lug nuts before raising the vehicle.
2. Raise the vehicle and support safely.
3. Remove the lug nuts and wheel from the vehicle.

To install:

4. Install the wheel and hand tighten the lug nuts until they are snug.
5. Lower the vehicle and torque the lug nuts EVENLY to 76 ft. lbs. in a criss-cross pattern.

INSPECTION

Before putting on wheels, check for any cracks on wheels or enlarged mounting holes, remove any corrosion on the mounting surfaces with a wire brush. Installation of wheels without a good metal-to-metal contact at the mounting surface can cause wheel nuts to loosen. Recheck the wheel nuts after 1,000 miles of driving.

Wheel Lug Studs

REPLACEMENT

Front Wheel

▶ **See Figure 2**

1. Raise and support the vehicle safely. Remove the front wheel.

2. Remove the front brake caliper and disc rotor.
3. Remove the hub bolt using a removal tool.

To install:

4. Install the new hub bolt and draw into place using the nut and a stack of washers. The new hub bolt must be fully seated in the hub assembly.
5. Install front brake disc and front brake caliper. Torque the brake caliper to 65 ft. lbs.
6. Install front wheel and lower the vehicle.

Rear Wheel

DRUM BRAKES

1. Raise the vehicle and support safely.
2. Remove the wheel.
3. Remove the brake drum from the vehicle.
4. Drive the lug bolt out of the axle hub using a stud removal tool.

To install:

5. Draw the lug bolt into the axle hub using the nut and a stack of washers.
6. Install the brake drum onto the vehicle.
7. Install the wheel and lower the vehicle.

REAR DISC BRAKES

1. Raise the vehicle and support safely.
2. Remove the rear wheel.
3. Remove the rear caliper and brake rotor.
4. Remove the wheel lug bolt by tapping bolt through hub with a hammer or using a stud removal tool.

To install:

5. Draw the new lug bolt into the hub using the nut and a stack of washers.
6. Install the brake rotor. Install rear brake caliper and torque to 25 ft. lbs. (14 Nm).
7. Install the rear wheel and lower the vehicle.

Fig. 1 Wheel nut tightening sequence

Fig. 2 Wheel stud removal tool

FRONT SUSPENSION

✳✳CAUTION

Exercise great caution when working with the front suspension. Coil springs and other suspension components are under extreme tension and result in severe injury if released improperly. Never remove the nut on the top of the shock absorber piston without using the proper spring compressor tool.

Spring and Shock Absorbers/MacPherson Strut

TESTING

Shock Absorbers

The purpose of the shock absorber is simply to limit the motion of the spring during compression (bump) and rebound cycles. If the car were not equipped with these motion dampers, the up and down motion of the springs would multiply until the vehicle was alternately trying to leap off the ground and to pound itself into the pavement.

Contrary to popular rumor, the shocks do not affect the ride height of the car nor do they affect the ride quality except for limiting the pitch or bounce of the car. These factors are controlled by other suspension components such as springs and tires. Worn shock absorbers can affect handling; if the front of the car is rising or falling excessively, the 'footprint" of the tires changes on the pavement and steering response is affected. The simplest test of the shock absorbers is simply to push down on one corner of the unladen car and release it.

Observe the motion of the body as it is released. In most cases, it will come up beyond its original rest position, dip back below it and settle quickly to rest. This shows that the damper is slowing and controlling the spring action. Any tendency to excessive pitch (up-and-down) motion or failure to return to rest within 2-3 cycles is a sign of poor function within the shock absorber.

While each shock absorber can be replaced individually, it is recommended that they be changed as a pair (both front or both rear) to maintain equal response on both sides of the car. Chances are quite good that if one has failed, its mate is weak also.

MacPherson Struts

▶ **See Figures 3, 4 and 5**

The struts are precise parts and retain the springs under tremendous pressure even when removed from the car. For this reason, several special tools and substantial specialized knowledge are required to safely and effectively work on these components. If spring and shock absorber work is required, it may not be a bad idea to remove the strut involved yourself and then consider taking it to a repair facility which is fully equipped and familiar with the car.

REMOVAL

▶ **See Figures 6, 7 and 8**

1. Under the hood, remove the 3 or 4 small nuts holding the top of the strut to the shock tower. DO NOT loosen the larger center nut.
2. Loosen the wheel lug nuts at the appropriate wheel.
3. Raise the vehicle and safely support it. It need not be any higher than the distance necessary to separate the tire from the ground. Do not place the jackstands under the control arms.
4. Remove the wheel. Install a cover over the driveshaft boot to protect it from fluid and impact damage.
5. On Nova vehicles:
   a. Remove the brake flex hose clip at the strut bracket.
   b. Disconnect the brake flex hose from the brake pipe at the strut. Remove the brake hose clips. Use a small pan to catch any leakage.
   c. Pull the brake hose back through the opening in the strut bracket. Plug the lines to prevent any dirt form entering.
   d. Remove the 2 brake caliper mounting bolts and remove the caliper. Hang it out of the way with a piece of wire. Do not allow it to hang by the flex hose and do not disconnect the hose from the caliper.
   e. Mark the position of the adjusting cam for reassembly.
6. On Prizm vehicles:
   a. Disconnect the brake hose from the brake caliper and drain the fluid into a small pan.
   b. Remove the clip from the brake hose and remove the hose from the bracket.
   c. Disconnect the ABS sensor wire from the shock absorber if so equipped.
   d. Use a sharp instrument or scribing tool to make matchmarks in all three dimensions on the steering knuckle. The strut must be reinstalled in its exact previous position.
7. Remove the 2 bolts which attach the shock absorber to the steering knuckle. The steering knuckle bolt holes have collars that extend about 5mm. Be careful to clear them when separating the steering knuckle from the strut assembly.

➡**Press down on the lower suspension arm in order to remove the strut assembly. This must be done to clear the collars on the steering knuckle bolt holes when removing the strut assembly.**

8. Remove the strut assembly. Remember that the spring is still under tension. It will stay in place as long as the top nut on the shock piston shaft is not loosened. Handle the strut carefully and do not allow the coating on the spring to become damaged.

1. Dust cover
2. Strut shaft nut
3. Strut support nut
4. Strut support
5. Spring seal
6. Spring seat
7. Spring bumper
8. Upper insulator
9. Coil spring
10. Lower insulator
11. Shock absorber/strut
12. Nut
13. Camber adjustment cam

14. Bolt
15. Steering knuckle
16. Ball joint nut
17. Lower ball joint
18. Dust deflector
19. Inner grease seal
20. Snapring
21. Front axle hub bearing
22. Outer grease seal
23. Wheel stud
24. Front axle hub
25. Brake disc
26. Hub washer

27. Nut
28. Cap
29. Cotter pin
30. Control arm nut
31. Bushing retainer
32. Bushing bracket
33. Bolt
34. Bushing
35. Bushing retainer
36. Lower control arm
37. Bolt
38. Bolt
39. Nut

Fig. 3 Front suspension — 1985-88 VIN code 4 engine

DISASSEMBLY

▶ See Figures 9 and 10

❊❊CAUTION

This procedure requires the use of a spring compressor; it cannot be performed without one. If you do not have access to this special tool, do not attempt to disassemble the strut. The coil springs are retained under considerable pressure. They can exert enough force to cause serious injury. Exercise extreme caution when disassembling the strut.

1. Place the strut assembly in a pipe vise or strut vise.

❊❊WARNING

Do not attempt to clamp the strut assembly in a flat jaw vise as this will result in damage to the strut tube.

2. Attach a spring compressor and compress the spring until the upper spring retainer is free of any spring tension. Do not over-compress the spring.

3. Use a spring seat holder to hold the upper support and then remove the nut on the end of the shock piston rod.

4. Remove the bearing plate, the support and the upper spring retainer. Slowly and cautiously unscrew the spring

1. Dust cover
2. Strut shaft nut
3. Strut support nut
4. Strut support
5. Support seal
6. Spring seat
7. Upper insulator
8. Coil spring
9. Lower insulator
10. Shock absorber/strut
11. Camber adjustment cam
12. Nut
13. Bolt
14. Nut
15. Steering knuckle

16. Lower ball joint
17. Dust deflector
18. Inner grease seal
19. Snapring
20. Front axle hub bearing
21. Outer hub seal
22. Wheel stud
23. Front axle hub
24. Brake disc
25. Hub washer
26. Nut
27. Cap
28. Cotter pin
29. Nut
30. Bushing retainer

31. Bushing bracket
32. Bolt
33. Control arm bushing
34. Bushing retainer
35. Lower control arm
36. Bolt
37. Nut
38. Bolt
39. Nut
40. Stabilizer bar retainer
41. Insulator
42. Stabilizer bar
43. Bracket
44. Bolt

Fig. 4 Front suspension — 1988 VIN code 5 engine

1. Strut rod piston nut
2. Suspension support
3. Dust seal
4. Spring seat
5. Upper insulator
6. Coil spring
7. Spring bumper
8. Lower insulator
9. Shock absorber
10. Brake line gaskets
11. Brake line to caliper bolt
12. Nut and bolt
13. Brake hose clip
14. Cotter pin
15. Ball joint castle nut
16. Ball joint
17. Nuts and bolt
18. Crossmember mounting nuts
19. Bolt
20. Crossmember mounting bolts
21. Suspension crossmember

Fig. 5 Front suspension — Prizm

compressor until all spring tension is relieved. Remove the spring and the dust cover.

➡**Do not allow the piston rod to retract into the shock absorber. If it falls, screw a nut onto the rod and pull the rod out by the nut. Do not use pliers to grip the rod as they will damage its surface, resulting in leaks, uneven operation or seal damage. Be extremely careful not to stress or hit the rod.**

INSPECTION

Check the shock absorber by moving the piston shaft through its full range of travel. It should move smoothly and evenly throughout its entire travel without any trace of binding or notching. Use a small straightedge to check the piston shaft

for any bending or deformation. If a Prizm shock absorber is replaced, the old one should be drilled at the bottom to vent the internal gas. Wear safety goggles and drill a small hole (2-3mm) into the base of the shock absorber. The gas within the strut is colorless, odorless and non-toxic, but should be vented to make the unit safe for disposal.

Inspect the spring for any sign of deterioration or cracking. The waterproof coating on the coils should be intact to prevent rusting. A quick check for a cracked spring is to hit the spring sharply with a small metal mallet or wrench handle. An intact spring will resonate, similar to a distant gong; a cracked spring will have much less resonance and a distinctly different sound.

Check the upper strut mount assembly for any abnormal noise, binding or restricted motion. Lubricate the upper bearing with multi-purpose grease before reinstallation.

Fig. 6 Upper strut retaining nuts. Nova with VIN code 5 engine has four, all others have 3 per strut.

Fig. 7 Use care in disconnecting the brake lines. Nova above, Prizm below

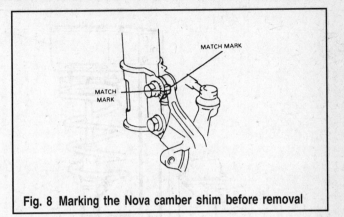

Fig. 8 Marking the Nova camber shim before removal

Fig. 9 Marking the Prizm steering knuckle before disassembly

ASSEMBLY AND INSTALLATION

▶ See Figures 11 and 12

❊❊WARNING

Never reuse a self-locking nut. Always replace self-locking nuts with new hardware.

1. Loosely assemble all components onto the strut assembly. Make sure the mark on the upper spring seat is facing the outside of the vehicle.

2. Compress the spring, carefully aligning the shaft guide rod with the hole in the upper mount. Align the lower spring seat. Do not over-compress the spring; compress it just enough to allow installation of the shaft nut.

3. Install the shaft nut and tighten it until the strut shaft begins to rotate.

4. Double check that the spring is correctly seated in the upper and lower mounts and reposition it as needed. Slowly release the tension on the spring compressor and remove it from the strut assembly.

5. Tighten the shaft nut to 34 ft. lbs.

6. On Nova vehicles, install the camber adjusting cam into the knuckle, observing the matchmarks made during disassembly.

Fig. 10 GM tools for compressing the spring and disassembling the strut. Equivalent tools may be rented from a reputable supply house.

Fig. 11 Make sure the upper strut seat marks face to the outside during reassembly.

Fig. 12 The strut to knuckle bolts must be set to the correct tightness.

7. Place the strut assembly in position and install the strut to knuckle attaching bolts. Tighten the bolts to the correct torque:

- Nova with VIN code 4 engine: 105 ft. lbs.
- Nova with VIN code 5 engine: 166 ft. lbs.
- All Prisms: 194 ft. lbs.

8. Using a floor jack and a piece of wood, gently elevate the control arm to the point that the upper mount can be aligned with the holes in the shock tower. Insert the bolts into the upper holes and install the nuts. Tighten the nuts to 23 ft. lbs. (Nova with VIN Code 4 engine) or 29 ft. lbs. (Nova with VIN code 5 engine and all Prizms).

9. Pack the shaft nut area with grease and install the dust cover.

10. On Nova vehicles, install the brake caliper and tighten the bolts to 65 ft. lbs. Pull the brake hose through the strut

bracket opening and connect the fitting. Tighten the fitting to 11 ft. lbs. Install the flex hose clip at the strut bracket.

11. On Prizm vehicles, install the brake hose in the bracket and install the clip. Connect the hose to the caliper and tighten the fitting to 22 ft. lbs. Connect the ABS sensor wire to the shock absorber, if so equipped.

12. Install the wheel and install the lug nuts snugly.

13. Lower the vehicle to the ground. Tighten the wheel lug nuts to 76 ft. lbs.

14. Bleed the brake system and top up the brake fluid level. Please refer to Section 9 for complete directions.

Lower Ball Joint

INSPECTION

Raise the front of the vehicle and safely support it on stands. Do not place stands under the control arms; the arms must hang free. Grasp the tire at the top and bottom and move the top of the tire through an in-and-out motion. Look for any horizontal motion in the steering knuckle relative to the control arm. Such motion is an indication of looseness within the ball joint. If the joint is checked while disconnected from the knuckle, it should have minimal or no freeplay and should not twist in its socket under finger pressure. Replace any joint showing looseness or free play.

REMOVAL & INSTALLATION

▶ **See Figure 13**

➡**The use of the correct tools is REQUIRED for this procedure. A ball joint separator is a commonly available tool which prevents damage to the joint and knuckle. Do not attempt to separate the joint with hammers, prybars or similar tools.**

1. Elevate and safely support the front of the vehicle. Do not place the stands under the control arms; they must hang free.

➡**Do not allow the driveshaft joints to over-extend. The CV joints can become disconnected under extreme extension.**

2. Install a protective cover over the CV boot.

3. Remove the wheel.

4. Remove the cotter pin from the ball joint nut.

5. Loosen the castle nut but do not remove it. Unscrew it just to the top of the threads and install the ball joint separator. (GM Tool 34754 or equivalent) Use the nut to bear on the tool; this protects the threaded shaft from damage during removal.

6. Use the separator to loosen the ball joint from the steering knuckle.

7. Remove the nuts and bolt holding the ball joint to the control arm.

8. Remove the ball joint from the control arm and steering knuckle.

9. When reinstalling, attach the ball joint to the control arm and tighten the 2 bolts and 1 nut to 105 ft. lbs. (Prizm) or 59 ft. lbs. (Nova).

10. Carefully install the ball joint to the steering knuckle. Use a new castle nut and tighten it to 94 ft. lbs. (Prizm) or 82 ft. lbs. (Nova).

11. Install the cotter pin through the castle nut and stud.

12. Remove the protector from the CV boot.

13. Install the wheel.

14. Lower the vehicle to the ground.

Stabilizer Bar or Sway Bar

REMOVAL & INSTALLATION

Nova with VIN Code 5 Engine

▶ **See Figure 14**

1. Disconnect the sway bar links from the lower control arms.

2. Disconnect the sway bar brackets from the body.

➡**CHILTON TIP: Check the bushings inside the brackets for wear or deformation. A worn bushing can cause a distinct bang or 'thunk" as the bar twists during cornering.**

3. Disconnect the exhaust pipe from the exhaust manifold.

4. Remove the sway bar from the car. Examine the insulators (bushings) carefully for any sign of wear and replace them if necessary.

5. To reinstall, place the bar in position and reconnect the exhaust system using new nuts. Tighten the nuts to 46 ft. lbs.

Fig. 13 Using the ball joint separator

Fig. 14 Front stabilizer bar link and bushings

6. Install both stabilizer bar brackets and tighten the bolts to 14 ft. lbs.

7. Connect the sway bar links to the control arms with the bolts, insulators and new nuts. Tighten the nuts to 13 ft. lbs.

1991-92 GSi Models

▶ See Figure 15

1. Raise and safely support the vehicle.
2. Remove the left stabilizer link from the stabilizer bar.
3. Remove the right stabilizer link from the stabilizer bar.
4. Remove the catalytic converter from the front exhaust pipe.
5. Remove the right stabilizer bracket from the floor pan.
6. Remove the left stabilizer bracket from the floor pan.
7. Remove the stabilizer bar from the vehicle. Remove the bushing brackets and retainers from the stabilizer bar.

To install:

8. Installation is the reverse of the removal procedure. Use the following torque specifications:

   a. Torque the bushing bracket retaining bolts to 29 ft. lbs. (39 Nm).

   b. Torque the left and right stabilizer link nuts to 26 ft. lbs. (35 Nm).

   c. Torque the left and right stabilizer bracket bolts to 94 ft. lbs. (127 Nm).

   d. Torque the left and right stabilizer bracket nut and bolt to 14 ft. lbs. (19 Nm).

9. To remove the stabilizer link, use the following procedure.

   a. With the vehicle still raise and safely supported, remove the stabilizer link from the stabilizer bar.

   b. Remove the stabilizer link from the control arm.

   c. Remove the stabilizer link from the vehicle.

10. Torque the stabilizer link nuts to 26 ft. lbs. (35 Nm).

Lower Control Arm

REMOVAL & INSTALLATION

1985-88 Nova

1. Raise and safely support the vehicle. Do not place the stands under the control arms.
2. Remove the nuts and bolts holding the ball joint to the lower control arm.
3. On 1988 vehicles with the VIN code 5 engine, remove the nut holding the sway bar link to the control arm and disconnect the link and bar from the control arm.
4. Remove the nuts and bolts holding the control arm to the body.
5. Remove the control arm from the car and check it carefully for cracks, bends or crimps in the metal or corrosion damage. Check the rubber bushing and replace it if any sign of damage or deformation is found.

6. Before reinstalling the arm, install or replace the bushing and tighten its retaining nut to 76 ft. lbs.

✴✴WARNING

Never reuse a self-locking nut; always replace the removed nut with a new one.

7. Position the control arm to the body and install the nuts and bolts. The front nut and bolt should be tightened to 105 ft. lbs. and the rear to 72 ft. lbs.
8. On 1988 vehicles with the VIN code 5 engine, reinstall the sway bar and link; tighten the nut to 13 ft. lbs.
9. Install the ball joint attaching nuts and bolts and tighten them to 59 ft. lbs.
10. Have the wheel alignment checked by a reputable facility.

1989-92

➡**Both lower control arms and the suspension crossmember must be removed as a unit even if only 1 arm is damaged.**

1. Raise and safely support the vehicle. Do not place the stands under the control arms or the suspension crossmember.
2. Remove the nuts and bolts holding the ball joints to the lower control arms.
3. Remove the nut and bolt holding the control arm rear brackets to the crossmember.
4. Place a floor jack under the suspension crossmember. Use a broad piece of wood between the jack and crossmember to evenly distribute the loading.
5. Remove the 6 bolts and 2 nuts holding the suspension crossmember. Carefully lower the crossmember (with the control arms attached) and remove from the car.
6. Remove the mounting bolt holding the control arm to the crossmember and remove the arm. Inspect the arm and bushing for damage, deformation or corrosion damage.
7. Install the control arm(s) to the crossmember and partially tighten the bolts. They should be tight enough to hold firmly, yet still be able to pivot when moderate force is applied.
8. Install the suspension crossmember and control arms to the body of the car and tighten the 6 nuts and 2 nuts.
9. Install the bolts holding the rear control arm brackets and partially tighten them.
10. Connect the ball joints to each arm and tighten the bolts to 105 ft. lbs.
11. Lower the vehicle to the ground. Bounce the front end up and down several times to stabilize the suspension. The partially tightened joints will flex and seek a 'normal" position.
12. With the vehicle on the ground (don't raise it or the suspension position will be lost), tighten the bolt holding the arm to the crossmember to 152 ft. lbs. Tighten the nut and bolt holding the rear bracket to the crossmember to 14 ft. lbs. and the rear bracket bolts to 94 ft. lbs.
13. Have the alignment checked by a reputable facility.

1993

▶ See Figures 16 and 17

➡**Both lower control arms and the suspension crossmember must be removed as a unit even if only 1 arm is damaged.**

1. Stabilizer bar
2. Stabilizer bar bracket bolt
3. Stabilizer bar bracket
4. Stabilizer bar bushing
5. Strut rod piston nut
6. Suspension support
7. Dust seal
8. Spring seat
9. Upper insulator
10. Coil spring
11. Spring bumper
12. Lower insulator
13. Shock absorber
14. Brake line gaskets
15. Brake hose clip
16. Strut mounting nut and bolt
17. Brake line-to-caliper bolt
18. Rear bracket bolt
19. Rear bracket
20. Rear bracket bolt
21. Ball joint castle nut
22. Ball joint
23. Ball joint retaining nuts and bolt
24. Crossmember mounting bolt
25. Crossmember mounting bolt
26. Control arm mounting nuts
27. Control arm through bolt
28. Crossmember mounting bolt
29. Crossmember mounting bolt
30. Crossmember mounting bolt
31. Stabilizer link nuts
32. Stabilizer link

Fig. 15 Front suspension — 1991-92 GSi models

1. Raise and safely support the vehicle.
2. Remove the front wheel assembly.
3. Remove the 1 bolt and 2 nuts and separate the ball joint from the lower control arm.
4. Remove the bolt and separate the rear transaxle mount from the suspension crossmember.
5. Place a floor jack under the engine crossmember.
6. Remove the bolt and separate the engine crossmember from the suspension crossmember.
7. Remove the nut and 3 bolts and loosen the right rear control arm bushing retaining bracket.
8. Place a floor jack under the suspension crossmember. Use a broad piece of wood between the jack and crossmember to evenly distribute the loading.
9. Loosen and lower the suspension crossmember from the body.
10. Remove the control arm to crossmember mounting bolt and remove the crossmember from the vehicle.
11. Clamp the lower control arm in a soft jawed vise, remove the retaining nut, bushing retainer and remove the bushing.

To install:

12. Install a new lower control arm bushing and bushing retainer. Do not tighten the nut fully at this time.
13. Install the lower control arm to the suspension crossmember and tighten the control arm to suspension crossmember bolt to 161 ft. lbs. (218 Nm) and rear bushing retaining nut to 101 ft. lbs. (137 Nm).
14. Install the suspension crossmember and tighten the 6 bolts to 152 ft. lbs. (206 Nm).
15. Remove the floor jack under the suspension crossmember.
16. Install the 3 retaining bolts and 1 nut to the left and right rear control arm bushing retaining brackets and tighten as follows (see illustration):
   • Bolt A to 108 ft. lbs. (147 Nm)
   • Bolt B to 37 ft. lbs (50 (Nm)
   • Nut C to 14 ft. lbs. (19 Nm)
17. Install the 4 nuts and bolt securing the engine crossmember and rear transaxle mount to the suspension crossmember and tighten as follows (see illustration):
   • Nut A to 35 ft. lbs. (48Nm)
   • Bolt B to 45 ft. lbs (61 (Nm)
   • Nut C to 45 ft. lbs. (61 Nm)
18. Remove the floor jack under the engine crossmember.
19. Install the ball joint to the to the lower control arm and tighten the bolt and nuts to 105 ft. lbs. (142 Nm).

20. Install the front wheel.
21. Lower the vehicle and check the alignment.

Knuckle, Hub and Wheel Bearing

REMOVAL, DISASSEMBLY AND INSTALLATION

✳✳WARNING

The use of the correct tools is required for this repair. These procedures require the use of assorted joint separators, slide hammers, bearing pullers, seal extractors/drivers and snapring pliers which may not be in your tool box. Do not attempt repairs or disassembly if the correct tools are not available; damage and/or injury may result.

Nova
▸ See Figures 18, 19, 20, 21, 22, 23, 24 and 25

1. Loosen the wheel nuts and the center axle nut.
2. Raise the vehicle and safely support it.
3. Remove the wheel.
4. Remove the brake hose retaining clip at the strut.
5. Disconnect the brake flex hose from the metal brake line. Use a small pan to collect spillage and plug the lines as soon as possible.
6. Remove the bolts holding the brake caliper to the knuckle; support the caliper with a piece of stiff wire out of the way.
7. Remove the brake disc.
8. Remove the drive axle nut. Use GM Tool J-25287 or equivalent to push out the drive axle.
9. Remove the cotter pin and the tie rod (steering rod) nut at the knuckle. Use a tie rod separator (GM Tool J-24329-01 or equivalent) to separate the joint.
10. Remove the nuts and bolt holding the ball joint to the control arm.
11. Matchmark the camber adjusting cam and the strut.
12. Remove the 2 bolts holding the knuckle to the strut. Remove the knuckle. The ball joint may be removed from the knuckle if desired.
13. Mount the knuckle securely in a vise. Use a screwdriver to remove the outer dust cover.

A. Bolt A to 108 ft. lbs. (147 NM)
B. Bolt B to 37 ft. lbs. (50 NM)
C. Nut C to 14 ft. lbs. (19 NM)
1. Bushing retaining bracket

Fig. 16 Rear control arm bushing retaining bracket bolt and nut locations

A. Nut A to 35 ft. lbs. (48 NM)
B. Bolt B to 45 ft. lbs. (61 NM)
C. Nut C to 45 ft. lbs. (61 NM)
1. Suspension crossmember

Fig. 17 Engine crossmember to suspension crossmember nut and bolt locations

1. Camber adjustment cam
2. Nut
3. Bolt
4. Lower control arm
5. Brake caliper
6. Lower ball joint
7. Ball joint nut
8. Drive axle
9. Brake disc
10. Lock nut cap
11. Cotter pin
12. Nut
13. Tie rod ball joint nut
14. Steering joint (tie rod joint)

Fig. 18 Nova front hub and knuckle assembly

Fig. 19 Removing the Nova driving axle

14. Using a slide hammer and puller (GM J-26941 or equivalent), remove the inner grease seal from the knuckle.
15. Remove the inner bearing snapring.
16. Remove the brake splash shield.
17. Remove the hub using an extractor such as GM Tools J-25287 and J-35378 or equivalent.

✲✲WARNING

Whenever the hub is removed, the inner and outer grease seals MUST be replaced with new seals. The seals are not reusable.

18. Use the same extractor to remove the outer bearing race from the hub.

19. Remove the outer grease seal with the slide hammer and puller.
20. Using a bearing driver of the correct size (GM Tools J-35399 and J-35379 or equivalent), remove the bearing assembly.

To install:

21. Clean and inspect all parts but do not wash or clean the wheel bearing; it cannot be repacked. If the bearing is damaged or noisy, it must be replaced.
22. Using a bearing driver of the correct size (GM J-8092 and J-35411 or equivalent), install the bearing into the hub.
23. Use a seal driver to install a new outer grease seal. (GM J-35737-1 or equivalent)
24. Apply sealer to the brake splash shield and install it to the knuckle.
25. Apply a layer of multi-purpose grease to the seal lip, seal and bearing. Install the hub with GM Tools J-8092 and J-35399 or equivalent.
26. Install the snapring.
27. Install a new inner grease seal using the correct size driver. (GM J-35737-2 or equivalent).
28. Install the outer dust cover (open end down) with GM Tool J-35379 or equivalent.
29. Install the lower ball joint to the control arm and tighten the nuts and bolt to 59 ft. lbs.
30. If the ball joint was removed from the knuckle, reinstall it. Install a new nut and temporarily tighten it to 14 ft. lbs. Back off the nut until clear of the knuckle and then retighten it to 82 ft. lbs.
31. Install the camber adjusting cam into the knuckle. Connect the knuckle to the strut lower bracket.

1. Dust deflector
2. Inner grease seal
3. Inner bearing race
4. Snapring
5. Wheel bearing (axle bearing)
6. Steering knuckle
7. Brake splash shield
8. Outer grease seal
9. Outer bearing race
10. Axle hub

Fig. 20 Nova hub and bearing assembly

Fig. 21 Removing the Nova inner grease seal

Fig. 23 Removing the Nova outer bearing race

Fig. 22 Removing the Nova hub

Fig. 24 Removing the Nova wheel bearing

32. Insert the bolts from rear to front and align the matchmarks of the camber adjusting cam and the strut. Tighten the nuts to 105 ft. lbs. (VIN code 4 engine) or 166 ft. lbs. (VIN code 5 engines).

33. Connect the tie rod to the knuckle. Install the nut and tighten to 36 ft. lbs. Install the cotter pin.

34. Install the driveshaft into the hub.

35. Double check the nuts and bolt holding the ball joint to the lower control arm. Correct torque is 59 ft. lbs.

36. Install the brake disc.

37. Reinstall the brake caliper. Tighten the bolts to 65 ft. lbs.

38. Connect the brake flex hose to the metal brake line. Correct tightness is 11 ft. lbs. Do not over-tighten this connection.

39. Install the wheel

40. Lower the car to the ground.

41. Tighten the wheel nuts to 76 ft. lbs.

42. Install the washer and nut onto the driveshaft end. Tighten the bolt to 137 ft. lbs. and install the cap and cotter pin.

43. Bleed the brake system, following directions in Section 9.

44. Have the alignment checked at a reputable facility.

Prizm

▶ **See Figures 26, 27, 28, 29, 30 and 31**

1. Loosen the wheel nuts and the center axle nut.

2. Raise the vehicle and safely support it. Remove the wheel.

3. Remove the ABS speed sensor, if so equipped.

4. Remove the center axle nut.

5. Remove the brake caliper and hang it out of the way on a piece of stiff wire. Do not disconnect the brake line; do not allow the caliper to hang by the hose.

6. Remove the brake disc.

7. Remove the cotter pin and nut from the tie rod end.

8. Remove the tie rod end from the knuckle using a joint separator (GM Tool J-6627-A or equivalent).

9. Remove the bolt and 2 nuts holding the bottom of the ball joint to the control arm and remove the arm from the knuckle.

10. Remove the 2 nuts from the steering knuckle. Place a protective cover or shield over the CV boot on the driveshaft.

11. Using a plastic mallet, tap the driveshaft free of the hub assembly.

12. Remove the 2 bolts and remove the axle hub assembly.

13. Clamp the knuckle in a vise with protected jaws.

Fig. 25 Installation of the Nova hub

14. Remove the dust deflector. Loosen the nut holding the ball joint to the knuckle. Use a ball joint separator (GM Tool J-35413 or equivalent) to loosen and remove the joint

15. Use a slide hammer/extractor (GM Tool J-26941 or equivalent) to remove the outer oil seal.

16. Remove the snapring.

17. Using a hub puller and pilot (GM Tools J-25287 and J-35378 or equivalents), pull the axle hub from the knuckle.

18. Remove the brake splash shield (3 bolts).

19. Use a split plate bearing remover, puller pilot and a shop press, remove the inner bearing race from the hub.

20. Remove the inner oil seal with the same tools used to remove the outer seal.

21. Place the inner race in the bearing. Support the knuckle and use an axle hub remover (GM Tool J-35399) with a plastic mallet to drive out the bearing.

To install:

22. Clean and inspect all parts but do not wash or clean the wheel bearing; it cannot be repacked. If the bearing is damaged or noisy, it must be replaced.

23. Press a new bearing race into the steering knuckle using a bearing driver of the correct size (GM J-8092 and J-37777 or equivalent).

24. Place a new bearing inner race on the hub bearing.

25. Insert the side lip of a new oil seal into the seal installer (GM J-35737-01 or equivalent) and drive the oil seal into the steering knuckle.

26. Apply multi-purpose grease to the oil seal lip.

27. Apply sealer to the brake splash shield and install the shield.

28. Use a hub installer (GM J-35399) to press the hub into the steering knuckle.

29. Install a new snapring into the hub.

30. Using a seal installer of the correct size, install a new outer oil seal into the steering knuckle.

31. Apply multi-purpose grease to the seal surfaces which will contact the driveshaft.

32. Support the knuckle and drive in a new dust deflector.

33. Install the ball joint into the knuckle and tighten the nut to 94 ft. lbs.

34. Temporarily install the hub assembly to the lower control arm and fit the driveaxle into the hub.

35. Install the knuckle to strut bolts, then install the tie rod end to the knuckle.

36. Tighten the strut bracket nuts to 194 ft. lbs. and tighten the tie rod end nut to 36 ft. lbs. Install the cotter pin.

37. Remove the old nut from the lower ball joint and install a new castle nut. Tighten the nut to 94 ft. lbs. and install a new cotter pin. (The old nut was used to draw the joint into the knuckle; the new nut assures retention.)

38. Connect the ball joint to the lower control arm and tighten the nuts to 105 ft. lbs.

39. Install the brake disc and the brake caliper and tighten the caliper bolts to 65 ft. lbs.

40. Install the ABS sensor and tighten the retaining bolt to 69 inch lbs. (88 Nm), if so equipped.

41. Install the center nut and washer on the drive axle and while applying the brakes tighten the locknut to 137 ft. lbs. (186 Nm) for 1989-90 and 159 ft. lbs. (216 Nm) for 1991-93.

42. Install the wheel

43. Lower the car to the ground.

1. Strut mounting nut
2. Tie rod end
3. Tie rod nut
4. Cotter pin
5. Brake rotor
6. Locknut cap
7. Washer
8. Driveshaft locknut
9. Ball joint mounting nut and bolt

10. Brake caliper
11. Caliper set bolt
12. Driveshaft
13. Dust deflector
14. Inner oil seal
15. Snap ring
16. Hub bearing
17. Steering knuckle

18. Dust cover
19. Outside bearing inner race
20. Axle hub
21. Wheel stud
22. Outer oil seal
23. Ball joint
24. Balljoint castle nut
25. Cotter pin
26. Inside bearing inner race

Fig. 26 Prizm hub and bearing assembly

Fig. 27 Removing Prizm oil seal

Fig. 28 Prizm axle hub removal

Fig. 29 Using split plate tool to remove Prizm outer bearing race.

Fig. 30 Removing Prizm inner bearing race

Fig. 31 Installing Prizm axle hub into steering knuckle

Fig. 32 Caster angle affects the tracking of the steering.

44. Tighten the wheel nuts to 76 ft. lbs. Install the cap and cotter pin.
45. Remove the protective cover from the CV boot.
46. Have the alignment checked at a reputable facility.

Front End Alignment

▶ See Figures 32, 33 and 34

Alignment of the front wheels is essential if your car is to go, stop and turn as designed. Alignment can be altered by collision, overloading, poor repair or bent components.

If you are diagnosing bizarre handling and/or poor road manners, the first place to look is the tires. Although the tires may wear as a result of an alignment problem, worn or poorly inflated tires can make you chase alignment problems which don't exist.

Once you have eliminated all other causes, unload everything from the trunk except the spare tire, set the tire pressures to the correct level and take the car to a reputable alignment facility. Since the alignment settings are measured in very small increments, it is almost impossible for the home mechanic to accurately determine the settings. The explanations that follow will help you understand the three dimensions of alignment: caster, camber and toe-in.

CASTER

Caster is the tilting of the steering axis either forward or backward from the vertical, when viewed from the side of the vehicle. A backward tilt is said to be positive and a forward tilt is said to be negative. Changes in caster affect the straight line tendency of the vehicle and the 'return to center" of the steering after a turn. If the camber is radically different between the left and right wheels (such as after hitting a major pothole or curb), the car will exhibit a nasty pull to one side.

Caster is not adjustable on either the Nova or Prizm. The camber angle is fixed by the proper location of all the suspension components. If caster is found to be incorrect, the cause must be determined through examination of the suspension and body parts. Bent, loose or worn components must be replaced. Recent body work must also be considered as a cause; if the shock tower is not correctly located, the camber will not be correct.

CAMBER

Camber is the tilting of the wheels from the vertical (leaning in or out) when viewed from the front of the vehicle. When the wheels tilt outward at the top, the camber is said to be positive. When the wheels tilt inward at the top the camber is said to be negative. The amount of tilt is measured in degrees from the vertical. This measurement is called camber angle.

Camber affects the position of the tire on the road surface during vertical suspension movement and cornering. Changes in camber affect the handling and ride qualities of the car as well as tire wear. Many tire wear patterns indicate camber related problems from misalignment, overloading or poor driving habits.

Camber is adjustable on the Nova and Prizm by turning the adjusting cam on each front strut. Anytime camber is adjusted, toe must be checked and reset if necessary.

TOE-IN

Toe is the turning in or out (parallelism) of the wheels. The actual amount of toe setting is normally only a fraction of an inch. The purpose of toe-in (or out) specification is to ensure parallel rolling of the wheels. Toe-in also serves to offset the small deflections of the steering support system which occur when the vehicle is rolling forward or under braking.

Changing the toe setting will radically affect the overall 'feel" of the steering, the behavior of the car under braking, tire wear and even fuel economy. Excessive toe (in or out) causes excessive drag or scrubbing on the tires.

Toe-in is adjustable on both Nova and Prizm, and is generally measured either in fractional inches or degrees. It is adjusted by loosening the locknut on each tie rod end and turning the rod until the correct reading is achieved. The rods left and right must remain equal in length during all adjustments.

Fig. 33 Camber is the inward or outward tilt of the wheel on the road.

Fig. 34 Toe in (or out) can affect tire wear and fuel economy.

FRONT WHEEL ALIGNMENT

Year	Model	Caster Range (deg.)	Caster Preferred Setting (deg.)	Camber Range (deg.)	Camber Preferred Setting (deg.)	Toe-in (in.)	Steering Axis Inclination (deg.)
1985	Nova	0.13P–1.63P	0.88P	0.75N–0.25P	0.5N	0.039	—
1986	Nova	0.13P–1.63P	0.88P	0.75N–0.25P	0.5N	0.039	—
1987	Nova	0.13P–1.63P	0.88P	0.75N–0.25P	0.5N	0.039	—
1988	Nova ①	0.13P–1.63P	0.88P	0.75N–0.25P	0.5N	0.039	—
	Nova ②	0–1.48P	0.74P	0.75N–0.25P	0.5N	0.039	—
1989	Prizm ③	0.58P–2.08P	1.33P	0.50N–1.00P	0.25P	0.039	—
	Prizm ④	0.67P–2.17P	1.42P	0.58N–0.92P	0.17P	0.039	—
1990	Prizm ③	0.58P–2.08P	1.33P	0.50N–1.00P	0.25P	0.039	—
	Prizm ④	0.67P–2.17P	1.42P	0.58N–0.92P	0.17P	0.039	—
1991	Prizm ⑤	0.61P–2.11P	0.75P	0.90N–0.60P	0.15N	0.04	—
	Prizm ⑥ ③	0.61P–2.11P	0.75P	1.02N–0.48P	0.27N	0.04	—
	Prizm ⑥ ④	0.70P–2.20P	0.75P	0.95N–0.55P	0.20N	0.04	—
1992	Prizm ⑤	0.61P–2.11P	0.75P	0.90N–0.60P	0.15N	0.04	—
	Prizm ⑥ ③	0.61P–2.11P	0.75P	1.02N–0.48P	0.27N	0.09	—
	Prizm ⑥ ④	0.70P–2.20P	0.75P	0.95N–0.55P	0.20N	0.04	—
1993	Prizm	0.58P–2.08P	1.50P	0.92N–0.58P	0.34N	0.08N–0.24P	11.83–13.35

N—Negative
P—Positive
① VIN Code 4 engine
② VIN Code 5 engine
③ Manual transaxle
④ Automatic transaxle
⑤ Base model
⑥ GSi model

REAR SUSPENSION

Spring and Shock Absorber/MacPherson Struts

REMOVAL & INSTALLATION

Nova
▶ See Figures 35 and 36

1. Working inside the car, remove the shock absorber cover and rear window shelf. On some models it is necessary to remove the quarter window trim panel and the rear shelf to gain access to the shock mounts. Remove the speakers and/or speaker grilles as needed.
2. Raise the rear of the vehicle and support it with jackstands. Remove the wheel.
3. Disconnect the brake line from the flexible hose at the mounting bracket on the strut tube. Disconnect the flexible hose from the strut. Reconnect the 2 brake lines to each other but not to the strut. This will prevent excessive leakage.
4. Remove the 2 lower bolts holding the strut to the axle carrier.

5. Remove the 3 upper strut mounting nuts and carefully remove the strut assembly.

✳✳WARNING

Do not loosen the center nut on the top of the shock absorber piston.

To install:
6. Place the complete strut assembly into the lower mount and pin it in position with the bolts.
7. Use a floor jack to gently raise the suspension and guide the upper strut mount into position.

✳✳CAUTION

The car is on jackstands. Elevate the floor jack only enough to swing the strut into position; do not raise the car!

8. Disconnect the flexible brake line and the metal pipe. Connect the flexible hose to the strut, then reconnect the metal brake line to the flexible hose.
9. Tighten the lower strut retaining nuts and bolts to 105 ft. lbs.
10. Tighten the 3 upper retaining bolts to 17 ft. lbs.
11. Install the wheel.
12. Lower the vehicle to the ground.
13. Reinstall the interior components as necessary.

14. Bleed the brake system. Please refer to Chapter Nine for complete directions.

15. Have the rear wheel alignment checked at a reputable facility.

Prizm

▶ **See Figures 37 and 38**

1. Elevate and safely support the vehicle on stands. Do not place the stands under the suspension arms.

2. Remove the wheel.

3. Disconnect the metal brake line from the wheel cylinder (at the backing plate) and from the flexible hose. Plug the lines as soon as possible to prevent leakage.

4. Remove the clip from the brake hose and remove the hose from the strut bracket.

5. Disconnect the sway bar link from the strut.

6. Remove the strut mounting bolts from the rear knuckle.

7. Remove the seat back side cushion (Sedan) or the rear sill side panel (Hatchback) to gain access to the upper strut mount.

8. Remove the 3 nuts holding the upper strut mount to the body. Do not loosen the center strut piston nut.

9. Remove the strut assembly from the vehicle.

To install:

10. When reinstalling, place the assembled strut in position and install the 3 upper retaining nuts, tightening them to 29 ft. lbs.

11. Reinstall the seat back side cushion or the rear sill side panel.

12. Install the strut into the rear knuckle assembly; install the bolts and nuts and tighten them to 105 ft. lbs.

13. Reconnect the sway bar link to the strut. Tighten the bolts to 26 ft. lbs.

14. Connect the flexible brake hose into the bracket and install the clip.

15. Connect the metal line at the flexible hose and at the wheel cylinder. Make certain the fittings are properly threaded before tightening them.

16. Bleed the brake system. Please refer to Chapter Nine for complete instructions.

17. Reinstall the wheel.

18. Lower the car to the ground.

19. Have the rear alignment checked at a reputable repair facility.

DISASSEMBLY

All Models

✳✳CAUTION

This procedure requires the use of a spring compressor; it cannot be performed without one. If you do not have access to this special tool, do not attempt to disassemble the strut. The coil springs are retained under considerable pressure. They can exert enough force to cause serious injury! Exercise extreme caution when disassembling the strut.

1. Place the strut assembly in a pipe vise or strut vise.

✳✳WARNING

Do not attempt to clamp the strut assembly in a flat jaw vise as this will result in damage to the strut tube.

2. Attach a spring compressor and compress the spring until the upper suspension support is free of any spring tension. Do not over-compress the spring.

3. Hold the upper support and then remove the nut on the end of the shock piston rod.

4. Remove the support, coil spring, insulator and bumper.

INSPECTION

Check the shock absorber by moving the piston shaft through its full range of travel. It should move smoothly and evenly throughout its entire travel without any trace of binding or notching. Use a small straightedge to check the piston shaft for any bending or deformation. If a shock absorber is replaced, the old one should be drilled at the bottom to vent the internal gas. Wear safety goggles and drill a small hole (2-3mm) into the base of the shock absorber. The gas within the strut is colorless, odorless and non-toxic, but should be vented to make the unit safe for disposal.

Inspect the spring for any sign of deterioration or cracking. The waterproof coating on the coils should be intact to prevent rusting.

✳✳CAUTION

Do not turn the piston rod within the cylinder if the piston rod is fully extended!

ASSEMBLY AND INSTALLATION

▶ **See Figure 39**

✳✳WARNING

Never reuse a self-locking nut! Always replace self-locking nuts with new hardware.

1. Loosely assemble all components onto the strut assembly. Make sure the spring end aligns with the hollow in the lower seat.

2. Align the upper suspension support with the piston rod and install the support.

3. Align the suspension support with the strut lower bracket. This assures the spring will be properly seated top and bottom.

4. Compress the spring slightly by pushing on the suspension support with one hand to expose the strut piston rod threads.

5. Install a new strut piston nut and tighten it to 36 ft. lbs.

STABILIZER BAR
ASSEMBLY (4A·GE)

1. Dust cover	12. Nut	22. Toe-in adjusting cam nut
2. Strut piston rod nut	13. Bolt	23. Toe-in indicator
3. Suspension support	14. Hub carrier and brake	24. Body
4. Upper insulator	drum assembly	25. Retainer
5. Coil spring	15. Strut rod	26. Cushion
6. Bumper	16. Nut	27. Sway bar link
7. Lower insulator	17. No. 2 arm (rearward)	28. Bushing
8. Strut	18. No. 1 arm (forward)	29. Collar
9. Brake line	19. Nut	30. Sway bar
10. Retaining clip	20. Bolt	31. Bushing
11. Flexible brake hose	21. Bushing	32. Bracket

Fig. 35 Nova rear suspension components

1. BRAKE LINE FITTING AT WHEEL
   CYLINDER
2. FITTING AT FLEXIBLE HOSE
3. FLEXIBLE HOSE
4. STRUT ASSEMBLY

Fig. 36 Nova brake lines and strut bracket

Control Arms

REMOVAL

1985-92

▶ **See Figures 35 and 37**

These models use two control arms on each rear wheel. To avoid the obvious confusion of referring to a 'front rear control arm", they are referred to as No. 1 and No. 2, with arm No.1 being the closest to the front of the car.

No. 1 Arm

1. Raise and safely support the vehicle.
2. Disconnect the sway bar link if so equipped.
3. Remove the bolt holding the arm to the body.
4. Remove the bolt holding the arm to the suspension knuckle.
5. Remove the arm.

No. 2 Arm

1. Raise and safely support the vehicle.
2. Observe and matchmark the position of the adjusting cam at the body mount.
3. Disconnect the bolt holding the arm to the suspension knuckle.
4. Disconnect the bolt holding the arm to the body.
5. Remove the arm.
6. Inspect the arms for any bending or cracking. If the arm is not true in all dimensions, it must be replaced. Any attempt to straighten a bent arm will damage it. Also check the bushings within the ends of the arms and replace any which are deformed or too spongy. If a bushing must be replaced, do not grease it before installation.

INSTALLATION

1. Place the arm in position, install the arm to body bolts and partially tighten them. If installing arm No. 2, make sure the matchmarks for the adjusting cam are aligned.
2. Install the arm to the knuckle and partially tighten the bolts.

3. Reconnect the sway bar link if it was removed. Use a new nut and tighten it to 11 ft. lbs.
4. Install the wheel.
5. Lower the car to the ground. Bounce the front and rear of the car several times to position the suspension.
6. Tighten the retaining bolts at the body and the knuckle: Nova, 64 ft. lbs. and Prizm, 87 ft. lbs.
7. Have the alignment checked at a reputable facility.

Lateral Links and Strut Rod

REMOVAL & INSTALLATION

1993 Models

▶ **See Figure 38**

1. Jack up vehicle and remove the rear wheel.
2. Remove the 2 bolts and nuts and remove the strut rod.
3. Remove the 2 nuts and washers and remove the lateral link.
4. Remove the 2 bolts and disconnect the resonator/intermediate pipe assembly and gasket from the catalytic converter.
5. Remove the 2 bolts and disconnect the resonator/intermediate pipe assembly and gasket from the muffler/tailpipe assembly.
6. Remove the 4 bolts retaining the muffler/tailpipe assembly to the body.
7. Remove the muffler/tailpipe assembly from the hanger.
8. Remove the 3 bolts and disconnect the intermediate pipe heat shield.
9. Support the suspension crossmember with a jack and remove the 6 bolts attaching the crossmember to the body. Lower the suspension crossmember.
10. Remove the 2 bolts and 4 washers and remove the front lateral link.

To install:
11. Install the 2 bolts and 4 washers and the front lateral link. Do not install the nuts until the rear lateral link is installed in the vehicle.
12. Raise the suspension crossmember with the jack and install the 6 bolts attaching the crossmember to the body. Tighten the bolts to 43 ft. lbs. (58 Nm).
13. Install the 3 bolts and connect the intermediate pipe heat shield.
14. Install the muffler/tailpipe assembly to the hanger and secure to the body with the 4 retaining bolts.
15. Install the 2 bolts and connect the resonator/intermediate pipe assembly and gasket to the muffler/tailpipe assembly.
16. Install the 2 bolts and connect the resonator/intermediate pipe assembly and gasket to the catalytic converter.
17. Install the rear lateral link and install the 2 nuts and washers. Do not tighten fully at this time.
18. Install the strut rod and secure with the 2 bolts and nuts but do not tighten at this time.
19. Stabilize the suspension by bouncing the vehicle up and down a few times.
20. Tighten the lateral link bolts and nuts to 87 ft. lbs. (118 Nm).

1. Fuel tank retaining strap
2. Tower cover
3. Strut piston rod nut
4. Strut
5. Toe-in adjusting bolt
6. Bolt
7. Nut
8. No.2 arm (rearward)
9. Nut
10. Bolt
11. Brake line
12. Brake drum
13. Brake assembly
14. Strut rod
15. Bolt
16. Bolt
17. Bolt
18. No.1 arm (forward)
19. Bolt
20. Bolt
21. Bracket
22. Bushing
23. Sway bar link
24. Sway bar link nut
25. Sway bar

Fig. 37 Prizm rear suspension components — 1989-92. All models use rear drum brakes except for the 1991 — 92 GSi models which have disc brakes, otherwise the rear suspension is identical

Fig. 38 Prizm rear suspension components — 1993

Fig. 39 Correct relationship of upper and lower mounts when reassembling Nova rear strut.

1. SUSPENSION SUPPORT
2. STRUT LOWER BRACKET

Fig. 40 Note the position of bushings when reassembling the Nova rear stabilizer bar.

21. Tighten the strut rod bolts and nuts to 67 ft. lbs. (91 Nm).

22. Install the rear wheel.

23. Lower the vehicle and check the rear wheel alignment.

Stabilizer Bar (Sway Bar)

REMOVAL & INSTALLATION

1985-88 Nova

▶ See Figure 40

1. Raise and safely support the vehicle

2. Remove the rear wheels.

3. Remove the nuts, retainers and cushions holding the sway bar links to the control arm.

4. Remove the bolts holding the stabilizer to the body.

5. Remove the bar with the links attached.

6. Remove and discard the bolts holding the links to the sway bar.

To install:

7. When reassembling, install new bolts to hold the links to the sway bar but do not tighten the bolts.

8. Place the bar in position and install but do not tighten the bolts holding the brackets to the body.

9. Connect the sway bar links to the control arms. Use new nuts and tighten them to 11 ft. lbs.

10. Tighten the bracket bolts to 9 ft. lbs. and then tighten the bolts holding the sway bar to the links to 22 ft. lbs.

11. Install the rear wheels.

12. Lower the car to the ground.

1989-90 Prizm

▶ See Figure 37

1. Using either a transmission jack or a floor jack with a broad piece of wood, support the fuel tank from below. Use care not to dent or deform the tank.

2. Remove the fuel tank retaining straps.

3. Disconnect the stabilizer links from the strut assemblies.

4. Disconnect the stabilizer bar bracket bolts.

5. Remove the bar.

To install:

6. Place the bar in position, attach the body retaining brackets and then connect the links to the strut on each side.

7. Tighten the body bracket bolts to 14 ft. lbs. and the link bolts (both ends) to 26 ft. lbs.

8. Reinstall the fuel tank straps and tighten the bolts to 29 ft. lbs.

9. Remove the tank support jack.

1990-92

▶ See Figure 37

1. Raise and safely support the vehicle

2. Disconnect the stabilizer links from the strut assemblies.

3. Disconnect the stabilizer bar from the bar links.

4. Disconnect the stabilizer bar mounting bolts and remove the stabilizer bar from the vehicle.

To install:

5. Position the stabilizer bar to the vehicle and install the stabilizer bar mounting bolts.

6. Connect the stabilizer bar to the bar links.

7. Connect the stabilizer links to the strut assemblies.

8. Tighten the stabilizer bar mounting bolts to 14 ft. lbs. (19 Nm).

9. Tighten the stabilizer bar to the bar link nuts to 26 ft lbs. (35 Nm).

10. Tighten the stabilizer link to the strut assembly nuts to 26 ft lbs. (35 Nm).

1993

▶ See Figure 38

1. Raise and safely support the vehicle and remove the rear wheels.

2. Remove the left and right stabilizer bar links.

3. Scribe matchmarks between the stabilizer bar bushings, stabilizer bar and body and remove the stabilizer bar bushings.

4. Remove the 2 bolts and disconnect the resonator/intermediate pipe assembly and gasket from the catalytic converter.

5. Remove the 2 bolts and disconnect the resonator/intermediate pipe assembly and gasket from the muffler/tailpipe assembly.

6. Remove the 4 bolts retaining the muffler/tailpipe assembly to the body.

7. Remove the muffler/tailpipe assembly from the hanger.

8. Remove the 3 bolts and disconnect the intermediate pipe heat shield.

9. Remove the right side fuel tank band.

10. Support the suspension crossmember with a jack and remove the 6 bolts attaching the crossmember to the body. Lower the suspension crossmember.

11. Remove the stabilizer bar.

To install:

12. Install the stabilizer bar.

13. Raise the suspension crossmember with the jack and install the 6 bolts attaching the crossmember to the body. Tighten the bolts to 43 ft. lbs. (58 Nm).

14. Install the right side fuel tank band.

15. Install the 3 bolts and connect the intermediate pipe heat shield.

16. Install the muffler/tailpipe assembly to the hanger and secure to the body with the 4 retaining bolts.

17. Install the 2 bolts and connect the resonator/intermediate pipe assembly and gasket to the muffler/tailpipe assembly.

18. Install the 2 bolts and connect the resonator/intermediate pipe assembly and gasket to the catalytic converter.

19. Install the stabilizer bar bushings to the stabilizer bar aligning the matchmarks.

20. Install the left and right stabilizer bar bushing retainers and tighten to 14 ft. lbs. (19 Nm).

21. Install the left and right stabilizer bar links and tighten the stabilizer bar link to strut assembly bolts to 33 ft. lbs. (44 Nm) and the stabilizer bar link to stabilizer bar bolts to 26 ft. lbs. (35 Nm).

22. Install the rear wheels.

23. Lower the vehicle.

Rear Wheel Bearing and Rear Axle Hub

REMOVAL & INSTALLATION

✳✳WARNING

The use of the correct tools is required for this repair. These procedures require the use of assorted bearing pullers, seal extractors/drivers and slide hammers which may not be in your tool box. Do not attempt repairs or disassembly if the correct tools are not available; damage and/or injury may result.

Nova

▶ **See Figures 41, 42 and 43**

1. Raise and safely support the vehicle.
2. Remove the wheel.
3. Remove the brake drum (VIN code 4 engine) or brake caliper and brake disc (VIN code 5 engine). If the caliper is removed, suspend it out of the way with a piece of stiff wire; do not let it hang by the hose.

✳✳CAUTION

Brake pads and shoes contain asbestos, which has been determined to be a cancer causing agent. Never clean the brake surfaces with compressed air! Avoid inhaling any dust from brake surfaces! When cleaning brakes, use commercially available brake cleaning fluids.

4. On VIN code 4 engines, disconnect the brake line from the wheel cylinder.
5. Remove the 4 bolts holding the axle hub/bearing assembly to the axle carrier and remove the hub and bearing assembly.
6. Remove the splash shield (VIN Code 5 engine) or the rear brake shoes (VIN code 4), then remove the O-ring. It must be replaced at reassembly.
7. Place the hub/bearing assembly in a vise with protected jaws. Do not clamp the hub any tighter than needed to hold it securely.
8. Remove the hub nut.
9. Using an extractor such as GM Tool J-25287 or equivalent, remove the bearing case from the axle hub.
10. Remove the inner race, the inboard bearing and the outboard bearing.
11. Use the extractor again to remove the inner race from the outboard bearing.
12. Remove the seal from the axle hub.
13. To remove the outer bearing race, install the outboard bearing inner race so that it pushes against the outer race. Use Tool J-35440 or similar to press the race free.

➡Whenever the bearing assembly is removed, it must be replaced with a new bearing assembly. Reuse of the bearing after disassembly is NOT recommended.

14. To reassemble, apply grease around the bearing outer race.

15. Press the new bearing outer race into the bearing case with Tool J-35400 or equivalent.
16. Install new bearings (inner and outer) and the inner races into the bearing case.
17. Lightly coat a new bearing seal with multi-purpose grease and install with a seal driver such as GM Tool J-35736 or equivalent.
18. Install the bearing case onto the hub with GM Tool J-35440 or equivalent.
19. Tighten the rear nut to 90 ft. lbs. and stake the nut with a chisel.
20. Install a new O-ring to the axle carrier.
21. Assemble the hub to either the brake backing plate (VIN code 4 engine) or the splash shield (VIN code 5 engine) and install. Tighten the bolts to 59 ft. lbs.
22. On vehicles equipped with the VIN code 4 engine, reinstall the rear brake shoes and connect the brake line to the wheel cylinder.
23. Reinstall either the rear brake drum or the brake disc and caliper.
24. Install the wheel and lower the car to the ground.
25. Refill the master cylinder and bleed the brake system, following instructions in Section 9.

Prizm

▶ **See Figures 44, 45, 46 and 47**

1. Raise and safely support the vehicle.
2. Remove the wheel.
3. Remove the brake drum and unbolt and disconnect the ABS speed sensor, if so equipped.

✳✳CAUTION

Brake pads and shoes contain asbestos, which has been determined to be a cancer causing agent. Never clean the brake surfaces with compressed air! Avoid inhaling any dust from brake surfaces! When cleaning brakes, use commercially available brake cleaning fluids.

4. Remove the 4 bolts holding the axle hub/bearing assembly to the axle carrier and remove the hub and bearing assembly.
5. Remove the O-ring from the backing plate.
6. Mount the hub/bearing assembly in a vise with protected jaws.
7. Use a hammer and chisel (not a screwdriver) to unstake the wheel bearing locknut.
8. Remove the locknut.
9. Using a split plate bearing remover, a race puller pilot and an axle shaft puller (GM Tools J-22912, J-38278 and J-8433 respectively), separate the axle shaft from the hub.
10. Using the same tools, remove the inner bearing race.
11. Use a slide hammer and seal puller to remove the oil seal from the axle shaft.
12. Press the inner race off with a bearing race remover such as GM Tool J-35400 or equivalent.
13. Clean all components thoroughly and examine for any signs of cracking, abrasion or corrosion. Whenever the wheel bearings are removed or disassembled, they must be replaced with new bearings. Reuse of the old bearings is NOT recommended.

201. Mounting bracket bolt 47 N·m (34 ft. lbs.)
202. Dust cover
203. O-ring
204. Bolt 80 N·m (59 ft. lbs.)
205. Axle hub
206. Disc
207. Caliper
208. Carrier assembly
209. Rear brake backing plate assembly
210. Rear axle hub assembly
211. Bolt 80 N·m (59 ft. lbs.)
212. Brake drum
213. O-ring
214. Bolt 142 N·m (105 ft. lbs.)
215. Nut 123 N·m (90 ft. lbs.)
216. Inner bearing inner race
217. Bearing outer race with bearing installed
218. Bearing case assembly
219. Outer bearing inner race
220. Seal
221. Axle hub

Fig. 41 Nova rear hub and bearing components

1. AXLE HUB BOLT ACCESS HOLES

Fig. 42 Removing the axle hub from the brake backing plate.

Fig. 43 Removing the Nova bearing case from the hub. Note that the tool is clamped in the vise, not the hub. The outboard bearing inner race is removed in the same fashion.

1. Wheel bearing locknut
2. Bearing inner race
3. Bearing outer race
4. Axle shaft
5. Hub bolt
6. Oil seal
7. Axle hub
8. Bearing

Fig. 44 Prizm hub and bearing components

Fig. 45 Unstaking the Prizm locknut

J 8433

J 38278

J 22912

Fig. 46 Removing the Prizm axle shaft from the hub. The inner race is separated from the axle shaft with the same tools.

J 35440

Fig. 47 Pressing the Prizm bearing race into the axle hub

To assemble:

14. Apply multi-purpose grease around the outer race of a new bearing and install the bearing into the inner race.

15. Using a seal installer and slide hammer, install a new oil seal onto the axle shaft.

16. Using the proper size installation tool, press the bearing and bearing outer race into the axle hub.

17. Press the bearing inner race into the axle hub.

18. Press the outer race onto the axle shaft.

19. Install a new wheel bearing locknut and tighten it to 90 ft. lbs. Use a hammer and chisel the stake the nut in place.

20. Install a new O-ring onto the knuckle.

21. Place the axle hub/bearing assembly in position, install the bolts and tighten them to 59 ft. lbs.

22. Reconnect and install the ABS speed sensor, if equipped and install the brake drum.

23. Install the wheel and lower the car to the ground.

24. Although this repair should not have affected the rear alignment, it is recommended that the alignment be checked and adjusted if necessary.

Rear Wheel Alignment

The proper alignment of the rear wheels is as important as the alignment of the front wheels and should be checked periodically. The rear wheels are adjustable for both camber and toe. If the rear wheels are misaligned, particularly a toe-in error on one side, the car will exhibit unpredictable handling characteristics. The usual symptoms include a different turning responses into left and right corners and difficulty in maintaining a straight path, both due to the rear wheels attempting to steer the car. This "rear steer" behavior is particularly hazardous on slick surfaces; the back wheels of the car may attempt to go in directions unrelated to the front during braking or turning maneuvers.

REAR WHEEL ALIGNMENT

		Caster		Camber			Steering Axis Inclination (deg.)
Year	Model	Range (deg.)	Preferred Setting (deg.)	Range (deg.)	Preferred Setting (deg.)	Toe-in (in.)	
1985	Nova	—	—	76N–14P	31N	1.57	—
1986	Nova	—	—	76N–14P	31N	1.57	—
1987	Nova	—	—	76N–14P	31N	1.57	—
1988	Nova	—	—	76N–14P	31N	1.57	—
1989	Prizm ①	—	—	0.8N–1.42P	0.67P	1.57	—
	Prizm ②	—	—	0.17N–1.33P	0.58P	1.57	—
1990	Prizm ①	—	—	0.8N–1.42P	0.67P	1.57	—
	Prizm ②	—	—	0.17N–1.33P	0.58P	1.57	—
	Prizm GSi	—	—	1.50N–0P	0.751N	0.16	—
1991	Prizm (Base)	—	—	1.33N–0.17N	0.58P	0.16	—
	Prizm (GSi)	—	—	1.43N–0.7P	0.68P	0.16	—
1992	Prizm (Base)	—	—	1.33N–0.17N	0.58P	0.16	—
	Prizm (GSi)	—	—	1.43N–0.7P	0.68P	0.16	—
1993	Prizm	—	—	1.67N–0.17N	0.75P	0.08–0.40	—

N—Negative
P—Positive
① Manual Trans.
② Automatic Trans.

STEERING

SERVICE PRECAUTIONS

❋❋CAUTION

The procedures in this section must be followed in the order listed to temporarily disable the Supplemental Restraint System (SRS) and prevent false diagnostic trouble codes (DTC's) from setting. Failure to follow procedures could result in possible air bag deployment, personal injury or otherwise unneeded SRS repairs.

The center sensor assembly can maintain sufficient voltage to cause a deployment for up to two minutes after the ignition switch is turned to **LOCK** or the battery is disconnected. Many service procedures require disconnection of the **IGN** fuse, **CIG** & **RADIO** fuse and the steering column circuit from the deployment loop to avoid an accidental deployment.

➡ **Refer to Section 6 for a more complete description of the SRS system and its precautions.**

DISABLING THE SRS

1. Turn the steering wheel so that the vehicle's wheels are pointing straight ahead.

2. Turn the ignition switch to **LOCK**.

3. Disconnect **IGN** fuse and **CIG** and **RADIO** fuse from junction block 1.2. Disconnect the connector position assurance (CPA) and disconnect the lower steering column (yellow two cavity) connector at the base of the steering column.

ENABLING THE SRS

1. Turn the ignition switch to **LOCK**.
2. Connect the lower steering column connector and secure with CPA.
3. Connect **IGN** fuse and **CIG** and **RADIO** fuse to junction block 1.
4. Turn the ignition switch to ACC or ON and verify that the air bag indicator illuminates steadily for approximately 6 seconds and then turns off. If it does not operate as described, "SRS Diagnostic System Check" will have to be performed by an authorized dealer.

Steering Wheel

REMOVAL & INSTALLATION

1985-92

▶ See Figures 48 and 49

✳✳CAUTION

Do not attempt to remove or install the steering wheel by hammering on it. Damage to the energy-absorbing steering column could result.

1. Disconnect the negative battery cable.
2. Loosen the trim pad retaining screws from the back side of the steering wheel.
3. Lift the trim pad and horn button assembly(ies) from the wheel.
4. Remove the steering wheel hub retaining nut and washer.
5. Scratch matchmarks on the hub and shaft to aid in correct installation.
6. Use a steering wheel puller to remove the steering wheel.
7. Installation is performed in the reverse order of removal. Tighten the wheel retaining nut to 25 ft. lbs.

1993

▶ See Figures 50 and 51

1. Disable the SRS as outlined earlier in this Section.

Fig. 48 Removing the steering wheel pad

2. Place the front wheels in a straight ahead position.
3. Remove the inflator module as follows:
   a. With the SRS disabled, remove the 2 side trim covers from the steering column.
   b. Remove the 2 Torx® head screws, release the connector position assurance (CPA) and disconnect the upper steering column connector.
   c. Remove the inflator module from the steering wheel.

✳✳CAUTION

When carrying a live inflator module, make sure the bag and trim cover are pointed away from you. When placing on a bench always face the bag and trim cover up, away from the surface of a bench.

4. Disconnect the horn electrical connector.
5. Place matchmarks on the steering wheel and shaft and remove the steering wheel retaining nut.
6. Remove the steering wheel, using a puller.

To install:

7. Install the steering wheel on the shaft, aligning the matchmarks. Tighten the retaining nut to 25 ft. lbs. (34 Nm).
8. Connect the horn electrical connector.
9. Install the inflator module as follows:

✳✳CAUTION

When carrying a live inflator module, make sure the bag and trim cover are pointed away from you.

   a. Install the inflator module to the steering wheel and connect the upper steering column connector and the CPA.
   b. Install the 2 Torx® head screws attaching the inflator module to the steering wheel and tighten to 78 inch lbs. (8.8 Nm).
   c. Install the 2 side trim covers to the steering column.
10. Enable the SRS as outlined earlier in this Section.

Combination Switch

REMOVAL & INSTALLATION

1985-92

▶ See Figures 52 and 53

1. Disconnect the negative battery cable.
2. Remove the lower dash cover and the air duct.
3. On Prizm vehicles, remove the upper and lower steering column covers. On Nova vehicles, remove the lower column cover; the upper cover will come off with the switch.
4. Remove the steering wheel.
5. Disconnect the wiring at the connector.
6. Unscrew the mounting screws and remove the switch. The Nova switch will come off with the upper column cover.

To install:

7. When reinstalling, place the switch in position and tighten the bolts.
8. Connect the wiring harness and reinstall the steering wheel.
9. Reinstall the column cover(s).

Fig. 49 Using a steering wheel puller to remove the steering wheel

Fig. 50 Removing the side trim covers — 1993 models

Fig. 51 Removing the inflator module from the steering wheel — 1993 models

10. Install the lower dash trim panel.
11. Connect the negative battery cable.

1993 Models

▶ **See Figure 54**

1. Disable the SRS as outlined earlier in this Section.
2. Remove the SRS coil assembly as follows:
   a. With the SRS disabled, remove the steering wheel.
   b. Remove the upper and lower steering column trim covers.
   c. Unclip and set aside the left front carpet retainer.
   d. Remove the 2 screws and disconnect the hood release lever from the knee bolster.

e. Remove the 2 trim caps and unbolt and remove the knee bolster from the instrument panel.
   f. Untape the SRS coil assembly harness from the combination switch harness.
   g. Disconnect the electrical connector from the SRS coil.
   h. Remove the 4 screws and remove the SRS coil assembly from the combination switch.
3. Disconnect the combination switch electrical connector.
4. Remove the 4 screws and remove the combination switch from the steering column.

To install:

5. Install the 4 screws and the combination switch to the steering column.
6. Connect the combination switch electrical connector.
7. Turn the spiral cable on the combination switch counterclockwise by hand until it becomes harder to turn. Then rotate the cable clockwise about 3 turns to align the alignment mark. The connector should be straight up.
8. Install the SRS coil assembly by reversing removal Step 2, above.
9. Install the steering wheel (align matchmarks) onto the shaft and torque nut to 25 ft. lbs. (34 Nm).
10. Enable the SRS as outlined earlier in this Section.

Ignition Switch/Ignition Lock

REMOVAL & INSTALLATION

▶ **See Figure 55**

1. Disconnect the negative battery cable.
2. Unscrew the retaining screws and remove the upper and lower steering column covers.
3. Remove the 2 retaining screws and remove the steering column trim.
4. Turn the ignition key to the **ACC** position.
5. Push the lock cylinder stop in with a small, round object (cotter pin, punch, etc.) and pull out the ignition key and the lock cylinder.

➡ **You may find that removing the steering wheel and the combination switch makes the job easier.**

6. Loosen the mounting screw and withdraw the ignition switch from the lock housing.

To install:

7. When reinstalling, position the switch so that the recess and the bracket tab are properly aligned. Install the retaining screw.
8. Make sure that both the lock cylinder and the column lock are in the ACC position. Slide the cylinder into the lock housing until the stop tab engages the hole in the lock.
9. Make certain the stop tab is firmly seated in the slot. Turn the key to each switch position, checking for smoothness of motions and a positive feel. Remove and insert the key a few times, each time turning the key to each switch position.
10. Reinstall the combination switch and the steering wheel if they were removed.
11. Install the steering column trim and the upper and lower column covers.
12. Connect the negative battery cable.

1. Column upper housing
2. Column lower housing
3. Upper bracket assembly
4. Main shaft bearing
5. Bearing retainer
6. Tube assembly
7. Column protector
8. Protector cushion
9. Main shaft bearing snapring
10. Shaft thrust stopper
11. O-ring
12. Hole cover clamp
13. Hole cover
14. Shaft snapring
15. Main shaft assembly
16. Pinch bolt
17. Sliding yoke
18. Break away bracket (Tilt)
19. Tilt lever lock bolt (Tilt)
20. Column ground cable (Tilt)
21. Plate washer (Tilt)
22. Tilt lever (Tilt)
23. Adjusting nut (Tilt)
24. Adjusting lever bolt (Tilt)
25. Lower support (Tilt)
26. Support tube bushing (Tilt)
27. O-ring (Tilt)
28. Pawl set bolt (Tilt)
29. Torsion spring (Tilt)
30. Nut
31. Wheel pad
32. Combination switch
33. Steering wheel
34. Return spring grommet.

Fig. 52 Nova steering column components

Steering Column

REMOVAL & INSTALLATION

Nova

▶ **See Figure 52**

1. Remove the steering wheel.
2. Remove the combination switch.
3. Loosen the hole cover clamp screw.
4. Remove the pinch bolt from the yoke.
5. Remove the yoke from the steering gear.
6. Remove the bolts holding the lower column mounting brackets.

7. Remove the bolts holding the upper column to the instrument panel.
8. Remove the column from the car.
To install:
9. When reinstalling, place the column assembly into position and install the upper and lower bracket nuts and bolts finger tight.
10. Position the column assembly so the end of the lower support holes touch the mounting bolts.
11. Tighten the upper and lower support nuts and bolts to 19 ft. lbs.
12. Install the yoke and tighten the pinch bolt to 26 ft. lbs.
13. Install the hole cover clamp.
14. Install the combination switch.
15. Install the steering wheel.

1. Hole cover
2. Intermediate shaft
3. Ignition harness connector
4. Lock cylinder assembly
5. Upper column cover
6. Multi-function switch
7. Wheel pad
8. Steering wheel
9. Steering column tube
10. Lower column cover
11. Lower instrument panel trim.

Fig. 53 Prizm steering column components — 1989-92

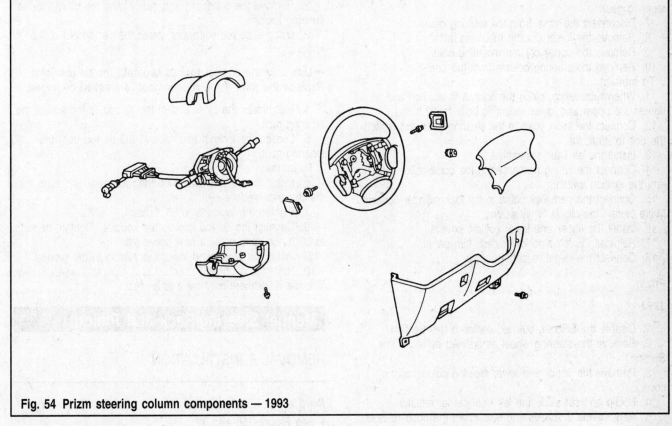

Fig. 54 Prizm steering column components — 1993

Fig. 55 Ignition switch removal — Prizm

Prizm

1989-92

➡While it is possible to remove the column with the steering wheel attached, it is much easier if the wheel is removed.

1. Disconnect the negative battery cable
2. Remove the left side lower dash trim panel; let it rest on the floor.
3. Remove the upper and lower column covers.
4. Disconnect the wiring harnesses to the combination switch and the ignition switch.
5. Disconnect the park/lock cable from the lock cylinder housing. (automatic transmission only)
6. Remove the air filter assembly to gain access to the steering gear.
7. Disconnect the yoke from the steering gear.
8. Remove the lower column mounting bolts.
9. Remove the upper column mounting bolts.
10. Remove the steering column from the car.
   To install:
11. When reinstalling, place the column in position and tighten the upper and lower mounting bolts to 19 ft. lbs.
12. Connect the shaft yoke to the steering gear and tighten the bolt to 26 ft. lbs.
13. Install the air filter assembly.
14. Connect the wiring harnesses to the combination switch and the ignition switch.
15. Connect the park/lock cable to the lock cylinder housing. Make certain the clip is firmly seated.
16. Install the upper and lower column covers.
17. Reinstall the left side lower dash trim panel.
18. Connect the negative battery cable.

Prizm

1993

1. Disable the SRS as outlined earlier in this Section.
2. Remove the steering wheel as outlined earlier in this Section.
3. Remove the upper and lower steering column trim covers.
4. Unclip and set aside the left front carpet retainer.
5. Remove the 2 screws and disconnect the hood release lever from the knee bolster.

6. Remove the 2 trim caps and unbolt and remove the knee bolster from the instrument panel.
7. Disconnect the steering column electrical connectors.
8. Disconnect the steering column pinch bolt.
9. Remove the 2 nuts and 2 bolts and disconnect the steering column from the instrument panel.
   To install:
10. Position the steering column to the instrument panel and tighten the 2 nuts and 2 bolts to 19 ft. lbs. (25 Nm).
11. Connect the steering column pinch bolt and tighten to 26 ft. lbs. (35 Nm).
12. Connect the steering column electrical connectors.
13. Install the upper and lower steering column trim covers.
14. Connect the hood release lever to the knee bolster.
15. Bolt the knee bolster to the instrument panel and install the 2 trim caps.
16. Install the left front carpet retainer.
17. Install the steering wheel as outlined earlier in this Section.
18. Enable the SRS as outlined earlier in this Section.

Tie Rod Ends

REMOVAL & INSTALLATION

▶ **See Figure 56**

1. Raise the front of the vehicle and support it safely. Remove the wheel.
2. Remove the cotter pin and nut holding the tie rod to the steering knuckle.
3. Using a tie rod separator, press the tie rod out of the knuckle.

➡Use only the correct tool to separate the tie rod joint. Replace the joint if the rubber boot is cracked or ripped.

4. Matchmark the inner end of the tie rod to the end of the steering rack.
5. Loosen the locknut and remove the tie rod from the steering rack.
   To install:
6. Install the tie rod ends onto the rack ends and align the matchmarks made earlier.
7. Tighten the locknuts to 35 ft. lbs.
8. Connect the tie rod joint to the knuckle. Tighten the nut to 36 ft. lbs. and install a new cotter pin.
9. Install the wheel and lower the vehicle to the ground.
10. Have the alignment checked at a reputable repair facility. The toe adjustment may have to be reset.

Manual Steering/Rack and Pinion

REMOVAL & INSTALLATION

Nova

▶ **See Figures 56 and 57**

1. Remove the cover from the intermediate shaft.

Fig. 56 Removing the tie-rod end from the steering rack

2. Loosen the upper pinch bolt. Remove the lower pinch bolt at the pinion shaft.

3. Loosen the wheel lug nuts.

4. Elevate and safely support the vehicle.

5. Remove both front wheels.

6. Remove the cotter pins from both ball joints and remove the nuts.

7. Using a tie rod separator, remove both tie rod joints from the knuckles.

8. Remove the nuts and bolts attaching the steering rack to the body.

9. Remove the rack through the access hole.

To install:

10. Install the rack through the access hole. Secure it with the retaining bolts and nuts and tighten them to 43 ft. lbs.

11. Connect the tie rods to each knuckle. Tighten the nuts to 36 ft. lbs. and install new cotter pins.

12. Install the front wheels.

13. Lower the car to the ground.

14. Install the lower pinch bolt at the pinion shaft. Tighten the upper and lower bolts to 26 ft. lbs.

15. Install the cover on the intermediate shaft.

Prizm

▶ **See Figure 56**

1. Remove the cover from the intermediate shaft.

2. Loosen the upper pinch bolt. Remove the lower pinch bolt at the pinion shaft.

3. Loosen the wheel lug nuts.

4. Elevate and safely support the vehicle.

5. Remove both front wheels.

6. Install an engine support and tension it to support the engine without raising it.

✴✴CAUTION

The engine hoist is in place and under tension. Use care when repositioning the vehicle and make necessary adjustments to the engine support.

7. Remove the 3 bolts holding the center crossmember to the radiator support.

8. Remove the covers from the front and center mount bolts.

9. Remove the 2 front mount bolts, then the center mount bolts.

10. Support the crossmember and remove the 2 rear mount bolts.

11. Remove the 2 bolts holding the center crossmember to the main crossmember.

12. Use a floor jack and a wide piece of wood to support the main crossmember assembly.

13. Remove the 8 bolts holding the main crossmember to the body.

✴✴CAUTION

When the fasteners are removed, the crossmembers are loose and free to fall. Make sure they are properly supported.

14. Remove the 2 bolts holding the lower control arm brackets to the body.

15. Slowly lower the main crossmember while holding onto the center crossmember.

16. Remove the cotter pins from both ball joints and remove the nuts.

17. Using a tie rod separator, remove both tie rod joints from the knuckles.

18. Remove the nuts and bolts attaching the steering rack to the body.

19. Remove the rack through the right side wheel well.

To install:

20. Place it in position through the right wheel well and tighten the bracket bolts to 45 ft. lbs.

21. Attach the tie rods to the knuckles. Tighten the nuts to 36 ft. lbs. and install new cotter pins.

22. Position the center crossmember over the center and rear transaxle mount studs; start 2 nuts on the center mount.

23. Loosely install the 3 bolts holding the center crossmember to the radiator support.

24. Loosely install the 2 front mount bolts.

25. Raise the main crossmember into position over the rear mount studs and align all underbody bolts. Install the 2 rear mount nuts loosely.

26. Install the 8 main crossmember to underbody bolts loosely.

27. Install the 2 lower control arm bracket bolts loosely.

28. Loosely install the 2 bolts holding the center crossmember to the main crossmember.

29. The crossmembers, bolts and brackets should now all be in place and held loosely by their nuts and bolts. If any repositioning is necessary, do so now.

30. On 1989-92 models, tighten the components below in the order listed to the correct torque specification:
- Main crossmember to underbody bolts: 152 ft. lbs.
- Lower control arm bolts: 94 ft. lbs.
- Center crossmember to radiator support bolts: 45 ft. lbs.
- Front, center and rear mount bolts: 45 ft. lbs.

31. On 1993 Models, refer to the appropriate illustration earlier in this section and torque the fasteners as follows:
- Main crossmember to underbody bolts: 152 ft. lbs.
- Nut A to 35 ft. lbs. (48 Nm)
- Bolt B to 45 ft. lbs (61 (Nm)
- Nut C to 45 ft. lbs. (61 Nm)

32. Install the covers on the front and center mount bolts.

33. Install the front wheels.

34. Lower the vehicle to the ground.

35. Connect the yoke to the pinion and tighten both the upper and lower bolts to 26 ft. lbs.

36. Install the yoke cover.

OVERHAUL

Disassembly

▶ **See Figures 57, 58 and 59**

1. Clamp steering gear housing in a vise. Matchmark and remove the tie rod ends from the housing.

2. Mark left and right boots for correct installation, remove the clamps then remove the boots.

3. Remove rack ends and unstake claw washers.

4. On 1985-92 models, remove the rack guide spring cap locknut and the spring and rack guide.

5. On 1993 models, remove the 2 bolts and the rack guide spring cover and the O-ring, compression spring, rack guide and rack guide seat.

6. Remove the pinion bearing adjusting screw locknut.

7. Remove the pinion bearing adjusting screw.

8. Remove the pinion with upper bearing.

9. Remove the rack from the pinion side.

Inspection

Check the steering rack for runout and for teeth wear or damage. The maximum runout is 0.012 inch. (0.3mm), for 1985-88 and 0.006 inch (0.15 mm), on later models. Replace the rack bushing, pinion oil seal or the rack assembly, as necessary.

Assembly

1. Grease all necessary parts upon installation. Install rack into the rack housing.

2. Install pinion into the housing.

3. Install pinion bearing adjusting screw.

4. Adjust the pinion preload (loosen or tighten pinion bearing adjusting screw). The preload (turning) specification is 2.0-2.9 inch lbs., for 1985-92 and 3.5 inch lbs. for 1993

5. Install pinion bearing adjusting screw locknut. Torque the locknut to 83 ft. lbs. (113 Nm)

6. Recheck the preload (turning) specification and adjust as necessary.

7. On 1985-92 models perform the following:

   a. Install the rack guide and spring.

   b. Install rack guide spring cap.

➡**When measuring the preload, measure within one rotation from the neutral position in both directions.**

   c. Center pinion by rotation. Adjust total preload by loosening the rack guide spring cap. The preload (turning) specification is 8.7-11.3 inch lbs.

   d. Install rack guide spring cap locknut. Torque the locknut to 51 ft. lbs. (69 Nm).

8. On 1993 models perform the following:

   a. Install the rack guide seat, rack guide, compression spring and O-ring.

   b. Install the rack guide spring cover and tighten the 2 retaining bolts to 106 inch lbs. (12 Nm).

   c. Install the center set bolt but do not tighten fully.

   d. Tighten the set bolt using a 4mm hexagon wrench.

   e. Measure and adjust the total preload. The total preload specification is 6.1-13.0 inch lbs.

   f. If the preload is less than specified, retorque the rack guide spring cover and return it approximately 12 degrees.

   g. If the preload is more than specified, slightly return the rack guide spring cover.

   h. Tighten the center set bolt nut to 15 ft. lbs. (21 Nm).

9. Recheck the total preload. Install rack ends and claw washers. Stake the claw washers.

10. Install rack boots and clamps.

11. Align matchmarks and install tie rod ends. Torque the locknuts to 35 ft. lbs. (47 Nm) for 1985-88 and 41 ft. lbs. (56 Nm) for 1989-93.

Power Steering Rack

The power assisted rack and pinion system has a rotary control valve which directs hydraulic fluid under pressure to either side of the rack piston. The piston uses this pressure to move the rack left or right. The rack then moves the tie rods and knuckles, which turn the wheels.

REMOVAL & INSTALLATION

Nova

▶ **See Figure 60**

1. Remove the intermediate shaft cover.

2. Loosen the upper pinch bolt and remove the lower pinch bolt.

3. Place a drain pan below the power steering rack assembly. Clean the area around the line fittings on the rack.

4. Loosen the front wheel lug nuts.

5. Safely elevate and support the vehicle.

6. Remove the front wheels.

7. Remove the cotter pins and nuts from both tie rod joints. Separate the joints from the knuckle using a tie rod joint separator.

8. Support the transaxle with a jack.

9. Remove the rear bolts holding the engine crossmember to the body.

10. Remove the nut and bolt holding the rear engine mount to the mount bracket.

11. Label and disconnect the fluid pressure and return lines at the rack.

12. Remove the 4 bolts and nuts holding the rack brackets to the body. It will be necessary to slightly raise and lower the rear of the transaxle to gain access to the bolts.

13. Remove the rack through the access hole.

   To install:

14. Place the rack in position through the access hole and install the retaining brackets to the body. Tighten the nuts and bolts to 39 ft. lbs.

15. Connect the fluid lines to the rack.

16. Install the nut and bolt holding the rear engine mount to the mount bracket. Tighten the nut and bolt to 29 ft. lbs.

17. Reinstall the engine crossmember bolts and tighten them to 29 ft. lbs.

Fig. 57 Exploded view of the Nova manual rack and pinion steering gear

18. Remove the jack from the transaxle.

19. Connect the tie rod ends to the knuckles. Tighten the nuts to 36 ft. lbs. and install new cotter pins.

20. Install the wheels and lower the vehicle to the ground.

21. Connect the intermediate shaft to the steering rack. Install the lower bolt; tighten both the upper and lower bolts to 26. ft. lbs. Install the intermediate shaft cover.

22. Add fluid and bleed the system.

23. Have the alignment checked and adjusted at a reliable repair facility.

Prizm

▶ **See Figure 61**

1. Place a drain pan under the steering rack.

2. Remove the cover from the intermediate shaft.

3. Loosen the upper pinch bolt. Remove the lower pinch bolt at the pinion shaft.

4. Loosen the wheel lug nuts.

5. Elevate and safely support the vehicle.

6. Remove both front wheels.

7. Install an engine support and tension it to support the engine without raising it.

❋❋CAUTION

The engine hoist is now in place and under tension. Use care when repositioning the vehicle and make necessary adjustments to the engine support.

8. Remove the 3 bolts holding the center crossmember to the radiator support.

9. Remove the covers from the front and center mount bolts.

10. Remove the 2 front mount bolts, then the center mount bolts and then the 2 rear mount bolts.

11. Remove the 2 bolts holding the center crossmember to the main crossmember.

12. Use a floor jack and a wide piece of wood to support the main crossmember.

13. Remove the 8 bolts holding the main crossmember to the body.

14. Remove the 2 bolts holding the lower control arm brackets to the body.

❋❋CAUTION

The crossmembers are loose and free to fall. Make sure they are properly supported.

15. Slowly lower the main crossmember while holding onto the center crossmember.

16. Remove the cotter pins from both tie rod ball joints and remove the nuts.

17. Using a tie rod separator, remove both tie rod joints from the knuckles.

18. Label and disconnect the fluid pressure and return lines from the rack.

19. Remove the nuts and bolts attaching the steering rack to the body.

20. Remove the rack through the right side wheel well.

To install:

21. Place it in position through the right wheel well and tighten the bracket bolts to 43 ft. lbs.

Fig. 58 Exploded view of the Prizm manual rack and pinion steering gear — 1989-92

22. Connect the fluid lines to the rack and tighten the fittings to 33 ft. lbs. Make certain the fittings are correctly threaded before tightening them.

23. Attach the tie rods to the knuckles. Tighten the nuts to 36 ft. lbs. and install new cotter pins.

24. Position the center crossmember over the center and rear transaxle mount studs; start 2 nuts on the center mount.

25. Loosely install the 3 bolts holding the center crossmember to the radiator support.

26. Loosely install the 2 front mount bolts.

27. Raise the main crossmember into position over the rear mount studs and align all underbody bolts. Install the 2 rear mount nuts loosely.

28. Install the 8 main crossmember to underbody bolts loosely.

29. Install the 2 lower control arm bracket bolts loosely.

30. Loosely install the 2 bolts holding the center crossmember to the main crossmember.

31. The crossmembers, bolts and brackets should now all be in place and held loosely by their nuts and bolts. If any repositioning is necessary, do so now.

32. On 1989-92 models, tighten the components below in the order listed to the correct torque specification:
   • Main crossmember to underbody bolts: 152 ft. lbs.
   • Lower control arm bolts: 94 ft. lbs.
   • Center crossmember to radiator support bolts: 45 ft. lbs.
   • Front, center and rear mount bolts: 45 ft. lbs.

15. O-ring
16. Rack guide spring cover
17. Set bolt
18. Inner tie rod
19. Locking washer
20. Steering rack
21. Outer tie rod
22. Tie rod locking nut

1. Boot clip
2. Steering gear rack boot
3. Boot clamp
4. Rack bushing
5. Steering gear rack housing
6. Pinion bearing adjusting screw
7. Pinion upper bearing
8. Upper pinion seal
9. Pinion upper bearing
10. Steering pinion
11. Pinion lower bearing
12. Rack guide seat
13. Rack guide
14. Compression ring

Fig. 59 Exploded view of the Prizm manual rack and pinion steering gear — 1993

33. On 1993 Models, refer to the appropriate illustration found earlier in this section and torque the fasteners as follows:
- Main crossmember to underbody bolts: 152 ft. lbs.
- Nut A to 35 ft. lbs. (48 Nm)
- Bolt B to 45 ft. lbs (61 (Nm)
- Nut C to 45 ft. lbs. (61 (Nm)
34. Install the covers on the front and center mount bolts.
35. Install the front wheels.
36. Lower the vehicle to the ground.
37. Connect the yoke to the pinion and tighten both the upper and lower bolts to 26 ft. lbs.
38. Install the yoke cover.
39. Add power steering fluid to the reservoir and bleed the system.
40. Have the alignment checked at a reliable repair facility.

OVERHAUL

Nova

▶ **See Figure 62**

DISASSEMBLY

1. Clamp steering gear housing in a vise.
2. Remove right and left turn pressure tubes. Matchmark and remove the tie rod ends from the housing.
3. Mark left and right boots for correct installation, remove the clamps then remove the boots.
4. Remove rack ends and unstake claw washers.
5. Remove the rack guide spring cap locknut.
6. Remove the rack guide spring cap.
7. Remove rack guide spring and rack guide.
8. Remove the rack housing cap.

Fig. 60 Nova power steering rack assembly

9. Remove self-locking nut while holding control valve in place.
10. Remove the control valve housing assembly.
11. Remove the cylinder end stopper.
12. Remove the rack bushing and rack.

Inspection

Check the steering rack for runout and for teeth wear or damage. The maximum runout is 0.012 in. (0.3mm). Replace the bushing, oil seals, teflon rings and O-rings if necessary.

Assembly

1. Grease or coat with power steering fluid on all necessary parts upon installation. Install rack into the rack housing.
2. Install rack bushing.
3. Install cylinder end stopper.
4. Install control valve.
5. Install oil seal.
6. Install dust cover.
7. Install control valve housing. Torque housing retaining bolts to 13 ft. lbs.
8. Install self-locking nut. Torque to 18 ft. lbs.
9. Install rack housing cap. Torque to 43 ft. lbs.
10. Install rack guide and rack guide spring.
11. Adjust total preload-tighten the rack guide spring cap. The preload (turning) specification is 7.8-10.4 inch lbs.
12. Install rack guide spring cap locknut. Tighten the locknut to 33 ft. lbs.
13. Recheck the preload (turning) specification which is 7.8-10.4 inch lbs.

14. Install rack ends and claw washers. Torque the rack ends to 53 ft. lbs. Stake the claw washers.
15. Install rack boots and clamps.
16. Align matchmarks and install tie rod ends. Torque the locknuts to 35 ft. lbs.
17. Install right and left turn pressure tubes. Torque tubes to 18 ft. lbs.

Prizm
▶ See Figure 63

DISASSEMBLY

1. Remove the power steering gear assembly from the vehicle as described earlier in this section. Mount the steering gear assembly into a vise. Place a piece of wood or soft metal between the steering gear assembly and the vise jaws to prevent damage to the steering gear.
2. Remove the right and left turn pressure pipes between the valve housing and the cylinder using a J 29698-A fuel line wrench, or equivalent. Loosen the locknuts and match the tie rod end marks to the tie rod marks.
3. Remove the locknuts and both tie rod ends.
4. Remove both rack boots, one retaining clip and one retaining clamp per boot. Unstake claw washers retaining both tie rods to steering rack.
5. Remove the tie rods and claw washers from the steering rack using a J 35414 tie rod housing wrench and a J 35418 steering rack end wrench or their equivalents.
6. Remove the steering rack guide cap nut, cap, spring, rack guide and seat using a J 35423 rack guide spring cap wrench and a J 35692 spring cap locknut wrench.
7. Remove the rack housing dust cover.

1. Mounting bracket
2. Cotter pin
3. Pressure and return lines
4. Column hole cover
5. Universal joint (yoke)
6. Intermediate shaft
7. Steering gear housing
8. Boot
9. Tie rod
10. Tie rod end
11. Engine mount
12. Grommet

Fig. 61 Prizm power steering rack assembly

8. Remove the housing snapring using snapring pliers.
9. Remove the housing cap.
10. Remove the lower valve nut, the lower bearing and spacer using a J 35428 pinion preload socket.
11. Remove the control valve using a J 35420 steering gear bushing installer or its equivalent.

❋❋WARNING

Do not remove the control valve by tapping it out of the housing; the valve may be damaged.

12. Remove the end stopper snapring using snapring pliers.
13. Remove the rack housing stopper and spacer.

14. Remove the rack and oil seal from the housing.
15. Remove the cylinder inner oil seal and spacer using a J 35434 rack cylinder seal remover or its equivalent.
16. Clean all disassembled parts. Do not use a wire brush.

ASSEMBLY

1. Install the new inner (teflon) and outer O-rings seals.
2. Install the new control valve (teflon) rings. Apply the power steering gear and pump fluid GM P/N 1050017, or equivalent, to a new housing oil seal.
3. Install the new housing oil seal.
4. Install the inner bushing to the valve housing using a J 35695 inner pinion bushing installer with a J 8092 driver

1. O-ring seal
2. Right side pressure tube
3. Left side pressure tube
4. Boot clip
5. Steering rack boot
6. Boot clamp
7. Pinion dust cover
8. Snap ring
9. Pinion upper seal
10. Upper pinion bearing
11. Control valve sealing ring
12. Pinion assembly valve
13. Snap ring
14. Cylinder end stopper
15. Outer cylinder end thick spacer
16. Outer cylinder end seal
17. Inner cylinder end seal
18. Inner cylinder end thin spacer
19. Rack housing
20. Lower pinion valve bushing
21. Pinion valve seal
22. Union seat
23. Rack guide seat
24. Rack guide
25. Rack guide spring
26. Rack guide spring cap
27. Rack guide locking nut
28. Pinion lower valve spacer
29. Pinion lower valve bearing
30. Pinion lower locking valve cap nut
31. Pinion lower valve cap
32. Ball joint inner end sub-assembly
33. Claw licking washer
34. O-ring ring
35. Piston sealing ring
36. Rack

Fig. 62 Nova power steering rack components

handle or their equivalent. The bushing must be installed to a depth of 2.736 inches (69.5 mm).

✳✳WARNING

If the bushing is pushed in too far, it will cause deformation of the housing. If it is not pushed in far enough, it will interfere with the pinion valve.

Apply power steering gear and pump fluid GM P/N 1050017, or equivalent, to control valve and inner bushing. Install the control valve and inspect for proper operation. Remove valve after inspection.

Clean the rack teeth, then cover the teeth with electrical tape. Tape both ends of the rack bar, especially the air bleed holes, to prevent damage to the oil seal lips.

Apply power steering gear and pump fluid GM P/N 1050017, or equivalent, to the cylinder bore and the new inner oil seal.

5. Install the new inner oil seal onto the rack lip end first.
6. Install a 0.079 inch (2 mm) cylinder spacer.
7. Apply electrical tape to the rack teeth. Apply power steering gear and pump fluid GM P/N 1050017, or equivalent, to a new cylinder outer oil seal.
8. Install the new outer oil seal onto the rack lip end first. Apply power steering gear and pump fluid GM P/N 1050017, or equivalent, to cylinder bore. Carefully install steering rack into cylinder. Push the inner oil seal, piston seal ring and outer oil seal into the bore. Be careful not to damage components on cylinder bore end or snapring groove.
9. Install a 0.236 inch (6 mm) cylinder spacer.

➡**Make sure to install spacer with shallow side facing out. Apply power steering gear and pump fluid GM P/N 1050017, or equivalent, to rack housing stopper.**

10. Install rack housing stopper onto rack and push into cylinder bore.
11. Install rack into cylinder. Tap the end of the rack with a fiber hammer to seat the inner seal and spacer. Seat the rack housing stopper using a J 35425 power rack pinion bearing and seal installer. The stopper should be in far enough to expose the snapring groove.
12. Install the snapring to cylinder end stopper. Inspect the inner and outer cylinder seal operation using a J 23738-A valve stem seal tester and a J 35376 cylinder pressure tester or their equivalents. Apply 15 in. Hg of vacuum. If vacuum does not hold for a minimum of 30 seconds, replace the faulty seals.
13. Install the control valve into the housing.
14. Install the rack housing upper bearing using a J 35425 power rack pinion bearing and seal installer or its equivalent. Apply the power steering gear and pump fluid GM P/N 1050017, or equivalent, to rack housing oil seal and snapring.
15. Install the rack housing oil seal and snapring.
16. Install the dust cover.
17. Install the spacer and lower bearing on the control valve shaft.
18. Install the new self-locking nut on the control valve shaft using a J 35428 pinion preload socket or its equivalent. Tighten the pinion shaft locknut to 43 ft. lbs. (59 Nm). Apply power steering gear and pump fluid GM P/N 1050017 or equivalent, to the threads of a new rack housing cap.

19. Install the new rack housing cap. Tighten the rack housing cap to 51 ft. lbs. (69 Nm). Stake the housing cap using a hammer and chisel.
20. Install the rack guide seat, the rack guide and the rack guide spring. Apply Loctite pipe sealant (with Teflon) GM P/N 1052080, or equivalent to rack guide spring cap.
21. Install the rack guide spring cap using a J 35423 rack guide spring cap wrench and a torque wrench. Tighten the rack guide spring cap to 18 ft. lbs. (25 Nm). Adjust the total preload. Turn the rack guide spring cap 15 degrees counterclockwise. Turn the control valve shaft right and left 1-2 times. Use a torque wrench and a J 35428 pinion preload socket to adjust the pinion valve to 7-11 inch lbs. (0.8-Nm).
22. Install the rack guide spring cap locking nut. Tighten the rack guide spring cap locking nut to 33 ft. lbs. (44 Nm). Inspect the final preload of pinion valve. If preload is not 7-11 inch lbs. (0.8-1.3 Nm), readjust the preload.
23. Install the tie rods and the new claw washers. Tighten the tie rods to 61 ft. lbs. (83 Nm). Using a brass bar and hammer, stake the claw washers. Important: Be certain that the air bleed hole is clear of grease and contaminants. Apply power steering gear and pump fluid GM P/N 1050017, or equivalent, to the inside of the steering rack boots' small end.
24. Install the steering rack boots to the steering rack. Do not twist the boots during installation.
25. Install the clips securing the boots to the steering rack with the open ends of the clips facing outward.
26. Install the locknuts and the tie rod ends onto the tie rods until the matchmarks are aligned. Tighten the tie rod locknuts to 41 ft. lbs. (56 Nm).
27. Install the left and right turn pressure pipes using a J 29698-A fuel line wrench and a torque wrench. Tighten the left and right turn pressure pipe fittings to 18 ft. lbs. (25 Nm).

Power Steering Pump

Both the Nova and Prizm use a 10-vane hydraulic pump to pressurize the system. The pump is driven by a multi-ribbed belt. The pump employs a flow control valve which is sensitive to engine rpm. As the engine speed increases, the valve reduces the pressure flow to the steering gear. When the engine is at low rpm or at idle, the valve delivers higher pressure to the rack, offsetting the higher resistance of a slow moving tire. This "variable ratio" power steering offers a combination of high power assist at low speeds, thus making parking and turning easier, as well as firmer, less sensitive steering reactions at highway speeds.

REMOVAL & INSTALLATION

Nova with VIN Code 4 engine
▸ **See Figures 64 and 65**

1. Place a drain pan below the pump.
2. Remove the air cleaner assembly
3. Remove the clamp from the fluid return hose. Disconnect the pressure and return hoses at the pump. Plug the hoses and suspend them with the ends upward to prevent leakage.
4. Loosen the pump pulley nut. Push down on the belt to keep the pulley from turning.

1. Right side pressure tube
2. Left side pressure tube
3. Union seat
4. Oil seal
5. Rack housing bushing
6. Upper bearing
7. Rack housing seal
8. Snap ring
9. Dust cover
10. Control valve
11. Control valve snap ring (Teflon®)
12. Pressure feed tube union seat
13. Rack guide cap locking nut
14. Rack guide spring cap
15. Rack guide spring
16. Rack guide
17. Rack guide seat
18. Screw
19. Boot clamp
20. Rack boot
21. Hose clamp
22. End stopper snap ring
23. Rack housing stopper
24. Spacer
25. Outer oil seal
26. Rack end
27. Claw washer
28. Teflon O-ring
29. Steering rack
30. Outer O-ring
31. Rack housing cap
32. Control valve locking nut
33. Lower bearing
34. Control valve spacer
35. Steering rack housing
36. Spacer
37. Inner oil seal

Fig. 63 Prizm power steering rack components

5. Remove the adjusting bolt.

6. Remove the pivot bolt and remove the drive belt.

7. Remove the pump assembly.

8. Remove the pump bracket.

9. Remove the pulley. Be careful not to lose the small woodruff key between the pulley and the shaft.

To install:

10. Place the pump in position and temporarily install the 2 mounting bolts.

11. Install the pump bracket and tighten the bolts to 29 ft. lbs.

12. Install the pump pulley and the woodruff key. Tighten the pulley nut to 32 ft. lbs.

13. Install the drive belt, making certain that all the grooves of the belt are engaged on the pulley. Adjust the belt to the proper tension.

14. Connect the pressure and return lines to the pump. Tighten the fittings to 33 ft. lbs. Install the clamp on the return hose.

15. Install the air cleaner assembly.

16. Fill the reservoir to the proper level with power steering fluid and bleed the system.

17. After the car has been driven for about an hour, double check the belt adjustment.

Nova with VIN Code 5 engine

▶ **See Figures 66, 67 and 68**

1. Place a drain pan below the pump.

2. Remove the air cleaner assembly.

3. Disconnect the return hose from the pump, then disconnect the pressure hose. Plug the lines immediately to prevent fluid loss and contamination.

1. Return hose
2. Pump assembly
3. Bracket bolt
4. Pump bracket
5. Adjusting bolt
6. Pivot bolt
7. Drive belt
8. Pulley nut
9. Pump pulley
10. Woodruff key
11. Gasket
12. Union bolt
13. Pressure hose

Fig. 64 Nova power steering pump components — 1985-88 VIN code 4 engine

RIGHT   WRONG   WRONG

Fig. 65 There is only 1 correct way to install the drive belt.

4. Remove the splash shield under the engine.

5. Remove the pulley nut. Push down on the drive belt to prevent the pulley from turning.

6. Loosen the idler pulley nut and loosen the adjusting bolt.

7. Remove the drive belt.

8. Loosen the pump pulley and woodruff key. Don't lose the woodruff key.

9. Remove the upper mounting bolt.

10. Loosen the lower mounting bolt and pivot the pump downward.

11. Disconnect the oil pressure switch connector.

12. Remove the pump bracket mounting bolts; remove the pump from the engine with the bracket attached.

13. Remove the pulley from the pump and the pump from the bracket.

14. Remove the idler pulley bracket.

To install:

15. Mount the pump on the bracket and loosely install the lower mounting bolt.

16. Temporarily insert the pulley onto the pump shaft without the woodruff key. The pulley cannot be installed after the pump is installed on the engine.

17. Install the pump and bracket onto the engine. Tighten the upper mounting bolts to 29 ft. lbs.

18. Connect the oil pressure switch connector.

19. Install the idler pulley bracket; tighten the 3 mounting bolts to 29 ft. lbs.

20. Tighten the lower mounting bolts to 29 ft. lbs.

21. Install the woodruff key into the pulley and install the drive belt. Make certain the ribs of the belt are properly placed on all the pulleys.

22. Tighten the pulley nuts on the pump and idler to 28 ft. lbs.

23. Connect the pressure hose and tighten its fitting to 33 ft. lbs.

24. Connect the return hose.

25. Install the air cleaner and install the lower splash shield.

26. Adjust the belt to the proper tension.

27. Fill the reservoir to the proper level with power steering fluid and bleed the system.

28. After the car has been driven for about an hour, double check the belt adjustment.

1989-90 Prizm

▶ See Figure 69

1. Place a drain pan below the pump.
2. Elevate and safely support the vehicle.

1. Oil pressure switch connector
2. Pump bracket
3. Bolt
4. Woodruff key
5. Return hose
6. Pump assembly
7. Pressure hose
8. Lower mounting bolt
9. Idler pulley bracket bolt
10. Idler pulley bracket
11. Idler pulley
12. Idler pulley nut
13. Splash shield
14. Pump pulley
15. Pump pulley nut
16. Drive belt
17. Upper mounting bolt

Fig. 66 Nova power steering pump components — 1988 VIN code 5 engine

Fig. 67 Idler pulley and adjusting bolt — 1988 VIN code 5 engine

Fig. 68 Removing the upper pump mounting bolt — 1988 VIN code 5 engine Location of oil pressure switch connector — 1988 VIN code 5 engine

3. Remove the right front wheel.

4. Place a floor jack under the engine block and support it. Use a broad piece of wood to spread the load evenly and prevent damage.

5. Remove the bolt from the right side engine mount and lower the engine about 50mm to gain access to the lower power steering pump through-bolt.

6. Working through the right wheel well, remove the lower pump through-bolt.

7. Disconnect the fluid lines from the pump and plug them immediately.

8. Remove the upper mounting bolt from the pump and remove the pump.

To install:

9. Place the pump in position and install the mounting bolts. Tighten them to 29 ft. lbs.

Fig. 69 Removing the pressure hose. The GM tool shown makes the job easier.

10. Raise the engine to its normal position and install the engine mount bolt, tightening it to 69 ft. lbs.

11. Connect the fluid lines to the pump and tighten the pressure hose fitting to 34 ft. lbs.

12. Install the belt and adjust it to the proper tension.

13. Install the right front wheel.

14. Remove the jack and drain pan from under the engine.

15. Lower the vehicle to the ground.

16. Fill the reservoir to the proper level with power steering fluid and bleed the system.

17. After the car has been driven for about an hour, double check the belt adjustment.

1991-92 Prizm

BASE AND LSi MODELS

▶ See Figure 70

1. Disconnect the negative battery cable. Remove the air cleaner.

2. Remove the power steering pump drive belt.

3. Loosen the power steering hose retaining clip and remove the return hose from the power steering pump.

4. Remove the pressure hose from the pump using a injection line wrench J-29698 or equivalent.

5. Remove the upper mounting bolt from the pump.

6. Remove the vacuum hoses from the power steering switch. Remove the 3 bolts retaining the pump bracket mount and the 2 from the engine block and the one from the engine mount.

7. Remove the lower mounting bolt and the power steering pump from the vehicle.

8. Installation is the reverse order of the removal procedure. Torque the power steering pump mounting brackets to 29 ft. lbs. (39 Nm). Connect the pressure hose to the power steering pump union bolt and torque it to 32 ft. lbs. (44 Nm). Adjust the belt tension and bleed the system.

GSi MODELS

▶ See Figure 71

1. Disconnect the negative battery cable. Place a drain pan under the vehicle.

2. Remove the windshield washer reservoir retaining bolt; position the reservoir out of the way.

3. Loosen the drive pulley retaining nut. Use a J-35416 or equivalent adjusting screw wrench to keep the pulley from turning while loosening the retaining nut.

Fig. 70 Power steering pump mounting — 1991-92 Base and LSi models and all 1993 models

4. Raise and support the vehicle safely. Loosen the jam nut on the idler pulley. Lower the vehicle and remove the power steering pump drive belt.

5. Remove the drive pulley retaining nut from the shaft and remove the pulley from the pump.

6. Remove the power steering pressure lines from the pump.

7. Remove the 2 power steering pump retaining bolts and remove the pump from the bracket.

8. Installation is the reverse order of the removal procedure. Torque the power steering pump mounting brackets to 29 ft. lbs. (39 Nm). Connect the pressure hose to the power steering pump union bolt and torque it to 32 ft. lbs. (44 Nm). Adjust the belt tension and bleed the system.

1993 VEHICLES

▶ See Figure 70

1. Disconnect the negative battery cable. Remove the air cleaner.

2. Remove the power steering pump drive belt.

3. Loosen the power steering hose retaining clip and remove the return hose from the power steering pump.

4. Remove the pressure hose from the pump using a injection line wrench J-29698 or equivalent.

5. Remove the upper mounting bolt from the pump.

6. Remove the vacuum hoses from the power steering switch. Remove the 3 bolts retaining the pump bracket mount and the 2 from the engine block and the one from the engine mount.

7. Remove the lower mounting bolt and the power steering pump from the vehicle.

8. Installation is the reverse order of the removal procedure. Torque the power steering pump mounting brackets to 29 ft. lbs. (39 Nm). Connect the pressure hose to the power steering pump union bolt and torque it to 32 ft. lbs. (44 Nm). Adjust the belt tension and bleed the system.

BLEEDING THE POWER STEERING SYSTEM

Any time the power steering system has been opened or disassembled, the system must be bled to remove any air which may be trapped in the lines. Air will prevent the system from providing the correct pressures to the rack. The correct fluid level reading will not be obtained if the system is not bled.

1. With the engine running, turn the wheel all the way to the left and shut off the engine.

2. Add power steering fluid to the **COLD** mark on the indicator.

3. Start the engine and run at fast idle for about 15 seconds. Stop the engine and recheck the fluid level. Add to the **COLD** mark as needed.

4. Start the engine and bleed the system by turning the wheels from left to right 3 or 4 times.

5. Stop the engine and check the fluid level and condition. Fluid with air in it is a light tan color. This air must be eliminated from the system before normal operation can be obtained. Repeat Steps 3 and 4 until the correct fluid color and fluid level is obtained.

1. Return hose
2. Pump bracket
3. Pump bracket bolts
4. Pump lower mounting bolt
5. Pump lower mounting bolt
6. Pump
7. Gasket
8. Pressure hose bolt
9. Pressure hose

Fig. 71 Power steering pump mounting — 1991-92 GSi models

TORQUE SPECIFICATIONS

Component	U.S.	Metric
FRONT SUSPENSION–1985–88 Vehicles;		
Ball joint to control arm:	59 ft. lbs.	80 Nm
Ball joint to steering knuckle:	82 ft. lbs.	111 Nm
Lower control arm bushing rear nut:	76 ft. lbs.	103 Nm
Lower control arm bracket bolts:	72 ft. lbs.	98 Nm
Lower control arm to body bolt:	105 ft. lbs.	142 Nm
Strut to knuckle nuts;		
VIN code 4 engine:	105 ft. lbs.	142 Nm
VIN code 5 engine:	166 ft. lbs.	225 Nm
Caliper bracket to knuckle bolts:	63 ft. lbs.	88 Nm
Upper strut to body nuts;		
VIN code 4 engine:	23 ft. lbs.	31 Nm
VIN code 5 engine:	29 ft. lbs.	39 Nm
Strut shaft to upper support nut:	34 ft. lbs.	47 Nm
Brake pipe to flex hose:	11 ft. lbs.	15 Nm
Wheel lug nuts:	76 ft. lbs.	103 Nm
Steering tie rod to knuckle nut:	36 ft. lbs.	49 Nm
Axle shaft nut:	137 ft. lbs.	186 Nm
Stabilizer bar to control arm nut:	13 ft. lbs.	18 Nm
Exhaust pipe to exhaust manifold:	46 ft. lbs.	62 Nm
Stabilizer bar brackets:	14 ft. lbs.	19 Nm
FRONT SUSPENSION–1989–92 Vehicles;		
Strut assembly to body nuts:	29 ft. lbs.	39 Nm
Strut assembly to knuckle nuts:	194 ft. lbs.	263 Nm
Strut rod piston nut:	34 ft. lbs.	47 Nm
Brake line bracket bolt:	22 ft. lbs.	30 Nm
Left and right lower arm bolts:	22 ft. lbs.	30 Nm
Rear bracket to crossmember bolt and nut:	14 ft. lbs.	19 Nm
Rear bracket bolts:	94 ft. lbs.	127 Nm
Shock absorber lower bracket nuts:	194 ft. lbs.	263 Nm
Tie rod end castle nut:	36 ft. lbs.	49 Nm
Ball joint to control arm:	105 ft. lbs.	142 Nm
Brake caliper to steering knuckle:	65 ft. lbs.	88 Nm
Wheel bearing locknut:	137 ft. lbs.	186 Nm
Ball joint steering knuckle castle nut:	94 ft. lbs.	127 Nm
Front lower arm bolt:	152 ft. lbs.	206 Nm
Control arm rear bracket bolts:	94 ft. lbs.	127 Nm
Control arm rear bracket to crossmember bolt and nut:	14 ft. lbs.	19 Nm
Control arm bushing nut:	101 ft. lbs.	137 Nm
Left and right stabilizer link nuts;		
1990–92 vehicles:	26 ft. lbs.	35 Nm
Left and right stabilizer bracket bolts;		
1990–92:	94 ft. lbs.	127 Nm
Left and right stabilizer bracket nut and bolt;		
1990–92:	14 ft. lbs.	19 Nm
FRONT SUSPENSION–1993 Vehicles;		
Strut assembly mounting nuts:	29 ft. lbs.	39 Nm
Steering knuckle to strut assembly nuts:	203 ft. lbs.	263 Nm
ABS wire harness bolt:	48 inch lbs.	5.4 Nm
Brake hose bolt:	21 ft. lbs.	29 Nm
Strut rod piston nut:	34 ft. lbs.	47 Nm
Control arm to suspension crossmember bolt:	161 ft. lbs.	218 Nm
Control arm rear bushing nut:	101 ft. lbs.	137 Nm
Suspension crossmember to body bolts:	152 ft. lbs.	206 Nm
Left and right rear control arm bushing retaining bracket bolts and nuts;		
*Bolt A:	108 ft. lbs.	147 Nm
*Bolt B:	37 ft. lbs.	50 Nm
*Nut C:	14 ft. lbs.	19 Nm

TORQUE SPECIFICATIONS

Component	U.S.	Metric
Engine crossmember to suspension crossmember bolts and nuts:		
*Nut A:	35 ft. lbs.	48 Nm
*Bolt B:	45 ft. lbs.	61 Nm
*Nut C:	45 ft. lbs.	61 Nm
Ball joint to steering knuckle nut:	87 ft. lbs.	118 Nm
Ball joint to control arm nuts and bolts:	105 ft. lbs.	142 Nm
Tie rod end castle nut:	36 ft. lbs.	49 Nm
Brake caliper to steering knuckle set bolt:	65 ft. lbs.	88 Nm
ABS speed sensor bolt:	69 inch lbs.	7.8 Nm
Driveshaft locknut:	159 ft. lbs.	216 Nm
Dust cover bolts:	73 inch lbs.	8.3 Nm
REAR SUSPENSION–1985–88 Vehicles;		
Strut rod to axle carrier nut:	105 ft. lbs.	142 Nm
Suspension support nuts:	17 ft. lbs.	24 Nm
Front suspension arm (rear) bolts:	64 ft. lbs.	87 Nm
Front suspension arm (front) bolts:	64 ft. lbs.	87 Nm
Stabilizer link to suspension arm nut:	11 ft. lbs.	15 Nm
Strut piston rod nut:	36 ft. lbs.	49 Nm
Stabilizer bar bracket to body bolts:	9 ft. lbs.	13 Nm
Stabilizer bar to stabilizer links:	22 ft. lbs.	29 Nm
Axle hub & rear backing plate to carrier:	59 ft. lbs.	80 Nm
Bearing case to hub:	90 ft. lbs.	123 Nm
Axle carrier to to strut nuts:	105 ft. lbs.	142 Nm
Wheel lug nuts:	76 ft. lbs.	103 Nm
REAR SUSPENSION–1989–92 Vehicles;		
Strut assembly to body nuts:	29 ft. lbs.	49 Nm
Strut assembly to rear suspension knuckle nuts:	105 ft. lbs.	142 Nm
Strut piston rod nut:	36 ft. lbs.	49 Nm
Strut rod to body nuts:	87 ft. lbs.	118 Nm
Strut rod to rear suspension knuckle nuts:	87 ft. lbs.	118 Nm
No 1 suspension arm to body nuts:	87 ft. lbs.	118 Nm
No 1 suspension arm to rear suspension knuckle nuts:	87 ft. lbs.	118 Nm
No 2 suspension arm to body nuts:	87 ft. lbs.	118 Nm
No 2 suspension arm to rear suspension knuckle nuts:	87 ft. lbs.	118 Nm
Stabilizer bar bracket mounting bolts:	14 ft. lbs.	19 Nm
Stabilizer bar to stabilizer bar link nuts:	26 ft. lbs.	35 Nm
Stabilizer bar link to strut assembly:	26 ft. lbs.	35 Nm
Axle hub mounting bolts:	59 ft. lbs.	80 Nm
Brake line to backing plate:	11 ft. lbs.	15 Nm
Wheel bearing lock nut:	90 ft. lbs.	123 Nm
REAR SUSPENSION–1993 Vehicles;		
Strut assembly to strut support mounting nuts:	29 ft. lbs.	39 Nm
Strut assembly to rear suspension knuckle:	105 ft. lbs.	142 Nm
Strut piston rod nut:	36 ft. lbs.	49 Nm
Strut rod bolts and nuts:	67 ft. lbs.	91 Nm
Stabilizer bar link to strut assembly:	32 ft. lbs.	44 Nm
ABS wiring harness bolt:	48 inch lbs.	5.4 Nm
ABS speed sensor bolt:	69 inch lbs.	7.8 Nm

TORQUE SPECIFICATIONS

Component	U.S.	Metric
Suspension crossmember to body bolts:	43 ft. lbs.	58 Nm
Lateral link bolts and nuts:	87 ft. lbs.	118 Nm
Fuel tank band bolt:	29 ft. lbs.	39 Nm
Stabilizer bar bushing retainer bolts:	14 ft. lbs.	19 Nm
Stabilizer bar to stabilizer bar link nuts:	26 ft. lbs.	35 Nm
Axle hub mounting bolts:	59 ft. lbs.	80 Nm
Brake line fittings:	11 ft. lbs.	15 Nm
Wheel bearing lock nut:	90 ft. lbs.	123 Nm
STEERING COMPONENTS–1985–88 Vehicles;		
Power Steering Pump;		
Pressure hose union bolt;		
1985–88 VIN code 4 engine:	34 ft. lbs.	47 Nm
1988 VIN code 5 engine:	33 ft. lbs.	44 Nm
Pump pulley set nut;		
1985–88 VIN code 4 engine:	32 ft. lbs.	43 Nm
1988 VIN code 5 engine:	28 ft. lbs.	38 Nm
Mounting bolts:	29 ft. lbs.	39 Nm
Flow control valve pressure port:	51 ft. lbs.	69 Nm
Return and pressure pipes to gear:	33 ft. lbs.	44 Nm
Manual Rack and Pinion:		
Intermediate shaft pinch bolts:	26 ft. lbs.	35 Nm
Tie rod to knuckle nuts:	36 ft. lbs.	49 Nm
Gear housing to body mounting nuts and bolts:	43 ft. lbs.	59 Nm
Tie rod end locking nut:	41 ft. lbs.	56 Nm
Inner tie rod to rack:	61 ft. lbs.	83 Nm
Rack guide locking nut:	51 ft. lbs.	69 Nm
Pinion bearing adjusting screw locking nut:	83 ft. lbs.	113 Nm
Upper and lower steering column support bolts:	19 ft. lbs.	25 Nm
Manual Rack and Pinion		
Steering gear bracket bolts:	45 ft. lbs.	59 Nm
STEERING COMPONENTS–1989–93 Vehicles;		
Power Steering Gear and Pump;		
Mounting bolts:	29 ft. lbs.	39 Nm
Yoke bolts:	26 ft. lbs.	35 Nm
Tie rod end locking nut:	41 ft. lbs.	56 Nm
Pressure hose fitting:	34 ft. lbs.	47 Nm
Pressure port union bolt:	33 ft. lbs.	44 Nm
Steering gear bracket bolts:	43 ft. lbs.	59 Nm
Pump pulley nut:	32 ft. lbs.	43 Nm
Manual Rack and Pinion;		
Steering gear bracket bolts:	45 ft. lbs.	59 Nm
Tie rods:	53 ft. lbs.	72 Nm
Tie rod end nuts:	36 ft. lbs.	49 Nm
Tie rod end locking nut:	41 ft. lbs.	56 Nm
Yoke bolts:	26 ft. lbs.	35 Nm
Steering wheel shaft nut:	25 ft. lbs.	34 Nm
Steering column attachment bolts:	19 ft. lbs.	25 Nm
SRS inflator module to steering wheel screws:	78 inch lbs.	8.8 Nm

* See illustration in section

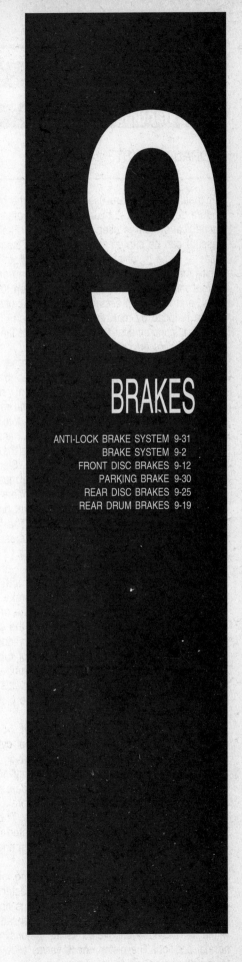

9

BRAKES

BRAKE SYSTEM

Understanding the Brakes

HYDRAULIC SYSTEM

Hydraulic systems are used to actuate the brakes of all modern automobiles. A hydraulic system rather than a mechanical system is used for 2 reasons. First, fluid under pressure can be carried to all parts of an automobile by small hoses — some of which are flexible — without taking up a significant amount of room or posing routing problems. Second, a great mechanical advantage can be given to the brake pedal, and the foot pressure required to actuate the brakes can be reduced by making the surface area of the master cylinder pistons smaller than that of any of the pistons in the wheel cylinders or calipers.

The master cylinder consists of a fluid reservoir and a single or double cylinder and piston assembly. Double type master cylinders are designed to separate the front and rear braking systems hydraulically in case of a leak. The master cylinder coverts mechanical motion from the pedal into hydraulic pressure within the lines. This pressure is translated back into mechanical motion at the wheels by either the wheel cylinder (drum brakes) or the caliper (disc brakes). Since these components receive the pressure from the master cylinder, they are generically classed as slave cylinders in the system.

Steel lines carry the brake fluid to a point on the vehicle's frame near each of the vehicle's wheels. The fluid is then carried to the slave cylinders by flexible tubes in order to allow for suspension and steering movements.

Each wheel cylinder contains 2 pistons, 1 at either end, which push outward in opposite directions and force the brake shoe into contact with the drum. In disc brake systems, the slave cylinders are part of the calipers. One or four cylinders are used to force the brake pads against the disc, but all cylinders contain 1 piston only. All slave cylinder pistons employ some type of seal, usually made of rubber, to minimize the leakage of fluid around the piston. A rubber dust boot seals the outer end of the cylinder against dust and dirt. The boot fits around the outer end of either the piston or the brake actuating rod.

When at rest the entire hydraulic system, from the piston(s) in the master cylinder to those in the wheel cylinders or calipers, is full of brake fluid. Upon application of the brake pedal, fluid trapped in front of the master cylinder piston(s) is forced through the lines to the slave cylinders. Here it forces the pistons outward, in the case of drum brakes, and inward toward the disc in the case of disc brakes. The motion of the pistons is opposed by return springs mounted outside the cylinders in drum brakes, and by internal springs or spring seals, in disc brakes.

Upon release of the brake pedal, a spring located inside the master cylinder immediately returns the master cylinder piston(s) to the normal position. The pistons contain check valves and the master cylinder has compensating ports drilled within it. These are uncovered as the pistons reach their normal position. The piston check valves allow fluid to flow toward the wheel cylinders or calipers as the pistons withdraw.

Then, as the return springs force the brake pads or shoes into the released position, the excess fluid in the lines is allowed to re-enter the reservoir through the compensating ports.

Dual circuit master cylinders employ 2 pistons, located one behind the other, in the same cylinder. The primary piston is actuated directly by mechanical linkage from the brake pedal. The secondary piston is actuated by fluid trapped between the 2 pistons. If a leak develops in front of the secondary pistons, it moves forward until it bottoms against the front of the master cylinder, and the fluid trapped between the pistons will operate the rear brakes. If the rear brakes develop a leak, the primary piston will move forward until direct contact with the secondary piston takes place, and it will force the secondary piston to actuate the front brakes. In either case, the brake pedal moves farther when the brakes are applied and less braking power is available.

All dual-circuit systems incorporate a switch which senses either line pressure or fluid level. This system will warn the driver when only half of the brake system is operational.

In some disc brake systems, this valve body also contains a metering valve and, in some cases, a proportioning valve. The metering valve keeps pressure from traveling to the disc brakes on the front wheels until the brake shoes on the rear wheels have contacted the drum, insuring that the front brakes will never be used alone. The proportioning valve controls the pressure to the rear brakes avoiding rear wheel lock-up during very hard braking.

DISC BRAKES

✳✳CAUTION

Brake pads contain asbestos, which has been determined to be a cancer causing agent. never clean the brake surfaces with compressed air! Avoid inhaling any dust from any brake surface! When cleaning brake surfaces, use a commercially available brake cleaning fluid.

Instead of the traditional expanding brakes that press outward against a circular drum, disc brake systems utilize a cast iron disc with brake pads positioned on either side of it. An easily seen analogy is the hand brake arrangement on a bicycle. The pads squeeze onto the rim of the bike wheel, slowing its motion. Automobile disc brakes use the identical principal but apply the braking effort to a separate disc instead of the wheel.

The disc or rotor is a 1-piece casting mounted just inside the wheel. Some discs are one solid piece while others have cooling fins between the 2 braking surfaces. These vented rotors enable air to circulate between the braking surfaces cooling them quicker and making them less sensitive to heat buildup and fade. Disc brakes are only slightly affected by dirt and water since contaminants are thrown off by the centrifugal action of the rotor or scraped off by the pads. Also, the equal clamping action of the 2 brake pads tend to ensure uniform, straight-line stops, although unequal application of the pads between the left and right wheels can cause a vicious pull under braking. All disc brakes are inherently self-adjusting.

There are 3 general types of disc brakes:

The fixed caliper design uses 2 pistons mounted on either side of the rotor (in each side of the caliper). The caliper is mounted rigidly and does not move. This is a very efficient brake system but the size of the caliper and its mounts adds weight and bulk to the car.

The sliding and floating designs are quite similar. In fact, these 2 types are often lumped together. In both designs, one is moved into contact with the rotor by hydraulic force. The caliper, which is not held in a fixed position, moves slightly, bringing the other pad into contact with the rotor. There are various methods of attaching floating calipers. Some pivot at the bottom or top, and some slide on mounting bolts. Many uneven brake wear problems can be caused by dirty or seized slides or pivots.

DRUM BRAKES

✳✳CAUTION

Brake shoes contain asbestos, which has been determined to be a cancer causing agent. Never clean the brake surfaces with Compressed air! Avoid inhaling any dust from any brake surface! When cleaning brake surfaces, use a commercially available brake cleaning fluid.

Drum brakes employ 2 brake shoes mounted on a stationary backing plate. These shoes are positioned inside a circular cast iron drum which rotates with the wheel. The shoes are held in place by springs; this allows them to slide toward the drum (when they are applied) while keeping the linings and drums in alignment. The shoes are actuated by a wheel cylinder which is mounted at the top of the backing plate. When the brakes are applied, hydraulic pressure forces the wheel cylinder's 2 actuating links outward. Since these links bear directly against the top of the brake shoes, the tops of the shoes are then forced outward against the inside of the drum. This action forces the bottoms of the 2 shoes to contact the brake drum by rotating the entire assembly slightly (known as servo action). When the pressure within the wheel cylinder is relaxed, return springs pull the shoes away from the drum.

Most modern drum brakes are designed to self-adjust during application when the vehicle is moving in reverse. This motion caused both shoes to rotate very slightly with the drum, rocking an adjusting lever, thereby causing rotation of the adjusting screw by means of a star wheel. This on-board adjustment system reduces the need for maintenance adjustments but most drivers don't back up enough to keep the brakes properly set.

POWER BRAKE BOOSTER

Virtually all cars today use a vacuum assisted power brake system to multiply the braking force and reduce pedal effort. Since vacuum is always available when the engine is operating, the system is simple and efficient. A vacuum diaphragm is located on the front of the master cylinder and assists the driver in applying the brakes, reducing both the effort and travel he must put into moving the brake pedal.

The vacuum diaphragm housing is connected to the intake manifold by a vacuum hose. A check valve is placed at the point where the hose enters the diaphragm housing, so that during periods of low manifold vacuum brakes assist will not be lost.

Depressing the brake pedal closes off the vacuum source and allows atmospheric pressure to enter on one side of the diaphragm. This causes the master cylinder pistons to move and apply the brakes. When the brake pedal is released, vacuum is applied to both sides of the diaphragm and springs return the diaphragm and master cylinder pistons to the released position.

If the vacuum supply fails, the brake pedal rod will contact the end of the master cylinder actuator rod and the system will apply the brakes without any power assistance. The driver will notice that much higher pedal effort is needed to stop the car and that the pedal feels 'harder' than usual.

Adjustments

DRUM BRAKES

▶ **See Figures 1 and 2**

The rear drum brakes are equipped with automatic adjusters actuated by the brake mechanism. No periodic adjustment of the drum brakes is necessary if this mechanism is working properly. If the pedal travel is greater than normal, it may be due to a lack of adjustment at the rear. In a safe location, drive the car backwards at low speed. While backing, pump the brake pedal slowly several times. (Neither the speed of the car or the speed of pumping the pedal has any effect on the adjustment. The idea is to apply the brakes several times while backing.) Drive forward and check the pedal feel by braking from moderate speed. It may take 2 or 3 passes in reverse to bring the pedal to the correct travel; each brake application moves the adjuster very little. It will take several applications to take up excess clearance.

If brake shoe-to-drum clearance is incorrect and applying and releasing the brakes in reverse does not adjust it properly, the parts will have to be disassembled for repair.

An alternate method of adjustment can be used when the brakes have been disassembled or when the reversing method does not work.

1. Elevate and safely support the vehicle. If only the rear wheels are elevated, block the front wheels with chocks. Once the vehicle is firmly on stands, release the parking brake.
2. Remove the rear wheels.
3. Remove the brake drum. It will not come off if the parking brake is applied.

✳✳CAUTION

Brake pads and shoes contain asbestos, which has been determined to be a cancer causing agent. Never clean the brake surfaces with compressed air! Avoid inhaling any dust from brake surfaces! When cleaning brakes, use commercially available brake cleaning fluids.

4. If the brake drum cannot be removed easily:

a. Insert a screwdriver through the hole in the backing plate and hold the adjusting lever away from the star wheel.

b. Using another screw driver or a brake adjusting tool, turn the wheel to reduce the tension (increase the clearance) on the brake shoes.

5. Use a brake drum measuring tool with both inside diameter and outside diameter capability (GM Tool J-22364-01 or equivalent). Measure the inside diameter of the brake drum and record the reading.

6. Measure the diameter of the brake shoe assemble at the friction surface. Use the adjusting wheel to adjust the brake shoes until the diameter of the shoes is either 0.60mm (Prizm) or 0.33mm (Nova) less than the diameter of the drum. This small clearance is important; over-adjusted brakes cause drag and premature wear on the shoes.

7. Install the brake drum(s) and install the rear wheel(s).

8. Apply the parking brake and lower the car to the ground.

BRAKE PEDAL

The correct adjustment of the brake pedal height, free-play and reserve distance is critical to the correct operation of the brake system. These 3 measurements inter-relate and should be performed in sequence.

Fig. 1 Measuring the diameters of the drum and shoe assemblies. GM tool shown.

Fig. 2 Backing off the adjuster

Pedal Height
▶ See Figure 3

1. Measure the pedal height from the top of the pedal pad to the floor. Correct distances are: Nova, 147-157mm, 1989-92 Prizm, 139-149mm and 1993 Prizm, 143.6-153.6mm.

2. If it is necessary to adjust the pedal height, loosen the brake light switch and back it off so that some clearance exists between it and the pedal arm.

➡**On Novas, it may be necessary to remove the lower dash trim panel and air duct for access.**

3. Adjust the pedal height by loosening the locknut and turning the pedal pushrod.

4. Return the brake light switch to a position in which it lightly contacts the stopper on the pedal arm.

Pedal Free-play
▶ See Figure 4

1. With the engine off, depress the brake pedal several times until there is no vacuum held in the booster.

2. The free-play distance is between the 'at rest' pedal position and the position at which beginning of pedal resistance is felt. This represents the distance the pedal pushrod moves before actuating the booster air valve. If there is no free-play, the car goes down the road with a slight vacuum leak and the brakes slightly applied. Correct free-play is 3-6mm for 1985-92 Nova and Prizm, and 1-6mm for 1993 Prizm.

Fig. 3 Pedal height

Fig. 4 Pedal free-play

3. If adjustment is necessary, adjust the pedal pushrod to give the correct clearance. After adjusting the pedal free-play, recheck the pedal height.

4. Double check the adjustment of the brake light switch; it should trigger the lights just at the end of the pedal free-play.

Pedal Reserve Distance

◗ See Figure 5

1. With the transaxle in **PARK** or **NEUTRAL** and the parking brake fully released, start the engine and apply normal braking effort to the pedal. Depress the pedal fully, but don't try to put it through the floor.

2. While the pedal is depressed, have a helper measure the distance from the top of the pedal pad to the floor, as illustrated. This distance is the extra travel available to the pushrod if it must work without vacuum assist or if the brakes

Fig. 5 Pedal reserve

are worn or severely out of adjustment. If the pedal height and pedal free-play are correctly adjusted, the pedal reserve distance must be at least 65mm for Nova or 55mm for 1989-92 Prizm and 70mm for 1993 Prizm. The reserve distance can be greater than specified but must not be less. If the reserve distance is less than specification, the brake system must be diagnosed for leaks or component failure.

Brake Light Switch

The brake light switch is located at the top of the pedal arm. It is the switch which turns the brake lights on when the brakes are applied. The plunger type switch is held in the off position by the normal position of the brake pedal; when the pedal moves during brake application, the switch plunger moves forward and the brake lights are brought on.

The switch is almost always the first place to look for the cause of the brake lights flickering over bumps or staying on without use of the brakes. If the brake lights fail to work with the brakes applied, check the fuse first and then check the switch.

REMOVAL & INSTALLATION

1985-92

◗ See Figure 6

1. Disconnect the negative battery cable.

2. Remove the wiring from the switch terminals. Put a piece of tape over each exposed wiring connector; 1 wire terminal may be 'hot' even though the ignition is off. If it accidentally touches metal, a fuse will blow.

➡**On Novas, it may be necessary to remove the lower dash trim panel and air duct for access.**

3. Loosen the locknut closest to the brake pedal arm. Unscrew the switch from the nut and remove it from the bracket.

To install:

4. Install the new switch and tighten the retaining nuts finger tight when the switch plunger is lightly compressed against the stopper on the pedal.

5. Connect an ohmmeter across the terminals of the switch. Move the brake pedal and check the on-off behavior of the switch. Adjust the switch so that the switch comes on at the bottom of the pedal free-play. This brings the brake lights on just as the brakes apply but no sooner.

6. Tighten the locknuts to hold the switch in position.

7. Remove the tape and connect the wiring to the switch.

1993

◗ See Figure 7

1. Disconnect the negative battery cable.

2. Slide the hood latch release cable sideways to release from the holder.

3. Disconnect the hood release cable from the hood latch release lever.

4. Remove the hood latch release lever from the knee bolster by removing the 2 retaining screws.

Fig. 6 Brake light switch — 1985-92

5. Remove the knee bolster from the instrument panel by removing the 2 cover plates, 2 screws, and four bolts.

6. Disconnect the left side ventilation duct from the left side duct outlet.

7. Disconnect the stoplamp switch electrical connector from the switch.

8. Loosen the stoplamp switch locknut and loosen the pushrod locknut and remove the switch.

To install:

9. Adjust the pedal height by turning the pushrod until the brake pedal height is within specification and tighten the pushrod locknut to 18 ft. lbs. (25 Nm). Refer the Pedal Height procedure earlier in the Section.

10. Adjust the stoplamp switch by turning it until the distance between the end of the stoplamp switch plunger and the end of the threaded portion of the switch is 0.02-0.09 inch (0.5-2.4 mm). Tighten the stoplamp switch locknut to 89 inch lbs. (10 Nm).

11. Connect the stoplamp switch electrical connector to the switch.

12. Connect the left side ventilation to the left side duct outlet.

13. Install the knee bolster to the instrument panel with the 2 screws and four bolts.

14. Install the 2 cover plates.

15. Install the hood latch release lever to the knee bolster with the 2 retaining screws.

16. Connect the hood release cable to the hood latch release lever.

17. Slide the hood latch release cable into the holder.

18. Connect the negative battery cable.

Fig. 7 Brake light switch clearance — 1993

Master Cylinder

REMOVAL & INSTALLATION

▶ See Figures 8 and 9

❉❉WARNING

Be careful not to spill brake fluid on the painted surfaces of the vehicle; it will damage the paint. If spillage occurs, rinse the area immediately with water. Handle the steel brake lines very carefully. Once they are bent or kinked, they cannot be straightened.

1. Disconnect the negative battery cable.

2. Clean the area at the reservoir and brake lines to prevent entry of dirt into the system.

3. Disconnect the wiring to the brake fluid level switch. Release the wiring from any clips.

4. On Prizm vehicles, remove the air intake duct.

5. Use a syringe to remove the fluid from the reservoir. Store the fluid in a clean glass jar with a lid.

6. Disconnect the brake lines from the master cylinder. Plug or tape the lines immediately to keep dirt and moisture out of the system.

7. Remove the retaining nuts holding the master cylinder to the brake booster.

8. Remove the 3-way union from the booster stud on vehicles not equipped with ABS or 2-way union with ABS.

1. BOOSTER
2. CONNECTOR
3. NUT 13 N·m (9 FT.-LB.)
4. MASTER CYLINDER
5. BRAKE TUBES 15 N·m (11 FT.-LB.)
6. GASKET

Fig. 8 Removing the brake master cylinder — 1985-92

1. Three-way proportioning valve
2. Master cylinder reservoir
3. Brake fluid level switch electrical connector
4. Vacuum booster
5. Two-way proportioning valve

Fig. 9 Removing the brake master cylinder — 1993 without ABS

9. Remove the master cylinder from the studs.

10. Remove the seal or gasket from the booster.

11. When reinstalling, always use a new gasket or seal and install the master cylinder to the booster. On Nova vehicles, confirm that the 'UP' mark on the master cylinder boot is in the correct position.

12. Install the 2 way or 3-way union bracket over the stud and install the retaining nuts finger tight.

13. Connect the brake lines to the master cylinder. Make certain each fitting is correctly threaded and tighten each fitting 1-2 turns. The job is made easier by having a small amount of movement available at the master cylinder mounting studs.

14. Tighten the master cylinder retaining nuts to 9.5 ft. lbs. (115 inch lbs.)

15. Tighten the brake line fittings to 11 ft. lbs. Do not overtighten these fittings.

16. On Prizm vehicles, install the air intake duct.

17. Connect the wiring to the brake fluid sensing switch and attach any wiring clips.

18. Fill the master cylinder reservoir.

19. Bleed the brakes.

20. Connect the negative battery cable

OVERHAUL

▶ **See Figures 10, 11, 12, 13, 14 and 15**

1. Remove master cylinder from the car. Remove the cap and strainer from the reservoir.

2. Remove the set screw and remove the reservoir.

3. Mount the cylinder in a vise.

4. Remove the 2 grommets from the cylinder.

5. Using a screwdriver or similar tool, push the pistons all the way into the bore and remove the piston stopper bolt with its gasket.

6. Hold the piston into the bore and remove the snapring with snapring pliers.

7. Place a rag on 2 wooden blocks. Remove the master cylinder from the vise and tap the cylinder flange between the blocks until the piston tip protrudes.

8. Remove the piston by pulling it straight out.

✳✳WARNING

If the piston is removed at an angle, the cylinder bore may become damaged.

9. Inspect all parts of the pistons, grommets and bore for any sign of wear, cuts, corrosion or scoring. Check the inlet port and return port for obstructions. Use compressed air to clear any dirt or foreign matter from the area.

To assemble:

10. Apply clean brake fluid to the rubber parts of the pistons.

11. Insert the 2 springs and pistons straight into the bore. Do not angle them during installation.

✳✳WARNING

Be careful not to damage the rubber lips on the pistons.

12. Install the snapring while pushing in the piston.

13. Push the pistons all the way in and install the piston stopper bolt and gasket. Tighten it to 7 ft. lbs.

14. Install the 2 grommets.

15. Install the cap and strainer onto the reservoir, then press the reservoir into position on the cylinder.

16. Install the set screw while pushing on the reservoir. Tighten the screw to 15 inch lbs.

➡**There may be a slight bit of play in the reservoir after the set screw is installed. This is normal and no washers or spacers should be installed.**

17. Reinstall the master cylinder.

Power Brake Booster(Vacuum Booster)

REMOVAL & INSTALLATION

▶ **See Figure 16**

1. Disconnect the negative battery cable.

2. On Prizm vehicles, remove the top of the air cleaner and the intake duct. Remove the charcoal canister mounting nuts.

3. Remove the brake master cylinder from the booster.

4. Remove the vacuum hose from the booster.

5. Inside the car, disconnect the pedal return spring. Disconnect the clip and the clevis pin.

6. Remove the brake booster retaining nuts. It will be helpful to have a helper support the booster while the nuts are loosened.

7. Remove the booster from the engine compartment.

8. When reinstalling, have a helper hold the booster in position while you install the retaining nuts. Tighten the nuts to 9.5 ft. lbs. (115 inch lbs.)

9. Install the clevis pin and clip, then install the pedal return spring.

10. Connect the vacuum hose to the booster.

11. Install the master cylinder onto the booster and tighten the nuts to 9.5 ft. lbs. (115 inch lbs.)

12. On Prizm vehicles, install the charcoal canister mounting bolts and install the air cleaner top and intake duct.

13. Connect the negative battery cable.

14. Bleed the brake system.

Brake System Valves

PROPORTIONING VALVE

▶ **See Figures 17 and 18**

The proportioning valve is located on the center of the firewall under the hood on all Prizms without ABS or attached to the hydraulic modulator on vehicles with ABS. Except for leakage or impact damage, it rarely needs replacement. If it must be removed, all 5 brake lines must be labeled and removed and the valve removed from its mount. Clean the fittings before removal to prevent dirt from entering the ports.

1. Strainer
2. Cap
3. Reservoir
4. Brake fluid switch wiring
5. No. 2 piston and spring
6. No. 1 piston and spring
7. Snapring
8. Seal
9. Cylinder housing
10. Reservoir set screw
11. Gasket
12. Piston stopper bolt
13. Reservoir grommets (seals)

Fig. 10 Master cylinder components — 1989-92

Fig. 11 Removing the stopper bolt

Fig. 13 Lightly tapping the flanges on protected blocks will release the pistons

Fig. 12 To remove the snapring, the piston must be pushed into the bore

15.2 IN.-LB.

Fig. 14 Removing the reservoir set screw

1. Master cylinder reservoir
2. Cylinder housing
3. Cap
4. Strainer
5. Seals

Fig. 15 Master cylinder reservoir assembly — 1993

After the lines are reconnected and carefully tightened to 11 ft. lbs., the entire brake system must be bled.

➡**On vehicles equipped ABS, refer to Hydraulic Modulator, REMOVAL & INSTALLATION procedure outlined in Anti-Lock Brakes at the end of this Section.**

VACUUM CHECK VALVE

▶ **See Figure 19**

The brake vacuum check valve allows vacuum to flow out of the brake booster but will not allow back-flow. This maintains a supply of vacuum within the booster during periods of low engine vacuum. The valve can be removed from the hose by hand. Once removed, the valve can be tested by gently blowing through it. It should allow airflow in 1 direction but not

the other. When installing a new valve, make sure it is positioned so that the air can flow from the booster to the engine. Most replacement valves have an arrow showing the direction of airflow.

Brake Hoses

INSPECTION

1. Inspect the lines and hoses in a well lighted area. Use a small mirror to allow you to see concealed parts of the hose or line. Check the entire length and circumference of each line or hose.
2. Look for any sign of wear, deformation, corrosion, cracking, bends, swelling or thread damage.
3. The slightest sign of leakage requires immediate attention.
4. Check all clamps for tightness and check that all lines and hoses have sufficient clearance from moving parts and heat sources.
5. Check that any lines passing through grommets pass through the center of the grommet and are not forced against the side of the hole. Relieve any excess tension.
6. Some metal lines may contain spring-like coils. These coils absorb vibration and prevent the line from cracking under strain. Do not attempt to straighten the coils or change their diameter.

REMOVAL & INSTALLATION

▶ **See Figures 20, 21 and 22**

1. Elevate and safely support the vehicle.
2. Remove the wheel.
3. Clean all dirt from the hose junctions.
4. Place a catch pan under the hose area.
5. Using 2 wrenches, disconnect the flexible hose from the steel brake line at the strut assembly.
6. If equipped with disc brakes, disconnect the brake hose union bolt at the brake caliper. If equipped with drum brakes, disconnect the hose from the steel pipe running to the wheel cylinder.
7. Remove the hose retaining clips and remove the hose from the vehicle.

Fig. 16 Power booster removal — 1989-92 models shown, other models similar

Fig. 17 Proportioning valve and master cylinder assembly

Fig. 18 Proportioning valve location on the center of the engine bulkhead

Fig. 19 Inspection of the vacuum check valve

Fig. 20 Removing the front brake hose

8. If the system is to remain disconnected for more than the time it takes to swap hoses, tape or plug the line and caliper to prevent dirt and moisture from entering.

9. Install the new brake hose into the retaining clips.

10. Connect the hose to the caliper (disc brakes) and tighten the union bolt to 22 ft. lbs. or connect the hose to the short line running into the wheel cylinder and tighten the fitting to 11 ft. lbs.

11. Connect the steel brake line to the hose at the strut. Start the threads by hand and make sure the joint is properly threaded before tightening. Tighten the fitting to 11 ft. lbs.

12. Install the wheel.

13. Bleed the brake system.

14. Lower the car to the ground.

LEFT REAR BRAKE HOSE

LEFT REAR BRAKE PIPE

Fig. 21 Rear brake hose connections

AD

Fig. 22 Front brake hose connections

Bleeding the Brake System

▶ See Figure 23

➡On vehicles equipped with ABS, the hydraulic modulator must be bled prior to the brake calipers and wheel cylinders. For complete ABS bleeding, refer to Anti-Lock Brakes at the end of this Section.

It is necessary to bleed the hydraulic system any time system has been opened or has trapped air within the fluid lines. It may be necessary to bleed the system at all 4 brakes if air has been introduced through a low fluid level or by disconnecting brake pipes at the master cylinder.

If a line is disconnected at 1 wheel only, generally only that brake needs bleeding. If lines are disconnected at any fitting between the master cylinder and the brake, the system served by the disconnected pipe must be bled.

✳✳WARNING

Do not allow brake fluid to splash or spill onto painted surfaces; the paint will be damaged. If spillage occurs, flush the area immediately with clean water.

1. Fill the master cylinder reservoir to the 'MAX' line with brake fluid and keep it at least half full throughout the bleeding procedure.

2. If the master cylinder has been removed or disconnected, it must be bled before any brake unit is bled. To bleed the master cylinder:

   a. Disconnect the front brake line from the master cylinder and allow fluid to flow from the front connector port.

   b. Reconnect the line to the master cylinder and tighten it until it is fluid tight.

   c. Have a helper press the brake pedal down one time and hold it down.

   d. Loosen the front brake line connection at the master cylinder. This will allow trapped air to escape, along with some fluid.

   e. Again tighten the line, release the pedal slowly and repeat the sequence (steps c-d-e) until only fluid runs from the port. No air bubbles should be present in the fluid.

   f. Final tighten the line fitting at the master cylinder to 11 ft. lbs.

   g. After all the air has been bled from the front connection, bleed the master cylinder at the rear connection by repeating steps A-E.

3. Place the correct size box-end or line wrench over the bleeder valve and attach a tight-fitting transparent hose over the bleeder. Allow the tube to hang submerged in a transparent container of clean brake fluid. The fluid must remain above the end of the hose at all times, otherwise the system will ingest air instead of fluid.

4. Have an assistant pump the brake pedal several times slowly and hold it down.

5. Slowly unscrew the bleeder valve (¼-½ turn is usually enough). After the initial rush of air and fluid, have the assistant slowly release the brake pedal. When the pedal is released, tighten the bleeder.

6. Repeat Steps 4 and 5 until no air bubbles are seen in the hose or container. If air is constantly appearing after

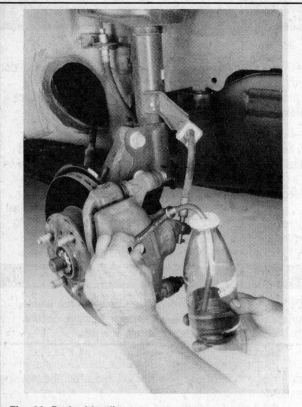

Fig. 23 Brake bleeding

7. If the entire system must be bled, begin with the right rear, then the left front, left rear and right front brake in that order. After each brake is bled, check and top off the fluid level in the reservoir.

❋❋WARNING

Do not reuse brake fluid which has been bled from the brake system.

8. After bleeding, check the pedal for 'sponginess' or vague feel. Repeat the bleeding procedure as necessary to correct.

repeated bleedings, the system must be examined for the source of the leak or loose fitting.

FRONT DISC BRAKES

❋❋CAUTION

Brake pads and shoes contain asbestos, which has been determined to be a cancer causing agent. Never clean the brake surfaces with compressed air! Avoid inhaling any dust from brake surfaces! When cleaning brakes, use commercially available brake cleaning fluids.

Disc Brake Pads

WEAR INDICATORS

▶ **See Figure 24**

The front disc brake pads are equipped with a metal tab which will come into contact with the disc after the friction surface material has worn near its usable minimum. The wear indicators make a constant, distinct metallic sound that should be easily heard. (The sound has been described as similar to either fingernails on a blackboard or a field full of crickets.) The key to recognizing that it is the wear indicators and not some other brake noise is that the sound is heard when the car is being driven WITHOUT the brakes applied. It may or may not be present under braking is heard during normal driving.

It should also be noted that any disc brake system, by its design, cannot be made to work silently under all conditions. Each system includes various shims, plates, cushions and brackets to suppress brake noise but no system can completely silence all noises. Some brake noise-either high or low frequency-can be considered normal under some conditions. Such noises can be controlled and perhaps lessened, but cannot be totally eliminated.

Fig. 24 Disc brake wear indicator

INSPECTION

▶ **See Figures 25 and 26**

The front brake pads may be inspected without removal. With the front end elevated and supported, remove the wheel(s). Unlock the steering column lock and turn the wheel so that the brake caliper is out from under the fender.

View the pads — inner and outer — through the cut-out in the center of the caliper. Remember to look at the thickness of the pad friction material (the part that actually presses on the disc) rather than the thickness of the backing plate which does not change with wear.

Remember that you are looking at the profile of the pad, not the whole thing. Brake pads can wear on a taper which may not be visible through the window. It is also not possible to

Fig. 25 Disc brake pad inspection

Fig. 26 Disc brake caliper assembly and pad inspection hole

check the contact surface for cracking or scoring from this position. This quick check can be helpful only as a reference; detailed inspection requires pad removal.

REMOVAL & INSTALLATION

▶ **See Figures 27, 28, 29, 30, 31, 32, 33, 34, 35, 36, 37 and 38**

1. Raise and safely support the front of the vehicle on jackstands. Set the parking brake and block the rear wheels.

2. Siphon a sufficient quantity of brake fluid from the master cylinder reservoir to prevent the brake fluid from overflowing from the master cylinder when removing or installing the brake pads. This is necessary as the piston must be forced into the cylinder bore to provide sufficient clearance to install the pads.

3. Remove the wheel, then reinstall 2 lug nuts finger tight to hold the disc in place.

➡ **Disassemble brakes one wheel at a time. This will prevent parts confusion and also prevent the opposite caliper piston from popping out during pad installation.**

4. Remove the 2 caliper mounting bolts and then remove the caliper from the mounting bracket. Position the caliper out of the way and support it with wire so it doesn't hang by the brake line.

➡ **It may be necessary to rock the caliper back and forth a bit in order to reposition the piston so it will clear the brake pads.**

5. Remove the 2 brake pads, the 2 wear indicators, the 2 anti-squeal shims (1985-92) 4 anti-squeal shims (1993), the 4 support plates (anti-rattle springs) and the 2 anti squeal springs, if so equipped. Disassemble slowly and take note of how the parts fit together. This will save much time during reassembly.

6. Inspect the brake disc (both sides) for scoring or gouging. Measure the disc for both thickness and run-out. Complete inspection procedures are given later in this section.

7. Inspect the pads for remaining thickness and condition. Any sign of uneven wear, cracking, heat checking or spotting is cause for replacement. Compare the wear of the inner pad to the outer pad. While they will not wear at exactly the same rate, the remaining thickness should be about the same on both pads. If one is heavily worn and the other is not, suspect either a binding caliper piston or dirty slides in the caliper mount.

8. Examine the 2 caliper retaining bolts and the slide bushings in which they run. Everything should be clean and dry. If cleaning is needed, use spray solvents and a clean cloth. Do not wire brush or sand the bolts-this will cause grooves in the metal which will trap more dirt. Check the condition of the rubber dust boots and replace them if damaged.

To install:

9. Install the 4 pad support plates (anti-rattle springs) onto the mounting bracket.

10. Install new pad wear indicators onto each pad, making sure the arrow on the tab points in the direction of disc rotation.

1. Mounting bolt
2. Dust boot
3. Collar
4. Slide bushing
5. Caliper housing
6. Piston
7. Piston seal
8. Boot
9. Set ring
10. Cap
11. Bleeder screw
12. Anti-squeal shim
13. Pad
14. Support plate
15. Wear indiactor
16. Mounting bracket
17. Anti-squeal spring

Fig. 27 Front disc brake caliper assembly — 1985-88

11. Install new anti-squeal pads to the back of the pads.

12. Install the pads into the mounting bracket and install the anti-squeal springs, if so equipped.

13. Use a caliper compressor, a C-clamp or large pair of pliers to slowly press the caliper piston back into the caliper. If the piston is frozen, or if the caliper is leaking hydraulic fluid, the caliper must be overhauled or replaced.

14. Install the caliper assembly to the mounting plate. Before installing the retaining bolts, apply a thin, even coating of anti-seize compound to the threads and slide surfaces. Don't use grease or spray lubricants; they will not hold up under the extreme temperatures generated by the brakes. Tighten the bolts to 18 ft. lbs (25 Nm) for 1985-92 and 25 ft. lbs. (34 Nm) for 1993.

15. Remove the 2 lugs holding the disc in place and install the wheel.

16. Lower the vehicle to the ground. Check the level of the brake fluid in the master cylinder reservoir; it should be at least to the middle of the reservoir.

17. Depress the brake pedal several times and make sure that the movement feels normal. The first brake pedal application may result in a very 'long' pedal due to the pistons being retracted. Always make several brake applications before starting the vehicle. Bleeding is not usually necessary after pad replacement.

18. Recheck the fluid level and add to the 'MAX' line if necessary.

➡Braking should be moderate for the first 5 miles or so until the new pads seat correctly. The new pads will bed best if put through several moderate heating and cooling cycles. Avoid hard braking until the brakes have

experienced several long, slow stops with time to cool in between. Taking the time to properly bed the brakes will yield quieter operation, more efficient stopping and contribute to extended brake life.

Brake Caliper

REMOVAL

1. Raise and safely support the front of the vehicle on jackstands. Set the parking brake and block the rear wheels.

2. Siphon a sufficient quantity of brake fluid from the master cylinder reservoir to prevent the brake fluid from overflowing the master cylinder when removing or installing the calipers. This is necessary as the piston must be forced into the cylinder bore to provide sufficient clearance to install the caliper.

3. Remove the wheel, then reinstall 2 lug nuts finger tight to hold the disc in place.

➡Disassemble brakes one wheel at a time. This will prevent parts confusion and also prevent the opposite caliper piston from popping out during installation.

4. Disconnect the hose union at the caliper. Use a pan to catch any spilled fluid and immediately plug the disconnected hose.

5. Remove the 2 caliper mounting bolts and then remove the caliper from the mounting bracket.

1. Anti-squeal spring
2. Inboard anti-squeal shim
3. Pad wear indicator plate
4. Support plate
5. Caliper carrier mounting bolts
6. Caliper carrier
7. Pads
8. Outboard anti-squeal shim
9. Piston
10. Piston seal
11. Piston boot
12. Caliper set ring
13. Dust boots
14. Caliper housing
15. Caliper slide bushings
16. Caliper housing mounting bolts
17. Bleeder screw
18. Cap

Fig. 28 Front disc brake caliper assembly — 1989-91

1. Inboard anti-squeal shim
2. Pad wear indicator plate
3. Anti-rattle springs
4. Caliper carrier mounting bolts

5. Caliper carrier
6. Brake pads
7. Inner outboard anti-squeal shim
8. Outer outboard anti-squeal shim
9. Piston
10. Piston seal
11. Piston boot
12. Caliper set ring
13. Dust boots
14. Caliper housing
15. Caliper slide bushings
16. Caliper housing mounting bolts
17. Bleeder screw
18. Cap

Fig. 29 Front disc brake caliper assembly — 1992

Fig. 30 You will need a short extension to remove the front caliper mounting bracket bolts

Fig. 31 Carefully remove the caliper assembly from the rotor

Fig. 32 Suspend the caliper assembly out of the way to avoid hanging from the hose

Fig. 33 Removing the outer brake pad from the caliper assembly

Fig. 34 Removing the inner brake pad from the caliper assembly

Fig. 35 Note the correct position support plates (anti-rattle springs)

Fig. 36 Exploded view of the brake pads, wear indicators anti-squeal shims and anti-rattle springs on a 1992 model

Fig. 37 Correct placement of the support plates (anti-rattle springs)

Fig. 38 Make certain the brake wear indicators are correctly installed

Fig. 39 Use just enough air to ease the piston out of the caliper. Keep fingers out of the way of the piston

Fig. 40 Using a large C-clamp to compress the piston back into the caliper bore

OVERHAUL

▶ See Figures 39 and 40

1. Drain the remaining fluid from the caliper.
2. Carefully remove the dust boot from around the piston.

3. Pad the inside arms of the caliper with rags. Apply compressed air into the brake line port; this will force the piston out.

❋❋CAUTION

Do not place fingers in front of the piston in an attempt to catch it or protect it when applying compressed air. Injury can result. Use just enough air pressure to ease the piston out of the bore.

4. Remove the seal from the inside of the caliper bore. Check all the parts for wear, scoring, deterioration, cracking or other abnormal conditions. Corrosion — generally caused by water in the system — will appear as white deposits on the metal, similar to what may be found on an old aluminum storm door on your house. Pay close attention to the condition of the inside of the caliper bore and the outside of the piston. Any sign of corrosion or scoring requires new parts; do not attempt to clean or resurface either face.

5. The caliper overhaul kit will, at minimum, contain new seals and dust boots. A good kit will contain a new piston as well, but you may have to buy the piston separately. Any time the caliper is disassembled, a new piston is highly recommended in addition to the new seals.

6. Clean all the components to be reused with an aerosol brake solvent and dry them thoroughly. Take any steps necessary to eliminate moisture or water vapor from the parts.

7. Coat all the caliper components with fresh brake fluid from a new can.

➡**Some repair kits come with special assembly lubricant for the piston and seal. Use this lubricant according to directions with the kit.**

8. Install the piston seal and piston into the caliper bore. This is an exacting job; the clearances are very small. Make sure that the seal is seated in its groove and that the piston is not cocked when inserted into the bore.

9. Install the dust boot and its clip or ring.

10. Install the slide bushings and rubber boots onto the caliper if they were removed during disassembly.

INSTALLATION

1. Use a caliper compressor, a C-clamp or large pair of pliers to slowly press the caliper piston back into the caliper.

2. Install the caliper assembly to the mounting plate. Before installing the retaining bolts, apply a thin, even coating of anti-seize compound to the threads and slide surfaces. Don't use grease or spray lubricants; they will not hold up under the extreme temperatures generated by the brakes. Tighten the bolts to 18 ft. lbs. (25 Nm) for 1985-92 and 25 ft. lbs. (34 Nm) for 1993.

3. Install the brake hose to the caliper. Always use a new gasket and tighten the union to 17 ft. lbs.

4. Bleed the brake system.

5. Remove the 2 lugs holding the disc in place and install the wheel.

6. Lower the vehicle to the ground. Check the level of the brake fluid in the master cylinder reservoir; it should be at least to the middle of the reservoir.

Brake Rotor

REMOVAL & INSTALLATION

1. Elevate and safely support the car. If only the front end is supported, set the parking brake and block the rear wheels.

2. Remove the wheel.

3. Remove the brake caliper from its mount and suspend it out of the way. Don't disconnect the hose and don't let the caliper hang by the hose. Remove the brake pads with all the clips, shims, etc.

4. Install all the lug nuts to hold the rotor in place. If the nuts are open at both ends, it is helpful to install them backwards (tapered end out) to secure the disc. Tighten the nuts a bit tighter than finger tight, but make sure all are at approximately the same tightness.

5. Perform the run-out and thickness measurements explained in 'Inspection'. Run-out must be measured with the rotor mounted on the car. Thickness measurements can be made either on or off the car.

6. Remove the 2 bolts holding the caliper mounting bracket to the steering knuckle. These bolts will be tight. Remove the 4 lug nuts holding the rotor.

7. Remove the bracket from the knuckle. Before removing the rotor, make a mark on the rotor indexing 1 wheel stud to 1 hole in the rotor. This assures the rotor will be re-installed in its original position, serving to eliminate minor vibrations in the brake system.

8. When reinstalling, make certain the rotor is clean and free of any particles of rust or metal from resurfacing. Observe the index mark made earlier and fit the rotor over the wheel lugs. Install 2 lug nuts to hold it in place.

9. Install the caliper mounting bracket in position and tighten its bolts to 65 ft. lbs. (88 Nm).

10. Install the brake pads and the hardware.

11. Install the caliper. Tighten the mounting bolts to 18 ft. lbs. (25 Nm) for 1985-92 and 25 ft. lbs. (34 Nm) for 1993.

12. Install the wheel and lower the car to the ground.

INSPECTION

Run-out

▶ **See Figure 41**

➡**Before measuring the run-out on the front discs, confirm that the front wheel bearing play is within specification.**

1. Elevate and safely support the car. If only the front end is supported, set the parking brake and block the rear wheels.

2. Remove the wheel.

3. Remove the brake caliper from its mount and suspend it out of the way. Don't disconnect the hose and don't let the caliper hang by the hose. Remove the brake pads with all the clips, shims, etc.

4. Install all the lug nuts to hold the rotor in place. If the nuts are open at both ends, it is helpful to install them backwards (tapered end out) to secure the disc. Tighten the

nuts a bit tighter than finger tight, but make sure all are at approximately the same tightness.

5. Mount a dial indicator with a magnetic or universal base on the strut so that the tip of the indicator contacts the rotor about ½ in. from the outer edge.

6. Zero the dial indicator. Turn the rotor 1 complete revolution and observe the total indicated run-out.

7. If the run-out exceeds 0.15mm (Nova) or 0.09mm (Prizm), clean the wheel hub and rotor mating surfaces and remeasure. If the run-out still exceeds maximum, remove the rotor and remount it so that the wheel studs now run through different holes. If this re-indexing does not provide correct run-out measurements, the rotor should be considered warped beyond use and either resurfaced or replaced.

Thickness

▶ See Figure 42

The thickness of the rotor partially determines its ability to withstand heat and provide adequate stopping force. Every rotor has a minimum thickness established by the manufacturer. This minimum measurement must not be exceeded. A rotor which is too thin may crack under braking; if this occurs the wheel can lock instantly, resulting in sudden loss of control.

If any part of the rotor measures below minimum thickness, the disc must be replaced. Additionally, a rotor which needs to be resurfaced may not allow sufficient cutting before reaching minimum. Since the allowable wear from new to minimum is about 1mm, it is wise to replace the rotor rather than resurface it.

Thickness and thickness variation can be measured with a micrometer capable of reading to one ten-thousandth inch. All measurements must be made at the same distance in from the

Fig. 41 Measuring the rotor run-out

Fig. 42 Measuring the rotor thickness

edge of the rotor. Measure at 4 equally spaced points around the disc and record the measurements. Compare each measurement to the minimum thickness specifications in the chart at the end of this Section.

Compare the 4 measurements to each other and find the difference between each pair. A rotor varying by more than 0.013mm can cause pedal vibration and/or front end vibration during stops. A rotor which does not meet these specifications should be resurfaced or replaced.

Condition

A new rotor will have a smooth even surface which rapidly changes during use. It is not uncommon for a rotor to develop very fine concentric scoring (like the grooves on a record) due to dust and grit being trapped by the brake pad.

This slight irregularity is normal, but as the grooves deepen, wear and noise increase and stopping may be affected. As a general rule, any groove deep enough to snag a fingernail during inspection is cause for action or replacement.

Any sign of blue spots, discoloration, heavy rusting or outright gouges require replacement of the rotor. If you are checking the disc on the car (such as during pad replacement or tire rotation) remember to turn the disc and check both the inner and outer faces completely. If anything looks questionable or requires consideration, choose the safer option and replace the rotor. The front brakes are a critical system and must be maintained at 100% reliability.

Any time a rotor is replaced, the pads should also be replaced so that the surfaces mate properly. Since brake pads should be replaced in axle sets (both front or rear wheels), consider replacing both rotors instead of just one. The restored feel and accurate stopping make the extra investment worthwhile.

REAR DRUM BRAKES

✳✳CAUTION

Brake pads and shoes contain asbestos, which has been determined to be a cancer causing agent. Never clean the brake surfaces with compressed air! Avoid inhaling any dust from brake surfaces! When cleaning brakes, use commercially available brake cleaning fluids.

Brake Drums

REMOVAL & INSTALLATION

1. Elevate and safely support the vehicle. If only the rear wheels are elevated, block the front wheels with chocks. Once the vehicle is firmly on stands, release the parking brake.

2. Remove the rear wheel.

3. Make an index mark showing the relationship between 1 wheel lug and 1 hole in the drum. This will allow the drum to be reinstalled in its original position.

4. Tap the drum with a rubber mallet or wooden hammer handle. Remove the brake drum. It will not come off if the parking brake is applied. If the brake drum cannot be removed easily:

a. Insert a screwdriver through the hole in the backing plate and hold the adjusting lever away from the star wheel.

b. Using another screw driver or a brake adjusting tool, turn the star wheel to reduce the tension (increase the clearance) on the brake shoes.

✷✷WARNING

Do not apply the brake pedal while the drum is removed.

5. Before reinstalling the drum, perform the measurements and adjustments explained in the 'Adjustments' section earlier in this Section.

6. Reinstall the drum, observing the matchmarks made earlier. Keep the drum straight while installing it; if it goes on crooked it can damage the brake shoes.

7. Install the wheel.

8. Lower the car to the ground.

9. Test drive the car at safe speeds and in a safe location to check the pedal feel and brake function. Adjust as necessary.

INSPECTION

1. Clean the drum.

2. Inspect the drum for scoring, cracks, grooves and out-of-roundness. Measure it to determine maximum diameter. A cracked drum must be replaced; do not attempt to weld a drum.

3. Light scoring may be removed by dressing the drum with fine emery cloth. If brake linings are replaced, always resurface a grooved drum.

4. Heavy scoring will require the use of a brake drum lathe to turn the drum.

➡**During manufacture, weights are used to balance brake drums. These weights must not be removed. After a drum is refinished or if there are vibration problems not traceable to wheel balance, the brake drums should be checked for balance. This can be done on most off-vehicle balancers; a bubble balancer is particularly handy for this check. If the drum is out of balance, it must be replaced.**

Brake Shoes

INSPECTION

◆ **See Figure 43**

An inspection hole is provided in the backing plate of each rear wheel which allows the brakes to be checked without removing the drum. Remove the hole plug and check the lining

thickness through the hole. If below minimum, the shoes will need replacement. Always replace the plug after checking and make certain it is properly seated and tight.

It should be obvious that this method doesn't provide a lot of information about how the brakes are wearing since it only shows one part of one shoe, but is a quick and easy first check. The only way to see the friction faces of the shoes is to remove the brake drums. No generalities can be drawn between the left and right side shoes, so both drums must be removed to perform a proper inspection.

With the drums removed:

1. Liberally spray the entire brake assembly with aerosol brake cleaner. Do not use other solvents, compressed air or a dry brush.

2. Measure the thickness of the friction surface on each shoe at several different locations. If any measurement is below the minimum thickness, replace all the shoes as a set.

3. Check the contact surfaces closely for any signs of scoring, cracking, uneven or tapered wear, discoloration or separation from the backing plate. Anything that looks unusual requires replacement.

4. If the shoes are in otherwise good condition except for glazing (a shiny, hard surface), the glaze may be removed by light sanding with emery cloth. Also lightly sand the inside of the drum to de-glaze its surface. Do not attempt to rub out grooves or ridges; this is best done with a resurfacing lathe. After sanding the components wash them thoroughly with aerosol brake cleaner to remove any grit.

REMOVAL & INSTALLATION

◆ **See Figures 44, 45, 46, 47, 48, 49, 50, 51, 52, 53, 54, 55, 56, 57, 58 and 59**

➡**The brake shoes can be removed and replaced using everyday hand tools, but the use of brake spring tools and assorted specialty tools makes the job much easier. These common brake tools are available at low cost and can greatly reduce working time.**

1. Elevate and safely support the vehicle. If only the rear wheels are elevated, block the front wheels with chocks. Once the vehicle is firmly on stands, release the parking brake.

2. Remove the rear wheel.

3. Make an index mark showing the relationship between 1 wheel lug and 1 hole in the drum. This will allow the drum to be reinstalled in its original position.

Fig. 43 One brake shoe on each rear wheel can be check through the inspection hole, but complete inspection requires removing the brake drums

4. Tap the drum with a rubber mallet or wooden hammer handle. Remove the brake drum. It will not come off if the parking brake is applied. If the brake drum cannot be removed easily:

a. Insert a screwdriver through the hole in the backing plate and hold the adjusting lever away from the star wheel.

b. Using another screw driver or a brake adjusting tool, turn the star wheel to reduce the tension (increase the clearance) on the brake shoes.

✳✳WARNING

Do not apply the brake pedal while the drum is removed.

5. Remove the return spring.
6. Disconnect and remove the retainers, hold down springs and pins.
7. Remove the anchor spring.
8. Use a pair of pliers to disconnect the parking brake cable from the parking brake lever.
9. Remove the adjusting lever spring.
10. Remove the shoes and adjuster as a unit.
11. Disassemble the adjustor, the parking brake lever and the automatic adjuster lever. The 'C' washer holding the shoe to the adjuster may need to be spread a little before removal.
12. Clean all the parts with aerosol brake solvent. Do not use other solvents.
13. Closely inspect all the parts. Any part of doubtful strength or quality must be replaced.

To install:

14. Before reinstallation, apply high-temperature grease to the points at which the brake shoes contact the backing plate and to both the contact and pivot points on the adjuster strut.
15. Install the parking brake lever and automatic adjusting lever to the rear (trailing) shoe.
16. Install a new C-washer and use pliers to close it. Do not bend it more than necessary to hold in place.
17. Install the adjuster (strut) and return spring in place on the rear shoe and install the adjusting lever spring.

✳✳WARNING

Do not allow oil or grease to get on the lining surface.

18. Using pliers, connect the parking brake cable to the lever.
19. Pass the parking brake cable through the notch in the anchor plate.
20. Set the rear shoe in place with the end of the shoe inserted in the wheel cylinder and the adjuster in place.
21. Install the hold-down spring, retainers and pin.
22. Install the anchor spring between the front (leading) and rear shoe.

23. Position the front shoe with the end of the shoe inserted in the wheel cylinder and the adjuster in place.
24. Install the hold-down spring, retainers and pin.
25. Connect the return spring.
26. Measure both the brake diameter and the drum diameter as explained in 'Adjustments' and adjust the brake shoes to the proper clearance.
27. Install the drum. Install the wheel.
28. Lower the car to the ground.
29. While not absolutely required, bleeding the brakes is recommended after replacing shoes.

Wheel Cylinders

REMOVAL & INSTALLATION

▶ **See Figure 60**

If wheel cylinders are leaking or seized, they should be replaced. The units are inexpensive enough to make replacement a better choice than repair. Even if the pistons and seals can be replaced, the internal bore can rarely be restored to perfect condition. A faulty repair can reduce braking effort on the wheel or cause a leak which soaks the brake shoes in fluid.

When inspecting the cylinders on the car, the rubber boots must be lifted carefully and the inner area checked for leaks. A very slight moistness — usually coated with dust — is normal, but any accumulation of fluid is evidence of a leak and must be dealt with immediately.

1. Remove the rear brake shoes and hardware.
2. Using a line wrench if possible, disconnect the brake line from the back of the cylinder. This joint may be dirty or corroded. Clean it off and apply penetrating oil if necessary. Do not allow the threaded fitting to twist the brake line. Plug or tape the brake line to prevent leakage.
3. Remove the 2 bolts holding the wheel cylinder to the backing plate. Loosen these gently to prevent breaking the bolts.
4. Remove the wheel cylinder from the backing plate. Drain the remaining fluid into a container.
5. Install the new cylinder onto the backing plate and tighten the mounting bolts to 7.5 ft. lbs. (90 inch lbs.).
6. Carefully reinstall the brake line and tighten it to 11 ft. lbs.
7. Reinstall the shoes and hardware.
8. Install the brake drum and wheel.
9. Bleed the brake system. Repeated bleedings may be needed to eliminate all the air within the line and cylinder.

1. Holddown pin
2. Plug
3. Inspection hole plug
4. Backing plate
5. Bolt
6. Wheel cylinder
7. Parking brake cable
8. Return spring
9. Front (leading) shoe
10. Rear (trailing) shoe
11. Strut (adjuster)
12. Anchor spring
13. Adjusting lever spring
14. Retainer
15. Hold down spring
16. "C" washer
17. Adjusting lever
18. Parking brake lever
19. Shim

Fig. 44 Rear brake components

Fig. 45 Backing off the adjuster

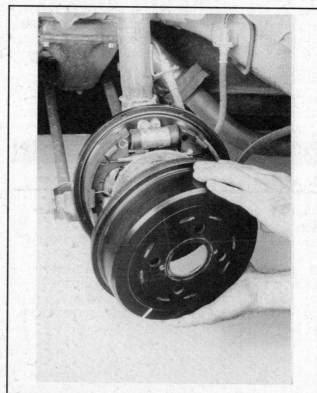

Fig. 46 After backing off the adjuster remove the brake drum

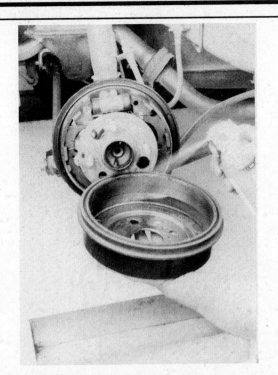

Fig. 47 Liberally spray the entire brake assembly with aerosol brake cleaner. Do not use other solvents, compressed air or a dry brush and always spray in a well ventilated area

Fig. 48 Removing the return spring with a T-shaped brake spring tool

Fig. 49 Use a pair of pliers and release the retainers on the hold down springs and pins

Fig. 50 After releasing the retainer with the pliers remove the retainers, hold down springs and pins

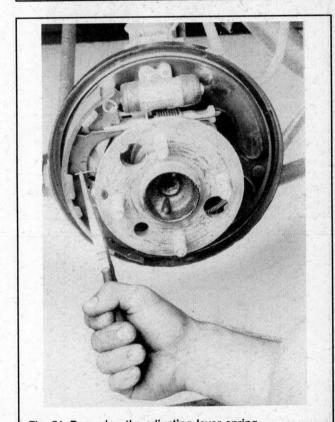

Fig. 51 Removing the adjusting lever spring

Fig. 52 Removing the hold down spring and pin and removing the shoe

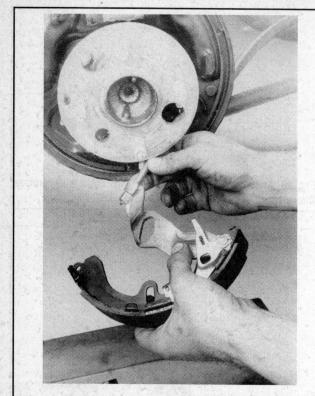

Fig. 53 Disconnect the parking brake cable and remove the shoe and parking brake lever

Fig. 55 Areas to be lubricated during reassembly

Fig. 54 Exploded view of the rear brake components

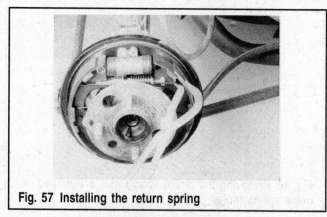

Fig. 57 Installing the return spring

Fig. 56 Installing the C-washer

Fig. 58 Adjust the strut length to the shortest possible amount

Fig. 60 Wheel cylinder components

1. Boot
2. Piston
3. Piston cup
4. Cylinder body
5. Spring

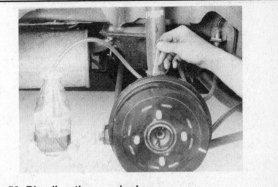

Fig. 59 Bleeding the rear brakes

REAR DISC BRAKES

✳✳CAUTION

Brake pads and shoes contain asbestos, which has been determined to be a cancer causing agent. Never clean the brake surfaces with compressed air! Avoid inhaling any dust from brake surfaces! When cleaning brakes, use commercially available brake cleaning fluids.

Brake Pads

INSPECTION

The rear brake pads may be inspected without removal. With the rear end elevated and supported, remove the wheel(s).

View the pads — inner and outer — through the cut-out in the center of the caliper. Remember to look at the thickness of the pad friction material (the part that actually presses on the disc) rather than the thickness of the backing plate which does not change with wear.

Remember that you are looking at the profile of the pad, not the whole thing. Brake pads can wear on a taper which may not be visible through the window. It is also not possible to check the contact surface for cracking or scoring from this position. This quick check can be helpful only as a reference; detailed inspection requires pad removal.

REMOVAL & INSTALLATION

▸ **See Figures 61, 62, 63, 64 and 65**

1. Raise and safely support the rear of the vehicle on jackstands. Block the front wheels.

2. Siphon a sufficient quantity of brake fluid from the master cylinder reservoir to prevent the brake fluid from overflowing the master cylinder when removing or installing the brake pads. This is necessary as the piston must be forced into the cylinder bore to provide sufficient clearance to install the pads.

3. Remove the wheel, then reinstall 2 lug nuts finger tight to hold the disc in place.

➡**Disassemble brakes one wheel at a time. This will prevent parts confusion and also prevent the opposite caliper piston from popping out during pad installation.**

4. Remove the lower mounting bolt from the mounting bracket. Do not remove the caliper main (upper) pin.

5. Lift the caliper from the bottom so that it hinges upward on the upper pin. Use a piece of wire to hold the caliper up. Do not allow the brake hose to become twisted or kinked during this operation.

6. Remove the brake pads with their shims, springs and support plates.

7. Check the rotor thickness and run-out following the procedures explained under Front Disc Brakes in this Section. Refer to the Specifications Chart at the end of this Section for the correct measurements.

8. Install new pad support plates to the lower sides of the mounting bracket.

9. Install new anti-rattle springs to the upper side of the mounting bracket.

To install:

10. Install a new anti-squeal shim to the back of each pad and install the pads onto the mounting bracket. Install the pads so that the wear indicators are on the uppermost side.

11. Use GM tool J-37149 or equivalent to turn the caliper piston clockwise while pressing it into the caliper bore. Proceed until it locks.

12. Lower the caliper so that the pad protrusion fits into the piston stopper groove. Install the mounting bolts and tighten to 14 ft. lbs. Install the rear wheel.

13. Depress the brake pedal until a firm pedal is obtained.

14. Repeat this procedure on the remaining caliper.

15. Pump the brakes until a firm pedal is felt. Lower the vehicle and fill the master cylinder reservoir to the correct level.

Fig. 61 Rear disc brake components

Fig. 62 Correct method for raising the rear caliper to gain access to the pads

Fig. 63 Installing support plates and anti-rattle shims

Fig. 64 Using the GM tool to retract the rear caliper piston

Fig. 65 Align the stopper groove with the pad protrusion

Brake Caliper

REMOVAL

1. Raise and safely support the rear of the vehicle on jackstands. Block the front wheels. Remove the rear wheel and install 2 lug nuts hand tight, to hold the rotor in place.

2. Place a container under the caliper to catch brake fluid that may leak from the brake hose as it is disconnected. Disconnect the union bolt holding the brake hose to the caliper. Once disconnected, plug or cap the brake hose to prevent excess brake fluid loss and possible system contamination.

3. Remove the clip from the parking brake cable and remove the cable. Remove the caliper bolt.

4. Swing the caliper up and remove the parking brake pin clip. Push on the parking brake crank (arm) to releave the tension and remove the pin.

5. Slide the caliper off of the upper pin. Remove the brake pads, springs and clips as required.

OVERHAUL

▶ **See Figures 66, 67, 68, 69, 70, 71 and 72**

❋❋WARNING

The use of the correct special tools or their equivalent is REQUIRED for this procedure!

Fig. 66 Removing the parking brake crank

Fig. 67 Removing the parking brake crank boot

Fig. 68 Install the stopper pin

Fig. 69 Installing the cable support bracket

Fig. 70 Installation of the parking brake strut

Fig. 71 Assembly of the adjusting bolt; GM tool shown

Fig. 72 Checking the parking brake crank

1. Remove the slide bushings and dust boots.
2. Remove the set ring and dust boot from the caliper piston.
3. Using GM Tool J-37149 or its equivalent, remove the caliper piston from the bore.
4. Remove the seal from the inside of the caliper bore.
5. Install GM Tool J-37150 or its equivalent onto the adjusting bolt and lightly tighten it with a 14mm socket. Do not overtighten the tool; damage to the spring may result.

✳✳WARNING

Always use this tool during disassembly. The spring may fly out, causing personal injury and/or damage to the caliper bore!

6. Remove the snapring from the caliper bore.
7. Carefully remove the adjusting bolt and disassemble it.
8. Remove the parking brake strut.
9. Remove the cable support bracket, then remove the torsion spring from the parking brake crank.
10. Remove the parking brake crank from the caliper.
11. Remove the parking brake crank boot by tapping it lightly on the metal portion of the boot. Do not remove the boot unless it is to be replaced.
12. Use a pin punch to tap out the stopper pin.
13. Check all the parts for wear, scoring, deterioration, cracking or other abnormal conditions. Corrosion — generally caused by water in the system — will appear as white

deposits on the metal. Pay close attention to the condition of the inside of the caliper bore and the outside of the piston. Any sign of corrosion or scoring requires new parts; do not attempt to clean or resurface either face.
14. The caliper overhaul kit will, at minimum, contain new seals and dust boots. A good kit will contain a new piston as well, but you may have to buy the piston separately. Any time the caliper is disassembled, a new piston is highly recommended in addition to the new seals.
15. Clean all the components to be reused with an aerosol brake solvent and dry them thoroughly. Take any steps necessary to eliminate moisture or water vapor from the parts.
16. Coat all the caliper components with fresh brake fluid from a new can.

➡**Some repair kits come with special assembly lubricant for the piston and seal. Use this lubricant according to directions with the kit.**

17. Install the stopper pin into the caliper until the pin extends 25mm.
18. Install the parking brake crank boot. Use a 24mm socket to tap the boot to the caliper.
19. Install the parking brake crank onto the caliper. Make certain the crank boot is securely matched to the groove of the crank seal.
20. Install the cable support bracket. Press the surface of the bracket flush against the wall of the caliper and tighten the bolt to 34 ft. lbs.
21. Check that the clearance between the parking brake crank and the cable support is 6mm.
22. Install the torsion spring.
23. Inspect the crank sub-assembly, making sure it touches the stopper pin.
24. Install the parking brake strut. Before adjusting the strut, adjust the rollers of the needle roller bearing so they do not catch on the caliper bore.
25. Install a new O-ring on the adjusting bolt.
26. Install the stopper, plate, spring, and spring retainer onto the adjusting bolt. Use Tool J-37150 and hand tighten the assembly. Make certain the inscribed portion of the stopper faces upward. Align the notches of the spring retainer with the notches of the stopper.
27. Install the adjusting bolt assembly into the cylinder.
28. Install snapring into the bore. Make certain the gap in the ring faces toward the bleeder side.
29. Pull up on the adjusting bolt by hand to make certain it does not move.
30. Move the parking brake crank by hand and make certain adjusting bolt moves smoothly.
31. Install a new piston seal in the caliper bore.
32. Install the piston into the caliper bore. Using Tool J-37149 or its equivalent, slowly screw the piston clockwise until it will not descend any further.
33. Align the center of the piston stopper groove with the positioning marks of the caliper bore.
34. Install the piston dust boot and its set ring.
35. Install a new boot on the main (upper) caliper pin. Use a 21mm socket to press in the new boot.
36. Install the slide bushings and boots onto the caliper.

INSTALLATION

1. Install the brake pads, springs and clips.

2. Install the caliper assembly to the main pin. Before installing the retaining bolts, apply a thin, even coating of anti-seize compound to the threads and slide surfaces. Don't use grease or spray lubricants; they will not hold up under the extreme temperatures generated by the brakes.

3. Install the caliper mounting bolt and tighten it to 14 ft. lbs.

4. Install the parking brake clip.

5. Install the brake hose to the caliper. Always use new gaskets and tighten the union to 22 ft. lbs.

6. Bleed the brake system.

7. To automatically adjust the parking brake, pull up on the lever several times, then release the lever and step on the brake pedal.

8. Double check that the parking brake crank touches the stopper.

9. Install the rear wheel and lower the car to the ground.

Brake Rotor

REMOVAL

1. Raise and safely support the rear of the vehicle on jackstands. Block the front wheels.

2. Siphon a sufficient quantity of brake fluid from the master cylinder reservoir to prevent the brake fluid from overflowing when removing or installing the brake pads. This is necessary as the piston must be forced into the cylinder bore to provide sufficient clearance to install the pads.

3. Remove the wheel.

➡**Disassemble brakes one wheel at a time. This will prevent parts confusion and also prevent the opposite caliper piston from popping out during pad installation.**

4. Remove the mounting (lower) bolt from the mounting bracket.

5. Lift the caliper from the bottom so that it hinges upward on the upper pin and slide the caliper off the pin. Use a piece of wire to hold the caliper out of the way. Do not disconnect the brake hose and do not allow the brake hose to become twisted or kinked during this operation.

6. Remove the brake pads with their shims, springs and support plates.

7. If the rotor is to be measured, install all the lug nuts to hold the rotor in place. If the nuts are open at both ends, it is helpful to install them backwards (tapered end out) to secure the disc. Tighten the nuts a bit tighter than finger tight, but make sure all are at approximately the same tightness. Follow the measurement and inspection procedures listed under 'INSPECTION'.

8. Remove the mounting bolts holding the mounting bracket to the rear axle carrier.

9. Remove the lug nuts and remove the rotor.

INSPECTION

Run-out

1. Mount a dial indicator with a magnetic or universal base on the strut so that the tip of the indicator contacts the rotor about ½ in. from the outer edge.

2. Zero the dial indicator. Turn the rotor 1 complete revolution and observe the total indicated run-out.

3. If the run-out exceeds 0.15mm, clean the wheel hub and rotor mating surfaces and remeasure. If the run-out still exceeds maximum, remove the rotor and remount it so that the wheel studs now run through different holes. If this re-indexing does not provide correct run-out measurements, the rotor should be considered warped beyond use and either resurfaced or replaced.

Thickness

The thickness of the rotor partially determines its ability to withstand heat and provide adequate stopping force. Every rotor has a minimum thickness established by the manufacturer. This minimum measurement must not be exceeded. A rotor which is too thin may crack under braking; if this occurs the wheel can lock instantly, resulting in sudden loss of control.

If any part of the rotor measures below minimum thickness, the disc must be replaced. Additionally, a rotor which needs to be resurfaced may not allow sufficient cutting before reaching minimum. Since the allowable wear from new to minimum is about 1mm, it is wise to replace the rotor rather than resurface it.

Thickness and thickness variation can be measured with a micrometer capable of reading to one ten-thousandth inch. All measurements must be made at the same distance in from the edge of the rotor. Measure at 4 equally spaced points around the disc and record the measurements. Compare each measurement to the minimum thickness specifications in the chart at the end of this Section.

Compare the 4 measurements to each other and find the difference between each pair. A rotor varying by more than 0.013mm can cause pedal vibration and/or front end vibration during stops. A rotor which does not meet these specifications should be resurfaced or replaced.

Condition

A new rotor will have a smooth, even surface which rapidly changes during use. It is not uncommon for a rotor to develop very fine concentric scoring (like the grooves on a record) due to dust and grit being trapped by the brake pad. This slight irregularity is normal, but as the grooves deepen, wear and noise increase and stopping may be affected. As a general rule, any groove deep enough to snag a fingernail during inspection is cause for action or replacement.

Any sign of blue spots, discoloration, heavy rusting or outright gouges require replacement of the rotor. If you are checking the disc on the car (such as during pad replacement or tire rotation) remember to turn the disc and check both the inner and outer faces completely. If anything looks questionable or requires consideration, choose the safer option and replace the rotor. The brakes are a critical system and must be maintained at 100% reliability.

Any time a rotor is replaced, the pads should also be replaced so that the surfaces mate properly. Since brake pads should be replaced in axle sets (both front or rear wheels), consider replacing both rotors instead of just one. The restored feel and accurate stopping make the extra investment worthwhile.

INSTALLATION

1. Place the rotor in position over the studs and install 2 lug nuts finger tight to hold it in place.
2. Install the mounting plate to the rear axle carrier and tighten the mounting bolts to 34 ft. lbs.

PARKING BRAKE

Cables

REMOVAL & INSTALLATION

▶ **See Figure 73**

1. Elevate and safely support the car. If only the rear wheels are elevated, block the front wheels. Release the parking brake after the car is supported.
2. Remove the rear wheel(s).
3. If equipped with drum brakes, remove the brake drum and remove the brake shoes.
4. If equipped with disc brakes, remove the clip from the parking brake cable and remove the cable from the caliper assembly.
5. If equipped with drum brakes, remove the parking brake retaining bolts at the backing plate.
6. Remove any exhaust heat shields which interfere with the removal of the cable.
7. Remove the 2 cable clamps.
8. Disconnect the cable retainer.
9. Remove the cable from the equalizer (yoke).
   To install:
10. Fit the end of the new cable into the equalizer and make certain it is properly seated.
11. Install the cable retainer, and, working along the length of the cable, install the clamps.

➡**Make certain the cable is properly routed and does not contain any sharp bends or kinks.**

3. Install the brake pads, springs and clips.
4. Carefully mount the caliper onto the upper slide pin.
5. Use GM Tool J-37149 or its equivalent to slowly turn the caliper piston clockwise while pressing it into the bore until it locks.
6. Lower the caliper so that the pad protrusion fits into the piston stopper groove.
7. Install the mounting bolt and tighten it to 14 ft. lbs.
8. Remove the lug nuts holding the disc, install the rear wheel and install all the lug nuts.
9. Depress the brake pedal once or twice to take up the excess piston play.
10. Lower the car to the ground and fill the master cylinder reservoir to the correct level. Final tighten the lug nuts.

12. Feed the cable through the backing plate and install the retaining bolts.
13. If equipped with disc brakes, connect the cable to the arm and install the clip.
14. If equipped with drum brakes, re-install the shoes. The cable will be connected to the shoes during the installation process.
15. Reinstall the wheel(s) and lower the car to the ground.

ADJUSTMENT

▶ **See Figure 74**

Pull the parking brake lever all the way up and count the number of clicks. The correct range is 4-7 clicks before full application. A system which is too tight or too loose requires adjustment.

➡**Before adjusting the parking brake cable, make certain that the rear brake shoe-to-drum clearance is correct.**

1. Remove the center console box.
2. At the rear of the handbrake lever, loosen the locknut on the brake cable.
3. Turn the adjusting nut until the parking brake travel is correct.
4. Tighten the locknut.
5. Reinstall the console.

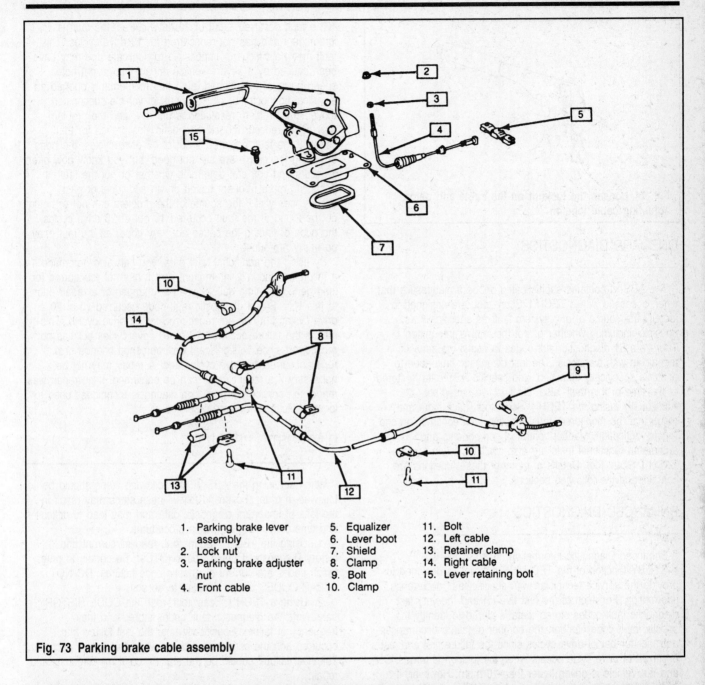

1. Parking brake lever assembly
2. Lock nut
3. Parking brake adjuster nut
4. Front cable
5. Equalizer
6. Lever boot
7. Shield
8. Clamp
9. Bolt
10. Clamp
11. Bolt
12. Left cable
13. Retainer clamp
14. Right cable
15. Lever retaining bolt

Fig. 73 Parking brake cable assembly

ANTI-LOCK BRAKE SYSTEM

DESCRIPTION

ABS-VI has been designed to improve the controllability and steerability of a vehicle during braking that would cause one or more wheels to lock. ABS-VI accomplishes this objective by controlling the hydraulic pressure applied to each wheel brake.

BASIC KNOWLEDGE REQUIRED

Before using this section, it is important that you have a basic knowledge of the following items. Without this basic knowledge, it will be difficult to use the diagnostic procedures contained in this section.

Basic Electrical Circuits - You should understand the basic theory of electricity and know the meaning of voltage, current (amps) and resistance (ohms). You should understand what happens in a circuit with an open or shorted wire. You should be able to read and understand a wiring diagram.

Use Of Circuit Testing Tools - You should know how to use a test light and how to use jumper wires to bypass components to test circuits. You should be familiar with the J 39200 digital multimeter. You should be able to measure voltage, resistance and current and be familiar with the meter controls and how to use them correctly.

Fig. 74 Loosen the locknut on the cable and before adjusting cable tension

ONBOARD DIAGNOSTICS

The ABS-VI contains sophisticated onboard diagnostics that, when accessed with a TECH I 'Scan' tool, are designed to identify the source of any system fault as specifically as possible, including whether or not the fault is intermittent. There are 51 diagnostic fault codes to assist the service technician with diagnosis. The last diagnostic fault code to occur is specifically identified, and specific ABS data is stored at the time of this fault, also, the first five codes set. Additionally, using the TECH I 'Scan' tool, each input and output can be monitored, thus enabling fault confirmation and repair verification. Manual control of components and automated functional tests are also available when using a TECH I 'Scan' tool. Details of many of these functions are contained in the following sections.

ENHANCED DIAGNOSTICS

Enhanced Diagnostic Information, found in the CODE HISTORY function of the TECH I 'Scan' tool, is designed to provide the service technician with specific fault occurrence information. For each of the first five (5) and the very last diagnostic fault codes stored, data is stored to identify the specific fault code number, the number of failure occurrences, and the number of drive cycles since the failure first and last occurred (a drive cycle occurs when the ignition is turned 'ON' and the vehicle is driven faster than 10 mph). However, if a fault is present, the drive cycle counter will increment by turning the ignition 'ON' and 'LOCK'. These first five (5) diagnostic fault codes are also stored in the order of occurrence. The order in which the first 5 faults occurred can be useful in determining if a previous fault is linked to the most recent faults, such as an intermittent wheel speed sensor which later becomes completely open.

During difficult diagnosis situations, this information can be used to identify fault occurrence trends. Does the fault occur more frequently now than it did during the last time when it only failed 1 out of 35 drive cycles? Did the fault only occur once over a large number of drive cycles, indication an unusual condition present when the fault occurred? Does the fault occur infrequently over a large number of drive cycles, indication special diagnosis techniques may be required to identify the source of the fault?

If a fault occurred 1 out of 20 drive cycles, the fault is intermittent and has not reoccurred for 19 drive cycles. This fault may be difficult or impossible to duplicate and may have been caused by a severe vehicle impact (large pot hole, speed bump at high speed, etc.) that momentarily opened an electrical connector or caused unusual vehicle suspension movement. Problem resolution is unlikely, and the problem may never reoccur (check diagnostic aids proved for that code). If the fault occurred 3 out of 15 drive cycles, the odds of finding the cause are still not good, but you know how often it occurs and you can determine whether or not the fault is becoming more frequent based on an additional or past occurrences visit if the source of the problem can not or could not be found. If the fault occurred 10 out of 20 drive cycles, the odds of finding the cause are very good, as the fault may be easily reproduced.

By using the additional fault data, you can also determine if a failure is randomly intermittent or if it has not reoccurred for long periods of time due to weather changes or a repair prior to this visit. Say a diagnostic fault code occurred 10 of 20 drive cycles but has not reoccurred for 10 drive cycles. This means the failure occurred 10 of 10 drive cycles but has not reoccurred since. A significant environmental change or a repair occurred 10 drive cycles ago. A repair may not be necessary if a recent repair can be confirmed. If no repair was made, the service can focus on diagnosis techniques used to locate difficult to recreate problems.

DIAGNOSTIC PROCESS

When servicing the ABS-VI, the following steps should be followed in order. Failure to follow these steps may result in the loss of important diagnostic data and may lead to difficult and time consuming diagnosis procedures.

1. Using the TECH I 'Scan' tool, read all current and history Diagnostic Trouble Codes (DTCs). Be certain to note which codes are current diagnostic code failures. DO NOT CLEAR CODES unless directed to do so.

2. Using a TECH I 'Scan' tool, read the CODE HISTORY data. Note the diagnostic fault codes stored and their frequency of failure. Specifically note the last failure that occurred and the conditions present when this failure occurred. This 'last failure' should be the starting point for diagnosis and repair.

3. Perform a vehicle preliminary diagnosis inspection. This should include:

   a. Inspection of the compact master cylinder for proper brake fluid level.

   b. Inspection of the ABS hydraulic modulator for any leaks or wiring damage.

   c. Inspection of brake components at all four (4) wheels. Verify no drag exists. Also verify proper brake apply operation.

   d. Inspection for worn or damaged wheel bearings that allow a wheel to 'wobble.'

   e. Inspection of the wheel speed sensors and their wiring. Verify correct air gap range, solid sensor attachment, undamaged sensor toothed ring, and undamaged wiring, especially at vehicle attachment points.

   f. Verify proper outer CV joint alignment and operation.

   g. Verify tires meet legal tread depth requirements.

4. If no codes are present, or mechanical component failure codes are present, perform the automated modulator test using the Tech 1 or T-100 to isolate the cause of the problem. If the failure is intermittent and not reproducible, test drive the vehicle while using the automatic snapshot feature of the TECH I 'Scan' tool.

Perform normal acceleration, stopping, and turning maneuvers. If this does not reproduce the failure, perform an ABS stop, on a low coefficient surface such as gravel, from approximately 30 - 50 mph while triggering on any ABS code. If the failure is still not reproducible, use the enhanced diagnostic information found in CODE HISTORY to determine whether or not this failure should be further diagnosed.

5. Once all system failures have been corrected, clear the ABS codes.

The Tech 1 and T-100, when plugged into the ALDL connector, becomes part of the vehicle's electronic system. The Tech 1 and T-100 can also perform the following functions on components linked by the Serial Data Link (SDL):
- Display ABS data
- Display and clear ABS Diagnostic Trouble Codes (DTCs)
- Control ABS components
- Perform extensive ABS diagnosis
- Provide diagnostic testing for 'Intermittent' ABS conditions.

Each test mode has specific diagnosis capabilities which depend upon various keystrokes. In general, five (5) keys control sequencing: 'YES,' 'NO,' 'EXIT,' 'UP' arrow and 'DOWN' arrow. The FO through F9 keys select operating modes, perform functions within an operating mode, or enter trouble code or model year designations.

In general, the Tech 1 has five (6) test modes for diagnosing the antilock brake system. The five (6) test modes are as follows:

MODE FO:DATA LIST - In this test mode, the Tech 1 continuously monitors wheel speed data, brake switch status and other inputs and outputs.

MODE F1:CODE HISTORY - In this mode, fault code history data is displayed. This data includes how many ignition cycles since the fault code occurred, along with other ABS information. The first five (5) and last fault codes set are included in the ABS history data.

MODE F2:TROUBLE CODES - In this test mode, trouble codes stored by the EBCM, both current ignition cycle and history, may be displayed or cleared.

MODE F3:ABS SNAPSHOT - In this test mode, the Tech 1 captures ABS data before and after a fault occurrence or a forced manual trigger.

MODE F4:ABS TESTS - In this test mode, the Tech 1 performs hydraulic modulator functional tests to assist in problem isolation during troubleshooting. Included here is manual control of the motors which is used prior to bleeding the brake system.

MODE F5:MOTOR REHOME - In this test mode, the Tech 1 commands the EBCM to rehome the motors on the hydraulic modulator assembly. This mode should always be used prior to bleeding the brake system.

DISPLAYING CODES

Diagnostic fault codes can only be read through the use of a bidirectional 'Scan' tool. There are no provisions for 'Flash Code' diagnostics.

CLEARING CODES

The trouble codes in EBCM memory are erased in one of two ways:
1. Tech 1 'Clear Codes' selection.
2. Ignition cycle default.

These two methods are detailed below. Be sure to verify proper system operation and absence of codes when clearing procedure is completed.

The EBCM will not permit code clearing until all of the codes have been displayed. Also, codes cannot be cleared by unplugging the EBCM, disconnecting the battery cables, or turning the ignition to 'LOCK' (except on an ignition cycle default).

Tech 1 'Clear Codes' Method

Select F2 for trouble codes. After codes have been viewed completely, Tech 1 will ask, 'CLEAR ABS CODES'; ANSWER 'YES.' Tech 1 will then read, 'HISTORY DATA WILL BE LOST. CLEAR DATA'? Answer 'YES' and codes will be cleared.

Ignition Cycle Default

If no diagnostic fault code occurs for 100 drive cycles (a drive cycle occurs when the ignition is turned 'ON' and the vehicle is driven faster than 10 mph), any existing fault codes are cleared from the EBCM memory.

INTERMITTENT FAILURES

As with most electronic systems, intermittent failures may be difficult to accurately diagnose. The following is a method to try to isolate an intermittent failure especially wheel speed circuitry failures.

If an ABS fault occurs, the 'ABS' warning light indicator will be 'ON' during the ignition cycle in which the fault was detected. If it is an intermittent problem which seems to have corrected itself ('ABS' warning light 'OFF'), a history trouble code will be stored. Also stored will be the history data of the code at the time the fault occurred. The Tech 1 must be used to read ABS history data.

INTERMITTENTS AND POOR CONNECTIONS

Most intermittents are caused by faulty electrical connections or wiring, although occasionally a sticking relay or solenoid can be a problem. Some items to check are:
1. Poor mating of connector halves, or terminals not fully seated in the connector body (backed out).

2. Dirt or corrosion on the terminals. The terminals must be clean and free of any foreign material which could impede proper terminal contact.

3. Damaged connector body, exposing the terminals to moisture and dirt, as well as not maintaining proper terminal orientation with the component or mating connector.

4. Improperly formed or damaged terminals. All connector terminals in problem circuits should be checked carefully to ensure good contact tension. Use a corresponding mating terminal to check for proper tension. Refer to 'Checking Terminal Contact' in this section for the specific procedure.

5. The J 35616-A Connector Test Adapter Kit must be used whenever a diagnostic procedure requests checking or probing a terminal. Using the adapter will ensure that no damage to the terminal will occur, as well as giving an idea of whether contact tension is sufficient. If contact tension seems incorrect, refer to 'Checking Terminal Contact' in this section for specifics.

6. Poor terminal-to-wire connection. Checking this requires removing the terminal from the connector body. Some conditions which fall under this description are poor crimps, poor solder joints, crimping over wire insulation rather than the wire itself, corrosion in the wire-to-terminal contact area, etc.

7. Wire insulation which is rubbed through, causing an intermittent short as the bare area touches other wiring or parts of the vehicle.

8. Wiring broken inside the insulation. This condition could cause a continuity check to show a good circuit, but if only 1 or 2 strands of a multi-strand-type wire are intact, resistance could be far too high.

Checking Terminal Contact

When diagnosing an electrical system that uses Metri-Pack 150/280/480/630 series terminals (refer to Terminal Repair Kit J 38125-A instruction manual J 38125-4 for terminal identification), it is important to check terminal contact between a connector and component, or between in-line connectors, before replacing a suspect component.

Frequently, a diagnostic chart leads to a step that reads 'Check for poor connection'. Mating terminals must be inspected to ensure good terminal contact. A poor connection between the male and female terminal at a connector may be the result of contamination or deformation.

Contamination is caused by the connector halves being improperly connected, a missing or damaged connector seal, or damage to the connector itself, exposing the terminals to moisture and dirt. Contamination, usually in underhood or underbody connectors, leads to terminal corrosion, causing an open circuit or an intermittently open circuit.

Deformation is caused by probing the mating side of a connector terminal without the proper adapter, improperly joining the connector halves or repeatedly separating and joining the connector halves. Deformation, usually to the female terminal contact tang, can result in poor terminal contact causing an open or intermittently open circuit.

Follow the procedure below to check terminal contact:

1. Separate the connector halves. Refer to Terminal Repair Kit J 38125-A instruction manual J 38125-4, if available.

2. Inspect the connector halves for contamination. Contamination will result in a white or green buildup within the connector body or between terminals, causing high terminal resistance, intermittent contact or an open circuit. An underhood or underbody connector that shows signs of contamination should be replaced in its entirety: terminals, seals, and connector body.

3. Using an equivalent male terminal from the Terminal Repair Kit J 38125-A, check the retention force of the female terminal in question by inserting and removing the male terminal to the female terminal in the connector body. Good terminal contact will require a certain amount of force to separate the terminals.

4. Using an equivalent female terminal from the Terminal Repair Kit J 38125-A, compare the retention force of this terminal to the female terminal in question by joining and separating the male terminal to the female terminal in question. If the retention force is significantly different between the two female terminals, replace the female terminal in question, using a terminal from Terminal Repair Kit J 38125-A.

Anti-Lock Brake System Service

Precautions

➡**Failure to observe the following precautions may result in system damage.**

• Before performing electric arc welding on the vehicle, disconnect the Electronic Brake Control Module (EBCM) and the hydraulic modulator connectors.

• When performing painting work on the vehicle, do not expose the Electronic Brake Control Module (EBCM) to temperatures in excess of 185°F (85°C) for longer than 2 hrs. The system may be exposed to temperatures up to 200°F (95°C) for less than 15 min.

• Never disconnect or connect the Electronic Brake Control Module (EBCM) or hydraulic modulator connectors with the ignition switch ON.

• Never disassemble any component of the Anti-Lock Brake System (ABS) which is designated non-serviceable; the component must be replaced as an assembly.

• When filling the master cylinder, always use Delco Supreme 11 brake fluid or equivalent, which meets DOT-3 specifications; petroleum base fluid will destroy the rubber parts.

Some ABS-VI components are equipped with electrical connectors using a Connector Position Assurance (CPA) lock.

Electrical Connectors

1. Remove the lock before separating the electrical connectors.

2. Be careful not to damage the locking pin during removal.

3. Make sure that the rubber connector seal is in place on the connector before and after connection.

4. Always install the lock after their connection is made.

ABS Hydraulic Modulator Assembly Bleeder Valves

REMOVAL & INSTALLATION

▶ See Figure 75

1. Place a shop towel or suitable container below the bleeder valve.
2. Unscrew the bleeder valve from the hydraulic modulator.
3. Install the bleeder valve but do not tighten fully. Bleed the brake system as outlined later in this section.
4. Tighten the bleeder valve to 80 inch lbs. (9 Nm).

Fluid Level Sensor

The fluid level sensor is serviced as a part of the master cylinder reservoir.

Enable Relay

REMOVAL & INSTALLATION

The enable relay is located on the right side of the engine compartment, bolted to the fender apron.

1. Disconnect the negative battery cable.
2. Disconnect the electrical connection.
3. Remove the 1 bolt and remove the relay from the fender apron.

To install:

4. Reposition the enable relay to the vehicle and connect the electrical connector.
5. Secure the enable relay to the vehicle with the bolt and tighten to 71 inch lbs. (8 Nm).

ABS Lamp Driver Module

The lamp module driver is located on the instrument panel harness attached to the back of the instrument panel.

1. Disconnect the negative battery cable.
2. Remove the instrument panel from the vehicle as outlined in Section 10.

3. Slide the glove box all the way out or remove it completely.
4. Disconnect the lamp driver module electrical connector and disconnect the module from the instrument panel harness.

To install:

5. Connect the lamp driver module electrical connector and connect the module to the instrument panel harness.
6. Install the instrument to the vehicle as outlined in Section 10.
7. Connect the negative battery cable.

ABS Hydraulic Modulator Assembly

REMOVAL & INSTALLATION

▶ See Figure 76

✳✳CAUTION

To avoid personal injury, use the TECH I Scan tool to relieve the gear tension in the hydraulic modulator. This is a function of the TECH I Scan tool and must be performed prior to removal of the brake control and motor assembly.

1. Disconnect the negative battery cable.
2. Disconnect the hydraulic modulator and solenoid electrical connectors.
3. Wrap a shop towel around the hydraulic brake lines and disconnect the 6 brake lines from the modulator.

➡**Cap the disconnected lines to prevent the loss of fluid and the entry of moisture and contaminants.**

4. Remove the 3 bolts attaching the ABS hydraulic modulator assembly to the vehicle.
5. Remove the ABS hydraulic modulator assembly from the vehicle.

To install:

6. Install the ABS hydraulic modulator assembly to the vehicle. Install the 3 attaching bolts and tighten to 48 inch lbs. (5.4 Nm).
7. Connect the 6 brake pipes to the modulator assembly. Tighten to 11 ft. lbs. (15 Nm).
8. Connect the hydraulic modulator and solenoid electrical connectors.
9. Properly bleed the system.
10. Connect the negative battery cable.

Hydraulic Modulator Solenoid Assembly

REMOVAL & INSTALLATION

▶ See Figure 77

1. Disconnect the negative battery cable.
2. Disconnect the solenoid electrical connector.
3. Remove the 2 Torx® head bolts.
4. Remove the solenoid assembly.

1. Bleeder valve
2. Hydraulic modulator
3. Solenoid electrical connectors
4. Hydraulic modulator electrical connector

Fig. 75 ABS-VI hydraulic modulator bleeder locations

Fig. 76 ABS-VI hydraulic modulator assembly removal

To install:

5. Verify that the solenoid lip seal is properly positioned on the new solenoid.

6. Position the solenoid so the connectors face each other.

7. Press down firmly by hand until the solenoid assembly flange seats on the modulator assembly.

8. Install the 2 Torx® head bolts. Tighten to 40 inch lbs. (4.5 Nm).

9. Connect the solenoid electrical connector.

10. Properly bleed the brake system.

11. Connect the negative battery cable.

Front Wheel Speed Sensor

REMOVAL & INSTALLATION

▶ See Figure 78

1. Disconnect the negative battery cable.

2. Raise and safely support the vehicle.

3. Remove the wheelhousing from the front wheelwell.

4. Disconnect the front sensor electrical connector.

5. Remove the 3 bolts retaining the front wheel speed sensor pigtail harness to the body and front strut assembly.

6. Remove the 1 bolt and remove the sensor from the knuckle assembly.

To install:

7. Install the front wheel speed sensor to the steering knuckle.

8. Tighten the bolt to 69 inch lbs. (7.8 Nm).

Fig. 77 ABS-VI hydraulic modulator solenoid assembly

9. Install the 3 bolts to retain the front wheel speed sensor pigtail harness to the body and front strut assembly and tighten to 48 inch lbs. (5.4 Nm).

10. Connect the front sensor electrical connector.

11. Install the wheelhousing to the front wheelwell.

12. Lower the vehicle.

13. Connect the negative battery cable.

Rear Wheel Speed Sensor Assembly

REMOVAL & INSTALLATION

▶ See Figure 79

1. Disconnect the negative battery cable.

2. Remove the rear seat cushion and side trim panel as outlined in Section 10.

3. Disconnect the rear sensor electrical connector.

4. Raise and safely support the vehicle.

5. Pull the rear wheel speed sensor pigtail harness out through the body, removing the grommet.

6. Remove the 3 bolts retaining the rear wheel speed sensor pigtail harness to the body and rear strut assembly.

7. Remove the 1 bolt and remove the rear wheel speed sensor from the rear suspension knuckle.

To install:

8. Install the 1 bolt retaining the rear wheel speed sensor to the rear suspension knuckle and tighten to 69 inch lbs. (7.8 Nm).

9. Install the 3 bolts and retain the rear wheel speed sensor pigtail harness to the body and rear strut assembly. Tighten the bolts to 48 inch lbs. (5.4 Nm).

10. Pull the rear wheel speed sensor pigtail harness in through the body, installing the grommet.

11. Lower the vehicle.

12. Connect the rear sensor electrical connector.

13. Install the rear seat cushion and side trim panel.

14. Connect the negative battery cable.

Electronic Brake Control Module (EBCM)

REMOVAL & INSTALLATION

1. Disconnect the negative battery cable.

Fig. 78 ABS-VI front wheel speed sensor installation

Fig. 79 ABS-VI front wheel speed sensor installation

2. Loosen the passenger compartment floor carpet from under the right side of the instrument panel. Pull the carpet back to expose the EBCM cover panel.

3. Remove the 4 nuts and remove the EBCM cover panel.

4. Disconnect the EBCM electrical connectors and remove the EBCM from the vehicle.

5. Installation is the reverse of removal.

ABS Bleeding System

➡Prior to bleeding the brakes, the front and rear displacement cylinder pistons must be returned to the top-most (home) position. Using a TECH 1 or T-100, select 'F5″ (motor rehome). Motor rehome function cannot be performed if current DTCs (Diagnostic Trouble Codes) are present. If DTCs are present, the vehicle must be repaired and DTCs cleared before performing the motor rehome function.

1. Raise and suitably support front end of vehicle so that the drive wheels are off the ground.

2. Start the engine, engage the transaxle and run the vehicle above 3 mph (5 km/h), for at least 10 seconds.

3. Observe the 'ABS' indicator. Make sure that the indicator goes out after approximately three seconds. If the 'ABS' indicator remains illuminated, a TECH 1 must be used to diagnose the malfunction. If the 'ABS' indicator goes out and stays off, stop the engine and repeat Steps 2 and 3.

4. Using a TECH 1 or T-100, enter the manual control function and 'Apply' the front and rear motors.

5. The entire brake system should now be rebled following 'Manual Bleeding' later in this section.

➡ Use only hydraulic brake fluid GM P/N 1052542, or equivalent DOT 3 brake fluid, from a clean, sealed container. Do not use fluid from an open container that may be contaminated with water. Do not use DOT 5 (silicone) brake fluid.

ABS Manual Bleeding Procedure

▸ See Figures 80 and 81

Brake Control Assembly

➡Only use brake fluid from a sealed container which meets DOT 3 specifications.

1. Clean the master cylinder reservoir and surrounding area.

2. Remove the master cylinder reservoir cap.

3. Inspect the brake fluid level; add clean hydraulic brake fluid GM P/N 1052542, or equivalent DOT 3 brake fluid if needed.

4. Install the master cylinder reservoir cap.

5. Prime hydraulic modulator.

a. Attach a clear plastic bleed hose to the rearward bleeder valve on the hydraulic modulator. Submerge the other end of the bleeder hose in a clean container partially filled with brake fluid.

b. Slowly open the rearward bleeder valve ½ to ¾ turn.

c. Have an assistant depress the brake pedal and hold until fluid begins to flow.

d. Close the bleeder valve and release the brake pedal. Repeat Steps B and C until no air bubbles are present. Tighten the bleeder valve to 80 inch lbs. (9 Nm).

e. Repeat procedure for forward bleeder valve.

➡Once fluid is seen to flow from both hydraulic modulator bleeder valves, the hydraulic modulator is sufficiently full of brake fluid. However, it may not be completely purged of air. At this point, move to the wheel cylinders/calipers and bleed them. This ensures that the lowest points in the system are completely free of air and then the hydraulic modulator can be purged of any remaining air.

6. Remove the master cylinder reservoir cover and inspect brake fluid level: add hydraulic brake fluid GM P/N 1052542, or equivalent DOT 3 brake fluid, if needed.

7. Install the master cylinder reservoir cover.

8. Raise and suitably support the vehicle.

➡Bleed wheel cylinders/calipers in the following sequence: right rear, left rear, right front, left front.

9. Bleed wheel cylinders/calipers in the sequence outlined above.

a. Attach a clear plastic bleeder hose to the bleeder valve on the wheel cylinder/caliper. Submerge the other end of the bleeder hose in a clean container partially filled with brake fluid.

b. Open the bleeder valve.

c. Have an assistant slowly depress the brake pedal.

d. Close the bleeder valve and release the brake pedal.

e. Wait 5 seconds, then repeat Steps B, C and D (including the 5 second waiting period) until the brake pedal

Fig. 80 Priming/bleeding the hydraulic modulator

Fig. 81 Bleeding the wheel cylinder/caliper

feels firm and no air bubbles are observed in the bleeder hose. Tighten the bleeder valve to 80 inch lbs. (9 Nm).

f. Repeat Steps A through E for the remaining wheel cylinder and calipers.

10. Lower the vehicle.

11. Remove the master cylinder reservoir cover and inspect brake fluid level: add hydraulic brake fluid GM P/N 1052542, or equivalent DOT 3 brake fluid, if needed.

12. Install the master cylinder reservoir cover.

13. Bleed the hydraulic modulator.

a. Attach a clear plastic bleeder hose to the rearward bleeder valve on the hydraulic modulator. Submerge the other end of the bleeder hose in a clean container partially filled with brake fluid.

b. Have an assistant depress the brake pedal with moderate force.

c. Slowly open the rearward bleeder valve ½ to ¾ turn and allow fluid to flow.

d. Close bleeder valve and release brake pedal.

e. Wait 5 seconds, then repeat Steps B, C and D (including the 5 second waiting period) until all the air is purged from the system. Tighten bleeder valve to 80 inch lbs. (9 Nm).

f. Repeat Steps A through E for the forward bleeder valve.

14. Remove the master cylinder reservoir cover and inspect brake fluid level: add hydraulic brake fluid GM P/N 1052542, or equivalent DOT 3 brake fluid, if needed.

15. Install master cylinder reservoir cover.

Inspect: With the ignition switch in **ON**, depress the brake pedal with moderate force and hold in position. Note pedal travel and feel.

If pedal feels firm and constant and pedal travel is not excessive, start the engine. With the engine running, re-check the pedal travel. If it is still firm and constant and pedal travel is not excessive, proceed with Step 16.

If pedal feels soft or has excessive travel either initially or after engine start, using the TECH 1, 'Release' then 'Apply' the motors three times and cycle the solenoids 10 times. Be sure to 'Apply' the motors to ensure that the pistons are in the home position. Repeat the bleeding procedure.

16. Road test the vehicle. Make several normal (non ABS) stops from a moderate speed to ensure proper brake system function.

BRAKE SPECIFICATIONS

All measurements in inches unless noted.

Year	Model	Master Cylinder Bore	Brake Disc Original Thickness	Brake Disc Minimum Thickness	Maximum Runout	Brake Drum Diameter Original Inside Diameter	Brake Drum Diameter Max. Wear Limit	Brake Drum Diameter Maximum Machine Diameter	Minimum Lining Thickness Front	Minimum Lining Thickness Rear
1985	Nova	—	0.531	0.492	0.0059	7.874	7.913	—	0.0039	0.0039
1986	Nova	—	0.531	0.492	0.0059	7.874	7.913	—	0.0039	0.0039
1987	Nova	—	0.531	0.492	0.0059	7.874	7.913	—	0.0039	0.0039
1988	Nova ①	—	0.531	0.492	0.0059	7.874	7.913	—	0.0039	0.0039
	Nova ②	—	0.531 ③	0.492 ④	0.0059	7.874	7.913	—	0.0039	0.0039
1989	Prizm	—	0.709	0.669	0.0035	7.874	7.913	—	0.0039	0.0039
1990	Prizm	—	0.709 ③	0.669 ④	0.0035 ⑤	7.874	7.913	—	0.0039	0.0039
1991	Base/LSi	—	0.709	0.669	0.0035	7.874	7.913	—	0.0039	0.0039
	GSi	—	0.709 ③	0.669 ④	0.0035 ⑤	7.874	7.913	—	0.0039	0.0039
1992	Base/LSi	—	0.709	0.669	0.0035	7.874	7.913	—	0.0039	0.0039
	GSi	—	0.709 ③	0.669 ④	0.0035 ⑤	7.874	7.913	—	0.0039	0.0039
1993	All	—	0.866	0.787	0.0035	7.874	7.913	—	0.0039	0.0039

① VIN Code 4 eng.
② VIN Code 5 eng.
③ Rear disc: 0.354 (GSi)
④ Rear disc: 0.315 (GSi)
⑤ Rear disc: 0.0039 (GSi)

DIAGNOSTIC PROCESS
(Page 1 of 3)

ABS CARTRIDGE SECTION	TECH 1 SCREEN DISPLAY
STEP 1 SELECT VEHICLE MODEL YEAR	MODEL YEAR: 1993
STEP 2 SELECT USAGE	"?" CAR
STEP 3 SELECT MODE (FIRST SCREEN)	

F0: DATA LIST

F1: DTC HISTORY — INFORMATION ABOUT PREVIOUS DTCs STORED

F2: SHOW DTCs — DTCs STORED AND CLEAR DTCs

F3: SNAP SHOT

F4: ABS TEST

F5: MOTOR REHOME

FRONT WHL SPEEDS
REAR WHL SPEEDS
VEHICLE SPEED
ABS INDICATOR LAMP
LF MOTOR COMMAND FWD/REV
LF MOTOR FEEDBACK
RF MOTOR COMMAND FWD/REV
RF MOTOR FEEDBACK
REAR MOTOR COMMAND FWD/REV
REAR MOTOR FEEDBACK
L FRONT SOLENOID
R FROM SOLENOID
BRAKE SWITCH
ENABLE RELAY COMMAND
BRAKE T-TALE COMMAND
BRAKE TELLTALE
ABS BATTERY VOLTAGE
ABS IGNITION VOLTAGE

SNAPSHOT OPTIONS
F0: REPLAY DATA
F1: MANUAL TRIG.
F2: AUTO TRIG.
F3: ANY DTC
F4: SINGLE DTC
F9: TRIGGER POINT

F0: BEGINNING
F1: CENTER
F2: END OF DATA

CONTINUED ON FOLLOWING CHART
(PAGE 2 OF 3)

REHOMES MOTORS PRIOR TO BLEEDING THE BRAKE SYSTEM.

Fig. 82 TECH 1 diagnostic process (1 of 3)

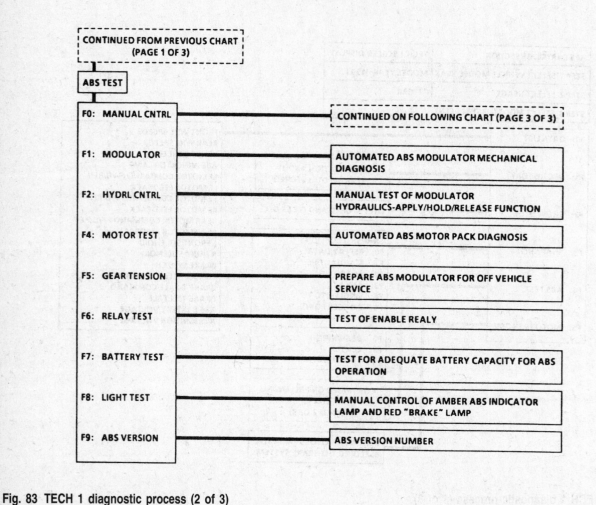

DIAGNOSTIC PROCESS
(Page 2 of 3)

CONTINUED FROM PREVIOUS CHART
(PAGE 1 OF 3)

ABS TEST

F0: MANUAL CNTRL — CONTINUED ON FOLLOWING CHART (PAGE 3 OF 3)

F1: MODULATOR — AUTOMATED ABS MODULATOR MECHANICAL DIAGNOSIS

F2: HYDRL CNTRL — MANUAL TEST OF MODULATOR HYDRAULICS-APPLY/HOLD/RELEASE FUNCTION

F4: MOTOR TEST — AUTOMATED ABS MOTOR PACK DIAGNOSIS

F5: GEAR TENSION — PREPARE ABS MODULATOR FOR OFF VEHICLE SERVICE

F6: RELAY TEST — TEST OF ENABLE REALY

F7: BATTERY TEST — TEST FOR ADEQUATE BATTERY CAPACITY FOR ABS OPERATION

F8: LIGHT TEST — MANUAL CONTROL OF AMBER ABS INDICATOR LAMP AND RED "BRAKE" LAMP

F9: ABS VERSION — ABS VERSION NUMBER

Fig. 83 TECH 1 diagnostic process (2 of 3)

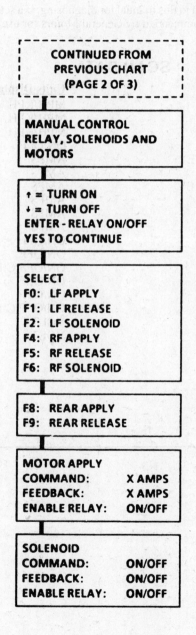

DIAGNOSTIC PROCESS
(Page 3 of 3)

CONTINUED FROM
PREVIOUS CHART
(PAGE 2 OF 3)

MANUAL CONTROL
RELAY, SOLENOIDS AND
MOTORS

↑ = TURN ON
↓ = TURN OFF
ENTER - RELAY ON/OFF
YES TO CONTINUE

SELECT
F0: LF APPLY
F1: LF RELEASE
F2: LF SOLENOID
F4: RF APPLY
F5: RF RELEASE
F6: RF SOLENOID

F8: REAR APPLY
F9: REAR RELEASE

MOTOR APPLY
COMMAND: X AMPS
FEEDBACK: X AMPS
ENABLE RELAY: ON/OFF

SOLENOID
COMMAND: ON/OFF
FEEDBACK: ON/OFF
ENABLE RELAY: ON/OFF

Fig. 84 TECH 1 diagnostic process (3 of 3)

DIAGNOSTIC CIRCUIT CHECK

The "Diagnostic Circuit Check" is an organized approach to identifying a problem created by an antilock brake system (ABS) malfunction. It must be the starting point for any ABS complaint diagnosis, because it directs the service technician to the next logical step in diagnosing the complaint.

The "Scan Data" listed in the table may be used after completing the "Diagnostic Circuit Check" and finding the on-board diagnostics functioning properly and diagnostic trouble codes (DTCs) displayed. **A TECH 1 THAT DISPLAYS FAULTY DATA SHOULD NOT BE USED, AND THE PROBLEM SHOULD BE REPORTED TO THE MANUFACTURER. THE USE OF A MALFUNCTIONING TECH 1 CAN RESULT IN MISDIAGNOSIS AND UNNECESSARY PARTS REPLACEMENT.**

Only the parameters listed below are used in this manual for diagnosing. If a scan tool other than TECH 1 is used and reads other parameters, the values are not recommended by General Motors for use in diagnosing.

SCAN DATA

Scan Position	Units Displayed
FRONT WHL SPEEDS	MPH/KPH
REAR WHL SPEEDS	MPH/KPH
VEHICLE SPEED	MPH/KPH
ABS INDICATOR LAMP	ON/OFF
LF MOTOR COMMAND FWD/REV	AMPS
LF MOTOR FEEDBAC	AMPS
RF MOTOR COMMAND FWD/REV	AMPS
RF MOTOR FEEDBAC	AMPS
REAR MOTOR CMD FWD/REV	AMPS
REAR MOTOR FDBK	AMPS
L FRONT SOLENOID	ON/OFF
R FRONT SOLENOID	ON/OFF
BRAKE SWITCH	ON/OFF/CIRCUIT OPEN
ENABLE RELAY CMD	ON/OFF
BRAKE T-TALE CMD	ON/OFF
BRAKE TELLTALE	ON/OFF/CIRCUIT OPEN
ABS BATT VOLTAGE	VOLTS
ABS IGN VOLTAGE	VOLTS

Fig. 85 Diagnostic circuit check

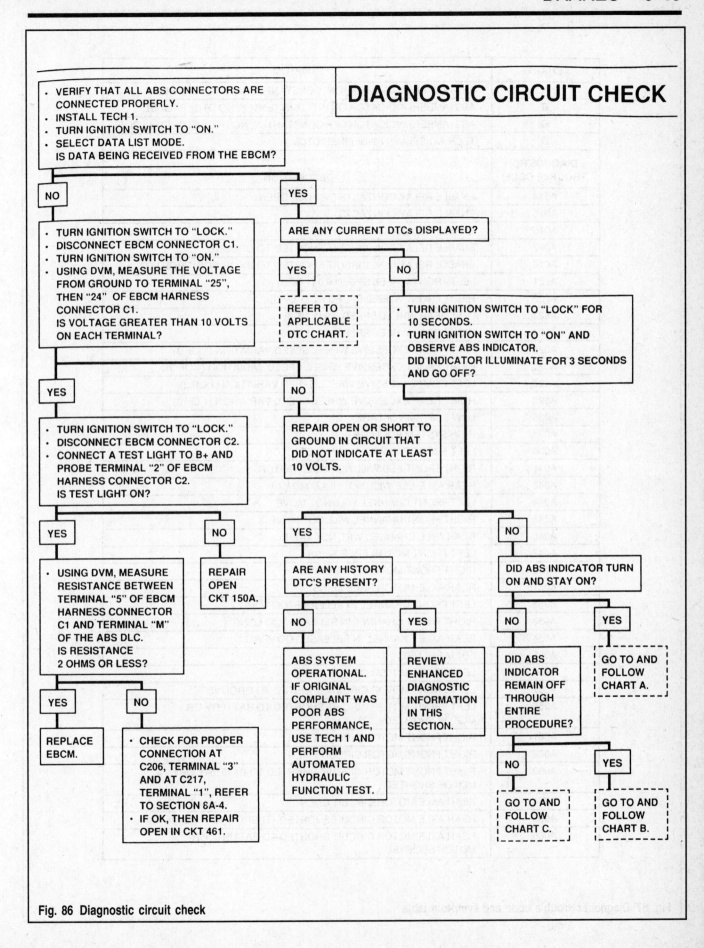

DIAGNOSTIC CIRCUIT CHECK

- VERIFY THAT ALL ABS CONNECTORS ARE CONNECTED PROPERLY.
- INSTALL TECH 1.
- TURN IGNITION SWITCH TO "ON."
- SELECT DATA LIST MODE. IS DATA BEING RECEIVED FROM THE EBCM?

NO

- TURN IGNITION SWITCH TO "LOCK."
- DISCONNECT EBCM CONNECTOR C1.
- TURN IGNITION SWITCH TO "ON."
- USING DVM, MEASURE THE VOLTAGE FROM GROUND TO TERMINAL "25", THEN "24" OF EBCM HARNESS CONNECTOR C1. IS VOLTAGE GREATER THAN 10 VOLTS ON EACH TERMINAL?

YES

- TURN IGNITION SWITCH TO "LOCK."
- DISCONNECT EBCM CONNECTOR C2.
- CONNECT A TEST LIGHT TO B+ AND PROBE TERMINAL "2" OF EBCM HARNESS CONNECTOR C2. IS TEST LIGHT ON?

YES

- USING DVM, MEASURE RESISTANCE BETWEEN TERMINAL "5" OF EBCM HARNESS CONNECTOR C1 AND TERMINAL "M" OF THE ABS DLC. IS RESISTANCE 2 OHMS OR LESS?

YES

REPLACE EBCM.

NO

- CHECK FOR PROPER CONNECTION AT C206, TERMINAL "3" AND AT C217, TERMINAL "1", REFER TO SECTION 8A-4.
- IF OK, THEN REPAIR OPEN IN CKT 461.

NO

REPAIR OPEN CKT 150A.

YES

ARE ANY HISTORY DTC'S PRESENT?

NO

ABS SYSTEM OPERATIONAL. IF ORIGINAL COMPLAINT WAS POOR ABS PERFORMANCE, USE TECH 1 AND PERFORM AUTOMATED HYDRAULIC FUNCTION TEST.

YES

REVIEW ENHANCED DIAGNOSTIC INFORMATION IN THIS SECTION.

YES

ARE ANY CURRENT DTCs DISPLAYED?

YES

REFER TO APPLICABLE DTC CHART.

NO

- TURN IGNITION SWITCH TO "LOCK" FOR 10 SECONDS.
- TURN IGNITION SWITCH TO "ON" AND OBSERVE ABS INDICATOR. DID INDICATOR ILLUMINATE FOR 3 SECONDS AND GO OFF?

NO

REPAIR OPEN OR SHORT TO GROUND IN CIRCUIT THAT DID NOT INDICATE AT LEAST 10 VOLTS.

NO

DID ABS INDICATOR TURN ON AND STAY ON?

NO

DID ABS INDICATOR REMAIN OFF THROUGH ENTIRE PROCEDURE?

NO

GO TO AND FOLLOW CHART C.

YES

GO TO AND FOLLOW CHART B.

YES

GO TO AND FOLLOW CHART A.

Fig. 86 Diagnostic circuit check

CHART	SYMPTOM
A	ABS (AMBER) INDICATOR "ON" CONSTANTLY, NO DTCs STORED
B	ABS (AMBER) INDICATOR ON INTERMITTENTLY, NO DTCs STORED
C	ABS (AMBER) INDICATOR OFF CONSTANTLY, NO DTCs STORED (1 OF 2)
D	TECH 1 DISPLAYS UNDEFINED DTCs

DIAGNOSTIC TROUBLE CODE	DESCRIPTION
A014	ENABLE RELAY CONTACTS OR FUSE OPEN
A015	ENABLE RELAY CONTACTS
A016	ENABLE RELAY COIL CIRCUIT OPEN
A017	ENABLE RELAY COIL CIRCUIT SHORTED TO GROUND
A018	ENABLE RELAY COIL CIRCUIT SHORTED TO B+ OR COIL SHORTED
A021	LEFT FRONT WHEEL SPEED = 0 (1 OF 3)
A022	RIGHT FRONT WHEEL SPEED = 0 (1 OF 3)
A023	LEFT REAR WHEEL SPEED = 0 (1 OF 3)
A024	RIGHT REAR WHEEL SPEED = 0 (1 OF 3)
A025	LEFT FRONT EXCESSIVE WHEEL SPEED VARIATION (1 OF 3)
A026	RIGHT FRONT EXCESSIVE WHEEL SPEED VARIATION (1 OF 3)
A027	LEFT REAR EXCESSIVE WHEEL SPEED VARIATION (1 OF 3)
A028	RIGHT REAR EXCESSIVE WHEEL SPEED VARIATION (1 OF 3)
A036	LOW SYSTEM VOLTAGE
A037	HIGH SYSTEM VOLTAGE
A038	LEFT FRONT ESB WILL NOT HOLD MOTOR
A041	RIGHT FRONT ESB WILL NOT HOLD MOTOR
A042	REAR AXLE ESB WILL NOT HOLD MOTOR
A044	LEFT FRONT CHANNEL WILL NOT MOVE
A045	RIGHT FRONT CHANNEL WILL NOT MOVE
A046	REAR AXLE CHANNEL WILL NOT MOVE
A047	LEFT FRONT MOTOR FREE SPINS
A048	RIGHT FRONT MOTOR FREE SPINS
A051	REAR AXLE MOTOR FREE SPINS
A052	LEFT FRONT CHANNEL IN RELEASE TOO LONG
A053	RIGHT FRONT CHANNEL IN RELEASE TOO LONG
A054	REAR AXLE CHANNEL IN RELEASE TOO LONG
A055	EBCM FAILURE
A056	LEFT FRONT MOTOR CIRCUIT OPEN
A057	LEFT FRONT MOTOR CIRCUIT SHORTED TO GROUND
A058	LEFT FRONT MOTOR CIRCUIT SHORTED TO BATTERY OR MOTOR SHORTED
A061	RIGHT FRONT MOTOR CIRCUIT OPEN
A062	RIGHT FRONT MOTOR CIRCUIT OPEN
A063	RIGHT FRONT MOTOR CIRCUIT SHORTED TO BATTERY OR MOTOR SHORTED
A064	REAR AXLE MOTOR CIRCUIT OPEN
A065	REAR AXLE MOTOR CIRCUIT SHORTED TO GROUND
A066	REAR AXLE MOTOR CIRCUIT SHORTED TO BATTERY OR MOTOR SHORTED

Fig. 87 Diagnostic trouble code and symptom table

DIAGNOSTIC TROUBLE CODE	DESCRIPTION
A076	LEFT FRONT SOLENOID CIRCUIT OPEN OR SHORTED TO BATTERY
A077	LEFT FRONT SOLENOID CIRCUIT SHORTED TO GROUND OR DRIVER OPEN
A078	RIGHT FRONT SOLENOID CIRCUIT SHORTED TO BATTERY OR OPEN
A081	RIGHT FRONT SOLENOID CIRCUIT SHORTED TO GROUND OR DRIVER OPEN
A082	CALIBRATION MEMORY FAILURE
A086	RED BRAKE WARNING LAMP ACTIVATED BY ABS
A087	RED BRAKE WARNING LAMP CIRCUIT OPEN
A088	RED BRAKE WARNING LAMP CIRCUIT SHORTED TO BATTERY
A091	OPEN BRAKE SWITCH CONTACTS DURING DECELERATION
A092	OPEN BRAKE SWITCH CONTACTS WHEN ABS WAS REQUIRED
A093	DTC A091 OR A092 SET IN CURRENT OR PREVIOUS IGNITION CYCLE
A094	BRAKE SWITCH CONTACTS ALWAYS CLOSED
A095	BRAKE SWITCH CIRCUIT OPEN
A096	BRAKE LAMPS CIRCUIT OPEN

Fig. 88 Diagnostic trouble code and symptom table (cont.)

Fig. 89 ABS circuit (1 of 2)

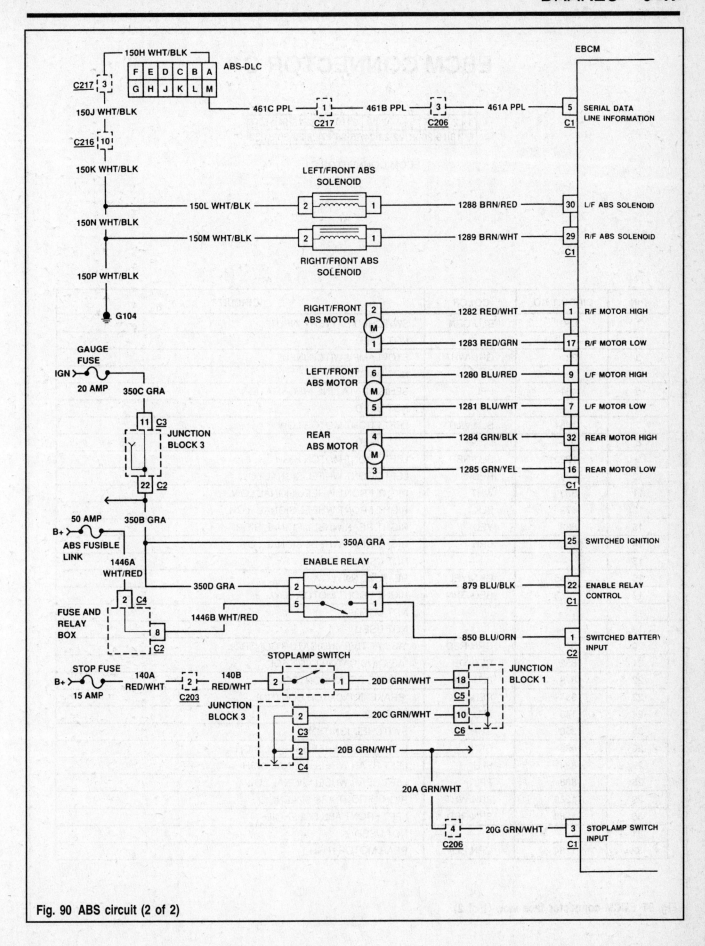

Fig. 90 ABS circuit (2 of 2)

EBCM CONNECTOR C1

EBCM CONNECTOR C1

PIN	CIRCUIT NO.	COLOR	CIRCUIT
1	850	BLU/ORN	SWITCHED BATTERY INPUT
2	—	—	NOT USED
3	20	GRN/WHT	STOPLAMP SWITCH INPUT
4	—	—	NOT USED
5	461	PPL	SERIAL DATA LINE INFORMATION
6	—	—	NOT USED
7	1281	BLU/WHT	LEFT FRONT MOTOR LOW
8	—	—	NOT USED
9	1280	BLU/RED	LEFT FRONT MOTOR HIGH
10	873	RED	LEFT FRONT WHEEL SIGNAL LOW
11	833	WHT	RIGHT FRONT WHEEL SIGNAL LOW
12	872	BLK	RIGHT FRONT WHEEL SIGNAL HIGH
13	882	YEL	RIGHT REAR WHEEL SIGNAL HIGH
14	883	BRN	RIGHT REAR WHEEL SIGNAL LOW
15	—	—	NOT USED
16	1285	GRN/YEL	REAR MOTOR LOW
17	1283	RED/GRN	RIGHT FRONT MOTOR LOW
18	—	—	NOT USED
19	—	—	NOT USED
20	34	GRN/RED	"ABS ACTIVE" INDICATOR CONTROL
21	852	RED/YEL	"ABS" INDICATOR CONTROL
22	879	BLU/BLK	ENABLE RELAY CONTROL
23	33	RED/BLK	"BRAKE" INDICATOR CONTROL
24	140	BLU/YEL	B+ FEED
25	350	GRA	SWITCHED IGNITION
26	830	GRN	LEFT FRONT WHEEL SIGNAL HIGH
27	884	BLU	LEFT REAR WHEEL SIGNAL HIGH
28	885	PPL	LEFT REAR WHEEL SIGNAL LOW
29	1289	BRN/WHT	RIGHT FRONT ABS SOLENOID
30	1288	BRN/RED	LEFT FRONT ABS SOLENOID
31	—	—	NOT USED
32	1284	GRN/BLK	REAR MOTOR HIGH

Fig. 91 EBCM connector face view (1 of 2)

EBCM CONNECTOR C2

PIN	CIRCUIT NO.	COLOR	CIRCUIT
1	850	BLU/ORN	SWITCHED BATTERY INPUT
2	150A	WHT/BLK	GROUND – G103

Fig. 92 EBCM connector face view (2 of 2)

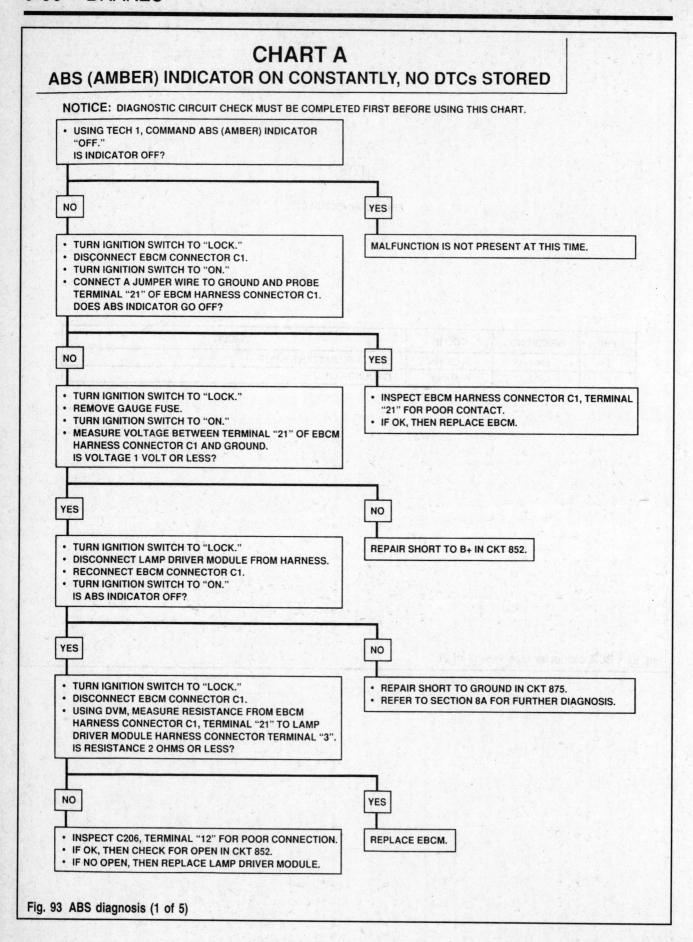

CHART A
ABS (AMBER) INDICATOR ON CONSTANTLY, NO DTCs STORED

NOTICE: DIAGNOSTIC CIRCUIT CHECK MUST BE COMPLETED FIRST BEFORE USING THIS CHART.

- USING TECH 1, COMMAND ABS (AMBER) INDICATOR "OFF."
  IS INDICATOR OFF?

NO

- TURN IGNITION SWITCH TO "LOCK."
- DISCONNECT EBCM CONNECTOR C1.
- TURN IGNITION SWITCH TO "ON."
- CONNECT A JUMPER WIRE TO GROUND AND PROBE TERMINAL "21" OF EBCM HARNESS CONNECTOR C1.
  DOES ABS INDICATOR GO OFF?

YES

MALFUNCTION IS NOT PRESENT AT THIS TIME.

NO

- TURN IGNITION SWITCH TO "LOCK."
- REMOVE GAUGE FUSE.
- TURN IGNITION SWITCH TO "ON."
- MEASURE VOLTAGE BETWEEN TERMINAL "21" OF EBCM HARNESS CONNECTOR C1 AND GROUND.
  IS VOLTAGE 1 VOLT OR LESS?

YES

- INSPECT EBCM HARNESS CONNECTOR C1, TERMINAL "21" FOR POOR CONTACT.
- IF OK, THEN REPLACE EBCM.

YES

- TURN IGNITION SWITCH TO "LOCK."
- DISCONNECT LAMP DRIVER MODULE FROM HARNESS.
- RECONNECT EBCM CONNECTOR C1.
- TURN IGNITION SWITCH TO "ON."
  IS ABS INDICATOR OFF?

NO

REPAIR SHORT TO B+ IN CKT 852.

YES

- TURN IGNITION SWITCH TO "LOCK."
- DISCONNECT EBCM CONNECTOR C1.
- USING DVM, MEASURE RESISTANCE FROM EBCM HARNESS CONNECTOR C1, TERMINAL "21" TO LAMP DRIVER MODULE HARNESS CONNECTOR TERMINAL "3".
  IS RESISTANCE 2 OHMS OR LESS?

NO

- REPAIR SHORT TO GROUND IN CKT 875.
- REFER TO SECTION 8A FOR FURTHER DIAGNOSIS.

NO

- INSPECT C206, TERMINAL "12" FOR POOR CONNECTION.
- IF OK, THEN CHECK FOR OPEN IN CKT 852.
- IF NO OPEN, THEN REPLACE LAMP DRIVER MODULE.

YES

REPLACE EBCM.

Fig. 93 ABS diagnosis (1 of 5)

CHART B
ABS (AMBER) INDICATOR ON INTERMITTENTLY, NO DTCs STORED

NOTICE: DIAGNOSTIC CIRCUIT CHECK MUST BE COMPLETED BEFORE USING THIS CHART.

- TURN IGNITION SWITCH TO "LOCK".
- DISCONNECT EBCM CONNECTOR C1. CONNECT A TEST LIGHT TO GROUND AND PROBE TERMINAL "24" OF EBCM HARNESS CONNECTOR C1. OBSERVE TEST LIGHT WHEN MOVING WIRE HARNESS AND CONNECTORS.
DOES TEST LIGHT REMAIN ON STEADY?

YES

NO

REPAIR INTERMITTENT CONNECTION IN CKT 140.

- CONNECT TEST LIGHT BETWEEN GROUND AND EBCM HARNESS CONNECTOR C1 TERMINAL "25". TURN IGNITION SWITCH TO "ON" AND OBSERVE TEST LIGHT WHEN MOVING WIRE HARNESS AND CONNECTORS.
DOES TEST LIGHT REMAIN ON STEADY?

YES

NO

REPAIR INTERMITTENT CONNECTION IN CKT 350A.

PROBLEM IS NOT PRESENT AT THIS TIME. INTERMITTENTS COULD BE CAUSED BY INCORRECT WIRING HARNESS ROUTING OR LOOSE GROUND CONNECTIONS.

Fig. 94 ABS diagnosis (2 of 5)

CHART C
(Page 1 of 2)
ABS (AMBER) INDICATOR OFF CONSTANTLY, NO DTCs STORED

NOTICE: DIAGNOSTIC CIRCUIT CHECK MUST BE COMPLETED BEFORE USING THIS CHART.

- TURN IGNITION SWITCH TO "ON."
- USING TECH 1, SELECT LAMP TEST AND COMMAND THE ABS INDICATOR "ON."
  IS ABS INDICATOR ON?

NO

YES

MALFUNCTION IS NOT PRESENT AT THIS TIME.

- TURN IGNITION SWITCH TO "LOCK."
- DISCONNECT LAMP DRIVER MODULE (LDM) FROM HARNESS CONNECTOR.
- TURN IGNITION SWITCH TO "ON."
- WITH A FUSED JUMPER, SUCH AS J 36169 WITH A 3 AMP FUSE, CONNECT TERMINAL "5" OF THE LDM HARNESS CONNECTOR TO GROUND.
  IS ABS INDICATOR ON?

NO

YES

- TURN IGNITION SWITCH TO "LOCK."
- DISCONNECT I/P CLUSTER HARNESS CONNECTOR C1.
- USING DVM, MEASURE RESISTANCE BETWEEN TERMINAL "5" OF THE LDM CONNECTOR AND TERMINAL "10" OF I/P CLUSTER HARNESS CONNECTOR C1.
  IS RESISTANCE 2 OHMS OR LESS?

- TURN IGNITION SWITCH TO "LOCK."
- CONNECT TEST LIGHT BETWEEN B+ AND TERMINAL "4" OF THE LDM CONNECTOR.
  IS TEST LIGHT ON?

YES

NO

REPLACE LAMP DRIVER MODULE.

- CHECK FOR PROPER CONNECTION TO JUNCTION CONNECTOR 3, TERMINALS "5" AND "14" AND TO JUNCTION CONNECTOR 1, TERMINALS "5" AND "6".
- IF OK, THEN REPAIR OPEN IN CKTs 150B, 150C OR 150D.

YES

NO

- INSPECT ABS INDICATOR BULB.
  IS BULB OPEN?

REPAIR OPEN OR HIGH RESISTANCE IN CKT 875.

NO

YES

REPLACE BULB.

- TURN IGNITION SWITCH TO "ON."
- CONNECT TEST LIGHT BETWEEN GROUND AND TERMINAL "5" OR THE LDM HARNESS CONNECTOR.
  IS TEST LIGHT ON?

NO

YES

GO TO FOLLOWING PAGE OF THIS CHART (PAGE 2 OF 2).

REPAIR SHORT TO B+ ON CKT 875. REPLACE LAMP DRIVER MODULE.

Fig. 95 ABS diagnosis (3 of 5)

CHART C
(Page 2 of 2)
ABS (AMBER) INDICATOR OFF CONSTANTLY, NO DTCs STORED

CONTINUED FROM CHART C (PAGE 1 OF 2).

- TURN IGNITION SWITCH TO "LOCK."
- RECONNECT LDM CONNECTOR AND I/P CLUSTER CONNECTOR C1.
- DISCONNECT EBCM CONNECTOR C1.
- TURN IGNITION SWITCH TO "ON."
  DOES ABS INDICATOR ILLUMINATE?

NO

YES

- CHECK FOR SHORT TO GROUND IN CKT 852 OR FOR OPEN IN CKT 39.
- IF OK, THEN REPLACE LAMP DRIVER MODULE.

REPLACE EBCM.

Fig. 96 ABS diagnosis (4 of 5)

CHART D
TECH 1 DISPLAYS UNDEFINED DTCs

🔔 **Important**

- USE THIS CHART IF ANY OF THE FOLLOWING UNDEFINED DTCs ARE SET - A012, A031, A043, A067, A068, A071, A072, A073, A074, A075, A083, A084, A085, A097, OR A098

• TURN IGNITION SWITCH TO "ON."
• USING TECH 1, CLEAR DTCs.
DOES UNDEFINED DTC RESET?

YES	NO
REPLACE EBCM.	MALFUNCTION IS NOT PRESENT AT THIS TIME.

Fig. 97 ABS diagnosis (5 of 5)

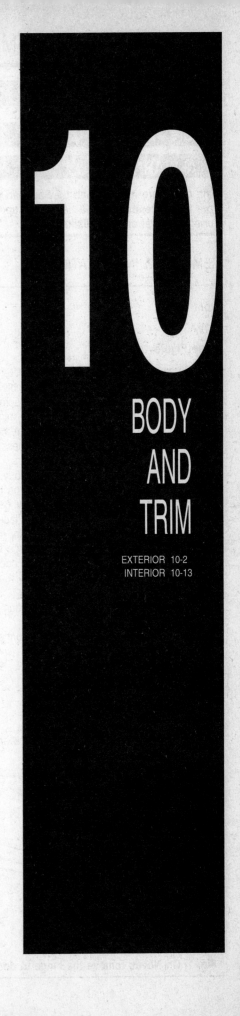

10

BODY

AND

TRIM

EXTERIOR

Doors

✳✳WARNING

The doors are heavier than they appear. Support the door from the bottom and use a helper to support the door during removal and installation.

REMOVAL & INSTALLATION

Front Doors

NOVA

▶ See Figure 1

1. Remove the door check pin.
2. Remove the rear view mirror assembly as follows:
   a. Remove the cover to expose the screw.
   b. Remove the screw and lift off the mirror assembly.
3. If equipped with power door locks, remove the door trim panel and disconnect the lock wiring harness.
4. Check for any other wiring (speakers, courtesy lights, etc.) running between the door and the body.
5. Carefully outline the hinge location on the door.
6. Support the door and remove the hinge-to-door bolts.
7. Lift the door away from the body. Place the door on cloths or an old blanket to protect the paint from scuffing.
8. Support the door and install the hinge bolts snugly.
9. Once the bolts are snug, move the door on the hinge bolts until the hinge aligns with the marks made during removal.
10. Support the door in its aligned position and tighten the hinge-to-door bolts.
11. Connect any wiring which was disconnected during removal.
12. Install the mirror assembly.
13. Install the door check pin.
14. Align the door.

PRIZM

1. Remove the pin from the door check arm.

Fig. 1 On Novas remove the hinge to door bolts

2. Disconnect any wiring running between the door and body. The door pad may require removal to gain access to connectors.
3. Inside the front wheel well, remove the screws holding the rear portion of the wheelhousing cover and remove the cover. This gives access to the inside rear of the front fender.
4. With the door supported from the bottom and held by a helper, remove the 12mm hinge-to-body bolts.

➡ **Unless the hinge is to be replaced, do not loosen the hinge-to-door bolts.**

5. Lift the door away from the body. Place the door on cloths or an old blanket to protect the paint from scuffing.
6. To reinstall, support the door in place and install the hinge bolts. Do not final-tighten any bolt until all are in place and snug.
7. Connect any wiring which was disconnected during removal.
8. Install the door check pin.
9. Install the wheelwell liner and install its screws.

Rear Doors

The rear doors on both Nova and Prizm are removed in approximately the same manner as the respective front door. On Novas, the hinge is disconnected from the door; on Prizms, the hinge is disconnected from the body. Don't forget to disconnect any wiring running from the door before removal.

ADJUSTMENT/ALIGNMENT

▶ See Figures 2 and 3

When checking for door alignment, look carefully at each seam between the door and body. The gap should be constant and even all the way around the door. Pay particular attention to the door seams at the corners farthest from the hinges; this is the area where errors will be most evident. Additionally, the door should pull against the weatherstrip when latched to seal out wind and water. The contact should be even all the way around and the stripping should be about half compressed.

The position of the door can be adjusted in 3 dimensions: fore and aft, up and down, in and out. The primary adjusting points are the door-to-hinge bolts. While the hinge is firmly mounted on the body, the door bolts may be loosened and the door repositioned. Once in the correct alignment, tighten the hinge bolts.

As explained above, the primary door adjustments are carried out at the hinge bolts at the forward end of each door. Further adjustment for closed position and for smoothness of latching may be made at the latch plate or striker. This piece is located at the rear edge of the door and is attached to the bodywork of the car; it is the piece the door engages when closed.

Although the striker or latch plate may differ on various models or from front to rear, the procedure for adjusting is the same:

1. Loosen the large cross-point screw(s) holding the striker. Know in advance that these bolts will be very tight; an impact

Fig. 2 Rear door adjustment

screwdriver is a very handy tool for this job-make sure you use the correct size bit.

2. With the bolts just loose enough to allow the striker to move if necessary, hold the outer door handle in the released position and close the door. The striker will move into the correct location to match the doorlatch. Open the door and tighten the mounting bolts. The striker may be adjusted towards or away from the center of the car, thereby pulling the door tighter to the body if needed.

➡**Do not attempt to correct height variations (sag) by adjusting the striker.**

3. After the striker bolts have been tightened, open and close the door several times. Observe the motion of the door as it engages the striker; it should continue its straight-in motion and not deflect up or down as it hits the striker.

Check the feel of the latch during opening and closing. It must be smooth and linear, without any trace of grinding or binding during engagement and release.

It may be necessary to repeat the striker adjustment procedure several times (and possibly adjust the hinges) before the correct door-to-body match is produced.

Hood

REMOVAL & INSTALLATION

▶ **See Figures 4, 5 and 6**

➡It is advisable to use two people while removing the hood from the vehicle. The hood is lightweight metal and can be easily damaged by twisting or dropping it.

1. Open the hood and support with the prop rod.
2. Mark the hinge location on the hood.
3. Disconnect the windshield washer lines running to the hood. Disconnect the under-hood light if so equipped.
4. Remove the bolts attaching the hood to the hood hinges.
5. Remove the hood assembly, lifting it off the hood prop.
6. Reinstall the hood by placing it in position and installing the hinge bolts. Tighten the bolts snug but not tight. Move the hood until the matchmarks made during removal align with the hinges.
7. Check the hood to fender alignment and adjust the hood position as needed. When the hood is properly positioned, tighten the hinge bolts.
8. Reconnect the washer lines and any wiring which was disconnected.
9. Check the hood latch operation and adjust as necessary. The closed height of the hood is adjusted by turning the rubber stoppers to raise or lower them.
10. When properly aligned, the closed hood has even seams on each side and sits at the same height as the fenders.

Fig. 4 Hood removal

Fig. 3 One method of adjusting the striker after the bolts are loosened

RUBBER
HOOD
STOP

Fig. 5 Front hood height adjustment

Fig. 6 Rear hood height adjustment

Fig. 7 Removing the hatchback support strut

Hatch or Trunk Lid

REMOVAL & INSTALLATION

▶ **See Figures 7 and 8**

In all cases the hatch or trunk lid is removed by separating the lid from the hinge. Certain rules must be observed:

1. Two people are absolutely required for safe and efficient removal. Some components are heavy and/or bulky. Damage or injury may result from improper removal.

2. Although the lid may be supported by springs or struts, always install a prop to support the lid.

3. On hatchbacks, the support (gas strut) must be disconnected from the lid before removal. The hatch is heavy; make sure an assistant supports it before removing the strut.

4. Trunk lid hinges are supported by 2 torsion rods (spring rods) running between the hinges. These rods SHOULD NOT BE DISCONNECTED during removal of the lid.

5. Outline the position of the hinge with pencil or marker. Pad or cover the surrounding area so that the paint is not damaged during removal.

6. Check carefully for any wiring harnesses or hoses running from the body to the lid and disconnect them before removal.

7. Make sure that both ends of the lid are well supported before removing the final bolt. The lid may slip and cause damage.

8. Place the lid on cloths or a padded surface to prevent scuffing. Do not stand a hatchback lid on edge and do not allow it to rest on the glass.

9. When reinstalling, position the lid to the car and install the bolts snug but not tight. Move the lid until the matchmarks made during removal align.

10. Tighten the mounting bolts.

11. If reinstalling a hatchback lid, connect the strut to the lid.

12. Connect the wiring and hoses as necessary.

13. Align the lid with the body.

ALIGNMENT

▶ **See Figures 9, 10 and 11**

With the trunk lid or hatchback down and latched, check the lid-to-body gap all the way around. It should be even in width

Fig. 8 Removing the hatchback lid-to-hinge bolts

and the lid should sit flush to the other body panels. Check the corners farthest from the hinges; this is where any errors will be most visible.

If adjustment is necessary, loosen the lid-to-hinge bolts and reposition the lid. Tighten the bolts and recheck alignment. If vertical adjustment is required, shims or washers must be added or removed between the lid and the hinge to raise or lower the lid.

The lid striker is adjustable. Loosen the nuts or bolts just enough to allow motion in the striker. Close the lid and let the latch move the striker into a matching position. Open the lid and tighten the striker. Double check the striker position by opening and closing the lid a few times. Chances are good that the striker adjustment will not come out right the first time. Continue adjusting it for the best feel when closing (no drag or grinding) and ease of release. The latch should hold to the

Fig. 9 Loosen the hinge bolts to adjust the trunk lid

striker without binding; there should be almost no tension on the key when used to release the lid.

Bumpers

REMOVAL & INSTALLATION

The bumpers, front or rear, are actually assemblies. The outer surface is the cover or fascia, behind which is found the absorbent material (foam block or honeycomb lattice) and the reinforcing steel bar. The components cannot be removed separately; the entire assembly must be removed from the car and then broken down into individual pieces.

✳✳CAUTION

The bumper assemblies are heavy. Always support the bumper from below in at least two places before removing the last bolts. Never lie under the bumper while removing it.

Front Bumper

NOVA

▶ **See Figure 12**

1. Remove the headlamp assemblies.
2. Remove the grille.
3. Remove the upper bumper retaining bolts.
4. Support the bumper.

5. Remove the lower bumper bolts and remove the bumper assembly.
6. The fascia may be removed by removing the nuts, bolts and lower retainer. Pay close attention to the location of any washers or shims during disassembly. They must be reinserted in their original location.
7. Inspect the reinforcing bar closely for any sign of twisting, crushing or deformation. Check the mounting bars for straightness. Do not attempt to straighten any bent metal components; they must be replaced.
8. Reassemble the fascia and absorber to the bar and tighten the nuts and bolts.
9. With a helper, place the bumper assembly on the supports and position it to the front of the car.
10. Install the lower bolts snug but not tight, then install the upper bolts snugly.
11. Check the bumper alignment in relation to the bodywork. Seams should be even all the way across the car and the bumper should be at the same height on both sides. Reposition the bumper as necessary and tighten the mounting bolts, lower ones first, to 70 ft. lbs.
12. Install the grille.
13. Install the headlight assemblies.

1989-92 PRIZM

▶ **See Figure 13**

1. At each wheelwell, remove the 2 screws holding the bumper cover to the fender.
2. Disconnect the turn signal wiring connectors.
3. Support the bumper.
4. Remove the 2 vertical 17mm bolts holding the bumper and remove the bumper from the car.

Fig. 10 Adjusting the hatchback striker

Fig. 11 Adjusting the trunk lid striker

1. Bumper cover (fascia)
2. Absorber
3. Reinforcing bar
4. Retainer
5. Reinforcement
6. Upper mounting bolts
7. Lower mounting bolts

Fig. 12 Front bumper components — Nova

5. To disassemble the bumper, remove the turn signal assemblies. Remove the upper bolts and the lower nuts from the edges of the bumper. Separate the assembly into its component pieces.

6. Inspect the reinforcing bar closely for any sign of twisting, crushing or deformation. Check the mounting bars for straightness. Do not attempt to straighten any bent metal components; they must be replaced.

7. Reassemble the fascia and absorber to the bar and tighten the nuts and bolts. Install the turn signal lamps.

8. With a helper, place the bumper assembly on the supports and position it to the body of the car.

9. Install the bolts snug but not tight.

10. Check the bumper alignment in relation to the bodywork. Seams should be even all the way across the car and the bumper should be at the same height on both sides. Reposition the bumper as necessary and tighten the mounting bolts to 70 ft. lbs.

11. Connect the turn signal wiring harnesses.

12. Install the 2 screws at each wheelwell.

1993 PRIZM

▶ **See Figure 14**

1. Disconnect the negative battery cable.

2. Remove the 4 screws from the front grille. Unclip and remove the grille from the vehicle.

3. Remove the 4 screws along the top of the front bumper fascia. Loosen the wheelhousings on both sides of the vehicle to gain access to two front bumper fascia upper support bolts.

4. Remove the two front bumper fascia support bolts, 1 on each side of the fascia.

5. Remove the 5 bolts from the bottom of the front bumper fascia. Pull the front bumper fascia forward, disconnect the turn signal and the side marker bulb sockets and remove fascia from the vehicle.

6. Remove the 4 plastic clips and the front bumper energy absorber from the vehicle.

7. Remove the 4 nuts retaining the front bumper impact bar.

8. Remove the front bumper impact bar from the front bumper impact arms.

To install:

9. Install the front bumper impact bar to the front bumper impact arms; secure with 4 nuts. Tighten the front bumper impact bar nuts to 33 ft. lbs. (45 Nm).

10. Connect the front bumper energy absorber to the vehicle; secure with 4 plastic clips.

11. Connect the front bumper fascia to the vehicle, connecting the turn signal and the side marker bulb sockets.

12. Connect the 5 bolts to the bottom of the front bumper fascia. Tighten the front bumper fascia bolts to 15 ft lbs. (20 Nm).

13. Connect the two bumper fascia upper support bolts, 1 on each side of the front bumper fascia. Tighten the front bumper fascia upper support bolts to 15 ft. lbs. (20 Nm).

14. Install the 4 screws along the top of the front bumper fascia. Clip the front grille into place; secure with 4 screws.

15. Connect the negative (-) battery cable.

1 FRONT FASCIA
2 HONEYCOMB ABSORBER
3 BUMPER
4 RETAINER

Fig. 13 Front bumper components — 1989-92 Prizm

1. Wheelhousing
2. Engine splash shield
3. Front bumper impact arm
4. Front bumper impact bar
5. Front bumper energy absorber
6. Front grille
7. Front bumper fascia side retainer
8. Front bumper fascia side support
9. Front bumper fascia
10. Front bumper fascia upper support

Fig. 14 Front bumper components — 1993 Prizm

Rear Bumper

NOVA

▶ **See Figure 15**

1. Open the trunk lid and lift the padding or carpet out of the way.

2. Remove the plugs to gain access to the bumper retaining bolts.

3. Support the bumper.

4. Remove the bumper bolts.

5. The fascia may be removed by removing the nuts, bolts and lower retainer. Pay close attention to the location of any washers or shims during disassembly. They must be reinserted in their original location.

6. Inspect the reinforcing bar closely for any sign of twisting, crushing or deformation. Check the mounting bars for straightness. Do not attempt to straighten any bent metal components; they must be replaced.

7. Reassemble the fascia and absorber to the bar and tighten the nuts and bolts.

8. With a helper, place the bumper assembly on the supports and position it to the body of the car.

9. Install the bolts snug but not tight.

10. Check the bumper alignment in relation to the bodywork. Seams should be even all the way across the car and the bumper should be at the same height on both sides. Reposition the bumper as necessary and tighten the mounting bolts to 70 ft. lbs.

11. Install the plugs over the bolts.

12. Reinstall the trunk mat.

1. Bumper cover (fascia)
2. Absorber
3. Reinforcing bar
4. Retainer
5. Reinforcement
6. Mounting bolts

Fig. 15 Rear bumper components — Nova

1989-92 PRIZM

▶ **See Figure 16**

1. At each wheelwell, remove the 2 screws holding the bumper cover to the fender.

2. Remove the 2 nuts on each side holding the bumper mounting posts to the bodywork.

3. Support the bumper.

4. Remove the 4 nuts (14mm) holding the bumper to the frame of the car and remove the bumper assembly.

5. To remove the bumper cover, remove the 7 nuts from the lower edge and remove the 6 bolts from inside the upper perimeter of the bumper.

6. Inspect the reinforcing bar closely for any sign of twisting, crushing or deformation. Check the mounting bars for straightness. Do not attempt to straighten any bent metal components; they must be replaced.

7. Reassemble the fascia and absorber to the bar and tighten the nuts and bolts.

8. With a helper, place the bumper assembly on the supports and position it to the body of the car.

9. Install the mounting bolts snug but not tight.

10. Check the bumper alignment in relation to the bodywork. Seams should be even all the way across the car and the bumper should be at the same height on both sides. Reposition the bumper as necessary and tighten the mounting bolts.

11. Install the nuts holding the mounting posts to the bodywork.

12. Install the 2 screws at each wheelwell.

1993 PRIZM

▶ **See Figure 17**

1. Disconnect the negative battery cable.

2. Open the deck lid. Remove the three plastic retaining clips along the top of the rear bumper fascia.

3. Remove the two bolts and the right-side rear wheelhousing.

4. Remove 1 rear bumper fascia support bolt from each side of the rear bumper fascia.

5. Disconnect the two bolts from the bottom of the rear bumper fascia.

6. Remove the two screws from the bottom of the rear bumper fascia.

7. Remove 1 nut from each rear combination lamp assembly (accessible from inside the luggage compartment.

8. Remove the two bolts from each rear combination lamp assembly and remove the lamp assemblies from the vehicle.

9. Remove 1 bolt from each side of the rear bumper fascia. Pull the rear bumper fascia rearward, disconnect license plate lamp bulb sockets and remove fascia from the vehicle.

10. Remove 1 plastic clip from each rear bumper energy absorber and energy absorbers from the rear bumper impact bar.

11. Remove the 4 nuts from the rear bumper impact bar and remove the impact bar from the vehicle.

To install:

12. Connect the rear bumper impact bar to the vehicle; secure with 4 nuts. Tighten the rear bumper impact bar nuts to 33 ft. lbs. (45 Nm).

13. Connect the rear bumper energy absorbers to the rear bumper impact bar; secure each with 1 plastic clip.

1 BUMPER
2 RETAINER
3 HONEYCOMB ABSORBER
4 REAR FASCIA

Fig. 16 Rear bumper components — 1989-92 Prizm

14. Connect the rear bumper fascia to the vehicle, connecting the license plate lamp bulb sockets.

15. Connect 1 bolt to each side of the rear bumper fascia. Tighten the rear bumper fascia bolts to 15 ft. lbs. (20 Nm).

16. Connect the rear combination lamp assemblies to the vehicle; secure each with two bolts and 1 nut. Tighten the rear combination lamp assembly bolts and nuts to 89 inch lbs. (10 Nm).

17. Connect the two screws to the bottom of the rear bumper fascia.

18. Connect two bolts to the bottom of the rear bumper fascia. Tighten the rear bumper fascia bolts to 15 ft. lbs. (20 Nm).

19. Connect 1 rear bumper fascia support bolt to each side of the rear bumper fascia. Tighten the rear bumper fascia support bolts to 15 ft. lbs. (20 Nm).

20. Install the right-side rear wheelhousing to the vehicle; secure with two bolts. Tighten the right-side rear wheelhousing to 89 inch lbs. (10 Nm).

21. Connect the three plastic retaining clips along the top of the rear bumper fascia. Close the deck lid.

22. Connect the negative (-) battery cable.

Grille

REMOVAL & INSTALLATION

1. Remove the screws retaining the grille to the vehicle.
2. Unclip and remove the grille from the vehicle.
3. Installation is the reverse of removal.

Mirrors

REMOVAL & INSTALLATION

▶ **See Figures 18 and 19**

1. Remove the screw holding the remote control knob to the shaft. The screw may be concealed under a cap which can be popped off with a small tool.

2. Use a flat-bladed tool to carefully pry off the triangular plastic cover. Don't damage the plastic and don't break the plastic clip underneath.

3. Support the mirror and remove the 3 bolts holding it to the door. Remove the mirror from the car.

To install:

4. Hold the mirror in position and install the 3 bolts. Before tightening the bolts, make certain the mirror is properly seated and mates flush to the door. The slightest gap will cause wind noise when the car is moving.

5. Install the triangular bezel.

6. Install the remote control knob and its retaining screw.

Fenders

REMOVAL & INSTALLATION

1989-92

1. Disconnect the negative battery cable.
2. Remove the 11 bolts and remove the wheelhousing.
3. Remove the 3 retaining bolts from the rocker panel forward of the front door.
4. Remove the 1 front retaining bolt from the front door jam.
5. Remove the 2 bumper fascia retaining bolts from the front of the wheelwell.
6. Remove the 1 retaining screw and pull the parking lamp forward, disengaging the retainer clip.
7. Remove the 4 bolts from the parking lamp assembly, securing the fender to the radiator support.
8. Remove the 4 upper fender retaining bolts from inside of the engine compartment and remove the fender from the vehicle.

To install:

9. Install the fender to the vehicle and from inside of the engine compartment install the 4 upper fender retaining bolts. Tighten the bolts to 15 ft. lbs. (20 Nm).

10. Install the 4 bolts to the parking lamp assembly, securing the fender to the radiator support.

11. Pull the parking lamp forward, engaging the retainer clip and the 1 retaining screw.

12. Install the 2 bumper fascia retaining bolts to the front of the wheelwell.

13. Install the 1 front retaining bolt to the front door jam.

14. Install the 3 retaining bolts to the rocker panel forward of the front door and tighten to 15 ft. lbs. (20 Nm).

1. Rear wheelhousing
2. Rear combination lamp assembly
3. Rear bumper impact arm
4. Rear bumper impact bar
5. Rear bumper energy absorber
6. License plate lamp
7. Rear bumper fascia

Fig. 17 Rear bumper components — 1993 Prizm

Fig. 18 Door mirror components — 1985-92

Fig. 19 Door mirror trim cover — 1993

15. Install the wheelhousing and tighten 11 retaining bolts to 15 ft. lbs. (20 Nm).

16. Connect the negative battery cable.

1993

▶ **See Figures 20, 21 and 22**

1. Disconnect the negative battery cable.

2. Remove the 10 bolts and 2 plastic clips and remove the wheelhousing.

3. Remove the 1 retaining screw and the side marker lamp assembly from the vehicle, disconnecting the bulb socket.

4. Remove the 1 retaining bolt and 2 screws from the headlamp assembly. Unclip the headlamp assembly and remove, disconnecting the headlamp bulb from the housing.

5. Remove the front bumper fascia.

6. Remove the 1 bolt securing the fender to the rocker panel.

7. Remove the 1 bolt securing the fender to the front door jamb.

8. Remove the 3 mounting bolts along the top of the front fender.

9. Remove the 1 mounting bolt located in the in the headlamp cavity.

10. Remove the 2 nuts securing the front fender to the front end support panel and remove the fender from the vehicle.

To install:

11. Secure the front fender to the front end support panel and with the 2 nuts and tighten to 15 ft. lbs. (20 Nm).

12. Install the 1 mounting bolt located in the in the headlamp cavity and tighten to 15 ft. lbs. (20 Nm).

13. Install the 3 mounting bolts along the top of the front fender and tighten to 15 ft. lbs. (20 Nm).

14. Install the 1 bolt securing the fender to the front door jamb and tighten to 15 ft. lbs. (20 Nm).

15. Install the 1 bolt securing the fender to the rocker panel and tighten to 15 ft. lbs. (20 Nm).

16. Install the front bumper fascia.

17. Connect the headlamp bulb to the housing and clip the headlamp assembly into place. Install the 1 retaining bolt and 2 screws to the headlamp assembly and tighten to 89 inch lbs. (10 Nm).

18. Connect the bulb socket then install the 1 retaining screw and the side marker lamp assembly to the vehicle.

19. Install the 10 bolts and 2 plastic clips to retain the wheelhousing.

20. Connect the negative battery cable.

Antenna

➡**The mast and cable are 1 piece. If the mast is damaged or broken, the entire antenna assembly including the cable must be replaced.**

REMOVAL & INSTALLATION

1985-92

1. Remove the console side panel, to the right of the accelerator pedal.

2. Disconnect the antenna cable from the radio by reaching through the back of the console and disconnecting the cable from its socket. If you can't quite reach or release the cable, the radio will have to be loosened in the dash and disconnected from the front.

3. Remove the 2 screws holding the hood release lever and move the lever out of the way.

4. Remove the lower left dashboard trim and disconnect the speaker wiring.

5. Remove the left side kick panel.

6. Remove the retaining screw and remove the left side cowl trim.

7. Attach a long piece of mechanic's wire or heavy string to the end of the antenna wire. This will track up through the pillar as you remove the old antenna and be available to pull the new line into place.

8. Remove the 2 attaching screws at the antenna mast. Remove the antenna and carefully pull the cable up the pillar. Use a helper to insure the end inside the car does not snag or pull other wires.

To install:

9. Remove the mechanic's wire or twine from the old cable and attach it to the new cable. Make sure it is tied so that the plug will stay straight during installation

10. With your helper, feed the new cable into the pillar while pulling gently on the guide wire or string. Route the antenna cable properly under the dash, making sure it will not foul on the steering column or pedal linkages. Route the cable high enough that there is no chance of it hanging around the driver's feet. Use tape or cable ties to secure it.

11. Remove the guide line from the antenna cable. Route the antenna into the radio and install the connector.

12. Install the attaching screws holding the mast to the pillar. Make sure the screws are properly threaded and that both the screws and their holes are free of dirt or corrosion. A poor connection at these screws can affect antenna and radio performance.

13. Install the left side cowl trim and the left side kick panel.

14. Connect the speaker wiring and install the lower left dashboard trim.

15. Install the hood release lever.

16. Install the console side panel.

1993

1. Disconnect the negative battery cable.

2. Remove the left side kick panel by disengaging the clips.

3. Disconnect the antenna cable from the antenna cable extension. Attach a piece of mechanic's wire to the antenna cable to assist in reinstalling through the A-pillar.

4. Remove the antenna base attaching screws from the roof and remove the antenna from the vehicle.

To install:

5. Remove the mechanic's wire from the old cable and attach it to the new cable.

6. Feed the new cable into the pillar while pulling gently on the guide wire. Use tape or cable ties to secure it.

7. Remove the guide line from the antenna cable. Route the antenna into the radio and install the connector.

8. Install the attaching screws holding the mast to the pillar. Make sure the screws are properly threaded and that both the screws and their holes are free of dirt or corrosion. A poor

Fig. 20 Engine splash shields and wheelhousings — 1993

1006

Fig. 21 Removing the front fender bolt from the rocker panel — 1993

FRONT FENDER

Fig. 22 Removing the front fender top bolts — 1993

connection at these screws can affect antenna and radio performance.

9. Install the left side kick panel.
10. Connect the negative battery cable.

Sunroof Panel

REMOVAL & INSTALLATION

1989-92

▶ See Figure 23

1. Remove the sun roof headlining, pull off of front clips and slide rearward.
2. Remove the front and rear shoe nuts.
3. Remove the sun roof panel.

To install:
4. Install the sun roof to the vehicle.
5. Install the front and rear shoes and nuts.
6. Install the sun roof headlining.

1993

▶ See Figure 24

1. Remove the headlining from the vehicle. Refer to 'Headliner' later in this section. Unclip the power sunroof interior trim from the power sunroof panel, slide rearward and remove from the vehicle.

➡Note the location and number of shims on either side of the power sunroof panel before removal.

2. Remove the 6 bolts and the power sunroof panel from the vehicle.

To install:
3. Install the power sunroof panel to the vehicle; secure with 6 bolts, but do not tighten fully.

Fig. 23 Sunroof panel removal — 1989-92 Prizm

4. Install the shims to the power sunroof panel. Adjust the power sunroof panel. Slide the power sunroof interior trim into position, making sure that the 2 guide pins slide into the interior trim brackets. Clip the power sunroof interior trim onto the power sunroof panel.

5. Install the headlining to the vehicle. Refer to 'Headliner' later in this section.

Fig. 24 Sunroof panel removal — 1993 Prizm

INTERIOR

Instrument Panel

REMOVAL & INSTALLATION

Nova

▶ See Figures 25, 26, 27, 28 and 29

1. Disconnect the negative battery cable.
2. Remove the steering wheel.
3. Remove the left side speaker grille. The grille may be attached with a clip (which must be pulled loose to remove the grille) or with screws.
4. Remove the lower trim cover from the steering column.
5. Remove the hood release lever.
6. Remove the heater duct assembly.
7. Remove the instrument hood. Remove the air conditioner outlet register, then remove the 4 screws and remove the hood.

8. Remove the 6 screws from the instrument cluster, and disconnect the speedometer cable and the wiring connectors. Remove the meter assembly from the instrument panel.
9. Disconnect the heating ducts to the dash vents.
10. Remove the finish panel on the end of the dash.
11. Remove the right side speaker grille.
12. Remove the right side speaker bracket with the speaker attached. Disconnect the wiring to the speaker.
13. Remove the glove compartment door with its reinforcement.
14. Remove the glove box door lock striker.
15. Remove the center trim panel over the console.
16. Remove the radio equipment and accessories.
17. Remove the lower center trim panel on the console.
18. Remove the heater control panel. Label and disconnect the electrical and vacuum connections to the panel.
19. Remove the side-window defroster nozzles. The grilles are snapped into place.
20. Remove the mounting bolts for the dashboard assembly and remove the dash from the car. Be careful of any wiring and/or hoses routed along the back of the dash. Do not

damage any other components while the dash is being removed from the car.

To install:

21. Position the dashboard in the car. Attach any wiring harnesses to the inside of the dash before securing the mounting bolts.

22. Install the side defroster nozzles.

23. Install the heater control panel and connect its wiring and vacuum lines. Install the trim panel on the lower console.

24. Install the radio and accessory equipment and install its trim panel.

25. Install the glove box door lock striker.

26. Install the glove box door with the door reinforcement.

27. Install the right side speaker bracket and speaker. Connect the wiring to the speaker.

28. Install the speaker grille.

29. Install the end trim panel.

30. Install the heater ducts to the dash vents. Make sure they are properly connected and will not come loose.

31. Install the instrument assembly, connecting the speedometer cable and the wiring connectors.

32. Install the hood for the instrument cluster and then install the air outlet grilles.

33. Connect the air ductwork to the grilles.

34. Install the hood release lever.

35. Install the steering column trim covers.

36. Install the left side speaker grille.

37. Install the steering wheel

38. Connect the negative battery cable.

Prizm

1989-92

▶ **See Figures 30, 31, 32 and 33**

1. Disconnect the negative battery cable.

2. Remove the hood release lever.

3. Remove the 4 screws from the lower left dash trim and pull the trim out.

4. Disconnect the wiring from the radio speaker.

5. If equipped with air conditioning, remove the ductwork from the lower air outlet and remove the trim panel from the car.

6. Remove the steering wheel.

7. Remove the upper and lower steering column covers.

8. Remove the 2 screws from the trim panel (bezel).

9. Pull the panel out, releasing the spring clips behind the dash. With the panel loose, disconnect the wiring to the dash switches.

10. Remove the switches from the panel.

11. Remove the 2 electrical connectors and the cigarette lighter from the trim bezel and remove the bezel from the car.

12. Remove the 4 screws holding the instrument cluster trim.

13. Disconnect the wiring from the hazard (4-way) flasher and dimmer switches.

14. Remove the cluster trim panel.

15. Remove the 4 attaching screws holding the cluster, move it away from the dash and disconnect the wiring harnesses and the speedometer cable. Remove the instrument cluster from the car.

16. Remove the cup holder.

17. Remove the radio. Disconnect the wiring and antenna cables.

18. Remove the glove box and trim assembly.

19. Remove the 4 screws holding the heater control panel and remove the panel.

20. Remove the screws from the center console trim panel and remove the panel.

21. Carefully pry the left and right side-window defroster vents loose from the dash.

22. Remove the 5 attaching bolts from the instrument panel.

23. Disconnect the 3 wiring connectors and the relay unit on the left side of the dash.

24. Disconnect the electrical connector on the right side of the dashboard.

25. Detach the defroster duct retainers behind the dash and remove the dashboard from the vehicle. Be careful of any wiring and/or hoses routed along the back of the dash. Do not damage any other components while the dash is being removed from the car.

To install:

26. Place the dash in position inside the car. Be careful to insert the defroster duct retainers into their bulkhead (firewall) clips.

27. Connect the 3 electrical connectors and the relay unit on the left side and the harness connector on the right side to their proper wire harnesses.

28. Install the dashboard mounting bolts.

29. Install the left and right side-window defroster outlets.

30. Install the center console trim panel.

31. Reinstall the heater control panel.

32. Install the glove box and trim assembly.

33. Install the radio and connect the electrical and antenna cables.

34. Install the cup holder and its attaching screws.

35. Connect the speedometer and electrical cables to the instrument cluster. Install the cluster and the 4 retaining screws.

36. Attach the wiring connectors for the hazard flasher and the dimmer switches.

37. Install the cluster trim bezel.

38. Place the dash switches in place on the lower trim bezel and connect the wiring to the switches.

39. Install the lower trim bezel, making sure all the clips engage.

40. Install the steering column upper and lower covers.

41. Connect the air conditioning ductwork to the lower air outlet if so equipped.

42. Attach the wiring to the radio speaker.

43. Install the lower left dashboard trim panel and its 4 screws.

44. Install the hood release lever.

45. Install the steering wheel.

46. Connect the negative battery cable.

1993

▶ **See Figure 34**

1. Disable the SRS (air bag) system as outlined in Section 6 and disconnect the negative battery cable.

2. Remove the A-pillar lower trim panel from both sides.

3. Remove 1 nut from each kick panel and panels from the vehicle.

4. Remove the steering wheel as outlined in Section 7.

1. Side defroster nozzle
2. Side defroster duct
3. Defroster nozzle
4. Dashboard
5. End trim panel
6. Center register
7. Side register
8. No. 3 heater duct
9. Duct
10. No. 2 heater duct
11. No. 1 heater duct
12. Column covers
13. Glove compartment door
14. Door lock striker
15. Speaker bracket
16. Speaker
17. No. 2 speaker panel
18. Glove door reinforcement
19. Heater control panel
20. Radio
21. Lower center cluster finish panel
22. Center cluster finish panel
23. Retainer
24. Ash tray
25. Hood release lever
26. No. 1 speaker panel
27. Speaker
28. Lower finish panel
29. Finish panel
30. Steering wheel
31. Combination meter
32. Meter hood
33. Lower register
34. ECT indicator (A/T)

Fig. 25 Instrument panel components — Nova

Fig. 26 Removing the radio speaker and bracket — Nova

Fig. 27 Removing the center trim panel — Nova

Fig. 28 Heater ducts — Nova

Fig. 29 Removing the side window defroster ducts — Nova

5. Remove the 5 screws and steering column upper and lower trim panels.

6. Remove the center console.

7. Remove the 2 screws and the instrument cluster trim panel, disengaging 2 lower clips.

8. Remove the 4 screws and the instrument cluster assembly, disconnecting 3 electrical connectors.

9. Remove the illumination control knob.

10. Remove 1 nut from illumination controller.

11. Remove the 4 clips and the instrument panel left side outlet trim bezel.

12. Remove the illumination controller electrical connector.

13. Remove the illumination controller from the vehicle.

14. Remove the 4 mounting bolts from the instrument panel.

15. Remove the instrument panel from the vehicle by lifting up and pulling toward rear, disengaging 5 clips.

16. Disassemble the ventilation and heater ducts as necessary by removing the retaining screws or clips.

To install:

17. Assemble the ventilation and heater ducts as necessary by installing the retaining screws or clips.

18. Install the instrument panel to the vehicle; secure with the 5 clips.

19. Install the 4 mounting bolts to the instrument panel. Tighten the instrument panel mounting bolts to 15 ft. lbs. (20 Nm).

20. Install the illumination controller to the instrument panel left side outlet trim bezel; secure with 1 nut. Tighten the illumination controller nut to 48 inch lbs. (5.4 Nm).

21. Install the illumination controller electrical connector.

22. Install the instrument panel left side outlet trim bezel, pushing in to engage the 4 clips and connect the 3 instrument cluster electrical connectors.

23. Install the instrument cluster assembly; secure with 4 screws.

24. Install instrument cluster trim panel, engaging 2 lower clips; secure with 2 screws.

25. Install the center console.

26. Install the steering column upper and lower trim panels; secure with 5 screws.

27. Install the steering wheel as outlined in Section 7.

28. Install 2 kick panels; secure each with 1 nut. Tighten the kick panel nuts to 48 inch lbs. (5.4 Nm).

29. Install 2 A-pillar lower trim panels.

30. Install the negative (-) battery cable. Tighten the negative (-) battery cable-to-negative (-) battery terminal retainer to 11 ft. lbs. (15 Nm).

31. Enable the SRS system as outlined in Section 6.

Front Console

REMOVAL & INSTALLATION

1985-92

▶ **See Figures 30, 33, 35 and 36**

The consoles on these models are simply removed by detaching the mounting screws. On the Nova models, many of these screws are concealed by plastic covers which may be popped off with a small screwdriver or similar tool. The

1. Defroster grille
2. Defroster duct
3. Center ventilation duct
4. Right ventilation duct
5. Brace
6. "A" pillar trim
7. A/C duct
8. Lower A/C deflector
9. Right ventilation deflector
10. Right window deflector
11. Cowl side trim
12. Instrument cluster
13. Cluster bezel
14. Gove box and trim assembly
15. Cassette box
16. Rear console
17. Shift lever boot (M/T)
18. Rear console
19. Front console
20. Ashtray
21. Retainer
22. Cup holder
23. Trim bezel
24. Center console triim
25. Hood release lever
26. Left lower dash trim
27. Scuff plate
28. Cowl side trim
29. Instrument panel
30. "A" pillar trim
31. Left window deflector
32. Left ventilation duct

Fig. 30 Instrument panel components — 1989-90 Prizm

consoles can be lifted over the shifter handle and removed from the car. Be very careful not to lose any small parts between the floor pan and carpet while the console is out.

Once the console is removed, take an extra moment to clean it thoroughly and apply a vinyl protectant. You can now get all the crevices that have been blocked by the seats and hidden by the carpet. When the console is reinstalled, make sure that any wires in the area are not pinched by the console or pierced by the mounting screws.

1993

▶ See Figures 34 and 37

1. Disconnect the negative battery cable.
2. Remove the ashtray from the ashtray guide by depressing the spring loaded tab and pulling rearward.

Fig. 31 Removing the center trim panel — 1989-92 Prizm

Fig. 32 Instrument panel retaining bolts — 1989-92 Prizm

1. Defroster grille
2. Brace
3. Right side window deflector
4. Instrument panel cluster
5. Right side cowl trim panel
6. Cluster bezel
7. Right lower trim bezel
8. Rear console
9. Front console
10. Ashtray
11. Ashtray retainer
12. Instrument panel trim bezel
13. Cup holder
14. Instrument panel to console trim bezel
15. Hood release lever
16. Left lower trim panel
17. Steering column trim covers
18. Left side cowl trim panel
19. Instrument panel
20. Left side window deflector

Fig. 33 Instrument panel components — 1991-92 Prizm

1. Center console trim panel
2. Knee bolster
3. Ashtray
4. Instrument panel left side outlet trim bezel
5. Instrument panel
6. Heater control assembly
7. Glove box assembly
8. Center console
9. Center console lower tray
10. Rear center console
11. Arm rest and storage compartment

Fig. 34 Instrument panel components — 1993 Prizm

3. Remove the center console trim bezel from the center console by prying with flat bladed screwdriver to release 6 clips.

4. Remove the cigar lighter, rear defogger switch and hazard switch electrical connectors.

5. Remove the cigar lighter and ashtray illumination bulbs from the center console trim bezel and remove bezel from the vehicle.

6. Remove the 4 screws and radio from the center console.

7. Remove the antenna, radio electrical connector and radio from the vehicle.

8. Remove the 3 bolts from the glove box assembly.

9. Remove 3 screws and 2 bolts from inside of the glove box and glove box assembly from the vehicle.

10. Remove the cover plates from knee bolster to gain access to bolts.

11. Remove 4 bolts and 2 screws from knee bolster.

12. Remove hood release cable and knee bolster from the vehicle.

13. Remove 2 screws securing the center console to rear center console.

14. Remove gear shift control lever upper boot from the center console (manual transaxle equipped vehicles).

15. Remove the center console lower tray by prying gently with a flat screwdriver (automatic transaxle equipped vehicles).

16. Remove 3 screws from rear tray of rear center console after removing felt liner (or arm rest/storage compartment if equipped) from tray. Raise the parking brake lever and lift the rear center console from the vehicle.

17. Remove the 2 screws and the center console from the vehicle.

To install:

18. Install the center console to the vehicle; secure with 2 screws.

FRONT CONSOLE   REAR CONSOLE

1. Cover
2. Cover
3. Bracket
4. Cover
5. Striker
6. Door
7. Stopper
8. Inner box
9. Stopper
10. Cover
11. Cover

Fig. 35 Console components — Nova

Fig. 36 Console (left) and console with cassette box — 1989-90 Prizm

26. Install 3 bolts to glove box assembly. Tighten glove box assembly bolts to 11 ft. lbs. (15 Nm).

27. Install radio to the vehicle, attaching antenna and electrical connector; secure with 4 screws.

28. Install cigar lighter and ashtray illumination bulbs.

29. Install cigar lighter, rear defogger switch and hazard switch electrical connectors. Press center console trim bezel into center console until clips engage. Slide ashtray into ashtray guide until spring loaded tab engages.

30. Install negative (-) battery cable. Tighten negative (-) battery cable-to-negative (-) battery terminal retainer to 11 ft. lbs. (15 Nm).

19. Install the rear center console to the vehicle, sliding down over the parking brake lever; secure with 3 screws in rear tray and 2 rear center console-to-center console screws.

20. Install felt liner (or arm rest/storage compartment, if equipped) to rear tray of rear center console.

21. Install the center console lower tray to center console (automatic transaxle equipped vehicles).

22. Install gear shift control lever upper boot to center console (manual transaxle equipped vehicles).

23. Install knee bolster to the vehicle, connecting hood release lever, secure with 4 bolts and 2 screws. Tighten the knee bolster bolts to 11 ft. lbs. (15 Nm).

24. Install cover plates to knee bolster over bolt head.

25. Install glove box assembly to the vehicle; secure with 3 screws and 2 bolts. Tighten the glove box assembly bolts to 11 ft. lbs. (15 Nm).

CENTER CONSOLE TRIM BEZEL   CLIP LOCATIONS

Fig. 37 Center console trim bezel clips — 1993 Prizm

Door Panels

REMOVAL & INSTALLATION

▶ **See Figures 38, 39, 40, 41, 42, 43, 44, 45 and 46**

1. Remove the small screw holding the plastic trim bezel at the inside door release. Slide the trim off the handle.

2. On Prizm models, disconnect the rod from the door handle and remove the handle. Before attempting to disconnect the rod, note that the retaining clip can be released from the rod and pivoted out of the way. The rod then lifts free.

3. If not equipped with electric windows, remove the window winder handle. This can be tricky, but not difficult. Install a piece of masking tape on the door trim panel to show the position of the handle before removal. The handle is held onto the winder axle by a spring clip shaped like the Greek letter omega: 'ω'. The clip is located between the back of the winder handle and the door pad. It is correctly installed with the legs pointing along the length of the winder handle. There are 3 common methods of removing the clip:

   a. Use a door handle removal tool. This inexpensive slotted and toothed tool can be fitted between the winder and the panel and used to push the spring clip free.

   b. Use a rag or piece of cloth and work it back and forth between the winder and door panel. If constant upward tension is kept, the clip will be forced free. Keep watch on the clip as it comes free; it may get lost as it pops out.

   c. Straighten a common paper clip and bend a very small J-hook at the end of it. Work the hook down from the top of the winder and engage the loop of the spring clip. As you pull the clip free, keep your other hand over the area to retain the clip.

4. Remove the armrest retaining bolts and remove the armrest. The bolts may be concealed under various trim pieces. On cars with power windows, the front part of the armrest is bonded to the door panel and cannot be removed.

5. On Novas, the outside remote control mirror must be removed before removing the front door panels.

6. Using a broad, flat-bladed tool — not a screwdriver — begin gently prying the door pad away from the door. You are releasing plastic inserts from plastic seats. There are 8-10 of them around the door.

7. When all the clips are released, lift up on the panel to release the lip at the top of the door. This may require a bit of jiggling to loosen the panel; do so gently and don't damage the panel.

8. Once the panel is free of all its mounts, check behind it before removing it from the door. Disconnect any wiring and then remove the panel.

✳✳WARNING

Behind the trim panel is a plastic sheet taped or glued to the door. This is a water shield and must be intact to prevent water entry into the car. It must be securely attached at its edges and not be ripped or damaged. Small holes or tears can be patched with waterproof tape applied to both sides of the liner.

To install:

9. Connect any disconnected wiring and align the upper edge of the panel along the top of the door first. Make sure its left-right positioning is correct and tap it into place with the heel of your hand.

10. Make sure that the plastic clips align with their holes. Use the heel of your hand to gently pop the clips into position.

11. Reinstall the armrest and tighten the bolts. Install the bolt cover (trim) pieces.

12. Install the window winder handle if not equipped with power windows. Place the spring clip into the slot on the handle. (Remember to position it so the legs point along the length of the winder.) Align the handle with the tape mark made earlier and put the winder over the end of the axle. Use the heel of your hand to give the center of the winder a short, sharp blow. This will cause the winder to move inward and the spring will engage its locking groove. The secret to this trick is to push the winder straight on; if it's crooked it won't engage and you may end up hunting for the spring clip.

13. On Nova models, reinstall the remote mirror. On Prizm models, reconnect the actuating rod to the door handle. Make sure the clip is installed properly.

14. Install the door handle trim bezel and its retaining screw.

Heater and Ventilation Ducts

REMOVAL & INSTALLATION

All heater and ventilation ducts are retained with screws and may be removed after instrument panel removal. Refer to instrument panel removal and installation procedure outlined earlier in this section.

Headliner

REMOVAL & INSTALLATION

1985-92

1. Disconnect the negative battery cable.
2. Remove the following:
   a. Sunshades
   b. Assist handles.
   c. Dome lamp
   d. Reading lamp and sunroof control assembly
   e. Rearview mirror
3. Remove the quarter window molding.
4. Remove the following interior garnish moldings:
   a. Windshield pillar
   b. Side roof moldings
   c. Front and rear roof moldings
5. Remove the fabric trim molding from sun roof opening (pull off, if so equipped).
6. Remove the headlining.
To install:
7. Install the headlining, securing with 4 perimeter moldings.
8. Install the quarter window molding.
9. Install the windshield pillar molding.

1. Mirror assembly
2. Window glass
3. Sash channel
4. Door belt molding
5. Door assembly
6. Outer handle
7. Door latch/lock assembly
8. Rear run channel guide
9. Window regulator
10. Inner handle
11. Hinge
12. Door check
13. Front run channel guide
14. Inner handle bezel
15. Lock knob
16. Door trim panel
17. Armrest
18. Window winder handle
19. Water deflector shield

Fig. 38 Front door components — Nova

WITH POWER DOOR LOCKS

WITH POWER WINDOW

A. Power lock solenoid
B. Power window regulator
1. Cover
2. Armrest
3. Inner door handle
4. Door trim panel
5. Rear lower door frame
6. Striker
7. Door latch/lock
8. Lock knob
9. Outer handle and lock cylinder
10. Window glass
11. Glass run
12. Door belt molding
13. Glass channel
14. Side mirror
15. Cover
16. Adjustment knob
17. Front lower door frame
18. Door hinge
19. Door check arm
20. Window regulator
21. Equalizer arm.
22. Water deflector
23. Plate
24. Spring clip
25. Window winder handle

Fig. 39 Front door components — 1989-92 Prizm

1. Kick panel
2. Armrest
3. Inside door handle bezel
4. Power window switch housing
5. Front door trim
6. Inner sealing strip
7. Water deflector
8. Inner door panel brace
9. Lock striker
10. Door lock
11. Rear window guide
12. Outside door handle
13. Window
14. Rubber window run channel
15. Outer sealing strip
16. Outside rearview mirror
17. Inner mirror garnish
18. Hinge
19. Door open stop
20. Front window guide
21. Regulator
22. Regulator handle

MANUAL WINDOWS

Fig. 40 Front door components — 1993 Prizm

10. Install the fabric trim molding to sun roof opening.
11. Install the following:
    a. Sunshades
    b. Assist handles
    c. Dome lamp
    d. Reading lamp and sunroof control assembly
    e. Rearview mirror

1993

▶ **See Figure 47**

1. Disconnect the negative battery cable.
2. Remove the inside rearview mirror bezel.
3. Remove the 2 screws and the inside rearview mirror.
4. Remove 2 screws from each sunshade and sunshades from the vehicle.

5. Remove 1 screw from each sunshade inner support and supports from the vehicle. Gently pry each A-pillar trim panel loose and remove panels from the vehicle. Gently pry each B-pillar lower trim panel loose and remove panels from the vehicle.

6. Remove 1 bolt from each front seat belt upper guide loop anchor. Gently pry each B-pillar upper trim panel loose and remove panels from the vehicle. Gently pry each C-pillar trim panel loose and set panels aside. Open screw cover on each assist grip, remove 2 screws from each grip, and remove grips from the vehicle (if equipped).

7. Remove 1 screw from each coat hanger, and remove the hangers from vehicle (if equipped). Gently pry dome lamp lens loose and remove.

8. Remove 2 screws and dome lamp from vehicle, disconnecting the electrical connector.

1. Window glass
2. Sash channel
3. Stationary window
4. Weather strip
5. Run channel guide
6. Door assembly
7. Outer handle
8. Inner handle
9. Door latch/lock assembly
10. Window regulator
11. Door check
12. Hinge
13. Lift arm bracket
14. Door belt molding
15. Water deflector
16. Trim panel
17. Inner handle bezel
18. Armrest
19. Window winder handle

Fig. 41 Rear door components — Nova

WITH POWER DOOR LOCKS

A

WITH POWER WINDOW

B

A. Door lock solenoid
B. Power window regulator
1. Cover
2. Armrest
3. Inner handle
4. Trim panel
5. Water deflector
6. Door latch/lock

7. Striker
8. Outer handle
9. Rear lower frame
10. Rear guide seal
11. Window glass
12. Glass channel
13. Belt molding
14. Glass run

15. Lock knob
16. window regulator
17. Hinge
18. Door check arm
19. Plate
20. Spring clip
21. Regulator arms

Fig. 42 Rear door components — 1989-92 Prizm

1. Regulator handle
2. Armrest
3. Inside door handle bezel
4. Rear door trim
5. Water deflector
6. Door lock
7. Lock striker
8. Outside door handle
9. Partition window
10. Center guide channel
11. Rubber window run channel
12. Window
13. Hinge
14. Door open stop
15. Regulator
16. Outer sealing strip
17. Inner sealing strip
18. Power window switch

MANUAL WINDOWS

Fig. 43 Rear door components — 1993 Prizm

Fig. 44 Connecting the Prizm door handle — 1989-92

Fig. 45 One method of removing the window winder clip

WITHOUT POWER WINDOW

WITH POWER WINDOW

Fig. 46 Removing the front door inner panels. Rear doors similar — 1989-92 Prizm

9. Remove 1 screw and gently pry bezel from power sunroof switch (if equipped).

10. Remove 1 screw and power sunroof switch from the vehicle, disconnecting the electrical connector (if equipped).

11. Remove 2 screws and headlining rear trim from the vehicle.

12. Remove the headlining from the vehicle (the headlining is attached to the roof with hook and loop fasteners).

To install:

13. Install headlining to the vehicle; secure hook and loop fasteners.

14. Install headlining rear trim to the vehicle; secure with 2 screws.

15. Install the power sunroof switch electrical connector (if equipped).

16. Install the power sunroof switch to the roof (if equipped); secure with 1 screw.

17. Install bezel to power sunroof switch (if equipped); secure with 1 screw.

18. Install the dome lamp electrical connector.

19. Install the dome lamp to the vehicle; secure with 2 screws.

20. Install the lens to the dome lamp.

21. Install the coat hangers to the vehicle; secure each with 1 screw.

22. Install the assist grips to the vehicle (if equipped); secure each with 2 screws; close screw covers.

23. Install C-pillar trim panels.

24. Install B-pillar upper trim panels to the vehicle.

25. Install the front seat belt upper anchor to B-pillar; secure each with 1 bolt.

Door Lock Cylinders

REMOVAL & INSTALLATION

Nova

1. Remove the door trim panel.

2. Carefully remove the water deflector shield from inside the door. Take your time and don't rip it.

3. Disconnect the link rod running between the lock cylinder and the lock/latch mechanism.

4. The lock is held to the door by a horse-shoe shaped retaining clip. Slide the clip free of the lock and remove the cylinder from the outside of the door.

To install:

5. Install the new cylinder and install the clip. The retaining clip has a slight bend in it and will install under tension. Do not attempt to straighten the clip.

6. Connect the link rod.

7. Install the water deflector shield, making sure that it is intact and firmly attached all the way around.

8. Reinstall the door trim panel.

Prizm

1. Remove the door trim panel.

2. Carefully remove the water deflector shield from inside the door. Take your time and don't rip it.

1. Sunshade
2. Inside rearview mirror
3. Inside rearview mirror bezel
4. Sunshade inner support
5. Power sunroof switch bezel
6. Power sunroof switch
7. Headlining
8. Headlining rear trim
9. Assist grip
10. Dome lamp
11. Dome lamp lens
12. C-pillar trim panel
13. B-pillar upper trim panel
14. A-pillar trim panel
15. Lower rear quarter trim panel
16. Rear sill plate
17. B-pillar lower trim panel
18. Kick panel
19. Front sill plate

Fig. 47 Headlining assembly — 1993 Prizm

3. Disconnect the link rods running between the lock cylinder and the lock/latch mechanism.

4. Remove the 2 bolts holding the door handle to the door and remove the handle and lock from the outside. On 1989-92 models, the cylinder and door handle are 1 piece and must be replaced as a unit. On 1993 models, the cylinder can be rotated counterclockwise and removed from the handle.

To install:

5. On 1993 models, rotate the cylinder clockwise and install to the handle. On all models, install the lock and handle and tighten the bolts.

6. Connect the link rods.

7. Install the water deflector shield, making sure that it is intact and firmly attached all the way around.

8. Reinstall the door trim panel.

Door Locks

REMOVAL & INSTALLATION

Front or Rear Doors

1. Disconnect the negative battery cable.
2. Remove the door panel and watershield. Remove the service hole cover.
3. Disconnect the door outside opening linkage. Remove the two mounting bolts and remove the door handle if in need of replacement.
4. Disconnect the lock cylinder control linkage.

5. Remove the lock knob and the child protector lock lever knob.

6. Remove the lock assembly retaining screws and remove the door lock. If equipped with power locks, disconnect the electrical connector.

To install:

7. Coat all the door lock sliding surfaces with multi-purpose grease.

8. Install the outside handle with the two retaining bolts, if removed.

9. Install the door lock solenoid linkage to the door lock.

10. Connect the link to the outside handle.

11. Install the lock knob and the child protector lock lever knob.

12. Install the door opening control link.

13. Install the door lock cylinder control linkage.

14. Install the door panel and watershield.

15. Reconnect the negative battery cable.

Tailgate Lock

REMOVAL & INSTALLATION

1. Disconnect the negative battery cable.
2. Remove the back door inside garnish trim.
3. Remove the trim panel.
4. Disconnect the links from the door control and door lock cylinder.
5. Remove the bolts and the door lock control with the solenoid.

6. To remove the door lock cylinder, remove the retaining screws and then remove the cylinder.

To install:

7. Install the door lock cylinder and secure with the retaining screws.

8. Install the bolts and the door lock control with the solenoid.

9. Connect the links to the door control and door lock cylinder.

10. Install the trim panel.

11. Install the back door inner garnish trim.

12. Connect the negative battery cable.

Sedan Trunk Lock

REMOVAL & INSTALLATION

1. Disconnect the negative battery cable.
2. Remove the inside trunk garnish trim.
3. Remove the bolts and the door lock assembly.
4. The installation is the reverse of the removal procedure.

Door Glass, Regulator and Motor

REMOVAL & INSTALLATION

Front Door Glass

NOVA

▶ **See Figure 38**

1. Remove the door trim panel.
2. Carefully remove the water deflector shield and lower the window glass fully.
3. Remove the outer weatherstrip.
4. Remove the sash channel mounting bolts.
5. Carefully remove the glass through the top of the door.
6. Remove the window regulator mounting bolts and remove the regulator
7. If the window glass is to be replaced:
   a. Remove the sash channel from the glass.
   b. Apply a solution of soapy water to the sash channel.
   c. Install the channel to the new glass using a plastic or leather mallet to tap the sash into place. Note that the sash channel must be exactly positioned on the glass or the bolt holes will not align at reinstallation.

To install:

8. Install the regulator and tighten the bolts evenly.
9. Install the window glass and install the sash channel mounting bolts.
10. Wind the window slowly up and down and observe its movement and alignment. The position of the glass can be adjusted by moving the equalizing arm bracket up or down. Make small adjustments and work for a perfectly aligned window.
11. Install the outer weatherstrip.
12. Install the water deflector, making sure it is intact and properly sealed.

13. Install the door trim panel.

1989-92 PRIZM

▶ **See Figure 39**

1. Disconnect the negative battery cable. Remove the door trim panel.
2. Carefully remove the water deflector shield and lower the window glass fully.
3. Remove the glass channel mounting bolts.
4. Remove the window glass by lifting it through the top of the door.
5. Disconnect the window regulator as follows:
   a. For power windows, disconnect the electrical connector and remove the 4 mounting bolts. The regulator will be removed with the motor attached.
   b. For manual windows, remove the 3 mounting bolts.
6. Remove the 2 mounting bolts holding the equalizer arm bracket.
7. Remove the window regulator.

✳✳CAUTION

If the motor is to be removed from the power window regulator, install a large stopper bolt through the regulator frame before removing the motor. When the motor is removed, the spring loaded gear will be disengaged, causing the gear to rotate until the spring is unwound. Install the stopper bolt to prevent possible injury by the spinning gear.

To install:

8. Before installing the regulator assembly, apply a light coat of lithium grease to the sliding surfaces and pivot points of the regulator. Do not apply grease to the spring.
9. Install the regulator:
   a. With power windows, install the 4 mounting bolts and connect the motor wiring.
   b. With manual windows, install the 3 mounting bolts.
10. Install the bolts holding the equalizer arm bracket.
11. Place the glass into the door and install the glass channel retaining bolts.
12. Adjust the door glass by moving the equalizer arm up or down as necessary to get the window level in the frame.
13. Install the water deflector, making sure it is intact and properly sealed.
14. Install the door trim panel.

1993 PRIZM

▶ **See Figure 40**

1. Disconnect the negative battery cable. Remove the door trim panel.
2. Carefully remove the water deflector shield and lower the window glass fully.
3. Remove the glass channel mounting bolts.
4. Remove the window glass by lifting it through the top of the door.
5. Remove the 4 bolts and one nut and remove the inner door panel brace from the door.
6. Disconnect the power window motor electrical connector, if so equipped.

7. Remove the 3 bolts and 3 nuts and remove the regulator from the door.

To install:

8. Before installing the regulator assembly, apply a light coat of lithium grease to the sliding surfaces and pivot points of the regulator.

9. Install the regulator to the door and tighten the 3 bolts and nuts to 62 inch lbs. (7 Nm).

10. Connect the power window motor electrical connector, if so equipped.

11. Install the 4 bolts and one nut and the inner door panel brace to the door and tighten to 11 ft. lbs. (15 Nm).

12. Install the glass channel mounting bolts and tighten to 62 inch lbs. (7 Nm).

13. Install the water deflector shield.

14. Install the door trim panel.

15. Connect the negative battery cable.

Rear Door Glass

NOVA

▶ See Figure 41

➡ **The movable window glass cannot be removed without removing the fixed glass.**

1. Remove the door trim panel.

2. Carefully remove the water deflector shield and lower the window glass fully.

3. Remove the outer weatherstrip.

4. Partially remove the door weatherstrip to remove the run channel guide upper retaining screw.

5. Remove the rubber or felt run channel.

6. Remove the 2 lower run channel guide bolts and remove the guide.

7. Pull the fixed glass forward and remove it. Place it in a safe and protected location, away from the work area.

8. Remove the sash channel bolts.

9. Carefully remove the glass through the top of the door.

10. Remove the window regulator mounting bolts and remove the regulator.

11. If the window glass is to be replaced:
   a. Remove the sash channel from the glass.
   b. Apply a solution of soapy water to the sash channel.
   c. Install the channel to the new glass using a plastic or leather mallet to tap the sash into place. Note that the sash channel must be exactly positioned on the glass or the bolt holes will not align at reinstallation.

To install:

12. Install the regulator and tighten the bolts evenly.

13. Install the window glass and install the sash channel mounting bolts.

14. Reinstall the fixed glass and make certain it is correctly positioned.

15. Install the run channel guide and install the 2 lower retaining bolts.

16. Install the felt or rubber run channel. Make certain there are no twists or kinks in the channel.

17. Install the top screw in the channel guide and secure the door weatherstrip.

18. Wind the window slowly up and down and observe its movement and alignment. The position of the glass can be adjusted by moving the equalizing arm bracket up or down.

Make small adjustments and work for a perfectly aligned window.

19. Install the outer weatherstrip.

20. Install the water deflector, making sure it is intact and properly sealed.

21. Install the door trim panel.

1989-92 PRIZM

▶ See Figure 42

1. Disconnect the negative battery cable. Remove the door trim panel.

2. Carefully remove the water deflector shield and lower the window glass fully.

3. Remove the glass from the regulator arm.

4. Loosen the window weatherstrip at the rear edge of the glass run channel.

5. Remove the screws holding the top and bottom of the rear channel guide.

6. Lift the door weatherstrip and remove the screws holding the (black) window filler panel.

7. Remove the door glass by pulling it upward.

8. If equipped with power windows, disconnect the motor wiring connector.

9. Remove the bolts holding the regulator and remove the regulator.

❊❊CAUTION

If the motor is to be removed from the power window regulator, install a large stopper bolt through the regulator frame before removing the motor. When the motor is removed, the spring loaded gear will be disengaged, causing the gear to rotate until the spring is unwound. Install the stopper bolt to prevent possible injury by the spinning gear.

To install:

10. Before installing the regulator assembly, apply a light coat of lithium grease to the sliding surfaces and pivot points of the regulator. Do not apply grease to the spring.

11. Install the regulator and tighten the mounting bolts evenly.

12. If equipped with power windows, connect the wiring to the motor.

13. Install the glass into the door and connect it to the regulator.

14. Install the black window filler panel and its 2 screws.

15. Install the rear glass guide channel.

16. Install the window weatherstrip.

17. Install the water deflector, making sure it is intact and properly sealed.

18. Install the door trim panel.

1993 PRIZM

▶ See Figure 43

1. Disconnect the negative battery cable.

2. Remove the door trim panel.

3. Carefully pull the water deflector far enough away to gain access to the center guide channel bolts. Loosen the rubber window run channel along the center guide channel.

4. Remove the 2 bolts and one screw and the center guide channel from the rear door.

5. Disconnect the power window motor electrical connector, if so equipped.

6. Remove the 4 bolts from the regulator and slide the regulator arm roller out of the window bottom channel.

7. Lift the window and remove from the door.

8. Remove the regulator from the door.

To install:

9. Before installing the regulator assembly, apply a light coat of lithium grease to the sliding surfaces and pivot points of the regulator.

10. Install the regulator to the door.

11. Install the window to the door.

12. Slide the regulator arm roller into the window bottom channel. Install the 4 bolts to the regulator and tighten the 4 bolts to 62 inch lbs. (7 Nm).

13. Connect the power window motor electrical connector, if so equipped.

14. Install the 2 bolts and one screw and the center guide channel to the rear door. Tighten the 2 bolts to 62 inch lbs. (7 Nm).

15. Press the rubber window run channel in place along the center guide channel.

16. Position the water deflector in place.

17. Install the door trim panel.

18. Connect the negative battery cable.

Windshield Glass

REMOVAL & INSTALLATION

Extreme care must be taken when removing, installing or resealing a windshield. The windshield will crack if a stress in the wrong direction is exerted, even if the pressure is very slight. Undesirable stress on the windshield could take place during a number of operations. Damage could occur days after the repair has been completed, caused by the body of the vehicle flexing during normal vehicle operation, or during the removal of the outer moldings before any repair work has been done. This should be realized before the job of removing a windshield is undertaken.

REMOVAL & INSTALLATION

▶ **See Figures 48, 49 and 50**

1. Disconnect the negative battery cable.

2. Remove the sunvisors, holders and the front assist grips.

3. Remove the inner rear view mirror.

4. Remove the front pillar garnishes.

5. Remove the hood, wiper arms and the cowl panel (louver).

6. Remove the hood weatherstrip by pulling upward. Take care not to tear the weatherstrip during removal.

7. Remove the retainer screws and the outside windshield molding.

8. Tape the end of a scraper and insert between the body and the upper windshield molding. Pry the molding upward and remove from the clips. Remove the molding from the vehicle.

9. Push piano wire from the interior of the vehicle outward and tie object to act as a handle to each end of the wire. Apply tape to the outer body surfaces to avoid scratching the finish. Cut the adhesive by pulling the piano wire, with the aid of a helper, around the windshield.

10. Carefully remove the glass from the vehicle.

To install:

11. Clean all adhesive off of the body of the vehicle. Clean all contact surfaces with an appropriate cleaner.

12. Remove old fasteners and replace with new.

13. Clean the removed glass of all adhesive and clean with an appropriate cleaner. Do not touch the contact area after cleaning.

14. Install new retainers to their original location. Install the spacer.

15. Position the glass onto the vehicle making sure all contacting parts of the glass are perfectly even and don't make contact with any fasteners.

16. Mark the position of the glass and remove.

17. Clean the contact surfaces of the glass.

18. Install the air dam with double tape making sure not to touch the glass.

19. Using a brush, coat the contact surface on the body with the appropriate primer according to manufactures instructions. Repeat the procedure using the appropriate compound on the glass.

20. Apply windshield adhesive to the contact points in a bead 0.39 inch (10mm) thick.

21. Install the glass aligning to the reference marks. Insure the correct sealing of the air dam. (lip curling downward and in the bead of sealer)

22. Apply a slight downward pressure on the glass to set into position. Using a spatula, apply adhesive to the outer rim of the glass.

23. Remove any excess sealer. Fasten glass securely until sealer sets. Water test once the sealer is fully dry.

24. If no leaks are present, carefully install the moldings, interior trim components, cowl panel, wiper arms and the hood.

25. Connect the negative battery cable.

Back Window Glass

REMOVAL & INSTALLATION

▶ **See Figures 51, 52 and 53**

1. Remove the rear seat and the rear cushion from the vehicle.

2. Disconnect rear window defogger electrical connection if equipped and follow the remaining steps. Remove the cover on the high mount brake light and remove the mounting bolts. Remove the brake light from the vehicle.

3. Remove the interior assist grips and the rear portion of the headlining.

4. Using a knife, remove the back window molding by cutting off lip portion of the molding which is over the glass.

MOLDING CLIP LOCATION

1. Windshield
2. Windshield side reveal mouldings
3. Windshield upper reveal moulding
4. Lower windshield moulding
5. Rubber spacers
5. Rubber spacers
6. Dam
7. Headliner front trim
8. Pillar garnish moulding
9. Inside rearview mirror
10. Wiper assembly

Fig. 48 Windshield assembly and mouldings — 1985-88 Nova

1. Side moulding
2. Upper moulding (non reusable)
3. Windshield glass
4. Dam (non reusable)
5. Inside rearview mirror
6. Headliner front trim
7. Sunshade support
8. Sunshade
9. Pillar garnish moulding
10. Cowl
11. Wiper arm
12. Spacer
13. Glass stopper

Fig. 49 Windshield assembly and mouldings — 1989-92 Prizm

Fig. 50 Windshield assembly and mouldings — 1993 Prizm

5. Remove the back glass in the same manner as the front windshield (using the piano wire) and remove the glass retainers.

To install:

6. Clean all adhesive off of the body of the vehicle. Clean all contact surfaces with an appropriate cleaner.

7. Remove old fasteners and replace with new.

8. Clean the removed glass of all adhesive and clean with an appropriate cleaner. Do not touch the contact area after cleaning.

9. Install new retainers to their original location.

10. Position the glass onto the vehicle making sure all contacting parts on the glass are perfectly even and don't make contact with any fasteners.

11. Mark the position of the glass and remove.

12. Clean the contact surfaces of the glass.

13. Install the air dam with double tape making sure not to touch the glass.

14. Using a brush, coat the contact surface on the body with the appropriate primer according to manufactures instructions. Repeat the procedure using the appropriate compound on the glass.

15. Apply the glass adhesive to the contact points on the body in a bead 0.39 inch (10mm) thick.

16. Install the glass aligning to the reference marks. Insure the correct sealing of the air dam. (lip curling downward and in the bead of sealer)

17. Apply a slight downward pressure on the glass to set into position. Using a spatula, apply adhesive to the outer rim of the glass.

18. Remove any excess sealer. Fasten glass securely until sealer sets. Water test once the sealer is fully dry.

19. If no leaks are present, carefully install the moldings, interior components, trim panels and the high mount brake light assembly and wiper arm if so equipped.

Quarter Window Glass

REMOVAL & INSTALLATION

1. Remove the rear quarter glass drip molding.

2. Using a scraper with the blade taped to prevent scratching the vehicle, pry off the window moldings.

3. Pull off, by hand, the belt molding.

4. Remove the rear seat back from the vehicle and all necessary interior components for access of quarter window glass.

5. Remove the rear inside upper trim panel and the rear pillar upper garnish.

6. Remove the window glass set nuts (remove all necessary trim panels and components) and remove the glass. Cut the sealer loose as required to remove the glass.

To install:

7. Clean all adhesive off of the body of the vehicle.

8. Clean all contact surfaces with an appropriate cleaner.

9. Clean the removed glass of all adhesive and clean with an appropriate cleaner. Do not touch the contact area after cleaning.

10. Using a brush, coat the contact surface on the body with the appropriate primer according to manufactures instructions. Repeat the procedure using the appropriate compound on the glass.

WEATHERSTRIP

REAR WINDOW GLASS

ROOF SIDE INNER GARNISH MOLDING

DEFOGGER WIRE CONNECTOR

HIGH-MOUNT STOP LAMP

COVER

WIRE CONNECTOR

PACKAGE TRAY TRIM

Fig. 51 Rear window glass assembly — 1985-88 Nova

1. Rear seatback and cushion
2. Roof headlining rear trim
3. Shoulder belt anchor trim
4. Roof side inner garnish
5. Dam (non reusable)
6. Rear window glass
7. Upper moulding (non reusable)
8. Lower moulding
9. Rear window shelf
10. Rear defogger connector

Fig. 52 Rear window glass assembly — 1989-92 Prizm

1. Rear window reveal moulding
2. Rear window
3. Rear window dam
4. Rear seatback-to-rear window trim panel
5. Center high mounted stoplamp bezel
6. Center high mounted stoplamp

Fig. 53 Rear window glass assembly — 1993 Prizm

11. Apply the glass adhesive to the contact points on the body in a bead 0.39 inch (10mm) thick and overlapping the bead approximately 2.0 inch (50mm).

12. Install the glass. Install the window glass set nuts.

13. Install the rear inside upper trim panel and the rear pillar upper garnish and the belt molding.

14. Install the rear seat back to the vehicle. Install all necessary interior components.

15. Install the window moldings.

16. Leak test the window when the sealer is completely dry.

Inside Mirror

REMOVAL & INSTALLATION

The inside mirror is removed by carefully prying off the plastic cover and removing the retaining bolts. The inside mirror is designed to break loose from the roof mount if it receives moderate impact. If the mirror has come off due to impact, it can usually be remounted by installing a new mirror base rather than an entire new mirror. If the glass is cracked, the mirror must be replaced.

Seats

REMOVAL & INSTALLATION

Front Seats

▶ **See Figure 54**

The front seats of both the Nova and Prizm are removed by disconnecting the 4 mounting bolts holding the seat to the floor rails. The bolts may be under plastic covers which can be popped off with a small tool. The seat assembly will come out of the car complete with the tracks and adjuster. When reinstalling the seat, make certain that the bolts are properly threaded and tightened to 27 ft. lbs. (34 Nm). Seat mounting and retention is a critical safety item. Never attempt to alter the mounts or the seat tracks.

Rear Bench Seat Cushion

1985-88 NOVA

▶ **See Figure 55**

1. Pull forward on the seat cushion releases. These are small levers on the lower front of the cushion.

2. Pull upward on the front of the seat cushion and rotate it free. It is not retained or bolted under the seat back.

3. To reinstall, fit the rear of the cushion into place under the seat back.

4. Push inward and downward on the front of the cushion until the releases lock into place. Make sure the seat is locked into place and the releases are secure.

1. Head restraint
2. Recliner mechanism
3. Recliner actuator handle
4. Seat adjuster

Fig. 54 Front seat components — 1989-92 Prizm

1. Rear seat back
2. Rear seat cushion
3. Seat cushion release
4. Seat back bolts
5. Seat back hangers

Fig. 55 Rear bench seat components — 1985-88 Nova

1. Rear seat cushion
2. Side hinge
3. Seat back
4. Center hinge

Fig. 56 Split/folding rear seat components — 1989-92 Prizm

1993 PRIZM

1. Pull forward on the seat cushion releases. These are small levers on the lower front of the cushion.

2. Pull upward on the front of the seat cushion and rotate it free. It is not retained or bolted under the seat back.

3. To reinstall, fit the rear of the cushion into place under the seat back.

4. Push inward and downward on the front of the cushion until the releases lock into place. Make sure the seat is locked into place and the releases are secure.

Rear Bench Seat Back

1985-88 NOVA

▶ See Figure 55

➡The seat bottom cushion need not be removed for this procedure, but access is improved with the cushion removed.

1. Remove the 2 lower bolts holding the seat back to the body.

2. Pull outward and push upward on the bottom edge of the seat back. This will release the seat back from the L-shaped hangers holding it.

3. Remove the seat back from the car.

4. When reinstalling, carefully fit the seat back onto the hangers.

5. Swing the back down and into place.

6. Install the lower retaining bolts and tighten them to 3.5 ft. lbs. (42 inch lbs.).

1993 PRIZM

60-40 Split Folding Rear Seatback

1. Raise the rear seat cushion at the front edge to disengage it from the retaining clips.

2. Slide the rear seat cushion over the seat belt buckles and remove the cushion from the vehicle.

3. Remove the 1 bolt from the rear seat side trim and lift and remove the trim from the vehicle.

4. Remove the 2 bolts from the seatback and remove the seatback from the vehicle.

5. Installation is the reverse of removal. Tighten the 2 seatback retaining bolts to 15 ft. lbs. 20 Nm).

Full-Width Rear Seatback

1. Raise the rear seat cushion at the front edge to disengage it from the retaining clips.

2. Slide the rear seat cushion over the seat belt buckles and remove the cushion from the vehicle.

3. Remove the 3 bolts from the rear seatback and lift the seatback from the vehicle.

4. Installation is the reverse of removal. Tighten the 3 seatback retaining bolts to 15 ft. lbs. 20 Nm).

Split/Folding Rear Seat Cushion

1989-92 Prizm

▶ See Figure 56

1. At the front lower edge of the seat cushion, remove the 2 bolts holding the seat cushion to the body. The bolts may be concealed under carpeting or trim pieces.

2. Pull upward on the front of the seat cushion and rotate it free. It is not retained or bolted under the seat back.

3. To reinstall, fit the rear of the cushion into place under the seat back.

4. Push inward and downward on the front of the cushion until it is in place and the bolt holes align.

5. Install the retaining bolts and tighten them.

Split/Folding Rear Seat Back

1989-92 Prizm

▶ See Figure 56

1. Push the seat back forward into a folded position.

2. Remove the carpeting from the rear of the seat back.

3. At the side hinge, remove the bolt holding the seat back to the hinge.

4. At the center hinge, remove the 2 bolts holding the seat back to the hinge.

5. Remove the seat back from the car.

6. Reinstall the seat back and install the bolts finger tight.

7. Tighten the side hinge bolt to 13 ft. lbs.

8. Tighten the center hinge bolts to 5.4 ft. lbs. (65 INCH lbs.)

9. Install the carpeting and trim on the rear of the seat back.

Seat Belt System

REMOVAL & INSTALLATION

Front Seat

1. Remove the trim cover at the upper shoulder anchor bolt.

2. Remove the anchor bolt.

3. Remove the lower cover on the outer retractor. Unbolt the retractor from the inner floor panel.

4. Remove the retractor portion of the seat belt.

5. To remove the buckle end of the seat belt, remove the cover on the base of the belt and remove the mounting bolt.

6. Installation of the belts is the reverse of the removal procedure. Torque the upper shoulder mounting bolt to 32 ft. lbs. (43 Nm), the lower retractor mounting bolt to 69 inch lbs. (8.0 Nm), and the buckle retainer bolt to 32 ft. lbs. (43 Nm).

Do not remove safety belts from any vehicle. Inspection of the seat belts for proper operation is recommended for the safety of the vehicle's occupants and is required in most states by law.

Rear Seat

1. Remove the trim cover at the upper shoulder anchor bolt.

2. Remove the upper shoulder anchor bolt.

3. Unbolt the outer belt anchor from the body panel. Removal of the rear seat is required. Unbolt the lower end of the belt under the retractor from the side panel.

4. Remove the retractor portion of the seat belt.

5. To remove the center belt buckle of the seat belt, remove the seat cushion and remove the center belt mounting bolt.

6. Installation of the belts is the reverse of the removal procedure. Torque all mounting bolts on the belt to 32 ft. lbs. (43 Nm).

TORQUE SPECIFICATIONS

Component	U.S.	Metric
Front Bumpers:		
1985–92 vehicles;	70 ft. lbs.	95 Nm
1993 vehicles;		
Impact bar nuts:	33 ft. lbs.	45 Nm
Fascia bolts:	15 ft lbs.	20 Nm
Fascia upper support bolts:	15 ft. lbs.	20 Nm
Rear Bumper:		
1985–92 vehicles;	70 ft. lbs.	95 Nm
1993 vehicles;		
Impact bar nuts:	33 ft. lbs.	45 Nm
Fascia bolts:	15 ft lbs.	20 Nm
Fenders:		
1989–93 vehicles;		
All bolts:	15 ft. lbs.	20 Nm
Front Seats:		
1989–93 vehicles;		
All bolts:	27 ft lbs.	34 Nm
Rear Bench Seat Back:		
1985–88 Nova		
Lower retaining bolts:	42 inch lbs.	4.75 Nm
Split/Folding Rear Seat Back:		
1989–92 Prizm		
Side hinge bolt:	13 ft. lbs.	17 Nm
Center hinge bolts:	65 inch lbs.	7.5 Nm
60-40 Split Folding Rear Seatback:		
1993 vehciles		
Retaining bolts:	15 ft. lbs.	20 Nm
Full-Width Rear Seatback		
1993 vehicles		
Retaining bolts:	15 ft. lbs.	20 Nm
Seat Belts:		
Front Seat;		
Retractor mounting bolt:	69 inch lbs.	8.0 Nm
Buckle retainer bolt:	32 ft. lbs.	43 Nm
Rear Seat:		
All mounting bolts:	32 ft. lbs.	43 Nm

GLOSSARY

AIR/FUEL RATIO: The ratio of air to gasoline by weight in the fuel mixture drawn into the engine.

AIR INJECTION: One method of reducing harmful exhaust emissions by injecting air into each of the exhaust ports of an engine. The fresh air entering the hot exhaust manifold causes any remaining fuel to be burned before it can exit the tailpipe.

ALTERNATOR: A device used for converting mechanical energy into electrical energy.

AMMETER: An instrument, calibrated in amperes, used to measure the flow of an electrical current in a circuit. Ammeters are always connected in series with the circuit being tested.

AMPERE: The rate of flow of electrical current present when one volt of electrical pressure is applied against one ohm of electrical resistance.

ANALOG COMPUTER: Any microprocessor that uses similar (analogous) electrical signals to make its calculations.

ARMATURE: A laminated, soft iron core wrapped by a wire that converts electrical energy to mechanical energy as in a motor or relay. When rotated in a magnetic field, it changes mechanical energy into electrical energy as in a generator.

ATMOSPHERIC PRESSURE: The pressure on the Earth's surface caused by the weight of the air in the atmosphere. At sea level, this pressure is 14.7 psi at 32{248}F (101 kPa at 0{248}C).

ATOMIZATION: The breaking down of a liquid into a fine mist that can be suspended in air.

AXIAL PLAY: Movement parallel to a shaft or bearing bore.

BACKFIRE: The sudden combustion of gases in the intake or exhaust system that results in a loud explosion.

BACKLASH: The clearance or play between two parts, such as meshed gears.

BACKPRESSURE: Restrictions in the exhaust system that slow the exit of exhaust gases from the combustion chamber.

BAKELITE: A heat resistant, plastic insulator material commonly used in printed circuit boards and transistorized components.

BALL BEARING: A bearing made up of hardened inner and outer races between which hardened steel balls roll.

BALLAST RESISTOR: A resistor in the primary ignition circuit that lowers voltage after the engine is started to reduce wear on ignition components.

BEARING: A friction reducing, supportive device usually located between a stationary part and a moving part.

BIMETAL TEMPERATURE SENSOR: Any sensor or switch made of two dissimilar types of metal that bend when heated or cooled due to the different expansion rates of the alloys. These types of sensors usually function as an on/off switch.

BLOWBY: Combustion gases, composed of water vapor and unburned fuel, that leak past the piston rings into the crankcase during normal engine operation. These gases are removed by the PCV system to prevent the buildup of harmful acids in the crankcase.

BRAKE PAD: A brake shoe and lining assembly used with disc brakes.

BRAKE SHOE: The backing for the brake lining. The term is, however, usually applied to the assembly of the brake backing and lining.

BUSHING: A liner, usually removable, for a bearing; an anti-friction liner used in place of a bearing.

CALIPER: A hydraulically activated device in a disc brake system, which is mounted straddling the brake rotor (disc). The caliper contains at least one piston and two brake pads. Hydraulic pressure on the piston(s) forces the pads against the rotor.

CAMSHAFT: A shaft in the engine on which are the lobes (cams) which operate the valves. The camshaft is driven by the crankshaft, via a belt, chain or gears, at one half the crankshaft speed.

CAPACITOR: A device which stores an electrical charge.

CARBON MONOXIDE (CO): A colorless, odorless gas given off as a normal byproduct of combustion. It is poisonous and extremely dangerous in confined areas, building up slowly to toxic levels without warning if adequate ventilation is not available.

CARBURETOR: A device, usually mounted on the intake manifold of an engine, which mixes the air and fuel in the proper proportion to allow even combustion.

CATALYTIC CONVERTER: A device installed in the exhaust system, like a muffler, that converts harmful byproducts of combustion into carbon dioxide and water vapor by means of a heat-producing chemical reaction.

CENTRIFUGAL ADVANCE: A mechanical method of advancing the spark timing by using flyweights in the distributor that react to centrifugal force generated by the distributor shaft rotation.

CHECK VALVE: Any one-way valve installed to permit the flow of air, fuel or vacuum in one direction only.

CHOKE: A device, usually a moveable valve, placed in the intake path of a carburetor to restrict the flow of air.

CIRCUIT: Any unbroken path through which an electrical current can flow. Also used to describe fuel flow in some instances.

CIRCUIT BREAKER: A switch which protects an electrical circuit from overload by opening the circuit when the current flow exceeds a predetermined level. Some circuit breakers must be reset manually, while most reset automatically

COIL (IGNITION): A transformer in the ignition circuit which steps up the voltage provided to the spark plugs.

COMBINATION MANIFOLD: An assembly which includes both the intake and exhaust manifolds in one casting.

COMBINATION VALVE: A device used in some fuel systems that routes fuel vapors to a charcoal storage canister instead of venting them into the atmosphere. The valve relieves fuel tank pressure and allows fresh air into the tank as the fuel level drops to prevent a vapor lock situation.

COMPRESSION RATIO: The comparison of the total volume of the cylinder and combustion chamber with the piston at BDC and the piston at TDC.

CONDENSER: 1. An electrical device which acts to store an electrical charge, preventing voltage surges.
2. A radiator-like device in the air conditioning system in which refrigerant gas condenses into a liquid, giving off heat.

CONDUCTOR: Any material through which an electrical current can be transmitted easily.

CONTINUITY: Continuous or complete circuit. Can be checked with an ohmmeter.

COUNTERSHAFT: An intermediate shaft which is rotated by a mainshaft and transmits, in turn, that rotation to a working part.

CRANKCASE: The lower part of an engine in which the crankshaft and related parts operate.

CRANKSHAFT: The main driving shaft of an engine which receives reciprocating motion from the pistons and converts it to rotary motion.

CYLINDER: In an engine, the round hole in the engine block in which the piston(s) ride.

CYLINDER BLOCK: The main structural member of an engine in which is found the cylinders, crankshaft and other principal parts.

CYLINDER HEAD: The detachable portion of the engine, fastened, usually, to the top of the cylinder block, containing all or most of the combustion chambers. On overhead valve engines, it contains the valves and their operating parts. On overhead cam engines, it contains the camshaft as well.

DEAD CENTER: The extreme top or bottom of the piston stroke.

DETONATION: An unwanted explosion of the air/fuel mixture in the combustion chamber caused by excess heat and compression, advanced timing, or an overly lean mixture. Also referred to as "ping".

DIAPHRAGM: A thin, flexible wall separating two cavities, such as in a vacuum advance unit.

DIESELING: A condition in which hot spots in the combustion chamber cause the engine to run on after the key is turned off.

DIFFERENTIAL: A geared assembly which allows the transmission of motion between drive axles, giving one axle the ability to turn faster than the other.

DIODE: An electrical device that will allow current to flow in one direction only.

DISC BRAKE: A hydraulic braking assembly consisting of a brake disc, or rotor, mounted on an axle, and a caliper assembly containing, usually two brake pads which are activated by hydraulic pressure. The pads are forced against the sides of the disc, creating friction which slows the vehicle.

DISTRIBUTOR: A mechanically driven device on an engine which is responsible for electrically firing the spark plug at a predetermined point of the piston stroke.

DOWEL PIN: A pin, inserted in mating holes in two different parts allowing those parts to maintain a fixed relationship.

DRUM BRAKE: A braking system which consists of two brake shoes and one or two wheel cylinders, mounted on a fixed backing plate, and a brake drum, mounted on an axle, which revolves around the assembly.

DWELL: The rate, measured in degrees of shaft rotation, at which an electrical circuit cycles on and off.

ELECTRONIC CONTROL UNIT (ECU): Ignition module, module, amplifier or igniter. See Module for definition.

ELECTRONIC IGNITION: A system in which the timing and firing of the spark plugs is controlled by an electronic control unit, usually called a module. These systems have no points or condenser.

ENDPLAY: The measured amount of axial movement in a shaft.

ENGINE: A device that converts heat into mechanical energy.

EXHAUST MANIFOLD: A set of cast passages or pipes which conduct exhaust gases from the engine.

FEELER GAUGE: A blade, usually metal, of precisely predetermined thickness, used to measure the clearance between two parts.

FIRING ORDER: The order in which combustion occurs in the cylinders of an engine. Also the order in which spark is distributed to the plugs by the distributor.

FLOODING: The presence of too much fuel in the intake manifold and combustion chamber which prevents the air/fuel mixture from firing, thereby causing a no-start situation.

FLYWHEEL: A disc shaped part bolted to the rear end of the crankshaft. Around the outer perimeter is affixed the ring gear. The starter drive engages the ring gear, turning the flywheel, which rotates the crankshaft, imparting the initial starting motion to the engine.

FOOT POUND (ft.lb. or sometimes, ft. lbs.): The amount of energy or work needed to raise an item weighing one pound, a distance of one foot.

FUSE: A protective device in a circuit which prevents circuit overload by breaking the circuit when a specific amperage is present. The device is constructed around a strip or wire of a lower amperage rating than the circuit it is designed to protect. When an amperage higher than that stamped on the fuse is present in the circuit, the strip or wire melts, opening the circuit.

GEAR RATIO: The ratio between the number of teeth on meshing gears.

GENERATOR: A device which converts mechanical energy into electrical energy.

HEAT RANGE: The measure of a spark plug's ability to dissipate heat from its firing end. The higher the heat range, the hotter the plug fires.

HUB: The center part of a wheel or gear.

HYDROCARBON (HC): Any chemical compound made up of hydrogen and carbon. A major pollutant formed by the engine as a byproduct of combustion.

HYDROMETER: An instrument used to measure the specific gravity of a solution.

INCH POUND (in.lb. or sometimes, in. lbs.): One twelfth of a foot pound.

INDUCTION: A means of transferring electrical energy in the form of a magnetic field. Principle used in the ignition coil to increase voltage.

INJECTOR: A device which receives metered fuel under relatively low pressure and is activated to inject the fuel into the engine under relatively high pressure at a predetermined time.

INPUT SHAFT: The shaft to which torque is applied, usually carrying the driving gear or gears.

INTAKE MANIFOLD: A casting of passages or pipes used to conduct air or a fuel/air mixture to the cylinders.

JOURNAL: The bearing surface within which a shaft operates.

KEY: A small block usually fitted in a notch between a shaft and a hub to prevent slippage of the two parts.

MANIFOLD: A casting of passages or set of pipes which connect the cylinders to an inlet or outlet source.

MANIFOLD VACUUM: Low pressure in an engine intake manifold formed just below the throttle plates. Manifold vacuum is highest at idle and drops under acceleration.

MASTER CYLINDER: The primary fluid pressurizing device in a hydraulic system. In automotive use, it is found in brake and hydraulic clutch systems and is pedal activated, either directly or, in a power brake system, through the power booster.

MODULE: Electronic control unit, amplifier or igniter of solid state or integrated design which controls the current flow in the ignition primary circuit based on input from the pick-up coil. When the module opens the primary circuit, the high secondary voltage is induced in the coil.

NEEDLE BEARING: A bearing which consists of a number (usually a large number) of long, thin rollers.

OHM:(Ω) The unit used to measure the resistance of conductor to electrical flow. One ohm is the amount of resistance that limits current flow to one ampere in a circuit with one volt of pressure.

OHMMETER: An instrument used for measuring the resistance, in ohms, in an electrical circuit.

OUTPUT SHAFT: The shaft which transmits torque from a device, such as a transmission.

OVERDRIVE: A gear assembly which produces more shaft revolutions than that transmitted to it.

OVERHEAD CAMSHAFT (OHC): An engine configuration in which the camshaft is mounted on top of the cylinder head and operates the valve either directly or by means of rocker arms.

OVERHEAD VALVE (OHV): An engine configuration in which all of the valves are located in the cylinder head and the camshaft is located in the cylinder block. The camshaft operates the valves via lifters and pushrods.

OXIDES OF NITROGEN (NOx): Chemical compounds of nitrogen produced as a byproduct of combustion. They combine with hydrocarbons to produce smog.

OXYGEN SENSOR: Used with the feedback system to sense the presence of oxygen in the exhaust gas and signal the computer which can reference the voltage signal to an air/fuel ratio.

PINION: The smaller of two meshing gears.

PISTON RING: An open ended ring which fits into a groove on the outer diameter of the piston. Its chief function is to form a seal between the piston and cylinder wall. Most automotive pistons have three rings: two for compression sealing; one for oil sealing.

PRELOAD: A predetermined load placed on a bearing during assembly or by adjustment.

PRIMARY CIRCUIT: Is the low voltage side of the ignition system which consists of the ignition switch, ballast resistor or resistance wire, bypass, coil, electronic control unit and pick-up coil as well as the connecting wires and harnesses.

PRESS FIT: The mating of two parts under pressure, due to the inner diameter of one being smaller than the outer diameter of the other, or vice versa; an interference fit.

RACE: The surface on the inner or outer ring of a bearing on which the balls, needles or rollers move.

REGULATOR: A device which maintains the amperage and/or voltage levels of a circuit at predetermined values.

RELAY: A switch which automatically opens and/or closes a circuit.

RESISTANCE: The opposition to the flow of current through a circuit or electrical device, and is measured in ohms. Resistance is equal to the voltage divided by the amperage.

RESISTOR: A device, usually made of wire, which offers a preset amount of resistance in an electrical circuit.

RING GEAR: The name given to a ring-shaped gear attached to a differential case, or affixed to a flywheel or as part a planetary gear set.

ROLLER BEARING: A bearing made up of hardened inner and outer races between which hardened steel rollers move.

ROTOR: 1. The disc-shaped part of a disc brake assembly, upon which the brake pads bear; also called, brake disc.
2. The device mounted atop the distributor shaft, which passes current to the distributor cap tower contacts.

SECONDARY CIRCUIT: The high voltage side of the ignition system, usually above 20,000 volts. The secondary includes the ignition coil, coil wire, distributor cap and rotor, spark plug wires and spark plugs.

SENDING UNIT: A mechanical, electrical, hydraulic or electromagnetic device which transmits information to a gauge.

SENSOR: Any device designed to measure engine operating conditions or ambient pressures and temperatures. Usually electronic in nature and designed to send a voltage signal to an on-board computer, some sensors may operate as a simple on/off switch or they may provide a variable voltage signal (like a potentiometer) as conditions or measured parameters change.

SHIM: Spacers of precise, predetermined thickness used between parts to establish a proper working relationship.

SLAVE CYLINDER: In automotive use, a device in the hydraulic clutch system which is activated by hydraulic force, disengaging the clutch.

SOLENOID: A coil used to produce a magnetic field, the effect of which is produce work.

SPARK PLUG: A device screwed into the combustion chamber of a spark ignition engine. The basic construction is a conductive core inside of a ceramic insulator, mounted in an outer conductive base. An electrical charge from the spark plug wire travels along the conductive core and jumps a preset air gap to a grounding point or points at the end of the conductive base. The resultant spark ignites the fuel/air mixture in the combustion chamber.

SPLINES: Ridges machined or cast onto the outer diameter of a shaft or inner diameter of a bore to enable parts to mate without rotation.

TACHOMETER: A device used to measure the rotary speed of an engine, shaft, gear, etc., usually in rotations per minute.

THERMOSTAT: A valve, located in the cooling system of an engine, which is closed when cold and opens gradually in response to engine heating, controlling the temperature of the coolant and rate of coolant flow.

TOP DEAD CENTER (TDC): The point at which the piston reaches the top of its travel on the compression stroke.

TORQUE: The twisting force applied to an object.

TORQUE CONVERTER: A turbine used to transmit power from a driving member to a driven member via hydraulic action, providing changes in drive ratio and torque. In automotive use, it links the driveplate at the rear of the engine to the automatic transmission.

TRANSDUCER: A device used to change a force into an electrical signal.

TRANSISTOR: A semi-conductor component which can be actuated by a small voltage to perform an electrical switching function.

TUNE-UP: A regular maintenance function, usually associated with the replacement and adjustment of parts and components in the electrical and fuel systems of a vehicle for the purpose of attaining optimum performance.

TURBOCHARGER: An exhaust driven pump which compresses intake air and forces it into the combustion chambers at higher than atmospheric pressures. The increased air pressure allows more fuel to be burned and results in increased horsepower being produced.

VACUUM ADVANCE: A device which advances the ignition timing in response to increased engine vacuum.

VACUUM GAUGE: An instrument used to measure the presence of vacuum in a chamber.

VALVE: A device which control the pressure, direction of flow or rate of flow of a liquid or gas.

VALVE CLEARANCE: The measured gap between the end of the valve stem and the rocker arm, cam lobe or follower that activates the valve.

VISCOSITY: The rating of a liquid's internal resistance to flow.

VOLTMETER: An instrument used for measuring electrical force in units called volts. Voltmeters are always connected parallel with the circuit being tested.

WHEEL CYLINDER: Found in the automotive drum brake assembly, it is a device, actuated by hydraulic pressure, which, through internal pistons, pushes the brake shoes outward against the drums.

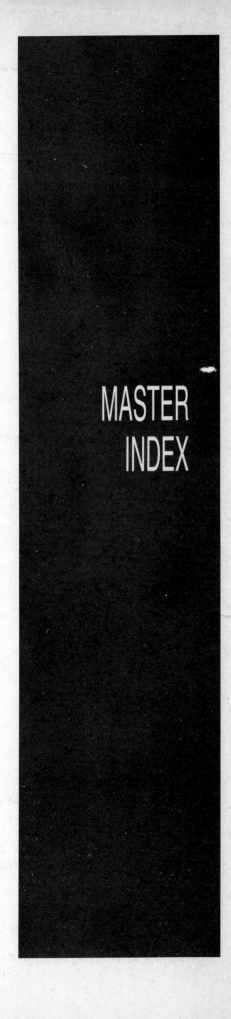

MASTER

INDEX